PSYCHOLOGY
The Science of People

Frank J. Landy

Pennsylvania State University

SECOND EDITION

PRENTICE-HALL, INC.
Englewood Cliffs, NJ 07632

Library of Congress Cataloging-in-Publication Data

LANDY, FRANK J.
   Psychology: the science of people.

   Bibliography
   Includes index.
   1. Psychology. I. Title.
BF121.L26 1987   150   86-30519
ISBN 0-13-732405-7

Credits
Art Director: Florence Dara Silverman
Development Editor: Maggie Murray
Photo Editor: Lorinda Morris-Nantz
Photo Research: Teri Leigh Stratford
Cover Art: SEF/Art Resource. Paul Klee: Port et voiliers (1937).
Cover Design and Interior Design Supervision: Anne T. Bonanno
Production Supervision: Martha Masterson
Copy Editor: Virginia L. McCarthy
Manufacturing Buyer: Barbara Kittle

Printed in the United States of America
10 9 8 7 6 5 4 3 2 1

ISBN 0-13-732405-7 01

Prentice-Hall International (UK) Limited, *London*
Prentice-Hall of Australia Pty. Limited, *Sydney*
Prentice-Hall Canada Inc., *Toronto*
Prentice-Hall Hispanoamericana, S.A., *Mexico*
Prentice-Hall of India Private Limited, *New Delhi*
Prentice-Hall of Japan, Inc., *Tokyo*
Prentice-Hall of Southeast Asia Pte. Ltd., *Singapore*
Editora Prentice-Hall do Brasil, Ltda., *Rio de Janeiro*

(Acknowledgments appear on pp. 643–644, which constitute a continuation of the copyright page.)

Brief Contents

Contents

Preface

Second editions of textbooks are more fun to write than first editions. In preparing a new text, there is a great deal of apprehension. The author is concerned about coverage and accuracy and writing style. The publisher is concerned about finding a new niche, about production problems, and about making sure that the appropriate package of supplementary materials has been prepared. Those apprehensions are greatly diminished in a revision. After a book has been on the market for several years, there is hard evidence about its acceptability by users. In addition, the sales figures and user reactions answer questions about its contribution. The decision to prepare a second edition means that the text has filled a gap in the market, that coverage is accurate and representative, that the book is "readable," and that the author and publisher have developed a good working relationship. Everyone can relax a little bit.

But relaxation does not mean standing still. The first edition of the book was well received by students and instructors alike. It was so well received that they were willing to take time to tell us how to make the book better. When they talked, we listened. As a result, the second edition represents a "fine tuning" of the first edition. The goals are the same as they were before. In the preface to the first edition, I set out to show how science could be applied in a way that would enhance our knowledge of the rich and complex phenomenon of human behavior. That is a primary goal of the second edition as well. In the first edition, I structured the book such that the first part was devoted to the "meat and potatoes" of the science of psychology—areas such as history, methods, sensation and perception, consciousness, physiology, and learning. The second part included the substantive areas of psychology—areas such as emotion and motivation, developmental, clinical, social and industrial/organizational psychology. It was my feeling that you needed a good understanding of the first part before you could fully appreciate the second part. I still believe that such a structure is appropriate, and the second edition has the same organization of chapters.

In the second edition, however, I did make some noticeable changes in format. For example, there were 25 chapters before. Now, there are 18 chapters. This was accomplished in two ways. First, the material in several chapters was integrated into other chapters. As an example, human sexuality represented an independent chapter in the first edition. In the second edition, that material is apportioned to the chapters on biology and behavior, developmental psychology, and social psychology. Similarly, the material from the testing chapter of the first edition now appears in chapters on language and thought, personality, and industrial/organizational psychology. I think that this helps greatly in illustrating the importance of these topical areas. In other instances, I felt that cohesion could be further improved by removing the boundaries between several two-chapter sequences. Thus, history and methods were combined into one chapter, as were the emotion and motivation chapters and the chapters on moderate and serious mental disorders. On the other hand, our users told us that it was a good idea to have separate chapters on sensation and perception, development in childhood and development in adulthood, and memory as distinct from other cognitive behaviors. In addition, they felt that the two learning chapters—theory and applications—served distinctly different purposes and should be left as two chapters. The result of these format modifications is a tighter, more coherent, and more flexible text.

In the first edition, I included some chapters that were uncommon in other, similar texts. These chapters included a stress chapter, a chapter on industrial and organizational psychology and an introductory "non"-chapter called "How to Study." The reactions of users has convinced me that these chapters make unique contributions to the introductory psychology students, so I have put them in the second edition as well. In a sense, they were experiments that turned out successfully.

There are other differences between the first and second edition in addition to the number of chapters. I have decided to include boxes in the second edition. Some of these boxes help me to expand my use of examples as pedagogical devices. Others highlight current issues or questions in psychology that help put the importance of research and theory in proper perspective. There are at least two boxes per chapter. In order to make room for this additional material, we have modified the running glossary. It has been moved to the bottom of the page and the pronunciation guide has been deleted. Other pedagogical devices have remained as before. I feel that the chapter opening questions and answers, the review questions in the chapter body, and the numbered summaries are important learning aids.

There are two other devices that I have continued to use in all of the second edition textual material. The first is the liberal use of everyday examples. Through a description of everyday examples, I hope to make it easier for students to appreciate research and theory in psychology—that has depended on experimentation, observation, and creative analysis. A second device I have retained has been the linking of material across chapters. Whenever possible, I remind the student about material that appeared earlier in the text. I have introduced this linking device to emphasize the fact that the same behavior can be viewed from many different perspectives and at many different levels.

One thing that users of the first edition will notice immediately is the new "look" of the book. The thematic colors have changed, we have gone to a full color layout for the book rather than using color only in selected sections, and the printstyle and page layout have been changed. This is more of the fine tuning that inevitably accompanies second editions. I am pleased with the results.

The most important difference between the first edition and the second edition is that the coverage in all topics has been updated. In addition new material has been added to each of the chapters. For example, there is new material on the revisions of the *DSM-III,* I have added new material on cognitive learning models, and I have deepened the discussion of stress and added material on stress and the immune system. I was gratified to find that the users and reviewers could identify no "big" areas or concepts that had been left out of the first edition. This meant that, for the most part, my job was to make sure that the latest research and theory in each topical area was presented. I have done that updating.

In addition to the text itself, the range of supplementary material to aid the student and instructor has been redone to accompany the second edition of the text. The Instructor's Resource Manual, written by Karen G. Duffy of SUNY, College at Geneseo, contains chapter outlines, suggestions for projects and papers, supplementary lecture and discussion material, essay questions, and lists of audio-visual aids and references. In addition, an introductory section on teaching and testing tips is provided.

The Test Item File, by Jesse B. Newkirk III, of Grossmont College, contains over 2000 multiple-choice questions, with every question page-referenced to the text. Some questions are conceptual, some factual, and some call for definitions. Test preparation and typing can be obtained through the Prentice-Hall phone-in testing service. A computer version of the Test Item File is available for many mainframe and personal computers.

The Student Study Guide with Practice Tests and Software Activity Accompaniment was prepared by Eliot H. Shimoff, B. A. Mathews, and A. Charles Catania, all of the University of Maryland, Baltimore County. It is designed to help students reinforce and supplement knowledge gained from class lectures and the text. For each chapter in the text there is a five-part chapter in the Study Guide that includes a chapter outline, key terms and concepts, short answer and fill-in-the-blank review questions, and a practice test.

In addition, the supplementary package has been expanded to include a computer-based set of experiments and demonstrations from which students can learn. This new element is called "Psychology on a Disk," and it was prepared by E. Shimoff, A. C. Catania, and B. A. Mathews to accompany the Student Study Guide.

Approximately 130 transparencies, many in full color, and 200 slides are also available to instructors for qualified adoptions. These include illustrations from the text as well as other non-text material.

In updating research material for all chapters of the second edition, I was greatly aided by Caran Colvin. In addition, Nancy Baker provided useful research reviews on several developmental topics. I am particularly indebted to two of my colleagues, Mel Mark and Jules Thayer. Mel worked with me on revising the social chapter. Jules aided in the revision of the stress chapter as well as in the integration and updating of the emotion and motivation material.

There were many outside reviewers for the first and second editions who provided insightful and indispensable suggestions at every stage of development. Both times the book has been greatly improved by these suggestions and I am indebted to the following for their help:

C. Berkeley Adams, Jamestown Community College; Patricia Barker, Schenectady County Community College; Roger Bernier, New Hampshire Vocational Technical College; John Boswell, University of St. Louis; John P. Brockway, Davidson College; David Brodzinsky, Rutgers University; Julia Carragan, Hudson Valley Community College; D. Bruce Carter, Syracuse University; Lorry J. Cology, Owens Technical College; William C. Crain, The City University of New York; Patricia Crane, San Antonio College; Robert DaPrato, Solano Community College; Stephen F. Davis, Emporia State University; Greg Dobbins, Louisiana State University; Karen Duffy, SUNY, College at Geneseo; William S. Edell, University of Massachusetts; Donald Elman, Kent State University; Kurt F. Geisinger, Fordham University; Pryor Hale, Piedmont Virginia Community College; Anne Harris, Arizona State University; Richard J. Harris, Kansas State University; Joseph Heller, California State University, Sacramento; Jill Hooley, Silver Spring, Maryland; Michael D. Hughmanick, West Valley College; George Janzen, Ferris State College; Paul Kaplan, Suffolk County Community College; Patrick A. Knight, Kansas State University; Thomas Leahey, Virginia Commonwealth University; Colin Martindale, University of Maine; Robert Mathews, Louisiana State University; Kathleen McCartney, Harvard University; Kathleen McNamara, Colorado State University; Gilbert Meyers, Illinois Valley Community College; Richard Miller, Western Kentucky University; Alan Monat, California State University, Hayward; Peter Murrell, Milwaukee Area Technical College; Sarah O'Dowd, Community College of Rhode Island; Thomas F. Oltmanns, Indiana University; John Pittenger, University of Arkansas; Steven J. Pollock, Moorpark College; Alan Randich, University of Iowa; Steven K. Reed, Florida Atlantic University; Edward C. Reid, Shelby State Community College; Howard M. Reid, SUNY, College at Buffalo; Damaris J. Rohsenow, University of Wisconsin; David Rubin, Duke University; Paula J. Schwanenflugel, Florida Atlantic University; Robert Seaton, College of DuPage; Stuart Solomon, Southern Connecticut University; W. Scott Terry, University of North Carolina, Charlotte; Roberta Weissman, Bethune-Cookman College; Jeremy Wolfe, Massachusetts Institute of Technology.

I would like to express my appreciation to one reviewer in particular, John Pittenger. He reviewed the entire manuscript of the second edition much as he did the first—with professionalism and a sense of concern for the students and instructors, who are the ultimate consumers of the text.

Finally, I am indebted to Prentice-Hall for its encouragement and assistance in producing the second edition. Since the time I first met John Isley, he has risen rapidly in the Prentice-Hall organization, assuming greater responsibility with each move. It has been my good fortune that John has never been able to get introductory psychology out of his blood. As a result, he has been as much a part of the second edition as he was of the first. As before, John's commitment has included the commitment of his able assistant Marilyn Coco. Her administrative skills and constant good humor help overcome even the most difficult obstacles. Others at Prentice-Hall who deserve praise include Martha Masterson, our production editor, whose hard work and enthusiasm carried us through a difficult production schedule; Anne Bonanno, who supervised the design and artwork; Lorinda Morris, photo editor, and Teri Leigh Stratford, photo researcher; Paul Rosengard and Carol Carter of College Marketing; and Sara Lewis, who has assisted us with the boxed features. I am also thankful to the many others behind the scenes at Prentice-Hall who contribute to the production and success of the book.

When I finished the first edition, I was in awe of the editorial skills of Susanna Lesan who had worked as the development editor on the text. She moved to another position in Prentice-Hall just as I began the second edition. I found the prospect of completing the revision without Susy disconcerting. My concern was groundless. Maggie Murray, the development editor for this edition, was as wonderful to work with as Susy had been. She has great editorial skill and a level of tolerance, calm, and patience that I have seldom seen elsewhere. This was a bonus for me since I now have a new friend at Prentice-Hall.

As far as a family dedication is concerned, my wife and children have become just as glassy-eyed and slack-jawed with my discussions of updated material as they were with my earlier first-edition discussions of new material. Nevertheless, they never left the room in mid-lecture (at least not suddenly and all together) and that is really what an author needs—someone to talk at during critical periods of integration.

F. J. L.

How to Study

QUESTIONS FOR THOUGHT

1. Is it better to stay up late to finish an assignment, or is it better to go to bed and get up early enough to finish the assignment in the morning?
2. How can you use chapter outlines and summaries before you even begin reading a chapter? How do they help you?
3. Why does asking questions before and as you read help you remember the material you read?
4. Would it help you to review material with a group of students rather than alone?
5. How can you narrow down your choices on an objective test?

The answers to these questions are at the end of the chapter.

Understanding is expensive; it costs dearly in terms of time and effort. The pursuit of understanding has left many a student (and instructor) depressed, anxious, tense, and tired. Comprehending the meaning of an abstract concept such as gravity, honesty, or vision is a complex task. One of the major distinctions between high school and college is the demand for a deeper understanding of the course material. It is no longer enough to remember and repeat rules, lists, and dates. It is now necessary to understand a concept well enough to use it in a creative way, to apply it to unusual situations, and to see how it connects to other concepts.

Some people think that comprehension or understanding is due to either luck or to inborn talents. Fortunately, this is not the case. Comprehension or understanding is not reserved for special people; it is available to all of us if we are willing to follow some rules. You know the general rule: Comprehension comes through study. But there are many different ways to study. You can cram or study systematically each day. You can study with someone else or alone. You can study by memorizing or by analyzing. As you must realize by now, some ways of studying are better than others. By "better," I mean that some methods lead to deeper understanding (and possibly higher grades!). In the following sections we will discuss a number of study methods and techniques that can be of use to you in this and other courses. But first we will take a look at the topic of memory—how it works and how you can make it work for you.

■ SOME THINGS YOU SHOULD KNOW ABOUT MEMORY

As you can see from the table of contents, there is an entire chapter devoted to memory later in the book. What you need to know now are some principles of memory and some techniques for studying that will make your memory more efficient and accurate.

Types of Memory

There are two kinds of memory that play a role in studying. The first is **short-term memory.** This is a form of temporary memory in which information is available for use for a short time only. When you hear a lecture about a particular topic, new terms are often introduced and then defined. It is necessary to keep the term in mind while listening to the definition. This is an example of short-term memory. Another example is dialing an unfamiliar phone number. After you look it up in the book, you must continue to repeat it to yourself until you have dialed the number. By repeating it, you are keeping the number available for use; otherwise you would probably forget it before you could dial it. The time span of short-term memory is very brief. Most of the material in short-term memory will be forgotten within a minute of when it was heard or seen.

The second type of memory is known as **long-term memory.** As the term suggests, material in

---

Short-term memory. A form of temporary memory that holds material for only a minute or two.

Long-term memory. A type of memory in which material may be held for long periods of time, even as long as a lifetime.

long-term memory lasts for extended periods of time (extended can mean a lifetime). Each of us has memories of early childhood—a favorite toy, a certain tune, a birthday party—and these memories will probably be with us until we die. Long-term memory is a very important part of learning. It is long-term memory that enables us to do well on tests covering material presented weeks before. Long-term memory allows us to build on what we have learned before. For example, after taking an introductory course you can go on to a higher level course without having to learn the basic information all over again.

It is clear how this affects studying—the problem is how to develop strategies for getting the material to be learned from short-term to long-term memory. Comparing this to the way a computer works is a good way to understand this kind of transfer. When you sit down at a computer terminal and type in some words or numbers, they will usually appear on the screen in front of you. This screen is like short-term memory—those words or numbers are available here and now. Assume that you have typed a long string of words or numbers. Feeling a little thirsty, you go off to get a drink of water. When you return, you find that someone else has taken over your seat and has begun to type in her own material. In order to do that, it was necessary for this other person to stop your job and begin her own. She probably accomplished this by simply typing some kind of END command. This told the computer to dump (or eliminate) the material that was on the screen (your material). In other words, the computer was told to "forget" what it had been working on and start to work on something else. Your material was in short-term memory. It is now gone and cannot be retrieved.

What you should have done before getting up to get your drink was to type some sort of SAVE command. This would have taken the material that was on the screen and put it in a permanent storage area (on a diskette or section of magnetic tape) so that when you came back, you could always ask for that material to be "remembered." In short, when you execute the SAVE command, you transfer the material from short-term to long-term memory. This is exactly what you want to do with material covered in coursework—execute some type of SAVE command. Unfortunately, doing that is slightly more complicated than pressing a button or punching the

word SAVE into your head. In this chapter we will discuss things you can do to SAVE course material in your long-term memory so that it can be retrieved at a later date, such as during an exam.

Getting Material In and Out of Long-Term Memory

Attention. You must pay attention to material if you expect to remember it. There are three things you can do that will help you pay attention to the material you read or hear. First, since you tend to pay closer attention to things that interest you than to things that don't, you can try to make the material more meaningful or interesting. One way to do that is to apply it to yourself or a friend. Try to think of examples of the material that can be tied to your everyday life. For example, in the sensation chapter we will discuss what causes seasickness. You will find this material much more meaningful if you think back to the time you were once seasick or if you make a note to pass this information on to a friend who is going to be sailing to Europe this summer.

The next thing you can do is to eliminate distractions from your environment. These distractions compete for your attention and "turn off" your memory for the material you are being exposed to. In later chapters, you will see that it is difficult for people to pay attention to several things at the same time. Instead, they usually switch back and forth, paying attention first to one thing and then the other. Unfortunately, any material that did not receive attention will not get into your long-term memory. This means that listening to the radio while you are studying, or reading the newspaper during a lecture is likely to leave gaps in your memory for the course material you are trying to learn.

Finally, you should avoid trying to learn or memorize material when you are tired. Fatigue often reduces the amount of course material that you can remember. This means that it might be better to get a good night's sleep and study in the morning rather than stay up a few hours extra and sleep late. You must have noticed how your attention wanders at 2:00 AM.

Rearranging and Recoding Material. In the last section I suggested that you could increase your attention to material by relating it to your everyday life. In addition to making the material more interesting, this has the effect of rearranging or recoding the material into more personal terms. Technically, this is called organization. Any organization that you can give to material will help you to rememeber it. Text material is organized to a certain extent for you in the form of headings. It is a good idea to list those headings on a separate piece of paper and use them for organizing your thoughts. Lectures are typically strings of words with an underlying organization. It is crucial that you make that underlying organization more obvious by using headings in your notes. This might mean that you must go back over your notes after lectures and fill in headings or rearrange certain information. This kind of effort is valuable.

Although organizing what you have heard or read will help you to remember the material, an even better idea is to organize *before* you are exposed to the material. This means going over assigned material before a lecture, or quickly skimming the major headings of a block of material to be read. This helps you to organize information as you encounter it.

Building Associations.   As you will see in the learning chapters, associations play an important role in behavior. This is particularly true with respect to memory. The greater the number of associations we make between what we already know and new information, the more likely it is that the information will be remembered. Associations can be thoughts of visual images. For example, when a waitress wants to remember who ordered what, she often creates some visual images to help. The overweight man ordered pork (pork comes from a pig). The sour-looking woman ordered fish in lemon-butter (lemon makes the mouth pucker). When it comes time to serve the food, it will be relatively easy to give the right dish to the right customers by simply looking at them. In the discussion earlier on attention, I suggested that material could be made more interesting by applying it to people you know, preferably people in your class. Later, just seeing those people or thinking about them will then help to trigger the association to the material to be remembered.

Memory Cues.   Sometimes, it is necessary to remember a series of names or dates or places. For example, in this course, it will be important for you to remember various theories of learning or personality. This type of memory can be accomplished through the use of certain mechanical aids or devices—tricks, in other words. This is often called **rote memorization**. The particular tricks or aids used in this type of memorization are called **mnemonic devices**. I will describe a few of the more popular mnemonic devices.

An **acronym** is a word formed from the first letters of a series of words. For example, FBI stands for the Federal Bureau of Investigation, and NASA stands for the National Aeronautics and Space Administration. If it is necessary to remember a string of words, it is often a simple matter to create an acronym that will help you to remember.

As a second mnemonic device, a series of words can be formed to produce a rhyme to help recall the information. The standard way for children to learn the number of days in each month is through the following rhyme:

Thirty days has September,
April, June and November,
All the rest have 31,
Except for February, which has 28,
Until leap year, when it has 29.

Even though the "rhyme" breaks down a little toward the end, it is very effective.

Timing.   Regardless of which techniques you use for arranging or rearranging material to go into long-term memory, an essential step is rehearsal. You must rehearse or repeat material in order to remember it. As a general rule, the more closely in time rehearsal follows the original presentation of the material, the more likely it is to be remembered. This means that it would be better to go over material immediately after class than to rehearse it later in the day. If that is not possible, it would still be better to go over the material that night than to go over it the next day; the sooner the better.

There are many other apsects of memory that are important for doing well in college courses, but

---

Rote memorization. Committing to memory a series of facts through the use of mechanical aids such as mnemonic devices.

Mnemonic devices. Memory aids used to string together a series of facts that have to be memorized.

Acronym. A word formed from the first letters of a series of words. Example: F.B.I. is an acronym for the Federal Bureau of Investigation.

rather than presenting them one after another, it might be best to examine a technique for studying that incorporates most of these principles.

■ A METHOD FOR STUDYING: SQ3R

As you can see, the name of the study method—SQ3R—is unusual. It may sound like a character from *Star Wars*, but it is actually a mnemonic device to help you remember some good study habits. The symbols SQ3R stand for SURVEY, QUESTION, READ, RECITE, and REVIEW. These five elements make up a set of study habits that almost guarantee success. The method was first described in detail by Robinson (1970), and is based on principles of learning and memory that we have been discussing. Let us now take a closer look at each one of these elements separately.

Survey

To survey is to find the limits or borders of an area. This course is a survey course, since you are being exposed to those topics that make up the discipline of psychology. When you are finished with the course, you will have a good idea of what topics are generally considered to be psychological in nature. In other words, you will have some idea of the borders of psychology.

Surveying the material to be studied is the first step in the SQ3R method. This is because it is important to find out what the limits or borders of the material are before studying it in depth. This step allows you to distinguish between important information and trivial detail.

The most obvious way to survey a body of information is to scan it from start to finish. By skimming over the pages, you will get an idea of what is to come. You will also get an idea of how long it will take to cover the material, which will help you to break the assignment down into reasonable time blocks. In most textbooks, this type of survey is made much easier through the presence of chapter outlines and chapter summaries. I have written this textbook in a way that should help you conduct your initial survey. By looking over each chapter outline and summary, you can get a quick view of the important parts or pieces of the chapter. If you look

at the chapter outline, you see that it is also broken down into smaller parts or pieces through the use of headings. Bold headings introduce big or important elements; smaller headings introduce sub-areas of these important elements. Thus the chapter outline can be an important roadmap through the chapter.

Let's take an example. If you were about to read Chapter 3, "Sensation," the first step would be to look over the chapter outline of headings (shown here in Table 1). Next, you should read through the summary of the chapter. These two things will give you a good survey of the material to be covered in this chapter, and you can then move on to the next major step in the SQ3R method.

Question

Most people need a reason to do things. In studying text material, a question becomes a reason. The same is true of information provided in a textbook format. If you have some questions to begin with, the material that you are reading will take on more life and be more meaningful.

TABLE 1.
Outline of Sensation Chapter

How We Measure Sensation
  Thresholds
  Psychophysical Functions
  Adaptation
Seeing
  The Characteristics of Light
  The Eye
  Eye Movement and Seeing
  The Brain and Seeing
  Color Vision
Hearing
  The Characteristics of Sound
  A Comparison of Hearing and Seeing
  The Ear
  The Brain and Hearing
  Hearing Loss
Other Senses
  Taste and Smell
  Balance
  Touch
Integration of the Senses
Extrasensory Perception
Summary

There are several ways to develop these questions. The first and most obvious way is to begin with the list of headings from the chapter outline. Write a question for each major and minor heading. In addition to these questions, which you can provide for yourself, in writing this book I have begun each chapter with a series of questions that you should be able to answer by the time you have finished the chapter.

Read

For most students, reading means the same thing as studying. When they say that they have studied the course material, they often mean that they have read it through several times. Obviously, reading is important, but it will be done more effectively when the survey and question steps have been completed.

Material should be read in chunks of a reasonable size. In other words, you should carve out a specific section that you will try to understand. (As mentioned earlier, when surveying the chapter you can get an idea of what these chunks might be.) A chunk might be all the material under a major heading. If the material under that heading runs for many pages, you might want to reduce the material to be understood to each of the minor headings taken one at a time. This doesn't mean that you should only read for brief periods of time. What it does mean is that you should not continue to read past one section until you understand that section. Many students set a time limit for their reading (for example, they decide to study for 2 hours) and quit no matter where they are at the end of that time. Other students define a reading block that is so large that it almost defies total understanding (for example, a 28-page chapter with many complicated sections). In the first strategy, the student tries to get through the material as often as possible in the allotted time. This does not help understanding. In the second strategy, the student often tries to read as quickly as possible in order to get the studying over with. This student is not likely to remember much from the reading.

The most effective way to pace yourself is to decide on the number of chunks that will be read (and understood) in a given study session. You can use the questions from the previous step as your definition of understanding—once you can answer the questions, you can move on to the next section.

Reading too much material in a study session, or reading it too fast, does not help understanding. The best approach is to read in chunks of a reasonable size and to check that you understand each section you read before moving on.

A good time to take breaks is between these sections, not in the middle of them. This might be a way of rewarding yourself for successfully completing the reading of each section.

It's important to make sure while you are reading that you are understanding the material. One way to do this is to look up the definitions of all new and unfamiliar terms. In this book, the glossary definitions appear on the text pages, close to where the term occurs, and are also listed, with corresponding page numbers, at the end of the book. In a course that uses a book without such a glossary, you should consult a dictionary to find the definitions of new terms.

Marking or Underlining. Another good way to make your reading time as useful as possible is to mark or underline the text while you are reading. This will make you a more active participant in the studying process. In addition, it will help you to focus on the major ideas and keep you from getting bogged down in details. This will also make it easier for you to review the material before a test, since you will have already given yourself some hints and associations that will aid in later recall.

In marking or underlining the text, you actually go through the text and underline key words and concepts that are important in understanding the material in the chunk you are reading. You might also make notes to yourself right on the text page. You can use the margins for these notes. If you choose to use the underlining and marking method, here are a few guidelines:

1. Read the whole section before doing any underlining or marking.
2. Don't mark or underline too much; the value of the technique lies in highlighting only the most important material.
3. Use ink if possible so that the underlining and notes do not disappear or become unclear in the course of studying.
4. Use symbols as much as possible. For example, use ? as a symbol for questions you have; use * to stand for a particularly important idea, and so on.

The act of choosing what is the most important material to highlight will make it easier for you to recall later the important material in the chapter.

Recite

Remember a time when you went to the store to buy several items? You didn't have time to write out a list, so you just repeated the items out loud several times on the way to the store. After several repetitions, you had memorized the list. If you had paid attention to what was happening, you would have realized that the act of reciting the list made the difference between remembering the list and forgetting it. This is just as true of course material as it is of shopping lists. **Recitation** is one way to establish information firmly in your long-term memory.

Recitation does not have to be out loud, but it should be formal. Don't just look over the information and say to yourself, "Now I know it." The point is that you should recite the information that you know. This can be done in several ways. One popular method is to close the book and try to repeat what you just have read. Then check to see if you were correct. A second way is to answer questions about the material you just have read. I have tried to make that easy to do in this book by providing review questions right in the body of the text. When you come to these questions you can use them to check whether you have learned the material in the section. If you have trouble answering the questions, you should go back and reread the parts you had a problem with.

It's very helpful to have a friend or classmate to recite with. You can ask each other questions about portions of the material, which will make you recite the material in a very formal way. It's not necessary to choose someone who is familiar with the material; your friend only has to be able to recognize that what you have said is what is written in the book or in your notes.

In order to be most effective, recitation should take place quite soon after you've first learned or read the material. This is important because, as we discussed earlier, the greatest amount of information is lost or forgotten right after you've first learned it.

Don't try to recite too much information at once. As we discussed earlier, depending on the number of pages covered, this might be all of the information in one major heading or even one subheading. A whole chapter is certainly too large a unit for recitation purposes.

Some sources (Pauk, 1974) suggest that the amount of study time given to recitation should depend on the nature of the material. For example, if you are dealing with unconnected pieces of information, as much as 90 to 95 percent of your study time might consist of recitation. This would include things like names, places, dates, formulas, or laws. On the other hand, if you are trying to learn abstract material that is well organized and nicely tied together by a general theme, only 10 to 20 percent of your time should be spent in recitation. For survey courses such as introductory psychology, Pauk estimates that about 50 percent of the study time should be spent in recitation.

Review

The last step of the SQ3R method is review. When you have finished studying a block of material such as a chapter, you should review or reconsider what you have learned. This can be done through reciting or through answering specific questions (as described above). The point is that you should go back over material once you think it has been learned. You should begin this review by reading the summary that appears at the end of each chapter. This will help you refresh your memory with respect to the major points of the chapter.

The second form of review is done just before beginning a new study session. In this form of review, you are actually preparing yourself for new learning by solidifying old learning. This makes sure that any old learning that is needed as a basis for new learning is correct and available. The final form of review is done before a test, as we will discuss in more detail later in the chapter. This review can be done quite effectively in a group with other students. This cuts down on some of the drudgery of pretest studying and also increases the meaningfulness of much of the information. This is because during the test you can more easily remember the information if you think back to who said what and how the review conversation went.

The SQ3R method of study is based on sound learning principles and gives the student a simple formula to follow. It provides both technical and motivational assistance in studying. I strongly recommend that you adopt this system or one very much like it in this introductory psychology course.

■ TAKING LECTURE NOTES

Taking a course is more than just reading the textbook. It involves supplementary reading, demonstrations, films, discussions, and class lectures. Of these elements, probably the most important is the class lecture. Since lectures aren't printed in textbooks, it is essential that the student develop some technique for storing information presented in a lecture. The most common method is notetaking.

Taking notes during a lecture is good for many reasons. The most obvious function of notes is to allow review and recitation of information that may not appear in the textbook. Another purpose note-taking serves is motivational; people seem to listen better when they are actively involved in the situation in which the listening occurs. When you take notes, you can't just copy down every word that comes from the instructor's mouth; there isn't enough time or space for that. As a result, you have to be selective about what is written down and what isn't. This selection and recording process turns you from a passive to an active participant in the listening process. Finally, note-taking is helpful because putting something in your own words aids comprehension and helps in storing and retrieving information from long-term memory.

Lectures can also provide a clue about the most important or difficult aspects of the topic under consideration. When preparing a lecture, most instructors concentrate on those points that are considered most central or important. This means that the lecture can act as an organizer for text material as well, pointing out the areas that are most important from the instructor's point of view.

How to Take Better Notes

As was the case with studying text material, there are some methods of taking notes that are superior to others. In this section you will find a few tips on establishing or strengthening your skills for taking lecture notes.

Preview. As is true in most learning situations, the best way to prepare for learning is to preview the material to be learned. In the case of lectures, this means reading text assignments before coming to class, which will give you an idea of where the lecture is going and what the important points will be.

Select. In spite of the fact that you should listen to everything in a lecture, you should only write certain things down. Some people feel that it is necessary to write every word and then go back later and decide what is important and what is trivial. This makes note-taking more difficult than it has to be. You can take in what is being said very quick-

---

Recitation. The act of repeating something out loud; a way to store information in long-term memory.

ly, much more quickly than it is being said; you often know what is coming at the end of a sentence before you hear it. This means that you have time to pick and choose what to write down as it is being said. Even while you are listening, there is plenty of time for taking notes and asking questions of yourself without losing track of what is being said.

When you first start taking notes on lectures, you may find yourself falling a little behind. Don't worry about it; simply stop and catch your breath and start again at a convenient point. You can get what you missed either from a classmate or the instructor later. Concentrate on the key ideas. To the extent possible, use a consistent set of headings and subheadings to write your notes. Three levels of heading should be enough—major headings, subheadings, and minor headings. If you were getting the information about note-taking from a lecture rather than from the text, your notes might look something like those shown in Table 2.

As you can see, there are three levels of headings—major headings (I,II), subheadings (A,B), and minor headings (1,2). These three levels are more than enough to give some structure to your note-taking activities. When the time comes to review those lecture notes, the identification of ma-

jor and minor headings will be a big help in remembering what was covered.

Question. As is the case when you are reading a textbook, in class you should always be asking yourself questions about the material. In a lecture, you have the added luxury of asking the teacher a question about something that was just said.

Organize. Lectures are unpredictable. Often, a teacher will switch topics abruptly, or forget to follow a particular line of thinking or digress for a brief period and then come back to the topic at hand. These behaviors make life difficult for the note-taker. It is important for purposes of study and understanding that the notes appear in a logical order. This means that it will be useful to go back over your notes after a lecture is over and rearrange or possibly rewrite them in a logical sequence. The best time to do this is immediately after class when the thoughts and words are still fresh. This has the added benefit of requiring you to read and review material—two Rs of the SQ3R method.

Review. As you read more in the text and of outside readings, you should add relevant information to your lecture notes. The best way to do this is to periodically review your lecture notes with an eye toward expanding and refining them.

TABLE 2.
Sample Lecture Notes

Introductory Psychology
Tuesday, Feb. 14.
Topic: Note-Taking in Lectures
Text Reference: How to Study
Outside Readings: None

I.   Lecture Notes—Importance
    A. Provide information
    B. Increase motivation
       1. Active participation increases motivation
       2. Process of selecting what to take notes on makes one an active participant
    C. Hint at most important areas
II. Improving Note-Taking Skills
    A. Preview
       1. Read text material
       2. Read any additional assignments
    B. Select
       1. Only make notes on main ideas
       2. Use three levels of headings for ideas

■ PREPARING FOR EXAMS

Cramming

A popular myth among college students is that weeks of inattention to a course can be wiped out with one "all-nighter." Using this strategy, students try to "cram" or stuff information into their memory just before an exam. This myth is reinforced by stories of fellow students who claim never to have opened the text until the night before the exam. If these claims are true, these fellow students are truly extraordinary and deserve the awe that they inspire; but under no circumstances should their strategy be adopted. Most of us are endowed with more ordinary skills and abilities and must use more conventional tactics for studying and learning.

The problem with **cramming** is that what is eventually learned through cramming is very quickly forgotten. This means that if you cram for a weekly test or even a mid-term, you are simply giving yourself a lot more work for the final exam. When it comes time to study for the final, the cramming you did several weeks before will not be any help; you will have to relearn the material from scratch.

What if you have not been able to keep up with the course material and the test is tomorrow? Should you cram? Of course. If there is *nothing* to recall, your test performance will be terrible. It's better to have some information than none. Fatigue is not a real issue here, since it can hardly interfere with performance when there is no information to recall. Besides, as you will see in the stress chapter, your anxiety level will keep you awake during the exam.

If you must cram, you should be discriminating in what you try to remember. You should survey the material and try to decide which topics are the most likely to appear on the exam. Discussions with classmates might help identify these topics. You should then concentrate on this reduced material. Trying to learn and remember every detail that was covered in the preceding weeks would be impossible. If you have time, a mini-version of the SQ3R method will help you to study this reduced information:

1. Read through the information once, making brief notes to yourself.
2. Develop questions on the material.
3. Read the material in chunks from start to finish.
4. Recite the material in either an outline form or as answers to questions you have prepared.
5. Review the material again to correct any errors that have intruded.

SQ3R works well for more normally paced studying, and there is no reason why it would not be a helpful strategy for cramming. Certainly, it is better than simply reading the same material over and over again until test time. Remember, if cramming must occur, the two keys are reducing the amount of information to key concepts or topics, and using a systematic strategy such as SQ3R for providing structure to the cramming.

A More Effective Way to Review

Instead of this extreme example of cramming, let's consider a better way to prepare for an exam. There is almost always some value in going over material one more time. Certainly, the closer your review of the material is to the time you take the test, the better. In addition, since there will be a broad range of material on the exam, covering several chapters and many lectures, this same broad range of material should be reviewed. If the SQ3R method has been used in the weeks before the exam, the last study session should be nothing more than the icing on the cake; the real work has already been done. A final substantial study session will also have positive effects on your motivation by increasing your confidence. This final session should not, however, be an "all-nighter." If the information is already in your head, fatigue will only interfere with your ability to recall material and answer test questions. The afternoon or early evening of the day before the exam would be a good time for the final review. You might even consider scheduling the final review for the morning of the exam, but this won't leave much time for checking out information you're unsure of. An important point to keep in mind is that new learning can interfere with old learning. This means that you should try not to put any other learning between your final review and the exam. If you have several subjects to study or work on before an exam, make sure that the subject matter you are going to be tested on is the last thing you study.

■ TAKING EXAMS

Before we discuss useful strategies to use in taking exams, it is important to distinguish between the two types of exams that you are likely to be faced with, essay exams and objective exams. Essay exams ask you questions that you are expected to answer in your own words with at least a few sentences, and at most several pages of an exam booklet. In answering the questions you must recall what you have learned about this topic, organize the information, and put it in complete sentences.

In an objective exam, you are asked to react to information that you are supplied with. Objective tests include multiple-choice items (in which you

---

Cramming. Trying to learn and memorize a large amount of material in one study period, usually just before a test.

It pays to take some time at the beginning of an essay exam to figure out how much time to allot to each question. It also helps to read each question thoroughly and organize your answer before starting to write.

choose the correct answer from a group of answers), true/false items (in which you say whether a statement is correct or incorrect), matching tests (in which you usually match a list of terms with a list of definitions), and fill-in-the-blank questions (in which you are asked to provide a word or phrase that will correctly complete a sentence).

These two types of exams call for different types of preparation and different strategies in taking them. We will discuss each separately.

Essay Exams

Essay exams require both recall and organization. Since the questions are usually broad and deal with concepts or theories rather than factual data, it is up to you to decide how the information will be presented. In fact, your success on this type of examination may depend as much on how well you organize your answer as on how well you know the material. The best way to prepare for an essay test is to develop a conceptual structure for large chunks of information. One way to do this is to develop and memorize an outline of topics so that you will be prepared to include all relevant material in your answer.

Most essay exams have more than one question, and the questions are often worth different point totals as well. The first thing you should do is divide your time in proportion to the value of each question. If there are four questions, each worth 25 percent, and 60 minutes provided to answer those questions, you should figure on 15 minutes for each question. If, on the other hand, 2 of the questions are worth 40 percent each, and 2 of the questions worth 10 percent each, you should allocate 24 minutes to each of the 40 percent questions and 6 minutes to each of the 10 percent questions. (This strategy also suggests that you bring a watch with you to the exam.)

Once you have decided how much time to spend on each question, you should decide which questions you know most about and which ones will be more difficult to answer. You should begin with the easiest questions and end with the most difficult one. But remember to keep to your time schedule no matter which question you start with.

When you have chosen the first question to answer, read it through thoroughly once. Then go back and underline the specific points to be addressed in your answer. Essay questions are often long and the sheer number of words can obscure the actual question. After underlining the important parts of the question, prepare a brief topical outline of your answer. You can use two or even three levels of headings in this outline. The outline should consist of key words or phrases which will guide you in actually writing your answer. The quality of this outline will determine the quality of your answer. Without some structure, you are bound to leave things out, mention the same point several times, or wander off the track and miss an important point in the question. With an outline of topics to work from, you can check off the points one at a time as you bring them up, and you can be sure that they are logical and completely cover the question. As an example, suppose you were asked the following essay question: How do you prepare for an exam? The topical outline for this question is shown in Table 3.

If you used this outline to structure your answer, it would be well organized and to the point, and you would waste much less time this way than you would with your pen poised over your paper as you tried to decide what to say next. From this outline, you should produce a series of full sentences and paragraphs that completely answer the question. Each main point (I,II) should begin a new paragraph. Depending on how much material is covered in the second level headings (A,B), you may want to begin each of these headings with a new paragraph as well. If it helps, you might want to actually list these headings in your answer.

TABLE 3.
Topical Outline for the Question:
How Do You Prepare for an Exam?

I. Daily Preparation
   A. Attend class
      1. Read material to be covered before class
      2. Take notes
   B. Review notes after class
      1. SQ3R method
II. Weekly Preparation
   A. Review sessions with classmates
      1. Prepare mock examination questions
      2. Begin with brief review of earlier material

When you have completed your answer, go back once more to the question. Look again at the parts you have underlined that represent the actual question to be answered. Now read what you have written one more time and make sure you have answered the question.

Objective Exams

Objective exams include multiple-choice items, true/false items, and matching tests. In this type of examination, you must recognize the correct answer in some larger group of answers. The best way to prepare for a recognition examination is to increase the number of associations you have with any particular piece of information. This can be done with the methods described in the earlier memory section: by studying with friends, making up applications of the facts, or even using mnemonic devices.

As was true of the essay exam, you should establish a rough time schedule of sorts. On an objective exam this usually means making sure that you don't spend too much time on any one item. Usually, each item is worth the same number of points, so it doesn't pay to spend a great deal of time on any one item. Check to see if the test instructions say anything about penalties for guessing. If there is no penalty for guessing, answer every question even if you are not completely sure of the answer.

If there are penalties for guessing, avoid those questions you are unsure of until you have answered those you know you will get correct. Then go back and answer those questions for which you can eliminate one or two alternatives as clearly incorrect. This means that you have a better than chance probability of getting the answer correct. For the questions in which each alternative seems as likely to be correct as any other, don't answer the question. The probability of getting it correct is not high and you will end up hurting your score unless you are very lucky.

After setting a rough time limit for each item, if possible, go through the entire test once, reading each question. Often, a word or phrase in one question or answer alternative will help you remember the answer to a different question. While you are reading through the exam, mark the items that you think will be difficult to answer so that you can answer them last. For some students, this is a luxury. If you are a slow reader or the test is particularly long and you don't have much time to complete it, you will not have time to go through the test before beginning to answer the items.

Read the first question that you will answer looking for words like *some, never, always, every,* and so on. Underline these words; they are often the key to the correct answer. In multiple-choice exams, there are usually four answers to choose from. Of these four, two are often considered **distractors.** These answers would usually distract or fool only the student who had not studied carefully. There is a third incorrect answer that is closer to the correct one and might fool even the student who has studied the material if the question and the answer are not read carefully. The fourth answer is the correct one. Knowing how the response choices are written suggests a strategy for answering the question. First, try to identify those choices that are clearly wrong and then choose the correct one from those that are left.

When you have finished answering all of the questions, go back and review each question and answer until time has run out. Don't jump up as soon as you have answered the last item and leave the test without having reviewed as many answers as possible before time runs out. Also, don't be afraid to change an answer if you think you were wrong initially. Some people are convinced that the first guess is the most accurate one. This is not true. There is research to show that students who carefully consider their original answer and then change it to one that seems more correct are likely to achieve higher scores.

The formula for good test performance is preparation and control. Preparation consists of weeks of class attendance, note-taking, regular review, and recitation. Control consists of a strategy for going through the examination. In an essay examination, this control is provided through outlining your answer prior to writing it. In objective examinations, control means reading all of the questions first, marking the difficult ones, identifying the distractor and the correct alternatives, and reviewing your answers.

In many of the chapters that follow, you will encounter the theory and research on which these study recommendations are based. These include learning principles, motivation principles, and principles of cognition and problem solving. These principles (and the study suggestions above) should prove useful to you not only in this course, but any time you must come to some understanding of a large body of information. The difference between doing well and failing is in study habits, not in "native ability."

■ SUMMARY

1. There are two types of memory that play a role in studying: *short-term memory,* in which information is available for only a few minutes, and *long-term memory,* in which information may last up to a lifetime. This chapter is devoted to a discussion of strategies for storing information in long-term memory so that it can be retrieved when needed.

2. There are several activities that enhance storage of information in long-term memory. Among these are focusing attention on what is being learned, rearranging and recoding while one learns, building associations between what is being learned and what is already known, using memory cues such as *acronyms* to memorize, and the timing of rehearsal of learning.

3. SQ3R is a mnemonic device that stands for some good study habits: *survey, question, read, recite, review.*

□ Survey: scan the chapter, using the chapter outline and summary to get an overview of the chapter before reading it.
□ Question: make up questions for each section before and while reading to become actively involved in what is being read.
□ Read: divide the material into manageable chunks to read and learn; use the glossary to learn the meaning of new or unfamiliar terms; mark and underline what you are reading to help focus on key ideas.
□ Recite: repeat what you've read after you finish reading each chunk, using review questions provided in the chapter; have a friend test you on what you have read.

Distractors. Two or more incorrect answers to a multiple choice question that are designed to fool the unwary or unprepared student and keep him or her from choosing the correct answer.

□ Review: again, use the review questions provided in the chapter, and also the summary. There are several types of review—after reading a chunk of text, before beginning the next study session, and before a test.

4. Taking lecture notes is helpful because the process of selecting what to take notes on and of putting them into your own words makes you an active listener and helps you remember what has been said. Some of the same principles of memory help in note-taking as well as in reading: it helps to preview what will be discussed in class, to select the important ideas to write down, to ask yourself questions about the material as you are listening, to organize your notes after the lecture, and to review lecture notes periodically.

5. *Cramming* should only be turned to if you haven't studied at all; it is a very inefficient way to learn material, and what little is learned is almost immediately forgotten, meaning that it all has to be done over again for the next test. If you must cram, try to reduce the amount of information to be learned to key concepts of topics and use the SQ3R approach to provide structure to the cramming.

6. There are two types of exams that students are usually faced with, essay exams and objective exams. In an essay exam you are asked to recall information and put it in your own words; in objective exams you are asked to recognize and react to information that is supplied to you. Each type of exam calls for a different strategy and different type of preparation.

7. In taking an essay exam, the first thing is to decide how much time to allow to answer each question, and start with the easiest questions, saving the hardest until the end. Next, underline the important parts of the question, then prepare a brief outline of your answer. This will let you check off the points as you cover them, so that nothing gets left out; it will also ensure that the points are covered logically and completely.

8. Objective exams include multiple-choice items, true/false items, matching tests, and fill-in-the-blank questions. It is important to make sure you don't spend too much time on any one item. With multiple-choice questions, it is helpful to identify the *distractors*, the possible answers that are obviously false, and thus narrow the choice to the most likely answers. When you have finished the test, go back and review each question and answer until the time is up.

■ ANSWERING QUESTIONS FOR THOUGHT

1. Fatigue tends to reduce the amount of material that you can remember, and your attention tends to wander late at night. For these reasons it is better to get a good night's sleep and study in the morning than to stay up late at night studying.

2. You can use chapter outlines and summaries in the survey phase of SQ3R, before you read the chapter. Reading through the outline of headings and the summary gives a quick overview of the main topics in the chapter, and helps you organize what you are going to be reading about before you get to it.

3. Asking questions—the question phase of SQ3R—before and as you read makes the material more meaningful and turns you into an active participant in the learning process.

4. Reviewing in a group with other students increases the meaningfulness of the material being discussed. This occurs because you build up associations during the discussion with the person who's talking, what's being said, and what other people added. Then when you are tested on this material you will have a number of memories of who said what in the group, and how the conversation went. These associations are very helpful in recalling the material that was discussed in the group.

5. In a multiple-choice test there is usually a choice of four or five answers. Some of these answers, called *distractors*, are obviously wrong. Key words in the question, such as *some, never, always,* and *every*, will help eliminate the distractors and will narrow your choice down to the more likely answers.

History and Methods of Psychology

QUESTIONS FOR THOUGHT

1. Why should I study psychology? What meaning could it have for my career and for my life?
2. What differences—if any—are there among a psychologist, a psychiatrist, and a psychoanalyst?
3. Why are the articles found in scientific journals so often much less exciting and dramatic than the science articles in the newspapers or magazines?
4. If I were to perform a psychology experiment, could I choose my ten best friends as subjects?
5. Do psychologists always work in the laboratory?

The answers to these questions are at the end of the chapter.

As you begin the study of a new field, it often helps to know something about how that field looked in the past as well as how it looks today. With this in mind, we will begin this chapter with a look at the past and present of psychology as a science. This background will include some of psychology's important names, concepts, philosophical orientations, and even controversies. In addition, since you may have some questions about how psychology fits into your daily life and future plans, it will include suggestions on how your interest in the field might be pursued—and used to advantage—in the years to come.

As a distinct field of study, psychology has a rather short past; it is scarcely more than 100 years old. Compared to sciences like physics, mathematics, chemistry, and biology, psychology is barely in its adolescence. In fact, until psychologists began gathering data from the "real world" through the observation of people, their mental life, and their behavior, psychology and philosophy were almost identical. It was the introduction of the scientific method that enabled psychology to break from philosophy and become a self-supporting discipline.

As you read about some of the most important influences on the way psychology looks today, keep in mind that this is intended as a brief overview, not a complete history. You will encounter many more of the names, dates, and events of psychology as we go along. In this early part of the course, you will be better off knowing *why* certain developments occurred than knowing all the people and events involved in those developments.

Psychology. The study of behavior and mental processes.

■ A DEFINITION OF PSYCHOLOGY

Psychology can be defined as the study of behavior and mental processes. The study of human behavior is emphasized in many areas of psychology, but a substantial number of psychologists study animal behavior. At a conceptual level this definition is enough to separate psychology from biology (the study of plant and animal life), chemistry (the study of the composition and transformation of substances), and physics (the study of inorganic matter and motion).

This simple definition also raises a number of interesting questions. In the first place, what do we mean by *study*? If you sit back and consider how colors affect your moods, have you *studied* color vision? Second, the definition makes a distinction between behavior and mental processes. Is this an important and necessary distinction? (Are dreams, for example, an instance of behavior or mental process?) Finally, I have indicated that some psychologists study animal behavior and some study human behavior. How do these two types of psychologists complement each other?

The questions raised here are very similar to those that spurred the development of modern psychology. Some early psychologists felt that the only legitimate method for the study of behavior was for a psychologist to study and describe his or her own behavior; others felt that there were forms of behavior that were unconscious and could not be described through self-study. Some psychologists felt that we should not study anything that could not be directly observed; others felt that observable behavior was less important than the mental events that occurred before those observable behaviors. Some psychologists felt that the study of animals was irrelevant; others felt that animals could provide the only "pure" information about certain forms of behavior.

After almost a century of struggle, certain conventions seem to be emerging about what psychology is and what it isn't. Modern psychology is heavily dependent on particular methods of examination. This means that a "study" has specific requirements. A study involves the scientific method, which we will discuss in detail later in the chapter. Today, we realize that it is not so easy to distinguish between behavior and mental processes. In fact, some psychologists prefer to distinguish between overt (observable) behavior such as talking and covert (unobservable) behavior such as thinking than to distinguish between behavior and mental processes.

In the psychology of the 1980's, a person's feelings, thoughts, intentions, attitudes, and expectations all are important topics for research and application. A good deal has been learned from studying both the behavior and the biological make-up of animals; it is fair to say that both animal and human behavior are legitimate for study by psychologists as long as the goal is a better understanding of behavior or mental processes.

■ THE DEVELOPMENT OF MODERN PSYCHOLOGY

As we have seen, there has been some disagreement throughout psychology's history about the definition of psychology, about methods of study and the proper organisms to study, and even about what can properly be considered behavior. In fact, the development of modern psychology can be traced rather easily by simply describing who disagreed with whom, when the disagreement occurred, and what the consequences of that disagreement were. Such disagreement is typical of science and, contrary to what you might think, normal, healthy, and almost always productive. Psychologists are no more (or less!) difficult to get along with than other scientists—disagreements are simply occupational hazards.

PSYCHOLOGY AND COMMON SENSE

There is one aspect of psychology that is unique when it is compared to other sciences like biology, chemistry, and physics. Unlike the practitioners of these other sciences, every human being is a psychologist. Each of us has the raw data and the laboratory necessary to develop theories and carry out research. Since each of us behaves in particular ways and is capable of guessing what the causes of those behaviors are, we each can function as a psychologist. The laboratory we use can be a subway, a restaurant, a classroom, or a football game. We carry out experiments almost from the day of our birth. For the most part they are lousy experiments, and they never appear in journals or books; nevertheless, we routinely analyze the behavior of others and try to predict what they will do in certain situations. In this way, we're doing just what the professional psychologist does, but our methods differ from theirs.

The theories that we "everyday psychologists" develop often go by the name of "common sense." But because of the way the information that helps form theories is gathered, psychology is more than common sense. The "man on the street" gathers information whenever he feels like it. He may tell others about this information or he may not; he may even forget some of it. This is how common sense comes about. Sometimes it is wrong and sometimes it is right. Common sense fails most often in *predicting* what someone will do in a given situation. It is more successful at explaining why someone behaved in a particular way after that behavior has occurred—that is, at *postdicting*. The Monday morning quarterback is never wrong; hindsight vision is 20/20. As you will see when we examine the experimental method, one of the strongest points of modern psychology is the manner in which data are gathered and used to form theories. This allows psychology to be more valuable in the long run than common sense.

People's feelings, thoughts, intentions, attitudes, and expectations are all topics for research by modern psychologists.

Schools of Thought

For all practical purposes, modern psychology appeared on the scene in the late nineteenth century—when Wilhelm Wundt in Germany and William James in the United States began research activities in special rooms or laboratories set aside for that purpose. At that time, there were only a small number of influences on what type of research was done. As a result, if you decided to pursue research in psychology, you usually identified with one or the other of these influences. This meant that you went to work in the laboratory of a particular person. For example, you might have gone to work with Wundt at Leipzig or with James at Harvard. Since there were only a few "brands" of psychology to choose from, these brands were given names that represented the philosophy or goals of the director of the laboratory. Many of these names ended with

the suffix *-ism*, which was meant to indicate that those who adopted this approach had adopted a doctrine or a system of thought. We will discuss four such isms: structuralism, functionalism, behaviorism, and humanism. In addition to the isms, four other important doctrines or systems of thought have influenced the development of modern psychology—Gestalt psychology, the psychoanalytic movement, cognitive psychology, and the biological approach. These eight influences cover over 100 years of psychology. The term *school* is also used in the historical context to identify a broad system or philosophical approach. Thus, instead of functionalism, you might see a reference to the functionalist school.

Structuralism. Wilhelm Wundt (1832–1920) was a physician by training. His major interest was in physiology, and he worked for a time in the laboratory of Hermann von Helmholtz, one of the pioneers in vision research. He became interested in consciousness, particularly the higher mental processes, and eventually wrote a ten-volume work on the topic. He was particularly interested in breaking consciousness down into its fundamental elements.

Since Wundt's laboratory in Leipzig, Germany, was the first of its kind, students from many countries came to study with him. One of these students was Edward Titchener from England. Shortly after receiving his degree from Leipzig, Titchener took a position as a professor of psychology at Cornell University where he remained until his death. Like Wundt, Titchener believed that mental processes could be best studied by looking at the fundamental elements of conscious experience: sensations, feelings, and images. These three elements provided the structure of conscious experience, thus giving rise to the term **structuralism**.

Structuralism did more than just concentrate on the elements of consciousness. It provided a set of procedures that were used to examine this structure. The most important of these procedures was called **introspection** (which means "looking inward"). Scientists were trained to report their conscious experiences while exposed to various sensory stimuli such as sounds, lights, and touches. The structuralists hoped to identify the elements of the mind by means of this guided tour of conscious experience. In the early days of structuralism, many experimenters acted as their own subjects. This avoided the problem of trying to deal with different reports of conscious experience that would come from different subjects.

There were several problems with structuralism. In the first place, there was disagreement about the value of introspection; some felt that it was too subjective because the results differed from person to person. In addition, even at this early stage of psychology, there were some people who wanted to *use* psychology to help the mentally ill, children, and the handicapped. Having to use the method of trained introspection meant that there was no way to learn about the consciousness of these groups. Finally, there were those who felt that the study of animals could provide rich information about how humans functioned, and trained introspection would be impossible with animals.

Functionalism. Like Wundt, William James (1842–1910) was trained as a physician and was interested in physiology. Unlike Wundt, he was more interested in why the mind or consciousness existed at all rather than in what its elements were. He saw the mind as ceaseless activity; it acquired and processed information about the internal and external environment and organized this mass of information. From James's work, **functionalism** emerged.

The views of William James were popularized by his students. Among those students were Edward Thorndike and James Angell. Thorndike was associated with a laboratory at Columbia University and made substantial contributions to learning theory by studying how animals solved problems such as escaping from cages or getting food. Angell founded a functionalist laboratory at the University of Chicago that came to be known worldwide for research and theory on education and educational strategies. In fact, the earliest applications of the functionalist approach were found in education, and the influence of the functionalists is evident in the development of various approaches to learning.

The functionalists' approach to psychological research was very different from the structuralists'. While the structuralists tended to view the individual as relatively passive, receiving stimulation from the outside and processing it almost automatically, the functionalists took a more aggressive view. They assumed that individuals actually sought out information, each individual combining it in a unique way that was more or less adaptive. In fact, there was a clear conceptual link between Charles Darwin, who had suggested that adaptation to the environment played a role in the survival of species, and the functionalists, who suggested that adaptation played a role in psychological processes.

The functionalists were not so much at odds with the structuralists, as they had different interests and lived in different environments. The Unites States was a young country where adaptation to the land was still a major issue for many families and "rugged individualism" was highly valued. It was natural, then, that in the United States adaptation should play a role in the theories and research of the behavioral sciences and that functionalism should thrive.

It is interesting to note that although neither the structuralists nor the functionalists wanted to study

A photograph of Pavlov (with the white beard) and his staff demonstrating an experiment conducted with a dog.

behavior *per se*, the functionalists eventually drifted toward a concern for actual behavior rather than mental processes. It was just this preference for the study of overt behavior rather than mental processes that gave rise to a new ism, behaviorism.

Behaviorism. At about the same time that Wundt and James were setting up their laboratories, Russian physiologists were busy examining a completely different type of behavior. Ivan Pavlov (1849–1936) was interested in chemicals that appeared in dogs' stomachs; in fact, he won the Nobel Prize for this research. In the course of conducting this animal research, Pavlov noticed that his dogs formed cer-

tain associations—for example, they would begin to salivate when they saw the lab assistants appear with food. This was the beginning of a line of research on associations and learning that still continues. Pavlov had no interest in either introspection or consciousness.

In the United States, John B. Watson (1878–1958) was also interested in observable behavior rather than consciousness. He was aware of Pavlov's work and was interested in the idea of associations. Watson, who was one of Angell's students and was thus a functionalist by training, proclaimed that consciousness had nothing to do with psychology (Murray, 1983). As far as Watson was concerned, consciousness was something humans had that was

---

Structuralism. One of the earliest movements of psychology; sought to study consciousness by breaking it down to basic elements.

Introspection. Means "looking inward"; early method in psychology in which trained subjects reported their conscious experi-

ence while in the process of perceiving or judging sensory stimuli.

Functionalism. Early movement in psychology claiming that consciousness actively seeks out and orders information, which is combined by each individual in a unique and more or less adaptive manner.

accidental to behavior. As a result, he was all in favor of studying animals and their behavioral patterns in order to compare them to the behavior of humans. This clearly left no room for psychological study through introspection.

Watson was particularly interested in explaining behavior by using associations learned from the environment. He felt that much, if not all, behavior was learned from environmental interactions. One of Watson's most famous quotes (and one that annoyed many people at the time) deals with the development of abilities in humans. He said:

Give me a dozen healthy infants, well-formed, and my own specific world to bring them up in and I'll guarantee to take any one at random and train him to become any type of specialist I might select—doctor, lawyer, artist, merchant-chief, and yes, even beggar man and thief, regardless of his talents, penchants, tendencies, abilities, vocations, and race of his ancestors. (In Murray, 1983, p. 278)

It was this emphasis on the relationship between environment and observable behavior that was responsible for the label **behaviorism**. Perhaps the best-known behaviorist of all is B. F. Skinner. In many respects, Skinner has not deviated at all from the original ideas of behaviorism. Like Watson, Skinner believes that the environment is mainly responsible for the differences in behavior that we observe in people, and like Watson, he has a unique view of mental processes. He feels that much of what is referred to as "thinking" or "creativity" is the result of interactions with the environment. In other words, it is learned like all other behavior. It is a response to environmental stimuli. To the behaviorists, language is simply another type of behavior and does not have any necessary relationship to abstract and nonobservable things such as thinking. As you will see, behaviorism is still a strong influence in modern psychology.

Gestalt Psychology. For the most part, the Gestalt psychologists were trained by German structuralists, although Gestalt psychology was very different from structuralism. The three major figures in this movement were Max Wertheimer (1880–1943), Kurt Koffka (1886–1941), and Wolfgang Kohler (1887–1967). Wertheimer performed a famous experiment using Koffka and Kohler as subjects; they were as impressed by the results as was Wertheimer. The experiment was a simple one. Wertheimer demonstrated that if you showed someone a single vertical line for a short period of time and then replaced it with a single horizontal line, the person did not report seeing two distinct lines but said that one line had moved from the vertical to the horizontal. This revolutionary experiment challenged both structuralism, because it meant that experience was more than a person's sensations, and behaviorism, because it suggested that something occurred in the brain to transform sensations into perceptions— something that smacked of "thinking."

Gestalt is the German word for *whole*. The point of the above experiment was to demonstrate that the whole (the experience of a moving line) we create by integrating separate parts (two lines—one vertical and the other horizontal) differs qualitatively from these parts. The resulting approach or school was called **Gestalt psychology** and it emphasized the way in which people perceive and experience the world as a whole.

Interest in this movement spread rapidly, and eventually the Gestalt approach was applied not only to sensation and perception but also to group dynamics, personality theory, and motivation theory. We will consider Gestalt psychology in some detail in Chapter 4 when we discuss perception.

Psychoanalytic School. The **psychoanalytic school** was founded by Sigmund Freud (1856–1939). Since the basic ideas of psychoanalysis still play a major role in many theories of normal and abnormal personality, as well as in methods of therapy, detailed descriptions of these methods and Freud's theory will be saved for the clinical chapters (Chapters 14–15). Nevertheless, it is important to know something about the differences between Freud's position and those of the structuralists and functionalists.

Freud lived most of his life in Vienna and was a physician by training and profession. Early in his career he became interested in abnormal behavior because of patients who came to him complaining of symptoms that seemed to have no physical basis. Since he was trained as a scientist, Freud had developed a healthy scientific curiosity and was interested in developing a general approach to understanding human behavior. Freud was familiar with Wundt's work, but while Wundt and his followers had set out to explore the conscious mind, Freud set out to explore the unconscious mind. He was convinced that he would never understand his patients if he concentrated on the realm of conscious experience. Freud proposed that the root of many of his patients' problems was to be found in the unconscious. This separated him from not only structuralism, but functionalism and behaviorism as well (although there was some possible connection to the Gestalt movement). Freud first attempted to examine the unconscious through hypnosis. He later came to depend on other methods, such as dream interpretation. The traditional experimental methods of Wundt and James were of little value to Freud, whose research was outside the laboratory. He conducted his studies with patients in his consultation room. Therefore, from a scientific perspective, **psychoanalysis** is a distinctly different brand of psychology that evaluates itself using rules very different from those of the typical scientist. This has created some problems over the years in judging its worth and development. What you should keep in mind is that the psychoanalytic school was not developed as a protest to any other movement, but as a way of dealing with issues that were not being adequately addressed by the schools or orientations then in existence.

Humanism. **Humanism** is a very current movement and one that developed to a certain extent as a protest against behaviorism and psychoanalysis (Leahey, 1980). It emphasizes the values that people hold, their ideals, and their aspirations. All people are considered to be unique and therefore better understood by examining their particular patterns of highs and lows, abilities and weaknesses, and likes and dislikes than by comparing them to others. The humanist movement concentrates on the power of people to affect their own behavior and downplays the role of environmental influences. In the history of psychology, this is a "newer" movement, appearing around 1940 in the writings of peo-

Freud, a physician by training, was the founder of the psychoanalytic school. This photograph was probably taken during one of his last years in Vienna.

ple like Abraham Maslow, Carl Rogers, and Gordon Allport. More will be said about this approach in the chapters on personality, abnormal psychology, and therapy.

Cognitive Psychology. An important recent influence on psychology in general is **cognitive psychology**. In certain respects, the cognitive approach is also a reaction against behaviorism, but it is much more than that. In keeping with earlier movements, it is concerned with the structure and function of mental processes—matters of no concern to behaviorists. Cognitive methods of study-

---

Behaviorism. Movement in psychology that focuses on the study of observable behavior rather than on mental processes.

Gestalt psychology. Studies the way in which people perceive and experience the world as a whole.

Psychoanalytic school. Studies the unconscious; focuses on abnormal behavior and treatment of it.

Psychoanalysis. Diagnosis and treatment of behavioral problems based on the principles of Freud and his followers.

Humanism. Movement in psychology that is interested in the unique qualities of individuals, their values and ideals.

Cognitive psychology. Movement in psychology that studies mental processes through experimentation; interested in language, problem solving, concepts, judgment, and other mental activities.

ing these processes include the introspection of the structuralist as well as the observation of both the functionalist and the behaviorist. In addition, cognitive psychology has devised ways to deal with events well beyond simple sensory processing, such as language, problem solving, concepts, and judgment. We will see more of the cognitive influence in later chapters.

The Biological Approach. Modern psychology has had much to gain from the many advances in the biological sciences. We now know, for instance, how genes can influence human development and functioning. We understand more about how substances such as alcohol, drugs, or even caffeine can influence behavior. We know more precisely how information is transmitted internally through the nervous system with the help of hormones. Not surprisingly, because of the growing appreciation of the potential influences of such chemical and biological variables on behavior, the **biological approach** has evolved. Conditions such as love, stress, obesity, mental illness, and aggression have been examined from the perspective of biology and chemistry. Further, there is a growing interest in bringing the biological approach to bear on higher mental processes such as thinking and creativity. We will consider this approach in some detail in Chapter 2.

The Importance of Isms and Movements. The controversy resulting from such movements as the eight described here are healthy. A science progresses not only by gathering followers and apostles, but also through differences of opinion. Having only one movement in psychology would be like living in a country with one political party—a large number of questions would be left unasked and unanswered.

These movements are also responsible, in one way or another, for the specialized areas of psychology that exist today. For example, functionalism led to the development of applied psychology, and perception research has made good use of the observations of the Gestalt psychologists. Our discussion to this point has been either historical or abstract. Now we will switch gears and examine exactly how psychologists act as scientists—what method they use and why it has proven so valuable in psychology. Let's start by considering the specific goals of science.

REVIEW QUESTIONS

1. Psychology can be defined as the study of _____ .
2. Most psychologists study the behavior of _____ , but many study the behavior of _____ .
3. Psychology became a discipline in its own right with the introduction of the _____ method.
4. Match the following terms with the correct definition:

___ structuralism   A. studies how people perceive and experience the world as a whole

___ functionalism   B. studies the unique qualities of individuals; emphasizes their values and ideals

___ behaviorism   C. studies consciousness by breaking it down into elements of sensation

___ Gestalt psychology   D. studies mental processes and functions through experimentation

___ psychoanalysis   E. studies only observable behavior; emphasizes how people learn

___ humanism   F. studies such areas as language, concepts, memory; interested in scientifically studying mental activity

___ cognitive psychology   G. studies the influence of biological and chemical factors on behavior

___ biological approach   H. studies the unconscious; focuses on treatment of patients rather than on research

5. Cognitive psychology differs from/is similar to behaviorism in its interest in mental activity; it differs from/is similar to structuralism and functionalism for the same reason.

Answers: 1. behavior and mental processes 2. people; animals 3. scientific 4. structuralism, C; functionalism, D; behaviorism, E; Gestalt psychology, A; psychoanalysis, H; humanism, B; cognitive psychology, F; biological approach, G. 5. differs from/is similar to

■ THE GOALS OF SCIENCE

Every science, whether it is biology, physics, chemistry, or psychology, has four goals. These are (1) description, (2) prediction, (3) control, (4) understanding.

Description

The simplest and least demanding goal of science is description: To describe reality in a way that can be understood by others. Description is a way of stating the existence of something. If something can't be described, we must question whether it exists. If it can be described and its description is accepted by others, we are more certain of its existence. For example, in Chapter 15, we will consider the descriptions of mental disorders provided by a reference manual used by clinical psychologists and psychiatrists when they try to determine the type of disorder a particular patient has. This manual consists of dozens of categories of mental disorders, each category described on the basis of observed behaviors. These descriptions can be extremely helpful in deciding on methods of treatment, but they are of little help in understanding why the disorder appeared in the first place. This does not mean that they're not valuable as descriptions.

Prediction

Observing and describing behavior leads to questions: What causes this behavior? Why does it happen? What would happen if. . .? These questions are then made more specific and turned into a **hypothesis**. A hypothesis is simply a question phrased as a statement and used by scientists as a way of launching an investigation or study. We might ask: *I wonder if watching violence on TV causes kids to hit each other?* As a hypothesis this might read: *Aggression in children is related to the amount of violence they see on TV.* This hypothesis is really a prediction. It is what an experiment is all about—predicting future events from past or present observations.

A hypothesis is usually stated in such a way that a choice is involved; the scientist must come to one

In our TV example there is a choice between two hypotheses: 1) Watching violence on TV increases aggressiveness in children, or 2) Watching violence on TV does not increase aggressiveness in children. Research allows the scientist to properly identify the correct hypothesis.

conclusion or the other. For example, you have already hypothesized that watching violent TV programs increases aggressive behavior in children. The results of your experiment may actually support either one of two conclusions:

A: Watching TV violence increases aggressive behavior, or
B: Watching TV violence does not increase aggressive behavior.

One of these two hypothesis must be correct; there are no other alternatives. Furthermore, if you accept one of these hypotheses, you must automatically reject the other. The problem for the scientist is to decide which one is correct and which one is incorrect. This problem is solved by doing research in a way that will allow you to identify the correct hypothesis. We will discuss research methods a little later in this chapter.

Control

After testing the hypothesis, the scientist knows whether or not the prediction was correct. Taking the example above, let's say that the hypothesis was supported: Children who watched violent TV pro-

---

Biological approach. Recent movement in psychology that studies the influence of biological and chemical factors on behavior.

Hypothesis. A question to be answered by investigation or study.

grams did hit other children more often. Simply knowing that relationship may help us at times to keep some kids from getting hit. In a Saturday morning play group, we can make sure that the children don't watch violent TV programs immediately before or during their play periods. In that way we can *control* a particular type of behavior—hitting. This control follows from the predictability of the behavior—if we could not predict it, we could not control it. As a matter of fact, a good deal of psychology is directed toward control. People are provided information about themselves that allows them to maintain control over their behavior and channel it in directions that they feel are appropriate.

Understanding

The most demanding scientific goal is *understanding.* This is the final objective of all scientific activity. First, the psychologist describes behavior and things that may affect it. Next, the psychologist carries out a study to see if the hypothesized relationships between the things and the behavior actually exist: Can behavior A be predicted from condition B? If this hypothesis is supported, then the psychologist may move on to a different type of activity—control. Finally, the psychologist could move to a higher or more abstract level of activity—understanding and explaining. Once the psychologist has successfully predicted and controlled the behavior, science requires an explanation of the relationship. This explanation is given in the form of a theory.

In a sense, hypotheses are the raw material for theories. A **theory** is a general principle, or a set of interrelated propositions, that is used to explain the phenomenon under consideration. Here, the phenomenon under consideration is aggressive behavior. While a hypothesis asserts a position, it does not help directly in understanding the behavior under consideration. In our TV example, even if the hyothesis is supported, we don't really know *why* watching TV violence increases aggressive behavior. We simply know *that* it does. Suppose we formed several more hypotheses on this same theme. Consider the following hypotheses:

▢ Children imitate behavior of adults.
▢ Aggressive children get more rewards in play groups.
▢ Children are rewarded by adults for being assertive.

If each of these hypotheses were supported, we would begin to see a more complex picture of TV and aggression. We might propose as a theory that children imitate what they see on TV, obtain rewards in their play groups for being aggresive, and are praised by adults who reward what they perceive as assertiveness (rather than aggressiveness). This theory would be a good deal more explanatory that any of the hypotheses taken individually. The interrelated propositions deal with imitation, rewards, and perceived assertive behavior. The theory ties them all together to explain aggressive behavior in children.

Characteristics of "Good" Explanations. The way a scientist communicates understanding is through explanation. The explanation may be in the form of a full-blown theory or in the form of a simple discussion of why and how one thing is related to another. But not all explanations are equally good. The "goodness" of an explanation depends on several characteristics, including simplicity, clarity, and breadth.

In general, simple explanations are preferred over complex ones, as long as the simplicity does not distort the view of the behavior or relationship being studied. Consider an explanation of why some children are better at computer games than others. Since children improve at playing computer games with practice, an explanation that included such things as room temperature, the height of the children, the ages of their cousins, and their preferences for certain foods would be unnecessarily complex and cluttered. On the other hand, an explanation that simply suggested that some children are born with the computer-game ability and that others aren't would not be enough to account for observable behavior.

The explanation should also be clear and unambiguous. Consider the following example. In our TV-aggression research, we might adopt a theory that aggression is caused by TV. This simple statement could, in fact, be hiding several theories. Some of them might be:

1. *All* forms of aggression are the direct result of watching TV.

2. In certain age groups, watching *any type* of TV program will lead to aggression.
3. In certain age groups, watching *violent* TV programs can lead to many forms of aggression.
4. In certain age groups, watching violent TV programs can lead to physical aggression directed toward children of the same age in the immediate vicinity.

As you can see, the original statement that TV causes aggression was not as clear as it might have been. You could easily have added another five theories to the four that were just stated. This is not good because everyone who reads the theory will have a different idea of what the theory actually says.

Finally, explanations that cover a wide range of behaviors or events are preferable to those that cover only a limited range of situations. The narrower the range of situations covered, the more explanations we need. This would ultimately violate the demand for simplicity. An explanation of aggressive behavior that could be applied to any sample of children between the ages of 5 and 9 would be more acceptable than one which applied only to 6-year-old white Catholic boys from affluent suburban homes in north-central Ohio.

Other characteristics of "good explanations" could be mentioned, but these three—simplicity, clarity, and breadth—should give you a feel for the difference between "good" and "bad" explanations.

■ COMMUNICATION IN SCIENCE

Science is a public activity. It is not done "in the privacy of your own home" for a few close friends. Science maintains its reputation for objectivity by allowing the results of studies and the statements of theories to be considered by anyone. This does not mean that the study is done at the largest intersection in the city at noon in front of several thousand spectators. Instead, it simply means that the procedures used in the study are spelled out. If a scientist is studying aggression, the way that aggression is measured must be completely described so that another scientist can check the results independently by following the same procedures. The way in which a particular variable is measured is called its **operational definition.** In our TV-aggression study, the operational definition of aggression might be how many times a child touches another child in a hostile manner. In addition to specifying the method for measuring aggression, the scientist must specify the conditions that were present when the study was done. These would include the number and type of subjects in the study, the conditions under which the observations were made, and any instructions that might have been given to the subjects.

As you can see, the public nature of scientific activity makes it difficult to "cheat." Since other scientists have the opportunity to repeat (or **replicate**) a series of observations, unsupported claims are more difficult to make. The publication of scientific results acts as a safeguard against fraud. A very famous case of such detection involved Cyril Burt, a once respected British psychologist who was known for his studies on intelligence. Over several decades, Burt had proposed that genetic inheritance was a stronger influence on intellectual ability than environmental factors. He claimed to have demonstrated this through a series of statistical analyses comparing identical twins raised together to twins raised apart. Eventually, a close inspection of these data turned up a number of curious characteristics. Perhaps the most curious was that the statistical estimates of the similarity of intelligence of the twin pairs did not change over a period of years, even though "new" subjects were presumably added to the analyses. Further checking revealed that no trace could be found of a woman who was supposed to have been a research collaborator of Burt's. In the end, it was concluded that Burt had made up his data to fit his beliefs about intelligence and heredity. While the basic honesty of the scientist is an important assumption of the scientific method, the public nature of scientific activity is further proof of its legitimacy. We will consider the related

---

Theory. A general principle, or set of interrelated propositions, that explains a phenomenon.
Operational definition. In an experiment, the way in which a variable, such as aggression, is defined and measured.

Replicate. To repeat; in science, to repeat an experiment under exactly the same conditions as the original to see if the results are the same.

TABLE 1-1.
Common American Phrases Used in Place of Exact Numbers, With Absolute Values Added.*

The nonspecific measures given below are often used to represent real quantities. Such measures violate the objectivity that is the aim of science.

Common Phrase	Absolute Value(s)
One	1
Only one	1
A couple	2 to 4
A few	3 to 5
Quite a few	3 to 6
Several	3 to 9
Many	3 to 8
Most ("most authorities")	4 to 6
Half a dozen	5 to 7
A lot	6 to 10
Quite a lot	7 to 11
A whole lot	8 to 17
Ten	9 to 11
Around ten	7 to 13
A dozen	11 to 13
About a dozen	9 to 15
A bunch	8 to 15
A whole bunch	9 to 19
A few hundred	75 to 125
A couple of hundred	99 to 139
Half a million: promoter's estimate of crowd size	90,000 to 125,000
A majority	50% + 1
A clear majority	51%
A vast majority	52% to 60%
An overwhelming majority	61% to 70%
Practically all/everyone	76% to 80%
All/everyone	81% to 85%
Absolutely all/everyone	86% to 90%
Street value: narcotic agent's valuation	Divide by 100 to find actual

*Named for technical writer Don Ried, who quantified the first values; usually called just "Ried's Table."
Source: Info World, December 6, 1982, p. 46.

issue of research ethics, including intentional scientific dishonesty, later in this chapter.

One aspect of scientific communication that distinguishes it from other forms of communication is its **objectivity**. Results of an experiment are not likely to be labeled "awesome" or "terrific"—instead, the scientist tries to report what was found with as little "editorializing" as possible. Readers or listeners can then form their own opinions about the results. Scientific communication can be done poorly, as evidenced by the reports of opinion polls that often appear in the popular press and on TV and radio. The reader or listener is told that a "substantial number," a "clear majority," or a "disappointingly small" number of people favor a candidate or have a particular opinion. A scientist would simply report the number of people, possibly compare that number to another number, and let the reader decide the importance of the number or the comparison. Table 1–1 shows some common "interpretations" of numbers and percentages. Scientists must avoid this type of exaggeration or distortion.

■ PSYCHOLOGICAL RESEARCH

Perhaps the best way to go about describing psychological research is to pose a few related questions. These questions are: *Whose behavior is studied? Where is behavior studied?* and *How is behavior studied?*

Whose Behavior Is Studied?

The issue of who will serve as a subject in a psychological study is based on the idea of a **sample.** When we take a sample of something, we use a small portion in order to make an evaluation of the whole portion. For example, when goods are manufactured, the finished product is "sampled" by quality control inspectors to make sure that it meets some standard of appearance or performance. If a certain percentage of "bad" units are uncovered, the entire production run may be discarded or examined. The inspector is not particularly interested in the units that make up the sample. These units are important only because they are thought to be representative of the entire production run. It is not practical to test every unit of production, but it is reasonable to make a guess or inference about every unit based on a representative sample of those units.

An example with which you might be more familiar is cooking. Typically, when you are preparing something like a stew, which requires just the right amount of seasoning, you continually taste the "product" while it is cooking. After tasting it, you might add a little salt or a dash of a particular spice. You sample the stew to make sure that it will meet your standards of taste. When you sample the stew, you stir it first and then take a spoonful from anywhere in the pot. You assume that the actual spoonful that you use as the sample is representative of any spoonful that could have been taken from any other spot in the pot.

The process of making a guess or inference from a sample is called **generalization;** a general statement is made from a specific piece of information. The general statement refers to the **population,** or all possible members of the group in question. This is where the link appears between the sampling process and the decision about "who" to study. Consider the manufacturing operation again. Suppose that the company made both bicycles and doorbells. It wouldn't make sense for the inspectors to pull a sample of bicycles for examination and, on the basis of their measurements, make a statement about the quality of the doorbells made that week. If you want to make broad or general statements about a particular population, you must sample from that population. In the stew example, if you simply took a spoonful from the top of the pot without stirring first, you could not really be sure if this spoonful fairly represented the taste of all of the stew (the population). In psychological research, this means that the subjects must be representative of the population of interest—the group to which we hope to generalize.

In deciding on a sample of subjects, the researcher faces a number of choices. The first choice is whether to use animals or humans, but there are other, less obvious, choices. If we decide that human subjects are appropriate, should we use males, females, or a mixture of males and females? Should we include subjects of all ages, or only those between the ages of 18 and 22? Does it matter if all of the subjects are volunteers from introductory psychology classes? These are important considerations, because the choices that are made will determine how widely the results of the research can be applied or generalized.

College students are the most widely studied group of human subjects. Over the years, concern has grown that many of our psychological theories are actually theories based on the behavior of college sophomores, which may have little relevance for other humans (or even for those same college students once they leave the college environment). In a recent review of the articles published in two psychology journals in the year 1981, Rubenstein (1982) found that 77 percent of the studies used college students as subjects. Approximately 26 percent of Americans between the ages of 18 and 24 were enrolled in college in 1981, and, as Rubenstein points out, a large number of those students were middle-class whites.

In considering the choice of subjects, an important distinction should be kept in mind. Some research is done with the intention of generalizing the result from the sample of subjects to the population in general. Other research studies are conducted to refine or develop a theory of behavior (Mook, 1983). For example, we may want to see if

---

Objectivity. Freedom from bias or self-serving interpretation.
Sample. A selected part or portion that represents a whole; in particular, one that represents the population being considered.

Generalization. Making a general statement from a specific piece of information.
Population. All possible members of a group being considered.

our theory holds up in the best and most controlled of circumstances (such as the laboratory with college-student subjects) before we try it out in a more demanding setting (such as a control tower with air-traffic-controller subjects). If our theory will not predict behavior in ideal circumstances, it can't possibly predict behavior in other settings.

It would be fair to say that in some circumstances the use of college students as subjects makes no sense while in other circumstances they are perfectly suitable subjects. Whether college students are appropriate subjects depends very much on the purpose of the research. If we are testing for normal night vision, students are as suitable as anyone else. If we want to generalize theories of substance abuse to a larger population, a different sample might be more appropriate.

The concept of generalization brings up the issue of animals and the extent to which research with animals can generalize to the behavior of human beings. Humans are unique in many respects, but they also share many characteristics with members of other species. These similarities include blood composition, organ structure, sensory apparatus, nervous system components, and reflexes. Given such similarities, it would seem reasonable to generalize to humans from the research on animals, but only when considering areas in which the two groups are similar. There are other characteristics that belong to only certain animals and generalizing to humans from those uniquely nonhuman characteristics would be illogical.

The way in which we pick subjects for research is related to the concept of bias in research. An important characteristic of scientific activity is that it is designed to be unbiased. To the extent that a particular sample of subjects distorts our view of how the population of interest behaves, the results of the research are biased. Through various safeguards, scientists try to control for or eliminate these sources of bias. There are many efficient techniques for such control, but none of these techniques can overcome the wrong choice of subjects.

Where Is Behavior Studied?

In psychological research, a distinction is usually made between the laboratory and the field. The **laboratory** means any controlled environment. It need not be a traditional laboratory with gauges, dials, burners, and sinks. As long as the environment can be controlled and distracting or distorting influences removed, any area—a classroom, a testing room, or even a coat closet—qualifies. For example, hearing is a complicated sensory process. It involves energy from the outside world (in the form of sound frequency and sound intensity), as well as receiving "equipment" on the part of the subject (outer ear, eardrum, auditory nerve, and so on). In order to understand hearing, it is important to control the conditions in which the study is carried out. We might use a special chamber that eliminates extraneous noises. We might use equipment that can be constantly monitored to ensure that differences are not a result of equipment malfunction. Or we might use earphones to present sounds in order to maintain the reliability of the stimulus.

Thus the laboratory is generally chosen as the research site when it is important to study some aspect of behavior, such as sensory mechanisms, in an environment free of distraction and distortion. Often, however, the psychologist is interested in how people behave in complex and less controlled environments such as work settings or city streets. In such cases, the results found in a laboratory might not be identical to those that would be found in the environment of interest, so the research is conducted not in the laboratory but in the **field,** where real-life conditions apply. A striking example of the need for field studies can be found in the United States' space program. Astronauts are subjected to intense laboratory study to determine their susceptibility to motion sickness. In spite of this screening, many astronauts experience motion sickness during the space mission. There is obviously something missing in the laboratory that is present in the actual space mission. This missing element seems to be related to motion sickness. Recently, NASA has begun sending physicians on space flights to conduct a study of motion sickness while it is actually occurring. From our perspective, this means that NASA has decided to add field studies to laboratory studies of motion sickness. While some behaviors are best studied in the laboratory, others must be studied in the field.

Field studies are difficult to conduct, but the results are worth the effort. As an example, consider the following field experiment conducted by Voevodsky (1974). If you have ever ridden in a cab in a large city, you may have wondered if these cabs are involved in many accidents. Well, they are. Not all of the time, but at a much higher frequency than normal passenger cars. An interesting aspect of this problem is that the cabs are hit in the rear end at a much higher rate than you might think. They get hit by other drivers more than they hit others (they are the "hittee" more often than the "hitter"). This makes some sense, since cabs start and stop quickly, often change lanes without signalling, and rapidly change speeds. They are not always predictable. In an attempt to reduce rear-end collisions, an experiment was conducted with 503 cabs in San Francisco. Of this group, 343 experimental cabs were equipped with large yellow brake lights on the surface of the trunk. This made their starting and stopping behavior much more apparent to other drivers. A control group of 160 cabs was not modified in any way. After 10 months, the two groups were compared with respect to the frequency and severity of accidents in which the cab was hit in the rear by another vehicle. There was a substantial difference. There were fewer rear-end accidents involving the experimental cabs; the experimental cabs were involved in 60 percent fewer accidents during those 10 months. As a budding psychologist, you might quickly argue that the cab drivers simply drove more safely because they realized they were subjects in the experiment. However, in this experiment it would have been difficult to keep the subjects unaware.

Fortunately, a clever data analysis was able to make this explanation less likely. It turned out that there was *no difference* between the experimental and control groups in other accident categories, in particular in "front-end" accidents where the cab driver hit another car. It seemed that the only variable affected was the behavior of the "other" driver, not the cab driver. It would be virtually impossible to simulate these conditions in a laboratory. Remember, the conditions included not only traffic density and driving controls (such as brake pedals, turn signals, and steering wheels) but also the mental and

physical characteristics of the respective drivers. There are many similar situations in which a field experiment is the best way to answer a question or solve a problem.

How Is Behavior Studied?

Behavior is studied in three basic ways: We attempt to change it, we watch it, or we ask about it. In an *experiment*, we attempt to change behavior; in *naturalistic observation* and *correlation*, we watch behavior; and in *surveying* and the *case study* method, we ask questions about behavior. Each of these methods is a legitimate way of understanding human behavior, and each has its own place in research.

The Experiment. In the physical sciences, understanding is achieved by looking for things that happen together. In chemistry, Boyle's Law, which describes the relationship between temperature and pressure, is based on the observation that under specific (controlled) circumstances, as temperature increases so does pressure. In fact, the scientist in this case is more than a simple observer; he or she actually does something that produces the observed relationship. In this case, the scientist may light a burner under a flask with a stopper in it; this in turn raises the temperature of the fluid in that flask. Readings of the pressure and temperature show that as temperature increases, so does pressure inside the flask. This is an **experiment.** One element is changed (temperature) to see if there are any effects on a second element (pressure). Since these elements can assume many different values, they are called **variables.** In other words, the values of temperature and pressure are not fixed and unmoving; they are free to vary. But in our experiment, one of these variables seems to control the other. We do not change pressure and measure temperature; we change temperature and look for its effect on pressure. In order to distinguish which variable has been changed by the experimenter, we attach

---

Laboratory. Any controlled environment in which research is conducted.

Field. Real-world conditions as opposed to controlled conditions in the laboratory.

Experiment. Under controlled conditions, changing one element in order to observe the effect on another element.

Variable. A quantity that may increase or decrease.

the label "independent" to that variable. The **independent variable** represents the change imposed by the experimenter. The other variable, the one that is measured in order to determine any effects of the independent variable, is called the **dependent variable.** In our chemistry experiment, temperature is the independent variable and pressure is the dependent variable.

In psychological experiments, behavior of one form or another is the dependent variable. In our example of studies of the effects of TV on aggression in children, watching violent shows on TV would be classified as the independent variable. Aggressive behavior would be the dependent variable. Experiments add to our knowledge by allowing us to notice that the changes in the independent and dependent variables seem somehow connected. When one variable changes, so does the other. When heat is increased, pressure also increases. In conducting experiments, it is important to eliminate any influences other than the independent variable that might affect the dependent variable. In our study of TV and aggression, we might want to make sure that the subjects were not looking for cues from the observer as to what they were "expected" to do. To control for this possibility, we might have the observer watch the children interact through a one-way mirror. If we want to control for possible socioeconomic characteristics (such as family education level or parents' income) that might influence the level or type of aggressive behavior a child engages in, we could limit our experiment to children with certain socioeconomic characteristics. In this case, we would be controlling the makeup of the sample rather than the behavior of the subjects in that sample or the behavior of the experimenter or observer.

The change made in the independent variable by the experimenter is actually a form of control—the experimenter controls the amount of that variable present in a given experiment. Another type of control that should be present in experiments is the inclusion of a control group. A **control group** is a group of subjects similar in composition to the group that experiences the change in the independent variable (called the **experimental group**). In the control group, however, the change in the independent variable is not presented to the subjects. For example, in the aggression experiment, we might com-

pare the level of aggressive play in children who saw a violent TV program and in children who engaged in another activity (such as playing with building blocks). The group that was not exposed to the independent variable (violent TV programs) would be the control group; the group that was exposed to it is the experimental group. If the level of the dependent variable (aggressive play) really depends on the level or presence of the independent variable (violent TV programs), then there should be no systematic change in the aggressiveness of the control group (since they were not exposed to the independent variable, violent TV programs).

Subjects may serve as their own control group. For example, we could measure the amount of aggressive play before seeing TV and after seeing TV and then compare the two levels. If violent shows on TV had an effect on aggressive behavior, we should notice that there was an increase in aggressive behavior above the **base rate** (the pre-exposure level of aggressive behavior). This type of experiment can be powerful since we can automatically control for differences between experimental and control group characteristics that might account for the observed differences in behavior. When subjects serve as their own control group, there *are* no such group differences.

Even with these various forms of control, scientists occasionally make mistakes. Sometimes these mistakes are random and sometimes they are not. Random mistakes include simple arithmetic errors, failure to correctly record what someone said, or misreading an instrument. In the TV-aggression study, for example, an experimenter might mistakenly record a behavior as aggressive when it is not, or place a code representing a behavior next to the wrong child's name. This sort of mistake is bound to occur now and then, no matter how careful the scientist is. We expect these random mistakes to cancel each other out over the course of the study.

Mistakes that are not random are harder to handle. Such mistakes include the systematic error or bias that can creep into a study through some behavior of the scientist. This is not intentional on the part of the scientist, but it causes problems just the same. The scientist has a hypothesis or guess about what is going to happen; as a result, he or she may be looking for certain behaviors more than for others. In the TV-aggression study, if the children

A NEW LOOK FOR AN OLD TEST

I like mechanics magazines.
I used to like the game "drop-the-handkerchief."
I like to take a bath.

These items are from a well-known test used to assess personality and mental health. The test, the *Minnesota Multiphasic Personality Inventory,* or *MMPI,* is one of the oldest and most widely used of psychological tests. Millions of people, ranging from U.S. job applicants to Soviet cosmonauts, have worked their way through its 550-item inventory. But users will soon be taking a new version of the 44-year-old test. One of the landmarks of psychology is undergoing a face lift.

The Minnesota Multiphasic Personality Inventory was first developed in the late 1930s to help identify those with psychological problems. During World War II the MMPI was widely used by military personnel to quickly spot attitudes toward authority and other potentially troubling characteristics of recruits.

To complete the new MMPI, subjects now have to answer a total of 704 questions about their attitudes, behaviors, symptoms, and beliefs using true-false or "cannot say" responses. The test is not scored item-by-item, however. Rather, the scores are summarized as a personality profile based on patterns of responses. One can then look in the MMPI manual for descriptions of personality characteristics associated with that profile.

The psychologists who are revising the MMPI are aiming to bring it up-to-date with modern attitudes, language, and professional needs. For some items on the test, answers once considered "abnormal" would now be mainstream by social standards. For example, a woman who answered "true" to the question "I like mechanics magazines" would not be automatically profiled as abnormally masculine. Other MMPI revisions will be simple and obvious. Dated references to a children's game like "drop-the-handkerchief" will come out. The item "I like to take a bath," which had been getting false answers from shower takers, will now read "I like to take a bath or shower." The new test will also include items that relate to contemporary problems such as eating disorders, drug abuse, and the Type-A personality.

One important change is that the new MMPI has separate evaluation scales for adolescents. The original test was not well adapted to adolescent psychology. In fact, in the old test, it was possible for a teenager temporarily caught in adolescent turmoil to fit a profile similar to the adult psychopath.

have just finished watching a violent cartoon the scientist may be looking very carefully for any signs of aggression. Sure enough, they pop up all over the place. The problem is that they may be more in the mind of the experimenter than in the behavior of the children.

Fortunately, there is a way out of this problem. The simplest thing to do is to hire data recorders who know nothing about the hypothesis or the variables involved. In the TV-aggression study, we could have the children watch TV in one room and then come into another room to play. In that other room would be an observer who has no idea what the children did prior to coming into the room or why they are being observed in the first place. The task of the observer would be to simply tally the numbers of different kinds of behavior for each child, and turn those tallies over to the scientist.

In addition to the scientist's or experimenter's expectations, subjects also may have expectations. It is common for subjects to want to "please" the experimenter or to make the study "turn out right." They can do this by trying to figure out how they should act if the hypothesis were true and then act-

Independent variable. In an experiment, the variable or element that is changed in order to see the effect on the other variables or elements.

Dependent variable. In an experiment, the variable that is measured to perceive any change as a result of changing the other (independent) variable(s).

Control group. In an experiment, a group that is similar to the experimental group that is not exposed to the independent variable.

Experimental group. In an experiment, a group that is exposed to the independent variable.

Base rate. In an experiment, the value or measure of the dependent variable before the independent variable is changed; the value or measure of the dependent variable before the experiment begins.

ing that way. In effect, the subject becomes a collaborator in the study rather than a randomly sampled subject. This type of bias can be handled in the same way as experimenter bias: The subject can be kept *blind* to the appropriate behavior. There are several ways to accomplish this. The most common is the **single-blind experiment**: Subjects in the control group are not told whether they are in the control group or the experimental group. This means that even if they wanted to help the experimenter, they would not know what behavior was appropriate. In drug studies, for instance, subjects in control groups are often given capsules that contain nothing but sugar or milk powder. These fake capsules are called **placebos** (a Latin word used in medical research to mean an inactive substance).

If we were concerned about possible bias on the part of both the experimenter and the subject, we might create what is known as a **double-blind experiment**. In this type of experiment, neither experimenter nor subject knows which subjects are "experimental" and which are "control."

Naturalistic Observation. It is often impossible to change the levels of an independent variable, for either practical or ethical reasons. For example, in the case of our TV-aggression study, if we have some evidence that watching violent shows on TV leads to aggression, it might be judged unethical to create conditions that would lead to antisocial behavior in children. Therefore, research in psychology is often accomplished through the process of **naturalistic observation**. Using this method, the researcher is more passive than he or she would be in an experiment. No changes are made in any independent variable. Instead, the researcher simply records various behaviors and environmental events. For example, a psychologist interested in aggressive

---

REVIEW QUESTIONS

10. Match the following terms with the correct definition:
    ___ sample
    ___ population
    ___ generalization

    A. all possible members of a group
    B. a selected part or portion that represents a whole
    C. an assumption about behavior of a group based on the behavior of part of the group

11. Studying behavior in the laboratory means studying it under _____ conditions; studying behavior in the field means studying it under _____ conditions.

12. The independent/dependent variable represents the change imposed by the experimenter; the independent/dependent variable is measured to see the effects of that change.

13. Match the following terms with the correct definition:
    ___ control group
    ___ experimental group
    ___ placebos
    ___ single-blind experiment
    ___ double-blind experiment
    ___ base rate

    A. fake capsules taken by the control group in drug studies
    B. a type of experiment in which neither the experimenter nor the subject knows who is in the control group and who is in the experimental group
    C. group not exposed to the independent variable
    D. a type of experiment in which the subjects do not know whether they are in the control group or the experimental group
    E. group exposed to the independent variable
    F. the value of the dependent variable before the experiment begins

14. In an experiment, the scientist watches/changes/asks questions about behavior.

Answers: 10. sample, B; population, A; generalization, C. 11. controlled; real-life 12. independent; dependent 13. control group, C; experimental group, E; placebos, A; single-blind experiment, D; double-blind experiment, B; base rate, F. 14. changes

behavior and its relationship to watching violent shows on TV may simply observe children at home or in play or school groups and record the types of TV programs they watched and the types of behavior that seemed to occur immediately after they watched various types of programs. The researcher hopes (hypothesizes) that the right variables were chosen for observation and recording. Even if a relationship is uncovered, the researcher still knows nothing about the *cause* of the behavior, only about the conditions that were there before and at the same time the behavior occurred.

As an example of a clever study based on naturalistic observation, consider the following research conducted by Barash (1974). He was interested in the behavior of people in the dentist's office. He recorded the behavior of both patients and nonpatients in the waiting room and noticed that patients were considerably more restless than nonpatients. This is not a surprise to anyone who has had a tooth pulled or filled; there is some apprehension involved in that wait. Nevertheless, from this simple observation, one might proceed to examine the restlessness of young vs. old patients, men vs. women, or patients on their first visit to this dentist vs. patients who have been treated on a regular basis. The point is that simple observation can provide a wealth of hypotheses to test. It is safe to say that many theories of behavior have developed from simple observation.

The Correlational Approach. Years ago, a sports writer noted wisely that "if you see a man with a spot on his tie, you don't need to look at his shoes—they're dirty too." Clever observers have always noted that certain events in life frequently occur together. For example, most of the people in my locker room know that if you are taking a shower and the water pressure drops suddenly, you should jump out from under the shower immediately because you will be scalded within seconds if you don't. The reason is that whenever a toilet is flushed

in the adjacent bathroom, the cold water coming into that section of the locker room is diverted to the bathroom to refill the toilet tank, leaving only hot water for the showers. Over the years, most of us have made the association between a drop in water pressure and an increase in temperature. We've learned to use the **correlational approach** in understanding our environment.

Researchers use the correlational approach in a more systematic way than do my locker room buddies, but the basic mechanism is the same—noting that two things appear together. The difference is that the researcher actually looks for variables that might appear together, and conducts an analysis to see if and how closely the variables are associated. A statistical index called a correlation coefficient is used to demonstrate the degree and direction of the relationship. This index is described in detail in the Appendix.

The correlational approach is most often used to examine the relationships among various characteristics of a single entity. For example, a researcher might want to examine the relationship between the job satisfaction of industrial workers and their productivity. This could be accomplished by administering a job satisfaction questionnaire to a sample of workers, getting a measure of their productivity, and calculating a correlation coefficient that would describe the extent to which satisfaction and productivity were associated. Suppose that we discovered that there was a substantial positive relationship between satisfaction and productivity. Could we then take the next step and say that satisfaction *causes* productivity? No, we could not. As with naturalistic observation, we must be cautious in making cause–effect statements. In the correlational approach, we know only that two variables are associated but we do not know if one causes the other. In this instance, it might be that the opportunity to be productive causes satisfaction. Many people report that they are satisfied when they have been able to accomplish a great deal at work. Alternative-

---

Single-blind experiment. A type of experiment in which subjects are not aware whether they are in the experimental group or the control group.

Placebo. In drug studies, pills made of nothing but sugar or milk powder; an inactive substance.

Double-blind experiment. A type of experiment in which neither the subjects nor the observers are aware of which subjects are part of the experimental group and which are part of the control group.

Naturalistic observation. A research method in which the scientist records behaviors and environmental events.

Correlational approach. Research method that looks to identify the degree of relation, or correlation, among two or more variables that appear together.

ly, it might be that both high productivity and high satisfaction are both caused by a third variable—high pay.

Although the correlational approach does not permit any firm statements about cause and effect, it can be extremely useful in pointing out basic associations that deserve closer investigation, perhaps in a laboratory experiment.

The Survey. In both the experiment and in naturalistic observation, the scientist observes how subjects behave. The experimenter in a sense "causes" changes in behavior; the observer notices changes. Sometimes, instead of watching subjects behave, a researcher can ask subjects how they might react in a given situation or how they feel about a particular set of circumstances. Most of us have taken part in market surveys in which an interviewer asks questions about preferences for certain items. What colors do we like most? Do we prefer fast cars or safe cars? Politicians are forever conducting opinion polls to estimate their "strength" (what percentage of the vote they can expect to get). Many psychologists also use surveys or questionnaires in their research. For instance, they ask subjects to answer questions about educational background, personality characteristics, or career goals. They may then compare these answers with reported leisure activities, marital difficulties, or choice of a college major in an attempt to uncover some possible explanations for behaviors such as jogging, fights with a spouse, or the decision to become a psychology major.

There are several advantages to **survey** research. It is often much easier to conduct than laboratory or field experiments. In addition, it allows the researcher to jump forward or backward in time by asking subjects what they did 6 months ago or what they might do 6 months in the future. But with these advantages come problems. First, the subjects might intentionally or unintentionally bias their answers. In political polling people will commonly say they plan to vote for candidate A but then actually vote for candidate B. Similarly, in psychological research, people may not want to admit to doing or thinking about certain behaviors (for example, being against the ERA or disliking members of certain minority groups) and, as a result, they may not answer questions truthfully.

A second drawback to survey research is having

In survey research, a questionnaire is designed and given to a sample of people. The usefulness of this method depends on interviewing a correct sample of people.

to make sure that the correct sample is questioned. This is no more serious a problem than in other methods of research, but it seems as if survey research often depends on convenience for subject selection rather than on developing a sampling plan based on the characteristics of the population of interest.

Finally, when we are questioning subjects about past events, we must often depend on their memory. As we will see in Chapter 8, memory is an ability on which people vary. Not every subject in a survey sample can be expected to have an equally good or reliable memory for events that occurred several months or years ago. To the extent to which remembered events differ from real events, the relationships under examination will be distorted.

Well-designed survey research can be very informative. For example, in 1975, the Institute for Social Research at the University of Michigan did a survey of high-school seniors on topics related to drug use (Johnston, Bachman, and O'Malley, 1980). They have repeated this survey each year since. Their sampling plan calls for first selecting particular geographic areas, then selecting high schools within those areas, and finally selecting individual seniors within those schools. This is done independently each year. The survey is administered in approximately 125 schools each year, with approximately 17,000 students completing the survey each year. As a result of the care with which the sampling methods were chosen and the questionnaires developed and administered, it has been possible to identify some important trends in drug use that have appeared during 1980 (as compared to earlier years). A sample of their findings includes the following:

□ Cigarette smoking has declined about 4 percent over that period.
□ Daily marijuana use among high-school seniors has dropped from 10.3 percent to 9.1 percent.
□ The percentage of high-school seniors who used some illicit drug other than marijuana increased from 28 percent to 30 percent.
□ From 1978 to 1980, there was an increase of 15 percent (from 35 percent to 50 percent) in the number of seniors perceiving regular marijuana use as potentially harmful.

These findings suggest many questions that could be studied by psychologists. As you will see in later chapters, the findings in survey research can be especially useful in identifying attitude change over time, differences among groups with respect to certain opinions, and the effects of certain environmental events (changes in laws, nuclear accidents such as the one that occurred in the Chernobyl nuclear power station in the Soviet Ukraine) on reported behavior. Even though it is seldom possible to draw any causal inferences from survey research, this method is an important tool in psychological research.

The Case Study. There is a final method of data collection that is often used by psychologists. The psychologist might spend a good deal of time examining one particular person or situation in order to get some ideas about what is going on. The **case study** is not really as valuable in answering questions as it is in helping the psychologist to ask questions. For example, a clinical psychologist might get a very detailed personal history from a patient suffering from anxiety attacks. Since the psychologist is not treating a population of people who have the same characteristics as this patient, there is no particular concern about sampling. On the basis of this history, the psychologist might write down three or four explanations that might account for the anxiety attacks; for example: Dissatisfaction with a marriage partner, an overbearing boss, or a fear of looking silly in public. The detailed case history helps to generate those alternative explanations. The psychologist can then go about exploring each of these possibilities until one seems to emerge as most likely.

Analyzing Results

The study may be completed and the observations or data in hand, but the researcher is hardly finished with the research. Two tasks remain—analysis and communication: The results must be analyzed and the conclusions stated. In the Appendix of this text you will learn about the common statistical procedures and terminology used in analysis. Here we will consider the role of analysis in the broader context of science. Remember, we began by pointing out that science, above all else, revolves around questions. The scientist develops a question (hypothesis) and carries out certain procedural and observational activities in order to answer that question. Does watching violent TV shows lead to increased levels of aggression in children? The analysis of the

---

Survey. Research method in which the scientist questions subjects about their behavior or attitudes.

Case study. Research method in which the scientist studies one person in depth. For example, in a case study a clinical psychologist would take a detailed personal history of each patient.

data should be directed toward an elimination of one of two competing hypotheses:

A: Watching violent shows on TV is related to increased aggression, or

B: Watching violent shows on TV is not related to increased aggression.

In order to see what really can be accomplished by analysis, it might help to consider the issue from a different perspective. In analyzing the results of a study, a scientist is really asking a very basic question: Is there a difference? In the case of an experiment, the difference that is examined is between an experimental group and a control group or between a sample of subjects before an event and after an event. In the case of naturalistic observation, the difference might be between the two groups observed (men and women, children and adults). In a survey, the difference might be between two groups questioned (democrats and republicans, heterosexuals and homosexuals).

A difference between groups has to be of a certain magnitude or size before we will accept that difference as "real" rather than as a result of some chance characteristic of the sample. In the terminology of research this magnitude takes the form of a **probability statement**. A scientist usually concludes that a difference of a particular magnitude is "significant at the .05 level of confidence." Translated into common terminology, this means that we would find a difference of this magnitude of chance alone only 5 times in 100. In other words, if we chose two samples of subjects 100 times, and took measurements on the behavior in question (the dependent variable) without presenting any independent variable (or experimental treatment), we would be likely to find a difference of this size or magnitude in only 5 cases. This is an indirect way of stating that something really happened. The non-scientist assumes that if an effect appears, it will always appear. The scientist is more cautious. Take a coin flip as an example. If you flip a coin once and it lands head up, would you conclude that it will always land head up? Probably not. Instead, you would flip the coin a number of times and consider the distribution of heads and tails for all flips. If a head appears on 99 of 100 occasions, then you may say with some confidence that there is a bias toward heads for that particular coin. If a head had appeared only 75 of 100 times, you would be somewhat less confident. The confidence of the scientist in the results of an experiment is similarly influenced. If the difference between two groups is great, there is more confidence that an effect really exists. If the difference is modest, there is less confidence that it exists.

We will explain some of these concepts in much greater detail in the Appendix. For the purposes of this chapter, however, keep in mind that a research study is not complete until the scientist comes to some conclusion about the differences between the groups. It is the presence or absence of this difference that tells the scientist something about the relationship (or lack of relationship) between the variables being examined.

When you start doing research studies you quickly discover that conclusions are not as easy to draw as you might think. The difficulty with drawing conclusions is well illustrated by a recent study of beer drinking (Geller, 1984). A psychologist decided to examine the relationship between the amount of beer consumed and the method by which it was served. He visited three bars close to the university where he taught. During those visits, he and his fellow researchers observed the beer drinking behaviors of 300 individuals. Using this data collection method, the psychologist discovered that serving from a pitcher was associated with higher beer consumption (on the average, 35 ounces) than serving single draft beers (12 ounces) or serving beer from a bottle (15 ounces). As a result of this association, the psychologist suggested that taverns could reduce drunkenness by no longer serving beer by the pitcher.

As you might expect, there was some skepticism concerning this association, and certainly the recommendation it inspired, among beer drinkers, particularly those who drank beer from pitchers. When the results of this research made the newspapers, I asked my introductory psychology class to interpret the results. The following is just a sample of the explanations that challenged the accuracy of the results (and the wisdom of the recommendations) provided by class members:

1. The choice of taverns was biased.
2. The choice of times to visit the taverns was biased.

3. The choice of days to visit the tavern was biased.
4. The age of the drinkers was not taken into account.
5. The observers were biased.
6. The size of the drinking groups was not taken into account.
7. No adjustment was made for how long the drinkers spent at the bar.
8. It was not clear whether people who drank beer by the bottle used a glass or not.
9. One cannot determine whether people who are light drinkers choose glasses and avoid pitchers on purpose.
10. Body size was not taken into account in analyzing drinking habits.

You can probably add some explanations or qualifications of your own to the list. An especially interesting explanation for the observed association was provided by a student who pointed out that there is an "ethic" to beer drinking. When you sit and drink with others, it is common for each individual to take a turn in buying a "round" of drinks. It is considered to be poor manners to leave without buying a round. As a result, in the name of "fairness" more beer than normal might be ordered. This explanation is supported, to some extent, by another finding of the study: Groups consumed more beer (27 to 33 ounces) than solitary drinkers (17 ounces). It is interesting to note that Geller did not suggest that group drinking be banned, even though that could be expected to have the same effect as banning pitchers of beer according to his data.

It should be obvious from this example that research studies are complex and that their conclusions are limited by the amount of control that can be exercised over the data collection. The greater the number of unmeasured variables that could affect the interpretation, the weaker the conclusion must be.

■ ETHICS

Because of the importance of the topics that scientists often study, it is tempting to think of any scientific activity as justified. To some it might seem as if the end (knowledge) justifies the means (scientific research), regardless of the means. This is not the case. In World War II, "scientific" experiments were carried out by the German researchers on prisoners of war, usually Jews. This research was "scientific" by every definition. It was also unethical by every definition. As with many other endeavors, in psychological research there are right and wrong ways to do things. In the previous sections of this chapter, *right* has meant efficient or unambiguous or representative. In this section we will consider *right* as it is defined by ethical principles.

Ethics, in science, has two concerns: Honesty and the rights of subjects. Both issues involve trust. The scientific community assumes that the research has been done in a manner identical to the published reports of that research. It is this assumption that allows for replicability and communication, as was discussed earlier. When data are falsified or when shortcuts in procedures are taken but not described, the whole body of knowledge in an area comes into question. As previously mentioned, it seems very likely that Sir Cyril Burt made up data to justify his belief that intelligence is inherited. When his fraud was uncovered, all of Burt's research and the studies that used this research as a point of departure came under question. This fraud has received a good deal of attention, not only because it points out that scientists are not always honest, but also because certain policies of the school system in Great Britain reflected Burt's "findings" (Kamin, 1974). In this case, it was not just the scientific community that was harmed by Burt's deception, but the entire British population as well.

Ethical Procedures in Human Research

The second concern of ethics in science, the rights of subjects, has received a good deal of attention in the past two decades. A case study may be instructive. Stanley Milgram conducted a series of classic experiments on the topic of conformity (Milgram, 1963). He was interested in seeing to what extent

---

Probability statement. A statement estimating the likelihood that an observed experimental effect was due to chance.

subjects would accept instructions to administer shocks to other "subjects." The individuals receiving the shocks were actually **confederates**, that is, they played the role of subjects but never really received any shocks. In some of the most extreme cases, the confederates screamed and shouted for the real subject to stop administering the shocks, but the experimenter urged and even demanded that the real subject continue with the experiment.

Milgram's research raised several questions. The first concerned what has come to be known as **deception research**. Whether such research should be conducted is debatable. In this type of research, the subject is fooled into believing something. Those in favor of deception research argue that it is the only way to establish the realistic conditions necessary for studying the behavior in question. Those opposed to deception research argue that the cost in terms of potential damage to subjects is not worth the benefits of the research, and that in most cases the research can and should be designed in a nondeceptive manner. Fewer deception studies are being conducted now than 20 years ago, but as long as they are being conducted, guidelines are necessary. Each proposed deception study should be carefully considered and approved only if deception is clearly the only way to examine the variable of interest. Even in those cases, care should be taken to debrief subjects so that they fully understand the purpose of the research and why it was necessary to deceive them.

Milgram's study of conformity raised another, more serious, issue that has had a substantial impact on the way research is conducted. It was obvious after his study that the scientist or researcher has awesome power in the eyes of the subjects. Subjects will do whatever the experimenter asks of them because of the trust they place in science and scientists. In Milgram's study, in order to get the real subjects to continue to administer the shocks, the experimenter told them that they would "ruin the experiment" if they didn't. In later discussions with the subjects, they confirmed that this argument had been persuasive. As a result of these disclosures, it became apparent that there was some need for a clear statement of what subjects' rights are in experiments and of how experimenters should conduct themselves. Thus, the notoriety of Milgram's study was due, in part, to its success. Milgram had

hypothesized that conditions could be created in which people would conform to suggestions to harm other people. His hypothesis proved correct. If it had not, it is unlikely that his study would be as well known as it is today. Almost by accident, it became apparent that experimenters wielded substantial power in dealing with subjects and that they should be concerned with their subjects' rights *before* an experiment is begun.

After a lengthy consideration of the needs of the researcher and the rights of the subject, the American Psychological Association (APA) published a list of principles to follow in conducting ethical research with human subjects. In most universities and research institutes, the process of subject protection has been taken a step further. Committees have been established to review research proposals involving the use of human subjects, and a group of fellow scientists actually reviews the proposed study in order to guarantee that ethical standards are maintained. It is the responsibility of the members of that committee to act as an advocate for the subject. They look for anything that might prove harmful to the subject and they require the researcher to eliminate the potential harm. Most government research grants require that such a review be made for every funded project.

While the value of these safeguards is obvious, there are also costs involved. There is some fear that if too rigid a view is taken of ethical behavior and subjects' rights, the results of the eventual research will be trivial or worthless. Gergen (1973) wonders if "informed consent" is really important in many experiments. As Gergen points out, the most harm that many experiments can do is to bore the subjects, and the APA does not yet consider inducing boredom as unethical. As an example, consider a traditional verbal learning experiment. The subject comes into a room, sits down, and is presented with a list of words to memorize. After a few minutes for memorization, the subject is then asked to recall the list. Perhaps the experimental manipulation was the length of the list; some subjects received longer lists and some received shorter lists. It is hard to see how this procedure could bring "harm" to the subject. Nevertheless, even though boredom may be the greatest danger, the subject must be given the chance to withdraw from the experiment at any time.

But should the subject be told about the hypothesis? Suppose we told the subjects in the verbal learning study what the hypothesis was. And suppose that just for the fun of it, some subjects decided to "screw up" the results, another group of subjects decided to "help out the experimenter," and a third group of subjects decided that the hypothesis was stupid and that they wouldn't really try at all. Under these circumstances, it is unlikely that the experimenter would learn anything about memory lists. Instead, a completely different hypothesis is being tested, that is, how subjects react to experiments in general.

An experiment with a hypothesis very much like this was actually carried out by Resnick and Schwartz (1973). Their experimental treatment was to tell one group of subjects what the hypothesis of a verbal learning study was and to withhold knowledge of the hypothesis from a second experimental group. The verbal learning hypothesis was that experimenter feedback would effect verbalization. Each time the subject used the words "I" or "we" to begin a sentence, the experimenter would say "ok" or "good." Previous studies had shown that this type of feedback does increase the frequency of the target words (I and we). In the Resnick and Schwartz study, the results obtained from the "uninformed" group were similar to those found in other studies. The results in the "informed" group were exactly opposite to the results of earlier studies. The subjects in this condition used the words "I" and "we" with a much lower frequency. It is hard to believe that the behavior of the subjects in the "informed" group was not a result of being told the experimental hypothesis. Therefore, if no harm is likely, the experimenter is not required to reveal the hypothesis (although the subject will still be given a form listing the right of subjects to withdraw from the experiment and the extent to which data are kept confidential).

Perhaps the simplest way of thinking about ethical conduct in human research has been suggested by Baumrind (1971). She suggests that we simply apply the Golden Rule: Do unto others as you would have them do unto you.

Ethical Procedures in Animal Research

In the same sense that human subjects do not exist for the convenience of the experimenter, neither do nonhuman subjects. It is common to use a wide range of animals in psychological research. To mention but a few species, research has been conducted with dogs, cats, rats, mice, monkeys, gerbils, pigeons, and fish. These subjects are even more at the mercy of the experimenter than human subjects. In 1977, the APA published a set of principles for the conduct of animal research. These principles require that scientists:

1. Be skilled in the care and treatment of laboratory animals.
2. Induce pain or discomfort in animals only when no other alternative experimental treatments are suitable.
3. Conduct surgery only when an animal has been appropriately anesthetized.
4. Take precautions to minimize infection or injury in animals.
5. Dispose of animals promptly and in a humane manner when such action is necessary.

Since animals cannot tell an experimenter of misgivings about the experiment, or express in any efficient way their displeasure with particular treatments, it is even more important that an experimenter keep in mind the principles that govern their treatment.

There is a second, more practical reason for taking proper care of animal subjects. Underfed, diseased, or otherwise distressed animals will not perform "naturally." You remember from our earlier discussion that the goal of sampling and experimentation is to generalize to a larger population of subjects from which the sample is selected. If we selected a sample of normal healthy white rats, and allowed them to catch diseases or become undernourished, we can hardly expect the results of our experiments with these animals to tell us much about how animals in a normal and healthy population might behave.

There is a final issue with respect to the ethical

Confederate. In an experiment, someone who assists the researcher in manipulating the behavior of the experimental subjects, often by posing as a subject and then acting in a way that will affect the behavior of the other subjects.

Deception research. Research in which subjects are fooled into believing that an experiment is about one thing when it is really about another.

conduct of animal research. The scientist does not relinquish membership in the larger community that makes up our world when he or she puts on a white lab coat. The principles that guide our daily life will also help us in deciding what is and what is not ethical in research settings. Most of us would consider it wrong to abuse a family cat or even a stray dog we might see on the street. There are certain obvious principles of right and wrong. The scientist is no less responsible to those principles than you or I.

Now that we know something about the scientific activities of psychologists, let's take a step back and look at psychology as a profession and the ways in which you might become involved in that profession if your interest in psychology broadens and deepens.

REVIEW QUESTIONS

15. Match the following terms with the correct definitions:

___ experiment

    A. research method in which the scientist studies one person or event in depth

___ naturalistic observation

    B. research method in which the scientist records behaviors and events

___ correlational approach

    C. research method in which the scientist attempts to change behavior

___ survey

    D. research method in which the scientist questions a sample about behavior and attitudes

___ case study

    E. research method in which the scientist observes that variables appear together

16. In science, there are two issues of ethics: _____ and the _____ of subjects.

Answers: **15.** experiment, C; naturalistic observation, B; correlational method, E; survey, D; case study, A. **16.** honesty; rights

---

■ PSYCHOLOGY TODAY

Most professions have an organization of some kind that speaks for them. This might involve statements of goals and acceptable procedures of the members of the organization, lobbying to get or maintain legislation favorable to the members of the organization, or simply educating the public through announcements, publications, and service to the community. Physicians have the American Medical Association, managers have the American Management Association, and psychologists have the American Psychological Association, or APA.

The APA is made up of various groups, or divisions, each one representing a specific area (such as clinical psychology), type of work or research setting (such as military psychology), or professional activity (such as the teaching of psychology). Table 1–2 lists the divisions of the APA. As you can see, the APA is quite a complex organization. Many members belong to more than one division, because they have more than one interest. For example, an industrial psychologist might be involved in constructing employment tests and thus belong to Division 5, and might also be a teacher in a university and thus belong to Division 2. Finally, since an industrial psychologist is probably interested in most of the topics in the subfield of industrial psychology, he or she may also belong to Division 14. Divisions are added as the interests and activities of the members develop.

Areas of Psychology

As you may have gathered from the list of APA divisions, there are several distinct areas of psychology. Figure 1–1 gives you some information about what percentage of APA members can be found in each of these areas. The list of divisions also suggests that psychologists can be found in many different settings performing many different kinds of activities. You can get some idea of the distribution of psychologists in different settings from Figure 1–2. The numbers in these charts tell us things about psychologists in the abstract. It might be helpful to take a look at what these people are likely to do in their jobs (American Psychological Association, 1982).

TABLE 1-2.
Divisions of the American Psychological Association.

1. General psychology	24. Theoretical and philosophical psychology
2. Teaching of psychology	25. Experimental analysis of behavior
3. Experimental psychology	26. History of psychology
5. Evaluation and measurement	27. Community psychology
6. Physiological and comparative psychology	28. Psychopharmacology
7. Developmental psychology	29. Psychotherapy
8. Personality and social psychology	30. Psychological hypnosis
9. SPSSI*	31. State psychological association affairs
10. Psychology and the arts	32. Humanistic psychology
12. Clinical psychology	33. Mental retardation
13. Consulting psychology	34. Population and environmental psychology
14. Industrial and organizational psychology	35. Psychology of women
15. Educational psychology	36. PIRI**
16. School psychology	37. Child and youth services
17. Counseling psychology	38. Health psychology
18. Psychologists in public service	39. Psychoanalysis
19. Military psychology	40. Clinical neuropsychology
20. Adult development and aging	41. Psychology and the law
21. Society of engineering psychologists	42. Psychologists in independent practice
22. Rehabilitation psychology	43. Family Psychology
23. Consumer psychology	44. Society for the psychological study of lesbian and gay issues

Note: There are no Divisions 4 or 11; they do not exist; they never have existed. The reason for this is not very interesting—it's better to simply accept it without pursuing the matter further.
*SPSSI = Society for the Psychological Study of Social Issues
**PIRI = Psychologists Interested in Religious Issues
Source: Vandenbos et al., 1981.

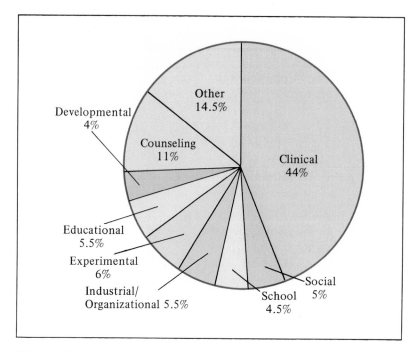

Figure 1-1
This chart shows the number of APA members who work in each of the eight major areas of psychology. *(Stapp et al., 1981)*

□ The *experimental pyschologist* is trained in designing and conducting research in such areas as learning, sensation, perception, human performance, emotion, motivation, language, thinking, and animal behavior.

□ The *clinical psychologist* specializes in the assessment and treatment of people with emotional or adjustment problems and is knowledgeable about the psychology of personality. He or she may also be involved in establishing community mental health programs.

□ The *social psychologist* studies the effects of groups on the behavior of the individual and may be involved in studies of attitudes, consumer research, prejudice, or conflict resolution.

□ The *personnel psychologist* focuses specifically on the hiring, training, assignment, and promotion of employees, using tools such as tests, interviews, and application blanks to predict success and happiness on the job.

□ The *human factors psychologist* designs environments in which people live and work and develops man–machine systems that take into account human capacities and limitations.

□ The *developmental psychologist* studies the patterns of change in human beings from conception to death and may be involved in developing activities and environments that are best suited for people of particular ages.

Figure 1-2
Psychologists work in a number of settings; the chart here shows where psychologists are employed. *(Stapp et al., 1981)*

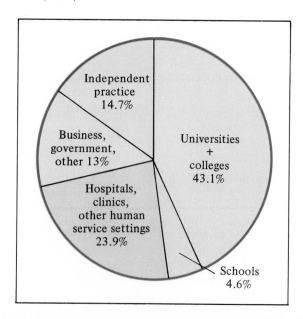

□ The *counseling psychologist* works with people in establishing more effective problem-solving skills and may use tests or other standard devices to provide people with information about themselves. Counseling psychologists are often found in school settings, rehabilitation centers, and community counseling agencies.

□ The *school and educational psychologist* analyzes educational achievement in order to identify individual differences in students or curricula that are associated with the success or failure of the students in that setting and administers tests of various types (intelligence, reading, eye-hand coordination) in order to identify possible problem areas.

The Differences between Psychology, Psychiatry, and Psychoanalysis

A common area of confusion when discussing psychology is the difference between psychology and psychiatry. Actually, the difference between the two is very simple. A **psychiatrist** is a medical doctor—an M.D.—who specializes in behavior. Other medical specialties with which you are familiar are surgery, pediatrics, dermatology, and internal medicine. Psychiatry is another type of specialty. The psychiatrist receives a medical degree with a special emphasis in the area of behavioral problems and receives advanced training in that area after the granting of the M.D.

The **psychologist**, by contrast, receives training in a university and, like an M.D., receives broad training first and specialized training afterward. The broad training includes topics such as experimental psychology, developmental psychology, research methods, and statistics. The specific training might be in the area of clinical therapy, social behavior, or ability testing.

The psychiatrist often deals with the same behavioral problems as the clinical psychologist. In other words, someone with a problem such as depression or anxiety might decide to visit either a psychologist or a psychiatrist. As an M.D., the

psychiatrist might choose to use drugs as a method of treatment. For example, the psychiatrist might prescribe a tranquilizer for the temporary control of anxiety. The psychologist, on the other hand, is not permitted to prescribe drugs. In some instances, psychologists and psychiatrists work together, so that the psychologist can refer a patient to a psychiatric colleague if a prescription is called for.

Another term that is often misunderstood is **psychoanalyst**. A psychoanalyst may be either a

---

Psychiatrist. A medical doctor who specializes in behavior.
Psychologist. Someone who has studied the general topics of psychology and then specialized in one of them; most, though not all, psychologists, hold Ph.Ds in psychology.

Psychoanalyst. May be either a psychologist or a psychiatrist who uses a technique of therapy based on Freudian principles (**psychoanalysis**) and who has been trained at a psychoanalytic institute.

clinical psychologist or a psychiatrist who has received special training at a psychoanalytic institute. Psychoanalysis is actually a "brand" of diagnosis and treatment of behavioral problems that is based on the principles developed by Sigmund Freud and his followers, which we discussed earlier. We will cover these principles in great detail in Chapters 15 and 16.

The Graduate Degree in Psychology

Graduate study in psychology (or in any field, for that matter) is a program of professional training. You could get the same training by putting together a series of night courses, volunteer activities, independent reading, and work experiences. Graduate study puts all of those things together in a limited period of time, and, by awarding a post-graduate degree, certifies that you have been exposed to and mastered certain skill areas.

There are different types of degrees for psychologists. There are three in particular that I will briefly describe: the Ph.D., the Psy.D., and the M.A. or M.S. The Ph.D. (Doctor of Philosophy) usually takes 4 to 5 years of course work, supervised research, and independent research (usually in the form of a doctoral dissertation or research project). In some Ph.D. programs there is a heavy emphasis on science and the scientific method. In others, the emphasis may be on acquiring practical skills.

In contrast to the Ph.D., the Psy.D. degree (Doctor of Psychology) concentrates on the *practice* of psychology rather than research in psychology. This does not mean that research is ignored in the Psy.D. program—far from it—it simply means that professional competence is achieved through practice in the *application* of particular behavior principles rather than through conducting research in these areas. The Psy.D. degree is relatively new; there are only a few schools that grant this degree at the present time, but this number is likely to increase steadily in the next decade.

The master's degree—either the Master of Arts (M.A.) or the Master of Science (M.S.)—includes course work and practice. It may or may not also have a research requirement, such as a master's thesis. A master's program usually takes about 2 years and is often geared to providing specific professional skills (for example, in the area of employment testing, counseling, or school psychology).

The APA publishes an excellent book, entitled *Graduate Study in Psychology* (APA, 1982), that can help you identify which schools have post-graduate degree programs that might interest you. In addition, every graduate program has its own descriptive material that you can get by mail.

The Undergraduate Major in Psychology

It is common for students to wonder about the value of their degree program. This is just as true for an associate degree as it is for a four-year B.A. degree, and just as true of students majoring in psychology as it is of those majoring in finance, engineering, or education.

Dr. Patricia Lunneborg has examined the typical career patterns of undergraduate psychology majors at the University of Washington and has found that these majors put their course work to a wide variety of uses. In Table 1–3, you will find an elaborate description of the jobs these majors found, the typical work activities in those jobs, and the requirements and any special preparation necessary to move into those areas. This information is encouraging; it suggests that there are many settings in which undergraduate psychology majors are valuable. This does not mean that just any set of psychology courses will do; the courses that make up the major should be carefully selected to meet your career goals. It should also be obvious that good grades in these courses imply better preparation (and greater likelihood of attractive employment) than poor grades.

In addition to the work of Dr. Lunneborg, the APA has also done several surveys of how people with a B.A. degree in psychology are employed. The findings are published in a book entitled *The Psychology Major* (Woods, 1979). Dr. Lunneborg has summarized some of the most relevant APA findings:

1. Since 1967, there has been a shift in entry level jobs away from education and human services toward business, professional, and trade jobs.
2. For all college graduates taken as a group, 50 percent began work at a level below that appropriate for a college graduate, such as accounting clerk,

equipment operator, or office worker. For psychology majors, however, at a point 10 years after graduation, 79 percent of those with a B.A. were in high-level positions such as counselor, school psychologist, computer analyst, lawyer, and physician. The other 21 percent worked in a position where the B.A. in psychology was an obvious qualification. These positions included psychiatric technician, employment interviewer, and personnel manager. The point here is that the B.A. in psychology is valuable in a broad number of ways—ways that are not always immediately obvious.

3. Between 50 and 75 percent of all of those with a B.A. said that they would major in psychology again if they had the chance.

In combination with Dr. Lunneborg's results from the University of Washington, these APA survey results paint a positive picture for the undergraduate psychology major—a picture worth your consideration.

Psychology for Nonmajors

In any college or university in which introductory psychology is offered, a very large percentage of students, regardless of their major, will take the course before they graduate. One of the reasons for this is the fact that most students see psychology courses as satisfying to both personal and professional goals. They want to know more about themselves and the people they will be dealing with throughout their lives, and they would like to develop habits, strategies, or ways of dealing with work-related problems that will help them in their careers. Both personal and professional goals can be met by psychology courses. Lunneborg (1978) has suggested that psychology courses are unique in some respects and that there are certain results that you can expect from taking these courses. These results are listed below.

General Preparation for Work. Many psychology courses (including introductory psychology) provide a good working knowledge of human relations. In most work settings, problems arise and challenges are met not only as a result of technical knowledge, but also as a result of the ability of people to get along with one another. This ability is not magical or inborn; it comes from understanding some basic principles of communication, personality, and motivation. Psychology courses can give that understanding.

Specific Preparation for Work. There are many popular majors or degrees that make use of particular combinations of psychology courses. Since there are as many combinations as there are majors, I will list only a few examples in Table 1–4. This is the kind of advice that your psychology teacher and advisor will be happy to give to you. Discuss your career plans with them, tell them the courses you have taken up to this point, and ask their advice in planning for additional course work.

Training in a Basic Skill. As you will be told over and over again, psychology is a science. As such, it has certain characteristics: There is a particular way of asking questions, of collecting data to answer those questions, and of communicating those answers to others. In short, there is the scientific way of doing things. By taking courses in psychology, you are exposed to this method of collecting and using information and will learn to think in that way. This mode of thinking will prove valuable in many other settings.

Understanding Yourself. There are few of us who completely understand why we do certain things. It is not that we don't recognize what we are doing; in fact, we can often predict that under certain circumstances, a certain behavior will occur. For example, you may be fully aware of the fact that you are impatient with old people or young children or your parents. The fact that you do things that you would rather not probably makes you uneasy. You tend to think that you are unique in this behavior and maybe even a little abnormal. Psychology courses help you to understand why these things occur and ease your fears about being abnormal. In fact, you usually find that you are behaving like most other people. To rise above that unwanted behavior is really the *abnormal* pattern. Understanding is the first step in change, and this goes for dealing with others as well as with yourself. Understanding why people behave in particular ways will help you to establish positive relationships with even the most difficult people.

TABLE 1-3. Job Opportunities for Psychology Majors

	Administration (Business and Public)	*Purchase and Sales*	*Interviewing*
Work activities	Program planning, allocating responsibilities, monitoring work, coordinating within an organization.	Applying knowledge of contracts, credit, marketing, and sales methods in a merchandising situation.	Interviewing people and evaluating their qualifications.
What's required of worker?	1. Ability to plan and carry out programs. 2. Verbal ability. 3. Math ability, to prepare and review financial reports. 4. Analytical ability to solve complex problems.	1. Ability to learn about contracts, marketing, credit, and sales psychology. 2. Ability to relate to people at all levels. 3. Power of persuasion, initiative, drive. 4. Verbal and in some cases math ability.	1. Verbal facility to converse with people at all levels. 2. Ability to put people at ease and gain their confidence.
How do college graduates enter this field?	1. On-the-job training. 2. Working your way up from lower level.	1. Formal on-the-job training, with classroom instruction. 2. Advancement from experienced merchandising position.	1. Minimal on-the-job training.
How should psychology majors prepare to enter this field?	1. Courses in business administration and accounting. 2. Summer or parttime work at low-level job in business administration. 3. Extracurricular activities that develop leadership and organizational ability.	1. Courses in business administration and marketing. 2. Volunteer experience selling or canvassing. 3. Extracurricular activities that develop outgoing personality.	1. Courses in personnel management, business administration, sociology. 2. Extracurricular activities that develop poise and verbal skills.
Sample job titles	Management analyst, college administrator, community relations officer, urban planning officer.	Advertising account rep, copywriter, marketing assistant, media buyer, sales rep, purchasing agent.	College admissions, customer service rep, resource specialist, recruiter.

Source: Lunneborg, 1982.

Supporting Other Life Goals. In the course of your life, you will find yourself in many situations that have been studied by psychologists. These situations include dealing with someone suffering from a mental disorder, a death in the family, a serious illness, substance abuse, establishing a lasting and intimate relationship, raising children, and so on; the list is almost endless. Courses in psychology can prepare you to face these challenges.

What's after Introductory Psychology?

Introductory psychology is usually called a "survey" course. This means that it presents the entire field

Counseling and Social Work	Rehabilitation	Education and Training	Scientific Research
Guiding people or groups to solve job, educational, personal, and social problems.	Planning and directing programs to aid physically or mentally handicapped.	Teaching, demonstrating, or tutoring individuals or groups.	Applying principles of natural and social sciences in basic and applied research.
1. Capacity for continued training and applying knowledge to diverse programs. 2. Empathy and ability to inspire confidence. 3. Organizational ability to plan and direct counseling programs.	1. Skill at planning and directing activities and evaluating programs. 2. Craft/arts skills. 3. Empathy with handicapped.	1. Ability to communicate ideas and relate to people. 2. Analytical ability to organize facts for program planning.	1. Intellectual capacity to absorb and interpret science theories and data. 2. Math ability. 3. Inquisitive mind, imaginative and thoroughness in detail.
1. On-the-job training. Beyond entry level jobs, master's degree in social work or counseling required.	1. Graduation or certification from special curriculum in therapeutic specialty.	1. State certification and bachelor's degree through secondary school level. 2. For in-service training in business, courses in personnel and human resource development.	1. On-the-job training.
1. Good grades in psychology. 2. Courses in sociology and social welfare. 3. Lots of different types of volunteer counseling work. 4. Extracurricular activities that develop confident speaking ability.	1. Courses in anatomy, physiology, nursing, arts/crafts. 2. Summer work supervising arts and crafts or sports activities. 3. Volunteer work in hospital, or home for aged.	1. Education courses. 2. Experience in helping college instructors teach courses. 3. Volunteer work in educational settings such as camps, recreation centers, etc.	1. Courses in math, physics, chemistry, computer programming. 2. Do as much research as possible in college. 3. Work at low-level job in scientific laboratory.
Case aide, mental health specialist, psychiatric aide.	Physical therapist, health care associate, learning disabilities teacher.	Day-care teacher, Head Start specialist, teaching assistant, Vista/Peace Corps volunteer.	Biofeedback technician, lab assistant, survey researcher, systems research analyst.

for your consideration. As a result of this exposure, you will probably identify some areas that you like better than others. In some schools, there is a second introductory course dealing with a slightly smaller chunk of the entire field. After the first introductory course, find a broad or survey course in the area that most interests you, then use that as the preparation for taking specialized courses in that area. After taking one or more introductory courses, you might decide that developmental psychology is pretty interesting. The next step would be to take a survey course in developmental psychology. This gives you an opportunity to see all the nooks and crannies in a smaller area of interest. When you have completed that survey course, you will be ready to take some specialized courses, such as language de-

TABLE 1-4. Psychology Courses Recommended for Different Majors.

Majors	Recommended Psychology Courses
Chemistry, biology nursing, pre-med	Personality and individual differences; human sexual behavior; racism and minority groups; deviant personality; deviant development; physiological psychology; introduction to clinical psychology
Business administration	Personality and individual differences; racism and minority groups; social psychology; human motivation; attitude change and persuasive communication; organizational psychology
Economics, political science	Elementary psychological statistics; social psychology; measurement and design in attitude research; attitude change and persuasive communication; organizational psychology
History	Elementary psychological statistics; social psychology; laboratory in social psychology; history of psychology; organizational behavior
English, communications	Social psychology; human motivation; human learning; cognitive psychology
Art, music, dance	Personality and individual differences; deviant personality; developmental psychology; social psychology; human learning; deviant behavior
Architecture	Social psychology; laboratory in social psychology; environmental psychology; perceptual processes
Modern languages	Racism and minority groups; social psychology; psychology of language; language development
Zoology, fisheries, forestry, oceanography	Comparative animal behavior; elementary psychological statistics; learning; laboratory in animal learning; laboratory in animal behavior; motivation

Source: Lunneborg, 1978, pp. 53-54.

velopment or moral development in children. This is probably the best way to proceed no matter what your interest area is. Your instructor in the introductory course can also give you good advice about how to pursue studies in your area of interest.

Finally, it's a good idea to try to get involved in research projects. Most psychologists at universities have several research projects going on at all times and would be happy to have motivated help on these projects. In this way you will learn about psychology from a very different perspective, and this research experience will help deepen your understanding of science, the scientific method, and psychology.

■SUMMARY

1. Psychology may be defined as the study of behavior and mental processes, but even this simple definition raises a number of questions: What do we mean by *study*, how are behavior and mental

processes distinguished, and how are the studies of human behavior and animal behavior related? Psychology began with the introduction of the scientific method, which helped it break from philosophy and become a self-supporting discipline.

2. Eight important schools of thought have influenced psychology's development over the last 100 years. These include the "isms"—structuralism, functionalism, behaviorism, and humanism—as well as Gestalt psychology, the psychoanalytic school, cognitive psychology, and the biological approach.

3. Wilhelm Wundt, founder of the first psychological laboratory, explored consciousness by focusing on immediate experience as people reported it. He sought to break down consciousness into its fundamental elements. One of Wundt's students, Edward Titchener, carried Wundt's thinking to America where it was a major force behind the structuralist movement. Titchener's belief that conscious experience is given structure by its fundamental elements—sensations, feelings, and images—gave rise to the name *structuralism*. Titchener and other structuralists studied consciousness

through *introspection,* a procedure in which trained scientists reported their conscious experiences while exposed to various sensory stimuli.

4. The American William James, the founder of *functionalism,* was more interested in why consciousness existed than in what its fundamental elements were. According to the functionalists, consciousness existed to actively seek out and order information, which was combined by each individual in a unique manner that was more or less adaptive.

5. *Behaviorism* started when Pavlov in Russia and Watson in the United States began studying observable behavior, rather than consciousness. Watson favored the study of animals, which eliminated the use of introspection as a research method. Like the original behaviorists, B. F. Skinner believes that the environment is mainly responsible for the differences that we observe in people. Skinner also views unseen mental processes, such as thinking, motivation, creativity, or attitudes, as forms of learned behavior.

6. *Gestalt psychology,* an outgrowth of German structuralism, sought to demonstrate that the whole of experience is more than just the sum of a person's sensations. This movement suggested that something goes on in the brain to transform sensations into perceptions, an idea that attacked the behaviorist school.

7. Freud, a trained physician and the founder of the *psychoanalytic school,* proposed that the root of many of his patients' problems was to be found in the unconscious. Freud's concentration was on treating patients, and he made use of a number of nontraditional methods. The absence of the scientific method from Freud's work has created problems in judging the worth and development of psychoanalysis. It's important to keep in mind, however, that psychoanalysis was developed to deal with problems that were not readily addressed by the existing schools of psychology.

8. *Humanism* is a current movement that developed in part as a protest against behaviorism and psychoanalysis. It emphasizes people's values, ideals, and aspirations. This movement focuses on the power of people to affect their own behavior and downplays environmental influences.

9. Like both structuralism and functionalism, *cognitive psychology* is concerned with the scientific study of mental processes. Some of the processes studied by cognitive psychologists include language, problem solving, concept formation, and judgment.

10. The *biological approach* has evolved because of the recognition that many biological and chemical variables influence behavior. Psychologists have used this approach to study such conditions as love, stress, aggression, and mental illness, and are now interested in using it to explore such higher mental activities as thinking and creativity.

11. The four goals that all sciences have in common are *description,* a way of showing that a particular thing exists; *prediction,* a declarative statement in the form of a *hypothesis* about a relationship between events; *control,* the ability to change an outcome based on whether or not the prediction was correct; and the overall aim of science, *understanding,* or the ability to explain the relationship between events.

12. A *theory* is a general principle, or a set or interrelated propositions, that is used to explain a phenomenon under consideration. Characteristics of a "good explanation" or theory are simplicity, clarity, and breadth.

13. Science is a public activity. Scientific procedures are explicitly spelled out so that they may be considered by anyone. The way in which a particular variable is measured is called an *operational definition.* Scientists must also specify the conditions under which their observations were made in such a way that other scientists can repeat the procedure. Results of experiments are reported in as objective a manner as possible.

14. Psychologists generally study *samples.* This means that they evaluate the characteristics of a whole *population* (all members of a group) by testing a small part of it. By testing the sample, scientists are able to make a *generalization,* or inference, about the population. Researchers must be careful to sample subjects who are in fact representative of the population of interest.

15. Some research is done with the goal of generalizing the result from the sample of subjects to the population in general. Other research is done to develop or refine a theory of behavior. The choice of subjects for study is significant and is related to the need to avoid bias in research.

16. *Laboratory studies* are those that are conducted in a controlled environment, away from distracting and distorting influences. *Field studies* are conducted in a natural setting when real-life con-

ditions are critical to the experiment.

17. The five ways of studying behavior are experiment, naturalistic observation, correlation, survey, and case study. In an experiment, scientists change behavior; in naturalistic observation and correlation, they observe behavior; and in surveys and case studies, they ask questions about behavior.

18. An *experiment* involves manipulating one element to see if a change is produced in another element. The variable that the experimenter manipulates is the *independent variable;* the variable measured to see the effect of manipulating the independent variable is the *dependent variable.* The *experimental group* is the group of subjects that experiences the change in the independent variable. The *control group* is similar in composition to the experimental group but is not exposed to the independent variable.

19. *Experimenter bias* occurs when the data represent the expectations of the experimenter rather than the behavior of the subject. *Subject bias* occurs when the subjects of a study behave according to their own expectations about the outcome of the experiment. Bias can ordinarily be avoided by using *single-blind experiments*—in which the subjects are not told whether they are in the control group or the experimental group, or *double-blind experiments*—in which neither the subjects nor the experimenters know which subjects are in the control group and which in the experimental group.

20. Researchers use *naturalistic observation* when practical or ethical considerations make it impossible to manipulate the independent variable. Using this technique, the researcher records behavior in the hope of finding a relationship between variables. Scientists using the *correlational approach* are also interested in the relationship between variables. They are particularly interested in seeing what variables appear together. In both these approaches, the researcher must be cautious in making cause–effect statements.

21. In a *survey study*, a researcher asks subjects how they might react in a given situation or how they feel about a particular set of circumstances. A *case study* is a method of data collection in which the psychologist examines one particular person or situation.

22. In analyzing the results of an experiment, the researcher is asking if there is a difference between the groups in the study or between the subjects before and after an event. The presence or absence of this difference tells the scientist something about the relationship (or lack of relationship) between the variables being examined. Through the *probability statement*, the scientist estimates the likelihood that this difference was due to chance.

23. The two issues of ethics are researchers' honesty and subjects' rights. When researchers falsify data or take shortcuts in procedures without describing them, the whole body of knowledge in an area of study comes into question. Those in favor of *deception research* argue that deception of subjects is necessary for realism; those who oppose such research procedures argue that the cost in terms of potential damage to subjects is not worth the benefits of the research. The fact that researchers have substantial power in dealing with subjects has made researchers aware of the need to inform subjects of their rights before an experiment begins. The American Psychological Association provides ethical guidelines for both human and animal research.

24. The American Psychological Association (APA) is made up of psychologists from many fields. Specialties in psychology include experimental, clinical, social, personnel, human factors, developmental, counseling, and educational psychology. A *psychiatrist* is a M.D. who specializes in behavior, whereas a *psychologist* has studied the general topics of psychology and then specializes in one of them. A *psychoanalyst* may be either a clinical psychologist or a psychiatrist who practices the diagnosis and treatment of behavior problems based on the principles of Freud and his followers, and who has studied at a psychoanalytic institute.

25. There are three different types of graduate degrees in psychology: the M.S. (Master of Science) or M.A. (Master of Arts), the Ph.D. (Doctor of Philosophy), and the Psy.D. (Doctor of Psychology). Graduate programs leading to the Psy.D. concentrate on the practice of psychology, while Ph.D. programs often stress research. Results of a recent survey indicate positive job prospects for people with B.A. degrees in psychology. By taking psychology courses, students who are not psychology majors can gain a good knowledge of human relations, an exposure to scientific method, greater self-understanding, and preparation for many life situations.

■ ANSWERING QUESTIONS FOR THOUGHT

1. There are a number of ways that a knowledge of psychology gained through even a few courses can help in personal and career goals. Among them are learning to use the scientific method, understanding your own and other people's behavior, learning how to get along with other people, and being better prepared for the challenges you will face after college.

2. A psychiatrist is a medical doctor who specializes in behavioral problems; a psychologist holds an academic degree rather than a medical degree and may deal with behavioral problems or go into one of the other areas of psychology; a psychoanalyst may be either a clinical psychologist or a psychiatrist who has received special training in Freudian methods of analysis.

3. Scientists try to report their findings as objectively as possible, without introducing personal comments or opinions. Adjectives and other descriptions that appear in newspaper or magazine stories have no place in scientific journals. While this may make for less sensational reading, it is an unbiased way to report results.

4. If a scientist wants to make a broad or general statement about a population, it is necessary to choose subjects that represent that population as a whole. Ten friends will probably not meet that standard.

5. Psychologists conduct research in a laboratory when a controlled environment is needed. This need not be what you would think of as a traditional laboratory—it can be any area in which standard conditions can be ensured. At other times psychologists work in the field, if real-life conditions are more critical to the experiment.

2 Physiology and Behavior

QUESTIONS FOR THOUGHT

1. **Why does a stroke that affects the right side of the brain paralyze the left side of the body?**
2. **Why do injuries to the spinal cord have such tragic consequences?**
3. **Why do football linemen wear padded collars?**
4. **What allows us to react so quickly in emergencies?**
5. **Why are you upset for a long time after an argument?**

The answers to these questions are at the end of the chapter.

In Hartford, Connecticut, a 29-year-old man is admitted to a hospital where he will undergo a highly unusual procedure to control his violent epileptic seizures. These seizures, which have plagued him since childhood, cause convulsions, tongue biting, uncontrollable urination, unconsciousness, and, finally, deep sleep. They have reached the point where drugs can no longer control them and the patient, a factory-production worker, can no longer do his job. From the evidence of earlier research with animals, the man's surgeons have hypothesized that the seizures originate in an area of the brain known as the hippocampus. Since drugs are no longer an effective form of treatment, the surgeons have recommended removal of the hippocampus as a way of bringing the violent epileptic seizures under control (Scoville and Milner, 1957; Penfield and Milner, 1958; Milner, 1959).

This operation actually took place over 30 years ago, and measured by its original purpose, it was a success. However, because of the striking side-effects of the surgery, the case has been written up many times in both medical and psychological journals. After the surgery, the patient, known as H. M., was no longer as plagued by epileptic seizures; they were much less frequent and less severe. But something serious had happened to his memory: Although he could still remember events that had taken place before the operation, events that occurred afterwards no longer became a part of his memory. For example, after the surgery he could not remember where the bathroom in his hospital room was (Scoville, 1954). Later, after moving to a new address, he could not find his way home from more than two blocks away (Milner et al., 1968).

After 30 years, H. M. continues to suffer from a specific inability to form new memories, even though he suffers no loss of general intellectual functioning. There has been no decline in his IQ or in his ability to use information he had acquired before the operation. Imagine what it would be like

to have H. M.'s problem. The meaning of what you are reading right now would slip away in minutes. You could, as H. M. frequently does, read the same magazine over and over again without realizing that you had already read it. Tomorrow you would not remember people you met today. In fact, H. M. does not recognize people who have visited him regularly over the years since his operation.

Damage to other areas of the human brain has had equally dramatic, although distinctly different, effects. Yin (1970) studied a large number of hospitalized patients with various types and locations of brain injuries. He noticed that a significant number of these patients could not identify pictures of familiar people's faces, although they had normal vision and had no problem recognizing other things. It was not the *identity* of the familiar person that was lost. For example, while these patients might not recognize their spouses' faces, they could immediately recognize the voices that came from the "strange faces" as those of their spouses. The disorder seemed to be confined to the ability to remember faces. Apparently, a particular area of the brain plays a role in the memory for faces and damage to this area can affect this ability.

As these examples demonstrate, damage to the brain can have serious effects on human behavior. The relationship between injuries to specific regions of the brain and the effects of those injuries on behavior is well documented. Based on observations of patients, we know that brain damage can cause blindness, amnesia, language difficulties (**aphasia**), and a host of other disturbances; what we still don't know is exactly *how* the brain is involved. One thing is certain from our observations of brain injuries: The injured brain provides a "natural laboratory"

Aphasia. Partial or complete loss of ability to use language, resulting from brain damage.

for answering questions about the intact brain. How, for example, is brain activity related to seeing and hearing, or to emotion and memory, or to thinking and acting?

These major questions cannot be answered by one psychological approach alone. Since the brain is composed of living matter and has physical weight and size, any consideration of these questions must incorporate a biological approach. The brain's physical properties affect its functions; behavior studied by psychologists is one of those functions. Thus, psychologists try to understand how the organization of cells in the brain allows us to learn and retain information, or how the brain system is built to permit recognition of familiar faces.

In this chapter we will examine the organization and functions of two of the body's major systems— the nervous and endocrine systems—and see how they interact to affect behavior. We will spend a good deal of time on the brain, since it is by far the most important element in determining behavior. We must remember, however, that the brain itself is part of the larger system that we call the **nervous system**.

■ THE ORGANIZATION OF THE NERVOUS SYSTEM

The nervous system is organized at several levels. Its basic unit is the nerve cell or **neuron**. Neurons act in groups. Within these groups, their interactions are complex. When several thousand neurons are interconnected in a specific way, they form a subsystem or specialized group of neurons. These subsystems of neurons might be compared to the various components of an automobile. We might describe an automobile as having a brake subsystem, an engine subsystem, and a drive-train subsystem. Each subsystem is intended to perform one function (e.g., stopping, supplying energy, or supplying motion). Further, the subsystems must all work together for the auto to function efficiently. The same is true with subsystems of neurons. For example, several neuron subsystems gathered together at the back of the brain process information from the eye. These neuron groups make up an area known as the *visual cortex*.

There are billions of neurons. Carl Sagan (1975)

has estimated that if all of a person's neurons were placed end to end, the chain would reach the moon and back. Each neuron has many complex connections to other neurons. It would be simple enough to say that behavior emerges out of all of these connections. But this doesn't really help us to understand why behavior is regular. Even Yin's patients and H. M. demonstrated a certain regularity of behavior. This regularity indicates that the brain has a specific *organization*; certain areas perform certain functions. Therefore it would be incorrect to say that behavior is *nothing more than* a collection of neurons or that a person is a simple sum of biological "parts." For example, look at the structure of water. It is made up of hydrogen and oxygen atoms, but these two elements together, as water, have very different chemical and physical properties than either one had alone. It is not just the sum of hydrogen and oxygen that makes water behave as it does. What is important is *how* these two elements are bound together. It is the workings of a complex brain, composed of billions of neurons arranged in complex but orderly ways, that *is* emotion, motivation, learning, perception, or memory.

Seen from this light, what we call the "mind" emerges from these complex interactions of the nervous system. The mind is not a place or thing that exists independently of the body. It is a set of processes, some familiar and others as yet unknown, accomplished by the cells that make up the nervous system. The purpose of these processes is communication.

In many sections of this book, you will see the term **neural** or the prefix **neuro-**. These terms will indicate that we are considering something that is related to neurons—our communications cells. A common mistake is to assume that *neural* means *brain*. It can, but neurons are found in many parts of the body other than the brain. The nervous system is simply a collection of cells with specific communication functions.

■ THE NEURON

We are now going to look at how neurons communicate with one another. Look carefully at Figure 2–1, which is a drawing of one type of neuron. First, notice the **dendrites**, the tiny fibers branching out

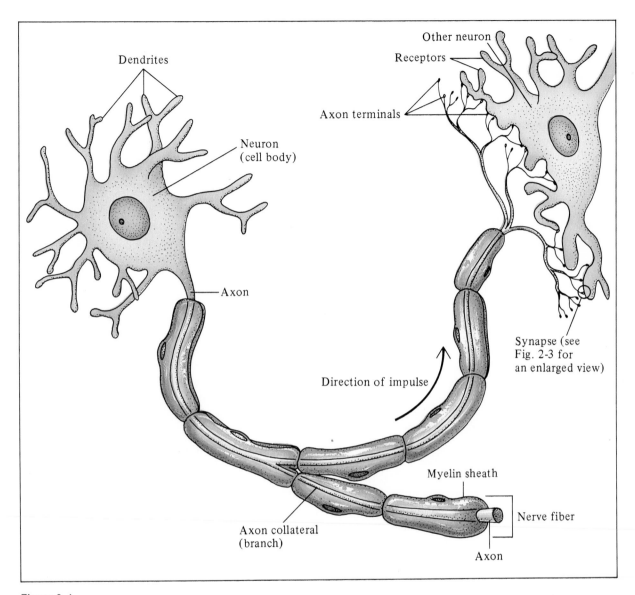

Figure 2-1
This is a drawing of one type of nerve cell, or neuron, which is made up of an axon,
a cell body, and dendrites. Neurons often have many dendrites, but only one axon.
The sausage-like covering around the axon is called myelin.

from the **soma**, or cell body. These dendrites perform a function similar to that of an antenna on a TV or radio: They pick up signals. In the case of the neuron, the signals come from other neurons, and instead of picking up electromagnetic waves in the air, they pick up chemical signals. Now look at the long, thin fiber called the **axon**. The function of the axon is to transmit messages to other neurons.

Nervous system. A collection of cells with specific communication functions; relays messages in the form of nerve impulses throughout the body.
Neuron. A single cell that is the basic building-block of the nervous system.
Neural, neuro-. Having to do with the structure or function of neurons.

Dendrites. The fibers of a neuron that pick up signals or impulses from other neurons and bring them to the cell body.
Soma. The cell body of the neuron.
Axon. The fiber of a neuron that carries signals or impulses away from the cell body to other neurons.

These messages move in one direction only, from the dendrites and cell body through the axon to the **axon terminals**, small bulblike branches at the ends of axons. Messages are then transmitted to other neurons, muscles, and glands. Neurons often have many dendrites, but only one axon. Since these many dendrites can provide a rather large surface area for receiving information, a single neuron is capable of receiving messages from many, even thousands, of other neurons.

Axons vary in length from very short to over three feet long. Even though there is only one axon per neuron, each axon has branches, and each of these branches is also capable of communicating with other neurons. Since there are 100 billion or more neurons in the nervous system, and since each one can receive messages from more than one nearby neuron, it is no wonder that each of us is capable of an almost infinite variety of behaviors.

Neurons differ from other cells in that they are specialized for communication. However, there is something other cells do that neurons cannot do: They cannot reproduce themselves. If you cut your hand, within several days the cells will reproduce themselves and the cut will heal, but if you destroy a neuron it will not be replaced. Therefore, neurons are particularly vulnerable to injury, though they can repair themselves or be aided in repair by surgically connecting severed nerves or even transplanting a segment of nerve from one area to another. It appears that the motor neurons—those whose axons terminate in muscle fibers—repair themselves somewhat more easily than those that make up the brain and spinal cord (Schneider and Tarshis, 1979). One of the most severe neural injuries is a severed spinal cord. Although, in principle, the neurons involved are capable of self-repair, this type of injury is apparently too traumatic for repair to occur.

At this moment, you have all the neurons you will ever have. In fact, since neurons cannot reproduce, you have fewer now than you had when you were born. It might interest you to know that during the 9-month period when you were a developing fetus, on the average 250,000 new neurons were appearing every minute. As we will see in Chapter 11, on human development, this explains the fact that the development of a fetus can be severely affected by substances such as drugs, alcohol, and nicotine. These substances are carried through the mother's bloodstream to the developing nervous system of the child, and can have very harmful effects.

In the normal wear-and-tear of living, neurons die off. In addition, some forms of malnutrition, as well as exposure to disease, to high concentrations of drugs such as alcohol, and to some environmental pollutants may injure neurons and cause them to die. There is some comfort in knowing that with 100 billion neurons and the astronomical number of interconnections of these neurons, we may not miss a few. The problem is that, as we saw earlier, specialized groups of neurons tend to be located together. Consequently, injury or disease may destroy a whole group of neurons that formed a local circuit. Thus, even though losing a few thousand neurons randomly located throughout the body may not result in behavioral change, losing those few thousand from one area may be serious.

Though the neuron illustrated in Figure 2–1 appears to exist in a vacuum, neurons are in fact surrounded by other cells called **Glial cells**. They fill the gaps around and between neurons, helping to insulate neurons from one another. In addition, they supply nutritional material for the cells and help in the repair of damaged neurons (Carlson, 1981). The Glial cells are also involved in the development of a type of covering around the axons of certain neurons. The covering, called **myelin**, dramatically increases the speed of neural transmission. When myelin degenerates, some serious problems result. An example is the disease known as multiple sclerosis (MS). Scattered myelin degeneration is thought to cause the impaired motor coordination that accompanies attacks of MS.

Each neuron is a little communication machine. It has the equipment to send and receive messages. But neurons are not always communicating; signals or messages are sent only under certain circumstances. Let's consider some of those circumstances.

The Action Potential

In physics, there are two kinds of energy. **Kinetic energy** is the energy of a moving body—a falling object, for example. **Potential energy** is the energy a body has as a result of its position or the arrangement of its parts. An object positioned on top of another has potential energy because if it were pushed off, its weight would cause it to gather speed.

Similarly, a coiled spring has potential energy because releasing it will produce motion. Neurons have potential energy; they are like coiled springs ready to be released. Each neuron has a small electrical voltage—about .10 volt. When a neuron is resting, its cell membrane forms a partial barrier between the semiliquid environments that are inside and outside the neuron. Both environments contain electrically charged particles. The environment outside the neuron contains mostly positively charged particles, while the environment inside is mostly negatively charged particles. Since there are relatively more negative charges inside the neuron than outside, a resting neuron (one in which the energy has not yet been released) is said to have a negative electrical charge. The fact that these two opposite charges exist close to each other causes the potential energy of the neuron. Whenever there is a significant change in the balance between these two opposing charges, a signal occurs. What happens is almost like a tug of war, with the forces inside the neuron tugging in one direction and forces outside the neuron tugging in another. If any significant additional force is added to the outside pull, something will happen. This something is usually referred to as a neuron "firing." When a neuron fires, a signal is sent through the axon to a dendrite of another neuron. This signal causes a change in the balance of charges in that neuron, causing it to fire, and so on. From this description, you can see that every neuron is "ready" to fire. This readiness is called **resting potential** (potential energy). The actual firing of the neuron, which is brought about by the change in the electrical balance between the inside and outside of the neuron, is called the **action potential** (the kinetic energy). Thus, when a neuron fires, its electrical status is changed from a resting potential to an action potential. This change can be measured.

Figure 2–2 illustrates the firing of a single neuron. As you can see, there are several phases. First the curve goes up, then it drops below the resting state (.10 volt), and then it returns to normal. When the curve drops below the resting state, the neuron is recovering and getting ready to fire again. The entire sequence of firing and recovery makes up the action potential.

This whole process occurs very quickly, even though there are some variations in the speed and distances that signals travel. You will remember that axons can be quite long. For example, in a giraffe a single neuron connects the spinal cord with the hoof. This means that within neurons, a signal must often travel a long way. Further, signals travel in an interesting manner. The part of the neuron that has been stimulated is responsible for the first impulse. This impulse then changes the electrical balance of the part of the neuron that is next to it, and so on. Thus, a rapid series or chain of impulses, rather than a single impulse traveling the length of an axon, is responsible for conducting the message. Think of a number of dominoes standing on end close to one another: Knock the first domino into the next one and a chain reaction begins. This chain reaction is what happens within a single neuron when it fires.

There is another fact to note about the action potentials of neurons: Each action potential is identical. It does not matter what message is being carried, or where the message originates; every action potential looks very much like the one illustrated in Figure 2–2. There is no way of telling, from this or any other action potential, whether it was recorded from a neuron in a worm, a whale, or a college sophomore, or whether it conveyed information about color, sound, or a command to turn the page. Action potentials in all neurons are the same.

Even though all action potentials are the same, there are various other differences in the activities of neurons. For example, some neurons fire more easily than others; others fire more frequently. Some stimuli result in many more neurons firing than do other stimuli. We will discuss these particular differences in the following three sections. The point to remember now is that these differences help explain how the brain can interpret the unending flow of messages arriving through the neural pathways. If

---

Axon terminals. Small bulblike knobs that form the ends of axons.

Glial cells. Cells in the nervous system that help to insulate neurons from one another. Also involved in the myelination of axons and in supplying nutritional material to the cells.

Myelin. A fatty covering surrounding some axons.

Kinetic energy. The energy of a moving body.

Potential energy. Anticipated energy, such as that of a coiled spring.

Resting potential. The potential energy contained in a neuron; the fact that it is ready to fire.

Action potential. The firing of a neuron resulting from a change in the electrical balance between the neuron and its environment.

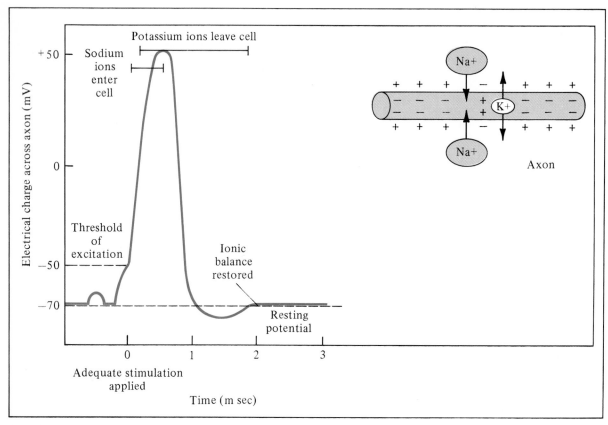

Figure 2-2
This figure shows what happens when a neuron fires, or goes from a resting potential to an action potential. Notice that after firing the curve drops below the resting
state and then returns to normal. When it drops below the resting state it is recovering and getting ready to fire again.

it were not for these differences in neural activity, there would be no way for the brain to distinguish one message from another.

Firing Threshold

As we have said, the only change of status occurring within a neuron is from a nonsignal condition to a signal condition. This change in status is determined by a built-in property of each neuron called its firing **threshold**. A threshold is the minimum amount of energy necessary to trigger a response. When input to a neuron is intense enough to reach its threshold, then an action potential will occur. When an action potential is produced, it begins at the end of the axon closest to the cell body and moves down the length of the axon through all its branches. This is the domino effect mentioned above. The fact that neurons can do only one of two things—either have an action potential or not—is known as the **all-or-none law**. Neurons have varying thresholds; some have lower thresholds than others. The fact that each neuron has its own threshold contributes to the type of message a neuron communicates. Some neurons have thresholds that require relatively little input to produce an action potential—for example, input from a very light touch on the skin might be enough. Other neurons have thresholds that require much more input. These neurons might be activated, for example, only when the skin is pinched. Thus, since some neurons fire more easily and others less so, a message might consist of the unique combination of the neurons that fired.

Frequency of Firing

Neurons differ in still another way. A neuron must recover before it can fire again, and some neurons recover more quickly after firing than others. The period of time necessary for recovery is called the **refractory period** for the neuron. This means that in a given time period, say 1 second, some neurons will fire more frequently than others. This difference in frequency produces different patterns of neuron firing. Each of these patterns represents a unique message. A group of elevators in an office building works on the same principle. Some go to higher floors (for example, floors 12–20) than others (for example, floors 2–11). If you are on the ground floor, you can push the "UP" button all you want, but the door will not open until the elevator arrives. Elevators that have traveled to the higher floors will take longer to come back than elevators that have gone up only a few floors. By looking at the panel of lights showing where those elevators are at any moment, you receive a message telling you which elevator will be going up next, and thus which door to stand in front of. Neurons are not elevators, but the principles governing neurons firing and elevator-doors opening are similar. They must both return to some beginning state (or ground floor) before they can be activated again.

Stimulus Intensity and Firing

Another way information is conveyed is by the *number* of action potentials that are produced by a stimulus. A weak stimulus will produce fewer action potentials; a stronger stimulus will produce many more. Stated in another way, a weaker stimulus will activate only those neurons whose thresholds are low. A stronger stimulus will activate all of these neurons, plus those with higher thresholds. After a certain point, further increases in intensity have no effect. This point is different for different neurons. Some neurons are capable of responding with as many as a thousand action potentials per second.

Neural Messages

At this point, you may still wonder how the same signal, an action potential, can be used to convey all the different information that your brain uses, such as sights, sounds, thoughts, and emotions. As we shall see, it is the organization of the nervous system that allows us to code this incredible variety of information. Stimulation from the outside world does not affect all neurons. Instead, we have specialized cells for receiving various types of stimulation. These cells, which are found in such organs as the eyes, ears, nose, and skin, send signals to particular regions of the brain. Thus, signals arrive at different locations. In addition, even neurons performing the same general function (for example, responding to visual stimuli) differ in their sensitivity to the stimulus and their rates of recovery. And stimuli themselves vary in their intensity. These factors produce all the diversity necessary to allow us to recognize and separate an almost infinite number of messages from our external environment. Each message has a unique aspect to it and is unlikely to be confused with any other message.

■ COMMUNICATION BETWEEN NEURONS

Up to this point, we have concentrated on the most elementary building-block of the nervous system, the single neuron, and you have become acquainted with the all-or-none nature of the action potential. The action potential, which normally travels the entire length of the axon, provides a means for getting a message to travel some distance *within* the neuron. When the action potential arrives at its final destination at the very end of the axon, the activated neuron will communicate with other neurons. However, because neurons do not directly touch one another, communication between neurons is performed by chemical messengers. This step, communication *between* neurons, represents another

---

Threshold. The minimum amount of energy necessary to trigger a neuron to fire. Below this amount of energy, the neuron will not fire.

All-or-none law. The fact that neurons can do only one of two things—either fire or not fire. There is no in-between.
Refractory period. The time needed for a neuron to recover after firing before it can fire again.

level of complexity in the nervous system. It also represents another level of organization.

Neurotransmission

Communication between neurons takes place at a site called a **synapse**. A synapse is actually a crossroad or junction between two paths. You can see from Figure 2–3 that a space exists between an axon and the dendrite of a nearby neuron. A synapse actually consists of the axon of one neuron, the dendrite of another neuron, and the space between them. An important physical feature of a synapse is the presence of **synaptic vesicles** at the ends of the axon terminals. These little ball-shaped containers hold the special chemicals used to transmit signals from one neuron to another. When an action potential arrives at the end of an axon, it causes the contents of some of the synaptic vesicles to be released into the synaptic space. The neighboring neuron may be activated (through its dendrite) by the chemicals released by the axon of the first neuron. Communication is always from axon to dendrite.

The dendrite of the receiving neuron is chemically-activated at a point called a **receptor**. The general process in which chemicals are released by

one neuron and activate an adjacent neuron is called **neurotransmission**. The chemicals that are used in this process are called **neurotransmitters**.

A number of different chemicals are used in neurotransmission. Several of the best-known neurotransmitters are listed in Table 2–1. One of the most prevalent neurotransmitters is **acetylcholine (ACh)**. ACh is an especially important neurotransmitter because of its effects on the skeletal muscles. In addition, ACh may be involved in memory and learning processes (Kalat, 1981). Interference with ACh mechanisms at the synapse can have very dramatic effects. For example, some drugs (such as curare, a plant poison) prevent ACh from being picked up or received by receptors in the skeletal muscles, resulting in paralysis. Other substances, such as botulinus toxin (the toxin in food poisoning) prevent the *release* of ACh. This also causes paralysis. **Catecholamine** is the name of another common class of neurotransmitters that includes *dopamine* and *norepinephrine*. Neurotransmitters in this class can be dramatically affected by drugs called amphetamines. When amphetamines are present in the body, the catecholamine level at various synapses temporarily increases. This increase results in the feeling of being "high." With so much additional catecholamine available, the body stops producing it in normal amounts. Several hours later, when the amphetamines have worn off, there is a "low" from the halt of natural catecholamine production (Kalat, 1981). Each of the neurotransmitters listed in Table 2–1 has specific effects on particular aspects of behavior. As you can see from the examples above, chemicals such as drugs can interfere with neurotransmission: They can block the release of a neurotransmitter, or block its reception at the synapse, or cause too much of a neurotransmitter to be available at the synapse. The ultimate effect the chemical will have on behavior depends on which type of disturbance it causes. We will look at these effects again in Chapter 5, when we consider the action of specific drugs.

The Lock-and-Key Model of Neurotransmission

Typically, a neuron releases the same neurotransmitter at all of the synapses formed by its axon. Since a neuron can have many dendrites, however,

Figure 2–3

The place where communication takes place between neurons is called a synapse. A synapse consists of the axon of one neuron, the dendrite of another neuron, and the space between them. When an action potential reaches the end of an axon, it causes the synaptic vesicles to release neurotransmitters into the synaptic space. These then activate the dendrites of the receiving neuron, which fires.

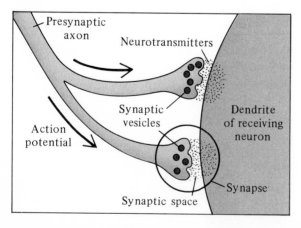

TABLE 2-1 Location and Effect of Some Neurotransmitters

Neurotransmitter	Location	Effect
Acetylcholine	Brain, spinal cord, autonomic ganglia, target organs of the parasympathetic nervous system	Excitation in brain and autonomic ganglia, excitation or inhibition in target organs
Norepinephrine	Brain, spinal cord target organs of sympathetic nervous system	Inhibition in brain, excitation or inhibition in target organs
Dopamine	Brain	Inhibition
Serotonin	Brain, spinal cord	Inhibition
Gamma-aminobutyric acid (GABA)	Brain (especially cerebral and cerebellar cortex), spinal cord	Inhibition
Glycine	Spinal cord interneurons	Inhibition
Glutamic acid	Brain, spinal sensory neurons	Excitation

Source: Carlson, 1981, p. 76.

it can receive stimulation from many different neurotransmitters. At each different dendrite of a neuron, different receptors can be found that recognize some neurotransmitters but not others. This is similar to a lock-and-key principle. An axon releases a neurotransmitter that has particular chemical characteristics. These characteristics are like the edges of a key. Dendrites are like locks; some keys can open them but others cannot. In other words, while each neuron may represent only one key, its dendrites represent many locks.

The important principles of neurotransmission are as follows:

1. Not every neuron releases the same neurotransmitter.
2. Different dendrites respond to different neurotransmitters.

These two simple principles add up to a rather complex matching system of neurotransmitters and receptors. Let's apply the analogy of the lock and key again. Only one key will open a lock. In the nervous system, the neurotransmitter is that key; the receptor site on the nearby neuron is the lock. When the "right" neurotransmitter appears at the receptor site, the lock is opened. Thus, by fitting "key" to "lock," a signal is transferred from the axon of one neuron to the dendrite of another. The message is accepted and is transported along the length of the receiving neuron to the end of *its* axon, where the lock and key procedure begins again.

In your everyday life, you must deal with many locks. Just look at your key ring. You have one or more car keys, an apartment or house key, a key that you use at your job, a key for your luggage, your bicycle, your safe deposit box, and so on. Similarly,

---

Synapse. A junction between two neurons, composed of the axon terminal of one neuron, the dendrite of the next neuron, and the space between them; site where communication occurs from one neuron to another.

Synaptic vesicles. Tiny ball-shaped containers near the end of the axon that hold the special chemicals used in neurotransmission.

Receptor. The place on the dendrite of a receiving neuron that picks up the neurotransmitter released by the axon of the activating neuron.

Neurotransmission. The process by which chemicals are released by one neuron and activate a nearby neuron.

Neurotransmitters. Chemicals released by the synaptic vesicles that carry messages from one neuron to another.

Acetylcholine (ACh). A prevalent neurotransmitter that affects skeletal muscles.

Catecholamine. A class of neurotransmitter that includes dopamine and norepinephrine.

in the nervous system many neurotransmitters are available. We know of more than 30, and it appears that there may be hundreds. Each of these neurotransmitters may be present in several different areas. For example, dopamine and norepinephrine can be found in many different sections of the brain. Thus, like a key that can be used to open many different locks, each of these neurotransmitters can find many different receptor sites. In this regard they are your house or car key. Your house key may be used to open both the front and the back door. Your car key may be used to start the car, open the door, open the trunk, and open the glove compartment. But just as your house key will not open the trunk of your car, so a neurotransmitter will not fit every receptor site. Figure 2-4 illustrates the lock and key principle.

Excitation and Inhibition

Although the chemicals used for neurotransmission vary widely, one of the fundamental aspects of this process is that all neurotransmitters do one of two things. In some cases, the action of a neurotransmitter on its receptor will bring a neuron closer to its threshold and increase the likelihood that an action potential will occur. When this happens, the receiving cell is described as being excited, and the neurotransmission is termed an **excitatory transmission**. On the other hand, if a neurotransmitter moves the cell away from its threshold, we say that the neuron has been inhibited and that neurotransmission is an **inhibitory transmission**. The presence of inhibitory neurotransmitters decreases the likelihood that an action potential will occur.

Excitatory transmission between neurons is clearly important for passing a message along the nervous system. Stopping your car at a red light, for example, requires that the message conveyed from your eyes be passed through many synapses to and in your brain. Through a series of connections between neurons, excitatory transmission can ultimately activate the neurons that control the muscles you use to apply the brakes.

Neural activity also needs to be regulated; thus inhibitory transmission is an important type of communication between neurons. Disturbances in inhibitory transmission can lead to chaotic neural activity, such as that seen in epileptic seizures. Seizures result from blocking of the reception of a

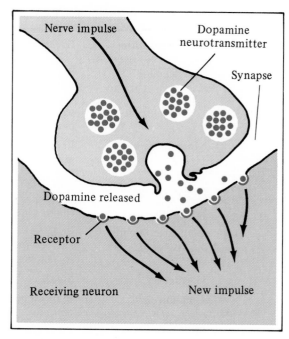

Figure 2-4
This figure illustrates the lock and key principle of neurotransmission. When the right neurotransmitter is received by the receptor sites on a nearby neuron, a signal is transferred from the axon of one neuron to the dendrite of another.

neurotransmitter that would prevent the seizures were it allowed to reach the dendrite. To return to the lock-and-key analogy, this is similar to inserting the wrong key in the lock. The key may go into the cylinder but not open the lock. Nevertheless, while the wrong key is in the cylinder, the correct key cannot be used to open that lock (Levinthal, 1979). The first key inhibits the action of the second. In an epileptic seizure, one neurotransmitter inhibits the action of another. Table 2–1 shows the inhibitory or excitatory effects of some neurotransmitters.

Some Common Neurotransmitters

Our understanding of the number and types of neurotransmitters involved in communication in the nervous system is increasing every day. At first, it was assumed that there were a few basic chemicals involved in synaptic transmission. It now appears that there may be hundreds of neurotransmitters in the nervous system. In many ways, research on neurotransmitters is in the same position as astronomy was when new and more powerful telescopes were being developed and astronomers were able to discover and name new stars on a regular basis. It is likely that the same will be true of neurotransmitters; as methods of detection and analysis improve, new chemicals will be identified.

Let's briefly consider several important neurotransmitters and their functions.

Dopamine is found in the brain areas that control muscles. This is because the neurons that produce dopamine at their axons are located in the basal ganglia of the brain. Disturbances of the basal ganglia result in motor disorders such as Parkinson's disease. When dopamine is present in enough quantity, we are able to move in a coordinated fashion. When dopamine production or reception is deficient, problems of movement occur. Medication (a substance called **L-dopa**) given to victims of Parkinson's disease is metabolized into dopamine and can sometimes eliminate the symptoms of the disease. You might wonder why the patient cannot be given pills or receive injections of dopamine, which would seem to be a more direct method. The reason is that the brain has a protective barrier around it, called **the blood-brain barrier,** that is intended to prevent poisons from reaching the nervous system. This barrier acts like a filter to prevent certain substances from reaching the brain. Dopamine is one of the substances that cannot pass the barrier. To get around the barrier, a chemical that can pass it (L-dopa) and then be metabolized into dopamine is used. The use of L-dopa is a perfect example of how increased knowledge of brain chemistry can lead to increasingly effective methods of treatment. Even large doses of dopamine would not pass the blood-brain barrier to combat the symptoms of Parkinson's disease. But small amounts of the drug L-dopa can be used effectively instead.

Another common neurotransmitter is **norepinephrine (NE)**. This substance is present in most areas of the brain and spinal cord. This means that there must be many NE receptor sites distributed throughout the nervous system and that NE must be involved in many different behaviors. NE is also produced by the neurons that make up the sympathetic nervous system (a part of the nervous system that controls the body without our awareness). Depending on its location, NE has different functions. In the brain, various concentrations of NE can affect states of consciousness. For example, NE has been implicated in states of excitement such as anger (Schacter, 1957) and pleasure (Stein, 1966). Insufficient NE is thought to be a cause of the disordered thinking of schizophrenics (Stein and Wise, 1973) and, possibly, of their inability to respond appropriately to pleasure. Once again, we can appreciate that our nervous system is like a small chemical factory, producing the chemical keys to open the chemical locks governing behavior.

Yet another group of neurotransmitters may play a part in the natural reduction of pain. In 1975, it was discovered that the brain contains naturally occurring substances that produce effects similar to the drug morphine (Hughes et al., 1975). These substances are referred to collectively as **endorphins**. Shortly thereafter it was discovered that the areas of the brain where these substances are found include those areas that are associated with the experience of pain. Endorphins were then recognized as neurotransmitters. The question was immediately raised whether these endorphins might normally serve the function of easing pain, and whether their release in the brain might be responsible for much of the placebo effect seen in pain studies. In this case, the **placebo effect**, as cited in Chapter 1, is the apparent reduction of pain experienced by a person, even when the person is taking a pill or injec-

---

Excitatory transmission. When the action of a neurotransmitter on a receptor brings a neuron closer to its threshold (and increases the likelihood of an action potential occurring).

Inhibitory transmission. When the action of a neurotransmitter moves a neuron away from its threshold (and decreases the likelihood of an action potential occurring).

Dopamine. A prevalent inhibitory neurotransmitter found in the brain areas that control muscles.

L-dopa. A chemical relative of dopamine that can pass through the blood-brain barrier and become metabolized into dopamine.

Blood-brain barrier. A barrier that prevents certain substances from reaching the brain.

Norepinephrine (NE). A common neurotransmitter found throughout the brain and spinal cord and implicated in many different behaviors.

Endorphins. Neurotransmitters apparently involved in easing pain.

Placebo effect. The apparent reduction of pain experienced by a person taking a pill or injection that contains no active ingredients.

tion that has only inactive or inert ingredients. The person, nevertheless, believes that a powerful drug is being taken and usually reports feeling decreased pain. It has been suggested that a release of endorphin occurs in response to taking the placebo, causing perceived reduction of pain.

The endorphins produced in the brain may play a role in extreme forms of exercise such as marathon running. Since painful stimuli apparently do result in the release of brain endorphins, this might result in some people developing a tolerance for pain. It has been suggested that marathon runners produce endorphins at greater than average rates as they run, enabling them to endure the pain that normally results from 26 miles of running. The hypothesized relationship between extreme physical exertion and the tolerance for pain may be too simple an explanation and may even be wrong. However, the prospect is interesting enough to stimulate research that will lead to a better understanding of the actual role of endorphins in both normal and abnormal behavior.

As we have already indicated, there are probably more than 100 neurotransmitters at work in the nervous system. The three we have considered—dopamine, norepinephrine, and the endorphins—were chosen because they are good examples of how specific neurotransmitters work to influence various forms of behavior. Table 2–1 lists some additional neurotransmitters and their influences on the body and behavior.

Individual Differences in Neurotransmission

Just as there are individual differences in hair color, eye color, and height, there are probably also individual differences in the neurotransmission system. Although you may not produce as much dopamine as the next person, you may produce more brain endorphins. These differences may be the result of heredity (the inheritance of certain neural characteristics from your parents), congenital factors (prenatal influences on the development of your central nervous system), or disease or injury that occurred after birth. What and when you eat can also have an effect on your neurotransmission system. The neurotransmitter known as **serotonin** is affected by levels of **tryptophan**, a substance derived from protein. In addition, serotonin levels change in response to blood sugar levels (Kalat,

1981). Fluctuations in serotonin have been implicated in behaviors as diverse as insomnia, mental disorders, and sensory perception, as well as in the regulation of body temperature. Not surprisingly, there may well be significant differences in serotonin levels, among people on a high-protein diet and those on a low-protein diet, that could affect their behaviors.

While the effects of general dietary habits on neurotransmission is still the topic of some debate, there is little doubt about the effects of alcohol and drugs on neurotransmission and resulting behavior. We will consider these effects in some detail in a later chapter.

■ AN OVERVIEW OF THE NERVOUS SYSTEM

Finally, we can outline a rather simple picture of the activity of the nervous system. All the capabilities of the brain are a product of vast numbers of neurons doing one of two things: being active or inactive. Many different types of chemicals are used as neurotransmitters, and those substances have either an excitatory effect or an inhibitory effect on the receiving neuron. Whether or not a neuron fires at any given moment depends on the relative amounts of excitatory and inhibitory neurotransmitters present at its many synapses. With these principles in mind, we can begin to look at the neural basis of behavior.

REVIEW QUESTIONS

1. Match the following terms with their correct definitions:

___ neuron

___ dendrite

___ axon

A. sends signals to other neurons

B. basic unit of the nervous system

C. receives signals from other neurons

2. The _____ _____ refers to the neuron's readiness to fire while the _____ _____ results from a change in the electrical

balance between the neuron and the environment.

3. Every action potential is the same—it does not matter what message is being carried, what part of the body the message is from, or even in what species it occurs.   T / F

4. The _____ law refers to the fact that an axon can either have an action potential or not have one—there are no halfway steps.

5. The fact that each neuron has its own _____ for producing an action potential can contribute to the type of message a neuron communicates.

6. Match the following terms with the correct definition:

___ synapse   A. chemical that activates neurons

___ synaptic vesicle   B. junction between two neurons

___ receptor   C. site that picks up neurotransmitters

___ neurotransmitter   D. contains neurotransmitter

___ excitatory transmission   E. prevents certain substances from reaching the brain

___ inhibitory transmission   F. neuron is moved away from its threshold

___ blood-brain barrier   G. neuron is brought closer to its threshold

Answers: 1. neuron, B; dendrite, C; axon, A   2. resting potential; action potential   3. True   4. all-or-none   5. threshold   6. synapse, B; synaptic vesicle, D; receptor, C; neurotransmitter, A; excitatory transmission, G; inhibitory transmission, F; blood-brain barrier, E.

■ FUNCTIONS OF THE NERVOUS SYSTEM

To understand the functions that communicating neurons perform, we will begin by looking at the organization of those neurons that process information. The billions of neurons in the human nervous system are divided into two large groups. One group is called the central nervous system and the other is called the peripheral nervous system.

The **central nervous system (CNS)** is composed of the brain and the spinal cord. It makes up the bulk of the nervous system, and it includes all of the complex interconnections that are used for interpreting the world around us and for directing our actions. The central nervous system, however, has no direct contact with the world or direct control over our movements; it relays and analyzes information. The **peripheral nervous system** is our link with the outside world. It is made up of all the nervous system components other than the brain and spinal cord. The peripheral nervous system receives information through the sense organs and transmits that information to the CNS. It then receives information from the CNS and takes appropriate action. In other words, the peripheral nervous system acts like a switchboard, relaying messages from the external world to the CNS for interpretation and from the CNS to various parts of the body for action. Figure 2–5 provides a diagram of the various parts of the nervous system that we will now consider. Notice the presence of the endocrine system, which is another communication system. We will consider the endocrine system later in the chapter.

■ THE PERIPHERAL NERVOUS SYSTEM

The peripheral nervous system is composed of two different kinds of neurons: those bringing information into the CNS and those carrying information out of the CNS. The neurons that bring information into the CNS are called **sensory neurons.** These neurons are activated by cells called **sensory receptors,** which are specialized to translate energy from the environment into electrical activity. As you will

---

Serotonin. A prevalent neurotransmitter implicated in such behaviors as insomnia, mental disorders, sensory perception, and regulation of body temperature.

Tryptophan. A substance derived from protein that affects serotonin levels.

Central nervous system (CNS). A division of the nervous system; composed of the brain and the spinal cord.

Peripheral nervous system. All of the nervous system outside of the brain and spinal cord.

Sensory neurons. Neurons that bring information into the central nervous system.

Sensory receptors. Cells that translate energy from the environment into electrical activity and thereby activate sensory neurons.

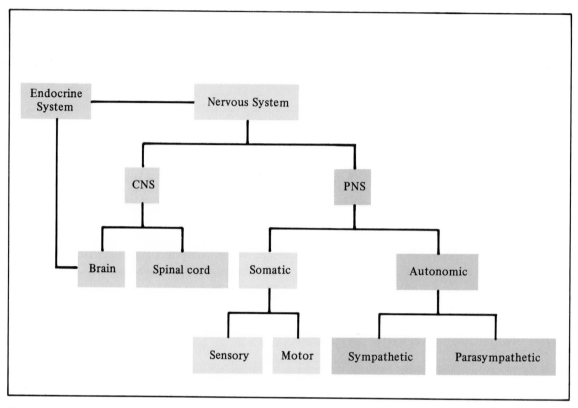

Figure 2-5
This is a schematic drawing of the divisions of the nervous system and their various subparts.

see in Chapters 3 and 4, "Sensation" and "Perception," you have different kinds of sensory receptors for receiving different kinds of information from the external world (such as light, sound, and so on). For example, the sensory receptors in the eye are tremendously sensitive to light but are relatively insensitive to other forms of stimulation, such as noise or physical pressure. The peripheral nervous system also has sensory neurons that are sensitive to various forms of activity inside your body. These neurons perform many tasks of which you are unaware, such as monitoring your blood pressure. Under some circumstances, however, you may become acutely aware of these sources of input. For example, if you are frightened by a sudden strange noise in the dark, you may feel your heart race and experience an unsettled feeling in your stomach. These experiences are brought to your awareness by sensory neurons in the peripheral nervous system, which convey their activity to the spinal cord and brain.

Another type of neuron found in the peripheral nervous system is called the **motor neuron**. These neurons carry information *out* of the CNS. Many motor neurons control the activity of our muscles and thereby direct our movements. These neurons form a part of the peripheral nervous system called the **somatic nervous system**. Other motor neurons control the activities of our internal bodily functions. In the example cited in the preceding paragraph, the noise in the dark produced bodily changes through the peripheral motor neuron activation of the heart and stomach. Because many of these changes in the activities of our internal bodily functions are automatic and, in many cases, are unnoticed, the part of the peripheral nervous system that controls these functions is commonly referred to as the **autonomic nervous system**. We will discuss each of these systems separately in the following sections.

Somatic Nervous System

The somatic division of the peripheral nervous system is more directly under our voluntary control than the autonomic division. It is the somatic division—the motor neurons that control our muscles—that we use to deliberately and knowingly direct our actions. Not all aspects of the somatic nervous system are under our control, however. In fact, an entire class of behaviors which involve muscle activity, called **reflexes**, occur automatically.

Reflexes. During a routine physical examination, your doctor may have tapped you just below the knee with a small hammer, and you may have noticed a small jerk in your lower leg in response to the tap. The doctor's hammer actually strikes a tendon that pulls a muscle, at first causing it to "stretch." This movement activates sensory neurons, which rush the message from the muscle all the way to the spinal cord. In the spinal cord, motor neurons are activated, and their messages travel back out to the muscles that control the knee joint, causing the "stretched" muscle to contract. This knee-jerk reflex occurs without any conscious direction on your part: The neural impulses travel from your muscle to your spinal cord and back to your muscle, without ever even reaching your brain. Many other reflexes are "wired" into the nervous system in this way, so that they occur automatically. These simple responses to input perform a host of helpful functions. In the case of the knee-jerk reflex, which is one of a class of stretch reflexes, these responses provide automatic adjustments for the changes in load to which our muscles are subjected as we move, lift, or carry objects. As a result of this automatic control of some aspects of behavior, we are free to direct our movements on a more general level; for example, we can avoid obstacles in our path or place the groceries where we want on the table.

Autonomic Nervous System

The autonomic nervous system is divided into two sections—the sympathetic and the parasympathetic systems. The **sympathetic nervous system** is geared to quick response in time of stress or excitement. It has direct connections with parts of the body that help us prepare for action. The **parasympathetic nervous system** acts as a control on the sympathetic nervous system. For example, it keeps the heart from accelerating to dangerous levels and acts to restore normal breathing. In other words, the sympathetic nervous system prepares us for action and the expenditure of energy, while the parasympathetic nervous system acts to conserve energy and brings us back to normal after the excitement is over. Figure 2–6 describes the various actions of the two parts of the autonomic nervous system.

Biofeedback involves using a machine that accurately measures and displays autonomic activity in order to learn to control specific bodily functions. For example, if you were attached to a machine that monitored blood pressure, you would probably find that with practice you could change your blood pressure on command, either raising or lowering it. Biofeedback has become useful as an aid to medical treatments for high blood pressure. Unfortunately, it appears that it is far easier to voluntarily raise blood pressure than it is to lower it. Biofeedback research has shown that people can gain some voluntary control over a number of autonomic responses (Shapiro et al., 1977). We will discuss biofeedback again later in the stress chapter.

Motor neurons. Neurons that carry information out of the central nervous system.

Somatic nervous system. The part of the peripheral nervous system that controls muscles; it is more directly under our voluntary control.

Autonomic nervous system. A part of the peripheral nervous system; controls internal bodily functions such as digestion, blood pressure, heartbeat, and so on.

Reflexes. Unlearned, automatic responses.

Sympathetic nervous system. A part of the autonomic nervous system; geared to quick response in time of stress or excitement; helps prepare us for action.

Parasympathetic nervous system. A part of the autonomic nervous system; acts to conserve energy (for example, slows heart beat).

Biofeedback. A way of controlling activity of the autonomic nervous system by using a machine that monitors and displays such activity. Providing people with feedback on such activity allows them to learn to control it.

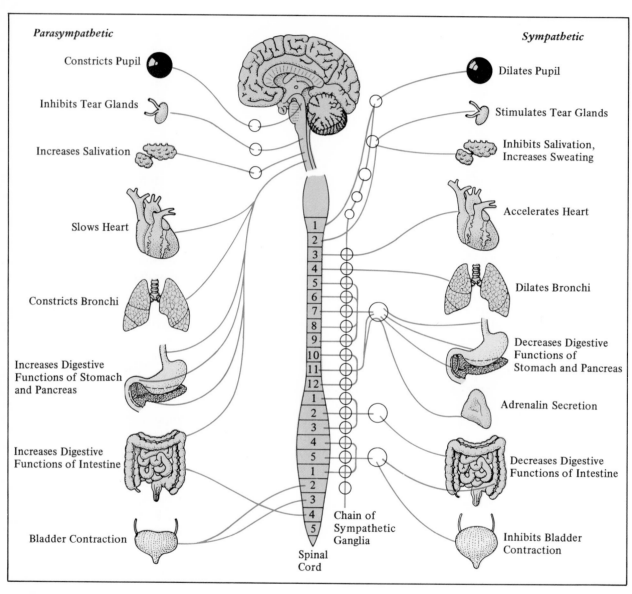

Figure 2-6

The autonomic nervous system is made up of two parts, the sympathetic and the parasympathetic. The sympathetic division generally acts to arouse the body, while the parasympathetic follows with messages to relax. The functions of each are shown in the figure.

REVIEW QUESTIONS

7. The central nervous system/peripheral nervous system has no direct contact with the world or direct control over our movements.

8. Sensory/motor neurons carry information out of the central nervous system; sensory/motor neurons bring information into the central nervous system.

9. The autonomic/somatic nervous system is under our direct or voluntary control; the autonomic/somatic nervous system affects heart rate, blood pressure, and digestion.

10. The sympathetic/parasympathetic subdivision prepares us for action in time of danger or stress; the sympathetic/parasympathetic subdivision brings us back to normal after the excitement is over.

Answers: 7. central nervous system *8.* motor; sensory *9.* somatic; autonomic *10.* sympathetic; parasympathetic

■ THE CENTRAL NERVOUS SYSTEM

The Spinal Cord

You were introduced briefly to the **spinal cord** in the discussion of the knee-jerk reflex. The spinal cord is covered by a set of hollow bones that reach from the base of the brain to a point about two-thirds of the way down the back. The tissue inside the spinal cord, like brain tissue, includes both neurons and non-neural cells. With the exception of sensations in the head, all sensations that come from the body enter the CNS through the spinal cord. Information relayed to the body from the CNS also passes through the spinal cord. In other words, everything that happens below the neck involves the spinal cord. Axons of sensory neurons enter the spinal cord at the rear and axons of motor neurons leave the spinal cord from the front.

Axons typically join one another outside the spinal cord and travel in a group commonly referred to as a nerve. There are 31 spinal nerves altogether, and the nerves that originate from different levels of the spinal cord are associated with different regions of the body. If a specific nerve is injured, sensation in the corresponding part of the body may be lost. Thus, when someone complains of numbness in an arm or leg, one possible explanation may be pressure on the spinal nerve that serves that area (this type of pressure is commonly referred to as a *pinched* nerve). The fact that particular nerves serve particular parts of the body can be used to advantage in the control of pain by surgical methods. Disrupting transmission of pain messages to the brain from the affected part of the body is called a *nerve block*.

Since a nerve contains both motor neurons and sensory neurons, a person's ability to use muscles in a body region may be affected when that nerve is damaged. For example, someone complaining of numbness in the left arm may also find that he or she can lift very little weight with that arm compared with the weight that can be lifted with the right arm. This is why injuries to the back and spinal cord can be so tragic. Since neurons do not reproduce themselves, once an area of the spinal cord is cut or injured, the loss of sensation and movement below the level of the injury is permanent—the brain can no longer communicate with the neural systems below the site of injury. This scenario may change in the future with the use of modern technology. The woman whose photo is on the next page was paralyzed from the rib cage down as a result of an automobile accident. Recently, by means of a special computer-driven apparatus, she has been able to achieve some measure of reflexive movement. The computer acts as a replacement for her spinal cord, electrically stimulating an artificial information flow between sense receptors near the skin and muscles groups in her legs. As you can see, she still requires elaborate aids to walk, such as a parachute harness and support bars. Nevertheless, such movement has never been possible before once the spinal cord was severed. She is not "cured," but this technological breakthrough may free her from her wheelchair.

In summary, the spinal cord is the part of the CNS that acts as a switchboard for sensory input and motor output for most of the body. As you will see, the information that enters the cord is dis-

Spinal cord. A cable of nerve fibers that runs from the brain to the lower back.

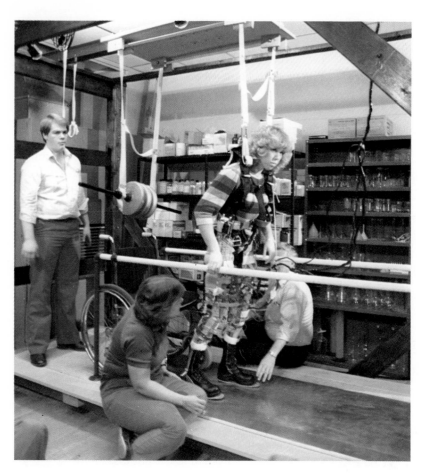

Nan Davis was paralyzed as a result of an accident. Here she is shown walking with the aid of a computer. The computer acts as a replacement for her spinal cord, artificially stimulating an information flow to her leg muscles.

tributed to a number of brain regions. Control over the activity of spinal cord neurons that send their axons out to muscles is also provided by a number of different brain regions.

The Brain

The Evolution and Development of the Brain. Like most mammals, the human being has a brain whose prominent features include an elaborately developed *cerebral cortex.* This cortex provides humans with a very powerful tool of organization. The cortex is intimately involved in sensation, perception, movement, and activities that generally fall under the heading of "thinking." Humans differ from other mammals in that our cortex is larger, affording more surface area. This expanded surface area means more cells, and more cells mean more power for information-processing, since the increased number of connections enhance efficiency (Kalat, 1981). If you are familiar with computer software, you know that some programs will run on very little "power" or storage area in the computer itself (e.g., 32K of memory) but others require a great deal of core storage or memory (e.g., 256K). These more "powerful" programs permit quicker and more sophisticated operations. Similarly, humans are capable of more sophisticated information-processing than other mammals with smaller cortical areas.

The brains of mammals were not always so arranged. It has been estimated that the human brain of today took several billion years to develop (Schneider and Tarshis, 1975). In the earliest stages of mammalian evolution, the brain was characterized by basic reflexive capabilities. Structurally, these capabilities were carried out by what is now referred to as the **hindbrain,** which is the portion of the brain closest to the spinal cord. Gradually, **midbrain** development occurred, allowing mammals to process information using both the hindbrain and the midbrain. Finally, the **forebrain** developed, and with it the cerebral cortex mentioned above. The development of each new brain structure (i.e., the midbrain and forebrain) did not make the hindbrain (or midbrain) useless or obsolete. Instead, with each new development the brain became more complex, with specific structures carrying out specific functions. The cortex, which developed most recently, seems more heavily implicated in behavior than the earlier structures. To return to our computer analogy, often if there are problems with our sophisticated software package, we can no longer do the simpler things that were possible with earlier and less sophisticated software. Similarly, the cortex now controls behavior that was once controlled by earlier structures. This may be one reason that head injuries are so serious. The forebrain, which now controls so much, is very likely to be involved in any blow to the head because of its prominent position.

Primates, and especially humans, are even further distinguished in terms of brain development. The brains of most mammals have two identical (or highly similar) halves. However, the primate brain has left and right hemispheres that perform different functions. Humans are described as having a **neocortex** ("new" cortex) that further segregates left and right hemisphere functions (Levinthal, 1979).

This evolutionary trend is most readily understood from a Darwinian perspective. Those members of a species who tended toward midbrain and forebrain development were more likely to survive (since they had information-processing capabilities superior to "average" members of the species). Thus, through various assortative and selective mating processes, brain structure continued to evolve. A few hundred thousand years from now, twentieth-century man may be viewed as primitive in respect to brain development. It may be that those individuals who have the most elaborate left/right hemisphere segregation of function are those most suited for survival in today's world and

are forming the foundation of continued neocortical differentiation. On the other hand, the environment might be radically altered (by a meteor shower or nuclear war) and other characteristics might be favored for survival. No matter what course the world takes for the next few hundred thousand years, however, we can safely assume that the brain will continue to evolve and change.

Roadmaps for Studying the Brain. The brain is extremely complex with highly differentiated structures and functions. There are many approaches to describing the brain. We could talk about it from an evolutionary perspective and consider the hindbrain, midbrain, and forebrain. We could break it down by function and look at the particular behaviors associated with various parts of the brain. We could look at the separate hemispheres of the brain (i.e., left and right). Finally, since we know that the cortex is such an important part of the human brain, we could look at subsections of the cerebral cortex.

It would be a kindness to the student if we could pick just one approach to the brain and stay with it. Unfortunately, that is not possible. The brain is so complex and so important that we must consider all these approaches. We can, however, begin with a primer on the various roadmaps that we will use. We can start with the evolutionary perspective. In Figure 2–7, you will see a picture of the brain as it is located in the skull. The areas that correspond to the hindbrain, midbrain, and forebrain have been indicated. Remember that the forebrain is the "newest" of the three areas and is characterized by a well-developed cortex. You can almost see how the human brain has "grown" over millions of years.

If we wanted to look at only the cortex of the brain, we could consider the two hemispheres separately, as illustrated in Figure 2–8, or we could further distinguish particular portions of the cortex called *lobes*, as in Figure 2–9. Finally, we could consider the various functions of parts of the brain. For

---

Hindbrain. Portion of the brain that is closest to the spinal cord.
Midbrain. Region between the hindbrain and forebrain.
Forebrain. Top part of the brain, including the thalamus, hypothalamus, and cerebral cortex.

Neocortex. Another term for the human cerebral cortex; the most evolved portion of the human brain.

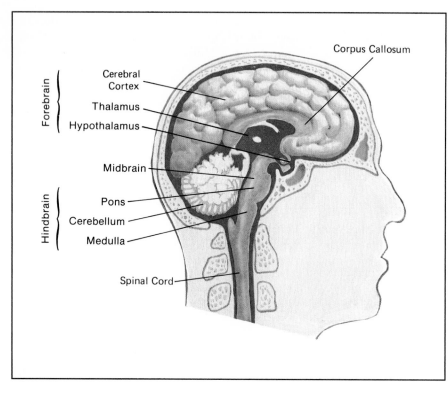

Figure 2-7
This is a picture of the brain that shows the hindbrain, midbrain, and forebrain areas. The hindbrain and midbrain are older in evolutionary terms; the forebrain is the "newest" part of the human brain.

Figure 2-8
The photograph of the brain clearly shows the split that separates the cortex into two hemispheres. The diagram shows the different functions performed by the right and left hemispheres of the brain.

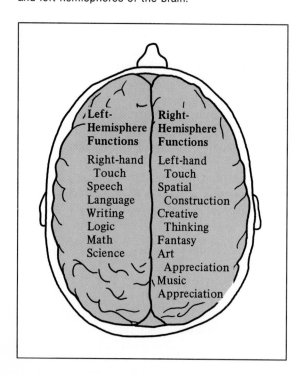

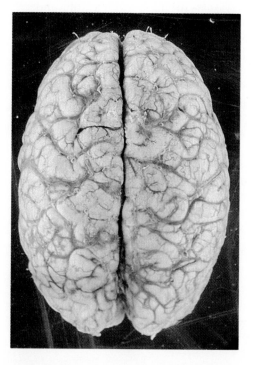

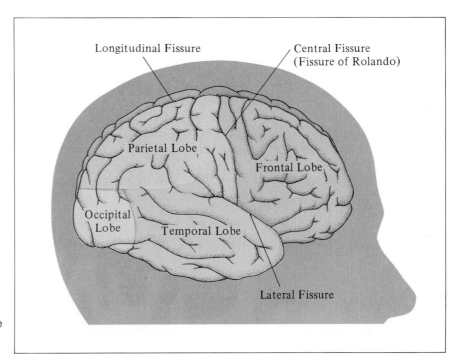

Figure 2-9
This is a side view of the brain, showing the four lobes of the cortex.

that purpose, we would need a roadmap that is more complicated, such as that illustrated in Figure 2–10. Even though we could use many different maps to travel through the brain, the important point is that each section deals with a different aspect of human behavior, regardless of which map we use. Just to make our exploration of the brain more orderly, we will start at the "bottom" of the brain and work up. As we get higher in the brain structure, things will get less orderly. As we have seen earlier, modern man is characterized by increasingly more complicated higher brain structures (and, as a result, is capable of increasingly complex behavior).

The Brainstem. As mentioned earlier, the hindbrain is considered the "oldest" section of the modern brain. It is located at the lower or bottom portion of the brain. The hindbrain (and in particular, the **medulla**) is implicated in some basic mechanisms such as breathing, heart rate, and blood pressure. In addition, balance and reflex movements

depend on the hindbrain structures. The **brainstem** can be thought of as the lower entryway to the hindbrain. The top end of the spinal cord enters the skull and attaches to the lower portion of the brain at the brainstem. The brainstem is like the spinal cord in several respects. Sensory and motor nerves connect to the brainstem as well. You will remember that the spinal cord has circuits that perform reflex actions (like the knee-jerk reflex). The brainstem has similar circuits, only they are much more important for survival. For example, breathing is controlled by groups of neurons in the brainstem, with the result that even minimal damage to some brainstem areas can be fatal. In recent debates about the death of boxers, the lower rope of the boxing ring has been implicated as a contributing factor. When a boxer falls backwards after being hit, his neck often hits the lower rope on the way to the floor, injuring the brainstem. If the injury is severe enough, vital functions like breathing stop and the boxer dies. In recent years, football helmets have been redesigned

---

Medulla. The hindbrain structure that controls functions such as breathing, heart rate, and blood pressure.

Brainstem. The top end of the spinal cord that widens to form the lower portion of the brain.

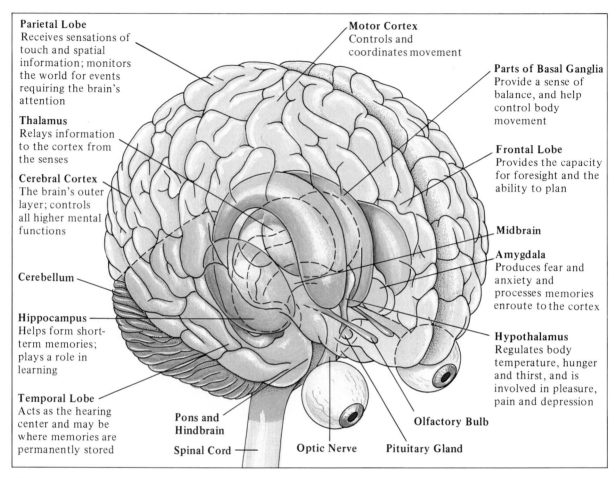

Parietal Lobe
Receives sensations of touch and spatial information; monitors the world for events requiring the brain's attention

Thalamus
Relays information to the cortex from the senses

Cerebral Cortex
The brain's outer layer; controls all higher mental functions

Cerebellum

Hippocampus
Helps form short-term memories; plays a role in learning

Temporal Lobe
Acts as the hearing center and may be where memories are permanently stored

Motor Cortex
Controls and coordinates movement

Parts of Basal Ganglia
Provide a sense of balance, and help control body movement

Frontal Lobe
Provides the capacity for foresight and the ability to plan

Midbrain

Amygdala
Produces fear and anxiety and processes memories enroute to the cortex

Hypothalamus
Regulates body temperature, hunger and thirst, and is involved in pleasure, pain and depression

Pons and Hindbrain

Spinal Cord

Optic Nerve

Olfactory Bulb

Pituitary Gland

Figure 2-10
This illustration brings together the anatomical structures and various functions of parts of the human brain.

to protect the brainstem area. Padding has been added to the back of the helmets at the base of the head. Many players, particularly linemen, also wear padded collars, which provide even greater protection.

The **reticular formation** is an area at the core of the brainstem that holds particular interest for psychologists. It is composed of large collections of neurons that receive input from a wide variety of sources, including all the sensory systems except the sense of smell. The reticular formation is heavily involved in regulating levels or states of consciousness. For example, the reticular formation is probably in-

volved in sleep states. We know from animal research (Moruzzi and Magoun, 1949) that a coma—a state similar to continuous sleep—can result from damage to some portions of the reticular formation. Damage to other areas in this region of the brainstem can produce a constant state of wakefulness. You may occasionally run into the term *reticular activating system* (RAS) to describe aspects of consciousness regulation. There is no difference between the reticular formation and the RAS. The former term emphasizes the area of the brain implicated in consciousness while the latter simply emphasizes the stimulating properties of the area.

The Cerebellum. Attached to the back of the brain-stem is a hindbrain structure called the **cerebellum**, which is involved in movement, particularly coordination and balance. People who suffer brain damage in this area often have an extremely un-coordinated gait and seem to be drunk. They also have difficulty reaching for objects; their hands either shoot past the object or bump into it.

As we can see, the various portions of the hind-brain such as the medulla, the cerebellum, and the reticular formation, are implicated in basic survival. They control the vital functions of breathing, blood flow, reflexes, and consciousness. Humans share these functions with other vertebrates. We often distinguish between "lower animals" and humans. We will see shortly that as we move "up" toward the cortex, the differences between humans and non-humans become more dramatic. Although the midbrain plays a role in such functions as hearing, sight, and the sensation of pain, its major function is to help transfer information to and from the fore-brain. Typically, forebrain functions are of greater interest to psychologists than either hindbrain or midbrain functions. For that reason, we will move immediately to a consideration of some of those forebrain functions.

The Hypothalamus and Thalamus. The hypo-thalamus and thalamus mark the boundary between the midbrain and the forebrain. They are both forebrain structures and, as such, are capable of complex functions.

As illustrated in Figure 2–7, the **hypothalamus** is found at the bottom of the forebrain. Neurons in the hypothalamus maintain optimal conditions in the body, such as body temperature as well as food and water intake, in accordance with biological needs. This function is sometimes referred to as

homeostasis. Depending on which part of the hypothalamus is injured, animals either are unable to stop eating, or do not eat at all and eventually starve. The hypothalamus is also implicated in emotional states characterized by pleasure, pain, or depression.

The **thalamus** sits in the middle of the brain above the hypothalamus and is made up of a number of different subregions. It is like a relay and coordinating station in the brain, preparing information for later integration by the cortex (a part of the brain we will examine in more detail shortly). In a sense, the thalamus acts like a projector, sending images to a screen (the cortex). It also deals with various types of sensory information independently, preparing each type for later processing by the cortex. There are distinct subregions of the thalamus that deal with the different senses; visual information passes through one subregion and auditory information through another.

The **basal ganglia** are interconnected structures in the forebrain that affect the control of motor responses. Patients with diseases that affect the basal ganglia do not become paralyzed, but do have movement problems. In **Huntington's chorea**, which is associated with the loss of neurons in the basal ganglia, patients have difficulty walking and speaking. As the disease progresses, memory loss, delusions, and hallucinations occur. The disease is almost always fatal, but before it kills it can debilitate its victims for 15 years or longer. One of the more famous victims of this disease was Woodie Guthrie, the noted folk singer and composer of the 1930s and 1940s. Huntington's chorea is an inherited disorder and a child of a Huntington's chorea victim has a 50 percent chance of developing the disease. In **Parkinson's disease**, which also involves the cells of the basal ganglia, movement becomes rigid and

---

Reticular formation. The area of the brainstem involved in regulating levels of consciousness; probably involved in sleep states.

Cerebellum. The area of the brain at the back of the brainstem, involved in movement, coordination, and balance.

Hypothalamus. A part of the forebrain; involved in regulating bodily conditions such as food and water intake. Active in both the nervous system and the endocrine system.

Homeostasis. The process of maintaining optimal bodily conditions, such as regulating body temperature, or food or water intake.

Thalamus. A part of the forebrain; serves to forward information coming from many different parts of the body.

Basal ganglia. Structures in the forebrain that affect the control of motor responses.

Huntington's chorea. A disease affecting the basal ganglia, in which patients have difficulty in walking and speaking, and also experience memory loss, delusions, and hallucinations.

Parkinson's disease. A disease affecting the basal ganglia; movement becomes rigid and difficult.

difficult. This is because the basal ganglia, together with the cerebellum, play a critical role in the movement of muscles and joints.

The Limbic System. Like the basal ganglia, the **limbic system** is made up of a set of interconnected structures. The **hippocampus,** an area of the brain involved in the sense of smell, emotions, and memory, and a few small regions of the thalamus and hypothalamus are included in the limbic system, and this set of structures forms a circuit. Since the limbic system appears to be heavily involved in emotions and memory, it is of interest to psychologists..

Many different memory disorders have been connected to limbic system damage (Rozin, 1976). The limbic system is illustrated in Figure 2–11.

You recall that we began this chapter with a description of H. M., who suffered the inability to form new memories following an operation that removed his hippocampus. Typically in such cases, a person can remember events that occurred before the damage. Thus, someone with limbic system damage might be able to tell you many recollections from childhood but fail to remember what happened yesterday. Cases such as these have led scientists to suspect that the limbic system is *not* used as a storehouse for memories. If that were the case, pa-

tients would not be able to recall *old* memories after injury to the limbic system. Intead, the limbic system appears to be important for *passing on* information that is then stored in other brain areas. This would explain why no new or recent memories are stored after damage to the limbic system—they don't get passed on.

The limbic system also plays a role in the regulation of emotions. It has been recognized for many years that damage to some parts of the limbic system can make normally ferocious animals quite tame and placid. In humans, damage to the limbic system often leads to inappropriate emotional responses (such as laughing at something sad or crying at something funny), or to appropriate but exaggerated responses (such as laughing loudly instead of simply smiling, or crying intensely instead of frowning).

■ THE CEREBRAL CORTEX

The **cerebral cortex** (also known as the **cerebrum**) covers the forebrain. It contains many folds, which give it a wrinkled appearance. This wrinkling allows an extremely large surface area to fit inside the volume of the skull. The cerebral cortex consists of two hemispheres, which can be subdivided into four smaller areas or lobes. The **occipital lobe**, located at the back of the brain, is associated with vision. The **temporal lobe**, next to the occipital lobe, controls hearing. The **parietal lobe**, above the temporal and occipital lobes, responds to touch, pain, and temperature. The **frontal lobe**, at the front of the brain as its name indicates, receives information from the other three lobes and communicates with the muscles and the limbic system. In the chapter on therapy, we will see that for a short period of time surgical experiments conducted with patients exhibiting severe emotional disorders involved severing portions of the frontal lobe in an attempt to reduce emotionality. The position of the frontal lobe made it possible to insert a scalpel through the eye socket or through a small hole drilled in the side of the skull.

In humans, the cortex contains 70 percent of all the neurons in the CNS (Nauta and Feirtag, 1979). Different areas of the cortex have distinct functions. We will now explore each of the areas in detail.

Figure 2–11
The limbic system includes the hypothalamus, part of the thalamus, and other forebrain structures. It is involved in two areas of interest to psychologists, emotion and memory.

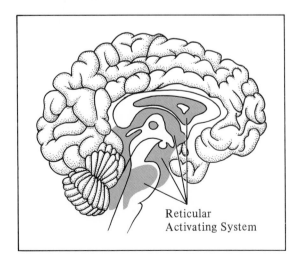

Reticular
Activating System

Motor Cortex

The **motor cortex** is involved in the control of movement. We now know that some neurons in the motor cortex send their axons all the way down to the spinal cord where they are capable of activating motor neurons. Thus the motor cortex, located at the very top of the brain, is actually only a synapse away from the motor neurons that control our muscles. The importance of the motor cortex can be seen when this system is damaged. A stroke victim may at first be left with paralysis or extreme weakness affecting some part of the body. The location of a motor disturbance in a limb will typically be found on the side of the body opposite to the site of damage in the brain. This is because the axons of neurons located in the motor cortex cross over to the opposite side of the brain as they travel down to the spinal cord. The same is true of the sensory cortex. Each half of the brain generally receives its information from the opposite half of the body.

In Figure 2–12 a map of the human body is laid out across the motor cortex. This map shows the location of the neurons in the motor cortex that control different parts of the body. The map may look strange to you, however, because the head—in particular, the face—is very large and distorted, and the hand looks out of proportion when compared with the foot. This reflects the fact that the highly skilled movements of human hands and the range of facial expressions we use for communication require more neurons, and that consequently a larger area of cortex is devoted to these body regions.

Sensory Cortex

The **sensory cortex** processes visual, auditory, and somatic (skin senses) information. There is a separate area of the sensory cortex for each of these

different types of stimulation. These areas are called, respectively, the visual cortex, the auditory cortex, and the somatosensory cortex. Input to each of these areas comes from a specific sensory receptor (such as the eye, the ear, the skin) through the thalamus.

In the **somatosensory cortex**, information about touch and movement arrives by means of neurons that originate in the skin and joints of the body. The right side of the cortex receives information from the left side of the body, and the left side of the cortex receives information from the right side of the body. If the somatosensory cortex is damaged, it will affect information from the opposite side of the body.

Within each hemisphere, a "map" of the opposite half of the body is found in the somatosensory cortex. This map can be seen next to the one describing the motor cortex (look at Figure 2–12 again). The body regions that appear enlarged in the somatosensory cortex are those that we would describe as the most sensitive. For example, our lips or fingers are much more sensitive than our forearms or backs, as the map reflects.

The **visual cortex** receives and processes information from the eyes. You can see how the cortex is arranged in Figure 2–13. With your head held in any steady position, all the area within your view is called your **visual field**. The visual pathway from your eyes is arranged so that all of the information from the left half of the visual field arrives on the right side of the brain in the visual cortex, and the left visual cortex receives the information from the right half of the visual field. Each half of the visual cortex contains a highly organized map of the opposite half of the visual field. Destruction of a small region of the visual cortex will produce blindness in one small part of the visual field.

Limbic system. The structures in the forebrain involved in emotions and memory.

Hippocampus. The area of the brain involved in the sense of smell, emotions, and memory; part of the limbic system.

Cerebral cortex or **cerebrum.** Covers the forebrain; divided into two hemispheres. Responsible for almost all higher-order or complex behavior.

Occipital lobe. A part of the cerebral cortex; responsible for vision.

Temporal lobe. A part of the cerebral cortex; responsible for hearing.

Parietal lobe. A part of the cerebral cortex; responds to touch, pain, and temperature.

Frontal lobe. A part of the cerebral cortex; receives information from the other three lobes and communicates with the muscles.

Motor cortex. A part of the cerebral cortex; involved in control of movement.

Sensory cortex. A part of the cerebral cortex; processes information from the eyes, ears, and skin.

Somatosensory cortex. A part of the sensory cortex; processes information about touch and movement.

Visual cortex. The area of the brain involved in seeing.

Visual field. All the area within view of the two eyes when the head is held in a steady position.

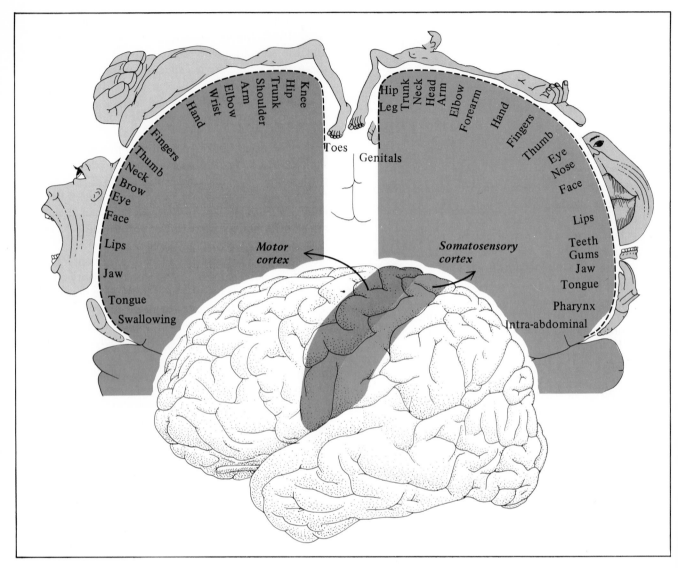

Figure 2-12
There are regions in the motor cortex and the somatosensory cortex that are
associated with specific parts of the body. The relationship between body parts and
areas of the cortex is shown in these two maps. Some body parts are shown larger
than others to reflect the fact that a larger area of the cortex is devoted to them.

To sum up, we have seen that different types of
sensory information are processed in separate
regions of the sensory cortex. Within these separate
regions, certain principles of organization apply. Inputs from the different senses to the cortex are
crossed, with each side of the brain receiving information that originates from the opposite side of
the body or visual field. A type of map exists for each

area of the sensory cortex, which shows an arrangement whereby neurons in the cortex are activated by the stimulation of corresponding locations
in the sensory receptors.

Now you can begin to appreciate the statements
made earlier in this chapter about how different
kinds of information are coded in the nervous system. Neurons do not use action potentials of var-

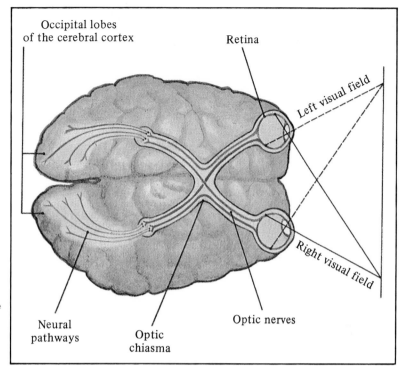

Figure 2-13
The visual cortex is arranged by area. All information from the left half of the visual field goes to the right side of the brain. Information from the right half of the visual field goes to the left side of the brain.

ious types to represent different stimuli such as sights and sounds. Instead, different neuron groups are involved in information exchanges about differing stimuli. Certain neuron groups (for example, receptors in the eye) carry messages to other neuron groups in the brain (for example, in the visual cortex). Moreover, these neuron groups carry and interpret messages of great variety. The variety is produced by the differing firing and recovery rates of the neurons involved, as well as by stimuli that vary in intensity.

The Association Cortex

Having described the motor and sensory cortexes, we find that there is still a good deal of the cortex left that we have not described. This is usually referred to as the **association cortex**. Some of the association cortex is devoted to the further processing of information from the various senses. Other areas of the association cortex are related to complex actions and motor performances. For example, the association cortex is involved in complex perceptual tasks such as recognizing objects and faces,

as well as in planning and executing complex sequences of behavior such as speaking.

For most right-handed people (approximately 95 percent), it is the left hemisphere that serves language. In left-handed people, the right hemisphere is used somewhat more frequently for language; but in over 70 percent of left-handed people, it is still the left hemisphere that serves their verbal abilities. Different areas of the association cortex contribute to different perceptual and motor aspects of language. Normal use of language requires the cooperation of several of these important areas of the cortex (see following box).

In the 1860s, Paul Broca proposed that damage to a specific area on the left side of the brain produced speech difficulty. Broca's area is identified in Figure 2–14. This region of the association cortex sits just in front of the part of the motor cortex that is related to the lips and the tongue, which explains why damage to this area causes problems in speech

---

Association cortex. The part of the cerebral cortex involved in complex perceptual tasks and complex sequences of behavior.

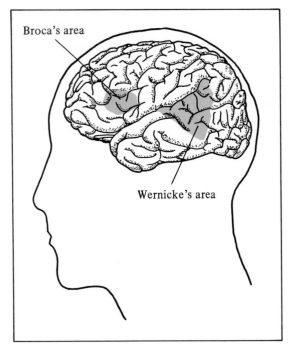

Broca's area

Wernicke's area

Figure 2-14
Damage to either Broca's area or Wernicke's area of the association cortex results in different types of aphasia, or difficulty in speaking and understanding language.

production. Patients with damage to Broca's area have great difficulty in speaking (*aphasia*) that is not due to paralysis. In contrast, damage to the same region of the cortex on the right side of the brain does not produce any disturbance in speaking, evidence that speech is generally associated with the left hemisphere.

In **Broca's aphasia**, speaking requires a good deal of effort and words are poorly articulated. Speech is also marked by grammatical errors. It is difficult for patients suffering from Broca's aphasia to form full sentences. Instead, their speech is characterized by single words and short phrases composed mostly of nouns. These patients are frequently described as using a "telegraphic" style of speech because what they say sounds like the contents of a telegram. However, they have little difficulty understanding language that is spoken to them in conversation.

A second type of aphasia was described by Carl Wernicke in 1874. This involves damage to a brain area called Wernicke's area, which is located in another region of the association cortex. (Wernicke's

area is also shown in Figure 2-14.) **Wernicke's aphasia** affects both comprehension and speech. Patients are able to produce many sentences that have a recognizable structure, and they articulate surprisingly well. It is the content of their speech that is frequently incomprehensible. Sometimes the wrong words are used, and sometimes nonsense words or syllables are used. At the same time, the disorder produces difficulty in understanding spoken conversation. In fact, Wernicke's aphasia patients have trouble understanding both written and spoken language. This region of the association cortex receives input from the auditory and visual cortexes. Thus, as in Broca's aphasia, there is some connection between the section of the cortex involved and the nature of the problem.

The Hemispheres of the Brain

The brain is divided into halves or left and right hemispheres. As we have indicated, in humans the left hemisphere performs perception and motor tasks that involve the use of language (see Figure 2-8). The right hemisphere performs a variety of functions that are nonverbal in nature. This does not mean that the right hemisphere is "illiterate," it just means that language skills are more developed in the left hemisphere. In Chapter 7, you will see that under certain circumstances, the right hemisphere can take over language skills if there are left hemisphere problems.

As you look at this page in your book, it is the left side of your brain that allows you to read the pattern of visual stimuli in your visual field that is provided by the print on the page. If you reach for a cup of coffee while you are reading, it is the right hemisphere that allows you to distinguish between the coffee cup and a flower vase next to it. Without a left hemisphere, you might be unable to read, but you could still identify the coffee cup by touch. Without a right hemisphere, you would not be able to use a map. When damage occurs to the left or right hemisphere, symptoms like these will be observed, but the exact symptoms will depend on the specific area of the hemisphere where the injury occurred.

Split Brain Research. Given that the brain is split into halves, it is natural to wonder if the two hemispheres are independent of one another. Normally,

IT TAKES MORE THAN AN EAR FOR LANGUAGE

The human brain is capable of numerous complex operations, including the use of language. Linguistic competence does not come easily, however; for us to speak and to understand what is spoken, many parts of the brain must work together. Consider what happens when you hear a word and repeat it (Figure 1). First, information from the ears is transmitted to the auditory cortex. But the word is not understood until this information is transmitted to Wernicke's area, where it is processed. If we want to repeat the word, it must somehow be represented in Wernicke's area; this representation is then transmitted to Broca's area via a group of nerve fibers called the *arcuate fasciculus.* There, a plan for its vocalization is formulated. This plan is passed on to the area of the motor cortex that controls the mouth, lips, tongue, larynx, and so forth. The proximity of Broca's area to the motor cortex makes this transfer easy. Both Wernicke's area and Broca's area are discussed in the text.

What if we want to read aloud a written word (Figure 2)? First, our eyes transmit information to the visual cortex. Now we have a visual representation of the word. This representation is transmitted to a part of the brain called the *angular gyrus,* which associates it with the corresponding auditory representation in Wernicke's area. Then, if the word is to be spoken, the processes described above must take place. Think of the number of transactions that must occur simply for you to read this sentence out loud.

Adapted from: Scientific American, Sept 1979. "Specializations of the Human Brain" by Norman Geschwind.

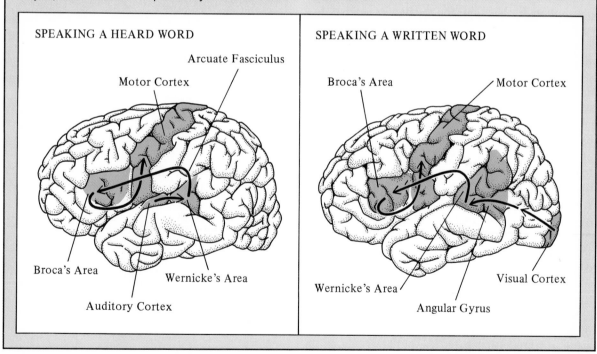

SPEAKING A HEARD WORD

Arcuate Fasciculus
Motor Cortex
Broca's Area
Wernicke's Area
Auditory Cortex

SPEAKING A WRITTEN WORD

Broca's Area
Motor Cortex
Wernicke's Area
Visual Cortex
Angular Gyrus

they are not. The two hemispheres of the cerebral cortex are connected by a structure known as the **corpus callosum** (See Figure 2–7). The corpus callosum is a neural pathway that allows information to move freely between the two hemispheres. The role of this structure was not well recognized before

---

Broca's aphasia. Difficulty in speaking that results from damage to an area on the left side of the brain; speech is marked by grammatical errors and incomplete sentence formation.

Wernicke's aphasia. A brain disorder that affects both speaking and comprehension; speech may show wrong choice of words or sometimes nonsense words and syllables.

Corpus callosum. A neural pathway that connects the two hemispheres of the brain.

research was done on epileptic patients. Research had suggested that epilepsy could be controlled in some patients by cutting the corpus callosum. It was felt that cutting it might reduce the occasional violent bursts of energy exchanged between the two hemispheres that seemed to be characteristic of at least some forms of epilepsy. Since there was concern about negative side effects that might be associated with this surgical procedure, studies were done anticipating the effects of such surgery on various aspects of patients' behavior. This surgery was later carried out and a battery of tests was constructed to determine the effects of this surgery (Gazzaniga, 1977). Before these tests, the prevailing view was that there would be no aftereffects to this surgery (Akelaitis, 1944). The prevailing view was wrong. There were a number of effects.

As described earlier, there is a crossing of the visual pathways from each eye, so that the images seen in the left visual field are projected to the right hemisphere of the brain, and the images seen in the right visual field are sent to the left hemisphere. The left hemisphere of the brain controls speech. If these surgical subjects were presented with a visual stimulus in their right visual field and asked to describe it, they had no problem doing so. But if the stimulus was presented to the left visual field, they could not describe it. In fact, they claimed that they had seen nothing but a flash of light. But if, instead of *describing* the stimulus, the subjects were asked to *point with the left hand* (the left hand is controlled by the right hemisphere of the brain and vice versa) to the object, they almost always pointed correctly, in spite of the fact that they just had claimed that there had been nothing but a flash of light! (Sperry, 1964). These tests showed that cutting the corpus callosum does cause side effects.

Another experiment showed even more clearly that the two hemispheres could no longer communicate if the corpus callosum was severed. If two different figures were presented simultaneously to the right and left visual fields, something interesting happened. Sperry used a dollar sign ($) on the left side and a question mark (?) on the right side. If the subject was asked to put the left-hand figure out of sight and draw what had been presented, the subject drew a dollar sign, the figure that was presented to the left visual field. If the subject was then asked what he or she just drew, the response was "a question mark," the figure that appeared in the right

visual field and was transmitted to the left or speech hemisphere. As you can see from these experiments, not only is the cortex of each hemisphere important for normal behavior, but so is communication between the two hemispheres.

REVIEW QUESTIONS

11. Once an area of the spinal cord is cut or injured, the loss of sensation and movement below the level of the injury may come back slowly, but it will eventually heal.   T / F

12. Breathing is controlled by groups of neurons in the _____ .

13. Damage to various areas of the brain result in certain behaviors; match the behavior with the area of damage associated with it:

___ damage to the cerebellum	A. overeating or undereating
___ damage to the hypothalamus	B. laughing at something sad; crying at something funny
___ damage to the hippocampus	C. lack of coordination and balance
___ damage to limbic system	D. loss of ability to process information to create new memories

14. The _____ _____ , which covers the forebrain, is divided into two hemispheres, each of which can be divided into four lobes. Match each lobe with its function.

___ occipital lobe	A. hearing
___ temporal lobe	B. vision
___ parietal lobe	C. processes information from other lobes
___ frontal lobe	D. touch

15. Input to each area of the sensory cortex comes from a sensory receptor through the _____ to the cortex.

16. In the _____ cortex, information about touch and movement arrives by means of neurons that originate in the skin and joints of the body.

Answers: 11. False 12. brainstem 13. damage to the cerebellum, C; hypothalamus, A; hippocampus, D; limbic system, B 14. cerebral cortex; occipital, B; temporal, A; parietal, D; frontal, C 15. thalamus 16. somatosensory

METHODS OF STUDYING THE BRAIN

Our consideration of damage to Broca's and Wernicke's areas brings us back to a point made at the beginning of the chapter: The injured brain provides us with a natural laboratory for learning about the intact brain. Fortunately, there are many ways now available besides surgery to study the brain and detect abnormalities. These techniques are highly refined and provide greatly detailed information.

CAT (Computerized Axial Tomography) scanners take X-rays of the brain at various levels (or X-ray "slices") and then combine those X-rays to produce a picture of the whole brain.

NMR (Nuclear Magnetic Resonance) is a more sophisticated form of the familiar X-ray. It depends on the use of magnetic fields to produce pictures of organs. The NMR technique is very successful in detailing the inner surfaces of the brain.

Both CAT and NRM techniques produce pictures of an organ in suspended animation. *PET* (Positron Emission Tomography) is specifically intended to portray a picture of the *working* brain. PET is based on the idea that as neurons in a given part of the brain fire, this part of the brain replenishes its energy supply by absorbing sugar from the blood. PET scanning maps the location in the brain of radioactively tagged sugar molecules that were injected into the patient for release into the bloodstream. By mapping the site of the brain's energy use, we can identify which parts of the brain are working normally and which are not.

EEG (electroencephalogram) is a method of studying the electrical waves produced by the brain under various conditions of stimulation. Cer-tain stimuli should produce one kind of brain wave and other stimuli should produce different brain waves. Electrodes are attached to various points on a person's scalp and the electrical activity is picked up by those electrodes and recorded on a chart. If the wrong type of waves are produced with a given stimulus, some possible problem is indicated. In Chapter 5, we will see how brain wave data are used to study sleep.

An EEG is a record of ongoing electrical activity in the brain. This activity might be monitored for an hour or more. Often, it is informative to watch how a person responds to a particular stimulus (e.g., a sound or a flash of light). This technique measures what is called the *evoked potential*, or the electrical response that was evoked (or caused by) a particular stimulus.

Cerebral Blood Flow is another potential indicator of brain abnormalities. As is the case with any organ of the human body, blood circulation is important for efficiency. It is possible to inject a dye into a person's circulatory system and watch the dye as it passes through various organs. An X-ray picture, called an *angiogram*, can be produced which outlines the circulatory system in the brain. If blood flow is reduced to one area of the brain, one would expect problems to arise. In fact, this is what happens when a person has a stroke—a portion of the brain is deprived of blood (and oxygen) and disordered behavior results.

Buchsbaum (1983) has made a good case for using many of these diagnostic techniques in combination when trying to understand how normal and abnormal brains function.

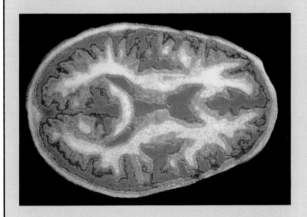

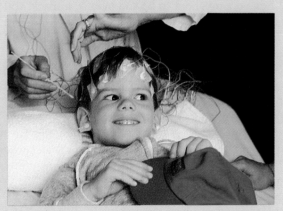

■ THE ENDOCRINE SYSTEM

In multicelled animals there are two communication systems. The first is the one we have just examined —the nervous system. In this system communication is electrochemical. The second communication system is the circulatory system. This system carries chemical messages through the bloodstream. These messengers are carried by substances called **hormones,** which have effects on various organs of the body. In the same way that synaptic vesicles release neurotransmitters, hormones are released by specialized organs called **glands.**

There are two different types of glands—the *exocrine glands* and the *endocrine glands.* Exocrine glands do not secrete hormones directly into the blood. Instead, these glands use special pathways or ducts. An example of an exocrine gland is the salivary gland, which sends hormones to the stomach through the digestive tract. Endocrine glands secrete hormones into the bloodstream, and the blood then carries these hormones to the various organs of the body, including the brain. This characteristic makes the endocrine system a communication system. Since the endocrine glands have a much greater impact on our behavior than the exocrine glands, we will examine only the **endocrine system.** Figure 2–15 illustrates the glands of the endocrine system and their relative positions in the body.

Why do we need two communication systems? Why not just have *either* the endocrine system *or* the nervous system? We need both of these systems because they serve different purposes. The nervous system is very rapid and is geared for quick action. When you are about to be run over by a truck, you want your eyes to communicate with your brain and your brain to communicate with your legs in a split second. The speed of transmission can be the difference between life and death. The endocrine system, on the other hand, is slower-acting and is intended to support sustained action of some type. There are some exceptions, however. For example, the adrenal glands act very quickly even though they are part of the endocrine system. This is because they are part of the stress-response mechanism that helps an individual prepare to fight or flee a threatening stimulus. As you will see in Chapter 12, "Motivation and Emotion," in many instances the endocrine system ensures that the body continues to react after the initial response of the sympathetic nervous system has ended. This means that the two communication systems—the nervous system and the endocrine system—work together to accomplish a goal. They are neither completely independent of one another nor redundant.

You have had first-hand experience with the relative speed of the two communication systems. You must have noticed that your emotions do not disappear when the stimulus that caused those emotions disappears. After an argument, it may be several minutes before you calm down. In the same way, after a very pleasant surprise (such as winning an award), the euphoric feeling may last for quite a while. In part, this is a result of the fact that your endocrine system is still carrying an "anger" or "joy" message to various parts of your body. As the hormones are absorbed and broken down into other chemical elements, their message fades and your body returns to normal.

The Hypothalamus

The keystone of the endocrine system is the *hypothalamus.* As you learned earlier, the hypothalamus is a part of the brain that is involved in maintaining a balanced internal environment for the body (through homeostasis). As part of the neural network, it carries out this function electrochemically. In addition to the role it plays in the neural-communication system, the hypothalamus also plays a major role in the endocrine system. It is the hypothalamus that stimulates the glands that, in turn, secrete hormones into the bloodstream.

The Pituitary Gland

While some glands have direct effects on particular areas of the body, some glands are important because of their capacity to stimulate other glands. For example, a hormone called **prolactin** causes an increase in the activity of the mammary glands of females, which results in the production of milk in the breasts. The **pituitary gland** secretes prolactin. This means that there is really a chain reaction in which the pituitary gland produces prolactin, prolactin stimulates the mammary glands, and the mammary glands produce milk. The pituitary gland is involved in the activation of many other glands,

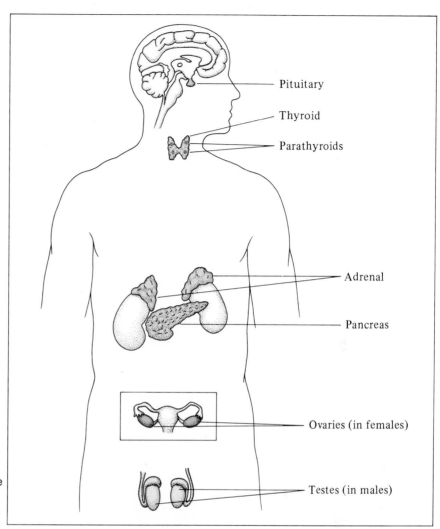

Pituitary

Thyroid

Parathyroids

Adrenal

Pancreas

Ovaries (in females)

Testes (in males)

Figure 2-15
This is a schematic drawing of the glands of the endocrine system that shows their relative positions in the body.

as well. For instance, it secretes a hormone that causes the male testes to produce testosterone and the female ovaries to produce estrogen and progesterone. It also secretes a growth hormone that aids in the development of muscle and bone. For this reason, the pituitary gland is often called the "master gland."

Table 2–2 lists some examples of hormones and their effects on specific glands and organs. This is really just a sample of hormonal action, not a complete listing. Nevertheless, it should give you some appreciation of the intricacy of the circulatory-communication system and the important role of the pituitary gland in that system. Let's consider some other glands that have direct implications for human behavior.

Hormones. Chemical substances produced by endocrine glands; regulate sexual development and the reproductive cycle, growth, fluid and food intake.

Glands. Organs in the body that produce various chemical substances, including hormones.

Endocrine system. A communication system made up of glands

that release hormones that help regulate bodily activities into the bloodstream.

Prolactin. A hormone produced by the pituitary gland; stimulates the mammary glands to produce milk.

Pituitary gland. The master gland of the endocrine system; involved in the activation of many other glands.

TABLE 2-2
Glands, Hormones, and Effect on Organs in the
Endocrine System

Gland	Hormone	Target or Function
Pituitary	Growth hormone	Growth
	Trophic hormones:	
	ACTH	Adrenal cortex
	TSH	Thyroid
	FSH	Gonads
	LH	Gonads
	Prolactin	Mammary glands
	Vasopressin	Kidney, blood pressure
	Oxytocin	Mammary glands, uterus
Thyroid	Thyroxine	Development, metabolic rate
Parathyroid	Parathormone	Calcium, phosphorous metabolism
Adrenal cortex	Sex hormones	(see below)
	Glucocorticoids	Metabolism of carbohydrates, protein, and fat
	Mineralocorticoids	Electrolyte, water balance
Adrenal medulla	Norepinephrine	Circulatory system, glucose release
	Epinephrine	
Pancreas	Glucagon	Glucose release
	Insulin	Glucose transfer and use
Ovaries	Estrogen	Development and
	Progesterone	maintenance of sexual anatomy,
Testes	Testosterone	physiology, and behavior

Source: Sommers, 1972.

The Thyroid Gland

The **thyroid gland** has two major influences on behavior. The first influence is on the development and maturation of the human body. As you will see in Chapters 10 and 11 on development, various systems of the body continue to develop after birth. This is particularly true of the nervous system. As a child grows, the nervous system unfolds. Neural pathways develop, the brain becomes increasingly complex, and organs develop, requiring greater control by the various parts of the nervous system. If the thyroid gland produces too little of its hormone (called **thyroxin**), development goes poorly, and there is substantial physical and mental retardation. This condition can be treated easily and effectively if it is diagnosed early in a child's development. Thyroxin injections can provide enough of the hormone to support normal physical and mental development.

The second major function of the thyroid gland is to control the speed at which the cells work (metabolic rate). In a sense, this works like the idling screw on a carburetor. It can be high, in which case the body's "engine" will run fast, or it can be low, in which case the "engine" will run slowly. Too little thyroxin in an adult causes sluggishness, difficulty in maintaining body temperature, and sometimes depression. Too much thyroxin produces difficulty in paying attention, excitability, and insomnia. A lack of thyroxin can be corrected by pills or injections; an overabundance of thyroxin is often corrected through surgery. A part of the thyroid gland is removed, thus reducing the amount of thyroxin produced (Levinthal, 1979).

The Pancreas

The **pancreas** is located between the stomach and the small intestine. It produces **insulin,** a hormone that aids in transporting **glucose** to the cells of the body. This activity is critical since glucose, a form of sugar, is the primary energy source for our cells. Without sufficient amounts of glucose, our cells will not function efficiently. When you eat, the food is broken down into a number of basic substances. As a by-product of digestive action, the pancreas is activated and produces insulin. This insulin then helps transport the glucose to the individual cells. The effect of improper pancreas functioning can be seen in the diabetic. When too little insulin is secreted, the glucose that results from the breakdown of food is not absorbed by the cells. This has two effects. First, it results in a great loss of water through urination, which leads to dehydration. This is one of the reasons that screening tests for diabetes often include questions about thirst. If a person is always thirsty, it may be because he or she is losing too much water as a result of a low insulin level. In addition to water loss and dehydration, the diabetic also becomes weak, since the cells are not receiving enough fuel to work efficiently. Diabetes is an internal form of starvation and has the same effect as depriving a normal person of enough food to support normal activity. In this instance, the diabetic gets enough food but cannot break it down and absorb it properly.

A malfunction of the pancreas can usually be corrected by insulin injections or pills. The treatment must be carefully regulated, however, since too much insulin will cause the cells to absorb too much glucose. This leaves insufficient glucose circulating in the bloodstream, thus depriving the brain of glucose. The result can be seizures or even, in an extreme case, a coma. Diabetics who have taken too large a dose of insulin by mistake can counteract the effects of this insulin by eating something sweet. This will increase the amount of glucose in the bloodstream, since sweet foods are easily converted to glucose (Levinthal, 1979).

The Adrenal Glands

The **adrenal glands** are located on the top of each kidney and are associated with many different behaviors, most notably stress reactions. The adrenal gland consists of two parts: the covering of the gland (called the **adrenal cortex**) and the body of the gland (called the **adrenal medulla**). The adrenal chain is somewhat complex. The hypothalamus stimulates the pituitary gland, which secretes the hormone ACTH. This ACTH, in turn, stimulates the adrenal cortex. Finally, hormones produced by the stimulation of the adrenal cortex (called steroids), activate the adrenal medulla and result in the secretion of the adrenal hormones epinephrine (or adrenalin) and norepinephrine (which also acts as a neurotransmitter).

The Physiology of a Complex Behavior

Since we have dealt with the nervous system and the endocrine system separately, it is tempting to think of them as functioning independently of one another. The simplest way to avoid this temptation is to examine a complex behavioral event that has a clear physiological foundation and to consider the interactions of the nervous system and endocrine system in that event. For that purpose, we will consider the physiological mechanisms that underlie the sexual response in humans.

Sexual Response. In humans, the physiological mechanisms involved in sexual activity include the hypothalamus, the endocrine system, and the peripheral nervous system. The pituitary gland is responsible for activating the gonads, the male and female sex glands, but it is the hypothalamus that initially activates the pituitary gland. Once stimulated, the gonads produce the sex hormones estrogen (in the female) and testosterone (in the male). These hormones enter the bloodstream and make

---

Thyroid gland. An endocrine gland that influences growth and development in humans; also affects the speed at which cells work (metabolic rate).

Thyroxin. The hormone produced by the thyroid gland; affects growth and development, and metabolic rate.

Pancreas. An endocrine gland that lies between the stomach and small intestine; as a by-product of digestive action, it is activated and produces insulin.

Insulin. A hormone produced by the pancreas; aids in transporting glucose, a form of sugar, to the cells of the body.

Glucose. A form of sugar that is the main source of energy for most of the body's tissues.

Adrenal glands. Endocrine glands consisting of the adrenal cortex and adrenal medulla; involved in many different behaviors, most notably stress reactions.

Adrenal cortex. Outer covering of the two adrenal glands that releases hormones that are important in the body's response to stress.

Adrenal medulla. Inner core of the adrenal glands that also releases hormones that are important in the body's response to stress.

their way back to the hypothalamus and play a role in actually initiating sexual activity.

The human sexual response can be initiated in several different ways. First, direct stimulation of the sex organs can set the chain in motion. In addition, sexual thoughts or dreams can begin the reaction. Finally, the secretion of sex hormones, for whatever reason, can also activate the response system. Thus, it is easy to see how closely the various physiological systems are interrelated in initiating the sexual response.

Once the sexual response has begun, other reactions take place in the peripheral nervous system. Masters and Johnson (1966) have identified the two basic processes that maintain the sexual response cycle. **Vasocongestion** is the engorgement of the blood vessels and corresponding flow of blood into the tissues of the genital region. The most obvious consequence of this process is the erection of the penis. Erection occurs when the arteries carry more blood to the penile tissues than the veins can take away. In females, vasocongestion occurs in the blood vessels and tissues surrounding the vagina. As a result, fluid seeps through the vaginal wall, producing lubrication. **Myotonia** is the contraction of the muscles in the genital region and in the rest of the body. Myotonia is most obvious during orgasm for both males and females and is responsible for ejaculation in males.

For ease of description, Masters and Johnson divided the sexual-response cycle into four stages. During the first (or excitement) stage, vasocongestion begins in response to sexual arousal. This stage follows the initiation of the hypothalamus-endocrine loop described above. At this point, the genitals become enlarged due to an increase in blood volume, as do the breasts. The nipples of the breasts become erect due to the onset of myotonia.

In the second (or plateau) stage, sexual arousal reaches its peak. Muscle tension (myotonia) increases throughout the body, heartrate and blood pressure rise, and a measles-like rash called a sex flush may appear on the abdomen and chest. This sex flush is a more common occurrence for females than males.

The third (or orgasm) stage, consists of a series of rhythmic contractions of the pelvic organs at approximately 1-second intervals. These contractions are accómpanied by a sharp increase in pulse rate, blood pressure, and breathing rate. Ejaculation usually occurs in the male. For both males and females, orgasm is accompanied by a release of sexual tension and subjective reports of intense pleasure.

During the fourth (or resolution) stage, the body gradually returns to its normal, pre-arousal state. Blood flows out of the blood vessels of the genital tissues, and the genital organs return to their normal size and position. Masters and Johnson noted that at this stage, males enter into the "refractory period," during which time they are incapable of further arousal to sexual stimulation. The refractory period is variable and may last from several minutes to hours. Some females, in contrast, can have multiple orgasms with little or no refractory period.

Masters and Johnson came to some important conclusions about the sexual response cycle. First, it appears that the physiological processes involved in orgasm do not depend on how the response cycle was initiated (e.g., by masturbation or intercourse). Second, the same physiological responses occur in response to both homosexual or heterosexual stimulation. Finally, the physiological responses of males and females are very much alike.

Thus, in examining the physiological foundation and mechanisms of the sexual response, we have an excellent illustration of not only the importance of several physiological mechanisms, but also the critical importance of the *interactions* of those mechanisms.

REVIEW QUESTIONS

17. Areas other than the motor and sensory cortexes, called the _____ cortex, are involved with further processing of information and complex behaviors.

18. In _____ aphasia, wrong words and sometimes nonsense words or syllables are used, but patients have no trouble speaking in complete sentences. In _____ aphasia, patients have difficulty forming full sentences—they tend to use single words and short phrases only.

19. The _____ hemisphere of the brain handles language and the _____ hemisphere handles nonverbal skills. The two hemispheres are connected by the _____ _____ .

20. Communication in the endocrine system is done by _____ , chemicals that circulate in the bloodstream.

21. Match the following terms with the correct definition:

___ hypothalamus   A. produces insulin, which transports glucose to the cells

___ pituitary gland   B. called the master gland because it is involved in the activation of many other glands

___ thyroid gland   C. active in both the nervous and the endocrine systems; maintains balanced internal environment

___ pancreas   D. influences growth and development in humans; also controls the speed at which cells work

___ adrenal glands   E. involved in stress reactions, among other behaviors

Answers: 17. association 18. Wernicke's; Broca's 19. left; right; corpus callosum 20. hormones 21. hypothalamus, C; pituitary gland, B; thyroid gland, D; pancreas, A; adrenal glands, E.

■ PHYSIOLOGY AND BEHAVIOR: A SUMMARY STATEMENT

By now you can appreciate the number and complexity of physiological factors that organize our behavior. As a final analogy, think of the largest computer you can imagine. There may be 1,000,000 electrical "connections" in that machine. Then think of a new computer that is 10,000 times larger (multiply the number of "connections" by 10,000). Now consider a plant that is capable of reliably producing several hundred different high-quality chemicals. Combine the computer and the chemical plant into a new "system" that fits in a space about the size of a cantaloupe. That is the human brain—an electrochemical system that organizes behavior.

Also from reading this chapter, you should have an idea of the role that physiological factors play in behavior. These factors represent the first or preliminary organizing influences on the behaviors we see; you have seen enough examples of behaviors that are not completely, or even substantially, explained solely on the basis of physiological factors to realize that behavior is not *just* cells or chemicals. Because behavior is the *interaction* of the organization imposed by physiological factors *and* experiences, the material that you have learned in this chapter will come in handy when we consider topics such as emotion, memory, and abnormal behavior. It seems fair to say that the biologist and the psychologist are really looking at the same behavior from different points of view. The biologist looks at human experience in terms of changes in body chemistry or electrical potential in cells. The psychologist looks at human experience in terms of behavior of various kinds. But neither the biologist nor the psychologist can do a satisfactory job of *understanding* behavior without the perspective of the other.

Regarding this chapter, you should especially remember two major points. The first is that all humans possess the systems that have been described here. We all have spinal cords, brains, neurotransmitters, and endocrine systems. Further, all of us have approximately 100 billion neurons communicating with each other. All of us—men and women, fat people and thin people, blacks and whites, old people and young people, short people and tall people—have the same structures. Consequently, we can count on these structures to remain stable parts of the behavioral systems that we will consider in the following chapters. This does not mean that we can take these biological circumstances for granted. Instead, it means that we should assume that they play some role in the behavior of all people. The second point to remember has to do with the organization of the nervous system. The 100 billion neurons do not interact randomly; they are organized to perform particular functions.

Vasocongestion. Part of the sexual response cycle. Refers to the engorgement of blood vessels and corresponding flow of blood into the genital region.

Myotonia. Part of the sexual response cycle. Refer to the contraction of muscles in the genital region and in the rest of the body most obvious during orgasm; responsible for ejaculation in males.

Groups of neurons form nerves that connect with particular parts of the body. These neurons permit us to take in information, analyze it, choose a course of action, and execute a response. Behavior is not *merely* the interaction of all these neurons. It is the interaction of *organized* neurons. Think of a football team with 22 of the biggest and most talented players available. If you gathered these 22 people together in a stadium one day and asked them to compete against a team of 22 different players, they might lose. Their abilities would be wasted if they were not organized into an offense of 11 players and a defense of 11 players. Furthermore, if the offensive team and the defensive team were not given any specific instructions (plays or defensive formations), even the basic organization they did have would not matter. The same is true of the body. It is how the body's energies and capacities are organized that makes the difference between ordered behavior and chaos. Any disruption of that organization will lead to a disruption of behavior.

■ SUMMARY

1. Though the body's nervous and endocrine systems interact to affect behavior, by far the most important element in determining behavior is the brain. The brain is a part of the *nervous system,* whose central unit is the nerve cell or *neuron.* Neurons act in groups. *Dendrites* are the branch-like parts of the neuron that pick up signals from other neurons. One *axon* per neuron transmits messages to other neurons. Unlike other types of cells, neurons cannot reproduce, so if one is destroyed it cannot be replaced. Neurons can repair themselves, but the neurons that serve the muscles repair themselves more easily than the neurons that comprise the brain and spinal cord.

2. A neuron's *resting potential* is its readiness to fire. A change in the electrical balance between the inside and outside environments of a neuron results in a sequence of firing and recovery, known as the *action potential.* An impulse travels along a neuron in a chain-reaction sequence: The part that has been stimulated first is responsible for the first impulse, which stimulates a second part, and so on. All action potentials take an identical form, but some neurons fire more frequently, more easily, or more rapidly depending on the stimulus—differences that

help the brain to interpret neural messages. The *threshold* is the minimum amount of energy necessary to trigger a response. The *all-or-none law* refers to the fact that neurons can do one of two things: They can fire or not fire. After firing, the period of time necessary for a neuron to recover before it can fire again is known as the *refractory period.*

3. The action potential of every neuron is identical. We are able to discriminate between action potentials, which serve as signals conveying information to the brain, because specialized cells for conveying this information have different endpoints in the brain, neurons performing the same function differ in their sensitivity, and stimuli vary in intensity.

4. The axon of one neuron, the dendrite of another, and the space between them make up the *synapse,* or the place where communication between neurons occurs. A *receptor* on the receiving dendrite picks up a chemical messenger, or a *neurotransmitter,* released by the axon of the neighboring neuron. Some of the most common neurotransmitters are *acetylcholine, dopamine,* and *norepinephrine.* Neurotransmitters can have either an *excitatory* effect on a neuron, bringing it closer to its threshold, or an *inhibitory* effect, decreasing the likelihood that the neuron will fire.

5. The *central nervous system (CNS)* consists of the brain and the spinal cord and includes all the complex interconnections that are used for interpreting our world and directing our actions. The *peripheral nervous system* is our link with the outside world and transmits information from our sensors to the CNS.

6. The peripheral nervous system is made up of *sensory neurons,* which receive stimulation from the environment in the form of electrical activity, and the *motor neurons,* which carry information out of the CNS and control the activity of our muscles. We use the *somatic nervous system* to control our actions, but many automatic behaviors, *reflexes,* are also part of this division. The *autonomic nervous system* is divided into two sections: the *sympathetic nervous system,* geared to quick response in time of excitement, and the *parasympathetic nervous system,* which acts as a control on the sympathetic nervous system.

7. One way to look at the brain is from an evolutionary perspective. In the earliest stages of evolu-

tion, reflexive capabilities were carried out by the *hindbrain,* the portion of the brain closest to the spinal cord. Gradually, the *midbrain* and then the *forebrain* developed. The forebrain is more heavily implicated in behavior than the earlier structures.

8. The *spinal cord* is the part of the CNS that acts as a switchboard for sensory input and motor output for most of the body. Severed nerves in the spinal cord can result in both a permanent loss of sensation and a loss of movement in a particular body area. The *brainstem* is the top portion of the spinal cord that widens to form the lower portion of the brain. Because this part of the CNS also contains some sensory and motor neurons vital to survival, severe damage to the brainstem can be fatal. An area of the brainstem, the *reticular formation,* is involved in regulating states of consciousness. Attached to the back of the brainstem is the *cerebellum,* which is involved in movement. Parts of the forebrain include the *hypothalamus,* which sustains optimal conditions for the body (homeostasis); the *thalamus,* which prepares information for later integration into the cortex; the *basal ganglia,* interconnected structures in the forebrain involved in the control of motor responses; and the *limbic system,* interconnected structures involved in emotion and memory.

9. The *cerebral cortex* covers the forebrain. The cortex is divided into a left and right hemisphere, each of which are further divided into four lobes: the *occipital lobe,* which processes visual information; the *temporal lobe,* which processes auditory information; the *parietal lobe,* which processes somatic information; and the *frontal lobe,* which receives information from the other lobes and communicates with the muscles and limbic system. In humans, association areas of the cerebral cortex in the left hemisphere perform perception and motor tasks that involve language; the right hemisphere performs a variety of functions that are nonverbal in nature. The two hemispheres are connected by the *corpus collosum,* which provides communication between the two hemispheres. The *motor cortex* is involved in the control of movement. In both the *sensory cortex* and the *motor cortex,* each half of the brain generally receives its information from the opposite side of the body.

10. For most right-handed people, it is the left hemisphere that processes language. Normal use of language requires the cooperation of several areas of the cortex including *Broca's area* and *Wernicke's area.* Damage to either area produces particular kinds of language problems, or *aphasia.*

11. In the *endocrine system, glands* release *hormones* to be carried through the bloodstream to various parts of the body, including the brain. The endocrine system is slower-acting than the neural system, and is intended to support sustained action of some type. The keystone of the endocrine system is the *hypothalamus,* which stimulates the glands to secrete hormones. Some of the important glands of the endocrine system are the *pituitary gland,* the *thyroid,* and the *pancreas.*

■ ANSWERING QUESTIONS FOR THOUGHT

1. Axons of neurons located in the motor cortex cross over to the opposite side of the brain as they travel down to the spinal cord. Thus, damage from a stroke to the left hemisphere will result in paralysis on the right side of the body.

2. Neurons cannot reproduce themselves—thus, if an area of the spinal cord is cut, there is no longer any way that the brain can communicate with the neural systems below the site of the injury.

3. Football linemen wear padded collars to protect the brainstem, an area of the brain at the base of the skull. An injury to this area will affect vital functions, such as breathing, and may result in death.

4. The sympathetic nervous system is geared to quick response in time of stress or excitement, and has direct connections with parts of the body that help prepare for action.

5. The endocrine system is slower-acting than the nervous system, and is intended to support sustained action of some type. Hormones circulate through the bloodstream, which takes much longer than neurotransmission. The reason it takes longer for your emotions to disappear after an argument is that your endocrine system is still carrying an "anger" message to various parts of your body.

3 Sensation

QUESTIONS FOR THOUGHT

1. Why does it take you a few minutes to be able to see well in a darkened movie theater? And why, after leaving the theater, does the sunlight make you squint your eyes?
2. Why can't you see colors in the dark?
3. How do you know what direction a sound is coming from?
4. Why do you lose your sense of taste when you have a head cold?
5. What causes seasickness? Is there anything you can do about it?

The answers to these questions are at the end of the chapter.

In Chapter 2 we saw the importance of the biological point of view to the psychologist's understanding of behavior. To understand the processes we will be examining next—how the senses take in information and how we process that information—we again have need of the biological viewpoint. Before focusing on sensory processes, let us look first at the human organism as a whole.

The human body consists of a series of interrelated subsystems. Each subsystem has a particular function and a specific relationship with other subsystems. For example, the sympathetic nervous system prepares the body for quick action while the parasympathetic nervous system compensates by letting the body rest after stress. We are not aware of many of these systems. Indeed, they work without any intention on our part. Once they are activated, a regular sequence of reactions occurs almost as if the body were on automatic pilot.

The very elaborate systems we have for collecting physical energy from the environment, transforming that energy into neural impulses inside the body, and translating those impulses into subjective experience are among the systems of which we are unaware. For example, it is difficult to ignore a flash of light or a loud bang. When such events occur, our senses are activated. Similarly, how we make sense of these sensations (that is, how we *perceive* events), does not seem to be something we control. Though we may "know" that the moon doesn't change in size, it is difficult for us to prevent it from looking larger when it is closer to the horizon than it does when it is high in the sky.

In this chapter we will consider **sensation**; we will see how information from the outside world gets inside the body. In the next chapter we will consider **perception**; we will discover what happens to that sensory information once it gets to the brain.

Sensation and perception don't really deal with different subject matter. Both processes require the stimulation of certain physiological equipment, with which most of us are born, that receives energy from the outside world and transforms it into neural impulses that are analyzed by the brain. Sensation and perception do differ, however, in which physiological mechanisms come into play and when they come into play. Figure 3–1 will give you a general idea of how sensation and perception are related. As you can see, the first thing that happens is an "event" in the outside world—a light, a noise, a jab in the arm. We see the light; we hear the noise; we feel the pain. If a firecracker went off ten feet from you, you would experience all the sensations of sight and sound and pain simultaneously. The senses involved would be vision, hearing, and touch. In the first second or two after the explosion, a physiological process would be activated. Your body would begin to prepare for action: Your heart would speed up, your breathing pattern would change, your pupils would dilate. Most of us would have no control over these sensations. At about the same time, a mental process would begin. You would try to make sense of or "interpret" the event. Was it a gunshot, a car backfiring, or a firecracker? The mental process involves matching the sight, sound, and feel with other sights, sounds, and feels you have experienced in the past in order to decide what has actually happened.

Sensation. The reception and transformation of physical energy from the outside world into neural impulses.

Perception. The interpretation of neural impulses sent to the brain by sensory receptors.

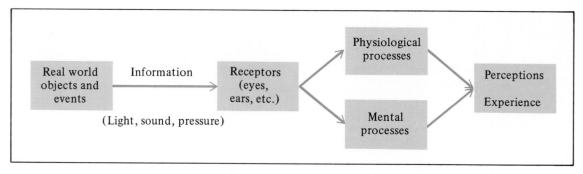

Figure 3-1

A diagram showing how sensation and perception are related. A chain of reactions begins when an event in the outside world engages certain receptors. This triggers physiological and mental processes that result in an interpretation of the event. The first part of this chain of reactions is what is usually referred to as sensation.

Your perception of the event is thus the result of a chain of reactions. It begins when something happens in the outside world, by which we mean outside the brain. As we shall see, muscles, tendons, and even the inner ear give information about body position and movement, so information can come from inside the body as well as from outside. The event engages certain **receptors**, as we call the equipment that receives energy from the outside world. Certain complicated processes—one physiological (in the peripheral nervous system) and one mental (in the central nervous system)—are triggered, resulting in translations of the outside events into what we call "experience." The first part of this chain reaction—the *reception* and *transformation* of physical energy from the outside world into neural impulses—is commonly referred to as "sensation." The second part of the chain—the *interpretation* of neural impulses—is what we mean by the term "perception." Perceptions play a major role in behavior. Most of our conscious actions depend upon our perceptions—our subjective impressions—of the outside world and not on its actual or objective characteristics. But before we discuss the final outcome of the chain of reactions we have been considering, let's go back to the beginning—to sensation, the point at which we become aware.

■ HOW WE MEASURE SENSATION

When we consider the physical energy we receive from the outside world, it is best to think in terms of stimulation. A specific instance of stimulation is called a **stimulus**, a psychological term that will become very familiar to you by the time this course is over. (In this chapter we will be dealing with physical stimuli, but later we'll see that ideas can also be stimuli.) Since stimuli represent the raw material from which perceptions are constructed, it is important to know something about their characteristics. In addition, you will also need to know something about the capacities and characteristics of receptors, since they are responsible for translating stimuli into neural impulses.

The nature of physical stimuli can be described by using some of the basic terminology and logic

The first thing that happens in sensation is an event in the outside world—an explosion, a burning fire. The way this event gets transformed into neural impulses and sent to the brain is the subject of this chapter.

of physics. Our capacity to receive these stimuli (that is, our receptors) can be described with the basic terminology and logic of physiology. When we combine the two disciplines of physics and physiology to study sensation and perception, we have a new field called **psychophysics.** Psychophysics is concerned with the measurement of sensations. By measuring sensations we discover not only how effective our sensory receptors are at receiving information, but also how effectively these senses convey physical reality in messages that our brains can comprehend. For example, the poor classroom performance of an elementary-school child could result from a number of things, including a defect in hearing or a dyslexia. Defective hearing is frequently a problem in receiving information. Dyslexia, a collective term for reading difficulties, is generally a problem in translating this information into perceptions. In order to help the child, we would need to identify the problem.

Thresholds

The lowest level of stimulation a person notices when none was noticed before, or the point at which a person notices that the level of stimulation has increased beyond a previous level, is known as a **threshold.** It would be nice and neat if each person always had the same threshold, but that is not the case for the following reasons:

1. Our thresholds are not fixed. Our sensitivity to particular stimuli varies, depending on circumstances.
2. Our senses are not all equally informative. Some senses, such as vision and hearing, provide high-quality, refined information. Other senses, such as touch, provide more general and limited information. As a result, we depend more heavily on some senses than on others. The two dominant senses in humans are vision and hearing.
3. Our senses are subject to sensory problems. Look around your classroom. The fact that some people wear glasses while others don't is testimony

TABLE 3-1.
Absolute Thresholds

Sense	Absolute Threshold
Seeing	Candle flame seen from 30 miles away on a clear dark night.
Hearing	A watch ticking under quiet conditions from 20 feet away.
Taste	1 teaspoon of sugar in 2 gallons of water.
Smell	1 drop of perfume diffused into the area of a three-room apartment.
Touch	A wing of a bee falling on your cheek from a distance of 1 centimeter.

Source: Adapted from Galanter, 1962.

to some common sensory problems. Some of us need a little help for our senses to work effectively.

These factors account for the differences between and within individuals in terms of what they see, hear, or feel at a particular time, but such differences usually occur within a fairly limited range. This means that it is possible to talk about the "average" person. For example, we know that most adults can hear sounds with frequencies of 20 to 20,000 cycles per second. The same kind of statement can be made for the other senses.

One way of describing the "average" capability of each of our senses is to identify the least amount of stimulation that will be noticed or sensed. Table 3–1 lists the smallest amount of stimulation needed to activate a particular sensory receptor. This minimum amount of stimulation is called an **absolute threshold.** Just as a threshold might separate one room from another, the absolute threshold separates sensation from nonsensation. In other words, at least this much stimulation is necessary before a person notices the presence of a stimulus such as a sound or an odor. If the strength or inten-

---

Receptor. Sensory mechanism that receives energy from the outside world.
Stimulus. Any change in physical energy that activates a receptor.
Psychophysics. A branch of psychology that deals with the measurement of sensation.

Threshold. The point at which a person notices stimulation when none was noticed before, or notices that stimulation has increased beyond a previous level.
Absolute threshold. The least amount of stimulation needed to produce a sensation.

sity of a stimulus is below this value, no sensation will be noticed by the person. To use the data in Table 3–1 as an example, if a candle is lit on a dark night and a person with "normal" vision is 30 miles away from that candle, he or she will be able to see a light in the distance. If the person is 40 miles away from the candle, he or she will not be able to see it.

As indicated above, the ability to sense a stimulus varies from person to person and even within the same person from time to time. As a result, a threshold has been traditionally defined as the value that will result in a positive report (the person reports the presence of a stimulus) 50 percent of the time that the stimulus is actually present. Therefore, you should think of a threshold as an average value, rather than a constant one, that applies to all people in all circumstances.

The absolute threshold is not the only type of threshold that exists. In fact, you are probably more familiar with the **difference threshold**. In contrast to the absolute threshold, the difference threshold represents the least or minimum difference between two stimuli that will be noticed. This minimum difference has been referred to as the **just-noticeable difference**, or *jnd* for short. To give you an example, think of a three-way light bulb that has a 50-watt, 100-watt, and 150-watt capacity. When the light switch is moved from the 50-watt to the 100-watt position, you can certainly notice the difference. But if the light had a 50-watt, 50.5-watt, and 51-watt capacity, you would not be able to tell if the switch were moved from the 50-watt to the 50.5-watt position unless you actually watched someone turn the switch. This means that the jnd for brightness must be more than the brightness produced by .5 watt, but less than the brightness produced by 50 watts.

Through carefully arranged experiments over the years, psychologists have been able to identify the jnd's for many common stimuli. During these experiments, something important was discovered about jnd's. They are not absolute values but proportional values. Consider the three-way light bulb again. At one time or another, you may have noticed that the difference between a 50-watt and a 100-watt light seems greater than the difference between a 100-watt and a 150-watt light. In other words, the increase in perceived light seems more dramatic when you go from 50 to 100 watts than it does when you go from 100 to 150 watts. This is

due to the unique proportional characteristic of jnd's. Experiments have shown that we notice changes in terms of *percentages* rather than absolute values. In the light bulb example, there is a 100 percent increase in light from 50 watts to 100 watts. We arrive at this percentage by dividing the change in intensity by the original intensity (50/50). Now look at what happens when we go from 100 watts to 150 watts: The increase is only half of the previous increase, or 50 percent (50/100).

This unique aspect of human sensation was recognized by an experimenter named Ernst Weber in the nineteenth century. Based on his work, it is possible to describe how sensitive various receptors are to *changes* in stimulation levels. Table 3–2 presents information about our sensitivity to changes in different types of stimulation.

Table 3–2 also provides us with dramatic evidence of the differences in the amount of information about the outside world that can be provided by the various senses. The value in the right-hand column is the percent of increase in a stimulus that is necessary before a difference in the level of stimulation would be noticed. Brightness differences of only 1.7 percent can be noticed, but the amount of salt in water would have to increase by 33.3 percent before it would be noticeable that the solution was "saltier." This helps to explain why we do not notice a change from 50 watts to 50.5 watts. The difference is only 1 percent (.5/50), a value below the difference threshold of 1.7 percent for brightness change. As was the case with absolute thresholds, these difference thresholds are average values and may vary between people and even within the

TABLE 3–2.
Weber's Functions for Certain Senses

Vision (brightness of a white light)	1.7%
Kinesthesis (lifted weights)	2%
Pain (aroused by temperature on skin)	3.3%
Hearing (middle pitch, moderate loudness)	10%
Pressure on the skin (pressure on a spot)	14%
Smell (odor of burning India rubber)	25%
Taste (table salt)	33.3%

same person in different situations. They can also be influenced by learning: Postal clerks, for example, are much better at estimating the weight of a letter than the average person.

Psychophysical Functions

S. S. Stevens, a modern psychologist, used the results of difference threshold experiments to study people's subjective experience of stimulation at all levels. He found that these difference thresholds were appropriate for middle ranges of stimulation, but were not always accurate at very high or very low levels. He showed that people tend to systematically overestimate certain stimulus intensities and underestimate others. For example, at high levels of stimulation we tend to overestimate the intensity of an electric shock but underestimate the intensity of the brightness of a light bulb. This is important information, because it tells us that our subjective experience depends to a great degree on the level of stimulation. At extreme levels, we tend to be less accurate. Nevertheless, on a day-to-day basis, stimulation seldom reaches extreme levels, so we are not greatly affected by these inaccuracies.

The relationships that Stevens studied are called **psychophysical functions**. They are called functions because an underlying mathematical function or equation can be used to describe the relationship between objective stimulus values and subjective experience. They are psychophysical because what is being studied is the relationship between the objective and subjective aspects of sensory stimulation. Figure 3–2 illustrates the psychophysical functions for several senses. As you can see, different stimuli elicit different reactions. As shock levels increase by very small amounts, the subjective response to each increase is much greater than the increase would seem to warrant. Conversely, as brightness increases substantially, the subjective response increases only modestly. As the length of a line increases, the subjective experience of that increase matches closely the increase in the outside world. This figure is a good illustration of the fre-

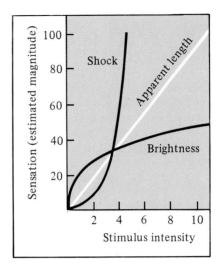

Figure 3–2
This graph shows the relationship between subjective experiences of stimulation and objective amounts of stimulation. The subjective response to even small increases in shock is much greater than the increases seem to warrant. The subjective response to increases in brightness is more modest. The subjective and objective experiences of apparent line length are the most closely matched.

quent disparity between the objective world and subjective experience.

Adaptation

There is one more thing to consider in our discussion of the measurement of sensation. We adjust to a particular level of stimulation after some period of time. For example, the first time you walk onto a factory floor, your ears are assaulted by the noise. Machines clack and whir, bells and horns ring, people shout, public address systems squawk. You doubt that you could survive an hour in such an environment. But several hours later, you are not as aware of the noise. Several days later, you are not only able to blot out the noise, but you are also able to hear your name called over the public address system. Your senses have adapted to the level of stimulation. This **adaptation** occurs in each of our

---

Difference threshold. The smallest or minimum difference between two stimuli that will be noticed by a person. Also called just noticeable difference (jnd).

Psychophysical functions. The mathematical functions or equa-

tions that can be used to describe the relationship between objective stimulus values and subjective experience.

Adaptation. A lessening of response over time to a constant level of stimulation.

THE TILT AFTEREFFECT

Spend a summer working in a factory and you will soon become accustomed to the noise of the machinery. Or take a job painting houses and soon you will hardly notice the smell of the paint. All of our senses adapt to a constant level of stimulation and subsequently become less responsive. They do so because the neurons supporting a particular sense mechanism become fatigued.

Adaptation explains an intriguing phenomenon called the "tilt aftereffect," a temporary change in how we perceive the orientation of lines. You can experience this phenomenon yourself by looking at the two circled sets of lines shown in this box. First look at the lines in the left-hand circle, which slant slightly counterclockwise. Really stare at the lines, letting your eyes wander around the circle. Now look quickly at the lines in the right-hand circle, which are vertical. You will notice that they appear to be slightly slanted clockwise. This effect will disappear quickly, but it is unmistakable.

What explains the tilt aftereffect? Apparently each cell in the visual cortex has a preferred orientation, that is, an orientation to which the cell responds best. For instance, a particular cell may respond to a line lying at a 45-degree angle; as the line moves away from that angle its responsiveness diminishes. Though the preferred orientations of cells in the visual cortex tend toward the

vertical and horizontal axes, all possible preferred orientations occur. If cells with a preferred orientation to a counterclockwise tilt are exposed for a length of time to lines that slant in that direction, they become fatigued. They will not be responsive, but cells with an opposing orientation will be, creating the momentary illusion that the vertical lines are slanted clockwise.

It is important to distinguish an aftereffect from an afterimage. Afterimages occur because cells in the retina become fatigued with prolonged stimulation. For instance, if you stare for a long time at a yellow circle and then glance quickly at a white surface, you will see a blue circle. This afterimage occurs because the red and green cones in your retina have become fatigued (yellow being a mixture of red and green). For a moment, only the blue cones are receptive. Aftereffects do not involve cells in the retina but cells in the brain. This is demonstrated by the fact that an aftereffect can be transferred from one eye to another. Prove this to yourself by looking at the left-hand circle with only one eye and then closing that eye and looking quickly at the right-hand circle with the other eye. This transfer could not be accomplished if it involved retinal cells only; such information cannot be transferred from eye to eye. Therefore, this information must be processed at a higher level—in the brain.

senses. For another example, paper mills produce a unique odor much like the smell of sauerkraut cooking. Many people find this smell unpleasant yet adapt to it after a short time and don't really notice it unless they leave the vicinity of the mill and then return. Such adaptations occur because the neurons that support the particular sense mechanism get fatigued. For the most part, these adaptations are automatic, and we seldom notice them. We will return again and again to these automatic reactions in our discussion of sensation and perception.

Research continues in the areas of absolute and

difference thresholds, adaptation, and receptor sensitivity. As a result of attempts to accurately measure the sensory capacities of both humans and nonhumans, the theories that attempt to explain sensation continue to improve. As we will see in many other areas of psychology, the very act of measurement plays an important role in understanding.

You now know something about sensation as a general process, but you still don't know how specific stimuli are received and recorded (that is, sensed). In the following sections, we will consider the most important characteristics of our senses. Because they are our dominant senses, we will spend most of our time on vision and hearing, but, as you will see, all of the senses operate in a similar manner.

REVIEW QUESTIONS

1. _____ is the reception and transformation of physical energy from the outside world into neural impulses; _____ is the interpretation of those impulses.

2. The least (or minimum) amount of stimulation needed to produce a noticeable sensation is called a(n) _____ _____ for that stimulus.

3. The least (or minimum) difference between two stimuli that will be noticed by someone is called a(n) _____ .

4. Thresholds are average values that differ for each person and even for the same person at different times.   T / F

5. The fact that our response to a constant stimulation lessens as time passes is called _____ .

Answers: 1. Sensation, perception 2. absolute threshold 3. difference threshold, or just-noticeable difference 4. True 5. adaptation

---

■ SEEING

People depend heavily on vision for dealing with the outside world. Obviously, it is possible to get by without perfect vision, or, in the case of blindness, without *any* vision at all. Nevertheless, life is easier if you can see well. Visual stimuli provide complex information about our world. Through such stimuli we can identify objects and make guesses about their size, weight, speed, distance, and direction. To understand how we see, we need to consider both the physical characteristics of light (the stimulus) and the physiological characteristics of our visual sense (the receptors). We will consider these two sets of characteristics separately.

The Characteristics of Light

What we call light is actually a wave of electromagnetic (EM) energy. As is the case with a wave in the ocean, a light wave has a height. Furthermore, a series of waves will have a number of different peaks, and the distance between these peaks can be measured. These two characteristics—height and the distance between peaks—are the most important physical characteristics of light waves. Each light wave has a specific height (amplitude) and a specific distance between its peaks (frequency). The intensity of brightness of a light is proportional to its amplitude, and color is related to the frequency of a particular light wave. The entire range of possible EM waves is called a wave spectrum. This spectrum ranges from cosmic rays and x-rays to FM and AM radio waves. Within this range of waves, we have the **visible spectrum**—the range of waves that humans can see. As Figure 3–3 shows, the visible spectrum is really very small compared to the existing range of EM waves. The visible spectrum is what we usually refer to as light.

Light comes to us in two ways. First, it can be directed toward our eyes by an energy source such as a light bulb. Second, it can come to us as a **reflection**, in which light waves that have come in contact with objects reach our eyes as a modified set

---

Visible spectrum. The range of light waves that humans can see.

Reflection. Occurs when light waves come in contact with objects and bounce off.

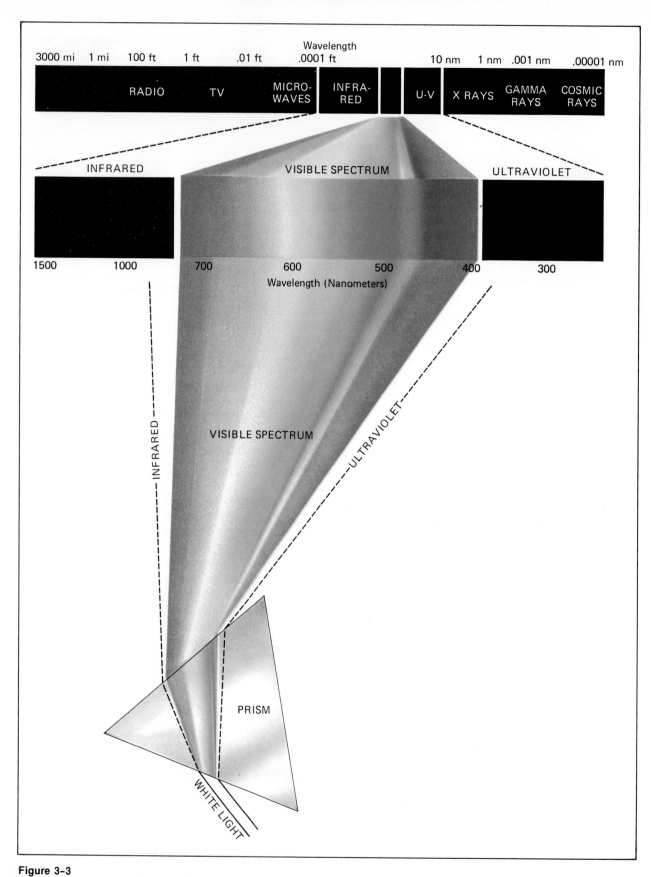

Figure 3-3
The visible spectrum, or the range of light waves that humans can see, is only a small part of the entire range of light waves. Each color shown here corresponds to a specific wavelength.

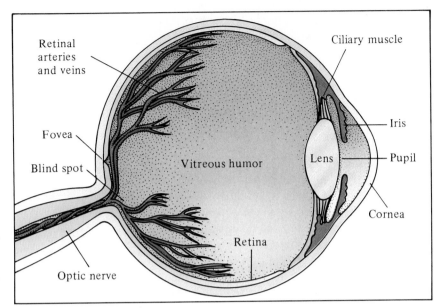

Figure 3-4

A drawing of the human eye. Light rays enter through the pupil, and are focused by the cornea and lens onto the retina. Receptors located on the retina transform the light rays into neural impulses, which are sent to the brain through the optic nerve.

of waves or signals. Reflected light is seldom exactly the same as the light from the original source, because some of the light rays are absorbed by objects and thus never reach the eye. Here is one example of absorption with which you are probably very familiar. Automobiles vary with respect to how hot they get in the summer. A black car gets very hot because most of the light rays from the sun are absorbed and turned into heat rather than reflected. In contrast, a white car reflects most of the rays that hit it and stays cooler. Generally, light-colored objects reflect light waves while dark objects tend to absorb them.

The Eye

The simple existence of light somewhere is not enough for you to see something. If someone directed the beam of a flashlight at the back of your head in a well-lit room, you would probably be unaware of the light waves from that source. For you to see, light rays must somehow come in contact with the appropriate area of your eye. The function of the eye, of course, is to get information to the brain; the complex construction of the eye (see

Figure 3–4) allows it to accomplish this function. As the figure indicates, the pupil controls the amount of light that enters; the cornea and the lens focus the light; the retina receives the focused light rays and transforms them into neural impulses; and the optic nerve transports these impulses to the brain. Now let's look at each of these parts of the eye.

The Pupil. The pupil and the iris form the opening of the eye through which light enters. The **iris** is the colored portion, corresponding to your eye color, that surrounds the opening of your eye. The muscles of the iris control the opening and closing of the pupil. The **pupil** is the dark portion in the center of the eye. This is the opening through which light actually enters.

The pupil works like one part of a camera system. On many cameras, the lens opening can be adjusted for different lighting conditions. When a lot of light is available, we usually "stop down," or narrow, the lens opening to avoid overexposing the film. When there is very little light available, we open up the lens to avoid underexposing the film. These adjustments affect not only the exposure but also the focus. With a constant amount of light and a narrower lens opening, more things will be in focus and

---

Iris. Colored portion of the eye that surrounds the black pupil in the center of the eye; color may be blue, brown, grey, green, etc.

Pupil. Dark portion in the center of the eye, the area through which light actually enters the eye.

vision will be "sharper." Wider lens openings mean that fewer objects will be in focus.

The eye works in a similar manner. When lighting conditions are poor, the pupil opens up, or dilates, allowing more light to enter and producing the sharpest vision possible under those conditions. When lighting is intense, the pupil closes down, or constricts, once again producing the best vision under the circumstances.

In addition to being affected by light, the pupil seems to be affected by variables such as interest and fear. Hess (1965) has shown that our pupils dilate when we are interested in an object. Similarly, it has been demonstrated that when we are afraid, our pupils dilate to allow more light to enter. This dilation is a function of the autonomic nervous system (ANS), which we discussed in Chapter 2. There is some speculation that when we perceive a threat in the environment, our bodies automatically prepare for action. Increasing visual acuity through increased light would be one possible preparatory step for coping with threat.

The Lens. After the **cornea** does some preliminary focusing of light, the lens refines that focus. The **lens** projects the image from the outside world onto a screen in the back of the eyeball, called the retina. The lens is the part of the eye most often responsible for the common visual defects of nearsightedness and farsightedness. For example, the shape of the lens may cause the image to be focussed at some point *behind* the retina. This condition is called **farsightedness**, because objects that are far away can be seen well, while things that are close up appear blurry without some correction to the lens, which is done by glasses or contact lenses. The opposite situation results when the image from the outside world is focussed at some point in *front* of the retina. This condition is known as **nearsightedness**, because objects that are nearby can be seen well, while things that are at a distance appear blurry. This condition can also be corrected by glasses or contact lenses. Figure 3–5 illustrates the mechanics of nearsightedness and farsightedness.

Another common problem of focus is called **astigmatism**. This condition occurs when the surface of the lens is not uniform. As a result, when a person with an astigmatism views a scene, some of that scene is in focus and other parts are out of focus.

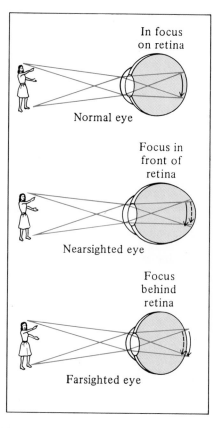

Figure 3–5

The normal eye is seen at top, with the focus falling directly on the retina. The middle figure shows the nearsighted eye, with the focus falling in front of the retina. At bottom is the farsighted eye, with the focus falling behind the retina.

The lens of the eye is not rigid, but is made of flexible tissue. In fact, a set of muscles in the eye stretches the lens, making it thicker or thinner depending on the light coming through the pupil. In theory, the lens should be able to adapt to lighting conditions to produce images in perfect focus through a process known as **accommodation**. However, not everyone has a lens that accommodates correctly. Some of us are born with lumpy or irregular lenses, a defect that can be corrected with glasses or contacts. We usually discover that correction is needed upon reaching the classroom, which is the first time that we are spending a good deal of time looking at objects close to our eyes (reading books) and far from our eyes (blackboards). The strain involved in trying to get things in focus often produces headaches, one of many clues leading to a diagnosis of poor vision. These clues are usually quickly and accurately recognized by teachers and physicians.

The lens can also change because of age. As we get older, the lens becomes less flexible. Consequently, accommodation becomes less and less efficient, and, as a result, vision gets poorer at particular distances. Many times both near- and farsighted symptoms appear. This is because the range of distances for which the lens can work efficiently becomes narrower and narrower. Within that reduced range, vision is fine. But on either side of that range, vision is poorer. In this situation, bifocal glasses are usually prescribed, with which two corrections can be made. One part of the lens, usually the upper part, corrects for nearsightedness, while the other part of the lens, usually the lower part, corrects for farsighted vision.

The Retina. The image brought into focus by the lens is projected onto the **retina**. The retina is the inner layer of tissue at the back of the eyeball and is covered with several different types of cells. Among the cells in the retina are two kinds of receptor cells: rods and cones. The rods and cones differ in function and number. The **rods** are sensitive to varying levels of brightness but are not responsive to color. There are approximately 120 million rods in each retina. The **cones** are sensitive to color differences. We have about 7 million cones in each retina.

Rods and cones are found in greater concentrations in different parts of the retina. Rods are found mostly around the edges of the retina and cones are found at its center. The greatest concentration of cones is in the **fovea**, a very small area at the center of the retina that is really the center of our visual screen.

The different roles played by rods and cones are determined by the amount of available light. During the day, the cones are more active. Stimulated by relatively bright light, they change chemically, and these changes produce neural impulses that are transmitted along the optic nerve to the brain. At night, the rods take over for maximum reception of light. Have you ever noticed that when you first walk outside on a dark night, you can't see much? You must also have noticed that your vision gradually improves after ten or fifteen minutes. This is an example of your rods and cones adapting to the light, with the rods taking the more active role because the amount of illumination is small.

Since rods are more sensitive to poor light conditions and, in addition, are more prevalent than cones around the edges of the retina, you are most likely to notice distant lights from "the corner of your eye." If you looked directly at the light source, "aiming" with your fovea, you would not see as well, because the fovea, with its high concentration of cones, functions poorly in low light conditions.

The retina is a complicated piece of equipment—far more complicated than the typical home movie screen—but it has one deficiency. At the point where the optic nerve leaves the eye on its way to the brain, there are no receptors. This is called the optic disc. Since there are neither rods nor cones on the optic disc, this area is incapable of stimlation from light sources. As a result, it has been referred to as the "blind spot" of the eye. This **blind spot** doesn't really cause a problem in day-to-day functioning, because we seem automatically to fill in the information that is missing—another ex-

---

Cornea. The outer, transparent coating of the eye.
Lens. Focuses or projects the image coming into the eye onto the retina.
Farsightedness. Difficulty seeing objects close up; occurs if shape of lens causes visual image to be projected behind the retina.
Nearsightedness. Difficulty seeing objects at a distance; occurs if shape of lens causes visual image to be projected in front of the retina.
Astigmatism. Defect in vision due to an irregularly shaped lens and creating a problem in focus.
Accommodation. The way the muscles in the eye change the shape of the lens in order to focus on an object.

Retina. An inner layer of tissue at the back of the eyeball; forms a screen-like surface on which the visual image is projected.
Rods. Cells concentrated on the edges of the retina, very sensitive to various levels of brightness. There are approximately 120 million rods in each retina.
Cones. Cells concentrated on the center of the retina, particularly on the fovea, responsible for color vision. There are approximately 7 million cones in each retina.
Fovea. Small area at the center of the retina. Contains greatest concentration of cones and thus produces our sharpest vision.
Blind spot. Area on the retina where optic nerve leaves the eye on the way to the brain. Contains no rods or cones, thus is not sensitive to light at all.

Figure 3-6

To locate your blind spot, close your left eye and stare at the X in the drawing. Hold
the book about a foot away from you and then slowly move it toward you and away
from you until the dot disappears.

ample of the automatic operations of the senses.
The missing information is apparently taken from
the visual material that surrounds this visual "hole."
The actual size of the blind spot is relatively small,
so not much information is really needed to complete the visual field. In Figure 3–6 you have an opportunity to demonstrate to yourself the presence

The eye chart is a test of visual acuity, or the ability to
distinguish fine details. "20/20" vision corresponds to
the smallest row of letters someone with average vision
can see at a distance of 20 ft.

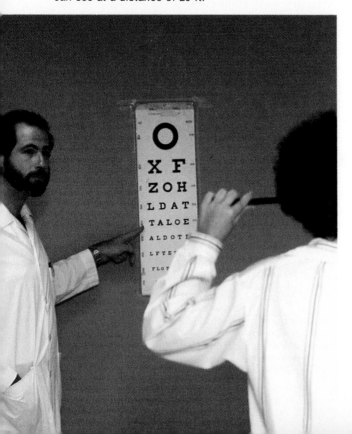

of the blind spot. We really are not aware of it unless
we set up specific conditions to illustrate its
presence.

Visual Acuity. The extent to which we can notice
fine visual details, or our **visual acuity**, varies in different areas of the retina. It is greatest when the image is focused on the fovea and drops off dramatically toward the edges of the retina. Of course, if
our lenses are uneven or our eye muscles fail to work
correctly, our ability to focus—and consequently our
visual acuity—is impaired.

Visual acuity is generally measured by an eye
chart of some type. The chart usually involves letters of various sizes that we are asked to read from
a distance of 20 feet. As we are asked to read smaller
and smaller letters, the task becomes more difficult.
When this method of testing was begun many
decades ago, individuals without any known eye
disease or vision problem were asked to read charts
and thus provide a standard for "normal" vision. At
a distance of 20 feet, they read lines of letters of decreasing size. A point was reached at which letters
of a particular height could only be read by 50% of
the subjects. This was designated as normal vision
and was assigned a value of 20/20. Subsequently,
individuals taking the same test who were able to
read the line of letters that could be read by 50%
of the "normal" subjects were said to have 20/20
vision. In other words, at 20 feet they could see as
well as individuals who were known to have no vision problems. Using 20/20 as an arbitrary "normal"
point, it was possible to identify some people whose
vision was better than normal (for example, someone
with 10/20 vision could read a line of letters at 20
feet that a "normal" person could only read at 10
feet) as well as some whose vision was worse than

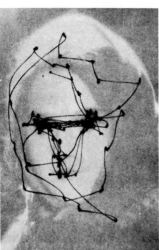

Figure 3-7
The network of lines shown here (right) is a pattern of eye movements made by someone looking at the photograph at left. The movements made by the eyes as they scan something are called saccades and are described in the text. (Yarbus, 1967)

normal (for example, someone with 20/30 vision could only read a line of letters at 20 feet that could be read by a "normal" person at 30 feet). Recent data suggest that young people should have better than normal vision (using 20/20 as the standard for "normal"). In fact, 20/20 vision is more characteristic of the 50-year-old than the 20-year-old, assuming that there are no unique problems with the various parts of the eye (Sekuler and Blake, 1985).

Eye Movement and Seeing

The eye moves in such a way that the retina and the fovea sweep back and forth across an object. This movement greatly enhances our ability to see, because the most sensitive area of the retina, the fovea, is more likely to make contact with the visual stimulus in this way. In addition to these small, automatic, and regular sweeping movements (called **pursuits**), we tend to scan the various parts of an object rapidly, picking up and processing bits and pieces of information. These scanning actions are called **saccades**. It may seem to you that you are not moving your eyes when you look at an object, but in fact you make rapid, darting movements from one

part of the object to another. Figure 3–7 was created by tracking for one minute the movements of both eyes of a person who was looking at a picture of a young girl. This gives you some idea of these scanning movements.

Recently, advertising agencies have begun experimenting with similar measurement procedures to determine how consumers choose among several brands of products. Russo has conducted several experiments (Russo and Rosen, 1975; Russo, 1977) in which he has studied the eye movements people make when considering a purchase. He has shown that these eye movements are not random; they have a specific sequence. This sequence has three phases: overview, comparison, and checking. In the overview phase, the person quickly scans the entire visual scene. In the comparison stage, he or she picks out one product from the many available on a shelf and then compares the other alternatives to it. The standard for comparison is usually the person's preferred brand. Even after a decision to purchase has been made, the person continues to check the alternatives; the individual is then likely to examine those alternatives that were ignored in the comparative phase. This area of research seems quite promising from both the marketing and the

---

Visual acuity. The ability to notice fine visual details.

Pursuits. Small, automatic, and regular movements of the eyes that help bring the fovea in contact with visual stimuli.
Saccades. Rapid, scanning actions of the eyes over an object.

psychological perspectives. There is still much to be learned about a wide variety of behaviors involving visual search patterns.

The Brain and Seeing

The **optic nerve** carries information to several portions of the brain. This information has two major destinations: a portion of the thalamus gland called the lateral geniculate nucleus and the visual cortex. The **lateral geniculate nucleus** is involved in determining the location of an object. The **visual cortex** plays a major role in determining the color, form, and pattern of visual stimuli. Certain cells in the retina help us to detect borders and edges, thereby allowing us to identify shapes. In addition, cells in the visual cortex help us identify such features as length, width, and angular characteristics of objects. An example that you are familiar with might help explain what these specialized cells do. When you check out at a supermarket or department store, the clerk often runs a light pen across a series of bars or lines attached by a tag, sticker, or label to the object you are buying. This light pen picks up specific information regarding product identification and cost that is used to compute your bill. In addition, this information may be stored in a computer memory that is used to keep track of inventory. The light pen functions as a **feature detector**. It tells the electronic brain (the computer) some very specific information. It does not care what other information may appear on the tag or label (such as fabric content or number of calories per serving) and it does not pick up information unless it "looks at" (is run across) the tag. The feature detector cells in our visual cortex work in a similar fashion.

It is possible to "map" the functions of neurons at various points in the visual cortex by recording the neural impulses that are stimulated by specific circumstances. Hubel and Weisel (1969) succeeded in mapping feature detector cells by measuring neural impulses in the brains of cats exposed to various visual stimuli. It was possible to determine which cells had fired in response to specific features and which ones hadn't. Later research has shown that the functioning of these cells can be affected by aspects of the animals' environment. For example, the feature detector cells of cats raised in a dark environment with no exposure to lines, edges, or angles do not work as efficiently as those of cats raised normally.

Color Vision

Let's begin our consideration of color vision with a brief illustration. Fixate on the black dot in either the top or the bottom panel in Figure 3–8 for about 15 seconds, then fixate on the black dot in the white center panel. You should notice something odd: There will be an afterimage that will have a color different from the color of the panel on which you originally fixated. If you stared at the red panel, the afterimage is green; if you stared at the green panel, the afterimage is red. This afterimage illustrates the complexity of color vision. Not only did we "experience" color when we were looking at a white stimulus, but the color was different from the one we had previously examined. Later in this section, we will see that the phenomenon of an afterimage

Figure 3–8

By staring at the black dot in the center of the red or green rectangle and then switching your gaze to the black dot in the white rectangle, you will see a negative-color afterimage.

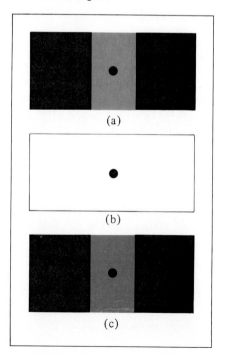

Psychologists have studied color vision for over 100 years, but there is still much to be learned about it. We can recognize hundreds of colors and enjoy using them in a variety of ways.

can be explained by a theory of color vision called the *opponent-process* theory. This theory proposes that the colors we experience are the result of the operations of several different color receptors working simultaneously.

As we showed earlier, color is related to wavelength. But wavelength actually represents only one aspect of color. Two other components of perceived color also play a role in color vision—brightness and **saturation**, or purity. Figure 3-9 presents the colors we can distinguish. There are three dimensions to this color sphere. As we go from top to bottom, the colors go from bright to dark; as we go around the circumference, the colors change in hue or wavelength; as we go from the center of the sphere to the edge, the colors become more saturated or

---

Optic nerve. Carries electrical impulses from the retina to the brain.

Lateral geniculate nucleus. Area of the brain that receives neural impulses from the retina and is involved with locating visual stimuli.

Visual cortex. Area of the brain receiving neural impulses from

the retina; plays a major role in identifying color, form, and pattern in what we see.

Feature detector. Cell in the brain that responds only to certain characteristics of objects—such as edges, corners, or certain angles.

Saturation. Refers to the purity of a color, whether it is a mixture of colors or one pure color.

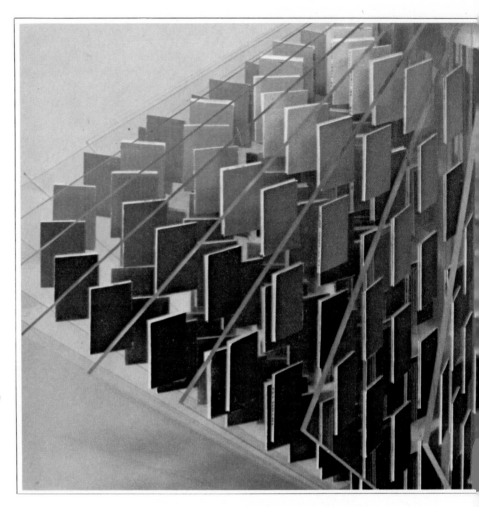

Figure 3-9
This color sphere contains all of the colors that we can distinguish. There are three dimensions to the color sphere: As you look from top to bottom, the colors go from bright to dark; as you look around the circumference, the colors change in hue or wavelength; and as you look from the center of the sphere to the edge, the colors become more saturated or pure. (Photo courtesy of Inmont Corporation)

pure. We can recognize hundreds of different colors, although we may only be able to name a few dozen. How do we distinguish one color from another?

In the nineteenth century, a theory explaining color vision was proposed by Thomas Young, and later refined by Hermann von Helmholtz. This theory (which is usually referred to as the **Young-Helmholtz theory**) was based on the fact that virtually any color on the visible spectrum can be produced by combining the three primary colors (red, green, and blue). It suggested that since these combinations could be made, the eye must have specific receptors for each of the three colors—one red receptor, one green receptor, and one blue receptor. Different colors are visualized when the brain receives a three-digit code, one digit coming from each of the three types of receptors (presumably cones

in the retina). This trichromatic theory was popular for many years, but a flaw in the theory became apparent in studying color blindness. According to the theory, yellow is a combination of red and green; but most people who could not see red or green could see yellow. (Color blindness will be discussed later in this section.)

In 1957, a new theory was proposed to explain color vision (Hurvich and Jameson). The theory, actually a revision of one proposed 75 years earlier by Ewald Hering, is called the **opponent-process theory** and is based on the notion that color receptors have the capacity to send to the brain one of two different messages about a stimulus. It proposes three sets of receptors, as does the Young-Helmholtz theory, but each receptor is responsive to not one but two colors: black-white, red-green, and yellow-blue. These receptors are considered

coding mechanisms rather than simply sensing mechanisms, as in the Young-Helmholtz theory. Each receptor registers the presence of the appropriate colors by turning "off" and "on." Since no cell can be "off" and "on" at the same time, the colors are said to "oppose" each other; hence the name of the theory. Each unique combination of "off" and "on" for all three receptors is thought to represent a different color.

Opponent-process theory stresses that the coding that comes from the retina is actually recoded in the visual cortex. In addition, it is generally accepted that the thalamus is involved in color vision. In experiments with monkeys, DeValois (1965) iden-

tified cells in the thalamus that correspond roughly to the black, white, red, green, yellow, and blue components proposed by opponent-process theory. The black and white cells did not seem to act in opposition to each other, but the remaining four cells did seem to pair up, as suggested by opponent-process theory.

Recent biochemical research (Wald, 1959; Mac-Nichol, 1964; Lewin, 1985; Sekuler and Blake, 1985) supports the early notions of Young and Helmholtz. Modern trichromatic theory is based on a technique called microspectrophotometry. By exposing sections of the retina to various wavelengths of light, this technique allows us to determine how much

---

Young-Helmholtz theory. Theory of color vision that proposes three different color receptors in the retina, each responsive to one of the three primary colors.

Opponent-process theory. Theory of color vision that proposes that the experience of color results from the operations of three sets of color receptors working simultaneously.

light is being absorbed by various cones. As a result of this research, three types of cones have been identified. Each type responds to a different range of the visible spectrum; hence, the three types are referred to as short-wavelength, medium-wavelength, and long-wavelength cones. The sensitivities of the three cone types are indicated in Figure 3–10. As you can see, the different types are not clearly distinguished; there is a good deal of overlap between them. This can be seen from the fact that the areas of the curves of sensitivity cross each other.

Color Blindness. Both the trichromatic and opponent-process theories seem to match some of the facts we know about color vision. We do seem to distinguish clearly among the groups of colors identified by the Young-Helmholtz theory as primary colors. In fact, some studies have shown that the abscence of certain chemicals in cones is associated with **color blindness** (Rushton, 1975). Nevertheless, people are not typically blind to only one color. If they cannot see red, then they usually cannot see green either; if they cannot see blue, they usually cannot see yellow either. Thus, the explanation for color blindness seems to involve a problem with either the red-green or the yellow-blue receptor.

There are simple tests for color blindness. An example of one of these tests appears in Figure 3–11.

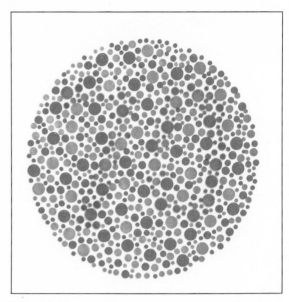

Figure 3–11

This figure is often used to test for color blindness. If you don't see a number in the circle, you have red-green color blindness. The number is printed in the review answers on page 111.

People with normal color vision can see a number in the circle; those who have red-green color blindness cannot. (The number you should see is printed in the review answers on p. 111.) Red-green deficiency occurs more commonly than other deficiencies, and color deficiency in general is more common in men (about 8 percent of the male population) than in women (less than 1 percent), leading researchers to conclude that color blindness is hereditary and tied to the same genetic code that determines sex. Color blindness is not necessarily an all-or-nothing situation; for instance, red-green color vision may be weak rather than missing. This would follow from the biochemical model of color vision since different individuals might possess varying amounts of the required pigment in each of the cone types.

There is still much to be learned about color vision. It has not even been determined if the experience of color is primarily a function of the retina, the thalamus, or the visual cortex. It would appear that the final explanation of color vision will combine the mechanics of the opponent-process theory with the results of the recent biochemical research on cone types (trichromatic theory).

Figure 3–10

The Young-Helmholtz theory of color vision is based on the existence of three types of cones. Each type of cone is particularly sensitive to a different range of the visual spectrum, as shown here. You can also see some overlap where the curves of sensitivity cross each other.

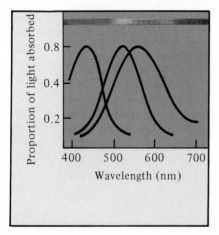

REVIEW QUESTIONS

6. The range of light waves that human beings can see is called the _____ _____ .

7. A dark car will be hot in the summer because it _____ light; a light car will be cooler because it _____ light.

8. Match the following terms with their definition.

____ pupil   A. your eye color

____ iris   B. screenlike inner layer of tissue at back of eyeball

____ lens   C. sensitive to color

____ retina   D. carries neural impulses from retina to brain

____ rod   E. works like a camera-lens opening

____ cone   F. greatest visual acuity possible here

____ fovea   G. works best in poorly lit environment

____ blind spot   H. place where optic nerve leaves the retina

____ optic nerve   I. focuses light on back of eyeball

____ lateral geniculate nucleus   J. involved in determining the color, surface, and pattern of visual stimuli

____ visual cortex   K. involved in determining the location of objects

9. Nearsightedness and farsightedness are caused by:
   a. the shape of the lens
   b. thickening of the retina
   c. lack of an iris
   d. malfunction of the cornea

10. The three types of cones in the opponent-process theory of color vision are red-_____ , blue-_____ , and white-_____ .

11. In modern trichromatic theory, three types of cones are identified, each sensitive to different _____ .

Answers: 6. visible spectrum **7.** absorbs; reflects **8.** pupil, E; iris, A; lens, I; retina, B; rod, G; cone, C; fovea, F; blind spot, H; optic nerve, D; lateral geniculate nucleus, K; visual cortex, J **9.** a **10.** green; yellow; black **11.** wavelengths. The number visible in Figure 3–11 is "70."

■ HEARING

It would be difficult to function efficiently with only our sense of vision. Our sense of hearing is also critical in identifying and locating objects around us. For example, consider a person's voice on the telephone. From its sound, we can usually tell the sex of the person, and we often can make a good guess as to age. From the caller's accent we may be able to tell where he or she grew up. Finally, we can pick up emotional overtones in the voice and identify feelings such as anger, fear, or elation. These types of judgments and identifications are quite complex, and only the brain seems capable of making them. No machines are able to distinguish emotions or age or accents.

As with the eye, the basic mechanical principles of the ear are easy to understand. When objects move, they produce a vibration in the air. This vibration is picked up by the ear, sent along an auditory pathway to the brain, and is interpreted by a particular area of the brain, the auditory cortex. Since different objects produce different vibrations, the brain is able to distinguish between objects on the basis of the sounds that they make. As an example, think of plucked guitar strings. When the lowest string is plucked, it sets up vibrations that are "heard" as an E note. When the next to the lowest string is plucked, different vibrations are produced, which we interpret as the note A. Thus, as with colors, each sound has its own unique character. Similarly, sounds, like colors, are created from mixtures of basic stimulus elements. Just as yellow can be created from mixing red and green lights, so can a musical chord be created from mixing individual vibrations. As an example, the C chord is composed of the notes C, E, and G.

The Characteristics of Sound

The best way to describe sound is with an analogy. Think of a bathtub full of water. Now imagine putting your hand in that water with the opened palm

---

Color blindness. Inability to see certain colors. A person can have trouble seeing reds and greens or blues and yellows. Red-green color blindness is most common; color blindness is more common in men than in women.

facing the bottom of the tub and pushing it up and down in the water. You will notice that the movement of your hand has created waves moving away from your hand in every direction. Now think of what these waves would look like if you varied your hand movements. For instance, if you pushed up and down more quickly, the waves would be closer together. If you pushed harder, the waves would have higher peaks and deeper troughs. If you used both hands instead of just one, there would be two sets of waves meeting each other at various times.

The tub example illustrates the two important characteristics of sound—frequency, or how close together the waves are, and amplitude, or how high the waves are. Frequency produces the subjective experience of **pitch**; high-pitched sounds have high frequencies and low-pitched sounds have low frequencies. Amplitude or intensity is generally what we experience as loudness.

Frequency. As with light waves, humans are aware of only a portion of the sound wave spectrum. Though the frequencies of sound waves can vary from very low to very high, humans are only aware of frequencies in the range of about 20 to 20,000 waves per second. Frequencies are usually not described in terms of waves per second, but as cycles per second or by the symbol **Hz** (for **hertz**). Table 3–3 will give you some examples of the frequencies of some common sounds.

Amplitude. When we classify sounds as either loud or soft, we are describing their amplitude or intensity. Amplitude is the physical characteristic of the

stimulus; loudness is our subjective experience of that stimulus. Amplitude is not related to frequency; the same note on a piano can be loud or soft depending upon how hard we hit the key. We usually measure the amplitude or intensity of sounds in **decibels (db)**. Figure 3–12 shows examples of the intensities of various sounds. As you can see, there is a level of intensity that produces both pain and damage that results in loss of hearing. We will discuss this type of damage shortly.

Complex Sound Waves. Just as colors can be combinations of lights of different wavelengths, sounds can be and usually are combinations of many sound waves. Consider, for example, the single note played by a full symphony orchestra. The sound made by a violin will be very different from the sound made by a French horn or oboe. A hundred different instruments will make a hundred different sounds, with no two exactly alike. Yet our ears will not be presented with a hundred individual sounds but a single, complex sound.

Most of the sounds that we hear in the course of the day are complex rather than simple. Nevertheless, our ears seem to work like little computers, breaking down these complex waves into their individual elements. This is actually what "hearing" is—breaking down and interpreting complex sounds.

A Comparison of Hearing and Seeing

In this discussion of hearing, we have made several comparisons between hearing and seeing. Both seeing and hearing are dependent on waves: In the case of seeing, these waves are electromagnetic; in hearing, they are pressure waves. In both cases, some part of the body "collects" these waves—the eye for seeing; the ear for hearing. In both cases, outside energy is translated into a series of neural impulses that are carried by nerve fibers to the brain. In both cases, we interpret information for identification purposes. It also appears that, in both cases, we have feature detectors that aid in identification. Just as there are certain cells in the retina and in the visual cortex that respond to edges, lines, and angles, so there seem to be similar specialized cells in the auditory system that respond to sounds like clicks (Masterson et al., 1968). It seems that these two systems are very similar in their physiology.

TABLE 3–3.
Frequencies of Common Sounds

Sound	Frequency (in Hz)
Limit of hearing (lower limit)	20
Lowest note on a piano	27
Middle C on a piano	262
Highest note on a piano	4,180
Limit of hearing (upper limit)	16–20,000

Source: Adapted from Deatherage, 1972.

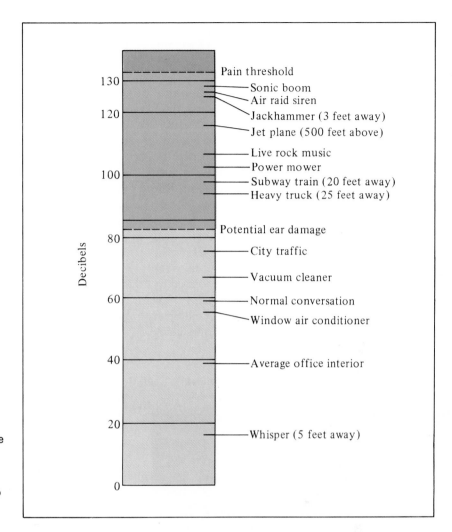

Figure 3-12

The graph shows the amplitude or loudness of a number of sounds, measured in decibels. Prolonged exposure to loud noises can result in damage to the ear. (Lindsay and Norman, 1972)

But in some ways these two senses are not alike, for electromagnetic waves and pressure waves are not entirely the same. Sound moves more slowly than light. A thunder and lightning storm is a good example of this principle. We see lightning before we hear the accompanying thunder. As a matter of fact, we often use this discrepancy to calculate how far away the lightning is. The less time between the lightning and the thunder, the nearer the storm. Sound waves also go around corners and through solid objects; light waves of the visible spectrum do not. We cannot see an object unless our eyes are at least directed toward that object, but we can hear sounds at any angle to our ears. These differences point out the fact that hearing is not completely similar to vision: Hearing tells us some things that vision does not.

The Ear

Like the eye, there are several parts in the ear that receive and transform outside energy into internal

---

Pitch. Subjective experience of hearing based on the frequency of sound waves: high-pitched sounds have high frequencies, low-pitched sounds have low frequencies.

Hertz (Hz). Term used to describe cycles per second of sound waves.

Decibels (dB). Term used to measure or describe the amplitude or intensity of sound.

electrical impulses. Figure 3-13 presents a basic diagram of the ear. There are three distinct sections to consider: the outside ear, the middle ear, and the inner ear. The outside ear is what is attached to the side of your head. This is known as the **pinna**. Sound waves are caught by the pinna and channeled through the **auditory canal** to the **eardrum**. These sound, or pressure, waves move the eardrum in and out. Each time the eardrum moves, the bones of the middle ear are moved. These bones in turn move the **oval window**, a membrane across the opening between the middle and inner ear. The inner ear is filled with fluid. When the oval window moves, this movement is transformed into waves that move through the inner ear, stimulating the **cochlea**. The **basilar membrane**, which contains the specific receptor cells that respond to sound frequencies, runs lengthwise through the middle of the snail-shaped cochlea. These cells are actually hair cells. These tiny hairs are bent by the waves being

We see lightning before we hear thunder because sound waves move more slowly than light waves.

transported through the fluid of the inner ear, which results in neural impulses that are picked up by the **auditory nerve** and transported by that nerve to the brain.

This description of the ear tells us something about the equipment needed to hear, but it really doesn't explain hearing. How is it that we can distinguish so many different sounds? That is, how does the system produce different neural responses for different sound frequencies? One explanation might be that the hair cells of the inner ear move at the same rate as a given sound wave. This would mean that for a sound corresponding to 12,000 Hz, the hair cells would move 12,000 times per second. This theory, proposed by a nineteenth-century physiologist named Ernest Rutherford, was called the *frequency theory*. However, after cell firings were measured, it became obvious that this theory was probably incorrect for frequencies above about 100 Hz; cells simply cannot fire much faster than that. It was then suggested that perhaps the cells do not respond all at once. Perhaps groups of cells "share the load," with each individual cell firing only once every tenth or seventeenth or hundredth stimulation. This was called the *volley theory* of hearing. Research demonstrated that cells did seem to work this way between 100 Hz and 5,000 Hz, but above 5,000 Hz, something different happened. In the higher frequency ranges, various parts of the basilar membrane seemed to respond differentially to different frequencies. This theory, called the *place theory* of hearing, was proposed by Helmholtz (the same person who studied color vision).

The most accepted theory of hearing is a combination of the three theories described above. At low frequencies, receptor cells fire at the same rate as the wave frequency. At middle frequency ranges, the cells fire in volleys. At high frequencies, specific spots or "places" on the basilar membrane are stimulated in unique ways. This is quite a complex process, but one that clearly gets the job done. In fact, we will see that this is often the case throughout psychology—numerous processes are needed to get the job completely done.

The Brain and Hearing

The auditory nerve leaves the cochlea and travels to the brain carrying the neural impulses that represent sound. These impulses are actually sent to two

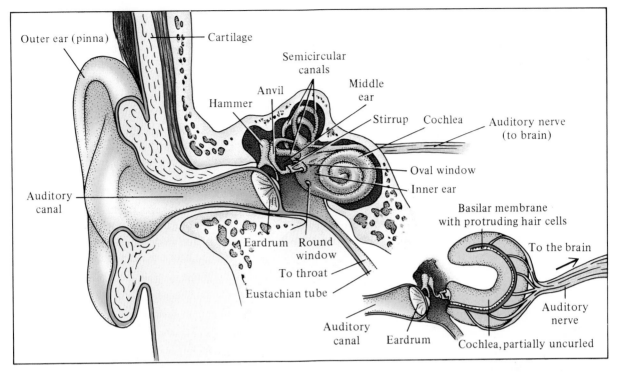

Figure 3-13
This is a drawing of the ear, showing the outside ear, the middle ear, and the inner
ear. The hair cells on the basilar membrane of the cochlea transform sound waves
into neural impulses, which are sent to the brain through the auditory nerve.

separate places. One area of the brain, a section of the thalamus called the **medial geniculate nucleus,** processes information dealing with the location of sound. You will remember that another section of the thalamus (the inferior geniculate nucleus) is involved in visual orientation. Thus, it appears that the thalamus is particularly important for the identification of the *source* of stimulation. The *interpretation* of auditory stimulation occurs in the **auditory cortex.**

Localization of Sound. The location or **localization** of sound is accomplished in a simple yet elegant way. That we have two ears rather than one makes localization possible. Since sound usually comes from a single source, it will not reach both ears at the same time unless the source is directly in front of or directly behind the head. In other words, the head gets in the way, and thus in most cases the sound reaches one ear before the other. If the sound is coming from the left side, it reaches the left ear

Pinna. Part of the outer ear; sounds are first caught by the pinna or ear flap and channeled into the ear.

Auditory canal. Part of the outer ear; channels sound from the pinna to the eardrum.

Eardrum. Part of the outer ear; a flexible membrane that vibrates in response to sound.

Oval window. Part of the middle ear; a flexible membrane that moves in response to the movement of the small bones in the middle ear, which are in turn moved by the vibration of the eardrum.

Cochlea. Part of the inner ear; contains receptor cells on the basilar membrane that respond to sounds.

Basilar membrane. Part of the cochlea in the inner ear; along

it are the receptor cells that produce the electrical impulses that we experience as sound.

Auditory nerve. Extends from the cochlea in the inner ear to the brain; transports electrical impulses from the cochlea to the brain.

Medial geniculate nucleus. Area of the brain that receives neural impulses from the basilar membrane and is involved with the localization of sound.

Auditory cortex. Area of the brain that receives neural impulses from the basilar membrane and identifies and interprets them.

Localization. Process through which we can tell from what direction a sound is coming, based on the fact that sound reaches one ear before the other.

unobstructed but must travel through and around the head to get to the right ear. The intensity of the sound on the right side is diminished both by the fact that it travels farther to get to the right ear and by the fact that it loses energy passing through the head. The brain is capable of using this intensity difference as information in locating the source of a sound. Movement of the head helps in this task enormously. In fact, when a sound is directly in front of or behind our heads, we often cock or move our heads in order to use the varying intensity information as a cue for locating its source.

Adaptation occurs in hearing just as it does in seeing. Just as rods and cones adapt to day and night conditions, the auditory system adapts to noise levels. This is good and bad. It is good in that we can become accustomed to certain noise levels and

be less annoyed or distracted by them. It is bad in that we can suffer significant hearing loss *because* the noise level is no longer painful or annoying, and thus we do not try to reduce its intensity.

Hearing Loss

There are two kinds of hearing loss or deafness: nerve deafness and conduction deafness. **Nerve deafness** is the result of damage to some part of the inner ear or basilar membrane. Such damage is very serious, since it prevents the neural impulses from reaching the brain. Trying to hear under such conditions is like trying to get a picture from a TV that is not plugged in. Nerve deafness cannot be treated in any efficient manner at this time. **Conduction deafness**, on the other hand, is the result of some

Prolonged loud noises can cause permanent damage to hearing. Industrial workers regularly wear some form of ear protection to reduce the danger.

damage or inefficiency of the outer ear or the middle ear. This would include a punctured eardrum or a defective bone in the delicate chain of bones in the middle ear. Conduction deafness can often be eliminated through the use of a hearing aid, which amplifies or exaggerates the sound waves so that they are more likely to reach the inner ear and, ultimately, the brain.

A wide range of studies of animals and humans leaves no doubt about the dangerous effects of loud noise on hearing (Fearn, 1973,1976, 1981). In many industrial settings, workers regularly wear ear protectors or ear plugs to reduce the danger. Rock concerts seem equally dangerous; studies have shown that it may take several weeks for the basilar membrane to recover from a two-hour rock concert, where noise levels are in the range of 100 to 110 db. As a result of such exposure, a member of the audience might notice a substantial hearing loss in the range of 2,000 to 8,000 Hz. He or she might not hear normal conversation, for this is the typical range of speech sounds. Such hearing loss can persist for days or weeks, depending on the number of prior exposures. Prolonged exposure may lead to permanent damage.

Musicians in rock bands are particularly vulnerable to such hearing losses. Jerger and Jerger (1970) studied a group of five musicians who had played for two years or more. These musicians showed losses of 30 to 50 db of hearing in the 2,000 to 8,000 Hz range for up to 4 hours following exposure. It is likely that the same effect can be produced by blasting music through headphones. Perhaps a warning should be included with every purchase of a stereo headphone set!

■ OTHER SENSES

Through our study of seeing and hearing, you should have a good basic understanding of how we "sense" the outside world. We have an external

---

Nerve deafness. Result of damage to part of inner ear or basilar membrane; means no electrical impulses can be sent to the brain.

Conduction deafness. Result of damage or deficiency in middle or outer ear, such as punctured eardrum, can be corrected by the use of a hearing aid.

REVIEW QUESTIONS

12. Although humans can see only part of the whole spectrum of light waves, they can hear the entire spectrum of sound waves.
    T / F

13. We measure the intensity or amplitude of sound in terms of _____ .

14. High-pitched sound waves have _____ frequency; low-pitched sound waves have _____ frequency.

15. Sound waves move more slowly than/faster than light waves.

16. Indicate, by numbering, the order in which a sound wave would reach the following parts of the ear.
    ___ cochlea
    ___ pinna
    ___ oval window
    ___ eardrum
    ___ auditory canal

17. Match the following terms with their proper location:
    ___ outer ear   A. cochlea, basilar membrane, auditory nerve
    ___ middle ear   B. pinna, auditory canal, eardrum
    ___ inner ear   C. oval window

18. Match the following theories with the correct description:
    ___ frequency theory   A. cells fire in groups, not each individually
    ___ volley theory   B. different parts of the basilar membrance respond to different frequencies
    ___ place theory   C. hair cells move at the same rate as the sound wave

19. Damage to the basilar membrane results in _____ _____ . Damage to the outside or middle ear, which results in _____ _____ , may be corrected with a hearing aid.

Answers: 12. False 13. decibels 14. high; low 15. more slowly than 16. (1) pinna, (2) auditory canal, (3) eardrum, (4) oval window (5) cochlea 17. outer ear, B; middle ear, C; inner ear, A 18. frequency theory, C; volley theory, A; place theory, B 19. nerve deafness; conduction deafness

mechanism of some kind—an eye or an ear. This mechanism gathers physical energy from stimuli in the environment and transforms it into neural impulses. These impulses are then transported along a neural pathway to the brain. In the case of the eye, the retina accomplishes the transformation. In the case of the ear, it is the eardrum, the bones of the middle ear, and the cochlea that make this transformation.

We have several other senses besides vision and hearing. These senses are taste, smell, balance, and touch. Each of these senses works in a way similar to seeing and hearing: For each sense there are specialized receptors that respond to a specific form of stimulation. These receptors in turn, transform the outside energy into neural impulses and move those impulses along to the brain. We won't discuss these other senses in the same detail as vision and hearing, but we will describe the function of each sense: the external stimuli, the receptors, and the results of those sensations.

Taste and Smell

Our senses of taste and smell are reactions to chemicals (as opposed to reactions to light waves or sound waves). Different chemicals lead to different patterns of receptor firings; in principle, this is how we distinguish one taste or smell from another. The sense of taste is aided by saliva, which helps dissolve substances. The odors necessary for smell are carried through the air.

The receptor cells for taste are in our **taste buds,** which are located in various sectors of our tongue (See Figure 3-14. There appear to be four different types of taste buds. These types correspond to the basic taste sensations of sweet, sour, salty, and bitter. More complex tastes are simply combinations of these four basic tastes. The four types of taste buds are concentrated on different parts of the tongue. For example, there are many sweet receptors on the tip of the tongue and few in the back. You can taste the effects of this yourself by comparing sugar on the tip of the tongue versus on the back of the tongue.

We are less sure about receptors for smell. We know which cells they are, and that they are located in the nasal cavity above the mouth, but we do not know how or why they are sensitive to specific

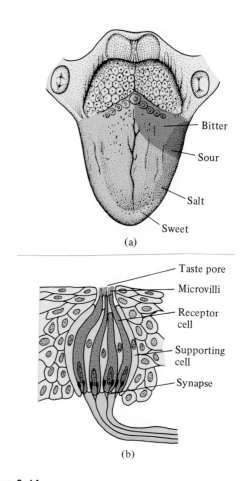

(a)

(b)

Figure 3-14

This drawing shows where the four types of taste buds are concentrated on different parts of the tongue. A taste bud consists of about a dozen individual taste cells clustered together.

chemicals. Neither are we sure exactly how many basic smells there are, or how these basic smells are combined to form complex smells.

Smells and tastes are as powerful in perception as sights and sounds. The smell of rain on a spring day or the taste or a particular type of candy you were fond of as a child can bring vivid memories flooding back in rich detail. Information coded by smell and taste clearly exists in the same detail and complexity as information coded by seeing or hearing.

Taste buds. Receptor cells for the sense of taste, located on various parts of the tongue.

THE LOCATION OF SMELL

When we discussed hearing, we saw how the existence of two ears makes it possible to locate the direction of a sound. If the same sound wave reaches both ears at exactly the same time, we locate it in a middle plane—either directly in front of or behind the head. However, if the sound wave reaches one ear before the other, the difference in arrival time produces a corresponding difference in sound intensity. The brain is able to use this difference in intensity as information about the source of a sound. Since we have two ears and two nostrils, it makes sense to wonder whether odors are located in a similar way. One of the principal investigators of this question is Georg von Békésy, who won a Nobel Prize for earlier work on hearing.

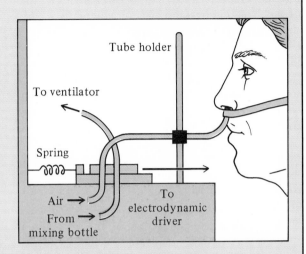

Under natural conditions, smell sensations are produced only during a flow of an odor through the entire nose. Closing off one nostril impairs the sense of smell severely, just as closing one ear impairs the sense of hearing. Also, in the process of sniffing, there is a certain time delay between the odor reaching one nostril and the other. To obtain these conditions experimentally, Békésy had to build a rather complicated piece of equipment.

Compressed air from a tank was humidified and adjusted to room temperature by bubbling it through a bottle where scent was mixed with air. This device controlled the concentration of odor in a stimulus. With the help of pulse generators and a control dial, Békésy could adjust the time delays between presentation of stimuli with precision. This was important in order to measure how accurately the olfactory nerves could discriminate the time difference between stimuli presented to each side of the nose. Two identical sets of apparatus were built for each side of the nose. The final outlet for the apparatus was a plastic tube that led directly to each nostril, where it was held in place with a rubber band around the head. Subjects would activate the driving unit when they inhaled in breathing (see the accompanying figure).

In one set of experiments, the focus was on observing what happened when odors such as benzol, eucalyptus, cloves, and lavendar were presented to one nostril before the other. The results were revealing. A time difference of as little as 0.3 msec was enough for subjects to observe a shift in smell sensation from one side of the nose to the other. Thus, in spite of the very small distance between the two nostrils as compared to that between the two ears, the direction of an odor can be determined with a precision close to that of hearing. This suggests that animals having a larger distance between the nostrils than man can locate an odor even better than humans can.

In other experiments, Békésy tested the sensitiviy of the nose to differences in odor intensity. It turned out that when the same level of stimuli was presented simultaneously to each nostril, this formed a sensation in the middle of the nose. However, even a small change in the concentration of odor on one side was enough to move the sensation from one nostril to the other. Thus, Békésy concluded that smell localization is probably accomplished by a combination of the time delay and the intensity differences produced between the nostrils during sniffing (Békésy 1964).

The discovery of a similarity between hearing and smelling is further evidence that the directional sense is a well-developed characteristic of the nervous system. Other researchers are now finding that taste and even skin sensations work in the same way. For example, a one msec time delay between two taste stimuli can move a taste sensation from one part of the tongue to another; an identical time delay between touch stimuli can shift a skin sensation from one point to another.

Taste and smell are closely linked in everyday life. As with color vision, we can recognize many more different characteristics than we can name. The role of smell in eating (and its enjoyment) is clearly demonstrated by the common cold. Think back to the last time you had a head cold. Your food tasted bland and you did not enjoy it as much as you would have if your sense of smell had not been impaired. If taste were simply the result of taste buds, there would be no reason for this to happen. We tend to think of taste and smell as signals of pleasant or unpleasant stimuli. The smell of fresh donuts may make you hungry, and you anticipate a pleasurable experience. But taste and smell play an important role in survival both for humans and for other animals. For example, you are unlikely to consume large amounts of a poisonous substance by mistake because of the way such substances taste (although there are certain exceptions to the rule, such as specific types of mushrooms). Female animals in heat often give off a chemical odor to signal their receptivity to mating. These chemicals, called **pheromones**, play a major role in ensuring the survival of a species. One of the most outstanding feats of chemical sensation is performed by the salmon. Salmon can follow a chemical trail from an ocean outlet more than 1,000 miles upstream. What happens is that the salmon follows the trail of chemicals unique to the stream in which it was born. This leads to the particular salmon's spawning grounds just as if a map were being used.

As with seeing and hearing, we adapt to various smells and tastes. Cooking odors seem to vanish quickly; the taste buds dull during the course of a meal. In summary, the senses of taste and smell are similar in many respects to the other senses we have discussed.

Balance

The sense of balance is clearly necessary to survive. This sense involves more than simply standing upright; it provides knowledge of how your body is positioned, regardless of whether you are standing, sitting, hanging upside down, or flying through the air. In addition to knowing where your body is relative to outside world, you need to know where the various parts of your body are and how they are positioned relative to one another. Balance can be divided into two parallel systems. One is called the vestibular sense and the other the kinesthetic sense.

The Vestibular Sense.   The stimulus for this sense is a change in position. Whenever you move your head, you receive some information about the position of your head relative to your body. This information comes from mechanisms within the ear called semicircular canals (see Figure 3–15). The **semicircular canals** are filled with fluid and are lined with hairs. These hairs are the receptors for the **vestibular sense**. Whenever you move your head, the fluid in the semicircular canals changes position and different hairs are bent by the fluid. As with the sense of hearing, these hairs are attached to a nerve that transmits this information to the brain. Thus they tell you if your head is rotating, tilting, moving forward, or moving backward, and also how fast it is moving in any of those directions. In this way the brain receives information about position and body movement.

The Kinesthetic Sense.   In addition to being able to sense where your body is relative to the outside world, you are also able to determine where your limbs are relative to each other without looking at them. This ability is often referred to as the **kinesthetic sense**. Receptors for joint motion and

Figure 3-15
The semicircular canals, shown here, are located in the inner ear. When your head moves, fluid in the canals changes position and bends the hair cells that line the canals. These hair cells send neural impulses to the brain, providing information about position and body movement.

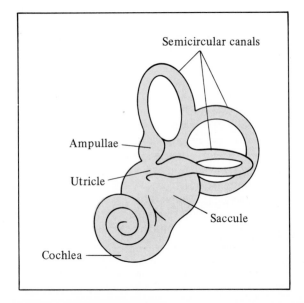

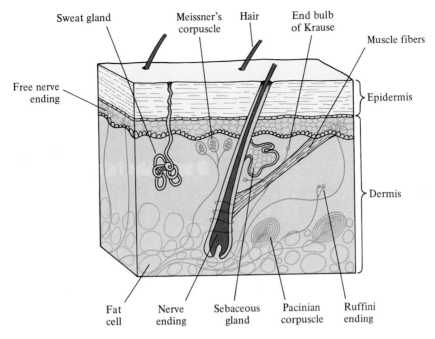

Figure 3-16
A schematic drawing of sensory receptors in the skin. Many different kinds of receptors have been located and not all are found in any one area of the skin. The nerve fibers from all of these receptors travel to the brain through the spinal cord.

for the stretching of muscles and tendons are located directly in the muscles, joints, and tendons. The brain receives neural impulses from these receptors, and you are thus made aware of the position of your limbs at any time, as well as their rate and direction of motion. Without this sense, it would be necessary to look at your arms or legs whenever you wanted to move or use them.

Touch

The skin senses, or sense of touch, provide you with information about things as varied as temperature, shape, and texture. We know little about this sense, but we do have some guesses about the distribution of receptors on the skin surface and on the surface of internal and external organs (see Figure 3-16). Table 3-4 and Figure 3-16 should give you some appreciation of the complexity of the skin and its role as a receptor. All we know for sure is that the skin receptors seem to serve the same function as

TABLE 3-4.
One Square Inch of Skin

In a square inch of skin, you will find:
20 blood vessels
65 hairs and muscles
78 nerves
78 sensors for heat, 13 for cold, 160–165 for pressure
100 sebaceous glands
650 sweat glands
1,300 nerve endings
19,500,000 cells

the receptors of other senses: They take in specific information, carry it along a neural pathway, and deposit it in the brain. It seems likely that our ability to distinguish shape and texture is related to the way the receptors in the skin are stretched and pushed.

Similarly, it is likely that the receptors that register temperature are somehow reporting the dif-

---

Pheromones. Chemicals given off by female animals in heat to signal receptivity for mating.
Semicircular canals. Located in middle ear; responsible for the vestibular sense. Respond to orientation and movement of head and limbs.

Vestibular sense. A sense of balance based on position of head and body movement.
Kinesthetic sense. Sense of balance based on movement of arms and legs.

ferences between the temperature of the skin and the temperature of the object being touched. This demonstrates another property of the sense of touch—like the other senses, it adapts. When you first get into a hot bath, it feels hot. As your skin temperature increases and the difference between the skin and the water temperature decreases, you begin to adapt to the temperature and feel more comfortable. It is not the water's cooling but the adaptation of your senses of touch that makes your bath more comfortable.

It is clear that touch is a very useful sense. Consider how you find the car key or front door key on a dark night: You recognize the shape with your fingers. Think about how you manage to find the bathroom in the middle of a dark night without turning on the light: You feel your way along a wall. Touch can also make up for permanent deficiencies in other senses. By using the **Braille alphabet**, people with defective vision can read using their fingertips instead of their eyes. Bumps on paper can be coded and translated into words by the brain just as surely as if the words had been heard or seen. Of course, reading in Braille is much slower than with normal visual methods, but to the blind person slow is much better than not at all. There are even Braille maps.

Our ability to feel physical pain is another example of the sense of touch. Pain can come from inside our body (a muscle cramp) or from outside our body (getting punched in the nose). Extremes of temperature or pressure and the overexertion of a muscle can also cause pain. Pain may be the result

Touch can make up for deficiencies in other senses. For example, using Braille letters, people with defective vision can read with their fingertips.

of the *extreme* stimulation of certain receptors rather than of specific pain receptors. This theory would explain why very bright lights or loud sounds produce the subjective experience of pain. The theories proposed to account for the phenomenon of pain are very complicated and often contradictory; we will leave the topic for another course.

■ INTEGRATION OF THE SENSES

In our study of what is traditionally considered the senses, we discussed them one at a time, almost as if they existed independently of one another. This is definitely not the case. For instance, the subjective experience of balance is usually a combination or interaction of several senses. Vision plays a major, even dominant, role in balance. For example, we tend not to notice upward movement in a smooth-riding elevator since we are looking at a wall or door that remains stationary. If we are stopped at a traffic light and the car next to us moves slightly forward, we often press harder on the brakes because we get a sensation of movement. The most painful example of the interaction of the senses is motion sickness. Many people become nauseated in cars, buses, planes, or boats. The most accepted explanation for this nausea is that the brain is receiving conflicting information from the senses (Reason and Brand, 1975). Consider what happens in a boat on a rough sea, particularly in an enclosed area. Your semicircular canals are signaling the brain that movement is taking place, but your eyes tell your brain that there is *no* movement because your eyes are usually fixated on some point that is moving in the same direction and at the same rate as your body. In your cabin, when the boat rises on a wave, the wall rises and you both rise at the same time. Reading in a car or traveling in a plane can induce the same feeling. The "therapy" for motion sickness is to try to fix your eyes on a surface that is not moving (like the horizon), or at least on a surface that is moving at a different rate than you. Unfortunately, this therapy only works on the first twinges of nausea. There is a "point of no return" in motion sickness, and once it has been passed, not much will help until the motion stops.

The motion sickness problems of our astronauts have become particularly troublesome. Even though they have been carefully screened during training, many astronauts experience motion sickness in space. This is probably due to the radically conflicting information that they receive from several senses. Since they are outside of normal gravitational forces, there is no longer any up or down, which modifies the information being provided by their vestibular sense. In addition, there is little feedback from bodily movement since there is no longer any weight to their limbs. More will need to be known about the interaction of our senses before these motion sickness problems can be eliminated.

The examples just given might lead you to believe that our senses are poorly coordinated and get in the way of each other. This is not true. These examples are exceptions, not rules. In most situations, our various senses work together as a *system*. They do not function independently or in opposition to

one another. They work together to present a coherent and complete picture of the world outside the body. A perfect example is eating. When you sit down to a meal at your favorite restaurant, your pleasure depends on a number of things. Obviously, the temperature, texture, and chemical properties of the food will affect you—but so might the smell, the color, and even the arrangement of the food. Similar integration of the senses happens continuously. We hear a noise and turn to look at an object. We combine visual cues with auditory cues to decide on distances and rates of speed of objects. This integration of the senses is the topic of the next chapter—perception.

■ EXTRASENSORY PERCEPTION

We have considered the five traditional human senses (vision, hearing, taste and smell, balance, and touch) by examining the manner in which the outside world is translated into an internal neural world. Some people have suggested that humans have more than just these senses. Attempts to describe and document the existence of additional senses belong to a field called **parapsychology**. The process by which individuals come to know the outside world through these additional senses has been labeled **extrasensory perception**, or **ESP**. Several varieties of ESP have been proposed. One known as **telepathy**, involves the sending and receiving of mental images by two or more people. A second form of ESP is **clairvoyance**, in which a person becomes aware of the characteristics of an object or a situation without using normal senses such as hearing or vision. For example, you might wake up "knowing" that someone close to you has just died. There is no "sender" involved in clairvoyance as there is in telepathy. A third form of ESP is known as **precognition**, in which a person can predict the outcome of an event or a future action.

At this time, there is no compelling evidence that

REVIEW QUESTIONS

20. The receptor cells for taste are located in the _____ _____ , and respond to the four basic taste sensations of _____ , _____ , _____ , and _____ .

21. The _____ sense, based on the position of the head, is a sense of balance that tells you about position and body movement; the _____ sense tells you about the relation of your limbs to one another.

22. The sense of touch, unlike our other senses, does not adapt—hot is hot and cold is cold, and we do not notice a difference over time.   T / F

23. Seasickness is often caused by conflicting information coming from our eyes and our _____ _____ .

Answers: 20. taste buds; sweet, sour, salty, bitter *21.* vestibular; kinesthetic *22.* False *23.* semicircular canals

---

Braille alphabet. An alphabet made up of raised dots that blind people can read by running their fingertips over the page.

Parapsychology. Field of psychology that investigates phenomena that apparently cannot be explained in terms of natural scientific laws.

Extrasensory perception. Receiving information by means other than our usual senses.

Telepathy. A type of ESP; involves sending and receiving mental images on the part of two or more people without using the senses.

Clairvoyance. Ability to know objects and events by some means other than the senses.

Precognition. Ability to predict the future; knowledge of future events.

ESP exists. It is difficult to even suggest what sensory mechanisms or receptors one might look for or where they might be found. Those supposedly possessing ESP (called sensitives) are rare, ESP "powers" are often weak and difficult to measure, sensitives have good and bad days so their power comes and goes. To make matters worse, sensitives cannot explain how they can perform acts of ESP. Scientists are skeptical of the research that claims to document ESP processes. Nevertheless, it is important to keep in mind that, traditionally, scientists are professional skeptics. In many instances, it is probably better to err on the side of skepticism than on the side of enthusiasm. For example, you would not want the scientists at the Food and Drug Administration casually approving a new drug without a complete knowledge of the possible side effects of that drug. But perhaps skepticism is not quite so important in considering ESP, since there is no obvious threat in admitting that it may exist.

By the same token, no evidence has been presented suggesting that ESP does *not* exist. Imagine for a moment a planet where all of the people are blind. They have eyes and retinas but their cones and rods are not functional. Once in a great while, however, some of the people have cells that suddenly function. They have the ability to see light during those periods, but this ability is rare, weak, and comes and goes; they cannot explain to others how they "see." If this type of planet existed, the physicists on that planet would not know anything about the experience of vision. The situation in which psychologists attempt to study ESP may be analogous to the planet of the blind.

■ SUMMARY

1. *Sensation* is the reception and transformation of physical energy from the outside world into neural impulses. *Perception* is the transformation of these neural impulses into subjective experiences.

2. The point at which a person notices stimulation when none was noticed before, or that stimulation has increased over a previous level, is known as a *threshold*. The *absolute threshold* refers to the smallest amount of stimulation that can activate a particular sense, while the *difference threshold* (usually called the *just noticeable difference*, or *jnd*) refers to the minimum difference between two stimulus intensities that will be noticed by a person. *Adaptation* is the tendency to become accustomed to a particular level of stimulation after some period of exposure.

3. Seeing depends on light, which is actually waves of electromagnetic energy. Each light wave has a specific height (its amplitude), which determines the brightness of the light, and a specific distance between peaks (its frequency), which determines color. The range of light waves that humans can see is called the *visible spectrum.*

4. The *pupil*, the dark center portion of the eye, is the area through which light enters. The *lens* projects the image from the outside world onto a screen (the *retina*) at the back of the eyeball.

5. The retina is covered with several different types of cells, including the *rods* and *cones*. The *rods* are sensitive to various levels of brightness, while the cones are sensitive to color differences. the *fovea* is a very small area in the center of the retina where the largest number of cones are concentrated. The greatest visual acuity, or the extent to which we can notice fine details, is found in the fovea. At night most of our vision depends on the rods, while in daylight the cones are more active.

6. Small, automatic, and regular sweeping eye movements (*pursuits*) enhance vision by making stimulation of the fovea more likely. In addition, we tend to rapidly scan the different parts of an object, picking up and processing bits and pieces from various portions. These scanning actions are called *saccades.*

7. The *optic nerve* carries information to the *lateral geniculate nucleus*, which is involved in determining the location of an object, and also to the *visual cortex*, which plays a major role in determining color, form, and the pattern of visual stimuli. Specialized cortical cells help to identify such features as the length, width, and angular characteristics of objects.

8. The color sphere shows three dimensions that enable us to distinguish among colors: *wavelength, brightness,* and *saturation.* The *Young-Helmholtz theory* of color vision states that there are three kinds of cones in the retina: one red receptor, one green receptor, and one blue receptor. The colors that we see are the result of stimulation of combinations of these three kinds of receptors. The *opponent-process theory* suggests that the three sets of color receptors

are each responsive to two colors: black-white, red-green, and yellow-blue. The receptors are thought to be able to register the presence of the appropriate colors by turning "off" and "on." Each unique combination of the "off" and "on" states of the three receptors represents a different color.

9. The *frequency* of sound refers to how close together the waves are; humans hear the range from about 20 to 20,000 waves per second. *Amplitude* refers to a sound's intensity or loudness.

10. Sound waves caught by the outer ear, or *pinna*, begin a chain of movement through the *auditory canal* to the *eardrum*, to the bones of the *middle ear*, to the *oval window*, and through the fluid of the inner ear to the *cochlea*. Specialized cells located inside the cochlea along the *basilar membrane* respond to various characteristics of sound. These cells, which are actually tiny hairs, transmit neural impulses via the auditory nerve to two areas in the brain: a section of the thalamus called the *medial geniculate nucleus* and the *auditory cortex*.

11. The currently accepted theory of hearing is a combination of three earlier theories: At low frequencies, receptor cells fire at the same rate as the wave frequency; at middle frequencies, the cells fire in volleys; and at high frequencies, specific places on the basilar membrane are stimulated in unique ways.

12. One kind of hearing loss is *nerve deafness*, the result of damage to some part of the inner ear or basilar membrane. *Conduction deafness* is the result of some damage or inefficiency of the outside or middle ear.

13. When we taste and smell, our sensory systems are responding to chemicals; different chemicals lead to different patterns of discharges or firings. Receptor cells for taste correspond to four basic taste sensations: sweet, sour, salty, and bitter. Less clear are the receptors and processes involved in smelling.

14. The sense of balance is made up of two parallel systems. The *vestibular system* tells us the body's position in space; the stimulus for this sense is a change in position, and its information comes from mechanisms in our ears. The *kinesthetic system* informs us about the position of our limbs without our looking at them. The receptors are located in our muscles, joints, and tendons.

15. The sense of touch, associated with the skin, gives us information about a variety of things, including temperature, shape, and texture. It also enables us to experience pain. We know very little about the sense of touch other than the fact that in many ways it functions like the other senses.

16. Attempts to document the existence of an additional sense, or *extrasensory perception (ESP)*, is known as *parapsychology*. No strong evidence has been presented either to support or to refute the existence of ESP.

■ ANSWERING QUESTIONS FOR THOUGHT

1. These are examples of adaptation, in which you become accustomed to a particular level of stimulation after some period of time.

2. The reason is that your cones, which are responsible for color vision, do not function well in the dark.

3. Because the sound reaches one ear before the other. This means that the intensity of the sound decreases by the time it reaches the other ear; the brain uses this intensity difference to locate the source of the sound.

4. Taste and smell are closely linked. Much of what we think of as the "taste" of food is really provided by our sense of smell, which is why food tastes very bland when you have a head cold and are congested.

5. Seasickness occurs because the brain is receiving conflicting information from the senses. Your semicircular canals are signaling the brain that movement is taking place, but your eyes tell your brain that there is no movement. The way to cure this is to try to get your eyes fixed on a surface that is not moving (such as the horizon), or at least on a surface that is moving at a different rate than you and the boat.

4 Perception

QUESTIONS FOR THOUGHT

1. Why can you hear (or overhear) someone mention your name from several feet away at a noisy cocktail party, even if you are talking to someone else at the time?
2. Why do we have a tendency to judge people by the company they keep or their racial and ethnic background?
3. How do artists produce a feeling of depth on a flat canvas?
4. What causes the "motion" in a motion picture?
5. What causes the visual illusions that make two lines of the same length appear to have different lengths, or two parallel lines appear not to be parallel? Are such illusions always harmless?

The answers to these questions are at the end of the chapter.

In the last chapter we considered how each of our senses conveys information from the outside (objective) world to the inside (subjective) world of the brain. In this chapter we will consider what happens to information once it enters that inside world. The behavior we observe in ourselves and others depends to a much greater extent on perceptions than it does on sensations. If we want to understand why people behave as they do, we won't get very far by simply measuring their physiological reactions to stimulation from the outside world. Instead, we need to consider what happens once stimulation is received and processed; that is, we must consider the nature of perception. **Perception** is the process that allows us to deal with a world of incomplete information. By means of various mechanisms and strategies, we take the raw material provided by our senses—those neural impulses carried to various areas of the brain—and create our subjective reality. There are a number of steps between "sensing" and "making sense."

Figure 4–1 presents three systems—search/attention, organization, and interpretation—that begin to function once sensations reach the brain. The result of their functioning is action. For simplicity, I have presented these systems in a straight-line model, but they do not always work in such an orderly way. For example, our interpretation often causes us to shift attention before taking any action. Similarly, a particular action may cause us to reinterpret some piece of information. Nevertheless, the figure gives you a general idea of the direction of the sequence of perception.

There is much more information out there in the world than we can ever hope to process. For example, you probably couldn't recall what color jacket or shirt the person next to you was wearing in one of your classes today. This might be true even if you spoke to this person before the lecture began. Your

Perception. The interpretation of neural impulses sent by sensory receptors to the brain; involves attention and search, organization, and interpretation.

FIGURE 4-1

The diagram shows the three basic elements of perception: search/attention, organization, and interpretation.

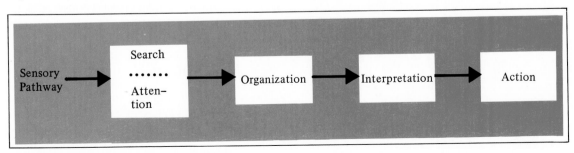

eyes received information about the color of the clothing; this information traveled along the visual pathway to the brain and may have even caused some neural activity in your visual cortex. Nevertheless, it never became a signal for action or even entered permanent memory, because you never paid attention to this aspect of the person. As this example shows, it seems that we either *actively search* for specific information or we *selectively attend* to some information at the expense of other information.

Once you begin searching for or paying attention to something, the information from this object comes to your brain as a disordered series of neural impulses. Somehow, you must re-collect or re-sort these impulses until they form a pattern that is recognizable or useful. A good example of this process is the way you sort the cards dealt to you in a poker or gin rummy hand. You may put all of the 10s and 3s and kings together. You may put together strings of cards that form an unbroken sequence of numbers—say, 3, 4, 5, and 6. You may put all cards of the same suit together. Each of these strategies involves the principle of *organization*. It is only after the cards have been rearranged or organized that you can get on with the game.

After elements have been organized, you still have to make sense out of them. Once you have arranged your cards, you decide if your hand is a good or a bad one. In poker, if you are dealt three of a kind or two pairs, you may decide that it is a good hand and bet on it. If you happen to get five un-

A good example of the way we go about sorting incoming information is the way we rearrange the cards we have been dealt in a card game.

connected cards with no useful pattern, you may decide that the hand is bad and drop out of the game for that round. In each case, you have *interpreted* your pattern of cards.

■ BASIC ELEMENTS OF PERCEPTION

Perceptual Guessing

Because we almost never have enough sensory information to be certain of the characteristics of a situation or an object, the process of perception involves guessing. For example, we make guesses about the motivations of someone we are arguing with, about whether we can make it across the street before an oncoming car hits us, about the probable ripeness of a tomato that we squeeze at the supermarket. Most of the time we aren't aware of such guessing; these guesses tend to be rapid, automatic, and unconscious.

Recent research considers perceptual guessing as cognitive in nature. While we are constantly being bombarded with sensory information, we frequently do not have information that tells us precisely what we need to know. Since our senses are not equipped to process so much incomplete information, we simply guess—but within reason. For example, think of the responses involved in driving home during the rush hour. As you drive along, you are aware that the highway traffic ahead is slowing down and that more and more cars are switching into your lane. You might guess that the slowdown is due to an accident up ahead, or to roadside construction, or simply to sheer volume of traffic—guesses that would hold until evidence proved otherwise. What you guess might even determine whether you exit and take a different route. Thus, the current point of view is that cognitive factors such as judgment and reasoning are involved in perceptual guessing (Pinker, 1984; Ullman, 1984). We will consider these cognitive factors in greater detail in Chapters 8 and 9.

Search and Attention

The term *search* suggests some active process in which we intentionally seek out critical information. You do this in several ways. The most obvious way is to orient or point your sense receptors toward a

This photo shows the frantic activity going on at the New York Stock Exchange. In such a situation, people are bombarded with stimulation of all kinds, and yet manage to pay attention to certain things and ignore others.

stimulus. When you hear a sound, you turn in the direction of that sound and try to see what caused it. If you are curious about the temperature of an object, you move your hand closer to it. If you are wondering whether or not you will enjoy a particular food, you may take a whiff of the odor coming from the pot or pan that holds it.

We search in other ways as well. In the last chapter we discussed how we "scan" a picture. We don't just look at various parts of the picture randomly; we have a pattern of search that seems geared to identifying particularly useful information (Yarbus, 1967). Since we are often interested in being able to recognize a person's face the next time we see it, it is not surprising that our search pattern emphasizes important facial features such as hair and eyes, for these characteristics help distinguish one person from another. This pattern of eye movements varies depending on what we are interested in. A dentist might well concentrate on teeth; a dermatologist, skin; and an ophthalmologist, eyes. Even though each of these patterns is different, there is *some* pattern; it is not just a collection of random glances. Turn back to Figure 3–7 on page 105 for an illustration of how that search goes on.

Even when we are not searching, we are still paying *attention*. That is, we are bombarded with stimulation—the sights, sounds, and smells that fill our environment. We don't have to search them out; they come to us whether we want them or not. It is often necessary to screen out some of this infor-

mation in order to concentrate on other pieces of information. Consider the atmosphere of the factory floor or the cocktail party: In both contexts, there are dozens of things that could draw our attention, but only two or three actually do so at any one time. This suggests that we somehow turn information channels on and off, and to a certain extent this may be true. However, though we do seem to concentrate on one stream of information at a time, this does not mean that we cannot become aware of other streams. For example, you can be talking to someone at a cocktail party and still hear your name spoken in a conversation several feet away (Moray, 1959). In the same way, you can be working on a noisy factory floor, absorbed in a job you are doing, yet still hear your name called over the public address system. This shows that we do not completely shut off information channels; instead, we turn them down. We refer to this phenomenon as **divided attention**.

The opposite type of situation occurs as well. Sometimes you find yourself needing to concentrate on one of two channels of information even though both channels are producing information. When answering the phone, you may ask others nearby to keep quiet so you can hear. Surely hearing is not the problem if you press the earpiece close to your ear. The problem is actually that the noise coming

---

Divided attention. Our ability to attend to two or three stimuli when many more stimuli could command our attention.

into the free ear interferes with concentrating on the voice on the telephone. This is a problem of **selective attention**. Several studies of selective attention have been carried out using a procedure called **shadowing**, in which a person is fitted with earphones and two different messages are presented—one through each earphone. The person is instructed to repeat, word for word, the message coming through the right (or left) earphone. Cherry (1953) found that under these circumstances people remember very little of the nonshadowed message (the message that was not repeated aloud). Though this seems to conflict with the "cocktail party phenomenon" in which you hear your name spoken across the room, there really is no serious conflict here. Apparently, you can *notice* a word on another channel even though you do not store that word in your memory (Glucksberg and Cowen, 1970). Usually, when you hear your name spoken in another conversation, you stop attending to the conversation in which you are currently engaged and try to listen to that other one. Therefore, although it seems that we are capable of monitoring or screening several channels of communication at once, we can really only pay close attention to one at a time.

Organization

Once we have completed our search or directed our attention to certain stimuli (noises, sights, smells), we must organize those various stimuli in a way that will help us to better understand what is happening in the outside world. We can organize information in several different ways, ways that even compete with one another. For an example, consider Figure 4–2. This figure could be seen either as a vase or as a profile of two faces on a background. If you look at it for a while, these two different possibilities will flip back and forth, in spite of the fact that nothing changes physically on the page. Each possibility is a different organization of the same information. This figure demonstrates an unusual situation in which you are confronted with an ambiguous stimulus and apparently have no rule for sorting out its various elements. But why should this situation be so unusual? We often don't have enough information—why, then, is perception so rarely ambiguous? The answer is that we usually do have rules for organizing information. In the poker game described earlier, ambiguity is reduced because you knew the rules of the game and were familiar with all 52 stimulus elements (the cards) that could possibly appear in your hand, so you organized your cards in groups that had the same value (pairs, three of a kind), or that represented consecutive strings of values (straights), or that carried the same symbol (hearts, diamonds, spades, or clubs). Our minds seem to work this way in most situations; we use a small set of principles to group or categorize stimulus elements.

Gestalt Psychology. From 1920 to 1940, a group of psychologists (Kohler, 1929; Koffka, 1935) proposed a theoretical framework to account for our organization of stimuli called *Gestalt theory*. The German word **Gestalt** means *whole*. Thus, this theory emphasized the understanding of perceived forms and events as whole units rather than as pieces of sensation. Another way of stating the underlying assumption of this approach is to say that the whole is greater than the sum of its parts. As discussed in Chapter 1, the Gestalt approach was opposed to the structuralist school of thought. The structuralists felt that behavior could be understood in terms of elementary sensations—patches of light, bursts of sound, areas of pressure on the skin. The Gestalt

FIGURE 4–2
This figure can be seen either as a vase, or as a profile of two faces against a background. If you look for a while, your perception will change back and forth.

approach emphasized the fact that we do not typically *experience* patches of light or bursts of sound; instead we experience spoken language, solid objects, and continuous motion. In short, everything that we become aware of has some form or unity to it. Our subjective experience or perception is not simply a collection of sensations.

An important concept of the Gestalt approach was the distinction between **figure** and **ground**. Our world is three-dimensional; what we see has height, width, and depth. As a result, when we look at two-dimensional pictures, we often make automatic depth estimates. That is, we try to separate the *figure* from the background, or *ground*, as it became known in Gestalt psychology. Look at Figure 4–3. There is no problem in organizing this figure: What is figure and what is ground are obvious. Now consider Figure 4–2 again. This example is partially organized. By applying rules we can narrow it down to two possibilities, but no further. Whether you see a vase or two faces in profile, depends on what you see as figure and what you see as ground, which in turn depends on how you identify the contours or edges of the figure. In a sense, you are trying to guess what object could produce the picture you are looking at. Apparently, some type of automatic mechanism is activated that helps us to identify the shape or contour of the object we are viewing in the picture, both by separating the figure from the ground and by trying to guess what kind of object would produce the given contour or shape.

There is good reason to believe that shapes or contours are important. In the last chapter, you learned that specialized cells called feature detectors, found in the retina and in the visual cortex, make borders and edges more distinct. Thus, what the Gestaltists noticed in the perceptions of people was later confirmed by studies of our physical makeup.

Figure 4–2 illustrates an important aspect of Gestalt theory: The figure is ambiguous, which

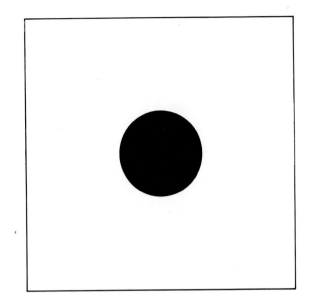

FIGURE 4-3
Gestalt theory emphasizes the role of figure and ground in reducing ambiguity. Unlike Figure 4–2, we can easily identify what is figure here from what is background.

means that it could represent more than one contour or shape, and the Gestalt psychologists dealt with understanding how people reduce ambiguity in the world. Their most general principle, called the **figure-ground principle**, stated that people try to identify a figure and separate it from a background. They suggested several other specific principles for understanding how a person might reduce the ambiguity in a stimulus. Figure 4–4 shows examples of these principles.

The **similarity principle** states that objects that appear to be similar tend to be grouped together. In Figure 4–4A, we can clearly separate the circles from the squares. We see one group of circles within a larger collection of squares.

According to the **proximity principle**, elements

Selective attention. The fact that we respond to certain aspects of the environment and ignore others.

Shadowing. Technique used in studying attention. Subject hears two separate messages delivered through earphones, one to each ear, and is asked to repeat one message word for word.

Gestalt. German word meaning "whole." Gestalt psychologists believed that we perceive whole units rather than pieces of sensation. Gestalt principles show how we group stimulus elements in whole perceptions.

Figure. Something that stands out against a background or

ground. On the page you are reading now, the words are the figure and the paper is the ground.

Ground. The background against which something is seen.

Figure-Ground principle. People tend to identify a figure and separate it from a ground or background; an important concept in Gestalt psychology.

Similarity principle. Gestalt principle that similar objects tend to be grouped together.

Proximity principle. Gestalt principle that elements close to one another tend to be seen as a single unit.

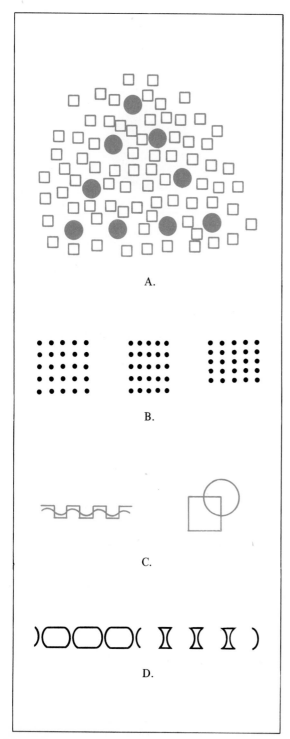

FIGURE 4-4

These are examples of the Gestalt principles of organization: A. the similarity principle, B. the proximity principle, C. the good continuation principle, and D. the closure principle.

that are physically close together will be grouped together and perceived as a single unit. In Figure 4-4B, your perception of the three groups of dots depends on how close the dots are to one another. On the left, they are equally distant from one another, so you see either rows of dots or columns of dots. In the middle, the dots are closer together on the horizontal dimension, so the figure appears to be horizontal rows of dots. On the right, the dots are closer together on the vertical dimension, so the figure appears as vertical rows of dots.

The **principle of common fate** highlights the fact that various stimuli that appear to be moving together are seen as bound together in a particular way. For example, if you are watching a runner on a track, you will see a body moving from point to point, not a series of limbs and a trunk and a head. All the parts move in unison and create a single object moving across the retina. The principle of common fate is most likely to apply when the object in question is in motion.

A related principle is known as **good continuation**. This principle says that independent elements that are arranged in a particular pattern are seen as related. This principle is illustrated in Figure 4-4C. The good continuation principle is the basis of most camouflage strategies. Consider the accompanying picture of a giraffe. Because the giraffe blends into the background, it is protected from many predators. In this instance, one principle of organization (good continuation) is actually counteracting another principle (figure-ground). The good continuation principle operates most often when an object is not in motion. In fact, as soon as the giraffe begins to move, the principle of good continuation is no longer an advantage to the giraffe; figure-ground will apply and the giraffe may become some predator's lunch.

The **closure principle** states that when there are gaps in a perimeter or border, we fill in those gaps to complete (or close) that border. An example of closure can be seen in Figure 4-4D. We recognize the figures as a circle and a square even though the borders are incomplete.

These examples are compelling evidence for the existence of the Gestalt principles. These principles could be said to be embodied in neural programs that are automatically activated when ambiguous stimulus elements are present. Figure 4-4 shows these principles as they apply to visual stimuli, but

The good continuation principle is the basis of camouflage. While at rest, the giraffe blends well into its background and is protected from many predators.

it is not hard to see how they could apply to a broad range of situations, including social ones. For example, the similarity principle suggests that we tend to treat blacks, or women, or senior citizens as members of a group rather than as individuals. Similarly, the proximity principle suggests that we tend to make judgments about people in terms of the company they keep. (Many a reputation has been lost on that basis.) The importance of the Gestalt approach is in showing that we have built-in perceptual mechanisms for reducing ambiguity that are automatic and often unconscious. The Gestalt theorists demonstrated dramatically that raw sensations are somehow organized in our brains and that what we perceive is the result of that organization, not the raw sensations themselves.

Interpretation

Search or attention produces information that is different from the raw sensations by reducing them. Organization produces information that is different in pattern from the original raw sensations by grouping or collecting them. One more operation is necessary before we finally "perceive" a stimulus. These sensations must be interpreted. The major principle governing interpretation seems to be the context in which the information is found.

Go back to the poker game for a moment. Regardless of your hand, you will interpret its value in terms of what cards the other people around you may be holding. If the person to your left seems anxious for the betting to begin, you may feel less confident about your cards. If the person to your right is hesitant in matching a bet, you may become more enthusiastic about your hand. In fact, most of the bluffing that goes on in poker is an active attempt to affect the context in which the other players evaluate or interpret their hands.

The act of interpretation is much like understanding a blueprint. You may recognize the lines and angles as belonging to some sort of object, but you really can't make sense out of it until you find out that you are looking at the blueprint of a four-bedroom split-level house. Only after you are told which view is the second floor, which is the first floor, and which is the front, can you perceive the blueprint as a three-dimensional object called a house. You have interpreted the organized information.

These three mechanisms—search and attention, organization, and interpretation—are actively involved in perception. We search for or attend to stimuli, we organize those stimuli into meaningful patterns, and we "make sense" out of those patterns in terms of the context in which they appear. Remember that in the absence of sense, your mind will produce sense. It seems as if the human mind strives for coherence and consistency, even when none exists. We are determined to make sense out of things. Search and attention, organization, and interpretation help us do it.

Principle of common fate. Gestalt principle that various stimuli that appear to be moving together are seen as bound together in a particular way.

Good continuation principle. Gestalt principle that elements arranged or arrayed in a particular direction are seen as related.
Closure principle. Gestalt principle that when a figure is incomplete we tend to complete it, making the figure whole.

REVIEW QUESTIONS

1. The three basic processes of perception are _____, _____, and _____.

2. The way in which we screen out noise when we want to concentrate on something is an example of _____ _____ . This has been studied using the technique of _____, in which a person hears two different messages through separate earphones, and is asked to repeat only one.

3. The word Gestalt means "_____ ." Gestalt psychologists state that perception is made up of entire units rather than pieces of _____.

4. Match the following Gestalt principles with their definitions:

___ proximity principle

___ similarity principle

___ principle of common fate

___ principle of good continuation

___ closure principle

A. when a figure is incomplete we tend to complete it, making it whole.

B. various stimuli that appear to be moving together are seen as bound together in a particular way.

C. elements close to one another tend to be seen as a unit.

D. objects that are like one another tend to be grouped together.

E. elements that are arranged in a particular direction are seen as related.

5. Gestalt principles can apply to social situations as well as to visual stimuli. For instance, according to the proximity principle, we would tend to make judgments about people according to:
   a. how they dress.
   b. their racial or ethnic background.
   c. the company they keep.
   d. our first impressions of them.

Answers: 1. attention/search; organization; interpretation 2. selective attention; shadowing 3. whole; sensation 4. proximity principle, C; similarity principle, D; principle of common fate, B; principle of good continuation, E; closure principle, A 5. c

■ VISUAL PERCEPTION

Visual information is the basis of much of our perceptual processing. Even so, we are not restricted to visual sensation. Depth perception and motion perception are two aspects of visual perception that reveal how perceptual mechanisms go beyond just "seeing." In the next section we will consider how depth and motion perception contribute to our understanding of the world.

Depth Perception

Depth perception is quite an accomplishment, since the eye itself is not perfectly designed for perceiving depth. The world is three-dimensional; images projected onto the screen-like surface of the retina have a height and width on the retina, but no depth. The third dimension is lost in the projection to the eye. Despite this limitation, we do perceive depth and distance. Two sets of factors help to produce the subjective experiences of depth and distance. One is based on our physiology, the other on the environment around us.

Physiological Cues to Depth. From the last chapter, you should remember that as we get closer to an object, our lenses change shape in order to keep that object in focus. A camera lens works the same way. We adjust the focus as we move toward or away from an object, and our brains are sensitive to that change in lens shape. The technical name for the change in the shape of the lens is **accommodation**.

As we look at an object, we make another adjustment. Our eyes **converge**, or turn in, as we move closer to an object and **diverge**, or turn out, as we move farther away from an object. Again, our brains use this information to help in determining the depth or distance of visual stimuli.

An additional physiological cue to depth is **retinal disparity**. Since our eyes are separated by 2 or more inches, each retina receives a slightly different view of a stimulus. You can demonstrate this for yourself. Hold 2 objects (your thumbs will do) in front of your nose, one about 12 inches away and the other at a distance about 18 inches away. Now alternate looking at them from the left and right eye, closing the eye not in use. If you pay close attention, you will notice that you get a slightly different view from each eye. These two different views reach the brain and are used as cues for depth. You will

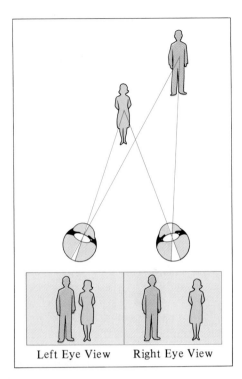

FIGURE 4-5
The left eye view of the man and woman is different
from the right eye view. The brain uses this disparity as
a depth cue. In this case, it indicates how far away
these figures are from the viewer.

retinas receive different images and disparity (and
in this case, depth) results.

Like convergence and divergence, retinal disparity is based on the interaction of both eyes; the brain
interprets the difference between the view from the
left eye and the view from the right eye in order to
estimate depth or distance. Consequently, all three
factors are known as **binocular cues.**

Environmental Cues to Depth. In addition to the
cues already mentioned, there is a set of cues called
monocular cues that help in depth perception.
These monocular cues affect each eye separately.
They are used by all of us, but are especially useful
for people who are blind in one eye and consequently cannot use binocular cues. You might try closing
one eye and looking around. This should make it
apparent that even without binocular cues, you can
still perceive depth.

Monocular cues are very different from binocular
cues. They depend more on past experience than
they do on the brain's interpretation of retinal
images. Monocular cues depend on familiar aspects
of the environment and associations between objects in that environment, like the depth of a scene,
the size of an object in the distance, or the distance
between two objects.

Interposition, in which one object partly blocks
a second object, is a powerful depth cue. Look at
Figure 4-6. Your first interpretation would probably
be that you are viewing three cards at different
distances, with the king of clubs interposed, or
placed in front of, a blank, in front of the king of
spades. As you can see from the right side of that
figure, your interpretation would have been wrong.
The king of spades is actually no further away than
the king of clubs. You made such an interpretation
because it is what you are used to seeing. But the
cards could have been unusual in some way, like the
ones on the right side of the figure. Usually, however, there are no "tricks"; the cue of interposition
is useful.

notice that if you hold the objects 2 or 3 inches from
your nose and alternate eyes again, the two views
will differ to a greater extent than when the objects
were 12 and 18 inches from your nose. You will see
the objects "move" or shift from side to side if you
alternate opening and closing your right and left eye.
The geometry of this phenomenon is illustrated in
Figure 4-5.

Retinal disparity is the basis of 3-D vision. In the
case of 3-D glasses, each lens (acting as a filter)
allows only certain wavelengths of light to reach the
eye. Two different images are then projected on a
movie screen, each composed of wavelengths that
are appropriate for one or the other eye. Through
this dual filtering and projection strategy, the two

Depth perception. The awareness of the distance between you
and an object.
Accommodation. The way the muscles in the eye change the
shape of the lens in order to focus on an object.
Converge. Our eyes turn inward as we get closer to an object.
Diverge. Our eyes turn outward as we move farther away from
an object.
Retinal disparity. The different view from each eye that is due
to the fact that our eyes are separated by 2 or more inches.

Binocular cues. Cues to depth that are based on the interaction
of both eyes; include convergence, divergence, and retinal
disparity.
Monocular cues. Cues to depth that work with each eye
separately.
Interposition. Monocular depth cue: If one object appears in
front of another, it will be perceived as being closer than the
other object.

FIGURE 4-6
One of the monocular cues to depth is interposition. At first glance (left) you probably think that you're seeing the king of clubs in front of a blank card and the king of spades behind it. Actually, as is shown on the right, instead of being placed one in front of the other, the cards have been notched to give this impression.

Another useful environmental cue to depth and distance is called **perspective**, and it refers to the apparent convergence of parallel lines as they approach the horizon. We have much real-world experience with this cue. A good example is shown in Figure 4–7, in which the two rails seem to come closer and closer together as the tracks get farther and farther away. Our knowing that the two rails are actually parallel helps us to interpret what we see as a signal for distance or depth.

Shading is another cue often used to judge distance or depth. Shading is actually not so much a cue for depth as a means of showing where a light source is. Nevertheless, it provides depth by suggest-

ing that an object has a third dimension; completely flat objects cannot produce such shading patterns. In art, we can produce many visual effects with shading; we can, for instance, give an object depth or height, depending on where the shading is placed (see Figure 4–8). Another common example of shading is the use of makeup to highlight cheekbones, making a face look longer and thinner.

The cue of **texture gradient** is similar to shading. Since objects of the same texture appear different farther away than they do closer up, experience tells us this difference is a cue for distance or depth. Figure 4–9 presents an example of this depth cue. Note that the texture of the image looks more compressed from a place far away than it does on a nearby part of the surface.

Artists use all of the monocular cues we have discussed so far to give a feeling of depth and distance to their paintings. It is not just the artistic use of environmental cues, but our familiarity with how these cues work, that enable artists to portray a three-dimensional world on a two-dimensional surface.

Relative motion, or **motion parallax**, is another cue that signals depth. If you are on a bus and looking out the window at some point between the bus and the horizon, the objects between you and your point of focus will appear to move in a direction *opposite* to your direction of movement (Figure 4–10).

FIGURE 4-7
Perspective is an important monocular cue, and one of the easiest ways to show it is with railway tracks. The fact that these two parallel lines seem to come together at the horizon is a strong distance cue.

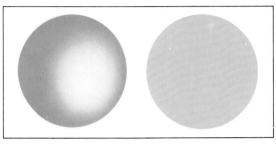

FIGURE 4-8
Shading on the outer edges of a spherical object, such as a ball, gives it a three-dimensional quality. Without shading, it might be seen as a flat disk.

The objects between your point of focus and the horizon will appear to move in the *same direction* as you are moving. You are not always paying attention to this phenomenon, but your brain is. This is a very powerful cue and is used to great advantage. The fact that objects between you and the horizon seem to move in two different directions implies that there is some distance between you and that horizon. Objects that seem to move in the same direction as you are moving are perceived as farther from you than objects that seem to move in the opposite direction.

In everyday situations, we do not depend on just one of these cues for determining depth or distance;

FIGURE 4-9
The texture of this sand dune looks more compressed in the distance than it does on a nearby part of the surface. A texture gradient like this is one of the monocular cues to depth and distance.

we use as many cues and perceptual mechanisms as we have available to us. There is a functional aspect to the use of many cues. Some research findings suggest that each additional cue available to us makes our depth perception that much more sensitive (Jameson and Hurvitch, 1959).

REVIEW QUESTIONS

6. Why is depth perception such an accomplishment? Because we experience a _____-dimensional world through our _____-dimensional retina.

7. One cue to depth is that our eyes _____ (turn in) as we move closer to an object and _____ (turn out) as we move farther away from it.

8. Since our eyes are separated by about 2 inches, each eye gets a different view of the world. This different view is called _____ _____ and is a powerful depth cue.

9. Next to each depth cue, put B if it is a binocular cue or M if it is a monocular cue:
__ retinal disparity   __ perspective
__ interposition   __ divergence
__ shading   __ texture gradient
__ convergence

10. One useful environmental depth cue is based on the fact that parallel lines seem to come together as they approach the horizon. This depth cue is called
    a. shading.   c. perspective.
    b. interposition.   d. texture gradient.

Answers: 6. three; two **7.** converge; diverge **8.** retinal disparity **9.** retinal disparity, B; interposition, M; shading, M; convergence, B; perspective, M; divergence, B; texture gradient, M **10.** c

---

Perspective. Monocular depth cue: the apparent convergence of parallel lines as they approach the horizon.

Shading. Monocular depth cue: Patterns of light and shadow on an object produce an effect of depth or height.

Texture gradient. Monocular depth cue: objects of uniform texture do not seem the same as they get farther away from us, which acts as a depth cue.

Motion parallax. Depth cue. Objects between you and your point of focus will seem to be moving in the direction opposite to yours, while objects between your point of focus and the horizon will seem to be moving in the same direction as you.

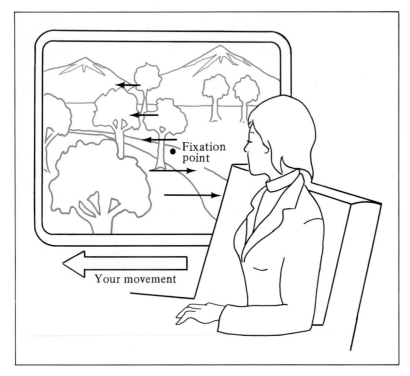

Fixation point

Your movement

FIGURE 4-10

This sketch shows how the principle of motion parallax works. When you ride in a car or train, objects between you and your point of focus will seem to move in the opposite direction to you. Objects between your point of focus and the horizon will seem to move in the same direction you are moving. The brain uses this as a cue to depth.

Motion Perception

Another vital function of our perceptual system is the detection of motion. Motion offers powerful clues about what an object is, where it is, and where it is going; in other words, motion is an important part of our perception of events. Two factors significantly influence the perception of motion. The first is that motion in the world causes motion on the retina of the eye. As you walk around, or as objects themselves move, the images on the retina change considerably. Yet you need to distinguish what is really moving from what is not. One theory is that just as there are line and angle detectors in the visual cortex that respond to specific features of an object, there also may be motion detectors that are uniquely sensitive to the movement of an object (Hubel and Wiesel, 1968).

The second significant factor is eye movement. When we considered depth perception, we discussed the role played by convergence and divergence (the movement of our eyes as an object gets closer or farther away). The same type of operation probably occurs in motion perception. The brain can estimate the motion of an object by using information from the rate of movement of each eye.

Since an object in motion moves across the retina, and since we strive to keep the image focused on the fovea at the center of the retina, we must move our eyes to accomplish this purpose. It is this tracking movement that provides a cue for perceiving motion. (Sherrington, 1906; Kasamatsu, 1976).

Motion Pictures. The "motion" that we perceive in motion pictures is achieved in several ways. One method is for the camera to produce effects of motion parallax for transfer to the screen: Near objects are filmed moving in the opposite direction and far objects are filmed moving in the same direction. In addition, the shooting can quickly interpose many different objects, giving an added feeling of depth. Similarly, the camera can be moved in many different directions and at many different speeds.

The illusion of movement can also be accomplished by using principles of **stroboscopic motion**. If you sit in a darkened room and look at two lights being turned on, one after the other, the light may appear to move. In other words, you won't see two bulbs being lit one after another; you will see one moving light. The critical variable is the amount of time that passes between the time the first light goes out and second light comes on. If that time is too

IT DEPENDS ON HOW YOU LOOK AT IT

Look at the picture in the box and describe what is happening. Undoubtedly, you will conclude that the hunter is trying to spear the antelope while an elephant stands placidly in the distance. Your conclusion may seem obvious to you, but in fact not everyone would describe the picture that way. In particular, members of remote, nonliterate tribes would be likely to assume that the hunter is trying to spear the elephant. Such a response indicates an inability to interpret pictures three-dimensionally. Can this be possible?

William Hudson had done work with South African Bantus that led him to question the ability of some primitive peoples to see pictures as three-dimensional. To test this hypothesis, he constructed a pictorial perception test using three cues to indicate depth: known size, interposition, and perspective. (One picture uses texture gradients as well.) When he tested African tribal subjects, he found that both children and adults had difficulty perceiving depth in the test pictures. Did the subjects perhaps have difficulty because they were not familiar with the content of some of the pictures? Further experimentation showed that this was not the case. Other subjects were tested

and defined as two-dimensional perceivers or three-dimensional perceivers. Then they were shown an abstract structure—two squares, one behind the other and connected by a rod—and asked to build models of what they had seen. More often than not, two-dimensional perceivers built a flat model, not a cube as the structure suggested.

Why did these subjects fail to see certain representations, such as pictures, as three-dimensional? A picture is a pattern of lines, forms, and shadings that must be organized and interpreted if the picture is to be meaningful. People who can't gauge three dimensions from two are seeing all those elements but failing to combine them properly. What does this inability mean? It implies that some familiarity with the pictorial conventions for representing depth—such as known size and interposition, as used in the figure shown here—may be needed for us to perceive a three-dimensional world on a two-dimensional surface. Thus what would seem to be a perfectly natural ability—so natural as to need no prior learning—is not entirely the case.

Source: J. B. Deregowski, "Pictorial Perception and Culture, *Scientific American* November 1972.

brief (less than 30 milliseconds), you will see the two lights come on together. If the interval is increased to 60 milliseconds, you are likely to see one light moving from one spot to another rather than see two lights. This principle is used to great advantage in movies. In this case what is presented to the retina is actually a series of still images that are illuminated in rapid succession. As these images are flashed by at a certain speed, the brain "fills in" the spaces.

It then uses the resulting motion cues to generate the subjective experience of motion. The apparent motion in motion pictures thus takes advantage of some unique characteristics of human perception and produces a very powerful illusion of external motion.

Stroboscopic motion. An illusion of movement caused by flashing lights on and off, one after another.

Constancies

Up to this point, we have considered many examples of how various automatic devices help us make sense of sensations from the outside world. This brings us to an interesting problem. According to our sensory information, the world is never the same from one second to the next. Our eyes (and retinas) bounce up and down as we walk, sounds made by a voice on the radio will differ from the sound of that voice in person, and the light waves reflected from an object at night are different from those that are reflected from the same object during daylight. Yet the world doesn't appear to move up and down as we walk, we would probably recognize Ronald Reagan's voice no matter where or how we heard it, and a red car is still perceived to be red whether parked on the street or in a dimly-lit parking garage. The way we accomplish this is through perceptual constancy.

Perceptual constancy means that we typically perceive objects as having a constant shape, size, and color no matter from what angle we view them, how far away from them we are, or under what lighting conditions we see them. In other words, no matter what the retinal image is, the perception remains constant.

For example, the farther away a person is, the smaller his image will appear on the retina. A man standing 5 feet away would cast an image on the retina that is twice as large as he would if he were standing 10 feet away (see Figure 4–11). Because of perceptual constancy, our perception of the man's size remains the same. Thus the size of the retinal image changes, and yet our perception of the person's size remains constant. This type of perceptual constancy is known as **size constancy**.

Size constancy is produced by our ability to integrate prior experience with distance cues. We know that people are about 5 to 6 feet tall, for example, and that they do not vary in height from 1 inch to 6 feet. Using this prior experience in combination with distance cues, the monocular and binocular cues that we discussed as part of depth perception, we could easily tell in the above example that in one case the man is near us and in the other that he is farther away. We interpret the retinal image in light of the perceived distance.

There are many other kinds of constancy. One of these is **shape constancy**. Figure 4–12 shows a coin being rotated through different angles. On our retinal field, the coin is changing in shape from a circle to an ellipse, yet we do not perceive it as changing. It remains a round coin. We have had enough experience with coins so that we assume that they do not easily change their contours. The elliptical shape is interpreted as a circular coin seen at a slant rather than an elliptical coin seen straight on.

FIGURE 4-11

This figure shows the relationship between the size of a retinal image and the distance between you and an object. An object 5 feet away from you will cast an image on the retina that is twice as large as the same object placed 10 feet away.

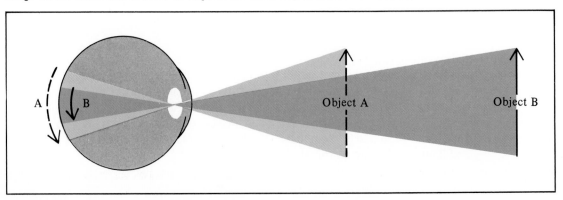

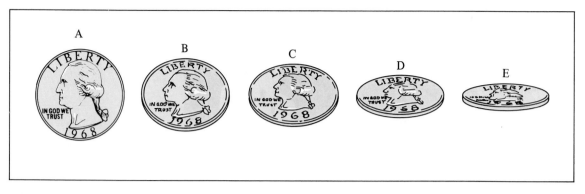

FIGURE 4-12

In this figure a coin is drawn at different angles to show the principle of shape constancy. Although the image on our retina changes from a circle to an ellipse, we continue to perceive it as a round coin.

Velocity constancy is another common experience. When we watch a car drive away from us at a constant speed, it might be expected to be perceived as slowing down, since it is covering a smaller distance across the retina as it gets farther away from us. In spite of the image on the retina, we perceive that the car maintains a constant speed. We do not see it as slowing down. Again, experience tells us that objects moving away from us *appear* to move slower. Experience wins out over sensation.

All constancies have two things in common: They tend to depend heavily on past experience, learning, or knowledge, and they are automatic. Constancies have been described as unconscious inferences or calculations (Hochberg, 1978); a person perceives the object that would have been most likely to produce a particular stimulus pattern. In the course of day-to-day activities, this perception turns out to be accurate much more often than it is wrong. Constancies permit us to take some things for granted, which frees mental energy so that it can be used in other ways.

Illusions

Sometimes our perceptions *are* wrong. They are wrong because we *misapply* constancies to particular objects or in certain situations. This is known as an illusion (Gregory, 1970). An **illusion** is a false impression of an object or the environment. Figure 4–13 is an illusion. After examining it, your first impression might be that the man on the left is a midget and the man on the right is a giant. But as you can see in the diagram, you were fooled by some distance cues. You assumed that the room was rectangular, in which case all three figures would be the same distance from you. It is not, and the man at the left is much farther away than he looks.

The illusion produced by this irregularly shaped room is quite different from size constancy, even though both compare a small and a large retinal image. When we see a person at a distance, we assume that the person is of normal height though our retinal image is small. The final perception of size is correct *in spite of* the objective sensation.

Perceptual constancy. Our perception of objects as having a constant shape, size, or color no matter what angle we view them from, how far away from them we are, or what lighting conditions we see them under.

Size constancy. The fact that we perceive objects as having a constant size no matter how far away we are from them.

Shape constancy. The fact that we perceive the shape of objects to remain constant no matter what angle we view them from.

Velocity constancy. The speed of an object seems to remain constant as it moves away from us, even though according to the stimuli we are receiving, it should be seen as moving more slowly.

Illusion. A false or mistaken impression of an object or the environment.

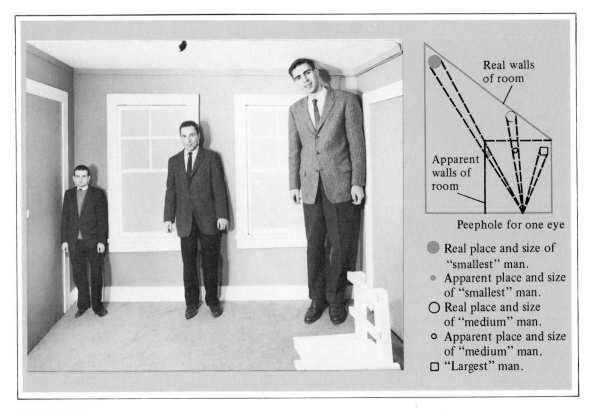

Real walls
of room

Apparent
walls of
room

Peephole for one eye

● Real place and size of
   "smallest" man.
• Apparent place and size
   of "smallest" man.
○ Real place and size
   of "medium" man.
∘ Apparent place and size
   of "medium" man.
□ "Largest" man.

FIGURE 4-13
The three men standing in this room appear to be of widely varying heights—the man on the left looks like a midget compared to the man on the right. Actually, as the diagram shows, you are being fooled by some misleading distance cues. The room is not a regularly shaped room, and the man on the left is really a lot farther away than he looks.

There are other illusions that are easy to demonstrate. Some examples appear in Figure 4-14. Each of these illusions depends on one or more of the perceptual cues or Gestalt principles that we considered earlier. There are some dangerous illusions that had not been recognized as illusions until recently. One is related to the judgments that people make about the relative speed and distance of moving objects. It might surprise you to know that almost 1,000 people are killed in the 12,000 car and train crashes that occur each year. As Leibowitz (1982) points out, this statistic is even more surprising when you consider the fact that every railroad crossing has a warning device that signals the approach of a train. Why, then, do these accidents occur? Perhaps people don't hear the train whistle or see the flashing lights, or perhaps there is no gate to prevent them from crossing the tracks while the train is approaching. But this is usually not the case. Analyses of accidents show that the victims probably saw the train coming and were aware of the warning signals. In fact, in some instances, drivers have even driven *around* barriers and then been hit by the train.

Leibowitz has considered these accidents from a perceptual standpoint and has suggested an intriguing explanation in which two aspects of motion perception play a role. The first aspect is the observation that large objects are perceived as moving more slowly than small objects. To prove this to yourself, simply watch two jet planes of different sizes take off or land. The smaller plane will seem to be moving faster than the larger plane, even

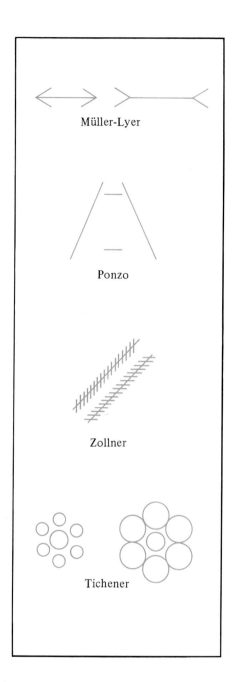

FIGURE 4-14

The illusions shown in this figure depend on one or more cues or Gestalt principles discussed in the text. In contrast to what the line drawings look like, the two horizontal lines in both the Müller-Lyer illusion and the Ponzo illusion are the same length; the oblique lines are actually parallel in the Zollner illusion; and the inner circles are the same size in the Titchener illusion. You may want to take a ruler and measure these lines to convince yourself that these really are illusions.

though they are actually moving at about the same speed. The second aspect is that an object seems to move more slowly when we track it or follow it with our eyes as opposed to keeping our head and eyes still. When these characteristics of motion perception are combined, the result is disbelief on the part of the driver at the train crossing. The driver thinks there is plenty of time to get across the tracks before the train comes. This illusion or false impression of speed may be responsible for the deaths of many motorists.

Another illusion has been identified as the cause of certain airplane accidents (Kraft, 1978). This type of accident usually occurs at night, in sloping terrain, and the pilot crashes at some point short of the runway. It seems that the pilot misjudges height; he cannot tell that the ground is sloping, since it is dark, and therefore assumes that the ground is flat. As a result, he is under the mistaken impression that the plane is actually higher than the altimeter indicates.

Research into such illusions can help us find ways to prevent accidents, such as lighting a runway differently or leveling the ground on the approaches to runways. The train-speed and plane-altitude illusions are misapplications of motion and speed cues with serious consequences. Until recently, accidents caused by these illusions have been attributed to human error, as if they were beyond prevention. Because psychologists have been able to correctly identify them as the results of illusions that are caused by a particular set of circumstances, it is more likely that these types of accidents can be reduced.

■ FACTORS INFLUENCING PERCEPTION

Learning

In many of the preceding explanations of constancies, illusions, depth cues, and so on, you ran across terms like "learning" and "experience." We must learn many complicated perceptions to get through each day. Children must learn to distinguish the letters p from q and b from d. Medical technicians must learn how to "perceive" an x-ray picture or electrocardiogram sheet. In our examples,

DANGEROUS ILLUSIONS OF NIGHTTIME DRIVING

Annual traffic fatalities are about four times higher for nighttime accidents than for daytime accidents. Two reasons frequently cited for this are the greater chances that a driver might be intoxicated or fatigued at night. These hazards are indeed to blame for at least an important percentage of nighttime traffic fatalities, but recently psychologists have been examining what they think is an even more critical factor—the human perceptual system.

We need two modes of vision to drive a car. One is a focal or recognition mode, or the ability to identify an object we are looking at. For example, you see that the sign in front of you is informing you of the speed limit. The second type of vision is a guidance mode, on which we base our judgments about how fast an object is moving or how far away it is. Under daytime conditions, we depend on both modes to operate with equally high efficiency. Under dim lighting conditions, such as those involved in driving at night, we tend to expect the same high level of perception. Unfortunately, while our guidance mode is not so seriously affected, our recognition abilities are drastically reduced. Psychologists believe that our confidence in the guidance mode—which allows us to steer a car just as well under bright or dim lighting conditions—also gives us a false sense of confidence in our recognition abilities, such as the ability to detect objects and our sensitivity to levels of contrast. Added to this confidence in our recognition ability is the fact that many of the visual guides that we depend on for night driving—dashboard instruments, road signs, and other vehicles—are enhanced with lights or reflective materials to compensate for our reduced perception. As a result, we get the impression that we see better than we actually can. The effects of alcohol present added dangers. An intoxicated person tends to have an inflated sense of self confidence, slower reaction times, and impaired judgment. It is not difficult to understand why drunk drivers contribute so heavily to the number of nighttime traffic accidents.

A typical example of a nighttime driving accident that results from reduced perceptual abilities is hitting a pedestrian in a spot where the driver does not expect one to be. When using low headlight beams, a driver can see a person dressed in dark clothing from a distance of about 100 feet. Driving at a speed of 55 miles per hour, however, it takes the average driver 317 feet to bring a car to a complete stop. While lower speeds, bright headlight beams, and light clothing worn by the pedestrian reduce the chances of an accident of this type, such traffic deaths are more likely than most drivers imagine and occur some 4,000 times per year. One particularly dangerous type of accident is known as an underride collision, which almost always happens at night and is usually fatal. In this kind of collision, the driver fails to see a larger vehicle ahead and actually drives the car underneath a tractor-trailer or some other type of large equipment. The sudden appearance of a disabled vehicle or an animal crossing the road are other examples of nighttime hazards that, because of reduced perceptual abilities, often cause nighttime driving accidents.

Among the suggested ways to reduce the number of traffic deaths, psychologists recommend the display of reflective material or illumination on all potential nighttime obstacles, such as pedestrians, trailers, trains, and disabled vehicles; lower speed limits for driving at night; and informing drivers about their reduced perceptual abilities in a darkened environment. (Leibowitz and Owens, 1986.)

learning was of a much more detailed and physical nature. We learn how our eyes "feel" when we are examining a distant object. We learn to "experience" movement with all of its related cues. We may even "learn" distance measurement through the changing thickness or accommodation of the lenses of our eyes. We will not consider learning in any great detail here; Chapters 6 and 7 are devoted to it. You should simply recognize the fact that a good deal of what we perceive is based on and can be changed through learning.

Maturation

Some of our senses seem to require maturation to function fully. **Maturation** is growth or physical development. Since we know that the human brain grows in complexity over time, and that our sense

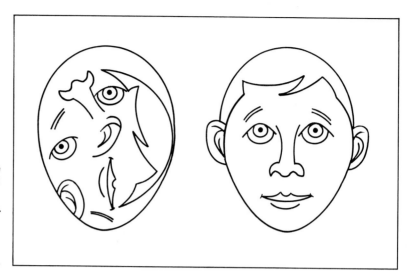

FIGURE 4-15

If the two faces pictured here are shown to children younger than 1 month, they will not show much preference for one over the other. As they get older, however, they begin to choose the regular face instead of the "scrambled" one. This is an example of maturation.

organs also improve to a point before they begin to degenerate, it should not be surprising that some aspects of perception are affected by simple maturation. The development of visual perception in infants affords us the best examples of the effect of maturation. Consider the two stimuli in Figure 4–15. Children younger than 1 month do not have any clear perference for the regular or the "scrambled" face, although they do seem to have some preference for facial features, regardless of how they are arranged (Hershenson, Kessen, and Munsinger, 1967). As children get older, a preference emerges for the regular face as opposed to the "scrambled" one. As research continues into the entire life span, a whole set of maturation changes in perceptual processes are being uncovered.

Another example of maturation occurs in the sense of taste. There is evidence that as we mature, the type and location of taste buds shift (Desor, Maler, and Turner, 1973), therefore, "tastes change." As young children we prefer sweet and lightly seasoned foods (Schiff, 1980), but as we get older our tolerance for "strange" and spicy foods increases, not soley as a function of habits or experience. Furthermore, older people actually have fewer taste buds than they had when they were younger. As a result, tastes may change even in the later stages of life.

Older people may also experience a different visual world as a result of maturational changes. For example, as people grow older, their pupils become smaller. Consequently, less light enters the eye and

the world is seen differently than it would be by a younger person or by the same person at a younger age. Similar changes occur in color vision and auditory acuity.

An interesting sidelight of maturation is the concept of a critical period. It appears that during the early stages of development, a certain amount of normal visual input is necessary for proper maturation of the visual system (Sekuler and Blake, 1985). This critical period extends to about age 4. If normal stimulation has not occurred by then, permanent abnormalities in the visual system result. Consequently, many of the cues used for depth and motion perception may never be available. This suggests that a developing child should be presented with a visually complex environment if perceptual abilities are to mature properly. It also suggests that any apparent problems in the vision of a young child should be investigated early and corrected, so that appropriate visual stimulation will occur during the critical period.

Inborn Tendencies

As we saw in the discussion of vision in Chapter 3, there seem to be specific feature-detector cells in the visual cortex that search for or respond to particular forms of stimulation. Are there any built-in, or innate, aspects to perception? Apparently there

---

Maturation. Growth or physical development.

are, at least with respect to depth. Almost from birth, infants are able to distinguish depth, as the **visual cliff** experiment shown in Figure 4–16 demonstrates. When crawling on the visual cliff, infants will avoid the deep side. This cannot really be used as evidence for inborn tendencies, however, since infants cannot crawl until they are four or five months old. Nevertheless, very young infants who cannot yet crawl will exhibit abnormal heart rhythms when they are placed on the deep side as compared with the shallow side of the visual cliff. The same kind of effects can be observed in many other animals—rabbits, mice, cats, and so on—with an interesting exception. Turtles and ducks show a *preference* for the deep side (Walk, 1962, 1964). One might

argue that their preference has some evolutionary significance. Water-based animals should have less to fear from depths than land-based animals (Coren et al., 1980). In addition, the deep side of the visual cliff may be more familiar to turtles and ducks, since they are used to looking at the bottom of a pond or lake through several feet of water. Thus, while it is clear that both maturation and learning play an important role in perception, it is interesting to note that certain perceptual tendencies seem to be present at birth.

There has been some suggestion that infants are also capable of perceiving biological motion at birth. Biological motion is the motion of living objects. In terms of evolution, it is reasonable to assume that

FIGURE 4–16
When placed on the visual cliff, babies will avoid the deep side, and will not cross it even to get to their mothers. This is evidence that infants can distinguish depth from an early age though not necessarily evidence that depth perception is inborn.

the capacity to distinguish between the movement of animate and of inanimate objects was critically important. A tree swaying in the breeze could not eat you but a prehistoric animal could. Research by Fox and McDaniel (1982) illustrates that infants prefer to watch biological rather than nonbiological motion. For this experiment infants of varying ages sat in front of two TV screens. On one screen, they could see white dots that represented a person running. On the other screen, the white dots moved randomly. An observer recorded how much time each infant looked at each screen. By 4 months, the infants appeared to favor the biological-motion screen over the nonbiological-motion screen. As with the visual cliff, this experiment does not prove that the preference for biological motion is inborn, since it does not appear strongly until 4 months of age, but the experiment cannot rule out this inborn tendency either. It may be that the visual system of the infant is not sufficiently developed to allow the preference to emerge, or that the musculature is not sufficiently developed to allow for effortless attention to the biological-motion screen, until 4 months of age. In any event, it does seem apparent that biological-motion perception does not require extensive experience.

Motivation

One final area needs some discussion. We have seen how learning and maturation affect perception; motivation can also have an influence. A simple example of motivation that appeared earlier in the chapter was selective attention. It is obvious that we can be instructed to perceive some particular stimuli at the expense of others. This is the same as saying that we can be motivated to perceive certain things. When you are in need of a restroom, you scan the environment for particular combinations of letters, such as *Men*, *Women*, and *Restroom*. You quickly dismiss from attention other collections of letters that might read *Exit*, *No Turn on Red*, or *Stairway*.

As you can see, perception is influenced by many things other than the simple stimulation of receptors. We will examine many of these influences in greater detail when we consider information processing, motivation, and interpersonal behavior.

Visual cliff. Experiment (or apparatus) used to test depth perception in infants (humans and animals).

REVIEW QUESTIONS

11. What we see in a movie is a series of still images that are illuminated rapidly one after the other. This effect is based on the principle of stroboscopic motion/motion parallax.

12. Size constancy is based on two things, _____ _____ and _____ _____ .

13. Kraft has made a study of airplane accidents and found that in many of them the cause of the crash is a visual_____ .

14. By the time they are 2 months old, infants
    a. get bored with a regular face and prefer to look at a scrambled face.
    b. perfer to look at a regular face rather than a scrambled face.
    c. can't seem to tell the difference between the two.
    d. prefer an abstract design to any kind of face.

15. The _____ _____ experiment has been used to show that depth perception is present in babies almost from birth. In this experiment, infants who can crawl will avoid the deep side/shallow side.

Answers: 11. stroboscopic motion   12. prior experience; distance cues   13. illusion   14. b   15. visual cliff; deep side

---

■ SUMMARY

1. The three components of *perception* are attention and search, organization, and interpretation. Through *perception* we make guesses about the physical world based on incomplete information.

2. Two strategies involved in the search process are orientation, or directing our receptors toward a stimulus, and the use of patterns of search that are geared to identify unique or particularly useful information. Attention patterns include *divided attention*, or attending to two or three stimuli when there are many more stimuli that could command our attention, and *selective attention*, or concentrating on one of two competing channels of communication (an example is listening to someone speak over the telephone when others are talking nearby). We are

capable of monitoring several channels of communication at once, but we can only pay close attention to one at a time.

3. An early theoretical account of the principles of perceptual organization was Gestalt theory, which emphasized the understanding of events as entire units, rather than as pieces of sensation. The underlying assumption of this theory was that the whole is greater than the sum of its parts. Gestalt principles of organization include the *figure-ground principle*, the *similarity principle*, the *proximity principle*, the *principles of common fate* and of *good continuation*, and the *closure principle*. Gestalt theory is important because it demonstrated that we have built-in, automatic, and often unconscious mechanisms to reduce the ambiguity of sensory information.

4. Physiological factors that allow the brain to estimate depth or distance are *accommodation, convergence, divergence,* and *retinal disparity.* The last three are called *binocular cues* because they depend on the use of both eyes.

5. Environmental factors also contribute to our ability to estimate depth and distance. These factors, called *monocular cues* because they depend on one eye only, include *interposition, perspective, texture gradient, shading,* and *motion parallax.*

6. *Motion parallax* is the tendency for objects between you and your point of focus to appear to be moving in the opposite direction that you are moving in, while objects between your point of focus and the horizon seem to be moving in the same direction as you are.

7. Motion pictures give the impression of movement through the simulation of *motion parallax* and other depth and distance cues. Because of the characteristics of human perception, stroboscopic motion can produce the perception of smooth, continuous motion.

8. *Perceptual constancies* allow us to understand that two very different images actually represent the same object. One example is *shape constancy:* The image of a rotating object or an object moving away from us changes shape on the retina, but we perceive it as maintaining its original shape. Other constancies are size constancy and velocity constancy. Constancies depend in part on experience, and they are automatic.

9. An *illusion* is a false impression about an object or the environment. Many illusions depend on Gestalt principles. One dangerous illusion is the tendency for people to misjudge the distance of large, moving objects, such as trains.

10. Some perceptual abilities develop as a result of physical *maturation.* Others appear to be inborn. One inborn human ability may be depth perception, as has been demonstrated in *visual cliff* experiments. Motivational factors can also influence our perceptions of the environment.

■ ANSWERING QUESTIONS FOR THOUGHT

1. This is a case of divided attention, in which you switch your attention from one channel (the conversation you are taking part in) to another (the conversation in which your name is mentioned), even if just very briefly.

2. Principles of perceptual organization can apply to social situations as well as to visual stimuli. For example, the Gestalt principle of proximity says that elements that are physically close to each other will be perceptually grouped together. In a social context, this would suggest that we judge people in terms of the company they keep—the people they have around them. The Gestalt similarity principle states that objects that resemble one another are likely to be perceptually grouped together—hence our tendency to regard individuals of a racial or ethnic group as group members rather than as individuals.

3. Artists use the various monocular cues we discussed in order to give a feeling of depth and distance to their paintings. These cues include perspective, interposition, shading, and texture gradient.

4. The "motion" in motion pictures is achieved in several ways: by producing effects of motion parallax (filming near objects moving in the opposite direction and far objects moving in the same direction); interposition (putting many different objects in front of one another to give a feeling of depth); and stroboscopic motion (illuminating a series of still images in rapid succession).

5. Visual illusions are the result of a false impression about an object or an environment—we are fooled by misleading depth and distance cues into seeing what isn't really there. Illusions can sometimes be dangerous. For example, visual illusions that affect judgment can play a role in certain kinds of automobile and airplane accidents.

5 Physiology and Consciousness

In the early 1950s, Aldous Huxley, the author of *Brave New World*, experimented with a then little-known drug called mescaline. Mescaline is the active ingredient of the peyote cactus. Huxley later wrote about his experience in a book called *The Doors of Perception*. The following are some of his impressions of the drug's effects on state of mind:

Thus it came about that, one bright May morning, I swallowed four-tenths of a gram of mescalin dissolved in half a glass of water and sat down to wait for the results. . . . Half an hour after swallowing the drug I became aware of a slow dance of golden lights. A little later there were sumptuous red surfaces swelling and expanding from bright nodes of energy that vibrated with a continuously changing, patterned life. At another time the closing of my eyes revealed a complex of gray structures, within which pale bluish spheres kept emerging into intense solidity and, having emerged, would slide noiselessly upwards, out of sight. But at no time were there faces or forms of men or animals. I saw no landscapes, no enormous spaces, no magical growth and metamorphosis of buildings, nothing remotely like a drama or a parable. . . . Space was still there but it had lost its predominance. . . . what happens to the majority of the few who have taken mescalin under supervision can be summarized as follows.

(1) The ability to remember and to "think straight" is little if at all reduced. (Listening to the recordings of my conversation under the influence of the drug, I cannot discover that I was then any stupider than I am at ordinary times.)

(2) Visual impressions are greatly intensified and the eye recovers some of the perceptual innocence of childhood, when the sensum was not immediately and automatically subordinated to the concept. Interest in space is diminished and interest in time falls almost to zero.

(3) Though the intellect remains unimpaired and though perception is enormously improved, the will suffers a profound change for the worse. The mescalin taker sees no reason for doing anything in particular and finds most of the causes for which, at ordinary times, he was prepared to act and suffer, profoundly uninteresting. He can't be bothered with them, for the good reason that he has better things to think about.

(4) These better things may be experienced (as I experienced them) "out there," or "in here," or in both worlds, the inner and the outer, simultaneously or successively. . . .

These effects of mescalin are the sort of effects you could expect to follow the administration of a drug having the power to impair the efficiency of the cerebral reducing valve. When the brain runs out of sugar, the undernourished ego grows weak, can't be bothered to undertake the necessary chores, and loses all interest in those spatial and temporal relationships which mean so much to an organism bent on getting on in the world. As Mind at Large seeps past the no longer watertight valve, all kinds of biologically useless things start to happen. In some cases there may be extra-sensory perceptions. Other persons discover a world of visionary beauty. To others again is revealed the glory, the infinite value and meaningfulness of naked existence, of the given, unconceptualized event. In the final stage of egolessness there is an "obscure knowledge" that All is in all—that All is actually each. This is as near, I take it, as a finite mind can ever come to "perceiving everything that is happening everywhere in the universe." (Huxley, 1954)

In just over 30 minutes, Huxley was introduced to a world he had never before encountered. It was a world that was both real and imaginary. He had perceptions seemingly unrelated to the direct stimulation of sensory receptors. This was the imaginary world. Yet he was still aware—his senses had not stopped functioning. This duality of experience can be understood only by considering the relationship between the brain and the experience of **consciousness**—the topic of this chapter.

We will begin by looking at drugs and how they affect the brain and behavior. Drug-induced states are the most direct and dramatic illustration of a consciousness unlike what we usually experience in our normal waking state. We will then look at sleep and dreaming and contrast them with two states of consciousness that we can experience with a special effort—meditation and hypnosis. Finally, we will look at some specialized brain functions and their implications for the study of consciousness.

■ CHEMICALS IN THE BRAIN

The use of certain substances for their effects on consciousness has a long history in human society. Alcohol, marijuana, cocaine, LSD, heroin, and even coffee are known to produce unusual sensations and alterations of behavior in people. All of the substances just mentioned are **drugs.** Many people tend to think of drugs as prescription medicines or illegal chemicals, without realizing that familiar substances such as alcohol, caffeine, and tobacco are also drugs. Technically, drugs are any substances that can produce alterations in our physical and mental functioning.

For most people, using drugs represents a deliberate attempt to change aspects of behavior. A person may have a drink to relax or go to a party to "get high"; many people have a cup of coffee in the morning believing that it gets their "internal motor" going. People often attribute irritability to "coffee nerves." A good part of the explanation for these effects on behavior can be found in the principles of neurotransmission. Most of these substances have their primary effects by interfering with, acting like, or exaggerating the effects of chemicals (neurotransmitters) that the brain already produces on a continuous basis. This means that the principles of neurotransmission that explain normal brain functioning also provide us with a foundation for understanding the effects of drugs.

Drugs and Neurotransmission

In Chapter 2 you were introduced to the "lock and key" principle of neurotransmission and you learned

about some of the more common neurotransmitters. Therefore, you now have a background to understand the action of drugs on behavior. Briefly, the lock and key principle describes the mechanism by which the right neurotransmitter fits the right receptor on a neighboring neuron the way a key fits a lock. The presence of drugs in the nervous system can interfere with normal neurotransmission in one or more of the following ways:

1. Drugs can act to decrease the amount of neurotransmitter that is released into the synapse. This limits the amount of neurotransmitter that can be picked up by receptors and the probability of an action potential (a "firing") is reduced in the nearby neuron. As you may recall from Chapter 2, botulinus toxin (the substance responsible for food poisoning) interferes with the release of the neurotransmitter ACh, leading to paralysis. Many drugs used to treat mental disorders, such as schizophrenia, work on the principle of reducing the outputs of certain neurotransmitters (such as dopamine).
2. Drugs can block the receptor sites on the receiving neuron so that a transmitter has no effect, even though it has been released. To recall an earlier example, the poison curare blocks the receptors of ACh, and this also results in paralysis.
3. Drugs can mimic neurotransmitters and, when in contact with the right receptors, produce effects similar to those that would have been produced by the naturally-occurring neurotransmitter. For example, the drug morphine can lock into the receptors for endorphins (the body's own painkillers) because it has a similar chemical structure. As a result, morphine has similar effects on pain perception. Members of the class of drugs called opiates often mimic the action of naturally produced neurotransmitters.
4. Drugs can prolong the release of a neurotransmitter at the synapse, causing the neurons to keep firing. This produces heightened activity levels and an euphoric mood for a short period of time. For example, amphetamines and other drugs classified as stimulants generally work to increase the amount of neurotransmitter (such as catecholamines) at a synaptic site. This often leads to heightened autonomic responses, such as increases in heartrate and respiration.

As you can gather from the above description, any drug that alters aspects of behavior probably does so by interfering with the process of chemical transmission in the brain. This is just as true of the nicotine in cigarettes (which alters the release of ACh at the synapse) as it is of LSD (which blocks the receptor sites for serotonin and may also mimic dopamine).

One of the problems in anticipating the effects of drugs is that all the possible side-effects of a particular drug may not be known. (Side-effects are effects in addition to those specifically being targeted.) The brain contains many widely-scattered receptor sites for various chemicals. Thus, any single drug has the potential to alter neurotransmission in many parts of the brain, not just in the target area. To give you an analogy, in the early days of automatic door openers, it wasn't unusual to drive down your street, push your automatic door opener, and see a neighbor's garage door begin to rise. The signal meant for your garage door had been picked up by the wrong receptor. The same thing can happen with drugs. A pain killer that is targeted to relieve pain can travel to other receptor sites where it has effects on heart-rate, blood pressure, and pupil size. Some drug side-effects are more serious than others. For example, a common side-effect of amphetamines is the feeling of panic. Some drugs used in the treatment of severe mental disorders are known to cause tremors and other problems in motor control.

One strategy that is frequently used in drug research is to introduce chemicals that are thought to be similar to neurotransmitters into certain areas of the brain and to observe their effects on behavior. For example, the hypothalamus is known to be involved in both eating and drinking behavior. When a chemical that is similar to the neurotransmitter ACh was injected directly into the hypothalamus of rats, rats that were not thirsty began to drink. When a chemical similar to the neurotransmitter norepinephrine was injected, rats that were not hungry began to eat. From this it was concluded that at least some of the brain circuits that control drinking use ACh as a neurotransmitter, and some of the circuits that control eating use norepinephrine (Grossman, 1967).

These various studies all point to the same general conclusions: Many behavior patterns are, at least to some extent, electrochemically based. This does *not* mean that our behavior is solely or simply a result of electrochemical action in the brain—there are obviously many other influences. A related point is that these electrochemical actions are highly organized, and even minute quantities of certain chemicals can cause changes in this organization. There is nothing simple about it. This combination of structural and chemical systems in the nervous system is one of the most elegant (if not *the* most elegant) organizations you will ever encounter. It is the underlying basis for behaviors such as learning, motivation, perception, and emotion. We will now look at how specific drugs affect the nervous system and cause changes in behavior.

REVIEW QUESTIONS

1. Using the lock and key model, the neurotransmitter is the lock/key that affects the receptor site, the lock/key on a nearby neuron.

2. A drug that alters behavior usually does it by interfering with the normal process of _____ in the brain.

3. Any single drug has the potential to travel to receptor sites in the brain besides those for which it is targeted. This may result in possible _____ , some of which are more serious than others.

Answers: 1. key; lock 2. neurotransmission 3. side-effects

■ PSYCHOACTIVE DRUGS

Drugs that affect the central nervous system and alter perception, mood, and behavior are known as **psychoactive drugs.** These drugs can be classified in many different ways: in terms of the chemical compounds that go into them or by the chemical

---

Consciousness. The normal waking state, when our mental abilities are fully available for use.
Drug. Technically, any substance other than food that can pro-

duce alterations in physical and mental functioning.
Psychoactive drugs. Drugs that affect the central nervous system and can alter perception, mood, and behavior.

formulas used to create them; in terms of the chemical actions that they produce in the body; or, in terms of groups or families of substances based on their effects on behavior, which makes the most sense from the psychological point of view. From this perspective, there are four major classes of psychoactive drugs: depressants, stimulants, hallucinogens, and psychotherapeutic drugs. A fifth category includes marijuana and other forms of cannabis. As we will see later, marijuana and related substances are treated as a separate category because of the complex nature of their psychoactive ingredient, TCH (or cannabis). Table 5–1 lists the most commonly used drugs, their chemical names, common names, and common effects.

Dependence on Drugs

People often associate the word *drug* with the word *addict*. An addict, by common definition, is someone who cannot function without the use of a particular drug because the body has somehow changed or adapted to the presence of the drug. More technically, addiction often means that the body has stopped producing a natural chemical that is important for some aspect of behavior because it is used to the chemical being supplied artificially by the drug. It is suggested that this is what happens with steady heroin use (Julien, 1984). As mentioned earlier, heroin and morphine mimic the neurochemical action of endorphins. As a result, when heroin is present in the body, the natural production of endorphins is reduced. This represents an attempt by the body to regulate itself, to keep its chemical system in balance—the more heroin present, the less natural endorphins are produced. Later, when the effect of the heroin wears off, the user is left with a depleted supply of endorphins. Since endorphins are involved in the body's natural toleration for pain, a net loss of endorphins results in great discomfort for the user. Stimulus levels of sound, color, or touch that may be "normal" and acceptable to you and me may become intolerable to the heroin user when the effect of the last injection has worn off. When viewed from this perspective, addiction is not particularly mysterious, but the seriousness of the problem is acute.

The term *addiction* has been historically used in connection with narcotics, a subcategory of depressants. The narcotics most people are familiar with are heroin and codeine and are what people usually think of when they hear the word addiction. Because of this, many professionals use the term *dependence* instead in referring to addictive substances. Dependence can occur with a wide range of substances and may involve a number of different effects.

Dependence. Continued use of certain drugs over a period of time can result in *dependence* on that drug. There are two different types of dependence—physical and psychological. In **physical dependence,** such as heroin addiction, a certain amount of the drug is needed just to maintain normal functioning. When the user is deprived of the drug (and thus cannot function normally) inevitable physical effects occur, such as muscle cramps, vomiting, and restlessness. These effects are called **withdrawal symptoms.** Withdrawal symptoms are the result of a reduction in the natural production of a neurotransmitter and the elimination of the artificial source of the neurotransmitter (the drug). When a person develops a **tolerance** to a drug, the body comes to depend more and more heavily on external sources of a substance that used to be produced internally and can *tolerate* increasingly larger doses. Over time, larger doses of the drug are needed to avoid withdrawal symptoms and to produce the same "high" or euphoric state that used to be possible with smaller amounts of the drug. Thus, the term tolerance is a description of the effects associated with a systematic decrease in the natural production of a substance (such as endorphins).

Increased tolerance is a problem with many drugs. One effect of the heavy and sustained use of alcohol is the gradual destruction of certain receptor sites at the synapses. As the number of receptor sites is reduced, the probability of certain neurons firing is reduced. However, as we saw in Chapter 2, the strength of a stimulus can affect the probability of a neuron firing. One way to make up for the gradual reduction of receptor sites is to gradually increase the "dosage" strength of alcohol. Thus, it might take four or five drinks for the alcoholic to feel the same effect a nonalcoholic feels after only one drink. Incidentally, this loss of receptor sites might provide a biological foundation for the Alcoholics Anonymous philosophy that once you are an alcoholic, you are always vulnerable to alcoholism.

Given the above, it is possible to see why this may be true. If the receptor sites are destroyed, it won't matter if you stop drinking for one week, one month, or ten years. You will still need more alcohol in your system to produce certain experiences than someone who was never an alcoholic and whose receptor sites remain intact and undamaged.

Psychological dependence is different from physical dependence, although it usually involves some behavioral consequences. We can become accustomed to the feeling that a particular substance gives us and come to crave that substance. For example, many people smoke to reduce tension; others can't do without a cup of coffee the first thing in the morning to get going. Both cigarettes and coffee contain substances that enter the bloodstream and produce noticeable changes in behavior. Cigarettes produce the change through *nicotine*, which enters the bloodstream through the lungs. Coffee has its effect through *caffeine*, which is processed through the digestive system into the bloodstream. If chain smokers or daily coffee drinkers are deprived of the substance they have become used to, there are likely to be unpleasant physical consequences (such as headaches or nervousness) for some period of time, but *not* because the body has adapted to the presence of the nicotine or the caffeine. This is an important distinction from true physical dependence. The smoker or coffee drinker's discomfort is more readily explained as the result of certain learned associations rather than any direct effect of withdrawal from the substance. As a rule, people who stop smoking notice that they experience the greatest discomfort right after a meal. This is probably because they associate the time right after a meal with smoking a cigarette. It doesn't mean that their bodies need or demand nicotine. Now that we have examined some general concepts related to drugs and neurotransmission, let's consider some specific drug groups or families and their effects on behavior.

■ DEPRESSANTS

Depressants derive their name from the fact that they depress the activity of the central nervous system. Behaviorally, the depressants reduce awareness of and response to stimuli from the outside (Schlaadt and Shannon, 1986). We will consider three of the most common depressants: sedatives, alcohol, and opiates (narcotics).

Sedatives

Sedatives are man-made drugs that may be used in low doses as tranquilizers to produce relaxation and as mild sedatives to reduce anxiety; or they may be used in higher doses as "sleeping pills." In low doses these drugs may decrease inhibitions and produce carefree, boisterous behavior. In higher doses there can be obvious sensory and motor effects—the person may stagger, slur speech, and show impaired judgment. In higher dosages these drugs also induce sleep. Because these drugs have a low threshold of dosage safety, higher dosages can lead to a **coma**— a sleep from which one cannot be aroused. These drugs all tend to slow respiration in the same way that heroin does, which under some circumstances may lead to respiratory failure. Psychological dependence is a large problem with these drugs, and substantial tolerances may develop in some users. The withdrawal symptoms associated with these drugs are especially unpleasant and potentially dangerous; they may sometimes include sudden convulsions that result in death.

Alcohol

Although many people think of alcohol as a stimulant, it really acts to *slow down* the central nervous system. A person who is drinking may appear to be more animated and sociable, but this is due

---

Physical dependence. The use of a drug becomes necessary for normal functioning and causes unpleasant physical effects when it is withdrawn or no longer used.

Withdrawal symptoms. Physical effects such as nausea, diarrhea, and itching that result from no longer taking a drug on which one is physically dependent.

Tolerance. A condition a person develops after repeated use of certain drugs; the person has to take a larger and larger dose in order to get the original effect of the drug.

Psychological dependence. Occurs when the effect of a drug becomes an important aspect of a person's life and is needed for the person to function.

Depressants. A class of drugs that act to slow the functioning of the central nervous system; includes opiates, sedatives, and alcohol.

Sedatives. Man-made drugs that may be used in low dosages as tranquilizers and in higher doses as "sleeping pills."

Coma. Sleep from which one cannot be aroused; can be caused by high doses of sedative drugs.

TABLE 5-1.   Drugs and Their Effects

Drugs	Often Prescribed Brand Names	Medical Uses	Dependence Physical	Potential: Psychological
Opium	Dover's Powder, Paregoric	Analgesic, antidiarrheal	High	High
Morphine	Morphine	Analgesic	High	High
Codeine	Codeine	Analgesic, cough suppressant	Moderate	Moderate
Heroin	None	None	High	High
Meperidine (Pethidine)	Demerol, Pethadol	Analgesic	High	High
Methadone	Dolophine, Methadone, Methadose	Analgesic, heroin substitute	High	High
Other Narcotics	Dilaudid, Levitine, Numorphan, Percodan	Analgesic, antidiarrheal, cough suppressant	High	High
Barbiturates	Amytal, Butisol, Nembutal, Phenobarbital, Seconal, Tuinal	Anesthetic, anti con-vulsant, sedation, sleep	High	High
Methaqualone	Optimil, Parest, Quaalude, Somnafac, Sopor	Sedation, sleep	High	High
Tranquilizers	Equanil, Librium, Miltown, Serax, Tranxene, Valium	Anti-anxiety, muscle relaxant, sedation	Moderate	Moderate
Cocaine	Cocaine	Local anesthetic	Possible	High
Amphetamines	Benzedrine, Biphetamine, Desoxyn, Dexedrine	Hyperkinesis, narcolepsy, weight control	Possible	High
Phenmetrazine	Preludin	Weight control	Possible	High
LSD	None	None	None	Degree unknown
Mescaline	None	None	None	Degree unknown
Psilocybin-Psilocyn	None	None	None	Degree unknown
PCP	Sernylan	Veterinary anesthetic	None	Degree unknown
Marijuana Hashish Hashish Oil	None	None	Degree unknown	Moderate

Source: Schlaadt and Shannon, 1982, pp. 260–262.

Tolerance	Duration of Effects (in hrs)	Usual Methods of Administration	Possible Effects	Effects of Overdose	Withdrawal Syndrome
Yes	3 to 6	Oral, smoked	Euphoria drowsiness, respiratory depression, constricted pupils, nausea	Slow and shallow low breathing, clammy skin, convulsions, coma, possible death	Watery eyes, runny nose, yawning, loss of appetite, irritability, tremors, panic, chills and sweating, cramps, nausea
Yes	3 to 6	Injected, smoked			
Yes	3 to 6	Oral, injected			
Yes	3 to 6	Injected, sniffed			
Yes	3 to 6	Oral, injected			
Yes	12 to 24	Oral, injected			
Yes	3 to 6	Oral, injected			
Yes	1 to 16	Oral, injected	Slurred speech, disorientation, drunken behavior without odor of alcohol	Shallow respiration, cold and clammy skin, dilated pupils, weak and rapid pulse, coma, possible death	Anxiety, insomnia, tremors, delirium, convulsions, possible death
Yes	4 to 8	Oral			
Yes	4 to 8	Oral			
Yes	2	Injected, sniffed	Increased alertness, excitation, euphoria, dilated pupils, increased pulse rate and blood pressure, insomnia, loss of appetite	Agitation, increase in body temperature, hallucinations, convulsions possible death	Apathy, long periods of sleep, irritability, depression disorientation
Yes	2 to 4	Oral, injected			
Yes	2 to 4	Oral			
Yes	Variable	Oral	Illusions and hallucinations (with exception of MDA); poor perception of time and distance	Longer, more intense "trip" episodes, psychosis, possible death	Withdrawal syndrome not reported
Yes	Variable	Oral, injected			
Yes	Variable	Oral			
Yes	Variable	Oral, injected, smoked			
Yes	2 to 4	Oral, smoked	Euphoria, relaxed inhibitions, increased appetite, disoriented behavior	Fatigue, paranoia, possible psychosis	Insomnia, hyperactivity, and decreased appetite reported in a limited number of individuals

to an initial depression of inhibition centers in the CNS. All alcoholic beverages have the same active ingredient, ethyl alcohol, but they don't all have it in the same concentration. Ethyl alcohol is produced when yeasts combine with sugar in a process called **fermentation.** Beer and wine are made in this way. **Distilled spirits** (hard liquors) are made by heating a fermented product so that the alcohol evaporates, but not the water. The alcohol vapor is then condensed to form a more concentrated alcohol solution. Whereas most beer is 4 percent alcohol and most wine is about 12 percent, whiskey, gin, and vodka are usually 40 to 50 percent alcohol. As with all drugs, the effect of alcohol depends on the amount of it in the body. The concentration of alcohol in the blood is usually estimated from its concentration in the air of the lungs. At a **blood alcohol level (BAL)** of 1/10 of 1 percent (0.10 percent), the average person's reaction-time and judgment are clearly impaired, and this level defines legal intoxi-

cation for driving purposes in most states. The effect of alcohol on an individual will depend on several factors. Three important factors are the amount of alcohol consumed, the weight of the person and the time period in which the alcohol was consumed. It is not much good to find out after it is too late that you are drunk. Since decision-making is impaired by intoxication, you may very well decide (incorrectly) that you are able to drive. Tables are available that allow you to estimate your BAL from your weight, the number of drinks you have had, and the number of hours that have passed since you started drinking. Figure 5–1 presents such a guide.

Since the concentration of alcohol in your blood can be accurately estimated from your breath, "breathalyzer" (or breath analysis) tests are used by law-enforcement agencies to identify drunken drivers. It would make sense to have these devices available in every place where alcoholic beverages are used or sold to allow people to get a quick

FIGURE 5-1

This chart allows you to estimate your blood alcohol level (BAL) based on your weight, the number of drinks you have had, and the number of hours that have passed since you started drinking. (Smith and Gay, 1972, p. 216)

Weight (lb)	Drinks: One drink equals 1 ounce of 80 proof alcohol; 12 ounce bottle of beer; 2 ounces of 20% wine; 3 ounces of 12% wine.									
	1	2	3	4	5	6	7	8	9	10
100	.029	.058	.088							
120	.024	.048	.073	.097						
140	.021	.042	.063	.083						
160	.019	.037	.055	.073	.091					
180	.017	.033	.049	.065	.081	.097				
200	.015	.029	.044	.058	.073	.087				
220	.014	.027	.040	.053	.067	.080	.093			
240	.012	.024	.037	.048	.061	.073	.085	.097		

CAUTION   DRIVING IMPAIRED

Alcohol is "burned up" by your body at .015% per hour, as follows:

No. hours since starting first drink	1	2	3	4	5	6
Percent alcohol burned up	.015	.030	.045	.060	.075	.090

Calculate your BAC
Example: 180 lb man – 8 drinks in 4 hours is .130% on chart.
Subtract .060% burned up in 4 hours. BAC equals .070% – DRIVING IMPAIRED.

reading on whether or not they should drive. This might have a much greater impact than TV, radio, and newspaper warnings against driving while intoxicated. People who are legally drunk are not often reading the newspaper or listening to the radio in a bar.

In terms of total cost in human misery, alcohol is by far the most deadly and dangerous drug. Violent crimes such as homicide, assault, rape, and spouse and child abuse are often associated with excessive alcohol use. Alcohol contributes to about 50 percent of the 50,000 annual traffic deaths, and plays a major role in home accidents, drownings, and fires from smoking in bed. As with sedatives, overdoses can kill by slowing respiration, and the withdrawal symptoms include convulsions that may lead to death. Combining alcohol with sleeping pills or tranquilizers kills hundreds of people each year in the United States, and the effects of long-term use of high doses of alcohol include damage to the liver, which is itself one of the leading causes of death among adults.

Clearly, heavy drinking is associated with negative effects on health and with increased mortality from several causes. However, most people who use alcohol keep their drinking within reasonable limits. There may even be some potential health benefit to moderate drinking. Recent tests have indicated that moderate daily drinkers (those who drink 2.5 ounces of alcohol per day) are likely to suffer from coronary artery disease (which often results in heart attacks) than nondrinkers (Julien, 1984).

Opiates

Opiates are derived from the opium poppy, which contains the chemicals *morphine* and *codeine* as psychoactive ingredients. As mentioned earlier, morphine mimics the action of endorphins in the brain. As a result, morphine can alter pain perception and produce euphoric states. Opium itself, a sticky substance that comes from the seed pod of the plant, has been used medically and recreationally for cen-

This device is used to identify drunken drivers. The concentration of alcohol in the blood can be accurately estimated from an analysis of the breath.

turies. These addictive drugs produce a dreamlike sleep and an intensely pleasurable sense of well-being or euphoria. Opiates are often referred to as narcotic analgesics, since they reduce the perception of pain without inducing unconsciousness. Although the external world becomes more remote to the person under the influence of opiates, the drugs do not alter motor functions such as walking and talking as alcohol does. Since opiates do reduce pain, they are attractive for controlled medical use. They can also control coughing and diarrhea. Codeine is a common component of prescription cough medicine.

When morphine was derived from opium in 1804, it was used extensively to treat pain. It was also believed not to be addictive. Unfortunately, it soon became apparent that morphine was just as addictive as opium. This led to a further search for artificial substances that would have the opiates' positive effects without producing dependence.

Around 1890 a drug was introduced that seemed to control coughing in hospitalized patients. It was administered orally and, in small doses, did not seem to result in physical dependence. The drug was

---

Fermentation. A process in which yeasts consume sugar and produce ethyl alcohol; the basis of alcoholic beverages.

Distilled spirits. Made by heating a fermented product to form alcohol vapor, which is then condensed to form a more concentrated alcohol solution.

Blood alcohol level (BAL). The concentration of alcohol in the blood; 0.10 is considered the legal definition of intoxication.

Opiates. A class of depressant drugs made from the opium poppy; includes morphine, codeine, and heroin.

heroin, and it was derived from morphine. It has since become clear that it was the way the drug was administered to these patients that accounted for the fact that they did not develop physical dependence—when injected in large doses, heroin produces a powerful physical dependence.

All opiates have a strong tendency to produce physical dependence. Users may develop substantial tolerances that lead to taking fairly large doses of these drugs. Overdoses of opiates can be very dangerous. An overdose can depress the respiratory system to a point where breathing actually stops. A large dose taken after a substantial tolerance has developed may not end in death, but the same size dose taken before tolerance has developed may be fatal. The withdrawal symptoms from opiates include a runny nose, cramps, vomiting, and diarrhea. Although the withdrawal experience is acutely unpleasant, it is seldom fatal.

Unlike heroin, **methadone** is not derived from morphine. Because methadone produces many of the same physical effects as heroin, it has been used to aid in withdrawal from heroin. One set of tolerances (to methadone) is simply substituted for another (to heroin). However, it is felt that it's better to be addicted to methadone than to heroin. One advantage of methadone is that it produces less of an euphoric experience and thus is less attractive to the user than heroin. Another advantage is that its effects are longer-lasting, and the physically-dependent person is able to function for longer periods of time before needing another dose. Methadone clinics have been established to help people gradually withdraw from heroin use. However, since methadone affects the CNS in the same way as morphine or heroin, death from an overdose of methadone is just as likely to occur as death from an overdose of heroin or morphine.

■ STIMULANTS

Stimulants act on the CNS by lowering the threshold for action potentials, thus making it more likely for neurons to fire. In addition, some stimulants (such as amphetamines) cause an increase of certain neurotransmitters (such as norepinephrine and dopamine) in the synapses of the brain. This also increases the probability that neurons will fire. The general effect of stimulants is to increase the arousal and general activity of the autonomic nervous system, including heartrate, blood pressure, and pupil dilation. Commonly used stimulants include cocaine, amphetamines, and caffeine.

Cocaine

Cocaine is a chemical found in the leaf of the coca plant, which grows wild in South America. Since prehistoric times the natives of Colombia and Peru have chewed coca leaves for their energizing properties. Cocaine powder, processed from the active ingredient in the plant, is widely used by many people and is the most powerful natural stimulant known. The original formula for Coca-Cola contained an extract from the leaf of the coca plant, including cocaine, which was later removed from the formula.

Cocaine acts as a blocker, preventing the reabsorption of three neurotransmitters—norepinephrine, dopamine, and serotonin. Because of its blocking effects, it also works as a local anesthetic. The same process—the blocking of neurotransmitters—can cause brain convulsions and increased heartrate and blood pressure, which may account for the occasional deaths of cocaine users from cardiovascular failure. This danger is greatest when cocaine is injected.

Part of the reason for the popularity of cocaine is that it is fast-acting, producing pleasurable effects within 10 to 15 minutes. This is even more true of crack, a highly potent form of cocaine that is smoked rather than sniffed (the usual method of taking cocaine). Crack also appears to produce addiction more rapidly than cocaine. Some users have reported becoming addicted to crack in a matter of days or weeks. (See the box for a more detailed discussion of crack.)

Methadone. A substance that is not derived from morphine that is used as a morphine substitute; frequently used to aid in withdrawal from heroin.

Stimulants. A class of drugs that act on the central nervous system by lowering the threshold for the firing of neurons; the general effect is to increase arousal. Includes cocaine, caffeine, and amphetamines.

Cocaine. Active ingredient of the coca plant from which cocaine powder is made; the drug cocaine is an extremely powerful stimulant.

THE DANGERS OF CRACK

Cocaine was once labeled "psychologically dependent," which separated it from the seemingly "harder" drugs, such as heroin, which were "physically addictive." Today experts regret that classification, as evidence mounts that cocaine is just as damaging to the lives and health of its users as any "harder" drug and can result in an equally severe physical dependence. Particularly in its newest and, to date, most potent form—crack—cocaine is indeed highly addictive and dangerous.

When users smoke crack, which is purchased in the form of concentrated pellets, the smoke fills the lungs, and the drug travels from there to the bloodstream. Users experience euphoria, or the pleasant feelings of increased energy, confidence, and enthusiasm. Because crack is concentrated (and usually smoked rather than snorted like conventional cocaine in powder form), the pleasurable effects are quicker and more intense. The after-effects are similarly strong. Following the high from crack comes a deep low, or "crash"—a depression that may result in users wanting just one thing: more crack. Thus begins a cycle of highs and lows. After long-term use of crack, the euphoric high is no longer attainable, and depression and anxiety are inevitable.

To understand how a physical addiction to cocaine occurs, we have to remember the effects the drug has on normal neurotransmission. As discussed in the text, cocaine blocks certain neurotransmitters from being reabsorbed by the sending neuron. These transmitters are dopamine, norepinephrine, and serotonin, which regulate mood and motor functions. Because cocaine interferes with the transmitters' retrieval process, there is a continual excitement of the neurons, producing the euphoric high. This high is followed by a depression or crash, because at some point there is a depletion of neurotransmitters. The body simply runs out of those chemicals, which results in the experience of depression and anxiety. Through extended or habitual use of the drug, the body cannot produce the transmitters as fast as they are required to excite neurons. At that point, there are no longer sufficient amounts of the transmitters present in the body to produce a high,

so that the habitual user will need cocaine just to experience a normal mood. Heavy users, then, no longer even get high but need the drug just to relieve depression. With crack, of course, this whole process is accelerated and intensified. A higher percentage of users become addicted to crack, experts believe, because the whole process is so intensified. Blockage of the neurotransmitters is also responsible for the brain convulsions, increased heartrate and blood pressure, and sudden heart attacks sometimes seen with cocaine and crack use.

In the year since crack first appeared on the drug market, it went from being virtually unknown, even in the big cities, to being available in many remote, rural areas. Getting the addict off cocaine or crack is proving every bit as difficult as any other drug addiction—with the added problem that more users become hooked. Some experts advocate extended drug-free hospital stays in conjunction with family therapy and participation in Alcoholics Anonymous-type groups. Others believe that antidepressant drugs should be used during the initial cocaine-free period. But just as in heroin or alcohol addiction, experts agree that the key ingredient to successfully breaking the crack habit is the addict's inner resolve to stay off the drug. The most challenging problem is keeping the addict off the drug for longer than the initial month or so of abstinence. At Phoenix House in New York, a program that has traditionally treated heroin addicts, cocaine addicts live in the facility for 18 months and participate in family and group counselling with former addicts. The counselling stresses treatment of addicts' underlying problems that may be linked to their drug use. In general, experts feel that no one program will be successful with all addicts, and they advise people hooked on cocaine to seek treatment programs that best suit their individual needs.

Sources: Erik Eckholm, "Ending the Cocaine Habit: Experts Differ on Methods," *The New York Times,* September 8, 1986 p. B 17.; Erik Eckholm, "Cocaine's Vicious Spiral: Highs, Lows, Desperation," *The New York Times,* August 17, 1986; William E. Schmidt, "Police Say Use of Crack is Moving to Small Towns and Rural Areas," *The New York Times,* September 10, 1986, pp., A16.

Amphetamines

Amphetamines are synthetic, or man-made, drugs, which were first manufactured in the 1930s. Some common amphetamines are *amphetamine*, trade-named Benzedrine; *dextroamphetamine*, trade-named Dexedrine, and *methamphetamine*, trade-named Methedrine. The availability and low price of amphetamines made them quickly replace cocaine as the drug addict's choice to mix with heroin in a so-called "speedball" injection (hence the street name "speed," originally applied to cocaine, was transferred to amphetamines).

Although amphetamines have much the same effect on mood as cocaine, they cause this effect by increasing the release of norephineprine (rather than by blocking its reabsorption, as cocaine does). People who take amphetamines soon develop a tolerance for it and need more and more pills to get the same effect. Chronic users ("speed freaks") may eventually need 200 or more times the initial dosage to produce the same high. Overdose can lead to death from respiratory failure or uncontrolled change in body temperature.

Caffeine

Caffeine is a chemical substance present in a surprising variety of different products. A cup of brewed coffee contains between 90 and 150 milligrams of caffeine. A chocolate bar may contain 25 milligrams of caffeine per ounce, and most cola drinks contain somewhere between 30 and 60 milligrams of caffeine. Even some over-the-counter pain medicines have caffeine as an ingredient. This in particular leads to some interesting problems. When people first cut caffeine out of their diet, they sometimes get headaches as a result of withdrawing from the substance. They might then take a pain reliever to cure the headache, and the headache goes away. Since the pain reliever may itself contain as much as 65 milligrams of caffeine, these people have actually reintroduced caffeine into their systems. This is partly why the headache disappears. However, not all pain relievers contain caffeine. If you plan to reduce or eliminate caffeine from your diet, in the event that you get a headache you must be certain that your pain reliever contains little or no caffeine. The cerebral cortex can be affected by doses of caffeine as low as 100 milligrams (or about

one cup of coffee). The effects of caffeine are increased alertness and clearer thinking. At low dosage levels, there is no major disruption of other functions such as motor coordination (Julien, 1984). At high levels, such as 1500 milligrams (or about 10 to 15 cups of coffee), the brainstem and spinal reflexes can be affected, resulting in high reactivity and jumpiness (often referred to as "coffee nerves").

All of these CNS stimulants act to produce a reversal of the effects of fatigue on both mental and physical performance. They don't improve performance in someone who is well-rested and alert, but they can improve the mental and physical performance of someone who is tired. They can also produce a heightened sense of confidence, in which people may feel that they are performing better than they actually are. The elevation of mood and increase in activity level produced by these drugs led to their early use in treating psychological depression. Freud proposed cocaine for this purpose in the late 1870s, and used it himself for many years, although he later changed his mind about this treatment. Amphetamines continued to be used to treat depression into the 1960s. However, these drugs produce only a short-term mood elevation (cocaine produces an even shorter effect than amphetamines), followed by a mood more depressed than before they were taken. As a result, they are seldom used for treating depression today. Amphetamines and related drugs have been used as "diet pills" to curb appetite, but they have only a slight effect, to which a tolerance develops within a week or two.

As a rule, the stimulant drugs have been less linked to death from overdose than the opiates. However, a stimulant overdose is possible. Those who frequently inject these drugs have reported suffering severe panic attacks in which they feel they are going to die. This is the result of the action of the stimulants on the CNS. Cocaine is somewhat more dangerous than amphetamines in that it may have an effect on the heart muscle. It is also more likely than other kinds of drugs to produce a serious allergic reaction.

Stimulants often lead to psychological dependence, particularly if they are injected. Although there is still some disagreement over whether physical dependence actually occurs, the sharp mood swings and periods of depression between doses of stimulants make this a particularly unpleasant and frightening form of dependence.

■ HALLUCINOGENS

Hallucinogens include *mescaline*, which is derived from the peyote cactus; *psilocybin* (PSB), derived from a Mexican mushroom; and LSD, ("acid") a synthetic drug. The chemical structures of LSD and mescaline are similar to those of certain natural neurotransmitters. As a result, these drugs can have complex and dramatic effects on neurotransmission in the brain.

LSD works as a blocker of serotonin, a neurotransmitter, for several hours, and may reduce serotonin production for several days (Jacobs and Trulson, 1979). It was originally thought that the blocking of serotonin caused the characteristic hallucinations of LSD use. However, LSD also mimics dopamine at the synapses, and the two effects together are thought to result in hallucinations (Kalat, 1981).

Other hallucinogens have similar effects on brain synapses. They produce major alterations in visual perception (for example, stationary objects may appear to move) and enhance emotionality. These effects, combined with possible increased suggestibility, lead to seeing ordinary scenes from a new perspective, accompanied by a sense of exaggerated emotion. The same scene may cause either joyous awe or terrible fright in an unpredictable fashion. These terrible fright reactions may lead to panic "anxiety attacks" in which the heart races and breathing becomes very rapid and shallow. These physical reactions are frightening in themselves, causing the panic to continue.

Tart (1977) has studied the varieties of experiences that seem to accompany particular drugs. During the height of the LSD era, in the late 1960s and early 1970s, hospital emergency rooms treated a number of these "fright" cases, often with tranquilizing drugs. As it became clear that these panics were not life-threatening and that people could be "talked down" in a calm, reassuring manner by reminding them that they were only experiencing a temporary drug reaction, newer treatment approaches appeared. Telephone "hot lines"sprang up in most large communities, and most emergency rooms stopped using tranquilizing drugs in these cases. LSD and similar drugs produce no apparent physical dependence, and psychological dependence on them is quite rare.

Angel dust, or PCP, is actually phencyclidine hydrochloride, a drug originally developed as an intravenous anesthetic to use during surgery. When it was tested in humans in the late 1950s, it produced a variety of bizarre psychological reactions, mostly involving altered perceptions of the body ("My arm feels like a telephone pole"). These experiments led to the drug being considered a hallucinogen and to restricting its use to veterinary practice. However, PCP is different from LSD in several ways. First, it reduces sensitivity to pain, so that if a person does something that results in tissue damage during the period of altered perception, pain does not perform its usual function of halting the damaging behavior. In addition, while LSD users are generally quite talkative about their experiences, PCP users are generally uncommunicative for long periods of time. Finally, many PCP users develop strong psychological dependencies and become daily users of the drug.

■ MARIJUANA AND HASHISH

As was indicated in the introduction to this section, *marijuana* and *hashish* don't fit neatly into any of the common categories of psychoactive drugs. This is because they have different effects at different dosage levels. Dosage levels are controlled by many different factors, including the form of the drug and the way it is taken. The active ingredient in both marijuana and hashish is called **tetrahydrocannabinol (THC)**. Since marijuana consists of the crushed leaves and flowers of a plant called *Cannabis sativa* (the hemp plant), the term *cannabis* is often used to refer to marijuana.

THC is commonly taken into the body in the form of marijuana, hashish, or hashish oil. Mari-

---

Amphetamines. Synthetic stimulants.
Caffeine. A chemical substance found in products such as coffee, tea, and chocolate; classified as a stimulant.
Hallucinogens. Any of a group of drugs that produce major

alterations in visual perception and enhanced emotional states; includes mescaline, psilocybin, LSD, and marijuana.
Tetrahydrocannabinol (THC). The psychoactive ingredient in both marijuana and hashish.

juana is now 2 to 7 times more potent than it was in the early 1970s. The concentration of THC in marijuana produced domestically has grown from an average of 0.5 percent in 1974 to 3.5 percent in 1985 and 1986 (Kerr, 1986). The concentration of THC has always been higher in hashish (from 5 to 20 percent) and in hashish oil (from 20 to 70 percent) (Julien, 1981). It follows, then, that the strength of the dose will depend on which substance is used and in what concentration. These differences are similar to the differences among beer, wine, and liquor with respect to the concentration of alcohol.

At low levels of ingestion, THC acts as a sedative and has effects similar to alcohol; but at high levels its effects more closely resemble that of the hallucinogens. The marijuana user of the past was more likely to experience sedative rather than hallucinatory effects, for several reasons. First, as suggested above, the concentration of THC in marijuana used to be at the low (0.5 percent), rather than high, end of the range. In addition, in the process of smoking the marijuana, a certain percentage of THC never reaches the lungs. Consider the effect of spilling part of a glass of beer in the process of drinking it. Also, the smoke has to be held longer in the lungs for a stronger effect. Thus, general smoking experience or "skill" can make something of a difference in concentrations and effects. As a result of all of these factors, most THC users of a generation ago experienced only a mild sedative effect. Very few users ever experienced the hallucinatory end of the continuum.

As far as neurotransmitters are concerned, we simply do not know much about how THC works. Its chemical structure is not like any of the known neurotransmitters. As a result, we don't know whether the effect at the synapses is one of blocking, exaggerating, or prolonging. We are not even sure where to start looking.

THC has effects on both the CNS and the cardiovascular system (Julien, 1984). It increases heartrate and decreases blood pressure. There are reports of euphoria and relaxation, but there are often reports of altered sensation and perception, nausea, and dizziness as well. One study being conducted by the National Academy of Sciences reports findings of short-term effects that include anxiety, confusion, and delirium. In terms of useful applications, it seems that THC has the potential for relieving pain, eliminating some symptoms of epilepsy, reducing vomiting in cancer patients undergoing chemo-

therapy, and treating certain diseases of the eye (such as glaucoma).

In terms of harmful or physically-damaging effects, there are several. THC affects motor coordination and reflexes. This means that skilled performance (such as driving or a sport such as tennis that requires coordination) suffers under the influence of THC. In addition, there are cognitive effects. Memory for material encountered while under the influence of THC is impaired—the greater the dosage, the greater the impairment. This means that going to class "stoned" is not likely to improve a student's grades. The higher potency marijuana now widely available is likely to intensify all these effects.

Is smoking marijuana dangerous to one's health? Yes. As in smoking tobacco, it can lead to various cancers, as well as to bronchitis. THC, like alcohol, can lead to auto accidents and other injuries resulting from diminished reflexes and coordination; like stimulants, it can place stress on the cardiovascular system. In addition, since we know so little about *how* THC works in the nervous system, we should be skeptical about using it. Finally, recent studies are pointing to growing evidence that there may be long-term health effects, including lung and immune-system damage.

Nevertheless, in the past the penalties for possession and use seemed greatly out of proportion to the threat posed by THC. Insofar as we now know it does not lead to physical dependency, it cannot cause death through CNS suppression, and (at least in the past) it seldom leads to bizarre hallucinatory experiences. As is the case with any substance that affects the CNS, the autonomic nervous system, and the endocrine system, marijuana and other substances containing THC should be considered dangerous; but there is no conclusive evidence that marijuana is *any more* dangerous than many other substances, such as alcohol or tobacco. Research will continue to consider the effects of the newer, greater potency marijuana.

■ PSYCHOTHERAPEUTIC DRUGS

In the 1940s and early 1950s, most seriously-disturbed mental patients were sent to mental hospitals for treatment, where they expected to remain for a long time. During this time, these hospitals experienced constant increases in the number of resident patients. Less than a decade later, this trend had reversed. By 1960, hospital populations were declining because more patients were being released and treated through outpatient community mental-health programs. This rapid change was a result of several factors, but the single most important factor was the introduction in the mid-1950s of **antipsychotic drugs,** such as *Thorazine*. Before this time, drug therapy for patients with serious mental disorders, such as schizophrenia, had been based on heavy sedation (often referred to as the "chemical straitjacket"). The new psychotherapeutic drugs were effective for calming patients without making them drowsy and unresponsive. Many research studies conducted over the past 25 years have shown the clear effectiveness of these drugs in producing improvement in the majority of schizophrenic patients (May, 1971; Kessler and Waletzky, 1981).

Soon after the antipsychotic drugs first appeared, **antidepressants** were discovered. These are drugs that help to improve mood in depressed patients but without being a CNS stimulant. An example is *Elavil*. These drugs are not as clearly or consistently useful in treating depression as the antipsychotic drugs are in treating schizophrenia, but most studies have found antidepressants to be significantly more effective than placebos (inactive drugs) (Veterans' Administration, 1970). Another important drug that has been introduced more recently is *lithium*. Originally shown to be useful in calming excited patients, it is now widely used to prevent the extreme variations in mood seen in some patients; thus it is considered a "mood stabilizer." We will discuss these drugs in more detail in Chapter 16 (Therapy).

REVIEW QUESTIONS

4. If a person is physically dependent on a drug and suddenly stops taking it, he or she will experience _____ _____; if the person builds up a _____ to the drug, it means that larger and larger doses have become necessary to produce the original effect of the drug.

5. Morphine, codeine, and heroin all belong to a class of drugs called _____; use of these drugs results in physical dependence.

6. At a blood alcohol level of _____ percent, a person's reaction time and judgment are clearly impaired; this level of alcohol in the blood is the legal definition of intoxication in most states.

7. _____ have been used to treat depression and as the main ingredient in diet pills, but they have been found to be of only short-term use in either case.

8. _____ cause major alterations in perception and enhance emotionality.

9. The active ingredient in both marijuana and hashish is called _____; it has _____ effects at low levels and _____ effects at high levels.

10. In the last 20 years the number of patients hospitalized for serious mental disorders has been declining because of the use of _____ drugs.

Answers: 4. withdrawal symptoms; tolerance 5. opiates 6. 0.10 7. Amphetamines 8. Hallucinogens 9. THC; sedative; hallucinogenic 10. antipsychotic

---

■ DRUG-TAKING BEHAVIOR

The idea of drug addiction (physical dependence) is frightening to most people. The costs to a person and to society can be high. There are many cases in which a drug seems to take complete control of a person's behavior, driving him or her to acquire it at any cost. Until recently, addiction was considered to be almost entirely a physical condition: The drug produced a physical need in the addict, and this need produced a behavior described as a "craving" for the drug. There is some truth to this model of addiction if the drug is an opiate. As described earlier, the regular use of opiates produces increasing levels of tolerance in a person's system; more and more of the drug must be taken just to

---

Antipsychotic drugs. Drugs used to treat patients with serious mental disorders such as schizophrenia.

Antidepressants. Drugs used to treat depressed patients; help to improve mood without acting as a CNS stimulant.

function normally. Physical dependence develops, and withdrawal symptoms appear when the drug is no longer used. In summary then, the following seem to be the mechanics of addiction: A person experiences some positive feeling from the first use of the drug. Desiring to produce that feeling again, the person takes the drug again. With repeated use, the positive reaction lessens, so the person increases the dose. Physical dependence is established, and the normal balance of the body now requires a constant level of the drug. According to this model of drug dependence, addiction is defined in terms of physical dependence.

Some years ago, certain drugs were said to be not really addictive because they produced *only* a psychological dependence. In recent years, it has become clear that this "mere" psychological dependence is much more important than had been realized. If psychological dependence didn't matter, how could one explain the fact that so many people who had been physically dependent and who had undergone complete withdrawal in treatment facilities chose to return to drug use? Largely because of animal research, some of the interrelated mechanisms of physical and psychological dependence are becoming known.

Schuster and Thompson (1968) connected monkeys to automatic injection devices; the monkeys could then get a small injection of morphine when they pressed a lever. The doses that were given were so small that they could never produce physical dependence. Therefore, the monkeys could not have been pressing the lever to avoid withdrawal symptoms. Instead, they must have been pressing the lever to receive the morphine as a reward. They were not "hooked" on the morphine in the physical sense, but they seemed to enjoy it and would work hard to get it. In fact, after learning the lever-pressing response, monkeys pressed on the lever hundreds of times for one small injection of morphine. This behavior occurred in spite of the fact that the dose was not increased (i.e., it remained the same dosage on every trial), and the monkeys never suffered withdrawal symptoms.

Once researchers in this area recognized the powerful rewarding effects of these opiates, they began to notice other things about human dependence on drugs. It has often been reported that an addict who is building up a tolerance that is be-

coming too expensive will voluntarily stop taking the drug and go through withdrawal in order to get back to an affordable dose level. In such cases, it is clear that the physical dependence is of secondary importance and the psychological dependence is of primary importance in maintaining the addiction. It is the positive experience that is sought rather than just an avoidance of a negative experience (withdrawal symptoms). If avoidance of discomfort were the only issue, an addict would never voluntarily undergo withdrawal as described here.

A behavior that is rewarded quickly will be learned faster than one that is rewarded only after some time has passed. Furthermore, once a behavior has been learned, rewards that closely follow the behavior will ensure that the behavior occurs very frequently. Thus, heroin that is injected and has a rapid effect is more addictive than heroin taken by mouth, which takes longer to have an effect. Other forms of drug use that are very likely to lead to dependence for those who try them and enjoy them are tobacco and cocaine. In each of these instances, the "reward" follows the behavior by a matter of seconds.

You might wonder why some people take certain drugs when it is clear that the drug will eventually produce undesirable consequences. As we have already seen, the formation of a drug habit can be largely analyzed and understood in learning terms: A drug produces positive consequences, making the drug-taking behavior increasingly likely to occur. In contrast, note that no one gets "hooked" on antibiotics. Thus, there are some types of drug-taking behaviors that are so immediately and consistently rewarding that almost anyone who performs them even a few times has good chance of developing a form of dependence. These behaviors include the intravenous injection of heroin, cocaine, or an amphetamine; either "snorting" (inhaling) or "freebasing" (a cocaine mixture that is smoked) cocaine; and smoking cigarettes. With other behaviors, either because the reward is somewhat delayed, weaker, or less predictable, serious dependencies are less likely to develop or may develop more slowly. These behaviors can include the oral use of narcotics, sedatives, and alcohol. For example, morphine dependency may develop in several days, but alcohol dependency may take several weeks, months, or even years. This is not to minimize the potentially negative aspects of these substances. As we will see in the following section, alcohol is in many ways the most seriously abused substance in our society.

Most of the research on this aspect of drug taking has been in relation to the illegitimate use of drugs rather than the legitimate use of prescription or over-the-counter drugs. Although there is some value in studying why some patients refuse to take their medication, or why some brands of aspirin are preferred over others, the most important and intriguing aspects of drug-taking appear in situations of illegal or abusive drug use.

Drugs and Cognition

One need not be an addict to suffer unwanted effects from drugs. As described earlier, most drugs work by changing the nature of neurotransmission in various parts of the brain. It is therefore not surprising that many drugs—including the body's own chemicals—have effects on problem-solving, memory, and other types of intellectual behavior. Let's use the endorphins as an example. It has been shown that injections of endorphins can have two significant effects on animals learning to avoid shock. The first effect is the blotting out of earlier learning. In a certain sense, this might be good, since it would prevent earlier learning experiences from interfering with an animal's attempts to escape the shock. The second effect is improved memory for those events that occur while the animal is under the influence of endorphins. Now consider the consequences for a person who takes a drug that mimics the action of endorphins. Because the endorphin-like drug would blot out earlier learning, the person would not be able to take advantage of previously-learned strategies for solving problems. In addition, memory for events that take place under the influence of the drug (including hallucinations) may become exaggerated, making it more likely that the person will remember these frightening experiences at a later time. In the chapter on memory, you will see that people do seem to remember certain emotional events in highly vivid detail. Most of us have a memory or two that we remember exactly and that will not go away—a time when we almost choked on a piece of food, an electric shock, an automobile accident. These memories seem to be the result of chemicals that occur naturally in response to

highly emotional experiences. At the time of the experience, the presence of high levels of endorphins might have led to the preservation of that memory for years to come. This suggests the possible consequences of drugs that are intended to copy or mimic the effects of these internal chemicals. If they are successful, they are likely to produce similar unwanted effects on memory and decision-making.

Alcoholism

Certainly the most studied form of drug use and misuse is the drinking of alcoholic beverages. One reason for this is that alcohol use is so common. Alcohol is legal, highly accessible, and widely advertised. Another important reason is that improper use of alcohol causes so many problems for our society. Recently, groups such as MADD (Mothers Against Drunk Drivers) have been formed to make the public in general and state legislatures in particular aware of the tragic consequences of driving while drunk. In addition to the consequences that drunk drivers inflict on innocent victims, they suffer death and injury themselves even more frequently. Recent statistics have shown that about half of all fatally injured drivers were driving while intoxicated (Ray, 1983). Notice that these statistics refer to those who use alcohol, not only to alcoholics who are addicted to alcohol. One does not have to be a veteran drinker to get drunk and kill someone with a car. Further, one does not have to be a certain age or drink certain things to become intoxicated. The effects of alcohol on coordination are just as predictable for the 18-year-old who has had too much beer as for the 45-year-old who has had too many cocktails. Driving is not the only problem—*walking* under the influence of alcohol can also be dangerous. Recent statistics from the state of Pennsylvania estimate that 75 percent of pedestrians fatally injured by automobiles in 1982 had been drinking (Nussbaum, 1983).

The problem of alcohol abuse and dependence, the most serious substance abuse in our society, is a very difficult one for researchers. After years of research, it has become clear that there is no simple way to define alcoholism; nor is there any clear dividing line beyond which alcohol misuse becomes alcoholism. In other words, it is not so simple to identify an addiction to alcohol. Also, many ques-

Driving while drinking is a leading cause of accidents and deaths. Groups such as Students Against Driving Drunk (SADD) have been formed to make people aware of the hazards of mixing alcohol with driving.

tions remain as to what factors contribute to alcoholism. Some research questions have dealt with the role of biological or genetic factors. Is alcoholism inherited? Are there inborn individual differences in alcohol tolerance? Other questions have to do with learning experiences. Do children learn alcoholic use (and misuse) from their parents or peers? To the nonscientist, "alcoholic" is a label applied to particular people. To the psychologist, the term is an invitation to theory and research.

Table 5–2 is a checklist of the generally-recognized symptoms of alcoholism. Not every alcoholic has every symptom, but any one symptom may be serious enough to warrant concern. However, even with this checklist it is impossible to say that the presence of one symptom is acceptable, that two symptoms represent pre-alcoholism, and that three or more symptoms describe alcoholism, since there are no clear breaks between the alcoholic and the nonalcoholic.

Treatment of Alcoholism

Problems in defining alcoholism are important because they influence beliefs about treatment. Alcoholics Anonymous (AA), founded in Ohio in 1935, has grown to be an international organization with over a million members. This organization of local groups has been and continues to be the single most popular approach to alcoholism treatment. This program assumes alcoholics are "different" from nonalcoholics, both psychologically and physically. In some ways, AA implies that alcoholics

are allergic to alcohol. This "allergy" may be the result of physical factors (such as the inability to metabolize or break down alcohol), psychological factors (a learned pattern of alcohol misuse), or a combination of both (the tendency to avoid anxiety by depressing the central nervous system). As a result, the treatment is total abstinence, which means giving up drinking alcohol entirely. In the same sense that someone who is allergic to penicillin can never take it in any form without great danger, this organization assumes that the alcoholic can never take even one drink.

Not everyone agrees with this view. In the first place, years of research have failed to detect a psychological or physical dividing line that can be used to distinguish someone who is alcoholic from someone who is not. You cannot have a blood test done to determine if you are an alcoholic. This may mean that the critical variable hasn't yet been discovered, or it may mean that it isn't there to be discovered.

A second problem with the Alcoholics Anonymous philosophy is that people may acknowledge that they have drinking problems but be unwilling to define themselves as alcoholics. Consider the person who drinks "only" on weekends, but on these days drinks to the point of unconsciousness. If this person finds it threatening to be labeled an alcoholic, he or she will avoid making the association with alcoholism. If you're not an alcoholic, why worry about "a few problems" associated with drinking, right? In other words, the socially-implied distinction between alcoholics and normal people may effec-

TABLE 5-2

There is no simple test to determine whether you or a loved one is an alcoholic, but the following set of questions can indicate whether someone is headed for trouble. They were prepared by the National Council on Alcoholism in collaboration with medical authorities.

1. Do you occasionally drink heavily after a disappointment, a quarrel, or when the boss gives you a hard time?

2. Have you noticed that you are able to handle more liquor than when you were first drinking?

3. Did you ever wake up the "morning after" and discover that you could not remember part of the evening before, even though your friends tell you that you did not "pass out"?

4. Are there certain occasions when you feel uncomfortable if alcohol is not available?

5. Are you irritated when your family or friends discuss your drinking?

6. Have you recently noticed an increase in your memory "blackouts"?

7. Do you often find that you wish to continue drinking after your friends say that they have had enough?

8. When you are sober, do you often regret things you have done or said while drinking?

9. Have you often failed to keep the promises you have made to yourself about controlling or cutting down on your drinking?

10. Do you eat very little or irregularly when you are drinking?

11. Do you sometimes have the "shakes" in the morning and find that it helps you to have a little drink?

12. Do you sometimes stay drunk for several days at a time?

13. Do you sometimes feel very depressed and wonder whether life is worth living?

14. Do you get terribly frightened after you have been drinking heavily?

tively encourage people to minimize their drinking problems until their problems become even more serious.

A third problem with the AA program is that an alcoholic's belief in a total "loss of control" if exposed to any alcohol may become a self-fulfilling prophecy: If an alcoholic that believes the Alcoholics Anonymous philosophy does take a little alcohol, he or she may just as well go all the way and go on a binge. Thus, the Alcoholics Anonymous approach may have theoretical and practical drawbacks.

In fairness, it must be recognized that as a system of treatment, AA has often been successful where other methods have failed. For that reason, it deserves careful attention. In addition, as was mentioned earlier, chronic alcoholics may very well have altered receptor sites in the brain that, for all practical purposes, make the AA concept of life-long alcoholism a distinct possibility.

There are serious questions about the best method of treatment for alcoholism. Certainly, the Alcoholics Anonymous approach guarantees success to those who abstain completely. However, there are many people who misuse alcohol and cannot seem to find the strength to completely avoid it. Are there any other methods that might reduce the severity of the problem and possibly even eventually cure it? This has been the subject of some controversy. There are those who suggest that alcoholics can effectively be taught "controlled" drinking. In one famous study conducted at a state hospital in California in the early 1970s (Sobell and Sobell, 1978), twenty alcoholics were exposed to a training program in which they were allowed to drink in a bar that had been set up in the hospital. As long as the drinkers ordered weak drinks, sipped them slowly, and did not order drinks too frequently, they could drink in peace. However, ordering straight drinks, gulping a drink, or ordering another drink too soon earned the drinkers electric shocks delivered through finger electrodes.

Another group of twenty alcoholics was given a more traditional treatment program that had abstinence as its goal. The early report of one- and two-year follow-ups indicated that the retrained social drinkers were more successful than the abstainers. However, recent long-term follow-ups conducted by others have revealed that most of the "social drinkers" have gone back to alcohol abuse. Ten years later, only one of the twenty alcoholics in the "social drinking" group is still drinking in a controlled manner. The others who are not now drinking heavily are either dead or have gone through other programs and become abstainers (Penderey, et al., 1982). This recent re-analysis has received a great deal of attention, since it is seen as a major failure of the behavioral psychology approach and as a vindication of the Alcoholics Anonymous philosophy. Scientific research is not free from values and beliefs.

The "Bottom Line" on Drug Use

We have come a long way from the opening discussion of neurotransmission to treatment programs for alcoholism. Simply summarized, alcoholism is a dramatic example of the effect that chemicals can have on long-term behavior. Alcohol is also an ordinary example of a chemical effect on short-term behavior. In both the long- and the short-term, behavior has been chemically influenced. In both instances, the normal organizing processes of the brain have been impaired. That is what all psychoactive drugs do—they change the action of the brain. Ultimately, it is up to the user to be aware of these effects and to decide what price he or she is willing to pay for this alteration.

REVIEW QUESTIONS

11. Recent studies have begun to show that it is an addict's _____ _____, or the positive effects of a drug, that is more important in explaining addiction than the avoidance of _____ _____.

12. The slower/quicker the effect of a drug, the more likely its use will lead to some sort of dependence.

13. Drugs that mimic endorphins seem to have two effects on mental processes: They block out earlier _____ and they improve _____ for what occurs while they are being used.

14. Alcoholics Anonymous's method of treating alcoholism is to encourage total abstinence/controlled drinking.

15. All studies of alcoholics and alcoholism seem to agree that there is a clear dividing line between misuse of alcohol and alcoholism.   T/F

Answers: 11. psychological dependence; withdrawal symptoms 12. quicker 13. learning; memory 14. total abstinence 15. False

■ VARIETIES OF CONSCIOUSNESS

Late in the 19th century, the eminent psychologist William James had this to say about consciousness: "Our normal waking consciousness is but one special type of consciousness, whilst all about it, parted from it by the flimsiest of screens, there lie potential forms of consciousness entirely different. . . . How to regard them is the question for they are so discontinuous with ordinary consciousness. Yet they may determine attitudes though they cannot furnish formulas, and open a region though they fail to give a map." (James, 1890).

From your reading of the chapter so far, you should have an appreciation for the variations in possible states of consciousness and the "maps" psychologists have uncovered to explore them. In the next section we will look at other instances of consciousness "discontinuous with ordinary consciousness." The first two, sleep and dreaming, are universal. As fascinating as they are, they happen every day. Two others, meditation and hypnosis, are also conditions in which people seem to lose normal consciousness. Unlike sleep and dreaming, however, they require some special effort and are not practiced by everyone. Meditation and hypnosis can be compared and contrasted in interesting ways to one another and to sleep and dreaming.

■ SLEEP AND DREAMS

Why should psychologists be interested in sleep and dreams? There are several reasons. The first, and most important, is that sleeping and dreaming are behaviors (just as seeing and hearing are behaviors), and psychologists are interested in understanding all behaviors. There is particular reason to be interested in sleep, since people spend as much as one-third of their lives sleeping. Also, there is a good deal that can be learned about consciousness, and in particular how the mind and the body interact, from studying sleep. Finally, sleep disturbances are also a behavior, and they represent a significant source of distress for many people. As students of behavior, psychologists are concerned with eliminating that source of distress.

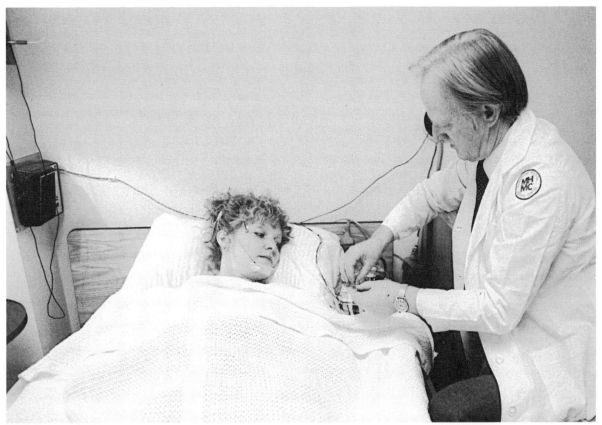

FIGURE 5-2
This person is about to begin an experimental sleep session. The wires attached to her skull monitor brain waves; the wires attached to her chin provide information about muscle tension in the face.

What Is Sleep?

To most of us, **sleep** seems like a relatively simple event. Our common-sense idea of sleep is that there comes a point in the course of a day at which fatigue overcomes us and we lapse into unconsciousness. The next morning we may or may not remember dreams that we had during the night, but for the most part it seems as if nothing much went on during our sleep. This view of sleep does not do justice to the intricacy of the sleep cycle.

When we look carefully at what actually happens during a sleep period, it is like looking at a drop of water under a high-powered microscope. The complexity and richness of what we see is astounding. We find that sleep is only vaguely related to fatigue; that one type of consciousness is replaced by another type; that our level of consciousness varies from minute to minute during the sleep period; and

that dreams may be the by-products of a very elaborate "house-cleaning" carried out by the brain.

A Typical Sleep Experiment. Sleep is one of those behaviors that almost has to be studied in the laboratory rather than in the field. As you will see shortly, different stages of sleep are defined by some very sophisticated measures of brain activity. These measures include patterns of brain waves, eyeball movements, and muscle tension. In the past, such measures have been difficult to obtain and even more difficult to interpret in a field setting. As a result, most research on sleep is now conducted in sleep laboratories, although this may change as a result of recent advances in equipment design. Figure 5–2 shows a subject about to begin a typical

Sleep. A state characterized by reduced consciousness, inactivity, and insensitivity to sensory stimulation.

experimental sleep session. As you can see, there are lots of wires attached to the subject's head. Each wire provides different information. The wires coming from the eyes provide information about eye movement during sleep, which provides important information about dreaming. The wires attached to the skull at various points provide brain-wave data. Other wires attached to the jaw provide information about muscle tension in the face, another indicator of certain types or stages of sleep. In addition to these most important measures, the experimenter may also monitor pulse, respiration, blood pressure, and body temperature.

Sleep Stages. Sleep consists of a sequence of stages that involves systematic changes in brain activity. In sleep research, a machine called an electroencephalograph (EEG) is used to monitor the ongoing brain activity of the subjects. Through a careful recording of brain waves, the various stages of sleep can be tracked. In addition to changes in brain waves, there are also changes in eye movements and face-muscle activity during sleep. Sleep stages begin with a pre-sleep phase that is generally referred to as "relaxed wakefulness." The two characteristic brain patterns in this pre-sleep phase are low voltage, high frequency brain waves (called **beta waves**) that are typical of normal wakefulness, and periodic, rhythmic **alpha waves** that are indicative of relaxed wakefulness. This stage is followed by four other stages. In Stage 2 sleep, the brain waves become less regular and sharp spikes begin to appear on the monitor. In Stage 3 sleep, even more wave irregularity begins to appear and in Stage 4, the deepest period of sleep, the brain waves are at their most irregular. The sleeper stays in Stage 4 for 15 to 30 minutes before the brain waves once again take on the characteristics of Stage 1 sleep. However, when the individual enters Stage 1 sleep for the second time, something new happens. The individual's eyes begin to move rapidly, there is a reduction of muscle tension, and dreaming occurs. This stage is referred to as **rapid eye movement (REM) sleep**. Unlike initial Stage 1 sleep, it is difficult to wake an individual in a REM sleep stage. In Figure 5–3, you can see the systematic changes in brain waves that occur as one progresses through the sleep stages. Note, as well, the changes that occur in eye movements in initial Stage 1 and subsequent Stage 1 sleep. Figure 5–4 will give you some idea of the relative duration of the various stages of sleep.

Periods of REM sleep recur throughout the night with various stages of non-REM sleep in between.

There are other physiological changes that occur in REM sleep. There is dramatically reduced muscle control in the neck and head. Heartrate, respiration, and blood pressure vary to a much greater extent in REM sleep than in other stages. Finally, in males, there is commonly an erection of the penis in REM sleep. Rather than discussing each stage independently, we will consider only two general categories of sleep: Stages 1, 2, 3, and 4, called **NREM or non-REM sleep**, and REM sleep.

Sleep Cycles. Sleep is a voyage through several stages. We move from drowsiness to NREM sleep to REM sleep. In fact, we make this trip several times during each sleep episode; the number of trips depends on how long we stay asleep. A typical trip through the stages takes about 90 minutes. As you can see from Figure 5–4, the time is not evenly distributed across the stages. Figure 5–4 also shows that REM periods gradually increase in length over the sleep period, starting off as relatively brief interludes and gradually lengthening to as much as an hour. In addition, as we get into the later periods of a sleep session, our excursions into sleep stages become more shallow, seldom dropping below Stage 2 after a few hours.

Young adults spend about 25 percent of sleep time in REM sleep and 75 percent in the other stages (Cartwright, 1978). It is interesting to note that infants spend almost twice as much time in REM sleep as young adults, and prematurely-born infants spend even more time in REM sleep than full-term babies. This has led to some speculation that REM sleep may play a role in learning or memory. The assumption is that information is transferred into permanent or long-term memory during

---

Beta waves. Low-voltage, high-frequency brain waves characteristic of normal wakefulness.

Alpha waves. Periodic, rhythmic brain waves characteristic of relaxed wakefulness.

Rapid eye movement (REM) sleep. Stage of sleep characterized by movements of the eye in quick and jerky patterns; stage during which dreaming occurs, also marked by varying heartrate, pulse, and blood pressure.

NREM or non-REM sleep. Stages 1–4 of sleep, which, along with REM sleep, occur in regular cycles throughout the sleep period. Characterized by steadier heartrate, pulse, and blood pressure than in REM sleep; dreaming does not usually occur in NREM sleep.

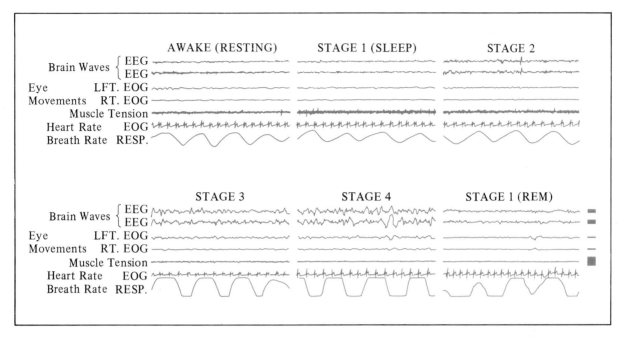

FIGURE 5-3

This figure shows the patterns of brain waves, eye movements, and other bodily functions during the awake resting state and during the various stages of sleep. If you look closely, you can see the changes that occur in eye movements in initial Stage 1 sleep and subsequent Stage 1 sleep. This subsequent stage is marked by the onset of rapid eye movements.

FIGURE 5-4

This figure shows the different stages of sleep as they occur in a cycle through the night. Note how REM intervals become longer and Stages 2 through 4 become shorter as the night progresses. (Dement, 1974, p. 114)

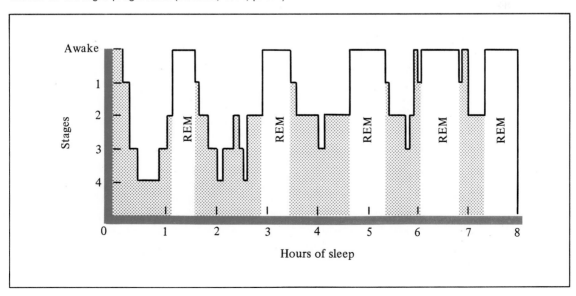

REM sleep. (Dewan, 1970). The hypothesis is that since infants must learn so much more each day than adults, their brains must sort through more information during sleep in order to separate what will be stored from what will be forgotten. There does seem to be a gradual reduction in REM sleep as people get older.

In addition to the 90-minute sleep cycle, there seem to be similar cycles, also about 90 minutes long, in waking states as well. Kripke and Sonnenschein (1978) discovered that people experience varying levels of arousal in 90-minute blocks throughout the day. Subjects also report fantasy or dreamlike thought patterns every 90 minutes. This has implications for a familiar time span—the 2-hour lecture period. During those two hours, your attention will wander at least once, possibly even twice. Add to this the possibility that the attention of the lecturer may also wander once or twice. Since your wandering attention and the lecturer's are not likely to travel down the same path, you may notice some gaps in your notes when reviewing them after class—not everything seems to fit together. You could fill in the gaps on your end by borrowing notes from a classmate. Or you could do it at the instructor's end by looking at the textbook for structure (provided the lecturer followed the text). A simpler solution is, of course, to shorten class periods to less than 90 minutes. This would reduce the probability of wandering consciousness on either end.

What Role Does Sleep Play?

As you have seen, sleep is a complicated pattern of psychological and physiological mechanisms. The intricacy of the pattern suggests that sleep has a critical purpose. Unfortunately, we still have no clear idea of why we sleep. There are several possible explanations, which will be presented in this section, but they are only guesses. We are not sure if sleep fulfills a critical function or if it is an evolutionary accident perpetuated through various survival mechanisms that played a major role in the early development of the species.

Restorative Hypothesis. The most obvious explanation for sleep is that it is a period of time when the body can recover from all the activities of the day. It is a time to give cells and organs a rest. It is a time

when various injuries are repaired by the body. This is an appealing explanation, but it does not match the facts. In the first place, there seems to be little relationship between the length of time spent awake and the "need" for sleep (as shown by how long people sleep after being awake). Many sleep researchers have noted that in a waking state, after a certain point is reached, people don't get more tired. Also, some people seem to require much more sleep than others, in spite of the fact that they are the same age and engage in many of the same activities on a daily basis. Finally, if the restorative explanation were true, people would require more sleep after very active waking periods than after less active periods; this does not seem to be the case.

Perhaps it is necessary to distinguish between rest and sleep. There are many periods of the day when our bodies are at rest even though we are not asleep. There is an opportunity during those periods for our bodies to engage in repair activities. A consideration of the difference between rest and sleep brings up another issue. REM sleep is anything but "restful." In fact, during REM sleep our minds seem to be engaged in some serious activity. It has been suggested that REM and NREM sleep serve different purposes. NREM sleep may help us to recover from the day's activities, since our blood pressure, heartrate, and respiration seem to be low during these periods. REM sleep, on the other hand, seems to involve intense mental activity of various forms, almost as if we are tidying up our memories and cognitive corners after a busy day interacting with reality. As already mentioned, this has been suggested as a possible explanation for the fact that infants spend more time in REM sleep than adults.

If this is the case, there should be some obvious effects of depriving subjects of the opportunity to enter into REM or NREM sleep periods. Depriving a person of REM sleep seems to result in longer REM periods in later sleep sessions. This is commonly referred to as the **REM rebound effect**. In some early sleep studies (Dement, 1960) it was shown that after being deprived of REM sleep for a period of time, subjects would spend a much greater amount of time in REM sleep in later periods, although the total number of hours the subjects slept did not change very much. There also have been studies with animals that have shown that REM sleep aids maze learning (Rideout, 1979); mice deprived of REM sleep learned much slower than a control group. On the other hand, several studies (Lucero, 1970; Block et al., 1977) have found that the percentage of REM sleep in animals increases as a result of maze-learning activities; the more time spent in maze learning, the more time spent in REM sleep. These studies seem to point to some relationship between REM sleep and the cognitive activity (i.e., the maze learning) that preceded it. It may be misleading to call the relationship a restorative one; it may be a supportive relationship, in which the work begun during a waking period is completed during a sleeping period.

But what happens when people are deprived of NREM sleep? There haven't been many studies of this type, but the few that have been done point to the restorative function of sleep. As was the case with REM sleep deprivations, there seems to be a rebound effect that occurs after NREM sleep deprivation. Subjects will spend more time in NREM sleep after being deprived of it (Agnew et al., 1964). As a result of NREM sleep deprivation, subjects occasionally show lethargic behavior, sometimes report symptoms of mild depression (Agnew et al., 1967), and are more likely to complain of stiffness and pain as well as to be more sensitive to pain generally (Moldofsky and Scarasbrick, 1976).

In summary, the restorative explanation of sleep needs more study before it can be accepted. Even if we are willing to accept the qualification that REM sleep serves cognitive purposes and NREM sleep serves physical purposes, we are still left with the problem of why physically active subjects don't require more NREM sleep than less active subjects. A good deal of research on this question lies ahead.

The Adaptive Explanation. Webb (1971) has offered another possible explanation for sleep. He believes that it is necessary for every organism to conserve energy or at least to exercise control over how that energy is spent. An efficient way to conserve energy is to enter a resting state at regular periods. Also, in prehistoric times people were more likely to survive if they stayed quiet at night, hidden from roaming predators and conserving energy for the next day's hunting. This suggests the development of sleep patterns that have nothing to do with restoration or repair. As Levinthal (1979) points out, this adaptive explanation might account for an interesting phenomenon. Researchers often find a negative relationship between the amount of time spent asleep and awake. In other words, even if we stay awake for long periods of time, say for several days, we don't need nearly an equal amount of sleep to make up for it—only a few hours extra at most. A simple restorative explanation, such as discussed earlier, would imply that there should be a positive relationship between the amount of time spent asleep and awake—that we need to match time asleep and time awake hour for hour. However, if we accept the possibility that negative sleep/wake cycles have come about through the daily cycle of light and dark, this relationship makes sense. It may mean that we have an internal or biological "clock" that controls our activity levels (and, to some extent, our states of consciousness). It also suggests that cycles play a part in many other aspects of human behavior. As you will see shortly, disturbing these sleep/wake cycles can have substantial effects on physical and psychological well-being. Shift work, jet lag travel, and all-night study sessions are a few common examples of disruptions to the sleep/wake cycle. These disruptions are closely tied to problems or disorders of sleep. Let's now consider sleep disorders in some detail.

REM rebound effect. Deprivation of REM sleep seems to result in longer REM periods in later sleep sessions.

REVIEW QUESTIONS

16. The sleep cycle begins with a presleep phase called relaxed wakefulness; the brain waves characteristic of this stage are called _____ waves.

17. REM/NREM sleep involves dreaming and variations in heart rate, breathing rate, and blood pressure.

18. Infants typically spend almost twice as much time in REM/NREM sleep as adults.

19. In terms of what function sleep serves, it has been theorized that REM/NREM sleep serves a physically restorative function, to allow us to recover from the day's activities, while REM/NREM sleep serves a mentally active, "tidying up" function, to allow us to straighten out our thoughts after a busy day.

20. People who have been more active during the day than usual will need more sleep.
    T / F

21. If you stay awake several nights in a row you will find that you do not have to make up that lost sleep hour for hour, but that there will be an effect on the amount of REM/NREM periods in later sleep sessions. This is called the _____ _____ effect.

Answers: 16. beta 17. REM 18. REM 19. NREM; REM 20. False 21. REM; REM rebound

Sleep Disorders

Sleep disorders fall into the categories of insomnia, or difficulty in falling asleep or staying asleep; narcolepsy, or difficulty in staying awake; and disorders of sleep/wake cycles.

Insomnia. **Insomnia** is defined as the chronic inability to obtain adequate sleep because of an inability to fall asleep, because of waking up frequently, or because of waking up early in the morning (Bootzin and Nicassio, 1978). Most people think of insomnia as a problem in falling asleep, but insomnia problems include getting to sleep *and* staying asleep. Because there are many forms of insomnia and many possible reasons for being unable to fall asleep or stay asleep, it is hard to find any single cure for the disorder (Borkovec, 1982).

Cartwright (1978) suggests that difficulties in getting to sleep may be caused by anxiety surrounding some specific problem. The anxiety causes arousal, which makes it difficult to fall asleep. After several sleepless nights, people become anxious about sleeping itself: "Will I be able to sleep tonight?" On the other hand, Cartwright suggests that waking up during the night and not being able to get back to sleep is the result of depression. Kales (1973) studied 220 insomniacs who had come to a medical center for treatment; many of them suffered from depression. We often begin to worry as soon as our thoughts are not taken up by immediate environmental events. We turn out the lights, pull up the covers, and flip on the worry switch. *What* we worry about may be a function of age or daily environment and *when* we worry may depend on how much of our attention is taken up by other stimulation. This is a good reason to wait until you are relaxed and ready to go to sleep before going to bed. Even watching an old movie on TV can distract you from worry and resulting sleep problems.

Many insomniacs are of the "mixed" variety, suffering from both difficulty in falling asleep and difficulty in staying asleep. There is still no complete picture of all the possible causes of insomnia, but at least some of the causes are clear. These include drugs, alcohol, worry, physical arousal, breathing difficulties, restless legs, heat, cold, and possible abnormalities in brain activity. Ironically enough, the "cure" most often taken for insomnia—the sleeping pill—is probably a *cause* of one form of the disorder. If you don't have a serious insomnia problem *before* taking sleeping pills for an extended period of time, you certainly will *afterwards*. This is due to the REM rebound effect described earlier. The effect of sleeping pills (and alcohol as well) is to cut down on the amount of REM sleep (Levinthal, 1977). As we saw in the REM deprivation studies, this seems to result in an increased demand for REM periods on following nights. Studies have shown that one of the side-effects of reduced REM sleep is an increase in awakenings during the night, almost as if REM activity is being demanded by the nervous system (Borkovec, 1982). These sleep disturbances are also rest disturbances. In order to stay asleep for longer periods of time, people continue to take the sleeping pills. Unfortunately, the effectiveness of these sleeping aids diminishes as their use continues. As you learned earlier in the chapter, our bodies develop a tolerance for certain chemicals. When the person stops taking the sleeping pills, the nervous system then begins to work even more vigorously, since it has adapted to the presence of the pills. After an extended period of use, the person will still suffer from night awakenings for sometime after the sleeping pills are discontinued. Most sleep researchers advise that sleeping pills should be used only as a last resort, and then only infrequently.

Treatments of Insomnia. There are two major treatments of insomnia—chemical and behavioral (Cartwright, 1978). As discussed above, the common chemical treatments cause more problems than they cure. A first step toward a cure for insomnia is to get the insomniac to give up sleeping pills. Alcohol is another chemical that might cause problems; insomnia is often an unrecognized side-effect of alcohol use. This can be a particular problem for those who work evening and night shifts. It is not uncommon for afternoon shift workers (working from 3 PM to 11 PM) to have a few drinks after work to relax. They then arise the next morning with the rest of the world. But from what we know of the effects of alcohol on REM sleep, their sleep will eventually be broken with awakenings. On the nights when they don't have a nightcap, things may be even worse if their systems have adapted to alcohol. The problem is even more difficult for workers on the night shift (from 11 PM to 7 AM). Since they are trying to get to sleep while the rest of the world is waking up, they might be tempted to take a drink or two to help them get to sleep. This almost guarantees later problems. As with sleeping pills, people quickly reach the point where they can't get to sleep without a drink and can't stay asleep if they have one.

Many sleep researchers believe that sleeping, like many other behaviors, is controlled by a series of habits. From this point of view, it stands to reason that the treatment for insomnia is to replace ineffective habits with better ones. This approach usually involves either relaxing or rearranging schedules or personal environments. Relaxation techniques will be discussed later on in both the stress and the therapy chapters, so there is no need to cover them at length here. Simply put, they involve a series of exercises that a person does before going to sleep. For example, you might systematically tense and relax various muscle groups. In addition, you might imagine a peaceful scene, such as sitting by a stream on a summer afternoon listening to your favorite music.

In addition to the relaxation techniques, physical environments, actions, and schedules can be rearranged. Bootzin has studied the behavioral aspects of sleeplessness and has made some suggestions for insomniacs (Bootzin and Nicassio, 1978). These include using the bed only for sleep or sex, not for working, watching TV, reading, or eating. In addition, he suggests that people get out of bed and do something else if they are not sleepy. He also sug-

gests that insomniacs rise each morning at the same time no matter how long they've slept so that a sleep rhythm is established. It goes without saying that insomniacs should avoid exercise, arguments, and caffeine immediately before going to bed, since all of these result in increased arousal.

Narcolepsy. The opposite problem to sleeplessness is **narcolepsy.** This disorder is characterized by falling suddenly asleep during the day—no matter what the time of day or the circumstances. Obviously, this can be embarrassing in some situations and even dangerous in others. The onset of sleep is often so sudden that it could easily lead to a serious automobile or industrial accident. It is also common for the attack to be preceded by some form of emotional experience (Cartwright, 1978). Levinthal (1977) estimates that approximately 100,000 people in the United States have narcolepsy. Even less is known about it than insomnia, although the best guess is that it is related to a neurological defect of some sort. Some researchers (Rechtschaffen et al., 1963) have studied narcoleptics and have found that during their sleep attacks narcoleptics are in REM sleep stages; in addition narcoleptics may begin normal sleep with a REM rather than a NREM sleep stage. As was mentioned earlier, people usually do not begin REM sleep until 90 minutes into the sleep cycle. This suggests that the mechanism responsible for REM sleep is also responsible for narcolepsy; but because REM sleep hasn't yet been fully explained, neither has narcolepsy. There has been some limited success in treating narcolepsy with antidepressants and stimulants (Browman et al., 1982). This is probably due to the fact that such drugs act to increase the activity of the central nervous system, making it less likely that sleep will occur. The tendency for narcolepsy to be inherited has been documented in both humans and animals, suggesting a genetic foundation for the problem (Baker and Dement, 1985).

Other Sleep Disorders. There are a number of other disorders associated with sleep and dreams. A few of them will be briefly described here.

Insomnia. Inability to obtain adequate sleep due to being unable to fall asleep, waking up frequently, or waking up early in the morning.

Narcolepsy. An inability to stay awake, no matter what the time of day or the circumstances.

NIGHTMARES AND CREATIVITY

If you dreamed that giant purple spiders were chasing you along a deserted beach, attacking with painful nips at your ankles, you would call your dream a *nightmare.* If you woke up screaming and convinced that you were covered with creepy, crawly bugs, dream researchers would call that a *night terror.* Psychologists who study dreaming draw a clear distinction between the two types of sleep experience. Although nightmares and especially night terrors are rare in adults, children, on the other hand, tend to have night terrors more often than nightmares. Among adults, only one in 500 averages one nightmare a week. Nightmares tend to be in full color and to include particularly vivid sensations, like pain, that are unlikely to appear in other types of dreams. Nightmares can have such a powerfully terrifying effect that memories of them can survive for many years.

Sleep researcher Ernest Hartmann has found that some people are particularly prone to nightmares and this tendency usually stays with them throughout their lives. Unfortunately, nightmares are even more common for these people when they are experiencing a particularly stressful period. Hartmann studied a group of nightmare sufferers and also found that they tended to be involved in some form of creativity, such as writing poetry, painting, or playing music. Hartmann fur-

ther characterizes nightmare sufferers as having what he calls "thin boundaries"—the tendency to be more emotionally sensitive and responsive to the feelings of others. An outlet for this sensitivity seems to be creativity in the form of artistic expression.

Supporting Hartmann's hypothesis about the connection between nightmares and creativity is the fact that some authors claim to have been inspired by especially vivid nightmares to create their best-known works. Robert Louis Stevenson's dream about a dapper Englishman transforming into a horrible monster was the germ of his novel, *The Strange Case of Dr. Jekyll and Mr. Hyde.* One of Mary Shelley's nightmares became the basis for her novel, *Frankenstein.* Hartmann is not surprised by the link between creative people and nightmare sufferers. He believes that a key element of the creative personality includes a heightened awareness of the individual's own "inner life," as well as the tendency to experience the everyday world quite fully. These creative individuals also tend to be those who, as adults, experience nightmares with some regularity.

Source: Dan Goleman, "Nightmares Are Linked to Creativity in New View," *New York Times,* October 23, 1983, p. C2.

Sleep apnea is a condition in which the sleeping individual stops breathing as a result of a build-up of carbon dioxide in the blood. The individual wakes gasping for breath. Some of us may have experienced this phenomenon at one time or another during sleep, particularly if we snore, or we may have heard a sleeper gasp in mid-snore. Sleep apnea has been implicated in the Sudden Infant Death Syndrome (SIDS) (Carlson, 1981). It is thought that some infants are without the mechanism that would awaken them when breathing stops. Death would be the inevitable result. Devices are now available that can signal to parents when an infant stops breathing.

Night terrors are often confused with night-

mares. Night terrors are predominantly physiological events that occur in Stage 4 or NREM sleep. They are characterized by many of the physiological elements of a strong emotion such as perspiration, trembling, and rapid heartbeat. The event usually begins with a loud shout or scream. The person experiencing a night terror can seldom identify the reason for the terror and is often unaware that the event has occurred. It is others, such as a spouse or parent, who are most aware of what has happened. Nightmares, on the other hand, occur in REM sleep stages and can usually be tied to particular dream content. It is not unusual for individuals to have recurring nightmares on the same topic. A major difference between the nightmare

Workers who are on steady evening and night shifts often have trouble with sleep disturbances.

and the night terror is that the night terror involves the autonomic nervous system and the nightmare does not.

Somnambulism (sleep walking) and **eneuresis** (bed wetting) also commonly occur during Stage 4, or deep sleep. Both of these disorders are characteristic of young children and often disappear as the nervous system of the child matures (Carlson, 1981). Bed wetting can be reduced through a combination of common sense (reminding the child to urinate before going to bed), training methods (using a specially-prepared sheet that signals when the first drops of urine are produced), and support (eliminating any sense of shame or guilt that the child may experience as a result of the problem).

Disturbances of Sleep/Wake Cycles. There are many times when our sleeping and waking cycles get out of synchronization. Some occasions are obvious: flights across time zones (jet lag), all-night study sessions, and temporary illnesses that create temporary sleep disturbances. There is one cir-

---

Sleep apnea. A disorder in which breathing stops during sleep and the sleeper wakes gasping for breath.

Night terrors. Predominantly physiological events that occur in Stage 4 or NREM sleep and are characterized by autonomic responses such as perspiration, trembling, and rapid heartbeat.

Somnambulism. Sleep walking. Commonly occurs during Stage 4 or deep sleep and is more likely to affect young children.

Eneuresis. Bed wetting. Also a disorder affecting young children and likely to occur during Stage 4 sleep.

cumstance that is more of a problem—shift work. Workers who are on steady afternoon and night shifts often report sleep disturbances. There are many reasons for this. As was described before, afternoon shift workers may take pills or alcohol in order to get to sleep when the rest of the world does—it is not easy for them to come home directly from work and go to sleep. Could you walk in from work at 5:00 P.M. and sleep for 8 hours? Sleeping during daylight hours also poses a problem. The rest of the world is awake and the environment is noisy and disturbing. Finally, biological cycles can also cause sleep disturbances. During the 24-hour day, body temperature, blood pressure, muscle tension, and brain waves change regularly. These changes are all related to the ease with which people can fall asleep. Lowered body temperature, lowered muscular tension, certain brain activity, and certain blood flow patterns make it easier to sleep. If we try to force ourselves to sleep during a period in which it is not appropriate, we may not be able to sleep because our biological clock gets out of step with the clock on the wall. Eventually, the biological clock adjusts itself, but this means that we are now out of step with some other aspect of the environment. It may be difficult to take part in family activities or to engage in certain leisure pursuits because of shifted physical cycles. Any adaptation to the afternoon or night shift represents a maladaptation to some other time of day.

Rotating workshifts can also cause sleep problems. In a rapidly-rotating shift, a person might work 2 days on a day shift, 2 days on an afternoon shift, take 2 days off, and then work 3 days on the night shift. Some people prefer the rotating shift because adaptation does *not* occur. This allows them to enjoy normal activities during their days off and day-shift periods.

Thus, as we have seen, sleep disturbances include a broad group of problems, and there is no single solution to them. As Borkovec (1982) notes, to discuss sleep disturbances in a general way is the same as saying that a psychiatric patient has a waking disturbance.

Dreams

Although dreams can occur in either REM or NREM sleep, they are much more common in REM sleep. The NREM-sleep dreams tend to be more abstract and perceptual, and less thematic in content, than REM-sleep dreams (Cartwright, 1978). An extreme example of the NREM dream might be the Stage 4 night terrors we discussed earlier.

Everyone dreams, but not everyone remembers those dreams. In the sleep laboratory, it is easy enough to wake a person in the middle of a REM period and get a vivid report of a dream. But in real life we don't always wake up in the middle or at the end of a REM-sleep period. If our alarm clock goes off in the middle of a NREM-sleep period, we are not likely to report a dream. As we know from the close association that exists between dreaming and REM sleep, we have many dreams each night. In the sleep lab, three, four, and sometimes five different dream reports can be collected from the same subject in the course of one night.

Dreams, like REM stages, can last anywhere from a few minutes to, toward the end of the night, almost an hour. Dreaming, like REM sleep itself, will increase and decrease based on how much REM sleep we have had. In normal circumstances, we tend to dream the same amount each night as long as we sleep the same amount of time.

Freud speculated on why dreams are not recalled. His view was that threatening or important dreams are repressed or kept out of consciousness because they would cause pain or difficulty for the waking mind. As to why dreams occur in the first place, Freud proposed that dreams are opportunities for the expression of impulses that could not be displayed in reality.

There have been many propositions regarding why we dream. We know too little at this stage to choose any of these explanations as "correct," but they are all interesting and worth considering until firm data are available to explain the function of dreams. Cartwright (1978) has identified many of these explanations. Several of them are listed below:

1. *Mental housekeeping:* Much that happens to us during the day is not worth keeping in long-term memory, and dreaming helps sort that which is to be kept from that which will be discarded.
2. *Self-stimulation:* Dreaming is a form of mental exercise that helps the brain develop. Thus, we find that infants and young children dream considerably more than adults.
3. *Continuity:* Dreams represent the attempt to continue working on information that was

presented in pre-sleep periods. This would account for the fact that many dreams are characterized by content that is easily recognizable as part of the events of the day preceding the dream.

4. *Self-protection:* Dreams serve to preserve our self-concept. In our dreams, we often play a role that we have been given by a social group or a role we aspire to. This may be the value of dream interpretation in Freudian therapy—the dream provides clues with respect to the individual's sense of identity.

5. *Problem solving opportunities:* Dream periods are, by definition, free of distractions from the external environment. As a result, they provide an excellent opportunity to devote unrestrained attention to difficult problems. It is likely that fresh ideas will appear in dreams that might not have appeared in waking periods.

6. *No function at all:* There is some speculation that dreams are simply neural activity—the firing of neurons and the action of neurotransmitters portrayed on the blank screen of sleep. We assume dreams have meaning when, in fact, they may not.

■ MEDITATION AND HYPNOSIS

There are two activities that are commonly recognized as affecting consciousness, yet which seem to be qualitatively different from sleep, chemically-induced states, or even fleeting daydreams. These two activities are meditation and hypnosis. Let's take a look at what is involved in each of these states.

Meditation

Meditation is an attempt to move from the kind of thinking that involves problem-solving or analysis to the kind of thinking that involves fantasy (Martindale, 1981). It is clear that as long as we allow the outside world to assault our senses, they will relay information to our brain which will, in turn, try to "make sense" of that information whether we want it to or not. Most methods of meditation involve radically changing the nature of outside stimulation. There are two ways of doing this: Outside stimulation can be "blocked out" or it can be made impossible to comprehend. Both of these methods are thought to "free" the consciousness from one type of thinking and allow free rein to another type, such as fantasy. We will consider the blocking-out approach first. From the behavioral viewpoint, the blocking methods vary mainly on the basis of execution. The types of meditation also often have unique religious and philosophical roots, but these underlying beliefs are not critical for a behavioral discussion of consciousness.

Restriction Through Adaptation. Using methods of adaptation, a person attempts to get the senses to adapt to (or *ignore*) certain outside stimulation. One form of this adaptation is called **concentrative meditation**. In concentrative meditation (Goleman, 1978), as the name suggests, the person concentrates on one particular thing. The thing concentrated on might be an object as mundane as a spot on the rug. In the practice of Zen, it might be a single breath or even the process of breathing (Naranjo and Ornstein, 1971). In a sense, the object is to fatigue or wear out the sensory receptors that carry information about that stimulus to the brain. Meditation is usually carried out in an environment free from distraction, and the meditator may be instructed in how to sit without movement (for example, on the floor with legs crossed); this further limits outside stimulation. Once the receptors have become fatigued, the problem-solving type of thinking is replaced with fantasy. You may remember the material dealing with the recovery period for neurons from the biology and behavior chapter. After neurons fire or discharge, there is a period when they must recover before firing again. The principle of restriction through adaptation seems to be based on a similar logic. Once the receptors are fatigued and cannot respond normally, other processes take over.

Meditation. Focusing on, or limiting one's thoughts to, a specific idea or stimulus in order to block out other sources of stimulation.

Concentrative meditation. An attempt to get one's senses to adapt to certain outside stimulation by concentrating attention on one particular stimulus, such as one's own breathing.

Most methods of meditation involve either blocking outside stimulation or making it impossible to comprehend.

Restriction Through Repetition. Another variation of adaptation is repetition. In this case, a stimulus is repeated over and over again until the sensory receptors wear down. The stimulus may be a visual one, such as a picture continually flashed on a screen, or an auditory one, the sound OM spoken over and over again. In meditation, this is called a **mantram** (plural is *mantra*). Mantra play a major role in **Transcendental Meditation (TM).** As we will see in a later section, repetition is a technique often used by hypnotists to induce a hypnotic state. The repetition may consist of a swinging medallion held

slightly above the eye level of the subject, or it may be the simple rhythmic repetition of a phrase or an instruction. Some researchers (Stroebel and Glueck, 1978) have suggested the possibility that there are particular physical characteristics of certain sounds that make them better for producing meditative or hypnotic trances (for example, sounds of particular intensities or frequencies), but such a relationship has yet to be proven.

Incomprehensible Stimulation. In Zen, a device called a **koan** (Naranjo and Ornstein, 1971) is used to free the meditator from outside stimulation. A koan is a logical impossibility cast in the form of a riddle. Since an analytic or problem-solving type of cognition cannot solve the riddle, it is thought that a fantasy-type of cognition is activated in its place. An example of a koan might be, "What is the sound of one hand clapping?" or, "What is the size of the real you?" (Naranjo and Ornstein, 1971, p. 148). There are no "correct" answers to these questions. If we are determined to solve them, it will take almost all of our mental energy, leaving none free to attend to outside stimulation. You must have had the experience at one time or another of being so absorbed with an idea that you did not notice someone enter the room; you looked up and were startled. The internal stimulation of what you were thinking about absorbed all of your attention, and you shut out the objective world.

Hypnosis

On the surface, **hypnosis** may appear to have little in common with meditation. But upon further study, there are some striking similarities. Both produce a state that is qualitatively different from normal, waking consciousness. Both achieve that state through some manipulation of sensory input, either directly or through instructions. And both have the capacity to leave people feeling better as a result of the experience. Of course, there are some substantial differences between hypnosis and meditation as well. Hypnosis is often used as a device to alter particular behaviors such as smoking or nail-biting. Meditation is used more often to produce a general state of calm and relaxation.

Hypnotic induction is a technique used to put someone into a hypnotic trance. The induction usually consists of a combination of relaxation techniques and focusing exercises, in which a person is first asked to listen carefully to the hypnotist.

The hypnotist then talks in a quiet, melodic way similar to the sound of the mantram in meditation, and suggests that the person is becoming tired. It will also be suggested that the person trust and obey the hypnotist. In effect, the person is told to stop evaluating actions and to begin acting in the way suggested. As you can see, these procedures could be made to fit nicely into the trance-inducing procedures of the meditator. There is nothing magical about the process, nor is there anything particularly mystical about the hypnotist.

There are several characteristics that are used as criteria for a hypnotic trance. Hilgard suggests that the following behaviors might characterize a person who has been hypnotized:

1. Increased suggestibility.
2. Improved visual imagery, particularly for past visual memories.
3. Decreased desire for self-initiation of action; preference for taking instructions rather than planning.
4. Acceptance of distortions of reality with ease (for example, hearing a song from an imagined loudspeaker or being told that ammonia smells like a rose).

The role of increased suggestibility in hypnosis is very important. In fact, it has been said that whether or not a person can be hypnotized at all depends upon how suggestible a person is. This is referred to as the **hypnotic suggestibility** of the subject and it can be measured by making a number of specific suggestions and seeing how many of these suggestions are acted upon by the hypnotized person.

Some have gone so far as to suggest that hypnosis is nothing more than suggestions made to suggestible people (Barber, 1972). The advocates of hypnosis (Orne, 1969; Hilgard, 1977) counter with dramatic examples of behavior that is difficult to explain by

---

Mantram. A word or sound used in Transcendental meditation that is repeated over and over to block other sources of stimulation.

Transcendental Meditation (TM). A form of Eastern meditation that relies on the repetition of a word or sound to block out other outside stimulation.

Koan. A logical impossibility cast in the form of a riddle. Used in Zen meditation to force a person into a fantasy rather than an analytical type of thinking.

Hypnosis. A trance-like state in which a person is very relaxed and susceptible to suggestion.

Hypnotic induction. Instructions given by a hypnotist to cause a person to go into a hypnotic trance. Usually consists of a combination of relaxation techniques and focusing exercises.

Hypnotic suggestibility. The willingness or tendency of a hypnotized person to carry out the suggestion of the hypnotist.

simple suggestibility. Hilgard (1975) has identified a strange circumstance of hypnosis called the **hidden observer effect,** discovered through the study of pain perception. A subject is hypnotized and the subject's hand is placed in ice-cold water. This is a painful experience, but subjects are given the suggestion that they will feel no pain. Throughout the period of hypnosis, they report no pain and seem not to be conscious of it. In addition to the suggestion to feel no pain, the subjects are also given the suggestion that the hand that is not in the water (called the *nonstressed hand*) will write about the extent to which pain is being experienced. The nonstressed hand acts as a sort of "hidden observer" of the situation. Hilgard reports that the nonstressed hand writes about pain and discomfort while the subjects are reporting verbally that they are experiencing no pain. This effect is more dramatic when compared with the behavior of people who are faking a hypnotic state. They are given the same suggestions (feel no pain and nonstressed-hand writing), but the nonstressed hand does not report as a hidden-observer hand does (Watkins and Watkins, 1979); there aren't two separate accounts of what is happening. Hilgard contends that this is ample evidence that hypnotic states represent unusual states of consciousness. Hidden observer effects are seen in very few people and only in those who are highly suggestible or hypnotizable, but the fact that very few demonstrate the effect is not really the issue. The fact that any subjects demonstrate the behavior is enough to make the case for hypnotic states as unique states of consciousness.

Orne has conducted a different type of experiment that also seems to indicate that hypnotic states are different from simple examples of heightened suggestibility (Orne, 1969). Subjects are hypnotized and asked to tap their feet to imaginary music. In the midst of this activity, there is a power failure. All the lights and equipment fail and the experimenter leaves the room to find out what is happening. In fact, the power failure was planned, and the subjects are closely observed after the experimenter leaves the room. It was found that much time passed before the hypnotized subjects became aware of their circumstances. They gradually became conscious of their surroundings but were disoriented and confused. A second group of subjects was instructed to simulate the behavior of a hypnotized subject. They were also subjected to the power

failure but they behaved very differently. Almost immediately after the experimenter left the room, they acted as anyone would when left alone. There was a dramatic difference between the behavior of the hypnotized subjects and those faking hypnosis. Once again, it seems as if there is some evidence for a unique state of consciousness that can be produced through hypnosis.

A common fear that people have about hypnosis is that they may be made to do something against their will by means of a suggestion or instruction they are given while in a hypnotic trance. For example, can a hypnotist plant the suggestion that you walk down the street and rip off all of your clothes when you see a bus? The answer is no. You are unlikely to do anything you believe to be wrong or dangerous. Nevertheless, people are more willing to believe that a particular statement is true when they are hypnotized than when they are not hypnotized. They seem to suspend the normal critical disbelief that they would have in a typical social setting. This is part of the increased suggestibility that seems to go along with the hypnotic state. If the hypnotist tries to convince you that ripping off your clothes at the sight of the bus is the latest fad, and if you are convinced that the hypnotist is telling the truth, and if you want to take part in the latest fad, you may very well end up in the newspaper—possibly even in the report of arrests for the week. A sadistic friend might be able to get you to do the same thing with a clever story or deception, but it would be a lot harder to fool you. Hypnosis in this case is not the critical factor—it is simply the opportunity for persuasion.

Hypnosis and Memory. Freud felt that hypnosis could be used to uncover memories of childhood that were critical in the treatment of mental disorders. Recently, hypnosis has been used to improve the memory of people who were victims of or witnesses to traumatic events. It is assumed that these people were greatly affected by the event and therefore are unwilling to remember the details because of the anxiety that the memory would cause. A recent case in point is the fire that occurred at a Stouffer's Inn on December 4, 1980. In that fire, 26 executives who were attending a management seminar were killed. Arson was suspected, and several of the people who had attended that conference were hypnotized in the hope that they would be able to remember details that might aid in the investigation. Using this method, two witnesses supplied details that pointed to a waiter who had served coffee to the seminar participants. In the trial that followed the investigation, Luis Marin, a 26-year-old Guatemalan, was charged with murder and arson. During that trial, a great deal of time was spent examining the validity of the testimony gathered through hypnosis. The prosecution argued that the witnesses were so upset by the fire that their memories of it could only be uncovered through hypnosis. The defense argued that the hypnotic experience actually *planted* memories for details in the witnesses; that before hypnosis, the memories had not existed. For example, in the course of the Stouffer's investigation, one of the seminar members was hypnotized and asked about the people who might have had access to the area around the fire. While the witness was in this hypnotic state, the head of the investigation leaned over to the hypnotist and said, "Get a better description of the Hispanic, he does not fit in with the description of our suspect." The defense claimed that the hypnotized witness probably overheard the comment and, from that point on, had the memory of an Hispanic employee who had been in the area. Luis Marin was Hispanic. Marin was eventually found not guilty, and the case raised serious questions about the role or value of hypnotically induced testimony.

Hypnosis poses some serious problems when it is used to aid memory. As you will see in later material on memory, it is not difficult for a person to add to or change the memories of another person through subtle forms of suggestion. And, as we have seen, increased suggestibility is identified as one of the common effects of hypnosis. Thus, hypnotized people should be the most vulnerable to the alteration of or addition to memories. Orne has studied hypnosis and memory extensively, and often testifies at trials such as the Stouffer's trial. He contends that once a person has been hypnotized, it is impossible to separate memories for real events from memories created during the hypnosis. Orne is also very much against allowing investigating officials to be present during sessions with hypnotized witnesses, because he feels that they are likely to ask leading questions or bias responses in other subtle ways. In the last several years, many court cases have excluded testimony gathered under hypnosis due to feelings that this testimony is somehow less reliable

and more prone to emotional distortion. On the other hand, Barber (1977), who argues that hypnosis is nothing more than suggestions made to suggestible people, does not believe that memories can be permanently altered by hypnosis. He sees no harm in the use of hypnotic techniques for investigations, since he does not accept the idea that hypnotized people are in some different state of consciousness.

One effect of hypnosis on memory seems to be that people feel more confident about what they remember than if they had not been hypnotized. Thus, the individual who might have been unsure of a face or a color or a sound prior to being hypnotized seems much more certain after hypnosis. This might be because the individual is now remembering a more recent and less confusing event—the hypnotic interview. As a result, it may be that hypnosis deprives some lawyers of an important tool—the uncertainty of a witness. In a trial during which a defense lawyer stresses the concept of "beyond the shadow of a doubt," uncertainty of a witness may greatly aid the defendant. If that uncertainty is removed, the defendant is in greater jeopardy.

Are Meditation and Hypnosis Different States of Consciousness?

One problem in studying hypnosis and meditation is that research studies have failed to show measurable physical differences (such as differences in brain-wave patterns) that would allow scientists to distinguish between control subjects and subjects in a meditative trance or under hypnosis. However, there are other indicators that do show differences; for example, it has been shown repeatedly that meditators can control many physical responses such as heartrate, respiration rate, and even skin temperature. The same can be seen in subjects who have been hypnotized. The problem is that many people can do the same things *without* meditating or being hypnotized (for example, through biofeed-

---

Hidden observer effect. While hypnotized, people seem not to be conscious of a painful stimulus applied to one hand, but with the other hand can write about the pain they are experiencing. It is as if there is a hidden observer, the other hand, that is conscious of the situation, though the subjects themselves do not seem to be.

back). In addition, since the brain seems so closely tied to other phenomena of consciousness, it is difficult to accept any state of consciousness that does not somehow involve differences in brain-wave patterns. This does not mean that the brain *is* consciousness, but it certainly makes sense to start looking for the key to understanding consciousness in the brain.

There are a number of possibilities to consider in dealing with the special circumstances of hypnosis and meditation. First, scientists may not have the necessary equipment or methods of analysis to correctly describe how the brain is functioning while a person is hypnotized or in a meditative trance. As little as 50 years ago, researchers had no inkling of the differences between sleeping and waking states, but this did not change the fact that the differences existed. The same may be true in the cases of hypnosis and meditation. It would be foolish to dismiss meditation and hypnosis as trivial variations of normal consciousness simply because we do not, at the present time, have the technology or methods to study them adequately.

Another possibility is that in considering hypnosis and meditation, we are considering emergent consciousness rather than some static condition. This means that perhaps consciousness is something that we develop over a lifetime rather than something that each of us "has" in some real sense. In fact, this is one of the claims of those who encourage meditation—that meditation systematically changes the nature (and possibly the extent) of consciousness.

An Explanation: Dissociation. There is the possibility that meditation and hypnosis don't really involve turning something *on*, like a switch on a brain-wave machine, but instead involve turning something *off*. In a sense, it may be that these two states help a person uncouple or **dissociate** from traditional, objective reality. Hilgard's hidden-observer effect is a perfect example of this dissociation. In many early studies of hypnosis, in which pain was used as the source of stimulation, hypnotized subjects were able to endure much higher levels of pain than those who were asked to fake hypnosis. The fakers reported pain at much lower levels of stimulation than those who had undergone real hypnotic inductions. In a sense, the hypnotized subject managed to dissociate one aspect of con-

sciousness (the sensation of pressure on certain nerve endings) from another (the experience of suffering). Another example is the reaction of hypnotized subjects to ammonia. If ammonia is waved under your nose, you will pull away immediately, unable to endure the strong and even painful odor. Hypnotized subjects can be instructed to treat ammonia as a pleasant substance and they will react accordingly. They will not pull away or grimace and can take several appreciative sniffs with no difficulty. Once again, clearly some dissociation has occurred.

Practiced meditators seeem capable of dissociating themselves from external reality on cue. They can substantially alter their metabolic rates and appear to be able to shut out many of the arousing aspects of their immediate environment. In some ways, they may have managed a much more effective compromise than the traditional sleeper, since they may not experience the same type of frantic mental activity that seems to characterize REM sleep.

REVIEW QUESTIONS

22. Sleep disturbances fall into several major categories. For example, _____ is the inability to go to sleep, and _____ is the inability to stay awake.

23. Not everyone dreams every night; if you don't remember any dreams the next day, it's probable that you didn't dream that night.   T / F

24. How easy you are to hypnotize depends on how _____ you are.

25. One of the reasons it is hard to understand the meditative and hypnotic states is because there are no identifiable changes in brain wave patterns.   T / F

26. The concept of _____ , which states that people are able to shut-off or separate one aspect of consciousness from another, might be a way of understanding meditation and hypnosis.

Answers: 22. insomnia; narcolepsy 23. False 24. suggestible 25. True 26. dissociation

■ THE BRAIN AND CONSCIOUSNESS

To a large extent, this chapter has been anchored in a physiological perspective on consciousness. We have looked at the specific effects of drugs on normal brain functioning. We have explored the physiological manifestations of other forms of consciousness: sleep, dreaming, meditation, and hypnosis. You probably recall from our study of the brain in Chapter 2 that the brain is organized to carry out very different and highly specialized functions. This phenomenon also has implications for consciousness. In this last section we will consider some further applications of physiological psychology to the issue of consciousness. We will begin with a brief account of consciousness research in psychology.

Research on Consciousness

From its beginnings, psychology has been interested in the study of consciousness. As you may recall from Chapter 1, Wundt and his followers trained themselves in the technique of introspection in order to get at the very elements of consciousness. They studied very specific examples of consciousness, expecting to find general rules or regulations for consciousness that would characterize all human beings. The Gestalt theorists had a very different view of consciousness. They believed that consciousness is something greater than the sum of its parts. They applied their ideas on consciousness to the Gestalt principles of perceptual organization that we discussed in Chapter 4.

Perhaps the best-known student of consciousness was William James. He was much more interested in the processes of consciousness than in its basic elements and he took a functionalist approach. James believed in the value of untrained observation and insisted that psychology should focus on everyday experiences.

Methods of studying consciousness have changed quite a bit since Wundt and James first considered the issue. For example, recall some of the brain studies done with patients that we discussed in Chapter 2. H. M. underwent radical surgery to reduce epileptic seizures; after surgery extensive testing showed that cutting his hippocampus had resulted in the loss of a portion of his consciousness. In Yin's patients, damage to the brain resulted in a loss of brain functioning that involved memory for faces. You encountered other examples of left- and right-brain functions and abnormalities in Chapter 2 as well. All these data suggest that investigations of consciousness should start with some consideration of the brain and its physical properties.

Split-Brain Research. Split-brain research was first mentioned in chapter 2. Sperry (1968) studied epileptic patients who had undergone surgery that cut the corpus callosum, thus severing the communication that would normally take place between the left and right hemispheres of the brain. After this operation patients are said to have a "split brain." One experiment by Sperry and his colleagues showed that the major effect of the separation of the two hemispheres occurs in speech and cognition, but not necessarily in emotion. If a subject with a severed corpus callosum is presented with slides showing a series of geometric figures with a slide showing a picture of a nude placed among them, and if this is presented to the left visual field, something unusual happens. If subjects are asked what they saw, they report that they saw nothing but a flash of light. But during the next few trials, they may grin or blush or giggle. If they are asked about the giggling or smiling, they have no idea why they are doing it. Sperry suggested that this emotion of embarrassment may be transmitted across the brainstem, but the cognitive component, which usually travels by way of the corpus callosum, cannot cross to the verbal hemisphere.

Implications of Split-Brain Research. The importance of this research for psychology is not that it presents a possible cure for epilepsy. In fact, since the technique was introduced, there have been only a few dozen such operations. Rather, this research supports a belief among some psychologists that the "mind" and consciousness emerge from the func-

---

Dissociate. Shutting out or separating one aspect of consciousness from another.

Split-brain research. Research done on subjects who, for medical reasons, have had their cerebral hemispheres surgically separated by cutting the corpus callosum; the unconnected cerebral hemispheres afterwards appear to function somewhat separately and differently.

tions of the brain. As demonstrated in Sperry's experiments, brain functions in specific hemispheres controlled what the person reported being aware of. This has led to the speculation that certain forms of mental disorders might be related to hemispheric differences. Since the left hemisphere of the brain seems closely linked to language and verbal/symbolic problem-solving skills, and since the behavior of schizophrenics suggest that many of their thoughts, words, and concepts have no real anchor in the physical world, they may be the victims of an over-aroused left hemisphere. This is just speculation, but it is a reasonable hypothesis given what we know about the two brain hemispheres.

Although results of the split-brain research might give you the idea that each hemisphere does something completely unique, that would be an oversimplification. Even though the right hemisphere does not ordinarily "speak" (a left-brain "function"), it does *understand* language. In the same way, while the right hemisphere might be the one that appreciates simple melodies, the left hemisphere is better suited to the analysis of complex music. There are differences between the two hemispheres when they are examined independently, as in split-brain research, but they are best characterized as interacting components. They do not work against each other or act in a parallel fashion. Normally, their actions are coordinated through the corpus callosum.

A Question of Dominance. The question that emerges from these applications is the possible dominance of one hemisphere over the other. Unless there has been some accident or illness, most of us have hemispheres that can communicate freely with each other. But there is still the distinct possibility that one hemisphere is more powerful or dominant than the other and that hemispheric dominance can vary among individuals. If that is the case, people would have different skills and preferences, depending on their dominant hemisphere. "Left-brain types" would be verbal, rational, abstract, and analytical; "right-brain types" would be visual/spatial, concrete, intuitive, and holistic (Bogen, 1977). A warning against such typecasting should be presented here. It is tempting to think that there are various independent "selves" bottled up inside each of us. In the simplest case, there would be the left-brain self and the right-brain self. This

type of thinking about "self" is not justified. The concept of self is tied to personality. As you will see in Chapter 13, a personality is, by definition, an integrated pattern of behavior. We are no more likely to have independent "selves" than we are to have multiple personalities. Split-brain research demonstrates very clearly that most of our behavior is the result of complex organization. When this normal organization breaks down, behavior changes substantially.

Levels of Consciousness

We have seen that there is nothing at all dull about the normal waking state. In this state, the two hemispheres of the brain are processing information in unique ways and are communicating through several pathways at the same time. We can think of this activity as characteristic of one level or state of consciousness; but in the course of a day we pass through many different states of consciousness, which can vary substantially.

Since consciousness plays such an important role in behavior, levels of consciousness have attracted the interest of many researchers. Some have suggested that consciousness is really on a continuum, which runs from very low levels of **arousal** to very high levels. Figure 5–5 presents an example of what such an arousal continuum might look like. As you can see from this figure, meditation is associated with low states of arousal and anxiety or schizophrenic behavior is associated with high states of arousal. You can also see that some types of behavior are more likely to occur in one state than in another. For example, we would expect creative thought to occur in states of heightened arousal. The nature and efficiency of our thinking seem to change with changing levels of arousal; this suggests that arousal level may somehow be involved in our experience of consciousness. You have certainly experienced the difficulty of concentrating when highly aroused, and can recognize that as a very different level of consciousness from the one you experience when you are sitting in a quiet room reading a novel.

This relationship between level of arousal and states of consciousness can also be seen in the *efficiency* of behavior. The connection was first noted

---

Arousal. General state of alertness.

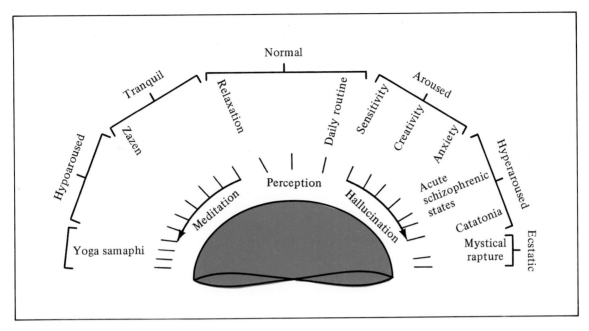

FIGURE 5-5

This figure shows the different levels of consciousness or arousal that a person can be in. It goes from the low levels of arousal achieved through different types of meditation, to the high levels of arousal characteristic of schizophrenic states. (Fischer, 1971)

FIGURE 5-6

This graph shows relationships between arousal and performance. In a difficult task, arousal is useful up to a point, but then it actually works against you and makes the task harder to do.

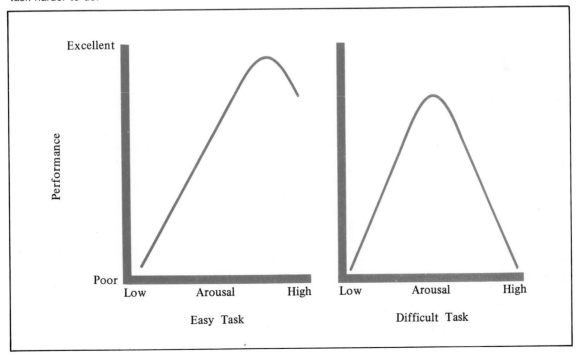

by Yerkes and Dodson in 1908. They had been experimenting with mice, teaching them to tell the difference between various shapes and to choose the correct one. They punished the mice with shock for making incorrect choices. Shock has a clear effect on arousal level; the more intense the shock, the higher the level of arousal. Yerkes and Dodson discovered that there was an upside-down-U shaped relationship between shock intensity and learning speed when the choice to be made by the mice was a difficult one. When the choice was an easy one, the relationship was a straight linear one. Figure 5–6 shows these relationships.

This graph shows that in difficult tasks, arousal is useful to a point, but then it becomes counterproductive. You must have noticed this effect in your own behavior. Think of a time when you were taking a difficult exam and were very anxious. You may have made some serious mistakes in judgment (such as the answer you chose) or neglected to do something simple but important (such as putting your name on the answer sheet or recording your answers to the last five questions). This was because your state of arousal had pushed you beyond a level of peak or optimal performance. In this case, the performance was cognitive (taking a test), but it easily could have been physical (a race, dart-throwing, or table tennis). Test anxiety is a very common example of the arousal/performance relationship among high-school and college students. The arousal is clearly the cause of the poor performance, since the student can answer the questions perfectly immediately after the examination. It seems as if sometimes we can be too aroused or motivated for our own good.

Research has shown that the effect of increased arousal on performance will depend on the difficulty of the task (Hokanson, 1969). We saw earlier that levels of awareness could be altered in epileptics through surgical procedures. Arousal theory proposes that levels of awareness or consciousness can vary for *any* individual on a daily basis, and that these variations have implications for behavior.

■ SUMMARY

1. *Drugs* are any substances that can produce alterations in our physical and mental functioning.

Familiar substances like caffeine, alcohol, and nicotine are drugs, as well as substances like marijuana, cocaine, and LSD. Drugs have their primary effects by interfering with, acting like, or exaggerating the effects of naturally-occurring neurotransmitters.

2. Drugs affect neurotransmission in one or more ways: They can (a) decrease the amount of neurotransmitter that is released; (b) block or clog the receptor site; (c) mimic or act as substitute neurotransmitters; and (d) prolong the release of neurotransmitters.

3. Five major classes of *psychoactive drugs* are depressants, stimulants, hallucinogens, marijuana and hashish, and psychotherapeutic drugs. When a person develops a *physical dependence* on a drug, a certain amount of a drug is needed to function normally; without the drug *withdrawal symptoms* occur. These can include muscle cramps, vomiting, and restlessness. A drug *tolerance* occurs when, with repeated use, the same amount of the drug will produce smaller and smaller effects. *Psychological dependence* occurs when a person has learned certain associations between the use of a drug and particular changes in the body.

4. *Depressants* reduce awareness of and response to outside stimuli. *Opiates* produce an intensely pleasurable sense of well-being, reduce pain, and control diarrhea and coughing. These drugs have a strong tendency to produce both psychological and physical dependence. *Sedatives* are man-made drugs that may be used in low doses to produce relaxation or to decrease anxious behavior. At higher doses they may be used as sleeping pills. Psychological dependence is common with these drugs. At *blood alcohol level (BAL)* 0.10 percent, the level defining intoxication in most states, the average person's reaction time and judgment are clearly impaired. Alcohol is by far the most dangerous drug, as it is associated with violent crimes and fatal accidents.

5. *Stimulants* work on the CNS by lowering the threshold for action potentials. Their effect is to increase the arousal and general activity of the autonomic nervous system. Common stimulants include *cocaine, amphetamines,* and *caffeine.*

6. *Hallucinogens* produce major alterations in visual perception and enhance emotionality. These drugs produce no apparent physical or psychological dependence, but they can cause terrible fright reac-

tions. Angel dust, or PCP, has more dangerous side effects, such as altered perception of pain and the tendency for users to develop psychological dependence.

7. Marijuana and hashish have different effects at different dosage levels: at low levels they have effects similar to alcohol, while at high levels their effects more closely resemble those of hallucinogens. THC, the active ingredient in these drugs, increases heartrate, decreases blood pressure, alters perception, and produces euphoria and relaxation. THC also affects motor coordination and reflexes, and impairs memory for material encountered under its influence.

8. Psychotherapeutic drugs—*antipsychotics* and *antidepressants*—have helped to reduce the resident populations of mental institutions.

9. Until recently only a physical dependence was viewed as a drug addiction. Research with both animal and human addicts has shown that physical dependence can be of secondary importance in maintaining a drug addiction.

10. Factors such as availability of a drug and social influences may be responsible for both first use and continued use of a drug during a person's history of drug use. Positive effects of the drug may be offset by other negative forces, including possible punishments.

11. Alcohol abuse is the most serious substance-abuse problem in our society and a particularly challenging one for researchers. There does not appear to be any clear dividing line between misuse of alcohol and alcoholism.

12. Alcoholics Anonymous (AA) is the most popular single treatment for alcoholism. The AA program implies that the alcoholic has a kind of "allergy" to alcohol that may include physical or psychological factors, or both. According to AA, the only treatment for alcoholism is total abstinence. A problem with the AA philosophy is that problem drinkers may not be willing to define themselves as alcoholics. Some critics feel the AA view may become a self-fulfilling prophecy for the alcoholic who believes he or she will experience a total "loss of control" when exposed to alcohol. Despite problems, AA is effective.

13. *Sleep* consists of a sequence of stages that involves systematic changes in brain activity. The first stage, relaxed wakefulness, is characterized by low-voltage, high-frequency brain waves called *alpha*

waves, and is in contrast to those typical of normal wakefulness, *beta waves.* Deep sleep is characterized by *rapid eye movements (REM),* which indicate dream activity. During each sleep episode, we pass through several cycles of drowsiness from *NREM (non-REM)* to REM sleep, each cycle lasting about 90 minutes. Research suggests that there may be similar 90-minute cycles in waking states that include daydreaming.

14. One explanation for the need for sleep is that it is a period when the body can recover from the day's activities. This explanation does not account for individual differences in the amount of sleep needed, the fact that longer periods without sleep do not result in the need for longer sleep periods, and the fact that after strenuous activity our need for sleep is no greater than after less strenuous activity. Depriving subjects of REM periods results in the lengthening of later REM periods, commonly referred to as the *REM rebound effect.* Also, there seems to be a relationship between cognitive activity and REM sleep. NREM sleep may have a physically restorative effect. These relationships need to be further researched, however.

15. The adaptive explanation for sleep suggests that a biochemical clock controls our activity levels so that consciousness occurs in cycles that correspond to light/dark cycles.

16. One sleep disturbance is *insomnia,* or the chronic inability to obtain adequate sleep due to being unable to fall asleep, to waking up frequently, or to waking up early in the morning. The effect of sleeping pills is to cut down on REM sleep, resulting in increased awakenings during the night. As the body becomes adapted to the pills, sleeping without them becomes more difficult. Behavioral treatments of insomnia involve using relaxation techniques before a sleep period, and rearranging the person's environment and schedule to make sleep more likely.

17. *Narcolepsy* is an irresistible urge to sleep no matter what the time of day or the circumstances. During narcoleptic attacks, the person is usually in a stage of REM sleep, so the cause of the problem may be connected to some mechanism responsible for REM. Full understanding and successful treatment have yet to be found.

18. Disturbance of sleep/wake cycles can occur because of flights across time zones, illness, and

working shifts that are in conflict with a person's biological clock.

19. Everyone has several *dreams* during the night, but not everyone remembers them. Freud's view was that threatening or important dreams are repressed because they would cause difficulty in the waking mind.

20. *Meditation* is an attempt to move from the kind of thinking that involves problem-solving to the kind of thinking that involves fantasy. *Concentrative meditation* involves focusing attention on one thing and blocking out distracting elements in the environment. The technique involved in *Transcendental Meditation (TM)* uses the repetition of the *mantram*, repeating one sound over and over again. The Zen meditation device is called a *koan*, a logical impossibility stated as a riddle used to free the mind for imaginative thinking.

21. *Hypnotic induction* is a technique that usually involves relaxation and focusing techniques and is used to put someone in a hypnotic trance. Characteristics used as criteria for the evidence of a hypnotic trance include increased *suggestibility*, improved visual imagery, decreased desire for self-initiation of action, and acceptance of distortions of reality. The existence of the *hidden observer effect* supports the view that hypnotic states represent unusual states of consciousness. One problem with the use of *hypnosis* to aid memory is that under hypnosis, a person is highly suggestible and the hypnotist may inadvertently alter the person's memory.

22. A problem in studying hypnosis and meditation is that studies have failed to show physiological differences that would allow researchers to distinguish between control subjects and those in a meditative trance or under hypnosis. This failure may be due to a lack of sufficient methods of measurement or analysis. Another possibility is that hypnosis and meditation may be states of emergent consciousness, rather than some static condition; or these two states may involve the individual's *dissociation* from traditional objective reality.

23. Split-brain subjects are subjects who, for medical reasons, have had their cerebral hemispheres cut at the corpus callosum and who subsequently show differences between the two hemispheres when these hemispheres are examined separately. *Split-brain research* demonstrates that most of our behavior is the result of complex organization and lends support to the belief that mind and consciousness emerge from the functions of the brain.

24. Some theorists suggest that consciousness is a continuum that runs from very low levels of arousal to very high levels. Arousal level is related to the efficiency of behavior in such a way that too high a level can be as counterproductive as too low a level.

■ ANSWERING QUESTIONS FOR THOUGHT

1. Withdrawal symptoms are physical effects, such as muscle cramps, vomiting, and restlessness, that occur when a person is deprived of a drug on which he or she has become physically dependent.

2. Amphetamines and related drugs have been used as "diet pills" to curb appetite, but they have only a slight effect, to which tolerance develops within a week or two.

3. A behavior that is rewarded quickly will be learned more quickly than one that is rewarded only after some time has passed. Thus, for example, heroin that is injected and has a rapid effect is more addictive than heroin taken by mouth, which takes longer to have an effect.

4. After a certain point is reached in a waking state, you don't get "more tired." And you can often make up for long periods of little or no sleep in one night. What happens during that make-up period of sleep is that you spend much more time in REM sleep than you usually would.

5. There are two major treatment approaches to insomnia: chemical and behavioral. Certain types of insomnia can be treated with specific drugs, such as antidepressants or progesterone. (This does not include sleeping pills, which generally create more problems than they solve.) The behavioral treatment involves learning relaxation techniques and better habits connected with sleeping. Some of these include using the bed only for sleeping, not going to bed until you feel tired enough to sleep, and getting up at the same time every morning so that a regular sleep rhythm is established.

6. This is a controversial issue. Some researchers say that the act of questioning a witness under hypnosis actually creates memories that did not exist before. The person will believe that he or she is tell-ing the truth, but in fact will be responding to the suggestions made while hypnotized. Others feel that memories cannot be permanently altered by hypnosis, and that it makes no difference whether a witness has been hypnotized or not.

6 Learning Principles

QUESTIONS FOR THOUGHT

1. Does learning always result in successful performance?
2. Why do you still get nervous in a dentist's waiting room?
3. Is spanking a child who has just fingerpainted the bathroom effective? Will it have any harmful side effects?
4. Why does money have such a powerful influence in our lives even though we can't drink it or eat it?
5. How do circus animals learn to jump through hoops and do other such tricks?
6. Why do people keep playing at slot machines and lotteries?
7. Is experience the *only* way to learn?

The answers to these questions are at the end of the chapter.

Several years ago in Milwaukee, a man splashed gasoline on his wife and set her on fire. After he was arrested, he explained that he got the idea from a TV movie called "The Burning Bed" in which a man had set his wife on fire. In Cathlamet, Washington, a young woman was driving friends home from a dance when her car veered off the road into a stream, landing on its roof in three feet of water. She could not open the door to escape but remembered seeing a similar incident on a television show called "CHIPS," a series about the California Highway Patrol, in which the victim opened the window and crawled out to safety. She used the same strategy and successfully escaped with her friends. While the first event is horrifying and the second is exhilarating, they both occurred as a result of learning. In this chapter, we will consider many of the principles that facilitate learning. In addition, we will consider a number of other examples that will help to illustrate the central role that learning plays in everyday behavior.

In a way, most of what you have read so far in this book has been a preparation for this chapter. Learning is involved in virtually every area of human behavior. For instance, as you discovered in the chapter on perception, we learn to perceive our environment in particular ways. Since our perceptual habits in turn affect what we choose to sense, learning affects sensation as well. As we will see, learning also plays a major role in the development of both children and adults and is at the root of many personality characteristics. In fact, most of our social behavior is learned. Consequently, clinical psychologists spend a good deal of time trying to get people to *unlearn* certain behavior patterns that produce anxiety, depression, and tension. Clearly, the process

by which we learn about ourselves and our environment is a key that unlocks the puzzle of behavior.

Like many other human characteristics, learning is vital for the preservation of the species: It is the basis for adaptability or flexibility in behavior. We need to be adaptable because for all practical purposes we do not have direct control over our environment. For example, we can't make it rain or snow, we can't effectively control whether a phone will ring, and we can't prevent a truck coming down the street from running over us while we wait to cross. Given that we can't make the world behave the way we want it to, the next best thing is to predict what will happen. Most of us can take advantage of the information provided by the weather report and carry an umbrella when rain is forecast. We also know that the best way to keep from hearing a phone ringing is to go where there are no phones. Most of us also realize that the probability of being squashed by a truck is reduced if we stand on the curb, not in the street.

All these predictions are instances of learning. We were not born with an innate understanding of phones or rain or trucks. Over some period of time we *learned* what kind of role each of these stimuli plays in our lives. Furthermore, we learned to adapt to their presence. We developed behavior patterns that help us survive and flourish in a world that has trucks, telephones, and rain.

The question is not really *if* we learn, it is *how* and *what* we learn. Many different theories have been proposed to explain learning. Since we find ourselves in many different situations with many different things to learn, these theories differ according to what is being learned. For example, theories that try to explain how we learn to swing a golf club will differ from theories that try to explain how we learn a foreign language. In this chapter, we will look at various learning theories. In the next chapter, we will consider some extensions and practical applications of these theories. These two chapters should provide us with the background and understanding necessary to consider issues such as cognitive development, stress, sexuality, personality, abnormal behavior, and just about every kind of behavior that is of interest to the psychologist.

■ CATS AND RATS AND PEOPLE

As we examine research and theories of learning, you will notice that most of the research is with animals. Some favorite animals in learning experiments are rats, pigeons, cats, dogs, and gerbils. (The animal of choice for human experiments seems to be the college sophomore, especially those taking Introductory Psychology.) Animals are used for many reasons. Most important, it is easier to control animals' experiences outside of the learning laboratory. The experimenter doesn't have to worry whether a rat just had a fight with its mate, or spent the previous evening drinking, or is trying to "outpsych" the experimenter.

In the 100 or so years during which learning research has been conducted, it has become obvious that many of the mechanisms that explain animal learning seem to apply to humans as well. This doesn't mean that humans are the same as rats or cats; it simply means that we can use what we know about animal learning as a point of departure for considering human learning. We will take this approach in this chapter.

Defining Learning

Before continuing, we had better define learning. One common definition that will serve us well is as follows: **Learning** *is a relatively permanent change in behavior potential that comes about through experience and is not a direct result of body states such as fatigue or illness.* Most experts on learning would accept this definition, although different experts might emphasize different aspects (Hall, 1982; Hergenhahn, 1982).

This definition has several important parts that

we should consider briefly. First, the definition specifies that learning is *relatively* permanent. That is to say, it is not a temporary phenomenon. This is an important distinction because we can think of temporary states that affect performance but have nothing to do with learning. Consider the example of dialing an unfamiliar phone number. Many people go through a predictable sequence to accomplish this task. They look up the number and—since there is never a pen or pencil around when you need one—repeat the number to themselves over and over until they successfully dial it. By repeating the number while dialing, they are able to "perform" the dialing task. It is tempting to assume that they "learned" the phone number. In most cases, this assumption is incorrect, because the next time it is necessary to dial that same number, they will probably go through the same process again. Therefore, the number wasn't learned. A brief rather than permanent change in behavior occurred.

The "relative" permanence of learning is important: We must be able to modify or change what has been learned for two reasons. First, as we will see shortly, we can learn things that are wrong or ineffective just as well or quickly as we can learn things that are correct. Therefore, it is important that we be able to change learned patterns. Second, some aspects of the environment change frequently. These changes require us to develop new or modified habits or behaviors to replace old ones that are no longer appropriate. You can imagine what the world would be like if once you learned some behavior, that behavior was then permanent! As an example, remember when you were a child and you learned to put your coat on by laying it on the floor, putting your arms in the sleeve holes, and flipping the coat over your head? That technique might draw some stares if you tried it at an exclusive restaurant after reaching adulthood. Therefore, the *relative* permanence of learning is essential, although it can have an inconvenient side—as we will see in the chapter on memory, we occasionally forget what we have learned!

A second part of the definition that we need to consider is the phrase "in behavior potential." We cannot see learning take place directly; in a sense, we must *guess* that learning has taken place from observing behavior. Contrast this with our earlier discussion of sensation. We can actually measure an electrical impulse traveling along the visual or

We cannot see learning take place directly; in a sense, we must guess that learning has taken place from observing behavior—in this case, a test.

auditory pathway to the brain; we can tell when a receptor has fired; we know when sensation occurs. We cannot measure learning in this way. Even if we had some magical machine such as a "learning meter," we wouldn't know where or when to hook it up! Instead, we look for changes in behavior as evidence that learning has occurred. Take your class as an example. Imagine that your instructor has given you a test of your knowledge about learning principles before presenting a lecture on the topic. After you have listened to the lecture, you are tested again on your knowledge of learning principles. The difference between your first score and your second score is used as proof that you have learned something (assuming that the second score is higher than the first). In this instance, we are inferring that learning has taken place from changes in your behavior (test performance), not by measuring the activity of some physical structure like an eye or an area of the brain. The tests tell us if and how much learning has occurred, which is why tests play such a large role in assessing the effects of various training and instructional methods. But even though someone has learned a response and is capable of executing it, it still may not occur. Thus, it is im-

portant to distinguish between behavior and behavior *potential*. We will consider this distinction in some detail when we discuss the difference between learning and performance.

The final part of the definition that we need to consider is the phrase "through experience." In considering learning, we will ignore things like reflexes. Sneezing is a reflexive behavior—that is, an automatic reaction to an environmental stimulus—that we do not normally learn how to do. We should also contrast this type of learning with strictly maturational changes—changes brought about by growth or physical development. By *experience* we mean trial, observation, practice, or rehearsal.

Learning and Performance

Let's return briefly to the distinction between behavior and behavior potential before we go on. Since we can only infer learning from behavior, the distinction between learning (behavior potential)

Learning. A relatively permanent change in behavior potential that comes about through experience and is not a direct result of body states such as fatigue or illness.

and performance (or behavior) is often fuzzy. But there is a difference. If performance is to be used as an indication of learning, the learning must come first. Learning and performance cannot be identical. In other words, learning is the precondition for many instances of performance. There are two things to keep in mind about this relationship: Not all performance is a result of learning, and not all learning will result in an observable performance. To return to the telephone example, the dialing task was not performed because the phone number had been "learned" (since it is not "permanent"). This is an example of performance without learning. Examples of learning not manifested in performance are common: On opening night, the actor is paralyzed by fear and cannot speak lines that he knows as well as his own name. He has studied them for 2 months and he delivered those same lines perfectly 15 minutes ago backstage. Similarly, students who have learned geometry theorems may "freeze" on a test of those principles and perform poorly. Learning occurred, but it is not obvious from the actor's performance or the student's performance. The point is that although we must infer learning from performance, the two should not be confused.

■ CLASSICAL CONDITIONING

Pavlov's Discoveries

Ivan Pavlov was a Russian physiologist who was interested in digestive systems. To examine the effect of salivation on digestion, he used meat powder to produce salivation in dogs. During the course of these experiments, Pavlov noticed that the dogs often salivated when they heard his footsteps. He reasoned that they made an **association** between his approach and the meat powder. Since footsteps accompanied his approach (and the presentation of the meat powder), the dogs came to associate his footsteps with meat powder, and thus salivated when they heard him approach. This was the same response (salivation) the dogs had originally shown to the presentation of the meat powder itself.

As a result of his observations of this "accidental" salivation, Pavlov set out to study more carefully the conditions under which this salivation occurred. He developed a special harness that held the dog still during the experiments, which were conducted in a quiet room to eliminate distractions (and unwanted associations as well). Since salivation was the behavior being examined, Pavlov surgically attached a tube directly to the salivary gland of the dog so that accurate measures of saliva flow could be taken. He also developed a device to dispense food to the food pan of the dog. Finally, he selected several different stimuli for these studies. The original stimulus that caused the dogs' response was the sound of footsteps. Instead of footsteps he substituted bells, buzzers, lights, and other physical stimuli. A drawing of the apparatus he used is shown in Figure 6-1.

In his first observations, Pavlov had identified several elements that seemed to play a role in this unexpected salivation. First, of course, there was the meat powder; in addition, there were the footsteps. But since the salivation could result from either the meat powder or the footsteps, he found it necessary to distinguish between the two different occasions for salivation (first to meat powder, then to the sound of footsteps). In his experiments, he came to think of stimuli as either unconditioned or conditioned. An **unconditioned stimulus (US)** was one that produced a reliable response of a particular kind every time the stimulus was presented. Thus, every time meat powder was placed in the mouth of a dog, salivation occurred. There were no (or at least few) conditions when this would not happen. The meat powder was the US. The salivation that occurred in the presence of the US was called the **unconditioned response (UR)**. In contrast, a **conditioned stimulus (CS)** was one that produced a response only in special conditions. In Pavlov's experiments, the condition that gave the footsteps their power was the repeated pairings between footsteps and meat powder. The footsteps represented the conditioned stimulus (CS). The salivation that was produced by the footsteps alone was called the **conditioned response (CR)**. **Classical conditioning** can be defined as learning that occurs through the repeated pairing of an unconditioned stimulus (US) (such as meat powder) with a conditioned stimulus (CS) (such as footsteps) to produce a conditioned response (CR) (such as salivation). This type of learning came to be called *classical conditioning* because it was the standard or classical way to study learning during the late-nineteenth century.

Pavlov's classical conditioning experiments were quite simple. He presented a specific sound—a

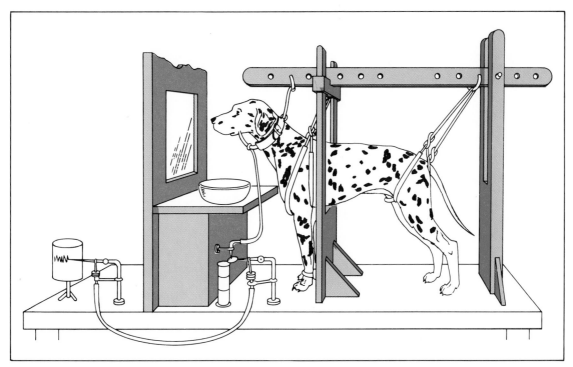

Figure 6-1
This is the apparatus used by Pavlov to study the classical conditioning of salivation in dogs. He devised a special harness to hold the dog quiet while the experiment was being carried out, and a special tube was attached to the salivary gland of the dog so that the amount of salivation could be measured.

bell—shortly before giving the meat powder to the dog. After he had done this many times, the dog began to salivate when it heard the bell—and *before* the meat powder was given. In these experiments, the meat powder was the US, the bell was the CS, the salivation to the meat powder was the UR, and the salivation to the bell was the CR. The bell and the meat powder were paired to cause the CR (salivation). Figure 6-2 sums up the results of Pavlov's experiments.

The procedure that Pavlov developed was both elegant and simple. Using it, he demonstrated that animals could learn to respond to what were originally neutral stimuli under specific conditions; they could be *conditioned*. Human beings can do the

same. Quite accidentally, we become conditioned to many stimuli that were originally neutral because these stimuli are connected in time or space with other stimuli. Consider some of the following examples (see Table 6-1):

1. A child winces when introduced to a new friend of the family who is identified as a dentist.
2. A driver who's been ticketed for speeding is fearful at the sight of a police car.
3. A person who loves pizza salivates at the sight of a neon sign advertising pizza.

Conditioning seems to play an important role in emotions and in abnormal behavior patterns. As a

Association. A connection between two stimuli (sometimes ideas), established through learning or experience.

Unconditioned stimulus. A stimulus that produces a response without learning having taken place.

Unconditioned response. A response to a stimulus that occurs without learning having taken place.

Conditioned stimulus. A neutral stimulus that, through repeated pairings with an unconditioned stimulus, comes to elicit a response when presented all alone.

Conditioned response. A learned response to a conditioned stimulus. Usually similar to, but not as strong as, an unconditioned response.

Classical conditioning. Learning that occurs through the repeated pairing of an unconditioned stimulus with a conditioned stimulus in order to produce a conditioned response.

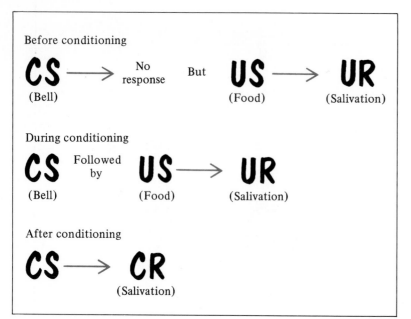

Before conditioning

CS ⟶ No response   But   **US** ⟶ **UR**
(Bell)   (Food)   (Salivation)

During conditioning

CS Followed by **US** ⟶ **UR**
(Bell)   (Food)   (Salivation)

After conditioning

CS ⟶ **CR**
         (Salivation)

Figure 6-2
A diagram showing the relationships between stimuli and responses that occurred during Pavlov's classical conditioning experiment.

result, the principles of conditioning are often used to diagnose emotional or behavioral problems and then to eliminate them. We will consider some of these procedures in detail in Chapter 16.

Making Conditioning More Effective

We do not associate everything in the world with everything else in the world. If we did, life would be one long stream of conditioned responses with no consistency or coherence. Since only *certain* associations tend to be made, there must be special circumstances that are more likely to lead to conditioning than others. The research that followed Pavlov's experiments identified the special circumstances under which effective conditioning

TABLE 6-1.
Some Examples of Common Conditioned Responses

US	CS	UR	CR
Drill	Dentist	Tension	Tension
Ticket	Police Car	Distress	Distress
Pizza	Neon Sign	Salivation	Salivation

might occur. Three conditions seem particularly important.

Frequency of US/CS Pairing. For conditioning to occur, the CS and the US should be paired with some frequency. If the CS is presented often without being paired with the US, or the US without being paired with the CS, conditioning will be reduced. Consider Pavlov's discovery of conditioned salivation. If Pavlov and his assistants had wandered in and out of the room where the dogs were caged 15 times every hour but only fed the animals once a day, footsteps would not have been a particularly important clue to the dogs that meat powder was coming. In this situation, the CS would have been presented many times without being paired with the US. Similarly, if meat powder had been available from an automatic dispenser attached to the wall of the dogs' cage and given out often without the presence of Pavlov or one of his assistants, footsteps would not have acquired any power to produce salivation. In this situation, the US would have been presented frequently without being paired with the CS.

After conditioning has taken place, the frequency of pairing plays a different role. Occasional pairing at that point can be enough to maintain a CR. But early in the conditioning process, frequent pairing of the CS and US usually leads to quicker and stronger conditioning.

Order of Presentation. For conditioning to occur, the CS must come *before* the US. In Pavlov's experiments, a cage with a dog in it could have been brought, by means of a conveyor belt, into a room where the experimenter was already seated. After placing meat powder in the mouth of the dog, the experimenter could then have then walked out of the room. Under these circumstances, footsteps would not have produced salivation in the dog no matter how many times they followed the presentation of the meat powder. Instead, the noise of the conveyor belt as it started up could have become a CS. The footsteps would not predict anything, but the conveyor belt noise would.

Timing of the CS/US Presentation. The best circumstance for conditioning to occur is if the conditioned stimulus is presented *slightly* before the unconditioned stimulus. The longer the interval between the two stimuli, the weaker the conditioning. In Pavlov's original observation, the time between the stopping of the footsteps and the placing of the food powder on the dog's tongue was perhaps a matter of seconds. If the lab attendant had walked into the laboratory and stood in front of the cage for several hours before giving the dog the meat powder, it is unlikely the dog would have associated footsteps with meat powder—possibly a bored look on the face of the assistant would have become the CS, but not footsteps.

Extinction and Spontaneous Recovery

Conditioned responses do not last forever. Eventually, a CS may lose its power to elicit a CR. When this happens, we say that the CR has been extinguished, and the process by which this occurs is called **extinction.** You saw that three elements are important for conditioning to occur: the frequency of CS/US pairing, the order of the CS/US presentation, and the time between the presentation of the CS and the US. These three elements can also be used to extinguish a CR. If we stop pairing the CS and US, if we reverse the order of the presentation of the CS and US, or if we insert long time periods

between the presentation of the CS and US, extinction will occur. In a sense, extinction occurs because one or more of the principles for effective conditioning has been violated.

You might think that extinction of a response means the response has been forgotten. This is not the case. In another of Pavlov's experiments, dogs that had originally devloped a CR of salivating to the sound of the bell were exposed to the bell alone for many trials. No meat powder followed the sound

---

Extinction. Eliminating the association between a conditioned stimulus and an unconditioned stimulus by no longer presenting them together, or by presenting the US before the CS.

of the bell. Eventually, the bell no longer resulted in salivating. In other words, the CR seemed to be extinguished. But then came the curious part. A period of time passed when *neither* the CS (the bell) nor the US (the meat powder) was presented. At the end of this period, if the CS (the bell) was again presented, a CR (salivation) would appear. Evidently the dogs had not forgotten that the US had *once* followed the CS. This reappearance of the conditional response was called **spontaneous recovery.**

It is not difficult to see examples of spontaneous recovery in everyday life. For instance, modern dentistry has elimanated a good deal of the pain that you may have experienced as a child. You may have had a number of dental visits with no pain (CS with no US). Nevertheless, if you have not been to a dentist's office for several years, when you first enter the waiting room (the CS), your stomach will probably feel as queasy (the CR) as it did when you were a child.

Stimulus Generalization and Discrimination

Often, conditioned responses are made to stimuli similar to the CS. In Pavlov's experiments, if a bell or buzzer with a different sound was used on one trial instead of the usual bell or buzzer, a salivation response occurred anyway. The response was not as intense as the one elicited by the usual bell, but it was a salivation response. In a sense, the dog was responding to a sound that had never really been paired with the meat powder. This is an example of **stimulus generalization.** Stimulus generalization is the appearance of a CR to a stimulus other than the CS. Stimulus generalization seems to depend on the similarity between the CS and the other stimulus. The more similar the other stimulus is to the CS, the more likely it is that a CR will appear when this other stimulus is presented.

You will remember from Chapter 1 that John B. Watson, one of the early behaviorists, was interested in the effect of environmental associations on learning. In pursuit of this interest, he conducted an experiment with a 11-month-old infant who has come to be known as "Little Albert" (Watson and Rayner, 1920). Watson was interested in demonstrating that emotional behavior was learned. He decided to do this by demonstrating that a neutral stimulus could become unpleasant or **aversive** through conditioning. The neutral stimulus was a white rat. Initially, Little Albert was not afraid of the rat; he showed a willingness to touch and play with it. The experiment consisted of standing behind Albert and hitting a steel bar with a hammer every time he reached for the rat. Needless to say, this came as something of a shock to the child. In fact, it was such a shock that the first time the pairing occurred, he fell forward on his face and began to cry. Each time Albert reached for the rat, the experimenter hit the bar with the hammer. Albert quickly decided that rats were not good playmates. Eventually, he would cry at the mere sight of the rat. So far, this was just another classical conditioning study (although somewhat more sadistic): the CS was the rat; the US was the sound made by striking the bar; the UR was the crying after the hammer struck the bar; and the CR was the crying in the presence of the rat. After the conditioning was completed, it was discovered that in addition to rats, Albert was afraid of a Santa Claus mask, a rabbit, a dog, a fur coat, and cotton. If any one of these wsa presented, Albert began to cry. Each of these stimuli had become a CS—a clear instance of stimulus generalization. Crying appeared in response to stimuli that had never been part of the conditioning experiment but were similar to the CS.

Stimulus generalization is part of our daily life. We often respond to a neutral stimulus as if it were a CS. In other words, we act as if we have had experience with the stimulus even though we have not. People with strong fears about broad classes of objects are thought to be the victims of stimulus generalization. A person who was once lost in a crowd as a child may remain uneasy in groups of people even as an adult. A person who was once stuck in an elevator for a long period of time may become uneasy in many different types of small closed spaces.

Some laboratory studies of stimulus generalization have come to the conclusion that generalization is really the failure to correctly make a **discrimination** between two stimuli (Kalish, 1956; Thomas and Mitchell, 1962). Thus, Little Albert failed to discriminate between a Santa Claus mask and a white rat; people afraid of closed spaces fail to discriminate between an elevator and other small rooms. But this explanation may be too simple. According to trichromatic theory, discussed in Chapter 3 in reference to color vision, specific chemicals in the eye react differently to various colors. In studies using color as a stimulus, the interaction of these chemicals would be part of the explanation of stimulus generalization. Thus, in the case of color perception, it would be incorrect to say that stimulus generalization was simply a failure to discriminate. Hall (1982) suggests at least three different explanations for stimulus generalization: (1) in some instances there is a physiological basis (e.g., color vision), (2) it is influenced by prior discrimination training, and (3) it may result from the method that subjects have learned to categorize stimuli (e.g., all orientals "look the same"; little Albert placed all white fur-like stimuli in the same category). It appears that stimulus generalization is a complex phenomenon, but one that is heavily involved in everyday learning and behavior.

REVIEW QUESTIONS

5. Extinction means breaking the association between which of the following:
   a. CS and the US   c. US and the UR
   b. CS and the CR   d. US and the CR

6. Even after extinction has occurred, a CS may still bring about a CR at a later time; this phenomenon is called _____ _____ .

7. Watson taught Little Albert to fear rats by pairing a loud noise with the sight of a rat. The fact that Little Albert, as a result of this conditioning, also feared rabbits, dogs, Santa Claus masks, and cotton is an example of _____ _____ .

Answers: 5. a **6.** spontaneous recovery **7.** stimulus generalization.

■ OPERANT CONDITIONING

Pavlov was a physiologist whose major interest was the digestive system. He designed his conditioning experiments using dogs as subjects. Although his research was thereby limited in nature, it nonetheless gave us important insights into how learning occurs. It showed us that animals are capable of forming associations between stimuli if those stimuli are presented one after another a number of times. This information is important, since much of our everyday life revolves around noticing relationships among objects and events. But in addition to simply noticing certain associations in our immediate environment, we also engage in particular behaviors that change it. These behaviors may be as simple as turning a doorknob to enter another room, or as complicated as instructing a stock broker to sell a block of stock if it reaches a certain value on the stock market. These attempts to "operate on" or change our environment (to change the room we're in or change the level of our bank account) are themselves opportunities for learning. It is this active kind of learning—not the passive learning of noticing associations—that we will look at now.

Because this type of learning focuses on the way people operate on and are active in the environment, it has been called **operant conditioning**. Sometimes it is also known as **instrumental conditioning** because the learned response is useful or instrumental in getting a reward. Like the original work of Pavlov that led to the development of classical conditioning principles, operant conditioning had modest beginnings. At the turn of the century, an American psychologist named Edward Thorndike was studying how animals solved problems. Like many American psychologists of that period, he was a functionalist. That is, he was interested in how organisms learned to adjust to environmental demands.

Thorndike began his studies using cats. He would place a hungry cat in a wooden box (called a "puzzle

---

Spontaneous recovery. The reappearance of a conditioned response after it has been extinguished.

Stimulus generalization. Responding in a similar way to stimuli other than the conditioned stimulus.

Aversive stimulus. An unpleasant or painful stimulus, such as an electric shock.

Discrimination. Learning to respond to only one of many similar stimuli.

Operant or **instrumental conditioning.** Learning that occurs as a result of association of a response followed by reinforcement.

box") and a piece of fish outside that box. The cat would then be faced with the challenge of getting out of the box in order to eat the fish. Different boxes had different ways for the cat to get out. In the box portrayed in Figure 6–3 the solution was for the cat to open the door by stepping on the wooden treadle. At first, the cat would try to push between the slats of the box. Then, it would bite or claw at the door. Eventually, it would investigate the treadle and push it. The door would open and the cat would leave the box and eat the fish. Having solved the problem once, the cat would quickly go to the treadle the next time it was put in the box.

Having watched cats solve many similar problems, Thorndike began to refer to this type of learning as trial and error learning. He developed some principles of learning that seemed to describe his observations. The best known of these has been called the *Law of Effect*. It can be stated very simply:

Responses followed by satisfaction will be more likely to occur again in a similar situation. Responses followed by dissatisfaction or frustration will be less likely to occur again in a similar situation. The greater the satisfaction, the greater the probability of the response occurring again in a similar situation. The greater the annoyance, frustration, or dissatisfaction,

the lower the probability of the response occurring again in a similar situation.

As you can see, Thorndike was just as interested in associations as Pavlov but studied them in a very different way. In Thorndike's research, the association was made between a situation (e.g., puzzle box) and an active response (e.g., pushing a treadle). It was this response situation that laid the foundation for operant conditioning theory. In addition, it provided the historical foundation for what is often referred to as S–R (stimulus–response) learning.

Association forms the backbone of trial and error learning. The association may be as primitive as the one made by a dog trying to avoid medication (see accompanying box) or the one made by a mechanic who uses the trial and error method of pinpointing a problem in your car's engine. The important point in operant conditioning theory is that once having *made* the association, the organism (dog or human or pigeon) subsequently *uses* that association to operate on the environment in order to receive a reward. Now let's consider operant conditioning from a more scientific perspective.

In the typical operant conditioning experiment, the subject responds freely to various stimuli in the environment. The best example of this type of experiment is one in which an animal (rat, pigeon, or fish) is placed in an experimental apparatus of some type and must learn how to get food. Figure 6–4 gives an example of an experimental compartment that is commonly used in operant conditioning studies with small animals. It is called a "Skinner box" after the person who developed the apparatus, B. F. Skinner. The learning task is to solve the problem of how to get food into the food cup, which can be done by pressing a bar on the cage wall. The animal (let's say, a rat) begins by simply exploring the new environment while the experimenter watches carefully. When the rat makes a move toward the wall where the bar is mounted, the experimenter presses a button and food drops into the cup. Since the rat has not had any food for some period of time before the learning session, this food is important to the rat. The rat now begins to pay closer attention to the food cup. Each time the rat approaches the food cup, another pellet of food is delivered. Eventually, the rat will not leave the area of the food cup. Now the experimenter provides food only when the rat looks at the bar. After the

Figure 6–3

A drawing of one of the original puzzle boxes used by Thorndike in his animal learning studies.

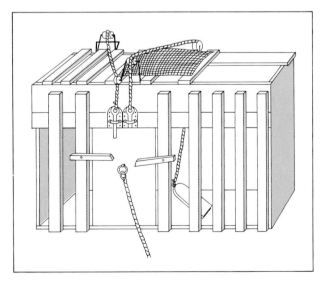

TAKE ONE OF THESE AND CALL ME IN THE MORNING

Thorndike noticed something that any animal owner can tell you: Animals are "clever"—sometimes more clever than their owners. Our dog is an outstanding example. She had developed in infection that required us to give her an antibiotic capsule three times a day. Dogs like to take pills about as much as I like lima beans—which is not at all. The vet tried to be helpful by suggesting that the simplest way to get the dog to take the pill would be to place it on the back of her tongue and hold her mouth closed. That advice avoided the more important issue—how to get her mouth open in the first place. Firefighters use a tool called the "jaws of life" to open car doors that have been buckled shut in auto accidents. "The "jaws of life" would not be able to open the jaws of our dog when she even suspected a pill was coming. We decided that the cleverest way to get her to take the pill would be bury it in some leftovers from the refrigerator. Since she never gets scraps of human food, this would be an unexpected treat.

Our ruse worked reasonably well for a week or so, but one day I ran out of leftovers and used the only food available—applesauce. I put the applesauce in a dish and imbedded the capsule in it. The dog lapped away at the applesause until she encountered the pill. She deftly moved the pill aside with a swipe of the tongue and finished the applesauce. I then made what I would later recognize as the "fatal error": I put *more* applesauce in the bowl and buried the pill once again. For a second time, the dog lapped the applesauce, found the pill, moved it, and finished the food. I gave up for that day, and the next day the supply of leftovers had been replenished. I buried the pill in the middle of a tasty meat and rice mixture, a strategy that had been 100 percent successful previously. The dog began immediately to search the food for the pill. She found it quickly, segregated it from the food, ate the food, and took a step back from the dish so that I could fill it again. I think she was also waiting for a pat and a "good girl" from me. That was the end of the clever pill-giving. From that day on, we had to open each pill and mix the powder with some food to get the antibiotics into her. Just for old times sake, about a week later I tried the "pill in rice" ploy again. She found the pill in no time, moved it aside, ate the food, and looked quite pleased with herself. I suspect that if I try to give her "pill in rice" ten years from now, she will find the pill immediately and move it to the side before eating the food.

Figure 6-4

A Skinner box, the basic apparatus used in operant conditioning. When the rat presses the bar located on the side of the box, the food is delivered to the cup.

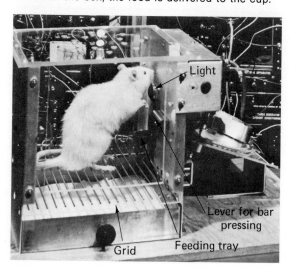

rat learns that response, food is given only when the rat touches the bar with a paw. Next, the rat may be rewarded only when the bar is fully pushed down. Finally, the rat may be given food only after pressing the bar five times rather than just once. At this point, the experimenter can sit back and relax, since the apparatus will automatically dispense the food when the rat presses the bar the required number of times.

In the course of these learning sessions, the rat has "learned" many things: that food is associated with a Skinner box, that food appears in a cup on the wall, and that pressing a bar will result in food appearing in the cup. After the rat has solved the problem of how to get food, it behaves in a very predictable way when placed in the Skinner box for a learning "session." As long as the rat has been deprived of food, it will move immediately to the bar and begin pressing it. Sophisticated rats (veterans of many learning sessions) will place one paw on the bar and press up and down while looking at the food cup to see when food arrives. Clearly the rat has learned, according to our earlier definition: There has been a relatively permanent change in behavior as a result of experience.

Let's look at an experience we humans are more familiar with, and then analyze how learning takes place. For many people, the first day on a new job presents a challenge similar to the one faced by the rat in the Skinner box. The new employee is often given only the most primitive information about the environment—what time to start work and when to stop. The employee shows up at the appointed time and then begins the frustrating task of learning about the environment without having to ask (and possibly looking "new" or stupid). Eventually, he finds the locker room and then the work station. He soon notices that people occasionally wander away for brief periods and then return to their work and assumes that access to the bathrooms is on an "as needed" basis. When the need arises, the employee wanders off in the same direction, only to find that he has discovered the route to the personnel office rather than to the bathroom. When he returns, his supervisor is waiting to find out why he left his machine without giving notice. The next several days include a mix of discovery and error. The supervisor comes around often and makes positive comments about how quickly the employee is learning little things about the job. Each day, the work environment and its procedures become a little more familiar through interaction with the environment. Now the supervisor stops only occasionally to check on the employee's progress and to give a small compliment. The employee has learned about his environment.

Shaping

There are several important things to notice about the "experiment" with the rat. First, the rat did not learn the bar-pressing response immediately. Instead, it learned responses that eventually led to bar pressing. First, it learned where the food was; next, it associated the bar with the food; last, it learned the bar-pressing response. This gradual process is called **shaping**. There are two important aspects to shaping. The first is called **differential reinforcement**. This simply means that certain responses are rewarded or reinforced and not others. In the rat experiment, movement toward the wall with the bar on it was reinforced, and movement away from that wall was not reinforced. Next the rat was reinforced for touching the bar, not for touching the food cup. The rat finally was reinforced for pressing the bar, not for just touching the bar. In each case, one response was reinforced and others were not reinforced.

A second important part of shaping is a process called **successive approximation**. This means that the response that is rewarded gets closer and closer to the desired final response. As you saw in the rat experiment, there was a kind of natural progression from approaching the bar, to touching the bar, to pressing the bar. Each rewarded response came closer to the one really wanted—pressing the bar. Most supervisors act the same way toward new employees. They usually praise even modest success by an employee in the early stages and try not to be too demanding about quality. Gradually, they increase the standard for acceptable work until the

Shaping is used to teach animals complicated tricks. The advantage of this technique is that animals learn quickly.

employee is praised only when he or she reaches a standard of performance that matches that of other experienced workers.

Shaping really has more to do with *how quickly* something is learned rather than *if* it is learned. In our rat example, we could have simply put the rat in the box and waited for it to press the bar. We could have continued to do this for many different learning sessions. Of course, it would have been necessary to keep the rat deprived of food. It might have taken 2 hours, 2 days, or 2 weeks before the rat pressed the bar, but rats, like the cats in Thorndike's puzzle boxes, are active and would continue to explore their immediate environment. Eventually, the correct response would have occurred. When the bar was pressed at last, it might have taken the rat another hour or so before it realized that food was available in the cup. This slow, clumsy process would have been repeated over hours and days and weeks, but eventually the rat would have learned to press the bar. In our other example, a supervisor can ignore new employees and just wait for them to learn on their own what is "acceptable" quality work. This might take several weeks or months instead of several days. The importance of shaping is that learning time is cut down dramatically. We will see other examples of the role of shaping in human learning shortly.

Reinforcement

When the rat presses the bar in the Skinner box, it receives food. This is an example of reinforcement (the food itself is called a "reinforcer"). **Reinforcement** is defined as any event that, presented after a response, increases the probability that the response will be repeated. The rat presses the bar, receives the reinforcer (the food), and as a result is more likely to press the bar again. The reinforcer

has thus increased the probability that the bar-pressing response will be repeated.

Primary and Secondary Reinforcers. There are two types of reinforcers: primary and secondary. **Primary reinforcers** have a direct effect on some physiological state. For example, food is a primary reinforcer, since it directly affects a physiological state called hunger. Water is a primary reinforcer, since it reduces thirst, and rest is a primary reinforcer, since it eliminates physical fatigue. A **secondary reinforcer** acquires power only by association with a primary reinforcer. After this association is built up, secondary reinforcers acquire the power to increase or decrease the probability that a response will occur. A good example of a secondary reinforcer is money. You can't eat dollar bills, but you can buy food (a primary reinforcer) with them. Money becomes a secondary reinforcer as a result of its association with various primary reinforcers.

Methods of Controlling Behavior: Positive Reinforcement, Negative Reinforcement, and Punishment. In operant conditioning there are three basic ways to influence response rate and probability: positive reinforcement, negative reinforcement, and punishment. **Positive reinforcement** means presenting a reinforcer after a particular response, which increases the tendency to make that response again. Praise is a good example of a positive reinforcer. A student answers a question correctly, a teacher praises the student, and the student is more likely to answer a question in the future. **Negative reinforcement** means *taking away* or *stopping* something and, as a result, increasing the probability that a particular response will be repeated. Nagging is a common example of negative reinforcement. The parent nags the child to pick up the toys and clothes; the child picks these things up and the nagging stops.

Shaping. A gradual learning process in which a series of responses are reinforced, each one being closer to the final, desired response.

Differential reinforcement. A technique of shaping in which desired responses are reinforced and others are ignored.

Successive approximation. A technique of shaping in which the response must get closer and closer to the final, desired response in order to be rewarded.

Reinforcement. Any event that, presented after a response, increases the probability that the response will be repeated.

Primary reinforcers. Reinforcers (such as food, water, rest) that

have a direct effect on a physiological state (such as hunger, thirst, fatigue).

Secondary reinforcer. A reinforcer (such as money) that has power only by association with a primary reinforcer (such as food).

Positive reinforcement. Presenting a reinforcer (such as food) after a response, which increases the probability that the response will be repeated.

Negative reinforcement. The stopping or taking away of a reinforcer (such as electric shock) after a response, which increases the probability that the response will be repeated.

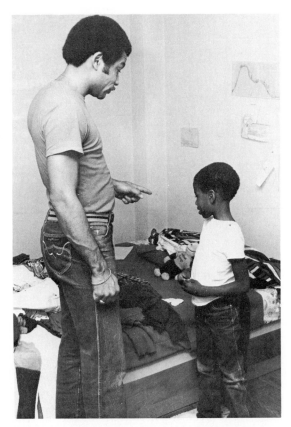

Nagging is an example of negative reinforcement. In this case the father will continue to nag until his son picks up his clothes and toys.

Presumably, the probability that the child will pick up the toys and clothes in the future has been increased. *Punishment* is the presentation of something that will decrease the probability that a particular response will be repeated. Thus, punishment is not a reinforcer at all since it *decreases* the probability of a particular response. When you are caught exceeding the speed limit by a patrol officer, you are issued a ticket. This ticket is an example of punishment, since it is intended to decrease the probability that you will speed in the future. (Punishment is also the taking away or stopping of something pleasant, which decreases the probability that a particular response will be repeated. Thus, in school a punishment for misbehaving might be having certain privileges cancelled for a week. This would have the effect of reducing the probability of misbehaving in the future.)

Each of these methods of controlling behavior—positive reinforcement, negative reinforcement, and punishment—is intended to affect the probability of a response being repeated. The goal in positive and negative reinforcement is to increase the probability; the goal in punishment is to decrease it.

One of the problems with punishment is that it really doesn't tell you what *to* do, it only tells you what *not* to do. So, as a learning mechanism, it is not as useful as either positive or negative reinforcement in pointing out desirable responses. Another problem with punishment is that it is often carried out ineffectively and can have harmful side effects. It can introduce strong, unpleasant emotions to a learning situation that interfere with thinking and remembering; as a result, learning is hampered. In addition, negative associations to the punisher are formed. Since the punishment is a US and will always produce certain emotional reactions (UR), and since the punisher appears slightly before the punishment, there is a pairing of the punisher and

---

REVIEW QUESTIONS

8. In operant conditioning, the learning task is not simply to make associations but to bring about some change in the environment.   T / F

9. One of the main principles of shaping is to reinforce certain responses and not others; this is called _____ _____ .

10. In one example, a rat was rewarded first for approaching a lever, and finally for pressing the lever. Getting the rat to press the lever is called shaping; rewarding each response that is closer to the final goal is called _____ _____ and is a basic principle of shaping.

11. The goal of both positive and negative reinforcement is to increase/decrease the probability that a response will be repeated.

12. Punishment doesn't tell someone what to do, it only tells them what not to do. T / F

Answers: **8.** True **9.** differential reinforcement **10.** successive approximation **11.** increase **12.** True

the punishment. The punisher thus becomes a CS and comes to evoke the same unpleasant emotions as the punishment itself. This is one of the reasons why people often have automatic fear reactions to the sight of a police officer—police are often cast in the role of the punisher.

Schedules of Reinforcement. An important aspect of operant conditioning is the frequency with which reinforcement is presented. In the early trials of the rat experiment, the rat was reinforced for *every* "correct" response. This is called **continuous reinforcement**. Then the rat was reinforced only every fifth time a "correct" response was given. Reinforcement in which only *some* correct responses reinforced is called **partial reinforcement**. An obvious choice that any experimenter, teacher, or instructor must make in aiding the learning process is how frequently to reinforce the learner. Common sense seems to tell us that lots of reinforcement early in learning will keep the interest level or motivation of the learner high. But what will happen if we decrease the rate of reinforcement? The program that decides the rate of reinforcement is called the **schedule of reinforcement**. We know a good deal about reinforcement schedules and their effects on learning and performance.

B. F. Skinner was one of the first to recognize the importance of reinforcement schedules, and he made the discovery because he was lazy! As a graduate student, he was responsible for doing learning experiments with rats. This research went on at all times of the day and night, including weekends. The rats were rewarded with food pellets for making correct responses. Since the rats learned well and responded frequently, close attention had to be paid to the food dispenser so that it would not run out of food. It was Skinner's job to make up the food pellets and put them in the food dispenser. On weekends, this was an inconvenience. He decided

to see if he could get away with rewarding the rats for every *other* bar press instead of every time they pressed the bar. This would solve two problems at the same time. In the first place, he would not have to make up so many pellets. In the second place, he might be able to spend a little more time away from the lab, since he could be gone twice as long before having to come in and fill up the dispenser. To his delight, not only did the rats maintain their response rate, they increased it to higher levels. As a result of this accidental discovery, Skinner began to seriously investigate the effects of different schedules of reinforcement on behavior (Skinner, 1959).

Four major variations of reinforcement schedules have been studied in learning research. The first two are based on the number of correct responses, and the last two are based on the passage of time.

1. *Fixed Ratio Schedules*: A **fixed ratio schedule** means that a reinforcer is given after a certain number of correct responses. The rat might have to make three correct responses in order to receive a food pellet. In this case, we would be using a fixed ratio (FR) schedule of three. If the rat had to make five correct responses before receiving food, it would be an FR5, and so on. This schedule would be "fixed"; every third or fifth correct response, for example, would be followed by a reward.
2. *Variable Ratio Schedule*: **Variable ratio schedules** also depend on the number of correct responses, but instead of a fixed number of correct responses leading to a reinforcer, the number varies from one time to the next. For example, we might reinforce the rat after three bar presses, then again after seven, then again after five.
3. *Fixed Interval*: Instead of rewarding on the basis of the number of correct responses, we could reward on the basis of time passed. We could decide to reinforce correct responses only after

Punishment. Presenting something that will decrease the probability that a certain response will be repeated.

Continuous reinforcement. A schedule of reinforcement in which every correct response is reinforced.

Partial reinforcement. A schedule of reinforcement in which only some correct responses are reinforced—for example, every third response or only after every five minutes.

Schedule of reinforcement. A program for deciding the rate of reward or reinforcement.

Fixed ratio schedule. A type of reinforcement schedule in which the learner is reinforced after making a certain number of responses—for example, after every 5 responses.

Variable ratio schedule. A type of reinforcement schedule in which the learner is reinforced after a certain number of correct responses, but the number varies from one time to the next—for example, being reinforced after 5 responses, then after 10, then after 2, etc.

2 minutes had passed since the response. If we did this in regular 2-minute blocks, the interval (2 minutes) would be "fixed," thus the name **fixed interval schedule**.

4. *Variable Interval*: As was the case with the ratio schedules, we could decide to be less predictable in our reinforcement. We might decide to use a different interval each time a reinforcer is to be given. We could reinforce the first correct response after 2 minutes had passed, the second after 7 minutes had passed, the third after 1 minute had passed, and so on. This would be called a **variable interval schedule**.

To appreciate the importance of schedules of reinforcement we must consider two separate issues—response rate and resistance to extinction. The number of bar presses that a rat makes in a minute is a way to measure the response rate of the rat. If you look at Figure 6–5, you will see what the response rates are typically like when the four different partial schedules of reinforcement are plotted on a graph. Fixed ratio gives the highest response rate, variable ratio the next highest, fixed interval the third highest, and variable interval the lowest response rate. There is one other interesting aspect to the graph. Look at the line representing the fixed interval schedule. Notice that it is uneven—it shows low response rates in the early part

of the interval and then high response rates toward the end of the interval. It seems as if even rats can tell time. They seem to realize that they will not be reinforced until enough time has passed and then begin to respond rapidly toward the end of the interval so that they will not "miss" the reinforcer.

Resistance to extinction is also affected by reinforcement schedules. The question here is now long the rat will keep pressing the bar after reinforcement is stopped. Remember how we used the term extinction in classical conditioning? It meant that we no longer presented the US and the CS together. It has the same meaning here, except that the bond or association we are trying to extinguish is between the response and the reinforcer. Generally, responses that have been continuously reinforced extinguish much more quickly than those that have been reinforced on some partial schedule. Furthermore, it seems as if responses that are on a fixed reinforcement schedule (either ratio or interval) extinguish more quickly than those that have been reinforced on some variable schedule. This makes sense; after all, fixed schedules are predictable. It is easier to realize when the reinforcement has stopped when you have been reinforced on a very regular basis. On the other hand, if reinforcement has been unpredictable (as is the case in a variable schedule), you can never be sure if reinforcement has stopped or not; it may simply be that the

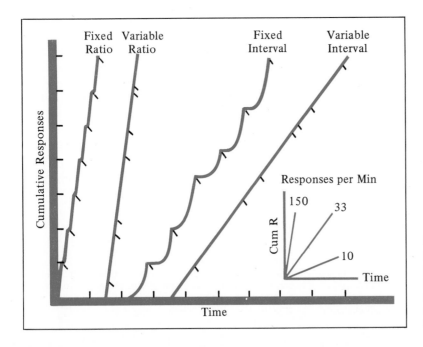

Figure 6-5

Examples of different types of responding for four types of reinforcement schedules: fixed ratio, variable ratio, fixed interval, and variable interval schedules. The slash marks show a reinforced response.

necessary number of correct responses or the time interval has been increased.

There are many examples of schedules of reinforcement in our everyday lives. Some of these examples have been listed in Table 6-2. We will consider some more elaborate examples of reinforcement patterns and their effects on behavior in the next chapter.

Escape and Avoidance Learning

In **escape learning**, a person or animal must learn a certain response to get away from or escape an unpleasant situation. This type of learning uses negative reinforcement, which, as we discussed earlier, is the taking away or stopping of something—such as a shock—to increase the tendency to repeat a certain response.

For example, rats are often placed in a long corridor called a runway and given an electrical shock through a grid on the floor (Trapold and Fowler, 1960). The only way to escape from the shock is to run to the other end of the corridor and through an exit. Similarly, in our earlier example of the child being nagged about clothes and toys, the best way to escape the nagging is to pick up the clothes.

The reinforcement here consists of stopping the shock or the nagging—and thus escaping from it. But notice that escape in this sense doesn't mean just running away—the rat and the child in these examples have to make a certain response to end the negative reinforcement.

In escape learning there is usually no way to prevent the unpleasant situation—the caged rat can't do anything before the shock begins, it can only respond after it begins. But in the case of the nagging parent, the child can learn to do something to avoid the situation—pick up the clothes before the nagging begins.

In **avoidance learning**, an experimenter might sound a buzzer 5 seconds before a shock is given. To avoid the shock, the rat must press a bar before the 5 seconds are up. Once the rat learns this sequence, it can, in theory, avoid the shock forever. To return once again to the child sitting in the middle of a pile of toys and clothes, the smart parent will begin to nag just as the child's favorite TV show is about to begin. This means that the clock can become an effective signal for the impending negative stimulus. As the theme for the TV show begins, the child can be seen scurrying around picking up toys and clothes. Most parents, however, have come to the conclusion that "neat" behavior must be incredibly complex, since it is learned so slowly (and sometimes never.)

Superstitious Behavior

At this point you might have the feeling that learning is a very complex and difficult activity. You are partially correct. It is particularly difficult to change other people's behavior, since you have to be able to manipulate their environment. But it does not follow from this that we don't learn very much—nothing could be further from the truth. We are learning constantly; as a matter of fact, occasionally we run into problems because we learn the wrong things or we learn too much.

You might remember from the perception chapter (Chapter 4) that humans try hard to make sense out of their world; take the Gestalt principles as an example. People seem naturally to group and arrange things in their minds. Occasionally, they group things together that may not belong together in a given situation, for example, all blacks, all women, or all teachers. It is not that these elements (blacks, women, teachers) are not similar in some respects. They obviously are. But in some circumstances those similarities are irrelevant.

As we discussed earlier in the chapter, this is called stimulus generalization—a failure to discriminate between stimuli that really are different. Sometimes, incorrect associations are built up between responses and reinforcements as well. We often pick

---

Fixed interval schedule. A type of reinforcement schedule in which the learner is reinforced for a correct response after a certain amount of time has passed—for example, being reinforced for a correct response after 5 minutes have passed, and then waiting another 5 minutes to reinforce the next correct

Variable interval schedule. A type of reinforcement schedule in which the learner is reinforced for a correct response after a certain amount of time has passed, but the amount of time keeps varying—first 5 minutes, then 10, then 2, etc.

Escape learning. A learning task that presents the learner with an unpleasant stimulus or situation (negative reinforcer) from which he or she can escape only by making the correct response.

Avoidance learning. A learning task in which the learner can avoid an unpleasant situation altogether (prevent the negative reinforcer) by making the correct response.

TABLE 6-2. Examples of Naturally Occurring Reinforcement Schedules

Continuous reinforcement (reinforcement every time the response is made)	□ Using a token to ride the subway. □ Putting a dime in the parking meter. □ Putting coins in a vending machine to get candy or soda.
Fixed ratio schedule (reinforcement after a fixed number of responses)	□ Being paid on a piecework basis—in the garment industry workers may be paid so much per 100 dresses sewn. □ Being allowed no more than five fouls in a college basketball game—in this case you are punished if you don't stick to the limit of five. □ Taking a multi-item test. This is an example of negative reinforcement—as soon as you finish those items on the test you can leave!
Variable ratio schedule (reinforcement after a varying number of responses)	□ Playing a slot machine—the machine is programmed to pay off after a certain number of responses have been made, but that number keeps changing. This type of schedule creates a steady rate of responding, because players know if they play long enough they will win. □ Hunting—you probably won't hit something every time you fire, but it's not the amount of time that passes, but the number of times you shoot that will determine how much game you are able to catch. And the number of times you shoot will no doubt vary—you won't hit something every time. □ Sales commissions—you have to talk to many customers before you make a sale, and you never know whether the next one will buy. Again, the number of sales calls you make, not how much time passes, will determine when you are reinforced by a sale. And the number of sales calls will vary.
Fixed interval schedule (reinforcement of first response after a fixed amount of time has passed)	□ You have an exam coming up, and as time goes by and you haven't studied you have to make up for it all by a certain time, and that means cramming. □ Picking up a salary check, which occurs every week or every two weeks. □ Going to the 7:00 show at the movies—again, the reinforcement occurs at a fixed time.
Variable interval schedule (reinforcement of first response after varying amounts of time)	□ Surprise quizzes in a course cause a steady rate of studying because you never know when they'll occur, and so you have to be ready (that is, prepared) all the time. □ Dialing a friend on the phone and getting a busy signal. This means that you have to keep dialing every few minutes because you don't know when they'll hang up. It doesn't depend on how many times you dial; it depends on dialing *after* the other person has hung up. □ Watching a football game, waiting for a touchdown. It could happen any time—if you leave the room to fix a sandwich you may miss it, so you have to keep watching continuously.

up extraneous pieces of behavior in a complex action and mistakenly assume them to be necessary for a "correct" response. To return to our rat learning to press a bar, it would not be unusual to find that in the course of learning this behavior the rat had picked up some unusual habits. These habits might include bobbing its head, sniffing, walking in a large circle, or any one of a number of activities that are unrelated to reinforcement. They are not unrelated activities to the rat, however. In one training session, the rat probably walked in a circle, or bobbed its head, or sniffed the air just before pressing the bar. Since the rat was immediately rewarded for pressing the bar, an association was built up between not only the bar pressing and the reinforcer, but also between many of the behaviors that immediately preceded the bar pressing. We call these unrelated associations **superstitious behavior**.

Human examples of superstitious behavior are numerous: The basketball player touches a good luck charm before attempting a foul shot; the baseball player scrapes the dirt exactly three times with his cleats before entering the batter's box; the actress wears a "lucky" ring for a first night performance. At one time or another, each of these actions was somehow related to a successful performance.

The Puzzle of Avoidance Learning and Superstitious Behavior

When reading the last two sections, you might have wondered why superstitious behaviors and avoidance responses persist since there seems to be no intentional pairing of a response with a reinforcement. In both cases, the critical pairings may occur infrequently but seem to influence behavior for long periods of time. One reason a response does not disappear may be that it's pairing with a reinforcement is sufficiently frequent that the association remains intact. For example, even a below-average major league baseball player gets a hit approximately once out of every four times at bat. Suppose such a player kicks the dirt exactly three times every time he goes to the plate. This means that the response (kicking the dirt) is followed by a positive reinforcer (a hit) on a variable ratio schedule of 4:1. Something similar happens with avoidance conditioning: The individual generally goes to great lengths to avoid the situation believed to be associated with aversive consequences, and so none of those aversive consequences arise. In this way, the association is maintained.

When an individual is *prevented* from making the avoidance response, interesting things happen. Consider the following case history. Until I was 37, I refused to get on a roller coaster. I was afraid of death or dismemberment. I made up all sorts of excuses not to ride on the terror machines. I would say my stomach was a bit upset or that I preferred to ride the ferris wheel; in my adult years, I would offer to hold the baby while my wife rode the rails. But on one particular day, there was no delicate way out of riding the terror machine without looking ridiculous. Surprisingly enough, I lived. In fact, I ended up enjoying it so much that I got right back

into line and rode it again. I have been riding roller coasters and other instruments of death since that day and loving every ride. Obviously, my expectations were radically altered by that maiden voyage. The point is that when an individual is faced with an objective reality that contradicts an expectation, the expectation changes and "learning" has occurred. In this instance an avoidance response has been replaced with one of approach. The trick to extinguishing an avoidance response is to get the individual to make the response he or she has been avoiding and then evaluate the consequences. Once this evaluation occurs, the avoidance response quickly disappears. For instance, children often avoid certain situations. Having been forced, coaxed, or tricked into approaching such a situation, the parent will say to the child "There! Now that wasn't so bad, was it?" Often, the child will agree.

Similarities Between Operant and Classical Conditioning

As you can see, associations and the circumstances in which they are formed play a major role in both operant and classical conditioning. Many of the concepts found in operant conditioning are found in classical conditioning as well. For instance, the concept of a schedule of reinforcement in operant conditioning is analogous to the concept of frequency or pairings in classical conditioning. Similarly, extinction, spontaneous recovery, stimulus generalization, and stimulus discrimination all appear in both classical and operant conditioning. If you repeatedly respond in a particular way and receive no reinforcement, you will eventually abandon the response. Most of us who have tried being nice to someone who refuses to reciprocate behave this way. Sooner or later we simply stop trying to be nice—a clear example of extinction. If this person happened to be a psychology teacher and we "stopped trying" with all teachers, this would be an example of stimulus generalization. If, on the other hand, we reacted this way to only psychology teachers, we might be showing signs of stimulus discrimination. Finally, if one day a teacher went out of the way to be nice to us

---

Superstitious behavior. Learning based on incorrect associations between a response and a reinforcement, in which someone assumes that a certain behavior was responsible for getting a reward when, in fact, it was not.

and we immediately began to make an effort with all teachers again, this might be an instance of spontaneous recovery. As these examples show, there are numerous important parallels between operant and classical conditioning. These parallels suggest that they are not really different processes but rather different ways of learning that occur in different situations.

Classical or Operant Conditioning: Which Do We Do Most?

If the difference between operant and classical conditioning is a difference between learning situations rather than learning processes, the answer to the question "which do we do most?" actually depends on the type of situations in which we generally find ourselves. For most people, a typical day consists of many different types of situations. In some of them, all we need to do in order to predict what might happen in the future is to notice certain regularities or associations: The boss looks angry, it looks like rain, the economy is getting worse. In other situations, we actually manipulate or operate on our environment. We study for an upcoming test. We wear our best clothes to a job interview. We put meat out to defrost before we leave home in the morning. In such situations, what we do affects whether we are reinforced or not. Eventually, we will probably turn associations we have received passively (about the boss, the weather, or the economy) into action patterns so they become operant responses as well. If the boss looks angry, better avoid him. If it looks like rain, better bring an umbrella. If the economy is getting bad, better sell stocks before their value drops.

Traditionally, the distinction between classically conditioned responses and operant conditioning has been maintained. But it makes sense, particularly in real-life situations, not to overemphasize the distinctions. Both types of conditioning result in learning and the two types undoubtedly interact. Consider an operant situation in which classical conditioning occurs, such as work. We choose to go to work to receive monetary rewards. Nevertheless, we come to associate certain elements in the work environment (smells, noises, and so forth) with fatigue, or happiness, or some other emotion. The association may be so strong that whenever or wherever we encounter that smell or noise, the paired emotion comes flooding back. Ultimately, it is less im-

portant for you to be able to distinguish what is operant from what is classical than it is for you to understand the principles supporting the formation and maintenance of associations.

■ COGNITIVE LEARNING THEORY

The various examples of learning that we've used in this chapter have included rats and cats in boxes, dogs in harnesses, children in cluttered rooms, and new workers trying to find the bathroom. Though simple and illustrative, these hardly capture the rich variety of experiences that we learn from each day—in some cases even without direct encounters. Consequently, some learning researchers and theorists feel that simple learning mechanisms, such as those described in classical and operant conditioning experiments, are not enough to explain the full range of learned human behavior.

In the chapter on perception (Chapter 4), we studied the work of the Gestalt psychologists, who believed that perception was aided by some complex, subtle human characteristics. In particular, they believed that we perceive whole units rather than bits of sensation, and that we group sensations according to such principles as continuity, common fate, and figure-ground. Gestalt psychologists also had an influence on learning theory. They believed that one could not explain learning by simply observing associations among stimuli, responses, and rewards. For example, they felt that the associationist explanation of Thorndike's cats did not do justice to what had occurred. The cat did not simply thrash around until the door opened. Further, after the cat had opened the door once, it did not continue to try other random solutions. For these reasons, Gestalt psychologists felt that the cat had demonstrated a capacity to solve problems, not just learn associations.

In the 1920s, Gestalt theorist Wolfgang Kohler began research with apes that was similar to Thorndike's research with cats. Kohler presented apes with a problem: He hung a banana from a rope so that the ape in each experiment could not reach it. In the immediate vicinity, however, he placed boxes and sticks. The apes learned to stack the boxes and use the sticks as tools to obtain the banana. Kohler considered their behavior to be dramatically dif-

CAN PIGEONS SOLVE THE BANANA AND BOX PROBLEM?

Recently, Robert Epstein of Harvard University and his associates found that pigeons can be every bit as insightful as chimpanzees. Epstein wanted to find out if a pigeon, given certain previous experiences, would be able to solve the banana-and-box problem in which Kohler's chimpanzees had so brilliantly succeeded. Kohler's chimps, when presented with a banana that they could not reach, eventually pushed a box beneath it, stood on the box, reached up, and snatched the banana. Epstein and his colleagues hypothesized that pigeons, as well as chimpanzees, could use what they had learned in the past to behave in novel ways.

In Epstein's experiment, the pigeons needed to learn two specific behaviors in order to solve the banana-and-box problem. First, they had to learn to push a box toward a specific target; second, they had to learn to climb up on a box to reach a banana. To train the birds to push a box, the experimenter placed a green spot at random positions in the training chamber. At first, the bird received reinforcement for aimless pushes at the box, then for pecking the spot, and finally for sighting the spot and pushing the box directly toward it. Epstein gradually increased the distance between the box and the green spot until the pigeon reliably pushed the box toward the spot, regardless of the location of either.

The second phase of learning involved training the pigeon to climb on the box, which was fixed in a stationary position, and peck a facsimile of a banana hanging overhead. At the end of this training period the bird had learned to climb up on the box and peck the banana to receive reinforcement. But when Epstein removed the banana and reintroduced the green spot, the pigeon would again push the box toward the spot. The birds were never reinforced for pecking or pushing the box when the banana was present. A final phase of the training process was to put the bird into the chamber with only the banana present until it no longer jumped or flew at it.

Next came the test phase to find out whether the pigeon could combine what it had learned in the two separate training sessions. The box and banana were both placed in the chamber, but this time they were kept some distance apart, with the banana well beyond the bird's reach. This was a situation the pigeon had not encountered before. When presented with this new condition, each pigeon at first appeared confused. It stretched its body toward the banana, turned around under it, looked at the banana, looked at the box, and looked back at the banana. Then, suddenly, each pigeon seemed to hit upon the solution. It began to push the box toward the banana, taking care to sight the banana between pushes and adjust its direction accordingly. When the box was positioned under the banana, the pigeon stopped pushing, climbed up on the box, and pecked the banana. Epstein's pigeons had struck upon precisely the same solution that Kohler's chimps had found over 60 years before.

Epstein also verified that the pigeons' insight was based directly on their previous learning experience. He trained two birds to climb on a box and peck a banana, but didn't train them to push the box. These birds failed to solve the problem because they didn't push the box. Two others were trained to push the box aimlessly and to climb on the box and peck at the banana. But because they had never learned to push a box in a specific direction, these pigeons also failed to solve the problem.

Epstein concludes that reaching an insightful solution to a problem depends—for animals as well as humans—upon combining the correct set of behaviors learned in past situations.

Source: R. Epstein, C.E. Kirshnit, R.P. Lanze, & L.C. Rubin, "Insight" in the Pigeon: Antecedents and Determinants of an Intelligent Performance, *Nature*, March 1, 1984 (vol. 308) pp. 61–62.

---

ferent from association learning, since the apes had never been exposed to this type of situation before.

In observations such as these, Gestalt psychologists did not see the plodding, torturous, trial-and-error learning that Thorndike described. Instead, they saw preliminary exploration and investigation, and then sudden and dramatic problem solving. They believed that animals solved the problems they confronted by manipulating the various stimulus elements (e.g., boxes and sticks) symbolically and then experiencing an "insight"; further, once the problem was solved, the animals were able to repeat the solution when placed in a similar situation at a later time. This approach, which emphasized the importance of mental events in learning, formed the basis of *cognitive theories* of learning.

Cognitive theorists don't deny that associations are important building blocks for learning; but they disagree that associations alone can explain learning. They believe that mental or cognitive operations play a role. These mental operations use basic sensory experiences as their "raw material," but much more than simple associations are produced. These operations include such things as memory, inductive and deductive reasoning, concept formation, and judgment.

Several chapters in this book are devoted to cognitive operations. Most cognitive operations have a place in a broader view of how people process information. In Figure 6-6, a simple model of information processing, as a cognitive learning theorist might see it, is presented. The information to be learned is organized, sent to short-term memory, rehearsed, coded, sent to long-term memory, and retrieved when needed for performance. Let's consider some evidence in favor of these cognitive operations.

Intentional Learning

One convincing demonstration of the effect of cognitive operations on learning can be seen in the use of instructions. If we tell people to pay attention to some particular aspect of a learning situation, they will learn faster than if we do not give any particular instructions. Giving instructions is, in a sense, like abstract shaping. We can instruct people with words and symbols; it is not necessary to give them practice trials. For example, Cook and Harris (1937) were able to classically condition a

physiological response to shock simply by telling the subject that a shock would follow the presentation of a light. Even after a number of light-shock pairings had occurred, the response to being told what would follow the light was as strong as the response to the light itself.

Blocking, Overshadowing, and Delay of Reinforcement

In various classical, operant, and stimulus discrimination experiments, a number of phenomena occurred that could not be easily explained by simple associationist principles. These phenomena—including blocking, overshadowing, and delay of reinforcement—indicate that cognition is involved in learning. Consider the following example of **blocking**. First a tone is paired with food powder in a classic Pavlovian experiment with dogs. Eventually, the tone will result in salivation. Next the tone is paired with a geometric pattern to produce a compound stimulus, that is, one with *two* important characteristics rather than one. Eventually, one would expect the geometric pattern alone to elicit the same response as the food powder. Experiments have shown otherwise (Kamin, 1969; Rescorla and Wagner, 1972). Instead, the prior association (between the tone and the food powder) seems to prevent or "block" the formation of a new association (between the geometric pattern and the food powder). No matter how often the compound stimulus is presented to the subject, the association

Figure 6-6

A model of information processing that is used by cognitive theorists in talking about learning.

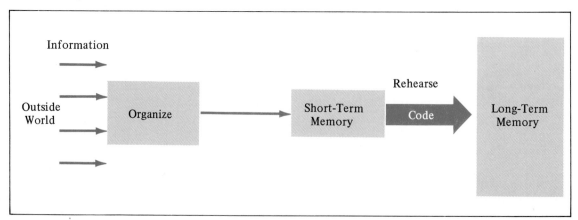

between the second stimulus characteristic—the pattern—and the food powder will not be formed. This phenomenon is difficult to explain using just the principles of association that are the basis of most classical and operant accounts of learning.

Wagner and Rescorla (1972) also describe a situation in which an organism is conditioned to two stimuli separately. For example, an association between a tone and food powder might be established, and separately, an association between a geometric pattern and food powder. *Then* the two stimuli might be paired to make a compound stimulus. According to the results of the research conducted by Wagner and Rescorla, in this situation the organism "expects" a stronger US (e.g., more food powder) as a result of the strength of the independent associations of each of the two stimulus elements—an expectation that would *not* occur if associationist principles alone applied. Also, after the presentation of the compound stimulus, the strength of the association with each of the separate elements will be reduced. Wagner and Rescorla suggest that this reduction is the result of the organism's "readjusting" expectations based on the strength of the compound stimulus. In other words, the organism becomes more "realistic" in its expectations based on the results of the compound stimulus presentation—a result that, once again, cannot be explained by associationist principles. We are accustomed to hearing discussions of "expectations" with respect to human behavior, but these experiments were conducted with rats!

Another phenomenon that a traditional associationist approach has difficulty explaining is known as **overshadowing**, in which one characteristic of a complex stimulus assumes greater influence over a particular response than another characteristic. Consider encountering a nasty, male psychology teacher. The association you make between psychology and nastiness may be stronger than the one you make between maleness and nastiness. If that were the case, it would take much longer to extinguish the connection between the first pair than between the second pair. There is no easy way to explain why one cue assumes greater influence than

another. Nevertheless, overshadowing is common in everyday life, and it cannot be explained by the traditional principles of association.

Taste aversion is a good example of an association that is made even though there is a long gap between a stimulus and its effect. This phenomenon is called **delay of reinforcement**. If we have a meal one night and wake up ill several hours later, we do not throw away our pillow or look at our sleep-mate for a causal explanation. Instead, we immediately associate our discomfort with the meal that we had several hours earlier. Further, if we had some exotic food for the first time, we may never eat it again. This association and the resulting behavior is not easy to explain in the absence of some cognitive mechanism that categorizes information, assigning various importance levels to various cues of a complex stimulus. (Taste aversion is discussed further in the next chapter.)

These three phenomena—blocking, overshadowing, and delay of reinforcement—all point to the importance of cognition in learning. They suggest that there is more to learning than associations built on frequent pairings or short intervals between stimuli.

Learning, Memory, and Reasoning

Perhaps the most dramatic evidence of the role of cognitive variables in learning is the simple *fact* of memory and of reasoning. Animals and humans can store information for long periods of time, using it later to solve problems. A police officer's work is a good example. The largest part of a police officer's job involves sorting information for later use. Consider the following incident: During a one-month period, a patrol officer answers several calls involving purse snatchings. The incidents usually occur at a fast-food restaurant at lunch or supper time. The victim reports noticing that her purse was missing shortly after talking with a stranger. In one case, the conversation involved a coat the victim was wearing; in another, it involved directions to a location not far from the restaurant. At some point, the patrol officer concludes that the purse snatcher is working with an accomplice who diverts the victim's

Blocking. Failure to make an association between the second stimulus characteristic of a compound stimulus and the unconditioned stimulus.
Overshadowing. The greater influence of one characteristic of

a complex stimulus than another over a particular response.
Delay of reinforcement. The making of an association despite a long gap between the presentation of a stimulus and a response.

attention so the partner can steal the purse. As a result, the patrol officer begins to look for a pair of thieves, not just one. The officer has "learned" a new behavior. You might argue that this is not learning; it is problem solving or reasoning. We will see in later chapters that separating learning from other processes, particularly mental operations, becomes very difficult. Nevertheless, if you consider our definition of learning as a relatively permanent change in behavior that comes about through experience, you will find that the patrol-officer example certainly fits the definition.

Social Learning Theory

One popular form of cognitive learning theory, proposed by Albert Bandura (1969), is called **social learning theory**. It is different from other theories in that it stresses the interaction among people as the occasion for learning. In addition, it suggests that factors other than those appearing in Figure 6–6 play a role in learning. These factors include motivation, emotion, expectations, and feelings of effectiveness.

Bandura suggests that there are many different ways in which we learn other than by doing. One of those ways is by just observing. In **observational learning**, we observe a model perform a particular activity and we rehearse those actions mentally until we have the opportunity to try them. In the process of trying to perform in the same way as the model, we compare our actions to the memory of the model's actions and make any necessary corrections.

Once again, a good deal of mental activity is im-

In observational learning, we observe a model perform some actions and then mentally rehearse those actions until we have a chance to try them.

plied. I once heard a discussion between my niece and her father that supports observational learning. My niece was 7 years old at the time and had just hopped into the car to travel with her dad to the store. She asked if she might drive and he said no. When she asked why, he said that she didn't know how. She respectfully disagreed and claimed that she did know. He asked her to describe how she would put the car in motion. She listed the following steps:

- get into the car on the driver's side
- put on the seatbelt
- put the key in the ignition
- light a cigarette
- turn the key and press the gas pedal
- pull the gear shift lever into the D position
- guide the car down the street

Needless to say, in many respects she did know how to drive, although she had learned one superstitious behavior—lighting the cigarette. Bandura suggests that this type of observational learning goes on constantly. We learn to walk, talk, and act like those we admire.

Are the Cognitive Theorists Right?

Do we come to an understanding of our environment and ourselves only through direct experience with stimuli, or do we use certain mental or cognitive operations such as reasoning or observation? This argument is what finally separates the cognitive learning approaches from the noncognitive, or associationist, approaches. The experiments of Pavlov, Watson, Skinner, and their followers have brought us much closer to an understanding of what learning is and how it is accomplished. Nevertheless, the failure of those approaches to adequately explain things such as learning through reasoning or observation, or the effect of instructions on learning, makes it clear that a complete explanation of learning must involve some cognitive variables.

As you saw in Chapter 1, American functionalists broke with the European structuralists on the issue of usefulness. The Americans wanted to *use* psychology. Learning theory, more than any other area in psychology, has produced useful information—something that B. F. Skinner, among other prominent learning researchers, has recognized. Recently, when he was asked why his research has remained popular in light of the newer cognitive approaches, he answered that it was because it is useful. Now that you have been exposed to most of the concepts and elements of learning from several different perspectives, it is time to see how they are used. In the next chapter, you will see how learning theory can be used to understand many of the more complicated behaviors that define being human.

REVIEW QUESTIONS

13. Match the following terms with the correct definition:

___ fixed ratio schedule

___ variable ratio schedule

___ fixed interval schedule

___ variable interval schedule

A. subject is rewarded after a varying number of responses—sometimes after the first, at others after the third, etc.

B. subject is rewarded for the first response after different amounts of time have passed—5 minutes, then 1 minute, etc.

C. subject is rewarded after a fixed number of responses.

D. subject is rewarded for the first response after a certain amount of time has passed.

14. In escape learning/avoidance learning it is possible to prevent the negative reinforcer by making the correct response.

15. In _____ _____ , we learn an activity by watching a model perform it first.

16. Blocking/overshadowing/delay of reinforcement, the failure to make an association between the second stimulus characteristic of a compound stimulus and the US, is one piece of evidence in favor of the _____ view that there is more to learning than making associations.

Answers: 13. fixed ratio schedule, C; variable ratio schedule, A; fixed interval schedule, D; variable interval schedule, B **14.** avoidance learning **15.** observational learning **16.** blocking; cognitive

---

■ SUMMARY

1. *Learning* is a relatively permanent change in behavior that comes about through experience and is not a direct result of body states such as fatigue or illness. Its "relative" permanence is important for two reasons: We need to be able to change learned patterns in case we've learned something that is wrong, and we need to be able to modify our behavior to match changes in the environment. The only way we can tell whether or not learning has taken place is by observing behavior. In considering learning, we ignore reflexive behavior.

2. Learning is the precondition for performance, though not all performance results from learning, and not all learning will result in performance.

3. In Pavlov's experiments with dogs, he noticed two occasions when salivation occurred: in the presence of an *unconditioned stimulus* (US), the meat powder, and in the presence of the *conditioned stimulus* (CS), the sound of Pavlov's footsteps as he entered the lab before a feeding. The US is a stimulus that produces a response of a particular kind every time it is presented. The salivation that occurred in the presence of the US was called the *unconditioned response* (UR). The CS is a stimulus that has been repeatedly paired with the US so that it produces a response similar to the UR, called the *conditioned response* (CR). The five elements that are critical to classical conditioning are the US, the CS, the UR, the CR, and the pairing of the US and the CS, which creates an association. All learning theories are based at some level on the concept of association.

4. The kind of learning that Pavlov demonstrated in dogs occurs in human beings, as well. We become conditioned to many stimuli that were originally neutral because these stimuli are connected in time or space with other stimuli. Three conditions seem

---

Social learning theory. A cognitive learning theory that stresses the interaction among people as the occasion for learning.

Observational learning. A type of learning in which a person watches a model perform a certain activity and then copies it. Learning by observing rather than by doing.

to be important for conditioning to occur: frequency of US/CS pairing (maximum information is provided when the two are consistently paired); order of presentation (the CS must predict, or come before, the US); and timing (the best circumstance for conditioning is a short interval, the time between CS and US).

5. *Extinction* is the process by which a CR is extinguished, or is no longer elicited by the CS. We can bring about extinction by presenting the US with the CS, by reversing their order of presentation, or by extending the interval between the presentation. *Spontaneous recovery*, or the reappearance of a CS after extinction has taken place, shows that extinction is not simply a process of forgetting. *Stimulus generalization* is the appearance of a CR to a stimulus similar to CS; it stems from a failure to correctly make a *discrimination* between two stimuli.

6. In *operant conditioning* rather than simply forming associations between stimuli, we learn that performing some action will achieve certain results. Since this action is useful or instrumental in getting some reward, this type of learning is also called *instrumental learning*. Much of operant conditioning theory is based on the work of Edward Thorndike, whose research on trial and error learning in animals showed that they made an association between a situation (e.g., a puzzle box) and a response (e.g., a way out of the box). In operant conditioning experiments, the subject can respond freely to the stimuli in the environment.

7. *Shaping* is the step-by-step procedure that psychologists use to train subjects to perform specific behaviors. Shaping involves *differential reinforcement*, or reinforcing certain responses and not others, and *successive approximation*, or reinforcing responses that are more and more similar to the desired response until only one correct behavior is rewarded. The importance of shaping is that it reduces the time it would take the subject to learn the behavior by simple trial and error.

8. *Reinforcement* is any event that, presented after a response, increases the probability that the response will be repeated. A *primary reinforcer* has a direct effect on some physiological state (an example is food), while a *secondary reinforcer* acquires power only by association with a primary reinforcer (an example is money).

9. There are three basic types of reinforcement

in operant conditioning: *positive reinforcement*, or presenting a reinforcer after a particular response to increase the tendency for that response to be repeated; *negative reinforcement*, or taking away something to increase the probability that a particular response will be repeated; and *punishment*, or presenting something that will decrease the probability that a particular response will be repeated. Punishment does not point out correct responses, only incorrect ones; it can also have harmful side effects, such as strong, unpleasant emotions and negative associations to the punisher.

10. A *schedule of reinforcement* refers to the frequency with which a behavior is rewarded: in *continuous reinforcement*, every correct response is rewarded, while in *partial reinforcement*, some correct responses are unrewarded. There are four major types of reinforcement schedules: (1) the *fixed ratio schedule* (FR), in which reinforcer is given after a set number of responses; (2) the *variable ratio schedule* (VR), in which the number of required responses varies from one reinforcement to the next; (3) the *fixed interval schedule* (FI), in which reinforcement depends upon production of a response after a set amount of time has passed; and (4) the *variable interval schedule* (VI), in which reinforcement depends upon production of a response after a time period that varies from one reinforcement to the next.

11. The different schedules of reinforcement have different effects on learning and performance. Response rate is highest for fixed ratio, next highest for variable ratio, next highest for fixed interval, and lowest for variable interval. Subjects on a fixed interval schedule learn to tell when the right amount of time has passed and respond more rapidly and more often toward the end of the interval.

12. In *escape learning*, the subject must learn a certain response to get away from an unpleasant situation. *Avoidance learning* is learning to perform a certain response to prevent an unpleasant situation.

13. *Superstitious behavior* occurs because an association is made between some action and a reinforcement when actually there is no relationship between the two. Laboratory studies show that animals as well as humans can exhibit superstitious behavior.

14. We must ask ourselves why superstitious behaviors and avoidance responses persist when there is no repeated pairing of a response with a re-

inforcement. One reason may be that the pairing is sufficiently frequent that the association remains intact.

15. Many of the concepts found in operant conditioning are found in classical conditioning as well. In fact, the distinction between the two types of conditioning is an historical accident. In real life, this distinction is a vague one based on when and how the learned behaviors are used, and both types are used constantly.

16. *Cognitive theories* propose that the concept of simple association is not enough to explain learning and that a series of mental operations also plays an important role. Evidence in favor of the cognitive view includes *intentional learning* (the fact that instructions can aid the learning process), *blocking* (failure to make an association between the second stimulus characteristic of a compound stimulus and the UC), *overshadowing* (in a complex stimulus, the assumption of greater influence by one characteristic than another over a particular response), *delay of reinforcement* (the fact that associations can be made despite a long gap between stimulus and response), and the fact that humans and animals are capable of both memory and reasoning.

17. *Social learning theory* is a cognitive view that emphasizes interactions among people as the occasion for learning. In addition, it suggests that factors such as motivation, emotion, expectations, and feelings of effectiveness play a role in learning.

18. *Observational learning* suggests that we can learn by watching models as well as by performing a behavior ourselves.

■ ANSWERING QUESTIONS FOR THOUGHT

1. Ideally, but not always. Other things may occur to keep you from performing what you've learned—the example given in the chapter was an actor who forgot his lines in the middle of a play. He had learned them, and was able to recite them beforehand, but that was not reflected in his performance on stage. You can probably think of other instances—failing your road test right after doing a perfect run-through with your driving instructor?

2. As a child, going to the dentist was probably a painful experience. In conditioning terms, the pain was the US, the dentist's office was the CS, and your anxiety was the CR. Even though things have improved in dentistry and it isn't likely to hurt that much anymore, your anxiety now is an example of spontaneous recovery of your old CR to the dentist's waiting room (CS).

3. Punishment is sometimes effective, but it quite often has harmful side effects. It tells people what *not* to do, but it doesn't tell them what to do. It also causes unpleasant emotions that can get in the way of thinking and remembering. Finally, negative associations are formed to the punisher, which can adversely affect parent-child relationships.

4. Money is a secondary reinforcer that gets its power through association with primary reinforcers. In fact, it is today the most common way to get many primary reinforcers, since most of us don't grow our own food any more.

5. Trainers use shaping techniques to teach animals complicated tricks. By rewarding animals for successive bits of behavior that come close to the desired one, the animals eventually learn the desired responses. The advantage of this method is that it cuts down on the time it would take the animals to learn the responses through simple trial and error.

6. Slot machines and lotteries are examples of naturally occurring variable ratio schedules. In this type of schedule, the number of responses necessary to gain reinforcement isn't constant. Because reinforcement is unpredictable, there's always the chance of hitting the jackpot, and the temptation to keep playing is great.

7. Cognitive theorists point out that we do not always have to learn the hard way—that is, by actually doing. We can also learn by watching someone else and through instructions, and we can learn by applying what we know in a later learning situation. We can also "learn to learn"—that is, we can learn a general strategy that can be applied in many situations.

7 Learning Applications

QUESTIONS FOR THOUGHT

1. **Why do some people get anxious and panic in test situations? Can anything be done to overcome it?**
2. **Why do people who have quit smoking say that the hardest time to resist a cigarette is right after a meal?**
3. **Can studying tapes or videos teach you how to improve your golf swing or be a better manager?**
4. **Can people who are shy be taught to overcome it?**
5. **Why do some people just seem to give up when they meet obstacles?**

The answers to these questions are at the end of the chapter.

It is common to see a newspaper article indicating that a reward is being offered for any information that might lead to solving a particularly puzzling or brutal crime. It is assumed that money might encourage reluctant witnesses to step forward or get people thinking creatively about a puzzling case. Recently, this type of strategy has become more institutionalized. For example, the city of Brunswick, Maine, has formed a nonprofit corporation called *Brunswick Crimeline, Inc.*, that offers cash for information leading to the solution of any crime that occurs in that city. The cash comes from donations made by local businesses.

Brunswick Crimeline, Inc., is a good example of the application of learning principles at an institutional level. The Brunswick police department would like the citizens of Brunswick to learn a new behavior. They would like them to learn to pick up the phone and provide information about crimes. To get citizens to learn this new behavior, the police must set up a situation in which citizens will respond freely. Citizens can call any time they want. If a response is "correct" (i.e., results in an indictment or an arrest), the individual is rewarded with cash. In other cities where similar systems have been tried, they have usually resulted in a core group of responders who actively seek information to provide to the police to earn money. These people have learned the response quite well. This type of response has always occurred at lower, unofficial levels. For example, most detectives rely on what is called a "snitch," a person they can count on to give them information in return for cash. The only difference between the snitch system and *Brunswick Crimeline, Inc.*, is that the latter is directed toward all citizens, not just a special few.

In this chapter, we will examine different applications of learning principles to real-world situations like the one just discussed. In this way, we can get a better idea of how and why learning principles are so important in understanding and affecting behavior.

In the last chapter we saw several different approaches to understanding how people learn. For the purposes of discussion, let's assume that each of these approaches is, to some extent, correct, and that the approaches should be combined. Under those circumstances, we might summarize what we know about human learning as follows:

People notice regular relationships in their environment. Sometimes these relationships are between two stimuli and sometimes they are between an action and an outcome. In addition to noticing these relationships, people remember them and combine them to form new and broader relationships that, in turn, affect future behavior.

This general statement is probably more applicable than any of the specific laws or principles of classical or operant conditioning to the circumstances of everyday living. As noted in the last chapter, the question of *which* set of learning principles govern human behavior is not the most important one. Our view is likely to change depending on what behavior we are looking at. For example, if we examined a behavior such as salivation we might conclude that classical principles are the governing ones; if we looked at bar pressing, we might decide on operant principles instead; if we considered still a third behavior, modeling, we might favor cognitive principles. But our environment, as we well know, makes more complex demands than ones that can be met simply by pressing a bar, salivating to the sound of a bell, or doing exactly as a model has demonstrated. The uses and applications of learning theory are much larger. For instance, we need to apply it to such questions as how children learn to read, why co-workers have trouble getting along, and why some people act in self-destructive ways. In this chapter we will consider some of the larger questions surrounding the human condition from the perspective of learning theory. Our objective is not to list every possible application of learning principles to behavior, but to show how learning principles are applied through the use of a few well-developed examples.

■ BIOLOGICAL INFLUENCES ON LEARNING

Perhaps the first and most basic question to ask about the application of learning principles is whether we should even try to apply these principles to humans, since they are based primarily on studies of animal behavior. The results of learning experiments using animal subjects do tell us something about human behavior—at least that has been the long-held assumption of researchers in the area.

To help us answer whether and how observations about one species can be used to understand the behavior of another, we will look first at biological influences on learning and the concept of preparedness.

Preparedness

In both classical and operant conditioning, the learning principles have traditionally been considered to be universally applicable no matter what the particular stimulus or response being studied. Hence, in Pavlov's experiments, the fact that a bell was the CS, meat powder was the US, and salivation was the UR and CR was not important. The same conditioning principles would have been uncovered using different variables—for example, if the US had been a poison of some kind, the CS had been a different type of food, and the UR and CR had been stomach cramps. Similarly, in operant conditioning experiments with rats, the studied response might be running instead of bar pressing; the particular reinforcer might be shock instead of food. A rat, it was believed, could just as easily learn to press a bar for food as it could learn to press a bar to terminate shock.

More recent research has begun to question this assumption. Seligman (1970), among others, has reviewed the literature on conditioning and found numerous examples of association and response patterns that do *not* follow the general laws of either classical or operant conditioning. He has proposed that a natural or biological preparedness helps both animals and humans to learn some things more easily than others. A striking example of preparedness, taste aversion, should help make this concept clearer.

Taste Aversion. If an animal just once tastes a food and later becomes ill, the animal may learn to avoid that food in the future. This is known as **taste aversion,** and is a well-developed response in rats. Garcia and Koelling (1966) have conducted some of the key research in this area. In their experiment, two groups of rats were trained to lick water from a bottle. The water given to both groups was flavored with saccharin and thus had a sweet taste. Also, each time a rat licked water from the bottle, lights would flash and a clicking noise was heard. The saccharin-water given to one of the groups also contained a tasteless poison that would make the rat sick. No poison was added to the water of the second group, but a shock was delivered to a rat's feet each time it licked from the bottle.

In this experiment, rats in both groups could have formed associations with either the noise/light cue, the flavor cue, or both. The results were surprising. The rats that received the poison formed an association with the saccharin-water and avoided sweet-tasting water in later trials. The rats that were shocked did not form this association and did not avoid saccharin-water in later trials. These results suggest that there is some "natural" relationship between taste and illness and that there is none between taste and shock or noise/light cues and illness. If this is true, then the principles of classical conditioning might not be as universally applicable as was once thought.

The literature on conditioning contains other examples of associations that are formed more easily than others. Konorski (1967) found it virtually impossible to teach a dog to yawn using food as a reinforcer. On the other hand, Brown and Jenkins (1968) found that pigeons would peck a lighted key even though the reinforcer (grain) came automatically, whether the pigeon pecked the key or not.

On the basis of his review of these and other examples, Seligman developed the concept of **biological preparedness** to explain the fact that some associations are formed more easily than others. According to this concept, for any subject (human or animal), three types of associations may be formed: the prepared association, the unprepared association, and the contraprepared association. A **prepared association** is one that is made easily because of certain native characteristics of the species in question. For example, rats have a highly developed sensitivity to taste, so in Garcia and Koelling's experiments taste/illness was a prepared association. Since pecking comes naturally to pigeons, Brown and Jenkins observed that pigeons were predisposed to peck a lighted key, despite the fact that pecking was unrelated to reinforcement. An **unprepared association** is one that is not necessarily favored by the characteristics of the subject but can be learned through a number of training trials. Bar pressing in rats and automobile driving in humans might be examples of unprepared associations. Nothing in the evolutionary history of rats would have favored those rats who were better bar pressers. Similarly, nothing in our evolutionary background might have given some advantage to good drivers. A **contraprepared association** is one that is difficult to make. In the case of Garcia and Koelling's rats, the taste/shock association was contraprepared, as was the noise-light/illness association.

Taste aversion in humans seems to function much the same way as taste aversion in animals. You have probably had an experience of being ill that has affected your eating patterns. Mine involved a turkey. We were invited to the home of a friend for Thanksgiving dinner. The turkey was stuffed with fruit and nuts, a stuffing I had never tasted before. It was delicious and I ate enthusiastically. Much later that night, I became very ill and I remained ill for several days. The illness involved all sorts of unpleasant stomach symptoms. To this day, I avoid

fruit and nut stuffing. It made no difference that there was a flu going around or that no one else who ate the stuffing became ill. In my mind, the association was (and is) between that stuffing and the illness. Notice that I did not form an association to any other new stimuli that might have been present, such as the dishes we ate from, the type of wine we drank, or the topic of conversation for the evening. Seligman would say that I was *prepared* to make the taste/illness association and either unprepared or contraprepared to make the others.

There are two other important aspects to this example of taste aversion. First, since I refuse to eat fruit and not stuffing, there is no opportunity for extinction of the response to occur. In classical conditioning, extinction occurs when the CS (stuffing) appears often without the UR (illness). In my case, extinction is not likely because I avoid the CS. This is a combination of a classically conditioned aversion supported by an avoidance response. The second is that one aspect of taste aversion seems to go against what we know about classical conditioning. This is the fact that the interval between eating the food (the CS) and becoming ill (the US) can be quite long and still conditioning can occur. In my case I formed an association between a food eaten earlier in the evening and the illness that happened much later that night. My own association is questionable (since no one else became ill), but the phenomenon has been genuinely demonstrated in rats. In one experiment with rats, the interval between eating a poisoned substance and the rats' becoming ill was a period of 12 hours, but the rats subsequently learned to avoid the food (Garcia, Hankins, & Ruisiniak, 1974).

A particularly distressing instance of taste aversion is related to chemotherapy treatments of cancer. Bernstein (1978) studied taste aversion in children undergoing chemotherapy. One side-effect of these treatments is nausea. Bernstein showed that children developed an aversion to the flavor of the ice cream they ate just before receiving a chemo-

---

Taste aversion. A dislike or negative reaction to a specific food; often because of an association between that food and a later illness, whether the food actually caused the illness or not.

Biological preparedness. The principle that for humans and animals some responses are easier to make than others and some associations are more easily formed than others.

Prepared association. According to Seligman, an association that is easy for a subject to make because of native characteristics of the subject; an example is taste-illness.

Unprepared association. According to Seligman, an association that is not necessarily favored by the native characteristics of the subject but can be learned over a number of trials.

Contraprepared association. According to Seligman, an association that is very difficult for a subject to make.

therapy treatment. This type of association can create a serious problem for cancer patients, who generally report a loss of appetite, perhaps partly due to conditioned aversions. Hall (1982) suggests that such associations be kept in mind when developing therapy programs. This means, among other things, that patients should eat only the blandest food prior to treatments and, foods that are an important part of the patient's diet should not be eaten immediately before a chemotherapy treatment.

Bolles (1970) offers a different perspective on the ease with which we make associations. According to Bolles, avoidance learning such as that illustrated by taste aversion is the result of species-specific defensive reactions. He suggests that certain associations are supported or encouraged by innate mechanisms that help animals survive. Taste associations are perhaps examples of such mechanisms. It is to an animal's advantage to learn to recognize dangerous or poisonous substances quickly. This may explain the phenomenon of overshadowing (discussed in the last chapter), in which some cues in a stimulus are more important than others. Viewed in these terms, the "preparedness" suggested by Seligman may actually represent biological limitations to learning. That is, some associations may be difficult to establish because they run counter to certain species-specific defense reactions. Although Bolles's concept differs from Seligman's, they both point to the same conclusion: Learning is not just the interaction of an organism with an environment. It also involves certain biological limitations or constraints that are part of that organism.

Recently, Best, Brown, and Sowell (1984) have demonstrated that food associations are much broader than previously thought. In their study, one group of rats were first given a saccharin solution in a distinctive cage. Next, they were given an injection of lithium, a substance that induces illness. Then they were put back into the cage with free access to plain water. A second group of rats went through the same sequence but in the first stage were given plain water rather than the saccharin solution. A third group of rats was simply exposed to the distinctive cage, then given the lithium injection and put back into the box with free access to water. The results were intriguing. The rats exposed to the saccharin solution drank very little water after they were returned to the cage. Remember, *all* of the rats

were given the lithium injection, so all were made ill in the distinctive cage. Nevertheless, only those rats that had been exposed to the "taste" stimulus (saccharin water as opposed to plain water or no water) seemed to act differently in the cage after the lithium injection and subsequent illness. It seems as if these rats associated the distinctive cues of the box with water that caused illness and the other rats did not.

This phenomenon, known as *potentiation*, describes a situation where one stimulus condition makes conditioning easier. Potentiation is almost the opposite of overshadowing. It suggests that taste is a very potent stimulus in our lives and, further, may explain why we form strong attractions or aversions to food. It may even explain why we develop preferences for types of restaurants or various ethnic foods. Consider the following situation. You go to a new Chinese restaurant for dinner and have Szechuan-style food for the first time. It is served on distinctive blue plates. It is very hot and spicy. Later that evening, you become severely ill. In fact, the illness is the result of a virus you picked up from a friend a day earlier. Nevertheless, you "learn your lesson" and never eat Szechuan food again. Furthermore, you begin to avoid Chinese restaurants and get an uncomfortable feeling eating from blue plates. On the same night that you are eating Szechuan food, a classmate is working as a waiter in that Chinese restaurant. He also becomes ill that night from the same strain of virus that affected you. Nevertheless, he comes back to work two days later, continues to work there and enjoy eating Chinese food, doesn't avoid eating in other Chinese restaurants, and has no reservations about eating from blue plates. The implications are intriguing. Consider the effect of forcing a child to eat something that he or she would rather not. What happens if the child becomes ill? What will be the effect on future "tastes"? Similarly, consider once again the chemotherapy example. Perhaps not only certain tastes but *all* distinctive tastes and environments that proceed treatment can become associated with the illness induced by chemotherapy. This suggests not only that patients should receive bland food, but also that they should eat in an environment that is completely different from the one in which they will usually have meals.

You should remember the concept of preparedness when you consider applications of learning theory to human behavior: Some forms of learning may be easier for humans than others. This means that while we can apply many of the principles of learning found in animal research to human behavior, we can't do it automatically. Humans are unique biological organisms with particular capacities and limitations, and learning occurs in the context of those unique capacities and limitations.

In the following sections we will consider some additional instances in which learning principles can help us to understand a complex behavior. For ease of discussion, these applications will be grouped under classical conditioning, operant conditioning, and cognitive learning. These headings are somewhat misleading, in that they imply that only classical, instrumental, or cognitive learning principles are involved in the application. But this is almost never the case. As pointed out in the last chapter, and as shown in the description of taste aversion in this chapter, most behaviors involve a complex combination of CS/US and response/reinforcement associations. With this idea in mind, let's consider some specific applications of learning principles.

■ CLASSICAL CONDITIONING APPLICATIONS

As you recall, classical conditioning procedures involve a pairing of an unconditioned stimulus (US) with a previously neutral or conditioned stimulus (CS) until that previously neutral stimulus produces a similar response to the one produced by the unconditioned stimulus. The new response is called the conditioned response (CR). As we saw in the last chapter, there are many simple and common examples of this process: signs advertising food, the sight of a police car. Other, more complicated examples seem to follow along the lines of a classically conditioned response. We will look at several of these more complicated examples.

Conditioned Emotional Responding

In the discussion of stimulus generalization in Chapter 6, you became acquainted with Little Albert, the infant who grew to dislike fuzzy white things (Watson and Rayner, 1920). In our earlier study of Little Albert, we concentrated on the fact that his fear of the white rat generalized to similar-looking stimuli, including stuffed animals, a Santa Claus mask, and even a ball of white cotton. Now we will concentrate on the fact that Albert came to be afraid of a *neutral* stimulus.

At first Little Albert was attracted to the rat and tried to play with it, so it was certainly not an unpleasant or aversive stimulus to begin with. Albert developed his fear of the white rat (CS) through its association with a loud noise (US); every time he reached for the rat, the experimenter hit a steel bar with a hammer and he learned to be afraid (CR, UR). Albert's fear of the rat became so strong that he tried to crawl away when it was placed in front of him. Thus Albert learned to fear a neutral stimulus, the white rat, and that fear generalized to other stimuli, such as a Santa Claus mask. As we shall see in the next example, the same pattern can be seen in the more complex and more realistic situations.

Test Anxiety—Little Albert in the Classroom. In our everyday lives, there are many examples of emotional responses that might develop as Little Albert's did. One response with which you may be painfully familiar is test anxiety. It is common for people to tense up or "choke" in high-demand performance situations like test-taking. You study for a week prior to an exam. You get plenty of sleep the night before. You arrive at the testing room early. You sit down. The test is passed out and your mind goes blank. Your heart races. Your palms get sweaty. Your breathing gets shallow and rapid. You have an overwhelming urge to get up and leave the room (just as Little Albert tried to crawl away from the rat). As a matter of fact, many students do just that. They hurry through the test and race for the door of the classroom.

By any standard you are experiencing an emotion. This sort of behavior can be understood in terms of classical conditioning of an emotional response. In the past, the classroom testing situation (CS) may have been an occasion for failure and criticism from parents or teachers (US). Everything was set up for effective conditioning. The CS came first, then the US, so they were in the correct order. Parents know when tests are given and usually ask how you did. This means that the CS and the US were paired frequently. It would have been an unusual circumstance if you were taking a test and there was no discussion of test performance, so the CS seldom appeared without the US. Finally, although the CS-US interval might seem long, we know from the taste aversion studies that the US can be separated from the CS by hours, so it is not unreasonable to assume that the period between receiving your test grade and receiving your criticism is short enough to allow for effective conditioning. As was the case with Little Albert, your emotional response can then easily spread to similar situations. Instead of responding emotionally to just one type of test (math), stimulus generalization occurs and you respond similarly to other types of tests (English, history, S.A.T., and so on). In Chapter 12, you will see that under many circumstances strong emotions inhibit intellectual activity. This means that your fear almost guarantees that your performance will be less than you are capable of, thus completing the circle. Your poor performance justifies the criticism of your parents and teachers, and that criticism guarantees continued poor performance.

The way out of this circle is through the same principles of conditioning that got you into it. One technique that has proven successful in overcoming test anxiety is called **counterconditioning** (Osterhouse, 1976; Meichenbaum, 1977). In counterconditioning, the person is taught an association that will interfere with anxiety. This means that the CS, the testing situation, is paired with a US that produces a relaxed state rather than an anxious state. First, the person is taught techniques of relaxation, which involve breathing exercises and concentration on tensing and relaxing special muscle groups. Next, the person is told to list the various test-taking situations from the least frightening (such as a small quiz that doesn't count toward the final grade) to the most frightening (such as a major exam that will cover all of the material in the course and count for 60 percent of the grade). Then, while the person is relaxed, the least threatening test-taking scene is visualized. Gradually, the person is asked to visualize more threatening situations while in a relaxed state. Eventually, the person has learned to associate tests with relaxation rather than anxiety. When the time to take the real test comes, the relaxation response replaces the tension response. If all goes well, the test performance will improve, the criticism will turn to praise, and the conditioned emotional response will disappear. Mechanically, there are now two classically conditioned responses: relaxation and anxiety. These two conditions cannot exist at the same time in the same person. You cannot be anxious and relaxed at the same time. This means that after counterconditioning is complete, when the CS (the testing situation) is presented, at the very least the relaxation CR will partially replace the anxiety CR. At the very most, relaxation will completely replace anxiety (see Figure 7-1).

There are other things to be done about test anxiety that also follow from conditioning principles. For example, you might explain to parents and teachers that criticism hurts your performance, and you would prefer that they offer help before exams but not criticism after exams. In this case, you are trying to set up a situation in which the CS will be presented without the US. You will remember that this is called extinction. Next, you might try taking practice exams and have a friend give you positive

Figure 7-1

This diagram shows how text anxiety can be treated through counterconditioning. In both cases the testing situation is the CS. At first the US is criticism from parents and teachers, and the UR and CR are anxiety. Through counterconditioning the US of criticism is replaced by a new US, the muscle and breathing exercises, which in turn produce a new UR and CR, relaxation instead of anxiety in the testing situation.

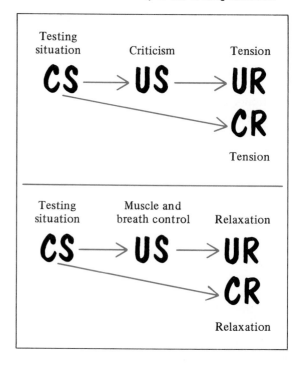

feedback about the amount of information you conveyed. In this case, you are replacing the US of criticism with the US of praise. Finally, you might make use of operant conditioning principles and see if any programmed instruction materials are available for the course you are taking. Programmed instruction usually involves answering questions on small chunks of information immediately after learning them. This means that the probability of getting each question correct is very high. Correctly answering these test questions should produce a positive feeling. Since tests are accumulations of single questions, the greater the success you have in answering programmed questions correctly, the less anxiety you will have during regular test con-

---

REVIEW QUESTIONS

1. _____ _____ is a dislike of a specific food because of an association between that food and a later illness.

2. Humans and animals find some responses easier to make than others, and form some associations more easily than others. This is called _____ .

3. One aspect of taste aversion seems to go against what we know about classical conditioning. This is the fact that the US/CS may be presented hours before the US/CS, and yet conditioning still occurs.

4. In the case of test anxiety, the testing situation is the CS/US/CR/UR, the criticism from parents or teachers is the CS/US/CR/UR, and the anxiety you feel when taking the test is the CS/US/CR/UR.

5. _____ is a technique based on classical conditioning principles and used to treat problems such as test anxiety. It involves substituting a new US (such as relaxation) for the old US (fear or anxiety).

Answers: 1. Taste aversion 2. preparedness 3. CS;US 4. CS; US; CR 5. counterconditioning

---

ditions. Once again, you have replaced one US with another. In every case, the CS remains the same—the test. (Programmed instruction will be discussed in greater detail under operant conditioning applications.)

Phobias. Students who experience test anxiety may be described as having an "irrational fear" of tests. While the term *fear* is accurate, the term *irrational* may at first strike you as inappropriate. It suggests that these students never had any reason for fearing tests when, in fact, test outcomes were probably the signal for punishment and, as such, deserved to be feared. But the term irrational is appropriate in other ways. It implies fear that is out of proportion to the object or situation. For example, there may be good reason to fear a snake while hiking in the woods, but there is less reason to fear a picture of a snake or a snake that is behind thick glass in a zoo. It also implies that there is no *apparent* reason to be afraid of a particular object or situation. Why *should* someone be afraid of something that most people find bearable? Thus irrational conveys the excessive and seemingly unreasonable nature of phobias.

Phobia is the clinical term used to describe irrational fears that people have attached to apparently harmless stimuli. Some common phobias are fear of airplanes, fear of reptiles such as snakes, and fear of heights. Some clinical psychologists (Wolpe, 1958) consider phobias to be the result of past associations. These past associations are examples of classically conditioned responses. Since the response (the CR) is fear or anxiety, and those emotions are unpleasant, people will try to escape from or avoid situations that produce those emotions. Thus, most phobias are a case of a classically conditioned association being protected by an operant response. The person has learned the association between making an escape (or an avoidance response) and making the negative emotion disappear. Since stimulus generalization is often involved in these phobic situations, the avoidance or escape response is activated for a wide range of stimuli. As a result, counterconditioning and various attempts to extin-

---

Counterconditioning. A technique using classical conditioning principles in order to treat a problem such as test anxiety. It includes substituting a new US (such as relaxation) for the old US (fear or anxiety).

Phobias. Irrational or exaggerated fears; examples are fear of snakes, fear of heights, fear of crowds.

Acrophobia is a fear of heights, such as a rooftop or the high floors of a building. Such phobias may be a result of a classically conditioned association being protected by an operant response. Counterconditioning and extinction are both used to treat phobias.

guish these associations may involve not only attention to the original fear-inducing stimulus, but also to the stimuli to which these characteristics have generalized.

The techniques for dealing with phobias are the same as those described for dealing with test anxiety. Counterconditioning and extinction are both popular strategies in which the person is taught to relax in the presence of the fear-inducing stimulus. Many treatment programs involve operant conditioning as well. For example, a person who is afraid of heights might be praised or rewarded by a counselor for looking out a second-floor window. If the counselor is correct in assuming that praise is a reinforcer, the probability that the person will look out a second-floor window again should increase. The counselor then requires greater and greater "brav-

ery" for awarding praise; the person is next praised for looking out a third-floor window, and so on. As you can see, the principle of successive approximation plays a role in the treatment.

Conditioned emotional responses such as fear and anxiety are complicated; they involve both classical and operant responses. Even though these emotions are often initially the result of CS/US pairings, a set of operant escape and avoidance behaviors are learned as a result of these associations. Therapy usually involves treating not only associations, but also overt behaviors. As you can see, a good deal is known about phobic reactions, and treatment programs that are successful have been developed (Bower and Hilgard, 1981; Walker et al., 1981).

Addictions

Drug and alcohol addiction are very difficult problems to treat effectively. People seem unable to do without certain substances, such as heroin, alcohol, nicotine, or caffeine, and require more and more of these substances as time goes by. Here again, learning theory can suggest approaches to treatment.

For the most part, addiction begins with an operant response rather than a classically conditioned association. At first, the person may use a substance to provide some form of stimulation, or may simply notice that the substance produces a good feeling of some kind. After that first experience, addiction depends on how often the substance is used. Even though classical conditioning may not be heavily involved in the initial development of the addiction, it may play a role in its maintenance.

One experience common to most addictions is "craving" for a substance at some point. At first, the substance produces a good feeling when it is used. As time goes on, the person not only feels good when the substance is used but bad in its absence: The alcoholic needs a drink to function normally; the cigarette smoker becomes increasingly agitated when kept from smoking. An interesting thing about many of these cravings is that they are often regular and predictable. Most people who have stopped smoking report having a tough time after a meal, for that is when they seem to crave cigarettes the most. Similarly, recovering alcoholics report that weekends, holidays, and social gatherings produce the most serious temptations.

Many cravings can be understood in the context of classically conditioned associations. Let's consider the smoker for a moment. Cigarettes are most commonly smoked after a meal. The plates are collected, the coffee arrives, and the cigarettes, cigars, and pipes are lit. In the early stages of addiction, plate clearing/coffee appearance represents the CS. The cigarette represents a US and has a predictable and pleasurable effect (the UR). In the later stages, however, the UR actually eliminates discomfort rather than producing comfort. That is, lighting a cigarette relieves an unpleasant feeling. As a result, the end of a meal becomes associated with an unpleasant feeling rather than a pleasant one. The operant response is to light a cigarette to relieve that feeling. It takes some time for the association between plate-clearing and discomfort to disappear. During this time, it is tempting to make the operant response that worked in the past—lighting a cigarette.

If you want to quit smoking, the most important association to break is the one between the response and the reinforcement; somehow you must stop yourself from lighting the cigarette. But remember that a number of CSs in the environment are adding to your problems. For this reason, many therapeutic programs for the elimination of smoking, drinking, or drug use stress the importance of breaking old associations; for example, don't linger at the table after supper, keep busy outside on weekends, don't get together with the people you are accustomed to drinking with, and so on. These classically conditioned associations make it that much more difficult to "kick the habit."

Many former addicts note that they experience withdrawal symptoms when they find themselves in areas where drugs are being used (O'Brien, 1975), just as former smokers feel tense when others are "lighting up." Because this reaction may influence the former addict to use the substance again to eliminate the aversive withdrawal symptoms, it is a potentially serious obstacle to recovery from addiction. A study by O'Brien, Testa, O'Brien, Brady, and Wells (1977) demonstrates just how serious an obstacle it is. The subjects in this study were eight former drug addicts who were enrolled in a residential methadone program. Each day for 21 days, subjects were given an injection of naxolone (a drug that counteracts the effects of heroin). One of the

side effects of naxolone is that it causes mild withdrawal symptoms, including tearing eyes, runny nose, yawning, chills, an increase in breathing rate, and an increase in heart rate. These symptoms represent an aversive situation. Shortly after they had received the naxolone injection, the subjects were presented with a tone and an odor (oil of peppermint). At first, the tone could barely be heard and the odor was very faint. The tone and the odor were then increased in intensity as the withdrawal symptoms increased in intensity. The stimulus intensity continued to increase for 18 minutes (which corresponded to the peak of the withdrawal symptom intensity) and then decreased until the tone was almost inaudible again and the odor was once more faint. The decrease period lasted for about 10 minutes.

In this experiment, the naxolone injection was the US and the combination of the tone and the odor was the CS. The UR was the collection of withdrawal symptoms. After repeated pairings, a series of test trials was presented. In these test trials, only the tone/odor CS was presented. In spite of the fact that no naxolone injections were given, withdrawal symptoms appeared in a majority of the subjects shortly after the tone/odor stimulus was presented. Thus, the "situation" (tone/odor) caused an appearance of withdrawal symptoms, which could now be categorized as a CR. One way to make those symptoms disappear would be to start using drugs again. These data add scientific credibility to the reports of the former addicts, demonstrating how difficult their battle against addiction can be. They also clearly point out the importance of breaking away from past acquaintances, "haunts," and habits in the battle against addiction. These principles are probably just as important for breaking a coffee, cigarette, or chocolate addiction as they are for fighting drug addiction.

■ OPERANT CONDITIONING APPLICATIONS

As we saw earlier, in operant conditioning the learner is free to make any of a number of different responses, and the association that is built up is between a response and reinforcement. In other words, the learner actually interacts with the environment rather than just passively recognizing certain associations between stimuli. Since our actions in the course of a day are so diverse and our environments so unpredictable, the opportunities for the applications of operant principles are also diverse. Most of these applications involve shaping and the use of different types of reinforcement schedules.

Shaping

In the last chapter, we identified shaping as a part of operant learning. Shaping involves reinforcing successive approximations of the desired behavior until the final desired behavior is achieved. The value of operant conditioning principles can be demonstrated by three particular instances of shaping: "pet control," programmed instruction, and behavior therapy.

Pet Control.   When we first got our dog, we ran into a problem. We wanted her to be a "house" dog, which meant we had to get up and walk her in the morning. Unfortunately her sleep schedule and ours did not coincide. She got up and was ready to go out at about 5:00 AM while we, on the other hand, got up at 6:00 and were definitely not enthusiastic about walking her any earlier. Each morning, she would awaken and begin to bark until we came to take her out. We tried to ignore her, but since her barking prevented sleep, we would eventually get up and walk her. If we tried waiting a little longer, she would simply bark a little longer. She always seemed to win the battle. Then, at last, inspiration struck. One night we put an alarm clock on a shelf near her bed in the basement. We set the alarm clock for 5:00 and the next morning, when it rang, went immediately to the basement and took her out for her walk. After doing this for several days, we reset the alarm for 5:15 and again, as soon as it rang, immediately took her out. Over a period of several weeks, we gradually moved the alarm later and later until it was set to ring at 6:00. Our idea worked like a charm. Shortly thereafter we dispensed with the alarm clock altogether. We had no more problems, as she would wait faithfully for the non-existent

WHEN THE BARK IS WORSE THAN THE BITE

Pet control needn't always be a matter of trial and error. Psychologist and animal trainer Daniel Tortora has applied learning theory principles to a commonplace problem with dramatically positive results. The problem is the dog that barks too much. This is not the trained pet that sounds the alarm when an intruder enters the yard. Nor is it the overly suspicious bowser who yaps a few times when new friends come to dinner. It's not even the rascal that intimidates the mailman every day. The problem barker is the dog that ceases to be anybody's best friend because its constant unprovoked noise-making disturbs a whole neighborhood of once-friendly people and frequently keeps its owners up at night.

According to Tortora, the reason this behavior is difficult for some petowners to extinguish, once it is established, is that they don't follow learning theory principles closely enough. While they may punish the dog for barking—by scolding, for example—often they don't build a strong enough association between the behavior and the punishment. Unless the punishment reliably occurs each time the dog barks, it may be completely ineffective. Or the dog may learn an association between the barking and punishment but only in the presence of a certain person. While the owner is away at work, the dog may take advantage of the absence of punishment and bark like crazy.

Tortora's solution is a special electronic collar. Each time the animal barks, the collar buzzes and administers a mild, harmless shock. By pairing the unwanted behavior with a consistent punishment, the dog quickly learns not to bark all the time. In fact, Tortora finds that barking diminishes considerably after only about thirty minutes. Three days of collar-wearing seem to ensure that the dog has kicked the constant barking habit for good. This may lead to a different problem, however. The dog's owner may wake up one day to discover that the family silver disappeared during the night while man's best friend stayed cool under the collar.

Adapted from Tom Dworetzky, "Old Dog, New Trick," *Discover*, January 1985, p. 57

alarm to ring before barking. I am both pleased and embarrassed to note that shortly after this successful shaping experiment, we became parents of a daughter who developed the same sleeping patterns as the dog. She wanted to "up and play" at 5:00 AM and we, needless to say, did not. Encouraged by our recent results, we dusted off the alarm clock and put it in our daughter's room. Soon our daughter, like our dog, learned to wait for the morning "alarm" before demanding attention.

Programmed Instruction. Many years ago, a device called a "teaching machine" was introduced (Pressey, 1929; 1950). This machine, shown in Figure 7–2, was intended to control the pace of learning so that the student progressed in small steps that could be

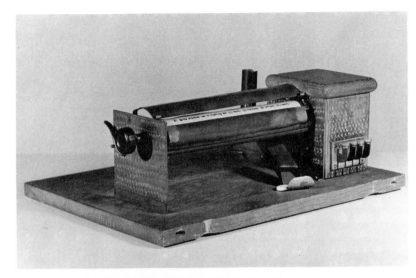

Figure 7–2
On the left is shown one of the first "teaching machines"; below, students use a computer-assisted instruction program. Both devices are based on the fact that the student progresses in small steps that can be easily mastered.

easily mastered. Eventually, the student successfully learned all of the material. This device was the forerunner of a method called **programmed instruction**. Programmed instruction is really self-instruction, with little direct participation of a human instructor (Landy, 1985). In a typical learning session, material is presented in small chunks. A relatively simple question follows immediately. Since little time has passed between receiving the information and having to answer the question, the learner has little opportunity to forget the information, and so usually gives the correct answer. For most people, being told that they are correct is a secondary reinforcer (in the past, correct responses have been associated with other more tangible rewards); thus the response (in this case the correct answer) is strengthened and is more likely to occur again in the future.

Gradually, more and more information is introduced and the questions become more involved. Since the information is introduced gradually and builds on earlier knowledge, fewer errors occur and the learner is less likely to be frustrated and discouraged by the learning experience. This, of course, is the reason for using shaping: to ensure that people are only asked to "perform" at a level appropriate to their knowledge or ability. It is through this successive approximation—the addition of more and more information in small steps—that the final goal or performance level is reached.

A simple version of programmed instruction is the typical "user friendly" computer-based information search system. Consider the simple interaction that occurs in Figure 7–3 between a person and an information network called THE SOURCE, a collection of up-to-date information put in various categories. In the process of using the system, the person doing the search learns a great deal about the internal structure of the search categories (such as news, business, education) as well as how to move through the system. As most seat-of-the-pants computer-users have discovered, the magic word is HELP. In most systems, if you type in the word HELP, you will be given detailed information about how to accomplish what you want with that system. If you are like most users, you will find yourself typing the word HELP less frequently as your experience with the system increases.

If events at Carnegie-Mellon University are any indication, in the next decade you can expect to see a good deal of computer-based learning at colleges and universities (Wall Street Journal, 1982). Students at Carnegie-Mellon are provided with computer terminals in their rooms that can be used for test-taking, self-study, language labs, and other forms of receiving instruction. Personal computers are making similar inroads in private residences. As the equipment becomes cheaper and more available, it is likely that many more people will be exposed to this particular form of learning.

As computer equipment becomes cheaper and more available, it is likely that many more people will learn how to use it.

```
THE SOURCE MAIN MENU

1 NEWS AND REFERENCE RESOURCES
2 BUSINESS/FINANCIAL MARKETS
3 CATALOGUE SHOPPING
4 HOME AND LEISURE
5 EDUCATION AND CAREER
6 MAIL AND COMMUNICATIONS
7 CREATING AND COMPUTING
8 SOURCE*PLUS

ENTER ITEM NUMBER OR HELP 1

NEWS & REFERENCE RESOURCES

1 NEWS AND SPORTS
2 TRAVEL AND DINING
3 GOVERNMENT AND POLITICS
4 CONSUMER INFORMATION
5 SCIENCE AND TECHNOLOGY
6 BYLINES NEWS FEATURES

ENTER ITEM NUMBER OR HELP 1

NEWS AND SPORTS

1 UPI NEWS SERVICE
2 THE EDITORIAL PAGE
3 UPI SPORTS

ENTER ITEM NUMBER OR HELP 1

KEY WORDS (PRESS RETURN FOR ALL STORIES):
   ZONING
```

```
ENTER STARTING & ENDING DATE—OR PRESS
   RETURN FOR TODAY: HELP

ENTER THE EARLIEST AND THE LATEST DATE
   FROM WHICH TO RETRIEVE STORIES IN THE FORM
   MM/DD/YY-MM/DD/YY. LEAVING OFF THE SECOND
   DATE IMPLIES SEARCHING THROUGH TODAY.
   ENTERING JUST A HYPHEN IMPLIES SEARCHING
   FROM EARLIEST ENTRY THROUGH TODAY.

ENTER STARTING & ENDING DATE—OR PRESS
   RETURN FOR TODAY:—

PICK A STARTING STORY NUMBER—FROM 1 (THE
EARLIEST) TO 3 (THE LATEST): 3

READ FORWARD IN TIME (RF), READ BACKWARD
   (RB), SCAN FORWARD (SF) OR SCAN BACKWARD
   (SB)? RB


1-20-83  10:59 AES

      TRENTON, N.J. (UPI)—THE NEW JERSEY SUPREME
COURT TODAY RULED THAT EVERY MUNICIPALITY
MUST PROVIDE A REALISTIC OPPORTUNITY FOR
DECENT HOUSING FOR AT LEAST SOME OF ITS
POOR RESIDENTS.
      IN SEVEN UNANIMOUS VOTES, THE STATE'S
HIGHEST COURT REAFFIRMED ITS STAND TAKEN IN
1975 THAT EXCLUSIONARY ZONING TO KEEP OUT
THE POOR WILL NOT BE TOLERATED....
```

Figure 7-3
A simple example of programmed instruction is a computer-based information search system. The figure shows the main menu of an information network called THE SOURCE. The main menu is a full listing of the search categories. It is the first in a series of progressive steps that will get you the information you need from the computer.

Behavior Therapy. When a client goes to see a clinical therapist, it is usually because of some behavior pattern that has become a problem. This problem may be anything from shyness to sexual dysfunction. The problem is usually long-term, and the behaviors that define it (such as avoiding elevators or excessive use of alcohol) are strong habits. It would be very difficult, if not impossible, to try to change the entire behavior pattern immediately. You can't just tell the person to "go out and act normal" and then reward the "normal" behavior when it occurs. Instead, the behavior therapist

usually works on one piece of the problem at a time. If the person is abnormally shy, the therapist might set as a first goal smiling at someone in a store or at work. The next step might be to make a simple comment such as "Nice day." Finally, the goal might be to engage a stranger in a brief conversation. At each step, the therapist verbally praises the client for successfully completing a "learning"

Programmed instruction. A type of self-instruction in which the material is presented in small chunks with positive reinforcement each time a correct response is made.

task. Once again, the final, desired behavior is approached through successive approximations. We will discuss this technique as it is used in therapy in Chapter 16.

Reinforcement Schedules

During early stages of shaping, reinforcement schedules are usually continuous—that is, every time a correct response is made, a reinforcer is given. What changes over the course of shaping is not the frequency or amount of reinforcement, but what a correct response is defined to be. This reflects an important assumption about operant learning—that the reinforcement must be connected to the response. The single most important proposition of operant learning theorists is that connected or **contingent reinforcers** are necessary for learning to occur. A second important assumption is that different schedules of reinforcement result in different behavior patterns. There is little doubt that contingent reinforcement affects behavior differently than no reinforcement or reinforcement that is not associated in any way with a response (Ferster and Skinner, 1957; Reynolds, 1975). But can this finding be used to any advantage in everyday life? We will examine three settings in which contingent reinforcement has been used to advantage—mental institutions, schools, and work settings.

Mental Institutions. Hundreds of published reports demonstrate the successful use of contingent reinforcement with mental patients in institutions. A typical example is similar to the one reported by Ayllon and Michael (1959). A female patient in a mental institution had a habit of talking nonsensically to such an extent that it frequently provoked her fellow patients to the point that they would beat her to make her stop talking. In order to stop this from happening, the nurses were instructed not to pay attention to the woman's nonsense talk—only to sensible or normal talk. As a result of this program, the patient's percentage of nonsense talk was reduced from 91 percent to 25 percent (Martin and Pear, 1978). Two things are obvious from this report. First, contingent reinforcement was effective in changing the patient's behavior. Second, any sort of attention seemed to be a reinforcer to this patient. Often, the problem in using operant learning procedures is not in applying the reinforcer but in identifying what serves as a reinforcer for that particular person.

An even more dramatic example of the effect of contingent reinforcers can be seen in Figure 7–4. This figure is taken from a study conducted with patients in another mental institution by Ayllon and Azrin (1965). The question addressed in this study was whether reinforcers had to be connected to behavior for a positive effect to be seen. The behaviors in question involved keeping the ward clean, dressing appropriately, and behaving in an "acceptable" manner. If the connection was unnecessary, then just providing rewards at any time during the experimental "session" should have the same effect as connecting the reinforcers to appropriate behavior. Figure 7–4 speaks for itself. When reinforcers were not tied to behavior, "correct" responses almost disappeared. When reinforcers depended on appropriate behavior, "correct" responses were frequent.

The use of operant principles in mental institutions has changed many aspects of patient care. In addition, such principles have been advantageous in directly treating symptoms of mental illness, such as an unwillingness to speak or act in a socially responsive manner (Isaacs et al, 1960; Kale et al, 1968).

Token Economies in Classrooms. A popular application of operant principles that has been tried in primary and secondary schools is known as the **token economy**. In this procedure, students are allowed to earn tokens (often poker chips or similar objects) that can then be traded in for other rewards such as candy, books, supplies, or the chance to play various games. Table 7–1, which was constructed from the description of a token economy study conducted by Packard (1970), illustrates such a system. This table presents two pieces of information that are important to the student: (1) how many tokens can be earned through particular behaviors, and (2) how many tokens must be used to "buy" certain desirable items.

Token economy techniques are often used to aid classroom management. Children can earn tokens by being quiet during special study periods, by keeping their desks clean, by walking in hallways instead of running (although most children seem prepared to run and contraprepared to walk), and by doing other things that either produce environments conducive to learning or eliminate distracting influences

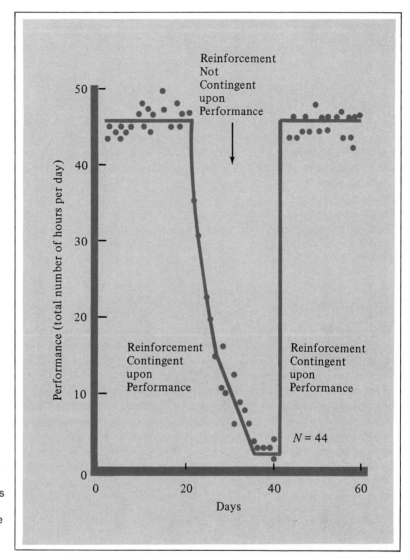

Figure 7-4

The graph shows the effect of contingent reinforcers. When patients in a mental hospital were reinforced for certain behaviors, such as keeping the ward clean or dressing appropriately, the rate of response was high. When reinforcers were just provided at any time, the rate of response dropped sharply. (Ayllon and Azrin, 1965)

in the learning environment. Tokens are secondary reinforcers; they have acquired power to affect behavior as a result of their association with primary reinforcers, such as candy.

Contingent reinforcement has also been effective in developing appropriate study skills in children and adults in school settings. These skills include such things as setting up a schedule for study, studying in a quiet area, accomplishing a set amount of reading during a study session, and so on. In the case of elementary school children, the reinforcement

can be tokens or points of some sort. In the case of older learners, the reinforcement may be self-administered, for example, watching a favorite TV program (Bower and Hilgard, 1981).

Work Settings. As in mental institutions and classrooms, contingent reinforcement can also be used to modify work activities or to "manage" the workplace. The clearest example of the effect of contingent reinforcement on work activities can be seen in piecework incentive schemes. In this type of ar-

---

Contingent reinforcers. Reinforcers that are dependent upon a correct response, that are connected to the response they follow.

Token economy. A system in which people are reinforced for correct response by receiving tokens that they can later trade for candy, books, supplies, free time, extra privileges, and so on.

TABLE 7-1. A Token Economy Study

Behaviors	Level of Performance Required for Reinforcement (3 tokens)	Typical Reinforcers— Tokens could be used to buy:
Acceptable	At the beginning, 12 minutes; gradually increased to 27 out of 30 minutes of class time	10 minutes' access to playing with electric typewriter
Sitting quietly Looking at and listening to the teacher Doing one's lessons	A cue light displayed on the teacher's desk told the class how they were doing. It was green when they were all paying attention, red when one or more were not paying attention	Sitting next to a friend in the next class period 15 minutes' playtime in the gym Serving as a teacher's assistant in the next period
Unacceptable		10 minutes' access to play on a piano
Standing up and walking around the classroom Talking to one's neighbor Singing Sleeping Doodling idly Making and throwing paper airplanes	A recording clock accumulated "attention time" toward the goal for the session	

Source: Adapted from Packard, 1970.

rangement, workers are paid according to how many units are produced. The schedule is usually a fixed-ratio schedule. For example, a worker's job may be glueing grips on pingpong paddles (Garson, 1975); this worker might be paid for every 5 boxes of ping-pong paddles sent to the shipping department.

In manufacturing and service organizations, contingent reinforcement is often in the form of bonus or incentive pay for above-average productivity. A worker may receive a set amount of money for each increase in productivity over the agreed-upon standard.

Another common example of reinforcement schedules in the workplace are annual pay raises, sometimes known as "merit" raises. Most workers know that performance is evaluated at a particular time during the year. Furthermore, they know that next year's pay will depend upon how their performance is evaluated. In other words, if they have performed well during the year, they will receive a raise. It follows that they will behave much more productively as the evaluation time approaches. If you made a graph of their productive efforts, you might see something similar to the curve in Figure 7-5. This curve looks a lot like the fixed interval curve we saw in the last chapter. Responding stays relatively low until just before the time for rein-

forcement, when it picks up, only to drop again after the reinforcement has occurred (in this case after the raises have gone through).

An example of a clever use of reinforcement principles to solve a problem in an industrial setting is supplied by Nord (1966). A hardware company was having a difficult time getting its employees to show up for work on time. To encourage the workers to show up on time, the company started a lottery. Each worker who arrived for work within 30 seconds of starting time every day for one month was eligible to win a $25 prize at the end of the month. There was one prize for every 25 employees in the company. Thus, each worker only had to worry about getting to work on time to have one chance in 25 of winning the prize. Each time another worker was late, it improved the chances to win, so there was a good deal of motivation to arrive on time. The company reported a dramatic increase in the number of workers who were on time for work.

Chaining

Before leaving this section on the application of operant techniques, there is one final topic that we should consider. Operant principles of learning suggest that a response is reinforced or strengthened

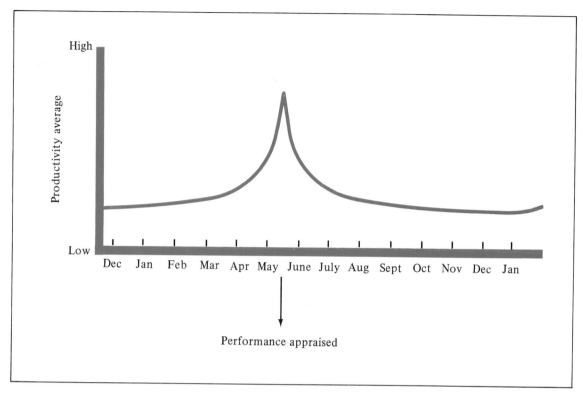

Figure 7-5
This graph is a curve of the performance of workers who are on a fixed interval
schedule of reinforcement (a yearly pay raise based on performance). As the time for
evaluation of performance approaches, in June, the workers' productivity rises
sharply, only to fall off again after the raises have gone through.

through rewards that are connected to making that response. But in our everyday behavior, most of our actions are complicated sequences of responses, not single responses. For example, consider the task of starting a car. We don't just push a start button. We must first place the key in the ignition switch. Next, we must be sure that the gearshift lever is in park or neutral (if the car has an automatic transmission). Then we must turn the key in a particular direction. Finally, we must depress the gas pedal just enough to provide the carburetor with sufficient fuel to mix with air and send to the cylinders. This is not as simple as it seems at first. Each of these actions is tied or chained in some manner to the others. If we press the gas pedal before turning the key, nothing happens. If we turn the key and don't have the car in park or neutral, nothing happens. If we put the gear lever in park, insert the key, and turn the key in the appropriate direction but do not push down the gas

pedal, the motor will turn but the car probably won't start.

Chaining is the technical term for linking several responses together in a sequence. Chaining of responses is most obvious in physical performance; the routine of a figure skater or gymnast is a perfect example. I can give another example from personal experience. As a graduate student with too much time on my hands, I joined two fellow students in teaching a Rhesus monkey to "play basketball." We found that the monkey enjoyed maraschino cherry juice. This became the reinforcer. First, we reinforced the monkey for picking up a ball bearing that was in a cup at the bottom of the cage. Next, we reinforced the monkey for carrying the ball

Chaining. The process of linking several learned responses together in a sequence. An example is starting a car, which consists of a number of connected responses that make up a complex action.

bearing around the cage for several seconds. Then we reinforced the monkey for approaching a plastic funnel attached to the upper bars on one wall of the cage, and next for dropping the ball bearing into that funnel. Since the funnel was connected by means of a plastic tube to the cup where the monkey originally found the ball bearing, it wasn't even necessary to worry about the "rebound." After that, it was simply a matter of reinforcing the monkey for throwing the ball bearing into the funnel from greater and greater distances. You should recognize this as an example of successive approximation. After the shooting response had been "shaped up," we switched to an automatic device for delivering the cherry juice on a VR (variable-reinforcement) schedule and sat back to watch the game. Betting was heavy on how many points would be scored in a 5-minute "quarter." We often regretted being too poor to afford another monkey. Some "one on one" might have given the betting a new dimension.

Sometimes a response chain can become unlinked and cause us problems. For instance, actors often study lengthy speeches in pieces—sentences or paragraphs. One sentence is cued by or chained to the preceding one. Therefore, when an actor forgets one sentence, it is often difficult to go on with the rest of the speech. In the same way, one of the cruelest things to do to a fellow actor is to change a line of yours that acts as a cue; without the proper cue, he will find it difficult to begin his lines.

There are any number of other examples of chained sequences in our daily behavior—making a meal, swinging a golf club, playing a tune on an instrument. In each case, the reinforcer comes only after the performance of a series of connected responses.

We have seen only a small sample of the applications of operant principles to real-world settings. These principles have an almost unlimited number

Most of our actions are complicated sequences of responses rather than single responses. *Chaining* is the term for linking several responses together in a sequence, which is what we do when we learn to start a car.

of such applications. Once again, the important thing to keep in mind is that people are constantly learning how to adapt to their environments. Operant principles are nothing more than descriptions of how this learning may take place. Therefore, we can use these principles to make learning and adaptation more efficient and complete.

REVIEW QUESTIONS

6. A phobia is a case of a _____ _____ association combined with an _____ response of escape or avoidance.

7. When trying to break a habit such as smoking, it is important to break old associations that act as CSs in the environment. T / F

8. Programmed instruction is based partly on the operant technique of _____; information is added in small steps, and people are gradually asked to perform at a higher level until the final performance level is reached.

9. A _____ reinforcer is a reinforcer that is connected to the response it follows.

10. A token economy is based on the power of _____ reinforcers. Thus, although tokens are not in themselves reinforcing, they can be traded in for something that is, such as candy or soda.

11. Match the following examples with the learning technique or principle each is based on:

___ starting a car   A. shaping
___ programmed   B. fixed interval schedule
     instruction   of reinforcement
___ piecework in   C. often treated by coun-
     factory   terconditioning
___ annual pay   D. fixed ratio schedule of
     raise   reinforcement
___ phobia   E. chaining

Answers: 6. classically conditioned; operant 7. True 8. shaping 9. contingent 10. secondary 11. starting a car, E; programmed instruction, A; piecework in factory, D; annual pay raise, B; phobia, C

■ LEARNING AS A COGNITIVE ACTIVITY

Up to this point, we have been examining applications of learning theory in terms of association. The association has been either between two stimuli (the CS and the US in the classical conditioning situation) or between a response and a reinforcer (as in operant conditioning). We have seen how these associations play a role in complicated everyday behavior. Cognitive activity, which we will consider at length in later chapters also has important applications for learning. But there are some instances in which basic associations interact with cognitive activities to yield some unusual behaviors. We will consider three of those instances briefly.

Learned Helplessness

Until now, we have been examining situations in which a subject learns a particular response to some environmental situation. But what happens when the learner's responses have no effect on the environment? In particular, what happens when a learner is punished and cannot escape that punishment? The answer seems to be that the learner gives up trying to learn. This answer is not startling in itself; what is startling is that this giving up is another kind of a learned response that shows up later when the learner is placed in similar learning situations. A suggested cause for this "giving-up" response has been labelled **learned helplessness,** and it has some important implications for understanding the behavior of depressed people.

Learned helplessness was examined by Seligman and Maier (1967), who conducted shock research with dogs. There were three groups of dogs. Each dog was suspended in a type of harness that kept it from moving around. In one experimental group, called the escape group, each dog was given a shock to its hind leg; however, the dog could shut off the shock by pressing a panel with its head. In the second experimental group, the non-escape group, each dog was also given a shock but could not shut it off, no matter what the dog did. A third group acted as

---

Learned helplessness. A response involving giving up to the feeling that your actions cannot affect an aversion or punishment environment or situation.

a control and received no shock at all but was simply suspended from the harness for periods of time equal to the other two groups. This was the "training" phase of the experiment.

After each dog received 64 training trials, the "test" phase of experiment began. In this phase, each of the animals from the three different groups was placed in one side of an experimental box with two chambers separated by a high partition. A test trial began when the lights were lowered in the experimental box. After 10 seconds, a shock was delivered through the floor of the box. The dog could escape the shock by jumping or climbing over the partition to the other side of the box. Eventually, the dog could learn to avoid the shock completely by simply climbing or jumping over the partition when the lights were lowered.

The performance of the dogs who had been in the non-escape training group was dramatically different from the other two groups. The results are presented in Figure 7–6. As you can see, the non-escape group *never* learned to escape from or avoid

FIGURE 7-6

This graph shows the result of Seligman and Maier's study of learned helplessness in dogs, which is described in the text. Dogs in the escape group, who in earlier trials had been able to cut off shock by making a certain response, here quickly learned how to escape shock by jumping over a partition in the cage. The same held true for the control group, which was not shocked in early trials but later also quickly learned to escape from shock by jumping over the partition. The nonescape group of dogs, however, who in early trials were shocked but could not shut it off, in later trials never learned to escape from the shock by jumping over the partition; in fact they never tried to escape the shock at all. This giving-up response is called learned helplessness. *(Adapted from Maier and Seligman, 1976.)*

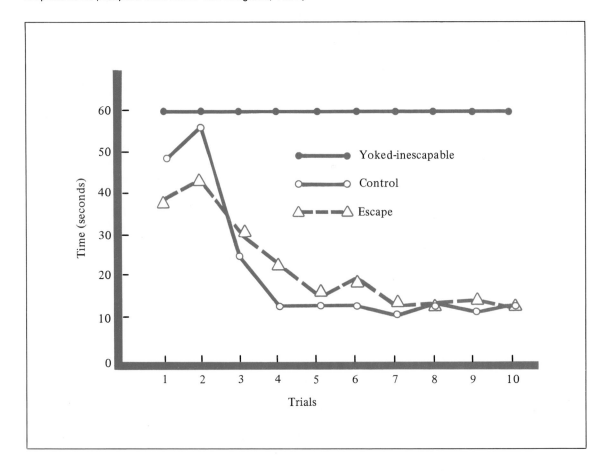

the shock. The other two groups learned rapidly and were seldom shocked.

Hall (1982) believes that the response of the non-escape dogs results from a cognitive operation. In a sense, on the basis of past experience with shock, the dog has assumed that no matter what it does, it cannot escape the shock. The previous association is preventing the formation of a new, more adaptive, association (that it can escape from or avoid the shock by jumping over the partition). In addition to the cognitive operation, Seligman and Maier also suggest that motivational and emotional factors are involved as well. Motivation to escape seems to be reduced in the non-escape group. In fact, the dogs eventually stop moving at all. There also seems to be an emotional change; fear seems to be replaced with what looks like depression.

Seligman (1975) has suggested that there are many parallels between the behavior of animal subjects in learned helplessness studies and humans who are severely depressed. Chronically depressed people show little enthusiasm, seem to be low on energy, are willing to let others decide what will happen to them, and seem unwilling to make a move in any direction. Abramson, Seligman, and Teasdale (1978) have proposed that in addition to a history of being unable to avoid or escape punishment, people who are depressed have certain beliefs that influence their behavior. For example, if people believe that success in the task at hand is a matter of skill and that they do not have that skill, it is likely that they will become depressed and adopt the learned helplessness pattern. This suggests that an effective form of therapy might include changing the beliefs of depressed people and giving them relevant skills to avoid punishment. Some of these strategies are described in Table 7-2.

There are endless opportunities for learned helplessness responses to develop—parents punishing children constantly for any offense, a spouse criticizing every attempt by a partner to be effective, a student poorly prepared to cope with a difficult and demanding course. When this is coupled with experiences that lead people to believe that they have no control over the environment, or that success is a matter of luck rather than skill, all of the ingredients for learned helplessness are there.

We will deal extensively with depression in the chapters dealing with emotion and abnormal behavior (Chapters 12 and 15). Not all depression

TABLE 7-2.
Strategies for Combating Learned Helplessness

Strategy A.

Change the individual's expectation about control of the situation from uncontrollability to controllability.

Specific Examples

1. Train the person in the necessary skills to attain his or her goal. These could include social skills, skills in resolving marital problems, or child management skills.
2. If the person already has the skills but doesn't believe this is so, use methods like assertiveness training and role playing to produce evidence of the skills and then reinforce the person for using them.

Strategy B.

Change unrealistic attributions for failure and success.

Specific Examples

1. It is not because you are incompetent but because the system is still closed to women. Or, the system is changing. Another opportunity will come if you keep looking.
2. He loves you not because he is insecure but because you are a warm appealing person.

Source: Adapted from Abramson, Seligman, and Teasdale, 1978, p. 69.

is the result of learned helplessness. Nevertheless, in dealing with a case of chronic depression, it is a good idea to look into the person's past for some inescapable punishment experiences that are combined with a set of beliefs about effectiveness. This is a dramatic example of how cognitive operations can *prevent* us from learning in certain situations.

Social Learning Theory

Social learning theory emphasizes the associations that are formed through observing the actions of others. As Bandura has suggested, we choose models, watch them perform, and then imitate their patterns of behavior, monitoring and correcting our actions until they match the model's actions as closely as possible. Bandura suggests that this observational learning is the way we learn many complex behaviors. If this is true, then it makes sense to

HE SAW IT ON TELEVISION

In what may go on record as the "youngest person to execute a life-saving maneuver," Brent Meldrum, aged 5, stopped Tanya Branden, aged 6, from choking on a piece of candy. Despite protests from his mother, Brent performed the tricky Heimlich technique on Tanya. He slipped his arms around her from behind, clasped his hands together, and squeezed, lifting the 41-pound girl off the floor. After he banged her on her feet a few times, she leaned over, coughed hard, and expelled the candy. A good story, surely, but how is this an application of learning theory?

Brent never used the term observational learning in the account he later gave to reporters. But as he explained, he knew what to do from having watched it done on *Benson*, a television show. 'I knew what to do. I saw this on Benson," said Brent. "Benson was choking. His cheek was blown up like a balloon and a different guy went behind him, put his arms around, squeezed him, lifted him up, and saved Benson."

Luckily for Tanya, Brent was not familiar with learned helplessness.

develop training (learning) programs based on the same principles.

Social learning theory is not radically different from the more traditional classical and operant approaches. In it, associations are important, as is reinforcement. The real difference lies in how the associations are formed and what type of reinforcement is used. In social learning theory, it is assumed that associations are made through observation. That is, they are formed through ideas and not just through exposure to two stimuli (as in classical conditioning), or by directly experiencing the relationship between a response and a reinforcement (as in operant conditioning). Social learning theory is therefore considered a cognitive theory. In addition, social learning theory emphasizes the importance of *social* reinforcement—praise and criticism—on learning. This sets it apart from a strict operant approach, which does not assume that one type of reinforcement is more or less important than any other type.

For over a decade, both General Electric and IBM have been using social learning theory to train first- and second-level supervisors in managerial skills and human relations (Burnaska, 1976). A typical training program consists of observing the behavior of a successful manager on videotape as he or she deals with human relations problems. Next, the trainee practices the behavior portrayed on the videotape by pretending to be the manager seen on the tape. The trainers or other trainees assume the roles of others who were involved in the taped se-

quence. The trainee then receives feedback on how well the behavior was learned and demonstrated. Finally, the trainee takes the behavior back to the real job and tries it out (Landy, 1985). Similar programs have been found to be successful in training managers in techniques of performance evaluation, work assignment, new employee orientation, and employee complaint management (Latham and Saari, 1978). These studies have shown that the observational or social learning approach is as effective as, and sometimes superior to, traditional classroom instruction.

Social learning approaches are also playing a substantial role in helping people overcome habits that they see as obstacles to a more pleasant and effective life. One popular area for social learning strategies has been assertiveness training. Many people feel that they are too submissive and that, consequently, others take advantage of them. One technique for increasing assertiveness is through studying and practicing the responses of a hypothetical individual, called a "model," who behaves correctly in a particular situation. In the case of assertiveness, this model might be firm without being nasty. Consider the person who is trying to change from being everyone's doormat to someone who can say "no" on appropriate occasions. Figure 7–7 provides a sample script for such learning experience. It is a fictitious conversation between someone who is trying to become more assertive (Maryellen) and a friend who has grown accustomed to taking advantage of her lack of assertiveness. This script can be used to pro-

1. Use assertive nonverbal behavior.
    —look directly at focal person when speaking
    —use gestures which are appropriate to verbal messages
    —use facial expressions which match the verbal message
2. Avoid adversive reactions.
    —such as: aggression
                slander (criticism of focal person)
                sarcasm
                over-apologizing
                threats
3. Use appropriate verbal behavior.
    —accept manipulative criticism yet maintain responsibility for your decision
    —calmly repeat a negative reply without justifying it
    —be honest about your feelings, needs, etc. (use "I" statements)
    —accept your faults calmly without apology

"Refusing Unreasonable Request" (Assertiveness) *Modeling Display Script*
    —*Boy Maryellen! Am I glad to see you! But I've got a problem and I was afraid I couldn't get anyone to help me out.*
Model—*Oh, yeah? What's the problem?*
    —*Well, I'd like to borrow your car this afternoon.*
Model—*Hum, that is a problem. I don't think I want to lend my car today.*
    —*Well, why not?*
Model—*I understand that you need it. I just don't want to lend my car today.*

    —*Well, do you have someplace to go?*
Model—*I might want to use it later.*
    —*You could just say when and I could bring it back to you on time.*
Model—*I know that you would. I just don't want to lend my car today.*
    —*I don't understand. You know whenever I've asked to borrow your car before you've always lent it to me.*
Model—*I know I did.*
    —*So what's the difference? Why won't you lend it to me today? I wouldn't do anything to your car.*
Model—*Oh, I know, Paul; and I can see that you're in a jam. But I just don't want to lend my car.*
    —*Come on Maryellen! I'm a good driver.*
Model—*I know, that's true; but when I lend my car I worry, and I just don't need that hassle today.*
    —*But I'm not going to wreck it or anything!*
Model—*I know, and it's probably dumb to feel this way, but I do.*
    —*Well, Maryellen, if it's so dumb, why won't you lend me your car?*
Model—*Because I just don't want to have to worry!*
    —*But, I wouldn't do anything wrong.*
Model—*I know, Paul. It's not you that's the problem, it's me; but I just don't want to lend my car because I worry—so I'm not going to lend it.*
    —*Okay, I can understand how you feel. If I had a car I probably wouldn't want to lend it out either . . . to have the worry and everything.*
Model—*Oh . . . well, thanks for understanding.*
    —*Oh, that's all right. Maybe I'll see you later, if I can find a car from someone else. Um . . . maybe at Phil's party?*
Model—*Okay . . . I'll see you then . . . bye-bye.*
    —*Okay . . . Bye, Maryellen.*

Figure 7-7
Social learning approaches are being tried in areas like management training and assertiveness training. The sample script shown here can be used in an assertiveness training session. A learning point (use appropriate verbal behavior) is identified, followed by a script that can be acted out and used as a video-taped modeling exercise.

duce a video-tape modeling exercise. First, the person is told what principles to follow. These are identified as the "learning points." Then the person is shown a scene in which Maryellen and her friend act out the script material. Following the brief taped sequence, there might be a discussion of exactly how and where the learning points were illustrated in the tape. The person might then practice playing this role with someone else. The person will receive praise for trying any or all of the assertive behaviors that Maryellen demonstrated.

Latent Learning

The experimental psychologist E. C. Tolman was an early advocate of the cognitive approach to learning. He believed that learning was more than just built-up associations. Much of his research involved

studying the way in which rats were able to learn the path through a **maze** (a system of pathways and blind alleys with one correct path leading to the goal). As a result of this research, he proposed that the rats actually formed a **cognitive map** or mental picture of the maze. He further claimed that this map would be formed whether or not the rat was rewarded with food for learning the way out of the maze. He used the results of an experiment to make this point. Tolman and Honzik (1930) provided one group of rats with experience in a maze. They were simply permitted to wander around the maze for a period of time although there was no reinforcement attached to this wandering. A control group was given no such "wandering" experience. Both groups of rats were then deprived of food. During the test phase, both groups were given food as reinforcement for successfully running the maze. The group that had "wandering" experience learned much more quickly than the group that had no such experience. Thus, as they wandered the rats must have learned something about the maze that they were able to use at a later time. A recent study by Menzel (1978) produced similar results. Chimpanzees were carried around a field and permitted to observe food being hidden there by the experimenter. The chimps were then returned to their cage and, after a time, released into the field. They were able to

find the food very easily. Even more interesting, they often took a more direct route to the hidden food than the experimenter had taken! In both the Tolman and Honzik study and the Menzel study, the learning that had occurred did not appear until a later time. As a result, this type of learning is called **latent learning.**

You have probably had a similar experience at some time as, for example, when it was necessary to find a building or a street in a particular section of a city with which you were only vaguely familiar. You may have been through that section once or twice before but only on your way to somewhere else. There was no reason to remember the details of that area. Nevertheless, in the course of looking for the building or street, you remember certain details—a one-way street, a swimming pool, a vacant lot. These details help you in finding your way. Obviously, you were able to learn some details without intending to do so. The learning that we actually use is probably only a small percentage of the learning that has occurred in our lifetimes.

Learning Without Awareness

Our last two examples were of learning that took place without obvious awareness. But, as we saw in Chapter 5, there are many different levels of aware-

REVIEW QUESTIONS

12. When you are in an aversive or punishing situation where you feel that nothing you do can affect what happens to you, the response is often a kind of "giving up" called _____ _____.

13. Many training seminars use videotaped programs in which a successful manager is shown dealing with various problems. This approach is based on _____ learning.

14. In social learning theory, it is assumed that associations can be made through _____ rather than through direct experience. It emphasizes the use of social _____ such as praise and criticism.

15. A group of rats were allowed to wander around a maze without receiving any _____ for it. In a later test, the fact that this group ran the maze so quickly means that they had formed a _____ _____ of the maze. The fact that they had learned their way around the maze earlier, but did not show this until they were reinforced later, is why this type of learning is called _____ learning.

Answers: 12. learned helplessness 13. observational 14. observation; reinforcement 15. reinforcement; cognitive map; latent.

ness. The question is *how* aware must we be to learn? Several psychologists have studied learning without awareness, and their results are quite interesting. In a typical experiment, the subject is asked simply to produce words one after another (Bower and Hilgard, 1981). The subject is led to believe that the research deals with the tonal qualities of speech. But while the subject is saying the words, the experimenter applies the "treatment," that is, begins the real experiment. Every time the subject uses a plural noun, the experimenter quietly mumbles "uh-huh" or "fine" or some other sign of approval. The result of these experiments is usually a significant increase in the number of plural nouns said by the subject, without any obvious awareness on the part of the subject that this is occurring. Over the years, there has been some disagreement about whether the subjects in these experiments are really unaware (DeNike and Spielberger, 1963), but learning without awareness has also been demonstrated in other types of experiments that are not so vulnerable to criticism (Hefferline and Keenan, 1963; Sasmor, 1966).

Learning without awareness has important implications for a wide range of behaviors. For example, it may be possible to influence the results of a telephone or face-to-face opinion poll through the selective reinforcement of certain comments. The interviewer could make supporting noises when the person being questioned discussed one candidate, and no noises or negative noises when the other candidate was discussed. The same procedure could be used when discussing products that are part of market surveys or advertising campaigns. Interestingly, the interviewer may be just as unaware of the "learning" as the person being interviewed. As we will see in the chapter on therapy (Chapter 16), clinical psychologists often use this technique on purpose to get clients talking about a particular subject or to stop them from talking about another. Remember our earlier example of the patient in the mental institution? The nurses were able to stop the patient from talking nonsensically by paying attention to normal talk.

What can we conclude from our discussion of learned helplessness, social learning theory, latent learning, and learning without awareness? For one thing, we can conclude that learning involves more than simple associations. It doesn't matter whether our associations are stimulus-stimulus or response-reinforcement; there is more to learning than just making connections. For another thing, we can conclude that learning can occur without any obvious reinforcer being involved. We can also conclude that learning resembles perception in that a number of processes seem to go on "automatical-

---

Maze. A system of pathways and blind alleys with one correct path leading to the goal. The objective in running a maze is to get from the starting point to the goal with the fewest possible errors.

Cognitive map. A mental picture. In the Tolman experiment, rats had learned the route that led to the goal and thus had a cognitive map of the maze.

Latent learning. Learning that occurs but is not apparent until a later time.

ly" without any obvious control being exerted by the learner.

The importance of associations as the building blocks of learning cannot be denied. As we have seen in this chapter, the knowledge of certain associations can be quite useful in solving some real problems that people encounter. Nevertheless, to understand the full range of learning tasks and behaviors, we must often add cognitive variables and processes to these principles of association.

Life is one long learning study. The opportunities to apply various learning principles are limited only by the hours in the day and the extent to which our environment does not change. In all the applications we have covered in this chapter, it should have become obvious that no one set of learning principles is sufficient to cover all our opportunities to learn. It is not likely that any one theory will ever be designated as the "correct" one.

■ SUMMARY

1. The aim of this chapter is to discover how learning principles find application in everyday life. The first question is whether principles arrived at through the study of animal behavior can apply to humans. We investigate this question by examining the concept of *preparedness*. Seligman conducted a review of learning experiments and found that some associations are formed more easily than others and that some responses are easier to make than others. Because of these findings, Seligman proposed that there are three types of associations: (1) the *prepared* association, one that occurs easily as a result of characteristics native to the subject's species; (2) the *unprepared* association, one that is not necessarily favored by the characteristics of the subject but can be learned; and (3) the *contraprepared* association, or one that is difficult to learn. In considering applications of learning theory, it is important to remember the concept of preparedness, since some forms of behavior may be easier for humans to learn than others.

2. One form of classical conditioning is the conditioned emotional response. Test anxiety is one instance in which a CS, the testing situation, becomes associated with a US, criticism from parents or teachers, resulting in a CR, anxiety. The CR might

become generalized and begin to occur in any kind of test situation.

3. *Counterconditioning* is a procedure used to extinguish behaviors like test anxiety. In this method, the person is taught an association that will interfere with anxiety. The person is first taught to relax and then, while relaxing, to visualize situations that would be increasingly more anxiety-producing. Eventually, the person learns to associate relaxation with the event that was once threatening.

4. *Phobias* involve fear that is out of proportion to the stimulus object or situation. Since emotional responses involve both classical and operant conditioning, treatment of phobias often includes counterconditioning, extinction, and successive approximation.

5. Addictions often involve classically conditioned associations. Treatment programs usually stress breaking those associations.

6. One application of operant conditioning is *programmed instruction*. Because information is introduced gradually and builds on earlier knowledge, fewer errors occur and the learner is less likely to be frustrated by the learning experience. Through the addition of more and more information, or successive approximation, the final performance level is reached. Behavior therapy also relies on operant conditioning procedures to change problematic behavior.

7. The most important principle of operant learning theory is that response and reinforcement are connected, or the reinforcer is *contingent* upon the response. Operant learning techniques are often used in mental institutions. As in other situations where operant conditioning is used, the reinforcer must be contingent on the performance of the appropriate behavior. The reinforcer must also be something that is desirable to the patient for operant conditioning procedures to be effective.

8. Operant learning principles have been used successfully in both the classroom and the workplace. In a *token economy*, a system often used in schools, particular behaviors earn tokens, which students can trade for rewards such as candy or books. The students need to know how many tokens a behavior will earn, and how many tokens they must earn to buy desirable items. In the work setting, the piecework incentive system is actually a fixed-ratio schedule. An example of contingent reinforcement is the practice of awarding bonus pay for perform-

ance of a particular task. Workers who receive raises at the same time every year tend to perform better around raise time, which is similar to the way that a subject on a fixed-interval reinforcement schedule increases responding around the end of the interval.

9. *Chaining* is linking several responses together in a sequence in order to receive a reward after the last response in the chain. Examples of chaining include making a meal, driving a car, and playing a tune on an instrument.

10. When no behavior brings about any relief from punishment the learner often stops trying to learn. This giving-up response becomes generalized to other situations and is called *learned helplessness*. Animal and human subjects who have repeatedly experienced an unpleasant stimulus over which they have no control display the emotional and motivational behaviors that we usually classify as depression. Some theorists argue that severely depressed people have certain beliefs about their skills and effectiveness that cause them to adopt patterns of learned helplessness. Effective treatment would therefore focus on changing beliefs as well as teaching skills that would help avoid punishment.

11. Social learning theory emphasizes the associations that are formed by observing others' behavior. This theory is considered a cognitive one because it assumes that associations can be made by observing, rather than actually experiencing, a behavior. Social learning theory emphasizes the role of praise and criticism as social reinforcers.

12. Learning that appears only after time has passed is known as *latent learning*. This type of occurrence is also called *learning without awareness* because the learner is not conscious of recording information until the time comes to use it.

■ ANSWERING QUESTIONS FOR THOUGHT

1. Test anxiety may be viewed as a classically conditioned emotional response, in which the testing situation is the CS, the criticism from parents or teachers is the US, and the anxiety is the UR and CR. One way of reducing test anxiety is to pair the testing situation with a new US (such as relaxation) through counterconditioning.

2. The most common time to light a cigarette is after a meal. For people who have been smoking for a long time, that association is hard to break. There are lots of other CSs in the environment right after a meal, such as clearing the table, having a cup of coffee, and so on, and in order to break the association it is best to avoid these situations or cut them short as soon as possible.

3. Yes, it is quite possible to learn a new skill through observational learning. This involves watching a model perform on a film or videotape and then imitating those actions, monitoring and correcting one's own actions until they match the model's as closely as possible.

4. Shyness can be treated through the operant technique of shaping. This starts by setting out small, easy tasks for a shy person to do, such as smiling at a stranger or saying "Nice day" to someone. By reinforcing these easy tasks and gradually demanding more difficult steps, the therapist builds up to the final desired goal.

5. This response arises in a number of ways, but it is common in cases in which people have been punished and have been unable to escape from that punishment. Then, just as in the case of Seligman's dogs, they learn to give up and stop responding, because they feel that no matter what they do it will have no effect.

8 Memory

QUESTIONS FOR THOUGHT

1. Some events are remembered for only a day or two, others for weeks, and still others for an entire lifetime. Why?
2. Is it better to be the first person called for a job interview or the last in line?
3. Why do some people remember faces better than others?
4. Is it possible to have a memory of something that never actually happened to you?
5. Eyewitness testimony is highly persuasive in the courtroom. Is it reliable?

The answers to these questions are at the end of the chapter

Recently an airplane left the Miami airport on a flight to the Caribbean. Shortly after take-off, one engine failed, then a second, and finally the third and last. The pilot turned back toward Miami, preparing to ditch the plane in the ocean as close as possible to land. The Coast Guard was standing by. Passengers were told to put on life vests and feared the worst as the plane dropped 20,000 feet in a matter of minutes. At an altitude of only 2,000 feet above the ocean surface, the pilot managed to restart one of the engines. The plane limped back to the Miami airport on one engine and landed safely. This near-tragedy was caused by two mechanics who forgot to replace a rubber washer on the oil plug of each of the engines. That day, a case of simple forgetting might have had serious results.

Contrast this failure to remember with the exceptional memory of S.F., an undergraduate who served as a subject in a memory study (Ericsson and Chase, 1982). By the time the study was completed, S.F. was able to recall a string of 82 randomly chosen numbers. To appreciate what an accomplishment that is, look at the sample memory exercise in Table 8-1. Study the 82 numbers for a minute or two and then have a friend choose either a row or a column at random and ask you to recite the numbers in it. How well did you do? S.F. was able to remember similar sets of numbers perfectly.

A third situation involving memory should be familiar to you from the introduction to Chapter 2, which described the case of H.M., an epileptic who underwent radical surgery to control his seizures. The operation was successful but there was a disastrous after-effect; following the operation H.M. could not form any new memories. He had no trouble retaining memories of events or things that had occurred before the surgery, but after it

he could not even remember how to get from the hospital corridor to his new room.

These are three extreme cases that call attention to memory. In the first example, we encounter a common occurrence—forgetting a small detail. In the second, we see a display of extraordinary memory. The third relates a situation in which memory appears to be permanently damaged. It is tempting to attribute these three cases to individual differences in memory. You might say that *you* would never forget to put the washer on an oil plug, but you probably have forgotten similar things. You may think that you couldn't memorize rows and columns of numbers as S.F. did, but you probably could—there was nothing special about S.F.'s intelligence aside from the fact that he *worked* at learning random sets of numbers for 230 hours. Since

TABLE 8-1.
Sample Memory Exercise

4	3	1	8	2	5
8	6	7	2	9	1
9	2	9	6	4	
1	8	3	4	7	
7	5	8	1	6	
5	9	6	5	3	
2	7	4	9	5	
3	4	5	7	8	
8	1	2	3	1	
6	2	7	9	3	
4	9	3	1	7	
2	4	8	5	2	
9	8	4	6	4	
5	3	2	2	8	
7	9	6	8	5	
1	5	9	3	9	

H.M. had an organic problem resulting from an operation, you might conclude that you would never have problems committing new information to memory, but you do. Chances are there have been times when you "studied" a chapter of a textbook for a long while and then couldn't remember many of the important facts you had just read. The point is that memory represents a collection of on-going processes in each of us. There are some instances in which the processes work poorly; others in which they work remarkably well. Both types of instances are evident in each of us. Either airline mechanic might have been able to tell you the current batting averages of the starting members of the New York Yankees to the third decimal place. S.F. might have had difficulty remembering the color of the room in which he spent the 230 hours memorizing strings of numbers. H.M. could easily recall details of his childhood.

Hermann Ebbinghaus, a German psychologist of the late nineteenth century, conducted the first systematic experiments on human memory.

Memory research has a long and distinguished history in psychology. Hermann Ebbinghaus, a German psychologist of the late nineteenth century, paved the way by studying how associations are formed and later retrieved. As you recall from Chapter 1, introspection was then a popular method of psychological research. Ebbinghaus used the introspective method to study his own memory. He set about describing how *he* formed associations between previously unassociated stimuli. It was obvious to him that he could not use words or symbols with which he was familiar, since these already had associations "attached," so he created a new set of stimuli that had no prior associations. These stimuli consisted of two consonants separated by a vowel and thus did not constitute a word: examples would be *zaf*, *mib*, or *tus*. These letter combinations are commonly referred to as "nonsense syllables." Nonsense syllables played a major role in early memory research. Over a period of years, Ebbinghaus systematically memorized several thousand lists of nonsense syllables, and in the process learned a great deal about how remembering and forgetting occur. He also developed a number of simple memory tasks and observed as people did them.

Memory research has grown considerably since the days of the nonsense syllable. In this chapter, we will consider the mechanics of memory and the implications of memory for other behaviors. To begin, we will outline the three major tasks in remembering. First, the information must be entered in memory. Next, it must be maintained or stored until the time comes for its use. Finally, it must be retrieved or taken out of memory and used in a particular situation. This sequence puts episodes of forgetting in a slightly different light. Consider the mistake made by the airline mechanics. They may have been new on the job and had never entered the information about replacing the washers into memory. Or, they may have initially entered but not maintained the memory, because they seldom worked on this type of airplane. (As you will see later, rehearsal or re-use of information can help to maintain it in memory.) Or, they may have stored the memory but failed to retrieve it for use in this situation. This last is the most likely explanation for the forgotten washers. In leaving out a major step in the memory process, the mechanics left out a step in the engine-assembly sequence.

■ A MODEL OF MEMORY

The major function of memory is to process information. You will recall from Chapters 3 and 4 that stimuli from the outside world are first picked up by sensory receptors and then transferred to the brain, where they are interpreted or perceived. These sensations and perceptions are the materials of memory. They can be held in memory for periods as short as 1/4 of a second—or as long as a lifetime. You were also introduced to the physiological structures and cognitive processes involved in sensation and perception. The structures are mechanisms such as sensory receptors and neural pathways. The processes are tendencies such as grouping and other Gestalt organizational principles. Memory is often conceived of in a similar way. The structures are components such as sensory memory, short-term memory, and long-term memory. The processes are mental operations such as rehearsal and coding. These structures and processes can be combined to create a model of memory like the one shown in Figure 8–1. Let's first look closely at the model and then relate the model to something with which you are familiar.

In the model, something that happens in the real world (environmental input) is held briefly as a sensory image (sensory store), is transferred and kept active temporarily (short-term memory or STM), is processed for current action (response output), is processed or transformed for later use (control processes), and is stored for later use (long-term memory or LTM). As you can see from the model, structures (sensory store, STM, and LTM) and processes (rehearsal, coding, retrieval, and so on) combine in memory.

This conceptual model is very similar to something with which you are probably familiar—the computer. The computer is often described as an information-processing model. You sit down at a computer keyboard and type in information (environmental input). This information is not usually sent directly to the computer as you hit each key. Instead, it is kept in an unanalyzed form in a buffer (sensory store) until you finish typing a line and hit a control key (such as a RETURN key). Computers often display the information in the sensory store or buffer on a screen. This is an aid to your memory. Nothing happens to this information until you send it from the buffer to the computer's central processing unit by hitting the control key. The central processor is similar to short-term memory, or STM. Material passes through the central processor on its

Figure 8–1
This figure shows the structures and processes of the Atkinson and Shiffrin model of memory. (Atkinson and Shiffrin, 1971)

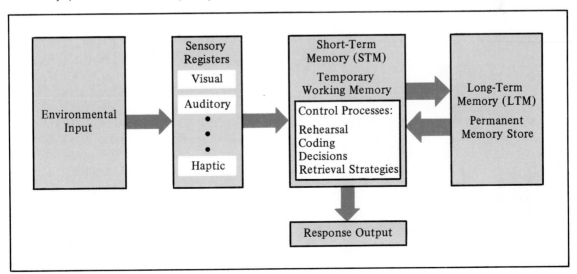

way to storage and is brought out of storage again into central processing. (In our conceptual model, material to be remembered comes from a sensory store into STM on the way to LTM. Material comes back out of LTM into STM for use in a current situation.) When you are finished typing on the computer, you make sure that the material is stored so that you can work on it again later. You store it by giving certain commands (for example, by typing SAVE on the keyboard). The material now exists permanently on a tape or a diskette (LTM). If you want to work on the material again tomorrow, you can call it back from the tape or diskette with another command (by typing GET and the name of the job). This is equivalent to a retrieval process.

An Overview of the Model

Let's now apply the conceptual model to the human memory system instead of a computer. Atkinson and Shiffrin, the researchers who developed the model, proposed that there are three different structures of human memory: sensory store, short-term memory, and long-term memory (1968). We will examine each one in detail, but first let's consider how they work together. A brief demonstration of their interaction may help make this clear. For our example, we will use a simple memory task such as those sometimes used in memory experiments. The model begins with environmental input.

Even though the human memory system is an internal one, it can be related to external memory systems, in particular computers.

Imagine that you are taking part in a psychology experiment, and the experimenter announces that a string of five unrelated letters will briefly flash on a screen in front of you. Your task is to write down the letters on a sheet of paper. If the letters are on the screen for only a very brief time—such as 1/100th of a second or 10 milliseconds (10 msec)—your performance will depend on whether you can preserve a sensory image of the letters long enough to recognize them. The lingering sensory image gives you additional time to recognize the letters. Visual images do appear to remain for some short period of time, about 1/4 of a second, after the actual stimulation disappears. This may not seem very long, but it is 25 times longer than the original stimulation (1/100th of a second). What is true for sight is also true for the other senses. A sound has an image—a sensory echo—that remains for a brief period; the same is true of touch. The important thing to keep in mind is that the sensory image remains after the stimulus itself is gone, allowing us to recognize even a brief stimulus. In the case of the 1/100th-of-a-second presentation of letters, without the lingering image you would not have enough time to recognize the letters before the stimulus disappeared.

Once you have recognized the letters in the sensory image, your next problem is to keep them in memory until you have a chance to write them down. People who participate in this kind of experiment typically report that they use **verbal rehearsal,** (repeating information over and over, silently or out loud) to remember the letters.

Verbal rehearsal works as a control process in two ways. One is to keep information in STM until we are ready to use it. This is hardly the most efficient way to remember something permanently, but it can be quite effective for a short while. For example, we often repeat a phone number to ourselves until we finish dialing it or rehearse a library call number until we locate the book. The other way verbal rehearsal functions is as a learning strategy used to transfer information from STM to LTM. Thus, even though the stimulus in our experiment only appeared for 10 msec, rehearsal keeps the stimulus "present" for considerably longer. Atkinson and Shiffrin argue that every time someone rehearses an item in STM, he or she is increasing the chances of transferring that item to LTM, where it will be permanently stored.

TABLE 8-2. Characteristics of the Three Types of Memory

	Sensory	*STM*	*LTM*
Introspection	Perception	Consciousness	Remembering
Maximum Duration	¼–2 seconds	30 seconds	Lifetime
Capacity	Very Large	7 ± 2 chunks	Unlimited
Coding	Sensory	Usually Verbal	Usually Semantic
Maintenance	Not Possible	Rehearsal	Occasional Use
Retrieval	Pattern Recognition	Not Needed	Search Process

Source: Adapted from Craik and Lockhart, 1972.

STM has two significant limitations as a memory store. One is that, as its name suggests, it doesn't keep items for very long. Without rehearsal, forgetting occurs in about 30 seconds. The other is that it cannot hold much information. (LTM has neither of these limitations. Forgetting occurs much more slowly from LTM and we don't have to worry about the amount of information, since LTM always has room.)

Even with its limitations, STM serves an important function. There are numerous occasions when we need to use information temporarily but do not need to remember it permanently. A good example is highway driving strategy. Before switching lanes, you usually take a quick glance in the mirror or over your shoulder at the position of cars in lanes behind you. If you decide there is enough room, you change lanes and move into a spot directly in front of another car. After that first glance, you probably don't look behind you again, but you have a good idea of where other cars are relative to yours. The image of the car now behind you was in STM during the period of switching lanes and you used it appropriately. It would have been dangerous to keep your eyes glued to the rearview mirror while actually making the move. This is true of many daily occurrences. We do not necessarily want to remember every phone number we dial or every shopping list we write down. As you will see later, this could lead to interference and make it difficult to remember the few phone numbers and other items that we use often.

Thus, each structure in our memory model serves a different but very important function. The sensory store preserves sensory images for a short period and gives us extra time to recognize a stimulus. STM lets us maintain information over brief periods of time and keep it active through rehearsal. LTM enables us to remember necessary information over longer time periods and permanently stores information that we have learned. As you can see, memory involves the interaction of structures and processes. Table 8–2 summarizes the major characteristics of each of these memories. The following sections discuss these and other characteristics of memory in more detail.

Characterizing Memory

There are many different ways to try to understand and characterize memory. One way is in terms of the structures and processes shown in our conceptual model. Another is to think in terms of the types of information we remember. In that case, we normally make a distinction between **episodic memory** and **semantic memory** (Tulving, 1972). Episodic memory, as the name suggests, is memory of real-life episodes—events that have taken place or will take place at a particular time and location.

Verbal rehearsal. Repeating information to be remembered (such as a telephone number) over and over, either silently or out loud.

Episodic memory. Memory of real-life episodes; stores specific information that has personal meaning.
Semantic memory. The collection of general facts and information stored in memory; forms our general knowledge.

Memories of your eighth-grade birthday party, the job interview you had last week, and the time you've agreed to play tennis tomorrow are all examples of episodic memory. It stores specific information that in one way or another has personal meaning for you.

Semantic memory, on the other hand, is the collection of general facts and information that we use every day. For example, we know without thinking that forests have trees and that Ronald Reagan is president. We know how to turn the stove on and we know the route we always take to drive to work. Perhaps the most dramatic and helpful of all such general knowledges is language, and we will see further evidence of this in the next chapter. Besides these major differences, there are also important differences in what happens to episodic and semantic memory over time. Semantic memory seems to be relatively invulnerable to decay or transformation. Episodic memory, on the other hand, is more vulnerable to transformation. This makes sense when you think about it. It is unlikely that your personal concept of a "dog" would change over time. It is likely, however, that your recollection of whether you or your brother won a childhood argument might change over time.

Another aspect of memory is retrieval. Each of us has had the embarrassing experience of being unable to remember someone or something's name in conversation. We think to ourselves, "I'll be able to recognize it when I hear it." We realize that we cannot *recall* the name without help but we could *recognize* it if we saw or heard it. We depend on recognition in a variety of memory situations. For example, multiple-choice tests and matching tests are considered recognition tests because they ask students to recognize and choose the correct answer from several alternatives that have been presented. Fill-in tests, short-answer tests, and essay questions, on the other hand, are examples of recall tests; they require students to retrieve information from memory rather than simply recognize it. Some memory experts have suggested that recognition is a more sensitive measure of memory, since individuals may recognize information that they cannot recall. Hall (1982) proposes that this is because recognition requires a single, relatively simple, cognitive operation, while recall requires greater cognitive effort. Recognition requires only the discrimination of relevant from irrelevant information. Recall, however, is a more active process, requiring both the generation of stimulus information and the discrimination of relevant from irrelevant information.

As you can see, the distinctions made above (episodic/semantic memory, recognition/recall) have some bearing on the study of memory. There has been a great deal of debate during the last 20 years about whether such distinctions are real or merely different ways of looking at the same process. Such a complex issue will not be resolved in an introductory textbook. For present purposes, it is sufficient that you are aware of the various phenomena associated with memory. We can now begin a more detailed consideration of the memory structures identified earlier in the chapter—sensory store, short-term memory, and long-term memory.

Sensory Store

As mentioned briefly in the discussion of our memory model (Figure 8–1), the **sensory store** is the entry point of environmental input into memory. The sensory store is distinguished from STM and LTM in that the environmental input still *seems* to be present, although what is being perceived is actually a lingering sensory image rather than the actual stimulus. The clarity of the sensory image quickly fades, so it is necessary to use the store very quickly. To demonstrate the sensory store, watch someone move a lighted cigarette rapidly in a circle in a dark room. The sensory store will preserve the sensory image long enough for you to perceive a continuous circle rather than separate points of light. The sensory store is useful in recognizing speech—individual sounds occur and fade very quickly; the sensory store briefly preserves them and gives us extra time to recognize individual sounds as parts of words.

There appears to be a separate sensory store for each sense. This is why there are different boxes, called sensory registers, in Figure 8–1. The sensory store is a general storage area; a sensory register is thought to be specific to the sense involved. The model suggests that even though a sound and a flash of light might both be maintained briefly in the sensory store, they are maintained independently of each other in separate registers or compartments. There they are preserved in distinct forms. The word *icon* means visual image, and the sensory memory for visual stimulation is known as **iconic** memory. Similarly, an echo is a preserved and repeated sound, and the sensory memory for hearing is **echoic memory**.

Recent research by Sakitt (1976) has suggested that iconic memory exists in the rods of the retina. Since the rods recover from stimulation more slowly than the cones, this makes some sense. The recovery period of the rods could account for the fact that an image remains after stimulation is over. These findings are important because they link the sensory stores to a particular physiological process. Once again, we recognize that the mind is not independent from the body—instead, the mind emerges from various physiological processes.

Short-Term Memory (STM)

We have mentioned that **short-term memory (STM)** is used to maintain verbal material through rehearsal, and that this material is quickly forgotten unless we keep rehearsing it. The rapid forgetting from STM was demonstrated in a now-classic experiment by Peterson and Peterson (1959), who measured how well undergraduates could remember three consonants over a short time period. The experimenters gave subjects a sequence of three consonants to learn, like CHL. The subjects then heard a three digit number and had to count backward by threes so that they could not rehearse the consonant sequence in STM. For example, they might hear the number 506 after learning CHL. They would then count backward by threes (for example, 503, 500, 497) until they saw a light that was the signal for recalling the three consonants. The light flashed either 3, 6, 9, 12, 15, or 18 seconds after the subject began counting. As Figure 8-2 shows, there was a rapid decline in the subjects' ability to remember the consonant sequence as the interval got longer. The longer the wait, the less likely subjects were to recall the consonants. These results offer strong evidence that unfamiliar material is

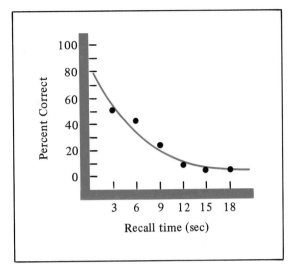

Figure 8-2
This experiment was set up by Peterson and Peterson to show the importance of rehearsal in maintaining material in STM. Subjects were given 3 consonants to remember, then asked to count backward by 3s from a 3-digit number, so that they had no chance to rehearse the consonants in STM. The longer the wait before reporting, the less likely the subjects were to recall the consonants. (Peterson and Peterson, 1959)

quickly lost from STM when people cannot rehearse it. The outcome of the experiment surprised even the experimenters.

Loss of Information in STM. What causes this rapid loss of information? The common term for failure to remember or failure to retrieve information from memory is **forgetting**. **Interference theory** proposes that various stimuli compete for a position in STM. The material that "wins" is remembered and the other information is lost. For example, consider the effect of being asked a question in the middle of dialing a telephone number you have just looked up. You will probably have to look the number up again, because the question took its posi-

---

Sensory store. One of three proposed structures of memory; enables us to preserve a sensory image long enough to perceive the stimulus.

Iconic memory. The brief memory of visual stimulation held in the sensory store.

Echoic memory. The brief memory of auditory stimulation held in the sensory store.

Short-term memory (STM). The second of three proposed struc-

tures of memory. Holds information for about 30 seconds with rehearsal; has capacity to hold about seven items of information at any one time; sometimes called consciousness or working memory.

Forgetting. Term generally used for the loss of information, or failure to retrieve information, from STM or LTM.

Interference theory. Holds that interference from other stimuli is the major cause of forgetting.

According to interference theory, the effect of being interrupted in a complex task, such as assembling an airplane engine, can be forgetting where you are in the sequence and skipping what you are supposed to do next.

tion in STM. Or, consider the effect of being interrupted while you are performing a complicated task, such as reassembling an airplane engine. When you return to the assembly task, you may forget where you were in the sequence and skip the step of putting the rubber washers on the oil plugs. One stimulus displaces another. In the Peterson and Peterson experiment, counting backward by threes interfered with the subjects' opportunity to rehearse the letters. The rapid memory fade in the Peterson and Peterson experiment also suggests that time itself has something to do with forgetting. According to **decay theory**, forgetting of the consonant sequence would still occur even if there were no other material to interfere with memory; it proposes that forgetting from STM is simply due to the passage of time.

Size of STM. Besides being limited in the length of time it can hold information, STM is also limited in the number of items that it can hold. The limited

capacity of STM was pointed out by Miller (1956) in a classic paper entitled "The magical number seven, plus or minus two: Some limits on our capacity for processing information." Miller noted as he read through the research literature that people seemed to be able to work with only about seven pieces of information at any one time. These pieces of information could be words, numbers, colors, or geometric patterns. There was, of course, some variation in this "magical" number. Some people could deal effectively with five or six items, some with eight or nine items. Nevertheless, the most common range of items that could be held in STM was between five and nine. This is how Miller's paper got its title. The common characteristic of many psychology tasks, Miller argued, is that they require the use of STM. If STM can hold only a

---

Decay theory. Holds that forgetting from STM is simply due to the passage of time.

"THAT REMINDS ME...,"

Do you sometimes find yourself holding the refrigerator door open, staring at the shelves, and thinking, "What am I doing here? What was I looking for?" Or do you find that, although you've been waiting to ask your psychology professor something for the last ten minutes, you suddenly realize that you've forgotten what your question was? Does it occur to you only a minute later that you had wanted to ask about the early signs for the onset of senility? Worry no more. Research on forgetting shows that these are two of the most common types of forgetting and that though they can be embarrassing and troublesome, they happen to most people from time to time.

Ulric Neisser, a cognitive psychologist at Emory University, and Douglas Herrmann, a psychologist at Hamilton College, have found that other common types of forgetting among healthy people include forgetting the name of a person just met at a party, vaguely recalling a dream but not being able to remember any details, and intending to make a certain point in a conversation and then forgetting to do so.

Cognitive psychologist Donald Norman of the University of California at San Diego has studied how people try to prevent forgetting. One way is by arranging objects—on a desk, for example—so that they will jog the memory. Placing a stack of files on the corner of a desk may not be a sign of disorganization, but rather, a way a person has devised to remember to do some pressing work. An envelope tacked to a bulletin board may remind you to pay a bill. Letters propped against the doorknob may remind you to drop them in the mailbox the next time you go out. Norman says that the more urgent it is that you remember an object, the more prominent you will make it visually.

A good deal of recent research refutes the common belief that forgetting increases dramatically with age. Harry Bahrick, a psychologist of Ohio Wesleyan University, tested what he calls "prospective memory"—the ability to remember to keep an appointment. Perhaps contrary to most people's expectations, older people between the ages of 65 and 75 were more likely to remember an appointment than college-age people. While only one of the older subjects forgot to make a telephone call at a prearranged time, 14 college students forgot. In another study, Bahrick looked at subjects who had learned Spanish in high school or college. He found that people did most of their forgetting in the first three to five years away from Spanish class. The Spanish they remembered after this initial period seemed to stay with them for at least the next twenty-five years. In a third study, Bahrick found that seventy-five-year-old professors remembered former students just as well as thirty-six-year-old professors.

Psychologist Yvette Tenney of the Boston Veterans Administration Hospital believes that some older people's forgetfulness isn't forgetfulness at all but simply misperception. For example, an older person looks for her housekeys. She thinks she left them on the coffee table, so she looks there first. When she doesn't see the keys on the coffee table, she searches the kitchen, bathroom, and her purse. Finally, she looks again on the coffee table and this time finds the keys. Tenney believes that the slight decline in older people's perceptual efficiency causes this kind of problem, which many people mislabel as forgetfulness. Dr. Neisser confirms Dr. Tenney's conclusions, saying that a "lost" object is often in exactly the place the person thought it was. During the search, however, the person sees it but fails to recognize it. Because of these misperceptions, according to Tenney, older people tend to regard themselves as more forgetful than they actually are.

Adapted from: Dan Goleman, "Forgetfulness Is Seen as Causing More Worry than It Should," *New York Times*, July 1, 1986, pp. C1, C9.

limited number of items (between five and nine), then performance in all tasks that require the use of STM should be limited.

You can demonstrate this limited capacity of STM for yourself by testing your ability to recall strings of letters in a memory-span test. Read each row of letters once, then shut your eyes and try to recall the letters in the correct order.

J Z N Q R L B
W Y P K V T L D R
X G B M H S Q C N
K Y C T M F J

The memory span for adults is typically around seven items. You were probably able to recall the seven letters in the first and last lines but found it difficult to recall the nine letters in the middle two lines. But an exception would occur if some of the letter sequences formed a familiar pattern. If a woman named Laura Dianne Roberts read the second line, the letters "LDR" would be a familiar sequence for her since those are her initials. Miller realized that in some circumstances we group and organize information to fit into meaningful units in STM. He called these units **chunks**. A chunk is familiar information that is already stored as a unit in LTM. The advantage is that each chunk will occupy only one space or slot in STM. The letter sequence "LDR" would occupy only a single slot in Laura Roberts' STM. As a result, she should find it easier to remember the second line than the third one, since the second line contains only seven pieces of information (that is, the first six letters and the chunk LDR). For another example, the letter sequences "LTM" and "STM" should by now occupy only a single slot each in your STM.

You can demonstrate the importance of chunks to yourself by asking someone to recall the following sequence of numbers: 12126786754. These numbers occupy 11 "slots" in STM. Arranged in that way, it would require some effort to memorize the list. If the numbers are rearranged, however, it is easier. Try this arrangement—1–212–678–6754. This is the format for dialing a long-distance call to a telephone in New York City. There are now four chunks to remember instead of 11.

Although it is very difficult to increase the limited capacity of STM, it is possible to use STM more effectively by creating more chunks. Chunks are created by combining individual items into groups

and storing these groups in LTM. This is in fact how the experimental subject S.F., described earlier in the chapter, managed to remember a string of 82 digits. Let's now consider LTM.

Long-Term Memory (LTM)

Processes. Atkinson and Shiffrin (1971) distinguished among several different control processes used for transferring material into **long-term** memory (**LTM**). Verbal rehearsal, as mentioned earlier, serves both to maintain items in STM (maintenance rehearsal) and to transfer information into LTM (learning). We transform material we want to remember by **coding** it, that is, by putting it into the context of other material that is easier to remember. For example, many of us learned the notes of the treble clef by remembering the sentence "*Every good boy does fine.*" We also code in visual form. **Imaging** refers to creating visual images to remember verbal material. We will say more about coding and imaging later in the chapter, but for now it is important to realize that coding helps us to transfer information into LTM.

Serial Position. The Atkinson-Shiffrin model specifies that the memory strength of an item in LTM is increased by rehearsing that item. Rundus (1971) tested this hypothesis by giving undergraduates a list of nouns, one word at a time. The words were given slowly enough so that there was time for the students to rehearse some of the words before the next presentation. They were allowed to rehearse any of the words on the list but had to rehearse aloud so that the experimenter knew which words were being rehearsed. Following the presentation of the entire list, the students tried to recall the words without putting them in order. Students were able to recall words at the beginning of the list better than words in the middle or at the end of the list. This illustrates the **serial-position effect**—the position of a word in a series of words will have an effect on the ability to remember it. This effect shows a relationship between recall and the amount of rehearsal. In the Rundus experiment, the words at the beginning of the list were rehearsed more than ones in the middle or at the end, probably because at the beginning there were fewer words to be rehearsed.

Serial position clearly has to do with retention. Interestingly enough, it also has to do with forget-ting. Let's go back again to the Rundus experiment. Here the serial position effect was a **primacy effect**, meaning that the higher recall of words was at the beginning of the list. But sometimes there is higher recall of words at the end of a list rather than at the beginning (Bower and Hilgard, 1981). This is known as the **recency effect** and it seems to contradict the primacy effect. One theory about the recency effect is that it results from the way STM works: Because the most recent stimulus elements may still be present in STM when the recall task begins, they can be retrieved more easily. Craik (1970) strengthened this explanation by inserting a 30-second distracting task between rehearsal of the end of a list and the beginning of recall. He found that the recency effect disappeared but the primacy effect remained.

The most recent thinking is that the two memory effects work together and sometimes simultaneously to meet the demands of the environment. There are many everyday examples of the primacy and recency effects. Think of the last frantic minutes before beginning an exam. As soon as the exam is handed out, you feverishly scribble down the last things you looked at before closing your notebook or text. You want to get these out of STM and onto paper before they are pushed out by something else. The material that you have rehearsed more frequently and that you feel you know well is safely tucked away in LTM. It needs less "protection".

A very interesting example of the primacy and recency effects is the employment interview. A number of studies have shown that applicants interviewed at the beginning or at the end of a long list are remembered best (Webster, 1980). This can work to your advantage if there is something positive to recall about you but can work to your disadvantage if there is something you would prefer that the interviewer forget. Similarly, the interviewer is more likely to remember what an applicant says early or late in the interview rather than what is said in the mid-

---

Chunks. Information already stored as units in LTM; allow STM to handle more information because each unit takes up only one slot.

Long-term memory. The third of three proposed structures of memory. Stores information permanently and has an unlimited capacity.

Coding. Transforming material we want to remember by putting it into the context of other, easier to remember, material.

Imaging. Creating visual images to remember verbal material.

Serial-position effect. The position of a word in a series of words will have an effect on the ability to remember it.

Primacy effect. Higher recall of words at the beginning of a list, probably due to more rehearsal.

Recency effect. Higher recall of words at the end of a list, probably because the latest stimulus items are still present in STM.

dle. Interviewers can easily overcome these problems of uneven recall. The most obvious way is to review the material on all applicants before evaluating any one candidate. For a single candidate, the interviewer should go back and review notes on all parts of the interview rather than trusting memory to fill in the missing details. This approach corresponds to a rehearsal strategy.

Retroactive and Proactive Interference

We first encountered the concept of interference when we discussed forgetting from STM. In STM, of course, we are looking at interference that involves very short time periods. But some of our memory loss happens over much longer periods of time—weeks, months, or even years. This too can be the result of interference. In fact, much forgetting in both STM and LTM can be attributed to various forms of interference.

Two partricular types of interference have received the most attention. **Retroactive interference** occurs when new information interferes with memory of something learned earlier. A good example is the dialing interruption described earlier: You are asked a question in the middle of dialing an unfamiliar telephone number, causing you to forget the rest of the number. A number of years ago Jenkins and Dallenbach (1924) conducted an experiment in which college students learned lists of nonsense syllables. After studying the lists, one group slept for eight hours while the other group stayed awake and active for eight hours. When both groups were later tested on recall, the sleepless group remembered far fewer syllables than the group that had slept. The difference was related to the fact that new learning can interfere with previous learning. **Proactive interference**, on the other hand, occurs when old learning in memory interferes with new learning. This happened to me when I tried to learn a new language. I was going to be living in Sweden for a while and in preparation I studied Swedish for several months. In high school, college, and graduate school I had studied German. My biggest problem with Swedish was interference from my knowledge of German. I was always substituting German words for Swedish ones. Something similar happens as you get used to driving a new car. You reach for controls or look for dials that were part of your old car.

These are examples of earlier information in memory interfering with remembering later information.

Proactive Interference in STM. Proactive interference, as stated above, is forgetting caused by the influence of earlier-learned information on newer information. It is logical that the more similar the old and new material, the more interference there will be. An interesting phenomenon that can be advantageous in studying and other learning tasks is known as *release from proactive interference*. This phenomenon seems more closely related to the way information goes into short-term rather than long-term memory. A number of experiments have demonstrated that subjects involved in word-recall tasks show improved performance when they switch to recalling numbers. Likewise, subjects in number-recall tasks do better when they switch to recalling words (Wickens et al., 1963). It seems that changing the material frees subjects from proactive interference because the new material is dissimilar to what has already been remembered. This dissimilarity can be in the physical features of the old and new material (such as upper-case vs. lower-case letters) or in the meaning of the material (such as words vs. numbers) (Hall, 1982).

Release from proactive interference also seems to apply to more complex material such as television news items. In two experiments (Gunter et al., 1980), it was shown that shifting coverage from sports items to politics improved recall of the actual items in the program. Most major TV-news shows have adopted this strategy. They present a piece of information from one category, such as finance (for example, the stock market report), and then shift to a crime report or the weather. If they have a second piece of financial news, they come back to it after presenting an item from a different news category.

This technique can help you in studying more effectively. You should arrange your study time so that you are not studying material from similar courses close together in time. Instead of studying psychology and then sociology, study psychology and then mathematics. If you have many similar courses, you should try to study the material for each course in a separate study session rather than in one single session.

REVIEW QUESTIONS

7. There are several processes used for transfering material into LTM; match the term with the correct definition:

___ verbal rehearsal   A. creating visual pictures to remember verbal material

___ coding   B. transforming material into an easier form to remember

___ imaging   C. repeating something over and over

8. When you learn many words in a list, you recall words at the beginning and end of the list better than those in the middle. This is called the _____ _____ effect. Better recall of words at the beginning of the list is due to the recency/primacy effect, and better recall of words at the end is due to the recency/primary effect.

9. An example of retroactive/proactive interference occurs if you're interrupted with a question while dialing a phone number and have to look it up again. An example of proactive/retroactive interference is the difficulty you may encounter in learning a new language, particularly if the language is similar to one you already know.

Answers: 7. verbal rehearsal, C; coding, B; imaging, A 8. serial position; primacy, recency 9. retroactive; proactive

■ ORGANIZATION AND MEMORY

When you go into a grocery store without a shopping list, you are likely to be challenged by the memory task ahead of you. There are a large number of items that you need and they are all different. You need paper towels and diet soda and meat and light bulbs and a dozen other things. How will you remember it all? Chances are that you will remember the items in categories rather than as individual units. Chances are, too, that you have stored those items in your memory in some particular way. For example, you may have stored cleaning products according to the layout of the store in which you will be shopping, or according to where in your house the items will be stored (e.g., kitchen, bathroom, laundry room). With food items, you might have arranged your mental list according to types of meals (e.g., breakfast, lunch, dinner, snacks) or by food category (e.g., meat, vegetables, fruit, drinks). The point is that *organization* can be a tremendous aid to memory. The interesting part of this process is that you may put the information *into* your memory randomly, that is, every time you run out of an item you may simply add it to your mental shopping list. Nevertheless, you recall it from memory by category. This organizational strategy is referred to as **clustering**.

As we saw in Chapter 4 (Perception), the Gestalt theorists proposed that perception is based on organizational principles. These principles were thought to be automatic processes that we engage in to help process the enormous amount of information that comes in from the outside world. Organizational principles play the same role in memory. They help us to reduce the information load. A little earlier in the chapter, we considered the problem of fitting a long string of numbers into short-term memory. We took the number 12126786754 and organized it into four chunks that made up a New York City telephone number: 1–212–678–6754. Alternatively, the number could have been organized according to the finishing places of four make-believe friends in the New York Marathon: One finished in position 1, the second in position 212, the third in position 678, and the fourth in position 6754. This illustrates another characteristic of storage and retrieval. It is "personalized." Since I am an avid runner and compete each year in the New York Marathon, I would be comfortable organizing that 11-digit number by

---

Retroactive interference. Occurs when new information coming into memory interferes with older information already in memory.

Proactive interference. Occurs when older information in memory interferes with new information entering memory.
Clustering. Organizational strategy by which information is recalled from memory according to category.

finish position. You, on the other hand, might choose to remember the number in quite another way, perhaps as a combination of your street address and the birthdates of you and a sibling—in other words, in a way that has meaning for you and will make it more likely for you to remember.

As the number of items to be remembered increases, so do our chunks. Finally, we reach a point where the number of chunks becomes unwieldy. The number of items within each chunk may become unwieldy as well. How do we keep chunking under control? It is generally accepted that our chunks or clusters are hierarchically arranged into subordinate (lower level) and superordinate (higher level) clusters. To return to our grocery list example, we may have superordinate categories labeled food, cleaning products, and paper products. Within each of these, we might have several subcategories. For example, within the superordinate category of food, we might have subordinate categories such as meat, vegetables, and fruit. Within meat, we may have subcategories of beef, pork, lamb, and chicken. As you can see, there is an almost limitless number of hierarchically arranged clusters or chunks that can be formed. In terms of this hierarchical perspective, Bower and Hilgard (1981) describe recall as an "unpacking" process. First we find the superordinate category (e.g., food) and "unpack" it into subordinate categories (e.g., meat, vegetables, fruit). From those we choose an even lower level category to unpack (e.g., fruit) and break it down into lower and lower level units (fresh and canned; apples, oranges, peaches, etc). This aspect of memory may remind you of a very rapid form of the old game of "20 Questions," in which an individual trying to find out something asks a series of "yes or no" questions until arriving at the correct answer. Likewise with memory—starting with the most superordinate category, we determine if the item to be remembered is in cluster A or B (meat or fish). Having answered "yes" to meat, the question may then shift to subordinate clusters (beef, pork, or chicken) and so on. Although we are rarely aware of this hierarchical process of remembering, it seems clear that this is how we "unscramble" or translate a flood of external information into a meaningful arrangement in memory.

In fact, we can think of this hierarchical process as an elaborate code that has a double advantage. We used the code not only to put information into

memory, but also to get it out. In the next two sections, we will look more closely at other forms of codes and see how they aid memory. Keep in mind that the effectiveness of memory codes depends on their efficiency in helping to form clusters or on the extent to which they help to keep the number of "chunks" under control.

Memory Codes

As we've seen, organization is an essential feature of memory. It helps in putting information into memory as well as in getting it out. A related line of research suggests that a *meaningful* form of organization, such as a code of some kind, makes a difference in memory. When we code a piece of information, we put it into a form that is different from the original but still conveys meaning. The degree of meaning retained in the code may relate to the wide variation seen in forgetting. How do we explain the fact that we are unable to recall all the information that we once learned or that some events are remembered for only a day or two, others for weeks, and still others for an entire lifetime? One possibility is that we form different kinds of memory codes for different events, and that more meaningful codes are more resistant to forgetting than less meaningful ones. Let's now examine some different types of codes that might be used in memory.

Levels-of-Processing

Many cognitive psychologists were unhappy with the Atkinson and Shiffrin model because it seemed to be too limited. It suggested that memories are *things* put in *places* and that memory is a process of transferring information from place to place. Craik and Lockhart (1972) proposed a very different approach to memory that tried to take into account the wide variation in the rate of forgetting. They introduced the term **depth-** or **levels-of-processing** to indicate the different levels at which people analyze information to be remembered.

Craik and Lockhart suggested three different levels of processing that correspond to three different ways of coding information: structural, phonemic, and semantic. When we first encounter a stimulus, we pay attention mostly to its physical characteristics—in other words, we try to determine its structure. This examination produces data or codes for the stimulus. For example, in looking at a building we might notice if it is made of brick or wood and how many stories high it is. A ten-story brick building looks different from a one-story wood building, and as a result the two have different codes. Craik and Lockhart have suggested that this initial and most superficial form of processing produces a **structural code** that contains the physical structure of a stimulus. This includes distinguishing physical features such as lines, angles, brightness, pitch, and loudness. After the first (structural) code is formed, a second and deeper level of analysis occurs. At this level of analysis, a name is attached to the stimulus. This name must already exist in memory, from which it is retrieved and attached to a new stimulus. Naming, then, represents a second code, called a **phonemic code**. A phonemic code consists of **phonemes**, which are the basic sounds of a language. In our example, the phonemic code might contain the names of the types of buildings (for example, the wooden building is a *garage* and the brick building is an *office building*). Now, in addition to having structural codes, we also have phonemic codes, which imply that the stimulus has been recognized as a member of a class of similar stimuli. It is this recognition that permits the processing to continue. With the addition of the phonemic code, the stimulus element becomes richer and has more characteristics than when it was defined exclusively by a structural code.

Once the stimulus is recognized, it may be coded at a still deeper level. This third form of coding involves meaning or semantics and is called a **semantic code**. To return to our building example, the garage may be where you store your convertible during the winter and the office building may be where you applied for a job last year. These buildings are not just *any* buildings. They have particular meaning to you. Thus, they have codes that are related to the meaning of the information to be stored. Semantic codes must play a role in the initial storage

of information in LTM, since most of the codes in LTM are semantic (as shown in Table 8–2).

Levels-of-Processing Theory. The **levels-of-processing theory** proposes that as processing levels become deeper, memories become more enduring. At the first (structural) level, the memory either quickly decays or becomes subject to interference (in our building example, you are likely to experience interference from other structural codes for similar buildings). Once the stimulus has been named (phonemic code), the memory is more definite. Finally, if the meaning of the stimulus is considered, the memory is at its most concrete. At the deepest level, forgetting occurs slowly. You may not remember all of the buildings you have seen in your lifetime, but you would certainly remember the building that protects your car or the building in which you applied for a job.

Bower and Karlin (1974) tested the levels-of-processing theory with memory for faces. The testing material consisted of slides made from yearbook pictures of the Yale graduating class of 1972. The subjects were Stanford undergraduates, who were unlikely to be familiar with any of the Yale graduates. Following a 5-second viewing of each slide, each subject was asked to make one of three types of judgments. The subject was asked to categorize the face in the slide as being either (1) male or female, (2) more likeable than average or less likeable than average, or (3) more honest than average or less honest than average. After the subjects had completed the judgment task with 72 slides, they were asked to view an additional 144 slides and simply indicate whether they had seen the slide before or not. The 144 slides consisted of the original 72 the subjects had made judgments about and a new set of 72 they had not yet seen. The two sets were combined randomly. There was a clear memory superiority for those slides that had been previously judged on likeability or honesty as

---

Depth- or **levels-of-processing.** The term used to describe the different levels at which people analyze or process information to be remembered.

Structural code. First level of information coding; produced by analyzing the physical structure of a stimulus—the physical features such as lines, angles, brightness, and so on.

Phonemic code. Second level of information coding; produced

when a stimulus is named and recognized as belonging to a class of similar stimuli.

Phonemes. The basic sounds of a language; English has about 40 phonemes.

Semantic code. Third level of information coding; produced when meaning is attached to a stimulus.

Levels-of-processing theory. Proposes that as processing levels become deeper, memories become more enduring.

compared to those that had been judged solely on gender. Eighty-one percent of the slides previously judged for honesty were correctly recognized; 75 percent of those judged for likeability were recognized; only 60 percent of the slides judged for gender were recognized. Bower and Karlin proposed levels-of-processing as the likely explanation for these results. Subjects clearly remembered faces that had been given some meaning (honesty or likeability) better than faces categorized on structure (gender) only. They concluded with the suggestion that if you want to remember someone's face, try to make a number of meaningful judgments about that face when you first see it.

Semantic Coding and Rehearsal. If a person simply rehearses information in a mechanical way without also attending to its meaning, the result will be a phonemic code that will be lost much more quickly than a semantic code. This can easily happen in reading. We have all experienced reading a page in a book while thinking about something else and then discovering at the bottom of the page that we couldn't remember anything that we had just read. We created a phonemic code of the words, but because we did not attend to their meaning, they were quickly forgotten.

Semantic Coding and Retrieval. The fact that there are qualitative differences in memory codes has implications for determining which retrieval cues will be most effective for recall. In general, the memory codes used to learn new material can also be used in retrieving what was learned. This is called the **encoding-specificity principle (ESP)** (Bower and Hilgard, 1981). Simply put, it means that the code we use to store information will be the most effective code for retrieving (remembering) that information. For example, if you are given a list of words to learn and on that list are the words "match" and "soccer," you may not recall that "match" was on the list or recognize it if it appears on a later list that includes the words "fire" and "cigarette." On the other hand, if the second list contains the word "tennis," chances are good that you will remember having seen "match" on the earlier list. The word that triggers the memory of the target word is called a *cue.* It seems that memory depends, to a great extent, on cues. The encoding specificity principle links storage cues and retrieval cues. It suggests that the cue is a key that opens the lock of memory. It also tells us something

practical—in order to find effective **retrieval cues,** we have to look to how the material was first coded.

Not long ago, I got a new combination lock for my gym locker. Naturally, I developed a strategy for remembering it. The lock combination was 33–12–24. My coding strategy was to say to myself, "When I was 33, I could run up 12 flights of stairs in 24 minutes." Shortly after I got the new lock, I went out of town for almost two weeks. When I returned and tried to open the locker, I had forgotten the combination. The person who had the locker next to me tried to help. He kept suggesting numerical codes: Was the first number half the last number? Were there any repeating digits? Was there a 9 in the first or last number? I couldn't remember. Then someone else walked by and made a disparaging comment about my performance as a jogger. I responded that I did fine for my age. This triggered the association between age and my locker combination. As a result, I remembered my coding strategy and the combination to my lock. If I had continued to use the codes suggested by my locker-neighbor, I might still be trying to figure out the right combination. Remembering was facilitated by the right retrieval cue.

What you now know about levels-of-processing should give you a very different outlook on memory. Instead of being things put in places, memories are better thought of as information-processing strategies applied to new input. In general, when these strategies are carried out with some deliberation, memory improves. When they are ignored or are used haphazardly, memory gets worse. It is now time to examine some special topics in memory with which you may be familiar. These include flashbulb memory, constructive memory, and eyewitness testimony.

REVIEW QUESTIONS

10. In the levels-of-processing approach to memory, there are different levels of memory codes—match each below with the correct definition:

___ structural code	A. attaching personal meaning to an object
___ phonemic code	B. emphasizing the physical features of an object
___ semantic code	C. giving a name to an object

11. The _____ theory proposes that memories become more enduring as we process information in more and more meaningful ways.

12. According to the _____ _____, the code we use to store information in memory will be the most effective code for retrieving it.

13. The word that triggers the memory of another word is called a _____ ____ _____ .

Answers: 10. structural code, B; phonemic code, C; semantic code, A 11. levels-of-processing 12. encoding-specificity principle 13. retrieval cue

■ SOME SPECIAL TOPICS IN MEMORY

Flashbulb Memory

On the morning of November 22, 1963, I was driving on the Pennsylvania Turnpike on the way to visit a friend at Pennsylvania State University. Shortly before noon, the radio program I was listening to was interrupted with a news bulletin announcing that John F. Kennedy had been shot in Dallas, Texas, and that the Texas governor, John Connally, had also been hit. The next hour was filled with confusing bulletins about the President's condition, about the possible motive for the shooting, about the condition of John Connally, and about possible suspects. The announcement was finally made that John F. Kennedy was dead.

As is the case with many of my generation, I can remember perfectly where I was and what I was doing when that tragic announcement was made. Younger generations have their own dramatic events to remember. My 18-year-old daughter remembers exactly what she was doing when it was

announced that Ronald Reagan had been shot by John Hinckley. One of my students in an introductory psychology class remembers when and where he heard that Roberto Clemente, the brilliant baseball player for the Pittsburgh Pirates, had died in an airplane crash. A friend of mine in his mid 30s remembers vividly the moment of learning about John Lennon's death. An event that is likely to rival the Kennedy assassination in terms of vivid recollection is the tragic explosion of the space-shuttle Challenger. Years from now, people who were of grade-school age or older will remember with precise detail where they were at 11:38 AM on January 28, 1986, when the shuttle exploded.

Events like these are emotional enough to be remembered by everyone, but it seems that each of us can remember some personal event or events in remarkable detail. This phenomenon is known as **flashbulb memory**, so called because the entire memory can be retrieved at once with little difficulty. The event is captured in memory like a scene is frozen in a flash snapshot. A time when we were in an accident, the funeral of a close relative, and being presented with an award are all events that may produce flashbulb memories. It seems that semantics play a role in this phenomenon; the personal meaningfulness of the event is critical to its memorability. As you learned above, this is due to the level of processing—the code used for storage.

Brown and Kulik (1981) used the Kennedy assassination to study flashbulb memory. They asked 40 white subjects and 40 black subjects to recall something about November 22, 1963. Only 1 of the 80 subjects was unable to report some detail of that day. The subjects were also asked to recall any details about the assassination of Martin Luther King. Seventy-five percent of the black subjects could recall in great detail how and when they learned of Dr. King's death. Only 33 percent of the white subjects could recall those details. In terms of the relative importance of each event in a list of nine events (including the Kennedy and King assassinations), black subjects rated the killing of Martin Luther

Encoding-specificity principle (ESP). States that the code used for storing information will be the most effective code for retrieving (remembering) that information.

Retrieval cues. Cues that lead to retrieval of information from memory; the most effective retrieval cue will be the same code that was used to store the information.

Flashbulb memory. A memory of a particularly striking event that can be retrieved at once in its entirety; often compared to a snapshot of a scene frozen in the light of a flashbulb.

King as the most important. The white subjects rated it fourth in importance. Brown and Kulik believe that the strength of this type of memory is closely related to the meaningfulness of the event remembered. Further, they suggest that unlike an actual photo, not every detail or fact about the event in question is remembered. Instead, we remember the details of the immediate or personal environment that were present when the event occurred. The ulimate explanation of flashbulb memory will most likely involve neurotransmission. The high level of emotion surrounding meaningful events such as assassinations is a sign that massive stimulation of the nervous system has occurred. As you discovered in Chapter 2, this stimulation produces the chemicals of neurotransmission as well as changes in the levels of hormones in the bloodstream. In a later chapter, you will learn more about the specific effect of emotions and mood on memory. Flashbulb

memory is not a case of extraordinary memory. It is an ordinary memory process responding in extraordinary circumstances to produce a memory of a special kind.

Constructive Memory

Jean Piaget, the renowned developmental psychologist, believed for a number of years that he had been kidnapped at the age of two. He "remembered" being out with his nurse and being forcefully snatched from her at the Champs-Elysées. In the struggle, the nurse's face had been scratched, and Piaget remembered the scratch in vivid detail. Thirteen years later, the nurse confessed that there had never been any kidnapping—it had all been a hoax. But the kidnapping story had been told so many times in Piaget's presence that it took on the characteristics of a memory. It was a vivid memory

Years from now, people will remember with precise detail where they were at 11:38 a.m. on January 28, 1986, when they heard about the explosion of the space shuttle Challenger.

and a detailed one—it simply did not relate the actual events. The memory was constructed from other pieces of information (Nelson, 1982).

Constructive memory involves adding information to a memory that was not part of the original stimulus or event. If you recall our discussion of perception, the possibility of constructed memories should not surprise you. In Chapter 4, you learned that minimal sensory information can be elaborated into meaningful and unified perceptions. Constancies and illusions are examples of such elaboration. The Gestalt principles of organization are further proof that perceptions can far outstrip sensations.

Eyewitness Testimony

In the movies and on TV, the murder trial usually climaxes with the testimony of a witness who observed the accused in the act of committing the crime. The prosecuting attorney asks the witness on the stand the critical question: "Is the person you saw commit this crime in this courtroom?" The witness slowly turns toward the defendant seated nearby, points an accusing finger in his direction, and says, "Yes, he is sitting there, there in the blue suit." The testimony of the eyewitness seals the verdict and draws the courtroom drama to a close.

Members of juries in actual courtrooms are just as impressed with eyewitnesses. They are swayed by the fact that the victim easily picked the assailant from a large group in a police line-up. They are convinced by the testimony of a trial witness that the defendant was the one responsible for the crime. In criminal proceedings, it is then up to the defense to establish that an error could have occurred in identification. Often, such defense takes the form of close questioning of eyewitnesses on particulars such as vision, confusion, lighting conditions, or length of time spent observing. In recent years, such lines of defense have become more sophisticated and more psychological in nature. Sometimes an expert on memory is called in to testify, and the memory of the victim or witness undergoes intense examination.

A fairly recent case in point is the Brink's armored truck robbery, which occurred on the afternoon of October 20, 1981. Two police officers and a Brink's guard were killed in the shootout that followed the $1.6 million robbery. There were witnesses to both the robbery and the shootout. One of the witnesses

testified that he had seen a particular defendant driving the getaway van. In the course of pretrial hearings, the way in which this identification was made came into question. The witness had been shown a number of photographs and asked to identify the person he saw driving the van. He picked out several people who might have been the driver. The witness was brought back again and shown a second series of photographs and was again asked to identify the driver of the van. Only one photograph from the original group was included in this viewing—that of the suspect. This time the witness identified the suspect as the driver of the van. The defense promptly raised the question of whether or not the "memory" and subsequent identification had, in fact, been created by the first photo-examination session. Clearly, if the question posed in the second photo session was, "Have you ever seen any of these men before?" the answer would have to be yes. At the very least, the witness *had* seen the suspect once before—in the first photo-examination session. At this point, the witness might have been unable to separate what was seen in the robbery from the first photo session. What is more, the witness, like Piaget, might have been totally unaware of the mix-up. In fact, the witness might remain extremely positive in his or her identification.

Earlier in this chapter, you read about Bower and Karlin's study of face recognition and how clear the results were. The probability of remembering a face was directly related to the way in which the face had been coded—by gender, likeability, or honesty. If the subject had been asked to make a semantic as opposed to a structural judgment about the face, the face was more likely to be remembered. Without semantic judgments, memory declined. Now consider criminal identifications such as the ones we've been discussing. In many cases the witness saw the suspect just before the crime was committed, but before being aware that a crime had occurred. At that point it is likely that if any coding was done at all, it was done at the structural level. This level of coding is often forgotten at a later time. Similarly, when victims or witnesses describe the circum-

---

Constructive memory. A memory of an event that did not really occur as remembered; consists of information added to a memory. An example is something you heard about as a child and later came to believe you'd actually experienced.

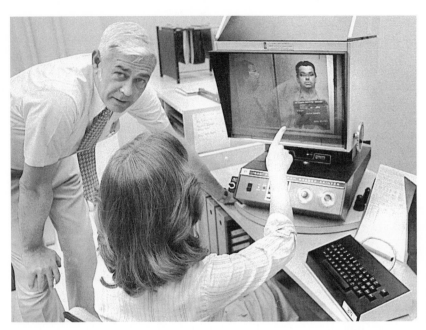

Serious questions have been raised about the methods used in eyewitnesses' identification of subjects. It may be that showing witnesses photos of possible subjects may actually create memories where none existed before.

stances of a crime, they often indicate being almost hypotized by a visible gun or other weapon—they reportedly "couldn't take their eyes off it." This is understandable, as the weapon represented the immediate danger in the situation. This raises the problem that the witness has either avoided studying the face of the criminal or has concentrated on structural rather than semantic features. Thus, the witness may be able to accurately recall structural details such as hair and eye color or visible scars, but not be able to recognize the face as a whole.

It has been shown that eyewitness testimony can also extend to nonexistent objects and events. Elizabeth Loftus, one of the leading researchers in eyewitness testimony and memory, has written a fascinating account of some of her findings (1979). Several of her studies reveal that information about nonexistent objects can be "added" to memory. In one study (Loftus, 1975), she demonstrated that asking a misleading question can help to rearrange or even create a memory. Subjects were shown a film of an automobile accident. Shortly after seeing the film, the subjects were asked one of two questions: "How fast was the white sports car going when it passed the white barn while traveling along the country road?" or, "How fast was the white sports car going while traveling along the country road?" In the film, there was *no* barn. One week later, all

subjects who had been asked the question mentioning the barn "remembered" seeing one. Fewer than 3 percent of the subjects asked the question omitting the barn remembered one in the film.

In another experiment, Loftus constructed the "theft" of a tape recorder from someone's bag at a bus station. Eyewitnesses sitting nearby later confirmed the theft, even adding detailed descriptions of the stolen item. However, there never was any tape recorder. As you can see from just this small sampling, memory can be changed or created after an event occurs.

■ THEORIES OF MEMORY

We mentioned that levels-of-proccessing was proposed as an alternative to structural models, which were considered too mechanistic. While the levels-of-processing approach of Craik and Lockhart has eliminated certain of these objections, it has raised others. For example, this approach minimizes the importance of rehearsal, but a number of studies have since demonstrated that rehearsal can have a positive effect on memory (Rundus, 1971). These two approaches continue to represent alternative points of view. Some psychologists (notably Atkin-

SOME THINGS YOU NEVER FORGET

You know that old expression about riding a bike—once you've learned to do it, you never forget how. But remembering other things, like who scored the first touchdown in Superbowl V or who the seventh U.S. president was, may be another matter. Researchers are finding that even patients with profound memory loss can still remember how to do things like riding a bike although their memory for facts may be severely impaired. By observing patients who suffer some type of severe memory loss as a result of illness, accident, or stroke, neuroscientists are finding that these two types of memory—memory for skills and memory for facts—may be parts of two distinct memory systems that may even be located in separate regions of the brain.

Dr. Daniel Schacter of the University of Toronto focuses his research on patients with *anthrograde amnesia*, or the inability to recall new facts introduced since the onset of the memory loss. At the same time, these patients are still able to use skills they had acquired earlier. With apparently one system intact and the other not functioning, these patients provide keys to understanding the two memory systems.

Dr. Schacter has conducted word-association experiments to compare people with normal memories to these amnesia patients. A list of word pairs that might include pairs such as *fish* and *scissors* is presented to subjects. An hour later subjects are given a recall test. When one word is presented, subjects are asked to provide the word that it was paired with. For example, the correct response for *fish* would be *scissors*. The same test is given again after a week. Just as you would expect, people with normal memories do better at recalling word associations after an hour than after a week. The amnesiacs, however, cannot learn the word pairs at all. The more surprising finding, though, is that in a word-completion test the two groups do equally well. Instead of being asked to supply the entire second word of the pair, this time subjects are given the cue *fish* followed by *sci_____*. The amnesiac group can complete as many of the second words as the group with normal memory. Dr. Schacter believes that these results demonstrate the operation of the two different kinds of memory. Word recognition appears to be an example of the fact memory, while word completion is an example of skill memory.

Dr. Larry Squire of the University of California and the Veterans Hospital of San Diego believes that the structure of the brain explains differences in the two types of memory. While a patient may lose all capacity for fact knowledge, some skill memory always remains. According to Dr. Squire, this indicates that skill memory is widespread over a number of parts of the brain and that fact memory is more narrowly located. A key location of the fact portion of memory is the hippocampus, where Squire believes facts are stored before they become associated with other knowledge and integrated into the cortex. The basal ganglia and cerebellum appear to be the centers of skill memory. These areas are also responsible for involuntary and habitual behaviors.

By comparing the memory systems of different kinds of animals, researchers observe that only animals with a large hippocampus have the fact portion of memory. Fact memory depends upon the formation of new brain-cell connections, or synapses, when new information is learned, says Dr. Squire. Stimulation of the hippocampus causes the formation of new synapses. The more learning that takes place, the more complex this system of synapses and nerve connections becomes. This is a continual, lifelong process which may account for the forgetting of facts as well as the learning of new ones. As the connections change, details once stored in fact memory become lost.

Adapted from: Sandra Blakeslee, "Clues Hint at Brain's Two Memory Maps," *New York Times*, July 29, 1986, pp. C1, C10.

son and Shiffrin) view memory as a structure located in a place. Others see memory as a complicated coding process. Still others view it as a combination of organizing principles applied to external events. Clearly, the Loftus data on eyewitness testimony strongly suggests that memory is constructive and active rather than descriptive and passive. The storage of a coded event (structural, phonemic, or semantic) is only the beginning of a process we call memory—not the end of it. This idea is central to the **constructive approach**, which states that memory is actively constructed from the raw material of external events. Constructive memory has received considerable attention in recent times (Bransford and Franks, 1971; Bransford and McCarrell, 1974), but the basic idea was introduced over 50 years ago by Bartlett (1932). A very recent approach to memory is the biological one (McGaugh, 1983), which assumes that memory is an elaborate chain of neural events that depends on specific axon/dendrite connections. In fact, Sakitt's research on the location of icons in the retina, which we discussed earlier, may be a step in the same direction. All these individual approaches will continue to influence future research on human memory. A more complete understanding of how we incorporate, maintain, and retrieve information will likely emerge from a combination of these theories.

■ MEMORY STRATEGIES

Every so often a new book appears on the market on how to improve your memory. Such books provide a variety of strategies for improving memory, but rarely provide any experimental data to support the claims that the strategies really work. Naturally, you might wonder if there is any evidence to support these claims. In fact, many memory strategies are *quite* effective and data do exist to support them. In this section, we will consider some of the tried-and-true strategies for improving memory: (1) use of acquired knowledge, (2) use of elaboration, (3) use of distinct memory codes, and (4) use of visual imagery. These four strategies are actually applications of principles discussed earlier in this chapter. Some

of the strategies were also discussed briefly in the introduction on "How to Study."

Use of Acquired Knowledge

Our success in learning new facts and concepts often depends on how well we can relate new ideas to knowledge that we have already acquired. If the material is totally unfamiliar it may be difficult to establish associations with old material, but whatever associations can be made should aid our understanding and memory. Read the passage that follows just once. After you have finished, close your book and try to remember as many different ideas from it as you can.

The procedure is actually quite simple. First you arrange things into different groups. Of course, one pile may be sufficient depending on how much there is to do. If you have to go somewhere else due to lack of facilities, that is the next step; otherwise you are pretty well set. It is important not to overdo things. That is, it is better to do too few things at once than too many. In the short run this may not seem important, but complications can easily arise. A mistake can be expensive as well. At first the whole procedure will seem complicated. Soon, however, it will become just another facet of life. It is difficult to foresee any end to the necessity for this task in the immediate future, but then one never can tell. After the procedure is completed, one arranges the materials into different groups again. Then they can be put into their appropriate places. Eventually they will be used once more, and the whole cycle will then have to be repeated (Bransford and Johnson, 1973, p. 400).

If you found it difficult to recall the ideas in this passage, you are not alone. In an experiment conducted by Bransford and Johnson (1973), people who were asked to read this passage recalled an average of only 2.8 ideas. The paragraph actually describes a familiar situation, but it is described so abstractly that most people cannot relate it to previously-acquired knowledge. However, when a second group of people were told *before* they read the passage that it was about washing clothes, they recalled 5.8 ideas. A third group that was given this information *after* reading the passage recalled only 2.7 ideas. This third group was actually a control group, and the fact that they did no better than the group with *no* information about what the activity was means that prior knowledge affects how material is *stored* but not how it is *retrieved*.

Providing a link between the abstract ideas and familiar knowledge improved recall, but only when the connection was established *before* people read the passage. Why wasn't the link useful when it was given after reading the passage? Bransford and Johnson suggested that the ideas were so abstract that people couldn't comprehend the passage to begin with. The result was that the ideas were forgotten so rapidly that most were gone from memory by the end of the passage. A potential retrieval cue—identifying the activity as washing clothes—was ineffective because there was so little information left in memory to retrieve.

Providing the cue before the paragraph was read enabled subjects to identify what was meant by the abstract ideas. The statement, "It is better to do too few things at once than too many," could then be interpreted to mean that it is better to wash white clothes and colored clothes separately rather than to combine them. When people were able to use their earlier knowledge to interpret the abstract ideas, the ideas became more concrete and could be related to one another. The result was the creation of a deeper semantic code that was easier to remember.

In the introductory section of this book, "How to Study," one of the suggestions was to survey the material before settling down to serious study. This survey process gives you a framework for comprehending what you will try to memorize; you know how each piece of information fits into the chapter or study unit.

Use of Elaboration

A second, and somewhat related, technique for improving memory is to use **elaboration**. Elaboration calls for associating additional information with material we want to remember. Since it often involves associating new material with earlier knowledge, this technique is related to how we coded the earlier knowledge.

As you learned in the section on memory codes, different levels of processing result in different rates of forgetting. But, there can also be different rates of forgetting within a particular processing level, depending on how much elaboration occurred within that level. Consider a task in which people judge whether a word fits into a sentence frame. The amount of elaboration can be varied by varying the complexity of the sentence frames. The following sentences illustrate three levels of complexity.

□ *Simple*. She cooked the _____.
□ *Medium*. The ripe _____ tasted delicious.
□ *Complex*. The small lady angrily picked up the red _____.

Craik and Tulving (1975) used these three different levels of complexity to test the hypothesis that recall would improve as sentence complexity increased. You should remember from earlier in this chapter that *recall* means remembering material without any prompts or cues other than the question—an essay test is a recall task. A recognition task, on the other hand, asks you to determine if a particular stimulus belongs to material that was previously learned—a multiple-choice test is a recognition task. In Craik and Tulving's study, after completing 60 judgments about whether words fit into sentence frames such as the above, subjects were unexpectedly asked to recall the words. Sentence complexity did not influence the recall of words that did not fit into the sentence frames (for example *cloud* would not fit in the above examples). However, sentence complexity did influence the recall of words that did fit into the sentence frames (such as *tomato* in the above examples). When words were consistent with the sentence frames, the more elaborate sentences resulted in better recall.

In the "How to Study" section, it is suggested that you apply principles described in this text to yourself or to situations with which you are familiar. This is an example of elaboration of knowledge; you are extending your network of associations by adding relevant examples and applications. For example, in remembering principles of taste aversion, you might recall a time when you become ill as a

---

Constructive approach. Proposes that memory is actively constructed from the raw materials of external events.

Elaboration. A memory strategy that consists of associating additional information with material we want to remember.

result of something you ate. It is also suggested that you ask yourself questions about the material in the text.

Use of Distinct Memory Codes

The first two memory strategies we have discussed, use of acquired knowledge and use of elaboration, require increasing the amount of material to be remembered. We do this by forming associations between acquired (old) information and the new information that we are trying to learn. An alternative approach is to create distinct memory codes that distinguish between new material and old material. The purpose of this strategy is to reduce forgetting by reducing interference, the major cause of forgetting.

Interference can be reduced by forming memory codes that make material as dissimilar as possible. A good demonstration of this technique is the example mentioned under the section on release from proactive interference. If you study psychology and mathematics in a single study session, you will be better off than if you study psychology and sociology in a single study session. The semantic codes for psychology and math are more distinct than the codes for psychology and sociology.

A particularly effective method for reducing interference is to store some items as a verbal code and some items as a visual code. A verbal, or phonemic, code is formed whenever we name items; a visual code is formed when we create a mental picture of an item's physical characteristics. It seems likely that items that are not easily named or verbally described are stored in memory as visual images or mental pictures. While studies have found that people tend to form verbal codes to maintain items in STM, most studies of this kind have used items that are easily named. An example of a memory task that emphasizes the visual characteristics of stimuli is one that requires subjects to remember a sequence of spatial positions. The task consists of presenting a random sequence of lights, to which subjects respond by pointing to the lights in the order of their appearance.

Although visual images are particularly useful when we want to remember visual information such as spatial locations, unfamiliar faces, and pictures, they can also help us remember verbal information.

It is not always possible to form a visual image to represent a word, but we will usually recall the word better if we create a visual code in addition to a verbal code. Thus, visual images are of distinct value as a memory code. This brings us to the final strategy—the use of visual images.

Use of Visual Images

It isn't hard to think of occasions when you might form two different codes to remember some piece of information. For instance, in order to remember that you need to buy milk at the grocery store you could rehearse the word *milk* and form a mental picture of a milk carton. The result would be two different memory codes—a verbal one created by pronouncing the word and a visual one created by mentally picturing the object. The advantage of having two memory codes is that recalling either the word *milk* or the visual image of a milk carton should remind you of your needed purchase. Paivio has obtained evidence that suggests that the verbal codes and visual codes are remembered independently of one another, implying that people have a better chance of remembering if they use both a verbal label and a visual image (Paivio, 1975). Paivio's theory of memory is called a **dual-coding theory** because it proposes that memory effectiveness is determined by whether someone is using a verbal code, a visual code, or both.

The positive side of these findings is that they demonstrate that we can improve our memory by forming visual images. The negative side is that it is very difficult to form images for certain words. If you want to remember Mr. *Brown*'s name, it is easy to visualize the color brown. If you want to remember Mr. *Gordon*'s name, it may be necessary to first associate *Gordon* with another word, such as *garden*, that is easier to translate into a visual image. The association of *garden* with *Gordon* represents a first step in using an effective memory strategy called the **key-word method**. *Garden* provides a key word that can be used to form an image. Retrieving the image serves as a reminder for *garden*, and *garden* serves as a reminder for *Gordon*.

Although the key-word method may sound complicated, it is nevertheless quite effective, as was demonstrated by Atkinson and Raugh (1975). The method was put to a particular challenging test—could it be used to help students learn the English translations of Russian words? The Atkinson and Raugh study divided the learning task into two stages. The first stage required associating a foreign word with a key word that sounded like some part of the foreign word. The second stage required forming a visual image that combined the key word with the English translation of the foreign word. For example, the Russian word for *building (zdanie)* is pronounced somewhat like *zdawn-yeh*, with the stress on the first syllable. In this case, one could use *dawn* as the key-word and imagine the pink light of dawn appearing behind a building.

Atkinson and Raugh tested the effectiveness of the key-word method by comparing the results of a "key-word" group and a control group. Both groups attempted to learn the English translation of 120 Russian words. After hearing each Russian word pronounced, students in the key-word group were given both a key word and the English translation and instructed to form an interactive image combining both words. Students in the control group were shown only the English translations and were instructed to learn the translations using whatever method appealed to them. After three study sessions, participants in both groups were tested on the entire 120-word list. Students in the key-word group learned the correct English translation for 72 percent of the Russian words, which was significantly better than students in the control group, who correctly translated only 46 percent of the words.

Other trials of the key-word method have followed the Atkinson study, including applications in classroom settings. The outcome has generally been encouraging, although research is continuing on refining the technique for potential classroom applications (Pressley et al., 1982). An interesting question for the future is whether students should be taught to use memory strategies as part of their usual classroom instruction. The accumulating evidence on the effectiveness of memory strategies should encourage students to apply these techniques when learning classroom material.

REVIEW QUESTIONS

14. Most of us have certain memories, either of national or personal events, that we can call up at once and in great detail, and will probably be able to do so the rest of our lives. Such memories are called _____ memories.

15. _____ memories are memories of events that we never actually experienced, although we think we did. An example would be something that you were told about as a child and that you later came to believe you had actually experienced.

16. One way to improve memory is to use _____, which means associating new material with something you already know.

17. Forming an association of a word with another word that can be translated into a visual image is an example of dual-coding theory/key-word method.

Answers: 14. flashbulb **15.** Constructive **16.** elaboration **17.** key-word method

Comparing Memory Strategies

We have considered a variety of memory strategies, including verbal rehearsal and elaboration, memory codes, and visual images. How do these strategies compare in their relative effectiveness? One way to go about answering this question is to assign groups of subjects the same learning task but different learning strategies and then to compare the groups to determine which strategy was most effective for a particular task.

This was the procedure followed in a psychology experiment in which students were asked to learn word pairs consisting of concrete nouns (Bower and Winzenz, 1970). Subjects in the *repetition* group were instructed to silently rehearse each pair. Subjects in the *sentence-reading* group read aloud a sen-

---

Dual-coding theory. Proposes that memory effectiveness is determined by whether someone uses a verbal code, a visual code, or both.

Key-word method. A memory strategy that calls for associating a word with another word that can be easily translated into a visual image.

tence in which the two words of a pair were capitalized as the subject and object of the sentence; the purpose of the sentence was to help associate the two nouns. In the *sentence-generation* group, subjects made up their own sentences to associate the two words in a meaningful way. Subjects in the *imagery* group were instructed to form a mental image that combined the two words in a vivid interaction. The average number of correct recalls was 5.6 for the repetition group, 8.2 for the sentence-reading group, 11.5 for the sentence-generation group, and 13.1 for the imagery group.

These results are especially revealing when placed in the context of the Atkinson-Shiffrin model discussed at the beginning of this chapter. As you recall, Atkinson and Shiffrin (1968) distinguished three different control processes: rehearsal, coding, and imaging. Their own work emphasized the importance of rehearsal in learning, but other research, such as the Bower and Winzenz study just mentioned, has shown that coding and imaging are more effective strategies. This study showed that forming visual images is particularly effective for a task that requires associating concrete nouns. However, the sentence-generation strategy is also effective and is easier to use for more abstract ideas.

Research on memory is continuing at a rapid pace. Most of this research is focusing on memory of material that is more complex and realistic in nature than the nonsense syllables that were used in earlier research. Experiments on such topics as memory for problem-solving and memory for written material are adding new insights into how we use memory in our daily activities. Current and future research will enable psychologists to extend current theoretical ideas into new areas and discover more about how people maintain and expand their knowledge of the world.

■ SUMMARY

1. The Atkinson and Shiffrin memory model consists of memory structures and processes: environmental input, sensory store, short-term memory (STM), response output, control processes, and long-term memory (LTM).

2. *Episodic memory* is of real-life events that have personal meaning. *Semantic memory* contains general facts and information. We are often unable to *recall* information in memory, but we are likely to *recognize* it when we hear or see it.

3. In the *sensory store*, images remain for a brief period of time after the actual stimulus is gone. Sensory memory for vision is called *iconic memory*; sensory memory for hearing is called *echoic memory*. The sensory store has a large capacity, but information disappears rapidly.

4. In *STM*, a limited amount of information can be stored for up to 30 seconds, or longer, using *verbal rehearsal*. STM is limited in the amount of information it can store and in how long it can store it.

5. *Interference theory* proposes that memory for other material or the performance of another task interferes with memory and causes forgetting. *Decay theory* proposes that forgetting would still occur even when no other information interfered with memory and that forgetting is simply due to the passage of time.

6. The number of items that adults can typically store in STM most commonly ranges from 5 to 9. *Chunks*, or familiar information already stored as units in the LTM, are each counted as one item.

7. *Imaging* refers to creating visual images in order to remember verbal material. The *serial-position effect* refers to the fact that when memorizing a list of items, people tend to remember the items at the beginning and the end best (due to the *primacy effect*—more rehearsal of the first items—and the *recency effect*—the last items still being present in STM).

8. Research has shown that interference is the cause of forgetting more often than the passage of time. *Retroactive interference* is caused by new information interfering with old information in memory. *Proactive interference* occurs when old information in memory interferes with new information.

9. Organization is a major factor in memory. We tend to organize information in hierarchically-arranged categories or *clusters*. The effectiveness of memory codes depends on their efficiency in organizing information and in keeping the number of chunks under control.

10. The Craik and Lockhart model describes

memory in terms of *levels-of-processing*. This involves three types of coding: *structural codes* (determining the physical characteristics of a stimulus), *phonemic codes* (naming and recognizing the stimulus), and *semantic codes* (attaching meaning to the stimulus). *Levels-of-processing theory* proposes that as processing levels become deeper, memories become more enduring. Repeating information without attending to its meaning produces a memory that is more easily lost than a semantically-coded memory. The *encoding-specificity principle* holds that the code we use to store information is the most effective code for retrieving that information. Memory is facilitated by the right *retrieval cues*.

11. A *flashbulb memory* is a memory of a particularly striking event that can be retrieved at once and with little difficulty. The meaningfulness of the event is an important factor in this type of memory. Although some details of the event itself may be lost, we remember many of the details of our own personal environment at the time the event occurred.

12. *Constructive memory* involves adding information to a memory that was not part of the original event. We can construct memories of things that never actually happened. Eyewitness testimony can include a detailed "memory" of events that did not occur. For example, Loftus has shown that a misleading question can change a memory. Research on eyewitness testimony has led to the suggestion that memory is constructive and active rather than descriptive and passive.

13. Strategies used to improve memory include acquired knowledge, elaboration, distinct memory codes, and visual imagery. The *key-word method* depends on forming associative images that are later used for retrieval. Coding and imaging appear to be the most effective methods of improving memory.

■ANSWERING QUESTIONS FOR THOUGHT

1. This is best explained by the fact that we process things and events in different ways. The more meaningful things and events are to us, and the more meaningful the ways in which we process them, the more enduring the memories we form of them.

2. Being either first or last is probably more effective when many people are being interviewed—the people in the center of the line tend to be forgotten. This is due to the primacy effect—those interviewed first will be longest in memory and so make a deeper impression, and the recency effect—those interviewed last will still be in memory when the final selection process begins.

3. Levels-of-processing determines how well we will remember faces. The way to remember a person's face is to make a number of difficult and meaningful judgments about it when you first see it, as was shown in the Bower and Karlin (1974) study discussed in the text. In this study, people remembered faces better if they had made judgments about them in terms of honesty or likeability as opposed to judgments made solely on gender.

4. Yes. The example given in the text is that Piaget remembered being kidnapped when he was very young, only to find out years later that it was a made-up story and had never really happened. This kind of memory is called constructive memory.

5. Eyewitness testimony is not considered as reliable as it once was. One reason for this is that we know more about memory and the ways in which a person's memory can be altered by investigative techniques and the way questions are phrased.

9 Language and Thought

QUESTIONS FOR THOUGHT

1. Why does a stroke usually affect a person's use of language?
2. Are all languages alike?
3. Can you know too much to solve a problem?
4. Is it true that two heads are better than one?
5. What kinds of problems can be solved by computers?

The answers to these questions are at the end of the chapter.

"We have no heading. We have no instruments." That is how the conversation between the pilot of Flight 797 and an air traffic controller at the Cincinnati airport began. Unknown to ground control, the Air Canada plane was on fire and the pilot was trying to get it down as quickly as possible. "I could hear in his voice that he wanted to get down pretty quickly," the controller said at a news conference. At one point, about 3-1/2 minutes before the plane landed, the controller was providing instructions that would put the plane in a position to land. The following dialogue was recorded between the pilot and the controller:

Pilot: *Canada 797. Where's the airport?*
Controller: *Twelve o'clock and eight miles, Air Canada 797.*
Pilot: *OK, we're trying to locate it. Advise people on the ground we're going to need fire trucks.*
Controller: *The trucks are standing by for you, Air Canada. Can you give the number of people and amount of fuel?*
Pilot: *We don't have time. It's getting worse here.*
Controller: *Understand, sir. Turn left now and you're just a half mile north of the final approach.*
Pilot: *OK, we have the airport.*

The plane landed a few seconds later. Even though 23 passengers died of smoke inhalation, 18 other passengers and the flight crew managed to escape. The pilot crawled out of the cockpit window with his pants on fire. Had it not been for the efficient communication between the pilot and the controller, everyone on the plane might have been killed. The actual words used by the controller and pilot were certainly important to their communication, but there was more to their communication pattern than just words. The controller could tell that the plane was in serious trouble and needed to land quickly. On the final approach, when asked for further information, the pilot said, "We don't have time. It's getting worse here." The controller replied, "Understand, sir,"—and it was clear that he did because he did not press the issue but returned to giving directions.

As we have just seen, one of the obvious uses of language is spoken communication. Language connects thought and action. In a quiet moment, try tuning in on your thoughts. You will find that a good part of your thinking goes on in words, phrases, and sentences. Occasionally we even speak these thoughts out loud—we talk to ourselves. The air traffic controller took the words of the pilot and added to them some mental images of the situation on the plane, some guesses about the condition of the pilot and crew, and a preliminary plan to get the plane safely to the ground. In his brief communications with the pilot, the air traffic controller was able to convey his comprehension of the situation to the pilot as well as give him instructions on how to land. Both the pilot and the controller were undoubtedly thinking many different things at the same time. Nevertheless, the language they used to communicate was the link between a set of internal thoughts (those related to a safe landing) and a set of actions (those that would place the plane in a position to land on the runway).

In this chapter we will examine some of the processes that make up what might be called *intellectual behavior*. These will include language, reasoning, problem solving, and judgment. We will also consider the development of intelligence testing and some important issues of the testing debate. This group of mental processes, along with memory, makes up what has come to be called "cognitive psychology". In earlier chapters we have encountered the cognitive aspects of other behaviors. We learned how cognition was involved in sensation and perception. We explored the relationship between biological processes and mental behavior. Finally, we considered the newer cognitive theories of learning. In this chapter we will deal directly with cognitive processes themselves.

■ COMMUNICATION AND LANGUAGE

Every living species has the capacity to communicate. Our family has had a dog for about 10 years. The family and the dog have come to know each other quite well. We can communicate with the dog and the dog can communicate with us. When she wants to go out to play, she has a low-pitched, sharp, and insistent bark. When she needs to urinate or defecate, her bark is high pitched and sporadic. When there is a stranger outside, her bark is of a medium pitch but continuous and menacing. When we want her to stop barking, we tell her in sharp but low-pitched commands to keep quiet. When we want her to get excited and jump up, we speak in high-pitched tones usually involving a question, such as, How are you? Do you want to play? Did you miss me today? We have worked out quite an efficient communication system. There are relatively few instances in which we do not correctly interpret each other. That is because neither the dog nor the members of the family are too ambitious in their attempts at communication. The dog cannot tell us with her bark that she is bored with the type of food we have been giving her and would prefer something with a touch of curry. We cannot make it known to our dog that we don't care for the way she walks, that we want her to walk straight rather than list to the left as she occasionally does. We are clearly limited to the present in our communications with the dog. She does not try to tell us about something that happened during the day while we were gone; we do not remind her of the time she put her paw in the fresh cement.

This interaction between dog and human highlights the difference between certain forms of communication and language. **Language** is a specialized communication system for expressing thoughts about internal and external events. We are the only animals with a communication system so flexible and creative that we can use it to build on our knowledge through time. Language provides not just the words and phrases we use, but also the ways in which we combine these words and phrases. As we will see, language serves our communicative and symbolic needs.

Biological Bases of Language

You may remember from the chapter on biology and behavior that the normal use of language requires the cooperation of different areas of the cortex. Further, it seems that the left hemisphere is often, *though not always*, the dominant hemisphere for language use for most people. One exception to this rule is the left-handed person. In left-handed people, the right hemisphere is sometimes the dominant language hemisphere (Foss and Hakes, 1978), and occasionally there is a situation called **bilaterality** (which means "two sides"), in which language functions are carried out by *both* the left and the right hemisphere. These data suggest that the two hemispheres are both capable of language function, but that in most people the left hemisphere serves as the dominant language area.

In Chapter 2 you learned about two brain areas associated with language—Wernicke's area and Broca's area. Injuries to these particular parts of the brain seem to lead to particular types of language problems. The general class of problem is called *aphasia*, but there are many different types. Injuries to Broca's area usually result in problems of speech production; injuries to Wernicke's area usually produce problems in comprehension. Patients who have suffered strokes often show symptoms of damage to Broca's area or Wernicke's area or both. In addition to paralysis of limbs or loss of other motor functions, stroke victims often have difficulty in speaking or understanding language. This may be the result of oxygen loss or hemorrhage in some portion of the left hemisphere. I once saw a startling and frightening demonstration of this effect. When my wife was seven months pregnant with our first child, she woke me one morning with a strange complaint. The clock radio had come on and she could not understand what the radio announcer was saying. She realized that he was talking but she could not recognize the sounds as words with any meaning. She knew that something serious was happening. I tried to calm her but that made matters worse—she couldn't understand what I was saying either. At the same time, she could feel nothing in her right arm or leg. As she dressed to go to the hospital, the right side of her tongue became paralyzed and her speech was slurred although I had no problem understanding what she was saying and the sentences were logical and appropriate. As we drove to the hospital, she began to understand what I was saying, she regained feeling in her limbs, and her speech lost its slur. By the time we arrived at the hospital, the symptoms had disappeared. The doctor diagnosed the problem as a minor stroke or a blood clot of some type. The point is that the loss of function involved language use and was confined to the left hemisphere of her brain. Fortunately, there was no permanent damage to my wife or my daughter, who she was carrying at the time.

■ WHAT IS LANGUAGE?

Language Universals

If you have traveled in a country where you didn't know the language, you may have felt that what you were hearing had nothing in common with English. It may even have sounded like a stream of gibberish rather than separate words and phrases.

Beneath what they sound like on the surface, all human languages share some fundamental properties, or *universals*. One is that meanings are assigned to words arbitrarily. This means that all languages have as many words as needed to serve their communicative and symbolic needs. Another similarity is that every human language has a structure of some type that allows for sequences of sounds and combinations. Further, all human languages are equally complex and equally grammatical. The language of a tribe in a remote jungle is just as complex as the languages of a city dweller in an industrialized nation (Greenberg et al, 1966). It is universal of all languages that they combine words in systematic ways to form sentences. Even though we may not know the vocabulary of another language, universal rules of language would enable us to grasp

that something is being done to someone, at some time, at some place, and by some means. Thus, all human languages have rules that are similar. These rules, or **grammar,** permit the creation of an unlimited number of allowable sentences.

Chomsky (1959) has proposed that language can be divided into two separate components. The first is called the **surface structure,** and this consists of the particular arrangement of words in a sentence. There are many different possible ways in which groups of words can be combined in a sentence and still convey the same thought or meaning. Consider the following four sentences:

☐ Gladys gave Chuck some advice.
☐ Chuck was given some advice by Gladys.
☐ Gladys gave some advice to Chuck.
☐ Some advice was given to Chuck by Gladys.

These sentences represent four different surface structures or arrangements of words and phrases together, but they all *mean* the same thing. The **deep structure** is the underlying meaning conveyed by the arrangement of words and phrases. In this instance, each of these sentences conveys the same meaning. The particular arrangement of words does not change the underlying meaning, so there is only one deep structure. Chomsky suggests that comprehension of the deep structure of sentences is something that each of us is capable of by virtue of innate or inborn knowledge of the rules of grammar.

Ambiguity, or confusion of meaning, arises when there is more than one possible deep structure of a sentence. Consider the following sentence:

☐ The president asked the police officers to stop drinking on campus.

This sentence has two possible deep structures or meanings. The president could have been asking the police officers to refrain themselves from drinking on campus, or the president could have been asking them to keep students from drinking on campus.

Language. A specialized communication system for expressing thoughts about events.
Bilaterality. Situation in which language functions are carried out by both the left and the right hemisphere of the brain.
Grammar. General rules of language; all human languages have rules that are similar.

Surface structure. The particular arrangement of words in a sentence; many different surface structures are possible to convey the same underlying meaning.
Deep structure. The underlying thought or meaning of a sentence.

Ambiguity can be better understood when surface structures and deep structures are compared. Take the following sentence:

□ Racing cars can be fun.

This sentence can be paraphrased in two different ways. Either

□ To race cars can be a fun thing to do.

or

□ Racing-type cars can be fun to drive.

This one sentence is really two different sentences that happen to have the same surface structure.

The rules that relate surface structures to deep structure are called **transformational rules.** These rules help to turn a thought (or idea) into language. When you want to express an idea you begin with the meaning to be conveyed or expressed. This meaning (or thought) is the deep structure of the sentence. Through a knowledge of grammar, vocabulary, and syntax, you produce a sentence with a particular surface structure that conveys this meaning. The surface structure is the written or spoken version of the deep structure.

Physical Characteristics of Language

Phonemes. As a physical stimulus, a sentence is extremely complicated. It consists of many components that are arranged in levels of increasing complexity. Sentences in any language are formed by combining basic speech sounds called **phonemes.** In English, there are about 45 such sounds. Sounds like *p, th,* and *s* are phonemes. Words are composed of phonemes. These sounds, in turn, are combinations of many different frequencies. As you may remember from the chapter on sensation, hearing depends on articulatory gestures and on the frequency and the amplitude of the sound waves. With our mouths, we produce sounds that vary in frequency and amplitude. Figure 9–1 illustrates the properties of sounds in terms of frequencies.

By most standards, speech is poorly produced. The movements inside one's mouth produce an infinite variety of frequencies piled on top of one another. In addition, there are often no physical separations, that is, silent periods, between sounds, words, phrases, and sentences. Thus, to interpret phonemes correctly, we need a context or a frame

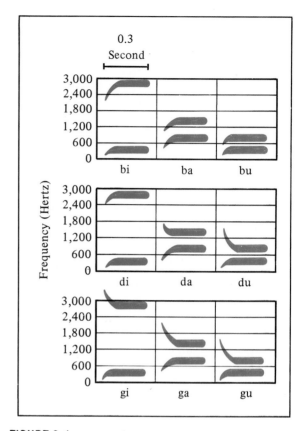

FIGURE 9-1

These charts show how different consonants and vowel combinations produce sounds at different frequencies. (Liberman, 1970)

of reference. Foreign languages are good examples of this difficulty: When we listen to someone speak French or German or Swedish or Arabic and we are not familiar with the language, we may hear what sounds like an undifferentiated stream of sounds. We don't know where words begin or end, and it is hard to make sense out of what we hear. When we learn a language, one of the first things we learn is to hear differences among the speech sounds that are important in that language.

Words. On the average, adults have over 100,000 words in their mental dictionary. Most of the time, when we decide on what meaning we want to convey, the form of the appropriate word comes to mind without much effort. Sometimes we get stuck. The word is on the "tip of the tongue" but it won't emerge. Other times, the word that is spoken is one that sounds somewhat like the one we're searching for but that has a different meaning (for example, saying *ravishing* instead of the intended *ravenous*).

Mistakes like these in the use of words are thought to be related to how they are stored in memory. We are looking for one word but retrieve another. The wrong word is not randomly chosen: When we mean to say *boat*, we may say *goat* but probably won't say *steamshovel*. There are usually similarities between the wrong word and the right one. Brown and McNeill (1966) have studied these types of mistakes by asking people to read a definition of a word and then name the word defined. For example, what's the word for a flat-bottomed boat used in China? Most people realize that a word for such a thing exists in English. They might say that the word sounds something like *sandal* or *sanddah* or *tincan*, but realize that none of those words was quite right. If the searched-for word came to mind they immediately recognized its correctness (for this definition it is *sampan*). The incorrect alternatives were often similar in number of syllables, pronunciation pattern, and in some of the phonemes. The form of words appears to be stored somewhat independently from the meaning. This should not be surprising, given what we know about encoding. As you learned in the chapter on memory, information can be encoded in several ways (Craik and Lockhart, 1972). The form of a word can be encoded *structurally* and the meaning of the word *semantically*. As a result, when we are searching for a particular word it may be that the cue we begin with determines which word will be retrieved. Semantic cues will encourage retrievals based on meaning, and structural cues (such as sounds, syllables, or particular letters) will encourage retrievals based on the physical characteristics of the word.

Many words have multiple meanings (for example, *can*, *bat*, and *bark*). This is known as **polysemy** (Anderson and Ortony, 1975). We usually can identify the meaning of the word from the larger context of the phrase or sentence. As an example, add the word *tin*, to *can*, or *at* to *bat* and the meanings of those words become clearer.

A friend of mine once broke the law because of polysemy. She had arrived in the U.S. from the Middle East and spoke little English. To improve her English rapidly, she enrolled in an intensive language course at an American university. There were several other students in the course with similar backgrounds in English. About four months after beginning the program, several of the students decided to try out their new competency in English by taking a weekend trip through the New England countryside. They had been driving for several hours through the mountains of New Hampshire when they were pulled over by a police officer. He asked them if they knew why he was stopping them. They replied that they did not. He asked them if they remembered throwing a bag full of sandwich wrappers and empty coffee cups out of the car window. They indicated that they did remember doing just that. The police officer then told them that he was issuing them a $25 ticket for littering. They protested that they had broken no law and recalled a sign they had seen that supported their claim. The sign read: Littering Fine! The officer looked at them long and hard, then smiled and told them that the word *fine* can mean many different things and that the sign was actually telling people that they would be subject to penalty if they littered.

Context. The context or frame of reference of a sentence is crucial for comprehension or understanding. "I'm on fire" may mean something different when you are sitting in a Mexican restaurant than it does when you are scrambling out of a burning car. A sentence such as, "The haystack was important because the cloth ripped" is grammatical but not meaningful without the necessary context cue—in this case *parachute* (Bransford and Johnson, 1973). The surface structure of a sentence is stored in short-term memory only until the meaning of the sentence is comprehended, then it is forgotten quickly (unless, of course, you have been explicitly instructed to remember the sentence in the exact form that you read or heard it). For example, when people are asked to remember that "John walked the

---

Transformational rules. The rules that help translate thought into language, or deep structure into surface structure.

Phonemes. Basic speech sounds that are combined to form words; in English there about 45 phonemes.

Polysemy. Occurs when a word has many meanings (examples are *can*, *bat*, or *bark*).

dog," they often find it hard to remember later whether they were told that "John walked the dog" or that "the dog was walked by John." We remember not the exact form of what people say, but what we have understood their message to mean. What we store in long-term memory is the meaning of a message, or its deep structure (Sachs, 1967). As we saw in the chapter on memory, semantic encoding—or coding in terms of meaning—is often critical for lasting memory. Memory and language are closely related concepts in psychology.

REVIEW QUESTIONS

1. The _____ hemisphere of the brain is usually the dominant hemisphere for language. One exception to this rule is people who are left-handed/right-handed.

2. All languages have similar rules, called _____ , that says how words are put together to form an unlimited number of sentences.

3. Chomsky has proposed that language can be broken into two separate components: surface/deep structure is the underlying meaning of the sentence; surface/deep structure consists of the way words and phrases are put together in sentences.

4. The rules that relate surface structure to deep structure are called _____ rules.

5. In English there are about 45 _____ , basic speech sounds that are combined to form words.

Answers: 1. left; left-handed 2. grammer 3. deep; surface 4. transformational 5. phonemes

---

■ HOW IS LANGUAGE LEARNED?

Theories of Language Development

As you have just seen, there is a good deal more to language than sounds or words. Sounds and words simply represent raw material rather than the finished product. Several approaches have been taken to explain where language comes from and how it develops to the sophisticated level usually seen in human communication. We will consider three of these approaches—learning, biology, and an interaction of learning and biology.

Learning Approach: The Behaviorist View. You saw in Chapter 6 that there are several ways for behaviors to be learned, ranging from classical conditioning to observational learning. The behaviorists see language as just another form of behavior—a verbal behavior. As such, they expect language to be subject to the same influences of learning, motivation, perception, and biology that govern other forms of behavior. For example, the behaviorists (Skinner, 1957) propose that language is conditioned in the same way as any other complex response. At first a mother smiles and hugs a baby each time the baby says "Mama." Gradually, the mother changes the schedule of reinforcement. The baby must say new words or make new combinations of old words to get the smile and hug.

According to the learning approach, words, phrases, and sentences are added to a child's linguistic tools through reinforcement, generalization (making old responses to new stimuli), and imitation of parents and other children. In adulthood, we see the results of the "reinforcing practices of verbal communities" (Skinner, 1957, p. 461).

This is a highly simplified description of the learning approach, but it includes the important elements. As Nelson and colleagues (1983) describe this type of approach, it assumes that the child interacts with "adults, and in particular mothers, [who] provide fine-tailored, well-adjusted input that is [perfectly] designed to facilitate progress of language in young children." If a child received selective positive reinforcement for his or her most successful imitative attempts at learning language, then a simple learning model might explain the child's gradual success in learning language.

The Biological Approach. Nelson and colleagues (1983) contrast the learning approach with a quite different one—one that holds that reinforcement has very little to do with the development of language in children. Perhaps the best-known biological theory is that of Noam Chomsky. Chomsky maintains that people are born with capacities to acquire a language, which he calls **language acquisition devices (LADs)**. These devices are inborn and universal. All humans have them at birth, and they develop over time, independent of experience or formal learning. A LAD is not a single thing but a collection of capacities that make language acquisition likely. Some of these capacities might involve basic brain organization, receptors that are sensitive to certain pitches and intensities (such as those peculiar to sounds produced by human vocal cords), and a memory that is responsive to various levels of encoding (for example, phonemic or semantic encoding). This is a strictly biological position. It says that language is a competency like vision and hearing and that even though there may be some individual differences in how *good* each of us happens to be in this compentency, our *basic* language skills are not very much affected by learning or experience (Fodor and Garrett, 1966).

People who agree with Chomsky's position look upon speaking and hearing language as observable behaviors (performance) that reflect an inborn knowledge of the general rules of language. These inborn rules of language can be thought of as principles of organization. Just as Gestalt psychologists proposed certain general principles of perception, such as similarity or contiguity, some language researchers propose certain general principles or rules of language use in humans. These rules of language allow us to generate and understand an infinite number of new phrases and sentences. The biological approach considers the existence of implicit rules the best argument against the learning approach to language (Chomsky, 1959). Look at the acceptable and unacceptable sentence categories in Table 9–1. Do you think that your parents, friends, or teachers taught you how to recognize correct and incorrect forms of sentences? Or did you discover them on your own? The advocates of the biological approach don't think your parents taught you those rules. They think these rules are programmed in some form into your brain at birth.

There are really four important components or processes to keep in mind. The first component is competence or knowledge about language. The biological approach suggests we are born with this competence. The second component is performance. Linguistic performance involves competence but also other variables in addition to knowledge; experience or exposure to certain models can influence performance. The third component is deep structure. This is the underlying

TABLE 9-1
Acceptable and Unacceptable Sentences

1. John didn't want to eat the goldfish at all.
   John wanted to eat the goldfish at all.

2. John didn't fall until yesterday.
   John fell until yesterday.

3. Max won't come, not even if you beg him.
   Max will come, not even if you beg him.

4. She wears her shoes inside out, doesn't she?
   She never wears her shoes inside out, doesn't she?

5. Students won't accept suggestions, and teachers won't either.
   Students won't accept suggestions, and teachers will either.

Source: Grinder and Elgin, 1973.

structure of the ideas to be expressed. The final component is surface structure. This is the way the underlying or deep structure appears in a sentence. Language is the result of the interaction of these four components.

The Interactionist Approach. Chomsky's biological approach emphasizes a language acquisition device—a collection of mechanisms or capacities built into each of us that gives us the power to use language. Chomsky assumes that LADs are inborn and universal because children develop creative and efficient language patterns at an early age—much earlier than an associative learning theory would suggest. Because Chomsky assumes that adults talk to children the same way they talk to other adults, he concludes that experience has little to do with language acquisition. Observation and research have shown that this last assumption is not true. Adults do *not* speak to children the same way they speak to other adults. Instead, adults often speak more simply, more slowly, and with a higher pitch when they are speaking to children (DePaulo and Bonvil-

Langauge Acquisition Devices (LADs). Term used by Chomsky to refer to what he calls inborn and universal capacities that all humans have to use language.

lian, 1978; Blount, 1981; Nelson and others, 1983). They do treat children differently, and this may well account for some variations in language development.

Recently, a new approach has emerged that concentrates on the linguistic relationships between children and adults and examines those relationships for clues to language development. This approach also stresses the interaction between physical growth and development and various language experiences. The key concept is **readiness**. This suggests that children are ready to profit from certain experiences at certain times but not at others. An experience when they are biologically *ready* will have a different effect than will a similar experience before they are ready. From this perspective, physical or biological capacities are necessary for language development, but a biological status cannot guarantee language development.

A good example of this approach can be found in the work of Nelson and colleagues (1983). They propose that learning a language is similar to breaking a code. The child examines the language environment with certain tools. These tools might be identical to those suggested by Chomsky. These tools change over time. In a sense, the child trades in some primitive tools for more sophisticated ones. But the task remains the same—to break the code of language that the child hears every day. Nelson has credited the mother as a primary source of supplying hints to the child searching to break the code. The mother can try to capture a child's attention when naming things. The mother can respond approvingly when the child associates words with the appropriate things. It is this method of parents responding to children that plays a major role in the speed and extent to which language skills develop. This approach does not ignore the powerful cognitive tools that the child beginning to talk already has. It is the presence of these tools (such as analyzing, recognizing, and remembering) that makes the hints of the mother valuable in language learning—thus, biology and experience interact.

Some categories of response that are available to the mother are simple rephrasing and complex rephrasing. The 24-month-old child might say, "She's funny." A simple rephrasing by the mother would be, "Yeah, she's pretty funny." A child might

Some theorists believe that it is the interaction between child and adult that sets the pace for language learning. One type of interaction is for the mother to respond with approval when the child names an object correctly.

say "It fell" and the mother might respond, "It fell off the wagon and rolled down the hill" (Nelson and others, 1983). This would be a complex rephrasing. Many other types of responses are available to the mother. These responses might involve continuing with a present topic or switching to a different topic, giving examples of the topic under discussion, or simply repeating or imitating what the child said. Nelson believes that it is the interaction between what the child says and how the mother responds that accounts for the pace of language development. Some types of response are more appropriate for one age or level of maturation than another. For example, it would not be effective to talk "baby talk" to a 5-year-old, nor would it be effective to continually change the topic with a 2-year-old.

The interactionist position is appealing. It allows for both biological development and environmental stimulation. It does not dismiss the learning and biological approaches but uses them to build on. The implications of this approach are particularly exciting for dealing with some types of language problems. Instead of drilling children on word skills or usages, it suggests a rather careful diagnosis to identify readiness levels and appropriate experiences. We will come back to this topic of readiness again in the first chapter on developmental psychology.

Learning and Maturation in Language Development

In the first chapter on developmental psychology (Chapter 10), you will learn that there are various patterns of change as people mature physically; physical development is accompanied by sensory, perceptual, cognitive, and other aspects of child development. Coordination and motor skills also improve substantially in the first few years after birth. If language is a competency like others that is built into the brain, it is reasonable to explore how it might be related to normal maturation as well as to abnormalities or injuries at various periods of development.

From Words to Speech. As you can see from Figure 9–2, children begin to develop an extensive vocabulary after the age of 2, and by the time they are 6 they know about 2500 words. Once children utter their first few words, parents and siblings begin

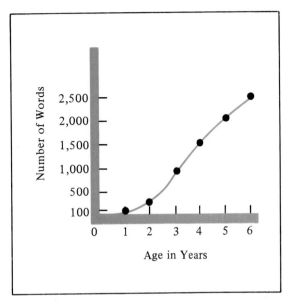

FIGURE 9–2

Children begin to develop a large vocabulary after the age of 2. By the time they are 6 they have a vocabulary of over 2,500 words. (Smith, 1926; Lenneberg, 1967)

to encourage meaningful linguistic interactions. The child may say "bear." The parent might respond, "Do you want your teddy bear?" As we saw above, the parent is likely to respond in a slow and deliberate way, often repeating the response several times.

As language develops in the child, there is a regular progression from single words, to two-word utterances, and eventually to complete sentences that are correct using the conventions of the English language. By the age of 4, many children communicate differently with adults from how they do with other children. They use longer and more grammatically complex sentences with adults than with 2-year-olds (Shatz and Gelman, 1973). This illustrates that the child has become proficient enough with the tools of language to use it in a way that is tied to the social context or environment.

The following is a characteristic pattern of language development:

Readiness. The concept that children are biologically ready to profit from certain experiences at certain times but not at others.

1. At 2 months, children make specific noises and faces in response to pleasant objects or familiar faces.
2. At 6 months, children begin to repeat the same phonemes. This is the characteristic babbling that appears in children of this age. Over the next few months, these sounds will begin to approximate the sounds of many words children hear from those in the immediate environment.
3. At 1 year, children will begin to utter single words.
4. At 15 months, children will begin to use single words as complex commands or requests. For example, they may say "wawa" to indicate that they would like some water. Similarly, they might extend their arms and say "up," indicating a desire to be picked up.
5. At 24 months, children form two-word sentences such as "see doggie" or "give candy" or "where ball?" (Slobin, 1971).

Critical Periods in Language Development. An important concept that relates the process of physical and psychological development to particular competencies is the concept of **critical periods.** This concept suggest that there are periods of development that are more important than others for the emergence of certain abilities or competencies. This seems to be the case with language ability. There are two lines of research that point to the importance of critical developmental periods. One line of research deals with injuries to the brain that occur at different ages. The second type of research examines people who have experienced unusual developmental experiences at particular times or periods.

As you learned in the chapter on biology and behavior, cells have the capacity to repair themselves. With respect to neuron damage (particularly damage to the left hemisphere), the developmental period during which the damage occurs seems to be an extremely important influence on the extent to which full recovery will be realized. There seem to be three general periods that can be identified in a discussion of brain damage and language deficit. These periods are from birth to about 4 years, from 4 to 11 or 12, and from 12 on through adulthood (Lenneberg, 1967; Bay, 1975). If an injury occurs in the first developmental period, recovery seems to occur quickly and language development picks up from the level

it had reached just before the injury (Foss and Hakes, 1978). The earlier that the injury occurs within this period, the more likely that recovery will be complete (Lenneberg, 1967). If an injury occurs during the second period (4 to 11), recovery is not as rapid and may not be complete (Foss and Hakes, 1978). If the injury occurs during the third and last period, the prognosis is not as promising. There is an initial period of improvement but this is often due to the fact that the injury is accompanied by swelling, infection, and other secondary problems. When the swelling disappears there is a quick improvement and then as the general condition stabilizes, improvement stops.

One interpretation of these data involves the issue of the two hemispheres of the brain. As Foss and Hakes (1978) suggest, at birth both hemispheres may be capable of supporting language functions. We know that this must be the case in at least some people since we know that some left-handers use the right hemisphere for language activities. It may be that the left hemisphere gradually assumes control over language and, in the process, the right hemisphere becomes less capable of language use. If this were the case, you would expect the right hemisphere to become less and less capable of picking up the language function as the individual matures. Finally, after puberty, the right hemisphere might have completely lost its capacity to process language. This is a reasonable explanation of the data on brain injury at various periods. It also fits with what we know about brain structure and function. Since the two hemispheres are similar anatomically, there is reason to believe that they *could* perform similar functions even though they may not at a given time.

■ CONVERSATION

Up to this point in the chapter we have been considering what language is and how it is learned. We are now going to look at some of the important uses of language. One of the most common forms of language use is communication with others. A con-

---

Critical periods. Periods of development that are more important than others for the emergence of certain abilities or competencies.

CRITICAL PERIODS OF SECOND LANGUAGE LEARNING

Up to this point, we have considered the problem of explaining how children develop a "first" or native language. This is one of the major tasks of early cognitive development. As Nelson suggests, "breaking the code" is an important goal for the child. You may not remember much about how you learned English. If the biological point of view is correct, there is not much to remember, since you never learned or encoded the rules of the language. They were there from birth. Learning to use a foreign or second language is another matter entirely. This often begins in junior high school or high school and you are face to face with the difficulties of language acquisition. Why do so many people find learning another language difficult if all the rules and processes for language development and use are programmed into humans?

The answer seems to be related to *when* second language learning begins. The difficulties that young adults and mature adults encounter in learning a foreign language may be due in part to factors similar to those that play a role in recovery from brain damage. As was suggested by the data on aphasia recovery, there seems to be a critical period for developing skill in a language—any language. This period for language acquisition is associated with a period of brain development and maturation. As you saw in aphasia, the later in development the damage occurs, the greater the difficulty in becoming skilled in the language. As you approach and pass puberty, the probability of developing normal language skills in spite of brain injury decreases. This maturational sequence may affect learning foreign languages as well.

In addition to possible biological obstacles, the *methods* by which first and second languages are acquired are qualitatively different. Krashen (1978) contrasts first language acquisition by children with the experiences of young adults trying to learn a foreign language. Young children's experiences of language involve social relations. Nelson's descriptions of mother-child interactions are examples. There is a social *exchange* between the two parties. This type of exchange seems to be a part of most communication involving children in real world situations. Through these communication (exchange) situations, first language skills are developed. In contrast, young adults learning a foreign language are usually given explicit drills in classroom situations or language laboratories for a few hours a week. They memorize foreign words and associate their meanings with equivalent words in their native language rather than to real world situations. They study rules for combining words and usually end up being able to read in the foreign language without developing communication skills.

There are other differences between children learning their native language and adults learning a second language. A major difference seems to be one of attitude or motivation. Children are motivated to communicate their wants, their desires, and their thoughts through the language system they are learning. They have no other language system to compare how well they are doing as they learn. They know less than adults, and so are not embarrassed or inhibited as they speak. Adults compare their native language competence to their attempts in speaking a new language and are likely to become embarrassed about their ignorance, and inhibited because of their mistakes.

Many people do speak more than one language with great skill. Often, this is because they grow up in countries where several languages are spoken, such as Canada, where both English and French are spoken. Many Canadians are bilingual. Most Dutch people usually are proficient in four languages; they speak Dutch, French, German, and English.

The conclusion that can be drawn from data and experience about second language learning is that it occurs more easily and completely if it begins at an early age and if the learning is tied to becoming a member of the foreign group. It is generally recognized that living in another country for extended period of time is an enormous benefit to learning that language. This is probably the result of the fact that there is no choice but to use the language for meeting almost all needs. One of the reasons why foreign immigrants to the United States seem to learn English so quickly is probably because few Americans speak the native language of the immigrant. There is no choice but to learn.

versation where one person speaks to another in a face-to-face encounter is the medium by which attitudes, ideas, solutions to problems, and intentions are exchanged.

As you saw earlier, when we construct a sentence we follow certain rules. We also follow certain rules when we engage in conversation with others. As was the case with sentences, the rules of conversation are for the most part unconscious. The conversational rules shared by a cultural group are mostly outside of the group's conscious awareness. Although the rules may differ across cultures, we expect that a speaker will attempt to make sense and will also try to be informative, relevant, and clear without the addition of unnecessary details. For example, suppose that in a casual conversation Blair asks Denise, "Where is the Statue of Liberty?" There are many possible answers. "It's in New York Harbor"; "It's in New York City"; "It's in the Northeastern United States"; or, "It's in the United States." Which answer Denise chooses depends on her guess about why Blair asked the question and how much he already knows. If Blair and Denise are in Germany, the last answer would probably be suitable. But if Blair asked the question while sitting in a car on the New Jersey Turnpike with a map in his hand, then the suitable answer would have to be more detailed than any of the above, indicating how to get from the New Jersey Turnpike into lower Manhattan.

There are also shared conversational rules about who has permission to speak next. This is called *turn-taking* (Weiner and Goodenough, 1977). For example, Speaker 1 has the option of designating the next speaker in a group. A second speaker will usually wait until the first speaker pauses. If Speaker 1 does not designate a next speaker, the next turn goes to the first person who speaks. Speaker 1 will get another turn after Speaker 2 pauses.

Turn-taking raises an interesting issue—interruptions. When you are speaking and someone interrupts you, it can be annoying. It is natural to wonder why they did not let you finish what you were saying, but you may have invited the interruption through your speech patterns. Margaret Thatcher, the Prime Minister of Great Britian, appears to have that problem. A research team of psychologists from Cambridge University set out to study Mrs. Thatcher's style of being interviewed. They examined televised interviews of Mrs. Thatcher that

included clear instances of interruptions by the interviewer. They found that in instances of interruption, Mrs. Thatcher had sounded and looked as if she were finished speaking when in fact she had not completed her answer. She suddenly dropped the pitch of her voice and looked straight at the interviewer as she did this. Both of these cues seemed to indicate that she had finished speaking (Nelson, 1983). To see if these observations were closely related to the interruptions, the research team showed film clips that included these interruptions to undergraduate students. They were asked to indicate when they thought Mrs. Thatcher was finished speaking. They came to the same conclusions as the researchers who had examined the videotapes: Mrs. Thatcher often appeared as if she had finished speaking when she had not.

Occasionally people use strategies that allow them to continue to speak *without* interruption, much to the annoyance of the other party who can't get a word in. These strategies involve raising rather than lowering pitch at the end of one thought and may also involve avoiding eye contact. Think about these techniques when you are engaged in a heated discussion. You may find that both you and the other party are making liberal use of these strategies in an attempt to control the outcome and direction of the discussion.

Rules also exist for opening and closing conversations. For example, when a telephone rings, the person receiving the call answers with "Hello," or, "Bill Moore speaking," or, "Extension 105," before the caller says anything to introduce the first topic of conversation. If these rules are violated the conversation doesn't work. For instance, if the person answering says nothing and waits for the caller to speak first, or if the person answering starts by introducing the first topic, both people will be confused (Clark and Clark, 1977). The most common leave-taking phrase for intimates (both male and female) is "Bye-bye," but most speakers are not consciously aware of this and may emphatically deny it (Labov, 1974).

Nonverbal Communication

The question of conversational rules touches upon another aspect of communication—the use of gestures, tones, facial expressions, and other cues

The significance of eye contact in conversation differs across cultures. Without awareness of such subtle differences in communication, foreigners may misread each others' nonverbal cues.

to convey information. This has traditionally been referred to as **nonverbal communication.**

In a typical two-person conversation, Birdwhistell (1974) estimates that more than 65 percent of the meaning is conveyed by nonverbal signals. Gestures, facial expressions, posture, eye behavior, touching, and spatial allowances all contribute to the social meaning of the spoken word. For instance, when a person about to make a speech says "I'm not nervous" but shows trembling hands and knees, beads of perspiration on the upper lip, and a furrow on the brow, the nonverbal cues convey more about how the person actually feels than his or her statement.

Although nonverbal cues can convey a great deal of meaning, it is possible to misread cues if one does not consider the context of the communication. For instance, crossing the arms in front of the body is

generally considered a barrier sign. But it is possible that rather than indicating a barrier, the person may be wearing short sleeves and is getting cold, and so is crossing the arms to preserve body heat.

Cross-cultural differences may also contribute to an inaccurate reading of nonverbal cues. For example, the significance of eye contact in conversation differs in different cultures. Two Americans in conversation will make eye contact according to whether they are speaking or listening. The speaker shifts gaze while talking, and periodically re-establishes eye contact with the listener to be sure he or she is still paying attention. Listeners keep their eyes on the speaker. We learn to do this as chil-

---

Nonverbal communication. The use of gestures, tones, facial expressions, and other cues to convey information.

dren when our parents say, "Look at me when I'm talking to you." In Japan, focusing one's gaze on another person's eyes is considered impolite. The Japanese gaze at the necks of their conversational partners (Argyle, 1975). An American in conversation with a Japanese may assume the listener is not interested and will pause until eye contact occurs, or will end the conversation. Arabs don't shift their gaze as they talk; they maintain eye contact and consider shifting the gaze away to be rude and disrespectful. Without awareness of these subtle cultural differences, Americans, Japanese, and Arabs may misread each other's nonverbal cues.

One fascinating aspect of nonverbal communication is *staring behavior*. Have you ever found someone staring at you? Or worse, been caught staring at someone else? Consider what you do in an elevator. You look hard at your fingers, the doors, or a paper you're carrying. This reduces the possibility of inadvertently making eye contact with a stranger. There is also the issue of the "staredown" (Collins, 1983). You are caught in a stare by a stranger who stares (or glares) back. Who will give in and break contact? Will you look away? Will he or she blink first? Staring is hardly a critical part of human behavior or communication; nevertheless, many messages fly back and forth across the 10 feet separating the combatants in a staredown. It is definitely a pattern of communication.

REVIEW QUESTIONS

6. Match the following theories with the correct definitions:

___ learning approach	A. emphasizes biological readiness and experience with others in the development of language ability.
___ biological approach	B. langue is acquired through reinforcement, generalization, and the imitation of others.
___ interactionist approach	C. people are born with the capacity to acquire a language independent of experience or formal learning.

7. At what age do children begin to form 2-word sentences, such as "see doggie"? 9 months/1½/2 years.

8. There are unstated rules of conversation, just as there are with the formation of sentences. One of these rules concerns who has permission to speak next—this is called _____ _____ .

9. A good way to avoid being interrupted in a conversation is to raise/lower your voice at the end of a thought and encourage/avoid eye contact with other speakers.

10. _____ _____ refers to the use of gestures, tones, facial expressions, and other cues to convey information.

11. People use similar gestures to mean the same things no matter what culture they are in.   T / F

Answers: 6. learning approach, B; biological approach, C; interactionist approach, A. 7. 2 years 8. turn-taking 9. raise; avoid 10. nonverbal communication 11. False

Language in Chimps

Nonhuman primates can communicate with one another but have not evolved a languagelike system in the wild. Are they capable of acquiring it with instruction? Can animals without a languagelike system reason or solve problems? Attempts to teach language to primates are seen as a test of how closely related our communication is to our thinking. Also, the idea of talking to other animals has interested humans for centuries. The first attempts to teach language to chimpanzees showed that these animals were intelligent but incapable of speech. Kellogg and Kellogg (1933) raised a chimp (named Gua) along with their own child. In her foster home, Gua learned to understand about 70 verbal commands, but she never imitated any vocalizations. She produced only the calls expressed by other chimpanzees. Her motor skills developed faster than those of the human child. For example, she learned to skip earlier. She also learned to perform socialized actions, such as learning to feed herself and to kiss to show forgiveness, earlier than her human sibling.

Hayes and Hayes (1951) also raised a chimp, named Vicki, in their home. They combined humanlike care with operant conditioning techniques of shaping and reinforcement. After intense efforts to teach Vicki to speak, she was able to produce approximations of only four words: *mama, papa, cup,* and *up.* She did show her intelligence in solving problems and in making distinctions among concepts.

Twenty years passed before researchers tried approaches other than spoken language. Because chimpanzees naturally gesture, one approach has been to teach hand gestures (signing) used by the deaf (American Sign Language). Gardner and Gardner (1975) encouraged signing in a homelike environment by modeling and imitation. They didn't try to teach any rules for recombining symbols into structured sentences. In contrast to Vicki, their adopted chimp, Washoe, learned the meaning of about 500 signs by the time she was 4 years old. She used these signs in general and abstract ways. For example, after learning the sign for *flower* with real flowers, she extended her use of the sign to pictures of flowers. When she encountered distinctive scents she would also sign *flower.* After learning to sign *open* to get her trainers to open a door, she extended her use of *open* to request that they open other containers (jars, boxes, drawers) and to turn on water faucets. As she looked through magazines, she would sign to herself, such as signing *drink* when seeing an ad for vermouth. She also combined signs, for instance, signing *gimme flower, come gimme*

open. When asked, "What's that?" when looking at a swan, she signed *waterbird.* Fouts (1973; 1975a; 1975b) found similar behavior in the learning of signs by a chimpanzee named Lucy. She invented the name *drink fruit* for watermelon.

Chimps have also shown that they can communicate their requests for goods and services that they need for their well-being on computer keyboards with a screen (Rumbaugh, 1974). On each key is a symbol representing a word and a symbol to ask a question. The messages appear on the screen, and the researcher can respond by typing messages onto the screen.

One chimp named Lana sometimes corrects the researcher's messages. For example, Lana typed, "?You put more milk in machine." The trainer typed back, "No milk in machine" (it was broken). Lana then typed, "You put more milk in cup." The trainer typed, "Yes" but didn't act because Lana forgot the question symbol. Lana then typed "?You give milk of," and then, "?You give cup of milk." The trainer typed, "Yes" and gave her the cup of milk (Gill, 1977, p. 1930; in Rumbaugh and Savage, 1978).

Considerable controversy exists over interpreting the languagelike behaviors of this group of primates (Savage-Rumbaugh, 1980). There is some agreement that they can use abstract symbols meaningfully to express intentions and emotions and that they can spontaneously combine words to form new words (Brown, 1973). But correct word order and general

The language capabilities of apes have yet to be unambiguously determined. Some chimps have been taught to use sign language meaningfully. Others have learned to communicate through a system of computer language.

grammar as well as interpretable vocalizations appear to be beyond their grasp (Premack, 1976; Terrace and others, 1979). For example, Terrace and colleagues analyzed three- and four-sign combinations and found a great deal of redundancy and repetition in the sequences. For instance, if a trainer failed to respond to the request signed by "eat drink," the chimp might attempt to gain attention and eye contact and would repeat the acts by signing, "eat drink eat drink." The repetitions add emphasis but no new meaning.

It seems as if these animals select symbols that have worked previously in similar situations and link them together. This is not the same thing as the symbolic use of language for the production of ideas and abstract concepts. For instance, a chimp signed a 16-sign request to get an orange when her trainer was trying to get her to imitate a comment about eating. The message was, "Give orange me give eat orange me eat orange give me eat orange give me you" (Terrace and others, 1979, p. 895). She couldn't grasp why new symbols were now necessary to get food when they had not been necessary before. Nonhuman primates appear to have great difficulty in grasping the creative and abstract value of language use.

Language and Thought

The research examining language use in animals introduces the next topic for consideration in this chapter—the relationship between language and thought. The experimenters in these studies were interested in the possible cognitive aspects of animal behavior. In this instance, language was being used as a "mirror of the mind." It is common to make inferences about thought processes from language. As you will see in a later chapter, one of the main symptoms of schizophrenia is disordered thought. This symptom is identified by the schizophrenic's use of strange language patterns. To be accurate, we should refer to this symptom as a language disorder rather than a thought disorder, but other symptoms make it obvious that the problem is much deeper than the inappropriate use of words and sentences. The schizophrenic is using a language pattern that indicates a unique thought pattern. In this case, it is assumed that disturbance of thought leads to disturbance of language.

A friend of mine puts the thought-language re-

lationship in a slightly different way. He once presented a paper entitled, "How do I know what I mean until I see what I say" (Weick, 196). What he meant was that he frequently writes out his thoughts and studies them, as one would a text written by someone else, in order to come to some understanding of what he is thinking. In this case, he uses language as a mirror to his own mind, a way of exploring thoughts that were not easily accessible before being turned into language. In fact, he is describing an extremely powerful interplay between language and thought. Although not many of us take the time to write out and formally consider our thoughts, most of us try to "think through" our logical positions before presenting them to others. In a sense, we rehearse how they will sound, sometimes even working out a script in our head of what the reactions will be to our position and how we might respond to those reactions.

Some researchers have suggested an even more radical relationship between thought and language. One theory—that language *determines* thought—was made popular by Benjamin Whorf (1956). Whorf made two related propositions. The first was called **linguistic determinism,** and it stated that the way we think is determined by the way we speak. The second was called **linguistic relativity,** and it stated that people who speak different languages think differently—that their thought patterns are affected by the structure of their particular language. This implies that a person from Japan has different thought patterns from a person from America or Germany. Whorf studied the languages of American Indians and gave as one example of his propositions the notion of time (Foss and Hakes, 1978). He suggested that because the Hopi Indian language does not have the tenses commonly found in English (for example, present, past, and future), then Hopi Indians who speak only Hopi do not have the same concept of time as speakers of English.

Whorf's two propositions have attracted much research attention along with strong criticism. Counter-examples are easy to find. An Eskimo dialect has many different single words to describe snow. But someone who lives in Minnesota may express the same differences with phrases (powder snow, corn snow, wet snow) instead of with single words for snow. It has also been shown in experiments that people who speak languages with very few names for colors can still recognize all of the colors that are recognized by those who speak languages with many color names (Heider, 1972; Rosch, 1973). On the other hand, Whorf may still be correct in pointing out that experience can help shape language, which in turn may help shape subsequent experience. In a sense, this brings us back to the proposition made earlier—that inborn capacities interact with experience to yield what we refer to as language.

As you will see more clearly later in the chapter, language, like memory, plays a role in complex cognitive activity. We assign meaning to many objects and events in our environment. What we "know" from experience is really an information network. This network consists of various meaning categories, which are tied together. These categories are called *concepts*. When we solve problems, reason, and judge, we are using concepts. As you can see, language and memory play a major role in these complex cognitive activities.

Let's now examine problem solving as an example of the complex cognitive activity. In the process, we will see how language and memory play a role in more elaborate mental operations.

■ PROBLEM SOLVING

Problem solving is readily seen as a cognitive activity. Its success depends on the efficiency with which a person carries out certain mental operations. Because these operations are mental, certain abstract tools are required. One very useful tool is *memory*. Can you imagine how much more difficult it would be to solve a problem if you could not take advantage of what you learned from earlier attempts? An example should show what this would be like. Each spring I bring my bike up from the basement to clean it for the new bicycling season. Each spring I try to remember the combination for the lock I use to keep the bicycle from being stolen. I remember that the first number is twice the last number, and I seem to remember that the first number is 19. In addition, it seems to me that the mid-

dle number is the age of one of my daughters. Then the ritual begins. I first try the combination 19-18-38. It doesn't work. Then I try 19-15-38 (I have two daughters). It doesn't work. Both of the attempts began with a clockwise beginning. It doesn't work. Now the fun begins. Did I try 19-18-38 clockwise? I can't remember, so I try it again. Did I try 19-15-38 counterclockwise? To be safe, I try it. Maybe the combination is 38-18-19. The possibilities begin to increase geometrically. Because I don't remember which possibilities I have tried, my efforts become more and more inefficient. I repeat some combinations five or ten times. Other possible combinations go untested because I "remember" trying them before.

This will give you just a small idea of what it would be like to try to solve problems without a memory. Any success would be accidental and would have no implications for future behavior. The next time you encountered the problem, you would have to solve it all over again. Incidentally, it may have occurred to you that the simplest solution would be to mark down the combination on a piece of paper and put it in a safe place so that the yearly ritual of trying to remember it is eliminated. That solution has occurred to me as well. Each year I do just that. Then I put the slip of paper in a "special" place so that it won't get thrown away. By the time the next year rolls around I have forgotten where I put the slip of paper, because there has been no reason to rehearse the location over the winter.

Problem Solving Examples

A few years ago in Phoenix, Arizona, a fire department dispatcher had a problem that he needed to solve quickly. He received a call for help from a woman who gasped "Rovey" and "41." She then passed out. The dispatcher began to follow normal procedure for getting a rescue squad to the woman immediately. But when he went to the fire department computer, he discovered that there was no 41 E. Rovey or 41 W. Rovey. Further, he discovered that there was no 4100 block of Rovey on the east side. He quickly dispatched a rescue squad

---

Linguistic determinism. Propostion by Whorf that the way we think is determined by the way we speak.

Linguistic relativity. Proposition by Whorf that people who speak different languages think differently—their thought patterns are affected by the structure of their particular language.

to the 4100 block of West Rovey and told them to sound their siren continuously as they went slowly down that block. Because the caller had not hung up the phone, the dispatcher was able to listen to the siren grow louder and softer and pinpoint the exact house from which the call was made. They found the caller in a very few minutes. She was unconscious but they were able to revive her and she was released from the hospital shortly after treatment. Most of us would call the dispatcher "clever" or "smart" or "bright." These are nontechnical terms. In psychological language, the dispatcher was engaged in "problem solving." To solve the problem, he used several different cognitive tools. Although psychologists do not usually study problem solving in as dramatic a context as that illustrated by the dispatcher, they do study the basic cognitive tools that the dispatcher used. Let us examine problem solving and the tools that are used to accomplish it.

Suppose that you were in a given situation—let us call that the *given state*—and you wanted to be in another situation—let us call that the *goal state*—but there was no obvious way of getting there. For example, you could be on one side of a busy street wanting to be on the other side, but without a direct crosswalk. You could have a paper due for a class but no idea about what to write. You could have a leaky faucet but know nothing much about plumbing. You could have the responsibility of dispatching a rescue squad to someone in trouble but not know where to send them. Each of these predicaments corresponds to the definition of a **problem**—wanting to get from a given state to a goal state but lacking a direct way of getting there.

Problem solving refers to the process of moving from the given state to the goal state of a problem. When I was in college I took a trip with some friends to a vacation area. While we were there, the transmission in my car decided to join us on vacation and stopped working. Because pieces of the transmission were lying on the ground under the car, it was obvious that it had to be replaced. I had the tools with me to complete the replacement and knew something about transmissions—at least enough to replace one with another. I called around and found a junk yard that would sell me a replacement transmission at a reasonable price. The problem was getting the old transmission out, because the weight of the engine rested on the back part of the trans-

mission. This meant that I could not simply unbolt the transmission and slip it out. Somehow, I had to get the weight of the engine supported so that I could slip the transmission out.

Now came the search for a solution. I first thought of a bumper jack, but I immediately realized that this would be useless because the weight of the engine would still remain on a portion of the transmission. The next solution I thought of was a floor jack that I could roll under the engine and raise. Because there were no garages or gas stations in the immediate vicinity, that solution would not work. I was stuck. I sat down on the curb trying to think of things I could do. As my gaze wandered around, I saw a pile of discarded bricks. The solution then occurred to me. I gathered up the pile of bricks, used the bumper jack to get the front of the car up in the air, placed a large column of bricks topped with a flat piece of wood under the bottom of the engine, and jacked the car down again. The transmission was now relieved of the engine weight. I had the old transmission out and the new one in within a few hours. Solving this problem involved more than simply finding the correct wrench or removing particular bolts. There were several discrete stages to the solution.

The problem-solving process can be seen as a series of steps. For example, Polya (1957, 1968) suggested the following four steps based on his observations as a teacher of mathematics:

- *Understanding the problem*—the problem-solver gathers information about the problem and asks, "What do I want? What do I have?"
- *Devising a plan*—the problem-solver tries to create a method of solution and asks, "Do I know a related problem? Can I restate the goal or the givens?"
- *Carrying out the plan*—the problem-solver tries out the solution plan.
- *Looking back*—the problem-solver tries to check the result and see how it all fits together.

Let us see if these stages can be applied to the way in which I solved my transmission problem. The first stage was *understanding the problem*. It became obvious very quickly that the problem was getting the weight of the engine off the back end of the transmission. Another part of defining the problem was realizing that I did not have the correct equipment to do this, and that it would be necessary to

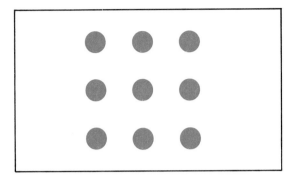

FIGURE 9-3
In the nine-dot problem, the task is to draw four straight lines that will cross through all nine dots—but you must do this without lifting your pencil from the paper.

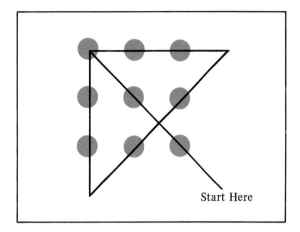

Start Here

FIGURE 9-4
This is one solution to the nine-dot problem. Many people are kept from reaching a solution by assuming that the four lines must be drawn within the boundary of the square formed by the dots.

use a substitute. The next stage was *devising a plan*. In my case, this meant recognizing that I could raise the car with a bumper jack, place a column of bricks under the engine, and jack the car back down, thus relieving the transmission of the engine weight. In my head, it worked perfectly. The third stage was *carrying out the plan*. I took the discarded bricks I had found, jacked up the car, placed a column of bricks topped with a flat wooden board under the engine, and jacked the car down. The final stage involved *looking back*. In this case, the solution worked perfectly and I filed it in my memory store of clever solutions. At least for my problem, Polya's description fit perfectly.

Approaches to Problem Solving

Creative Problem Solving. Sometimes we are required to solve poorly defined problems using any method we want as long as it solves the problem. Because this often involves looking at a problem in a new way, it is referred to as *creative problem solving*. Solving this type of problem often includes such strategies as rearranging elements in the problem or coming up with as many different and unique solutions as possible.

Consider the problem shown in Figure 9-3. You are given nine dots arranged in a square. Your job is to draw four straight lines, without lifting your pencil from the paper, which will cross through all nine dots. This is called the *nine-dot problem*.

Adam (1974) has noted that people often have "conceptual blocks" because they tend to limit the problem area too narrowly. If you are suffering from a "block," take a rest for a minute and then return to the problem. This rest period is called **incubation,** because the solution may be developing in your mind. Now try to look at the problem in a new, less limiting, way. For example, some people assume that the lines must be drawn within the boundary of the square. However, if you let your lines extend beyond that boundary you may suddenly realize a solution such as that shown in Figure 9-4. Another limitation that some people impose on the problem is that they believe the lines must cross through the center of each dot. However, if you free yourself from that self-imposed limitation, you may be able to solve the problem by using only three lines, as shown in Figure 9-5.

Problem. State of wanting to get from a given state to a goal state without a direct way of getting there.
Problem solving. The process of moving from the given state to the goal state of a problem.

Incubation. A rest period in problem solving during which one hopes the solution is developing in one's mind.

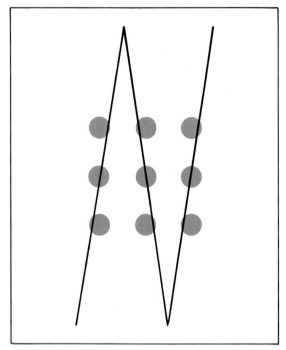

FIGURE 9-5
This is another solution to the nine-dot problem. There is nothing in the statement of the problem that says that the lines must cross through the center of each dot—by angling the lines in a slightly different way this solution can be reached.

Overcoming a fixed way of look at a problem involves what the Gestalt psychologists called insight. **Insight** means a sudden reorganization of a problem so that the inner structure of the problem becomes clearer. As you may remember from the chapter on history and methods, the Gestalt psychologists (Kohler, 1925; Katona, 1942; Wertheimer, 1959) were convinced that certain built-in principles of organization played a large role in perception. As a result, they felt that many problems were the result of incorrect or inefficient organizational principles. They believed that this could account for the experience of insight—what is sometimes referred to as the "ah ha" phenomenon or the feeling that you have just "seen the light." As soon as the correct principle of organization is applied, the problem almost solves itself. Creative problem solving often involves this flash of insight—a sudden realization of how the elements in the problem can be organized to fit together.

Productive Thinking vs. Reproductive Thinking. One of the major contributions of the Gestalt approach to problem solving is the distinction between two kinds of thinking—productive thinking and reproductive thinking. In **productive thinking,** the problem-solver must develop a new answer or approach to a problem that he or she has never seen before. For example, if you had never seen the nine-dot problem before, then you had to engage in productive thinking to solve it. In the same way, I doubt that I had ever before seen anyone remove a transmission without the right equipment. This type of thinking is called productive because the problem-solver must produce a new solution. This would include solving an old problem with a new or unorthodox solution or solving a new problem with an adaptation of an old (but unorthodox) solution. In **reproductive thinking,** the problem-solver can solve the problem by using a procedure or facts that are already in the problem-solver's past experience. For example, if you used the procedure involved in the nine-dot problem to solve a similar kind of problem, then you engaged in reproductive thinking. You simply reproduced a procedure for solving the problem that was already known to you. In reproductive thinking, a clear link exists between a problem and a solution that has previously worked to solve that problem. If I had been able to secure a floor jack, I would have reproduced a solution that I had seen work on many similar occasions.

Rigidity in Problem Solving. A major obstacle to productive thinking occurs when a problem-solver relies too heavily on past experience. For example, suppose that you need a stick to stir a can of paint, but that no stick is available; even though a pencil is nearby, you may fail to realize that you can use the pencil to stir the paint. The Gestalt psychologist Duncker (1945) termed this phenomenon **functional fixedness**—the function or use of an object becomes fixed in one's mind so that new, less common ways of using the object are not easily found. Because the normal use of a pencil is "to write with," it is difficult to use it in a new function such as "to stir with."

In an experiment, Duncker (1945) asked subjects to hang a decoration from an eyelet screwed into an overhead beam; although no "S" hook was provided, the subjects did have access to paper clips. The solution was to bend a paper clip into an "S" shape and then use that as a hook to hang the decoration from the eyelet. Some subjects had just used paper clips to attach pieces of paper together; these subjects had much more trouble solving the problem than subjects who did not have this previous experience. Apparently, previous experience in using paper clips helped to produce functional fixedness, for example, thinking of the function of paper clips as "to hold pieces of paper together" rather than less common functions such as "to serve as a hook."

As another example of rigidity in problem solving, consider the water jar problem summarized in Table 9–2. In this problem you are to suppose that you are given three jars and an unlimited amount of water, and that your job is to figure out how to obtain a certain amount of water. For example, if you had jars that hold 21, 127, and 3 units of water, you could obtain 100 units by filling the 127 and then dipping out 21 and 3 and 3. As you can see in Table 9–2, each of the first five problems (labeled E1 through E5) can be solved using the procedure B–A–2C. The same procedure can be used on subsequent problems, C1 through C4, although each also has a more direct solution procedure; for example, problem C1 can be solved using the long procedure, 49–23–3–3 or by a more direct procedure, 23–3.

In a series of experiments involving over 900 subjects, Luchins (1942) found that if a subject was given problems E1 through E5, the subject would almost always use the long procedure for solving subsequent problems C1 through C4. Luchins called this phenomenon **problem-solving set** because subjects' prior experience with the first five problems created a mental set—a way of looking at the problem—that was used on new problems even when a more efficient way of looking at the problem was possible. In contrast, subjects who did not have to solve problems E1 through E5 tended to use the more direct solutions for problems C1 through C4. Apparently they were more efficient, because

TABLE 9–2
The Water Jar Problem

	Given			Find
	a	b	c	
E1	21	127	3	100
E2	14	163	25	99
E3	18	43	10	5
E4	9	42	6	21
E5	20	59	4	31
C1	23	49	3	20
C2	15	39	3	18
—	28	76	3	25
C3	18	48	4	22
C4	14	36	8	6

Source: From Luchins, 1942.

they lacked the problem-solving set built up from earlier experience.

Studying Problem Solving By Computer. Suppose that you were asked to solve the problem shown in Figure 9–6. You are given three pegs, labeled A, B, and C. On peg A there are three disks: large, medium, and small. Your job is to move only one disk at a time, and you may never place a larger disk on top of a smaller disk. You can try this problem by using a penny, nickel, and quarter as the three disks, and three spaces on a table or desk as the pegs.

The problem that you have just dealt with is called the *disk problem* or the *Tower of Hanoi problem*. This is an example of a *well-defined problem* because the following three things are given to you in the problem statement:

Insight. A sudden reorganization of a problem so that the inner structure of the problem becomes clearer.

Productive thinking. Type of thinking that involves developing a new answer or approach to a problem you've never seen before.

Reproductive thinking. Type of thinking that involves solving a problem using a procedure or knowledge from your past experience.

Functional fixedness. Occurs when the usual function or use of an object becomes so fixed in one's mind that new, less common ways of using the object are not seen.

Problem-solving set. Occurs when your past experience with a problem creates a mental set—a way of looking at the problem—that is used on new problems even when a more efficient solution is available.

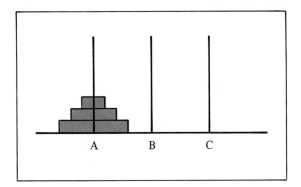

FIGURE 9-6
This is called the Tower of Hanoi problem. The task is to get all three disks in peg C, but you must move only one disk at a time and you may never place a larger disk on top of a smaller one.

- □ *Given state*—a clear description of the given state of the problem; all three disks are on peg A.
- □ *Goal state*—a clear description of the goal state of the problem; all three disks should be on peg C.
- □ *Legal operations*—a clear description of the legal moves that can be used for going from one state of the problem to another; you can move one disk at a time but can never place a larger disk on top of a smaller disk.

Well-defined problems, such as the Tower of Hanoi problem, can be solved by computers. In addition, computer programs are available that can do the following: solve algebra story problems, geometry proofs, logical proofs, and deductive and inductive reasoning problems; choose moves in chess and checkers; answer intelligence test items; and complete a medical diagnosis.

A person who writes a computer program for solving problems may have either one of two goals: computer simulation or artificial intelligence. In **computer simulation**, the goal is to make the computer go through the same thought process and the same performance (including errors) as a human problem-solver. In **artificial intelligence**, the goal is to make the computer solve the problem, without concern for whether it uses the same processes as humans. In general, psychologists are most interested in computer simulation of thought, because this approach allows for testing of theories of human thinking (see the box on computer simulation and thinking-aloud protocol). In contrast, designers of automatic systems such as robots may be more interested in artificial intelligence.

Brainstorming vs. Groupthink

Many people have noticed that groups can often solve problems more effectively than one person alone. In other words, if we take four people and put them together to solve a problem, the problem will be solved more quickly than if we ask each one to work on the problem alone. There may be some good reasons for this group advantage. As you just saw, one of the problems we often encounter in searching for solutions is that we become fixed or tied to one type of solution. One way of avoiding this fixedness is to ask a group of people to get together and come up with a lot of possible solutions. This assumes, however, that the problem is already defined for the group.

An advertising executive named Alex Osborn described a method of running a group meeting that could improve the chances of solving a given problem. He called his method **brainstorming**. It consists of thinking up many different solutions to a problem without stopping each time to criticize and evaluate. As you will see shortly, a group setting is not critical to the production of many different solutions, but it can help. The logic is that the greater the number of proposed solutions, the more likely it is that one will work.

Hayes (1981) has suggested that the most important principle underlying the effectiveness of brainstorming is the separation of the step of thinking up ideas from the step of evaluating those ideas. Group members are encouraged to produce as many solutions as possible and are discouraged from criticizing the solutions of others until all of the suggestions have been made. During this idea phase all criticism is withheld until a formal evaluation phase; ideas are encouraged and welcomed no matter how

---

Computer simulation. Computer programming that is designed to make the computer go through the same thought process and the same performance (including errors) as a human problem-solver.

Artificial intelligence. Computer programming that is designed to have the computer solve the problem, without concern for whether it uses the same problem-solving processes as humans.

Brainstorming. Problem-solving approach in which a single person or group of people is asked to come up with a lot of solutions without immediately evaluating them as good or bad.

THINKING ALOUD FOR BETTER PROBLEM SOLVING

In order to develop a computer-simulation program, the first step is to determine how humans go about solving the problem or problems. Establishing a *protocol* is a first step in this—a protocol is nothing more than a description of the steps that someone goes through in solving a problem. One way of arriving at protocols involves verbal descriptions by people as they are trying to solve problems. It is as if a gymnast or baseball player were asked to do a play-by-play description of his or her own performance. This type of protocol has been labeled a *thinking-aloud protocol*—a person's description of what is going on inside his or her head during the problem solving. This may seem unusual to you, but it is something you have often done yourself while watching someone else perform what seems to be a complicated task or while teaching another person how to perform that task. As a trainer, you describe what you are doing as you do it. In fixing a 10-speed bike for a friend who would like to learn how to fix it himself, you might describe in great detail what you are doing. "The first thing to do is make sure that the chain is not caught between two gears. Take the chain and gently pull it away from the gear area. If it's stuck, pick up the rear wheel and turn it by hand. That should free it. If that doesn't work, move the pedals in a clockwise direction very gently. After you are sure the chain is free...."

In the process of telling the person how to fix the bike, you are trying to anticipate problems that might arise and prepare your friend for dealing with those problems (such as a chain wedged between gears).

You have also probably been on the other side of this type of interaction more than once. On a new job, the supervisor shows you how to start a machine. You may ask for a second, slower description and, in the course of that description, stop the supervisor and ask for a more detailed description of one or more pieces of the action sequence. As you can see, the thinking-aloud technique is not just for the use of computer programmers trying to simulate problem solving. Some have suggested that the think-aloud technique should be taught in school, so that students learn how to instruct others in problem solving and how to benefit from watching others solve problems (Whimbey and Lockhead, 1980).

Once developed, a protocol is edited or cleaned up to eliminate unnecessary or irrelevant information, and then a computer program is written to simulate what is described on the protocol. After the program is written, it can be run and the output or results compared with the results of the human problem-solver. If they are very similar, including getting stuck in the same places, then it can be concluded that the program is a good simulation of human thought (Newell and Simon, 1972).

Computer simulations of problem solving using thinking-aloud protocols have confirmed that the two major phases of problem-solving activity are *problem definition* and *search for solutions* (Hayes, 1981). The value of computer simulations of problem-solving behavior is this: If the program "works," then we have the beginning of a theory of human problem solving. Once we develop a theory of how people actually solve problems, it is possible to teach them how to solve problems more efficiently. We can take the computer, reprogram it so that the problem is solved with fewer steps, and then develop a training or educational program to provide humans with that new and better program for problem solving. One of the things that has become obvious from the attempts to develop computer programs of human problem solving is the enormous complexity of human problem-solving operations. Because many of these occur in fractions of a second, we are often not aware of all the different cognitive operations we engage in while solving a problem. Protocol analysis has served to remind us of the power and complexity of human problem-solving capabilities.

ridiculous they may seem; members are praised for producing many ideas; members are encouraged to build on or use earlier ideas or solutions as a point of departure; the group is kept intact and subgroup formation is discouraged; and one person is assigned the role of recording the ideas or solutions (Hayes, 1981).

In group brainstorming sessions, one person's idea often stimulates related but different ideas from the other members of the group. In addition, social reinforcement for thinking up ideas motivates each person to continue producing ideas. An additional advantage is that brainstorming rules actively discourage criticism during the idea phase; a study by Stein (1975) found that more ideas are produced when groups do not evaluate ideas as they are produced.

Brainstorming seems best suited for two kinds of idea production. The first is in generating ideas that might be followed to achieve a certain goal (for example, how to get rid of graffiti on building walls). The second is in identifying all of the possible consequences of a particular action (for example, the effects of canceling the food stamp program).

It appears as if brainstorming groups can aid in problem solving, but the real test of the method is to compare the total number of ideas produced by people alone with those produced by the same people in a group. This is a more accurate test of the value of group brainstorming than comparing the productivity of any one person with that of a group. Lamm and Trommsdorf (1973) reviewed research on group brainstorming and found that the sum of the unique solutions of a given number of individuals working alone was greater than the total number of unique solutions that would have been produced by those individuals in a group.

This suggests that brainstorming might be effective for single individuals as well and for the same reasons. As in group brainstorming, it is important to instruct individuals not to evaluate their ideas until they have finished producing as many as possible. Taylor, Berry, and Block (1958) found that the ideas of individuals working alone were often superior to those produced in a group setting. One conclusion that might be drawn from these results is that the old saying "two heads are better than one" is correct, but the two heads don't have to be talking with each other. If you want a large number of new solutions to a problem, have a large number

of people go off and work on solutions independently and submit them when they are finished. The people might then be formed into a group to evaluate each of those possible solutions.

Brainstorming is not the equivalent of group problem solving. It means nothing more than the attempt to produce multiple solutions before evaluating them. It is only accidental that brainstorming is usually done in groups and, unless some care is taken, group brainstorming may even turn out to be counterproductive. Let us examine one of those counterproductive situations.

Groupthink: Inhibiting Problem Solving. If a group consists of people who know one another well, like one another, and are committed to solving a particular problem, each member may be reluctant to criticize a solution suggested by another group member during an evaluation stage. The mutual respect each member has for the other makes criticism seem inappropriate and counterproductive. Instead, one person makes a suggestion and the rest of the group says, "Great! Let's do it!" Janis (1972) has referred to this as **groupthink**—the tendency to accept the suggested solutions of other group members without proper evaluation. Janis gives as an example of this process the Bay of Pigs invasion that was hatched during John F. Kennedy's presidency. A number of high-level officials in the Kennedy administration joined with the President in devising a plan to invade Cuba and overthrow Fidel Castro. Later examination showed that many aspects of the plan were ridiculous and that what passed for planning and problem solving was only slightly removed from fantasy. The real problem was that the uncritical acceptance of strategies allowed for no checking or evaluation of those strategies. For example, it was assumed that, should the invasion fail and the invaders have to escape, they could run into the Escambray Mountains and seek refuge with the anti-Castro rebels. Everyone thought that was a great idea. No one bothered to check the maps. If they had, they would have realized that the Escambray Mountains were 80 miles from the invasion point and separated by swamps and marshes that made travel almost impossible (Janis, 1972).

As you can see, producing and evaluating ideas can be a fragile process. Other people may help or hinder the process. In the Bay of Pigs fiasco, a session of brainstorming followed by critical evaluations might have helped to avoid the groupthink tendency. It might at least have encouraged evaluation on a more comparative basis. As you will see in a later chapter, group therapy is also based on the notion that others can make suggestions that can help *you* solve problems. On the other hand, if the issue is simply thinking up as many solutions as possible, individual brainstorming may be the most effective way to begin solving the problem.

■ REASONING

Suppose you were asked to solve the problems at the top of Table 9-3. You are given a series of statements; assuming they are all true, which of the conclusions can you be sure is correct? This task requires a type of thinking that is called **deductive reasoning**. In deductive reasoning you are given all the necessary information and your job is to reach a logical conclusion.

Now suppose that you were asked to solve the problems at the bottom of Table 9-3. You are given a series of numbers or letters, and your job is to determine what will come next in the series. This task requires a type of thinking that is called **inductive reasoning**. In inductive reasoning you are given incomplete information from which you must come up with a general rule. Let us consider these two different types of reasoning separately.

Groupthink. The tendency shown by a group to accept the suggested solutions of other group members without proper or adequate evaluation.

Deductive reasoning. A type of reasoning in which you are given all the necessary information and are supposed to reach a logical conclusion.

Inductive reasoning. A type of reasoning in which you are given incomplete information from which you must come up with a general rule.

Groups can often solve problems more effectively than one person alone. However, groups have to guard against the tendency to accept the suggested solutions of group members without proper evaluation.

TABLE 9-3
Some Reasoning Tasks

Deduction

Which conclusions can you be sure of?
All P are M; All S are M. Therefore

1. All S are P.
2. Some S are P.
3. Some S are not P.
4. All S are not P.
5. Can't be sure of any of these.

Induction

What letter comes next?
a m b m c m d m —

Deductive Reasoning

When you go to a doctor, you are asked to report your symptoms. Have you been running a fever? Do your joints ache? In addition, the doctor examines you for other symptoms. Your eyes, throat, ears, and reflexes may be checked. When the doctor is finished gathering this information, a preliminary diagnosis is made. In a sense, the doctor has been looking for a category for you. Flu is one category. Cancer is another. Liver disease is a third. There are hundreds of categories available for the doctor to use. The problem is one of applying a set of rules (those that permit placement in one or another of those categories) to your symptoms. You bring to the doctor all of the information that is needed. This includes your self-report, the doctor's observations, and the results of various tests (for example, blood tests and X-rays). Once the appropriate category has been found, once you have been correctly diagnosed, the solution to the problem is the simple application of known remedies such as rest or an antibiotic or a change in diet.

The point is that the doctor's task was to reconcile your symptoms with a known set of principles. In other words, the conclusion (your diagnosis) was deduced. There are many instances of deductive tasks in everyday life. The most obvious recent examples for you might be a geometry class. You are given theorems to use in solving geometry problems. Your task is to apply these general theorems (rules) to particular examples and thus solve the problem.

Many jobs involve this type of reasoning as well. A good example is the police officer. In enforcing the laws, the police officer must often choose which set of rules is applicable in a given circumstance. The most obvious choice that the officer must make first is whether any law was broken at all. After deciding that a law has been broken, the next decision is *which* law has been broken. This could become critical later in the event of a trial. If the defendant is charged with breaking the wrong law, the case could easily be dismissed.

Let us take one example. A police officer is called to an office building where the security guard has detained a man who was wandering around an upper floor and walked into and quickly out of an office. In his jacket, the man has a list of items—radio, cassette tape recorder, short fur jacket, and so on. In a paper bag, the man has an electric drill, some drill bits, and an extension cord. The officer must decide whether to charge the man with attempted burglary, with possession of burglary tools, with trespassing, with all three of those charges, or to set the man free. After some serious thought, the police officer lets the man go. He could not be charged with burglary because none had occurred. He could not be charged with possession of burglary tools because his tools could be used for purposes other than burglary. He could not be charged with trespassing because the office was entered during the regular working hours, anyone could enter the office if he or she chose to, and there was no warning not to enter the office.

The point of this example is that the officer is required to take some set of universal principles called laws and apply them to a specific instance. The laws are not variable; they do not change. The task is to link the action of the man with a potential violation. In this case, no clear link could be made; some of the critical aspects that defined each of the violations (such as burglary tools or no-trespassing signs) were missing. As a result, the conclusion was that no law had been broken.

To reason deductively means to derive a conclusion from some given propositions or statements called **premises.** You assume that the premises are true and then apply the rules of deduction. Geometry proofs and simultaneous equations are examples of deductive-reasoning tasks that are formally taught in schools.

Research on deductive reasoning indicates that some errors are regular and systematic, particularly by the person who does not use formal rules for drawing conclusions (Nisbett and Ross, 1980). This is good news, because it should mean that reasoning can be improved with training. Most junior high schools and high schools now include formal training in deductive reasoning. This usually occurs in mathematics courses in the form of "truth tables." This training is an attempt to improve deductive reasoning.

Inductive Reasoning

Inductive and deductive reasoning differ in terms of how much information is available. Deductive reasoning involves logically deriving a conclusion from some statements you assume to be true. If you know everything you need to know and it is just a matter of applying a set of rules to that information, the reasoning is *deductive*. If, on the other hand, information is limited and it is necessary to discover the rule that will allow you to understand that information and supply the missing information, the reasoning is *inductive*. Inductive reasoning is an ability necessary in many occupations.

But it is not only occupational tasks that require inductive reasoning. For example, in school a child may use words like *runned* or *taked* or *eated*. Use of these words indicates that the child has induced the rule, "To use past tense add *-ed* to the verb." Other examples of situations involving induction include **series-completion tasks**, such as shown in Table 9–3. In these tasks, the reasoner must induce a rule that will predict what will come next.

Simon and Kotovsky (1975) found that problems that required long descriptions of the underlying rule were more difficult than those that could be expressed easily. Also, Holzman, Glaser, and Pellegrino (1976) used Simon and Kotovsky's analysis to train elementary-school children to solve series-completion problems. The training focused on formulating and applying rules. The results showed a large improvement in performance for the trained students but not for an untrained control group. Ap-

parently training in inductive reasoning can be successful.

Sternberg and Ketron (1982) trained college students in the process for solving analogy problems (for example, refrigerator is to food as wallet is to _____). The training focused on how to induce rules and apply them to come up with answers. Students given training greatly improved their performance, even if they had first scored low in general reasoning ability. In another study it was found that a seven-hour training course in how to solve analogy problems improved performance by about 60 points on the GRE-Analytic Test, as compared to a control group (Swinton and Powers, 1983). These results encourage the idea that inductive reasoning processes can be taught.

Reasoning: General or Specific?

There is some question as to whether reasoning is a general ability or, instead, an ability that is limited to a particular knowledge area (Glaser, 1984). These two positions can be termed the *general* and the *specific* positions. The general position assumes that an ability such as deductive reasoning or inductive reasoning exists regardless of what problem it is applied to. Thus, in our example of the fire dispatcher, the general position would predict that the dispatcher would show high levels of reasoning in any problem situation. The specific position would say that the dispatcher was knowledgeable about city streets and rescue operations and that this knowledge permitted him to use his abilities but would predict that he might not be able to use those abilities in a situation that was unrelated to rescue work.

The issue of general versus specific abilities is not a trivial one. It has important implications for cognitive training in educational systems. In the past it has been assumed that any training in reasoning will be useful in developing general reasoning skills and that these general reasoning skills can be applied to solving any problem. Recent research (Glaser, 1984) suggests that this is a dubious assumption. The implication of this research is that reasoning cannot and should not be taught on some general level.

Premise. A given proposition or statement that is asserted to be true.

Series completion tasks. Tasks or questions in which you are supposed to figure out the general rule that governs the series and, based on this, decide what should come next in the series.

Rather, training in reasoning and judgment should occur only in the context of some particular knowledge base. In other words, the reasoning skills of auto mechanics can be improved by teaching reasoning in the context of diagnosing automobile malfunctions. High school students might learn more about reasoning and problem-solving strategies if presented with problems related to after-school jobs, school dances, and student politics than with traditional mathematics "word problems" that deal with the number of pennies, nickels and dimes that comprise a sum of money.

A general consensus seems to be emerging (Sternberg, 1985; Glaser, 1985) that reasoning and problem solving require both knowledge and ability. On the one hand, it seems clear that simply accumulating more knowledge does not guarantee that a problem will be solved or an advance made (Sternberg, 1985). On the other hand, it seems equally clear that people who are familiar with the context in which a problem arises are quicker at suggesting solutions for that problem than those who have never before seen that problem (Glaser, 1984). It is probably fair to say that an individual's reasoning ability is most likely to appear in areas where that individual is knowledgeable. This does not mean that reasoning is solely dependent on knowledge. It simply says that reasoning is not as likely to appear in a situation of which the individual is ignorant as opposed to one for which the individual possesses a good deal of knowledge.

Nevertheless, this position still allows for individual differences in reasoning ability. In other words, if two individuals have the *same* amount of knowledge about a particular area, the individual with more reasoning ability will be more likely to solve the problem than will the individual with less reasoning ability. The implications for training are equally clear. If you want to improve an individual's reasoning ability, give that person some knowledge base on which to apply that ability. Trying to improve someone's ability to reason in the abstract is like trying to sharpen a knife without something to sharpen it with.

Concepts

There is one form of inductive reasoning that plays a major role in all of our lives—concept formation.

As I suggested earlier in the chapter, **concepts** are meaning categories. We form them easily and use them constantly. Consider the following statements:

- A *corplum* may be used for support.
- *Corplums* may be used to close off an open space.
- A *corplum* may be long or short, thick or thin, strong or weak.
- A wet *corplum* does not burn.
- You can make a *corplum* smooth with sandpaper.
- The painter used a *corplum* to mix her paints. (Werner and Kaplan, 1950)

You probably had no difficulty in deciding that a corplum was a stick. Corplum is now a concept because it is a meaning category that includes a broad range of possible members. You are not likely to store this concept for later use, for you already have a more than adequate concept (such as a stick or piece of wood) to deal with objects described in the sentences above. Nevertheless, this gives you an idea of how concepts are formed. You will note that you formed this concept using induction, not deduction: You were not given a rule that defined a corplum; you were given examples of various corplums and you figured out the rule from considering those examples. Concept formation is a critical part of language learning and thinking in general. In our interactions with people and the environment, we create categories of meaning. These categories are used in later cognitive operations. Once we have developed a rule that covers category membership, we use that rule to place unfamiliar objects in categories. To the young child who has just experienced a visit to Santa Claus, every man with a white beard becomes Santa, at least for a few weeks. In fact, as you will see in the chapter on child development, some psychologists have described cognitive development as a process by which meaning categories are formed to help the child deal with environmental objects and events. As the child encounters new stimuli, new categories or concepts of meaning are formed (Piaget, 1970).

Theories of Concept Learning

Psychologists have offered three major types of theories of how people learn concepts: *continuity theory, noncontinuity theory,* and *prototype theory.*

In the past, continuity theory and noncontinuity theory have been pitted against each other; thus, we will consider them first and then examine prototype theory.

Continuity vs. Noncontinuity. The **continuity theory** views concept learning as an extension of operant conditioning as described in Chapter 6. Each time you see a stimulus and are told which category it belongs to, you strengthen the association between each feature in the stimulus and the category name (as a response). Thus, concept learning involves a process of continuously and gradually building stimulus-response links. A child sees an old Volkswagen beetle go down the street and hears a parent say, "They were interesting cars." The next day, the child sees an Edsel parked by the curb and hears the parent say, "I wish I had bought one of those cars when they were new." On a third day, the child is crossing the street with the parent just as a big Pontiac goes racing by. The parent says aloud, "Wow! That car was really moving." The concept "car" now includes a Volkswagen, an Edsel, and a Pontiac. Gradually, many other examples are added to the concept "car" almost as if it were a snowball rolling down a hill and picking up more snow with each turn. It is important to note that in the continuity approach, the child must be exposed to clear connections between the concept label (car) and examples of that concept. These connections can come from parents, friends, or TV commercials, but the formal associations must be made in the presence of the child.

In contrast, **noncontinuity theory** views concept learning as inducing rules or hypotheses and testing them. If a rule is successful in getting the correct answer, it is retained; otherwise, a new hypothesis is generated. In this case, concept learning is noncontinuous; it is an active "all-or-none" process in which the learning either has found the correct hypothesis or has not. From this perspective, the presumed interaction between the child and the cars described above is quite different. After having been exposed to the Volkswagen and hearing the parent comment about the fact that it is an interesting *car*, the child forms a hypothesis: Things with wheels that are found on the street are called *cars*. The next day the child is with the parent when they pass the Edsel. The child then waits for the parent to confirm that hypothesis. The parent says, "I wish I had bought one of those cars when they were new," and this supports the hypothesis. The next day, the encounter with the Pontiac provides further confirmation for the preliminary concept *car*. On later occasions, the child may seek even further confirmation by pointing to a Toyota with a questioning look. The parent will most likely respond to the implied question "What is that?" with confirming or nonconfirming information. A *car* response would support the hypothesis.

Which of these two theories best describes human concept learning? To help answer this question, several studies (Bower and Trabasso, 1963; Trabasso and Bower, 1964, 1968) gave college students a concept-learning task. The stimuli consisted of cards that contained line figures varying in color, size, shape, number, position, and shading. For each card, the experimenter asked the subject to tell whether it belonged to category 1 or category 2, and then the experimenter gave the correct answer. For one group of subjects, the same rule was used throughout the entire experiment (for example, *red* is category 1, *blue* is category 2). For another group, the rule was reversed as soon as the subject made an early error. According to continuity theory, the group in which the rule was reversed should learn much more slowly than the group in which the rule stayed the same, because old associations must be unlearned and new ones relearned. According to noncontinuity theory, the two groups should learn at about the same rate because the group in which the rule had been reversed had not yet learned anything (that is, an error indicates that the subject had not yet found the correct hypothesis). This theory assumes that the subject does not remember past hypotheses, but just makes a new hypothesis after

---

Concept. An abstract category that includes a broad range of possible members. An example is money—the concept "money" includes coins and bills of many denominations.

Continuity theory. The view that concept learning involves gradually building up stimulus–response links.

Noncontinuity theory. The view that concept learning is a matter of inducing rules or hypotheses and testing them.

each error. Trabasso and Bower found in this instance that the two groups took about the same amount of time to learn, which added support for the idea that noncontinuity theory best describes human performance.

Prototype Theory

Data relating to continuity and noncontinuity theory have most often been gathered in the laboratory. A small number of characteristics (such as color, size, shape) of objects were involved in these studies. In many respects, these studies were very artificial. In real life, we are confronted with stimuli more demanding than simple red squares or green triangles. Instead, everyday categories include such things as animals, furniture, teachers, and jobs. Rosch (1972) has pointed out some differences between concepts as they are studied in the laboratory and the way they are used in real life. She suggests that concepts are understood and used by people in terms of representative examples of those concepts rather than in the form of categorization rules or lists of characteristics (Rosch, 1975). She suggests that we form concepts by identifying and visualizing good examples of the categories in question. For example, when you think of the concept *bird*, the image of a model bird (usually a robin or a sparrow) comes to mind. You don't say to yourself, "A bird is something that has wings and flies."

The example of the concept that most easily comes to mind is called the **prototype** of that concept. If Rosch is correct, this must mean that some examples of a concept are better than others. In other words, some examples seem more clearly to belong in the category or concept than others. When you heard the word *bird*, you did not immediately think of an ostrich or a pelican (Bourne et al., 1979). This does not necessarily mean that the prototype must be an actual bird you have seen. It might be your version of a "typical" bird. It might just be a nondescript brown bird of no particular species.

Several studies seem to support Rosch's propositions. Consider the data in Table 9-4. Subjects were asked to judge the extent to which the objects listed were "good" examples of the respective categories. There was general agreement that a chair was a better example of the concept *furniture* than a bed, and that an automobile was a better example of the concept *vehicle* than a cable car. Further, there was high

TABLE 9-4
Judging Examples of Four Categories

Goodness of example		Goodness of example	
Member	*Rank*	*Member*	*Rank*
Furniture		*Vehicle*	
Chair	1.5	Automobile	1
Sofa	1.5	Station wagon	2
Couch	3.5	Truck	3
Table	3.5	Car	4
Easy chair	5	Bus	5.5
Dresser	6.5	Taxi	5.5
Rocking chair	6.5	Jeep	7
Coffee table	8	Ambulance	8
Rocker	9	Motorcycle	9
Love seat	10	Streetcar	10
Chest of drawers	11	Van	11
Desk	12	Honda	12
Bed	13	Cable car	13
Fruit		*Weapon*	
Orange	1	Gun	1
Apple	2	Pistol	2
Banana	3	Revolver	3
Peach	4	Machine gun	4
Pear	5	Rifle	5
Apricot	6.5	Switchblade	6
Tangerine	6.5	Knife	7
Plum	8	Dagger	8
Grapes	9	Shotgun	9
Nectarine	10	Sword	10
Strawberry	11	Bomb	11.5
Grapefruit	12	Hand grenade	11.5
Berry	13	A-bomb	13.5
		Bayonet	13.5

Source: Rosch, 1975.

agreement among subjects about the extent to which objects belonged to a particular category—their *degrees of category membership* (Rosch, 1975). In a later study, Rosch examined the impact of these differences in category membership (Rosch, 1975). She hypothesized that it should take longer to decide if a weak-membership object belongs to a category than it would to make that judgment about a strong-membership object. This is exactly what happened. For example, it took less time for a subject to decide that an orange was a member of the category *fruit* than it took to make the same judgment about a grapefuit or a berry.

These data seem to show that concepts are arranged around prototypes or good examples of the category rather than around lists of characteristics or features. This raises another question, however. Where do these prototypes come from? What makes them "better" examples? Rosch believes that examples can assume their "prototypicality" in several ways. In her study of concepts for colors, she found that regardless of culture, all subjects identified the same shade of *red* as the best example of the color red. It did not matter whether the subject was a college student or a member of a primitive tribe in New Guinea. In spite of the fact that the Dani people of New Guinea have only two words for all colors, they still remembered one shade of red better than other shades. Rosch explains this biologically. She suggests that the human visual system is more sensitive to particular wavelengths than others. It would follow that these "sensitive" wavelengths would be the prototypes for certain colors.

Rosch also suggests that categories or concepts are not arbitrary in the sense that they represent accidental combinations of physical characteristics. This is because the world contains natural categories of things (concepts) that are separate or independent from other categories of things (other concepts). For example, in nature, things that have feathers are far more likely to have wings and fly than things that have fur (Bourne and others, 1979). The category or concept of *bird* is found in nature with certain combinations of physical characteristics.

It may appear that we have drifted far afield from problem solving but we really haven't. Rosch assumes that making sense of the infinite numbers and types of stimuli with which we come in contact is a form of problem. One strategy for solving that problem is collecting or categorizing information—forming concepts. This allows us to deal more efficiently with external stimuli. In this respect, Rosch's ideas are similar to both the continuity and noncontinuity theorists. All would agree that concepts are formed to help process information more efficiently. Where she differs is in suggesting that concepts exist in the form of examples of those concepts and that some concepts are more easily or naturally formed than others.

■ JUDGMENT

One final type of cognitive activity that we engage in frequently deserves at least some brief consideration. We are often called upon to make evaluations of, or judgments about, other people, objects, or situations. Supervisors judge the quality of a subordinate's work. Teachers judge the extent to which students have learned. Consumers make judgments about the value of goods for sale. But just as is the case in deductive and inductive reasoning, errors commonly occur in judgment as well. This should not be surprising, for judgment is really a form of reasoning. For example, in deciding whether an employee is productive, you may engage in inductive reasoning, deductive reasoning, or both. If you collect a great deal of information about the employee, sift through that information and try to come to some conclusion about whether those data represent a pattern of productivity, you are actually trying to induce a rule that can adequately explain that person's work activities.

On the other hand, if you have an idea of what the characteristics of a productive and a nonproductive employee are, you may simply be trying to place this employee in one of those two categories. This might be considered an example of deductive reasoning—trying to choose the correct classifica-

---

Prototype theory. The view that concepts are arranged around representative examples, or prototypes, rather than around lists of characteristics.

Prototype. The example of a concept that most readily comes to mind.

tion rule for dealing with complete information. Actually, in everyday instances such as employee evaluation, the judgment has both inductive and deductive aspects. Because we seldom have *all* of the relevant information about the employee, there must be some induction involved. In addition, because the supervisor has had experience with productive and nonproductive employees before (and probably has a prototype for those categories), there is a certain amount of rule-applying going on.

Judgment processes have been studied extensively by psychologists. These studies have identified many different strategies that people use for making judgments. These strategies have a double-edge to them. Sometimes they are effective and help the person rise above incomplete information to make a good judgment. At other times they interfere with information processing and result in a bad judgment. This circumstance is similar to constancies and illusions as they were defined in the chapter on perception. In the same sense that illusions represent misapplied constancies, inaccurate judgments often represent misapplied information-processing rules.

Heuristics

Heuristics are "quick and dirty" rules that are used in problem solving and decision making. They help in limiting the amount of information that needs to be considered and in bringing solutions in closer reach (Bourne, Dominowski, Loftus and Healy, 1986). For example, a football coach might tell the defense to guard against a pass on third down. Use of this rule greatly reduces the burden of analyzing the arrangement of offensive players. Other heuristic devices can be easily seen in card games such as bridge. People use systems for deciding how much to bid. Having so many aces, so many kings, and so many cards of one particular suit leads to one bid. A different arrangement leads to another bid. The system that players use helps them to deal with what would otherwise be an overwhelming amount of information. In gambling casinos, some professional card players use counting systems to keep track of which cards have been played and which ones have not yet appeared in the game "21" or blackjack. This is a tremendous advantage in deciding whether to take additional cards or how much to bet. This counting system is a heuristic device.

In the examples above, certain automatic strategies work to the advantage of the person using them. These strategies limit the number of alternatives that have to be considered simultaneously. As such, they improve the efficiency of reasoning and problem solving. But there are other occasions when heuristics work against the person using them and lead to inaccurate decisions or judgments. Tversky and Kahneman (1974) have identified two such heuristic devices that we commonly use in making judgments.

The first of these is called the **representativeness heuristic**. People are notoriously inaccurate at correctly estimating certain probabilities. They make these errors because they have a preconception of some sort. For example, if I flip a coin 10 times and the first nine flips result in heads, what would you estimate the probability of flipping a tail on the tenth flip to be? Many people would guess 60 percent, 80 percent, or even 90 percent. In fact, the probability is 50 percent—exactly the same as it was on the first, fifth, or ninth flip. These people have a preconception of how many heads and how many tails should appear in a series of 10 flips. It is this preconception that is distorting their judgment. This error is known as the "gambler's fallacy" because it influences the betting behavior of many amateur or novice gamblers. Professional gamblers "play the odds" and are unaffected by these "chance" variations in outcomes.

Another way of describing the representativeness heuristic is that it turns similarity into likelihood. Let us say that a teacher has had good educational experiences with children from a particular family. When the youngest child comes along and enters that teacher's classroom, the teacher assumes that this child will be a good student as well because this child comes from the same family. Judgments about the quality of this child's school work may be due more to the fact that the teacher has placed the child in the "good performer" category than to the child's actual performance; but the child was placed in this category only because of superficial similarities to "good performers." Many industrial supervisors use similar heuristics in categorizing employees. They may feel that secretaries who keep their work area neat or machine operators who keep their tools polished are effective. The best way to get a ride if you need to hitchhike is to dress in your best clothes. Drivers are less likely to believe that

The "gambler's fallacy," an error in judgment, influences the betting behavior of many amateur or novice gamblers. Professional gamblers use heuristic devices such as counting systems to keep track of the odds.

you are a threat because they place you in a "safe" group as a result of your appearance.

A second heuristic device described by Tversky and Kahneman is called the **availability heuristic.** Using this heuristic, we assume that what we see on any one occasion is what happens most often. Would you buy a car that would not start when the salesperson turned the key? Definitely not. Would you get on a flight to Houston after hearing that the last flight to Houston had crashed? Probably not. You would assume that the same thing would happen to you after you bought the car or boarded the plane. When people must estimate how often an event will occur, they may depend on inaccurate information or memory to make that estimate. Combs

and Slovic (1979) demonstrated that probability estimates of causes of death are notoriously biased and inaccurate. Further, they demonstrated that these inaccuracies may be the result of media coverage. It seems that people overestimate the number of deaths that occur from events widely covered by the media and underestimate the number of deaths from less widely publicized causes. For example, strokes kill almost twice as many people as car accidents, yet the average person believes that car accidents kill 25 times more people than strokes. Similarly, asthma causes 20 times more deaths annually than tornadoes, yet the average person believes that tornadoes causes three times the number of deaths as asthma. Seldom will you see a description of an asthma death or a stroke death on the front page of your newspaper or on the evening TV news; but you will see lengthy descriptions of a tornado or a traffic accident, often with vivid pictures and first-person interviews. This is a good example of how the availability heuristic works to produce an inaccurate base of information.

Let us return to the case of a supervisor and a subordinate. The manager at McDonald's happens to walk by just as the new cashier is told by the customer that the order is messed up—she didn't order a Big Mac; she ordered a fish fillet. The manager mentions to the assistant manager that they may have trouble with the new employee. But if the manager had carefully observed all of the cashiers, she might have discovered that the new person made considerably fewer such mistakes than any of the long-term employees. The fact is that everyone makes these errors occasionally. The issue is to estimate correctly the relative frequency of the behavior.

This discussion of heuristics has just brushed the surface of research and theory in judgment processes. The point I wanted to make was that judgment and reasoning—like language comprehension, memory, perception, and other psychological processes—is often affected by certain rules of organization. These rules most often work to our advantage and help us make up for the fact that we

---

Heuristics. Quick judgment rules that are used to process information and bring solutions within closer reach.

Representativeness heuristic. A preconception, based on wrong estimates of probability, that often leads to inaccurate decision making.

Availability heuristic. A preconception, based on the idea that what we see on any one occasion is what happens most often, that often leads to inaccurate decision making.

cannot possibly gather all of the information we need to make an absolutely accurate decision or judgment. Nevertheless, sometimes these strategies, or heuristics, work against us.

REVIEW QUESTIONS

12. A problem can be defined as wanting to get from a _____ state to a _____ state without a direct way of getting there.

13. There are four stages in problem solving: _____ the problem, devising a _____ , _____ _____ the plan, and _____ _____ .

14. _____ problem solving involves looking at a problem in a new way. If you have a block when you try to solve something like the 9-dot problem in the text, a rest period, called _____ , may help you to approach a solution in a different way.

15. _____ is involved in much problem solving, and involves a sudden reorganization of the problem so that the inner structure of the problem becomes clearer.

16. In reproductive/productive thinking, people must come up with new approaches to a problem they've never seen before. In reproductive/productive thinking, people can solve the problem with a procedure or facts they already know.

17. _____ is a technique for solving problems that involves two separate phases: thinking up as many ideas as possible and then evaluating the ideas.

18. One problem with group problem solving has been called _____ . It usually occurs in a group of people who know each other well and are reluctant to criticize one another's ideas.

19. In inductive/deductive reasoning, you are given all the necessary information and you must logically reach a conclusion. In inductive/deductive reasoning you are given incomplete information and you must extract a rule from it.

20. Rosch suggests that we form a concept by identifying a good example, or _____ , of the category in question, not from a list of characteristics.

21. Using the _____ _____ , we assume that what we see on any one occasion is what happens most often. Using the _____ _____ , we make decisions based on wrong estimates of probability.

Answers: **12.** given; goal **13.** understanding; plan; carrying out; looking back **14.** Creative; incubation **15.** Insight **16.** productive; reproductive **17.** Brainstorming **18.** groupthink **19.** deductive; inductive **20.** prototype **21.** availability heuristic; representative heuristic

■ A GENERAL COMMENT ABOUT COGNITIVE OPERATIONS

I have presented a selective sampler of cognitive operations that all of us engage in daily. To present all of the relevant and current information in the field of cognitive psychology would take all of the pages of this book and many more. You can explore these topics more deeply in another psychology course. Nevertheless, there is a theme that pulls together operations as different as language, problem solving, concept formation, reasoning, and judgment. The theme is *organization*. The speed and accuracy of our attempts to solve problems will depend, at least in part, on how we organize or lay out the problem and the alternative solutions. Our reasoning capacity depends to some extent on how premises are organized and analyzed (deductive reasoning) and on how incomplete information is ordered or presented (inductive reasoning). The formation of concepts seems to depend on a regular ordering of objects from most typical (prototypic) to least typical. In addition, some categories or concepts seem to occur in nature, where they have certain combinations of physical characteristics. Finally, there seem to be certain automatic solution strategies (heuristics) that come into play in making judgments, sometimes for the better and sometimes for the worse. The cognitive operations we have examined in this chapter are ample testimony to the elaborate organization of biological processes, learning experience, memory, and language capacities that make the human organism unique.

In the final section of this chapter we will consider the subject of intelligence, as it is generally assumed that the energy that flows into cognitive activity is intelligence. It is assumed that more intelligent people are better able to carry out cognitive operations than less intelligent individuals.

■ INTELLIGENCE TESTING

To be described as intelligent is commonly considered a compliment, for intelligence often represents success in formal education, a wide range of knowledge, and skill at solving problems. There even are clubs for people who meet a particular standard of intelligence; the *Mensa* organization limits its membership to those who have intelligence scores (frequently referred to as IQs) of one hundred thirty-five or above.

A Brief History of Intelligence Testing

The birth of intelligence testing in 1904 was a modest attempt by the French Ministry of Public Instruction (the National Board of Education) to identify children who did not have the mental ability to benefit from traditional schooling. A physician, Alfred Binet, had been developing tests of intellectual ability in children for many years before the French school system requested his services. He had discussed the mental abilities of students with their teachers and had observed his own children. Binet had become convinced that one of the important characteristics about intelligence was the fact that, in the normal child, it systematically increases with age. This relationship suggested that a good way of identifying students with mental handicaps was to examine mental growth rates. This could be done by comparing each child with a norm or reference group of children who were all at the same age level; the handicapped child would have a difficult time completing mental tasks that the normal child could complete.

Binet felt that intelligence was a single capacity that appeared in almost every mental task. Thus, he made his test a combination of many types of mental tasks arranged in order of increasing difficulty. The test score was a combination of the performance on all of these different types of items

measured against what the normal average child could do at each age level.

Binet's concept of intelligence was a broad one in the sense that he did not use his tasks to identify specific factors of intelligence. In the early 1900s a British psychologist named Charles Spearman redefined Binet's concept somewhat. While Spearman, like Binet, felt that there was a general intelligence factor (called *g*), he also felt that there were some specific factors as well. These factors (called *s* factors) could be very specific and useful in only one task (such as remembering strings of numbers), or broader and involved in several tasks (such as being able to understand mechanical relations). These broader *s* factors were called *group factors* because they were involved in a whole group of tasks.

In the United States, L. L. Thurstone went a step further. A general intelligence factor such as *g* had no place in his theory of intelligence. He felt that mental activity or intelligence was described completely by a small set of primary abilities or group factors. These were called the *primary mental abilities*; they include spatial abilities, perceptual abilities, numerical abilities, verbal relations, words, memory, and induction abilities. Thurstone developed a series of tests for measuring each of these abilities.

The movement away from a view of intelligence as a single capacity has continued. J. P. Guilford (Guilford, 1967, 1968) has suggested that what we see in intelligence test performance is actually a combination of three distinct components. Guilford's theory, called the *structure of the intellect*, is presented graphically in Figure 9–7. The first component consists of the type of test item the person is asked to complete. This is labeled "contents" in Figure 9–7. The test item can be figural, symbolic, semantic, or behavioral. Guilford felt that each different type of item required a different type of mental ability. The second component consists of the various mental operations necessary to work on the particular test item. The third component consists of the products that result from the various mental operations used to answer the various test item types. The center section in Table 9–5 provides examples of these contents, the top section presents operations, and the bottom section shows products. When you combine four types of content with five operations and six possible products, you get 120 dif-

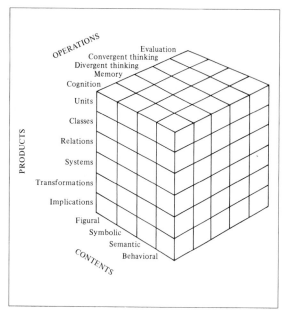

FIGURE 9-7
The diagram here shows what Guilford refers to as the structure of the intellect. It is possible to combine 4 types of content, 5 operations, and 6 possible products in different ways to get 120 different mental abilities. (Guilford, 1961)

ferent mental abilities. This is quite different from the idea of a single factor called *g*.

From this brief history, two views about intelligence should be apparent. First, the field has moved from a concept of intelligence as one factor to a view of a complex or multifaceted concept. Second, there is a much greater tendency now to view intelligence as a process rather than as a trait—intelligence is seen as the way people solve problems, not what native capacities they have (Sternberg, 1970). This is a very optimistic position, for it suggests that people can be made more intelligent as a result of training or instruction in basic mental operations or skills. Remember, however, that there is some debate regarding the nature of that training or instruction. Some psychologists think that the training can occur only in the context of some specific knowledge base (Glaser, 1984, 1985). Others see mental abilities as more general and not quite so dependent on specific knowledge bases (Sternberg, 1985).

Intelligence Tests

A wide variety of tests is available for estimating people's intelligence. It may be surprising to hear that

the very first intelligence test, the Binet test, has gone through several revisions and is still a popular and widely used test. As theoretical shifts have occurred in the idea of what intelligence is, there have been changes in intelligence tests as well. Thurstone developed a collection of tests to measure primary mental abilities, and Guilford has devoted many years to creating various tests that enable him to isolate the various mental abilities of his theory. He has identified 90 of his 120 abilities in test performance (Hopkins and Stanley, 1981). In the sections that follow we will look briefly at some of the most commonly used intelligence tests.

The Stanford-Binet. Terman, a psychologist at Stanford University, adapted Binet's intelligence test for use with American children. The test was called the **Stanford-Binet test**. The adaptation involved administering the exam to groups of children of various ages. These age groups were arranged by year and month. Thus, 9–4 would mean an age of 9 years and 4 months. Terman used this age scale to develop what is now known as the **intelligence quotient**, or IQ. He did this by constructing a ratio of a person's chronological age to his or her mental age. **Chronological age** is the number of years and months since birth—the common meaning of age. The idea of mental age was introduced by Binet. **Mental age** is identified by comparing a person's performance on a test to the performance of various other children in specific age groups (the norm groups). Because the test had been previously administered to large samples of children of various ages, the average performance of various age groups was known. By finding the group that most closely approximated the person's performance, the person could be assigned a mental age the same as the chronological age of that group. In other words, if a child performed like the average 10-year-old, then the child was assigned the mental age of 10. The intelligence quotient or IQ was figured by dividing the mental age by the chronological age and multiplying by 100 (so that there wouldn't be any fractions). This can be shown through the following equation:

$$IQ = \frac{MA}{CA} \times 100$$

As you can see, if the mental age is greater than the chronological age, the IQ score will be greater than

TABLE 9-5   Explanations and Examples of Guilford's Categories

Mental Operations	1. Evaluation. Deciding how appropriate or significant an object, event, or idea is. Example: Ranking the solutions to a problem in terms of their effectiveness.
	2. Convergent Thinking. Sorting information to arrive at the correct solution to a problem. Example: Listening to two sides to a dispute and deciding which is accurate.
	3. Divergent Thinking. Using information to discover a variety of ideas or solutions to a problem. Example: Listing as many uses for a brick as you can think of.
	4. Memory. Retaining information. Example: Remembering the combination to a lock.
	5. Cognition. Being able to organize information in different contexts. Example: Being able to explain the rule that governs right turns on red lights.
Contents	1. Figural. Directly perceived objects or events. Example: Completing a jigsaw puzzle.
	2. Symbolic. Letters, numbers, and other signs. Example: Using a code number from a mail order catalogue to order an item.
	3. Semantic. Meanings of words. Example: Answering questions about word meanings.
	4. Behavioral. Social situations. Example: Introducing one friend to another.
Products	1. Units. Single items of information, such as numbers, letters, and words. Example: Recognizing individual letters or numbers.
	2. Classes. The sorting of units according to common characteristics. Example: Identifying concepts or categories of objects.
	3. Relations. The factors that connect things to one another. Example: Being able to apply "greater than" and "less than" rules to objects.
	4. Systems. The patterns in which things are organized. Example: Arranging groups of people according to assigned duties, supervisors or pay levels.
	5. Transformations. The changing structures of patterns. Example: Changing weight from pounds to kilograms or volume from quarts to liters.
	6. Implications. Additional factors suggested by all of the above with reference to planning and selecting an appropriate course of action. Example: Using stock market data from the past month to decide whether a stock is a "good buy." Or looking at game films of an opposing team to plan a successful offense or defense.

100. A child with a chronological age of 8 who performs as well as the average 10-year-old on the test has an IQ of 125. A 10-year-old who performs as well as the average 8-year-old has an IQ score of 80. This means that at any chronological age, a score of 100 is average or "normal."

Ever since the Stanford-Binet test was first introduced in 1916, there have been two major revisions of test items, and, in 1972, new norms were established by administering the test to people of varying ages and recording their performance. Items similar to those found on the current version of the Stanford-Binet appear in Table 9–6.

The procedures for administering the examination are very specific, and anyone who gives the exam must practice and study these procedures exten-

---

Stanford-Binet test. An intelligence test first devised by Alfred Binet and later revised at Stanford by Lewis Terman.
Intelligence Quotient (IQ). The number arrived at by dividing mental age by chronological age and multiplying by 100.

Chronological age. The number of years and months since birth.
Mental age. A person's score on the Stanford-Binet test.

TABLE 9-6
Sample Test Items at Three Different Levels of the Stanford-Binet Test.

Year Two

1. Put a circle, triangle, and square in proper place in a formboard.
2. Identify by name toys representing common objects such as a cat, a button, a cup, etc.
3. Identify parts of the body: Show the hair, mouth, ears, and hands on a doll.
4. Identify pictures of objects such as a shoe, a table, a flag, etc.

Year Six

1. Define such objects as an orange, an envelope, a straw, etc.
2. Reproduce from memory a pattern of seven beads on a string.
3. Identify missing parts from a picture, such as a wheel off a wagon.
4. Give the examiner the correct number of blocks up to 10.
5. Identify the figure that is different from four other figures (four chairs and a table are shown).

Year Ten

1. Define such words as "roar," "muzzle," and "haste."
2. Read a standard paragraph and be able to recall the major ideas.
3. Name 28 words of any type in 1 minute.
4. Repeat correctly a sequence of six digits.

Source: Adapted from Terman, 1937.

sively before administering the test. This is critical; if the scores are to be of any value, the conditions under which a child receives the test must be identical to the conditions under which the norm group performed. The test is always administered to one child at a time, never in a group.

There are different tests for each age level. The test begins by finding the lowest test level the child can pass. The examiner then gives higher and higher level tests (tests for older and older children) until the child fails all of the test items. The test is then stopped. The scoring consists of giving the child credit for the items that were passed. After the various item credits are combined, the child is assigned a mental age. It is this mental age that represents the IQ of the child. The mental age is no longer divided by the chronological age to obtain the IQ score. This is because the range or variability of performances within an age group is different from one age to another. As a result, a person's IQ changes as he or she moves from one age group to another, even though the person's ability remains constant. You can see an example of this type of problem in academic testing. If you received a test score of 70, its interpretation depends on how the other students in the class scored. In intelligence testing, a similar effect occurs when you move from one age group to another. Different age groups represent different standards for comparison. To overcome this problem, a statistical technique is used to equate the range of performance for various age groups. Today, IQ scores are determined by using tables describing levels of performance for each age group. This new measure is called the **deviation IQ** because it corrects for the deviation, or variance, of scores within an age group.

Criticisms of the Stanford-Binet Test. In spite of the popularity of the Stanford-Binet intelligence test, there are some problems with it. In the first place, it was developed for children. This makes its use with adults awkward; many of the items are not suitable for adults. In addition, adults often read too much information into the questions, giving responses that are more complex than necessary; in spite of the creativity or complexity of these responses, they are marked wrong. There is also the problem of norm or reference groups. The items have been extensively tested on specific age groups of young children and adolescents, but there are few systematic studies of the performance of adults on the items. This means that adult performance is interpreted with references to nonadult norm groups, and this causes problems.

In developing the original test, Binet assumed that intelligence was a broad and general trait that showed up in almost all intellectual tasks. But the work of Spearman, Thurstone, and others suggested that this might be too broad a view of mental abilities. At the very least, there is the possibility that there are differences between verbal abilities (such as analogies and information tasks) and performance abilities (such as perceptual and spatial tasks). There is no way to get separate verbal and performance scores using the Stanford-Binet test; only one score is produced, which represents intelligence.

The Wechsler Test. Wechsler set out to develop a new intelligence test that would correct some of the problems with the Stanford-Binet test. He was successful and developed a series of tests that are widely used today for assessing the intellectual capacities of both adults and children. There are three tests. The first is called **WAIS** or **Wechsler Adult Intelligence Scale.** This test is intended to be used with people between the ages of 16 and 60. Next, he developed a test for use with children between the ages of 6 and 16, called the **WISC** or **Wechsler Intelligence Scale for Children.** Finally, in 1967, he developed a test for use with very young children between the ages of 4-½ and 6. This was called the **WPPSI,** the **Wechsler Preschool and Primary Scale of Intelligence.**

The WISC and WAIS tests have both been revised since then and are now known as the WISC-R and WAIS-R to indicate this revision. Revisions were necessary for several reasons. In the first place, items that were appropriate 20 years ago might no longer be useful or even have the same meaning today. Secondly, it is important to develop new norms; because the whole logic of intelligence testing depends on comparing the performance of one individual with the performance of a reference group, the reference or norm group must be an appropriate one. Today, almost every elementary-school child and young adult is familiar with standardized testing, but this was not true as recently as 20 years ago. A score that was thought outstanding a generation ago may be just slightly above average today; everyone may be scoring higher as a result of different learning experiences and more experience with testing. As an example, the prevalence of video games may have had a dramatic effect on the average child's spatial and perceptual abilities. If this average child is compared to the child of 20 years ago, his or her levels of spatial ability might seem extraordinary. Compared with a group of children

tested today, the same performance might seem quite ordinary. Thus, the child would seem either very talented or average, depending on which norms were used.

The Wechsler tests also introduced a distinction between intelligence as measured verbally and as estimated by nonverbal methods. There are actually 11 different subtests in the test as a whole. Of these, six of the subtests are called *verbal subtests* and five are *performance subtests.* The verbal subtests include items on general knowledge of society, arithmetic and vocabulary items, and reasoning items. The performance subtests are distinct from the verbal subtests in that they require the subject actually to manipulate symbols such as picture puzzles or blocks and do not require a verbal response of any kind. The test results include a separate score for each of the 11 subtests, a verbal score, a performance score, and a total (or "full scale") score. As you can see, the Wechsler test gives considerably more detailed information than the Stanford-Binet test.

Group Intelligence Tests. The Stanford-Binet and Wechsler tests are examples of individual intelligence tests; they are taken by only one person at a time. In addition, the recent versions of these tests include performance subtests requiring demonstration and timed administration, conditions that are impossible in group settings. Besides this, skilled examiners are necessary for the administration of these individual intelligence tests. As a result, a modification of intelligence tests that allowed for group administration was begun in the very early stages of intelligence testing. This was fortunate, because a national need for quick screening appeared in the form of World War I. When the United States entered the First World War it became obvious that there was a need to determine which recruits were capable of command positions and which ones were not. An effort was made to develop an intelligence test that could be used to classify the almost 2 million recruits in the armed services. The new exam, called the *army Alpha test,*

Deviation IQ. Standard score on an intelligence test such as the Stanford-Binet test; corrects for variance of scores within an age group.

Wechsler Adult Intelligence Scale (WAIS). Intelligence test by David Wechsler for testing adults, ages 16–60.

Wechsler Intelligence Scale for Children (WISC). Intelligence test developed by David Wechsler for testing children ages 6–16.

Wechsler Preschool and Primary Scale of Intelligence (WPPSI). Intelligence test developed by David Wechsler to test very young children, ages 4½–6.

The World War I army tests showed dramatic differences in scores between native-born Americans and newly arrived immigrants who could not understand English.

closely resembled the verbal sections of the Stanford-Binet test. It had items dealing with such tasks as completing number series, unscrambling sentences, answering informational questions, and following directions. The revolutionary aspect of the army Alpha test was that it could be given to hundreds of recruits at once in a relatively short time and scored by clerks. The test was ultimately administered to 1,250,000 recruits and scored by over 350 enlisted men at 35 different locations.

Shortly after beginning their group testing program, the armed services realized that the army Alpha test was inappropriate for many recruits who were not fluent in English. The decades before World War I had seen a great influx of immigrants to the United States; as a result, many of the recruits could not speak English well and thus could not read the test questions. It was obvious that they would all receive scores considerably below their mental ability level only because of their language problems. Consequently, the army *Beta* test was created. This test was intended to parallel the army Alpha exam, but it was specially prepared for those who could not read and those who had difficulty with the English language.

Following World War I, there was a rapid growth of group testing in school and industrial settings. Several tests were developed that could be quickly and cheaply administered to large groups of candidates and scored by clerks. The development of multiple-choice tests and machines to score answer sheets made group testing even more attractive. Group tests are still commonly used in school and industrial settings; for example, your exams in this course are group tests. Today, most group tests focus on special abilities, like mechanical comprehension or spatial relations. We will examine several of these specific tests shortly. Other tests that are concerned with academic achievement, such as the SAT, are also group tests.

In spite of the advantages of group tests, the Stanford-Binet and Wechsler scales remain popular individual methods for measuring intelligence in several settings. Clinical psychologists often gather data on the intelligence of their patients as an aid in determining potential causes and side effects of mental disorders. In order to collect such information, it is often better to administer an individualized test rather than an impersonal paper-and-pencil exam. This enables the administrator to keep the motivation of the person being examined high, and to handle any problems of communication or administration on a person-by-person basis. In addition, it is often useful to have performance information about the person in question: for example, how good they are at manipulating objects, such as blocks, with designs on them. Finally, many people who take tests (for example, children or mentally impaired individuals) cannot easily follow standardized instructions for taking tests. For all of these reasons, there will always be a need for individually administered intelligence tests.

Group Differences in Intelligence

The army quickly recognized that there were differences between native-born and foreign-born recruits on the army Alpha test. The army further recognized that these differences had little or nothing to do with the mental capacity of those recruits. The issue was not terribly complicated; the intention was to give a test of intelligence, not a test of English. To the extent that the scores represented language ability rather than intelligence, they were of little value. If proficiency in English was the object of testing, a brief conversation would probably have sufficed.

After World War I, data gathered from the testing of recruits was used to develop immigration policies. In fact, the low average IQ score of the various immigrant groups was used as evidence that many were feebleminded or retarded. Because people from southeastern European countries (Jews, Poles, Italians, and Russians) scored on the average lowest, the numbers of immigrants of those nationalities admitted to the United States was kept low. Immigrants from England, Scotland, and Canada typically scored higher. As a consequence, many more were admitted to the United States. In this way, it was assumed that the national intelligence could be kept high. Psychologists were heavily involved in advising Congress on immigration laws based on tested intelligence (Goddard, 1917; Yerkes, 1921; Brigham, 1923). This is an unfortunate chapter in the development of psychological testing and one that is well documented (Fancher, 1985; Gould, 1981).

Over the years of intelligence testing, many group differences have emerged, and these differences have been used as ammunition in some very serious social and political controversies. At one time or another, claims have been made that blacks, Hispanics, senior citizens, and physically handicapped people are not as intelligent as the comparison group. The assertion that these differences exist was serious, because these alleged differences were then used to justify discrimination in employment, voting rights, and education on the grounds that certain groups could not perform "adequately" in these areas.

Americans occasionally find themselves compared unfavorably to other nationalities in productivity, creativity, or attitudes. Lately, there has been a nagging doubt about the capacity of the United States to compete with Japan in various commercial markets. The Japanese seem to produce more and better cameras, high-technology equipment, and automobiles. In addition, their methods of management seem to be more enlightened than those of American managers, with a greater concern for the employee as a resource (Ouchi, 1981). It is tempting to think of these differences in behavior as due to differences in intelligence. In other words, it is tempting to view the Japanese as more intelligent. This would conform to the assumption that intelligence results in "success." In fact, one recent study seems to confirm that possibility. A British psychologist recently reported the results of a comparison of the performance of Japanese and American children on the WISC. Lynn (1982) administered a translation of the WISC to 1100 Japanese children. In comparing the scores of the Japanese children with American data, Lynn found that the average IQ score for the Japanese children was 111, compared to an average score of 100 for the American children.

Some have argued that the difference in scores is due to the difference in genetic makeup between the Japanese and Americans. Many reject the genetic explanation. It is instructive to consider this study and the acceptability of the genetic explanations because in considering alternative explanations, many of the pitfalls in test score interpretation become apparent. Let us consider some of these alternatives to a genetic explanation.

The Differences Are Due to the Home Environment. In Japan, students have to pass an exam every year in order to move on to the next grade. As a result, there is a great deal of stress put on school work in the home. This starts at a very early age, before first grade. It may be that because of this Japanese children are exposed to a more challenging intellectual climate in their home than are American children of the same age.

The Differences Are Due to Better Schooling. In examining the results of Lynn's research, it has been suggested that in the last generation there has been an extraordinary upgrading of educational opportunities and programs in Japan (Anderson, 1982). In contrast, improvements in American schools and curricula have been less dramatic. Since comparisons were made between Japanese and American children between the ages of 6 and 16, the Japanese sample would have been exposed to a different "treatment" than the American sample. Once again, the environment could play a major role.

Japanese Children Take Even More Exams than American Children. As indicated earlier, there is a strong emphasis on taking tests in Japan, and youngsters there take many tests between the ages of 6 and 16. As we will see shortly, people who are used to taking tests often outperform others of equal abilities who are less familiar with tests and taking tests. To the extent that the Japanese sample had greater experience in taking tests, their scores would be higher.

The Samples Were Different in Some Important Respects. The Japanese sample was selected from special schools that were often connected to universities. This implies that the students in these schools were being groomed to do well in those very abilities measured in the test.

The Nature of the Test Items Favored the Japanese Sample. Many of the WISC test items are nonverbal. They involve shapes, blocks, the rearrangement of picture parts, and the completion of mazes. In fact, the Japanese children did best on these items. The Japanese alphabet depends heavily on shapes and angles of connected lines. Once again, this would suggest that Japanese children are performing better as a result of experience rather than any genetic difference.

These are just some of the possible reasons for the differences found between the two samples. It is not certain that a genetic explanation is wrong, but there are several other possible explanations as well. In addition, as you saw earlier, the fact that the average score for the two groups was different says nothing about the capabilities of the individual members of the groups. There also were many American children who scored substantially higher than Japanese children. Thus, even if genetics played a role, it would only describe the extent to which the children's intelligence is transmitted from the parents' genetic material, but would not necessarily have any implications for the differences between races or nationalities.

This comparison of American and Japanese children's intelligence scores is a good example of the kind of debate that surrounds almost every aspect of ability testing. Intelligence testing is simply one variation of the debate. The same arguments and counterarguments are heard in discussions of differences between male and female samples, black and white samples, old and young samples. Furthermore, these debates rage around just about every type of test. For example, women (on the average) do more poorly than men on tests of strength and agility and are often denied opportunities for employment as police officers on that basis. Blacks and Hispanics (on the average) often do more poorly than whites on tests measuring verbal skills and, as a result, are denied opportunities for both employment and education on that basis. Recently, the NCAA passed a rule requiring certain minimum scores on the SAT for athletes who are being recruited by universities. The presidents of some predominantly black universities argue that this is an attempt to keep blacks off the teams of white universities. Those in favor of the new rule claim that they are trying to protect the black athlete from being exploited by making sure that the athlete has the basic ability to get a college degree. Thus, there is no area of testing that has not had its share of debate about the use of tests for making decisions.

Culture-Reduced Tests

The debate about the role of test scores in making decisions about people is not likely to go away in your lifetime. The arguments are influenced both by values and by actual data. Tests were originally developed to identify merit, to prevent important decisions from being made on the basis of favoritism, whims, or prejudices. But the very groups who should have been protected by the tests now claim that they are the victims of them. They claim that the tests have been created to favor those who come from a particular culture. In Lynn's study on the difference between Japanese and American children, it might have been argued that the test favored the Japanese culture (because so many of the test items were nonverbal) and, as a result, Japanese children scored higher. The same argument is often made with respect to the differences between black people and white people on particular ability tests. Critics argue that the tests favor peo-

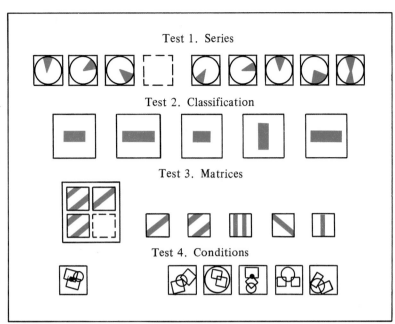

FIGURE 9-8

These are sample items from a culture-fair intelligence test developed by the Institute of Personality and Ability Testing. In Test 1 you must select the item that completes the series. In Test 2 you must mark the one item in each row that does *not* belong with the others. In Test 3 you must mark the item that correctly completes the matrix or pattern shown. In Test 4 you must put a dot in one of the designs on the right so as to meet the same conditions shown in the design on the left (in other words, the dot must be in the two rectangles, but not in the circle). (Institute of Personality and Ability Testing, 1961)

ple who are white and come from middle-class homes. This argument about favoritism is based on test elements such as grammar, vocabulary, and the types of questions asked.

Several ways exist to reduce the effect of culture on test scores. The first way is to create a test that minimizes cultural advantage. Many have suggested the use of nonverbal test items to accomplish this. In Figure 9-8, you can see examples of some nonverbal test items that have been proposed for measuring mental abilities. In particular, these items are concerned with relationships or abstract principles of order. But as we saw in the Japanese/American example, even these items might be biased toward one culture or another. For instance, children who can afford elaborate video games might score much better on nonverbal tests than those who cannot afford them. Another problem with the notion of reducing the cultural influence on test scores by using nonverbal items is the fact that we have already seen that there is a connection between language and thought. In many instances, the only thing nonverbal about the item is the way it is presented. It may still require verbal skills in order to answer correctly the question or solve the problem. To the extent that the thought process involves concepts, labels, or linguistic categories, differences might still emerge from nonverbal items.

Another way of reducing the effect of culture on tests scores is to use the same items but develop separate norms for separate groups. You will remember that this is exactly how age norms were developed for intelligence tests. A sample of children in one group (for example, 8-year-olds) was given the test, and the percentages of children passing each item were calculated. This became the average or the standard to which other scores were compared. Your own intelligence score depends on how well you do relative to others in your group. The same might be done with men and women or blacks and whites. For example, the test scores of blacks and women would be compared to other members in their own group (blacks or women), and not to scores of those in other cultural groups (whites or men). This creates something of a problem, however. We really end up with separate rankings for the various groups, and there is no way of knowing how the highest scorer in one group compares to the highest scorer in the other group. In other words, this method works *within* groups but not *across* groups.

A final method that has been suggested for reducing cultural influences on tests is to develop completely different strategies for making decisions about members of different cultural groups. In fact, this approach is being used today in admissions to some graduate and professional schools. In some schools, when white applicants are evaluated, greater weight is placed on GRE scores and lesser weight on the number of courses in the major area of study. In contrast, when black applicants are evaluated, greater weight may be placed on the number of courses, and lesser weight on the GRE scores. In a sense, this says that the things that predict success for black applicants are different from the things that predict success for white applicants. In fact, many studies have attempted to show that different prediction systems are appropriate for white and black applicants. However, most of these studies have failed to demonstrate the difference (Landy, 1985). Currently, the prevailing opinion is that the same things that predict success for whites predict success for blacks and Hispanics. Similarly, the same things that predict success for men predict success for women.

Most professionals who are engaged in developing tests are well aware of the potential for bias in their tests. Thus, they spend a good deal of time developing test items that are fair to all subgroups. This is accomplished by pretesting items on samples of people selected from different cultural or racial groups. In addition, items are examined to make sure that all biased language and examples have been removed. For example, as recently as 10 years ago, most tests used the pronoun *he* rather than using a neutral form or alternating *he* with *she*. But bias in test items will continue to be a problem because subgroup cultures are constantly changing.

Heredity vs. Environment

At the heart of much of the testing debate is the issue of *heredity versus environment*. To what extent does a test score represent genetic inheritance, and to what extent does it represent the accumulation of experiences and environmental influences since birth? It is a fact that group differences in test scores do exist; the question is why do they exist?

Most often cited to support the argument that abilities are inherited is a comparison of the intellectual performance of identical twins. You will remember that identical twins have exactly the same genetic material. As a result, any differences in their test scores must reflect the effect of different environmental experiences, not different genes. By examining the different combinations of genetics and environment, it is hoped that some estimate can be made of how various genetic factors interract with various environmental ones. The highest correlations or matches in test scores are usually between identical twins raised in the same household. The lowest correlations or matches are between unrelated individuals raised in completely different environments. This implies that environment is less important than heredity. If environment were very important, then all of the correlations in the instances where individuals were raised together would be high. This is not the case.

On the other hand, the few studies that have been done of identical twins reared apart (an extremely rare event) show that the environments they are adopted into tend to be more similar than one would expect. For example, in cases of adoption from an adoption home or foster home agency, it is very likely that there would be standards for placement. Foster or adopted parents would have to meet certain educational, emotional, and economic standards. This would inflate the correlations between the test scores of the twins because they would be exposed to similar environments. In turn, this would inflate the estimates of the contribution of heredity. In the same way, there is good reason to believe that the environments and experiences of identical twins may be more similar than regular sibling combinations or even fraternal twins. Identical twins are often treated identically—they are dressed the same, taken out together constantly, and, as they mature, often spend a good deal of time with each other. In effect, their environments are being held constant. Under these circumstances, the observed similarities seem to be the result of biological makeup, but we cannot separate the biological makeup from the uniform environmental treatment that twins receive.

As you can see, serious problems exist in conducting a fair or good study of the influence of heredity on intelligence. Even if the perfect study could be done and it were possible to get accurate estimates of the contribution of environment and genetic inheritance, we would still know little that would help us predict or understand the observed levels of intelligence in human beings. This is because it is the *combination* or *interaction* of heredity and environment that is responsible for observed abilities. An example will illustrate this point. Suppose that you decide to grow some tomatoes in your dorm room. You buy some seeds very cheaply. The package warns you that some of the seeds are better than others, that their quality differs from good to poor. You decide to plant two trays of seeds, and you split the packet of seeds between these two trays. But you only have enough room on your window sill for one of the trays. The other tray must be placed on the desk, some distance from the window. You carefully tend these two trays. After one month, the average height of the plants in the tray on the window is 4 inches. The average height of the plants in the tray on the desk is 2 inches. There is a clear difference between one group of plants and the other. But let us look at the differences between the heights of the plants *within* each tray. In the tray on the window sill, the heights vary from 2¼ inches to 5½ inches. In the desk tray, the heights vary from 1½ inches to 4¼ inches. There is considerable variability within a tray as well as between the trays. The sun interacted with the quality of the seeds, producing observable differences. The final height of any plant was the result of the interaction between the quality of the seed from which it came and the amount of sunlight it received. Now, let us consider a variation on our plant-growing experiment. Let us assume that we had seeds of a uniform quality. They were identical in every respect. In that circumstance, we might (incorrectly) conclude that all variation in plant height is due to sunlight (environmental factors). Now let us assume the opposite condition. The seeds varied dramatically in quality, but both trays were placed in identical lighting conditions. We might then (incorrectly) conclude that all variation in plants was the result of seed (genetic) composition. As you can see, both of these conclusions are inappropriate. In fact, when we hold one of the factors constant, variation can *only* be due to the other factor. This makes the factor that varied seem of tremendous importance.

It is very likely that human abilities are the result of similar interactions. In samples of people with similar environments, heredity factors may appear very important. In samples of people with similar heredity, environmental factors may appear very important. With the exception of identical twins, every person has a unique genetic makeup. In addition, each of us is exposed to a different external environment. Further, our cognitive and biological processes give each of us an individual perspective on that external environment. Under these circumstances, it becomes somewhat silly to identify *the* contribution as heredity. In fact, viewed this way, the study of the intelligence of identical twins is largely irrelevant, for the results can be generalized only to a very small population—identical twins.

The Social Implications of Tests

To the extent that test scores are inaccurate or distorted, actions based on them will be inappropriate and may lead to unfair discrimination of several varieties. Distorted test scores can unfairly limit access to employment or education or act as labels for people that will affect how others respond to them (for example, "bright" or "underachiever"). Distorted test scores can even change the way people evaluate themselves. If you receive a test score that says you are bad in math, you are inclined to believe it.

Despite their limitations, many tests of mental abilities do a good job of predicting school performance. They do a good job of predicting academic success in the form of grade point average. The SAT can predict college grades. Tests of reasoning can predict law school grades. The problem with tests arises as we get further removed from a learning or conceptual environment. Using an intelligence test to hire an unskilled laborer doesn't make much sense. Using the same test to admit an applicant to a university may be appropriate. Tests are neither good nor bad; uses of tests are appropriate or inappropriate.

The Stability of Intelligence

Another aspect of the heredity versus environment issue is the extent to which mental abilities change over time. In other words, can you become more (or less) intelligent? There is no doubt that scores change over time; this is to be expected. Every test score is only a guess about your true ability. The better the test, the more reliable the guess, but it is still a guess.

It has often been suggested that intelligence declines after young adulthood—that an inevitable consequence of aging is the general loss of mental ability. This is an illusion created by the way in which studies were conducted in the past. If a researcher were to go out and collect a sample of 1,000 people from the street and give them a test of a mental ability (say, reading comprehension), the scores would suggest a decline in intelligence after the age of 25. Each age group would score more poorly than the next younger age group. We have to remember, however, that when we compare the performances of these older and younger people, we are comparing people of different generations. Subjects born at different times would be exposed to different educational and cultural experiences. Successive generations may do better for many reasons. Nutrition can make a difference, as can test sophistication or motivational factors. But if the *same* sample of people were tested at 10-year intervals, the decline in test scores would be much less severe and would start much later. If we only look at a cross section of the population, we cannot separate changes that have occurred within an individual over time from those that characterize the differences between generations. There are some practical social implications for this phenomenon. Older applicants for jobs will often get lower test scores than younger applicants. This is interpreted as meaning that the older applicants are less talented, when in fact the test scores simply reflect differences in test sophistication between younger and older generations. Both the younger and the older applicant may have equally good chances of being successful at the job.

A Concluding Comment

We have covered a number of important topics in this chapter. It should be apparent that it is virtually impossible to separate langue from thinking. Further, it should be apparent that intelligence is a very complex concept, not a unitary inherited trait. Every individual can be characterized as a unique combination of various intellectual capabilities. Tests of intellectual capabilities can capture only a small part of that complexity. Moreover, particular tests have a tendency to emphasize one or a small number of these capabilities rather than providing a more balanced picture. For all of these reasons, it might be best to stop thinking of people as "intelligent" or "unintelligent" and, instead, start thinking about the particular strengths and weaknesses that appear in the cognitive processes of individuals that distinguish them from other individuals. As we will see later in this book, these differences in cognitive operations have implications for many different kinds of behavior—work behvior, social behavior, stress, and the behavior that characterizes mental illness.

REVIEW QUESTIONS

22. _____ _____ is the number of years and months since birth; _____ _____ is measured by the level on the Stanford-Binet test the person was able to pass.

23. The army Alpha test discriminated against newly arrived immigrants to this country because of their lack of knowledge of _____ ; the army Beta test was designed for those who could not _____ and could not speak _____ .

24. The question of intelligence often involves the question of what has a greater effect on IQ, _____ or _____ . The answer must always involve both of these elements, not just one.

Answers: 22. Chronological age; mental age 23. English; read; English 24. heredity; environment

---

■ SUMMARY

1. *Language* connects thought and action. Human language is a specialized communication system for expressing thoughts about events.

2. Both brain hemispheres are capable of language function, but in most people the left hemisphere becomes the dominant language area.

3. All human languages consist of similar rules, or grammars, that permit the creation of an unlimited number of allowable sentences. People are often able to use a language correctly without knowing how to describe its principles of organization.

4. *Phonemes* are basic speech sounds used to form words; there are about 45 phonemes in English. Most adults have over 100,000 words stored in memory. Mistakes in word use seem to be related to how words are stored in memory; there are usually similarities between the right word and one that is used by mistake. *Polysemy* is the term for words having multiple meanings. Context, or frame of reference of a sentence, is crucial for comprehension. We remember meaning or *deep structure*, rather than word sequence or *surface structure* of sentences.

5. Behaviorists believe that we learn language as we learn any other behavior, through reinforcement,

generalization, and imitation. The biological view holds that people are born with a capacity to learn langauge. Chomsky suggests that humans are born with *language acquisition devices (LADs)*, collections of devices that make language acquisition likely, and that experience is not the most important factor in language learning. Chomsky proposed that language can be broken into four components: surface structure, or the arrangement of word sequences that actually occur; deep structure, or the underlying meanings of words and phrases; competence, inborn knowledge about language; and performance, influenced by competence as well as variables such as experience.

6. The interactionist approach stresses *readiness*, or the idea that children can learn language from certain experiences at some times but not at others. This approach allows for both biological development and environmental interaction.

7. The concept of *critical periods* suggests that there are periods of development that are more important than others for the growth of certain competencies. When brain injury occurs, recovery is more complete if the person is young, suggesting that at birth both hemispheres may be capable of supporting language functions.

8. The rules of conversation, like the rules of constructing sentences, are often outside of our consciousness. In mental disorders, the normal communicative agreements in society often break down. *Turn-taking* involves the conversational rules about who has permission to speak next.

9. *Nonverbal communication* includes the use of gestures, tones, facial expressions, and other cues to convey information. Misreading of cues can occur if one does not consider the context of a conversation. Cross-cultural differences in nonverbal communication can cause inaccurate reading of nonverbal cues.

10. Nonhuman primates can learn to use abstract symbols meaningfully to express intentions and emotions. But correct word order and general grammar as well as interpretable vocalizations appear to be beyond their grasp.

11. *Linguistic determinism* is the view that the way we think is determined by the way we speak. *Linguistic relativity* is the view that thought patterns are affected by the structure of the particular language a person speaks.

12. *Problem solving* is a cognitive activity that in-

volves language and memory. Problem solving refers to the process of moving from the given state to the goal state of a problem. The problem-solving process involves a series of steps: understanding the problem, devising a plan, carrying out the plan, and looking back.

13. Creative problem solving, looking at a problem in a new way, often includes such strategies as rearranging elements in the problem or coming up with as many different and unique solutions as possible. *Incubation* is a rest period in problem solving in which a solution may be developing in the person's mind. *Insight* is a sudden reorganization of the problem so that its inner structure becomes clearer. *Productive thinking* requires that the problem solver develop a new answer or approach to a problem that he or she has never seen before. In *reproductive thinking* the problem solver can find a solution in a procedure or facts that are already in the problem solver's past experience.

14. Learning by understanding, or learning to use insight, results in the ability to transfer learning to new situations. *Functional fixedness* occurs when the function or use of an object becomes fixed in one's mind so that new, less common ways of using the object are not easily found. A *problem solving set* occurs when a person's prior experience with several problems creates a mental set that is used on new problems, even when a more efficient way of looking at the problem is possible.

15. A well-defined problem gives the given state, goal state, and legal operations in the problem statement and can be solved by a computer. Computer problem-solving has either one of two goals: *computer simulation*, or making the computer go through the same thought processes as a human problem solver; or *artificial intelligence*, having the computer solve the problem without concern for whether it uses human processes.

16. Groups can often solve problems more effectively than one person alone. *Brainstorming* consists of thinking up many different solutions. Group members are encouraged to think up as many ideas as possible without criticizing them. Brainstorming seems to work best for suggesting steps to achieve a certain goal and in identifying all the possible consequences of a particular action. One person alone can also use brainstorming techniques to work toward a solution to a problem. *Groupthink* is the tendency to accept the suggested solutions of other

group members without proper evaluation. The group, in this instance, hinders the problem-solving process.

17. In *deductive reasoning* a person is given all the necessary information and must logically reach a conclusion; in *inductive reasoning* a person has incomplete information from which he or she must come up with a general rule. *Premises* are given statements that are assumed to be true and used in deductive reasoning.

18. *Series completion tasks* require a problem solver to induce a rule that will predict what will come next. Training in inductive reasoning tasks can improve performance.

19. *Concepts* are meaning categories that include a broad range of possible members. *Continuity theory* is the view that concept learning involves continuously or gradually building stimulus–response links. *Noncontinuity theory* views concept learning as inducing rules or hypotheses and testing them. Research has supported the noncontinuity view as the better explanation of concept learning. *Prototype theory* proposes that concepts are arranged around prototypes, or good examples, rather than around lists of characteristics. One researcher believes that examples become prototypes because our perception systems are more sensitive to some characteristics than others.

20. Judgment is a form of reasoning that involves both deductive and inductive processes. Inaccurate judgments often represent misapplied information-processing rules. *Heuristics* are judgment rules that are used to process information. The *representativeness heuristic* is an inaccurate judgment of the probability of an event based on previous observations of its occurrence. Using the *availability heuristic* we assume that what we see on any one occasion is what happens most often.

21. The history of intelligence testing shows that the field has moved from a concept of intelligence as a single trait to a current view of intelligence as a multifaceted problem-solving process.

22. One currently used mental test is known as the *Stanford-Binet test,* an adaption of the first intelligence test that was based on the comparison of a child's test performance and test performances of children in various age groups. The *deviation IQ,* the measure currently in use, is determined by using tables describing levels of performance for each age group and corrects for the variance of scores within the group. The *Wechsler Adult Intelligence Scale (WAIS)* is used for people between the ages of 16 and 60; the *Wechsler Intelligence Scale for Children (WISC)* is for those between ages 6 and 16. The army Alpha test is a group intelligence test that was developed to screen large groups of World War I recruits in a short time.

23. Group differences in intelligence test performance have been used to justify voting, employment, and education discrimination on the grounds that, in these areas, some groups' performance is inferior to a comparison group. One explanation for the differences in Japanese and American children's IQ test performance is that there is a genetic difference between groups that makes Japanese children perform better. Alternative explanations point out some pitfalls in test score interpretation: (1) differences may be due to home environment; (2) differences may be due to better schooling for Japanese children; (3) Japanese children take more exams; (4) the samples were different in some important respects; (5) the nature of the test items favored the Japanese children.

24. Critics of many ability tests argue that they favor people from the white middle class. Methods of reducing the effect of culture on test scores include the use of nonverbal test items, the use of separate norms for each group, and the development of different methods for making decisions about members of different cultural groups.

25. The testing debate is tied to the issue of heredity versus environment. The highest correlation in test scores is between identical twins raised in the same household, while the lowest correlation is between unrelated people raised in different households. Human abilities are probably due to interactions between heredity and environment.

26. Distorted, inaccurate, or invalid test scores can limit access to employment or education; attach labels to people that will affect how others respond to them; and change the way people evaluate themselves. To be fair and valuable, test scores must be used with an understanding of their strengths and limitations.

27. A person's test scores change over time. Older people may not score as well on tests because they lack the test sophistication of younger people.

■ ANSWERING QUESTIONS FOR THOUGHT

1. If a stroke affects the left hemisphere, which in most people is the dominant language hemisphere, a person's use of language will be affected. This can be seen in any one of a number of different types of aphasia caused by damage to Broca's area or Wernicke's area. The damage by the stroke is usually caused by the loss of oxygen or bleeding in these areas.

2. All languages have a structure, and the structures of all languages are similar. Some languages may have larger vocabularies in certain areas than others (for instance, Eskimos have many more words for *snow* than we do), but basically any idea can be expressed in any language, and in this all languages are alike.

3. Sometimes, if you've solved a problem a certain way a number of times, you get stuck with that solution and can't see beyond it when a similar problem comes along that calls for an entirely different solution. This is called a problem-solving set. Another case in which your prior knowledge or experience might get in the way of solving a problem is the case of functional fixedness, when the function of an object becomes fixed in your mind so that new ways of using it are not easily found.

4. Groups can often solve problems more quickly than one person alone, if brainstorming is used. The effectiveness of this method is that the step of thinking up ideas is separated from the step of evaluating the ideas. This leads to a lot of possible solutions, which can then be evaluated by the group. Another reason that a group may come up with more answers than one person alone is that a person alone may tend to get stuck on one way of looking at a problem, while in a group there are likely to be several different approaches to the problem.

5. Computers can solve well-defined problems. As you recall from the text, well-defined problems are those in which the problem statement contains: 1) a clear description of the given state, 2) a clear description of the goal state, and 3) a clear description of the moves allowed in going from one state of the problem to another. Problem-solving computer programs can, for example: solve algebra story problems, geometry proofs and logical proofs; choose chess and checker moves; and answer intelligence test items. Computer programs are also available that can complete a medical diagnosis.

10

Life-Span Development I: Infancy and Childhood

DEVELOPMENTAL ISSUES
The Study of Life-Span Development □ Individual Differences □
Prenatal Development □ Genetic Transmission □
Dominant and Recessive Genes □ Genotype and Phenotype □
The Prenatal Environment

CHILDHOOD DEVELOPMENT
Physical Development □
Sensory and Perceptual Development □ Cognitive Development
   An Adult Conservation Task
Social Behavior
   Day-Care Centers
Bonding □
Prosocial and Antisocial Behavior in Children
   Why Children Talk to Themselves
Erikson's Theory of Psychosocial Development □
Moral Development □ Gender-Role Development □
Biology of Gender □ Sex-Role Development

SUMMARY

QUESTIONS FOR THOUGHT

1. **How are characteristics passed on from parent to child?**
2. **Whose genetic contribution determines whether the child will be male or female—the mother's or the father's?**
3. **Do infants have a functioning memory?**
4. **Do very young children have any understanding of gender roles?**
5. **When do children begin to realize the difference between right and wrong?**

The answers to these questions are at the end of the chapter.

In every chapter of this text thus far, you have seen examples of change. Learning is an example of relatively permanent change. So is the development of language, memory, and problem solving. Other examples involve states of consciousness, such as changes in sleep/wake patterns and associated brain waves as a child matures physically. Strange as it may sound, change is one of the most stable aspects of behavior. In this chapter and the following one, we will examine the extent and varieties of change that can be seen in human behavior during a lifetime. Traditionally, this area of study has been called **developmental psychology.** You may remember our definition of developmental psychology from Chapter 1 as the study of patterns of change in human beings from conception to death. These patterns include both physical maturation and psychological development.

It is traditional for psychologists to distinguish among various temporal stages of development: infancy and childhood, adolescence, and adulthood. We will follow this tradition and devote this chapter to infancy and childhood. The next chapter will consider adolescence and adulthood.

■ DEVELOPMENTAL ISSUES

The Study of Life-Span Development

The brief introduction to this chapter should have given you a feel for the dynamic character of human development. Something is always happening. The conclusion to be drawn from this is that between conception and death, something is always changing. There is never a period in which change does not occur.

Twenty years ago, the terms *developmental psychology* and *child psychology* were almost synonymous. It almost seemed as though psychologists believed that no development took place after adolescence. In recent times, there has been a growing recognition that development does not stop at adolescence. In order to emphasize this broader approach, a new phrase has appeared to replace the term developmental psychology. This phrase is **life-span psychology.** Life-span psychology considers the ways in which various aspects of behavior change over the entire life of an individual. This approach encourages a consideration of the continuity of behavior and development. It suggests that behavior unfolds and evolves rather than abruptly appearing and disappearing.

Individual Differences

A particular age or chronological period has no fixed or intrinsic developmental importance—just that it is more important for the development of some aspects of behavior than another period. Another reason for not strictly categorizing particular ages with respect to their developmental importance is because people develop at different rates. It is reasonable to say that language development comes

---

Developmental psychology. Traditionally, the study of patterns of change in human beings from conception to death, including both physical maturation and psychological development.

Life-span psychology. Term now used in place of "developmental psychology" to recognize a broader approach to development; considers the ways in which various aspects of behavior change over the entire life of an individual.

after the development of sensory mechanisms and comes before the development of moral values. It is less possible to fix that development at a particular chronological age. Some children walk at 10 months and others not until 18 months. Some children speak in sentences at 20 months and others do not show this competency until 36 months. Keep these variations in mind when I say that certain behaviors appear or change at particular ages. I am really speaking here of an "average" age. The same behavior may be shown by some children at an earlier age and by others at a later age.

Many possible reasons exist for individual differences to appear in the rate of development. A basic reason is *genetic.* The genetic material we inherit is more than just a biochemical substance; it is a message that is programmed to last a lifetime. Furthermore, it is known that a genetic message need not be immediately or fully apparent. In some cases, the expression of a message can be delayed until later in life. Consider the example of "male pattern baldness." A son whose father was bald at an early age has a predisposition toward early baldness himself. But the son doesn't begin to lose his hair at age 8 or 14, or even at 23. Much like his father, the son's hair begins to thin in his late 20s, until by age 35 there is only a fringe of hair remaining. This is a case of a genetic message that took a long time before the trait it governed was expressed. Similarly delayed messages might be involved in the development of physical and cognitive skills.

Another possible reason for different rates of development is *nutrition.* Cell development and function depend on the availability of nutrients in the bloodstream. If a particular vitamin deficiency occurs, cognitive or physical development may be retarded, regardless of any genetic message present. Such a deficiency might either accelerate or delay a genetic message. Suppose your genetic material carried a message for rapid development of brain areas that support language skills. A perfect diet might allow for an extremely rapid development of these skills. A poor diet might delay language development well past the time suggested by the genetic code.

Still another reason for varied rates of development is the social environment. For example, consider the case of the child who did not speak until age 6. Her parents took her to specialists who could find nothing wrong with her neural functions or speech mechanisms. Nevertheless, the child did not speak. One day at the dinner table, the child spoke her first words. She said, "The soup's cold!" The parents were flabbergasted and asked her why she had never spoken before. She shrugged and answered, "So far everything's been okay." As you will see in the chapter on motivation, needs and incentives play a major role in behavior. An environment that is full of stimulation, uncertainty, stress, or love will produce different behaviors from one that is dull, predictable, calm, or full of hate.

These three factors—genetic transmission, nutrition, and social environment—interact with one another to yield different rates of development. Sometimes one factor may be more important than the others for particular behaviors. In the development of moral values, for example, environment plays a larger role than either nutrition or genetic transmission. In the development of skilled physical performance, all three factors may be equally important but may have their influence at different times.

Prenatal Development

From a strictly biological point of view, life begins when a sperm fertilizes an egg. This signals the beginning of development. The period from conception to birth is known as the **prenatal period.** It typically lasts for 40 weeks. As you can see from the panel of pictures in Figure 10–1, rapid physical growth and development characterize this period. Throughout this period of development, the consequences of many events are obvious. If a mother-to-be acquires certain diseases (such as measles), has an accident, or introduces certain substances into her body (such as alcohol or narcotics), serious implications await the unborn child. Less obvious, but equally important, is the effect of a deficient diet or chronic stress during pregnancy on a child's development prior to birth. This may cause the genetic material itself to develop abnormally, resulting in abnormalities. We will now consider some possible influences on development that occur in the prenatal period. The first such influence is the actual genetic material contributed through the sperm of the father and the egg of the mother.

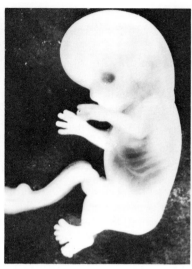
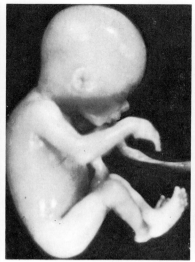
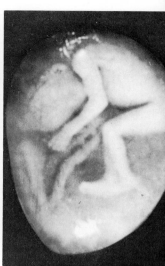

FIGURE 10-1
These photographs show an embryo (far left), followed by a fetus at three different stages of development. A protective fluid sac is formed around the fertilized egg in the first 2 weeks after conception.

Genetic Transmission

In this century, substantial advances have been made in understanding how the human body grows and develops. This has been possible because of what is now known about a molecule called **deoxyribonucleic acid** (or **DNA**). DNA is a chemical. Segments of this chemical are linked together in a series of chains. Each chain of DNA is called a **gene**. The basic building block for our consideration of genetic transmission is the chromosome. A **chromosome** is a collection of genes or DNA chains. Each chromosome carries about 20,000 genes. In a sense, the chromosome is the boxcar carrying the instructions for human development. Genes, or the chromosomes in which they are carried, represent the blueprint for how our body will develop. The genes carry information about hair color, weight, size, sex, eye color, and so on. Look around you. You will see quite a few different blueprints. A child represents a combination of two different blueprints—the genetic contribution of the mother and the genetic contribution of the father. This is where the chromosomes come in. The genes of the mother do not directly connect with the genes of the father. Instead, the two sets of chromosomes unite to form the master blueprint that will result in the child.

The mother's genetic blueprint is carried in the ovum or egg, the father's in the sperm. The sperm and the egg are unique cells in certain respects. Most human cells carry 23 matched *pairs* of chromosomes. The sperm cell and the egg cell are different. They each contain 23 *single* chromosomes. The sperm carries 23 single chromosomes, which represent the genetic contribution of the father. The egg carries 23 single chromosomes, which represent the genetic contribution of the mother. The pairing of these two sets of 23 single

---

Prenatal period. The period from conception to birth.
Deoxyribonucleic Acid (DNA). A chemical molecule that forms the basis of genes.
Gene. Made up of DNA molecules; transmits the blueprint or

information that determines many of our characteristics, such as eye color, sex, hair color, and so on.
Chromosome. A collection of genes (about 20,000 genes per chromosome). Each parent contributes 23 single chromosomes to the child—thus, we have 23 pairs of chromosomes.

chromosomes accounts for the joint contribution of the mother and father. If there are 20,000 genes in a chromosome and 23 chromosomes contributed by the father and the mother, there are approximately 1,000,000 pieces of information (or parts of the genetic instructions) present when the sperm and egg unite. Because the mother and father each contribute separate halves of the code, each baby born to them will be different from either of them. Moreover, the specific 23 single chromosomes that are contributed by the mother and father will change with each uniting of sperm and egg. This accounts for the fact that you do not look exactly like all of your brothers and sisters. At a much simpler level, this accounts for the fact that not all boys or girls are born in a given family. If the same 23 single chromosomes were contributed by each sperm or egg cell, there could only be all male or all female children in a given family.

Once this pairing has occurred at conception, the process of growth is not complicated. Through a mechanism called **mitosis,** the 23 pairs of chromosomes duplicate themselves, and each of the two 23-pair sets moves to opposite sides of the cell. The cell then divides, yielding two cells, each with identical genetic compositions. Each of those two cells then duplicates itself and splits. This duplication and splitting continues and is the biological definition of growth. To give you some feel for the scope of this development, consider the fact that when the baby is born, it will be made up of 10,000,000,000,000 (10 trillion) individual cells, each containing the same genetic information or blueprint as the very first cell. As an adult it will have about 300,000,000,000,000 (300 trillion) cells. As you learned in the chapter on biology and behavior, billions of neurons are being formed during this period, at an average rate of 250,000 per minute. Cells that make up other organs and bodily systems are being produced at a similar rate.

Each chromosome pair is important for development, but there is one pair in particular that stands out—the 23rd pair. (Scientists have given numbers to the pairs so that their individual contributions can be discussed.) The 23rd pair is of special interest because it differs for males and females. Gender—that is, chromosomal gender—is determined by the combination of chromosomes in the 23rd pair. A female has two X chromosomes, a male has an X and a Y chromosome. Since a female always has two X's in the 23rd pair, the chromosome contributed by the father ultimately determines the sex of the child. Because the father has an X and a Y chromosome for the 23rd pair, he can contribute either an X or a Y. If he contributes an X chromosome, the child will be female. If he contributes a Y chromosome, the child will be male.

Dominant and Recessive Genes

As you have already seen, chromosomes are made up of genes. Genes are not all equal. Some are more powerful than others. This relative power has its effect when the genes of the mother combine with the genes of the father. Powerful genes are called **dominant genes.** Weaker genes are called **recessive genes.** Whenever a dominant gene is present, its message will control the appearance of a physical characteristic. This characteristic might be eye color or hair color or physical size. Consider the case of eye color. Look at Figure 10–2. There you see the transmission of eye color from parents to their offspring. Brown eye color is the result of the action of a dominant gene. As you can see, both parents have brown eyes because they both possess the dominant gene (B). Both parents also have a recessive or weaker blue eye gene (b). When the genetic material of the mother and father combines, there are four possible genetic combinations—BB, Bb, bB, and bb. In only one of those combinations—bb—will the resulting child have blue eyes. In the other three combinations, since at least one B is present, brown eyes will result. The actions of dominant and recessive genes account both for the similarity and the dissimilarity of brothers and sisters. Consider Figure 10–2 again. Assume that the four combinations of genes on the bottom row are actually four children of the same parents. Three of those children will share a family resemblance—brown eyes. That is attributable to the effect of the dominant gene B. One child has blue eyes. This is the result of the chance combination of the two recessive blue eye genes of the parents. So, in spite of the fact that each parent contributes a very complex and different genetic pattern to each child, the action of dominant and recessive genes can superimpose some regularity among the children.

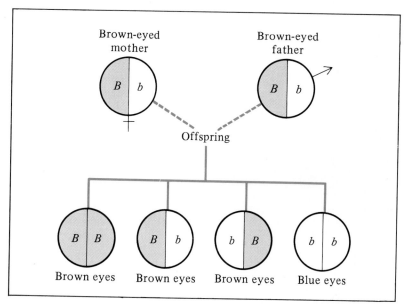

Brown-eyed mother

Brown-eyed father

Offspring

Brown eyes   Brown eyes   Brown eyes   Blue eyes

FIGURE 10-2
This diagram shows how eye color is transmitted from parents to their offspring. The gene for brown eyes is dominant, and is marked B; the gene for blue eyes is recessive, and is marked b. Since the parents here have both dominant and recessive genes, there are four possible genetic outcomes for their children: BB, Bb, bB, and bb. Only one combination (bb) results in blue eyes; the other three result in brown eyes.

Genotype and Phenotype

The discussion of dominant and recessive genes brings up a related topic—the relationship of physical characteristics to genetic characteristics. The outward or physical appearance of someone is called the **phenotype.** The genetic makeup of an individual is called the **genotype.** As you can see in Figure 10-2 above, there are four genotypes (BB, Bb, bB, and bb) but only two phenotypes (brown eyes and blue eyes). The phenotype is what you see when you look at someone. It is the hair color, eye color, and other distinguishing characteristics. At the level of genetic material, when you are looking at the outward appearance of someone, you are see-

ing only part of the story. What you actually see may come from several different combinations of genes. Any physical characteristic might have come from a combination of two dominant genes or one dominant and one recessive gene. You cannot tell from looking at the person exactly what his or her genetic blueprint is.

The example of eye color has greatly simplified the process of genetic inheritance. In fact, most characteristics that we observe in humans are combinations of many genes, not just two or three. It is this fact that, in part, accounts for the seemingly endless variety of appearance and behavior. People are not either tall or short—they vary in height. People are not either intelligent or unintelligent—they vary along an intelligence continuum. Modern psy-

---

Mitosis. The splitting of the 23 pairs of chromosomes in a human cell after conception.
Dominant genes. Genes that control the appearance of a physical characteristic.

Recessive genes. Weaker genes that only determine the appearance of a physical characteristic if the dominant gene is not present.
Phenotype. A person's outward or physical appearance.
Genotype. A person's genetic makeup.

chology has accepted the concept of **polygenic** (that is, many genes) **inheritance** in the discussion of phenotypic differences.

REVIEW QUESTIONS

1. The period from conception to birth is known as the _____ period; it usually lasts for _____ weeks.

2. Match the following terms with the correct definitions:
   ___ DNA   A. molecule that is linked together in chains
   ___ gene   B. every human has 23 pairs
   ___ chromosome   C. carries the blueprint for our physical characteristics

3. The _____ pair of chromosomes is important in that it determines gender. A female will have XY/XX chromosomes and a male will have XY/XX chromosomes.

4. It is the chromosome of the father/mother that determines the gender of the child.

5. When a dominant/recessive gene is present, its message will control the appearance of a physical characteristic, such as eye color.

6. The outward or physical appearance of someone is called their _____ ; the genetic makeup of someone is called their _____ .

Answers: 1. prenatal; 40 2. DNA, A; gene, C; chromosome, B 3. 23rd; XX; XY 4. father 5. dominant 6. phenotype; genotype

---

The Prenatal Environment

For a period of about 40 weeks after conception, the developing child is completely dependent on the mother's body for protection and growth. Within 2 weeks of conception, the fertilized egg, or **zygote,** implants itself in the wall of the mother's **uterus.** For the next 4 to 5 weeks (the period of the **embryo**),

major body systems begin to appear, such as the skin, the nervous system, respiratory system, and the limbs. The period of the **fetus** begins at 9 weeks and ends at about 40 weeks, when birth occurs. During this period, further development and refinement of each of the major systems occur. The critical period for survival of the baby is encountered at about 26 weeks. It is at this point that the respiratory system is developed to a point at which it can sustain a life outside of the mother's body. Babies born before this time seldom survive without elaborate medical support.

After the fertilized egg has implanted itself in the wall of the mother's uterus, a protective fluid called the **amniotic sac** is formed around the zygote. This sac acts like a shock absorber for the next 38 weeks. In addition to this sac, two other structures appear that aid in development. The **placenta** is formed on the wall of the uterus where the zygote is attached and quickly develops into a network of blood vessels and membranes that permit the baby to share the biological systems of the mother. The baby is attached to the placenta by the **umbilical cord.** The umbilical cord is actually a three-lane highway: Two lanes carry waste material back to the placenta to be expelled through the body of the mother, and one lane carries nutrients to the baby.

It is chiefly through this physical or symbiotic relationship to the mother that an unborn child becomes vulnerable to damaging effects from the outside world. Many changes in the mother's body chemistry, whether a result of nutrition, disease, drugs, or even prolonged stress, are carried to the fetus directly through the placenta. Of course, other factors can cause damage, such as a direct blow to the abdomen. Another potential danger is radiation. Radiation can pass through the protective amniotic fluid that surrounds the child and can cause **mutation**—spontaneous change in the genetic message of the chromosomes. Mutation usually results in a birth defect of some kind. Although mutations can happen on their own without any apparent external cause, the likelihood is greater if the developing child is exposed to radiation. Pregnant women are given X-ray examinations only when such techniques cannot be avoided (to identify a broken bone, for example). Nonetheless, the greatest potential threat to a child is from harmful substances in the blood of the mother. The mother passes the toxic effects of such things as alcohol, narcotics, medications, and a variety of other chemicals through the umbilical cord into the placenta.

A new field of study has grown up around the subject of abnormal prenatal development. This field is called **teratology**. One of the things we have learned from studies in this field is that the timing of attacks on the fetus seems to be critical in determining what the resulting effects will be (Moore, 1974). In Figure 10-3, you can get an idea of what effects are associated with particular developmental periods. As you learned in the chapter on biology, hundreds of thousands of cells are being formed (on the average) during every moment of development after conception. Certain cells with certain functions are being formed at one time and other cells with a different function at another time. This means that whenever a damaging agent is introduced into the bloodstream of the mother, it is likely to affect the particular cells that the child is forming at the time. As you can see from Figure 10-3, the central nervous system is vulnerable almost from the point of conception. On the other hand, the teeth, palate, and genital organs are not vulnerable until the beginning of the seventh week after conception.

A dramatic example of the effects of a damaging agent can be seen in cases of mothers who took the drug *thalidomide*. Thalidomide is a mild tranquilizer that was given to thousands of women in the 1950s to reduce the nausea and insomnia that occasionally accompanied pregnancy. The drug was widely prescribed in Europe but was used less frequently in the United States. Thalidomide had very specific effects, which depended on when during pregnancy it was taken (Saxon and Rapola, 1969). If the drug was taken in the sixth week after conception, the baby might be born without ears; if it was taken late in the sixth week or in the seventh week after conception, the baby might be born without arms. If the drug was taken in the eighth week after conception, there might be no damage to the child at all. It became clear that *when* the drug was taken was a crucial factor in determining its effects. As you can see, there appear to be certain **critical periods** in development. They are called critical because during the period in question, the presence of an external stimulus or event will have a different effect than if it were present at an earlier or later period of time.

As we saw in Figure 10-3, it is the period of the embryo (or the period from 3 to 8 weeks) that seems to be most critical for major problems. Problems appearing after that time seem to be more specific. This means that mothers must be particularly cautious during that period. Although thalidomide is no longer used, some other more common substances can be just as dangerous. These substances are alcohol and drugs.

Alcoholic mothers may give birth to children who are underweight, premature, and who suffer from various aspects of physical or mental retardation or both. This is known as the **fetal alcohol syndrome (FAS)**. It also often results in distinctive facial features in the child, including strangely proportioned features and eyes set wide apart (Jones, 1975). Abel (1981) reviewed research on FAS and concluded that a strong link exists between alcoholism in mothers and mental retardation in the children they bear, although there is still confusion about why some alcoholic mothers do not give birth to defective children. Many studies have concentrated on levels of alcohol consumption by prospective mothers, but the fact is that there is really no safe level of alcohol consumption during pregnancy. FAS

Polygenic inheritance. Inheritance of traits that depend on the interaction of many genes, not just one gene.

Zygote. A fertilized egg, created by the joining of sperm and egg.

Uterus. The womb of the mother, in which the child is carried for 9 months.

Embryo. Term for a developing child from the time the fertilized egg is implanted in the wall of the uterus until the beginning of the third month.

Fetus. Term for a developing child from 9 weeks until birth.

Amniotic sac. A protective fluid that surrounds the zygote and acts as a shock absorber until birth.

Placenta. Forms on the wall of the uterus and develops into a network of blood vessels and membranes that allow the baby to share the biological systems of the mother.

Umbilical cord. Link between the baby and the mother's placenta, through which nutrients are brought to the baby and waste material is removed.

Mutation. A spontaneous change in the genetic message of the chromosomes.

Teratology. The study of abnormal prenatal development.

Critical periods. Periods during which the presence of an external stimulus or event will have a different effect than if it were present at an earlier or later period of time.

Fetal Alcohol Syndrome (FAS). Causes child to be born underweight, premature, and physically and mentally retarded; a result of the mother drinking excessively during pregnancy.

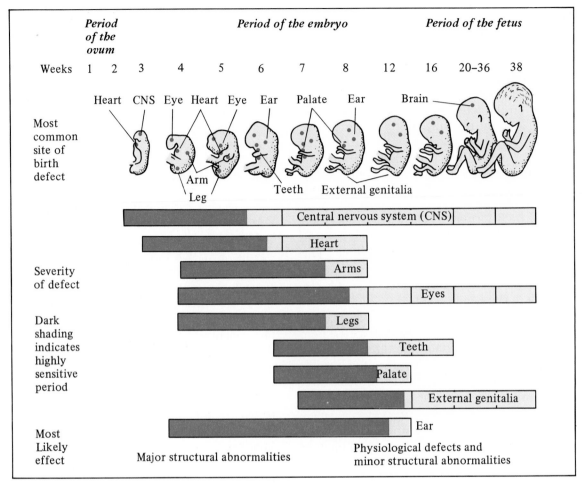

FIGURE 10-3
The timing of attacks on the fetus is critical in determining the developmental effects of such attacks. The central nervous system is vulnerable almost from the point of conception, but certain organs are not vulnerable until the seventh week.

is not an all-or-nothing type of event. More limited alcohol use by the mother is likely to have less dramatic effects on the prenatal development of the child; more intense use is likely to have more dramatic effects.

Drugs such as heroin can also have dramatic effects on the fetus. As the mother becomes addicted and develops a physical dependence on the drug, so does the child. This is because the child's developing neurotransmitter and circulatory systems are just as responsive as the mother's. If a child is born to a mother who is physically dependent on

a narcotic, the child will suffer immediate and life-threatening withdrawal symptoms. These babies are also usually underweight and commonly born with malformations of various types (Abel, 1981).

These various threats to normal development can be frightening. It might even sound as though giving birth to a normal child is unlikely. This is certainly not the case! The incidence of abnormal development is quite low. In one study of 50,000 pregnancies, Heinonen (1976) found structural abnormalities in only 6 percent of the children born. Nevertheless, these figures mean nothing if *your* child is one of the 6 percent. Some abnormalities of development can be avoided and some cannot. It is important to know what steps one can take to deal with the avoidable ones.

CHILDHOOD DEVELOPMENT

After a child is born, there are many different types of development going on at the same time. In order to make sense of all this change, we will consider development in several broad areas. These areas include sensory and perceptual development; physical and cognitive development; social-emotional development, moral development, and sex-role development. Furthermore, we will track this development over three time blocks—infancy (0–2 years), early childhood (2–5 years), and late childhood (5–12 years). Related treatments of these topics appear in the chapters on biology and behavior, sensation and perception, emotion and motivation, and language and cognition. This chapter will show you how these various activity patterns *change* over time.

Physical Development

At birth, the infant possesses a series of specific responses called **reflexes**, as well as certain muscles, certain skeletal characteristics (such as bones and cartilage), and a certain size (height and weight).

Changes in motor behavior result from a combination of muscular and skeletal development, learning, brain development, and changes in body proportions. For example, even if the baby had the muscles and bone structure needed to walk the day after birth, it would still be enormously difficult,—the baby's head is so large and heavy compared to the rest of its body that it would be falling over all of the time. The infant's center of gravity would be around its neck. In other words, the newborn's body proportions would not necessarily allow for that type

of locomotion. But as body proportions change and muscles develop, walking gradually becomes possible. The baby learns first to do push-ups to look around, then to raise itself to a sitting position, then to crawl, and finally to walk.

Inborn reflexes are very important for a number of reasons. Reflexes do not involve cognition and do not require an elaborate mechanism such as the cerebral cortex in order to happen. As you learned in the chapter on biology, reflexes are automatic adjustments that the nervous system makes to outside stimulation. For example, the knee-jerk reflex is a very specific spinal cord reflex. At birth, infants have a full range of reflexes that can act as adaptive mechanisms until the cortex develops to the point where complex voluntary actions become possible. When you get something stuck in your throat, you often voluntarily try to cough to dislodge it. Although voluntary coughing may not seem like a complex action, it is. It involves the cortex, as does any voluntary action. The infant is born with a cough and a sneeze reflex intact. This enables the baby to clear the respiratory passages of annoyances without involving the cortex.

In the same way, the **rooting reflex** results in a baby turning its head toward anything that touches its cheek. This is very functional in the first few months of life. It has the immediate result of positioning the baby's mouth near the nipple of a bottle or breast. Other reflexes include the **sucking reflex** (which results in sucking when the baby's lips are touched), the **grasp reflex** (which causes the baby's fingers to close around an object that touches a palm), and the **Moro** or **startle reflex** (which causes a brief motor action or jerk of the arms and legs when a sudden noise is heard or when there is a sudden loss of support). Most of these inborn reflexes gradually disappear after the first few months of life. In fact, their disappearance is used as an indication of normal nervous system development. If certain reflexes do not disappear, this is an indication of a neurological problem. As an example, the Moro reflex should disappear by about 5 months of age if development is normal. Because voluntary con-

---

Reflexes. Automatic, uncontrolled muscle responses.
Rooting reflex. Causes baby to turn its head toward anything that touches its cheek.
Sucking reflex. Causes baby to suck when its lips are touched.

Grasp reflex. Causes baby's fingers to close around anything that touches its palm.
Moro (startle) reflex. Causes baby to jerk arms and legs when startled.

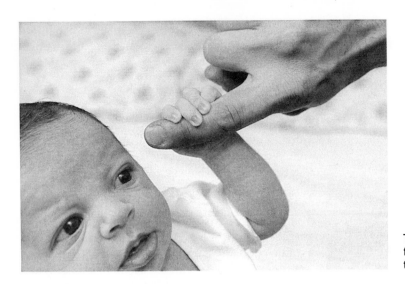

The grasp reflex causes the baby's fingers to close around an object that touches a palm.

trol begins to appear for many environmental reactions, the reflexes are no longer as important as they were at birth. Of course some reflexes, like the knee-jerk reflex, stay with us throughout life.

A concept that is traditional in the discussion of the physical and motor development of children is **maturation**. This concept refers to the almost automatic changes that occur in both the size and shape of the developing child and in the various physical capacities of that child. In some respects, this change is so regular that parents can be advised to look for certain milestones that signal this maturational sequence. The most obvious of these milestones are those relating to the child's ability to move from one place to another. Consider the sequence of activities that are illustrated in Figure 10-4. Although not every child reaches each milestone at the same time, there is a great deal of regularity, nevertheless.

The major physical accomplishments of the infant stage are lifting the head, rolling over, sitting, standing with support, crawling, standing alone, and walking. This sequence is controlled by simple maturation and physical development and is universally recognized in children regardless of environment. What is not universal is the *rate of progress* through the sequence. In addition, there is some variation in *when* these behaviors appear in different cultures (Elkind and Weiner, 1978), for they appear early in some cultures and late in others. This seems to imply that *when* particular levels of proficiency

appear in a behavior pattern is not just a matter of heredity. Environment makes a difference too.

As the infant enters the preschool years, gross motor skills involving the use of arms and legs and whole bodies improve substantially, but finer skills—finger dexterity and carefully coordinated eye-hand movements—are still poor. Children of this age much prefer less skilled games such as tag than those involving small, fine movements. By the end of this period (at about 5 years of age), it is usually clear whether the child will be left- or right-handed. There are no clear implications to be drawn from handedness other than that it should be allowed to develop naturally because it is likely to be part of a genetic code (Fincher, 1977). Toilet training can be successfully accomplished during this period because the child is able to communicate to the parent when the need arises to use a toilet. In addition, the child is now able to control the muscles of the bowel and bladder and to remove clothing when necessary. Toilet training should not begin until enough of these muscle and communication systems have developed adequately.

During the early school years, gross movement patterns become quite well controlled. This allows the child to experience success in many common sports that involve running, jumping, and throwing.

Maturation. Regular changes in the process of physical and motor development; also the concept that developments in behavior are made possible solely on the basis of physical growth.

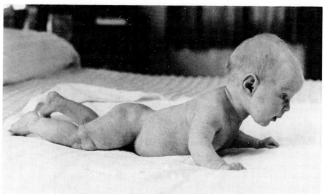

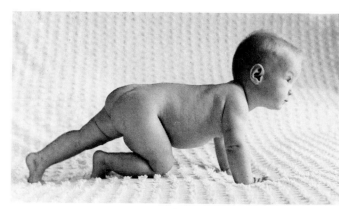

FIGURE 10-4
The normal sequence of motor development. Newborn babies are only capable of inborn reflex movements. At about 1 month infants begin to lift their shoulders. They start to crawl at about 4 to 6 months. By 9 months they are able to sit up by themselves. At about 10 months babies can stand upright, and at about 13 months they begin to walk.

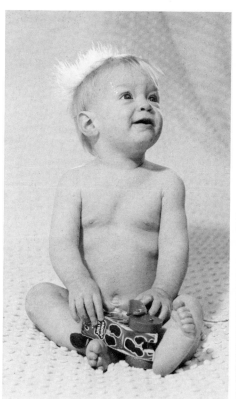

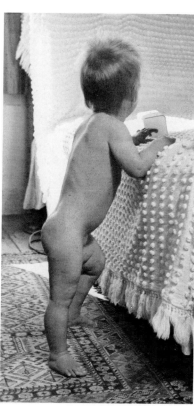

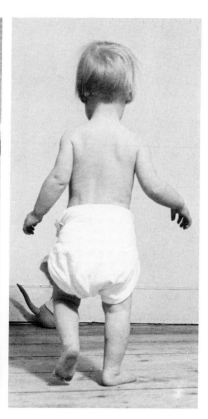

Much of this skill is a result of improved eye-hand and eye-foot coordination. Moreover, practice at tasks such as writing, sewing, and drawing helps to improve fine motor skills and eye-hand dexterity. Minor differences exist between boys and girls at this age in terms of skill levels. Boys seem to have greater forearm strength and girls seem to have greater flexibility, but for the most part the two sexes are equal (Elkind and Weiner, 1978).

REVIEW QUESTIONS

7. Match the following terms with the correct definition:

___ zygote	A. developing child from third month until birth
___ embryo	B. a fertilized egg
___ fetus	C. where the child develops for 9 months
___ uterus	D. delivers nutrients from the mother and removes waste from the child
___ placenta	E. developing child from 2 weeks to beginning of third month
___ umbilical cord	F. network of membranes and blood vessels between mother and child

8. If radiation passes through the fluid surrounding the child in the womb, it can cause _____, or a spontaneous change in the genetic message of the chromosomes. This usually results in a birth defect of some kind.

9. A new field of study of abnormal prenatal development, called _____, has emphasized that the timing of attacks on the fetus seems to be critical in determining what the resulting effects will be.

10. Babies are born with certain reflexes that disappear after a few months. One of the most functional is the _____ reflex, which causes the baby to turn its head toward anything that touches its cheek, thus positioning its mouth near the nipple of a bottle or breast.

Answers: 7. zygote, B; embryo, E; fetus, A; uterus, C; placenta, F; umbilical cord, D. 8. mutation 9. teratology 10. rooting

Sensory and Perceptual Development

The newborn's hearing is better than its vision. It seems to be able to distinguish between particular sounds quite well (Eimas, 1975). Mills and Milhuish (1974) were able to show that infants only 20 days old could tell the difference between their own mother's voices and the voice of a stranger.

By the time the child enters the preschool years (2–5), the senses are already well developed. Changes that occur now are in the perceptual rather than sensory area. This is particularly true of attention. The child now begins to show more purpose in examining the environment, and perception is dominated less by the obvious features of a stimulus than it is for an infant. For example, place a small, attractive toy in each hand of a 12-month-old infant. Then offer a third, equally attractive, toy. One of the original two toys will be dropped in favor of the new toy. The 3-year-old is not so easily seduced. The older child will either compare the toys in the hand to the toy being offered or, more likely, will tuck one of the original toys safely under an arm and reach for the third.

Perceptual development becomes more rapid during the school years (5–12). In part, this is due to learning and greater exposure to environmental objects. This makes sense. We know that perception depends heavily on learned cues. For example, the school-age child can identify an entire picture when only certain parts are visible—something a younger child cannot do. The school-age child uses scanning and search patterns different from those of the 3- or 4-year-old when visually inspecting an object (Zaporozhets, 1965). There is less variability and more structure to the scanning patterns of the older child. These patterns are better adjusted to get the information needed for current purposes out of the stimulus available.

Many of these developments in sensory/perceptual mechanisms can have a significant effect on the child's ability to succeed in school-related tasks. The most obvious of these tasks is reading. Reading is a very complex activity involving vision, hearing, memory, perceptual mechanisms, and environmental exposure. Stimulation from the environment seems to play a substantial role on the development of perceptual mechanisms that are present at this point. Because parents have some degree of control over the child's environment at this age, it is possible to provide experiences that may contribute to the development of efficient perceptual mechanisms for reading.

Cognitive Development

We have already considered some aspects of cognitive activity in earlier chapters. Cognitive operations involve complicated abstract operations such as concept formation, reasoning, and association. Children are not born with these capabilities. Cognitive development, like perceptual and physical development, occurs over time, not all at once.

The most popular view of cognitive development is that proposed by the late Swiss psychologist Jean Piaget. He suggested that the main task of every human was to make sense of the world. For Piaget, making sense involved two different operations—*organization* and *adaptation*. The child has certain information about the world, and this information must be organized. It is sorted and grouped according to certain principles. Organization makes it easier to use the information efficiently. Adaptation is a general term for the process by which the child deals with new information. It actually consists of two separate cognitive operations—assimilation and accommodative operations. **Assimilation** is a matter of putting new information into an existing view that the child has of the world. For example, a young child may have had a pleasant experience playing with a kitten. As a result, the next time the youngster sees a kitten, the child reaches out to stroke it. When the kitten scratches the child's finger, it comes as quite a surprise. The information presented by the presence of the kitten had been assimilated into an existing view of kittens. The scratch changed that. Now the child needs to develop a slightly altered view of the world—there are nice kittens and there are nasty kittens. A new category called *nasty kittens* has been formed. **Accommodation** is a matter of creating new categories or altering an existing view of the world. These principles of cognition—assimilation, accommodation,

and organization—are *how* an individual comes to know his or her environment.

In Piaget's view of cognitive development, there are a series of stages through which children pass. Responding to the environment is quite important to this progression. Each of Piaget's stages represents a cognitive scheme or network that the child uses to account for happenings in the outside world. How elaborate or rich those schemes are will depend on how complicated the outside world is. If the world presented to the child is slow and simple and uncomplicated, then the corresponding schemes will be sparse and simple. If the outside world is complicated and filled with objects and relationships, then the mental world of the child will require more complicated schemes as well. Piaget's theory says that the developing child is always reaching for a state of **equilibrium**, or balance, so that the inside schemes match the outside facts. This balance is accomplished through assimilation and accommodation. The mismatch of internal schemes with outside facts spurs or motivates cognitive growth. If the child is presented with many new stimuli that do not fit easily into some existing concepts or categories, new categories will be formed. The greater the stimulation from the environment, the more extensive the development of the child's cognitive framework.

From Piaget's perspective, the child begins with unconnected bits and pieces of information from the outside world. Gradually, these bits and pieces become connected and form larger chunks of information. These larger chunks take on a meaning broader than any single element in them. As you learned in the last chapter, another word for this larger category is a *concept*. Concepts then become connected to form networks of associated information. These networks, or schemes, are then used to sort future information.

Assimilation, accommodation, and organization are processes that are assumed to be present and operating throughout the entire life of an individual. Piaget proposed that the information these

---

Assimilation. A cognitive activity discussed by Piaget; consists of putting new information into already existing mental categories.

Accommodation. A cognitive activity discussed by Piaget; con-

sists of creating new mental categories for new information that will not fit into existing categories.

Equilibrium. A term used by Piaget to refer to a kind of mental balance in which a child's inner schemes or categories match outside facts.

processes work on changes during the course of human development. He maintained that a child is capable of understanding at successively more abstract levels as the child grows. These levels were thought to be tied roughly to chronological age. Thus, we have the characteristics of a stage theory of development, which in this case is a theory of cognitive development.

After observing and carrying out experiments with children for many years, Piaget proposed that there were four stages that could be used to describe cognitive development. The first stage is called the **sensorimotor stage**, and it lasts from birth to 2 years of age. Early in this period, the child uses the reflexes it was born with to categorize objects and events in the outside world. Later in this period, the child will use voluntary movements to gather and store useful information about the environment. As the term sensorimotor implies, the child uses motor responses to explore and create sensory experiences. The child sucks, bangs, babbles, listens, looks, and feels. To some observers, these might appear as random and uncontrolled movements. To Piaget, these movements represent the first attempts of the organism to learn about and gain control over the environment.

One of the most important accomplishments of the sensorimotor stage is the development of **object permanence**—the realization that objects in the real world have a permanent existence. Just because an object is out of sight does not mean that it has ceased to exist. This concept develops over the course of the sensorimotor period. There seems to be no object permanence before about 4 months of age. If you place a toy in front of a 3-month-old, the child will play with it. If you then put a screen in front of the toy, the child will act as if the toy never existed. Gradually the child develops an awareness

The sensorimotor stage lasts from birth to 2 years of age. Later in this stage, the child will use motor responses to gather and create sensory experiences.

FIGURE 10-5
In the conservation task, children are asked to judge whether or not the amount of something changes when the shape of the container changes. To test this, water is poured from a short wide glass into a tall narrow glass, and the child is asked if the amount of water is the same as it was before.

of where objects go that are taken out of the line of vision. Between 4 to 8 months of age, the child may visually search for the object that has "disappeared." Between 8 and 12 months, the child will physically search for the object. In our example, the child might knock down or reach behind the screen to retrieve the toy. By 24 months, the concept of object permanence is well developed. The child might search a number of locations where an object had previously been in an attempt to find it. It is obvious that the child knows the object exists *somewhere*, even though it is not in sight.

Piaget's second stage is called the **preoperational stage** and lasts from age 2 years to 7 years. In this stage, the child rises above simple sensory ex-

periences. Because the child has become capable of using symbols, language communication is possible. Words can be used as symbolic representations of objects and events. Children in the preoperational stage tend to be egocentric. They cannot distinguish between themselves and the outside world and have a difficult time putting themselves in the place of others. For example, a child might say, "Mommy, I'm so sorry for baby horses—they cannot pick their noses" (Chukovsky, 1968).

The term *preoperational* derives from the fact that the child at this stage does not seem capable of certain logical operations. A common example of this problem is seen in a task known as **conservation**. Consider the two beakers in Figure 10–5. Both are

---

Sensorimotor stage. First stage of Piaget's theory of cognitive development; lasts from birth to 2 years. Child uses motor responses to explore and create sensory experiences.

Object permanence. Realization that occurs during sensorimotor stage—child learns that an object still exists even if it is hidden from sight temporarily.

Preoperational stage. Second stage of Piaget's theory of cognitive development; lasts from age 2 to age 7. Child can use symbols (words) to represent objects, but is not yet able to perform certain logical operations, such as conservation.

Conservation. Child's ability to realize that the amount of something is not changed by pouring it into glasses of different shapes; test devised by Piaget.

full and both contain the same amount of water. The child in the preoperational stage would say that the tall beaker had more water in it than the short beaker. In fact, even if the child were to watch you pour water from the short beaker into the tall beaker, the judgment would be the same in spite of the fact that the child has seen the water transferred. Conservation-type problems can often create problems for both adults and children. In the box below, consider the difficulties that the waitress has as a result of her belief that the two cups hold identical amounts of liquid.

There are other noticeable cognitive characteristics of the preoperational child. For example, the child tends to think that many more things are alive than would an older child or adult. It is common for the child to carry on a conversation with a stuffed animal. The preoperational child has diffi-

culty forming concepts to represent complex events such as death and divorce. Further, because the child is egocentric, there is a tendency to blame oneself for the event.

In the stage of **concrete operations** (age 7 to 11 years), the child is able to perform many of the reasoning tasks that were not possible in the preoperational stage. Conservation is no longer a problem, and the child correctly concludes that when the water is poured from one beaker to another, the amount of water remains the same. Children in this stage are also capable of **seriation**, or the ordered arrangement of objects. They can be given a large number of objects, for example, pencils of different lengths, and can perfectly arrange the pencils according to length after simply looking at the entire collection. The preoperational child is more likely to use a trial-and-error method and to

---

AN ADULT CONSERVATION TASK

I'm a man of bad habits, one of which is reading the newspaper while eating. Since I don't have time for either activity, each one provides a good excuse for the other. The result is that I eat too much, and probably read too much, with the deep pollution of mind and body that those excesses cause.

The other day, spreading my newspaper across the empty counter at the local Drug Fair, I asked the waitress for a cup of coffee. Large, I specified. The company had recently supplied cups that were larger than the old ones but kept the price of a cup the same. I like coffee (another bad habit) and had learned to ask for the larger cup: otherwise, I'd be given the smaller one, which was in greater supply.

The waitress, who was not the usual one serving my favorite counter bay, said that there was no point specifying the larger cup. "They're both the same," she said. "They hold the same amount of coffee." She seemed annoyed; other customers, too, had been rejecting her small coffee cups.

Now, I respect experts, and that waitress was certainly an expert in coffee and cups. And I remember how many times I've been fooled by optical illusions. So, responsible scientist that I am, I proposed a test.

"Could you fill the large cup with water?" I asked the waitress.

She complied but filled it only three-quarters full. I poured the water into a small cup, quickly filling it to the brim. I tipped the large cup to show her the water remaining at its bottom. She made no effort to look.

"They're not the same," I said triumphantly.

"They are to me," she replied.

Stubborn man that I am (another bad habit), I proceeded to pour the rest of the large cup's water into the already full small cup, flooding her counter and my newspaper.

"What are you doing?"

"Nothing."

"What do you mean, nothing? You're pouring water all over the place!"

"No I'm not," I said, continuing to pour. "There's no water coming out. It all went into the small cup. Unless you're wrong; unless the two cups aren't the same."

"They are to me," she said, glowering, as she wiped up the spill and reality with it.

(Source: *Thoughts Over Coffee,* by Walter Reich, originally published in *The New York Times.* Reprinted by permission.)

try different arrangements until the pencils are finally ordered correctly.

The major limitation of the child in this stage is dealing with abstract relationships. Appropriately, the label for this stage is *concrete operational—concrete* means "here and now." The child deals with what is reality, with what is immediately present and not mere possibility (Inhelder and Piaget, 1958). A good example of this limitation is the child's approach to a balance problem. It is interesting to watch young children try to solve the problem of balancing a seesaw with children of different weight on each end. Younger children often give up after trying things like pushing harder or gripping the bar more intensely. Older concrete-operational children may realize that more or less weight is needed and may choose a different partner or ask someone to add their weight to one end of the seesaw. The child in the *formal operational* stage might easily realize that it is simply a matter of moving the heavier person closer to the center of the seesaw.

The **formal operations stage** begins at age 11 years and continues through adulthood. Much of what we examined in Chapter 9 was formal-operational thought. Formal operational thought is abstract reasoning. It is the capacity to form hypotheses to deal with future events—to generate theories of why certain events occur. Because this stage brings us into adolescence, we will postpone a discussion of cognitive development in this stage until the next chapter.

An Evaluation of Piaget's Theory. Strictly speaking, most of what has been described here does not represent a theory. More accurately, it is a description and listing of the observable capacities and activities of the developing child. Piaget's *theory* is that these stages are ordered in the same way for every child, that the successful completion of one stage prepares the child for the successful completion of the next stage, and that learning and adaptation are predominantly biological rather than environmen-

tal realities. The most serious criticism of Piaget's approach is that he has underestimated the influence of environment on cognitive development (Bruner, 1973). The demands of the environment may influence cognitive development in ways not accounted for by Piaget. In some respects it might be better to see Piaget's theory as a model or ideal, rather than a real, picture of cognitive development. It should also be evaluated in terms of its usefulness. There is no disagreement here. Piaget's propositions and observations have been enormously valuable in understanding the development of cognitive operations in children.

Other Cognitive Variables in Development. Piaget's theory is a very popular and useful approach to the subject of cognitive development. Nevertheless, there are some other variables that we might also label *cognitive* that can be considered separately in a chapter on human development. One of these variables is *memory*. Experiments with newborn infants have demonstrated that they do have a memory and that the memory is related to action. For example, babies will often begin to make sucking movements when they see a bottle being taken out of the refrigerator. This demonstrates a functioning memory with a connected response system.

As the child enters the preschool period, recognition memory becomes quite good, although problems with recall memory still persist. The child between 2 years and 5 years of age makes little use of strategies for remembering things. As the child progresses through the age range from 5 years to 12 years, the use of deliberate strategies to remember things appears. An interesting sidelight to the issue of memory is something called **metamemory**. Metamemory is the awareness a person has of the process of committing information to memory. For example, when you sit down to review this chapter at exam time, you will be conscious of trying to remember it in preparation for a test. You will also

---

Concrete operations stage. Third stage of Piaget's theory of cognitive development; lasts from age 7 to age 11. Child is able to perform many more reasoning tasks and deal with more than one dimension at a time but cannot yet deal with abstract relationships.

Seriation. The ordered arrangement of objects.
Formal operations stage. Final stage of Piaget's theory of cognitive development; lasts from age 11 on. Person's ability to deal with abstracts, to hypothesize.
Metamemory. The awareness a person has of the process of memorizing.

have some idea of when you have reviewed sufficiently. This appreciation for the memory process develops in the period from age 5 years to 12 years. Flavell and Wellman (1976) showed that younger children (in kindergarten and first grade) could not realistically assess when they had memorized some information. Children in higher grades could make these assessments. The development of metamemory has important implications for all cognitive operations that involve memory. The absence of metamemory represents an obstacle to complicated cognitive operations in young children because they seldom know when they have actually committed an important piece of information to memory. In addition to the development of memory, a major cognitive accomplishment for the developing child is language development. The details of that development were presented in the chapter on language.

Social Behavior

Most parents think of a baby's smile as a social action—an attempt to communicate happiness to another person. Crying, too, is often interpreted socially—the baby cries in order to get the parent or caregiver to do something. More objectively, smiling has been interpreted as simply an imitation of what the baby sees the parent doing. In fact, some studies have shown that infants can imitate facial expressions quite well (Meltzoff and Moore, 1977). But smiling must be more than simple imitation because blind babies also smile (Bower, 1977). A reasonable guess as to how and why smiling develops in children as a social tool is that it begins as a reflex but its development and refinement is aided by social stimulation. This could be just as true of the blind child as the sighted child, because parents are just as likely to respond to the smile of a blind child.

The best term to describe this interaction between an infant and those who care for it is **attachment**. Babies become attached to parents or other primary caregivers. Caregivers, in turn, become attached to those who depend on them. Ainsworth (1973) defines attachment as an emotional tie between one person and another that endures regardless of the passage of time or physical distance between the two parties. The bond between a parent and a child, or between marriage partners, siblings, or even close friends, is a unique type of social connection. In the case of the newborn in-

fant, who is totally dependent on others, this attachment is critical. It forms very early in life and seems to be the basis for certain motivated behavior. For example, a child will cling to the mother and resist being taken out of the arms of the mother, particularly by a stranger. Attachment seems to play a very important role in activity patterns of the child. In the presence of the mother, the child will explore an environment freely (Ainsworth, 1974). Srouge (1978) has suggested that when a solid attachment develops between the young child and the mother, the child is likely to mature more rapidly and explore more fully. There are similar motivational effects on parents. They are more concerned with the well-being of their own children than of other children. They will gladly sacrifice personal comfort for the comfort of their children. It is clear that both parties receive emotional satisfaction from this type of attachment.

In the infant, attachment forms early and remains a strong force until midway through the second year. By the time a child is 24 months, the emotional aspects of the bond have weakened somewhat. When the mother leaves a 2-year-old, the distress shown by the child is usually mild (Serifica, 1978). In contrast, if the mother leaves a 12-month-old child, the youngster may cry uncontrollably. Similar attachments form between father and child (Kotelchuck and others, 1975), although the kinds of interactions between father and child may differ from those between mother and child. One study (Clarke-Stewart, 1978) found that children responded more actively to play activities with the father than with the mother. This suggests that play is a more familiar pattern of interaction with fathers. As Berger (1980) points out, the implications of the attachment studies are clear. The period between 9 months and 18 months is not conducive to separation of child from parent. This means that special care should be taken in the choice and introduction of babysitters and day-care centers. Everything should be done to make the transition as painless as possible. The strength of attachment during this period of 9 to 18 months may also account for what has been called "stranger anxiety." Many parents have noted that their children become anxious and may cry and act fearful when a stranger approaches. It may be that the child is anticipating separation from the mother and reacting in advance. As you have seen in other examples, the child is quite capable of developing learned responses, even at this early age.

The majority of attachment studies have been observational—that is, children being watched in their environment by trained observers. A series of laboratory experiments conducted by Harlow examined the consequences of attachment relationships (or the prevention of such attachments) in monkeys. Harlow took newborn monkeys from their mothers and raised them in several different situations. Some monkeys were raised in isolation whereas others were raised with other infant monkeys. Some monkeys were provided with terry-cloth "mothers" they could cling to and others with wire "mothers" (see Figure 10–6). The results of these studies reveal a number of important things about attachment and parenting. Even though the infant monkeys were adequately fed, some of them raised in isolation died. In addition, those that survived were abnormal—they were antisocial and withdrawn and unable to relate with other monkeys later on. The monkeys raised by terry-cloth mothers were also negatively affected. They grew up to be maladjusted monkeys. In some cases, female monkeys raised on terry-cloth mothers were unable to show care to their own infants later on. They

Infants between the ages of 9 months and 18 months are strongly attached to their parents. They will become anxious and may cry when approached by others, particularly by a stranger.

Attachment. Emotional tie or bond between one person and another that endures over time and in spite of physical separation. Usually forms between baby and parents or caregiver.

DAY-CARE CENTERS

In the past few years a vigorous debate has been waged about the effects of day care on the development of children. The day-care advocates say that there are no harmful effects of good day care and that often the social benefits to the developing child are greater than he or she might experience at home. The opponents of day care contend that the separation of a child from its mother at early developmental periods can be damaging to a child's social, cognitive, and emotional development. Given the seriousness of the issue, there has been a good deal of recent research on the topic. This research has been summarized in several sources (Kaplan, 1986; Liebert, Wickes-Nelson, and Kail, 1986). Kagan, Kearsley, and Zelazo (1980) compared infants from ages 3 months to 30 months who attended day-care centers with infants of the same ages who did not attend day-care centers. The results showed no substantial differences between the two groups of infants on measures of cognitive or language development. Further, the day-care children maintained strong relationships to their mothers and clearly preferred their mothers to other adults. Similar results have been reported by several other research groups as well (Watkins and Bradbard, 1984; Clarke-Stewart and Fein, 1983; Belsky and Steinberg, 1978).

This is not to say that all day-care programs are of equal quality. Most of the research has probably been carried out in good day-care centers rather than poor ones. As Kaplan (1986) points out, good day-care centers are often more expensive than poor ones so there is a preselection of the subjects in these studies as well—they tend to come from more advantaged families. Although we cannot draw any general conclusions about day care, we can say that there is little data to suggest that good day-care centers do substantial harm, particularly when the parent-child relationship at home is good.

FIGURE 10–6
Harlow found that a monkey separated from its mother at birth would attach itself to a terrycloth "mother" over a bare wire mother. However, even those monkeys "raised" by the terrycloth mother showed problems of adjustment later on.

refused to nurse their offspring and sometimes even neglected them. It thus appears that contact between mother and child is important in and of itself, not just for the purpose of getting food (Harlow and Harlow, 1962). It also suggests that learning behaviors from one's own species is a necessary part of social development. In addition to the isolation of child from mother, Harlow also suggested that isolation from peers can be damaging. Some research (Novak and Harlow, 1975) seems to indicate that the damage can be corrected with later exposure to peers. Nevertheless, early social support and affection seem important for later adjustment.

Bonding

Bonding is a relatively recent concept that has become associated with the process of attachment.

It has been proposed (Klaus and Kennell, 1976) that the period immediately following birth is critical for later cognitive and emotional development in the child. This period is believed to last anywhere from minutes to hours, but it is thought that a child who does not have immediate and extensive contact with the mother and father will not experience optimal development later on. These propositions were based on both human and animal data.

A social side effect of the bonding discussion has been an emphasis on encouraging fathers to be in the delivery rooms, allowing mothers a greater role in planning the delivery process, and closer contact of mother, father, and infant in the minutes immediately following delivery. In support of bonding, there is a strong argument that this change in the delivery process (what Lamb and Hwang, 1982, refer to as the "humanizing" of delivery) has been a decidedly positive one. Nevertheless, data provide little support for the process of bonding. Lamb and Hwang (1982) published a review of bonding studies and concluded that there was no evidence for the existence of any such effect. Further, they criticized the bonding advocates for inappropriately applying the results of specialized animal studies to human behavior.

Prosocial and Antisocial Behavior in Children

As the child encounters peers in preschool and school settings and develops a greater capacity to speak and act, we see the emergence of prosocial and antisocial behavior. **Prosocial behavior** can be defined as actions performed to benefit someone else without any reward expected for performing the action. This type of behavior begins to appear at age 6 or 7 years. By this time, the child has become less egocentric and more aware of other children. Other children make for powerful models. Being of the same relative size and appearance, the child finds it easy to copy other children's behaviors in dealing with new situations. Moreover, at school there are adult models in addition to their parents to observe in imitating behavior patterns. But this simply means that the child *can* perform prosocial acts, not that these acts *will* be performed. It seems as if prosocial behaviors are heavily influenced by environmental variables. In the chapter on motivation and emotion, striking examples are presented that indicate that positive events in the environment encourage prosocial behavior. It may be that examples of prosocial behavior in school-age children are more the result of these favorable environmental events than of physiological or psychological maturation.

The opposite type of social behavior—**antisocial behavior**—also begins to emerge after the age of 5 years. Most often this behavior is learned from others and takes the form of aggression. Bandura and Walters (1959) conducted a series of studies that showed dramatically how aggressive behavior patterns are picked up by children. The top row of

Figure 10-7 contains a series of pictures showing an adult "beating up" a rubber toy. Below that is another series of pictures showing the behavior of children who watched the adult's behavior on film. They learned quickly and accurately how to behave like adults. As a result of this research by Bandura, it became clear that models exert a strong influence on children's behavior. Once again, we are left with the conclusion that learning plays a major role in social behavior. Furthermore, this type of evidence also argues for a broader cognitive view of learning rather than a simple response/reinforcement approach. Observational learning plays a large role in the developing social patterns of the child.

This leads to the consideration of a concern of many parents and educators. Can the social behavior of children be influenced by models they observe on television? Can watching violence on TV and in the movies lead to aggressive behavior in children?

Psychologists do not fully understand the effects of TV viewing on children. A good deal of research supports the view that television has a negative impact on children's behavior (Leifer and Roberts, 1972; Friedrich and Stein, 1973; NIMH, 1982). However, this same research also supports the idea that television can have a positive influence by teaching prosocial behavior (Stein and Friedrich, 1975). The point is that parents should be aware of the powerful influence that television can have on the social development of their children. Parents can then act on the basis of their awareness in deciding what TV shows their children should watch.

Erikson's Theory of Psychosocial Development

One of the best known and most comprehensive theories that attempts to explain how social behavior develops has been proposed by Erik Erikson (1963). Erikson considered life to be segmented into a series of crises that the individual has to resolve. These crises are thought to appear during particular

---

Bonding. Term used to refer to the attachment formed in the period immediately following birth; depends upon immediate and extensive contact between child and mother and father.

Prosocial behavior. Actions done to benefit others or society in general.

Antisocial behavior. Actions intended to harm another person or society in general.

FIGURE 10-7
These photos were taken during a study of how children pick up aggressive behavior patterns. In the top row, children watched an adult beat up a rubber toy (called a Bobo doll). The photos in the two rows below show the behavior of the children when they were later allowed to play with the toy.

developmental periods, making Erikson's theory, like Piaget's, a stage theory. Erikson proposed eight stages, ranging from shortly after birth to old age. The first four of these stages are relevant for our discussion of childhood development. The last four stages will be discussed in the next chapter. The relevant stages and their descriptions are as follows:

Trust vs. Distrust (Year 1). The basic crisis the child must resolve is developing some form of trust of people and the world. Birth is a shock. The child comes from the warmth and security of the womb to a more disturbing environment. Erikson assumes that this change fosters distrust in the newborn. The child must learn to trust as a result of interactions with the mother. Trust is built as the parents regularly satisfy the comfort needs of the child as well as talk to, caress, and smile at the child. It is the regularity or predictability of these caregiving activities that is critical. If the interactions are minimal or deficient, it is assumed that trust does not develop normally.

Autonomy vs. Shame and Doubt (Year 2). The crisis here is to assert some independence. The child has been dependent only on adults so far for survival, particularly the parents. In this stage, the child must learn to be autonomous and self-directing. The caregivers can help in resolving this crisis by providing opportunities and support for competent behavior. These opportunities might involve toilet behavior, eating, or language usage. As an example, parents who act disgusted when their children soil their diapers or pants are likely to suppress in their children feelings of independence and to create a sense of shame in their children. The same result might occur from excessive concern over how children should act at mealtime. On the other hand, a supportive atmosphere in which children are praised for success in toilet training or eating activities and consoled when minor failures or setbacks occur will lead to independence.

Initiative vs. Guilt (Years 3–5). The crisis in this stage involves more complex activities. Children

WHY CHILDREN TALK TO THEMSELVES

If you've been around young children, you've probably heard them talking aloud to themselves. You may even have noticed some variation in these utterances, depending on the child's age and on what he or she happened to be doing at the time. For example, 3-year-old Billy wanders around the preschool classroom repeating two or three words over and over to himself. His sing-song sounds a little like a chant. Carla, a first-grader, talks to no one in particular while she works on a drawing: "I think I'll draw a house. I think I'll draw my house. I think I'll draw the house next to ours, too." Joey, a third grader, talks so quietly to himself that he can barely be heard. But his lips and mouth are moving, and he is counting to himself as he works out the solution to a math problem. These are just a few examples of what psychologists call childrens' "private speech." It is believed to be a large part of the language used by preschool and elementary school children (Berk, 1986).

Some very prominent psychologists have been fascinated by this behavior and have offered different explanations. Piaget thought that it was egocentric behavior and that it served no social purpose. Vygotsky, a Russian psychologist, disagreed. He considered talking aloud an important form of social communication that children need to gain control over their behavior. Some very recent studies have tended to support this view.

Berk (1986) conducted a series of observations of 75 first and third graders while they worked alone at math problems without any teacher assistance. She found that the children's use of private speech was extremely high and that it was related to their success at solving the math problems. She also observed a pattern of moving from audible speech in the first grade to completely internalized speech by later in the third grade.

Thus it may be that private speech is a means by which children organize, understand, and exercise control over their behavior. As such, it may also be an important aid in childhood learning. Psychologists have noted that children who talk problems over with themselves appear generally attentive and task-oriented. They also tend to use other problem-solving behaviors as well, such as using a pencil to read a line or nearby objects to count with.

These findings suggest that some children may need learning environments in which they can talk aloud more freely. Providing a classroom study corner where this can happen is one possibility. Encouraging more play experiences is another. The give-and-take that occurs as children play together seems to help children develop their language and problem-solving abilities.

make occasional mistakes in assessing their competencies, and failures result. Parents can help resolve this crisis by encouraging initiative on the part of the child. Parental punishment for initiative is thought to lead to guilt. For example, the 5-year-old decides to make breakfast for Mom and Dad. Breakfast consists of pieces of chocolate candy and some orange juice. On the way up the stairs, a glass of juice gets spilled. The parents can react either by telling the child that he or she is too young to carry glasses on a tray, or by thanking the child for the thoughtfulness and giving some tips about how to carry glasses filled with liquid.

Industry vs. Inferiority (*Years 6 through puberty*). In this stage, children attempt to develop competencies outside of the home environment. New environments include school and outside play settings. Feelings of competency or inferiority develop based on interactions with peers. When the child accumulates failures or experiences of incompetency, guilt develops. Accumulations of success build feelings of competency. The 7-year-old builds a lemonade stand, the 9-year-old is picked for the school kickball team, the 11-year-old has a paper route in the neighborhood. All of these situations are opportunities for the development of feelings of industry.

As you can see, in Erikson's theory the parents can play an enormous role in determining what type of social behavior patterns develop in the child. One set of responses (demanding, suspicious, punishing) by the parents might lead to the development of a mistrusting, tentative, and guilt-constrained child.

A different set of responses (accepting, rewarding, encouraging) will result in a child who is confident, independent, and high in initiative. In addition, interactions with peers can result in feelings of competence or inferiority. We will return to Erikson's propositions in the next chapter.

Moral Development

Moral behavior is a complex interaction of cognitive activity, learned associations, and emotional response. When a child faces a choice between the "right" behavior and the "wrong" behavior in a given situation, several systems are brought into play. In the first place, the child must consider the general meaning of right and wrong. This means that morality is a concept. Next the child must identify the alternative courses of action correctly, that is, label one action as "right" and the other as "wrong." Having labeled the alternatives, the child must now cope with the conditioned emotional responses to the two alternatives being considered. In the past, engaging in "right" behaviors has resulted in certain outcomes (rewards) whereas doing something "wrong" has resulted in other outcomes (punishment). Furthermore, the child has observed brothers, sisters, and other models being rewarded and punished for certain behaviors.

As a result of the apparent involvement of cognitive activity in moral behavior, many theories of moral development are linked with theories of cognitive development. Piaget's theory of moral development has two stages. In the first stage, the child applies rules within the limits of knowledge of those rules because rules or laws are considered sacred and not to be violated. In the second stage (which accompanies advanced stages of cognitive development), actions are judged more in terms of what was intended by those actions. Rules are modified to fit situations. What is "right" and "wrong" is defined more by peer expectations than by the "authorities." Seen in this light, morality is really an extension or example of some combination of social and cognitive development. Moral behavior in the first stage is concrete. In the second stage, moral behavior is more abstract, involving general rules or theories of moral behavior.

The predominant theory of the development of moral reasoning in the past several decades is one suggested by Lawrence Kohlberg. Like Piaget,

Kohlberg believed that moral reasoning develops in stages. Kohlberg (1958) developed his theory on the basis of interviews he conducted with children and adults of various ages. His method was to describe dilemmas such as the one that appears below and ask for a yes/no response.

A woman was dying of cancer, but the doctors said there was one drug that might save her. A druggist in the same town has recently discovered this drug, but he was charging 10 times what it cost him to make it. The sick woman's husband, Heinz, tried to borrow the money, but he could only borrow half as much as he needed for the drug. He told the druggist that his wife was dying and asked him to sell it cheaper or let him pay later. But the druggist said: "No, I discovered the drug and I'm going to make money from it." So Heinz broke into the store and stole the drug for his wife. Should Heinz have done that? (Adapted from Kohlberg, 1963, p. 19)

Kohlberg was chiefly interested in the reasoning that went into the answer than in whether the answer given was yes or no. This is similar to the idea of a protocol or the "think aloud" technique described in the chapter which dealt with problem solving. Moral reasoning is an example of problem solving; it is a matter of deciding which is the correct action to take.

Kohlberg developed a series of questions that could be used in the interviews to identify the reasoning behind the particular answer. Based on this type of data-gathering procedure, Kohlberg proposed that there were six different types of thinking or reasoning that are used in solving moral problems. Further, he suggested that these six types of thinking were ordered or arranged in stages so that some levels were more abstract or representative of mature thinking than others. He believed that children passed through these stages on their way to adulthood. The six stages and their descriptions appear in Table 10–1.

As was the case with Piaget, there have been many critics of Kohlberg and for many of the same reasons. Many think that the idea of a rigid sequence of developmental stages is inappropriate. They believe that Kohlberg may be describing the developmental sequence of some children but not others. There have also been criticisms of Kohlberg's samples, his techniques of data collection, and his methods of analysis (Kurtines and Greif, 1974), as well as considerable resistance to his proposition that

TABLE 10-1.
Kohlberg's Stages of Moral Reasoning

I. Preconventional Level

Rules are set down by others.
Stage 1. Punishment and Obedience Orientation
Physical consequences of action determine its
goodness or badness.

Stage 2. Instrumental Relativist Orientation
What's right is whatever satisfies one's own needs and
occasionally the needs of others. Elements of
fairness, reciprocity are present, but they are mostly
interpreted in a "you scratch my back, I'll scratch
yours" fashion.

II. Conventional Level

Individual adopts rules, and will sometimes
subordinate own needs to those of the group.
Expectations of family, group, or nation seen as
valuable in own right, regardless of immediate and
obvious consequences.
Stage 3. "Good Boy–Good Girl" Orientation
Good behavior is whatever pleases or helps others and
is approved of by them. One earns approval by
being "nice."

Stage 4. "Law and Order" Orientation
Right is doing one's duty, showing respect for
authority, and maintaining the given social order for
its own sake.

III. Postconventional Level

People define own values in terms of ethical
principles they have chosen to follow.
Stage 5. Social Contract Orientation
What's right is defined in terms of general individual
rights and in terms of standards that have been
agreed upon by the whole society. In contrast to
Stage 4, laws are not "frozen"—they can be
changed for the good of society.

Stage 6. Universal Ethical Principle Orientation
What's right is defined by decision of conscience
according to self-chosen ethical principles. These
principles are abstract and ethical (such as the
Golden Rule), not specific moral prescriptions (such
as the Ten Commandments).

Adapted from Kohlberg (1969).

there are such things as universal standards of right
and wrong. (This is the implication of stage 6.) Other
researchers have come to quite different conclusions
(for example, Gibbs, 1977). They cite the failure to
find examples of the reasoning characteristic of

stages 5 and 6 in certain cultures as evidence that
these stages are *not* universal. Once again, a
reasonable conclusion is that Kohlberg's theory has
been valuable in clarifying some of the processes involved in moral reasoning and changes in these
processes over a lifetime. As a theory, it is better to
think of it as an ideal rather than a "true" picture
of moral development. Most psychologists agree that
cognitive activity becomes more complex as the
child develops into an adult and as the adult accumulates new experience. To the extent that moral
problem solving involves cognitive activity, it will
become more complex over time. This is a far cry
from saying that children are biologically programmed to pass through stages of moral reasoning
on the way to some universal final stage. As was the
case with Piaget, this simply leaves too little room
for individual differences and environmental
influence.

Gender-Role Development

Our discussion of genetics earlier in the chapter considered only one aspect of gender—chromosomal
gender. But **gender** is a good deal more complicated
than just the pattern of chromosomes in the 23rd
pair. Gender involves the interaction of both physiological and psychological factors. For the psychologist, there are two important and interrelated issues
to deal with. The first is *gender identity*, or the conclusion that an individual comes to with regard to
whether he or she is male or female. The second
is that of *sex role*. The sex role consists of the attitudes, behaviors, and interests that are associated
with males or females (Liebert, Wickes-Nelson, and
Kail, 1986). Thus, the gender-identity process followed by the sex role acceptance (or rejection) process
plays a major role in the social and emotional
development of the child. As a result, we will consider this developmental experience in some detail.

Instead of thinking of gender as a given, it can
be thought of as a conclusion a person comes to
about some complicated aspect of his or her identity. This conclusion does not always follow the environmental or physiological "facts." It might be
more appropriate to consider gender identity as a
problem that the child must solve. It is not neces-

Gender. One's sex, involving both anatomical characteristics and
psychological factors.

sarily a traumatic or stressful type of problem (although it can be in some instances). It is more like the problem that the child faces in learning language. It is a matter of "breaking the code," or solving a riddle. As was the case with language, some of the tools necessary for breaking this code are internal. These internal tools include hormones and sex characteristics (both primary and secondary). These are also external sources of information for breaking the code or solving the riddle. These sources are environmental interactions. They include watching models (observational learning) as well as interacting with others (friends, parents, and strangers). Let us begin our consideration of the gender-identity process with some consideration of the biology of gender.

Biology of Gender

Money and Ehrhardt (1972) have identified five biological components of gender that unfold in a series of developmental stages, beginning at the moment of conception.

Chromosomal Gender. In terms of a time sequence, the first stage at which gender is influenced is at conception. As you learned earlier in this chapter, all human beings, male and female, start out as a single cell, the fertilized egg. This cell contains 23 pairs of chromosomes, one member of each pair contributed by the mother and the other member of the pair contributed by the father. The chromosomes contain all the genetic information necessary for the biological development of an adult man or woman. Of these 23 pairs, the final pair determines the gender of the developing organism. By convention, these chromosomes are identified as either X or Y chromosomes because of their shape. If the chromosomes are both X (XX), the embryo will develop as a female. If one is an X and the other is a Y (XY), the embryo will develop as a male. The mother contributes an egg (ovum), which *always* contains an X chromosome. The father contributes a sperm, which may contain *either* an X *or* a Y chromosome. Thus, it is the father who determines the biological gender of the child. It is ironic that over the centuries, many women have been blamed for not bearing a son. This has been particularly true in royal families in which only a male child is permitted to rule. In fact, if the woman could bear children at all, then the sex of these children was clearly due to the king, not the queen.

It would seem that nature's basic gender blueprint is female. The presence of a Y chromosome is crucial for male development; if it is absent, the embryo will develop as a female.

Gonadal Gender. Following conception, the cell formed by the egg and the sperm begins to divide and multiply. This is the second point at which gender development is influenced. Anatomical structures begin to form. By the fifth or sixth week after conception, the embryo has developed the beginnings of a reproductive system: a pair of gonads (which will eventually become testes, or ovaries), two sets of ducts for secreting hormones (which will be either testosterone or estrogen), and rudimentary external **genitalia** (which will become either a penis or a vagina). In the first few weeks after conception, these structures are identical for males and females. During the seventh week after conception, the sex chromosomes begin to direct a process of prenatal sexual differentiation. From this point on, the structures will develop in a distinctly male or female direction. If a Y chromosome is present, the gonads will develop into testes (testicles). If the Y chromosome is absent, the gonads will develop into ovaries.

Hormonal Gender. Once the testes and ovaries have developed, they begin to manufacture sex hormones. This is the third step in the development of gender. As you saw in Chapter 2, hormones are chemical messengers that travel through the bloodstream, carrying information from one part of the body to another. Sex hormones play a major role in gender development and also in sexual behavior. The differences in hormone production become critical as secondary sex characteristics develop in puberty. In addition, these hormonal differences will influence sexual behavior. At the prenatal stage of development, the production of the male and female hormones set the stage for the development of the genital system, a primary rather than secondary sex characteristic.

Internal Genital Organs. The sex hormones direct the development of the rest of the sexual and reproductive system. As was the case at the time of

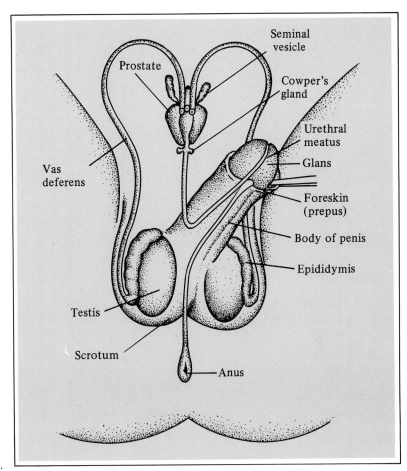

FIGURE 10-8
Male genital organs.

conception, nature's basic blueprint seems to be female. The blueprint can be altered only by the presence of large amounts of testosterone. If a large enough quantity of testosterone is present, the ducts through which the hormones are secreted will develop into the structures that form the route traveled by sperm in the male (see Fig. 10–8). If there is not enough testosterone present, whether or not female sex hormones are present, the ducts will develop into the structures that form the route traveled by ova in the female (see Fig. 10–9).

External Genital Organs. The external genitalia also develop in response to the sex hormones. If enough testosterone is present, the rudimentary external genitalia will develop into a penis and a scrotum. Otherwise, they will develop into a clitoris and inner and outer lips (labia).

Other sexual and reproductive organs develop from the urinary system. Although the genital organs of adult males and females appear to be quite different, it is useful to keep in mind the similarities of their origins.

A second period of sexual differentiation occurs during puberty, sometime in early adolescence. Again in response to the sex hormones, the genitals grow and assume their mature size, shape, and position. Sufficient amounts of estrogen in females and testosterone in males will result in normal development of secondary sex characteristics.

In addition to the five biological variables of gender just described, Money and Ehrhardt (1972)

Genitalia. Sex organs.

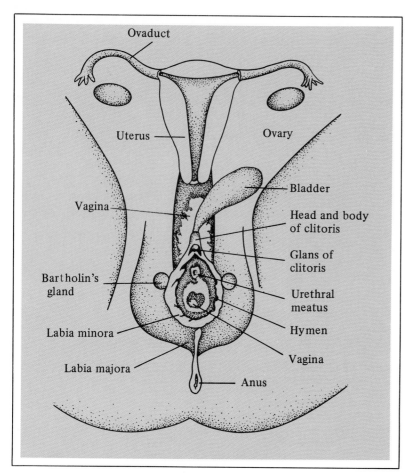

Ovaduct

Uterus

Ovary

Bladder

Vagina

Head and body
of clitoris

Glans of
clitoris

Bartholin's
gland

Urethral
meatus

Labia minora

Hymen

Labia majora

Vagina

Anus

FIGURE 10-9
Female genital organs.

also defined two social variables of gender. **Assigned gender** is the gender the baby is pronounced to be, usually by the physician attending delivery, after an examination of the external genitalia. This is the gender the parents believe the child to be and in which the child is usually raised. Note that there is no check of hormones, chromosomes, or internal organs. The announcement follows an external examination. **Gender identity** is the gender the individual eventually considers himself or herself to be. This is a private conclusion rather than a public announcement, a personal sense of being male or female. If all goes well, all seven variables of gender will be consistent. For example, an "announced" female will have XX chromosomes, ovaries, and other appropriate internal and external organs, and will eventually consider herself to be a female. In some cases, however, contradictions can arise.

Hermaphroditism is a contradiction among the biological components of gender. A true hermaphrodite has both rudimentary ovaries and testes. A pseudohermaphrodite may have any combination of male and female reproductive organs, for example, ovaries and a small penis and scrotum. The situation arises as a result of abnormal levels of sex hormones present during the critical period of prenatal sexual differentiation.

Transsexualism is a contradiction between biological gender and gender identity. The transsexual believes that he or she is trapped in a body of the wrong gender. For example, a person who considers herself to be a female may find herself housed in a male body. This invariably leads to psychological problems and abnormal behavior resulting from the stress, frustration, and personal confusion created by this contradiction. Such people may be candidates for sex-change surgery, which is accompanied by hormone therapy and psychological counseling. Tennis player and author Renee Richards (formerly Richard Raskind) is a well-known example of someone whose psychological gender and biological gender did not match, at least until she had surgery to correct the inconsistency.

Sex-Role Development

The Psychoanalytic Model. There are many views of how and why male and female children develop different behavior patterns (or gender roles). An early popular view was proposed by Sigmund Freud and is still accepted by the psychoanalytic school.

Freud proposed that personality and behavior patterns emerge as the child goes through a series of psychosexual stages of development. Each stage is characterized by a major conflict that is primarily sexual in nature. According to Freud, the child is capable of deriving sexual pleasure from a variety of sources, including the mouth, the anus, and the genitals. At each stage of psychosexual development, the sexual energy or libido is attached to or associated with one of these highly sensitive parts of the body, called **erogenous zones**. A conflict between the child and parents arises at each stage. If the conflict is properly resolved, pleasure from the activities of that stage will be repressed and will no longer be a source of sexual gratification. If, on the other hand, the conflict is not fully resolved, some psychic energy will remain invested in the activities of that stage. In Freud's terminology, the individual will become **fixated** at that stage of development and will continue to derive sexual pleasure from an immature activity.

According to Freud, there are five stages of psychosexual development. The first three stages, which occur during the first five or six years of life,

are critical for the development of the adult personality. By the end of the third stage, the individual's behavior patterns have been formed for life and will be extremely difficult to change.

The first stage is the **oral stage**, in which the child derives pleasure from stimulation of the mouth, most often by sucking and chewing. The primary conflict during this stage of development is weaning or being separated from a bottle or breast that had been the primary source of nourishment since birth. If weaning is a traumatic event for the child and the conflict is not resolved, the individual will be fixated at the oral stage as an adult. A preference for oral activities, such as eating, smoking, and drinking, may result from this fixation.

The second stage is the **anal stage**, in which the child derives sexual pleasure from the expulsion and retention of feces. The major conflict of this stage is toilet training. Fixation at this stage may result in an adult who is overly concerned with either messiness or cleanliness.

The third stage is the **phallic stage**, in which the child derives pleasure from manipulating the genitals. This stage is crucial for the formation of gender identity and for the acquisition of gender-appropriate patterns of behavior. The primary conflict of this stage is different for boys and girls. Boys must resolve the **Oedipus complex**, named after the Greek king who killed his father and married his mother. During this stage, the young boy develops sexual desires for his mother and views his father as a rival for her affection. He secretly wishes to kill his father, but he fears retaliation. So he represses his sexual urges toward his mother and imitates his father. In so doing, he adopts his father's moral values as his own, including his father's gender identity and appropriate behaviors.

Assigned gender. The gender a child is pronounced to be at birth after an examination of the external genitalia.

Gender identity. The gender an individual considers himself or herself to be.

Hermaphroditism. A contradiction in the biological components of gender in which an individual has both rudimentary testes and ovaries or some combination of male and female reproductive organs.

Transsexualism. A contradiction between biological gender and gender identity; the transsexual believes that he or she is trapped in a body of the wrong gender.

Erogenous zones. Highly sensitive parts of the body that, when stimulated, give rise to sexual feeling.

Fixated. In Freud's theory, occurs if a person does not resolve

a conflict at one of the five psychosexual stages and thus continues to derive sexual pleasure from an immature activity.

Oral stage. Child gets pleasure from sucking and chewing; primary conflict occurs through weaning child from breast or bottle.

Anal stage. Child gets sexual pleasure from expulsion and retention of feces; major conflict of this stage is toilet training.

Phallic stage. Child gets sexual pleasure from manipulating the genitals; primary conflict is Oedipus complex for boys and Electra complex for girls.

Oedipus complex. Conflict on part of a boy in the phallic stage between fear of his father and desire for his mother.

Girls must resolve the **Electra complex**, which is essentially the reverse of the process boys go through. The young girl develops libidinal desires for her father and views her mother as a rival for his affection. Knowing that her sexual wishes will never be fulfilled, she abandons her sexual urges toward her father and imitates her mother. In so doing, she adopts her mother's moral values as her own, including her mother's gender identity and appropriate behaviors. Failure to resolve these conflicts adequately results in confusion concerning gender identity and may result in the appearance of inappropriate gender-related personality traits, interests, and behavior patterns.

The fourth stage, which the child enters at about age 5 and which lasts for eight years, is the **latency stage**. Freud assumed that during this stage, all sexual activity is repressed and that the child has no sexual desires of any kind.

The last stage, which occurs during puberty, is the **genital stage**. Here, as during the phallic stage, sexual pleasure is derived from manipulating the genitals. However, the child is no longer content to produce such pleasure from masturbation alone. Rather, he or she turns to a partner of the opposite gender in order to obtain sexual fulfillment. According to Freud's model, normal adult sexual activity is restricted to heterosexual intercourse. Sexual pleasure obtained from any other source is immature and represents a fixation at a pregenital stage of development.

The Freudian view is that children initially develop a deep love for the mother. This love results in different conflicts for male and female children. The female child is angered at the mother for the absence of a penis. She blames the mother for this lack. On the other hand, she admires and desires the father. Eventually, she realizes that it is impossible to possess the father in the same way as he is possessed by the mother and must choose alternative love objects. The male child sees the father as a competitor for the mother's love and is caught in a bind between love for the mother and fear of the father. This bind, or conflict, is eventually resolved in different ways by the male and female child. In Freudian theory, it is this resolution that produces sex roles and identities. The male child identifies with (or acts like) the father in order to win the mother's love or the love of someone similar to the mother. The female child identifies with (or acts like)

the mother in the hope of being equally successful in attracting a male partner. If these conflicts are not adequately resolved, the Freudians predict disturbances of identity and abnormal behavior. The conflicts will be examined in greater detail in the chapter on personality. For the Freudians, the critical period for the development of sex role identity is the age period from 3 years to 6 years.

The Learning Model. A second view of gender-role development uses more of a learning approach. It is assumed that mothers and fathers behave differently toward children and that children learn to behave in particular ways in order to receive praise and/or avoid criticism (Kagan, 1971; Parke, 1979). Girls are praised for being pretty, verbal, and well-behaved. Boys are praised for being successful, forceful, and problem-oriented. The phrases "act like a man" and "behave like a lady" capture the flavor of this view of gender-role development. Observational learning or modeling plays a major role in this approach as well.

This second point of view—the learning approach—seems more plausible than the first, in part because gender-role stereotypes appear in children at a very early age. Kuhn, Nash, and Bruckin (1978) demonstrated that 3-year-olds have firm stereotypes of what behavior might be expected from a boy and a girl. Their data were gathered by asking male and female children to consider two paper dolls and respond to a series of statements by indicating which doll would do or say something indicated in the statement. The results appear in Table 10–2. As you can see, these stereotypes are uncomfortably close to some similar stereotypes held by adults. Because the Freudians would expect gender roles to develop as a result of the resolution of conflicts (Oedipus and Electra complexes) that occur much later in development, it is difficult for them to account for these stereotypes. Social learning and reinforcement mechanisms are more likely explanations for the development of these stereotypes and, by extension, for the beginnings of gender-role development in children.

In this first developmental chapter, we have considered some general examples of the ways in which behavior patterns change over the period bounded by birth and adolescence. In addition, we have considered some of the prenatal influences that might play a role after birth in observed behavior. Having

TABLE 10–2.
Gender-Role Stereotypes in 3-Year-Olds

Both boys and girls held the following stereotypes:

Girls Are More Likely To

play with dolls
help mother
talk a lot
never hit
say "I need some help"
clean the house
become a nurse

Boys are More Likely To

help father
say "I can hit you"
become a boss
mow the grass

Source: Kuhn, Nash, and Bruckin, 1978.

explored the period of childhood, in the next chapter we will consider the adolescent and adult phases of the human life span.

REVIEW QUESTIONS

11. Assimilation/accommodation means creating new mental categories for new information; assimilation/accommodation means putting new information into already existing mental categories.

12. Match the following terms with the correct definition:
___ sensorimotor stage
___ preoperational stage
___ concrete operations
___ formal operations

A. child can deal with abstract relationships
B. child can perform reasoning tasks and deal with more than one dimension at a time
C. child uses motor responses to explore and create sensory experiences
D. child can use symbols (words) to represent objects, but cannot perform other logical operations, such as conservation

13. _____ is the emotional tie between one person and another that endures over time and in spite of physical separation.

14. Match the following stages of Erikson's theory wtih the correct definition:
___ trust vs. distrust
___ autonomy vs. shame and doubt
___ initiative vs. guilt
___ industry vs. inferiority

A. child learns trust through interactions with parents
B. child works at developing competency outside of home, through interactions with peers.
C. child learns to be self-directing and independent through a supportive attitude of parents
D. child engages in more complex activities, gains confidence through parental encouragement to try new activities

15. _____ is more than one's anatomy, it is the interaction of both physiological and psychological factors. Sex role stereotypes appear in children before 3 years/between 3 and 6 years of age.

Answers: 11. Accommodation, assimilation 12. sensorimotor stage, C; preoperational stage, D; concrete operations stage, B; formal operations stage, A. 13. Attachment 14. trust vs. distrust, A; autonomy vs. shame and doubt, C; initiative vs. guilt, D; industry vs. inferiority, B. 15. Gender; before 3 years

■ SUMMARY

1. The *developmental psychologist* studies the patterns of change in human beings from conception to death and considers the issues of both physical maturation and psychological development.

Electra complex. Conflict on the part of a girl in the phallic stage between desire for her father and anger at her mother.
Latency stage. A dormant period of about 8 years in which all sexual activity is repressed.
Genital stage. Period after the latency stage, in which people reestablish heterosexual relations through adult urges for intercourse, procreation, and individual sexual pleasure.

A new term for this branch of psychology is *life-span psychology*, a term that emphasizes the fact that changes occur from conception through death. Individual differences exist in rates of development that may be caused by genetics, diet, or environment.

2. The first developmental stage is the 40-week *prenatal period*. Genetic material, or chromosomes, exist in molecules of *DNA*. Through *mitosis*, the 23 pairs of chromosomes duplicate themselves and each of the two 23-pair sets moves to opposite sides of the cell. The duplication and splitting continues and is the biological definition of growth. The 23rd pair of chromosomes determines a person's sex. The actions of dominant and recessive genes account for both the similarity and dissimilarity between brothers and sisters. *Phenotype* is a person's outward physical appearance, while *genotype* is a person's genetic makeup. Phenotypic characteristics are combinations of many genes.

3. The *placenta*, formed on the wall of the uterus, becomes a network of blood vessels and membranes that permit the prenatal baby to share the biological system of the mother. The *umbilical cord* attaches the baby to the placenta. *Mutation* is spontaneous change in the genetic message of the chromosomes that can be caused by radiation and usually results in a birth defect of some kind. *Teratology* is the study of abnormal prenatal development. Genetic abnormalities can result from attacks on the fetus during *critical periods* in development. The mother's use of alcohol or other toxic agents during pregnancy may also cause defects in the baby.

4. At birth the infant possesses *reflexes*, which are automatic adjustments the nervous system makes to the outside world. Reflexes provide the earliest interactions between the infant and the environment. The major physical accomplishments of the infant stage (lifting the head, rolling over, sitting, crawling, standing, and walking) occur in a sequence that is controlled by physical *maturation*. The sensory mechanisms develop rapidly during the infant period. As early as 20 days after birth an infant can distinguish the sound of the mother's voice from the sound of a stranger's. In school-age children, the environment is very influential on perceptual mechanisms. Reading abilities are related in part to perceptual development, and perceptual problems may cause difficulties in reading.

5. Piaget suggested that the main task of every human was making sense of the world through organization (sorting and grouping information) and adaptation (dealing with new information). Two cognitive operations that are part of adaptation are *assimilation*, putting new information into an existing view of the world, and *accommodation*, creating new categories or altering an existing view of the world.

6. In Piaget's theory, children seek an *equilibrium*, or balance, between their view of the world and outside facts. Piaget proposed that there are four stages of cognitive development. In the *sensorimotor stage* (birth to 2 years) children use motor responses to explore and create sensory experiences. In the *preoperational stage* (2 to 7 years), children become capable of using symbols, tend to have difficulty putting themselves in others' places, and are not capable of logical operations. In the *concrete operations stage* (7 to 11 years), the child is able to perform more complex reasoning tasks but cannot deal with abstractions. The fourth stage is *formal operations* (11 years to adulthood) and is characterized by abstract reasoning. Piaget's theory is that these stages are ordered in the same way for every child and that learning and adaptation are predominantly biological, rather than environmental, realities.

7. Smiling probably occurs first as a reflex but is developed and refined as a social tool through social stimulation. *Attachment* is an emotional tie between two people that endures regardless of the passage of time or physical distance between them. Attachment develops early in infancy and plays an important role in the motivation patterns of the child and may be responsible for stranger anxiety. With exposure to peers, *prosocial actions*, performed to benefit someone else, and *antisocial behavior* begin to emerge. Models play an important role in the development of both types of behavior.

8. Erikson considered life to be segmented into a series of crises that the individual has to resolve. The first four stages are *trust vs. distrust* (year 1), *autonomy vs. shame and doubt* (year 2), *initiative vs. guilt* (years 3 to 5), and *industry vs. inferiority* (years 6 through puberty).

9. Many theories of moral development are linked with cognitive development. Kohlberg suggested that moral reasoning develops in a series of six stages that become progressively more abstract and representative of mature thinking. Many resear-

chers believe that Kohlberg's theory overlooks the influence of culture on moral reasoning.

10. *Gender-role development* is based on internal sources including hormones, sex characteristics, and external sources, or environmental interactions.

11. Money and Erhardt have identified five biological components of gender that unfold in a series of stages beginning at conception: *chromosomal gender*, determined by the 23rd pair of chromosomes (if both are X, the embryo develops as a female, and if one is X and the other is Y, the embryo develops as a male); *gonadal gender*, the development of a pair of gonads during the 5th or 6th week after conception; *hormonal gender*, the production of testosterone by the testes for males, and estrogen and progesterone by the ovaries for females; *internal genital organs*; and *external genital organs*.

12. According to the psychoanalytical model, the libido is an instinct for sexual gratification that constantly seeks expression but is also controlled by societal rules and moral codes. In this theory there are five stages of psychosexual development during which children receive gratification through the stimulation of a particular *erogenous zone*. In each stage a particular conflict arises between parent and child and must be resolved or the child will remain *fixated* at that stage.

13. Expectations about the ways men and women should behave also play a part in gender-role development. The learning model holds that observational learning and reinforcement mechanisms are likely explanations for the beginnings of gender-role identity in children. This model offers a plausi-

ble explanation for why gender-role stereotypes appear in children at a very early age.

■ ANSWERING QUESTIONS FOR THOUGHT

1. Characteristics are passed on from parent to child through genes, which carry information about hair color, weight, size, sex, eye color, and so on. A child represents a combination of two sets of genes, one from the mother and one from the father.

2. The father's genetic contribution determines whether the child will be male or female. If the father contributes an X chromosome from the 23rd pair, the child will be female; if the father contributes a Y chromosome, the child will be male.

3. One study showed that infants only 20 days old could tell the difference between their own mother's voice and the voice of a stranger. This tells us that babies are able to remember the sound of their mother's voice and thus do have a functioning memory from a very early age.

4. Gender role stereotypes appear in children at a very young age. One study cited in the text showed that 3-year-old children have firm stereotypes of what behavior might be expected from a boy and a girl.

5. By the age of 7, most children have reached stage 1 of Kohlberg's six stages of moral reasoning. In this stage the child obeys rules to avoid punishment and thus knows according to the rules what is right and wrong.

11

Life-Span Development II: Adolescence, Adulthood, and Aging

In the last chapter we examined the course of childhood development in different age ranges. We first examined prenatal development, followed by development in infancy (birth–2 years), early childhood (2–5 years), and later childhood (5–12 years). This chapter will also be divided into subsections that represent some broad age ranges. But these age ranges involve longer spans of time and include adolescence (12–20 years), young and middle adulthood (20–60 years), and older adulthood (over 60 years). As was indicated at various times in the last chapter, it is important to remember that nothing about these time periods is sacred or definitive. They provide convenient categories in which to organize information related to development after childhood.

ADOLESCENCE

The stage of life called **adolescence** does not "begin" on a particular day in a particular year after birth. It is typically defined in terms of other time periods, such as the period between childhood and adulthood. From another perspective, we might say that adolescence begins at puberty and ends when the individual assumes "adult" responsibilities. This leaves room for considerable variation. Some children do not begin puberty until they are 14 or 15. By this is meant that until then there are no apparent changes in secondary sex characteristics. Others begin to mature at the age of 10.

Consider the other—that is, adult—end of the adolescent age range. In most major cities, there are instances where 10- and 11-year-old children are responsible for making enough money to feed themselves and sometimes their brothers and sisters as well. In El Salvador, Cambodia, Lebanon, and Northern Ireland, children barely into their teens are actively engaged in guerrilla warfare and may kill others or die themselves as a result of that activity. There is thus ample evidence that some children assume "adult" responsibilities at a very young age. All of these examples make the point that the beginning, end, and duration of adolescence varies dramatically from child to child and from culture to culture.

Perhaps the reason that adolescence is so difficult to define is that it is not a period at all. It is the transition from childhood to adulthood. It is exactly that fact that makes adolescence an appropriate concept for discussion in the context of developmental psychology. Some of the changes that occur are obvious and immediate. There is a growth spurt that adds inches, pounds, and contours. Secondary sex characteristics appear. In addition, new behavior patterns emerge that had been absent earlier. The most obvious is the pattern that defines sexual behavior. Other changes are less obvious and have long-term implications. Values that will later help define the adult personality are being formed. Plans that will culminate in an occupation are made. Cognitive strategies for solving problems are developing. Many of these changes may not be obvious for many years or may be obvious only under the right set of circumstances. Obvious or not, many changes are occurring all at once in the period called adolescence.

Physical Development

Most of the physical changes in males and females during adolescence can be easily identified. Many of them are obvious externally. In the female, the

---

Adolescence. Time period between childhood and adulthood.

external physical changes include a growth spurt, the development of breasts, and the widening of the hips. Some internal biological changes also occur. In this stage of development, the gonadal hormones (which have been present since birth) have specific effects, including the appearance of erotic sexual feelings and secondary sex characteristics as well as ovulation in the female and sperm production in the male. Ovulation in turn produces the characteristic menstrual cycle that is tied to the production of eggs, or ova. Increases and decreases in estrogen levels are responsible for the menstrual cycle. Progesterone prepares the wall of the uterus to accept a fertilized ovum. It is interesting to note that the age at which menstruation begins has been getting earlier over the past hundred years. The average girl began menstruation at age 14 in 1910; at 13.4 years in 1930; and at 13.3 years in 1940 (Malina, 1979). The average age of the onset of menstruation is now 12.8 years and appears to be stable for the time being (Tanner, 1970). This is probably the result of improved nutrition represented by diets lighter in starch and heavier in protein (Victor, 1980).

In males, equally noticeable physical changes oc-cur, although on the average they begin almost two years after the changes in females. The external changes include a growth spurt similar to that seen in females, a deeper voice, an increase in the size of the penis and testes, and the appearance of facial hair. Internally, these changes are being brought about by increased levels of androgens, in particular, testosterone. Just as the female begins to secrete hormones that produce ovulation and changes in the uterus conducive to pregnancy, the male begins to produce sperm capable of fertilizing a female egg. After the appearance of secondary sex characteristics, desires for sexual gratification appear in both males and females.

Although it is true that both males and females experience a growth spurt in adolescence, there are wide differences in the timing of that spurt. Figure 11–1 gives an idea of the changes that occur in size and proportion from infancy through adulthood in both sexes. Figure 11–2 shows growth rates and sexual development of both sexes during puberty, along with the average age at which boys and girls begin and complete the events of puberty. Again, this is to illustrate that age categories are general indicators, not definitive indicators of stages.

FIGURE 11-1
This figure shows the physical changes in size and proportion that occur from in-fancy through adulthood.

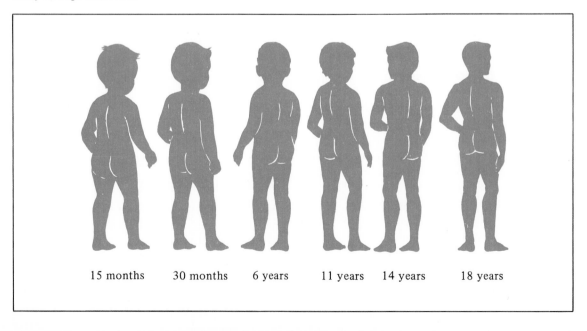

| 15 months | 30 months | 6 years | 11 years | 14 years | 18 years |

Both males and females experience a growth spurt in adolescence, but as evident in the photo, there are wide differences in the timing of that spurt among individuals.

Sexuality

Sexual behavior is a second issue that arises in adolescence. After puberty, the extent to which the adolescent is able to experience pleasure from stimulation of the genital organs increases. A study by Miller and Simon (1974) found that approximately 50 percent of both adolescent males and females engaged in light petting prior to the age of 16. Only 25 percent had engaged in heavy petting by the age of 16. As adolescents get older, they engage in heavy petting with increasing frequency. As you might expect, there is a similar increase in the frequency of intercourse as a function of age. A study by Zelnick and Katner (1977) was conducted with 4,000 teenage women between the ages of 15 and 19. In 1976, 18

FIGURE 11-2

This chart shows growth rates and sexual development of both sexes during puberty. The bars represent the average age at onset and completion of the events of puberty. (Tanner, 1973)

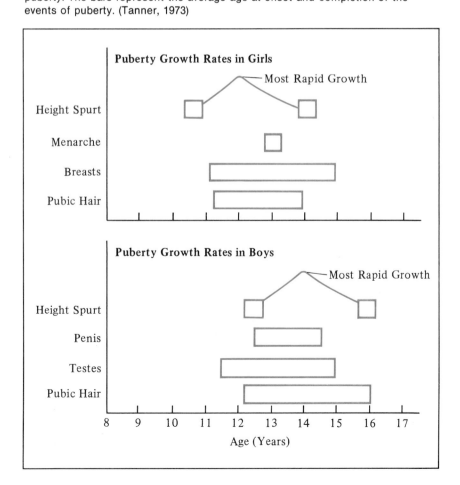

percent of the unmarried 15-year-olds and 55 percent of the unmarried 19-year-olds had engaged in intercourse. This shows that a majority of unmarried women have intercourse before the age of 20. Similar percentages have appeared in other surveys. Male adolescents seem to engage in intercourse at a more frequent rate than females. Brown, Lieberman, and Miller (1975) surveyed male and female adolescents and found that 67 percent of the males and 45 percent of the females had engaged in intercourse by the age of 17. Again, we see the gradual behavioral changes that accompany changes in age.

A recent book dealing with adolescent sexuality (Chilman, 1983) provides interesting data on the differences between males and females with respect to the factors that seem to contribute toward premarital sexual activity in adolescents. Consider the data in Table 11–1. These data indicate that nonmarital intercourse in adolescents is the result of a complex constellation of environmental, cognitive, and social factors.

Traditionally, marriage and sexual behavior have been linked. As we saw above, sexual behavior is beginning earlier and earlier. What about marriage? Interestingly, an opposite trend is occurring. Recent census figures reveal that among males between the ages of 20 and 24, 75 percent are unmarried. This compares with figures of 69 percent in 1980 and 55 percent in 1970. The same trend seems to be true for females. Recent census figures indicate that 57 percent of women between the ages of 20 and 24 were unmarried. This compared with 50 percent in 1980 and 36 percent in 1970. It would appear that for many young people the bond between sex and marriage is growing weaker.

Social-Emotional Development

Identity Development. One of the most important approaches to the process of identity development is that of Erik Erikson (1963, 1968). As you learned in Chapter 10, Erikson suggested eight stages in social-emotional development. In Chapter 10, we examined the four stages that are associated with social-emotional development in the childhood years. Of the remaining four stages, one stage in particular is relevant to the adolescent years. As you remember, Erikson suggested that the various stages of development were characterized by crises—

dilemmas to be solved. He considered the crisis of the adolescent years to be one of identity versus role confusion.

The establishment of an identity is a gradual process. As you saw in the previous chapter, the process begins at birth. In Erikson's theory, the child has already encountered four crises before reaching adolescence. If all has gone well, the child has developed into a trusting, autonomous, motivated, and self-confident person. A temporary identity has been established. But this identity is disturbed by the onset of adolescence. Confusion arises and the adolescent must establish a revised identity. Two types of information are used in establishing this new identity. The first type includes new physical information, such as size, appearance, and evidence of hormonal changes. The second type includes the new expectations of parents, friends, teachers, and strangers.

Some recent research has examined how this identity crisis is resolved during the adolescent years. Marcia (1966, 1976) has proposed that the adolescent might meet the crisis with one of four responses. These responses vary considerably. Table 11–2 presents the four responses and the characteristic behaviors of those who choose each type of response. As you can see, some adolescents meet the crisis head on, some are plagued by doubt and indecision, some hold fast to the values of childhood, and some may simply not care. The adaptive solution is the **achievement response**. The adolescent develops an identity that is compatible with both the past and the future. For example, the Boy Scout becomes a Boy Scout leader. The young girl who liked to play nurse volunteers to help at a nursing home one day a week. In this way, new relationships are formed and old ones are maintained. At the same time, social values are endorsed and occupational experiences sampled—all in all, an adaptive solution.

The other three responses are not so adaptive. The **moratorium response** simply postpones the resolution of the crisis but does not relieve the anxiety created by competing demands of parents,

---

Achievement response. In Erikson's theory, the most adaptive solution to the problem of establishing an identity in adolescence.

Moratorium response. In Erikson's theory, postponing the establishment of an identity; creates anxiety.

TABLE 11-1 Summary of Major Factors Apparently Associated with Nonmarital Intercourse among Adolescents

Factors	Males	Females
Social Situation		
Father having less than a college education	unknown	yes, especially for blacks
Low level of religiousness	yes	yes
Norms favoring equality between the sexes	probably	yes
Permissive sexual norms of the larger society	yes	yes
Racism and poverty	yes	yes
Migration from rural to urban areas	unknown	yes
Peer-group pressure	yes	not clear
Lower social class	yes (probably)	yes (probably)
Sexually active friends	yes	yes
Single-parent (probably low-income) family	unknown	yes
Residence in western states	unknown	yes (for whites)
Psychological		
Use of drugs and alcohol	yes	no
Low self-esteem	no*	yes*
Desire for affection	no*	yes*
Low education goals and poor educational achievement	yes	yes
Alienation	no*	yes*
Deviant attitudes	yes	yes
High social criticism	no*	yes*
Permissive attitudes of parents	yes*	yes*
Strained parent-child relationships and little parent-child communication	yes	yes
Going steady; being in love	yes*	yes*
Steady love partner with permissive attitudes	—	—
Risk-taking attitudes	yes*	yes*
Passivity and dependence	no*	yes*
Aggression; high levels of activity	yes	no*
High degree of interpersonal skills with opposite sex	yes*	no*
Lack of self-assessment of psychological readiness	no*	yes*
Biological		
Older than 16	yes	yes
Early puberty	yes	yes

*Variables supported by only one or two small studies. Other variables are supported by a number of investigations.
Source: Chilman 1983, p. 99.

TABLE 11–2.
Four Responses to the Identity Crisis

Achievement	Moratorium	Foreclosure	Diffusion
Crisis has been experienced and commitment made	Ongoing crisis indecision and struggle about alternatives	Static position with maintenance of childhood values without crisis	Commitment lacking: crisis may or may not have occurred
Achievement oriented	High anxiety	High authoritarianism	Withdrawn; lack of intimate relationships
Socially adaptive	High conflict with authority	Close to parents	
High levels of intimacy in relationships	Low authoritarianism	High need for social approval	Somewhat conforming
High levels of moral reasoning, need for complexity, cultural sophistication	Relate to parents with guilt and ambivalence	Low autonomy	
		Low anxiety	

Source: Adapted from Bourne, 1978b.

teachers, friends, and memories of the past pleasures of childhood. The **foreclosure response** is really a form of surrender to the parents and society in general. The adolescent simply accepts all of the values of parents and others in authority without serious consideration of their suitability for his or her particular situation. The adolescent who chooses this response to the crisis identifies closely with the parents, goes where they go, values what they value, and seeks the approval of others in authority. The **diffusion response** is best characterized by the word *apathy*. The adolescent simply withdraws from social interaction. This is the simplest and most direct way to eliminate competing demands.

Like most stage theorists, Erikson proposed that later stages could not be successfully dealt with unless earlier identity stages were completed successfully. Thus, for Erikson, the period of adolescence was another of the critical periods for the development of an effective pattern of social-emotional behavior.

REVIEW QUESTIONS

1. _____ can be defined as the period between childhood and adulthood.

2. One of the most noticeable physical changes in this period is the development of _____ _____ characteristics.

3. One of the major developmental tasks for the adolescent is establishing a stable _____ . Erikson called this life crisis _____ versus _____ .

4. Match the following terms with the correct definition:
   __ achievement response
   __ moratorium response
   __ foreclosure response
   __ diffusion response

   A. putting off the problem of establishing an identity
   B. withdrawing from social interaction rather than dealing with problem of establishing an identity
   C. adaptable response to problem of establishing an identity
   D. giving in to parents and society, taking on their values without question

Answers: 1. Adolescence 2. secondary sex 3. self-concept or identity; identity; role confusion 4. achievement response, C; moratorium response, A; foreclosure response, D; diffusion response, B.

Cognitive Development

In the last chapter you were introduced to Piaget's theory of cognitive development. Basically, this theory suggested that as people mature physically, and as they accumulate greater experience with the real world, certain intellectual abilities begin to emerge. In late childhood and early adolescence, those abilities termed **formal operations** make their first appearance and continue to develop over the first part of adolescence. As indicated in the earlier discussion of formal operations, the most significant characteristic of this stage is the capacity to hypothesize, to consider a range of possible explanations for an event. In the previous stage of cognitive development, namely, concrete operations, the child deals with what is observable but has difficulty in considering abstract ideas or things that are not present.

As is the case with every aspect of development, the change from concrete to formal operational

---

FORMAL OPERATIONS HITS THE BULL'S-EYE

Recently, I had an opportunity to see concrete and formal operational thought in action. I have two daughters. At the time this was written, one was 11 and the other 15. The 15-year-old had just completed a geometry course. Here was my problem. I had bought a dart board and wanted to hang it in the basement. Being a stickler for detail, I wanted to place the line from which the darts are thrown at the "correct" spot on the floor. The instructions that came with the dart board included two pieces of information: The dart board should be positioned at a point such that the bull's-eye is exactly 5½ feet above the floor; in addition, a diagonal line from the bull's-eye to the spot from which the darts are thrown should measure 9 feet. From this information, one is expected to solve the problem of where to put the correct spot, or line, on the floor. The instructions did *not* tell me exactly where to put that line. I was to deduce the answer from the two line lengths given. I asked my 11-year-old how she would determine that distance. She wasn't sure, but she thought I should first hang the board at a height of 5½ feet, then get my tape measure, use it to cut a piece of string exactly 9 feet long, and stretch that string from the bull's-eye to the floor. Wherever the string touched the floor, that would be where the line should be placed. I asked my 15-year-old where to place the line. She turned and left the room. I assumed she was stumped or uninterested or both. She returned a minute later with her math book, paper, and a pencil. She sat down and calculated the distance from the wall to the throwing line using the Pythagorean theorem, which states that the square of the length of the hypotenuse of a right or 90° triangle equals the sum of the squares of the lengths of the other two sides ($a^2 + b^2 = c^2$). Because she knew the length of the hypotenuse (9 feet) and one of the sides (5½ feet), it was a simple matter to calculate the length of the other side (the distance from the wall to the line). Unfortunately she made a minor error in calculation, which would have placed the line approximately 71 feet from the board rather than 7 feet 1.4 inches (the correct distance), but the method of solving the problem was a clear illustration of formal operational thought. Incidentally, the instructions that came with the dart board instructed the purchaser to use the method suggested by my 11-year-old. I still wonder why they did not just tell you to place the line 7 feet 1.4 inches from the wall, which is the correct distance! It was also interesting to note that both the 11-year-old and the 15-year-old thought the other's solution was "stupid," and each was equally pleased at having solved the problem.

Foreclosure response. In Erikson's theory, a form of surrender to parents and society in general—the adolescent simply accepts values from outside without questioning.

Diffusion response. In Erikson's theory, a withdrawal from social interaction rather than trying to establish an identity in adolescence.

Formal operations stage. Final stage of Piaget's theory of cognitive development; usually begins in adolescence and lasts throughout life. Signifies the capacity to hypothesize and reason abstractly.

The development of formal operational thought makes possible the pursuit of a number of new subjects in high school, such as chemistry and physics.

thinking is not abrupt. It occurs gradually and is often complete by the age of 16 (Coleman, 1974). Nevertheless, some individuals never develop formal operational thinking.

Egocentrism. One other aspect of adolescent thought deserves some attention. Elkind (1967) has suggested that adolescents assume that they have some special insight into the world around them. Further, they assume that their insight is correct or valid and that others around them "don't understand" certain situations or feelings. Elkind calls this tendency **adolescent egocentrism**. It is a way of thinking that appears in adolescence and gradually disappears in young adulthood. This egocentrism leads adolescents to feel that they are the center of attention in the environment. They feel they are

constantly being watched and evaluated. As a result, they often "preview" their actions and try to anticipate how others will react. This has been referred to as the creation of an **imaginary audience**. This kind of cognitive activity is made possible by formal operational capacities. It is an abstract activity that takes place without the physical presence of others. Nevertheless, it can substantially affect actual behavior. It often leads to the construction of a **personal fable**, or script, for future events that the adolescent uses to make plans or choose between alternative courses of action. Elkind (1967) gives the following example:

The imaginary audience. . . seems often to play a role in middle-class delinquency. . . . As a case in point, one young man took $1,000 from a golf tournament purse, hid the money, and then promptly revealed *himself. It turned out that much of the motivation for this act was derived from the anticipated response of "the audience" to the gutsiness of his action. In a similar vein, many young girls become pregnant because, in part at least, their personal fable convinces them that pregnancy will happen to others but never to them. . . . (Elkind, 1967, pp. 1031–1032)*

■ YOUNG AND MIDDLE ADULTHOOD

As a person leaves adolescence and enters the adult years, change and development become less a matter of change in structure (brain, hormonal system, limb length) and more a matter of adapting to new situations or the application of knowledge, process, or skills. Researchers have pointed out that in childhood a strong association exists between the development of a physiological structure and the appearance of a particular behavior (Flavell and Wohlwill, 1978; Schaie, 1982). Reflexes appear at birth and disappear as the central and peripheral nervous systems develop. In the same way, as the brain develops in size and complexity, there is a corresponding increase in cognitive ability. As the gonadal system of the child entering puberty becomes active, various aspects of sexuality emerge.

When a person enters the adult years, the structure/behavior relationship becomes much weaker. An example of this is Piaget's stage of formal operations (Schaie, 1982)—reaching this stage does not seem to depend on any obvious changes in physiological structure. The same is true of the more specific examples of reasoning that appear in various settings such as school or work.

Adulthood is also a time when undesirable behaviors are modified and the range of behaviors used to solve problems or control situations increases (Baltes and Schaie, 1976). One of the reasons for the increased range and complexity of behaviors is that adults have the power to change or adopt life-styles that, in turn, require the development of different skills or response patterns (Gribbin, Schaie, and

Parham, 1980). The 20-year-old decides to spend several months in Europe; the 30-year-old decides to end a marriage and live alone; the 40-year-old decides to quit the job at the publishing company and open a grocery story in northern Maine. These are changes that are self-induced and not possible for a child or an adolescent.

For the reasons presented above, discussions of adulthood usually abandon the traditional structure of physical change, cognitive change, changes in sexuality, and social-emotional change. Adulthood is more obviously a time when situations or environments change than a time when structures change. Thus, it makes some sense to order a discussion around the topics of vocational behavior, marriage, parental roles, and so forth. This discussion of adulthood will spend some time on major life events but will not completely abandon the earlier developmental topic areas. Erikson has suggested that three of the eight developmental stages he proposes are active in the years following adolescence. Two of these stages are relevant for a discussion of the adult years between adolescence and old age. Our consideration of adulthood will begin with a discussion of those two stages.

Social-Emotional Development

Before discussing Erickson's crises of adulthood, it might help to review the earlier crises of childhood and adolescence. During the preadolescent years, the child is faced with the dilemma of trust versus mistrust, autonomy versus shame and doubt, initiative versus guilt, and competence versus inferiority. The extent to which these dilemmas are resolved will depend on the responses that parents and friends make as well as on certain environmental events. In adolescence, the major crisis or dilemma is that of identity. As you saw, there are many possible responses that the adolescent might make to resolve the identity dilemma and reduce role confusion.

Adolescent egocentrism. The feeling by adolescents that they are the center of attention in the environment, that they are constantly being watched and evaluated.

Imaginary audience. Cognitive activity on the part of adolescents in which they "preview" their actions and try to anticipate how others will react to them.

Personal fable. In adolescents, a script for future events that is used to make plans or choose between alternative courses of action.

"STORMY" ADOLESCENCE—DOES THE LABEL REALLY FIT?

Early psychologists characterized adolescence as a period of extreme turbulence and highly charged, changeable emotions. G. Stanley Hall, who in 1904 published the book *Adolescence*, was the first to label the period a time of "storm and stress." In Hall's view, adolescents typically go from one extreme of behavior and feeling to another—from energetic activity to lethargy, from cruelty to sensitivity, from diligence to laziness. Freud described adolescence in much the same way, maintaining that the physical changes, a surge of sexual energy, and the need to become independent from parents produce many adolescent conflicts. Erickson also believed that adolescence was particularly charged with stormy conflict over the development of an appropriate identity. Adolescence still carries with it the "storm and stress" label. But are adolescents as full of turmoil as these theorists suggest?

Some recent studies indicate that adolescence is not necessarily such a turbulent period. Elizabeth Douvan and Joseph Adelson (1966) studied 3,500 adolescents and found that relatively few experience the emotional turmoil described by the theorists. Daniel and Judith Offer (1974) observed 73 middle-class adolescent boys for a period of ten years. Only one quarter of the boys fit the traditional view that adolescents experience stormy periods dominated by crisis and conflict. In a follow-up study, only about 20 percent of the boys

had a "tumultuous" pattern of development from adolescence to adulthood. Offer, Ostrov, & Howard (1982) also studied the responses of 20,000 teenagers to a self-image questionnaire. The adolescents in this research were from three groups, including normals, disturbed young people, and delinquents. Among the normal teenagers, the authors found that satisfaction with their physical changes, enjoyment of sexuality, and minimal conflict with parents were typical.

In another study, Csikszentmihalyi and Larson (1984) had high-school students carry beepers that went off at random two-hour intervals. When the beeper went off, the students filled out questionnaires concerning their moods, arousal level, and level of motivation at that moment. The researchers found that the adolescents they studied could swing from being very happy at one time to feeling discouraged and bored two hours later. These waverings, however, did not seem to result in unmanageable mood swings. In general, adolescents learn to temper these changes in mood by choosing activities that they enjoy and that help advance their development. Thus in light of these recent studies, the more traditional view of adolescence as filled with "storm and stress" may need to be revised. Probably for most young people, the transition is not without conflict but is smoother than the early theorists believed.

Young Adulthood: Intimacy vs. Isolation. In the years of young adulthood, the person faces the challenge of developing intimate relationships with others. Remember that the person just finished developing a self-image through the resolution of the identity crisis. Now the dilemma is whether to make a commitment to another person or to remain isolated with no bonds or constraints. Erikson proposed that this crisis cannot be addressed until the person has a firm hold on his or her identity. The notion of stages comes to the forefront very clearly here. Establishing a bond or an intimate relation-

ship with another person would simply add to the role confusion unless a person has established a firm self-image or identity. This is because intimacy involves accepting or sharing the values of another person.

Although intimate relationships are most often developed with persons of the other sex in the young adult years, Erikson thought that there was considerably more to resolving the intimacy crisis than finding a sexual partner. He believed that if a person failed to develop an intimate relationship with another, a pattern of isolation would result.

Isolation was thought to produce highly stereotyped and mechanical interpersonal relations. It may take many years before a truly intimate relationship is developed by a young adult. As far as Erikson was concerned, until and unless this crisis is resolved, the person cannot continue to develop socially and emotionally. Continued isolation over long periods of time is assumed to eventually lead to serious emotional problems and abnormal behavior.

Middle Adulthood: Generativity vs. Stagnation. After the intimacy crisis is resolved, the next dilemma facing the adult is whether to be active in establishing new links with the world that exists outside of the intimate relationship or to stagnate and become inactive and unproductive. The most obvious generative behavior in the early years of middle adulthood is developing a family as a social unit. Many adults in the later years of middle adulthood describe themselves as being in a "rut"—doing the same things, seeing the same people, endlessly repeating the same behaviors. Erikson proposed that this is the result of an inappropriate response to a crisis. The appropriate response is to widen a circle of friendships, begin new activities, and help other people. One example of generative activity might be helping with a youth group at church or in the community.

Stagnation is thought to be accompanied by various counterproductive behavior patterns such

According to Erikson, the most obvious generative behavior in the early years of middle adulthood is developing a family as a social unit.

as a growing concern for personal health and comfort, an increase in self-centered thinking, and an increase in self-indulgence. This can have particularly devastating effects on the children of those adults because it is the parent who is primarily responsible for helping the young child resolve the crises of trust versus mistrust, autonomy versus shame, and initiative versus guilt. If the parent is self-centered and self-indulgent, it is unlikely that the child will receive the support necessary to resolve successfully those crises of childhood. Thus, there may be the beginning of several generations of poor social and emotional development.

Levinson's Stages of Adulthood. Erikson's stages are reasonable descriptions of the challenges of the adult years. They are not explanations but they do provide a broad framework for considering many of the events that characterize an entire life span. Others have suggested adult stages with a good deal more detail than the two suggested by Erikson. Levinson and his colleagues (Levinson and others, 1978) have proposed a framework for considering early and middle adult years that was developed through interviews with adult men. Levinson and his co-workers conducted extensive interviews on

several occasions with men in four specific occupations: industrial workers (both white- and blue-collar workers), business executives, scientists in universities, and novelists. These individuals were encouraged to talk about their values, interests, lifestyles, social networks, and anything else that they felt was an important part of their personality. On the basis of these interviews, Levinson identified several distinct periods of development. These periods and the associated age ranges appear in Table 11–3. As you can see, Levinson's approach is somewhat different from other stage theorists in that he specifically identifies overlap between stages. In fact, it is the overlap that is the critical part of his theory. He calls the overlap between one stage and another a **transition period**. A transition period is similar in meaning to a life crisis as described in Erikson's stage theory. They are considered to be naturally occurring events that represent changing expectations of people and the social environment in which they find themselves.

From Levinson's point of view, many people don't really *choose* to enter the adult world. Adulthood is thrust upon them. The fact is that it becomes more difficult to live at home and maintain the behavior patterns of an adolescent. Your

TABLE 11-3
Periods of Development of Men During Early and Middle Adulthood

Periods of Development	*Ages*
Leaving the Family Transition effort to establish oneself independent of the family	16–18 to 20–24

Getting into the Adult World
    a new home base
    exploration and commitment to adult roles
    fashioning an initial life structure
	early 20s to 28

Age Thirty Transition reassessment of life structure	28 to 30

Settling Down
    establishing a stable niche
    making it: upward strivings
    becoming one's own man: giving up mentors
    emphasizing parts of the self and repressing others
	early 30s to 38

The Mid-Life Transition reassessment of life structure	38 to early 40s
Restabilization to Middle Adulthood	middle 40s

Source: *From Levinson, Darrow, Kleirt, Levinson, and Braxton, 1974.*

parents won't allow it; your friends won't allow it; society in general expects you to begin acting differently; and new standards are applied to your behavior. The same is true of the Age Thirty Transition and the Mid-life Transition (Table 11–3). These are not things that one can do anything about.

Levinson's suggestions are interesting and plausible. In addition, they fit with other theories and what people report as personal experience. There are other appealing aspects of Levinson's approach when contrasted with other stage theories. He specifically proposes that stages overlap. This suggests gradual rather than abrupt movement. In addition, he places equal emphasis on the person and the environment. The fact is that the crises or transitions are not simply a function of changes in the individual. The expectations of others and of society in general play a significant role. Finally, the stages are quite flexible in terms of chronological age. The person's age is only a rough guideline in this theory; it is not a hard and fast boundary. Nevertheless, Levinson does suggest that the order of the stages is set. It is not likely that someone would experience a mid-life transition before an early adult transition. This may provide an interesting backdrop for evaluating certain dramatic life changes such as remarrying and starting another family. What happens when a person has successfully navigated a transition and is thrust back into a pretransition role? Must they begin the whole sequence again?

As you can see, many opportunities exist for the continuing development of adult social and emotional behavior after adolescence. Because the environment we live in does not remain static, nor do the expectations of those around us, there will always be pressure for development and change. Moreover, our self-image changes over time. Our needs, skills, and preferences evolve. All of these forces contribute to the continued change in our personalities over the adult years.

REVIEW QUESTIONS

5. In terms of cognitive development, adolescence is the time that most people enter what Piaget called the _____ _____ stage.

6. One of the life crises of young adulthood, according to Erikson, is _____ versus _____. The dilemma at this stage is whether to make a commitment to another person or remain without bonds or constraints.

7. Levinson's study of adulthood focused on _____ _____, which are similar to Erikson's life crises. They are naturally occurring events that represent changing expectations of the person and a changing social environment.

8. The final stage of courtship is called the _____ stage, in which each of the parties tries to anticipate what it will be like to be married to the other person.

9. For Erikson, parenthood represents a chance to resolve the _____ versus _____ crisis.

Answers: 5. formal operations 6. intimacy; isolation 7. transition periods 8. role 9. generativity; stagnation

■ SEX ROLES IN ADULTHOOD

As children learn society's expectations concerning gender-related behavior, they strive to fulfill them. The psychoanalytic and behaviorist models offer different accounts of how these expectations are conveyed to the child. According to the psychoanalytic model, gender-appropriate behavior develops through identification with a parent of the same gender and internalization of that parent's moral values. This is an outcome of the resolution of the Oedipus and Electra complexes and occurs when the child is about 5 or 6 years old. Once a gender identity has been formed and gender roles have been acquired, they are highly resistant to change. According to the behaviorist model, gender-appropriate behavior develops through observational learning and through the administration of rewards and punishments contingent upon gender-related

---

Transition period. In Levinson's theory, a period of overlap between one stage and another—similar to a life crisis in Erikson's theory.

behavior. From the behaviorist perspective, gender identity and gender roles are the products of learning and thus may be modified at any point during the individual's life.

One study measured people's gender-role expectations (Broverman and others, 1972). The researchers asked people to list the characteristics that distinguish the average man from the average woman. They found that the average woman was described as warm, expressive, emotional, illogical, and lacking in competitiveness. These traits are thought to be consistent with the female roles of wife and mother. The average man, on the other hand, was described as competent, logical, independent, objective, and competitive. These traits are thought to be consistent with the male role of wage-earner. Of course, these results reflect people's stereotypes about what males and females are like psychologically.

Research on *actual* differences between males and females (MacCoby and Jacklin, 1974) reveals that such differences are limited to a small number of areas and, even then, the differences are small. Perhaps the largest and most consistent difference is in aggressiveness. At all ages, males are more aggressive than females. This difference is also reflected in the preferences young boys and girls have for toys. Although there are no overall differences in intelligence, there are some gender differences with respect to specific intellectual abilities. Males tend to do better on tasks requiring mathematical and spatial skills, whereas females tend to do better on tasks requiring verbal skills. These differences in abilities are quite small, and the distribution of males and females possessing each skill overlaps considerably.

Androgeny. In light of the small gender differences in actual behavior, researchers have recently begun to investigate the potential *similarities* between males and females and to challenge stereotypes about masculinity and femininity based on presumed *differences*. Until recently, research on gender roles was based on the assumption that masculinity and femininity represented opposite ends of a single continuum. Falling at the masculine end were people whose personality traits, abilities, and behaviors reflected competence and independence. These people were generally assumed to be males. Falling at the feminine end were peo-

ple whose characteristics reflected warmth and expressiveness. These people were generally assumed to be females. According to this viewpoint, the more masculine characteristics one possessed, the fewer feminine characteristics one would have. Thus, by behaving competently and aggressively on the job, a woman would be viewed as incapable of behaving with warmth and tenderness in the bedroom and she would be seen as less feminine. It was assumed that masculinity and femininity were negatively related. The more masculinity you had, the less femininity, and vice versa.

The clearest example of this type of thinking can be seen in the methods used in the past to measure masculinity and femininity. A single set of questions would be asked. Some answers were considered masculine answers and others were considered feminine. On the basis of answers to particular questions, a person was assigned a score that indicated a position at some point along the line representing the masculinity/femininity continuum. Consider Table 11-4, which lists five questions and the answers to those questions provided by two hypothetical subjects, one male and the other female. Assume that True answers are feminine answers. Thus, person M(ale) would be seen as slightly feminine and person F(emale) as slightly masculine.

Now consider a second possibility. What if masculinity and femininity are not opposites but instead are two separate traits or styles of reaction or response? In other words, suppose that you could be *both* masculine and feminine at the same time.

TABLE 11-4
Sample Items on a Test for Masculinity/Femininity

Items	Person M	Person F
I prefer a shower to a bath.	True	True
I think it is important to be assertive.	False	False
A person should defend his or her beliefs	False	True
I am an analytical person.	True	True
I like to lead groups	False	False
	M: 2	F: 3

TABLE 11-5
Examples of Items on the Masculinity and Femininity Scale of Bem's Androgyny Test

Note: On the test the items are mixed together. For each item the subject is asked to describe himself or herself by marking the appropriate number.

Masculine Items	Feminine Items
Acts as a leader	Affectionate
Analytical	Compassionate
Competitive	Feminine
Forceful	Sympathetic
Individualistic	Gullible

1	2	3	4	5
Never or Almost Never True	Usually Not True	Occasionally True	Usually True	Always or Almost Always True

Person M: 15 masculine, 15 feminine **Person F:** 7 masculine, 7 feminine

Source: Adopted from Bem, 1974.

Suppose that you could be *neither* masculine *nor* feminine but somehow "neutral." (This brings to mind a term that has been reserved for exactly this possibility—the term *neuter*, meaning *without gender*.) If we consider masculinity and femininity as *separate* dimensions, we get a very different view of sex roles. Let us consider a different test of masculinity/femininity. This time, let us use some questions that measure masculinity and others that measure femininity. Table 11-5 presents some hypothetical questions for the two different dimensions. Instead of receiving just one score, our two hypothetical subjects, M and F, receive two scores, one for masculinity and one for femininity. As you can see, they seem a good deal farther apart than they did in Table 11-4. Now, M seems to be *both* highly masculine *and* highly feminine, whereas F seems to be only slightly masculine and slightly feminine.

This new way of looking at sex roles has been receiving quite a bit of attention in recent years. Bem (1974, 1978) has proposed just such an approach. She believes that masculinity and femininity are better thought of as two separate dimensions rather than as endpoints on a single continuum. That is, a person may possess any combination of masculine and feminine traits. She suggested that there are really four kinds of people: people who possess few of either kind of trait, people who possess many masculine but few feminine traits (and these may be either males or females), people who possess many feminine but few masculine traits (again, these may be males or females), and people who possess many of both kinds of traits. This latter group of people Bem calls **androgynous**.

According to Bem, androgynous people are at an advantage because they have a large number of potential behavioral responses from which they can choose. Thus, they can vary their behavior according to the demands of a particular situation. In other words, an androgynous person, of either gender, can behave competently and aggressively on the job and with tenderness and warmth at home. Table 11–6 illustrates the various characteristics that Bem has suggested as representing the masculine and feminine gender. You have probably encountered many people, both male and female, who seemed

Androgynous. Word used to describe people who have many masculine and feminine traits.

TABLE 11-6
Items on Bem's Sex Role Inventory Scale

Feminine Items	Masculine Items	Neutral Items
Affectionate	Acts as a leader	Adaptable
Cheerful	Aggressive	Conceited
Childlike	Ambitious	Conscientious
Compassionate	Analytical	Conventional
Does not use harsh language	Assertive	Friendly
Eager to soothe hurt feelings	Athletic	Happy
Feminine	Competitive	Helpful
Flatterable	Defends own beliefs	Inefficient
Gentle	Dominant	Jealous
Gullible	Forceful	Likable
Loves children	Has leadership abilities	Moody
Loyal	Independent	Reliable
Sensitive to the needs of others	Individualistic	Secretive
Shy	Makes decisions easily	Sincere
Soft spoken	Masculine	Solemn
Sympathetic	Self-reliant	Tactful
Tender	Self-sufficient	Theatrical
Understanding	Strong Personality	Truthful
Warm	Willing to take a stand	Unpredictable
Yielding	Willing to take risks	Unsystematic

Source: Bem, 1974, Table 1, p. 156.

to have *both* characteristics of the following pairs: affectionate-ambitious; compassionate–self-sufficient; shy-athletic; loves children–willing to take risks. Similarly, you have probably encountered people who were neither cheerful nor forceful, neither sympathetic nor independent, neither tender nor self-reliant. The actual characteristics are not really important. We are not trying to define the perfect masculine or feminine role; we are trying to point out the advantages of considering masculinity and femininity as two separate dimensions. This two-dimensional conceptualization conforms more closely to actual behavior patterns that we see in people we know.

From this perspective, gender-specific behaviors can be seen as competencies, as skills that can help a person adapt to various situations. People who have developed neither masculine nor feminine competencies are at an extreme disadvantage in dealing with others because they seem to be missing many of the traits that define efficient social interaction. Those who have developed one of those competencies but not the other are still at a disadvantage, though not so severely as those with neither competency. The person most capable of dealing with a wide range of situations is the one who has developed both competencies. Surveys in popular magazines concerning the characteristics of most preferred sexual partners often conclude that the "perfect" woman is capable of both independence *and* warmth. The "perfect" man can be assertive and sensitive at the right times. The trick for both sexes is to use those two different competencies at the right time.

Some Life Events in Young and Middle Adulthood

Each of our life histories is different. No two of us have the same set of experiences over a lifetime. Nevertheless, many of us have experiences that are similar in nature. We may each handle these experiences differently but we are exposed to them in a similar manner. It might be useful, then, to consider briefly some of these events and associated behavior patterns.

Marriage. Marriage is a prime concern in early adulthood. Whether or not to marry, whom to marry, and when to marry are important questions to many developing adults. Older theories of how marriage decisions are made usually assumed that one factor was of primary importance in the decision. That factor might be a physical one (such as attractiveness) or a personality factor (such as aggressiveness). As an example, one theory proposed that a dominant person would choose a submissive person for a marriage partner (Winch, 1955, 1958).

Single-factor theories are now considered too simplistic for explaining a relationship as substantial as marriage. Some specific variables have been identified in the development of friendship, romantic love, and sexual relations, but marriage is a qualitatively different type of relationship (even though it includes all three of these other kinds of relations). Marriage is much more clearly a *decision* than are other forms of interpersonal relations.

Recently, the theories of how people make this decision have become more detailed and include several factors instead of only one. As an example, one approach is called the *stimulus, value, and role approach* (Murstein, 1976, 1979, 1982). This approach assumes that both parties consider the pluses and minuses of each other in a particular sequence. The theory emphasizes a courtship period and breaks this period into three stages, corresponding to a stimulus stage, a value stage, and a role stage. Each stage derives its name from the fact that the

name of the stage reflects the important variables in it. Murstein describes courtship as "a slowly accelerating conveyor belt whose destination is matrimony" (1982, p. 659). This implies that the early stages move more slowly than the later stages.

In the *stimulus stage*, first impressions are formed based on such things as attractiveness, temperament, and desire for sexual activity. In addition, there are less observable but equally important stimulus characteristics, such as reputation, professional aspirations, and past accomplishments. In the sense, a perfect "10" on a stimulus scale applied to males might be a male who is tall and muscular, pleasant, sensitive to the sexual desires of his partner as well as enthusiastic about sexual activity generally, respected in the community, studying to be a neurosurgeon, and the captain of the varsity football team. Similar characteristics could be suggested for the female stimulus scale.

The *value comparison stage* follows the stimulus stage. Murstein proposes that each of the parties somehow adds up his or her personal stimulus characteristics and then the characteristics of the prospective partner. If these sums are roughly equal, then the relationship moves to the next stage. In the value comparison stage, each party compares and contrasts his or her own interests, values, needs, and preferences with those of the other. Murstein believes that this is most often accomplished through simple verbal interaction. This seems to fit everyday experience. In most courtships, there is a period in which the parties seem to talk with each other endlessly, filling in missing background information about themselves, revealing tragic and joyful events in their past, and sharing views on current events. All of this conversation has the effect of transmitting information about values. During this stage, partners make a preliminary judgment about compatability, trying to determine if they can live with the value patterns of the other person.

The final stage is called the *role stage*. During this final courtship stage, each of the parties tries to anticipate in some detail what it will be like to be married to the other person. Often the conversation turns to, "What would you do if I . . ." topics. One method for exploring these roles is living together before marriage; many young people have chosen this method of exploration in recent years. Up to this point, the courtship has been general. In this stage, it becomes quite specific. Both partners are trying to anticipate the concrete satisfactions and dissatisfactions of marriage. In terms of cognitive operations, this is quite a complex task. It involves dealing with many abstractions, the most important of which is the future. As a result, cognitive skills such as those described by Piaget in the formal operations stage are critical to anticipating these role-related variables. This might be an explanation for why very young people often are unable to make good decisions regarding marriage. They have not yet developed the formal logical skills (such as reasoning) necessary for considering future roles.

Murstein's theory is an interesting one. Because marriage is best thought of as a motivated act, any reasonable theory of marriage choice should be compatible with a motivational interpretation. Stimulus-value-role theory fits quite well with what we know about adult motivation. In addition, this theory allows for a flexible interpretation of stages— a very important characteristic considering the wide individual differences in courtship and marriage decisions.

Divorce. As Murstein suggests, courtship is a moving conveyor belt that more often than not ends up in marriage. Information produced at any of the three stages might result in stopping or reversing the conveyor belt. The stimulus characteristics of the other party might not be sufficiently compelling, the values might not match, or the roles envisioned might not be compatible. Occasionally, information provided at one of those stages is inaccurate or incomplete. There can be two consequences of this information problem. The first, perhaps less bothersome in the long run, is to stop the conveyor belt. You may decide that marriage is not appropriate. This may be a mistake—you may have not accurately determined the values of the other person or you may have collected insufficient role information. This type of mistake is not always obvious and is seldom identified as a mistake by the people involved, who may spend the rest of their lives still believing that they made the correct decision in not marrying a particular person. The other type of mistake is more obvious and more bothersome and damaging—incorrectly deciding to marry. This mistake often involves a chronic state of argument, frustration, anxiety, and disappointment—all negative emotional events. Such mistakes frequently end in divorce and, in the process, there is substan-

tial anguish for the partners as well as any children they may have.

Parenthood. After the transition from an unmarried to a married state, the next major transition that young adults face is the transition from childlessness to parenthood. Even before marriage, the concept of parenthood is very real for most young adults.

There have been some interesting changes in parenthood trends in the years since the turn of the century. The first change is in the percentage of childless couples. In the early 1900s, 21.7 percent of marriages were childless. In the 1970s, this figure had dropped to 10.4 percent (Glick, 1977). Many possible reasons account for this change. First, many problems in fertility have been solved through new methods of treatment. In addition, the life expectancy of females has increased over this time span (Doherty and Jacobson, 1982). Even this current percentage does not do justice to the motivations of the potential parents. Over the past 20 years, the number of women expecting not to have children in their lifetime has varied between 3 percent and 5 percent (U.S. Bureau of the Census, 1978).

From a broad perspective, both Erikson and Levinson have something to say about parenthood. For Erikson, parenthood represents an opportunity to resolve the generativity versus stagnation crisis. Having children is one rather substantial way of making sure that one stays out of psychological ruts. Parenthood provides an opportunity to guide, nurture, and invest oneself in another person—one's child. It is an extension of the successful resolution of the earlier intimacy versus isolation crisis of the young adult years. In Levinson's framework, the first child represents an active step in making the transition into adulthood. The child then helps to define the new life structure. Instead of simply husband or wife, man or woman, the new life structure becomes mother or father.

There are, of course, both advantages and disadvantages to parenthood. There is no doubt that bearing a child has a profound effect on both the mother and father. A new sense of responsibility arises, a new need for financial security, an increasing awareness of the future, and a sense of self-sacrifice that would have been unlikely without a child to sacrifice for. It is hard to tell whether these behaviors are caused by or are the causes of the evolution of stages such as those described by Erikson and Levin-

Parenthood places a couple at the beginning of a new cycle, the family cycle.

son. In some respects, it doesn't really matter; the fact is that children play an important role in adult development.

The critical aspect of the first child is that it signals the beginning of a new social unit—the family. This places the couple at the beginning of a new cycle—the family life cycle. This is superimposed on the individual life cycles of the mother and father.

Many other important events occur in the young and middle years of adulthood. First and subsequent jobs, the illnesses and death of friends and parents, remarriage, grandparenthood, and many other events have profound effects on psychological and physiological well-being. I have simply highlighted a few of the more common events of the adult years. Many cognitive, physical, and physiological changes are occurring as well, changes that also affect behavior. Unfortunately, in a chapter that must cover the years from adolescence to death, many of these significant aspects of change must go unexplored.

■ THE LATER YEARS

In a guest column in the *New York Times*, June Wilson described some emotional aspects that she felt were representative of the later years of adulthood.

I have been growing increasingly irritable. My whole family has declared me a shrew. It's as if my senses had lost their protective insulation and keep short-circuiting. When they suffer an insult they scream. . . .

Irritability works on three levels: the senses, the emotions and the intellect. Hearing is my most vulnerable sense. Rock music drives me into paroxysms of irritability; so does bubble gum, the rustle of candy wrappers at a concert and the gunning of motorcycles. In the area of sensory feeling, heat and cold trigger my shrewishness because my physical thermostat has gone awry and no longer adjusts to temperature changes. Overheated spaces in winter, excessive air conditioning in summer, drafts at any time cause acute misery. . . .

This vulnerability works both ways. The nose quivers like a rabbit's at the smell of freshly baked bread. The eye revels in an October sunset over Central Park. The feel of a baby's bare bottom is profoundly satisfying as is a headlong dive into breaking surf. . . .

Irritability between people involves emotions. The workplace encourages rivalries, territorial squabbles, perceived injustices. (Who gets the office with the window?) (I did all the work and he gets all the credit.) Aging couples are subjected to the unremitting intimacy of post-retirement. Irritability lies just below the surface, ready to explode. It feeds on conflicting attitudes and habits, on abused nerves. Sure-fire irritants include: apportioning blame (I knew this was the wrong house when we bought it), money (I suppose your account is overdrawn again), friends (what do you see in those people), food (you know I like my meat rare), alcohol (you shouldn't try to tell a story when you've been drinking) and health (you'd be all right if you had taken your pills). (New York Times, June 16, 1983, p. C2)

Wilson's firsthand description of how aging has affected her points out many of the puzzles of aging. She describes a change in sensation rather than a loss of sensory capacity. The pleasing sights and sounds are more pleasing; the things that annoyed her before now enrage her. Similarly, she describes not so much a change in emotional level as a change in circumstance or environment that leads to a greater demand on the emotional system. Retired couples spend many more hours with each other than they ever had before. Is this so different from the annoyance that forms as a result of prolonged and intense interaction between middle-aged or younger adults? Perhaps not. There is a story about a man and a woman who had been married to each

other for 50 years. The woman was asked if she had ever considered divorce. She answered, "Divorce? Never! But I did consider *murder* a few times."

There are many stereotypes of older people. Widely held beliefs concern changes in personality, changes in physiology and biological function, and changes in cognitive abilities. Many people assume that aging is a process of degeneration and that older people are frail, feebleminded, and unpredictable. These stereotypes are nonsense. In a recent Boston Marathon, the winning time for the "Veterans" category of runners (age 60+) was 2 hours and 31 minutes. This time was approximately 24 minutes slower than the world's record (and 25 minutes *faster* than the best time for the now 43-year-old author of this book!). Vladimir Horowitz, the classical pianist, recently performed spectacularly on a concert tour in Russia. Horowitz was born in 1904. Ronald Reagan, born in 1911, is still vigorous and uses contact lenses and a hearing aid to compensate for slight impairments of his senses. Aging does not imply inevitable performance decline. It simply implies what other phases of the life span imply—change. The last section of this chapter will cover a sample of changes and events that occur in the later years.

Physiological Changes

Over the years, a good deal of research has been done on the topic of changes in sensation and perception that correlate with increased age (Birren, 1983). Two areas that have received great emphasis are vision and hearing. Figure 11–3 provides data on visual and auditory impairment as a function of age. Note that we are only considering the percentage of people who report *any* difficulty in seeing or hearing. This does not mean that the respondents are blind or deaf, only that they don't see or hear as well as they had at one time.

Many of these changes are understandable and predictable. For example, Fozard and colleagues (1977) have demonstrated that the lens of the eye thickens and yellows with age. This change is most prominent after the age of 40, and its effect is to reduce the amount of light reaching the retina as well as to eliminate certain wavelengths from the visible spectrum. For example (Schaie, 1982), older persons often have difficulty in discriminating between blue and blue-green, or blue-green and violet.

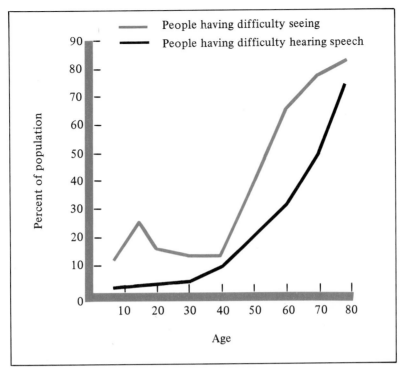

FIGURE 11-3
People's vision and hearing may become impaired as they get older, as shown in the graph here. Many of these problems can be corrected by eyeglasses and hearing aids, however.

This produces problems in dealing with prices stamped in blue on green backgrounds at a store. Similarly, certain computer screens that use these colors are difficult for older people to work with. In addition to the effects on light reaching the retina in the lens of the eye, changes also occur in the eye's capacity to accommodate to distances. This results from the thickening of the lens as well as a certain loss of flexibility, and leads to problems in both near and far vision. Most of these problems can be corrected by bifocals and modified lighting.

Hearing loss begins as early as age 32 in men and age 37 in women (Rebo and Reddell, 1972). This hearing impairment can take two forms. The first is a loss of acuity in the high-frequency ranges, particularly for consonants such as *s* and *t*. This can be particularly annoying and troublesome because speech consists of many high-frequency sounds. The result is that many words that sound alike are confused. This has the effect of making the person seem intellectually rather than physically impaired.

The second effect is a more general loss of sensitivity. These range losses need not be actual handicaps if the speaker would take the time to enunciate clearly and to present visual cues to the listener by not turning away and using accompanying relevant gestures and nonverbal cues when possible.

Cognitive Changes

Another popular area for research in aging has been examining changes in cognitive capacities. There has been a general misperception of the extent to which cognitive abilities change with age (Schaie, 1982). Actually, no general decline takes place. Rather, some changes in particular intellectual abilities may occur. For example, it is generally acknowledged that memory declines for older people. This is true for some people but it is not universal, as was noted earlier regarding changes in sensation and perception. More importantly, the decline in memory seems tied to the type of memory

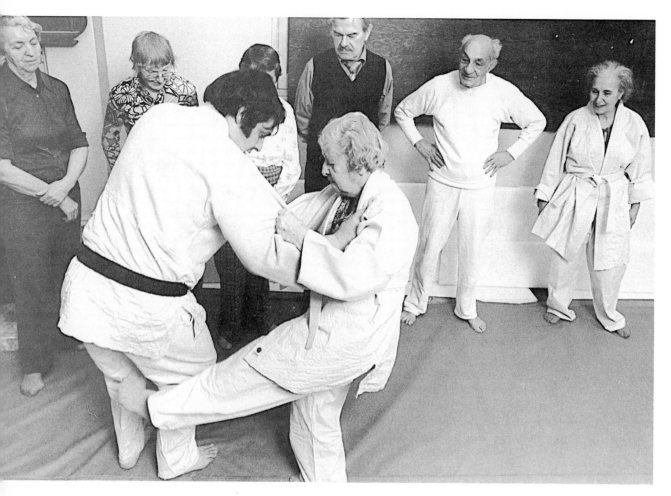

Although there are some changes in physical and cognitive abilities as people age, such changes do not keep older people from practicing old skills or learning new ones.

task that is required. Recall performance suffers to a much greater extent than recognition performance (Schaie, 1980). Data suggest that apparent decline depends on the task involved. Schaie draws an interesting conclusion: "Obviously, these data have substantial implications for the adult educator, both with respect to memorization strategies and for the design of examinations; contrary to folk wisdom, older learners are likely to do better on multiple choice than on essay examinations!" (Schaier, 1980, p. 15). The point is that older people might learn just as efficiently as younger people but may require a different type of test in order to demonstrate that learning.

Personality Changes: A Special Problem

One of the puzzling problems of aging is disease-related personality change. In earlier years, such changes were said to be the result of senility; but we have since come to realize that the label is not particularly useful because it implies that, eventually, all older persons become senile. This is certainly not the case. **Senility** is a disease; it is not part of the normal process of aging. Senility is actually a collection of symptoms that add up to a state of mental confusion. In describing these symptoms, it is important to be precise in both labeling and description. The most common form of the disease is known as **senile dementia**. The symptoms usually first appear after age 65. Often the first symptom to appear is memory loss. Then come

subtle personality changes, such as the development of apathy, lack of spontaneity and a quiet withdrawal from social interactions. Individuals usually remain neat and well-groomed and, aside from an occasional irritable outburst, are cooperative and behave in a socially appropriate way. With progression to the middle stages of the disease, various cognitive disturbances become quite apparent, and behavior and personality are more obviously affected. By the late stage, the individual may be completely mute and inattentive. At this point, he or she is totally incapable of caring for himself or herself. This stage leads inevitably to death. With senile onset, the average duration of symptoms from onset to death is about 5 years. (DMS–III, p. 125)

All forms of senility are disorders of the brain.

Delirium and Alzheimer's Disease. Another brain disorder in older persons is called **delirium**. This disorder appears quite suddenly and involves problems with attention and confusion and often includes visual hallucinations. It may result from poor nutrition, inappropriate dosage levels of medication, or similar kinds of problems. As you may remember from Chapter 2, neurotransmission is a very sensitive process. It is likely that the process becomes even more sensitive as a brain ages. This results in the increased vulnerability of the brain actions to outside influences such as prescription drugs.

Alzheimer's disease is still another form of brain disorder. This disease involves a gradual destruction of neurons in the brain and leads to the symptoms of senility as well as other symptoms that are not characteristic of the senile person (such as speech problems, convulsions, and hyperactivity). Because it is a physical deterioration of cells, it is not reversible. Alzheimer's disease can appear in a person as early as age 40. It has been estimated that be-

tween 2 and 4 percent of people over the age of 65 suffer from the type of dementia characteristic of Alzheimer's disease (DSM-III, 1980). A woman is three times more likely to get Alzheimer's disease than a man.

Recently, a great deal of research has been initiated in the diagnosis and treatment of Alzheimer's disease. Recent reviews of research (Khachaturian, 1985; Crook and Miller, 1985; Katzman, 1983) have provided direction for investigation of the disease. Unfortunately, we don't know a great deal yet. We suspect that there is a hereditary component, but there are also indications that infections might be involved (Khachaturian, 1985). The good news is that the federal government seems committed to funding the research necessary to solve the riddle of Alzheimer's disease (Heckler, 1985; Rickards, Zuckerman and West, 1985).

Yet another threat to brain functioning are strokes. Strokes result from a lack of oxygen to the brain; they can also cause small patches of neurons in the brain to die. From your knowledge of brain chemistry and brain function, you should be able to guess the effect of these neuron losses. The effects will be specific to the areas of the brain affected. Because the probability of stroke increases with age, older people may have several small strokes, separated by time, that give the appearance of a gradual deterioration such as might be seen in senile dementia or Alzheimer's disease. In fact, they are simply showing the accumulation of a series of discrete events. Brain disorders of an older person can be difficult to diagnose from simple observation. Correct treatment will depend heavily on correct diagnosis. The thing to keep in mind is that senility and brain disorders do not occur in the majority of older people. Similarly, a single symptom, such as memory loss, does not justify the label *senile*. As we have already seen, this could be simply a difficulty of recall that disappears when a recognition task is presented.

Senility. A disease that causes mental confusion, withdrawal, and personality change.

Senile dementia. A category of senility; long-lasting, irreversible brain disorder.

Delirium. Brain disorder that appears suddenly and can often be reversed; causes confusion and often visual hallucinations.

Alzheimer's disease. Form of brain disorder; causes a gradual destruction of neurons leading to symptoms of senility as well as other symptoms (for example, speech problems, convulsions).

Social and Emotional Changes in the Later Years

Let us return once more to Erikson's theory of social and emotional development over the life span. We have examined seven of his eight stages, or crises. The eighth and last crisis is *integrity versus despair*. Erikson proposed that even in later years, people continue to develop and change. As you saw earlier, a crisis is the catalyst for change. In the later years, the crisis appears in the form of an evaluation of one's life span up to that point and a realistic view of what is to come—a confrontation with the reality of death. There are two extremes to resolving this crisis. The first is acceptance and understanding of the role that death plays in the cycle of life. The person is able to integrate past experiences and come to an understanding of what his or her life span represents. The other extreme is despair and disgust. The person wants more time to try different things, to reach goals that have been elusive to this point. This unsuccessful resolution often leads to feelings of disgust and dissatisfaction with people and events. Nevertheless, even in the last period of life, change occurs.

Earlier, you read June Wilson's account of increased irritability. Social patterns change substantially as grandchildren arrive, children move far away and become absorbed with their own families, friends and spouses die, and retirement approaches. All these events precipitate changes in people's lives. These events occur earlier in some lives and later in others. Sometimes they do not occur at all. But one event does occur in everyone's life cycle—death. Death is something each of us considers, and this consideration often influences our actions, attitudes, and health. The last section of this chapter considers the implications that death and dying have for personal change in the later years.

Death and Dying. The last crisis in Erikson's theory brings us to the logical conclusion of the life span—death. As you might expect, old people think about death more often than young people (Cameron, 1973). That is not to say that these thoughts are necessarily negative. As Erikson suggests, the successful resolution of the integrity versus despair crisis implies a positive or neutral consideration of death.

Death and dying are separate issues in many ways. To contemplate death is to consider a future state of some type. To contemplate dying is to consider a process that may be frightening and painful. Kastenbaum (1979) examined the way old people prepare for death and suggested that this preparation has three components:

1. *Validation* involves people recalling past instances of effectiveness or competency. This has the effect of maintaining a positive self-concept and giving them the security necessary for the adaptations that will be required in their last years. This may also provide the impetus necessary to maintain skills or even develop new ones.

2. *Boundary setting* involves a conscious effort on the part of the person to identify clearly those things that belong to the past. As an example, older people often change residences, moving from the house in which they spent most of their adult years raising a family to a smaller residence or nursing home. Leaving the house requires leaving many fond memories. It is another indication that the last life segment is being played out. This is clearly a challenge that requires a cognitive response on the part of the person. This individual must find a compromise between the validation activities described above and the boundary-setting activities that represent objective reality.

3. *Replaying* involves recollection of particular events of the earlier years that brought pleasure. This is critically important because many direct opportunities for reinforcement and gratification are no longer available to the older person. There are few children who have not engaged in conversations with their older parents that begin, "Do you remember the time. . . ?" It is interesting that replaying is not confined to older people. It is often done by school-age children in the process of trying to understand or integrate new and old learning.

These three processes—validation, boundary setting, and replaying—are natural cognitive events that occur frequently in the later years. They are attempts by the person to cope with or adjust to a new status; they represent change. Being aware that these activities will occur and knowing why they occur may help you to deal more effectively with older friends and with your own parents. It would be useful to help them carry out these activities by reminiscing with them. It would be counterproductive to tell them to stop living in the past or to ignore their efforts to integrate past experience with present status.

Death is abstract; dying is concrete. The cognitive and emotional changes that occur when it is clear that the process of dying has begun are quite different from those described above that were related of death. Kübler-Ross (1975) has studied the manner in which people deal with dying. She conducted interviews with people who were dying and was able to identify several distinct stages that seem to occur frequently. As was the case with other stage theories, it is best to think of this theory as a general one that might apply to the "average" person (who does not really exist). Not everyone goes through these stages, and the stages may not be in the same order for those who do go through them. Nevertheless, Kübler-Ross's description is a valid one for many people who are dying, no matter what their age. The stages and their descriptions appear in Table 11–7.

These stages clearly represent attempts by the person to deal with the massive anxiety created by impending death. In fact, as a group, these reactions do not differ appreciably from a group of strategies called *defense mechanisms* that people of every age use to cope with stress. We will further examine defense mechanisms in Chapter 14 (Stress). The point is that these responses are clear attempts by the person to adapt to an external threat. That death may be inevitable for the person is irrelevant to the fact that these strategies for dealing with the anxiety will be activated. There is no such thing as "accepting" imminent death. Adaptation will take place in one way or another. As we saw in the chapter on perception, many cognitive processes are involuntary—they begin with an event and continue until the new event is integrated into some conceptual network.

A Final Comment

It has been a long journey from birth to death. If you come away impressed with one thing, it should be the fact that development and change continue over the entire life span. There is no period that is completely stable or unchanging. One aspect—such as sensory capacities—may have stabilized, but

TABLE 11–7
Kübler-Ross's Stages of Adjustment to Death

Denial	The person denies the possibility of death, will not believe it can happen to him or her, and searches for other, more promising opinions and diagnoses.
Anger	Once the person realizes he or she will indeed die, there is anger, resentment, and envy. The person is frustrated in that plans and dreams will not be fulfilled.
Bargaining	The person looks for ways to buy time, making promises and negotiating with God, doctors, nurses, clergymen, or others for more time or relief from pain and suffering.
Depression	When the bargaining fails or time runs out, hopelessness and depression take hold. The person mourns both for the losses that have already occurred and the death and separation from family and friends to come.
Acceptance	The person accepts and awaits his or her fate quietly.

Source: Kübler-Ross, 1969.

other aspects—such as motivational patterns—are still developing. In addition, because the real world continues to change at a rate that cannot always be controlled or even anticipated by the individual, adaptation is constantly required during every phase of life. Psychology may be unique among the sciences in its capacity to deal with and understand these adaptations.

REVIEW QUESTIONS

10. The lens of the eye thickens and yellows with age. This causes people to have difficulty discriminating among the colors _____ , _____ , and _____ .

11. One form of hearing loss that occurs with age is a loss of hearing in the high/low frequency ranges. This can be very troublesome because _____ consists of sounds in this frequency.

12. Senile dementia/delirium is long-lasting and seldom reversible once it begins.

13. _____ _____ is another form of brain disorder. It involves a gradual destruction of neurons in the brain and leads to the symptoms of senility as well as other symptoms.

14. Erikson's last stage of life crisis, which usually occurs in old age, is _____ versus _____ .

15. List the five stages of adjustment to death as defined by Kübler-Ross:
    1. _____
    2. _____
    3. _____
    4. _____
    5. _____

Answers: 10. blue; green; violet 11. high; speech 12. Senile dementia 13. Alzheimer's disease 14. integrity; despair 15. denial; anger; bargaining; depression; acceptance

■ SUMMARY

1. *Adolescence* is said to begin at puberty and end when the individual assumes adult responsibilities, but the beginning, end, and duration of this period vary considerably from person to person and from culture to culture. Adolescence is the transition from childhood to adulthood.

2. Physical changes in adolescence include the development of secondary sex characteristics, hormonal changes, and a growth spurt. These developments, on average, occur two years later in boys than in girls. These physical changes also alter the adolescent's self-concept and may require adjustments in coordination.

3. After entering puberty there is an increase in the extent to which the adolescent can experience pleasure from stimulation of the genitals. Sexual attitudes differ among adolescents in different age groups. A majority of unmarried females have had intercourse by age 20. Males tend to have inter-

course at an earlier age.

4. A major task for the adolescent is developing a self-concept, or a set of beliefs and evaluations about one's own abilities, personal characteristics, and behavior. Erikson considered the crisis of adolescence to be *identity versus role confusion.* Two sets of new data must be used in establishing the new identity: new physical information and new expectations of others. Marcia proposed that the adolescent might have one of four responses to the identity crisis: *achievement, moratorium, foreclosure,* or *diffusion.* These responses tend to change over time.

5. The adolescent develops *formal operations,* including the ability to hypothesize. *Adolescent egocentrism* is adolescents' feeling that they alone have special insight into the world and that they are the center of attention.

6. According to Erikson, a crisis in young adulthood is *intimacy versus isolation.* A commitment to another person cannot occur until one has a firm grasp on his or her own identity. This crisis of middle adulthood is *generativity versus stagnation,* or whether or not to be active in establishing new links with the world outside of the intimate relationship. Levinson identified several stages overlapping in transition periods in which the person must decide whether to keep an old identity or develop a new one.

7. One theory of how people decide to marry, the *stimulus-value-role* approach, assumes that both parties consider the assets and liabilities of each other in a particular sequence of stages: the stimulus stage, the value-comparison stage, and the role stage. A mistake in marrying may be the result of gathering inaccurate or incomplete information before the marriage. After the marriage, one partner may change in any one of the variable sets, and divorce may result.

8. Stereotypes about old people include notions that aging is a process of degeneration and that older people are frail, feebleminded, and unpredictable. The later years represent another segment of the life span that includes both physiological and cognitive changes. *Senility,* a disease that affects a percentage of older people, is a collection of symptoms that add up to a state of confusion. Three types of senility are *senility dementia, delirium,* and *Alzheimer's disease.*

■ ANSWERING QUESTIONS FOR THOUGHT

1. Adolescents do tend to assume that they are constantly being watched and evaluated and that they have a special insight into the world around them. This way of thinking, which has been called *adolescent egocentrism*, appears in adolescence and gradually disappears in young adulthood.

2. Yes, they do. At adolescence people become capable of *formal operations*, which is the ability to hypothesize or to consider a range of possible explanations for an event. In the previous stage of cognitive development, children have difficulty in considering abstract ideas. This marks a major difference between the way adolescents and children think.

3. One approach to analyzing the influences on a decision to marry has been termed the *stimulus, value, and role approach*. In the stimulus stage, first impressions are formed on the basis of attractiveness. In the value-comparison stage, each partner compares his or her interests, values, needs, and preferences with those of the other. The final stage is the role stage, during which partners try to anticipate in some detail what it will be like to be married to the other person.

4. The role of parent is an important one in adult development because it helps define a new life structure—one is now a mother or father instead of simply a woman or man, wife or husband. It is also the beginning of a new social unity—the family—and the beginning of a life cycle that is imposed on each partner's individual life cycle.

5. Reminiscing is one way for older people to prepare for death and to adjust to change at this stage of their lives. It helps them retain a positive self-concept as they recall past accomplishments; it also allows them a kind of indirect gratification by remembering pleasures from earlier years.

12 Emotion and Motivation

QUESTIONS FOR THOUGHT

1. Are emotions the same all over the world? Are they expressed the same way?
2. Does anxiety have the same efffect on everyone?
3. Is laziness a lack of motivation?
4. How can boredom motivate you?
5. Why do some people enjoy things like riding on roller-coasters or climbing high mountains?

The answers to these questions are at the end of the chapter.

"Have a nice day." This simple phrase has practically become a slogan of the times in America. One person wishes another person peace, tranquility, joy, and a day free of aggravation. Translated into psychological terms, the message might be: Have a day of positive emotions.

Emotions of every kind play a major role in our day-to-day activities. Feeling shy might cause us to avoid talking to someone. Being curious might help us decide where to go on our next vacation. The shock of surprise may leave us temporarily speechless even though the English vocabulary is full of words to describe emotions. Consider Table 12–1, which is only a partial listing of the many labels we have available for distinguishing among emotional experiences.

In some cases, as when we wish someone else a nice day, these labels represent goals to be achieved. It is certainly the goal of filmmakers, performers, and other kinds of artists to try to create feelings of intense fear, amusement, or anger in you. That is the *purpose* of their work—to create an emotional experience that was not present before the particular film, performance, or artwork was seen.

Purpose, or motivation, is present along with emotion in our daily behavior. A psychologist once said of behavior that it "reeks of intention and purpose" (Tolman, 1932). We may not always be aware of that purpose or it may not be obvious, but there is a purpose nonetheless. The study of motivation is an attempt to understand the purpose that underlies behavior.

In this chapter we will examine both emotion and motivation. Emotion and motivation are two closely related concepts. Over the years, theories have depended heavily on emotions as an energy source of motivation. Many, if not most, theories of human motivation begin with the idea that certain experiences are emotionally pleasant and others emotionally unpleasant, and that people try to increase emotional pleasure and decrease emotional pain. In fact, one psychologist (Tompkins 1970) asserts that emotion is *the* primary innate biological motivating mechanism. Because many psychologists consider emotion to be central to a conception of motivation, we will begin our discussion with a definition of

TABLE 12-1.
Emotions

Serene	Indignant
Cheerful	Jealous
Timid	Bitter
Panicky	Annoyed
Shy	Outraged
Embarrassed	Grouchy
Terrified	Greedy
Humiliated	Boastful
Nervous	Curious
Sad	Proud
Remorseful	Ecstatic
Worried	Hopeful
Gloomy	Enthusiastic
Despairing	Joyful
Discouraged	Pleased
Bewildered	Sympathetic
Amazed	Trusting
Disgusted	

emotion. An **emotion** is a reaction or experience made up of both cognitive and physiological elements. As we will see later, the physiological element usually involves the central and peripheral nervous systems. It is this combination of the physiological and cognitive components that distinguishes emotion from other concepts we have considered. To give you an example, sensation is directly activated by our sensory receptors, but there is little overall cognitive activity involved. Perception involves mental processes, but the autonomic nervous system plays no important role. It is this combination of changes in our physiological status and our cognitive interpretations of bodily as well as environmental changes that are linked to "feeling" good or bad. Thus an emotion is a **psychophysiological** event.

■ INDICATORS OF EMOTION

Like many of the topics of psychological study (such as learning, memory, or perception), emotion cannot be observed directly. Emotions may be inferred from things that can be observed, called *indicators*. In the study of emotion, most researchers agree that there are three broad classes of indicators: verbal reports, expressive reactions, and physiological reactions. In this section we will examine each of these classes of indicators in turn.

Verbal Reports

Most people are capable of describing how they feel at a particular time. While watching a football game, you might describe yourself at various points as excited, apprehensive, enthusiastic, or depressed. At work, you might describe yourself as bored, nervous, annoyed, or proud. Just before a test, you might tell a friend that you are confident, terrified, nervous, or distracted. On any or all of these occasions, a researcher could give you a checklist of words and ask you to put an X next to those that describe how you are feeling right then. Several dozen other people in a similar situation could be asked to fill out the same list. This list might contain words like *sad, surprised, guilty, delighted,* and *astonished*. By averaging these responses, a researcher can make some guesses about the "average" or typical reaction of

people to particular situations. He or she would then look at average or typical reactions across many situations and come to some conclusions about smaller or basic sets of reactions or emotions. This smaller set outlines the specific feelings of average people with respect to a particular situation. One example of a basic set has been suggested by Marshall and Izard (1972):

—joy	—fear
—surprise	—distress
—interest	—contempt
—disgust	—guilt
—anger	—fatigue
—shame	

Having people describe their emotions in words has been a very popular method for studying emotions. However, since this method is heavily dependent on a person's concepts (and vocabulary), it is not well-suited to the study of the universal nature of emotions. As a simple linguistic example, there are not nearly as many terms for emotional experiences in the Swedish language as there are in the English language. This does not mean that Swedes have fewer emotions, but it does mean that an analysis of verbal reports might yield different "basic" emotions. One way around this dilemma is through the observation of expressive reactions. This type of emotional display is nonverbal and presumably should present fewer problems than the verbal report method.

Expressive Reactions

A second way to study emotions is to observe people who are "having" emotions. For example, in a laboratory setting several dozen people might be exposed to a variety of sensory and cognitive stimuli—such as smells, sounds, pictures, and verbal descriptions—or be asked to imagine themselves in a given situation. Pictures could be taken of the subjects' faces while they were being exposed to the stimuli. Presumably, if the range of stimuli is broad enough, we should see all of the basic emotions in these people's faces.

This approach assumes that the face is critically tied to emotions. In fact, Charles Darwin suggested just that over a hundred years ago in his book *The Expression of Emotion in Man and Animals* (1862). He wrote that a natural link exists between emotions and facial expressions and that human facial expressions have their origins in the facial expressions of animals. Assuming Darwin's observations to be true, it would be a simple matter to use facial expressions to draw an emotional map of a human being.

One of the most active of modern researchers in this area has been Paul Ekman. He has conducted research on facial expressions throughout the world, often by asking people to identify emotions from the faces shown in photographs. Ekman has also included as his subjects primitive tribesmen who had never been exposed to the various models for emotional expression that exist in newspapers, magazines, or TV. Figure 12–1 presents a series of photographs he took in an experiment that asked New Guinea tribesmen to feign certain emotions. After a review of his own research and the research of others, he has come to the following conclusions about the facial expression of emotion (Ekman and Oster, 1979):

1. The labels that are attached to emotional expressions are universal and do not depend on specific cultural interpretation.
2. When asked to produce a particular emotional expression (such as anger or joy), members of different cultures will produce identical expressions.
3. People from one cultural group can recognize and correctly label the emotions expressed by members of a different cultural group. (It is possible for us to label what kinds of emotions are being expressed by the New Guinea tribesmen pictured in Figure 12–1.)

Darwin suggested that there is a natural link between emotions and facial expressions and that human facial expressions have their origins in the facial expressions of animals.

Emotion. A reaction or experience made up of both cognitive and physiological elements.

Psychophysiological. Having both a psychological and a physical, or physiological, effect—for example, an emotion, which involves both psychological and physiological elements.

FIGURE 12–1
Members of the Fore tribe of New Guinea were asked to show on their faces the appropriate expression for each of several emotion stories. From the left, the emotion stories were: "Your friend has come and you are happy"; "Your child has died"; and "You are angry and about to fight."

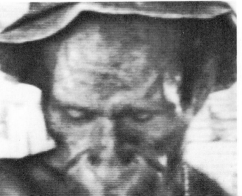

4. There appear to be at least six basic emotions: anger, disgust, happiness, sadness, fear, and surprise. There may be other basic emotions as well, but there are at least these six.

As you can see, there is some agreement between the verbal-report method and the facial-expression method that basic emotions can be identified. This is added support for the idea that there are some common or standard emotional categories. In both the verbal-report method and the facial-expression method, it is assumed that the person acts like an "emotion meter," giving the researcher a reading of how much or what type of emotion he or she is experiencing. In some respects, the person is viewed as part of a very basic input–output system: a stimulus comes in, affects the person emotionally, and the person reports it verbally or shows it by facial expressions. While this basic input–output system is a good model of emotional behavior most of the time, sometimes the emotion that a person reports or shows is not the emotion that the person is experiencing. Sometimes people may try to hide or deceive others about their real feelings. Because verbal reports and facial expressions may not always give an accurate reading of a person's emotions, researchers have suggested that physiological reactions may serve as a third class of emotional indicators.

REVIEW QUESTIONS

1. An emotion is a reaction or an experience made up of both _____ and _____ elements.

2. There are three indicators that can be used in the study of emotion: _____ _____, or statements by people about how they feel; how people appear to others, their _____ _____; and _____ _____, changes in internal bodily state.

3. Ekman found that members of primitive tribes, who had not been exposed to models of facial expressions in the media, had quite different expressions than we do for such basic emotions as anger, fear, and surprise.

T / F

Answers: 1. cognitive; physiological   2. verbal reports; facial expressions; physiological reactions   3. False

---

Physiological Reactions

As you will see shortly, physiological reactions are included in most theories of emotion. However, for over a hundred years the exact role of physiological reactions in emotion has been debated. Some theorists, such as William James, for example, have argued that each emotion has its own specific pattern of physiological reactions. Other theorists, such as Cannon, have argued that every emotion is accompanied by the same basic physiological reaction. In any case, it is agreed that physiological reactions serve as important indicators of emotions.

The idea that each emotion has its own specific pattern of physiological reactions has recently received some support. Ekman, Levenson, and Friesen (1983) had subjects perform deliberate facial actions as a way to investigate the physiological-reaction patterns for six different emotions. Subjects in this study were directed muscle by muscle into showing the facial expressions for surprise, disgust, sadness, anger, fear, and happiness. Figure 12–2 illustrates this procedure for the facial expression of fear. It is important to remember that the subjects were not told to produce an emotional expression but only to perform certain muscle actions. When each subject had performed all the muscle actions for a particular expression, their faces were videotaped and second-by-second averages for four physiological measures were recorded: heartrate, finger temperature, skin resistance, and forearm muscle tension. Figure 12–3 shows a decision tree for discriminating emotions based on two of these measures: heartrate and skin temperature. These results suggest that at least some emotions are associated with specific patterns of physiological reactions.

■ THEORIES OF EMOTION: PAST AND PRESENT

It is sometimes difficult to separate theories in psychology from the methods used to investigate them. This is certainly true in the area of emotion. As you have seen, verbal reports, expressive reactions, and physiological reactions are three popular methods for studying emotion. At the same time, they are the basic elements of every past and present theory of emotion. The major theories of emo-

FIGURE 12-2
Ekman had subjects perform deliberate facial actions for six different emotions. This
series of photos shows one subject's performance for the facial expression of fear.

tion represent either some combination of those elements or an emphasis on one element over the others.

James-Lange Theory

The first modern theory of emotion was proposed by William James. You may recall from Chapter 1 that James was among the first to rebel against the psychology of structuralism. James and other American functionalists were far less interested in the elements of consciousness than in the way consciousness functioned in on-going behavior. In James' view, consciousness involved ceaseless activity, a constant processing of internal changes. James' theory of emotion is based on this principle. According to James, an external stimulus causes arousal and internal (physiological) changes in our bodies. Emotion is the result of our awareness of changes in our bodily state. In other words, we notice this new state and report an emotion. A car (external stimulus) rushes toward us; we jump back and our hearts race (arousal and physiological change); we report that we are afraid (emotion). Figure 12–4 presents this sequence graphically. Similar propositions were made around the same time by a Danish psychologist named Lange. Thus, this approach came to be known as the **James–Lange theory** of emotion.

Cannon-Bard Theory

The James-Lange theory was attacked almost immediately upon reception. A physiologist named Cannon was able to show that a number of emo-

---

James-Lange theory. States that a stimulus event causes arousal and internal bodily changes, which are interpreted by us and reported as emotion.

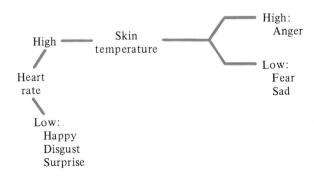

FIGURE 12-3
This is a decision tree for discriminating emotions in Ekman's directed facial action task. The distinctions are based on heart rate and skin temperature differences.

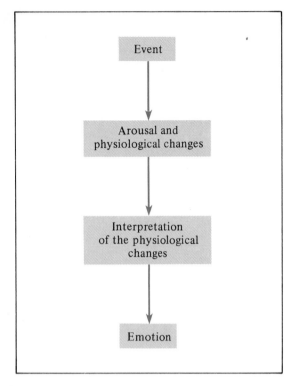

FIGURE 12-4
This diagram shows the James-Lange theory of emotion: An event causes arousal and physiological changes, which are interpreted by the person and reported as an emotion.

tions are identical physiologically, so a person's physiological state cannot provide information specific enough to account for the variety of emotions that are experienced. In addition, Cannon noted that emotions in response to an event often occur immediately, while bodily changes follow some seconds later. Finally, Cannon was able to show that animals whose neural pathways were severed so that their brains could not receive information from their internal organs still showed emotional behavior. As a result, Cannon suggested that an event gives rise to both physiological reactions (arousal) *and* the perception of an emotion. These reactions occur close in time but are both by-products of the external stimulus and are not directly related to each other. Cannon's research was followed up by Bard (1934), who was primarily interested in the neural aspects of emotion. Since that time, the theory has become known as the **Cannon-**

Bard theory of emotion. It is shown graphically in Figure 12-5.

However, there was one aspect of emotion on which the James–Lange and Canon–Bard theories agreed. Both proposed that arousal is involved in emotion. James felt that the pattern of arousal *was* the emotion. Cannon felt that the pattern of arousal occurred at the same time as the feeling, but was not otherwise connected. As was pointed out earlier, it is this element of physical arousal that helps to separate emotional experience from other types of experience.

The early history of research on emotion suffered many problems, some procedural and some conceptual. To begin with, it was not then possible to carefully measure many of the physiological systems that are now believed to play a role in emotional experience. More importantly, the many findings failed to distinguish between animal research and human research. Strongman (1978) points out that most of Cannon's objections to James' theory have been effectively refuted by modern research. But even though the Cannon-Bard theory now appears to be essentially incorrect, it is important in that it still represents one of the major physiologically based theories of emotion.

FIGURE 12-5
The Cannon-Bard theory of emotion says that an event gives rise to both physiological changes and the perception of an emotion.

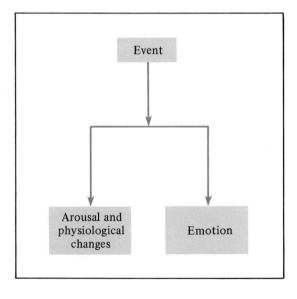

Schachter-Singer Theory

In 1962, a study was conducted by Schachter and Singer to test a new theory of emotion. This theory suggested that thought processes played a major role in the experience of emotion. Schachter and Singer proposed that a person is aroused by an outside stimulus, notices that arousal, looks to the environment for clues as to why the arousal has occurred, and picks an emotional label that fits the clues. The **Schachter-Singer theory** appears in graphic form in Figure 12-6.

In an experiment, groups of students were given injections of epinephrine. Epinephrine is a stimulant that produces increased heartrate, sweating palms, and fast breathing, among other symptoms. One group of subjects was told to expect these symptoms as a result of the injection; another group was told nothing. The hypothesis was that there would be a difference between the two groups in reported emotion. It was expected that the group that had been informed about the effect of the drug would not report any particular emotion, although they would be aware of the increased arousal. Since they had been told that the arousal would occur, there would be no need to look further than the drug injection for an explanation of this arousal. The uninformed group was expected to look for an explanation, since they were not aware of the effect of the injection. Also, the particular identity of the "emotion" experienced by the uninformed group was expected to be tied to social cues in the immediate environment. The uninformed group subsequently was broken down into two smaller groups. After the injection, one of these groups was exposed to a "subject" who acted silly. This "subject" (who is usually referred to as a *confederate*) was really an experimental assistant playing a role. The real subjects were led to believe that the confederate had also been given an injection. In this case, the real subjects also started to act silly and reported feeling "happy." The second group of real subjects was exposed to a confederate who acted angry. The confederate complained about filling out a questionnaire, ripped it up, and stalked out of the room. The real subjects in this situation then acted irritable and reported feeling angry.

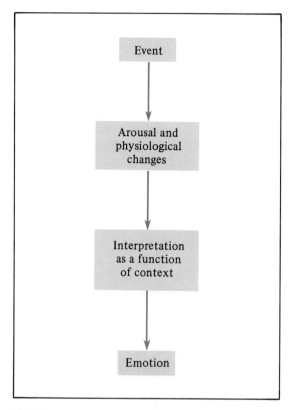

FIGURE 12-6

In the Schachter-Singer theory of emotion, an event causes arousal and physiological changes, which are noticed by the person, who looks to the environment for clues as to what caused the arousal and then picks an emotional label that fits the clues.

Schachter and Singer's results suggest that the most important components of emotion are arousal and cognition. An external event produces arousal and this arousal is given meaning by cues from the evironment. This should come as no surprise. For example, in the perception chapter we saw many examples of the meanings people give to sensations. This was the interpretation component of our model of perception (see Figure 4-1 in Chapter 4). In the case of emotion, rather than simply interpreting information from the environment, a person must integrate that external information with an internal state of arousal.

Schachter and Singer's theory of emotion is not

Cannon-Bard theory. States that a stimulus event gives rise to both physiological changes (arousal) and to the perception of an emotion.

Schachter-Singer theory. Proposes that a person is aroused by a stimulus event, looks to the environment for clues as to why arousal has occurred, and then labels the emotion.

THE RELATIONSHIP OF POSITIVE EMOTIONS TO NEGATIVE EMOTIONS

In our theories of emotion, we have been assuming that specific emotions are the result of unique combinations of levels of arousal and external stimuli. From this point of view, certain combinations should consistently lead to certain emotional experiences. But we know from personal experience that this is not the case. Our emotions change over time, even when the external stimulation stays the same. The layman's explanation for this is that we "get used to" the stimulus. This is not a satisfactory explanation for the scientist. *How* does someone "get used to" something? Does arousal decrease? Do we change the cognitive labels that we apply to arousal? Do we stop attending to the stimuli?

Solomon has suggested a theory of emotion that tries to explain the fact that what stimulates us today will bore us tomorrow. He calls his theory the *opponent-process theory* (Solomon and Corbitt, 1973, 1974; Solomon, 1980). This theory proposes that emotions represent a departure from some balanced state of the body. Emotions are accompanied by changes in the sympathetic nervous system, changes in blood composition, and changes in various organs of the body (eyes, lungs, heart, and skin). In fact, the parasympathetic nervous system seems to monitor changes of the sympathetic nervous system and has a controlling influence on bodily changes. In this sense, the parasympathetic nervous system opposes the sympathetic nervous system; it is automatic and is activated whenever the sympathetic nervous system is activated. Using the same logic, Solomon proposes that whenever we are presented with an arousing stimulus, our body begins to oppose the physical changes brought about by that stimulus. This opposing force (which Solomon calls an opponent process) gets stronger and appears quicker each time the arousing stimulus is presented. The opponent process is slow to disappear and remains active for some period of time (minutes or even hours) after the arousing stimulus has gone. Eventually, the opposing force appears shortly after arousal. This has the effect of canceling the arousing effect of the external stimulus and bringing the body back in balance. This accounts for the fact that we no longer feel "stimulated" or aroused by the stimulus. This is what we call boredom. Here is where the sluggish disappearance of the opponent process becomes important. After the stimulus is taken away, our emotional reaction is *exactly the opposite* of the initial emotional reaction to the object in question!

Let's look at a concrete example. You meet a person of the opposite sex and are very attracted to him or her. You spend every free moment with that person in the next few weeks. Initially, your heart was pounding and your palms were sweating when you were in the company of that person. After repeated "exposures" to the person, you begin to calm down. Your emotional reaction seems less extreme. Eventually, you even become "used to" this person. There doesn't seem to be any emotional reaction to that person any longer. But consider what happens if that person is suddenly unavailable. You will probably "miss" him or her terribly. You will experience the emotion of sadness. An extreme example of this is the grief that is experienced at the sudden death of a loved one. In spite of the fact that we may have taken people for granted, their absence shows that emotional systems are still active.

The implications of Solomon's theory for understanding emotions are profound. For one thing, it suggests that objects in the real world have no absolute power to please or displease. Anything that produces a pleasant feeling today in its presence will produce an unpleasant feeling tomorrow in its absence. Another implication is that we are not always aware of physiological systems that are at work balancing our bodily states. Many researchers have noted that departures from a normal or neutral state can be physically and psychologically damaging to a person.

Solomon also makes a very convincing argument that many addictive behaviors (such as smoking, drinking, and drug dependency) can be best understood as examples of opponent processes at work. At first, the stimulus (the cigarette or the drink) produces a positive feeling. After many exposures to that stimulus, its absence now produces the opposite emotional reaction—pain. This accounts for the craving that seems to motivate the addict to use the substance again. But now it is used to eliminate pain. George Bernard Shaw made a similar observation in *Man and Superman.* He said, "There are two tragedies in life. One is to lose your heart's desire. The other is to gain it."

without its critics. Their theory, like other cognitive theories of emotion as well as the Cannon–Bard theory, presumed that the physiological reaction was the same for all emotions. Ekman and his colleagues have produced data that question this assumption. Any modern theory of emotion must therefore explain how the three indicators of emotion—verbal reports, expressive reactions, and physiological reactions—interact with one another in our experience of emotion.

■ EMOTIONALITY AS AN INDIVIDUAL DIFFERENCE

We sometimes refer to emotional people as "high strung." This is a way of saying that some people are more easily aroused than others. Since arousal seems to be central to emotions, easily-aroused people might be reasonably referred to as emotional. There could be a number of physiological reasons for this. Easily-aroused people might have sensitive limbic systems that are easily activated; or they might have very active adrenal or pituitary glands that produce above-average amounts of hormones;

or they might have cortexes that do not have as much inhibitory control over their emotions. Whatever the reason, some people do seem to be more emotional than others.

There is one emotion that seems particularly subject to these individual differences—anxiety. Many people can be reliably classified as either high or low in anxiety (Levitt, 1980). Anxiety can have serious effects on intellectual performance. A demonstration of the negative effects of anxiety was shown in a study involving students in an introductory psychology class similar to the one that you are taking (Paul and Eriksen, 1964). The students in the course were given a typical class exam. A few days later, they were given a second exam covering the same material and made up of the same type of questions. The second time the students took the exam they were told that it would have nothing at all to do with their grades—it was just being administered for experimental purposes. The students had already filled out a questionnaire that enabled the experimenters to identify those students who were high in anxiety. On the first exam, the one that "counted," there was a negative correlation between anxiety scores and test scores. This means that those students who were classified as anxious scored more

Test-taking offers evidence of individual differences in anxiety levels and of the effect of emotions on performance.

poorly, and those who were low on anxiety scored well. On the second test, there was no correlation between anxiety and test performance; there were just as many high-anxious students who scored well as who scored poorly. Similarly, there were just as many low-anxious students among the low scorers as there were among the high scorers. Furthermore, the mean or average test score for the two tests was equal. This means that on the second test many of the high-anxious students improved their test scores, and many of the low-anxious students did more poorly than on the first test. You probably have noticed that many people perform better when there is no pressure. Other people thrive on pressure and do much better when they are anxious. Both of these circumstances are evidence of individual differences in anxiety levels and of the effect of emotions on performance.

A study involving verbal problem-solving showed similar results (Harleston, 1962). The subjects were asked to solve anagrams. This is a task in which scrambled letters must be rearranged into meaningful words. For example, the stimulus word might be *levos*, and one correct solution is *solve*; another is *loves*. There were both easy and difficult anagrams in the experiment. In addition, the subjects were categorized as either low, medium, or high in anxiety. The results of the study appear in Table 12–2. As you can see, difficult problems took their toll on the high- and medium-anxious subjects. On the other hand, there were only slight differences in the performances among the groups when the problems were easy.

Another study looked at the effect of anxiety on the ability of people to communicate. It has often been noted that when people are excited or aroused,

they don't communicate effectively. Gynther (1957) categorized subjects as high-anxious and low-anxious. She then examined the ability of the subjects to communicate effectively in stressful and nonstressful situations. She found that both groups communicated more effectively in the nonstressful situation; and in both the stressful and nonstressful situation, the low-anxious subjects communicated more effectively than the high-anxious subjects. Nunnally (1961) also examined the effect of anxiety on people's ability to understand. He found that messages that were stress-provoking were less well understood than messages that provoked little stress for anxious subjects. The implications of these studies for daily behavior are clear. Both verbal expression and verbal comprehension are inhibited by anxiety. If we are chronically anxious, the effects of stress on expression and comprehension seem to be even greater.

TABLE 12-2.
Number of Anagrams Solved as a Function of Anxiety-Proneness

	Type of Anagram		
Anxiety Group	*Easy*	*Hard*	*All*
Low	155	118	273
Medium	151	89	240
High	147	88	235

Data from Harleston (1962).

REVIEW QUESTIONS

4. Match the following names with the theory connected to them:
   ___ James-Lange   A. stimulus causes both changes in bodily state *and* perception of an emotion at about the same time.

   ___ Cannon-Bard   B. stimulus causes arousal; we notice the arousal and look to our environment for clues to label the emotion.

   ___ Schachter-Singer   C. stimulus causes changes in bodily state; we notice the new state and report it as an emotion.

5. Some people are more easily aroused than others, and consequently are more emotional than others.

   T / F

6. Studies show that both verbal _____ and verbal _____ are inhibited by anxiety.

Answers: **4.** James-Lange, C; Cannon-Bard, A; Schachter-Singer, B. **5.** True **6.** expression; comprehension

■ MOOD

When you think of emotional experiences, it is likely that you think in terms of happy–sad or pleasant–unpleasant feelings. The term **mood** is often used to characterize the general pleasantness or unpleasantness of a particular emotional experience. Pleasant emotional experiences are associated with happy, good, or positive moods. Unpleasant emotional experiences are associated with sad, bad, or negative moods. Recently, a good deal of research has been done to see if positive and negative moods have different effects on behavior. In this section we will consider the effects of positive and negative moods on two aspects of behavior: memory and prosocial behavior.

Mood and Memory

Let's begin with psychologist Gordon Bower's account of Sirhan Sirhan's recollection of events surrounding the assassination of Robert Kennedy. The assassination had been recorded on videotape and Sirhan Sirhan was charged and eventually convicted of killing Kennedy.

Sirhan had absolutely no recollection of the actual murder, which occurred in the small kitchen of the Ambassador Hotel where he pumped several bullets into Kennedy. Sirhan carried out the deed in a greatly agitated state and was completely amnesiac with regard to the event. Hypnosis helped Sirhan to reconstruct from memory the events of that fateful day. Under hypnosis, as Sirhan became more worked up and excited, he recalled progressively more, the memories tumbling out while his excitement built to a crescendo leading up to the shooting. At that point Sirhan would scream out the death curses, "fire" the shots, and then choke as he reexperienced the Secret Service bodyguard nearly throttling him after he was caught. (Adapted from Bower, 1981, p. 129)

Bower, an experimental psychologist interested in learning and memory, was intrigued by this and similar incidents of selective memory. It seemed to him that the extent to which people recalled something depended on the mood they were in at the time the event occurred and the mood they were in when they tried to recall the event. He called this **mood-dependent memory.** Bower launched a series of experiments to test this hypothesis.

In one of his first experiments (Bower et al., 1978), Bower hypnotized college students and asked them to imagine themselves in either a happy or a sad situation. When they had successfully established this mood, the students were asked to memorize a list of 16 words. After the list had been learned, the students were asked to switch to the opposite mood. If they had been happy at first, they now became sad. After the mood was switched, the students memorized a second list of words. At a later time (either 10 minutes or 1 day later), the students were asked to recall words from the first list. Before beginning the recall task, students were once again put in a happy or a sad mood. The results of the recall attempts are shown in Figure 12-7.

The results showed that people remembered the word list better when they were in the same mood they had been in when they originally learned the list. The results are clear-cut and dramatic, although,

---

Mood. A mild, usually transitory emotion; often used to describe the general pleasantness or unpleasantness of a particular emotional experience.

Mood-dependent memory. Memory may be better if the person is in the same mood at the time of recall as he or she was when the event occurred or the material was learned; thus, one's memory may depend on one's mood.

FIGURE 12-7
This graph shows the effect on recall attempts of the match between learning mood and recall mood. Subjects could recall many more items if the subjects were in the same mood in which they first learned the items. (Bower et al., 1978)

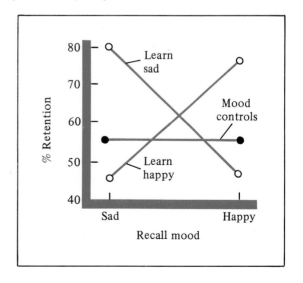

as you will see, they are open to several possible interpretations. There was another finding of the study that Bower had found repeatedly in similar experiments—there is no particular advantage to being in one mood or another when either learning or recalling. In other words, there does not seem to be any particular advantage in being happy or in a "positive state of mind" for either initial learning or later recall. What does seem to make a difference is the similarity of the mood when learning and recalling; that is, memory is better when the learning and recall moods are matched. If you learned material when you were happy and attempted to recall that material when you were sad, your recall would be worse than if you tried to recall the same material when you were in a happy mood.

This was a nice demonstration of the effect of mood on memory for lists of words, but learning lists of words is an uncommon event in the real world. It might be argued that this effect is limited to meaningless lists and would not be found in real situations. Bower's next experiment (Bower and Gilligan, 1979) dealt with a person's capacity to remember personal experiences while in positive and negative moods. People were asked to keep diaries of emotional events that occurred over the course of a week. For each emotional event, the subjects were asked to list the time and place of the event, who else was involved, and the details of what occurred. They were also asked to rate the event on a 10-point scale that ranged from pleasant to unpleasant. A week after the people turned in their diaries, they were asked to recall the events that had been recorded in their diary. Before beginning the recall task, hypnosis was used to put 50 percent of the people in a positive emotional state. The other 50 percent were hypnotized into a negative emotional state. The results appear in Figure 12–8. As was the case with the word lists, mood made a difference in recall. The people who were in a positive mood recalled proportionately more positive events than negative events. People in a negative recall mood recalled proportionately more negative events.

In his next experiment, Bower asked subjects to recall events from childhood. Through hypnosis, one group of subjects was put in a positive mood before beginning the recall task and a second group was put in a negative mood. A day after producing these childhood recollections, subjects returned and

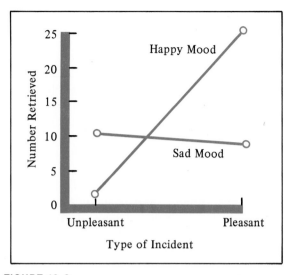

FIGURE 12–8
In this experiment, mood also had an effect on recall. If subjects were hypnotized and put in a positive mood, they recalled more positive events than negative events; if put in a negative mood, they recalled more negative events. (Bower and Gilligan, 1979)

rated these recollections on the 10-point pleasant–unpleasant scale. The results of the third experiment were similar to those of the first two experiments: Subjects in positive moods recalled a larger number of positive events and subjects in negative moods recalled a larger number of negative events.

In every one of Bower's studies mood seems to play a role in recall. In many respects, however, these studies are imprecise. As you saw in the memory chapter, there are several different mechanisms involved in memory. Two of the most important are encoding (storage) and retrieval. Given what we know about memory, the most likely explanation for Bower's results is that the mood that someone is in when they encounter information plays a role in determining how that information is encoded, particularly with respect to semantic (or meaning) encoding (Craik and Lockhart, 1972). In the chapter on memory, you learned that semantic encoding plays a major role in memory. If we look at Bower's results in this light, this means that it is not necessarily helpful for people to be in the same mood when they recall something as they were when they first learned it. Instead, it means that semantic cues will help in retrieving this information. To the extent that the hypnosis method of establishing mood also brings out semantic cues, a person's memory for previously-learned material improves. This makes the interpretation of Bower's results much more cognitive and less physiological. In addition to the issue of the theoretical explanation for Bower's results, there is also some question about positive versus negative moods. It seems that the results differ somewhat. Bower's results have been confirmed in positive-mood states more often than in negative-mood states (Nasby and Yando, 1982). Future research is necessary to settle the issue of *why* Bower obtained his results.

The implications of these findings for many different behaviors are important and don't really change if the explanation of Bower's results is cognitive rather than emotional. In clinical psychology, one of the most serious problems to treat is depression. Depression is considered a negative mood. Bower's findings suggest that people who are depressed are more likely to remember sad or unhappy events, which has the effect of deepening the depression. In the same way, people who are anxious are more likely to remember events that produce fear or apprehension. These memories probably have the effect of raising or maintaining the anxiety level. Natale and Hantas (1982) confirmed Bower's findings about the effect of negative-mood states on recall and extended them to include self-conceptions and self-esteem. Subjects in a hypnotically-induced negative mood tended to describe themselves in more negative terms than did subjects in a hypnotically-induced positive mood. Children's memories also seem to be somewhat affected by mood. A study of fifth-grade children (Nasby and Yando, 1982) showed that positive mood improved their recall for emotionally-positive words, although the same was not true of negative moods and emotionally-negative words. It is clear that the effects Bower finds are complicated and probably depend on many factors in addition to mood. These factors might include type of task, type of subject, and the manner in which the mood is created. Nevertheless, his research suggests several avenues of application.

Depression and anxiety have often been described as vicious circles. Bower's concept of mood-dependent memory may prove valuable in understanding how the circle is formed and pro-

tected. Bower's data suggest that one form of therapy might involve trying to change the way depressed people think about events. As you will see in Chapters 15 and 16, this technique has been used in treating depression (Beck, 1976). Depressed people are trained to break out of the vicious circle by interjecting either neutral or positive thoughts whenever a negative mood begins to arise. This prevents them from recalling depressing events from the past. Bower's data suggest that if positive thoughts are substituted for negative ones, a positive emotional state will result and may help the recollection of positive past events. The combination of Bower's research findings and strategies discovered in clinical research and practice provides a perfect example of the connection between science and application. As a result of research such as Bower's, it may be possible to refine and extend the therapy strategies currently in use.

There is a second area of application of Bower's results that may have more direct implications for everyday behavior. Some of the studies described above indicate that what we remember may depend on the mood we are in when we are required to recall the information. If we are in a good mood, we will remember good things. If we are in a bad mood, we will remember bad things. There are many everyday judgments that depend on memory. To mention just two, grades assigned by teachers and ratings of employee performance by supervisors depend to varying extents on recollection of instances of behavior. In spite of the fact that test scores play a role in determining grades, teachers often exercise personal discretion in assigning final grades. They consider all of the elements of student behavior, including attendance, class participation, and so on, and combine these recollections with test grades when making a final decision. Bower would predict that these teachers may remember one set of events when they are in a negative mood (unpleasant interactions with the student in question) and another set of events when they are in a positive mood (pleasant interactions with the student).

The same mechanism might be involved in supervisory ratings of workers' performance on the job. If the supervisor is in a good mood, good things will be recalled about the subordinate. If the supervisor is in a bad mood, examples of ineffective performance may be recalled. The situation becomes even more complex if we consider the mood we are in when we originally observe the behavior in question. Bower's data may mean that how we encode (store) information depends on mood as well. A general summary of this speculation is that whenever one person evaluates another and whenever this evaluation depends on memory, there is the possibility that mood states will affect that evaluation.

Mood and Prosocial Behavior

There seems to be sufficient evidence to suggest that positive and negative moods have an effect on intellectual activity. The literature on anxiety documents the effect of stress on problem-solving and communication skills. The research done by Bower points to the effects of positive- and negative-mood states on memory. There is an additional line of research that shows the effects of mood states on prosocial or helping behavior.

The Warm Glow of Success. Why do some people stop and offer assistance when your car stalls? Why do some people hold the door for you? Why do some people help you pick up the pile of papers that you just dropped? Each of these instances is classified as prosocial behavior. Isen (1970) suggested that this type of behavior may be the result of mood. Simply put, people who are in a good mood are more likely to help another person than people who are in a bad mood. She designed a clever experiment to test this hypothesis. The subjects in the experiment were teachers in a suburban school district. They were asked to take a series of tests that identified relationships between perceptual-motor skills and creativity. After completing the tests, they were told how well or how poorly they did, but in fact what the subjects were told had nothing to do with their real scores or performances. One randomly selected group of the subjects was told that they had performed well above average and another group was told that they had performed well below average. It was expected that the performance feedback would create feelings of success (which would be emotionally positive) or failure (which would be emotionally negative).

The tests were administered on a hot summer day in an air-conditioned library of a senior high school. When they had completed the tests, each subject received $1 in change as a reward for participating in the study. After the subjects had received their success or failure feedback, they were asked to wait for a brief period while the test administrator retrieved some forms in another room. While they were waiting, a door opened and a person came into the room carrying a can with the label "Junior High Air Conditioning Fund." The person with the can explained that the junior high school building was *not* air-conditioned and that it was felt

What leads one person to offer help to another? Helping behavior may be the result of mood—people who are in a good mood are more likely to help someone else than people who are in a bad mood.

that the best place to collect money might be in the air-conditioned library of the senior high school. The can, containing $2 in change, was then left on the table and the subjects were once again left alone in the room. The results of the study were clear-cut. Subjects who had experienced "success" put an average of 46¢ in the can. Subjects who had experienced "failure" averaged 7¢ in donations.

A second study was conducted with similar subjects in a similar situation. This time, instead of a person entering the room with a can for charitable donations, a person entered the room with an armful of books and managed to drop one. The variable of interest was whether or not a subject would pick up the book for the person who had dropped it. As was the case in the first experiment, those subjects who had experienced success helped more frequently than those who had experienced failure. This is what Isen referred to as the "warm glow of success." She had demonstrated that success and failure seem to affect people's willingness to help.

In a follow-up to the library study, Isen (1972) showed that prosocial behavior was not just the result of success, as might have been the case in the library study. Instead, prosocial behavior seemed to result from receiving an unexpected reward or present. In this follow-up study, some subjects unexpectedly received a cookie and their prosocial behavior was compared to other subjects who did not receive a cookie. Those who received the cookie were more likely to engage in prosocial behavior than those who did not. There was, however, the possibility that the prosocial behavior could be the result of imitation. A stranger had come by and done something nice—given them a cookie. Perhaps the subjects decided to try out the same behavior and see what happened. For this reason, they volunteered to do something nice.

The "Dime" Study. In order to eliminate any modeling or imitative effects, Isen designed a study called the "dime" study. This time, the study took part in an urban shopping mall. The subjects were 24 randomly-selected males and 17 randomly-selected females who happened to make calls from a particular phone booth. In order to create a positive mood, a dime was left in the coin return of a phone booth after the experimenter made an incomplete call. In the control condition, the experimenter was unable to complete the call but took

the dime out of the coin return. Thus, a subject was any person who entered the phone booth immediately after the experimenter had left the booth. In half of the trials, a dime was left in the return. In the other half of the trials, the dime was taken out by the experimenter. If the person who followed the experimenter into the booth did not look in the coin return, he or she was no longer considered a subject and no further data were gathered.

After the subject completed a call and had left the phone booth, an experimenter began to walk in the same direction and slightly ahead of the subject. At a designated point, the experimenter dropped a manilla folder filled with papers, which spread across the floor. The measure of prosocial behavior was whether or not the subject stopped and helped the experimenter to pick up the papers. Once again, the results suggested that a positive mood led to prosocial behavior. Of the 16 subjects who found a dime in the coin return, 14 stopped and helped. Of the 24 who did not find a dime in the coin return, one helped to pick up the papers. These data are about as convincing as any could be that the simple pleasure of an unexpected reward can be converted into prosocial behavior. Both modeling and task success can be discounted as explanations.

The issue of why a positive-mood state leads to helping behavior is still open to question. A recent study (Batson et al., 1980) suggests that receiving a reward increases arousal, which in turn leads to an increase in many behaviors, including helping another person in need. Ultimately, the answer may be found in blood chemicals or neurotransmitters. The important point is that positive moods seem to lead to helping behavior. This is another of the many implications that emotions hold for common behavioral patterns.

In some recent studies, Isen has shown that the good feeling and the resulting helping behavior do not last very long (Isen et al., 1976), perhaps less than 20 minutes. This may be explained by hormonal action. As you learned in the chapter on biology and behavior (Chapter 2), hormones are slow-acting and remain in the bloodstream after an arousing stimulus has disappeared. If the stimulus was a mild one (such as receiving a free gift of cosmetics), the chemical effect might be mild as well, disappearing within a few minutes. In terms of a sequence of physiological events, this means that after the hormones stopped flowing into the bloodstream the neurotransmitters stopped stimulating the sympathetic nervous system, arousal level declined, and behavior returned to normal (control) levels.

Isen's data provide confirmation of something that you may have suspected: If you plan to ask people for a favor, it is best to get them into a good mood first. The knowledge that hormones affect the time-span of an emotion extends this application. Not only should you get them in a good mood, but you should ask them for the favor *quickly*. The suggestion to "strike while the iron is hot" may be based on this idea.

REVIEW QUESTIONS

7. The term _____ usually is used to describe the general feeling of pleasantness or unpleasantness of an emotional experience.

8. Bower theorized that people would remember things better if they were in the same mood/in a different mood as they were when the events occurred.

9. Another line of research on the effects of mood has studied the effects of mood states on _____ behavior.

10. Isen has found that a good mood makes people more/less willing to help others than a bad mood.

Answers: 7. mood **8.** same mood **9.** prosocial **10.** more

■ THE RELATIONSHIP BETWEEN EMOTIONS AND MOTIVATION

As you have seen, emotions are very complicated psychophysiological events. We have also seen that emotions can have profound effects on our daily activities. As suggested at the beginning of this chapter, many psychologists believe that emotions are central to motivation and that in fact motivation relies on emotion to supply the energy that turns motives into action. Tompkins (1970) brings the relationship between emotion and motivation into sharp focus with the following illustration:

Consider anoxic deprivation. Almost any interference with normal breathing will immediately arouse the most desperate gasping for breath. Is there any motivational claim more urgent than the demand of one who is drowning or choking to death for want of air? Yet it is not simply the imperious demand for oxygen that we observe under such circumstances. We are also observing the rapidly mounting panic ordinarily recruited whenever the air supply is suddenly jeopardized. The panic amplifies the drive signal, and it is the combination of drive signal and panic which we have mistakenly identified as the drive signal. We have only to change the rate of anoxic deprivation to change the nature of the recruited affect which accompanies the anoxic drive signal. Thus, in the Second World War, those pilots who refused to wear their oxygen masks at 30,000 feet suffered a more gradual anoxic deprivation. They did not panic for want of oxygen. They became euphoric. It was the affect of enjoyment which the more slowly developing anoxic signal recruited. Some of those men, therefore, met their deaths with smiles on their lips (p. 101–102).

■ APPROACHES TO MOTIVATION

Motivation consists of the circumstances surrounding the beginning, direction, intensity, and the ending of behavior (Vinacke, 1962). In other words, why do people act the way they do?

Over the years there have been many suggestions about what motivates people. One of the earliest-suggested reasons was instinct. It was believed that each person was born with a set of preprogrammed urges to behave in particular ways. These urges were labeled **instincts**. Furthermore, the early theorists believed that all humans had the same set of instincts. These instincts were thought to be at the core of motivated behavior—when certain stimuli were present these instinctive behaviors were activated.

Another approach to understanding behavior has been the biological one, in which hunger and thirst are two good examples of motivators. Biological approaches to motivation propose that a person has certain physical needs that must be met. For example, we know that cells need nutrients to function. When nutrients are absent, the cells have a **need**. Drive is thought to be a condition that results from need. **Drive** is a mobilization of energy or resources directed toward meeting a particular need. People are "driven" to satisfy needs. In a sense, needs are thought to charge or energize people. Since need and drive are such closely-connected concepts, the terms are often used interchangeably.

As we saw in the chapters on learning, associations play an important role in behavior. The concept of association plays an important role in motivation as well. Some approaches to motivation emphasize the fact that people form associations in the process of satisfying biological needs. These associations are between stimuli that directly satisfy the need (food, which satisfies hunger) and stimuli that are indirectly related to the satisfaction of the need. For example, some people act as if they have a need for money. They work hard to get it, they save it, they count it, they are upset when they lose it. This need for money seems to operate like the need for food or water; the difference is that the need for money is an acquired or learned need. In Chapter 6, we learned to distinguish between a primary and a secondary reinforcer: a primary reinforcer has an immediate and automatic effect on some biological state of the person. Shock reduction is a good example of a primary reinforcer. A secondary reinforcer has its effect only through its association with a primary reinforcer; the power of the secondary reinforcer is acquired or learned. The same sort of distinction has been applied to motivation analysis. **Primary needs** or drives are those needs that are directly related to some bodily state, and **secondary needs** or drives are those needs that have arisen as a result of an association with a primary drive. For example, let's examine sexual activity. Sex might be considered a primary drive that results in sexual activity. This does not explain why we are sexually attracted to certain people and not to others. Why do some women find the "strong, silent type" particularly attractive? Why do some men prefer blonds? These are both examples of secondary drives. There is no biological reason why strong men or blond women are more satisfactory in meeting sexual needs.

Still another approach to understanding motivation is called the *incentive approach*. This approach concentrates on the characteristics of the goal that pulls us toward it. This is in contrast to need theories, which have more of a "pushing" quality to them. For example, put an average child in a room with an electric typewriter and the child will type. There is no clear "need to type" or "typing drive" that can be biologically identified. Instead, it seems almost as if the stimulus characteristics create the behavior. The presence of the typewriter is an incentive to action, and in particular, a main source of pulling behavior. Incentive theory and need or drive theory have often been contrasted as the carrot and the stick approaches, respectively. This refers to the problem of moving a mule that is too "stubborn" to move on its own. One person might suggest jabbing the mule with a pointed stick (creating a need state that must be satisfied, such as the need to reduce pain). Another person might suggest tempting the mule with a carrot (presenting an incentive to move).

Need and incentive approaches do not emphasize cognitive variables. Primary needs are assumed to be biological realities, and secondary needs are learned through association with biological conditions. Incentives have a power of their own to elicit certain behavior. In none of these approaches is it important that the person think, decide, or judge. The person responds to a need or to a stimulus. A final class of motivational approaches emphasizes thinking and cognition. These approaches suggest that the beginning, the direction, the intensity, and the ending of behavior can best be understood by knowing what plans the person has, what beliefs he or she holds about the results of certain actions, and even how confident he or she is that a particular action will have a particular effect.

Remember that motivation is different from learning. Learning provides us with the skill or in-

---

Motivation. What makes people behave the way they do; more technically, the circumstances surrounding the start, direction, intensity, and end of behavior.

Instincts. Complex, unlearned responses that are characteristic of a given species.

Need. A physical necessity, such as food, water, or air.

Drive. A condition that results from need—a mobilization of energy directed toward meeting a particular need.

Primary needs. Needs that are directly related to some bodily state, such as hunger or thirst.

Secondary needs. Needs that are not directly related to a bodily state, but have arisen as a result of an association with a primary drive—examples would be the need to have a large bank account or a brand new car.

formation necessary to perform a particular action, but it does not explain *why* we perform that action. Recall the study of latent learning in Chapter 7, in which animals were carried from one place to another and watched food being hidden (Menzel, 1978). If those animals were later allowed to explore the environment, their exploration patterns would depend to a certain extent on their hunger (primary need state) and the incentive value of the food. If they had been deprived of food, they would go directly to the hiding places as they did in the experiment. On the other hand, if they had just been fed, their pattern of behavior would be very different and they might not go to the hiding places at all. In the same way, if the animals were in a new environment in which they had never seen food being placed, they might not act "hungry" or explore for food. Learning provided the potential or precondition for behavior, but learning was not responsible for the food-searching behavior. The process of motivation in this case is quite distinct from the process of learning.

In the same way, motivation can be distinguished from emotion. An emotion suggests a particular bodily state (such as arousal) and a particular interpretation of that state. This emotion may represent a need state (for example, fear) with implications for energy expenditure (for example, flight), but the emotion is independent of the energy expenditure. The process by which a bodily state was created (emotion), and the process by which that bodily state is dealt with (motivation), are quite different. It is not that they are unrelated, it is just that they are unique psychological concepts. In most motivation theories, emotions play an important role in the intensity and direction of behavior. It is the desire to attain a good feeling or avoid a bad feeling that is the basis of many of the motivation theories we will examine.

In summary, motivation theory attempts to explain the fact that two different people with the same biological status and equal learning experiences might behave differently. For example, both you and a friend are offered an opportunity to make a little extra money by working overtime. You accept the offer and your friend turns it down. How can the difference between the two of you be explained? Motivation theories aim at explaining such differences.

There are literally dozens of motivation theories. It is neither necessary nor appropriate to present all of these theories in an introductory psychology course. Instead, we will study some examples of different types of theories. We will start with a consideration of two common biological need states.

■ NEEDS

Hunger and Thirst: Biological Needs

When you go for a long period of time without water, you get thirsty. The longer you are without water, the thirstier you become. Up to a point, the same seems to be true of going without food. In the early periods of food deprivation, hunger seems to increase with time. In the case of hunger, however, a point seems to be reached where it no longer seems to increase. These two conditions, hunger and thirst, are related to particular kinds of behavior—eating and drinking. When you are hungry and food is available, you eat. When you are thirsty and water is available, you drink. In these two circumstances, your body has a particular biological status. For example, in the case of hunger, your blood-sugar may be low and your stomach may be empty. If possible, you look for restaurants. You may look for them in the phone book or you may walk up and down the streets, but your behavior has begun, is directed, and is maintained by a combination of a biological condition (low blood-sugar and an empty stomach) and the anticipation of food. Once you have found something to eat and you consume it, your biological condition changes once again. For one thing, your blood-sugar goes up. This new biological condition is no longer related to the search for food. Instead, it may be related to resting and digesting. According to our definition, the search for food is a motivated behavior. It appears, is directed, and is maintained for some time before disappearing.

Eating and drinking are good examples of motivated behaviors with biological influences. It has been known for some time that the hypothalamus is directly involved in the regulation of eating behavior. Lesions or injuries to different parts of the hypothalamus result in changes in eating behaviors.

If one part of the hypothalamus is injured, eating is slow to begin, no matter how long it has been since the last meal was eaten (Anand and Brobeck, 1951; Carlson, 1981). If another part of the hypothalamus is injured, eating is excessive, no matter how much food has already been eaten (Hetherington and Ranson, 1940; 1942; Carlson, 1981). These two sections of the hypothalamus seem to have different primary functions—one to start eating and the other to stop eating. The two sections may not be completely independent of one another but their primary functions can be distinguished. The process is much more complicated than this (Grossman, 1979) and probably involves sensory mechanisms, hormones, metabolic levels, and additional brain areas, but for the sake of the present discussion, we can assume that eating and drinking behavior are influenced by biological structures.

It has been shown that injuries to the hypothalamus have strong effects on the level of stored fat in an animal. This has led some researchers (Keesey and Powley, 1975) to propose the concept of a *set point*. A set point is similar to a thermostat that monitors the temperature in a room and signals the heating system to turn on when the temperature falls below a certain point, or to turn off when the temperature goes above that point. The **set point theory** of eating proposes that when stored-fat levels drop below a certain point, eating begins. When the stored fat levels go above a certain point, eating behavior stops.

You may have noticed that after introducing this section with the terms *hunger* and *thirst*, they weren't mentioned again. Instead, you read about the interaction between biological conditions (blood-sugar and stomach status), the availability of certain reinforcers (food), and certain behaviors (eating). It was not necessary to introduce the concept of a need or a drive. This is a major distinction between modern motivation theory and classical motivation theory. In earlier years, motivation theory was dominated by the biological approach. More recently, the role of the environment has become more important in motivation theory. For this reason, the emphasis has changed from a straight biological approach to what might be called a **biosocial approach**, which considers the interaction of biological status and environment. A good example of the biosocial approach is the psychological research on obesity.

Obesity. Overeating is assumed to lead to excessive body fat. The condition of being overweight is called **obesity.** As we saw in the above-mentioned studies of the hypothalamus, there seems to be some involvement of biological structures in eating behavior. In addition, there may be other motivational variables of a nonbiological nature involved. Schachter (1968) has proposed a theory of obesity based on incentive theory. He suggests that obese people are motivated by external cues to a much greater extent than nonobese people. The sights and smells of food presumably have a much greater pulling-power on some people than on others. It is this incentive motivation that increases food consumption and leads to obesity. In an early experiment (Schachter and Rodin, 1974), it was discovered that obese people overeat when food is easily available and attractively presented. On the other hand, when effort is required to get the food or when it is not attractively presented, obese people tend to eat less than others.

Other studies have shown that eating by obese people is affected by the taste of the food and the time of day. These are also external cues rather than internal states. It does seem as if food has come to have an incentive value for certain people that is only loosely related to a biological condition. This brings to mind Seligman's (1970) concept of preparedness and long-term taste aversion. At the root of the problem, we may very well find that learning mechanisms interact with biological mechanisms to produce the circumstance of obesity. At the very least, we can say that food is a stimulus that has great incentive value for some people. In these cases, hunger is only peripherally involved.

Set point theory. A theory of eating proposing that when stored fats drop below a certain set point, eating begins; when they go above a certain point, eating stops.

Biosocial approach. An approach to motivation that focuses on the interaction of biological status and environment.
Obesity. The condition of being substantially overweight.

Need for Arousal

In the chapter on consciousness and in our earlier discussion of theories of emotions, the concept of **arousal** was mentioned. Arousal also plays a major role in drive theory. It is assumed that needs arouse people, and that this arousal is the drive. Duffy (1962) suggests that arousal is a need of its own and that people differ in terms of the strength of that need. For example, let's look at the state of boredom. All of us have been in situations in which we were bored to the point of pain. In other words, we were under-aroused or seemed to need arousal. In these circumstances, a person usually does something to increase arousal. While listening to a boring lecture, you doodle; at a boring formal dinner, you create patterns in your mashed potatoes; on a boring assembly line, you let the line get ahead of you and see if you can "catch up." In each of these cases, you are seeking sensation in order to change a biological situation. Relieving boredom is just one example of the importance of stimulation. Other examples of stimulation include speeding along winding roads, riding roller-coasters, or climbing mountains.

If stimulus variation is related to some basic need or preference, we might expect to find that being deprived of such variation can have an effect on behavior. This has been found in both animal and human studies. Several studies have shown that animals will work harder to produce stimulus change after they have been deprived of this change. The longer the period of deprivation, the harder the animals work to produce change (Butler, 1957; Fox, 1962; Levison et al., 1968). Studies of stimulus variation in humans have taken the form of **sensory deprivation**, in which people are put in environments that greatly minimize any outside stimulation. An early series of studies was carried out with college students (Bexton et al., 1954). These studies showed that when the students were deprived of sensory stimulation for several hours, they had difficulties in paying attention and solving problems. In addition, even basic perceptions, such as the position of lines or the stability of objects, were distorted.

One popular current device for accomplishing sensory deprivation is a tank of warm water in which a person is immersed. Most of the sensory information that people typically receive can be held constant or eliminated while they are in this tank. There

are no sounds, no light reaches the retina, there is no feedback from the sense of touch, no changes in temperature, no smells, tastes, or pain. After extended periods of time, the effects can be quite dramatic. In an early sensory-deprivation study using a quiet chamber (rather than a tank of water), Heron (1957) reported that subjects saw animals climbing on the walls and dots of nonexistent light. One subject reported, "My mind seemed to be a ball of cotton wool, floating over my body."

Sensory-deprivation studies do seem to point to some human need for stimulation, but they don't really tell us how this need works or how it might affect more common behavior. The daily implications of this research have more to do with the concept of sensation-seeking than with the condition of sensory deprivation. Zuckerman (1974) proposes that sensation-seeking is a combination of a characteristic of the person and a characteristic of the environment in which the person is found. It is assumed that everyone has a particular (or optimal) arousal level. Any time we are aroused to a significantly greater or lesser extent than our optimal level, we are uncomfortable. In order to eliminate the discomfort, we engage in appropriate action. If we are under-aroused, we will seek stimulation; if we are over-aroused, we will try to reduce stimulation. The environment we are in determines how much stimulation we are receiving. When we combine the personal factors and the environmental factors, we have an explanation of why some people seek stimulation and others don't. If you have a characteristically low arousal level (that is, if it does not take much to arouse you), you will be happy in low-stimulation environments and uncomfortable in high-stimulation circumstances. On the other hand, if you have a high arousal level, you may become easily bored, even in environments that seem interesting or stimulating to others. These differences in arousal level may account for the wide variations in reactions to sensory deprivation. You would expect those who have high arousal levels to experience greater "deprivation" in an isolation tank or room than those with low arousal levels. For the person with a high arousal level in an environment with low stimulation the choices are simple—create stimulation or change environments. The reported hallucinations and extreme reactions by people in experimental conditions may be the body's way of creating stimulation. For example, as you may have noticed

		Environment	
		Low Stimulation	High Stimulation
Person	High Arousal	Agitated Seeks arousal Seems tense Poor attention Makes mistakes	At ease Pays attention to several tasks simultaneously Performs well
	Low Arousal	At ease In control of task Performs well	Tense and irritable Distractible Makes mistakes Can't keep up with work schedule

FIGURE 12-9

This chart shows the relationship between level of arousal in a person and amount of stimulation in the environment. People have different arousal levels and thus seek different levels of stimulation in their environments.

Sensation-seeking seems to be an example of a biological condition that interacts with environmental stimuli to produce motivated behavior.

in your own experience, in the moments before a movie begins you will see some people reading the small print on the popcorn box in an effort to relieve the boredom of this low-stimulation environment. Figure 12–9 presents these proposed relationships graphically.

Zuckerman has shown that people can be categorized as high- or low-sensation seekers (1974a, 1974b). In Figure 12–10 you will find some questions he uses to identify the two different groups. There are undoubtedly many complicated biological mechanisms involved in sensation-seeking; these include autonomic responses, hormone production, and brain excitation. It is not necessary to explore those connections here; it is enough just to make the point that sensation-seeking seems to be an example of a biological condition that interacts with environmental stimuli to produce motivated behavior.

Some applications of this relationship come readily to mind. Infants will explore more or less of their immediate environments depending on the amount of stimulation that they find satisfying. Some children will be happier with a complex and cluttered crib; others may prefer only a few objects to investi-

---

Arousal. A state of generalized physical excitation, involving heartrate, sweating, and other autonomic-response mechanisms.

Sensory deprivation. The state of being cut off from all outside stimulation.

I. A. I would like a job that requires a lot of traveling.
   B. I would prefer a job in one location.

2. A. I would prefer living in an ideal society in which everyone is safe, secure, and happy.
   B. I would have preferred living in the unsettled days of our history.

3. A. I sometimes like to do things that are a little frightening.
   B. A sensible person avoids activities that are dangerous.

4. A. I would like to try parachute-jumping.
   B. I would never want to try jumping out of a plane, with or without a parachute.

5. A. I enter cold water gradually, giving myself time to get used to it.
   B. I like to dive or jump right into the ocean or a cold pool.

6. A. When I go on a vacation, I prefer the comfort of a good room and bed.
   B. When I go on a vacation, I prefer the change of camping out.

7. A. People who ride motorcycles must have some kind of unconscious need to hurt themselves.
   B. I would like to drive or ride a motorcycle.

FIGURE 12-10
Zuckerman has shown that people can be categorized as high- and low-sensation seekers. This chart shows a few of the questions he has used to identify the two different groups.

Some children are happier with a complex and cluttered environment, while others may prefer only a few objects to investigate at one time.

gate at one time. Adults with little need for stimulation will avoid crowded, noisy, and confusing environments; for example, a low-sensation seeker is not well-suited for a job as a police officer or goalie on a hockey team.

Need Theory

Many motivation theories are based on the concept of need. Even in our everyday conversations, we speak of people being motivated by needs such as the "need for achievement" or the "need for power." We are told to ignore children who are acting badly because they are simply showing a "need for attention." In both our everyday descriptions and in the psychological literature, these need theories are presented within the traditional "drive" framework. It is assumed that the person "needs" something (for example, attention, power, or a feeling of accomplishment), is aroused by that need, and directs energy toward satisfying or eliminating that need. When the need is met, other needs may become more important and urge or compel another behavior in the same way.

Many motivational theories are built around the interplay of various needs. One of the first of these theories was proposed by Murray in 1938. Murray suggested that there are a fixed set of needs that are inborn in human beings. These needs vary in importance for each person. Unfulfilled needs are the most important and demand the most attention; needs that have been fulfilled are less important and demand little attention. Thus, Murray's theory was that people direct their behavior (or are driven) toward meeting unfulfilled needs.

Maslow's Hierarchy of Needs. Maslow has a modern need theory that is based on a similar foundation. Maslow has proposed that people have five basic needs: physical, security, love, esteem, and self-actualization. *Physical* needs are just what the name implies; they are needs for food, water, warmth, rest, and other circumstances that guarantee the immediate survival or physical comfort of the person. In most industrialized nations these physical needs are met, at least at some minimal level, for most adults, but there are temporary circumstances in which these needs become important (such as lack of water on a hot day at the beach, or getting caught in a snowstorm without

warm clothing). *Security* needs are like physical needs, but they have a future orientation—they represent the person's need to protect against deprivation in the future. We buy food to store in the refrigerator; this ensures that we will not go hungry tomorrow, or next week. We save money to make sure that we can eat at a later time. Security needs represent a type of safety margin guaranteeing that physical needs will be met in the future. *Love* needs are a desire to have a personal relationship with another person. Love is not used here in the romantic sense but in the more general, social sense; Maslow assumed that people have a basic desire to love others and to be loved by them. It is important that there can be no conditions on this love; people need to be loved simply for what they are, not for what they can do for others. *Esteem* needs represent a desire to be respected for a particular quality or skill. Most people have some talent they are proud of. Maslow suggested that this is not an accident; that it is part of human nature to want to be good at something and to be respected for this skill. **Self-actualization** needs are the highest level in Maslow's hierarchy. These needs represent the desire all people have to develop themselves to the greatest extent and to be the best they can be. This is different from an esteem need because the goals for improvement are internalized; people answer to themselves, not to others.

In addition to specifying these five categories of needs, Maslow also proposed that one set of needs in the hierarchy must be satisfied before the next set of needs can be met. Figure 12–11 illustrates the proposed hierarchy; this figure suggests that physical needs must be met before security needs, security needs must be met before love needs, and so on. This seems to correspond to everyday experience. When you are cold, hungry, or in pain, you spend energy to get warm, find food, or end the pain. You do not spend energy making new friends, seeking recognition for accomplishing a difficult task, or learning to master the 12-string guitar. As a general statement, Maslow's theory proposes that people will spend energy trying to meet the needs of the lowest unsatisfied level. In our motivational terms,

---

Self-actualization. Maslow's term for people's desire to develop themselves to their fullest potential; represents the highest level of Maslow's hierarchy of needs.

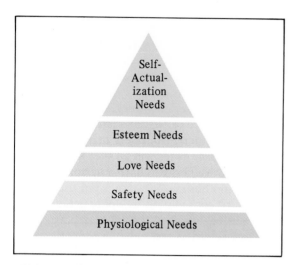

FIGURE 12-11
Maslow proposed that there are 5 basic types of needs, arranged in a hierarchy, as shown here. He also proposed that the lower categories of needs in the hierarchy must be satisfied before the higher levels can be.

you will begin, direct, and maintain certain behavior patterns until your particular lowest-level need has been met.

There is one other aspect of Maslow's theory that has made it popular; a distinction is made between deficiency needs and growth needs. Physical needs, security needs, love needs, and esteem needs are considered **deficiency needs**; that is, when these elements are gone we are driven to replace them. When we have enough to eliminate the need, we no longer seek the things that satisfy that need. For example, when we are hungry we eat; when hunger has been eliminated, we stop eating; we do not continue to eat until we collapse. Self-actualization, on the other hand, is a **growth need**. We can never get enough of it. We will continue to seek increased self-actualization as long as the lower four need levels are satisfied.

From a motivational standpoint, Maslow's theory is fairly simple. It states that everyone has five energizers of behavior (the five need categories). At any given time, one or more of those energizers is controlling behavior. If there are some deficiency needs that are not met, we will spend energy to meet those needs. If all the deficiency needs have been met, we will spend energy in meeting self-actualization needs.

When we combine Maslow's ideas with learning

theory, we have a good basic description of some circumstances that might lead to particular behaviors. People can be motivated to perform a particular action by learning that certain actions will result in the satisfaction of important (unfulfilled) needs. For example, if people have unsatisfied esteem needs, they will learn behaviors that will lead to satisfying those needs. A student who is striving to meet esteem needs will work hard in order to be recognized as a "top student." A manager with an unsatisfied esteem need will stay after work and come in on Saturdays hoping for a promotion. To take this one step further, teachers praise students who do well; companies promote managers who work hard. The student and the manager have learned that working hard is useful in meeting esteem needs. The teacher and the boss have recognized that certain rewards (the label of "top student" or a promotion) can be used to activate behavior in certain people (to fulfill esteem needs) and that people can learn to make the necessary association between hard work and reward.

Maslow's theory has a lot of appeal, but it seems applicable only to humans—we don't usually think of gerbils as having esteem or self-actualization needs. In addition, the growth need of self-actualization has a positive connotation that suggests an optimistic and self-controlled view of the human organism. As a result, Maslow's theory has been associated with the humanist movement, which we discussed in Chapter 1. It suggests that people are capable of much more than is observable at any one time. It suggests a psychology of the possible rather than the probable.

REVIEW QUESTIONS

11. Biological approaches to motivation propose that a person has certain physical _____ that must be met.

12. If you're trying to get a mule to move, jabbing it with a stick would be an example of the _____ approach and offering it a carrot would be an example of the _____ approach.

13. Injuries to the _____ result in either overeating or undereating.

14. The _____ _____ theory of eating proposes than when stored fat levels drop below a certain point, eating begins, and when they go above a certain point, eating stops.

15. Cutting out all sources of stimulation, which is done in _____ _____ studies, causes problems in attention and problem-solving as well as basic perceptual distortions.

16. Maslow's hierarchy of needs has five categories of needs: _____ , _____ , _____ , and _____ needs are deficiency needs; _____ is a growth need.

Answers: 11. needs 12. drive or need; incentive 13. hypothalamus 14. set point 15. sensory deprivation 16. physical; security; love; esteem; self-actualization

■ INCENTIVE MOTIVATION

One of the usual characteristics of motivated behavior is the presence of something called a goal object—what we strive to obtain. This might be money, a good grade, or a position of importance. The important characteristic of this goal object is that it is anticipated—it relates to the future, not the present. This future-oriented aspect of a goal object has been viewed as a "pulling" force on behavior. This is what an **incentive** is—a characteristic of a goal that draws a person toward it. This is in direct contrast to drive theory, which suggests that people are "pushed" toward a goal.

Unlike need motivation, incentive motivation is learned and is not present because of biological circumstances. We *learn* the association between certain behaviors and desirable goal objects. A lot of advertising is built on that principle—advertisers want people to make an association between their product and some desired state of affairs. The designer's label or brand name is associated with sophistication or respect: If you wear our jeans, you

will be noticed; if you wear our aftershave lotion, women will fall at your feet; if you eat our cereal, you will run faster. Thus we don't always go out and buy new jeans simply because our old ones are worn out. There is no present biological need that can account for the purchase (the motivated behavior)—we don't walk into the store naked from the waist down, suffering from exposure to intense cold or heat.

The behaviorists consider rewards to be stimuli that strengthen the relationship between a stimulus situation and a response (learning). In this sense, rewards are really past-oriented. They refer back to something that has already occurred. Incentive theory, on the other hand, holds that certain stimulus conditions are necessary in order to turn learning into performance. Consider once again the research of Menzel with the chimpanzees (Menzel, 1978). The fact that food was "out there," hidden under leaves and in holes, provided the incentive to search. Thus, incentive theory places a greater emphasis on the characteristics of external stimuli (the incentives) than on internal stimuli (needs). An example of this difference of approaches can be seen in explanations of obesity. One point of view is that obesity is the result of a greater hunger drive in obese people. An alternative incentive view has been suggested by Schachter (1971). He suggests that obese people may be more sensitive to the incentive cues of food than other people.

You have seen that incentive theory is different from drive theory in several important respects; the theories explain motivation in two different ways. In the next two sections we will discuss how two types of experiments using rewards have shown these differences. The first type of experiment involves variations in the amount of reward that is provided for the activity; the second type of experiment deals with qualitative differences between rewards.

Amount of Reward

Drive theory predicts that performance will change gradually as a result of changing reward levels. One

---

Deficiency needs. Part of Maslow's hierarchy of needs; these are physical, security, love, and esteem needs.

Growth need. Part of Maslow's hierarchy of needs; a need that can never be entirely satisfied. The need for self-actualization is a growth need.

Incentive. A characteristic of a goal that draws a person toward it; money is a common incentive.

assumption of drive theory is that an animal receives information from changing levels of blood-sugar or other chemicals in the bloodstream. However, these changes are gradual; we would not expect an animal to react immediately to changes in the amount of the reward. For example, if an animal has been rewarded with a certain amount of food for moving down a runway and then the amount of food is cut in half, the animal should only gradually learn a new association and reduce its running speed. This is not what occurs, however. In one experiment (Crespi, 1942), different groups of rats were given different numbers of food pellets at the end of a runway. The greater the amount of food, the faster the rats ran. The number of pellets was then changed and running speed was reduced. If more food was obtained, running speed increased. This shift was too quick to be accounted for by new internal information related to drive levels. Crespi concluded that the amount of the reward affected the "eagerness" (motivation) of the rats.

Quality of the Reward

Several studies have shown that performance seems to be greater when preferred rewards are available. As an example, Simmons (1924) studied the speed with which rats ran through a maze and found that the rats performed better when the reward was bread and milk than when the reward was sunflower seeds. The same principle seems to apply to most human behavior. For example, there was a case of a company that was having a hard time motivating employees to perform a dirty job—cleaning out large ash furnaces every few weeks. The first strategy was to offer a higher rate of pay—those people who did furnace-cleaning tasks would be paid at a higher rate than other workers. There was little enthusiasm among the workers in response to this offer. The company then proposed a different kind of offer. They knew that under present conditions it usually took 8 hours for the furnace-cleaning task to be accomplished. They offered to pay employees for 8 hours of work no matter how long it took them to clean the furnace. Many employees accepted this offer: The furnaces were now cleaned in about 2½ hours and the workers left with a full day's pay. The important point was that a potential reduction in working time was offered as the reward rather than

just money. The quality of the reward made an immediate and dramatic difference.

Rewards vs. Interest: A Dilemma

The point of the preceding sections seems obvious: Rewards can produce motivated behavior. More recently, it has been suggested that while rewards can produce one kind of motivated behavior, they can destroy another kind. Over the years, there has been discussion about the effects of different kinds of rewards. **Extrinsic rewards** are thought to be those rewards that you get from someone else. They would include money, praise, grades, and so on. In each case, someone else must provide the reward. **Intrinsic rewards**, on the other hand, seem to appear from inside yourself without any necessary activity on the part of another person. Often after completing a difficult task successfully, you feel proud of yourself. You feel pleased (rewarded) in spite of the fact that no one else has praised you. Similar feelings arise from playing a musical instrument well or even completing a long run by yourself. No one else has to be there to recognize the accomplishment; the fact is that when you have been effective, you are pleased.

Since it is generally assumed that rewards can increase motivation, it would logically follow that a combination of extrinsic and intrinsic rewards would result in a higher motivation level than if only one type of reward were used. Although this may be a logical assumption, some studies have shown the opposite effect. In certain circumstances, it appears that adding extrinsic reinforcement to an intrinsically-interesting task may actually reduce intrinsic motivation in the long run. We can illustrate this with a little anecdote (Zimbardo, 1974). There was an old Italian shoemaker who moved into a new neighborhood and set up shop. Shortly after opening, some local teenagers decided to have some fun at his expense. They stood outside of his shop one afternoon cursing and insulting him and his customers. He came out and tried to reason with the teenagers, but that only made them curse louder. This went on for several days. One day, the teenagers arrived and the shoemaker came out to meet them and told them they were in luck. He had been very successful that day and had made a good deal of money. As a result, he could afford to pay them to curse. He gave each of them a dollar and they cursed with new enthusiasm. He did the same thing each day for several days—paying them to curse. One day when they arrived, he told them that he had hit a slump and could only pay them 50¢ to curse. They grumbled about the "rip-off" but cursed, although for a shorter period than on previous days. This 50¢ payment continued for several more days. One day when thay arrived, he told them that business was so bad that he could only pay them 10¢. They looked at him in shock and told him they were not about to perform for 10¢ when they were used to getting $1. They stalked off and never came back.

The point of this little story is that behavior that had been intrinsically interesting or rewarding (the cursing) had been extrinsically rewarded (first with $1 and then 50¢). Eventually, the intrinsic interest faded, and when extrinsic rewards were diminished, motivation decreased as well.

Deci (1972) conducted an interesting study with college students. He had students come for an experiment in which they were to try to solve puzzles. Before the experiment began, the students waited in a room and were permitted to play with the puzzles. Most of the students found the puzzles intrinsically interesting and devoted a good deal of attention to them. When the experiment began, some subjects were paid for every puzzle they completed. Other subjects were paid hourly, regardless of how many puzzles they solved. After the puzzle-solving session was over, the subjects were asked if they would like to continue solving puzzles on their own time for no pay. The subjects who had been paid for each puzzle they solved were much less interested in continuing than the subjects who had been paid hourly.

Many explanations have been offered for results such as these (deCharms and Muir, 1978). One popular explanation is that the person feels externally controlled when extrinsic rewards are present and this has an effect on motivation. In this case the cues or incentives come from outside, and motivation is reduced when they are taken away (Deci, 1975). The assumption is also made that people have

a need to feel effective or competent with respect to their environment (White, 1959) in order to experience a positive emotional state. In contrast, when the environment seems in control of the person, no such positive state is felt. In the studies described above, it is assumed that when rewards are extrinsic and are tied to performance the person is made to feel controlled rather than controlling. This produces a negative emotional state, and an association is made between this state and the task (such as puzzle solving). Since the task now has negative associations, it is avoided.

These experiments lead to the conclusion that a person's belief about his or her effectiveness can influence both behavior and emotional states. Incentives do not exist in a vacuum outside of the person; the person superimposes interpretations on the situation that may change the meaning of those incentives. In this case, the person previously saw him- or herself as being in control of the environment. When the reinforcement became extrinsic, the person's perception changed. The person now perceives him- or herself as *being controlled by* some external force. Once again, we encounter the idea of cognition. We will now consider two theories of motivation that have clear roles for thinking in motivated behavior.

REVIEW QUESTIONS

17. _____ are characteristics of a goal that pull us toward it.

18. An intrinsic/extrinsic reward would be a bonus for doing a good job; an intrinsic/extrinsic reward would be a feeling of pride for doing a good job.

19. Some studies have shown that adding extrinsic rewards to an intrinsically interesting task may increase/reduce intrinsic motivation in the long run.

Answers: 17. Incentives 18. extrinsic; intrinsic 19. reduce

Extrinsic rewards. Those rewards that someone else gives you, such as a bonus or a medal.
Intrinsic rewards. Rewards that you give yourself or that exist

in the nature of the activity itself. Examples are a feeling of pride on completing a task, or enjoyment in doing something for its own sake (such as playing a musical instrument).

■ COGNITIVE APPROACHES TO MOTIVATION

The concept of anticipation runs through much of motivated behavior. For example, when a pouting child cries, "That's not fair!", the implication is that there is some discrepancy between what was anticipated and what actually occurred. The issue of anticipation was first raised in the section on incentive theory, but we will now consider it in greater detail. In motivation theories, the term **expectancy** usually is used in place of anticipation. An expectancy is a belief about the probability of a particular outcome or event. The rat scurrying down the runway has an expectancy about the presence of food in the goal box, just as the student studying late in the library has an expectancy about the probability of getting a good grade on a test. This expectancy, or belief, about food or grades seems to play a role in the behavior of both the rat and the student. It seems to act as an incentive, drawing out certain behaviors (running and studying). It should be clear that an expectancy is an idea. In earlier chapters, whenever you encountered the term *idea*, it was usually in the context of a cognitive theory of some kind. The same is true here with regard to cognitive motivation theories. There are two types of theories that we will examine. One type emphasizes the effect of other people, and the other type emphasizes probabilities. Let's look at the "people" theory first.

Equity Theory

Most of us have developed some notion of social justice. We have an idea of what is fair and just. For example, the phrase, "a fair day's work for a fair day's pay," suggests a social contract between employer and employee. The employee invests effort and skill and expects payment in return. The employer invests money and machinery and expects acceptable and reliable production in return. Each party puts something in (which we will call input) and gets something out (which we will call outcome). One approach to motivation involves this basic input/outcome relationship. It is called **equity theory** because it emphasizes the motivating characteristics of exchange relationships. Unfair or inequitable relationships are thought to be motivating. In particular, these inequitable exchange relationships are

assumed to energize the person and lead to action of some sort. An example might make the point a little clearer. When I was growing up I lived in Philadelphia, which got its share of snow each winter. Being the industrious type, I would often shovel the snow off sidewalks in order to make spending money. On one particular day, I entered into an agreement with a homeowner to clear a stretch of sidewalk and some steps of snow. The agreed-upon price for the job was 25¢ (which, in those days, would buy 5 candy bars or 1 rubber-band airplane). I worked hard and cleared the sidewalk in about 35 minutes. When I went to the door for my pay, the homeowner told me that he had reconsidered the deal and felt that I was overcharging for the amount of work. As a result, he would pay me 20¢ rather than the agreed-upon 25¢. I accepted the money and waited for him to go back inside the house. I then proceeded to shovel 5¢ worth of snow back on the sidewalk. By any standard, I was motivated in that second burst of shoveling. I can even say that I enjoyed returning the snow onto the sidewalk and steps. I enjoyed it so much I may have even put *more* than 5¢ worth of snow back. When I was finished, I felt that the contract was once again a fair one. We were even.

Equity theory (Adams, 1965) proposes that people strive for cognitive balance between inputs and outcomes in their environment. Whenever inputs are greater than outcomes, there is an imbalance or inequity. The same is true when outcomes exceed inputs. Presumably, the emotion that is experienced in the former case is annoyance or anger; in the latter case, the emotion is guilt. In either case, the theory says that actions will be taken to bring the cognitive system back into balance. Let's consider the possible alternative actions for bringing the two different inequitable situations back into balance. In the case of inputs exceeding outcomes, the person can either try to reduce inputs or try to increase outcomes. Inputs include such things as energy, skill, quality or quantity of work, experience, loyalty, and attention. Outcomes are rewards. In the case of my snow-shoveling experience, I reduced my inputs (in particular the quality and quantity of my work) to match my outcome (20¢). I could have argued with the homeowner for the full 25¢, but something told me I would not win the argument. Let's consider the opposite situation. Suppose the homeowner had given me 50¢ instead of the agreed-

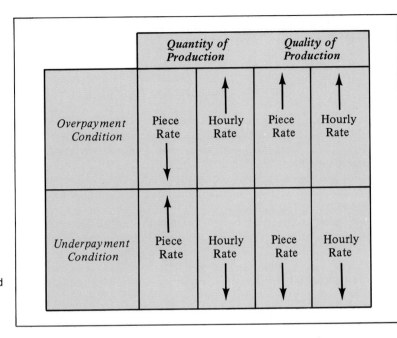

FIGURE 12-12
The chart here shows the predicted effects of inequity on quantity and quality of performance. (Landy and Trumbo, 1980)

upon 25¢. Now my outcomes would be larger than my inputs. Once again, I would have had two choices. I could have refused to accept the extra 25¢, or I could have increased my inputs by clearing the back walk to the garage in addition to the steps and sidewalk.

Equity theory has been a popular way of considering motivation in work settings. The predictions about the effect of various forms of inequity on effort and performance are fairly obvious. Look at Figure 12-12. There are two different conditions shown—overpayment (which means greater outcomes than anticipated) and underpayment (less outcomes than anticipated). There are also two different types of behavior to consider—the quality of performance and the quantity of performance. In an industrial setting, quality means number of errors and quantity means production rate. There is one more variable that must be considered, however. We must know if the worker is paid by the hour or by the piece. The arrows in each cell of the figure represent the predictions from equity theory.

For example, if a person is overpaid and is on an hourly wage, the quantity and quality of production should go up. This would relieve the guilt caused by the overpayment. If the person is on piece rate, quality will go up but quantity will go down. If quantity went up, inequity would increase even more, since outcomes would also go up. The same logic can be used to make predictions in each of the other cells of the figure.

This basic equity model has been expanded to include the perceptions of the inputs and outcomes of other people in the environment. It has been suggested that people tend to compare themselves to others around them in evaluating how fairly they are being treated. Thus, you may not mind receiving outcomes that are lower than you anticipated as long as everyone else also receives reduced outcomes. To use the classroom as an example, if you study hard and do poorly on a test, you may be upset, but you will probably calm down if you find that the rest of the class also did poorly. If you find that the rest of the class did well, you may appeal

---

Expectancy. A belief about the probability of a particular outcome or event.

Equity theory. Proposes that inequities in exchange relationships are motivating; also stresses the process of comparison and the importance of other people in motivational decisions.

PUTTING THE THEORY TO THE TEST

What would you think if your employer made the following offer: "Decide what you think you *ought* to be paid, and tell the bookkeeper to put it in your pay check next week." You might respond as did the 15 employees of Friedman Co. who received this offer—in disbelieving silence. But Arthur Friedman, the owner of Friedman Appliance Co., was serious; he had a theory about motivation in the workplace that he wanted to try. His basic idea was to allow employees to decide for themselves what they should get paid. In addition, employees were free to set their own hours, take vacations when they wished to, and borrow from the company cash box in times of need. In exchange for these allowances, Friedman expected increased skill and effort in work performance.

If the terms of Arthur Friedman's proposal sound familiar to you, it is probably because they illustrate a model of motivation that you have been reading about—equity theory. Equity theory, as you know, emphasizes the motivating characteristics of exchange relationships; it assumes that actions will be taken to keep an exchange such as that between employer and employee in balance.

How successful was this application of equity theory at Friedman Appliance Co.? According to Friedman himself, his employees showed remarkable restraint in asking for pay raises. The increases in wages that they demanded were just slightly higher than the scale of the union to which they all belonged. The worker who demanded the highest pay raise—$100 a week—showed a matched improvement in work performance. "He had been resentful about his prior pay," explained Friedman. "The raise made him a fabulous employee." Interestingly, some of Friedman's employees who were making less than their co-workers did not insist on equal pay. When asked why not, one worker replied, "Because I don't want to work that hard."

There were other changes in the workplace as well. During the five years in which Arthur Friedman's system was in effect, there was no turnover in employees. Work was done on time. It was rare that anyone was late for work; there was almost no absenteeism. As for the business itself, net profits increased. While the changes resulted in lower volume and higher overhead costs, Friedman felt that greater productivity and efficiency more than made up for it.

In case you're wondering what happened to Arthur Friedman and his business, there is a sequel. Friedman, who is a talented cook, eventually sold his general appliance business to open a microwave-oven store. From the start he applied the same principles of motivation that had been so successful in his appliance store. Within a couple of years he opened five more microwave-oven stores. Each year the business doubled. At last report, management procedures were exactly the same. Employees still set their own wages and work hours. People are still given keys to the company cash box. While we'd have to say that Friedman's system of management is unique, it is a good demonstration of how a motivational principle can be applied successfully.

Sources: The Washington Post, February 23, 1975; Landy, 1986.

---

your grade to the teacher in an effort to get it raised.

The introduction of the significant other person into the basic equity equation enriches it greatly and makes it more suitable for dealing with social behavior. The theory now emphasizes the exchange relationship between two people or among members of a group. The theory suggests that people will spend energy (that is, be motivated) to maintain a balance in these relationships between their own inputs and outcomes and the inputs and outcomes of "significant others." Goodman (1974) has found that

significant others don't even have to be real; they may be idealized others. A student may ask the question, "Is this how you should treat a college student?" In this case, a comparison is being made between the particular student and the average college student.

Equity theory suggests the importance of the process of comparison in decision-making and energy expenditure. There was no such process involved in need theory or incentive theory. This process of comparison is the cognitive component

TABLE 12-3. Examples of Combining Valences

Action Contemplated	Positive	Negative	Action taken
Go to class?	Learn	Boredom	Go to class
	See friends	Miss lunch	
	Get grade from last test	Sit next to person with bad breath	
	Get money owed by classmate		

of the theory. In addition, equity theory stresses the importance of other people in motivational decisions. This agrees with the emphasis of social learning theory on other people as sources of information for learning. Equity and fairness relationships are found throughout work, school, leisure, and love. This seems to be a fruitful way of looking at motivation in social settings.

Expectancy Theory

One variation of cognitive motivation theory deals with expectations and their role in starting and guiding behavior. Logically enough, it is called **expectancy theory**. The basic form of the theory is presented graphically in Figure 12–13. Simply, the theory states that there are two beliefs, or cognitions, that play a role when we are deciding on a course of action. The first cognition is called **valence**. This represents our preference for certain outcomes or rewards. You can think of this as similar to the valence of an element in chemistry—a positive valence is an attracting force and a negative valence is a repelling force. In expectancy theory, certain outcomes are considered desirable and have a positive valence; examples of these outcomes are money, good grades, or a promotion. Other outcomes have negative valences; examples might be criticism, failure, or loss of a job. The theory states that people try to consider the valences of all of the possible outcomes; the person must combine these various outcomes and come to some bottom-line

decision about whether the average of the outcomes is positive or negative. Table 12-3 gives an example of this averaging process.

Valence is only one of the components in motivation, however. The second is called **instrumentality**. This component has to do with a belief about the probability of certain outcomes. For example, when you buy a lottery ticket, you have some estimate of your chances of winning first prize. The estimate may be one in a million, one in a thousand, or one in ten. Instrumentality is an estimate of the probability that you will actually receive desired outcomes (those with positive valences) if you make an effort. Your teacher may tell you that hard work will lead to good grades, but if you know that this teacher does not easily give out high grades, and that only 10 percent of the grades are likely to be As and Bs,

FIGURE 12-13
The expectancy theory states that there are two beliefs that play a role in motivation. The first is valence, or our preference for certain outcomes or rewards. The second is instrumentality, or our belief about the probability that our effort will bring about desired outcomes. These two beliefs are multiplied to get motivation.

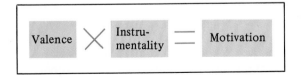

Expectancy theory. States that there are two beliefs that play a role in motivation: preference for certain outcomes and belief about the probability of certain outcomes.
Valence. The psychological attractiveness of objects. Examples

of objects with positive valence would be money, good grades, or a promotion; objects with negative valence would be criticism, failure, or loss of a job.
Instrumentality. A belief that an action will lead to an outcome.

you may not believe that hard work, by itself, is likely to lead to a good grade. In other words, hard work is not useful in getting good grades. As you can see, instrumentality is a form of expectancy; it is the expectation that an action on your part will lead to a particular outcome. Thus, it is called an *action-outcome expectancy*.

One important aspect of the theory that you should note is the fact that valence and instrumentality are multiplied to get motivation; thus, if either of the values is zero, motivation will also be zero. This makes sense: If you don't believe that you will receive a reward for your effort, it doesn't really matter how much of that reward is promised. In the same way, if someone offers you a reward that you don't value or prefer (such as 500 lbs. of old telephone books), the expectancy that this reward will follow effort doesn't matter—you still won't put forth the effort.

When we combine these two elements, we can make the following prediction from the theory. If desirable outcomes in a situation outweigh the undesirable outcomes and you believe that effort will yield these desirable outcomes, then you will put forth that effort. In this theory, the mental operations are not as closely tied to comparisons (social or nonsocial) as they were in equity theory. The emphasis here is on people's tendency to estimate future probabilities. This type of approach is appealing because it gives some explanation as to why behavior is started in the first place. It also fits neatly with the incentive principles that were covered earlier. It gives certain "pulling" properties to stimuli and also allows for cognitive interpretation of these properties.

This theory has appeared in many different forms over the years (Peak, 1955; Rotter, 1955). It has received a great deal of attention in work settings because of its implications for work motivation (Vroom, 1964). One popular version of the theory is presented in Figure 12–14. As you can see, this model covers more than just motivation; it carries the sequence of motivation to its conclusion in performance. Nevertheless, the full model is worth examining because it points out another interesting aspect of motivation—it can rise and fall depending on interactions with the environment. This can be seen in the two arrows that run from rewards to valence and instrumentality. For example, if you expect to get a reward and don't, your belief in the

probability that effort will be followed by reward should drop. This, in turn, suggests that the next time you are deciding whether or not to expend effort, you will be less likely to do so. This is another way of saying that you learned something about the effort/reward association. In the same way, if you receive a reward but it isn't as great as you thought it would be, the valence element might change. As an example, you may have thought that a promotion would be terrific, but after being promoted you realized that the demands were greater, the hours longer, and the opportunity for maintaining friendships less. As a result, the next time a promotion is offered as a reward, its valence may be less (see Table 12–4).

In industrial settings, studies support the basic relationship between beliefs and actions (Porter and Lawler, 1968; Mitchell, 1974; Campbell and Pritchard, 1976). Since expectancy theory avoids the prob-

TABLE 12–4.
Leadership Table

Theory	Actions of Leader
Need	Find out what need level each employee occupies and supply appropriate rewards, for example, praise for someone at *esteem* level, group activity for someone at *love* level.
Incentive	Determine what employees consider to be rewards. Create conditions conducive to effective work (for example, right tools and materials and instructions). Reward when the person produces at correct level.
Equity	Determine what the person's expectancies are with respect to rewards. Determine what the person's inputs are (as perceived by the person). Make sure that everyone is rewarded using the same input/outcome ratio.
Expectancy	Determine valences for alternative rewards. Determine valences for possible negative outcomes. Increase positive valences and decrease negative valences for outcome. Increase person's expectancy of reward.

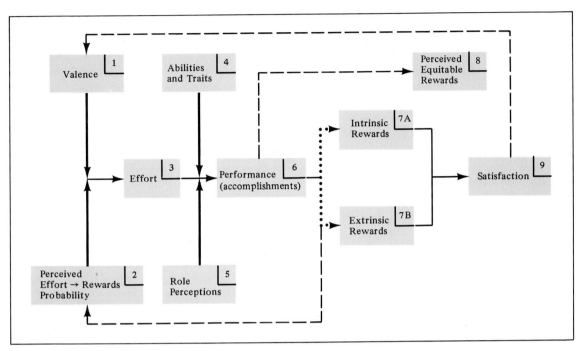

FIGURE 12-14
This is a model of expectancy theory. It has received a great deal of attention in work settings because of its implications for work motivation.

lems of drive theory, takes advantage of the incentive properties of stimuli, and emphasizes the cognitive interpretation that people place on events and stimuli, it is appealing as a way of understanding human motivation in a wide range of settings.

■ MOTIVATIONAL PROBLEMS

Since motivation concerns the start, direction, intensity, and ending of behavior, any problems of motivation must be related to one of these four aspects. The start or beginning of behavior is not normally a problem, in spite of the widespread use of the term *lazy*. Teachers, parents, and supervisors on the job often identify laziness as a characteristic of those in their charge, but there is seldom any justification for the label. Laziness implies a lack of energy, but if you observe the supposed "lazy" person, this often turns out not to be the case (Kelly, 1955). I once suggested to a supervisor that he take notes on the behavior of an employee whom he thought was lazy. He smiled and said that wouldn't

be hard—there wouldn't be anything to record. Two days later, he had changed his mind—his notebook was full of behaviors performed by this worker. They included numerous trips to the water fountain and rest room, constant casual conversations with nearby workers, trips around the office to collect money for a football pool, calls to friends and acquaintances, and the seemingly-endless reading of newspapers, circulars, and magazines. In short, the employee was a beehive of activity; this is usually the case. It is safe to assume that healthy and fully conscious people are usually engaged in one kind of behavior or another. Thus, starting behavior is not a problem; the problem usually turns out to be the direction the behavior takes.

There can be a motivational problem related to intensity, or the rate of activity. This is the clinical problem of depression, which is characterized by low levels of activity. In Chapter 7, you read about the state of learned helplessness. This condition could be interpreted as a lack of motivation. Certainly, it is a problem in the rate or amount of activity of a person. Seligman's (1975) interpretation of learned helplessness in humans was that it involved depression and a set of beliefs that people held about their power to change their environment. We will consider the problem of depression in some detail in Chapters 15 and 16, so we won't cover it here. The point is that the rate or amount of activity is a problem only in certain limited cases.

Motivation theory is about the choices we make of how to expend energy. In instances in which the choice is especially difficult to make, the direction of activity is more of a problem. These situations are usually called **conflict** situations. In these circumstances, there are competing goals that make the choice a difficult one. There are four common conflict situations.

In each case the person faces contradictory forces. In the **approach/approach** case the person is equally attracted to two different and mutually-exclusive goals. For example, when you have to choose between two different automobiles and they seem equally attractive, it often takes quite some time to make a decision. In the same way, in the **avoidance/avoidance** case you are looking for the lesser of two evils. The defendant in a plea-bargaining situation often has such a choice—plead guilty to a reduced charge or stand trial on a more serious charge with greater possible penalties. The **approach/avoidance** situation is also quite common. In this instance a goal has both positive and negative aspects. Marriage is an opportunity to spend unlimited time with a desired person, but it also reduces personal freedom. A new car is great fun, but it may mean no vacations for a year or two. Since most activities involve many different goals, the most common situation in everyday life is the **double approach/avoidance** conflict. In this case the person is faced with choosing between two or more goals, each of which has both desirable and undesirable characteristics. You might have to choose between working late and going to the movies with a friend. It would be great to work late and make extra money. On the other hand, you may have worked eight hours already and need to rest. It would also be fun to be with your friend, but the movie didn't get a good review in the paper, and you might not like it. The decision will require you to balance the attracting and repelling characteristics of the two alternatives.

Conflicts can have serious consequences. They often lead to maladaptive behavior patterns such as aggression or self-delusion. We will cover these

consequences in greater detail in the chapters on stress and abnormal behavior. The interesting thing to note here is a concept known as **goal gradient** (Hull, 1943; Miller, 1959). Think of a magnet with a positive and a negative pole. The closer a metal object gets to the positive end, the stronger the pull. The closer the metal object gets to the negative end, the greater the repelling force. Goal gradient means that the power of a reward or a punishment becomes greater as the goal object gets closer. If you think of a goal as having these attracting and repelling forces at the same time (the approach/avoidance situation described above), then there must be a point when the attracting and repelling forces are equal and the person hesitates, unable to decide between moving toward the goal or moving away from it. It has been further suggested that the strengths of these two opposing forces are not equal. As a goal with both attracting and repelling forces gets closer, the repelling force becomes stronger than the attracting force. This accounts for wavering or see-sawing back and forth. The person approaches the goal until the strength of the repelling force overcomes the strength of the attracting force. The person then retreats until the attracting force once again becomes stronger, causing the person to approach once again. Figure 12–15 graphically demon-

FIGURE 12-15

The graph shows approach and avoidance tendencies as one nears a goal. Both curves increase the closer you get to the goal, but the avoidance curve increases more rapidly.

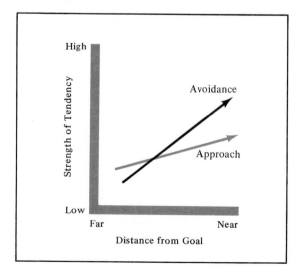

strates how these forces work. There are many examples of this type of behavior in what we see every day. A child cannot decide between riding on the roller-coaster and watching from the sidelines; he wants to ride it but is also fearful; he gets in line and then runs out of line. The bride eagerly anticipates the wedding day, but announces 15 minutes before the ceremony is to begin that she cannot go through with it. The motivational moral to this story is that when you see people wavering, it may be a good indication that they are motivated to move in two directions at the same time. The problem can be solved by changing either of the two forces involved. The child sees people get off the roller-coaster in one piece and laughing; this increases the positive valence and decreases the negative valence. The bride's mother assures her that marriage is not the end of the world, and reminds her of the exciting honeymoon trip that is planned.

Our range of behaviors is extraordinarily large. Some of these behaviors are motivated and others are reflexive or habitual. Even within the motivated behaviors there are differences. Some involve other people and some do not; some involve long-range plans and others involve present situations; some stimuli are stronger incentives than others. It is unlikely that any one theory of motivation will be proposed that can cover all of these situations. Incentive theory is well-suited to describe spontaneous and short-term behavior. Expectancy theory seems appropriate for longer-range intentional behavior. Equity theory seems like a good approach for explaining motivated behavior when interpersonal relations are involved. In extreme cases of motivational problems, such as addiction (to food as well as other substances), it may be better to deal with specific behaviors rather than to try and fit them into a broader theory of motivation. We will consider these problems at greater length in the chapter dealing with abnormal behavior.

REVIEW QUESTIONS

20. An _____ is a belief about the probability of a particular outcome or event. It seems to act as an _____ , pulling out certain behaviors from people.

21. _____ theory focuses on the basic input–output relationship involved in any social exchange. An unfair balance of input or output is thought to motivate people to take action of some sort.

22. The cognitive element in equity theory, which is not present in need theory or incentive theory, is the process of _____ of one's own situation with that of others in the environment.

23. There are two beliefs that play a role when we are deciding on a course of action; one is _____ , our preference for certain outcomes or rewards; the other is _____ , the belief that we will actually achieve the desired rewards if we make an effort.

Answers: 20. expectation; incentive 21. Equity 22. comparison 23. valence; instrumentality.

■ SUMMARY

1. An *emotion* is a reaction or experience with both cognitive and physiological components usually involving the central and peripheral nervous systems. The fact that emotion is a *psychophysiological* event distinguishes it from other psychological processes.

2. One method of studying emotions is to ask subjects to describe how they feel. This method is heavily dependent on the individual's concepts and

---

Conflict. A situation involving incompatible or competing goals, needs, demands, or opportunities.

Approach/approach. A conflict that results from being equally attracted to two different and mutually exclusive goals.

Avoidance/avoidance. A conflict that results when you have to choose between two undesirable possibilities.

Approach/avoidance. A conflict that results when a goal has both positive and negative aspects to it.

Double approach/avoidance. A conflict that results when we need to choose between two goals, each of which has both positive and negative characteristics.

Goal gradient. A graded difference in the strength of motivation as a goal is neared. There can be both approach and avoidance gradients.

vocabulary so that it may not be a reliable guide in determining basic emotions.

3. Some conclusions from the study of the relationship between emotions and facial expressions are: (a) the labels attached to emotional expressions are culturally universal; (b) when asked to produce a particular emotion, members of different cultures will produce identical expressions; (c) people from one culture can correctly identify the emotions of those of another culture; and (d) there seem to be six basic emotions: anger, disgust, happiness, sadness, fear, and surprise.

4. The *James-Lange theory* suggested that emotion is the recognition of some internal bodily state. The *Cannon-Bard theory* suggested that a stimulus event gives rise to both physiological changes (arousal) *and* to the perception of an emotion. These events occur close in time but are not directly related to each other. The *Schachter-Singer* theory proposes that a person is aroused by an external stimulus, notices that arousal, looks to the environment for clues as to why the arousal occurred, and labels the emotion. Any modern theory of emotion must explain how the three indicators of emotion interact with one another in our experience of emotion.

5. One emotion particularly prone to individual differences is anxiety. Studies show that while some people perform better under pressure, others perform more poorly. Research has also demonstrated that both verbal expression and comprehension are inhibited by anxiety.

6. The term *mood* is used to describe the general pleasantness or unpleasantness of a particular emotional experience. Bower's experiments show that the extent to which people recall an event depends on their mood at the time of the event and at the time of recall, a concept known as *mood-dependent memory*. Memory seems to be better when a person's learning and recall moods are similar. The clinical implication of these results is that if positive thoughts can be substituted for negative ones, the vicious circle of depression or anxiety may be broken. In school or employment settings, or whenever an evaluation depends on memory, there is a possibility that the evaluator's mood-states affect the evaluation.

7. In a "warm glow of success," or a good mood induced by positive performance feedback, people are more likely to offer help to others. Also, people who have received an unexpected reward are more likely to show *prosocial behavior.*

8. *Motivation* is the study of the circumstances surrounding the start, direction, intensity, and end of behavior. One approach is the biological explanation, or the idea that motivation comes from people's *drives* to satisfy biological *needs*, such as hunger and thirst. The incentive approach is an approach that concentrates on the properties of various stimuli to pull people into a particular form of behavior. The cognitive approach suggests that motivation is based on people's thoughts, plans, and beliefs about their actions.

9. Eating is an example of a motivated behavior with a biological influence. Some theorists believe that brain areas may initiate eating behavior based on fat levels in the body. A modern motivation theory, the *biosocial approach*, stresses the interaction between biological states and the environment. *Obese*, or extremely overweight, people appear to be more motivated by external cues to eat than nonobese people. The drive theory, or the view that a person is compelled to act, has two problems: (a) studies do not always show a strong relationship between a need and a particular behavior; and (b) there is no evidence of the drive in the absence of a stimulus.

10. Many studies show that animals and people will work to produce stimulus change after they have been deprived of it. Each person may have a different optimal arousal level: If we are underaroused we will seek stimulation, and if we are overaroused we will try to reduce stimulation.

11. Murray's early theory of motivation was that people direct their behavior toward meeting unfilled needs. Maslow proposed that people have five basic needs: physical, security, love, esteem, and *self-actualization*. Maslow's theory proposes that you will expend energy trying to meet the needs on the lowest unsatisfied level (starting with physical needs). An important aspect of this theory is that it distinguishes between *deficiency needs* (physical, security, love, and esteem) and *growth needs* (self-actualization). In this view, one or more of the need categories energizes behavior at any given time.

12. One characteristic of motivated behavior is the presence of a goal object, or an *incentive*, that has a "pulling" effect on behavior, drawing a person toward it. Two types of experiments demonstrate differences in drive and incentive theories'

predictions and their relation to actual behaviors. One type of study shows that the amount of reward available immediately affects behavior, in contrast to drive theory's prediction that such changes should be gradual. Another type of experiment shows that performance is greater when preferred rewards are available.

13. *Extrinsic rewards* are those provided by someone else, while *intrinsic rewards* come from inside ourselves. Contrary to what we might expect, in some circumstances adding extrinsic rewards to intrinsically interesting tasks reduces motivation. One explanation for this tendency is that with extrinsic rewards the person feels controlled, producing a negative emotional state that becomes associated with the task.

14. An *expectancy* is a belief about the probability of a particular outcome or event. *Equity theory* stresses the importance of the process of comparison in decision-making and energy expenditure, a cognitive component of motivation theory. This process was not included in either incentive theory or in drive theory. Another key factor in equity theory is the importance of other people in motivational decisions.

15. *Expectancy theory* states that there are two beliefs or cognitions that play a role when we are deciding on a course of action: *Valence* represents the positive or negative value we place on outcomes or rewards; *instrumentality* represents belief about how much our efforts will influence an outcome. These two components are multiplied to get motivation. If either equals zero, motivation is also zero. Expectancy theory is appealing because it avoids the problems of drive theory, takes advantage of the incentive properties of stimuli, and emphasizes the cognitive interpretation that people place on events.

16. *Conflict* situations occur when competing goals makes a choice difficult: In an *approach/approach* conflict the person is equally attracted to mutually exclusive goals; an *avoidance/avoidance* conflict occurs when both choices are negative, an *approach/avoidance* conflict occurs when a situation has both negative and positive aspects; and a *double approach/avoidance* conflict occurs because a person is faced with choosing between two or more goals, each of which has both desirable and undesirable characteristics. The *goal gradient* is the concept that the power of a reward or a punishment becomes greater as you get closer to the goal object.

■ ANSWERING QUESTIONS FOR THOUGHT

1. Six basic emotions—anger, disgust, happiness, sadness, fear, and surprise—seem to be universal. People all over the world use the same facial expressions when feeling these emotions, and use the same labels when they see others expressing these emotions.

2. No, anxiety is one emotion that seems particularly prone to individual differences. People can usually be classified as being high or low in anxiety. Anxiety itself can have different effects on performance. You probably know some people who thrive on pressure and others who perform much better when the pressure is off.

3. Laziness is usually the lack of desired behavior rather than the lack of any behavior at all. People who are called lazy by supervisors, for example, are often very active. The problem is that they are not busy working, they are busy doing other things. Except in the case of depression, there is usually not a problem in initiating behavior; the problem is in directing behavior.

4. Boredom is a state of under-arousal, and some researchers have theorized that we have a need for a certain amount of arousal. Thus, when we are bored, we are motivated to increase arousal.

5. People have different optimal levels of arousal—if you have a high arousal level, you may seek out more stimulating situations than those with low arousal levels. Riding on a roller-coaster or climbing a mountain appeals to people with a high arousal level.

13 Personality

QUESTIONS FOR THOUGHT

1. Is personality the way we *think* or the way we *behave*?
2. Why is it that at a certain age boys want nothing to do with girls, girls want nothing to do with boys, and strong attachments are formed with friends of the same sex?
3. Do people's expectations and beliefs have anything to do with their personalities? What about their feelings regarding how rewards are achieved?
4. How does one "pass" a personality test?
5. How accurate are questionnaires as personality tests?

The answers to these questions are at the end of the chapter.

How often have you heard people make comments like these: "She's not my kind of person"; "I'm always like that first thing in the morning"; "My sister's the athletic type"; "All the kids in that family have great personalities"? What you are hearing in each case is an observation about one's own, or someone else's, style of behaving. You might describe a new acquaintance as mean, pleasant, funny, or timid. You might describe a close friend as highly motivated and imaginative, intelligent, stubborn, loyal, and energetic. Observations like these come naturally to us; in everyday conversation, such descriptions are taken to represent aspects of personality. As you are well aware, we each have a personality, and personality affects everyone. There are even tests that you can buy in a bookstore that claim to tell you something about your personality. People sometimes take these tests to see if they have a "good" personality. The problem with attaching the adjective "good"—or any adjective, for that matter—to personality, is that what you might consider a "good" feature someone else might consider "bad."

■ WHAT IS PERSONALITY?

We've talked in general terms about personality, but we haven't yet answered the question "What is personality?" The concept of personality has always been associated with the uniqueness of an individual. An individual's **personality** is what helps to distinguish one individual from another. Further, personality is a combination of the many different aspects of the individual. These aspects include emotions, motivations, learning capacities and experiences, perceptual mechanisms, thought patterns, and even biological

capacities. The point is that each of us possesses a unique combination of these various elements and each of us is made unique by virtue of these particular combinations. Thus, the best answer to the question "What is personality?" is that it is the total organization of the various behavior aspects of an individual. Personality does not exist independently of motivation, emotion, learning, or biological mechanisms. It depends on *all* these aspects for its meaning.

■ THEORIES OF PERSONALITY

Given this definition of personality, it isn't surprising that personality theories are somewhat different from other types of theories. Theories of emotion, motivation, or learning set out to explain how or why some specific behavior occurs. The issues of personality are somewhat different. Since each of us has a personality, the real issue for personality theorists is what components or processes should be included or emphasized in a theory of personality. As we will soon see, some theories emphasize the role of thinking and conscious behavior, others emphasize learning capacities and experiences, and still others emphasize motivations and drives. It is very important to remember these differences in emphasis when considering the major personality theories. Each theory represents a position, chosen by the theorist, about what should be included in a theory of personality.

Personality. The uniqueness that helps distinguish one individual from another; an integration of components such as motivation, emotion, learning capacity and experiences, perceptual mechanisms, biological capacities, and thought patterns.

Our personality helps to distinguish us from other people; each of us is a unique combination of emotions, motivations, learning capacities, and many other characteristics.

Despite these differences in emphasis, personality theorists agree that their observations need objective verifications. Thus, the study of personality also involves the different ways that psychologists go about measuring aspects of personality. This chapter will therefore discuss both personality theories and personality measurement. We'll begin with a basic question for all personality theorists—the implications of personality for behavior.

■ THE IMPLICATIONS OF PERSONALITY FOR BEHAVIOR

Historically, the understanding of personality has been closely tied to thinking about abnormal behavior. This is a topic for further exploration in Chapter 15 (Abnormal Psychology). For the moment, however, it is important to remember that the origins of personality theory lie in observations of individuals, frequently those experiencing problems in day-to-day functioning. The practice of clinical psychology and psychiatry is directly concerned with improving the functioning of those who have poorly-organized behavior. As a result of their need to diagnose and treat abnormal conditions, clinicians have been responsible for many innovations in personality theory and personality measurement.

From a strictly theoretical viewpoint, personality is sometimes seen as a machine that consists of many working parts. From this perspective, abnormal behavior occurs when there is a malfunctioning of one of those parts, just as a car that has perfect tires, transmission, and shock absorbers won't move if the carburetor is clogged.

Another view of the relationship between personality and behavior is that personality is a framework like the steel understructure that supports a building. When this structural framework weakens or disintegrates, outward behavior crumbles with it. This is a somewhat static view of personality that implies the importance of stability or endurance for well-organized behavior.

The study of personality ties in with thinking about abnormal behavior in another way as well. Consider the meaning of the term *abnormal*. It means "out of the ordinary." In statistical thinking, "out of the ordinary" simply means "at a distance from the average." When someone behaves in an unusual or inappropriate way, it is logical to search for some aspect of personality in which that person is distant from the "average" or "normal" person. One way of searching for this aspect is to use personality tests of various kinds. When such an aspect is found, it becomes a possible candidate for the diagnosis and treatment of abnormal condition.

When we consider the implications of personality for behavior, we must keep in mind that there are (by definition) many more "average" or "normal" people than "abnormal" people. For this reason, personality theories need to be just as concerned with normal processes as with abnormal ones. In the next sections, we will be discussing some of the more important theories of personality that have emerged. As you read through them, you should evaluate how each theory deals with the relationship between personality and the normal and abnormal processes of behavior. Remember what was said earlier: Each of these theories represents one person's idea of what

"makes up" the individuality of each of us. The theorists are attempting to answer many questions, all of them attempts to account for the individuality, or uniqueness, in human behavior.

■ FREUD'S PSYCHODYNAMIC THEORY

Although personality theories can be traced to the ancient Greek physician Hippocrates, as far back as 400 B.C., modern personality theory begins with the work of Sigmund Freud. Freud proposed the first comprehensive and influential theory of personality and its influence can still be felt today. Based on his theory, he developed a special technique, or therapy, to deal with abnormal personality. We will discuss Freud's therapy and other kinds of therapies in Chapter 16.

Freud was trained as a physician and he started his clinical-neurology practice in Vienna in 1881. He became acquainted with another physician, Joseph Breuer, and the two began collaborating in treating patients with symptoms of what was then called *hysteria* (physical problems that have no obvious organic cause). Breuer was convinced that upsetting memories were at the root of hysteric symptoms and was using hypnosis to try to uncover them. In one case, a patient (known as Anna O.) was afraid to drink from a glass. Using hypnosis, Breuer uncovered the fact that the young woman had once seen a dog drinking from a glass and had been disgusted by what she had seen. She had forgotten the incident at one level but it remained elsewhere in her consciousness. After undergoing hypnosis and recognizing the cause of her fear, Anna O.'s problem disappeared. Freud was greatly impressed with the effect on the patient of both hypnosis and talking about the trauma. From this and other single case histories, Freud developed a construct of personality and a theory about what produced behaviors like those shown by Anna O.

Levels of Consciousness

Before Freud, psychology had focused on consciousness—the thoughts, feelings, and memories of which we are actively aware. Freud proposed a radically new view of consciousness. It seemed to him that some part of the mind is open to conscious awareness because many events are easily and accurately remembered, and that some part of the mind is hidden from conscious awareness because other events *cannot* be easily brought to mind. Freud eventually came to the conclusion that consciousness has three levels. The **conscious** level consists of material that a person is actually aware of at any one time. According to Freud, the conscious level is relatively small—in his words, rather like the tip of an iceberg that floats above the surface of the water. The second, or **preconscious**, level consists of whatever thoughts the person might not be aware of at a particular instant, but could become aware of with little difficulty. For example, you don't have your telephone number in mind constantly, but if someone asks you for it you become conscious of it quickly. The third level is the **unconscious**. This consists of material that is not readily accessible—like the submerged portion of the iceberg— that one becomes aware of only with great difficulty. Anna O.'s traumatic memory of the dog drinking from the glass was presumably in her unconscious.

As tempting as it may be, we must be careful not to think of these three levels as things or places, because that is not what Freud intended. Instead, these terms refer to special processes that operate both together and individually to influence personality and behavior. Just as there are other kinds of processes of which we are generally unaware, such as constancies in perception and coding in memory, so too these levels of consciousness are processes of the mind, not locations in the mind.

Structures of Personality

Along with the three levels of consciousness, Freud proposed that there are three distinct systems that function at the same time in the personality. These are called the *id*, the *ego*, and the *superego*. Once again, these terms do not describe things or places, but are meant to describe processes. The first, the **id**, is a wishing or desiring process that is continually seeking satisfaction. The id represents the drives that provide the energy for behavior. There are two id drives that Freud particularly emphasized—the **pleasure drive** and the **destructive drive**. The pleasure drive is related to sexual impulses of a broad variety. The energy from the pleasure drive is called the **libido**, or **libidinal energy**. The destructive drive

is expressed in behavior that is aggressive and often has the appearance of being self-destructive. Thus, the id and its drives are a basic source of psychic energy.

The instinctive nature of the id is modified by the ego. The **ego** is a cognitive or reasoning process that helps reconcile the basic needs of the individual (as defined by the id) with the demands posed by the environment. It serves to protect the individual from the possible dangers involved in indiscriminate satisfaction of the drives of the id. Insofar as the ego acts to control the ways in which needs are satisfied, it is a tie with external reality that the id alone does not have.

The third process, the **superego**, consists of standards against which actual and potential behaviors are evaluated for moral correctness. Freud believed that people form a set of internal standards, and that self-perceived failure to meet these standards produces feelings of guilt and shame. What Freud called the superego we might call the conscience.

In Freud's view, the id is always unconscious—it is never directly accessible; the ego and superego, on the other hand, are partially accessible. Figure 13–1 pictures the three systems of personality existing at the different levels of consciousness.

Freud thought that these systems act in opposition to one another in ways that are often not obvious to the individual. For example, the unconscious id could be opposed to the fully conscious portion of the ego (since the ego is involved in controlling the drives of the id). This opposition is a critical concept in Freud's thinking and is one reason the term **psychodynamic** is often used to describe Freud's theory. The dynamic element of behavior comes from these opposing processes. Also, there are the opposing processes of the destructive drive and the pleasure drive. According to Freud, these are the beginnings of individual differences: People are unique and vary in their behavior as a result of the relative strengths of their drives and the relative strength of their id, ego, and superego. The behavior that we observe in someone is one product of the interaction of these personality processes. For a very simple example, suppose the id "demands" the pleasure afforded by eating. The superego, on the other hand, shows concern for what others might think about unrestrained eating. As a result, the ego settles on a compromise.

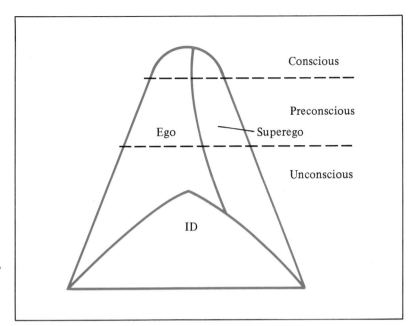

FIGURE 13-1

According to Freud, there are three processes of personality: id, ego, and superego, and three levels of consciousness: conscious, preconscious, and unconscious. The chart here shows how the three processes exist at the different levels of consciousness.

The person decides to make dinner for the family and to taste various dishes as they are being prepared. This is an oversimplified example, but it gives you a feel for the dynamic interaction. More serious conflicts are not settled so easily and, as we will see, can cause ongoing personality difficulties.

Stages of Development

For various reasons, Freud thought that experiences in early childhood are critical to the development of the adult personality. In the first place, he be-

lieved that the id is present at birth but that the ego and the superego start to develop once the child begins to grow. This implies that opposing forces will become more and more prominent as the ego and superego emerge. In addition, Freud believed that particular zones of the body are sensitive at different stages of maturation, and that libido and satisfaction of the pleasure drive will be concentrated in these sensitive zones. Freud outlined five stages of development, which were introduced in Chapter 10 (Development). To review, these stages, called **psychosexual stages of development,** involve

---

Conscious. Freudian concept; the level of consciousness consisting of material that a person is aware of at any one time.

Preconscious. Freudian concept; the level of consciousness consisting of material that a person might not be aware of at any one moment but could become aware of without difficulty.

Unconscious. Freudian concept; the level of consciousness consisting of material that is not readily accessible and that a person can become aware of only with great difficulty.

Id. One of three processes of personality theorized by Freud; made up of drives, including the pleasure and destructive drives, that are constantly seeking expression. Operates on the level of the unconscious.

Pleasure drive. Freudian term for the id drive that is related to satisfying sexual stimulation of a broad nature; a basic source of psychic energy.

Destructive drive. Freudian term for the id drive that seeks expression in aggressive behavior and may have the appearance of being self-destructive; a basic source of psychic energy.

Libido or **libidinal energy.** Freudian term; the energy derived from the pleasure drive of the id. The source of pleasure is sexual stimulation.

Ego. One of three processes of personality theorized by Freud; helps reconcile basic needs of the person (as defined by the id) with opportunities to safely satisfy them in the environment.

Superego. One of three processes of personality theorized by Freud; corresponds to the conscience. Concerned with moral standards of behavior.

Psychodynamic. Term used to describe Freud's theory of personality. Refers to the dynamic opposition of the processes of id, ego, and superego, as well as the opposition of the pleasure and destructive drives of the id; out of this opposition emerges a unique personality.

Psychosexual stages of development. Freud's five stages of development; called psychosexual stages because they involve psychological development of the personality as well as changing areas of sexual sensitivity.

both psychological development of the personality and changing areas of sexual sensitivity. Remember that Freud's concept of sexual pleasure is a very broad one, similar in meaning to the term *gratification*. In the description of the stages that follows, keep in mind that the ages given are approximate; it is thought that some children enter stages earlier and others later. Also, movement through the stages is assumed to be influenced by a combination of things—physical growth and development, the passage through earlier stages, and environmental experiences.

The Oral Stage (Birth to 1½ Years). In the oral stage the mouth is the area of greatest sensitivity. In this stage children get pleasure from stimulation of the mouth through activities such as sucking, eating, and making noises. It is during this stage that they are weaned from the bottle or their mother's breast and encounter social rules for eating. In addition, children may be stopped from thumb-sucking or placing foreign objects in their mouths. This represents a conflict between desires and control that the child must deal with.

The Anal Stage (1½ to 3 Years). In the anal stage the anal area is particularly sensitive. This means that activities involving elimination become pleasurable to the child. It is also at this stage that the child is toilet-trained, which is a restraint on the pleasure of elimination. This represents another potential conflict for the child.

The Phallic Stage (3 to 6 Years). In the phallic stage the genital area becomes the focus of attention. Children begin to explore their genital organs and find them pleasurable. Parents, on the other hand, are often critical of this exploration and may try to stop it in various ways. This curtailment may take the form of direct control ("Don't do that") or indirect criticism ("Good little boys don't do that," "That is not what nice little girls do"). Once again, there is a conflict between activities that bring pleasure and activities that bring approval.

Freud believed that both boys and girls were deeply in love with their mothers, since their mothers had always satisfied all of their needs. He also believed that boys deal with this feeling in a different manner than girls. During the phallic stage,

In the oral stage children get pleasure from the stimulation of the mouth through thumb sucking, eating, and making noises.

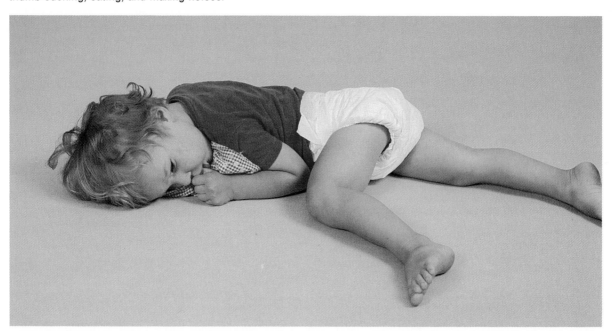

the boy develops sexual desire for his mother. Even to a young boy, it is obvious that the father will not allow this desire to be fulfilled. This realization leads, in turn, to a fear of the father—a fear that the father will cut off the boy's penis to prevent fulfillment of the desire. Finally, the young boy resolves this desire/fear conflict by accepting the father as a role model and getting pleasure from acting like him. In boys, this conflict between fearing the father and desiring the mother is known as the **Oedipus complex**.

The young girl also experiences changing feelings toward her mother during the phallic period. When the girl realizes that she does not have a penis, she becomes angry at the mother, blaming her for the missing organ. As a result, she transfers her love feelings to the father, who has a penis. Since she cannot lose a penis, she suffers less fear of punishment than the boy. As a result, the phallic period is thought to be less traumatic for girls than for boys. In girls, the desire/anger conflict is called the **Electra complex**. There is still some conflict for the girl, since it is obvious to her that she cannot sexually possess her father. Resolution of this complex for the girl occurs when she successfully transfers her feelings toward her father to other males.

Freud thought that the successful resolution of these conflicts of the phallic stage corresponds to the first serious development of the superego in children.

The Latency Stage (6–12 Years). Freud considered the latency stage to be a dormant period characterized by rapid growth of the superego. Because the libido is being controlled by the superego at this stage, there is no particularly sensitive bodily zone that brings pleasure. Following the successful resolution of the Oedipus and Electra complexes, children form strong attachments to playmates of their own sex and may shun playmates of the opposite sex.

The Genital Stage (13 Years through Adulthood). During the genital stage, the person must establish heterosexual relations once again. Now the conflict is between the controls of the superego, which were developed in response to the desire for the same-sex parent, and the reawakened sexual urges of the phallic stage. The desires that emerge now are more readily recognizable as adult urges for intercourse, procreation, and individual sexual pleasure.

As you will see in the chapters on abnormal psychology and therapy, Freud believed that behavioral problems arise from unresolved conflicts at one or more of these stages. When this happens, the person is said to have a **fixation** or to be **fixated** (or stuck) at the stage that is associated with the conflict. Since the person did not successfully complete that stage, behavior is likely to involve a continued seeking of gratifications that are appropriate for that stage.

Before taking leave of Freud, it is appropriate to consider how successful his theory has been. The theory clearly satisfies the goal of a personality theory—to account for the uniqueness and complexity of human behavior. Its ideas about sexual energy, personality processes, and the role of the unconscious were revolutionary for its time and had a major impact on all theorists and theories that followed it.

A Synthesis and Some Variations

Recall that we began this chapter by suggesting that personality is the combination of processes that helps to define individual uniqueness. Freud identified three separate sets of processes in personality. These include processes of awareness (the conscious, preconscious, and unconscious), processes of desire and control (the id, ego, and superego), and processes of change and development (the psychosexual stages). His theory, then, suggests that personality is unique as a result of different interactions among these three sets of processes. In one person, the ego may devise certain strategies for meeting particular needs of the id or for avoiding guilt caused by comparisons of behaviors to superego standards.

Oedipus complex. According to Freud, the conflict a boy experiences during the phallic stage involving fear of his father and desire for his mother.
Electra complex. According to Freud, the conflict a girl experiences during the phallic stage involving anger at her mother and desire for her father.

Fixated or fixation. Occurs when a conflict associated with a certain psychosexual stage is unresolved and the person remains stuck in the stage at which the conflict occurred, continually seeking gratifications that are appropriate for that stage.

In another person, conflicts that appeared at particular stages (such as between desires for oral gratification and controls over eating behaviors) may have been only partially resolved and, as a result, play a role in later behavior. Each of us has certain "equipment" (such as levels of consciousness and id, ego, and superego processes) and certain experiences. The interactions of this equipment and these experiences result in the uniqueness of personality.

Since the original publication of Freud's theory there have been numerous variations offered by those wishing to stress one aspect or process over another as an influence on personality. In general, the generation of thinkers that followed Freud (the so-called "Neo-Freudians) have had different views from Freud on what creates conflict and motivates personality. Some have modified his theory in very interesting ways. For example, Carl Jung (1875–1961) agreed with Freud about the role of the unconscious, but he chose to break the unconscious down further into two more components. One he called the **personal unconscious**, consisting of all the things that were once known to the individual but have now been forgotten, and the other is the **collective unconscious**, the memory trace laid down through the whole of human history and shared by all people. According to Jung, the collective unconscious is independent of anything in the personal life of the individual.

Another important follower of Freud was Alfred Adler (1870–1937). Adler differed from Freud in his theory of the major energy source of behavior. In place of the libidinal energy that is so stressed by Freud, Adler proposed that feelings of inferiority as a child evoke later desires for excellence. In Adler's view, it is an upward striving for self-improvement and perfection that is the motivating force of behavior.

■ TRAIT THEORIES

Freud had very specific ideas about the makeup and mechanics of personality and about the opposition dynamic that forms the adult personality. He came to his conclusions largely on the basis of careful thought, knowledge from his medical training, and his personal observations and work with patients.

This is one way to construct a theory, but there is another way to go about it, one that is more common in science. As we discussed in Chapter 1, this other method avoids personal observations and instead depends on systematic observation and categorization. The researcher first describes all the varieties of the object (or subject) of interest, then classifies these many varieties into a smaller subgroup, then develops a rule for this classification, and finally uses this rule as the basis of a theory. This method has proven successful in biology (for example, the phylogenetic scale, which is used to order various species of life) and in chemistry (the periodic chart, which is used to order elements by their atomic weight), and also represents a common approach to the development of personality theories. Personality theories that use this type of systematic approach are called **trait theories**. A **trait** is a predisposition within the individual to respond in characteristic ways to various kinds of stimuli (Hjelle and Ziegler, 1981). Trait theories maintain that characteristic patterns of behavior are a result of a person's traits.

The method used to devise a trait theory is not complicated. If the purpose of any personality theory is to provide a framework that can account for the diversity of behavior, then the first step of a trait theory is to catalogue or describe this diversity. This can be accomplished in several ways: We can talk to people directly, or we can ask them to respond to standard stimuli.

Most of the terms that you use every day to describe personality are examples of traits: *Friendliness, openness, excitability, humor,* and *carelessness* are all terms that suggest a style or manner of behavior that is unique in some respect. A full list of such terms is potentially limitless, and researchers have worked at paring it down. Instead of dealing with thousands of adjectives, modern trait theorists have generally settled on some basic dimensions that can be used to describe variations in personality.

Many theories of personality depend on just a small number of dimensions or characteristics to account for individual differences in behavior. Freud's theory was an early example of this tendency. It consists of a very few basic elements—levels of consciousness (conscious, preconscious, unconscious) and personality processes (id, ego, superego). Biological growth and interaction with environment add complexity to this basic framework.

An extravert is outgoing, likes stimulation, and enjoys being around people.

Eysenck's Trait Theory

Hans Eysenck (1916–   ) is a modern personality theorist who also proposes three basic factors to explain personality. He arrived at these basic factors after years of careful research using many different types of tests to measure personality traits. By means of statistical methods, he then combined these many and varied personality characteristics into three major dimensions. He found that with just three dimensions, he could account for all of the complexity in behavior shown in individual test responses and

---

Personal unconscious. Term used by Jung to refer to things that were once known to the individual but have now been forgotten.

Collective unconscious. Term used by Jung to refer to memories laid down through the whole of human history and shared by all people; independent of anything personal in the life of the individual.

Trait theories. Approaches to personality that maintain that unique characteristics of personality are a result of a person's predispositions or traits.

Trait. An enduring predisposition within the individual to respond in characteristic ways to various kinds of stimuli. Examples of traits are extraversion and introversion.

other measures of personality (Eysenck, 1975). These three dimensions are introversion/extraversion, stability/neuroticism, and psychoticism.

Eysenck proposes that people vary along these three dimensions, and that the particular combinations of various levels of introversion/extraversion, stability/neuroticism, and psychoticism result in the different patterns of behavior that we call personality. Let's consider these dimensions one at a time. The **introvert** is thought to be quiet and reserved, striving for control and the suppression of excitement. The **extravert**, on the other hand, is outgoing, does not worry about things, likes stimulation, and dislikes being alone. The **stable** person is calm and does not become emotional very often or easily. The **neurotic** person is easily excited and tends to be moody or "touchy." The individual who scores high on **psychoticism** is withdrawn, solitary, and uncaring, while the individual who scores low on psychoticism is easy to get along with, pleasant, and sensitive to the needs of others. Psychoticism is an aspect of personality that primarily applies to people with severe mental disorders. Eysenck suggests that the many *specific* personality traits that we attribute to people every day can be described based on variations of the levels of the other two dimensions—introversion/extraversion and stability/ neuroticism. As an example, someone who is seen as outgoing and sociable scores high on extraversion. Figure 13–2 demonstrates what might be expected from various combinations.

Cattell's Trait Theory

Eysenck's theory is extremely compact, suggesting only two basic dimensions in the normal personality. Cattell, on the other hand, feels that there are considerably more than two basic personality dimensions. Like Eysenck, Cattell has used many different types of tests to measure personality traits. He decided on 16 factors that he felt were the most basic dimensions on which people differ. These 16 factors, which he believes can account for the many personality differences we observe, appear in Figure 13–3. As was the case with Eysenck's theory, people can occupy various levels on each of Cattell's personality dimensions. This makes the number of variations in personality almost limitless. Cattell's theory includes some dimensions that are common to all people, as well as some dimensions that are unique to individuals. Research on Cattell's theory continues today.

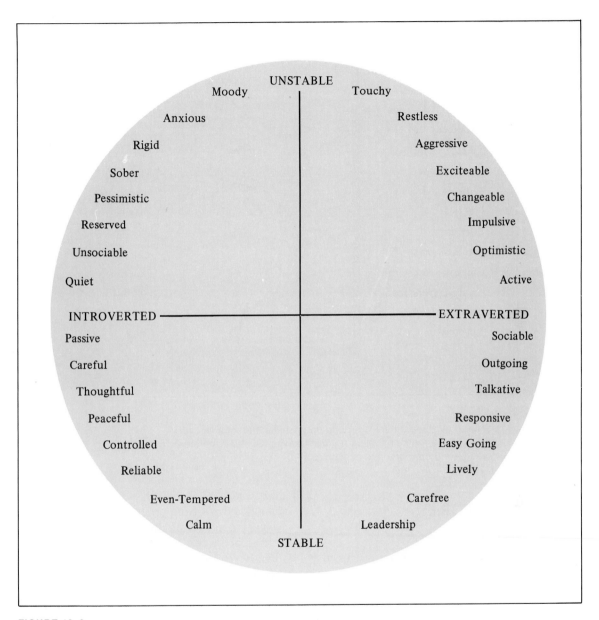

FIGURE 13-2
Eysenck proposes that many different personality traits can be described in terms of
two dimensions, introversion/extraversion and stability/neuroticism (or instability, as
shown in the chart here).

Introvert. Term used by Eysenck to describe someone who is
quiet and reserved, always striving for control and suppress-
ing excitement.

Extravert. Term used by Eysenck to describe a person who is
outgoing, unworried, likes stimulation, and dislikes being alone.

Stable. Term used by Eysenck to describe a person who is calm
and does not become emotional often or easily.

Neurotic. Term used by Eysenck to describe a person who is
easily excited and tends to be moody or "touchy."

Psychoticism. Term used by Eysenck to describe the personality
of an individual who is withdrawn, solitary, and uncaring.

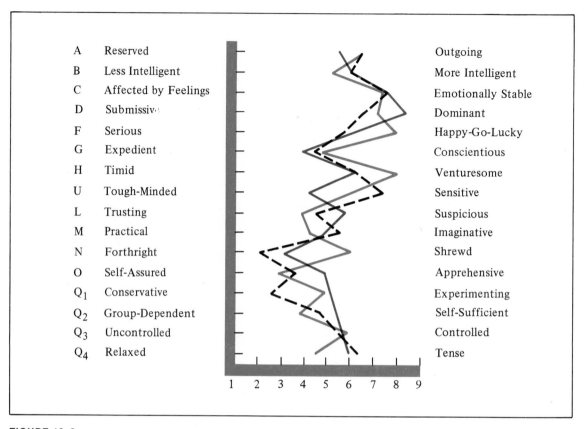

FIGURE 13-3
This shows scores made by three different groups on Cattell's 16-factor questionnaire: Olympic athletes, clergymen, and sales representatives (Olympic athletes are
the red line, clergymen are the broken line, and sales representatives are the
blue line). (Cattell, 1965, pp. 242, 347)

■ HUMANIST THEORIES

Both Freudian theories and trait theories stress the
idea that personality consists of parts or elements
that interact. In Freudian theories, these interacting parts include the levels of consciousness and the
processes of the id, ego, and superego. In trait
theories, the respective traits are the parts.
Humanist personality theories have a very different
emphasis. They see personality as an integrated
system, not one that is broken down into elements
such as traits or processes. In the same sense that
you would not talk about a car as a vehicle containing only a muffler, the humanists feel that a personality contains everything of importance to
human functioning. This includes, among other
things, intelligence, values, habits, and goals.

Another aspect of humanist theories that

separates them from other approaches is that they
see personality as intentional. They believe that the
individual is a controlling and active part of the personality. In contrast, the individual in Freudian
theory is controlled by forces of the id, ego, and
superego; in trait theories, predispositions or traits
determine the way a personality is expressed.
Humanist theories assume that an individual's personality grows and emerges throughout life and is
characterized by purpose and intention; it is not a
product of other controlling forces such as personality processes or traits.

There is one final aspect of humanist theory that
distinguishes it from other approaches. Humanist
theories emphasize those characteristics and processes that make humans different from other
animals. As a result, humanist theories concentrate
on aspects such as language, future planning, logical thought, self-control, and rationality.

Carl Rogers' Self Theory

Carl Rogers (1902–   ), a famous humanist, developed a theory in which the self plays a central role in the formation of personality. He saw personality as resulting from the interaction of a person's self-concept with his or her actual experience. Each of us has a self-concept, or a view of ourself. You may see yourself as kind, tough, bright, or afraid. In addition, each of us is viewed in a particular way by others we meet. Some people take you seriously, others think you are a fool, still others think you are too practical.

The real issue for Rogers was how people can reconcile the concept that they have of themselves with the ways they actually behave as well as with the ways others view them. Let's take an example. You may think of yourself as bright and informed, but in a group of friends you may be treated as a clown and not as the intelligent person you consider yourself to be, because you are always making wisecracks and playing the fool. When you say something intelligent, your friends pass it off as a lucky mistake. This lack of correlation between your view of yourself and the impression that your friends have of you may eventually create problems. At some point, you may become angry or distressed because your advice is consistently ignored as "foolish."

In this example the results of the discrepancy may not be significant, but discrepancies can cause more serious problems. Most people think of themselves as adults who are competent in their work. Some supervisors may have the opposite opinion of employees. They may think of workers as childish, unintelligent, and irresponsible. Supervisors who think this way may treat workers like children, making all decisions for them, scolding them when something goes wrong, and treating them as being generally incapable of complicated mental activity. At some point, this discrepancy will have to be resolved. Workers will have to either change their self-concepts or change their supervisors' concept. Often what happens is that workers begin to act in the childish and irresponsible way they are "expected" to act. From the supervisors' point of view, the behavior then confirms their existing beliefs about the traits of workers. In a similar way, some adolescents, convinced equally of their own trustworthiness and of their parents' lack of trust, begin to behave in a way that upholds their parents' suspicious attitudes. Again, a discrepancy has been resolved, but in a way that causes the individual more problems. Eventually, anxiety appears as a result of the discrepancy between self-concept and actual experience and leads to further denial and distortion in behavior.

It is the inconsistency between self-concept and real-world experience that Rogers feels produces variations in personality (and behavior). As you will see in Chapter 16 on therapies, a therapist who accepts Rogers' concept of personality will try to help the client develop a self-image that is more in line with his or her behavior. In effect, this will be an attempt to close the gaps between a person's experience and self-image.

From Rogers' point of view, personality is a very fluid thing, always changing and emerging. Because we find ourselves in constantly changing situations, we consequently see ourselves behaving in many different ways. In addition, according to Rogers, our self-concept is affected by our behavior, and our behavior is influenced by our self-concept. As a result, a person is always evaluating consistency between self-image and behavior.

Another important aspect of Rogers' theory has to do with motivation. Rogers believes that there is a universal need for acceptance by other people. This need, in turn, affects a person's self-concept, since the extent to which a person is accepted by others is a measure of self-worth to that person. Thus, self-concept develops from interactions with others. In our earlier examples, the workers might try harder to please their supervisor in order to obtain the supervisor's respect, or the adolescent might try to remove any suspicions that the parents may have. In each case, the person is acting to receive or maintain the acceptance of others. This may also create problems. We may find ourselves acting in a way that will please others but that is not true to our self-image. When a bright person plays the fool for a group of friends, there are times when it is painful. According to Rogers, this is an instance of a disorganized or unintegrated personality—some parts don't match; behavior does not correspond to self-concept.

It is this interaction between self-concept and experience that defines personality growth for the humanist theories. Thus, in humanist thinking, the personality of the healthy individual should be just as dynamic as the personality of the disturbed or troubled person.

■ LEARNING APPROACHES

In a sense, behaviorists believe that what you are is what you *do*, and that what you do is learned. Thus, from the learning viewpoint, it is not necessary to propose a "trait" such as introversion, or a process such as the ego, or an idea such as a self-concept. The variations in personality can be explained as variations in learning experiences and the resulting associations. As you saw in Chapter 6, Learning Principles, there are differing viewpoints on how learning is accomplished. In the same way, different learning theorists have differing viewpoints and place emphases on different aspects of learning that influence personality.

Skinner's Behaviorism

Skinner would not think of himself as a personality theorist. In the first place, he would reject the existence of a personality as a controlling element in behavior. On the other hand, if we consider a person's personality to be a pattern that might be used to describe the unique but reliable aspects of that person's behavior, then Skinner would agree that learning theory can be used to account for both the uniqueness and the regularity of behavior. So, for the purposes of this chapter, we will look at personality in terms of Skinner's learning theory.

For Skinner, the uniqueness of personality is the result of several different factors. These include schedules of reinforcement that are currently operating in the person's environment, past associations between responses and reinforcers, and the relationships that have been formed between primary and secondary reinforcers. For example, Skinner might account for aggressive behavior in a child by identifying past instances in which aggressiveness was reinforced, current partial reinforcement schedules that maintain aggressive behavior at a high rate, and secondary reinforcers in the environment that have assumed the power of primary reinforcers. Thus, the young boy who has been praised for "acting tough" at home might act aggressively in the classroom in an attempt to get praise and good grades from the teacher. Skinner would certainly dismiss any consideration of an id, superego, and ego as factors in aggressiveness. Similarly, he would probably say that explaining a child's aggressiveness as resulting from the trait of aggressiveness is circular and invalid reasoning.

Two other key factors in personality development from the learning perspective are the processes of generalization and discrimination. As you remember from the chapter on learning principles, stimulus generalization means responding in a similar way to stimuli other than the conditioned one. Such generalized responses are what is thought to give personality its broad consistency in many different situations. On the other hand, generalized responses are not always rewarded; they might even be punished or ignored. This would result in a type of discrimination learning, or learning to respond to a specific stimulus, and would give personality some unique and specific aspects. Thus, in learning terms, personality is formed of a series of associations, some of which are general and some of which are unique.

Thus, in the case of learning theory, we have a whole system of elements (schedules of reinforcement, secondary reinforcement, response/reinforcement associations, and generalization/discrimination processes) to account for the diversity and uniqueness of behavioral patterns. In short, however, Skinner would probably claim that differences in personality are simply reflections of differences in environments.

Social Learning Theory

We first encountered expectancy theory in the chapter on emotion and motivation. It is the cognitive theory that people expend energy according to their beliefs about how much they will enjoy a particular outcome and whether their efforts will actually lead to that outcome. One point we mentioned only briefly was the fact that people *vary* in both preferences and beliefs about outcomes. Julian Rotter was one of the first psychologists to emphasize the importance of preferences and beliefs in the development and expression of personality. In addition, he proposed another key variable as part of personality—a variable he called **locus of control**. This is a type of belief, but it is not connected with the probability of getting a reward. Instead, it has to do with a person's broader view of how rewards are achieved—through luck or through effort. Those who believe in an **external locus of control** think that rewards are controlled by someone besides themselves or else are a function of luck. Those who believe in an **internal locus of control** believe that reinforcements are a result of their own hard work and skill. In Rotter's view, the variables of locus of control, expectancies, and preferences combine to yield a wide variety of potential behaviors that make for uniqueness of personality. In other words, our personalities are unique because our beliefs are unique.

Bandura (1977) has expanded locus of control to a broader concept he calls **perceived self-efficacy**. This concept includes the feelings that someone has about his or her capabilities, especially those skills and abilities necessary to complete a particular task. Feelings of self-efficacy can be affected by a number of variables (Hergenhahn, 1984). One is the individual's past history of accomplishment. When you stand on the starting line of your first race next to the person who is the defending champion, you are likely to feel at a disadvantage. Consequently, your behavior (i.e., your finishing time) might be affected by your feeling of inadequacy. Perceived self-efficacy can also be affected by the comments of others. Most of us respond to being told to "Go for it!" as we are about to tackle something difficult. Another influential variable is the behavior of others we see as being similar to ourselves. For example, you might feel reluctant to sign up for a particular class because you think it will be too difficult. You then discover that a friend you consider similar to yourself in intellectual ability took that class last semester and did well in it. You may then decide that you can do well after all and sign up for the class.

Feelings of self-efficacy operate in many different circumstances. I take part in many road races. The distances vary from 5 miles to the 26-mile marathon. Invariably, as I line up for the start of the race, I look around at my fellow runners and want to crawl in a hole. Every one of them looks leaner, stronger, faster, and more at ease than I. If it were not for the fact that my family *expected* me to start and finish the race, I might very well make my way back to my car by a side street and drive home. After the race starts, these uneasy feelings start to

Feelings of self-efficacy can be affected by a number of variables, including the comments of others. Runners usually respond to crowd urgencies to "go for it" in finishing a difficult race.

Locus of control. People's beliefs about whether rewards are achieved through luck or through hard work and skill.

External locus of control. Belief that rewards are controlled by someone or something else or are a function of luck.

Internal locus of control. Belief that rewards come as a result of hard work and skill, and thus are entirely controlled by oneself.

Perceived self-efficacy. Bandura's idea that a person's expectations about having the abilities and skills needed to complete a task can strongly influence accomplishment; can be affected by several variables, including a personal history of accomplishment and the comments of others.

diminish because I find that I am passing many of the people who looked so strong and fast. These feelings of inadequacy are also less intense if there are people in the race that I have run with before, in training or in other races. It should be clear by now that locus of control or feelings of self-efficacy could be responsible for widely varying behavior patterns in the same individual on different occasions or in different individuals on the same occasion.

From the learning perspective, the important thing to remember is that preferences, beliefs, and expectancies can all be affected by experience. In other words, they can all be products of associations of one type or another. The term *social learning* has been proposed by Bandura, because much of what we learn is affected by other people. The above examples all involved other people in one way or another. We imitate the behavior of others; we learn expectancies from watching and listening to others; we develop our locus of control beliefs largely in response to our relationships with other people.

■ THE INTERACTION OF TRAITS AND SITUATIONS

It should be apparent by now that there are differences of opinion among personality theorists with respect to the importance of characteristics of the person and characteristics of the environment. The trait theorists attach great importance to the characteristics of the person, but the learning theorists believe that the situation or environment has a stronger affect on behavior. The trait theorists cite the consistency of behavior over long periods of time and in a large number of situations as evidence that internal factors play a greater role in behavior than external ones (Block, 1971). In the chapter on stress (Chapter 14), we will see an example of a trait called "Type A" behavior. This trait implies a hard-driving, competitive, time-urgent style of behavior. My wife and I were out to dinner one evening with a friend and his wife. This friend is widely recognized to be a "Type A." When his wife took up golfing, he immediately took it up as well and quickly worked to become more proficient. If she began reading a new book, he would buy it as well and finish it before her. On this particular evening, we were eating our salad and he leaned over to his wife and

whispered something in her ear. She threw her fork down on the table and exclaimed, "For God's sake, Don, what difference does it make that you finished your salad before I finished mine!" This is the type of consistency that trait theorists point to in behavioral sequences.

Those more in favor of situational explanations cite the inconsistency of behavior as evidence against the prominence of traits in understanding personality (Mischel, 1968). For example, many boxers are mild-mannered, pleasant, and considerate when they are not in the ring fighting an opponent, yet once they step into the ring they are ferocious. I am also reminded of an interview I saw with a professional linebacker about pregame activities. He quietly described the pregame prayer at breakfast, the hour of quiet meditation following breakfast, and the brief team prayer that preceded the actual game. The interviewer asked the next question, "Then what do you do?" The linebacker responded, "I go out and try to kill the quarterback of the other team." These are examples of what some people think of as situationally-determined behaviors. Most likely neither the boxer nor the linebacker would try to knock down a cashier in a restaurant or a child in a playground.

Rorer and Widiger (1983) suggest that personalities are most likely influenced by *both* traits and situations:

It is clear that one does not go to a restaurant to get one's hair cut. One does not have sexual intercourse in church during church services. It is unusual to find anyone reading a book during a movie. People at football games do not usually sleep. If this is what behaviorists mean when they say that behavior is primarily determined by situations, then they are correct and we have never heard of a trait theorist who disagreed. On the other hand, one's traits may determine whether one goes to a movie or to a football game or stays home and sleeps or reads a book. (p. 446)

The fact that certain behaviors are more likely to occur in one situation than another seems to suggest that traits and situations interact. In other words, certain behaviors seem to require appropriate circumstances. This point of view has been called the *interactionist position*. This is very much like the interaction between biological circumstances and environmental stimuli that defines the incentive theory of motivation discussed in Chapter 12. Biological circumstances without appropri-

TABLE 13-1.
An undergraduate female's description of her traits, feelings, and behavior in four different situations. As with other subjects, her behavior was consistent in a given type of situation but quite different in dissimilar situations.

Type of situation	Examples	Traits associated with situation	Feelings	Behaviors
Interacting with males	On a date; Talking to a fellow student; At a friend's party	Easygoing, sociable, light, friendly, intellectual	Fun, ok. mature	Enjoying, laughing, interested, honest, extraverted
At work or interacting with strangers	Working in Washington; Doing research in Boston; In a large, new group	Difficult, tiring, demanding, intimidating	Shy, inadequate, overwhelmed, quiet	Listening, fearful, polite, cool, aloof, introverted
Interacting with supportive others	In a counseling session in a therapy group; Talking with mother	Unique, special, personal, important	Love, sadness, gratitude, tenderness, closeness	Loving, hopeful, questioning
Family relationships	At home; Being with relatives; Fighting with mother; Interacting with brother; Drinking alone	Defensive, unaware, closed, lonely, familiar	Want attention, frustrated	Demanding, exploding, expecting too much

Source: Based on Pervin, 1976, p. 470

ate stimuli do not produce motivated behavior. In the same way, appropriate stimuli in unfavorable biological circumstances do not produce motivated behavior. Recall the incentive theory of motivation as applied to eating behavior. If a person is hungry, certain cues in the environment (food) will act as incentives for certain types of behavior (eating). If the biological circumstances are wrong (if the person just ate 15 minutes ago) or the cues are not there (if the person is at a class lecture), then the particular behavior (eating) will not occur.

Interactionist theories of personality (Mischel, 1973; Endler and Magnusson, 1976) propose that certain traits are expressed only in certain situations. The shy student becomes the aggressive tennis player; the friendly salesperson becomes the hostile customer. In interactionist terms, a trait becomes a predisposition to respond in a particular way in the presence of a particular stimulus. This could easily account for the seeming inconsistency of behavior in different situations—behavior is only con-

sistent to the extent that situations are perceived as similar by the person. This further implies that it is the *meaning* a person places on a situation, not just the physical characteristics of the situation, that is important. Table 13-1 gives some examples of the subtle interactions among traits, situations, and feelings that might explain apparent "inconsistency" in a particular individual's behavior.

REVIEW QUESTIONS

6. In Rogers' view, the acceptance by others important to us is necessary for us to develop a positive _____.

7. In the learning approach, variations in personality can be seen as variations in _____ experiences and the _____ one forms as a result of those experiences.

8. Freud would see the problem of a child behaving aggressively in school as a conflict of id, ego, and superego; Skinner would see it as a question of _____ and _____ _____ schedules.

9. If you think that the good grades you get in school are due to your own hard work, you have an internal/external locus of control; if you think good grades depend on the whim of the teacher or on luck, you have an internal/external locus of control.

10. The _____ position says that personality is influenced by both one's personality traits and the situations one finds oneself in.

Answers: 6. self-concept 7. learning; associations 8. reinforcement; reinforcement 9. internal; external 10. interactionist

■ THE ASSESSMENT OF PERSONALITY

Next to intelligence assessment, personality assessment may be the psychological technique most familiar to the public. At one time or another, most people have heard about or taken an "inkblot" test or have answered a questionnaire asking about unusual behaviors or thoughts. A description of a person in terms of a characteristic pattern of behavior is known as a **personality assessment**. Although the term *measurement* is also used, the term we will use here is assessment. Measurement implies ratings of some kind—good or bad, high or low, right or wrong; assessment simply implies description without an accompanying evaluation.

In order to answer the question, "How is personality assessed?", we should first ask, "Why is personality assessed?" There are two basic reasons. The first is a practical one. Most approaches to abnormal behavior and therapy concentrate on recurring patterns of behavior or a particular style of behaving that seems to be causing problems. As pointed out earlier, there are basic connections between personality and behavior. It is natural, then, to look to aspects of the personality for answers to questions about abnormal behavior. For these purposes, particular aspects of the personality are examined. The choice of aspects will depend, to some extent, on the viewpoint of the assessor. For example, Freud-

ians might be especially interested in examining ego processes. Social-learning advocates might be most interested in the person's belief about locus of control. A humanist who agrees with Rogers' self theory might concentrate on uncovering areas of inconsistency between self-image and behavior. In each case, it is not the entire personality that is being assessed, but some particular aspect.

The second reason for assessing personality is to further understanding of what personality is, the extent to which traits and situations play a role in the organization of behavior within a person, and the characteristics of personality on which people differ significantly. In other words, personality is assessed for research purposes. When personality is assessed in the context of abnormal behavior, the assessment devices are usually quite specific and focus on specific areas. When personality is assessed for research purposes, many different devices may be used at the same time. These devices are often broader, with the intention of covering several traits or processes of personality. Even in the research context, however, the number of traits measured is usually far fewer than the number that might actually make up personality. (Two notable exceptions to this "limited range" approach are Cattell and Eysenck, who usually deal with dozens of traits in their research.) Taken as a whole, however, personality assessment offers a wide variety of information, since each researcher tends to be interested in different aspects of personality. It is important to keep in mind that when assessment devices are used for a particular purpose (such as to identify possible causes of abnormal behavior or to screen applicants for employment), personality is not being assessed in any broad sense, but rather, some particular aspect that seems important in that context is being evaluated.

There are many different techniques for assessing personality, but they are usually placed in one of three categories. Personality can be assessed through observations, through interviews, or through questionnaires or tests. Over the years, certain measurement techniques have become associated with certain theoretical approaches. For example, Freudians generally emphasize talking rather than observing or analyzing responses to questionnaires. For Freudians, it is important to use techniques that bypass the reality processes of the ego. These "bypassing" techniques include free association (or expression of thoughts as they occur), discussions of dreams, and discussions of the meaning of daily events. Behaviorists such as Skinner, on the other hand, would be far more interested in what is revealed by behavior than by words. What circumstances are currently associated with aggressive behavior in the child? What reinforcers in the environment might be maintaining certain behavior patterns? Humanists would prefer an interview or discussion that would lead to the identification of self-concepts and allow the person to become more actively involved in the assessment process. Social learning theorists would examine the person's beliefs through questionnaires as well as examining the environment for possible models. Trait theorists would concentrate on obtaining accurate assessments of a person's position on one or more personality dimensions (high, low, or average). Thus, the different orientations of researchers usually suggest particular methods of assessment.

Observation

Personality assessment using observational techniques can take several forms. The most obvious is to simply watch someone behave. One type of observation, that was originally developed for screening candidates for the Office of Strategic Services (intelligence officers), is called the assessment center. The assessment center may be more broadly used to screen applicants for upper-level managerial positions. The technique consists of observing the performance of various exercises that are intended to reveal particular personality characteristics. These characteristics usually include empathy, aggressiveness, creativity, and sociability. One common exercise is called the leaderless group, in which a small number of applicants are brought together to discuss a particular issue or solve a problem. As applicants go about solving the problem, they are observed by trained assessors who make notes or may even give ratings on the particular characteristics in question (for example, empathy). After the group exercise is completed, the trained assessors usually meet to compare notes and to arrive at an assessment of the individuals in question. The results of their observations and discussions are then combined with personal interviews for a total assessment of the particular personality characteristics thought to be relevant to the job in question. The final assessment is written up as a lengthy prose descrip-

TABLE 13-2.
Sample Leaderless Group Problem

Name _____   Group Number _____

NASA MOON PROBLEM

Your group is a space crew originally scheduled to meet with the mother ship on the lighted surface of the moon. Due to mechanical difficulties, however, your ship was forced to land at a spot some 200 miles from the meeting point. During re-entry and landing, much of the equipment was damaged and, since survival depends on reaching the mother ship, the most critical items available must be chosen for the 200 mile trip. Below, you will find a list of 15 items which were intact and undamaged after landing. You should rank order these items in terms of their importance for helping the crew to make it to the meeting point 200 miles away. Place the number 1 next to the most important item, the number 2 next to the second most important item and so on until you have ranked all 15 items. Take 2 or 3 minutes to decide on your ranks then record them on this sheet.

1. Box of matches _____
2. Food concentrate _____
3. 50 feet of nylon rope _____
4. Parachute silk _____
5. Portable heating unit _____
6. Two .45 caliber pistols _____
7. One case of dehydrated milk _____
8. Two 100 lb. tanks of oxygen _____
9. Star map of the moon's constellations _____
10. Life raft _____
11. Magnetic compass _____
12. Signal flares _____
13. 5 gallons of water _____
14. First aid kit containing injection needles _____
15. Solar powered FM receiver-transmitter _____

tion. Table 13–2 is an example of a leaderless group problem.

There are some problems with observations, however. Potentially the most significant is that observers may see more or less than is actually present

---

Personality assessment. The description made of an individual in terms of his or her characteristic pattern of behavior; involves description alone without any accompanying evaluation of whether that pattern is "good" or "bad."

THE SELECTION OF A JURY

In a recent case involving a man charged with the bombing murder of his mother and adopted brother, the defense lawyers commissioned a jury survey and hired a professional jury consultant to pick sympathetic people. Based on the consultant's recommendations, the lawyers created a questionnaire that would elicit attitudes (such as opinion on the death penalty) and personal details (such as favorite television show) about prospective jurors. The defense believed that knowing the backgrounds and personal interests of the jurors could mean the difference between a conviction or a non-guilty verdict for their client. The lawyers and their consultant also carefully observed behaviors, body movements, style of dress, and casual comments that might provide useful information about the prospective jurors' personalities.

In the end, the attorneys decided on a jury made up of 10 women and 2 men. The group included a fashion coordinator, nurses, homemakers, an industrial engineer, secretaries, a construction site inspector, and a hairdresser. The attorneys also hired six "shadow" jurors, who were similar in politics and views to the real jurors. These hired jurors sat among the spectators in the courtroom, and provided the defense attorneys with a daily review of their performance.

In this particular case, the strategy of picking a panel of jurors most likely to sympathize with the defendant did not work out favorably. After a full day of deliberation, the jury turned in a verdict against the defendant of guilty of first-degree murder. According to newspaper reports, the "shadow" jury had given signs to the defense attorneys of the negative outcome ahead. Four of the six shadow jurors had voted in an unofficial poll to convict the defendant.

in the situation. In other words, there can be bias or systematic inaccuracy in perception. For example, an assessor might have read in advance the personnel file of the person being observed. The assessor might then be looking for certain behaviors more than for others. If the candidate's file contained comments about "aggressiveness" or a "tendency to step on toes," the assessor might look for this type of behavior in the group exercise. Observers must be careful to guard against such possible distortions of perception.

Another problem is that there is not always a good sample of the person's behavior to observe. For example, if you were to judge your classmates' sociability by watching them on the day before a course examination, you might include that they are antisocial, since they seemed to avoid each other and concentrated only on their lecture notes and books. On the other hand, if you observed the same people right after the exam, you might conclude that they are extremely sociable, since they sought out and seemed to enjoy talking with classmates.

A recent application of the use of observation and interviews to assess personality can be found in jury selection. There have been instances in which consulting firms have advised lawyers concerning which prospective jurors might be sympathetic or hostile to clients. Following jury selection, they have sometimes advised lawyers on what persuasion techniques might work best with particular jurors. Most of this advise is based on the assumed personality traits of the jurors (Starr and McCormick, 1985). In the accompanying box, consider the strategies used by defense attorneys to assess the personalities of prospective jurors in a murder trial.

The procedures used in the selection of jurors are a good example of the use of interviewing and observation for personality assessment. It also happens to be a heated issue. In fact, personality assessment in jury selection has become so controversial that the matter has reached the Supreme Court. One source of contention is a concept known as the "death qualified" jury. In states that have the death penalty, in cases of crimes that might warrant a death sentence it is common for the prosecution to exclude individuals from juries who might be opposed to the death penalty. In addition to general questioning of jury candidates about the death penalty, it has become increasingly common for lawyers to engage psychologists to assist in identifying prospective jurors who may have particular biases for or against the death penalty. Psychologists provide this assistance by preparing questions that can be legally asked of the prospective jurors, studying the way they act in the courtroom, and examining the background characteristics of these individuals. Some defense lawyers have argued that individuals who have no reservations about the death penalty are more likely to convict defendants. As a result, they would like to be able to systematically eliminate such individuals from juries. Recently, the Supreme Court ruled that such individuals could not be excluded simply because they did not oppose the death penalty.

The very act of being observed may create some problems. When you are made "self-conscious" by knowing that someone is watching you, you may not perform normally. You may behave according to what you think is "expected" of you by the observer, rather than behaving in the way you would naturally. People are often more cautious in their driving when a patrol officer is following them than when they are alone on the road. The patrol officer might assume that they are perfect drivers, which is exactly the impression they would like that officer to have. Interestingly enough, patrol officers are learning that one of the tell-tale behaviors of the drunk driver is being *too* careful. This includes stopping overly long at stop signs, staying in the exact center of the road, and driving below the speed limit. Thus, some people who are driving the way it says to in the drivers' training manual are finding themselves being given breathalyzer tests for possible intoxication.

Observation can be a very useful technique, but only when the conditions of observation are carefully controlled and when care is taken to specify what exactly will be observed and interpreted.

Interviews

The interview is a commonly-used assessment technique. Interviews can be either structured or unstructured. In the **unstructured interview**, the person is asked to talk freely about any experiences, feelings, and attitudes. As the person speaks, the interviewer observes the person and may ask questions about points being raised. Ideally, the interviewer should try to direct the conversation over a wide range of topics, but in many respects, the person being interviewed is in control of the conversation. The conversation follows the track laid down by the person being interviewed.

A second type of interview is the **structured interview**, in which the person is asked a specific set of questions in a specific order. Follow-up questions are also determined beforehand and the interview is usually not over until all of the questions have been asked. The person may be allowed to diverge from the question momentarily, but the interviewer will repeat the question, if necessary, before moving on.

The structured interview is often preferred when it is necessary to compare one individual with another on personality characteristics. Since the same questions are asked of everyone, it is easier to compare answers and come to a conclusion. It is even possible to go one step further and specify which types of answers are more or less desirable for certain purposes. For example, it is assumed that certain personality characteristics are desirable for positions in industry and government. Interview questions that seem likely to produce responses related to these personality characteristics are developed in advance. Answers are then prepared that would correspond to varying degrees of the personality characteristic in question. After the interview has been conducted, the candidate's answers are compared to the predetermined answers in order to determine how much of the particular personality characteristic the applicant possesses.

Unstructured interview. Interview in which a person is asked to talk freely within any one of a broad range of topics. Interviewer's questions or interruptions are suggested by the comments of the person being interviewed, not planned beforehand.

Structured interview. Interview in which a person is asked a specific set of questions that are determined beforehand. Follow-up questions are also planned beforehand, and the interview goes on until all questions have been asked.

As with observations, interviews can sometimes provide distorted information about personality. This can be a problem on both ends of the interview. People being interviewed usually prefer to put themselves in the best possible light, and this means that their answers are not always accurate representations of their feelings, thoughts, or past behaviors. In addition, it is well known that interviewers make errors in asking questions and evaluating answers. For example, it has been shown that interviewers form opinions about the person being interviewed early on, and then look for information to confirm that impression.

Personality Tests

The term *test* is often used to describe personality-assessment techniques. Conceptually, a test is just a standardized sample of behavior. In that sense, the term test is probably accurate in the personality context, because an attempt is being made to sample a person's behavior using standard devices. Unfortunately, sometimes personality tests are confused with tests of academic knowledge. There is a big difference. In knowledge tests, there is a "right" answer that can be verified. In personality tests, there is no right or wrong answer. At best, the answer can be compared to the answers of other groups of people (such as 40-year-old male high-school principals, prisoners in a maximum-security facility, or randomly selected college students) and some statement about whether the responses are "average" can be made. What must be emphasized is that "average" does not mean "right" and "not average" does not mean "wrong." One does not "pass" a personality test. One set of responses might

The interview is a basic tool of personality assessment. An unstructured interview flows freely, while a structured interview follows a fixed content and order of questioning.

PERSONALITY ASSESSMENT FOR THE 1-MINUTE MANAGER

Psychologist James H. Johnson, president of Human Edge Software, believes he has created a high-tech answer to everyday personality assessment. Take the selection of a marriage partner, for example. Johnson points out that, judging by the high divorce rate, it's obvious that many people are choosing partners who are not at all matched to their own personalities. With Johnson's software program, *Mind Prober*, and a home computer, people can assess the personality of a potential spouse before it's too late. Instead of dating a man for a few months, observing him in a variety of situations, and finally deciding whether he is a suitable partner, Johnson suggests that a woman might make a quicker and, in his opinion, more reliable judgment by using *Mind Prober*. For around $50, you can buy this program to assess the personality of a prospective employee, date, roommate, babysitter, or jogging partner.

To use *Mind Prober*, you first input your subject's age and sex. You are then presented with a list of sixty adjectives to which you would respond "yes" if they applied to the subject or "no" if they did not. On this list are such terms as *goal-oriented, loyal, silly,* and *trusting*. Based on your yes or no responses, the program prints out a personality assessment of your subject that covers several dimensions: attitudes toward work, coping with stress, personal interests, attitudes toward sex (or toward school, if the subject is

under 18), and what makes him or her tick. Reviewers note that *Mind Prober* works best when you know your subject quite well. With only slight knowledge of your subject, *Mind Prober's* output can be ambiguous. In this, the program seems to fall short of its main purpose: To gain an understanding of people's personalities when you know little about them.

Critics argue that assessment software has the potential to infringe on people's privacy. Some people might not want their minds probed, particularly without their knowledge. With this objection in mind, several distributors sell assessment programs only to mental-health professionals. However, software like *Mind Prober* has been created to be used by anyone with a home computer. Human Edge has advertised *Mind Prober* in *Playboy* and other mass-market magazines. One of the product's distributors is Wham-O, the toy distributor, and Dr. Johnson has said that he hopes to sell *Mind Prober* in Toys R Us™ toy stores.

Mind Prober is well suited to game stores. Mass market computer programs for personal analysis are seldom developed in any careful or scientific way.

Sources: Denis Caruso, "Software Probes the Mind," *Infoworld*, September 24, 1984, pp. 34–39; Tony Lima, "Mind Prober, the More You Know, the Better It Works," *Infoworld*, December 17, 1984, pp. 48–49.

lead to one conclusion about personality and another set of responses might lead to quite another conclusion. The object of the test is to accurately assess personality, not to pass, fail, or assign a letter grade to people as is done in academic testing.

Questionnaires. Both observation and interviewing have disadvantages as methods of personality assessment; they are time-consuming, require trained people, and are subject to distortion unless careful controls are used. A method that avoids many of these problems is assessment by means of questions that may be answered by choosing one answer from

a set of alternatives. These alternatives may imply various degrees of agreement with a statement (such as strongly agree, agree, neutral, disagree, or strongly disagree), may be simple "yes" or "no" answers, or may ask the person to report the frequency with which certain behaviors or thoughts occur. The questions and answers have usually been developed using a particular strategy. One method is to develop the questionnaire to fit a theoretical orientation. One hundred or more questions might be asked in order to assess a person on various needs, such as the Maslow needs you learned about in Chapter 12. When the questionnaire has been scored, the person is described according to these need categories.

Another way of developing a personality questionnaire is to look for items or questions that distinguish among individuals on certain characteristics. Since personality is closely tied to the notion of the uniqueness of the individual, any set of questions that can help to distinguish one person from another would presumably be related to personality. When this approach is taken, there is usually no particular theory that guides the selection or writing of questions. Instead, a large number of questions are prepared, and those that adequately distinguish among a group of individuals or between one group of people and another become permanent parts of the questionnaire. Those questions that don't help to distinguish among individuals or between groups are eliminated.

One example of this type of questionnaire is the **MMPI (Minnesota Multiphasic Personality Inventory)**. Examples of the MMPI items appear in Table 13–3. This questionnaire consists of 550 statements to which the person responds "True," "False," or "Cannot Say." The original version of the MMPI was developed by comparing the responses of people who had been diagnosed as having particular psychological problems (such as paranoia) to the responses of people who were not known to have any specific symptoms or disturbance. Those questions on which these two groups differed were retained, and those questions that did not show differences between the groups were eliminated. As a result, each response to each item could be scored with respect to abnormality. If the person answered with the same response as the one given by a group with a particular problem (paranoia), this response was "scored" as indicating that this person might also have the same problem. The MMPI produces scores on 10 different aspects of personality. There is a much greater emphasis on abnormal behavior than is the case with many other personality questionnaires. The MMPI is used extensively to determine specific aspects of a behavioral problem. It is often used, along with other information gathered from interviews and observation, to develop a diagnosis of the problem.

Since its introduction, the MMPI has been widely used to study both abnormal and normal behavior. It is a very sophisticated and complicated instrument

and requires a great deal of training before it can be used accurately for the assessment of personality.

Currently, the MMPI is being revised to make sure that the language in which questions are asked and the comparison group are up to date.

Like other techniques, questionnaires have their weaknesses. There is the obvious problem of intentional distortion. Many questionnaires are transparent and it is relatively simple to determine the most "socially desirable" answer. For example, if you are applying for a job as a bus driver, it is unlikely that you would agree with the statement "Time schedules make me nervous." To counteract such influences, many questionnaires have certain questions built into them that can help to determine if someone is intentionally distorting his or her responses. This detection can be accomplished by comparing the individual's response pattern to a pattern produced by someone who was instructed to intentionally distort the answers in a self-serving manner. If there is a close match, there is a strong possibility that the person in question is not answering the questions truthfully. Unfortunately, this does not solve the problem. It simply tells us that the answers to the questions are not trustworthy. It does not provide us with more trustworthy information about the person.

Projective Tests. Personality questionnaires depend on the ability and willingness of a person to respond to a series of statements about styles of behaving and thinking. There is another method of assessment that assumes that people are unable or unwilling to respond to these types of statements accurately. For example, from the Freudian perspective personality is defined by the completely uncon-

TABLE 13–3.
Sample MMPI questions

I do not tire quickly.

Most people will use somewhat unfair means to gain profit or an advantage rather than to lose it.

I am worried about sex matters.

When I get bored I like to stir up some excitement.

I believe I am being plotted against.

Source: *The Psychological Corporation, 1970.*

scious process of the id, as well as the partially unconscious processes of the ego and superego. A questionnaire is likely to deal with only conscious aspects of thought and behavior, and to leave the important unconscious aspects of personality unexamined. However, a method has been developed that is intended to avoid this problem. Instead of well-developed, easily understood statements or questions that require choosing among a limited number of alternatives, some assessment devices consist of ambiguous stimuli with a free-response format. If the stimuli have no clear meaning, then the way you interpret them may have more to do with you than with the stimuli. This is called the **projective hypothesis** (Anastasi, 1982). It is assumed that a person's response to an ambiguous stimulus represents an important and stable personality characteristic. If the projective hypothesis is correct, projective tests represent an opportunity to examine a person's principles of organization or perception.

The stimuli used in these assessments are often visual rather than verbal, although simple word-association exercises can also be considered projective devices. The person is expected to project or display certain deep personality processes onto these ambiguous stimuli in much the same way as a picture is projected onto a blank movie screen; therefore these devices are called **projective tests**.

Two of the most popular projective tests are the Rorschach inkblot test and the Thematic Apperception Test (TAT). The **Rorschach inkblot test** was developed by a Swiss psychiatrist named Hermann Rorschach (1921) for the purpose of clinical diagnosis. He asked groups of people with particular psychiatric symptoms as well as groups of normal people to describe in their own words what a specific inkblot meant to them. Their responses were then recorded and later analyzed in an attempt to identify particular responses that helped to distinguish

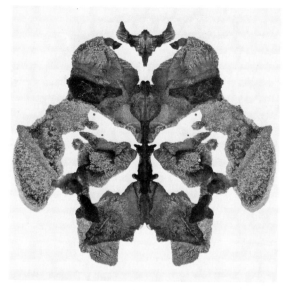

FIGURE 13-4

This is an example of the type of inkblots that are used in the Rorschach test.

among different psychiatric groups, as well as between psychiatric patients and normal people.

Figure 13-4 is an example of a Rorschach inkblot. There are 10 such inkblots, and each one is presented to the individual for consideration. In addition to verbal responses to the card, a record is also kept of other verbalizations, how the person acted when responding (Did they turn the cards around?), and how long it took the person to respond to the particular inkblot. The inkblot test is used to elicit a wide range of behaviors to create an opportunity for behavior observation.

There are several scoring systems that have been developed to help interpret inkblot test responses. For example, if someone were to say that the ink-

---

MMPI (Minnesota Multiphasic Personality Inventory). A questionnaire consisting of 550 statements to which people respond "True," "False," or "Cannot Say." Generates scores on 10 different aspects of personality and is used frequently for diagnostic purposes in clinical practice.

Projective hypothesis. The assumption that a person's response to an ambiguous stimulus may have more to do with the person than with the stimulus; the response is thought to represent an important and stable personality characteristic.

Projective test. An assessment device that consists of ambiguous stimuli that a person is supposed to identify or make up a story about, in the process displaying certain elements of personality.

Rorschach inkblot test. Projective test used in clinical diagnosis. The test consists of 10 inkblots, which people are asked to look at and describe in their own words.

blot looked like "big eyes staring at me," the interpretation might be that the person is insecure and afraid of being criticized. Similarly, if a person reported that the inkblot looked like a "fight between two animals in which they are clawing at each other and bleeding," the interpretation would likely include some assumption of hostility and aggression on the part of the individual.

Early in the development of the Rorschach inkblot test, both scoring and interpretation were subject to personal viewpoints, thus reducing the value of the test. Some standard scoring methods and keys were developed by Klopper and his colleagues (Klopper et al., 1954). In recent years, the scoring and interpretation have become even more standardized (Exner, 1978; Wiener-Levy and Exner, 1981). This is an important development; many users objected to the Rorschach test because of the subjective nature of its interpretation.

Another common projective device is the **Thematic Apperception Test (TAT)**, developed by Murray (1938). The TAT consists of 20 drawings of people in ambiguous settings or situations. The person being assessed is asked to consider the picture and then to make up a story about it. The story should include (1) what led to the event in the picture, (2) what is happening in the picture, (3) what the people in the picture are feeling, and (4) what the outcome of the situation will be. There are four different subsets or combinations of cards that are used with different subgroups of people: one for adult males, one for adult females, one for male children (under 14), and one for female children (under 14). The person's responses are analyzed in light of categories that Murray developed and a profile of the personality is developed.

The TAT is commonly used for diagnosis purposes in much the same way as the Rorschach inkblot test. The person's responses are considered by the clinical psychologist or psychiatrist in order to diagnose or classify the person's symptoms. The accuracy of this diagnosis, as is the case with any diagnosis, will depend to some extent on the experience of the person administering the test. The logic of the TAT is simple: If you respond to a TAT picture in the same way as a diagnosed phobic might have responded, then you may be having phobic problems as well. Like the Rorschach test, there are scoring schemes and interpretation suggestions

available for evaluating TAT responses, and a good deal of training and sophistication is necessary to use the device effectively.

In my graduate training, I had occasion to use the TAT for a research project on the effect of a father's absence on the development of his children. We asked college students to fill out questionnaires about their families and any period of their lives when their fathers might have been absent (in the service, in jail, as a result of a divorce, and so on). Part of the data we collected came from the students' responses to a TAT picture that shows a man in a room. As I read the stories that the students developed about this picture, I began to notice a recurring theme in some of these stories. The theme was one of a man coming home from working the night shift to find that his wife had been killed by a criminal. A second, though less frequent, theme was that the man had come home from working the night shift to find his wife in bed with another man. Both of these themes seemed to imply that the man was being punished for working the night shift. In a subsequent data-collection session, we asked the students who had completed these TAT stories if their fathers worked on fixed or rotating work shifts. We discovered that most of the stories with the "punishment" theme had been written by students whose fathers had worked the afternoon (3 PM- 11 PM) or night (11 PM-7 AM) shift for an extended period while the student was growing up. This led to some extensive research dealing with the effect of a father's work shift on a child's development (Landy, Rosenberg, and Sutton-Smith, 1969).

As you saw above, the value of projective tests such as the Rorschach inkblot test or the TAT depends on the projective hypothesis. There is some reason to question this hypothesis. Even among those who are in favor of the use of projective tests, it is recognized that the situation in which these tests are administered can have a substantial effect on the responses of the person in question. For example, if the person being assessed does not have positive feelings about the person doing the assessment, the pictures will look different than they would if the two parties had good rapport (Hamilton and Robertson, 1966; Klinger, 1966). Similarly, responses can be affected by sleep loss, anxiety, drugs, and a number of other factors (Anastasi,

1981). These influences weaken the assumption that projective tests can identify stable underlying aspects of personality.

In summary, projective tests represent a theoretical assumption about the process of personality. Improvements in administration and scoring will not alter that assumption. On the positive side these methods may provide an avenue for exploring aspects of personality that is not provided by other observational techniques, interviews, or personality questionnaires. This can be important for the clinical psychologist or psychiatrist who has the difficult task of diagnosis or treatment. In this regard, projective tests may provide some ideas about which aspects of the person should be pursued with other assessment techniques. On the other hand, the use of projective tests in making specific decisions involving the comparison of two or more people (as might be the case in deciding who to hire) is inappropriate. These techniques were never intended for that purpose and to use them in that way would put them in the category of the type of test that you "pass" or "fail." You know already that personality is not that type of concept.

REVIEW QUESTIONS

11. Personality assessment differs from intelligence testing in that there are no "right" or "wrong" scores or answers
T / F

12. In the _____ group exercise, people who are being assessed are brought together to solve a problem. As they do this, they are rated by trained assessors. This type of assessment is called _____ .

13. In the structured/unstructured interview, the person who is being interviewed actually controls the interview; in the structured/unstructured interview, a list of predetermined questions or topics controls the interview.

14. In _____ tests, people are shown ambiguous stimuli and asked to describe them or make up a story about them.

Answers: 11. True 12. leaderless; observation. 13. un-structured; structured 14. projective

Some Assessment Issues

Since the various techniques described in the last section are intended to provide information about individuals, it is reasonable to consider the extent to which that information is trustworthy. Just as a manufactured item must go through a quality-control examination, it is appropriate to perform quality-control inspections of tests. Even though there are many different types of tests, there are certain minimum requirements that every test must meet to be of any value, no matter what testing method is used or what variable is being tested. These requirements include standardization, reliability, and validity.

Standardization. To standardize something is to make it uniform. Can you imagine the result if each person in the class received a final exam with a different number of questions? At the very least, it would be difficult to compare the performance of one person with the performance of another. Even if scores were calculated as percentages of correct items, students who had more items on their tests might be more affected by fatigue than those who had fewer items. The point is that if a test is to be used as a yardstick, that yardstick must have the same characteristics every time it is used. It cannot be one length one day and another length the next.

Standardization ensures that tests are always given under the same circumstances every time. This means that each person should receive the same instructions, the same test materials, the same time limits, and, to whatever extent possible, the same physical environment. If these procedures are not standardized, we cannot be sure whether differences in scores are due to real differences in the characteristic being measured or to differences in administrative procedures.

Another aspect of standardization is the develop-

Thematic Apperception Test (TAT). A projective test developed by Murray. Consists of 20 pictures of ambiguous stimuli, which people are asked to look at and make up stories about; like the Rorschach, is commonly used in clinical diagnosis.

Standardization. The principle of administering tests under the same conditions every time (using the same instructions, the same test materials, the same time limits, and so on). Also, the development of norms against which to compare scores.

ment of norms or standards against which to compare scores. This is actually a calibration or an adjustment of scale rather than a standardization. Norms allow relative judgments about how high or low a score is. An example with which you are familiar is a score on a course examination. When a person is told that he or she scored 70 on a test, what does that mean—is it good or bad? If everyone else in the class obtained scores in the 50s and 60s, the score of 70 is excellent. On the other hand, if everyone else scored in the 80s and 90s, the score of 70 is a disaster. The interpretation of the score depends on a comparison to a norm or standard.

It is important that tests be administered under the same conditions in which the norms were established. If the testing procedures used for the normative sample or reference group in establishing the standard differ from the procedures subsequently used to test individuals, it will be impossible to accurately interpret the scores because they could have been influenced by the different testing conditions. A good example of this might be a make-up test that you take because you were absent on the day of a test. When you come to the instructor's office to take it, you are told that the only place available for taking the test is a noisy and drafty waiting room. You sit at a cluttered table and try to concentrate on the examination questions as people wander in and out talking, laughing, and occasionally shouting to others in the next office. The comparison between your score on this make-up exam and the scores of the other class members will not be a fair one. Their scores were established in a quiet environment suited to test-taking. Your test score will probably be lower as a result of the distractions in the environment. Standardization is critically important for accurate interpretation. Unless the comparison is to an appropriate norm group, the score is not fair.

Reliability. In order to be of any value, measurements must be consistent. Consider the bathroom scale. If and when you begin a diet program in preparation for appearing in your new bathing suit, the scale in your bathroom will become a very important testing device. It will tell you how effective your diet is. But it often seems that, in spite of cutting down on calories the day before, you have actually gained a pound or so the next day. This can be very depressing. This "gain" may actually be an

instance of unreliability or inconsistency in your measuring instrument. In fact, if you weighed yourself 10 times in 15 minutes, you might very well get 10 different readings. The difference between the lowest and highest weight could be as much as 2 pounds. The variability will depend on the quality of the scale; the better the scale, the less the variability. The same thing is true of tests. The better the device (whether it is a paper-and-pencil test or a performance test), the greater its **reliability**. There are several types of reliability, each measured in a different way. First, in order to show that a test produces consistent results no matter when it is administered, the same test could be administered to the same sample of people on two different occasions (separated, let's say, by a one-month interval) and the scores could be compared. If the same people scored high, medium, and low on both occasions, the conclusion would be that this test produced reliable scores. Since giving the same test at different times proves whether the test is consistent or reliable, this type of reliability is called **test-retest reliability**. This is only one of several kinds of reliability.

Another type of reliability is the agreement between two people looking at the same event or object. Gymnastics judges or diving judges are a good example. To the extent that there is variability in their judgments or awarding of points, there is inconsistency or unreliability. It may seem as if this type of unreliability is really a part of being human—people are just not perfect judges. To a certain extent, this may be true. Some people are better than others at making certain types of judgments. But this inconsistency between judges can be dramatically reduced if all judges agree to use the same measurement scale. In the diving and gymnastics examples, there are certain standards that must be met for a high score, and certain agreed-upon deductions for mistakes. These standards or conventions guarantee some consistency among judges. But, the fact that there is more than one judge is testimony to the unreliability of the process. If the judgments were perfectly reliable, there would not be a need for more than one judge. In many cases, the assessment process consists of two components—the assessment device or test, and the assessor or judge. Each of these components contributes to the final reliability.

Studies have been done on the reliability of tests

that are used to measure mental abilities, personality, special interests, and perceptual skills. Most of the tests that are commercially available have good reliability. But, no tests are perfectly reliable. This means that every test score has some built-in variability or uncertainty. This is important to remember when you are interpreting a test score. The less reliable the test, the less certainty there is about what the true score actually is.

Validity. In addition to reliability, another extremely important characteristic of a test is its **validity.** A test is considered to be valid if it measures what it is intended to measure. For example, consider the concept of intelligence. Most definitions of intelligence emphasize the person's ability to learn. If, for some reason, height was measured and this measure was used to represent intelligence, some people (particularly people of below-average height) would object. They would point to the definition of intelligence and claim that the measuring process or device had nothing to do with that definition. In technical terms, they would be claiming that the assessment procedure had no validity. Notice that the test—measuring height—would probably be perfectly reliable (that is, people would measure the same height on every test), but it would be a terrible test because it lacked validity (height is not a measure of intelligence). Reliability without validity is useless.

Many tests are criticized for lacking validity. Students often claim that a course exam is poorly constructed and as a result does not measure their knowledge of the course material. They are attacking the validity of the test. On a much broader scale, the college-admissions tests are often attacked as being invalid. The argument is that they don't really measure the things most necessary for success in college, such as motivation or social skills.

As was the case with reliability, studies have been done of the validity of commercially-available tests. Validity is demonstrated in several ways. The first is through predictions. For example, mental-ability test scores should show some relationship to performance on tasks that require those mental abilities. In this case, the scores of individuals on a mental-ability test would be compared with their degree of success on a task requiring mental abilities. If high test scores were associated with successful performance, the conclusion would be that the test is valid. In fact, many mental-ability tests do a good job of predicting success in educational programs. This is the basis for the claim that they are valid measures of mental abilities. This type of validity is called **criterion-related validity,** because there is a comparison between the test and some criterion of excellence—actual performance. SAT scores are used to predict whether or not a student can earn a college degree or maintain a required minimum grade-point average. In this case, the SAT score is the predictor, and the awarding of the degree or the grade-point average is the criterion.

There are other types of validity that emphasize other characteristics of the tests in question. For example, validity might be established by showing that experts agree that the test questions measure the ability being examined. This is called **content validity.** Another method of establishing validity is by showing that the scores on the test in question are positively related to scores on other tests that are intended to measure the same or similar abilities. This is called **construct validity.** An example would be a driver's examination. If you took a driver's test in New York and passed, you would expect to pass on a test given in Pennsylvania or Connecticut. If driving skill and knowledge were truly being measured, the actual details of the test should not matter.

Standardization, reliability, and validity are all important characteristics of tests, and they affect

Reliability. A measure of consistency—a test has reliability if a person's score is about the same no matter how many times the test is taken.
Test-retest reliability. A kind of reliability that occurs if a test taker receives the same score on the same test taken at two different times.
Validity. The extent to which a test actually measures what it was intended to measure. If a test is supposed to measure future performance in school, it has validity if people who do well on the test go on to get high grades in school.

Criterion-related validity. A type of validity based on comparison between a test and some standard (or criterion), such as performance in a certain task.
Content validity. A type of validity based on the items on a test having been drawn from the performance area being assessed.
Construct validity. A type of validity based on the positive relationship between one test and another test measuring the same skill.

one another. The lower the reliability of a test, the lower its validity. On the other hand a reliable test with no validity is useless. A test that has not been standardized is not likely to be reliable (or, as a consequence, valid). Those who develop tests as well as those who take tests need to be informed as to what extent a particular test meets the requirements of standardization, reliability, and validity.

REVIEW QUESTIONS

15. _____ tests are tests that are given under the same conditions every time and whose scores are compared against norms.

16. _____ tests are tests that tend to yield a consistent score no matter how many times you take them.

17. _____ tests are tests that measure what they are intended to measure. If a test is intended to measure performance in school, then people scoring high in such a test should get high grades in school.

18. Match the following terms with the correct definitions:

___ criterion-related validity	A. logical relationship between one assessment and another test or type of procedure measuring the same skill.
___ content validity	B. a comparison between a test and some standard, such as performance in a certain task.
___ construct validity	C. test containing items that have been drawn from the performance area being assessed.

Answers: 15. Standardized 16. Reliable 17. Valid 18. criterion-related validity, B; content validity, C; construct validity, A.

Validity and Reliability in Personality Assessment

Validity. We have just seen that validity is defined as the extent to which a test is successful in measuring what it intended to measure. In personality assessment, validity presents something of a prob-

lem. In the first place, most devices for personality assessment deal with particular aspects of the personality, rather than with the personality in its entirety. Also, many devices are really intended to test a theory of personality functioning rather than to get an accurate measure of a trait. Thus, the question about validity becomes, "Valid for what purpose?" The question of validity is a particularly thorny problem in personality assessment, since personality can be stable even though behavior varies. For example, a device might consistently show that a particular person desires respect. In one situation, respect can be achieved by keeping quiet; in a different situation, respect might be obtained by expressing an opinion. This means that a device is not necessarily lacking in validity just because it cannot accurately predict future behavior.

The most serious problem with many forms of personality assessment is not so much the validity of the test or device itself, but the validity of the *use* of that device. In every instance of personality assessment that we have examined in this chapter, interpretation of some kind on the part of the person doing the assessment has been involved. This interpretation must be valid as well. The numbers produced by the test might be perfectly accurate representations of traits or processes, but if these numbers are misinterpreted by the assessor they will yield a summary statement about personality that lacks validity. The most valid personality test will be one which is developed from a particular theoretical framework and is examined for its ability to distinguish among individuals or groups who display differing patterns of behavior organization in particular situations. The overriding purpose of a personality-assessment device is to capture the uniqueness of an individual's total behavior pattern. If the assessment device does not accomplish this, it cannot be considered valid.

Reliability. A second important aspect of personality assessment is reliability. As you discovered earlier in the chapter, a measure of something should not vary dramatically from one time to another or from one situation to another. Many definitions of personality assume that the processes or structures of personality are stable over time, and that they will have consistent effects on behavior in situations that the person perceives as similar. This is true of the psychodynamic, trait, and interactionist approaches to personality. On the other hand, some approaches assume that personality is not stable but changes as a result of reinforcement (the behaviorists), modified beliefs (social learning theory), or personal growth (the humanists). So, some theorists look for stability and others look for change. This presents something of a dilemma: The process of assessment seems to demand reliability, while some theoretical positions demand change. As a result, the issue of reliability must be qualified. If a number produced as a result of an assessment device is to be used to predict some future occurrence (such as job or school success or the capacity to function normally in the community), that number should not be easily influenced by passing or situational variables. This means that the reliability should be high in the traditional sense. On the other hand, if the number produced by the assessment device is to be used together with other information to produce a psychological "snapshot" of the personality processes of the individual here and now, consistency of the moment is much less important.

Even though there are matters in which it is not important that a person's response be consistent from one time to the next, this does not mean that the concept of reliability is unimportant. There should always be some type of assurance that the interpretation of information does not change with changes in interpreters. For example, if I gave someone the Rorschach inkblot test today and interpreted the results as showing some evidence of anxiety, and then looked at the same results a month from now and interpreted them as evidence of anxiety-free patterns of thought and behavior, it would be questionable whether the results are more indicative of the person being assessed or the person doing the assessment. Similarly, if two different people look at the same response and conclude two very different things from that response (one sees anxiety and the other sees freedom from anxiety), again it would not be clear exactly what is being measured. In other words, the interpretation lacks reliability or consistency. Achieving this type of reliability has been one of the most serious problems in actually using the results of personality-assessment procedures for making practical decisions about people.

Since personality includes patterns of reactions, motives, learned associations, perceptions, skills, and communication, it is one of the broadest and most inclusive of all psychological concepts. Personality may legitimately be seen as an umbrella covering many important aspects of behavior. It is for this reason that disorders of the personality—problems in the organization of behavior—are so serious. In the next several chapters, we will examine various types of personality disorganizations (the effects of stress and abnormal behavior) and techniques for reestablishing organization (therapy).

■ SUMMARY

1. *Personality* is the total and unique organization of various behavioral components of the individual that include motivations, emotions, learning capacities and experiences, perceptual mechanisms, biological capacities, and thought patterns. Personality theories are attempts to account for uniqueness in human behavior.

2. After observing patients under hypnosis, Freud proposed that there are three levels of consciousness: the *conscious* level, material that a person is currently aware of; the *preconscious* level, material that the person could become aware of with little difficulty; and the *unconscious* level, material not readily available that the person can only reach with great difficulty. In Freud's theory, three distinct processes function simultaneously within the personality: the *id*, containing the drives, including the pleasure drive and the aggressive drive, which produce the energy for behavior; the *ego*, or the cognitive process that helps reconcile an individual's needs and the possibilities supplied by the environment; and the *superego*, a set of standards against which actual and potential behaviors are evaluated for moral correctness.

3. Freud felt that early experiences were critical in the development of the adult personality. Through five stages of psychosexual development various zones of the body become the focus of sensitivity. The stages are the *oral stage*, the *anal stage*, the *phallic stage*, the *latency stage*, and the *genital stage*. Freud felt that behavioral problems arise from unresolved conflicts at one or more of the stages in which the person becomes *fixated*, or stuck. In Freud's theory, personality is the result of unique interactions of the id, the ego, and the superego.

4. A *trait* is a predisposition within the individual

to respond in characteristic ways to various kinds of stimuli. Eysenck's theory states that individual personalities are the result of variations along three trait dimensions: introversion/extraversion, stability/neuroticism, and psychoticism. Cattell's personality theory is based on 16 trait dimensions on which people differ.

5. *Humanist personality theories* view personality as an integrated system rather than a number of interacting elements. Another important factor in humanist theories is an emphasis on intentional behavior and natural personal growth, in contrast to the idea of personality as the product of controlling forces such as personality structures or traits. A third feature of humanist theories is an emphasis on characteristically human processes such as language, future planning, and rationality. Carl Rogers believes that people universally need to be accepted by others. Inconsistencies between self-concept and the way others view us can cause behavioral problems.

6. Learning theorists view personality as the result of variations in learning experiences and resulting associations. Skinner would view personality as the result of schedules of reinforcement and past associations between responses and reinforcers. Another key factor in the learning perspective is the importance of generalization and discrimination.

7. Social learning theorists, particularly Rotter, have stressed the importance of preferences, beliefs, and ideas about locus of control in development and expression of personality. Locus of control refers to people's beliefs about whether outside forces control rewards (external locus of control) or whether rewards are the result of a person's own efforts (internal locus of control). Unique personalities result from people's unique expectancies and beliefs.

8. The interactionist position points out that certain behaviors are more likely to occur in one situation than another. According to this view, a trait is a predisposition to respond in a particular way in the presence of a certain stimulus.

9. Personality assessment is the description of an individual in terms of characteristic patterns of behavior and is used to look at behavioral problems and as a research tool for developing a better understanding of behavior. Observations, interviews, and questionnaires or tests are the three main methods of personality assessment.

A recent and controversial application of techniques of personality assessment is found in jury selection. The Supreme Court has ruled that individuals cannot be systematically excluded from a jury, simply because they are not opposed to the death penalty.

10. By observing behavior in a particular situation, evaluators can judge whether a job applicant has the personality characteristics needed for a particular job. Two problems with this technique are that observers tend to be biased in their perceptions and that there is not always a good sample of the person's behavior to observe.

11. In unstructured interviews, the person is asked to talk freely within any one of a broad range of topics. In the structured interview a person is asked a specific set of questions and follow-up questions. Evaluators then compare the answers to those of others. Two problems with this type of test are that people try to present themselves in a good light and that interviewers can make errors in questions and evaluations.

12. Personality tests provide a sample of behavior; there are no right or wrong answers to the test items. Questionnaires require a choice between a number of alternative answers to a question. Often researchers develop questionnaire tests that fit a particular theoretical orientation.

13. Projective tests consist of ambiguous stimuli and a free-response format. Use of this kind of test is based on the idea that if the stimuli have no clear meaning, then the way you interpret them says more about you than about the stimuli. Two of the most popular projective tests are the Rorschach inkblot test and the Thematic Apperception Test (TAT). Though standard scoring procedures have been established for these measures, situational factors during testing can influence people's responses.

14. The overriding purpose of a personality-assessment device is to capture the uniqueness of an individual's behavior pattern; if a test fails to accomplish this, then it is considered *invalid*. *Reliability* of personality tests depends upon how they are used: If the test is used to predict stable behavioral characteristics (such as school performance), test-retest reliability should be high; if it is used in conjunction with other information to produce a picture of an individual at this moment, test reliability is less important.

■ ANSWERING QUESTIONS FOR THOUGHT

1. Personality is *both* the way we think and the way we behave. It is the combination of various elements, such as motivation, emotion, learning capacity and experiences, perceptual mechanisms, behavior, biological capacities, and thought patterns.

2. According to Freud, this type of behavior is characteristic of the latency period, which lasts from about age 6 to age 12. During this period, children lose interest in sexual behavior and neither sex takes much interest in the other. This stage comes after the appearance of the Oedipus or Electra complex, which children successfully resolve by identifying with the same-sex parent and forming attachments to friends of the same sex.

3. People vary in their expectations and beliefs about desirable outcomes and the efforts made to achieve them. In the view of social learning theory, these expectations and beliefs are important in the development and expression of personality. According to psychologist Julian Rotter, people also differ in their feelings about how rewards are achieved. Some people believe that rewards are a matter of luck—an external locus of control. Other believe that rewards result from their own hard work and skill—an internal locus of control. Rotter believes that locus of control beliefs are an important part of personality and combine with other variables to produce certain behaviors.

4. One doesn't "pass" a personality test. In tests of knowledge there is a right answer that can be verified. In personality tests, there is no such thing as a right or wrong answer. The object of a personality test is to assess personality as accurately as possible, not to pass, fail, or grade people as is done in academic testing.

5. Questionnaires are considered to be very accurate as personality tests, but that accuracy depends on the assumption that people are willing to tell the truth about themselves. Questionnaires generally require a choice between a number of alternative answers to a question. Sometimes the most desirable answers are transparent and the test-taker may intentionally distort his or her responses. To counteract this, some tests contain built-in validity scales that help detect this distortion. However, these scales tell us only that answers are untrustworthy; they do not provide trustworthy information about personality.

14 Stress

When the chase started, it was just growing dark. Moments before, the police officer had pulled over a car after watching the driver go through a yellow light. As the officer walked toward the car, it abruptly took off. He followed in the patrol car onto the expressway. Meanwhile, he learned over his radio that the car in question was stolen and the driver considered dangerous. The fleeing driver had managed to get a lead, but then something strange happened—the car began to slow down and move toward the shoulder of the road. By the time the officer caught up with the car, it was stopped all the way on the right shoulder. The officer could see no sign of the driver through the rear window. He approached the car in a crouch with his gun drawn, shouting for the driver to show his hands. Finally he came even with the window, and in an instant caught a glimpse of the driver reaching for a gun in the glove compartment. The officer fired four shots in rapid succession. Three of them hit the suspect—one in the head. Shortly thereafter, an ambulance arrived and took the suspect away. He was dead.

Later that evening, the police officer was telling his version of the event to an investigative unit at police headquarters. A detective asked the officer to describe what had happened in the moments following the chase. He described approaching the car and seeing the driver reaching for something—probably a gun—in the glove compartment. The detective stared at the officer with a strange look on his face. The officer asked what was wrong. The detective answered that the man could not have been reaching for anything. He had died of a heart attack before the car had even come to a stop on the shoulder of the road. The coroner was certain that the man had been dead before the police

officer shot him. There was no way the man could have moved.

This is an extreme example of the effects of stress on behavior. The police officer had chased the suspect for almost 20 minutes. It could safely be said of both individuals that sensation was affected, perception was affected, psychological arousal was affected, motor responses were affected, and in the officer's case, cognitive processes were affected. An event in the external environment had placed a tremendous load on some internal systems of the body and, as a result, dramatically affected behavior. Few of us experience the extreme environmental demands or loads that the police officer experienced—at least not regularly. Our stress experiences are typically milder and may have cumulative rather than immediate effects. Furthermore, stress is not necessarily bad (in spite of its consequences on behavior in the example above) or to be avoided. In fact, many people actively seek to increase stress rather than decrease it. Finally, it is practically impossible to avoid stress altogether. In the course of a week at school or work, you experience—and handle—many different types and levels of stress. In this chapter, we will consider the types of events and stimuli that can place loads or demands on internal systems (that is, produce stress). In addition, we will consider how these internal systems respond or adapt to the demands of stress.

◼ WHAT IS STRESS?

Stress means different things to different people. Some people define stress in terms of external

---

Stress. A state of strain, either mental or physical.

demands or stimuli—in other words, "things" in the environment cause stress. Others define stress as a person's reaction or response to such stimuli. A third definition brings together aspects of both stimuli and responses—stress is seen in terms of a particular response to a particular stimulus. These three types of definitions—stimulus specific, response specific, and interactional—are the most common (Cox, 1978). Let's consider them one at a time.

Stimulus Definitions of Stress

Whether one is talking about the stress of noise, crowding, computers, or major life changes, the stimulus definition assumes that stress is inherent in the stimuli. Thus, people who adopt this approach refer to the stimuli themselves as **stressors**. This is a very environmental, almost physical, view of stress. In physics, stress is defined as subjecting an object to pressure from external forces. That definition is similar to the stimulus definition of stress. Also in physics, it is assumed that too much stress will produce strain or deformation. For example, if too much stress (or load) is applied to a metal, some

permanent damage will result. Instead of bending (or adapting), the metal may crack or develop a stress break. Similarly, psychological stressors are thought to be capable of producing strain reactions in people. It is assumed that if extreme stress is applied to a person, the individual may fail to bend and instead may "crack," perhaps developing an illness or depression of some kind.

While stimulus definitions emphasize the kinds of situations that people generally find stressful, they must depend on the existence of some "average" person who represents the "average" response to a stressor. A problem arises here. It is readily apparent that there are individual differences in reactions to the same level of stress. Stimulus definitions of stress assume that external events or physical conditions are roughly equivalently stressful for all people, and this is clearly not the case.

Response Definitions of Stress

Response definitions of stress emphasize psychological and physiological reactions to environmental demands (stressors). The most notable example of

There are several different approaches to stress: Some define stress in terms of stimuli; some define it in terms of our psychological and physical reactions during stress; and some define it in terms of how people perceive a stressful situation or what they tell themselves about it.

this approach to stress is the work of the Canadian physiologist Hans Selye, often considered the father of stress research. Selye described stress as "the nonspecific response of the body to any demand made upon it" (Selye, 1976). He used the term "non-specific" (or common) because many and very different stimuli can trigger a stress reaction.

The body's reaction to stressors is a complex one, involving a cluster of responses that we have already examined in the chapters on biology and consciousness. These responses include autonomic nervous-system responses (increased heartrate and respiration), hormonal responses (increased secretion by the endocrine glands), and neurotransmitter responses (the release of certain neurotransmitters). According to Seyle, the stress response changes in a predictable fashion as the person attempts to adapt to a prolonged or severe level of stress. One of his major concerns was understanding how this adaptation takes place. We will take this up later when we consider physiological reactions to stress.

Interactional Definitions of Stress

The third definition of stress assumes that stress is neither specifically in the stimulus nor specifically in the response to the stimulus. Rather, stress arises out of an interaction of the two—our perceptions and cognitions of events interracting with our physiological state. This should sound familiar; it is the definition we arrived at for an emotion. As you may remember from Chapter 12, some theorists claimed that emotions were the result of stimuli; others claimed that emotions were the result of internal physiological states. The best explanation of emotion turned out to be that it is the result of both our interpretation of the environment (perception) and our pattern of internal changes (physiological response). From this perspective, psychological stress may be thought of as a special case of an emotional event. The experience of stress may be more intense than that of a typical emotion; furthermore, it may be longer-lasting and have more serious implications for physical and psychological well-being. Nevertheless, the interactional definition of stress,

which emphasizes both internal (physiological and cognitive) and external (situational) variables offers more than either the stimulus or the response definition alone.

The interactional approach is not without problems. For example, simply accepting that stimulus variables and internal variables interact does not help us to understand why some stimuli produce more stress than others. In the same way, the issue of exactly which internal changes qualify as stress responses is not resolved. In the next two sections, we will cover stimulus and response aspects of the stress experience in more depth.

■ STRESSFUL STIMULI

Many situations have been identified as being stressful. In a general sense, there are physical stressors (such as heat and cold), psychological stressors (such as fear of failure), and social stressors (such as interpersonal conflict). Let's look more closely at three specific stressful stimuli that affect all of us at least some of the time: crowding, noise, and particular life events.

Crowding

Under the right circumstances, large masses of people can be stimulating and pleasurable. Going to a rock concert can be fun, living in a large city can be exciting, and the thrill of being in a packed stadium watching a winning team is hard to beat. Yet, crowding is also known to affect people negatively, creating unpleasant physiological reactions as well as having the potential to cause physical illness. What is it about crowding that makes it stressful?

Let's start by considering a distinction between crowding and density (Dubos, 1965; Stokols, 1978). **Density** is an *objective* term referring to the number of people (or animals) in a particular spatial or physical setting—for example, the number of people in a particular section of a football stadium. A group of 300 people would be lower in density than

---

Stressors. Stimuli that cause stress, such as noise, crowding, heat, cold, and so on.

Density. The number of people in a particular spatial or physical setting.

People in a packed stadium at a sports event do not usually feel crowded—it is possible to have a highly dense situation that is not a crowded or stressful one.

a group of 3000 in the same space. **Crowding**, on the other hand, is a *subjective* term referring to the psychological factors or personal experiences in a situation—for example, a person's perceptions that too many people are present or that there is too much activity. An acquaintance of mine moved from New Mexico to Montana because he felt "crowded." His definition of "crowded" was the fact that on the first day of the fishing season he actually saw another angler a mile upstream. He wanted to fish in a stream that, in his mind, wasn't crowded. He felt that Montana could provide such protection.

While studies of animals clearly suggest that they suffer from crowding (Calhoun, 1962, 1971), the same cannot be said of humans living in high-density situations. One need only to look at high-density cities such as Hong Kong and Tokyo to see that density alone is not necessarily to be associated with adverse effects. For example, despite its high density, Hong Kong has a relatively low crime rate—the rate of serious crime is less than half that of comparable cities in the United States (Tanner, 1976). In general, studies correlating density and measures of "social pathology" (such as admissions to mental hospitals, suicide rates, and crime and juvenile delinquency) find either a modest or low positive association (Altman, 1975) or none at all (Freedman, 1975).

Thus, research suggests that defining crowding in terms of density may not be appropriate. That is, a highly dense situation may not be a crowded one. People in a packed football stadium (or a disco) typically report that they do not feel crowded (often in spite of the fact that they will say that the stadium or disco was "packed"). This points to the possibility that density may be a necessary but not sufficient condition for feeling crowded. It appears that other variables must be present along with density in order to produce the feeling of crowding. Examples of those other factors are information overload (too many people talking or acting at once), behavioral interference (group size getting in the way or preventing the carrying out of a particular action, such as getting to the water fountain), or the loss of personal control (being swept along in a mass of people toward an exit).

Noise

Beyond the physical damage it can do to hearing, does noise have adverse effects? The answer seems to be a clear "yes"; noise does have the potential to be a stressor. Physiologically, noise has been shown to cause stress reactions such as increases in sweating, blood pressure, and levels of adrenaline (Cohen et al., 1980). Noise has also been linked to nervousness, insomnia, digestive disorders, heart disease, and admissions to mental health hospitals (Jones and Cohen, 1968; Welch, 1979).

Behaviorally, noise has been shown to affect us in many ways. For example, in the laboratory and in real life, people exposed to high levels of noise are less likely to help others in need (such as helping to pick up dropped books or other objects) than those exposed to low levels of noise (Mathews and Canon, 1975). This ties in with the research on mood and prosocial behavior discussed in Chapter 12. There we saw that prosocial behavior (helping someone else) is associated with positive moods. Thus, it seems logical to conclude that negative emotions (such as stress) might have the opposite effect; that is, they might lead to an unwillingness to help. In addition, noise often increases tendencies toward aggression, particularly if the individual is already angered or in a heightened state of arousal (Geen and O'Neal, 1969; Donnerstein and Wilson, 1976).

A number of fascinating studies have documented adverse effects of noise on young children. In 1973, Cohen, Glass, and Singer reported the effects of excessive traffic noise on children's reading abilities and overall hearing. These children had lived for at least four years in a New York City high-

rise apartment complex, which was built over a 12-lane expressway. The lower apartments were noisier (because of the heavy traffic going underneath) than those on the upper levels. Children living in the noisier apartments were less able to recognize differences between similar-sounding words—such as "sick" and "thick" or "map" and "nap"—than were children living in the less noisy apartments on the upper floors. The reading ability of those children residing in the noisier apartments suffered as well.

Cohen and colleagues (1980) studied blood pressure and task persistence of third- and fourth-grade children whose elementary schools were along the flight path of Los Angeles International Airport. There are over 300 flights a day over these schools, approximately one every 2½ minutes during school hours. A group of children from schools in relatively quiet locations was used for comparison. All testing was done in a quiet setting; therefore the study was actually concerned with the after-effects of noise, or what happens to a person after exposure to noise has ceased. The findings were revealing. Children from the schools along the flight path had higher blood-pressure levels and were more likely to give up on a task (solving moderately difficult puzzles) than children attending schools in quieter neighborhoods. Furthermore, the children from the noisy schools who *did* complete the puzzles took longer to do so than the children from the quieter schools. On the average, the effect was greater for students who had been enrolled in the noisy schools for over 3½ years. This finding (and others from the study) suggests that children do not get used to noise and that its impact may cause them to suffer, at least cognitively and motivationally, from its effects.

Why does noise affect behavior and health in such negative ways? It seems that noise is particularly disturbing when it is *unpredictable* and *uncontrollable* (Cohen and Weinstein, 1981). In some respects, these variables are similar to those that seem to turn density into crowding (e.g., personal control). The effects of predictable versus unpredictable noise were tested in several studies. Glass and Singer (1972) proposed that even though it is

---

Crowding. A person's subjective feeling in a particular spatial or physical setting—an uncomfortable feeling that there are too many people in that space.

sometimes possible to adapt physiologically to noise, that adaptation uses up energy. This leaves less energy for dealing with additional stress, thus making the person more vulnerable to negative after-effects following the occurrence of noise.

To test this hypothesis, Glass and Singer first exposed subjects to either predictable or unpredictable noise while they were completing various tasks. Later, in a quiet environment, all subjects were asked to complete two tasks: a set of unsolvable puzzles and a proofreading assignment. Subjects in the unpredictable-noise group showed the most dramatic after-effects from noise exposure. In particular, the unpredictable-noise subjects gave up more quickly on the puzzles than subjects in the predictable-noise group; they also made more errors on the proofreading task compared with subjects in the predictable-noise group.

Glass and Singer reasoned that unpredictable noise made subjects feel that they had no control over their environment, resulting in feelings of helplessness. Because they lacked a sense of control over the noise, the subjects simply gave up on the tasks—or at least, they did not try as hard as those with a sense of control over the noise.

REVIEW QUESTIONS

1. There are three basic theories of what causes stress: a _____ , a _____ , or a combination of the two (the _____ theory).

2. A _____ is a specific stimulus, such as heat, cold, or pain, that causes stress.

3. _____ is the number of people in a particular space; _____ is a personal reaction to the number of people in a space—one's perception of space or lack of it.

4. In humans, there is a direct relationship between high-density areas such as cities and adverse effects such as high crime rates. T/F

5. Two elements that are important in both crowding and noise as stressors are _____ and _____ . If neither of these two elements are possible, it increases the amount of stress caused by crowding and noise.

Answers: 1. stimulus; response; interactional 2. stressor 3. Density; crowding 4. False 5. prediction; control

---

Stressful Life Events

Noise and crowding are two stressors that all of us come in contact with at various times in our lives. They are not peculiar to a particular developmental stage or circumstance. Neither are they related to any particular activity that we engage in regularly. In general, they are accidental characteristics of certain environments in which we may find ourselves. There is another class of stimuli that is also capable of producing stress, and these stimuli are more related to happenings in our lives at particular times. They are not accidental aspects of events—they are the events themselves. They are called life events and are thought to be directly related to the body's overall resistance. It has been proposed that as life events add up they can affect the immune system and make the body more vulnerable to illness. A direct relationship between physical and psychological well-being is proposed.

A life event is essentially any event that requires a significant adjustment in circumstances, such as the death of a spouse, the birth of a child, a jail term, or getting a promotion. In 1967, Holmes and Rahe published a list of major life events, ordered in terms of the extent to which they believed the events disrupted someone's life. They attached values to each of these events, making it possible to consider the cumulative impact of several of these events within a specified time period. Thus, if only one life event occurs during the year, the threat to health (that is, the extent to which resistance is lowered) is considerably less than if two events of the same magnitude occurred. The values are in the form of points called **life-change units (LCUs)**. The **Social-Readjustment Rating Scale (SSRS)** (see Table 14–1) allows us to add up the point values of all the life events occurring within a fixed time period. The most common time period considered is one year. The higher the score, the greater the likelihood of developing an illness of some kind in the near future. Scores from 150 to 199 are considered to represent a "mild life crisis"; from 200 to 299, a "moderate life crisis"; and from 300 up, a "major life crisis." For example, if your spouse died (100 LCUs), you were fired from your job (47 LCUs), and one of your parents died (63 LCUs) all in the same year, you would be characterized as having a moderate life crisis during that period (a total of 210 LCUs). If, in addition to those misfortunes, you also changed jobs (36 LCUs), had a close friend die (37

TABLE 14-1.

Social-Readjustment Rating Scale

Rank	Life Event	Mean Value
1	Death of spouse	100
2	Divorce	73
3	Marital separation	63
4	Jail term	63
5	Death of close family member	63
6	Personal injury or illness	53
7	Marriage	50
8	Fired at work	47
9	Marital reconciliation	45
10	Retirement	45
11	Change in health of family member	44
12	Pregnancy	40
13	Sex difficulties	39
14	Gain of new family member	39
15	Business readjustment	39
16	Change in financial state	38
17	Death of close friend	37
18	Change to different line of work	36
19	Change in number of arguments with spouse	35
20	Mortgage over $10,000	31
21	Foreclosure of mortgage or loan	30
22	Change in responsibilities at work	29
23	Son or daughter leaving home	29
24	Trouble with in-laws	29
25	Outstanding personal achievement	28
26	Wife begins or stops work	26
27	Begin or end school	26
28	Change in living conditions	25
29	Revision of personal habits	24
30	Trouble with boss	23
31	Change in work hours or conditions	20
32	Change in residence	20
33	Change in schools	20
34	Change in recreation	19
35	Change in church activities	19
36	Change in social activities	18
37	Mortgage or loan less than $10,000	17
38	Change in sleeping habits	18
39	Change in number of family get-togethers	15
40	Change in eating habits	15
41	Vacation	13
42	Christmas	12
43	Minor violations of the law	11

Source: Holmes and Rahe, 1967.

Moving is an example of an event that most people find stressful. Stressful life events are thought to be related to the body's overall resistance to disease.

LCUs), and stopped smoking (24 LCUs), you would be described as having a major life crisis.

While major life events can obviously be seriously stressful, it is also possible that more minor, daily frustrations can produce stress. Lazarus (1981) has noted, for example, that college students experience stress from everyday "hassles" such as anxiety over

---

Life-change units (LCUS). Point values assigned to major life events, such as divorce, death of spouse, marriage, and so on.

Social-readjustment rating scale (SRRS). A scale developed by Holmes and Rahe that makes it possible to add up the point values of the life events that have occurred during a fixed time period—the higher the score, the greater the likelihood that the person will develop an illness of some kind in the near future.

wasting time, meeting high standards, and being lonely, while middle-aged people complain about economic concerns and having too many things to do. Lazarus describes hassles as petty annoyances, irritations, and frustrations. Some researchers believe that frequent exposure to such hassles may be an even better predictor of disease than major life events (DeLongis et al., 1982). Other examples of hassles are concern about weight, yard work, rising prices, and a malfunctioning car.

There is really no contradiction between the life events scale of Holmes and Rahe and the hassle concept of Lazarus and his colleagues. Life events tend to occur sporadically or infrequently; hassles occur every day. However, even if these hassles are only worth 1 or 2 LCUs each, it does not take long for the total "exposure" to exceed 300. The differences between life events and hassles are in terms of both frequency and the demand for readjustment, but the mechanism by which they affect health is assumed to be the same.

Work life is rich in hassles and LCUs. Some jobs are considered more stressful than others because they offer little in the way of personal control or opportunity to make decisions (an aspect that also seems to moderate the effects of noise and crowding). Other jobs are stressful because they place a high demand on the capacities of the person. A recent study of heart disease that compared Swedish and American men (Theorell and Schwartz, 1981; Karasek, 1982) indicates that the most stressful jobs are those that are characterized by low control and high demand. Figure 14–1 shows where some familiar jobs fall in this framework.

■ RESPONSES TO STRESS

Stress has a direct effect on the person experiencing it, and usually an indirect effect on others with whom that person comes in contact. The range of effects is quite broad and cuts across many of the systems we have studied in other chapters. Emotional reactions to stress may include anxiety, guilt, and loneliness. Cognitive reactions may result in an inability to concentrate, frequent forgetting, and being overly sensitive to criticism. Sometimes unwanted and unpleasant images may intrude during

either wakefulness or sleep, making concentration difficult, if not impossible. Physiological and health-related symptoms include muscle tension, headaches, dryness in the mouth, sweating, troubled breathing, frequent urination, diarrhea, loss of sexual functioning, and internal hormonal changes.

Physiological Reactions to Stress

The body's physiological response to stress appears to be regulated by the endocrine system. You may recall from Chapter 2 that the endocrine system is made up of a series of glands that secrete chemical messengers (hormones) directly into the bloodstream. These hormones go on to affect particular organs and muscles in the body, such as the heart and liver. The principle is simple but the system in action is quite complex.

To illustrate, let's consider the adrenal glands and hormones. There are two **adrenal glands**, one on top of each kidney. These glands secrete critical hormones that help the body mobilize its resources under stress. Actually, each adrenal gland is made up of two sections—an inner portion, or medulla, and an outer portion, or cortex. The hormones secreted by each portion are quite different.

The **adrenal medulla** secretes two hormones. One, **adrenalin**, acts through the liver to produce glucose for energy. **Noradrenalin**, the second hormone, acts mainly to constrict the blood vessels of the skin to divert more blood to the underlying muscles. Adrenalin and noradrenalin both cause an increase in the amount of fat circulating in the bloodstream.

The **adrenal cortex** secretes a number of hormones. Some, like **cortisol**, help the body meet stress by increasing the production of glucose for energy and by reducing inflammation associated with stressors like muscle injury. A second kind of hormone is involved in maintaining the mineral content of the body, particularly sodium salt. These hormones are known to heighten the body's inflammatory response, helping to build a protective barricade against further invasion of foreign agents (like bacteria or viruses).

The adrenal cortex is part of a chain-reaction system formed by the hypothalamus, pituitary gland, and adrenal glands. Selye, the leading investigator of the stress response, emphasized this chain-

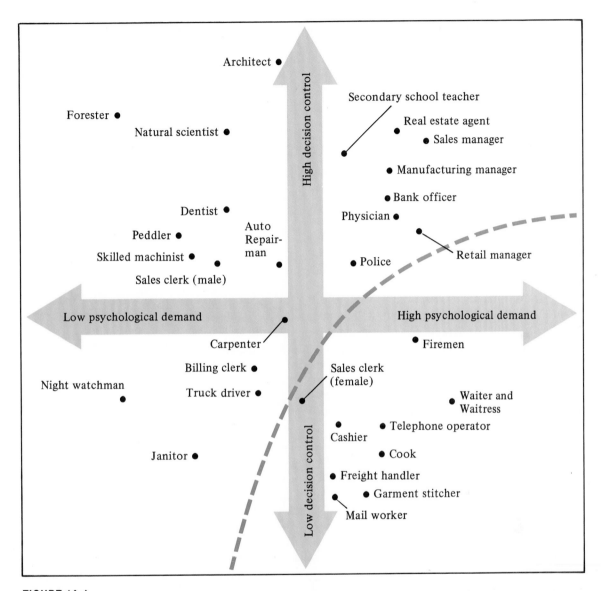

FIGURE 14-1

Some jobs are considered more stressful than others. The chart shows a number of familiar jobs and how they would be rated in terms of control or ability to make decisions and in terms of the demand on the person. The most stressful jobs are those shown in the lower-right area of the chart. These jobs are characterized by low control and high demand. (Columbia University Department of Industrial Engineering and Operations Research, 1983)

Adrenal glands. Part of the endocrine system located above the kidneys; produces hormones that help the body mobilize its resources under stress.

Adrenal medulla. Inner portion of the adrenal glands; produces adrenalin and noradrenalin.

Adrenalin. Hormone that acts through the liver to produce glucose for energy; also increases heartrate.

Noradrenalin. Hormone that constricts the blood vessels of the skin to divert more blood to the muscles.

Adrenal cortex. Outer portion of the adrenal gland; secretes hormones that increase the production of glucose, and that either increase or decrease the body's inflammatory response.

Cortisol. Hormone secreted by the adrenal cortex that helps the body meet stress; increases the production of glucose.

reaction system. He labeled the reaction the **general adaptation syndrome (GAS)** (A **syndrome** means a collection of events or reactions as opposed to a single specific reaction.) Selye proposed that although each stressor has specific effects on the body (like cold causing shivering and heat causing perspiring), the general effects of the syndrome are common to all stressors and should be regarded as the body's definition of "stress."

Recently Marianne Frankenhauser, a leading Swedish stress researcher, has found that not all hormones respond the same way to all stressors. She proposes a model she calls the **Effort–Distress Model** to understand these differing responses. In this model effort and distress may be experienced either separately or together; moreover, effort and distress seem to be associated with different hormones. Frankenhauser (1983), notes that *effort without distress* is a pleasant or joyous state which is accompanied by the secretion of the hormones adrenalin and noradrenalin from the adrenal medulla. *Effort with distress* is likely to be associated with daily hassles and is accompanied by secretion of the adrenal medulla hormones as well as secretion of the adrenal cortex hormone cortisol. *Distress without effort* is an unpleasant state characterized by feelings of helplessness and accompanied by secretion of the adrenal cortex hormone cortisol.

This model strongly suggests that it is important to minimize feelings of distress. In the following two sections we will examine some ways of minimizing distress and achieving effort without distress.

REVIEW QUESTIONS

6. A _____ _____ is anything that happens to you that requires a significant change in your circumstances. The cumulative effect of such occurrences can be measured by assigning points called _____ _____ _____ .

7. The most stressful jobs are those that are characterized by low _____ and high _____ .

8. The body's physiological response to stress seems to be controlled by the _____ _____ . Two glands that have a major

role in the body's response to stress are the _____ glands.

9. Selye labeled the body's response to stress the _____ _____ _____ . He said that there are three stages to this reaction: the _____ _____ , _____ and _____ .

10. Frankenhauser has found that differing responses to stress seem to be associated with different hormones. In her model, _____ _____ _____ is a pleasant state characterized by the secretion of the hormones adrenalin and noradrenalin.

Answers: 6. life event; Life Change Units (LCUs) 7. control; demand 8. endocrine system; adrenal 9. general adaptation syndrome (GAS); alarm reaction; resistance; exhaustion 10. effort without distress

■ MODERATORS OF RESPONSES TO STRESS

Personal Control and Responses to Stress

One important moderator you are already familiar with is *personal control*. Earlier in the chapter we saw how the loss of personal control in combination with density can lead to the feeling of crowding. We also saw how unpredictable noise leads to feelings of helplessness. Frankenhauser has done much work looking at the effects of personal control on responses to stress. Two experiments from her laboratory (1980) help illustrate how personal control can moderate responses to stress. In one experiment a situation of "effort *with* distress" was constructed. This low-control situation consisted of a one-hour vigilance task in which the subject had to press a key in response to the randomly changing intensity of a weak light signal. In the other experiment a high-control situation was constructed. This situation was designed to elicit "effort *without* distress." It consisted of a choice-reaction task in which subjects were allowed at the start of the experiment to choose how fast the stimuli would appear. In addition, every five minutes the subjects were allowed to adjust the stimulus rate so that they maintained a comfortable pace for the entire one hour session. Subjects were asked after each experiment to rate their feelings of effort and distress, and

WORK AND STRESS

Marianne Frankenhauser and her associates, who developed the Effort-Distress Model, have also studied stress conditions outside the laboratory. Using physiological and biochemical techniques, these stress researchers can measure the effects of various work conditions. When a person experiences stress, certain hormones, such as adrenaline and cortisol, are secreted into the bloodstream. By taking a blood or urine sample, researchers can measure the amounts of the hormones present and determine subjects' stress levels.

As you know from reading the text, a key factor in the moderation of stress is the element of personal control. Frankenhauser (1980) found that when workers can choose their work pace, the work is less stressful than when the pace is set by an outside control, such as a machine or another worker. Conditions known as underload and overload were also found to be critical to stress at work. Both an excess of stimulation (too much work) and a lack of stimulation (too little work) have been found to have negative effects. At low workload levels, people become bored and easily distracted. When overload occurs, the central nervous system becomes overaroused and tense, thinking becomes fragmented, judgment is impaired, and initiative is reduced. Other factors that may contribute to a stressful work setting are a lack of variety in the tasks that workers are asked to perform and limited social contact with co-workers.

A work setting that combines many of these potentially stressful elements is the Swedish sawmill. The work pace for grading timber is set by a machine. In addition, workers must make judgments about timber quality very quickly—sometimes in less than five seconds—before the next piece comes along. There is little variation in the task, and interaction with other workers is severely limited. Sawmills are also very noisy—another stressful factor. Frankenhauser compared adrenaline levels of workers in this type of job with a control group made up of other workers in the same sawmill. The control group worked under conditions of greater personal control and fewer restrictions. She found that, among the workers in the high-stress condition, the adrenaline level was very high, and it increased during the course of the workday. The control group had a moderate adrenaline level. Frankenhauser's findings were supported by interviews in which a large number of workers in the high-stress condition reported that they were unable to relax after work. They also reported feeling that their work was monotonous and repetitive and that they experienced considerable physical strain.

In another study, Frankenhauser (1981) looked at the stress of commuting to and from work by train. During a gas rationing period in Sweden, there was an increase in the number of passengers commuting by train from Swedish suburbs into a major city. Frankenhauser hypothesized that the more crowded trains would add to the stress of commuting. She measured the adrenaline levels in the same group of passengers under two different conditions of crowdedness. On both occasions there were enough seats for everyone but on the second ride passengers were much more restricted as to their choice of seat. Measuring adrenaline excretion, Frankenhauser found that the passengers' stress levels rose as their choice of seats became more limited. They had lower stress levels on the first ride than on the second one with more restricted seating. Further, passengers who boarded the crowded train early and were able to choose where they sat had a lower stress level than passengers who boarded later and had little control over where they sat. Thus, although the early-boarding passengers had a longer commute, it was less stressful for them because they had some control over seating.

measures of adrenaline and cortisol were taken. Figure 14–2 shows the results. Subjects in both experiments reported high levels of effort but only the low-control subjects reported high levels of distress. These two groups of subjects also differed in their levels of adrenaline. These experiments help show how personal control can alter our appraisal of the situation as well as our physiological response. (The accompanying box describes the results of stress studies conducted outside the laboratory.

General adaptation syndrome (GAS). Selye's term for a chain-reaction system made up of the adrenal glands, pituitary gland, and the hypothalamus; forms the body's response to stress.
Syndrome. A collection of events or reactions.

Effort-distress model. A model developed by Frankenhauser that proposes that different combinations of effort and distress are associated with different hormones.

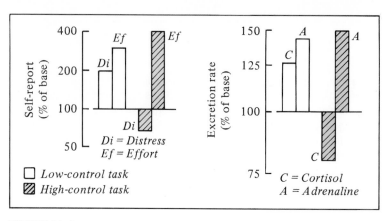

FIGURE 14-2

This graph shows the results of a study testing the effects of personal control on stress. One group of subjects performed a low-control task designed to produce "effort with distress." Another group of subjects performed a high-control task designed to produce "effort without distress." After each task, subjects were asked to rate their feelings of effort and distress, and measures of adrenaline and cortisol were taken. Both groups of subjects reported high levels of effort, but only those in the low-control situation reported high levels of distress. The two groups of subjects also showed differences in their levels of adrenaline. (Frankenhauser, Lundberg, and Forsman, 1980)

Social Supports and Reponses to Stress

Pain is a strange phenomenon. Most of us have childhood memories of a parent kissing a scraped knee or rubbing a banged head to make it feel better. The actual blood or bruise did not disappear, but the pain certainly seemed to diminish. The stress produced by an outside stimulus was reduced. On a broader level, the same can be true of adults suffering from misfortune or illness. It often appears that a willing ear and a gentle hand can make the sickest person feel a little better. It is even possible to console people who have just experienced the death of a loved one or other misfortune, and thereby ease their anguish.

Death and illness are extreme examples of life event stressors as we saw in the SRRS. But what about the accumulation of small irritations or hassles, which Lazarus refers to? Here, too, it seems as if the stressful effects of even little hassles can be reduced somewhat by consideration from another person. Our experience instinctively tells us that the way we handle stress can be affected by the relationships we have with those around us.

The process described here is one of social support (and by implication, the lack of it). A person is said to enjoy **social support** when he or she has relationships with others (family members, friends, co-workers) characterized by a sense of acceptance and love, and a willingness to give assistance (emotional and practical) in times of need. Having a

social-support network to rely on can lead to fewer perceptions of stress, better coping when stress is experienced and, in general, better health and performance.

Why does social support reduce stress? Probably for several reasons. For example, if you have the support of fellow workers in the workplace, you are like-

The support of other people is one of the best defenses against stress. On the other hand, social rejection can increase levels of felt stress.

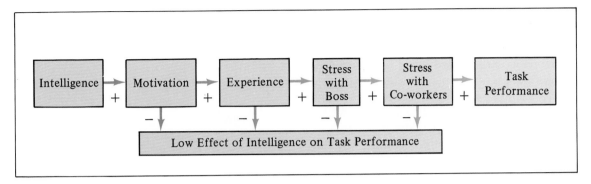

FIGURE 14-3
This is the multiple screen model of the effect of various factors on intelligence in job performance. Stress with the boss and with co-workers are two of the factors that can interfere with one's intelligence and thus with one's job performance. (Fiedler and Leister, 1977)

ly to perceive less stress on the job—perhaps because of reduced interpersonal pressures and heightened good feelings about yourself (McLean, 1974). Also, supportive others may provide needed information and practical problem-solving guidance to help you meet the demands of on-the-job stress. Encouragement and reassurance are also important qualities provided by social supports.

In addition to the personal control and social support variables, some researchers have suggested that there are major differences among individuals in terms of their capacity to tolerate stress. In fact, it has been suggested that some people even seek out stressful situations.

Responses to the Stress of Interpersonal Conflict

A team of psychologists (Fiedler and Leister, 1977) has developed an interesting model that suggests that stress can neutralize the effects of intelligence in certain settings. Indirectly, stress can have an effect on ultimate job performance—even in normal circumstances not related to the source of the stress. This model is known as the multiple screen model and it is illustrated in Figure 14-3. As you can see, it assumes that the person begins with some fixed amount of cognitive skill (called intelligence in this model). In theory, this intelligence should make a direct contribution to task performance. Brighter people should do better on the task as long as it re-

quires intellectual skills. According to the model, however, the problem is that intelligence must pass through a series of screens or filters before it has its effect. Each screen has the power to reduce (but not increase) the effect of intelligence. For example, low motivation will reduce the effect of intelligence, and inexperience will have a similar effect.

It is the last two screens—stress with the supervisor and stress with co-workers—that interest us in this section. Fiedler and Leister propose that stress resulting from poor interpersonal relations at work can actually suppress intellectual ability. As mentioned earlier, some of the cognitive effects of stress are inability to make decisions, problems in concentration, lapses of memory, and overreaction to criticism. Fiedler and Leister have presented some preliminary data gathered from military officers that seem to support this model. They have been able to show that when interpersonal stress is high, intelligence will not contribute to intellectual performance or problem solving.

Fiedler and his colleagues (Barnes, Potter, and Fiedler, 1983) have also presented data to show that interpersonal stress may have a substantial effect on the extent to which intellectual abilities can be

---

Social support. A network of friends, family members, or co-workers that can be relied upon in times of stress.

brought to bear on college studies. They found that under conditions of interpersonal stress in the college environment, Scholastic Achievement Test (SAT) scores do not predict grade point averages (GPA) very well. Put another way, this means that intellectual achievement (measured by GPA) failed to match the performance predicted by the SAT exam. On the other hand, when stress is low, SAT scores do a reasonable job of predicting GPA. The implications of these findings for school settings are important. Bright children may be hampered in learning and performance in nonsupportive classroom environments. At the same time, children with poorly developed cognitive skills may be able to develop them to more adaptive levels in supportive environments. Keep in mind that this model and these data relate to intellectual performance or tasks that require cognitive skills. For motor performance, the relationship may not exist or may even be opposite. It may be that stress can increase arousal and, in turn, improve the performance of a well-developed motor skill. For example, many athletes work hard to develop antagonistic relations with opponents; witness the required insults and staredowns that commonly accompany the preliminaries to a boxing match. Obviously, social-support variables can have a broad effect on the efficiency with which people handle stress. In some cases, such as those described by the multiple screen model, the reverse of social support—social rejection—can actually increase levels of stress and interfere with intellectual performance.

■ COPING WITH STRESS

As you have probably gathered from the preceding discussion, dealing with stress seems to be more a matter of management or organization than a simple matter of reduction of physiological arousal. How stress is managed has to do with how stress is perceived. Top-level athletes, such as gymnasts, swimmers, or runners, are not interested in totally eliminating anxiety and arousal. In fact, they worry about *not* being anxious enough before a competition and try to develop strategies for making arousal work to their advantage. This is one way of managing stress—turning a weakness into a strength. Generally speaking, the process of managing stress is called **coping**. The implication is that a stressor will not necessarily go away by itself and that it is up to the individual to develop some method of dealing with the cognitive, emotional, physiological, and behavioral consequences of perceived stress.

Over the years, stress-management skills have

PILOT UNDER STRESS

The passengers and crew of an Eastern Airlines flight from Atlanta to Pensacola and Tampa recently experienced a series of delays. The galley door wouldn't shut, there was a fuel shortage, and finally they faced a long wait for takeoff behind a number of other jets.

Passengers reported that the pilot came on the intercom and complained about the delay on the runway. "We're going to be stuck out here for twenty minutes," the pilot was quoted as saying. A few minutes later, his announcements began to sound peculiar and inappropriate to passengers. He said, "You know, they say when you die you have to change in Atlanta." Some passengers grew concerned about the pilot's ability to safely fly the plane. Then he announced that he was "sick and tired of the delays, the waiting." He told passengers that he wouldn't be flying anymore and walked off the plane. The airline found another pilot for the flight, which took off two hours late. The following day, the flight's original pilot requested and received voluntary early retirement.

Spokespeople for the airline blamed stress for the pilot's behavior. A series of environmental stressors, over which the pilot had no personal control, seemed to have caused a breakdown of his stress management system to such an extent that he felt his only alternative for reducing stress was to remove himself from the environment.

been developed to help people learn to reduce the undesirable stress in their lives and to prevent and treat stress-related symptoms and diseases. Because stress comes from many sources, stress management is likely to be most effective when approached from several different perspectives rather than from one viewpoint. These perspectives include the alteration of environments and life-styles, personality traits, and physiological response systems. We will now consider each of these possibilities in some detail.

Altering Environments and/or Life-Styles

Social Supports. As stated earlier, one of the best defenses against stress is a social-support network. Do not hesitate to enlist the aid of others. If you do not have much of a social-support network, develop one. This can usually be accomplished by joining a group of people who have similar stressors in their lives. Examples are single-parent-family groups, senior-citizens groups, and arthritis-support groups. The community section of the local newspaper is a good place to start, since it usually carries announcements of future metings or reports on past meetings. As an example of the effects of such social-support networks, research clearly shows that the support of others reduces depression and even physical complications during pregnancy (Nuckolls et al., 1972).

Nutrition, Alcohol, Smoking, and Exercise. Many aspects of current life-styles may contribute to excessive stress reactions. Making alterations in patterns of living may be difficult and require substantial efforts at times, but the efforts will undoubtedly pay off in the long run.

Proper nutrition is essential for combating the effects of stress. For example, too much salt may contribute to high blood pressure, especially in people predisposed to this disease. Alcohol and refined white sugar deplete the body of the B vitamins essential in managing stress. Both caffeine and nicotine can induce the "fight or flight" body response, resulting in a highly awake and alert (aroused) state; heavy coffee-drinking or smoking can substantially increase heartrate, blood pressure, and respiration,

release fats in the blood, stimulate the adrenals, and deplete the body of vitamin B.

A related problem is that most of us do not get proper exercise. This is unfortunate because exercise, and physical activity in general, are excellent ways of discharging or using up stress products, such as excessive adrenalin, noradrenalin, and sugar. There are some things to consider in choosing exercise, however. It is best to choose activity that is not likely to make you overconcerned about "winning." As Girdano and Everly (1979) caution, highly competitive activity may contribute to stress rather than help dissipate it. A sensible stress-prevention plan should probably include (Davis et al., 1982):

1. a variety of foods;
2. reduced amounts of fats and fatty foods, sugars and sweets, and alcohol;
3. exercise.

Altering Traits and Perceptions

Defense Mechanisms. There appear to be some common psychological processes which people employ to manage the emotional reactions to stress. These processes have been labeled **defense mechanisms**, since they have the effect of defending against the anxiety or otherwise aversive emotional consequences of stress. Another way to describe them is as strategies, or coping mechanisms, that seem to be activated without any conscious effort. This does not mean that they are "unconscious" in the sense that Freud used the term. It simply means that, over time, these strategies have assumed some automatic properties. When stress starts to build, one or more of these mechanisms "kicks in" as a sort of pressure-relief valve.

Defense mechanisms are sometimes thought of as aids in self-deception. In other words, they protect the person emotionally against threat, without actually altering or affecting the (external or internal) stressor itself. Defense mechanisms involve cognitive rather than motor performance. A number of possible defense mechanisms have been identified by psychologists over the years. Some of the more common mechanisms and examples of their

---

Coping. The process of managing stress.
Defense mechanisms. Cognitive processes used for managing

the emotional reactions to stress, especially in defending against the anxiety caused by stress.

Exercise, and physical activity in general, can help to dissipate stress. Another defense against stress is proper nutrition.

use appear in Table 14–2. There are an infinite number of possible examples for each one, because for each of us there are an infinite number of situations in which we might find ourselves using defense strategies. A few examples might help you to understand how these strategies are used. In **denial,** the person tells himself or herself that something is not true or is not happening. For example, the cancer victim insists that "I am not dying of cancer"; the alcoholic feels that the problem is under control; the smoker refuses to believe that smoking *causes* cancer, pointing to the fact that research has demonstrated only a *correlation* between smoking and cancer. In each of these instances, the threat or demand of the environment is reduced.

As another example, consider **intellectualization**. This defense mechanism has the effect of

changing the nature of the demand or stressor by changing the focus to an exaggeration of thought over feeling. For example, people who have just had an illness diagnosed as cancer might avoid making the difficult choice between surgery, radiation therapy, or chemotherapy by concentrating on learning all there is to learn about cancer. They go off to the library and read, they talk with cancer specialists (not about their case but about the nature of cancer in general), and they redefine their problem as one of learning as much as possible about a biological condition. In fact, this not only helps them deal with the emotional aspects of the disease by putting them in the background, but it also helps to increase feelings of control and competency to deal with the stressor. In that sense, intellectualization can be more adaptive in the long run than

TABLE 14-2.
Common Ego Defense Mechanisms

___

Repression—excluding unacceptable impulses, ideas, or feelings from consciousness. For example, in repression, feelings of hatred or lust toward one's parents are blocked from awareness.

Regression—returning to a less mature level of adaptation, especially under extreme frustration or stress. For example, regression may be seen in the fired executive who begins to act in an extremely dependent and helpless fashion, requiring relatives to attend to his or her every need.

Projection—attributing unacceptable ideas or impulses to others rather than acknowledging them as one's own. For example, unconscious homosexual impulses may be projected upon others, so that now the person is troubled by the homosexual behavior of other people and not by his or her own desires.

Rationalization—justifying an act or idea that is unacceptable because it is unreasonable, illogical, or inconsistent. For example, the individual who fails to achieve a much-desired and hard-fought-for goal then decides that failure really was "for the best" or "a blessing in disguise."

Reaction Formation—transforming dangerous or painful urges into their opposite forms, though the original urges persist unconsciously. The transformed urges often are felt or expressed in excessive and exaggerated ways, for example, a mother's hatred of her child is transformed into maternal oversolicitousness.

Denial—rejecting or distorting those aspects of reality which consciously are unacceptable. For example, the person maintains that the death of a loved one "just did not happen."

Sublimation—modifying unacceptable impulses into socially acceptable activities. For example, sexual impulses may be channeled into painting or sculpturing nudes, while aggressive tendencies may be discharged by choosing to become a movie critic.

Displacement—shifting impulses and feeling about one person or object toward a safe or less dangerous person or object. For example, aggressive feelings toward the boss are totally inhibited, but expressed later toward family members, pets, or furniture.

Intellectualization—removing or isolating feeling from a thought so that the thought can remain conscious without the associated affective charge. Thinking about impulses to murder someone without getting upset or anxious, or talking in a detached way about a recent divorce or personal failure without feeling the disappointment and hurt are common examples.

Identification—incorporating the thoughts, feelings, and actions of another to increase one's sense of worth or to reduce threat from powerful others. The child acquires parental standards and values partly through identification with its parents.

___

Source: Lazarus and Monat, 1979, p. 163.

denial, since it reduces the discrepancy between the environmental demand and the person's perceived capacity to deal with that demand. Denial is seldom adaptive in the long run.

Stress Inoculation Training. This technique (Meichenbaum and Cameron, 1974; Meichenbaum, 1977) involves training people to monitor the triggers for stressful thoughts and feelings, learning and rehearsing new coping skills or thoughts, and applying these skills or thoughts. The following stress-coping statements are examples of neutral or positive thoughts that may be substituted for negative ones in stressful situations and, as a result, may provide relief from stress reactions:

☐ There's nothing to worry about.
☐ I'll jump in and be all right.
☐ I can do this, I'm doing it now.
☐ I can get help if I need it.
☐ It's okay to make mistakes.
☐ Relax now!
☐ I've survived this and worse before.
☐ I did all right. I did well.

___

Denial. Defense mechanism that consists of telling oneself that something is not true or is not happening in order to reduce the threat or demand posed by the environment.

Intellectualization. Defense mechanism that works to change the focus of a response to a problem from an emotional one to an intellectual one.

These or similar thoughts must become routine and automatic, so that when stress occurs in real life they will come to mind at the first sign of tension and anxiety. Learning and using these coping skills can be difficult, but considerable success has been noted for those persistent enough to master them.

Altering Physiological Responses to Stress

Progressive Relaxation. An excellent technique for reducing the body's stress response is based on deep-muscle relaxation exercises (Jacobson, 1938). These exercises have been shown to reduce pulse rate, blood pressure, sweating, and breathing rate.

As described by Wolpe (1958), progressive relaxation is aimed at the awareness of tense muscles and learning a way to relax them. Relaxation training progresses from one major muscle group to another, until total muscle relaxation has been achieved. The progression might go something like this: You first get into a comfortable position (lying down or sitting) and let yourself relax. As you relax, clench your right fist, tighter and tighter, and observe the tension. Notice the tension in your fist, hand, and forearm. Now relax and let the fingers of your right hand become loose. Then do the same with your left fist; then your elbows and biceps, and so on. Finally, after doing the hands, forearms, and biceps, practice tensing and relaxing the following major muscle groups: head, face, throat, and shoulders; chest, stomach, and lower back; and thighs, buttocks, calves, and feet.

Relaxation is a skill that must be rehearsed regularly. Relaxation training serves not only as an excellent emotion-focused coping technique, but also as an aid in using other stress-management techniques, particularly when tension and anxiety are so great that utilization of these other techniques is hindered.

Biofeedback. Many of the body's stress reactions have long been assumed to be largely regulated by the "involuntary," or "autonomic," nervous system, and thus outside the realm of personal control. In recent years, however, researchers have done studies in which both humans and animals have learned to control certain activities of the autonomic nervous system. **Biofeedback** techniques have emerged to help people learn to regulate bodily processes such

as heartrate, blood pressure, and brain waves. These techniques involve using instruments to inform people about some biological response over which they want to gain control. The person can then use this information (feedback) to improve control over the response. The techniques require discipline and practice, but they have the advantage of placing the control of bodily reactions, which include stress reactions, in the person's own hands.

Meditation. A coping strategy that you may find effective is the regular practice of some form of meditation. Millions of people throughout the world use Zen, Yoga, or Transcendental Meditation, for example, to combat the effects of stress and to promote personal growth. (The general strategies of the various techniques were described in the chapter on consciousness.)

The physiological effects of meditation are decreased heartrate, blood pressure, muscle tension, oxygen consumption, and breathing rate. Benson (1975) calls this set of meditation-induced responses the **relaxation response**.

Benson has studied the relaxation response extensively and has developed a westernized form of meditation to elicit this response. His simple meditative technique has four major components: 1) a *quiet environment*; 2) a *mental device* such as a repetition of a sound or word (known as a "mantra" in most meditative techniques); 3) a *passive* ("let it happen") *attitude* toward distracting thoughts; and, 4) a *comfortable position* that can be maintained for about 20 minutes without undue muscular tension.

REVIEW QUESTIONS

11. One important moderator of a person's response to stress is _____ _____, the opportunity to make one's own decisions about a situation. Another important element in a person's ability to resist stress is the _____ _____ one gets from family members, friends, and co-workers.

12. It has been suggested by Fiedler and Leister that when interpersonal stress is high, it reduces the effects of _____ on performance or problem solving.

13. The process of managing stress is called _____ . This involves developing methods to deal with the cognitive, emotional, physiological, and behavioral aspects of stress.

14. Proper _____ can help to combat the effects of stress. Eating a variety of foods, and reducing intake of fats, sugar, sweets, alcohol, and caffeine should be part of a sensible stress prevention plan.

15. _____ _____ are cognitive processes people engage in for managing stress. Two examples discussed in the text are _____ and _____ .

16. _____ _____ , a technique based on deep muscle relaxation exercises, has proven effective in reducing the body's response to stress.

Answers: 11. personal control; social support 12. intelligence 13. coping 14. nutrition 15. Defense mechanisms; denial; intellectualization 16. Progressive relaxation

■ STRESS AND ILLNESS

As we have said, stress and disease appear to be related, although exactly how they are linked is largely guesswork at this time. Psychological factors in general have only recently been implicated as a susceptibility factor to illness. We do not yet know whether it is stress alone that wears down immunity, or whether and to what extent stress, life-styles, and maladaptive personalities are interrelated in susceptibility to disease. It may be that the answer is different for different disorders. Nevertheless, there is a growing realization in both the psychological and medical communities that psychological health and physical health are closely connected. Some examples of this relationship have been carefully

studied and offer ideas about how psychological and physical health might be related. One such example is the so-called Type A behavior.

Type A Behavior and Heart Disease

Heart disease is a major killer in the United States. About 1½ million Americans are expected to have heart attacks in 1987; one third of these victims will die as a result. Over 4½ million Americans today have a history of heart disease (*The World Almanac*, 1981, p. 95). Men are twice as likely as women to have heart disease, though women's rates are on the rise. About 25 percent of all victims are under the age of 65.

The chief biological risk factors in heart disease appear to be high blood pressure, high levels of fats (especially of cholesterol) in the blood, and heavy cigarette smoking. In addition to these, however, it is now well documented that another risk factor is the style of behavior known as **Type A behavior pattern**.

The Type A behavior pattern is defined by an intense striving for achievement, competitiveness, impatience, a sense of time urgency, abrupt gestures and speech, overcommitment to a profession, and excess drive and hostility. According to Friedman and Rosenman (1974), the two medical researchers who first identified this pattern, Type A individuals are always battling multiple deadlines, obstacles, and harrassments. Cluttered calendars are reminders of their incessant, compulsive strivings. The Type A individual is locked in a never-ending struggle to complete the greatest number of tasks in the shortest amount of time. Such people perceive a great environmental demand yet feel that they have insufficient resources to meet that demand. In particular, they see themselves as having too little time to accomplish certain tasks.

Type B people behave in an opposite way. They are much more relaxed and easy-going than Type As. They cope with stress in a less frantic manner—with less hostility and competitiveness—than Type

---

Biofeedback. Use of equipment to provide immediate feedback to a subject about the activities of his or her body's autonomic nervous system; the information provided allows the subject to control activities such as heartrate or brain waves.

Relaxation response. Technique developed by Benson that combines meditation with muscle relaxation to ease stress.

Type A behavior pattern. A type of behavior that involves intense striving for achievement, competitiveness, impatience, a sense of time urgency; people with Type A behavior pattern run a higher risk of developing heart disease.

As. Type Bs rarely try to do two or more things at the same time, as Type As often do, and job and recreational pursuits are managed more casually.

Using either a standardized interview or a questionnaire to assess the Type A behavior pattern, many studies have supported the proposed link between this behavior and coronary heart disease. Table 14–3 presents a portion of a commonly used questionnaire for assessing Type A behavior. Friedman and Rosenman have reported data showing that Type A men are two and a half times more likely to develop heart disease than Type B men. In addition, Type As are more likely than Type Bs to suffer recurrent heart attacks.

The physiological basis for the greater coronary risk of Type A is still not clear, but Friedman and Rosenman suggest that the behavior leads to an excessive outpouring of certain hormones. These hor-

mones are known to increase the amount of fats circulating in the bloodstream, which in turn contribute to a narrowing of the blood vessels, making blockage more likely.

Can anything be done to modify Type A behavior? Probably, but research has only recently begun to address this important question. Whether inherited or learned (and most believe it is primarily learned), the Type A behavior pattern seems to be deeply ingrained. The Type A person has a very strong need to control his or her environment (Glass, 1977) and probably a strong, though often inhibited, need to argue, persuade, and otherwise try to help people who have not even requested aid (McClelland, 1979). It may be that this strong need to control is at the root of Type-A stress. Most of us realize, if reluctantly, that many events are out of our control. We cannot stop the rain, make the

The Type A individual is locked in a never-ending struggle to complete the greatest number of tasks in the shortest amount of time.

TABLE 14-3.
Sample Items from a Questionnaire
Used to Assess Type A Behavior

1. Do you ever have trouble finding time to get your hair cut or styled?
   A. Never
   B. Occasionally
   C. Almost always

2. When you are under pressure or stress, what do you usually do?
   A. Do something about it immediately
   B. Plan carefully before taking any action.

3. Ordinarily, how rapidly do you eat?
   A. I'm usually the first one finished
   B. I eat a little faster than average.
   C. I eat at about the same speed as most people.
   D. I eat more slowly than most people.

4. How often do you find yourself doing more than one thing at a time, such as working while eating, reading while dressing, or figuring out problems while driving?
   A. I do two things at once whenever practical.
   B. I do this only when I'm short of time.
   C. I rarely or never do more than one thing at a time.

5. When you listen to someone talking, and this person takes too long to come to the point, how often do you feel like hurrying the person along?
   A. Frequently
   B. Occasionally
   C. Almost never

6. Would people who know you well agree that you enjoy a "contest" (competition) and try hard to win?
   A. Definitely yes
   B. Probably yes
   C. Probably no
   D. Definitely no

Source: Jenkins et al., 1979.

subway run on time, or prevent a younger sister from using our new cassette tape player. It may be that the Type As are simply unwilling to admit that some things are naturally out of their control.

Psychoneuroimmunology

In recent years an interdisciplinary area called **psychoneuroimmunology** (Ader, 1981) has emerged. Research in this area is helping us to better under-

stand the connection between psychological factors—particularly stress—and disease. A strong immune system is important in combating the disease-carrying micro-organisms that cause infectious diseases such as colds. It also appears to be important in the development and progress of cancers. Researchers have found that distress weakens the immune system, making the body more susceptible to infectious diseases.

Stressors such as loss of a loved one, surgery, and sleep deprivation have been found to lower the responsiveness of the immune system. In most cases, however, the immune system eventually returns to a normal level of functioning. Short-term (acute) distress can alter the immune response by temporarily reducing the number of lymphocytes (cells which attack invading cells) or lowering the level of interferon (a substance believed to inhibit some cancers). Long-term (chronic) distress may permanently alter these disease-control mechanisms as well as cause damage to tissues that help the immune system to function efficiently.

Current research is focusing on how stress alters immune functioning. It has been suggested that the adrenal hormones of adrenalin, noradrenalin, and cortisol are the primary causes of immunosuppression (Stein, 1983). If this is true, Frankenhauser's Effort-Distress Model may be very important in helping us explain the link between stress and disease.

REVIEW QUESTIONS

17. The clearest connection between stress, coping, and disease can be seen in the connection between heart disease and the behavior pattern known as _____ _____ .

18. Current research is focusing on how stress lowers the responsiveness of the _____ system, thus making us more susceptible to infectious disease.

Answers: 17. Type A 18. immune

Psychoneuroimmunology. Interdisciplinary area of research that studies the connection between psychological factors and disease.

■ SUMMARY

1. A stimulus definition of stress assumes that *stressors* are inherent in the environment. Response definitions emphasize psychological and physiological reactions to stressors. According to the interactional definition, stress is determined not solely by the situation but also by the person's perception of the situation as stressful. Also, the degree of stress will depend to some extent on the person's perception of his or her capabilities to cope with the situation's demands.

2. One potentially stressful situation is *crowding*. In addition to *density*, other variables must be present for a crowding situation to become stressful: information overload, behavioral interference, or loss of personal control. Noise is particularly stressful when it is unpredictable and uncontrollable. Both positive and negative life events, or any event that requires a significant change in circumstances, can be stressful and can increase vulnerability to health problems. Daily hassles also increase stress.

3. The body's physiological response to stress is regulated by the endocrine system. One example of how this system works is the adrenal glands on the kidneys. These glands mobilize our resources under stress. From Frankenhauser's studies of humans under different combinations of effort and distress, she concluded that the physiological response to stress is not a simple one. She described a model with three different patterns of responses: effort without distress, effort with distress, and distress without effort.

4. The effects of stress can be reduced through social support, or a relationship with others that is characterized by a sense of acceptance and love and a willingness to give assistance. On the other hand, social rejection can increase levels of felt stress.

5. Some people seem to seek stress, while others try to avoid it. The two factors that determine these individual differences in response to stress are a belief about whether one's skills are sufficient to cope with demands, and perceived control, or people's belief about whether or not the situation is within their control.

6. *Coping* is the process of managing stress. Learning stress-management skills helps people to reduce undesirable stress and to prevent and treat stress-related symptoms and diseases. Methods of changing the environment to reduce stress can include developing social supports, regulating diet, not smoking cigarettes, and exercising.

7. *Defense mechanisms* are common cognitive processes for managing emotional reactions to stress through altering the perception of the stressor; two examples discussed in the text are *denial* and *intellectualization*. Stress inoculation training can also reduce stress. Altering biological responses to stress can involve progressive relaxation, meditation, and *biofeedback*.

8. Stress and illness appear to be related. One example is the fact that Type A people—those with intense striving for achievement, competitiveness, impatience, and excessive drive and hostility—are particularly vulnerable to coronary heart disease.

■ ANSWERING QUESTIONS FOR THOUGHT

1. People do not always suffer from crowding in highly dense situations—other elements besides density must be present in order to produce the feeling of crowding. These other elements include information overload, behavioral interference, or the loss of personal control.

2. Major life events occur infrequently, while smaller hassles occur every day. Thus, over a year's time, the smaller hassles may amount to more cumulative stress than one or two major life events and have the same long-term effect on health.

3. As noted in the chapter, cognitive effects of stress are an inability to make decisions, problems in concentration, lapses in memory, and overreaction to criticism. These reactions to stress have been noted on the job and in school. The effects of stress on intellectual functioning have been explained on the job by the multiple screen model, in which various screens (such as stress with co-workers or with the boss) get in the way of a job performance.

4. Denial is one of the defense mechanisms discussed in the text; it helps us protect ourselves against the emotional consequences of stress. Denial can be helpful in maintaining a sense of hope under

threatening conditions when no direct action is possible. However, if it keeps us from dealing directly with a problem when we are able to, then it becomes a maladaptive reaction.

5. Proper nutrition is very important in combating the effects of stress. For example, alcohol and refined white sugar deplete the body of B vitamins, which are essential in managing stress. Heavy coffee drinking or smoking induce the "fight or flight" body response, releasing fats in the blood and depleting the body of vitamin B.

Abnormal Psychology

QUESTIONS FOR THOUGHT

1. Can you diagnose a mental disorder the way a physician diagnoses a physical illness?
2. Why do people have fears of things like heights, elevators, or snakes, even though they've never had a bad experience involving them?
3. Why are college students particularly vulnerable to some types of depression?
4. What are delusions? What are they a symptom of?
5. What does it mean to be paranoid?
6. Does severe depression commonly end in suicide?

The answers to these questions are at the end of the chapter.

In Chapter 14, we considered some of the stresses that are part of human life. These stresses—death of a loved one, illness, marital discord, promotion to a more demanding job—cause emotional reactions and often lead to temporary changes in behavior. We might become quiet, sullen, loud, forgetful, or impulsive for a while, but eventually our behavior returns to normal. In this chapter, we will deal with abnormalities of a more persistent and troubling nature. These abnormalities may involve unusual thoughts, unusual behaviors, or both. Very often they lead to the involvement of a clinical psychologist or psychiatrist.

As you will see shortly, there is a wide range of abnormal behavior to consider. Generally speaking, this range is divided into two classes of problems. The first class is milder and often treated on an outpatient basis (treatment that seldom involves hospitalization). The second class of problems is more serious and disruptive and often involves treatment in an institutional setting, such as a psychiatric hospital. In this chapter, we will be considering both classes of problems.

■ A WORD OF CAUTION ABOUT SELF-DIAGNOSIS

One of the interesting aspects of an introductory psychology course is being able to notice and explain your own behavior from examples and principles provided in class and in your text. You now understand why you can hear your name spoken in a conversation across the room, why large objects seem to move more slowly than small objects, and why you still get nervous at the dentist's office. Similarly, as we examine some abnormal behavior patterns in this chapter, you might see aspects of your own behavior. Of course, this is true for each of us; we all have our unusual or extreme behaviors. The important difference between your unusual behavior and the abnormal patterns described here is that your behavior probably does not cause any significant problem for you or for others around you. In addition, some of the things that you identify as unusual behavior on your part are transient—they appear and disappear quickly. Finally, the fact that you recognize instances of "abnormal" behavior in yourself makes you an unlikely candidate for concern. The point is that you should not be overly concerned if you see some examples of problems here that strike close to home. Truly abnormal behavior is persistent, troubling, and frequently ignored or denied.

■ MODELS OF ABNORMAL BEHAVIOR

The first issue that must be addressed in a chapter on abnormal behavior is how we will define "abnormal." There is no single, universally accepted definition of abnormal behavior; its meaning changes from one era to another and even from one culture to another. Nevertheless, there are four basic models that can be used to define "abnormal." Each has its advantages and disadvantages.

The Statistical Model

One commonly used statistic is the mean or "average"; it is useful for making comparisons. We might use the concept of an "average" person to define abnormality, with "average" meaning "in the normal range." In these terms, anyone who departs significantly from the average on one or more aspects of behavior is considered abnormal. The advantage of the statistical definition is that it is specific and can be communicated easily; the disadvantage is that it ends up including just about everyone. In the chapter on personality, it was suggested that each of us is unique in some way—each of us has a unique personality. That being the case, each of us probably is significantly above or below average on one or more values. You may be extremely intelligent; someone else may be extremely anxious; the woman down the street may be exceptionally funny. Under this definition, we are all abnormal.

The Medical Model

The medical model follows from the nineteenth-century approach of seeing abnormal behavior as symptomatic of an underlying disease—as some type of "mental illness."

There are some advantages to the medical model. In the first place, it recognizes the concept of sickness and the need for appropriate treatment. Another advantage is that it encourages careful examination and diagnosis before treatment. The medical model has led to the classification of symptoms and the naming of mental disorders. But there are also disadvantages to this model. The most serious of these is that nonphysical causes are harder to detect than physical causes. When a person goes to a doctor complaining of aches, pains, and sluggishness, the doctor can collect information on blood pressure, body temperature, and muscle tone. There are no equivalent physical measures that can be taken from someone complaining of tension or fear and who is behaving in a bizarre manner. Being labeled "sick" might also discourage people from taking any personal responsibility for behavior or behavior change, since they might then feel it's beyond their ability to cope with it because it is due to an illness they have "caught." Finally, the medical model might encourage the use of drugs when nonphysical therapies might be more appropriate.

The Cultural Model

This definition of abnormal behavior depends heavily on your particular culture. For example, homosexuality was not only tolerated but encouraged in ancient Greece. However, there are many groups in Western society that consider homosexuality of any kind abnormal.

The advantage of the cultural model of abnormal behavior is that the context of behavior is taken into account. It also acknowledges that abnormal behavior is at times a relative issue; for example, laughing out loud at the movies is "normal," but laughing out loud in the middle of a funeral service is not. The problem with this model is in the definition of "culture." Where are the boundaries drawn? The culture could be Western, American, urban, black, young, high school, or any combination.

The Adaptive Model

A recent point of view regarding the definition of abnormal behavior rests on the issues of coping and well-being. Coleman and his colleagues (Coleman et al., 1980) consider normal behavior as behavior that fosters the well-being of the individual and the group. Using this definition, many behaviors seen as "normal" by other models would here be seen as abnormal. For example, Coleman suggests that conforming behavior, considered normal in some models, can be maladaptive or harmful to both the individual and the group and thus be abnormal in the adaptive model. Two vivid examples of this are the Nazi war crimes and the My Lai massacre. The overriding question for the adaptive model is whether or not the person is coping adequately with his or her environment. Recently, there has been a great deal of discussion about the coping abilities of "street people." In the dead of winter, they can be found sleeping in doorways, in cardboard boxes, or over steam or subway grates. One line of thought holds that such people are mentally ill and should be placed in overnight shelters whether they want to go in those shelters or not. The opposing line of thought is that they are capable of coping with their environment and should not be deprived of the right to decide where they will spend the night. The adaptive model would suggest that at least some of these people should not be considered abnormal simply because they choose to sleep on the streets.

■ DIAGNOSING ABNORMAL BEHAVIOR

In the case of physical illness, diagnosis is the first step toward a cure. A patient reports his or her symptoms, the physician gathers various data (such as blood pressure, temperature, and reports of pain in response to probing), diagnoses (that is, identifies) the cause of the symptoms, and selects a method of treatment that has proven effective in treating that particular problem in the past. The treatment may involve a change in diet, medicine, surgery, or simply bed rest.

In dealing with abnormal behavior, the problem is somewhat more complicated. In the first place,

as was suggested above, there are seldom any clear-cut physiological causes for particular types of abnormal behavior. In fact, some psychologists (the behaviorists) believe that the symptoms *are* the problem. They believe that people act abnormally as a result of being reinforced for acting that way.

There is another problem with diagnosing abnormal behavior. When the physician gathers data, there is usually no disagreement or ambiguity about the meaning of those data. When information about temperature is required, a thermometer is used. Can you imagine the problems if each physician used a different method of gathering temperature data? One doctor might use the traditional thermometer, a second might place his or her fingers on the forehead of the patient. Based on the methods of

The adaptive model looks at whether or not the person is coping adequately with his or her environment. This model would suggest that at least some homeless people are coping adequately and should not be considered abnormal because they choose to sleep on the streets.

measurement used, we might justifiably expect some differences of opinion with respect to whether a patient had a temperature or not.

Body temperature is a reasonably well-understood mechanism. Physicians know something about the acceptable limits of body temperature. For adults, temperatures below 88°F and above 104°F can cause serious problems. These problems can be described and have been documented. To use the terms of measurement, under certain circumstances (when accompanied by other symptoms) body temperature is a valid measure of some biological condition of the person. In addition, when a standard measuring device is used (such as a thermometer), it is also a reliable measure of the biological condition. If temperature is taken once and then again in five minutes, it will most likely be the same.

Related problems in the diagnosis of abnormal behavior are issues of reliability and validity, which we considered in the personality chapter. Three different people looking at the same behavior might describe it in three completely different ways. Often, this is a result of the different theoretical viewpoints of the observers. For example, in Table 15–1 look at the phrases used to describe an interviewee who had been identified as a "patient" to both a behavior therapist and a psychodynamic therapist. The same behavior receives dramatically different descriptions. In other words, there is a difference of opinion about what the behavior represents—this raises questions about the validity of the observation.

From one perspective, the problems of the psychologist seem considerably greater than those of the physician. Reliability and validity of diagnostic devices or categories can be questioned. In another respect, however, the physician and psychologist have similar problems. When abnormal behavior occurs, the psychologist must determine why it has appeared and how to treat it. The same problem confronts the physician who successfully (i.e, in a valid and reliable manner) assesses the temperature of a patient. *Why* does she have a temperature of 103° and how should it be treated?

The Effect of Labeling

In Table 15–1 you saw that a difference in orientation led to a difference in interpretation. In that particular study, the "patient" was not a patient at all but a confederate in the experiment. In fact, in

TABLE 15-1.
Interviewee Labeled as "Patient"

Behavior Therapists	Psychodynamic Therapists
"Relatively bright"	"Considerable hostility, repressed or channeled"
"Responsible"	"Tight defensive person"
"Easy manner of speaking"	"Conflict over homosexuality"

Based on Langer and Abelson, 1974.

another phase of that study, different behavior therapists and psychodynamic therapists saw the same videotaped interview, but this time were told that the individual was applying for a job. Look at the agreement in descriptions between the two observers in Table 15–2, and compare them with the ones in Table 15–1. In addition to the differences in interpretation that might have occurred as a result of the differences in orientation of the therapists, it seems as if there was also a difference as a result of the label "patient" or "job applicant."

Rosenhan (1973) carried out a dramatic field study that showed similar effects of labeling. As part of the study, a number of psychology students and mental-health professionals had themselves admitted to various mental hospitals by complaining of hearing "voices" saying words like *hollow* and *thud*. This was the *only* symptom that they reported. They wanted to see how long it would take to get out of the hospitals once they had been admitted. In the first interviews, the new "patients" accurately reported their past behavior and family history, although they did not reveal anything about their involvement in the study or their status as psychology students or professionals. Almost all the

TABLE 15-2.
Interviewee Labeled as "Job Applicant"

Behavior Therapists	Psychodynamic Therapists
"Realistic"	"Attractive"
"Pleasant"	"Conventional looking"
"Fairly sincere"	"Straightforward"

Based on Langer and Abelson, 1974.

"patients" were diagnosed as schizophrenic. Immediately after being admitted to the hospital, the fake patients stopped talking about the voices and acted as normal as possible (although there was some apprehension and anxiety about being in this new and somewhat frightening environment). They then concentrated on getting out of the hospital. Their average stay was 19 days before they were released. In some cases, it was 1½ months before the patient was discharged. During their stay, almost everything the "patients" did was interpreted in light of their being diagnosed as schizophrenics. For example, when one "patient" was being interviewed by a psychiatrist, he decided to keep notes. The psychiatrist assured the "patient" in a soothing tone that notes were unnecessary—the psychiatrist would remind the "patient" of anything that he forgot (Ullman and Krasner, 1975). Eventually, every "patient" was released but was characterized as still having schizophrenia, which was dormant (or in remission) for the time being. No one on the hospital staff suspected that the patients were fakes. Interestingly enough, several genuine patients recognized the deception. This suggests that the perceptions of the staff were distorted by the label.

In a follow-up phase of the study, Rosenhan warned a hospital psychiatric staff that a number of phony patients would try to have themselves admitted to the hospital in the following 3 months. During that period, 193 patients were admitted. Of that number, 41 were identified by at least one member of the psychiatric staff as a fake patient, and 19 were suspected of being phony by a psychiatrist and one other staff member. None of the patients was a fake. The work of Rosenhan points to clear problems in diagnosis and labeling.

It would be unfair to conclude, however, that staff in mental hospitals are incompetent at diagnosis. There were some obvious limitations to Rosenhan's study. In the first place, the admitting staff in a psychiatric institution has no reason to suspect that a person asking to be admitted for a particular problem is telling a lie. Under the same circumstances, you and I might have admitted Rosenhan's colleagues. Another weakness of the study was the choice of symptom—the auditory hallucination. This is one of the easiest of symptoms to fake. Other symptoms—such as anxiety, compulsive behaviors, or strange speech patterns—are not as easy to mimic; had one of these other symptoms

been used, the results might have been very different. In spite of these limitations, Rosenhan's study did point out a problem in diagnosis. At the time when the study was done, the tools available to help in diagnosis were not as sophisticated as they are now. (In the next section, you will read about the system that is currently used for diagnosis.) Rosenhan's experimenters might not have been admitted to the hospital if the study were done today. Nevertheless, these results still apply to the problem of labeling. Once a diagnosis has been made and a disorder has been identified, it may be difficult for the patient to shake that label.

The DSM-III

As was pointed out in the earlier example of the physician taking body temperature, the use of a standardized measuring and labeling instrument, called a thermometer, makes for valid and reliable measurement. For many years, it was suspected that the problems with the validity and reliability of abnormal-behavior diagnosis could be traced to the fact that the labeling system then in use was not adequate. In 1952, the American Psychiatric Association published a manual to be used for diagnosing abnormal behavior. The manual was called the **Diagnostic and Statistical Manual,** or **DSM** for short. In 1969 this manual was revised as the *DSM-II*. In 1980 the most recent version, called the *DSM-III*, was published by the American Psychiatric Association. It is considerably more detailed than its predecessors, the *DSM* and the *DSM-II*. It includes diagnostic categories based primarily on behaviors shown by the individual, rather than on categories based on some underlying cause or disease. There are, however, provisions for information beyond just behavioral data.

When the *DSM-III* system is used to diagnose or classify, the person is actually considered on five different dimensions or aspects (called *axes* in the *DSM-III* system). The first two axes are the most important, since they really deal with the actual behavior in question. Axis I concentrates on the par-

---

Diagnostic and statistical manual (DSM). A manual used by clinicians for diagnosing abnormal behavior; the third edition was published in 1980 by the American Psychiatric Association.

TABLE 15-3.
Selected categories of DSM-III

Category	General Description	Example of Specific Disorder
1. Organic mental disorder	Mental or behavioral abnormalities associated with dysfunction of the brain, either temporarily or permanently.	Senile dementia
2. Substance use disorder	Undesirable behavioral changes because of the effect of drugs on the central nervous system.	Alcoholism Marijuana abuse or dependence
3. Schizophrenic disorders	Serious alterations of thought and behavior involving a split from reality.	Paranoid schizophrenic reaction
4. Affective disorders	Pervasive mood disturbances that affect one's life as a whole.	Depression
5. Anxiety disorders	Disorders reflecting the individual's attempts to cope with intense anxiety.	Phobias Obsessive-compulsive disorder
6. Factitious disorders	Physical or psychological symptoms willfully produced by patient, often involving deceit.	Factitious disorder with psychological symptom
7. Somatoform disorders	Characterized by physical symptoms with no known physical cause, often resulting from stress.	Conversion disorder
8. Dissociative disorders	Characterized by a split in consciousness or identity.	Multiple Personality
9. Personality disorders	Rigid or maladaptive patterns of behavior.	Antisocial Personality
10. Psychosexual disorders	Disturbances of sexual identity or behavior.	Exhibitionism Transvestism
11. Disorders usually arising in childhood or adolescence	Disorders which first manifest themselves at this stage of development	Hyperactivity Mental retardation
12. Disorders of impulse control	Difficulties with control of one's emotions or behavior	Kleptomania Pathological gambling

ticular behavior that is causing the problem. Table 15–3 presents examples of the major categories of disorders found in the *DSM-III.*

Axis II deals with habitual or inflexible ways of dealing with a broad range of situations. Axis II is more closely related to what we think of as consistent aspects of the personality, rather than to temporary responses or responses that occur only in certain situations. This is an important distinction, since a behavioral problem could be either a manifestation of some stable personality characteristic or a result of some specific circumstance or situation. By evaluating a person on both Axis I and Axis II, this critical distinction can be made.

Axis III provides an opportunity to mention any physical problems that may be related to the abnormal behavior. Examples of relevent information on this axis would include nutritional deficiencies, neurological disorders, or recent illnesses and physical diseases. This axis is included so that any physiological factors that have an influence on the behavior in question will be considered. In this way, the various axes make sure that all potentially relevant information is considered.

Axis IV includes recent life events that might be related to the behavior in question, and also involves a rating of how stressful these events might have been to the person. Events that would be included in this category are divorce, death of a loved one, and retirement or being laid off from work. These events are "major," as we saw in the chapter on stress, and there is every reason to believe that any one of them might be related to the behavioral problem. The diagnostician is supposed to consider the type of events that occurred in the person's life in the past year and assign a rating on the basis of an estimation of the stress the person experienced. Table 15–4 shows the Axis IV rating scale.

Axis V represents a judgment about how effectively the person has been functioning in the past year. This would include a wide variety of settings including school, work, and other social environments. Table 15–5 shows the Axis V rating scale.

As you can see, the *DSM-III* provides a detailed framework for collecting most of the relevant information about a pattern of abnormal behavior. This should reduce the types of errors and biases in classification that were found to exist by Rosenhan. The *DSM-III* provides clear rules for diagnosis,

TABLE 15-4.
Axis IV: Scale for Rating Severity of Psychosocial Stressors.*

1	None—no apparent psychosocial stressor.
2	Minimal—minor violation of the law; small bank loan.
3	Mild—argument with neighbor; change in work hours.
4	Moderate—new career; death of close friend; pregnancy.
5	Severe—serious illness in self or family; major financial loss; marital separation; birth of child.
6	Extreme—death of close relative; divorce.
7	Catastrophic—concentration camp experience; devastating natural disaster.
0	Unspecified—no information, or not applicable.

*Compare this scale with the Life-Change Units Scale presented in Chapter 14.
Adapted from American Psychiatric Association (1980), p. 27.

TABLE 15-5:   Axis V: Scale for Rating Level of Functioning.

Levels	Adult examples
1 SUPERIOR—Unusually effective functioning in social relations, occupational functioning, and use of leisure time.	Single parent living in deteriorating neighborhood takes excellent care of children and home, has warm relations with friends, and finds time for pursuit of hobby.
2 VERY GOOD—Better than average functioning in social relations, occupational functioning, and use of leisure time.	A 65-year-old retired widower does some volunteer work, often sees old friends, and pursues hobbies.
3 GOOD—No more than slight impairment in either social or occupational functioning.	A woman with many friends functions extremely well at a difficult job, but says "the strain is too much."
4 FAIR—Moderate impairment in either social relations or occupational functioning, or some impairment in both.	A lawyer has trouble carrying through assignments; has several acquaintances, but hardly any close friends.
5 POOR—Marked impairment in either social relations or occupational functioning, or moderate impairment in both.	A man with one or two friends has trouble keeping a job for more than a few weeks.
6 VERY POOR—Marked impairment in both social relations and occupational functioning.	A woman is unable to do any of her housework and has violent outbursts toward family and neighbors.
7 GROSSLY IMPAIRED—Gross impairment in virtually all areas of functioning.	An elderly man needs supervision to maintain minimal personal hygiene and is usually incoherent.
0 UNSPECIFIED	No information.

Adapted from American Psychiatric Association (1980), pp. 29–30.

rather than general descriptions to be used at the discretion of the person performing the diagnosis.

REVIEW QUESTIONS

1. Match the following models of abnormal behavior with the correct description:

___ statistical model

A. emphasizes the context in which behavior occurs.

___ medical model

B. anyone who departs from the average in behavior is considered abnormal.

___ cultural model

C. abnormal behavior is an illness; emphasizes examination and diagnosis before treatment.

___ adaptive model

D. abnormal behavior means the person is not coping well with the environment; involves well-being of the group as well as the individual.

2. In 1980 the American Psychiatric Association issued a manual to be used for diagnosing abnormal behavior. It is commonly called _____ , and lists the various categories and circumstances to be taken into account in diagnosing abnormal behavior.

3. Match the following dimensions of *DSM-III* with the correct definition:

___ Axis I

A. recent stressful life events that might relate to abnormal behavior.

___ Axis II

B. names of categories of behavior considered abnormal.

___ Axis III

C. judgment about how effectively a person has been functioning for the past year.

___ Axis IV

D. habitual ways of dealing with situations.

___ Axis V

E. physical problems connected with abnormal behavior.

Answers: 1. statistical model, B; medical model, C; cultural model, A; adaptive model, D 2. *DSM-III* 3. Axis I, B; Axis II, D; Axis III, E; Axis IV, A; Axis V, C

■ A RECENT CONTROVERSY ABOUT DIAGNOSIS

Although the *DSM-III* has generally been seen as a major improvement over the *DSM-II*, it is clear that there is still room for improvement of diagnostic categories. As a result, the American Psychiatric Association has been in the process of preparing another revision of these diagnostic guidelines, the *DSM-III-R* (the R stands for "revised"). As part of this revision, over 200 changes and additions to diagnostic categories have been proposed. Several of the proposed changes have been branded as having an anti-woman bias (Fisher, 1986). The categories include the "premenstrual dysphoric disorder," the "sadistic personality disorder," and the "self-defeating personality disorder." It is charged that the introduction of these categories would stigmatize and endanger women from several perspectives. For example, the "premenstrual dysphoric disorder" might be used to label women who are experiencing pre-menstrual tension as mentally ill. Similarly, since the "self-defeating personality disorder" is partially defined by the tendency to remain involved in abusive relationships, this might imply that women beaten by their husbands are suffering from a form of mental illness. Finally, the "sadistic personality disorder" would address the problem of the rapist. It has been charged that this category of disorder would provide a tailor-made defense for the rapist, who would claim that he was mentally ill and not responsible for his actions. The opponents of this last category fear that such a "defense" would increase the frequency of rapes.

The final version of the *DSM-III-R* has recently been approved. The three disputed categories have been left in, although the "premenstrual dysphoric disorder" has been changed to the more technical label "periluteal phase dysphoric disorder." In an attempt at compromise, the committee responsible for the revision agreed to downplay these disputed disorders in contrast to the more serious disorders of depression and schizophrenia. This controversy helps to point out the problems of determining what is and what is not a "disorder."

These are only a few of the changes represented by the *DSM-III-R*. It is likely that revisions will now occur with more regularity than has been true in the past.

Specific Categories of Moderate Disorders

In the following sections, using the *DSM-III* as a guide, we will consider some patterns of abnormal behavior. For the most part, we will use the major categories of the *DSM-III* for the discussion, but on a few occasions we will discuss an area that relates to a particular problem (such as *anorexia nervosa*) or complaint (such as worry) even though that problem is just one example of a larger diagnostic category. As was indicated early in this chapter, our discussion of abnormal behavior will be divided into those that are moderate and do not usually require hospitalization and those that are more severe. The following section will discuss those patterns that fall in the moderate category.

■ ANXIETY DISORDERS

Anxiety State

Before the introduction of the *DMS-III*, abnormal behavior was usually classified as either neurotic or psychotic. In this scheme, neurotic behaviors were considered less serious or severe; psychotic disturbances were thought to be more severe, since the person often loses contact with reality. The *DSM-III* has abandoned the term *neurosis*. Now the focus is on a more exact list of symptoms. Many of the mild disorders are classified as **anxiety disorders.**

Anxiety is a generally unpleasant feeling that something bad is about to happen. Of course, there are real reasons for fear. If a bus is about to run you down, if you are about to undergo a serious operation, or if someone is holding a knife to your throat and asking for money, you have every reason to be afraid. Anxiety states involve a fear that is inappropriate or excessive given the nature of the external threat.

As we discussed in Chapter 12, anxiety involves a state of heightened arousal. The most extreme variation of this state of heightened arousal is called

TABLE 15-6.
Ten Most Common Symptoms in Anxiety Disorders*

Symptom	Patients	Controls
Palpitation	97	9
Tires easily	95	19
Breathlessness	90	13
Nervousness	88	27
Chest pain	85	10
Sighing	79	16
Dizziness	78	16
Faintness	70	12
Apprehension	61	3
Headache	58	26

*Figures indicate the percentage of patients diagnosed as anxiety disorders and control subjects who showed the symptoms. *Based on Marks and Lader, 1973.*

panic. The *DSM-III* describes panic as involving several of the following symptoms: shortness of breath, rapid heartbeat, chest pains, a choking sensation, dizziness, tingling hands or feet, profuse sweating, trembling, and the sensation of losing control over actions.

Anxiety is usually associated with one or more unpleasant physical symptoms. Table 15–6 illustrates some common physical symptoms of anxiety. The difference between these reactions and what was just described as panic is only in number and severity. The range of physical reactions is identical for anxiety and panic. The person often engages in a particular action (operant response) in order to escape these symptoms.

We will now examine some types of disorders that represent different responses to anxiety.

Phobic Disorders

Often, anxiety has a specific focus. When irrational anxiety is connected to a particular person, object, or situation, it is called a **phobia.** There are long lists

---

Anxiety disorders. A category of the *DSM-III* that includes moderate disorders such as phobias and obsessive-compulsive disorders.
Anxiety. A vague, unpleasant feeling that something bad is about to happen.

Panic. An extreme state of heightened anxiety and arousal.
Phobia. Fear of a specific object, event, or situation, such as snakes or heights; the fear is out of proportion to the danger involved.

CASE STUDY OF A PHOBIC

Unlike most New Yorkers, I am not afraid of falling objects. I am afraid of becoming one. I am a phobic. When I moved to New York from San Francisco in 1977, I knew that living here would be harder for me than most newcomers. For almost ten years now, severe height phobias have made it impossible for me to do some things unescorted—cross high bridges, go above the fourth floor, travel on elevated highways—without experiencing acute, paralyzing panic. . . .

My phobias began when I was a reporter for the San Francisco *Examiner* and was going through a series of family, job, and love problems. I had a walking nervous breakdown in which I experienced deep depression, fluctuating despair, and frequent outbursts of panic during which I thought I would start screaming. I started analysis four days a week, took Valium, and saturated myself in introspection. . . .

Then, one day about a month later, driving my normal route from my apartment in Berkeley to my job in San Francisco, I stopped at a tollbooth on the Bay Bridge and suddenly froze. For the first time, I really looked at the bridge, and I felt completely out of control: What if I crashed and fell? What if the bridge collapsed? What if I got out of my car and jumped? I was seized with a panic so strong I couldn't breathe. I was literally paralyzed with fright. . . .

I woke up in the passageway that runs beneath the tollbooths. I had passed out and been carried down there by an attendant. I gathered my strength, drove back home, and boarded the bus for work. I felt that nothing could happen to me in a bus full of people.

That day I was to interview Vice-President Gerald Ford in his suite on the top floor of the St. Francis Hotel. Everything went fine until the vice-president decided to show me the terrace. Suddenly, it occurred to me that I could panic and jump off skyscrapers as well as off bridges. For the second time in my life, I felt real fear.

I had to excuse myself and go to the bathroom to down some Valium and do breathing exercises. As I stood there taking deep breaths, I realized that strangely enough at that moment I felt no anxiety about the rest of my frazzled and confusing life. I suddenly understood exactly what I had done to myself: Because I found the floating anxiety about my life too devastating to deal with, I had localized it. My phobias now contained my overall fears, but they also nearly ruled my life.

Nothing has really changed since that day—despite my best efforts. I've spent years in psychoanalysis. I've devoured all available literature on phobias and tried a great variety of treatments. . . .

But for now, I have accepted that, for whatever reason, this is the way I handle stress—or don't handle it. And I have not allowed my weakness to hold me down. . . .

Reluctantly, I brought this emotional baggage here with me, and I decided to look at life in New York as a series of phobic challenges. I devised strategies that have allowed me to live and grow here—and for the most part they have worked.

I have committed to memory the window types of a vast number of buildings: which ones are hermetically sealed (and safer) and which ones can be opened (and leaped from). I have formulated intricate plans to get around town and out to the airports without crossing bridges, taking expressways, or going on the subway (I'm afraid I might leap onto the third rail). I have been able to find most important services—doctors, lawyers, shopping—on low floors, and when it is absolutely necessary to be above fourth-floor level, I bring along a large, strong person who can hold me back if I try to jump. I have never let my phobias interfere with my ability to do a good job, develop close friendships, and enjoy life. I just have to work a little harder at all three.

If you have to be phobic, there's no better place to live than New York. The city is filled with other phobics. I have met performers afraid to perform, people terrified of heights or open spaces (including those who are so scared they cannot leave their apartments), people afraid of such things as spiders, straight edges on buildings, radiator steam, or showers, and one woman who freezes if a pigeon comes near her. I talk often with my fellow phobics in the hope that we can help one another.

(From "Phobic in New York," by Susan Berman, *New York Magazine*, January 24, 1983.)

of phobias that describe irrational fears of everything from snakes to classrooms. Since it is likely that phobias are based on learned associations, there are as many potential phobias as there are objects. Keep in mind that phobias involve a feeling of anxiety that is tied to a specific stimulus (person or object) and that is out of proportion to the danger represented by that stimulus. Phobic reactions are particularly troublesome, since they often lead to operant responses. Consider the person described in the case study of a phobic. This woman has developed a rather bizarre and elaborate style of behavior in order to cope with the many anxieties she experiences because of her environment.

Obsessive-Compulsive Disorders

Anxiety can also be associated with both thoughts and actions. **Obsessions** are persistent thoughts that cause anxiety. A common obsession is the impulse to jump off a high building. **Obsessive fears** are persistent thoughts that you will do something wrong or dangerous. For example, you may be overly concerned about picking up some disease from glasses in restaurants. **Obsessive images** are persistent imagined scenes. Parents may be terrified by a recurring image of their child being hit by a car; travellers often have images of their airplane crashing on take-off or landing.

Compulsions are not thoughts; they are behaviors. The behavior occurs over and over again and is vaguely directed toward relieving anxiety. Davison and Neale (1982, p. 173) describe a patient who washed her hands 500 times each day. Even though this constant washing led to painful sores, she could not stop it. She was desperately afraid of germs, and this was her way of temporarily relieving that anxiety. Another example of a compulsion that is related to an obsession is checking on the alarm-clock. Some people might lie in bed all night worrying about whether the alarm had been set while others get up a dozen or more times to check

the alarm button. Years ago, there was a tennis player known as "the tapper." He became very anxious if he could not tap his opponent on a part of the body as they changed sides on the odd games. He always arranged to brush or touch his opponent. This compulsion became known after a while and his opponents made it increasingly difficult for him to touch them. They would start toward the referee's chair on the change of side, and after "the tapper" had committed himself in the same direction they would turn and cross on the other side of the net. They often used the referee chair as an obstacle as well. Eventually, the ritual began to take on the appearance of a bizarre game of tag, with "the tapper" pursuing his opponent around the net and the referee's chair. His opponents were well aware of the effect of this compulsion on his game and took full advantage of it.

As you can see from the examples above, obsessions need not involve compulsions, but compulsions are usually responses to obsessions of one kind or another.

Post-Traumatic Stress Disorder

Often, an event or situation in the environment is so stressful or **traumatic** that it leaves a state of anxiety in its aftermath. If this anxiety lasts for a short period of time after the event, it is called **acute distress**. If it persists for a long period of time (more than 6 months), it is called **chronic distress**. The most significant event in the lives of many young men in the 1960s and 1970s was the Vietnam War. They saw friends killed and wounded before their eyes. Many of those young men came home to find that the minor stresses of everyday life were almost unbearable, causing chronic anxiety. Just driving down a highway was an ordeal.

There are many events in the course of a lifetime that might result in extreme stress levels. In addition to wars and nuclear accidents, there are more common but equally stressful catastrophes such as

---

Obsessions. Persistent thoughts that cause anxiety.
Obsessive fears. A type of obsession that involves persistent thoughts about doing something wrong or dangerous.
Obsessive images. A type of obsession that involves persistent imagined scenes.
Compulsions. Actions that a person repeats over and over again—are vaguely directed toward relieving anxiety.

Traumatic. Extremely painful or upsetting.
Acute distress. Anxiety that lasts for a short period of time after a stressful event.
Chronic distress. Anxiety that persists for a long period of time after a stressful event.

floods, fires, plane crashes, and automobile accidents. The event can be on a smaller scale (such as being mugged or raped), affecting only one person, and still produce post-traumatic stress disorders.

Explanations of Anxiety Disorders

We have considered several types of anxiety, ranging from the generalized anxiety state to very specific conditions associated with phobic objects, or fear-including situations accompanying worry. In Chapter 13, it was pointed out that most theories of personality include explanations of abnormal behavior. Freudian theory suggests that inner conflict involving the id is critical to understanding abnormalities. The humanistic propositions of Rogers suggest that inconsistency between self-image and behavior is the cause of abnormal behavior. Learning theorists look to the environment for clues about which reinforcers might be operating to maintain the abnormal behavior. In the following two sections, we will consider two common approaches to understanding anxiety that leads to abnormalities of thought and/or action. We will apply Freud's psychodynamic theory as well as various aspects of learning theory. These applications are just examples and are not intended as preferred explanations. For comparative purposes, we will stick with two particular abnormal patterns—phobic and obsessive-compulsive behaviors.

Psychoanalytic Explanations. Freudians have specific explanations for the various forms that anxiety may take. The explanation for a phobia, for example, is different from the explanation for obsessive-compulsive states. Nevertheless, all explanations involve the three basic elements of Freudian theory: levels of consciousness (unconscious, preconscious, conscious); structures of personality (id, ego, superego); and psychosexual stages (oral, anal, phallic, latency, and genital).

Phobias are thought to result from unacceptable id processes. It is assumed that an ego process develops to control this id process. The ego process is then translated into a particular behavior, which helps to decrease the anxiety caused by the id process. As an example of this mechanism, Coleman and his colleagues (1980) suggest a husband who develops a great fear of lakes and swimming pools

as a result of persistent thoughts about drowning his wife. In this instance, the superego is opposed to the contemplated act of violence. Since this thought is more likely to intrude on some occasions than others (for example, when the man is actually near the water with his wife), a mechanism (such as fear of water) which is easily understood and accepted by others is a perfect way out. The man does not have to admit to a violent urge and he can avoid the occasions for that urge. The fear of the impulse is moved or displaced to the fear of a body of water in which the drowning might occur. In fact, the process of displacing fear from the real object of fear (the thought or impulse) to another object (a lake or swimming pool) is central to a Freudian explanation of phobias.

Another example of the application of Freudian theory to abnormal behavior is provided by obsessive-compulsive behavior. For instance, consider a person who is compulsively neat. A psychoanalytic explanation would suggest that the person has an unresolved conflict that arose in the anal stage of psychosexual development. As you may remember, anal activities provide erotic pleasures between the ages of $1\frac{1}{2}$ to 3 years. This is also the time when toilet training is generally begun. In effect, a conflict arises because the child is being prevented from engaging in a pleasurable activity. In Freud's theory, the unconscious is the storehouse for unresolved conflicts. Thus, the compulsively neat person is thought to have experienced unpleasant toilet training (perhaps the parents were harsh and punitive whenever the child soiled his or her clothes). As a result, the conflict between seeking pleasure and accepting control was never successfully resolved. As an adult, the desire to be "dirty," to soil and mess the environment, continues to intrude from its unconscious location. In defense, an ego process exactly opposite to that desire emerges—compulsive neatness. The person engages in this compulsive behavior to ward off the anxiety that the "impulse to soil" creates.

There are similar explanations for a great variety of abnormal behaviors. These explanations may emphasize one or another of the elements of the Freudian approach (such as a psychosexual stage or an ego process), or combinations of those elements, but the explanations will always be consistent with Freud's theory of personality and its development.

Learning Explanations. From the learning perspective, phobias can be explained in several ways. One popular concept is conditioned fear, much like Little Albert's fear of furry objects that developed as a result of associations with loud, startling noises. As you saw in Chapter 6, every time Little Albert reached for the rat, a steel bar was struck with a hammer, scaring the child. Shortly, a fear of the white rat and other white, furry objects developed. The conditioned fear was followed by an operant behavior—escape; Little Albert would crawl away from the furry object as fast as he could. One could describe the child's behavior as phobic—an inappropriate fear of a particular stimulus object. Even though we understand *why* Little Albert was afraid of white furry objects, the fact remains that the objects were not directly responsible for the discomfort—the steel bar and hammer actually produced the aversive sound. Thus, the person afraid of elevators may have once been trapped in a small, hot room and developed a fear of being trapped again. As a result, the person now actively avoids elevators—places where people occasionally get stuck for some period of time. This type of explanation can be used in some cases, but may not be enough to account for all phobic reactions. Many people who have frightening experiences do *not* develop phobic patterns, and, on the other hand, many people with phobias do not seem to have had one of those frightening experiences in their past or at least cannot recall them.

Another learning explanation of phobias is modeling or social learning. My father was a plumber and early in his training he received a severe electrical shock while working on some pipes that came in contact with an electrical source. From that point on, he avoided doing anything electrical, even around our own home. When anything electrical had to be done (such as changing a wall switch), he called an electrician. I spent many years working with him in the homes of his customers as well as in our own home. He would always caution me not to touch anything electrical, suggesting that I would be risking harm or death. This was often done while we watched an electrician perform the simple operations that we were avoiding! To this day, I have serious reservations about doing any electrical work in my own home.

As was the case with conditioned fear, some phobias can be explained through modeling or social learning experiences, but many cannot. The point is that phobias may develop in many different ways, but various aspects of learning theory can be applied as explanations that do not depend on the unconscious, the id, or a particular stage of psychosexual development (as does Freudian theory).

As we saw in the case of compulsive behaviors that accompany obsessions, the short-term effect of the compulsive behavior is to relieve the discomfort of anxiety. Washing one's hands relieves, at least temporarily, the fear of infection. Thus, the com-

One learning explanation for phobias is the idea of a conditioned fear followed by an operant response. A person who is afraid of heights may once have been trapped in a high place and now tries to avoid all high places.

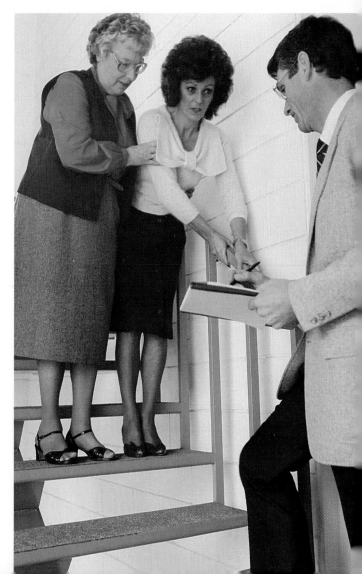

pulsive behavior can represent either an escape response, an avoidance response, or both. Regardless of which type of learning it represents, the behavior is controlled by negative reinforcement, since performing the act eliminates a negative state. As a result, the response of hand washing is strengthened—it is more likely to occur again. Studies have shown that people who engage in compulsive behaviors report less anxiety right after completing the compulsive act (Hodgson and Rachman, 1972) and, in fact, some of the psychophysiological symptoms that characterize anxiety are also reduced (Carr, 1971). Learning theory is attractive as a general approach to explaining the behavior that characterizes and results from anxiety.

REVIEW QUESTIONS

4. When anxiety has a specific focus, such as an object or a situation, it is called a _____ _____. This type of fear is basically rational/irrational in proportion to the danger involved.

5. If you stay awake all night because you're worrying about whether the alarm clock will go off tomorrow morning, you might be called _____ ; if you get out of bed 10 times during the night to check that the alarm is set, you might be called _____.

6. Often an event or situation is so stressful that is creates anxiety afterward. If that anxiety lasts only a short time it is called acute/chronic distress; if it is long-lasting it is called acute/chronic distress.

Answers: 4. phobic disorder; irrational 5. obsessive; compulsive 6. acute; chronic

---

■ DEPRESSION

Depression is a feeling or emotion that involves sadness, feelings of worthlessness, and even guilt. This feeling often is accompanied by a desire to be alone rather than with others, and by disturbances of appetite, sleep, and general activity (Davison and Neale, 1982). There are three types of depression.

One type might be characterized as "normal." It is the emotional state that appears following a major life event such as the loss of a loved one, or the failure to achieve a strongly-desired goal or objective (such as admission to a college or selection for an athletic team). This type of depression is clearly tied to an event in the environment—we usually know why we are depressed, we usually talk to others about it, and we take steps to get out of it. Grief or disappointment are words that are sometimes used to describe this type of depression. It disappears eventually, and there are seldom any lingering effects on state of mind.

Major depression, on the other hand, is a state in which people have given up trying. The view people have of themselves in this type of depression is uniformly negative; they feel that life is meaningless and that nothing can be done to improve the situation. This major form of depression frequently involves thoughts of suicide. Severely depressed people may be hospitalized for various periods and may be given potent drugs or electroshock treatments to normalize their moods.

There is a third type of depression that is more intense and longer lasting than disappointment, but less severe than the numbing state of major depression. It might be referred to as "the blues." A psychologist would call it a depression of mood. It may last anywhere from several days to several months. This type of depression can be quite unsettling; when in this state, people cannot come up with enough enthusiasm to begin or maintain important activities such as studying or working at a job. They may be unwilling to try anything new or risky, since they are convinced they will fail. They feel that they cannot do anything right and that they have certain negative qualities that will make it impossible for them ever to be successful. This description may sound familiar to you. This condition was alluded to when we discussed Seligman's research on learned helplessness in Chapter 7. Seligman suggests that depression in humans is like learned helplessness in animals, and may be the result of past learning experiences combined with beliefs about personal effectiveness.

Beck has studied this third type of depression in college students (Beck and Young, 1978). He estimated that in a 9-month period (the school year) of 1978, 78 percent of the students enrolled in college would suffer some symptoms of depression. In

1978, over 53 million people suffered from symptoms of depression.

Beck believes that college students are particularly vulnerable to this type of depression for several reasons. In the first place, they have left behind many family support systems to attend college; thus, their personal cheerleaders are not there to encourage them when obstacles arise. In addition, typical college students may have been among the brighter members of the graduating high-school class. They now find themselves among several thousand bright students; they are no longer the exception. There are also pressures of grades, career choice, and establishing loving relationships. According to Beck, these pressures can be overwhelming to students of this age and can lead to feelings of helplessness and powerlessness that characterize depression. As a result of these feelings, the student becomes increasingly withdrawn and self-critical, and apathetic about events in the environment. Even though Beck emphasizes the vulnerability of college students, the fact that over 53 million people may suffer from symptoms of depression at any given time suggests that depression is not exclusive to college students.

Beck maintains that this form of depression is a result of irrational thought: People "get down" on themselves, and a vicious cycle of negative thinking, emotions, and actions results. Depression of this sort can become a serious problem. As self-doubt and apathy grow, actual behavior becomes maladaptive—classes are cut, opportunities for social interaction and support are ignored, and realistic strategies for improving circumstances go unrecognized. Most of us will encounter one or more of these depressed episodes in our lifetime; this is why depression is often referred to as the "common cold" of abnormal behavior. Therapy in the early stages of depression can reduce the serious consequences, but since the problem is usually not recognized by outsiders, the depressed person has to be ready to take the first step.

■ SOMATOFORM DISORDERS

While shopping for Christmas presents, a 40-year-old man goes completely blind. Let's consider what in his background might have caused this to hap-

Beck believes that college students are particularly vulnerable to depression of mood. This may result from a combination of many pressures and inadequate social supports when starting college life.

pen. He had lived with a demanding wife and mother-in-law for twelve years. He had a history of eye problems and had lost partial vision in one eye as a result of an infection. Just prior to the onset of blindness, he was under heavy pressure from his wife and mother-in-law to perform various household duties. His blindness now made it impossible for him to be employed or to help around the house.

Depression. A feeling or emotion that involves sadness, feelings of worthlessness, and even guilt. There are several types of depression—major depression, a more serious disorder, is defined under affective disorders.

He received a disability pension from the army and financial support from the community and his family. There was no apparent physical cause for his blindness (Ullman and Krasner, 1975).

A 19-year-old woman loses her hearing. By way of background, there were many tensions in her family before the appearance of her problem. In particular, her mother would commonly "nag" her about behavior, dress, and other issues. There did not seem to be any obvious damage or degeneration of the auditory pathways or structures of the ear. Nevertheless, she did not seem to respond normally to loud noises. Careful testing, however, revealed that she did have muscle contraction to loud noises, which were similar to those that a person with normal hearing might have (Malmo, 1970).

Somatoform disorders are physical complaints that have no apparent physical or organic cause. The prefix *soma* means "body." In order to be considered abnormal, the symptoms must persist over an extended period of time. A headache that appears unexpectedly in the middle of the afternoon does not imply abnormality. However, a headache that appears regularly at the same time of day or before a particular activity (such as going to work), and defies diagnosis and treatment by a physician, may be an instance of a somatoform disorder. There are many different types of somatoform disorders. The two cases above are what is known as a **conversion disorder**. This is a very specific set of complaints that usually involves loss of a particular physical function. There is also a more general category called **somatization disorder**, which involves many varied complaints of distress such as blurred vision, pain, diarrhea, and other symptoms. No single set of symptoms invariably characterizes a somatization disorder. A diagnosis of a somatization disorder requires the presence of 12 or more physical complaints from a list of 37 in *DSM-III*.

There are certain characteristics that help distinguish conversion disorders from true physically based disorders. One common characteristic is that the person does not seem anxious about the disorder. The person seems to be "resigned" to the problem and does not mind talking about it. In fact, people often go on at great length about the disorder and may even suggest theories (almost always involving physical disease or injury) to account for it. This characteristic also helps distinguish somatoform dis-

orders from simple malingering, or conscious lying about symptoms. Malingerers are often very reluctant to talk about their symptoms since they may slip and give a "wrong" description or symptom. As you learned in the chapter on biology, behavior is very complex, and impairment might result from a malfunction of the nervous system, a disturbance of neurotransmitters, or a hormonal imbalance. Nevertheless; when none of these physical malfunctions can be detected, the diagnosis of a somatoform disorder is a reasonable possibility.

Explanations of Somatoform Disorders

There are two common frameworks that are applied in explaining these disorders. The first is the psychoanalytic orientation and the second is the learning model.

The Psychoanalytic Explanation. Historically, the psychoanalytic school was the first to recognize and confront the problem of somatoform disorders. As you may remember from chapter 13, Freud dealt with a number of patients who complained of hysterical symptoms. The term *conversion* was originally used by Freudians to describe the disorder. They believed that tension or anxiety was "converted" into a physical disorder. This was a socially acceptable way for dealing with anxiety—a reasonable compromise of the id, ego, and superego.

Since the psychoanalytic school places a great emphasis on psychosexual development, conflicts that arise during one or more of the psychosexual stages are seen as the root of somatoform disorders. The most likely stage in which these conflicts begin is the phallic stage, since the conflicts embodied in the Oedipal and Electra complexes represent the most significant potential obstacle to the healthy psychological development of the child. Less orthodox psychodynamic theories allow for causes other than conflicts of the phallic stage. In our earlier examples, a psychodynamic explanation might be that the ego develops a mechanism (blindness or deafness) to cope with the anxiety being caused by external stimuli (such as pressure from the wife and mother-in-law to help around the house in the case of the blind man, or demands for perfection from the mother of the deaf woman).

The Learning Explanation. It is relatively easy to demonstrate that physical symptoms have the potential of keeping punishment away. A good example of this mechanism is the child who becomes ill just before it's time to go to school for the first time. The child has been dreading the first day of school for some time. It will mean meeting certain standards of performance, playing with strange children, and leaving the comfort of home and mother. There is nothing abnormal about the child's feelings of apprehension and this apprehension may well lead to physical symptoms, such as a headache and an upset stomach. Not surprisingly, the combination of excitement, apprehension, and an enormous breakfast causes the child to vomit and the mother reluctantly keeps the child home from school that first day. This association is not lost on the child, and the foundation is laid for an operant response. The child may well try this strategy again at some future point. If being sick again results in being allowed to stay home, the mother is in for a difficult period until the child's response has been extinguished. The understanding and attention of both the mother and the teacher will be needed to accomplish this extinction.

An important thing to remember about somatoform disorders is that the person is actually experiencing the symptoms. The headache or stomach upset is real and not imagined. As a result, the accusation "It's all in your head" is misguided and not particularly helpful. From the learning perspective, this might even signal that the symptoms will have to be intensified. For short-term relief of the physical symptoms associated with somatoform disorders, learning approaches seem particularly suitable for the development of treatment strategies. For example, in the case of the illness-prone first grader, the strategy would be to clean up the vomit, clean up the child, and send the child off to school (assuming that there are no other symptoms of illness, of course).

■ DISSOCIATIVE DISORDERS

In Detroit, a man walks into a police station and asks for help. He is reasonably well dressed although disheveled. He seems confused and in distress. He is clearly worried that he has "lost his mind," since he cannot remember who he is or how he got to Detroit or to the police station. A physician examines him and can find no evidence of a head injury. There is no apparent evidence of drug or alcohol abuse, and his reflexes and vital signs are normal.

Sara and Maud are two very different people. Maud is outgoing, happy, and adventuresome. She likes outlandish clothes and uses a good deal of makeup to highlight her features. She is particularly partial to vivid red lipstick and nail polish. She is a compulsive smoker and does what she wants, when she wants. Sara is almost the opposite; she is quiet and depressed. She wears plain clothes and uses no makeup. She does not smoke and is very concerned about morality and doing the "right" thing. It is not surprising to meet two people as different as Sara and Maud. It is unusual when these two "people" are actually two personalities that appear in the same person. Maud and Sara existed in one body (Lipton, 1943).

These two examples describe instances of abnormal behavior called **dissociative disorders**. The *DSM-III* describes a dissociative disorder as a sudden interruption in normal everyday consciousness. This may involve the loss of memory for events, for identity, or both. As is the case with most of the major categories of disorders, the symptoms vary greatly. The man in Detroit was suffering from what is known as a **psychogenic fugue**. *Fugue* means "flight." In his case, it was a flight from a stressful event or circumstance, possibly a traumatic situation in his marriage or his work. This type of fugue is also accompanied by **amnesia**, or the loss of memory. The different personalities of Maud and

---

Somatoform disorders. Physical complaints that have no apparent physical or organic cause.

Conversion disorder. A specific set of physical complaints that usually involves loss of a particular physical function, such as sight or hearing. The complaints have no apparent or organic cause.

Somatization disorder. Many varied physical complaints, such

as blurred vision, pain, diarrhea, and other symptoms, all without apparent physical or organic cause.

Dissociative disorder. A sudden, temporary disorder involving loss of memory for events or identity or both.

Psychogenic fugue. A dissociative disorder that involves amnesia, or loss of memory, and flight to another city or country to avoid a stressful event or circumstance.

Amnesia. Loss of memory.

Sara represent a disorder known as **multiple personality**.

Both psychogenic fugue and multiple personality are rare disorders. Nevertheless, when they do occur they are dramatic and receive a good deal of attention, especially since the symptoms appear in such extreme form. A more commonly-occurring problem of this type is **depersonalization disorder**. This disorder does not involve a clear loss of memory for events, so there is some question about whether it is a dissociative disorder, but since the *DSM-III* places it in this group of disorders we will discuss it here. The primary symptom of the depersonalization disorder is a feeling of unreality. Often, this takes the form of a perception that a limb is no longer a part of the body, or that the mind has left the body and is somewhere outside looking in. You may have had the experience of an arm or leg going numb from sitting or sleeping in an awkward position. In spite of knowing *why* the limb is numb, it still feels strange psychologically. You are dragging around this "thing" that you know is part of you, but it doesn't *feel* as if it is part of you. This experience is only mildly annoying or may even be amusing. We know why it is happening and that it will shortly disappear. In a depersonalization disorder, the same type of feeling may appear suddenly without any warning or obvious cause. Under these circumstances it can be frightening and can cause other disordered behavior. In its most extreme form, this disorder may result in people reporting that they "left their body" for a brief period (5 or 10 minutes) and traveled to another location.

Explanations of Dissociative Disorders

Dissociative disorders are usually set off by a particular stressful event. One such event is war, and there were many reported instances of such disorders during conflicts such as World Wars I and II, the Korean War, and the Vietnam War. As was the case with the somatoform disorders, the two most common explanatory approaches are the psychoanalytic and the learning frameworks.

The Psychoanalytic Explanation. In psychoanalytic thinking, dissociative symptoms are thought to represent the mechanism of **repression**. The mind is protecting itself from anxiety by blotting out memory or identity. As is the case in all applications of traditional psychoanalytic thought, the basic conflict is thought to be the result of sexual desires that emerged in childhood, particularly in the phallic stage. Again, the Oedipus and Electra complexes are assumed to be heavily involved. Ordinarily, simple repression is effective enough for dealing with a conflict; the person simply forgets that a particular event occurred. It is assumed that in the case of dissociative reactions, the conflict is so severe and the anxiety so massive that only a complete split from consciousness will work.

The Learning Explanation. To the behaviorist, fugue, multiple personality, and depersonalization disorder are all examples of escape or avoidance learning. By assuming a different identity, or at least by abandoning a current identity, the person avoids punishing situations, if only for a brief period. The behavioral explanation seems weak, however, when applied to the understanding of dissociative reactions. How was this strategy (fugue or depersonalization) chosen? Did the person see someone else use it successfully or was he or she reinforced by parents or friends for acting this way? Both possibilities are unlikely. Since memory seems to be involved in the disorder, there may be some value in examining the relationship of memory to anxiety. You may remember that we discussed the dynamics of memory and emotion in Chapter 12. Some experiments (Bower, 1981) seem to indicate that our emotional state can have a substantial effect on what and how much we remember. There has been no formal examination of the more traditional cognitive learning mechanisms in this disorder, but it seems to be a good possibility for research. We simply don't know much about why this type of disorder arises or how to treat it. Often the symptoms disappear as quickly as they appeared, no matter what treatment method is used.

■ ANOREXIA NERVOSA AND BULIMIA

On April 12, 1980, a young nurse named Bernadette Gillcrist died of cardiac arrest. At the time of her death, she was acting as a subject in a sleep experiment that was being carried out at the National Institutes of Health. She had arrived at the laboratory at 9:30 on the evening of April 11, and when the experimenter checked on her the next morning at 5:15 AM, she was dead (Kolata, 1980). Ms. Gillcrist was not a victim of an experiment nor a victim of a congenitally-weak cardiovascular system. She was suffering from a condition known as **anorexia nervosa**. People with this disorder have serious eating problems. All sufferers of this disorder have a common goal—the reduction of weight. Sometimes the strategy involves self-imposed starvation; the person stops eating or eats only a minimal amount and, as a result, suffers an extreme loss of weight. A related disorder is called **bulimia**. The bulimic person is characterized by periods of bingeing in which enormous amounts of food are consumed, followed by self-induced vomiting to get rid of the food and thus avoid weight gain. Bernadette Gillcrist had adopted a vomiting strategy. A side effect of frequent self-induced vomiting is a chemical imbalance in the stomach. Hydrochloric acid is lost as a result of the vomiting and, in certain circumstances, this chronic and extreme loss of hydrochloric acid leads to cardiac arrest. Unfortunately, the independent variable in the sleep experiment was the drug lithium, and lithium creates circumstances in which the loss of hydrochloric acid from the stomach can lead to cardiac arrest. Of course, the experimenter knew nothing of Ms. Gillcrist's anorexia; she had lied about her medical history.

Although Bernadette Gillcrist's case was extreme by any standard, anorexia and bulimia are serious problems for many adolescent and post-adolescent women. A more recent example of the problem was the death of a popular singer Karen Carpenter. She had been struggling with anorexia for many years and finally died of cardiac arrest—which often happens in advanced cases of the disease. The problem is considerably more prevalent among women than men. Some reports (Crisp et al., 1978) suggest female to male ratios of as high as 20 to 1. The problem often appears first in the high-school and college years. Crisp and his colleagues estimate that as many as 1 out of every 200 school-age girls suffers from anorexia.

Anorexic and bulimic people show many of the same psychological characteristics that accompany depression. These characteristics include low self-esteem, severe and persistent doubts about personal effectiveness, and a belief that they cannot meet the high standards of performance and appearance that others (particularly their mothers) have set for them. There is an inordinate fear of body fat and, as a result, of the caloric composition of food. It is as if they need to control *something* in their environment and that something is their bodies, and particularly their body weights. In anorexics, the severe nutritional deficiency invariably interferes with sexuality. Menstruation usually stops, and there is a delay in the appearance of secondary sex characteristics in adolescents. This interruption of sexuality could play a role in either a psychoanalytic or a learning explanation of the phenomenon. From the psychoanalytic viewpoint, the starvation is a response to unacceptable sexual urges. It is a mechanism that can reduce the anxiety that may be caused by the emergence of secondary sex characteristics and menstruation in young women. By putting a temporary halt to manifestations of sexuality such as menstruation, the need to resolve the Electra complex may also be postponed. This might explain both why the disorder is more common in women than men, and why it first appears in the adolescent years. From a learning perspective, if there is some fear associated with menstruation, sexual activity, or the appearance of secondary sex characteristics, starvation turns out to be an excellent way of avoiding that anxiety. We are still left with the problem of explaining how the person discovers the starva-

Multiple personality. A dissociative disorder in which a person is split into several separate (and often quite different) personalities.

Depersonalization disorder. A dissociative disorder; the main symptom is a feeling of unreality, in which either a part of your body goes numb and seems not to belong to you, or your mind seems to leave your body and be outside of you looking in.

Repression. A term used by Freud to refer to the way events or memories are blotted out—kept from conscious awareness.

Anorexia nervosa. A disorder that mostly affects females, usually beginning during the teenage years. This disorder consists of vigorous dieting to the point of starvation and is accompanied by low self-esteem and a distorted body image.

Bulimia. A disorder mostly affecting females, usually beginning in the teenage years. This disorder consists of periods of bingeing or overeating followed by self-induced vomiting to get rid of the food and thus avoid weight gain.

tion/menstruation relationship in the first place, but it is easy enough to see how an operant approach could account for the continuation of the self-starvation once it begins.

In the case of the bulimic person, there is obvious ambivalence; bingeing is followed by vomiting. As a result, guilt and shame most likely play a role in bulimia. The anorexic, on the other hand, is less ambivalent. She sees herself as "fat" and simply disregards disconfirming statements of friends and acquaintances. In fact, she can look in a mirror and see a person who weighs 85 pounds—someone who is nothing more than skin and bones—and still insist that she is overweight.

Since these eating disorders tend to first appear in the adolescent years, there is speculation that family dynamics may be involved in the problem. The mothers of anorexics tend to be characterized as domineering and unreasonably demanding. The fathers, on the other hand, tend to be seen as "emotional absentees" (Coleman et al., 1980). This leaves the mother as the major punisher in the household. As is the case in other disorders, there is an equally good likelihood that internal conflict is involved. In this case, the conflict is likely to be between a desire to be independent and a fear of failing in that role (Palazzoli, 1978). As a result, the symptoms often appear when a new life challenge is introduced—going off to school, taking a new job, getting married (Coleman et al., 1980).

Anorexia and bulimia are extremely complex disorders that are difficult to treat. Nevertheless, they do seem to involve distorted standards and self-images and many treatment programs concentrate on improving self-esteem, making self-images more realistic, and countering unrealistic fears. In the case of the bulimic person, attempts are also made to deal with accompanying feelings of shame and guilt. Like depression, these disorders are seldom obvious to outsiders. A physician will usually suspect a problem when there are unexplained disorders of the menstrual cycle in women. (As was indicated earlier, this is one of the side effects of anorexia.) Another common characteristic is a denial that anything is wrong. This means that patterns can be well established before any intervention takes place, making treatment that much more difficult. As with depression, if you or someone you know seems to be developing these inappropriate eating patterns, seek professional help immediately.

REVIEW QUESTIONS

7. In _____ disorders, there is evidence of some physical incapacity without any physical or organic cause.

8. In a somatization/conversion disorder, there is a very specific complaint involving loss of a particular physical function (such as loss of sight); in a somatization/conversion disorder there are many varied complaints, such as blurred vision, pain, diarrhea, and other symptoms.

9. A _____ disorder is a sudden, temporary loss of memory for events or for identity.

10. Match the following terms with the correct definitions:
___ psychogenic fugue — A. disorder in which someone's consciousness is split into several separate personalities.
___ multiple personality — B. flight from a stressful event, accompanied by loss of memory.
___ depersonalization disorder — C. feeling of unreality—limbs go numb and seem not to belong to the body; mind seems to leave the body and be outside looking in.

11. There is a disorder that involves problems in eating among mostly females and often begins in the teenage years. One type of problem, called _____ _____, involves self-starvation. The other type, called _____, involves overeating followed by self-induced vomiting.

Answers: 7. somatoform 8. conversion; somatization 9. dissociative 10. psychogenic fugue, B; multiple personality, A; depersonalization disorder, C. 11. anorexia nervosa; bulimia

■ PSYCHOSEXUAL DISORDERS

Psychosexual disorders cause moderate discomfort in an individual. There are two classes of these disorders: gender-identity disorders and paraphilias (unusual means of obtaining sexual arousal).

Gender-Identity Disorders

There are two predominant but related forms of **gender-identity disorders**—transsexualism and gender-identity disorders of childhood. **Transsexuals** are people who are unhappy with their anatomical sex. Transsexuals should not be confused with homosexuals; what makes transsexualism a disorder is the unhappiness with anatomical gender. As a result of the conflict between an objective circumstance (anatomical gender) and a desired circumstance (the opposite of the current anatomical gender), anxiety and depression often accompany transsexualism. It is this anxiety and depression that leads to the "abnormal" classification, not just the desire to be of the opposite sex.

These patterns of thought and desire do not develop overnight. In most cases, there were identity problems and confusion that appeared in childhood. These problems may have involved expressions of disgust with genital organs (for example, a boy expressing disgust for his penis). The disorder may also include patterns of behavior suitable for opposite-sex children, or even a preference for the clothes of the opposite sex. This does not mean that a young boy who likes to put on dresses or a young girl who hates skirts will grow up to be an adult transsexual; the point is that, in retrospect, it is often easy to see hints of dissatisfaction with anatomical sex in the case histories of transsexuals.

Paraphilias

The prefix *para* means deviation, and the word *philia* means attraction. In combination, then, **paraphilia** means a sexual attraction to a deviate object or action. The *DSM-III* describes this disorder in the following manner:

Unusual or bizarre imagery or acts are necessary for sexual excitement. Such imagery or acts tend to be insistently or involuntarily repetitive and generally involve either (1) a preference for the use of a non-human object for sexual arousal, (2) repetitive sexual activities with humans involving real or simulated suffering or humiliation, or (3) repetitive sexual activity with nonconsenting partners. . . . In varying degrees, [these paraphilia] may interfere with the capacity for reciprocal affectionate sexual activity (DSM-III 1981).

Paraphilias are more common among men than women and can be found in both heterosexuals and homosexuals. Some of the more common forms of paraphilia are **fetishism** (sexual arousal from an inappropriate object such as a piece of clothing), **transvestism** (sexual arousal from dressing in the clothes of the opposite sex), and **voyeurism** (sexual arousal from watching others disrobe or engage in sexual awareness).

Explanations for Psychosexual Disorders

The causes of all of these problems are poorly understood. This makes treatment even more difficult. As was the case with other patterns of abnormal behavior, a learning or psychoanalytic explanation could be easily developed, but there are very few good studies on these subjects.

The Psychoanalytic Explanation. The psychoanalytic explanation for many of these disorders, and in particular the gender-identity disorder, is a sexually-based conflict that is associated with the unsuccessful resolution of the Oedipus and Electra complexes in the phallic stage that are thought to involve some complicated emotional displacements (such as displacement of love for the father to love for other men in girls; displacement of love for the mother with respect for and identification with the father in boys). It would make sense that poor or

---

Gender identity disorders. Disorders in which there is a basic confusion about or dissatisfaction with one's anatomical gender.
Transsexuals. People who are unhappy with their anatomical sex and may seek a sex-change operation.
Paraphilia. Sexual attraction to an unusual object or action.

Fetishism. Inappropriate sexual arousal from an object rather than a person.
Transvestism. Deriving sexual pleasure from dressing in the clothes of the opposite sex.
Voyeurism. Deriving sexual pleasure from watching someone undress who is unaware of being watched.

misdirected displacements, transferences, or identifications could easily lead to psychosexual disorders at a later time. Many of the psychosexual disorders appear early in adolescence. This gives added weight to the notion that early experiences play a significant role. This, of course, does not confirm the existence of the Oedipus or Electra complexes. It simply says that childhood experiences may play a role in adult disorders.

The Learning Explanation. According to learning theory, it is easy to see how a particular sexual practice is learned. Sexual gratification is its own reward, thus, events or objects that become associated with that gratification assume both classical and operant characteristics. The same is true for the failure to receive gratification; this may function as a punishment and discourage certain kinds of future behavior.

On a more cognitive note, models play an important role in sexual activity and adaptation. A child learns sexual practices from others; sometimes these "others" are friends and sometimes they are strangers in books or in films. Many of these practices may bring pleasure. Since sexual gratification can be intensely pleasurable and is always immediate, associations form quickly.

At this point, relatively little is known about the sources of sexual disorders. There are many possible explanations, but further research is needed to determine if one explanation is better than any other.

The abnormal behavior patterns that have been described in this section vary from mildly to moderately disruptive for the individual. Almost all of these disorders can be treated without hospitalization. In the next section, we will consider the more serious disorders.

■ SPECIFIC CATEGORIES OF SERIOUS DISORDERS

Several years ago, I arrived at work early one morning to find my secretary waiting at the elevator to tell me about a student who had come to see me. He had arrived 30 minutes earlier and had asked the secretary if he might have a cup of coffee while he waited for my arrival. She said that the coffee was for the faculty and staff but he could probably have

a cup if he wanted. He became very agitated and sarcastic, offering a continuous string of mock apologies for having requested the coffee. He then took out a handful of change and threw it at the secretary. He went out into the hallway and threw more change on the floor. By the time I arrived, the secretary was terrified. I found the student waiting by my door. He was calm and smiling. He asked if I had a minute to talk about his schedule for the next academic term. I said "sure" and he came in and sat down. We talked about a particular course for a few minutes and then he asked me if I knew anything about numbers. I answered that I didn't know that much, and he proceeded to describe a theory that he was working on that assumed that numbers were "causal" agents; the number 3 caused storms, the number 7 caused conflict between people, and the number 46 was closely tied to academic success. He then became very excited and anxious. He closed my door and began to whisper. He told me the local telephone company was secretly manipulating the number system so that they could take over the world; since they could issue numbers they could control events. I told the student that it would be a good idea to talk with someone at length about his concerns. I suggested that since he was worried about the situation, the best thing to do was to talk it out and get some advice about what to do. As he seemed quite pleased with that idea, I then suggested we walk down to the psychology clinic where someone would be available for a chat. We walked downstairs and into the reception area of the clinic. The student went over and sat in the lap of the receptionist, put his arms around the receptionist's neck, and began to cry. The student was hospitalized that morning and institutionalized several weeks later, at his request.

I had been an adviser to this student for two years. He had always seemed a little "eccentric" and I knew that he was under pressure at various times. Whenever I had asked if I could help, he had usually replied that he would be ok when he had finished the term paper or when the test was behind him. Most people did not seem to recognize that he was under any unusual pressure. He had acted "normally" until the morning he had come to my office and this disorganized behavior appeared. Everyone noticed it—the secretary, a colleague in the office down the hall, the people in the reception area. There was no mistaking the disordered behavior.

This is the type of behavior that we will consider in this section: substantial and consistent patterns of disorganized behavior. In this student's case, the eventual diagnosis was schizophrenia. Although I did not know it at the time, he had been hospitalized twice before with the same diagnosis.

As you saw in the chapter on stress, it is virtually impossible to avoid pressure of one kind or another. Broken love affairs, the illness of a friend, changing jobs or houses—all of these events put pressure on us. Most of us learn to deal with these transient pressures on an event-by-event basis. We adopt certain strategies to cope with this short-term stress. Sometimes, the strategies appear even when there is no external stressful event. Sometimes we have no strategies to help us cope with situational stress. Under these circumstances, moderate behavior disorders arise. In the last section, the disorders we described were those that caused some problem for the person. They were accompanied by reported anxiety or discomfort, as well as somewhat disorganized behavior and thought. The symptoms that we will examine in this next section are of a considerably more severe nature. Depending on the disorder they include hallucinations, bizarre speech patterns, a lack of awareness of the environment, and substantially distorted moods or emotional states. The student's actions that I just recounted are an example of the extent to which behavior can become seriously disordered.

■ CONTROVERSIES ABOUT MAJOR MENTAL ILLNESS

A debate has been waged over the last two decades with respect to serious mental disorders. On one side, there are those who contend that mental illness is a myth. They claim that with a few exceptions—since there is no medical or biological foundation that can be found for the behaviors in question—the term "illness" should be dropped. Szasz (1960) suggests that mental illness represents a combination of the moral, social, and ethical problems of living. The issue is really how different people solve these problems. In other words, what we call sickness is better labeled "maladaptive" behavior. By using the term "sickness" we encourage

continued bad behavior and free the person from any responsibility for that behavior.

R. D. Laing (1964) believes that mental illness does not exist. Laing suggests that patients with severe disorders such as schizophrenia are doing the only reasonable thing—they are withdrawing from reality. This point of view implies that the external world—particularly the interpersonal aspects of it—is responsible for the symptoms. Friends and associates make competing demands, the environment gives conflicting signals, predictability is impossible. In these circumstances, the path to sanity is found in withdrawal, not in interaction.

The differences between these two positions are not simply philosophical; there are serious implications for treatment. If you take the approach of Szasz, then the mentally ill must "face the music" and accept the social and legal consequences of their behavior. As you will see shortly, this is at the heart of the current debate on insanity as a legal defense for criminal behavior. Is it "right" for a person convicted on multiple occasions of brutal rape to be sent to a hospital for a brief period and then released, possibly to rape again, simply because he was judged insane at the time of the rape? The counterargument is that to ignore mental status is to return to the days when the disturbed were killed or persecuted as witches or as people possessed by demons. Laing suggests that instead of treatment we should offer the schizophrenic the privileged status of an artist at work, sculpting a new reality from the shattered remains of an old one. He suggests that the best treatment is no treatment—to leave the person alone to get on with the work of art. It was interference by the outside world that caused the problem in the first place. Laing's suggestion is intriguing, but it is counterintuitive in some respects. Many seriously disturbed people seem to be in a great deal of pain and often ask for help. Is it fair to allow their suffering to continue without some attempt to help? Most professionals feel that some intervention is appropriate.

As is the case in most such debates, the truth probably lies somewhere in the middle of these positions. There is little doubt, as you will see, that environments can "cause" mental disorders; in that sense, Laing may be partially correct. Similarly, as you will see in the chapter on therapy, certain "bad" behaviors can be effectively eliminated without any regard for the "cause" of the disorder; thus Szasz may have a point. There is, however, one additional point that should be made. There seems to be a universality to some of the more serious forms of mental disorders. For example, in an international study of schizophrenia supported by the World Health Organization (1973), it was found that this particular disorder appears in nine different cultures. It does not matter if the culture is Western or Eastern, rural or urban, industrialized or nonindustrialized. This study shows that schizophrenia is, at the very least, not peculiar to Western cultures. This argues against a purely arbitrary or cultural interpretation of mental disorders. The conclusion that can be drawn from this debate is that serious disorders have some other foundation than just a cultural one, and that the problem of labeling can be solved with a better descriptive system. The *DSM-III* represents an improved system of classification that should help reduce the type of findings found in the Rosenhan study, which you read about earlier in the chapter. There is reason to believe that these disorders have causes, that these causes can be discovered, that people suffering from these disorders should be given help in eliminating them, and that psychologists, among others, are capable of providing such help.

Mental Disorders and the Law

To many people, mental disorder implies danger. This danger might involve the patient—as in the case of suicide or self-mutilation—or it might involve another person—as in rape or homicide. In terms of dealing with the disordered person, there are two different types of fears that people experience. People are often uneasy in dealing with those suffering from mental disorders because of the assumed unpredictability that accompanies the disorder. They are uncomfortable interacting with someone who may not be consistent or who may not subscribe to accepted standards of behavior.

The other fear associated with mental disorders is one of criminal behavior. There is the general feeling people have that they have more to fear from discharged mental patients than from the population at large. Rabkin (1979) has surveyed studies of criminal behavior in discharged mental patients and concluded that these former patients are no more likely than the public at large to be involved in serious forms of crime. On the other hand, they are

no *less* likely to be involved in crime either. Some studies have shown that former mental patients are more likely to engage in criminal acts, but in most of these studies it was also true that these patients had arrest records *before* entering the psychiatric hospital. This seems to indicate that psychiatric hospitals are being used as alternatives to prisons. As an example Rabkin cites the statistics from New York State. In the past 30 years, the proportion of patients with arrest records who entered state psychiatric facilities has increased from 15 percent to 40 percent. Given this fact, it is surprising that former mental patients are *not* more dangerous than the public at large. Rabkin suggests that former mental patients are actually composed of two subgroups. One group is composed of people with previous arrest records, histories of substance abuses, and other criminal or antisocial activities. These people are dangerous, but not necessarily because of their status as former psychiatric patients. The other group consists of people with the more traditional mental illnesses, such as schizophrenia and depression. These people are considerably less likely to be involved in violent or dangerous activity than the public at large. These data are presented graphically in Figure 15–1.

Commitment

People who are considered dangerous can be placed in hospitals against their will in two ways. **Civil commitment** can be carried out when people are considered threats to themselves or to someone else and will not enter the hospital voluntarily. It can be initiated by anyone, but ordinarily it is done at the request of a relative or friend. A court order is obtained, the person is given a psychiatric examination to determine mental status, and if the examination bears out the concern of the person initiating the action, commitment takes place.

The process of **criminal commitment** is begun through the commission of a crime. In these instances, a person might be committed by a judge to a psychiatric hospital rather than to a prison. It is this process, criminal commitment, that raises a hotly debated topic—the insanity plea.

Insanity and the Law. **Insanity** is a legal term that is used to describe a person who is unaware of the meaning of criminal behavior or who is unable to

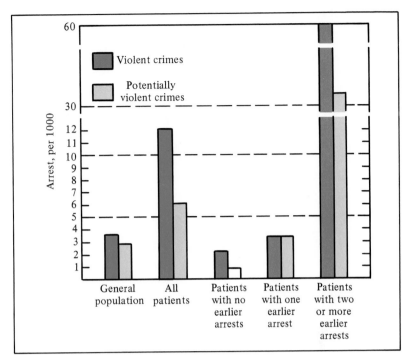

FIGURE 15-1
One study suggests that former mental patients can be divided into two groups, those that have previous arrest records and those that don't. The first group of people is dangerous, but not necessarily because they have been psychiatric patients—they have a history of drug and alcohol abuse and criminal or antisocial activity. The second group is no more dangerous than the general population and, in fact, is less likely to commit a violent crime.

conform to models of noncriminal behavior at the time a crime is committed. Insanity deals with the issue of accountability or responsibility. Can people be held *responsible* for their actions? Did they know that what they were doing was wrong? Thus, it is possible for criminal defendants to argue that they were innocent by reason of insanity of an action that everyone, including the defendant, agrees that the defendant carried out.

Before entering such a plea, a preliminary procedure must be completed to determine if defendants are competent to stand trial. In order to be judged competent, people must be able to understand the charges against them, must be able to understand how the legal system works (including the functions of the judge, jury, defendant, and prosecutor), and must be able to help their lawyer prepare a defense. If people are judged not competent

to stand trial, they are usually committed to a psychiatric hospital until the conditions of competence described above can be satisfied. It has been estimated (Davison and Neale, 1982) that ten people are committed to hospitals as a result of being judged incompetent for every one that is committed by reason of being judged insane.

If people are judged competent to stand trial, they may be found innocent by reason of insanity if it can be established that they did not understand the criminality of their action *at the time the action took place*. There must be some evidence of insanity other than the criminal action for which they are being prosecuted. For example, if they had been under the care of a psychologist or psychiatrist for the treatment of hallucinations or disordered behavior *before* the criminal action, that could be used as evidence of a prior condition. In the case of an

---

Civil commitment. A legal process by which a court order is obtained to commit someone to a mental hospital and the decision is based on determination of the person's mental status.
Criminal commitment. A legal process by which someone is hospitalized because of having committed a crime.

Insanity. A legal term used to describe a person who was unaware of the meaning of criminal behavior or unable to conform to models of noncriminal behavior at the time a crime was committed.

PSYCHOLOGICAL EXAMINATION OF THE SUSPECT IN A CRIMINAL CASE

A clinical analysis of abnormal behavior and its careful diagnosis can sometimes be critical—even a matter of life or death. In a criminal case, in which an individual is accused of a violent crime, systematic psychological examination of the suspect may determine whether or not he or she is competent to stand trial and whether or not a sentence such as the death penalty may be imposed.

In the late 1970s, Kenneth Bianchi was accused of the rape and strangulation murders of two young female victims in Bellingham, Washington. Because of fingerprints and other strong evidence, the same man was thought to be responsible for 13 similar killings in the Los Angeles area. None of Bianchi's alibis for the time of the murders could be confirmed. As the evidence against him increased, his attorney sought to prove that Bianchi was insane under Washington state law and that instead of receiving a possible death penalty, he should be treated in a psychiatric institution.

The attorney for Bianchi proposed that his client was suffering from a multiple personality disorder. In this disorder, as you read earlier in the chapter, more than one personality exists within the same individual. When the dominant personality is presenting itself, the person may seem agreeable, friendly, and sociable. On other occasions, however, the same person can be hostile, aggressive, and belligerent. These personalities are so distinct that changes in mood or circumstance do not account for the differences.

In Bianchi's case, a second personality seemed to emerge while he was in prison and under hypnosis with an examining clinician, an expert for the defense. This alter personality, "Steve," was as macho and belligerent as Bianchi's dominant personality seemed pleasant and cooperative. "Steve" admitted to the two Washington murders, providing many grisly details of what he had done.

Among the experts for the prosecution was Dr. Martin T. Orne, an authority on hypnosis. One set of examination procedures was designed to determine whether Bianchi were actually hypnotized when the "Steve" personality came through, or if he were simply acting. Bianchi appeared highly hypnotizable, as are most people with multiple personality disorder. One of Orne's tests involved suggesting to Bianchi while he was hypnotized that his lawyer was sitting in a chair in front of him. The lawyer was actually in a different chair at the time, but Bianchi appeared to "see" him under hypnosis. Then Bianchi was instructed to turn around

and face the actual lawyer, who was sitting in a chair previously outside Bianchi's view. Bianchi reacted in a puzzled manner, confused as to how there could be "two" of his attorney. This response was not at all typical of truly hypnotized people, who tend to willingly accept under hypnosis that one person can be in two places. Bianchi was also asked to describe the suggested hallucination of his attorney. His response here was also atypical of the truly hypnotized person. He seemed surprised that Orne could not also see the hallucination. Truly hypnotized people tend not to question the hypnotist in this way but to simply describe their hallucinations as they have been instructed.

Also inconsistent with true multiple personality cases was the fact that Bianchi seemed to develop an additional personality at the suggestion of the prosecution's hypnotist. Orne suggested to Bianchi that having just two personalities was unusual for multiple personality disorder. If Bianchi were faking, Orne hypothesized, he could be expected to suddenly produce another personality after this suggestion. This is, in fact, just what happened. Immediately following this conversation, Bianchi's third personality, "Billy," a 9-year-old boy, emerged.

Orne also reports that none of the people who knew Bianchi well had ever observed him behaving as one of the alter personalities, which is highly unusual for a multiple personality with a lifelong history of the disorder. From a large body of this kind of evidence, Orne and his colleagues concluded that Bianchi was not a true multiple personality case but had adopted the symptoms specifically to avoid the most severe punishment for the murders. (Orne, Dinges, & Orne, n.d.)

The clinical experts did not, of course, conclude the Bianchi was free of mental illness. In fact, the diagnosis was that Bianchi had a psychopathic or sociopathic personality, or the antisocial personality disorder as defined by *DSM-III*. This disorder includes such symptoms as failure to accept social norms with respect to lawful behavior. Working as a security guard, Bianchi often stole from stores he was hired to protect from thieves. Another symptom was his pattern of lying to others for personal gain.

Though these disorders were indeed pronounced and severe, under Washington law Bianchi was considered sane and fit both to stand trial and to receive punishment as a criminal. The reason was that Bianchi knew the difference between right and wrong; he simply chose to ignore it.

insanity plea, several things could happen. First, the person might be judged guilty and sent to prison; second, the person might be judged not guilty by reason of insanity and sent to a hospital; finally, the person might be judged not guilty of performing the action and set free, as is the case in any criminal trial regardless of an insanity plea. An interesting sidelight of the insanity plea is that a person can be judged insane at the time a crime was committed, but may be judged sane at the time of the trial. Under these circumstances, it is possible to find the defendant not guilty by reason of insanity. This is an extremely rare outcome.

On March 30, 1981, John Hinckley waited outside a Washington, D.C. hotel and shot President Ronald Reagan, his Press Secretary James Brady, and a Washington police officer. On June 21, 1982, after eight weeks of testimony including the opinions of psychiatrists called as expert witnesses for both the prosecution and the defense, Hinckley was found not guilty by reason of insanity. This stirred up a controversy that had been simmering since Sirhan Sirhan had invoked the insanity defense when he was charged with the assassination of Robert F. Kennedy. Sirhan's defense was unsuccessful and he was sentenced to life in prison for his crime.

Following both decisions, movements surfaced to abolish the insanity plea. The insanity issue is a legal one, not a psychological one; it is a decision made by a judge. No particular diagnosis leads to the decision of insanity. Regardless of the defense offered, the fact is that ruling on disordered behavior is involved. Treatment might be carried out in a hospital or in a prison. The criminal action might be judged to have been a transient occurrence with little likelihood of reoccurring, in which case no treatment may be indicated at all, although the person might be hospitalized for some period of time for observation to make sure that the behavior is not an enduring pattern.

Civil commitment and criminal commitment are two sides of the same coin. Civil commitment is a legal action taken before the fact, usually as a result of a fear that a person might hurt himself or others. Criminal commitment occurs after a criminal action has occurred. Both represent legal actions taken in response to the behaviors (anticipated or actual) of someone suffering from a serious mental disorder.

■ SCHIZOPHRENIA

There is a common misconception that schizophrenia means "split personality." This is because various books, movies, and TV programs have applied the term to cases of what actually turn out to be multiple personality rather than schizophrenia. The prefix *schizo* does mean "split," but the term was introduced by Eugen Blueler in 1911 to describe a circumstance where intellectual functions are separated or split from emotions. You remember from the chapter on personality that personality is an intergrated whole. In fact, it is this integration or organization that accounts for the uniqueness of behavior. The term **schizophrenia** was chosen to emphasize the lack of integration in the personalities of some people. For example, their emotional lives were not integrated or matched to their intellectual lives and they laughed at sad events, or their intellectual lives were not integrated with their senses, and they heard voices in the absence of direct sensory stimulation. Blueler listed four problem areas that characterize the schizophrenic. Each of these symptoms is a variation of poor integration of the personality:

1. The loose association of, or loss of the logical connection between, ideas.
2. Inappropriate emotional responding. This could be either the absence of emotional response when one might be expected, or the presence of an inappropriate emotional response (laughing at a sad event).
3. Autism, which consists of a refusal to share a generally accepted sense of reality and a refusal to define or describe the private reality sensed by the patient.
4. The presence of strong and opposite feelings about the same person. (Blueler, 1911).

Symptoms of Schizophrenia

The most common behavioral symptoms of schizophrenia fall into five distinct categories: hal-

---

Schizophrenia. A mental disorder marked by a lack of integration or organization of personality. This may appear as a split between mental and emotional processes or between mental and sensory processes.

lucinations, delusions, formal thought disorders, motor disturbances, and emotional symptoms.

Hallucinations. **Hallucinations** are perceptions that are not based on any outside stimulation and tend to be either auditory (the patient hears voices), visual (the patient sees distorted images such as a face melting), or olfactory (the patient becomes aware of certain smells). Visual and auditory hallucinations are more frequent than olfactory ones. These hallucinations tend to be persistent and may go on for hours or days. When the person hears voices, their appearance and content seem to be unrelated to the mood of the patient. In addition, these voices talk in entire sentences rather than in just single words or phrases. The voices may talk about the patient in the third person: *He* should do this or *she* should do that. It is not uncommon for multiple voices to be speaking at the same time, sometimes even arguing. Mellor (1970) provides some dramatic examples of hallucinations:

☐ One patient heard a voice two feet above her head that repeated her every thought. She would think, "I must put the kettle on," and the voice would say, "I must put the kettle on."

☐ Another patient reported hearing an argument between two voices in an empty office.

☐ A third patient reported hearing a voice that described everything that she did as if describing these actions to someone else. "She is peeling potatoes, got hold of the peeler, she does not want that potato. . ."

Delusions. Hallucinations are perceptions without sensations; **delusions** are false beliefs. Delusions are disorders of the *content* of thoughts. There are several common types of delusions. One of these is called *thought withdrawal* or *insertion*. In this delusion, patients believe that some external force is stealing from and/or inserting thoughts into their mind. A woman reports that while thinking of her mother, a mental vacuum cleaner comes in and sucks those thoughts out of her mind (Mellor, 1970). A second type of delusion is called the *thought broadcast*. In this case, the patient believes that his or her thoughts are broadcast so that others are aware of them. A young man describes a mental ticker-tape in his mind that transmits his thoughts to the ticker-tape machines in the heads of others (Mellor, 1970).

Delusions of control are beliefs that an outside force or personality has replaced the patient's own will or personality. A young woman claims that she is a puppet manipulated by cosmic strings. When those strings are pulled, her arms and legs move accordingly; she cannot prevent the movement (Mellor, 1970).

Formal Thought Disorders. Thought disorders involve serious problems in communication. The observable symptom of a thought disorder is disordered language. They are called thought disorders because of the inference that disordered language implies disordered thought. There are several types of thought disorder. In **loose associations**, things are said together that do not obviously belong together, for example: "I hate cars, bottles, grass, chickens." **Neologisms** are made-up words that commonly appear in the speech of the schizophrenic but that have no meaning to the listener, for example: "I am an infrapine discortic." **Incoherence** appears in sentences that consist of unconnected phrases or thoughts, for example: "The pope can't be newer if the building has broken its time." In **clang associations** rhyming words are used in place of words that logically go together, for example: "A dime in time is fun to run if the back is slack."

Motor Disturbances. In addition to cognitive symptoms, schizophrenics sometimes display unusual movement patterns. These motor disturbances include **catatonic immobility**, in which a person assumes a position or posture and holds it for hours. While in these positions, the limbs of the schizophrenic can often be moved about by someone else. When they are moved to this new position, the limbs will then remain in the new position unless they are moved again. There may be contorted facial expressions and strange hand movements as well.

Emotional Symptoms. The schizophrenic will often laugh at something sad or cry at something funny. In addition, the swing from happiness to sadness may be rapid. Sometimes the person displays what is referred to as "flat" affect or emotion—very little emotional response of any kind to things in the outside world.

Types of Schizophrenia

Schizophrenia is not characterized by a single set of symptoms. The disorder appears in several forms. The *DSM-III* lists four subtypes of schizophrenia: disorganized, catatonic, paranoid, and undifferentiated.

Disorganized schizophrenics are characterized by apparently random delusions and hallucinations that do not appear to be consistent with any particular theme. Emotionally, these people often act silly and express inappropriate emotions (such as laughing at the death of a close relative). Occasionally, there is childlike behavior.

Catatonic schizophrenics act in one of two ways. They are either immobile, showing the strange posturing described earlier, or they act wild and excited. Often these patterns alternate, with the person shifting abruptly from immobile to frenzied activity.

Paranoid schizophrenics have delusions, usually involving jealousy (believing a lover is cheating) or persecution (they have been singled out for assassination). They feel that bits and pieces of innocent conversations are somehow related to them. The thought patterns of paranoid schizophrenics are often better organized than other schizophrenic patients, making it easier for them to hide the distortion of their thoughts.

The **undifferentiated** subgroup shows a mixture of many different symptoms of schizophrenia, including delusions, hallucinations, disorders of thought, motor disturbances, and emotional disturbances. One of the most common symptoms is

simply confusion and turmoil. In some cases, this may describe a person on the way to one of the more specific forms of schizophrenia described previously (see the case study of a schizophrenic).

Causes of Schizophrenia

There are many alternative points of view that can be adopted in trying to explain *why* a disorder such as schizophrenia appears and continues. Some alternatives you are familiar with are the psychoanalytic explanation and the learning explanation. Unfortunately, there is no one explanation that is suitable for all serious disorders, because the disorders are all so different. Here the most promising or likely explanations for what could be causing the disorder will be identified.

The Developmental Approach. There are two aspects of this approach; the first one is physiological. There has been some suggestion that complications during pregnancy and birth may lead to neurological damage (Pollin et al., 1969). It is this damage that eventually leads to the symptoms that appear. As you saw in the chapter on biology and behavior, during the 9 months before birth an average of 250,000 neurons develop each minute. Thus, there is plenty of opportunity for nervous-system damage to occur.

The second aspect is related to family dynamics. Fontana (1966) has studied the parents of schizophrenic patients and found that there is more

---

Hallucinations. Perceptions that are not based on any outside stimulation—false perceptions. In schizophrenics, such events are often auditory (hearing voices), visual (seeing distorted images), or olfactory (being aware of certain smells).

Delusions. False beliefs. Several different types of delusions may occur in schizophrenia, including delusions of control, or beliefs that an outside force or personality has replaced the person's own will or personality.

Loose associations. A characteristic of schizophrenic thought and speaking, in which the person groups things that do not go together.

Neologisms. Made-up words that commonly appear in the speech of schizophrenics but have no meaning to anyone else. Example: "I am an infrapine discortic."

Incoherence. Producing sentences that consist of unconnected phrases or thoughts.

Clang associations. The use of words that rhyme rather than words that logically go together. Example: "A dime in time is fun to run if the back is slack."

Catatonic immobility. A motor-disturbance association with a type of schizophrenia in which the person sits in one position or posture without moving for hours on end.

Disorganized schizophrenic. A type of schizophrenic who has random delusions and hallucinations, often acts in a silly way, and expresses inappropriate emotions.

Catatonic schizophrenic. A type of schizophrenic who varies between sitting motionless for hours or acting wildly and excitedly.

Paranoid schizophrenic. A type of schizophrenic who suffers from delusions of being betrayed by those close to them or that strangers are out to get them.

Undifferentiated schizophrenic. A subgroup showing a mixture of many different symptoms of schizophrenia.

CASE STUDY OF A SCHIZOPHRENIC

As a girl, Judy was smart and pretty. She grew up in the Midwest, where she worked on her high-school year book, was a member of the National Honor Society and church choir, and married a young man from one of her town's prominent families. Her mother recalls that as a young wife, Judy was an excellent housekeeper and had a knack for entertaining.

Today Judy is homeless, a street person. During the day, she sits on a plastic garbage bag on Lexington Avenue and 63rd Street in New York. At night, she goes to a bank's doorway on Second Avenue and 64th Street. Neighbors report that during the night, she sometimes screams obscenities for several hours at a stretch. Other times, she seems to adopt an alternate personality, a male, with whom she appears to have loud arguments.

Judy has been diagnosed as a paranoid schizophrenic. She often hallucinates and has lost contact with reality. Questioned by a neighbor about her yelling one night, Judy stated that "They've got my brain in Washington, and I have all these transistors in my head." On other occasions, she has told people that her father was King Albert of Belgium and that she owned all the land in the neighborhood where she lives, pulling a copy of a document written in Latin out of a bag as "proof." At other times, though, Judy can communicate rationally.

Early signs of Judy's schizophrenia went unrecognized. Judy's mother now recalls that as a teenager, Judy seemed to have another personality that would emerge for a day or two. At the time, though, Judy's mother didn't recognize this as anything more than a rather nasty mood. Judy's first husband recalls that she was hard to beat in a discussion, backing up everything she said with facts. Much later, he realized that Judy was inventing these "facts."

Several years ago, after failed attempts to commit her to a mental health institution for treatment, Judy moved to New York, where, her mother guesses, she was seeking anonymity. Judy's street life includes many routines. One is Judy's washing ritual, which she performs every morning, in public, on Second Avenue. She brushes her teeth, washes her face and her body underneath her many layers of clothes with a bar of soap kept in a plastic box and bottled water, washes her hair, and puts on antifungial solution on her feet. She buys coffee at the same cafe every morning and buys a newspaper. For dinner, she has meat loaf and onion rings. While she will not accept food handouts, Judy refuses to pay sales tax on the food she buys. Once a week, she calls her mother collect from a pay phone. A neighbor accepts packages for Judy, which are usually clothes sent by her mother.

Many neighbors have adopted a protective attitude toward this woman with obvious mental illness. They give her dollar bills as they pass her on the street, and these handouts help her to feed herself. But her family and neighbors alike agree that she needs help and that the streets of New York are no place for her. Unfortunately, no one has yet come up with a way to administer that help.

Source: Deirdre Carmody, "The Tangled Life and Mind of Judy, Whose Home Is the Street," *The New York Times*, December 17, 1984, pp. B1, B16.

conflict between them than is found between the parents of normal children. In addition, the communication between the parents of schizophrenics seems to be less efficient. The problem is whether or not these patterns of conflict and inefficient communication arose *as a result* of having a schizophrenic child rather than being the *cause* of the schizophrenia itself (Liem, 1974). One study (Brown et al., 1966) has shown a clear family involvement in the continuation of schizophrenic symptoms. Families of schizophrenic patients were characterized as either high or low on expressed emotion. Expressed emotion involves making comments, criticizing, and being heavily and vocally involved in the symptoms of the patient. Of the patients from high expressed emotion families, 58 percent returned to the hospital within 9 months of discharge. Of those from low expressed emotion families, 10 percent of the patients returned to the hospital. These data suggest the possibility of family involvement in causing or maintaining schizophrenia, but the relationship is not yet well understood.

Genetic Approach. Some researchers have suggested that schizophrenia has a genetic basis. As was true of studies of intelligence, the subjects for this type of research are identical twins and fraternal twins who have been separated at birth and raised with different families. If both identical twins develop the symptoms of schizophrenia, it would seem that genetics must be involved, since family patterns are no more similar for identical than fraternal twins raised apart. In fact, the incidence of symptoms is much higher in identical twins than in fraternal twins. Thus, supporting data exist for the genetic approach but still leave room for the influence of other factors.

Another type of study that has shed some light on the possible genetic explanation of schizophrenia is research involving adopted children. Heston (1966) identified 47 children who had been born to schizophrenic mothers and adopted shortly after birth. He also selected a control group of adopted children who had been born to nonschizophrenic mothers. The results were clear. In later psychiatric examinations, 66 percent of the adopted children of schizophrenic mothers were diagnosed as having symptoms of the disorder. Only 18 percent of the adopted children of nonschizophrenic mothers were seen as having symptoms. Of the 47 children of schizophrenic mothers, 16 percent were diagnosed as schizophrenic. Of the 50 control children, none were diagnosed as schizophrenic.

Both the twin studies and the adoption studies suggest some genetic involvement. It seems clear that genetic inheritance plays a role. Nevertheless, it is just as inappropriate to say that schizophrenia is genetically determined as it is to say that intelligence is. A more reasonable point of view might be that there are some genetic **predispositions** toward the development of schizophrenic symptoms. The actual appearance of symptoms may depend on

One symptom of schizophrenia is called catatonic immobility, in which a person holds one position or posture for hours on end.

many factors, including nutrition, environmental stress, and learning experiences.

Biochemical Approach. In light of evidence of a genetic factor in schizophrenia, it has been argued that the inherited characteristics may have something to do with brain chemistry. As we saw in Chapter 2, psychological processes such as sensation, perception, language, thinking, and emotion depend heavily on brain processes. This being the case, it is logical to explore the possibility that psychological problems characteristic of schizophrenia may be symptoms of some neurochemical disorder. This possibility is supported by the fact that certain drugs are effective in relieving many of the symptoms of schizophrenia. Since we know that drugs affect the neurotransmitters of the brain, the effect of drugs on symptoms leads to the conclusion that schizophrenia may be due to a faulty neurotransmitter system. Since the drugs used to control schizophrenic symptoms act as blockers for the neurotransmitter *dopamine*, this chemical may be somehow involved in the disease. Specifically, it may be that schizophrenia results from too much dopamine. Further evidence is provided by studies of the effects of amphetamines. Sometimes amphetamine users report symptoms similar to those

---

Predisposition. A hereditary characterisic that favors the development of a certain trait.

of schizophrenia. Since amphetamines increase dopamine in synaptic areas, this further supports the theory that schizophrenic symptoms are the result of too much dopamine. Dopamine blockers such as phenothiazine are effective in reducing schizophrenic symptoms.

As was the case with the genetic approach, some caution is in order here. In the first place, it is often hard to tell if there is an excess of dopamine *before* the onset of the symptoms or whether it is a by-product of the disease. In other words, it is hard to tell if the level of dopamine is a cause or an effect. In addition, the drugs used to treat schizophrenics do not work equally well on all patients, nor do they eliminate all symptoms of schizophrenia. Once again, it is safe to conclude that biological factors probably play some role in schizophrenia, but how much of a role is still an unanswered question.

Stress/Vulnerability Approach. In the chapter on personality, you read about an approach called interactionism. This was a point of view that combined traits and situations to account for behavior. Personality was seen as the manifestation of certain enduring characteristics in particular situations. The interactionist approach can be applied to schizophrenia as well by combining the concepts of biological predispositions (possibly inherited) with environmental stress. Put in simple terms, this theory proposes that some people have biological systems that are vulnerable to the development of schizophrenic symptoms under the right circumstances. For example, one hypothesis is that people differ in the extent to which dopamine is present at their synapses in times of stress. Some people have neurons that produce too much dopamine, and others have neurons that produce just the right amount to deal with the communication demands of a stressful situation. The cause of this might be a neuron with a larger than average number of dendrites (so more dopamine is picked up from other firing neurons), a neuron with a lower than average threshold (so the neuron produces dopamine more frequently than similar neurons in "normal" or nonschizophrenic people), or a neuron that has a shorter refractory period than the neuron of a normal person (so the neuron that is releasing the dopamine will fire more frequently than it should). There are

many other possible neural differences that could be considered, for example, the efficiency of the axon in carrying the impulse along its length, but each of these explanations involves a biological characteristic of the schizophrenic patient. As you saw earlier, neurons do not fire or release neurotransmitter chemicals randomly; they require stimulation of some kind.

The second part of the stress/vulnerability approach suggests that different events in the outside world induce different amounts of stress (Zubin and Spring, 1977). As we saw in Chapter 14, various life events can be arranged in the order of their capacity to induce stress. A death is more stressful than a divorce which, in turn, is more stressful than losing a job. The stress/vulnerability hypothesis says that some people are more vulnerable to stress. People with certain biological characteristics (e.g. the tendency to overproduce dopamine) display behavior that is more disorganized under circumstances of stress than under nonstress. Furthermore, these people have a greater tendency to display disorganized behavior in reaction to less stressful events than do nonschizophrenics.

As you can see, there is no lack of possible approaches to explaining why schizophrenic behavior patterns appear. Of these, the most compelling are those that take into account biological factors. The data gathered from drug studies, twin studies, and adoption studies are impressive. Nevertheless, the fact that not all the children of schizophrenic parents develop schizophrenia, the fact that drugs cannot control all symptoms of schizophrenia or any one symptom in all patients, and the fact that different schizophrenics develop different symptoms, points to the possible role of learning, environmental factors (including perceived stress), and social/emotional factors in schizophrenic behavior patterns. In the past, schizophrenia has been characterized as a lifelong illness with periods of particularly intense symptoms. This notion is gradually changing. Zugin and Spring (1977) have described schizophrenia as a temporary disability but containing lifelong vulnerability. This fits nicely with the stress/vulnerability approach that was just described. The appearance of stressful events might account for the temporary nature of the disability; genetic or biological circumstances would account for a lifelong vulnerability. The stress/vulnerability model is probably the best single explanation at this point.

Treatment of Schizophrenia

At the present time, the treatments for schizophrenia are mainly directed toward symptom relief rather than "cure." Research persists, but no "cure" is on the horizon. Until we understand why schizophrenic symptoms appear, we will not find a permanent "cure." In the meantime, attempts are made to keep the person free of undue stress and possible injury while the symptoms are present. Drugs are used to relieve symptoms so that the person might be released back into the community without danger to self or others. After release, there is usually a continuing program of daily medication. In addition, there is often some attempt to work with the family of the schizophrenic patient. The family may play a role in determining if the patient eventually returns to the hospital. Family members are taught to be supportive, to keep from getting overinvolved in the symptoms, and to keep from being overly intrusive in the life of the patient at home.

Therapeutic drugs have enabled many patients to be treated outside of the hospital environment. This is probably a good idea, since life on a psychiatric ward is painful at best. In hospitals, there is often little formal "treatment" besides drugs, and the patient often has no sense of personal control over his or her own life. The patient is a member of a community that is not normal by any standards. The psychiatric ward of a hospital is a poor training ground for developing strategies to deal with the pressures of normal living.

An understanding of why schizophrenia develops and how it can be reversed is desperately needed. Traditional psychotherapies, such as psychoanalysis or counseling, which rely on clear communication between therapist and patient, are ineffective in dealing with the schizophrenic patient who is exhibiting disordered thought. Chemical therapy, since it is directed toward influencing neurotransmission, has side-effects that tend to disorganize behavior in a different way, thus replacing one set of symptoms with another. Thus institutions may well do more harm than good. At present, it is reasonable to say that treatment of schizophrenia has on-

ly a minimal effect. Patients can be made more "manageable," but they are not likely to be "cured."

12. _____ refers to a lack of integration of personality. This may mean a split between mental and emotional processes, or between mental and sensory processes.

13. _____ are made-up words that schizophrenics often use, which have no meaning in the real world. _____ _____ are a use of words that rhyme rather than words that logically go together.

14. The _____ approach to explaining schizophrenia looks at the general pattern of communication between parents and children and family involvement in schizophrenic symptoms.

15. The _____ approach to explaining schizophrenia looks at studies of identical twins who are separated at birth and raised apart, and compares the incidence of schizophrenia in adopted children and in both their adopted and biological parents.

16. The _____ approach to explaining schizophrenia focuses on hormonal imbalances in the brain. This approach suggests that the presence of too much dopamine/serotonin/norepinephrine in the brain causes schizophrenic symptoms.

17. The _____ approach combines the concepts of biological predispositions in the schizophrenic person with the stressful life events that happen to that person.

Answers: 12 Schizophrenia 13. Neologisms; Clang associations 14. developmental 15. genetic 16. biochemical; dopamine 17. stress/vulnerability

■ INFANTILE AUTISM

Schizophrenia involves, among other things, language and communication problems. With the adult schizophenic, these problems emerge over time and often as a result of long-term stress. In some children, a pattern of symptoms involving communication and language disorders appears very early in development, often prior to age 30 months. The major symptom in **infantile autism** is a failure to relate to other people, including parents, siblings, and playmates. Language problems are central in this disorder. The child simply may not speak. If the child does use language, it may be very disordered and may not function as communication. One example is known as **echolalia**, in which the child simply repeats everything that someone else says. In addition to the language problems, there is often a desperate desire to keep things the same, including schedules and environments. Consider the following example:

A beautiful girl of five, with autism, finally made contact with her teacher. Each morning she had to be greeted with the set phrase, "Good morning, Lily, I am very very glad to see you." If even one of the words was omitted or another added she would start to scream wildly. (Diamond, Baldwin, and Diamond, 1963, p. 304 cited in Davison and Neale, 1982, p. 512.)

Autism develops so early that there is a strong likelihood that biological factors are involved. Nevertheless, there are curious psychological aspects as well. For example, Colby (1968) worked extensively with autistic children and found that they could be taught language by means of a computer. They would come each day and sit at a terminal with a screen and enthusiastically answer questions by pressing keys on the keyboard. Eventually, some could communicate with the computer using words, phrases, sentences, and even entire paragraphs. Nevertheless, they could not or would not communicate with humans in the same environment. This means that autism is not a simple matter of retardation or organic malfunction. Another person triggers reactions that a machine does not.

Since there is confusion about what autism is and why it appears, there is no standard treatment. There have been attempts to modify the behavior of autistic children using drugs, counseling, behavior modification principles, and psychoanalysis. None of these approaches has been particularly effective. Fewer than 25 percent of autistic children improve sufficiently to be considered "adjusted" by adulthood (Davison and Neale, 1982). Nevertheless, some improvement can be noticed through treatment, and while the children may never be self-sufficient, neither are they invalids. In fact, Kanner (1973) reports on several cases in which the children were gainfully employed outside of the home as adults.

The major symptom in infantile autism is a failure to relate to other people.

■ AFFECTIVE DISORDERS

One large class of mental disorders involves emotion or mood. Another word for emotion is **affect**. As a result, disorders that are characterized by unusual emotional levels or inappropriate moods are known as **affective disorders**. As you may remember from our consideration of moods and emotions, there are two extremes to mood—positive (happiness, excitement, elation) and negative (sadness, unresponsiveness, depression). If we think of moods as falling on a scale that runs from positive to negative, we can think of the extremes of this scale as poles, like the poles or opposite ends of a magnet. Affective disorders, then, are considered either **unipolar** (involving only one extreme) or **bipolar** (involving both extremes). The excited end of the emotional scale is often referred to as **mania**. In popular literature, you occasionally encounter the term *maniac*. It usually describes someone running around in a disorganized and wild manner. The other pole, the unresponsive or unexcited end of the scale, is referred to as **depression**. Depression most often occurs by itself without any accompanying mania. On the other hand, mania is almost always accompanied by depression in the form of emotional changes or swings from one extreme (depression) to the other (mania). For this reason, the affective disorders are broken down into two categories, unipolar (depression) and bipolar (depression and mania). I will refer to the unipolar disorder by its more common name—depression.

Depression

In 1973, it was estimated that at any one time, 15 percent of the population will display symptoms of depression (Secundo et al., 1973). The *DSM-III* estimates that 18 to 23 percent of all females and 8 to 11 percent of all males will suffer a major depressive episode at some point in their lives. Of this number, 6 percent of the females and 3 percent of the males will require some period of hospitalization (APA, 1980). The group most likely to suffer depressive symptoms falls in the age group 18 to 29 (Secundo et al., 1973). This makes college students a high-risk subgroup. One study (Craighead et al., 1982) reports that 10 to 12 percent of a college sample were moderately depressed, and that 4 to 5 percent were severely depressed. Remember that these percentages reflect only those students who ap-

peared as subjects or as patients requesting help; there are probably at least as many college-age students experiencing depression who are never seen professionally. The high rate of depression makes some sense given the substantial changes experienced by those of college age and slightly older. People in this age group complete college, marry, have children, take jobs, plan careers, and establish independence from parents. There is a good deal of pressure involved in getting from 18 to 29. Pressure can cause depression, and depression may result in thoughts of suicide. In fact, one of the most serious aspects of depression is that which relates to suicide. It has been estimated that 15 percent of severely depressed people commit suicide (Robins and Guze, 1972), and that 80 percent of those who commit suicide were depressed at the time. (Flood and Seager, 1968). The *DSM-III* lists eight major symptoms of depression. These symptoms are given in Table 15–7. A diagnosis of depression is given if four of the eight symptoms are present nearly every day for at least two weeks.

Many theories exist to explain depression. One approach is more common than others. The *learning/cognitive* approach is represented in the work of Seligman (1975) and Beck (1976). As you may remember from Chapter 7, Seligman's research suggests that dogs learn to act in a helpless way when they cannot escape from or avoid an aversive stimulus such as a shock. Furthermore, this helplessness carries over into other situations in which they could but do not take action to avoid the punishment. Seligman proposed that human depression is similar to the learned helplessness that he observed in animals. He reasoned that depressed patients may have encountered situations in their past where they were regularly punished and could not escape the punishment. As a result, they act helpless in many situations. To this basic learning approach, a cognitive mechanism was added (Abram-

---

Infantile autism. A disorder involving communication and language that appears at a very early age. The major symptom is an inability to relate to other people in any way.

Echolalia. Disordered use of language that often occurs in infantile autism; consists of simply repeating everything someone else says.

Affect. Another word for emotion and/or the expression of emotion.

Affective disorders. Mental disorders involving emotion or mood;

includes unipolar (depression) and bipolar (depression and mania) disorders. A category of *DSM-III*.

Unipolar disorder. An affective disorder involving depression.

Bipolar disorder. An affective disorder involving both mania and depression, usually in alternating cycles.

Mania. Excited, disorganized, wild behavior; part of a bipolar disorder along with depression.

Depression. Unresponsiveness, lack of activity, negative outlook. When it occurs with mania it is part of a bipolar disorder; when it occurs alone it is called a unipolar disorder.

TABLE 15-7.
Eight Major Symptoms of Depression

1. Poor appetite or significant weight loss (when not dieting) or increased appetite or significant weight gain (in children under six, consider failure to make expected weight gains)

2. Insomnia or hypersomnia

3. Psychomotor agitation or retardation (but not merely subjective feelings of restlessness or being slowed down) (in children under six, hypoactivity)

4. Loss of interest or pleasure in usual activities, or decrease in sexual drive not limited to a period when delusional or hallucinating (in children under six, signs of apathy)

5. Loss of energy; fatigue

6. Feelings of worthlessness, self-reproach, or excessive or inappropriate guilt (either may be delusional)

7. Complaints or evidence of diminished ability to think or concentrate, such as slowed thinking, or indecisiveness not associated with marked loosening of associations or incoherence

8. Recurrent thoughts of death, suicidal ideation, wishes to be dead, or suicide attempt

Source: DSM-III, 1980 p. 214.

son et al., 1978). A condition for helpless (depressed) behavior in humans is that the person must believe that it is possible to control the environment, but that he or she does not have the necessary skill, ability, or power to exercise that control.

Beck (1976) emphasizes the cognitive components of depression to a greater extent. He suggests that depressed patients have illogical thought patterns. They tend to take the blame for everything bad that happens and take no credit for anything good. As you saw in the last chapter, Beck's method of treatment is to help patients to adopt different ways of thinking; in other words, he asks people to learn different thinking patterns. Both Seligman and Beck see learning and cognition as possible causes of depression; but each emphasizes one component more than the other.

Bipolar Disorder

As was indicated earlier, bipolar disorder involves basic manic and depressive symptoms. They often alternate, but there is typically a neutral or normal emotional period between the two extreme periods. The symptoms of mania may include restlessness, increased talkativeness, inflated self-esteem, decreased need for sleep, and distractability. This disorder is defined as the alternation of the two sets of symptoms—the depressive set and the manic set.

While the learning/cognitive approach attempts to explain depressive disorders, the genetic/biological approach is more common in attempting to explain bipolar disorders. With respect to this approach, several theories involving neurotransmitters and hormones are receiving attention. One suggestion is that the absence of *serotonin*, a neurotransmitter discussed in Chapter 2, produces a tendency for the appearance of affective disorders. It has been shown that a significant number of depressive patients have lower than average amounts of serotonin in their cerebro-spinal fluid. This deficiency of serotonin in combination with high or low levels of *norepinephrine*, another neurotransmitter, may produce manic or depressive behavior. In the absence of enough serotonin, high levels of norepinephrine are responsible for mania, and low levels of norepinephrine are responsible for depression (Prange et al., 1974).

As was the case with other disorders, biology and genetics are not *the* answer. Instead, they can be identified as pieces of the puzzle. But there are people who suffer from affective disorders, particularly depression, who do not have unusual levels of chemicals such as serotonin and norepinephrine. In addition, there are many who have unusual levels of these chemicals who do not display the symptoms of affective disorder. Even for those who do show both symptoms and abnormal levels of chemical substances, there is still the problem of identifying cause and effect. It is not clear if the excess or the deficiency of the chemical caused, or was the result of, the abnormal behavior. We seldom see an "experimental group" (schizophrenics, depressives, and so on) until *after* the symptoms have appeared.

The most common treatment for severe affective disorders is drug therapy. Lithium is used to control manic-depressive behavior. Other drugs are used to affect levels of norepinephrine in depressive conditions. Psychoanalytic and cognitive therapies are occasionally helpful with moderate levels of these disturbances, but these traditional psychotherapies are relatively useless with the severely disordered person.

■ PERSONALITY DISORDERS

Schizophrenia, affective disorders, anxiety, phobias, and so on, all seem to have one characteristic in common—the periods of disorder come and go. The symptoms may last a lifetime, but there are periods of **remission** when the symptoms are not there. A **personality disorder**, on the other hand, indicates a long-standing and permanent pattern of inappropriate behavior. Personality disorders represent one of the axes or diagnostic categories of the *DSM-III*, but there is a good deal of disagreement about the existence of any types of people who fit the descriptions. Table 15–8 presents two common descriptions.

Let's look at another of these disorders in greater detail. The **narcissistic personality disorder** is characterized by a feeling of great self-importance. The person typically acts as if he or she is the center of the universe. This disorder includes such symptoms as an exaggeration of talents or achievement, and

TABLE 15–8.
Descriptions of Two Personality Disorders

1. *Paranoid personality*—Unwarranted suspiciousness shown by expecting trickery, hypervigilance, secretiveness, avoidance of accepting blame, questioning others' loyalty, overconcern with hidden motives, intense jealousy. Supersensitive to slights and ready to counterattack. Restricted affect: cold, unemotional, and excessively rational, lacking real sense of humor or tender feelings.

2. *Schizoid personality*—Cold and aloof, lacking warm feelings for others, indifferent to praise, criticism or other peoples' feelings, very few close friendships.

a preoccupation with fantasies revolving around fame and fortune. The person demands constant attention and admiration and reacts poorly to criticism, sometimes responding with indifference and other times with rage. The person expects to be treated as "special," but would not think of treating others similarly. This type of person is often described as a "manipulator," using interpersonal relationships to his or her advantage. Above all, there is a shallowness in interpersonal relations. This type of person finds it difficult to appreciate the distress of others (*DSM-III*, 1980). The point to keep in mind about this personality disorder and the others listed in Table 15–8 is that they represent long-standing and habitual ways of behaving. These disorders are not patterns that appear suddenly when stress is unusually high. The behavior described here is typical, not unusual. This is what distinguishes these disorders from the symptoms usually examined on Axis I of the *DSM-III*.

Another characteristic that is said to separate these disorders from the others we have examined is that the *patient* does not regard his or her behavior as a disorder, and could not imagine living his or her life any other way. It might be tempting to characterize people you know using these labels, but that would be a mistake. Most people who act in ways

---

Remission. A period in a physical illness or a mental disorder during which the symptoms of the illness or the disorder disappear, usually only temporarily.

Personality disorder. Long-standing, permanent pattern of inappropriate behavior.

Narcissictic personality disorder. Characterized by a feeling of being the center of the universe. The person demands constant attention and admiration and is often described as a manipulator, using relationships with other people to his or her advantage.

similar to these descriptions would prefer to act differently if they simply knew how. In addition, most of the people you know would only act this way when they were in particular situations. In contrast, personality disorders are thought to represent collections of enduring trait-based behaviors that appear in all situations.

■ SUBSTANCE USE DISORDERS

We have covered these disorders in detail in Chapter 5. Since substances such as drugs or alcohol have direct effects on neurotransmission, it is not surprising that they often produce disordered behavior. Sometimes the disorders are intellectual, at other times they are motor, and at still other times the problem is with emotional control. The particular effect will depend on which receptor sites in the brain are involved. Depressive symptoms may appear in one case; manic symptoms may appear in another; in a third instance, the paranoid symptoms of schizophrenia may be present. Often, the more serious problems for disordered behavior result from physical and psychological dependence. These circumstances produce a pattern of behavior that is directed toward only one end—the creation of a different state of consciousness at any cost.

■ ORGANIC DISORDERS

Schizophrenia, affective disorders, and personality disorders are also called **functional disorders**. They may have a biological foundation, but we don't understand it well enough to completely explain the disorder on that basis. **Organic disorders** are different. In these cases, there is a clear, central-nervous-system explanation for the disturbance. Signs of organic disorders include:

1. Disorientation with respect to place, time, or people.
2. Memory loss, particularly for recent events.
3. Serious problems with planning, judgment, or learning.
4. Changeable emotions or lack of emotion.

The tests that are typically used to confirm or rule out organic disorders are EEG recordings (brain waves), CAT scans (three dimensional brain X-rays), tests of spinal fluid for poisons or infections, and neuropsychological testing (for example, performance subtests of an intelligence test). In addition, neurological examinations are also commonly performed. These include checking various reflexes, such as the knee-jerk reflex, as well as examining the retina of the eye for signs of damage to blood vessels. These tests might also involve testing coordinated movement, such as touching the tip of your nose with your index finger while both eyes are closed.

You have now been exposed to the minor and major categories of mental disorders. We have given brief descriptions of treatment approaches for each of these classes of disorders. In the next chapter, we will examine the technique and logic behind the various treatments of mental disorders.

■ SUMMARY

1. There is no universally-accepted definition of abnormal behavior because values change from one era to the next and from one culture to another. *The statistical model* uses the concept of "average" to distinguish between normal and abnormal behavior, but fails to make distinctions between desirable and undesirable behaviors and between important and trivial behaviors. The *medical model* views abnormal behavior as symptomatic of some underlying disease. The *cultural model* takes into account the cultural context in which the behavior occurs, so that abnormal behavior is relative to the norms of the society. The *adaptive model* views normal behavior as that which fosters well-being, while abnormal behavior does not.

2. Diagnosing abnormal behavior is difficult because there are seldom clear-cut causes for particular types of abnormal behavior. Diagnosing abnormal behavior can also present both validity and reliability problems: Different observers can vary in their descriptions of the same behavior and also tend to classify it differently. Once a diagnosis has been made, people tend to interpret all the patient's behaviors as being part of this disorder.

3. *The Diagnostic and Statistical Manual III*, or *DSM-III*, is a manual for diagnosing abnormal behavior. Using this system, the person is considered

on five dimensions, or axes, that provide a detailed framework for collecting most of the relevant information about a pattern of abnormal behavior. The *DSM-III* represents an effort toward improving the reliability of the classification of such behaviors.

4. In *DSM-III,* many of the mild disorders are classified as anxiety disorders. *Anxiety states* are fear states that are inappropriate or excessive given the nature of the external threat; they involve heightened arousal. The most extreme arousal of this type is called *panic.* A *phobia* is an inordinate amount of anxiety focused on a particular person, object, or situation. *Anxiety* is usually associated with one or more unpleasant physical symptoms. *Obsessions* are persistent thoughts that cause anxiety. *Compulsions* are actions that a person performs over and over again in an effort to relieve some anxiety. One post-traumatic stress disorder is *acute distress,* a state of anxiety that continues for a short time after a traumatic event; *chronic distress* is anxiety that continues for a long time after the event.

5. In the psychoanalytic view, specific forms of anxiety such as phobias and obsessive-compulsive behavior are thought to result from unacceptable id processes. To control the unacceptable thoughts or desires, an ego process develops and is then translated into a particular behavior.

6. The learning explanation of phobias is often based on the concept of conditioned fear, resulting from an association between a particular stimulus and a frightening event. However, this view presents problems: Many people have frightening experiences but do not develop phobias, while many people with phobias do not seem to have had particularly frightening experiences. Another learning view is that phobias develop from modeling or social learning.

7. Depression is a feeling or emotion that involves sadness, feelings of worthlessness, and even guilt. There are different types of depression: "normal," an emotional state that occurs after a negative life event; major depression, a state in which the person gives up and has a uniformly negative self-concept; and a depression of mood that may last several days to several months. Beck views depression as a thought disturbance involving a vicious cycle of negative thinking, emotions, and actions.

8. A *somatoform disorder* consists of physical complaints with no apparent physical or organic cause. A *conversion disorder* usually involves the loss of a particular function. A *somatization disorder* involves many varied complaints of distress. A characteristic of these disorders that helps to distinguish them from physically-based disorders is low anxiety about the symptoms. The psychoanalytic explanation is that tension or anxiety is converted into a physical disorder. A learning explanation is that somatoform disorders provide reward and/or avoidance of punishment or an unpleasant situation. With somatoform disorders, the person actually experiences the symptoms, even though the cause is not physical.

9. A *dissociative disorder* is "a sudden, temporary alteration in the normally integrative functions of consciousness, identity, or motor behavior" (*DSM-III,* p. 253). A *psychogenic fugue* can involve a flight from a stressful event or circumstance through a loss of memory. A *multiple personality* disorder occurs when a person behaves as more than one distinct personality. A more common problem is a *depersonalization disorder,* in which the primary symptom is a feeling of unreality. The psychoanalytic explanation of these disorders is that the symptoms are thought to represent the mechanism of repression when a conflict and anxiety are extremely severe. The learning explanation is that these disorders are examples of escape or avoidance.

10. *Anorexia nervosa* and *bulimia* are severe eating disorders in which people become so extremely preoccupied with weight loss that they will adopt dangerous strategies, such as starvation and self-induced vomiting. The psychoanalytic view of *anorexia nervosa* is that starvation is a response to unacceptable urges. Bulimia, a disorder involving eating binges followed by vomiting, seems to involve ambivalent feelings, while the anorexic is less ambivalent. Treatment involves improving self-esteem, making distorted self-images more realistic, and countering unrealistic fears.

Functional disorders. Disorders that may have a biological foundation, but are not yet well enough understood to be explained on that basis. Presently includes schizophrenia, affective disorders, and personality disorders.

Organic disorders. Disturbances of thought caused by a malfunction of the central nervous system; causes disorientation, memory loss, and other difficulties.

11. Psychosexual disorders include *gender identity disorders, paraphilias* (unusual means of sexual gratification), and disturbances of normal sexual functioning. *Transsexuals* are individuals who are unhappy with their anatomical sex and may undergo surgery to reverse their sexual identity so that it matches their sense of gender. The psychoanalytic explanation for these disorders is sexually-based conflict associated with unsuccessful resolution of the Oedipal and Electra complexes. The learning explanation is that events or objects that become associated with sexual gratification function as both classical and operant reinforcers.

12. Theorists differ in their opinions of the way in which we should view mental disorders. Szasz believes mental illness is an inappropriate term for what would best be labeled maladaptive behavior. Laing believes that the external world is responsible for creating symptoms in some people, and that the path to sanity for these people is found in withdrawal. Some forms of mental illness, such as schizophrenia, seem to be universal.

13. People can be placed in mental hospitals against their will by *civil commitment,* or on the basis of being a potential threat to themselves or to someone else, or by *criminal commitment,* which is initiated through the commission of a crime.

14. *Insanity* is a legal term applied to a person who was unaware of the meaning of criminal behavior or unable to conform to models of noncriminal behavior at the time the crime was committed. Before entering an insanity plea, the defendant must go through a preliminary procedure to determine whether he or she is competent to stand trial. Several outcomes are possible with an insanity plea: The person can be judged guilty and sent to prison, not guilty by reason of insanity and sent to a hospital, or not guilty and set free.

15. Bleuler introduced the term *schizophrenic* to describe a disorder in which intellectual functions were separated from emotions, and patients' personalities lacked integration. Bleuler listed four characteristics of these patients: (a) loose association or loss of logical connection between ideas; (b) inappropriate emotional responding; (c) *autism,* or a refusal to share a generally accepted view of reality and a refusal to describe the private one; and (d) the presence of strong opposite feelings about the same person. The most common schizophrenic symptoms are *hallucinations, delusions,* formal-thought disorders, motor disturbances, and emotional symptoms. Subtypes of schizophrenics distinguished by *DSM-III* include *disorganized, catatonic, paranoid,* and *undifferentiated.*

16. The developmental approach to explaining schizophrenia suggests that neurological damage before birth may lead to the disorder. Another developmental view is that schizophrenia is caused by certain types of family dynamics. Some studies have suggested that genetic inheritance plays a role in schizophrenia. The biochemical approach argues that the disorder has to do with brain chemistry or hormonal imbalances. A final view, the stress/vulnerability approach, proposes that some people have biological systems that are likely to produce schizophrenic symptoms, given the right circumstances.

17. Treatments for schizophrenia are mainly directed toward symptom relief rather than cure. Drugs are used to relieve symptoms so that the person can be released back into the community. After release, medication and work with the patient's family continue.

18. *Infantile autism* develops around age 2 or earlier and includes failure to relate to others, severe communication problems, and often a strong desire to keep things the same. There is a great deal of confusion about this disorder, and there is no standard treatment.

19. *Affective disorders* involve inappropriate or unusual levels of emotion or mood and are either *unipolar* (involving one extreme) or *bipolar* (involving both extremes). At the two opposite ends of the emotional scale are *depression* and *mania.* Depression is a widespread disorder, and the group of people most likely to suffer from depression are between the ages of 18 to 29.

20. The learning/cognitive approach suggests that depressed patients have been in many situations in which they were helpless to escape punishment, and that they now act as though they are helpless in most situations. Beck suggests that depressed people have illogical thought patterns and that the method of treatment should be to teach these patients to adopt new ones.

21. The bipolar disorder is an alteration between depressive and manic symptoms. The genetic/biological approach is the most common explanation:

Possibly a *predisposition* for this disorder is inherited, making some people vulnerable during certain stressful life events or biological disturbances.

22. A personality disorder is a longstanding and permanent pattern of inappropriate behavior. The narcissistic personality disorder is characterized by a feeling of great self-importance.

■ ANSWERING QUESTIONS FOR THOUGHT

1. Yes, to a certain extent you can. The DSM-III (discussed in text) lists descriptions of symptoms that can be used in classifying the particular mental disorder. The very act of classification can provide a beginning for treatment. Unlike physical illness, however, there are no equivalent physical measures (such as temperature and blood pressure readings) that can be used in the diagnosis of a mental disorder.

2. Phobias may be the result of generalization. You come to fear an object like the one you have had an unpleasant experience with. Thus, the person who is afraid of elevators might have been trapped once in a small room and after that be afraid of all small, enclosed places. Another way that a fear may be learned without actually experiencing the object of the fear is through observational learning—hearing or seeing someone express or show great fear of something.

3. To begin with, college students leave behind a number of social support systems, such as friends and family, when they go away to college. They also find themselves surrounded by other equally bright students rather than being the exceptions in their class, as they may have been in high school. There is also the pressure of grades, choosing a major and eventually a career, and establishing loving relationships. All of these factors may make college students more vulnerable to depression.

4. Delusions are false beliefs, and they are one of many thought disorders common in schizophrenics. An example given in the text is the delusion of control, or the belief that an outside force or personality has replaced the patient's own will or personality—for instance, that the patient is a puppet being controlled by someone else.

5. This is a subtype of schizophrenia in which patients have delusions that they are being betrayed by those close to them, or that strangers are out to do them harm. They often turn quite innocent remarks and conversations into evidence that supports these delusions.

6. Many depressives have thoughts about suicide, but not all depressives are suicidal and not all suicides are the result of depression. Thus, while there is reason to be concerned about the possibility of suicide with a severely depressed person, suicide is far from a normal or common expression of depression.

16 Therapy

QUESTIONS FOR THOUGHT

1. Do people's expectations have any effect on therapy?
2. Is any one type of therapy more effective than the others?
3. Is abnormal behavior a symptom of an underlying problem, or is the behavior itself the problem?
4. Can you cure a mental disorder just by talking about it?
5. What benefits are there to taking part in group therapy rather than individual therapy?

The answers to these questions are at the end of the chapter.

In Minneapolis, a patient in a psychiatric hospital is handed two pills. He takes the pills as a nurse watches, then moves back to the day room to watch TV. In Miami, a woman is given a mild electrical shock to her brain. This leads to a brief but strong convulsion that is followed by deep sleep. In Santa Fe, a young boy begins another weekly discussion with a clinical psychologist about his problems with his parents. In Seattle, a young girl talks with a psychologist from the school system about peer pressure from her friends. They are giving her a hard time because she refuses to drink alcohol at weekend parties and she wants advice on how to handle the situation.

All these people have something in common. Each of them is having an experience directed toward solving a problem or relieving discomfort. Each of them is receiving therapy.

■ WHAT IS THERAPY?

You may recall from Chapter 13 that Freud developed a theory of personality and a treatment approach (psychoanalysis) to go along with it.

Since Freud first introduced psychoanalysis, therapy has branched out in many different directions. Three of these major directions are: insight therapies, behavior therapies, and somatic therapies. **Insight therapies** are directed toward giving people a better or clearer understanding of their feelings, thoughts, and behaviors. **Behavior therapies** aim at changing behavior patterns directly, usually through the application of learning principles. **Somatic therapies** have a biological basis and assume that a change in a person's physical status will result in a change in behavior. The physical change may be brought about through drugs, shock, or surgery. It is unfortunate that many people think in terms of which type of therapy is "best." This way of thinking implies that one type of therapy works best for all people or that only one type of therapy should be used per patient. But this isn't true of therapy. What works "best" has to do with the patient, the kind of problem, and even the therapist. As you've already seen in the chapter on abnormal psychology, one approach may be better for one type of problem and another approach may be better for another problem. In addition, it is often the case that even within a particular problem area (such as drug abuse or excessive anxiety), one therapeutic approach works better with one individual and another approach works better with someone else. Finally, even within a single problem area and a single treatment approach, some people profit more than others from the same therapist. For all these reasons, we should avoid the question of which therapy is "best." They all have strengths and weaknesses; there is no clear "winner." This isn't to say that no one is interested in the relative effectiveness of various therapy techniques. In fact, many such

---

Insight therapy. A type of therapy directed toward giving people a better understanding of their feelings, thoughts, and behaviors.

Behavior therapy. A type of therapy that aims at changing behavior patterns directly, through the application of learning principles.

Somatic therapy. A type of therapy that has a biological basis, assuming that a change in a person's physical status will result in a change in behavior.

studies have been done and we will review some of their results later in the chapter.

Sometimes there is good reason to consider a combination of therapeutic approaches rather than one alone. For example, it is unlikely that 50 minutes of quiet discussion with a manic-depressive patient in a psychiatric hospital will be very helpful to that patient. It doesn't matter whether these discussions continue for a week, a month, or 10 years. On the other hand, it might make sense to first prescribe a drug that will help bring mood problems under control and enable the patient to move out of the institution—an abnormal environment by any standard—and then to begin a program of regular interactions with a psychotherapist aimed at helping the patient develop a more normal life-style. Can you imagine either of these approaches being truly effective without the contribution of the other approach? Unless the mood swings are brought under control, it is not possible for the patient to function effectively in the world outside the hospital. Unless the patient is exposed to normal environments, most of that patient's efforts are devoted to coping with or adapting to the abnormal environment of the hospital. Unless the patient has help in understanding why certain behavior patterns have developed, it is unlikely that the "problem" of adapting to normally-changing environments can be solved.

The combination approach to treatment is made easier by the fact that all therapies have the same goals. Coleman, Butcher, and Carson (1980) have listed the following general goals:

1. Changing maladaptive behavior patterns.
2. Trying to get rid of environmental conditions that may be causing or maintaining such behaviors.
3. Improving interpersonal skills.
4. Resolving handicapping or disabling inner conflicts and easing personal distress.
5. Modifying people's inaccurate assumptions about themselves and their world.
6. Fostering a clear-cut sense of self-identity.

The differences among the various therapies are really a matter of which goal (or goals) is emphasized. Despite these differences in emphasis, there is no attempt to belittle or criticize other therapeutic goals. At the very worst, the advocates of one approach might consider the goals of another approach unattainable or irrelevant to "recovery."

The Placebo Effect

Before we discuss therapies, you need to understand a phenomenon that can make it difficult to evaluate therapeutic effects. Have you ever noticed how valuable a good listener can be? When you have something on your mind, you often seek out another person to listen to you. You don't really want them to do anything or even say anything, you just want them to listen. After they've listened, you feel better—you have gotten something off your chest. In spite of the fact that they may have said almost nothing over a 30-minute period, you may tell someone else that you just had a great discussion. This session with the sympathetic listener can probably qualify as therapy, since it achieved several of the goals listed earlier.

In formal therapies, a similar event often occurs. It has been called the **placebo effect**. As you saw in earlier chapters, expectations play a major role in behavior. This seems to be particularly true of people who seek help from therapists. The fact that people go to therapists expecting to be helped has a positive effect. This is not particularly surprising: By the time most people make formal contact with a therapist, they have usually tried the remedies suggested in popular magazines, talked with sympathetic friends, and maybe even tried various creative solutions they thought up on their own. It is usually after all of these strategies have failed to solve the problem that they contact a therapist. They are *ready* for help. The very act of placing themselves under the care of professionals can relieve anxiety. In many circumstances, the particular orientation of the therapist may matter very little; what does matter is the person's belief that the therapist can help. Rogers and Dymond (1954) gathered data that showed that improvement actually begins before there has been any direct contact between therapist and client—improvement begins almost from the moment that the first appointment with the therapist is made. The reason for calling this phenomenon the "placebo" effect is that the necessary ingredient for improvement is a person's commitment to a therapeutic relationship, rather than the particular approach used by the therapist. This means that for all practical purposes, the therapist is an "inert" substance in the change (which is our previous definition of the term *placebo*). Actually, the use of the term "placebo" in this context is somewhat misleading. Although the type of therapy and the exact behaviors of the therapist may be unrelated to the cure, the *fact* of therapy and the expectations of the patient are not. There is nothing "inert" about the situation (Wilkins, 1986). As we will see when we compare the relative effectiveness of various forms of psychotherapy, these expectations and the "readiness to be cured" on the part of the patient may be *the most active* ingredients in psychotherapy.

Unfortunately, there are two sides to this coin. If a person believes that therapy is a waste of time, or that there is no problem, or that the therapist is taking the wrong approach, then he or she may not benefit from therapy no matter how effective the approach or how skilled the therapist. Forcing someone to enter a therapeutic relationship is seldom effective. Until and unless the person believes that the therapy may help solve the problem, little progress is likely to be made.

Is this an argument against therapy? No. It just means that a particular therapy may owe its success with a particular patient to a generalized belief the patient holds rather than to anything special about the therapy (Stiles, Shapiro and Elliott, 1986). From a strictly physiological point of view, the fact that anxiety is reduced is a major step forward. As you may remember, anxiety involves arousal. This arousal is often excessive. Since excessive arousal has negative effects on intellectual performance (as you saw in the chapter on stress), reducing anxiety (and arousal) can improve the course of therapy by allowing the person to engage in more effective self-evaluation, information processing, and problem solving. Thus, most therapies start from a position of advantage; the question then becomes whether or not the therapy improves on that position.

■ INSIGHT THERAPIES

Insight therapies are based on the idea that the goals of therapy are best served by helping people understand their current behaviors, why these behaviors may have developed, and how to change unwanted behaviors. There are literally hundreds of insight therapies, each one slightly different in emphasis or procedure from the others (Goldfried, 1980; Parloff, 1976).

Coleman (1980) has identified some key characteristics that may be used to distinguish among insight therapies. The therapy may be individual (one therapist and one client) or in a group (one therapist and a few clients). It may aim at cognitive change (such as increasing self-esteem) or at behavior change (such as getting a client who is afraid to fly to use air travel). The therapy may be directive (the therapist asks questions and offers interpretations) or nondirective (the therapist offers no advice, focusing instead or getting the client to clarify how he or she is feeling). The therapy may be aimed at developing an inner control mechanism or an outer control mechanism for certain behaviors. Inner control might involve changing a client's values with respect to a particular behavior (for example, getting the client to minimize the importance of minor disagreements with a spouse). Outer control emphasizes the use of environmental rewards to maintain a particular behavior (for example, promising yourself a night out at the movies if you go a full week without overeating). The therapy may be long-term (often 5 years or more) or short-term (about 10 hours). Finally, the therapy may focus on the past (your feelings as a child) or the present (your feelings today).

By combining just these six characteristics of psychotherapy on an either–or basis, there are 64 different possible therapies. For example, consider the following combination: individual, behavior change, directive, outer control, brief, here-and-now. This might be a program of treatment to help someone overcome an irrational fear of heights. It would fall into the class of therapies known as behavior modification. In contrast, consider a second combination: group, cognitive change, nondirective, inner control, long-term, historical focus. This might describe a therapy program for helping anorexic women to overcome their obsession with weight and their compulsion to diet through group discussions. Some treatment programs may be mixed, involving both group and individual sessions and both histori-

---

Placebo effect. In therapy, the fact that the person expects to be helped has a positive effect, no matter what the therapist does or doesn't do.

cal and here-and-now aspects. This should give you an idea of how many different *possible* types of insight therapy exist. We'll now see details of a number of important and widely used types of insight therapies.

Psychoanalysis

As you may remember from the personality chapter, Freud believed that unresolved conflicts are largely responsible for various mental disorders. As a result, his methods of treatment were tied to uncovering these conflicts and bringing them to the patient's awareness. Freud also thought that many such conflicts are left over from earlier stages of psychological development. The person failed to resolve these conflicts at the appropriate stage and they reappear later, causing anxiety and other problems. Psychoanalysis works at uncovering these conflicts in several ways. The two most common methods are free association and dream analysis.

Free Association. In the technique of **free association** people are asked to allow their minds to run free and to talk about their ideas or associations as they arise. They are asked not to avoid painful or embarrassing topics or to edit their comments in any way. The orthodox approach to free association is

In psychoanalysis, a client may lie on a couch with the therapist sitting behind or to the side, out of the client's line of vision.

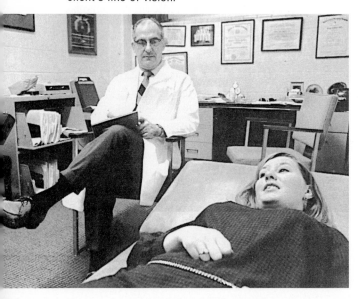

to encourage people to say anything and everything that comes to mind, regardless of how illogical or inappropriate it seems. This is harder to do than it sounds, and it takes time to learn the skill. This is one reason psychoanalysis takes longer than many other forms of insight therapy. The client is not simply resolving conflicts; new skills are being developed.

Free association depends on the absence of outside distractions. To facilitate this, clients often lie on a couch or sit in a comfortable chair. The therapist stays out of the line of vision, behind or to the side. This eliminates people's natural tendency to concentrate on the therapist's reactions to their comments. Freud had additional reasons for developing this technique—he did not find it pleasant to be stared at for eight hours a day (Jones, 1955).

It is assumed that in the course of freely associating, unconscious conflicts will emerge in the flow of comments and images. The therapist records the comments and interprets them in the context of conflict. You may recall the "hidden observer" technique used by Hilgard in his hypnosis experiments (see Chapter 5). Free association is somewhat similar—unconscious conflicts are allowed to emerge through mental associations in the same way that acknowledgments of pain are allowed to appear through the nonaffected hand ("the hidden observer") of the hypnotized person.

Dream Analysis. In Chapter 5, we considered the idea that sleep and dream states are different from the normal waking state. Psychoanalysts would strongly agree. They suggest further that one of the side effects of sleep is the relaxing of the ego defenses that are present during normal conscious experience. You may remember from the chapter on stress that ego defense mechanisms are habitual cognitive processes that we use to reduce the stress that results from conflict in the unconscious. This means that dreams—ideas and images produced during sleep—may also be free from the influence of the ego defense mechanisms. If this is the case, the underlying conflicts causing the problem might be revealed in dreams.

Freud felt that some conflicts were so deep that they could not be allowed to surface even in dreams. For this reason, he suggested that dreams really exist at two levels. The first level consists of the surface elements of the dream (who was involved, what action took place, what was the outcome). This is called the **manifest content** of the dream. Beneath this surface, however, is the more important dream material. This deeper material is more closely connected to the conflict. This deeper meaning is called the **latent content**. The therapist and the client examine and discuss the manifest content of the dream and interpret or analyze it in an attempt to identify the latent content. It is almost as if the manifest content is a code and the therapist is trying to help the client break that code and understand the meaning of the message. The concepts of manifest and latent content are strikingly similar to the concepts of surface and deep structure that we considered in the chapter on language. In the same way that a single thought (deep structure) can be expressed in many different ways (surface structure), so can a single conflict (latent dream content) be expressed in many different dreams (manifest dream content). The manifest content may be influenced by the events of the day, but these events are only triggers that release a more basic source of tension produced by an underlying conflict.

Resistance. In the view of the psychoanalyst, the single most important indicator that the person is beginning to identify underlying conflicts is the person's **resistance** to talking about certain topics or feelings. It would seem as if the ego is defending itself against anxiety by refusing to talk or think about those occasions that give rise to that anxiety. It is assumed that the greater the reluctance to talk about something, the more central it is to the conflict. Seen in this light, both free association and dream analysis are opportunities for the person to unknowingly reveal sources of sensitivity. By expertly exploring those areas, the psychoanalyst can gradually remove the layers of denial and defense that have acted to mask the anxiety. This process is not very different from the part of a general physical examination in which your physician pokes, pushes, and pulls until you wince or gasp. Your reac-

tion is a clear indication that a sensitive area has been found—one worthy of further exploration. In the context of either free association or the discussion of a dream, resistance may take the form of an abrupt change of topics by the person, a significant pause, or a quick comment to the effect that the material is "not important" or "silly."

Transference. Another important type of event in psychoanalysis is known as **transference**. This means that the emotions the patient feels for those involved in the conflict or anxiety become attached to the psychoanalyst. This provides the therapist with an excellent way to turn back the clock. In transference, the patient begins to respond to the psychoanalyst as if the therapist were the patient's mother, father, or sibling. Patients get angry, depressed, afraid, or elated as a result of interactions with the therapist in exactly the same way as they originally did as children with their mothers, fathers, or siblings. Once this happens, the psychoanalyst can point out the irrationality of the client's reaction. The therapist is *not* the parent or sibling, so it is irrational for the client to behave in a childlike manner. When transference occurs and these irrational reactions emerge, they can be used as material for learning and discussion (insight). Some people have the idea that the patient and therapist should avoid becoming emotionally involved. But treatment actually *depends* on this involvement, at least with respect to the emotional involvement of the patient. When the patient begins responding in this way, it is a signal that the therapist can begin helping the person to work through the unresolved conflicts of the past.

We have discussed free association and dreams as the raw material of psychoanalysis, and identified resistance and transference as indicators of progress. The therapist has another indispensable tool in psychoanalysis. This tool is interpretation. The psychoanalyst collects the past experiences of the patient using the methods described earlier, and

---

Free association. Freudian technique in which people are asked to allow their minds to run free and to talk about their ideas or associations as they arise.

Manifest content. The surface elements of a dream—the people and events involved in the dream.

Latent content. The deeper meaning of a dream, usually connected to an unconscious conflict of some sort.

Resistance. Freudian term for the unwillingness to talk about topics connected to a source of conflict. Resistance may be conscious or unconscious.

Transference. In psychoanalysis, the process by which the conflicted or anxious emotions the patient feels toward others become attached to the analyst instead.

then sorts and groups these experiences until they form a theme and make sense. The organizing principles that the psychoanalyst uses are the propositions of Freud's theory. These propositions include levels of consciousness, cognitive operations, and psychosexual stages.

Evaluation of Psychoanalysis. Luborsky and Spence (1978) have reviewed the strengths and weaknesses of the psychoanalytic approach and have drawn some conclusions. The first is that psychoanalysis is poorly suited for dealing with serious mental disorders such as schizophrenia or major depression. This is because the method depends heavily on verbal skills and sound reasoning capabilities, while serious disorders are often characterized by disturbances of communication and thought. It has also been shown that educated patients show greater progress than uneducated patients; this is undoubtedly the result of the effect of education on both verbal ability and reasoning skills. A third conclusion is that no firm judgment can be made about the effectiveness of psychoanalysis. As you will remember from the introduction to this chapter, there has been a tendency to

THE 50-MINUTE PSYCHOTHERAPY HOUR

When Sigmund Freud was first developing psychoanalysis, there was no such thing as an hourly treatment session. He could afford to spend time with each patient as needed and to ignore the ticking of the clock. For example, when the composer Gustav Mahler came to see Freud, he received just one treatment—a session that lasted a full six hours. But as the number of patients grew, the luxury of unlimited time soon became a thing of the past, even for Freud. To accommodate an increasing clientele and still maintain the quality of treatment, Freud devised what he called the "fifty-minute psychotherapy hour." This grew out of his belief that the therapist should not take notes during the time spent with the patient. Thus patients were given 50 minutes of a session to talk, and the therapist used the remaining ten minutes to make notes before seeing the next patient. In time, Freud's fifty-minute hour became a standard for clinical practice. Although today some therapists have shortened the hour even further (to 45 minutes), surveys shows that 50 minutes is still the norm. Interestingly, too, researchers find that the session tends to follow a pattern of exchange between therapist and client.

As in other types of conversation, sessions generally start off with a few pleasantries. While to the client these opening remarks may seem of no particular significance, to the therapist they may contain significant, underlying meaning.

Small talk over the next few minutes allows the therapist and client to become comfortable with one another and may set a session off in a particular direction. During the next 30 to 35 minutes, the client brings up pressing issues, often expressing deep feelings and going into great detail. This corresponds to the main theme of the session. Several minutes before the end of the session, intensity either builds to a resolution, or simply to the release of feelings. In the remaining few minutes, clients tend to try to compose themselves before returning to the outside world. They may need this time to cool down after a period of emotional intensity. The final moments are again filled with seemingly casual remarks by the client from which experienced therapists may draw deeper meanings.

This breakdown of a 50-minute psychotherapy session is, of course, an ideal picture. Not all sessions will, or necessarily should, fit into this model. Sometimes clients feel frustrated by these arbitrary time limits when important matters cannot be satisfactorily resolved within the time allotted. In practice, the 50-minute hour represents an attempt to strike a compromise between the needs of individual clients and the demands of a busy clinical schedule.

Adapted from: Daniel Goleman, "Therapy: Critics Assail 'Assembly-line Sessions,' " the New York Times, April 17, 1984, pp. C1, C11.

pit one therapy against another to try to answer the question of which one is best. In that sense, psychoanalysis cannot be demonstrated to be any more effective than many other approaches. The belief system of the patient as well as the skill of the therapist play roles in the ultimate effectiveness of therapy. If the patient is forced into psychoanalysis or does not believe it will work, the approach is not likely to be effective. In the same way, psychoanalysts vary in effectiveness; some are better than others. You would expect the effectiveness of the approach to depend, at least to some extent, on the skill of the therapist.

When differences in the clients' beliefs and expectations and therapist skills are coupled with the heavy dependence of psychoanalysis on verbal skills and thinking, it is not surprising that evaluations of many therapists, many patients, and many problems show no clear advantage for psychoanalysis. This failure to demonstrate clear superiority is not enough to dismiss the psychoanalytic approach as useless. One common way of evaluating the success of therapy is asking people how they *feel* afterward. Reports of reduced anxiety and increased positive feelings are just as likely to result from psychoanalysis as from the other insight therapies. In many cases, this might well be considered an enormous success.

Humanistic Therapies

The humanistic approach emphasizes the uniqueness of human experience, the importance of the present, the potential of each person for growth and development, and the significance of the interactions with the therapist that occur in the course of therapy. There is an interesting parallel between Freudian psychoanalysis and humanistic approaches. Both theories stress the importance of people's capacity to consider and evaluate both past and anticipated behaviors. Both theories suppose that the mind can consider itself. In Freudian theory, the id, ego, and superego processes interact. This interaction often results in conflict between what the id wants, what the ego can do, and what the superego will allow. In humanistic theory, there is an interaction between what the person is now and what the person would like to become. These two images are compared and contrasted, and these comparisons and contrasts play a major role in the course of therapy. In both humanistic and psychoanalytic theory, dialogues—created by the fact that two conflicting ideas exist in the mind at the same time—are critical.

Person-Centered Therapy. Carl Rogers is a prominent humanist. He developed a theory of personality and therapy that has come to be known by various names such as person-centered, client-centered, nondirective, or reflective therapy. His therapy is based on the following assumptions (Ford and Urban, 1963; Davison and Neale, 1982):

1. The only "real world" for the therapist is the world as perceived by the client. It is the way in which the person sees events or people that is critical, not how the therapist interprets those events.
2. People are capable of being aware of both their behavior and their motives.
3. People are, by definition, good and effective. Problems arise only as a result of faulty learning.
4. People are self-directing. They do not simply respond to their environment (as behaviorists would suggest) or to hidden inner drives (as Freud suggested).
5. Therapists should set up an environment in which people can learn more about themselves and, as a result, grow and change from that

Carl Rogers believes that certain characteristics of the therapist, especially openness, unconditional positive regard, and empathy, are important for progress to occur in therapy.

knowledge. It is this growth that represents a "cure" of the problems that led to treatment.

As suggested in the earlier review of Rogers' theory of personality (see Chapter 13), people are constantly assessing the match between how they see themselves and how they behave or are viewed by others. There are often discrepancies between self-image and behavior. You may think of yourself as a generally pleasant and accepting person. Thus, after an argument with a friend in which you intentionally said some unkind things, there is a discrepancy in your mind that must be resolved. Why would you say things to hurt someone, particularly a valued friend, if you were a "nice" person? It is through the consideration of these contradictions that progress or growth is realized.

Rogers believes that certain characteristics of therapists are important for their clients' progress. These characteristics are *openness, unconditional positive regard*, and *empathy*. Openness by a therapist is demonstrated in interactions with the client. The therapist must not be guarded or dishonest in discussing personal details, thoughts, and desires. In this way, the client sees a significant person acting in an honest and open way and, in so doing, the therapist acts as a model. **Unconditional positive regard** means that the therapist places no conditions on respecting the client. The client is considered important not because of what he or she does or says, but because he or she is a human being. There are no strings attached to valuing the person. The opposite of this would be a therapist who shows conditional regard—who withholds approval or support until the person behaves "better" or changes a behavior pattern.

According to Rogers, part of the problem that brings a person to therapy is the realization that there is no opportunity to try out or explore new ways of behaving because there is almost always the fear of others' disapproval. People need approval to feel accepted. Think of a friend or relative with whom you are particularly close. In many instances, this person is someone you can be honest with. You don't have to hide weaknesses or doubts; you don't have to fear looking stupid in front of them. They will love you regardless of the way you behave. It is important for a person to have this type of relationship with someone and definitely with the

therapist. This type of relationship occurs most commonly in parent/child interactions, but, even in that context, problems arise when parents become demanding and use love as a reward for success, beauty, or acceptable behavior. The same problem arises outside of the family with friends and employers. An unstated question that is sometimes asked by supervisors in supervisor/subordinate relationships in work settings is, "What have you done for me lately?" The relationship between the therapist and client must be completely free of demands and conditions.

The final characteristic of an effective therapist that Rogers emphasizes is empathy. This means that the therapist tries to see the world as the client does. Instead of telling people how they *should* view a situation, the therapist makes an effort to understand how they actually are feeling. For example, a client might say, "I saw my mother today and she seemed in a hurry to get away from me. I think she really dislikes me." It might be tempting for a therapist to respond, "You are misinterpreting what you saw. She was probably late to an appointment of some kind. You shouldn't read so much into situations like that." A Rogerian response might be, "Her behavior made you feel that she has no use for you." This type of response provides the person with a chance to explore the emotions of the situation in greater detail without feeling stupid or trivial. You may remember from Chapter 9 that the value of brainstorming depends on creating as many innovative solutions as possible before beginning to critically evaluate them. The Rogerian approach is similar in some respects. The quickest way to cut down on the active exploration of emotional problems is to criticize, evaluate, or to reinterpret them.

Most of us have had some experience with a person who is open, consistently supportive, and empathic rather than self-centered. It is difficult to deny the positive effect this type of person can have on our emotions and behavior. It is equally difficult to ignore the likelihood that person-centered therapy can be effective in many situations. As is the case with psychoanalysis, however, it is not likely that this approach would be effective in addressing serious mental disorders. Humanists rely heavily on reasoning, verbal interactions, and common frames of reference. It would be difficult for a therapist to experience the emotions of a manic-depressive patient, and it would be almost impossible for a therapist to communicate with a schizophrenic in a language pattern or conceptual network that both could understand.

Gestalt Therapy. Another humanistic approach to treatment is Fritz Perls' **Gestalt therapy**. Gestalt therapy stresses the examination of the person's perceptions of the world. In the chapter on perception you learned that people often view the world in terms of figure–ground relationships. This was a proposition of the Gestalt school of perception. Applied to therapy, Gestalt therapists see a person's dominant needs or motives as the figure, and the various situations in which they find themselves as the background or ground. As a result, the aim of therapy is to help people separate the figure from the ground and, as a result, better understand the influence that certain needs and motives have on their behavior. Gestalt therapy aims to uncover distortions in perceptions. Since the progress of this treatment approach is thought to depend on the person's awareness of his or her feelings and actions, the techniques often involve role playing, in which the client acts out a particular role and then steps back and examines the behavior and emotions that were just portrayed. This is one way to separate the figure from the ground.

There are many other forms of humanist therapy, but they all share the same emphasis on the worthiness of all human beings, the capacity of people to cure themselves, and the importance of self-examination.

■ COGNITIVE THERAPIES

Several approaches to abnormal behavior concentrate on the cognitive operations of the person. This is not to say that psychoanalysis or person-centered therapy ignore cognition; they obviously don't. After all, free association and dream recall are cognitive activities, and exploring emotions with an uncon-

In Gestalt therapy an important technique is role playing, in which a person acts out a particular role and then steps back and examines the behavior and emotions that were just portrayed.

ditionally supportive therapist requires powers of reasoning. Cognitive therapies assume that problems arise from the way people think and the images they use to represent events in their memories. There is a heavy emphasis on the examination of irrational beliefs.

One of the popular forms of cognitive therapy has been developed by Beck (1976). Beck often asks patients to keep diaries or running accounts of various thoughts involving depression and anxiety. He then uses those recorded observations as the raw material for therapy sessions. Discussions revolve around the relative rationality of those thoughts and concerns. For example, in the week before the therapy session, the client might have been depressed by the thought of not receiving an invitation to a party. In the therapy session, this thought is explored. The client lists the perceived consequences of not receiving the invitation: Everyone will wonder why he wasn't at the party; he will be

---

Unconditional positive regard. The acceptance and love shown toward another person regardless of that person's behavior; in therapy, the idea that the therapist places no conditions on respect or admiration of a client.

Gestalt therapy. A type of humanistic therapy that stresses the examination of a person's perceptions of the world.

left alone on Saturday night with nothing to do; others may decide that he is not part of the "in" crowd and he won't receive invitations to other parties in the future. The client is then assisted in reevaluating those perceived consequences and coming to more realistic conclusions. As a result, the client may realize that few will really notice his absence since many people will come and go over the course of the evening. Further, there are others who will not be going to the party because they don't know the host and he can arrange to do something with one of those people. Finally, there are few people who carry past guest lists around in their heads and use them to determine the guest list to their own parties. Thus, each of the perceived negative consequences becomes less negative.

Beck feels that there are certain automatic operations that people often go through that maintain or exaggerate feelings of anxiety or depression. These feelings, in turn, lead to behaviors directed toward eliminating or reducing them. These behaviors might be withdrawal, phobic fears, or generalized anxiety. It is assumed that therapy consists of replacing maladaptive automatic thought processes with other thought processes that are more rational and more likely to lead to constructive actions (normal behavior) on the part of the patient. As a result of comparing irrational and rational interpretations of events, both past and future, the patient comes to an understanding of the causes of the behavior problem. Since an old behavior (the irrational analysis of situations) is being replaced by a new behavior (a rational analysis of situations), cognitive therapy is often considered a particular form of behavior modification. We will return to certain aspects of cognitive therapy in the next section, which deals more directly with learning and reinforcement principles in therapy.

As you can see, there are many links among the various forms of insight therapies. These links include an emphasis on the verbal exploration of thoughts, moods, and motivations and a dependence on the cognitive skills of the therapist to recognize significant events and to explore them more fully when they appear in the course of therapy. Now let's consider a somewhat different approach to treating abnormal behavior—one which places greater emphasis on the nonverbal behavior of the patient. This class of treatments has been labeled behavior therapy.

REVIEW QUESTIONS

1. Match the following terms with the correct definitions:

___ insight therapies   A. focused on changing a person's physical status in the belief that this will result in a change in behavior.

___ behavior therapies   B. aimed at changing people's behavior through the application of learning principles.

___ somatic therapies   C. directed toward giving people a clearer understanding of their feelings, thoughts, and behaviors.

2. The _____ effect is an important element in the success of therapy—if people are ready for help and believe that therapy will help them, they are much more likely to make progress in therapy.

3. Match the following terms with the correct definitions:

___ free association   A. ego defending itself against anxiety by refusing to think about certain topics or feelings.

___ transference   B. analyzing the latent content that is connected to an underlying conflict.

___ resistance   C. allowing your mind to run free and saying whatever comes into your head.

___ dream analysis   D. attaching emotions you felt as a child to the therapist, instead of to the person who caused them (parent, sibling, and so on).

4. An important quality in Rogers' person-centered therapy is the fact that the therapist accepts the person and values him or her with no strings attached. Rogers refers to this as _____ _____ _____ .

5. In _____ therapy, the aim is to help people separate the figure/ground (their

> needs or motives) from the figure/ground (the situations they find themselves in), and thus better understand the influence that various motives have on their behavior.
>
> 6. _____ therapies in general assume that problems arise from the way people think and the images they use to represent events in memory. There is a heavy emphasis on examining irrational beliefs.
>
> *Answers:* 1. insight therapies, C; behavior therapies, B; somatic therapies, A. 2. placebo 3. free association, C; transference, D; resistance A; dream analysis, B. 4. unconditional positive regard 5. Gestalt; figure; ground 6. Cognitive

BEHAVIOR THERAPY

Behavior therapy, or **behavior modification**, as it is often called, differs from the insight therapies in some very basic ways. Behavior therapy and behavior modification are the same thing (Craighead et al., 1976)—the only difference is that behavior therapy refers to a therapy process, and behavior modification refers to the goal of that process. The behavior therapist assumes that almost all behavior of significance (other than certain simple reflexes such as coughing and sneezing) is learned. Further, it is assumed that maladaptive or abnormal behavior is learned in exactly the same manner as normal behavior. It follows from these assumptions that the only "tools" necessary for treatment are principles of learning. As a general strategy, maladaptive behaviors are eliminated and replaced by more effective behavior patterns. This is certainly an attractive possibility. You have seen in earlier chapters that we know a good deal more about learning than we do about emotions, cognitions, or alternate states of consciousness. As a result, we proceed on firmer ground when we attempt to apply learning principles to the treatment of abnormal behavior.

The main principle for the behavior therapist is one of conditional or contingent positive regard. The therapist provides rewards in keeping with the behavior of the person. To be fair, the behavior therapist tries to set up situations in which the person can only succeed, thus in practice the rewards (such as praise from the therapist) occur just as fre-

quently in behavior therapy as they do in person-centered therapy. Nevertheless, there is a real difference in theory. In person-centered therapy the positive regard is unconditional; in behavior therapy there are conditions imposed on praise and support.

Behavior therapy, in contrast to Freudian theory, has no concern for the unconscious or for conflicts between the ego and id. Certainly, there is a ready acceptance of the importance of past events on present behavior, but this importance is tied to learning experiences, not to unresolved conflicts at critical periods (such as the oral stage of psychosexual development). In behavior therapy, there is no attempt to identify underlying causes of maladaptive behavior. The behavior is not seen as a symptom—it is seen as the problem. If the behavior is changed, the problem has disappeared.

You have already seen that maladaptive behavior can result from many different learning experiences; these include both operant and classical conditioning experiences. Since the inappropriate learning might have developed in many different ways, there are many different approaches to behavior therapy. There are, however, some basic approaches that can be described. These approaches account for most of the individual types of behavior therapy.

Applied Behavioral Analysis

The basic principle of Skinner's behaviorism is that the probability of a behavior is directly related to the nature of the environmental consequences that follow that behavior. All of the other aspects of operant conditioning (such as schedules of reinforcement, shaping, successive approximation, and so on) are really just refinements of that basic principle.

A general example of the application of applied behavioral analysis to abnormal behavior is seen in wards of psychiatric hospitals that are run on a token-economy system (which we discussed in relation to schools in Chapter 7). The types of behaviors that are rewarded include keeping the ward clean, not assaulting other patients, not inflicting self-injury, decision making, communicating with other patients, dressing, grooming, and not exhibit-

---

Behavior modification. The goal of behavior therapy, in which maladaptive behaviors are eliminated and replaced by more effective behavior patterns.

ing hallucinatory and hysterical behaviors. A checksheet is used to record which patients have performed which behaviors; the form used is very much like a financial balance sheet. There are earnings that are accumulated through appropriate behaviors, there are expenditures of the credits earned for food and activities, and there is a running balance of credits available for spending. There is a wide variety of opportunities to spend the credits earned. This is important, since not every patient enjoys the same activities or reinforcers. This type of reinforcement system has proven effective in eliminating certain undesirable behaviors and replacing them with more adaptive actions. Successes with severely disturbed patients have been reported by Ayllon and Azrin (1965) and Paul and Lentz (1977).

A question remains, however. Have these seriously disturbed patients been cured or simply made easier to manage? There is some doubt about the answer to the first part of the question. If you consider schizophrenia to be nothing more than disordered language or inappropriate emotional expressions, then there has been some success in curing schizophrenics. But schizophrenia seems to be a more general and serious disorder than the uttering of strange words and inappropriate giggling or crying. In the last chapter we saw the numerous symptoms that are characteristic of the disorder. At best, it might be said that certain symptoms of certain patients have been eliminated. With respect to the second part of the question, the answer is clearer; even severely disturbed patients can be taught adaptive or constructive behavior. They can

In a token economy system a patient can earn credits or tokens by performing certain behaviors, such as keeping the ward clean, dressing and grooming themselves, and communicating with other patients.

improve to the point where it is possible to discharge them from psychiatric institutions into residential homes, such as half-way houses or shelters. Even though this may not be a cure, it is certainly an improvement.

As is the case in any learning experience, efforts can occasionally be ill placed. It is important to make sure that the correct behaviors are reinforced. Mahoney (1974) describes a humorous (and fic-titious) example of misapplied behavioral reinforce-ment resulting in inappropriate learning. A mother had two young children who had developed a habit of frequent cursing. This was quite an embarrass-ment and she consulted a behavior therapist for guidance. The therapist suggested that she severe-ly punish the child who cursed next, and, if it were possible, allow the nonpunished child to observe the punishment (this was a combination of contingent

A BEHAVIOR MODIFICATION CONTROVERSY

There has been a good deal of discussion, much of it emotionally charged, regarding the use of punishment therapy with autistic patients. (Strictly speaking, punishment therapy falls into the category of behavior modification even though many behavior therapists strongly disavow the use of punishment techniques.) Autism is a severe disorder that appears early in life, and may include a variety of specific behavioral symptoms, such as speech defects, self-abusive behavior (e.g., head-banging), and instances of aggression against others. Autism has defied effective treat-ment by conventional therapies. The most com-mon approach involves institutionalization and drug therapy.

A treatment center in Providence, Rhode Island, has recently instituted principles of behavior modification to deal with the most severe autistic symptoms. As in other applied behavior modifica-tion systems (e.g., token economies in school systems), positive reinforcement is the key. Pa-tients can "cash in" good-behavior credits for gifts and opportunities to engage in leisure activities. Controversy has arisen, however, from the treat-ment center's use of a class of reinforcers called "aversives." The aversives are used to stop the pa-tient from engaging in disruptive or potentially dangerous activities. Aversives include pinching, noise loud enough to be painful, water sprays in the face, and spankings (Butterfield, 1985). Ques-tions about the acceptability of this type of treat-ment began after a 22-year-old male patient died following the administration of loud noise through a helmet-like device. Following his death, state authorities sought court orders banning therapies that involved "aversives."

The average individual who has had no ex-posure to an autistic child or young adult would probably cringe at the description of the "therapy." It sounds cruel and primitive, like something left over from the asylums of earlier centuries. Many of the parents of children treated by this method, however, feel differently. From their perspective, the alternatives are considerably worse. These alternatives include doing nothing and allowing the individual to continue a pattern of self-injury and uncontrollable social interaction or institutionalizing the person and controlling these unacceptable behaviors through the use of tranquilizers. Many parents feel that it is better to allow the use of these "aversives" than to have their children go through life in a state of heavy sedation.

The issue of punishment therapy in this ex-treme form is difficult to deal with. The fact that aversives have such dramatic effects on the target behavior may make them seductively attractive and may discourage attempts to uncover less radical forms of treatment. Perhaps the first step to take in resolving this controversy is to examine the relative effectiveness of this form of therapy compared to other forms of treatment for autistic patients. Most of the evidence currently available is in the form of case studies of success. The scientist would require more thorough evidence, carefully gathered and analyzed. including ex-amples of punishment therapy that did *not* have the intended effect. As much as one might sym-pathize with the parents of autistic children, public policy involving the acceptability of aversive treat-ment should be based on careful research and analysis, not testimonials. Therapies with the potential of causing anguish, pain, and possibly death need to be scrutinized very carefully.

punishment and observational learning). The very next morning an opportunity arose. Both children came into the kitchen for breakfast. The mother asked the first what he would like. He replied, "Give me the damned cheerios." The mother reached across the table and hit the boy so hard she knocked him from his chair to the ground. As he lay there dazed and bewildered, she turned to the second child and asked what *he* would like. He answered, "You can bet your sweet ass it isn't cheerios." It was clear that he had learned something, but not the right thing.

Systematic Desensitization

Systematic desensitization attempts to break associations between certain stimulus objects and negative emotional responses. Gradually the person is taught to replace fear and anxiety with relaxation in the presence of certain stimuli. It is assumed that the anxiety leads to escape and avoidance responses. As a result, eliminating or reducing the anxiety should lead to a reduction in the response. This is an attempt to reverse the original association that was inappropriately learned. This is somewhat different from concentrating on only correct or adaptive behavior. Desensitization is considered necessary because the person is not initially likely to engage in the appropriate behavior because of the fear or anxiety associated with a particular stimulus. This anxiety must be addressed directly before any progress can be made. It is almost as if a period of unlearning is required before new learning can take place.

The techniques that make up desensitization were developed most completely by Wolpe (1958). There are two major elements in Wolpe's program of treatment. The first element is identifying a hierarchy of threat. The patient is asked to describe events or situations that represent various points on a stress continuum. This hierarchy includes some events that are only mildly stressful, others that present real discomfort, and still others that result in near panic. For a person with a fear of closed spaces, a mildly stressful situation might be a large auditorium with exits spaced 20 feet apart along the length of every wall. An uncomfortable environment might be a classroom with one exit in the front and one in the rear. A terrifying situation might be a

crowded elevator going directly to the top floor of a skyscraper.

The second element of desensitization is training in relaxation. The patient is taught various techniques for controlling breathing, relaxing muscles, and generally reducing physical tension. These techniques often make use of hypnosis or imagery. For example, the person might be asked to imagine sitting on a grassy bank near a gentle stream on a pleasant summer afternoon.

The final step in the treatment is to link these two elements together by asking people to practice their new relaxation skills in the presence of some level of the threat hierarchy. The technique is called *systematic desensitization* because the therapy starts with the least threatening level of the fear stimulus. In the previous example, this would be the large auditorium with lots of exits. The person is asked to imagine that scene while relaxing. Often, the scene is presented visually by using a slide projector and screen. While viewing the scene, the patient relaxes. The treatment proceeds through the stress hierarchy, eventually pairing the most stressful image with the relaxation. When the hierarchy has been successfully completed, the person has managed to replace one emotional response (panic) with another more appropriate response (problem solving and rational analysis permitted by the greatly reduced stress level).

A general conclusion that might be drawn from this approach is that systematic desensitization can be very effective in dealing with specific instances of anxiety associated with particular objects or events. Nevertheless, Wolpe's technique is only one of many that have proven equally successful. There has been some success with just exposing the person to the fear-inducing stimulus for extended periods of time. This is called **flooding.** Similarly, Paul (1966, 1969) has suggested that relaxation is not really critical, nor is the stress hierarchy. Just repeated exposure is enough to bring about a reduction in anxiety.

Cognitive Behavior Therapy

This approach assumes that thought processes are aspects of behavior and can be modified just like any other behavior. The therapy in this case involves replacing one way of thinking with another. As is the case with other forms of behavior therapy, the emphasis is on *how* the person behaves (thinks) in particular situations rather than *why* the person developed this way of thinking. In Beck's approach to therapy, the person is taught to analyze situations more rationally or reasonably, with particular emphasis on identifying and eliminating fears that are out of proportion to the object or situation.

An example may help you come to a better understanding of the technique. As you saw in the chapter on abnormal behavior, a difficult problem for certain people is the recurrence of unwanted thoughts. The label for this is *obsessive thought*. One simple technique that is suggested to patients is to begin saying, "No. No. No..." or "Stop. Stop. Stop..." as soon as the thought begins. The technique has been referred to as **thought stopping** (Walker, et al., 1981) and it is learned gradually. First, the patient is instructed to summon the unwanted thought. When it occurs, the patient indicates the presence of the thought by raising a finger. The therapist immediately shouts "No!" or "Stop!" or "Get out of here!" The patient lowers the finger when the thought disappears. Eventually, the patient is asked to join in the shouting and the therapist gradually allows the patient to do more and more of the shouting. Finally, the patient learns to repeat the command silently whenever the unwanted thought occurs. In this way, the patient has learned to control irrational thinking. Walker and his colleagues report successful treatment of a man with an obsessional fear of germs carried by a neighbor. These disturbing thoughts had been occurring for over 7 years. The obsession led to extreme compulsive behaviors as well, such as wearing gloves and a leather jacket in the presence of the neighbor and refusing to touch anything that the neighbor had handled. After 10 forty-minute sessions of thought stopping, the obsession and compulsive behaviors were greatly reduced and therapy was ended. One year later, a check of the man's status indicated that neither the obsession nor the compulsion had returned.

The important aspects of both Beck's approach to depression and Walker's treatment of obsessional thinking are teaching new patterns of thinking and offering a measure of self-control. This is quite different from the insight therapies. It is assumed that the person must develop new *habits* for dealing with anxiety. In this approach, progress is not necessarily the result of reasoning; instead, progress depends on practice. Another substantial difference is that the client can actually practice dealing with anxiety between therapy sessions. In most insight therapies, the client must wait until the next session to deal with the anxiety. In cognitive behavior therapy, if a person were abnormally anxious about an upcoming test, he or she might sit down with a piece of paper and list all of the feared consequences of poor performance. Then, each of these consequences would be considered more rationally and the anxiety could be reduced. In the traditional insight therapy, the client might make a call to the therapist and ask to arrange a special session, or the person might just try to live with the disturbing anxiety until the next scheduled insight-therapy session.

What distinguishes the work of people like Beck and Walker from earlier behaviorist thinking is the issue of self-control (Thoresen and Mahoney, 1974). The final step in cognitive behavior therapy is the transfer of control of behavior from the environment to the client.

Social Learning

Primarily the work of Bandura (1969), the *social learning approach* to behavior modification is actually the broadest of the behavioral therapies. It includes aspects of all three of the previously described approaches: applied behavioral analysis, systematic desensitization, and cognitive behavior modification. The social learning approach assumes that inappropriate learning can occur by any of the following means: classical conditioning, operant conditioning, or the development of incorrect cognitive habits. This approach also assumes that the learner

---

Systematic desensitization. A type of behavior therapy that seeks to break associations between certain objects or stimuli and negative emotional responses.
Flooding. A technique sometimes used in behavior therapy—

consists of exposing the person to the fear-inducing stimulus for long periods of time.
Thought stopping. A technique used in cognitive behavior therapy to stop obsessive thoughts.

(the patient) has a much more active role in treatment than is true within the applied behavior analysis approach of contingent reinforcement.

A critical part of the social learning approach is the cognitive interpretation that the person applies to particular interactions with the environment. In addition, modeling (practicing the behaviors displayed by others) and observational learning (watching others have success and failure in particular situations) play a major role in treatment. For the most part, the modeling and observational learning elements are peculiar to the social learning approach. They are not found in applied behavior analysis, systematic desensitization, or the more narrowly defined cognitive approach described above.

In many respects, it is difficult to distinguish between Bandura's notions of social learning and certain aspects of cognitive behavior control. Both emphasize learning from cognitive rather than actual experience. For example, consider the technique known as **covert modeling**. A patient is asked to imagine the behavior of a friend or acquaintance. The patient is presented with a "script" or outline very much like the one presented in Table 16–1.

After imagining how the friend would feel in this situation, the patient is then instructed to take the place of the friend and practice (in imaginary terms) going through the same sequence of actions. The patient is told to imitate the model in the script. Once the patient has successfully modeled the behavior in imagination, details are added to personalize it. The patient is encouraged to make the scene more relevant to his or her own situation.

■ DIFFERENCES BETWEEN INSIGHT THERAPY AND BEHAVIOR THERAPY

One clear difference between the insight therapies and behavior therapy is the way in which they originally developed. Insight therapies arose in the context of clinical settings, in attempts to alleviate symptoms or complaints of patients who were in distress. Behavior therapy, on the other hand, developed from laboratory research on learning principles. This research was extended to cover the area of abnormal behavior, but the principles had been uncovered long before they were so applied. As a

TABLE 16–1.
A Sample Script Used in Covert Modeling

The street scene

(Setting)

Imagine a person whom you highly admire *(name of specific person)*, walking down a street in your city *(specific place)*. The street is busy and many people are walking up and down the street as it is late in the afternoon and many are on their way home after work.

(Approach behavior)

As your "model" *(specify person)* walks down the street for two blocks ... he or she has a slight smile ... walks with head erect and at a comfortable pace ... As people approach ... he or she looks them in the eye and with a slight nod of the head says, "Hello," or "Hi," or "Good evening," to the various passers-by.

(Reinforcement)

Also, imagine a pleasant reply from each of these people to your model. Each exchange of greetings was well received and indicated acceptance by each person.

Source: Walker et al., 1981, pp. 254–255.

result of these differences in development, behavioral researchers have concentrated on changes in behavior as evidence of the success of the therapy. Insight therapists, on the other hand, have tended to concentrate on the self-reports of patients. If a patient reports feeling better, the therapy is considered successful.

Behavior therapists also try to specify in great detail exactly what the nature of the problem is and to develop a very specific and well-described treatment strategy. This is what you would expect from a scientist: good operational definitions, clear identification of procedures, and everything necessary for replication and hypothesis testing. Insight therapists have been less concerned with hypothesis testing than with helping patients. As a result, they have been less concerned with precise definitions and descriptions of procedures.

Another difference between behavior therapies and insight therapies is the amount of time necessary for change to occur. As was shown earlier in the thought-stopping example, only 10 weeks passed before the obsessional thought disappeared. It is inconceivable that the patient could have completed a course of treatment with a psychoanalyst in that period of time. Nevertheless, it cannot be concluded that the patient would not have derived some benefit from several years of psychoanalysis that went well beyond the problem of the obsessional thought.

There are several other differences between behavior and insight therapies, but it is not necessary to detail them here. The main differences are that they come from completely different traditions, for the most part they use different terminology, and they accept different definitions of success. There is simply no adequate way to compare their relative effectiveness. Behavior therapists typically treat different problems than insight therapists, the confidence of the clients in the therapy may vary, and the skills of the therapists might differ substantially both between and within the different approaches. Thus, it makes no sense to try to keep score. The fact is that both approaches work better than no treatment, and that people who are engaged in either form of therapy report that they feel better.

Although this section has focused on differences, we'll conclude with one characteristic that the insight and behavior therapies share. They are both generally unsuccessful in "curing" serious disorders such as schizophrenia and major depression. There are some instances of specific behavior changes, but these changes seldom represent a cure in the sense in which the term is commonly understood.

REVIEW QUESTIONS

7. The behavior therapist assumes that almost all behavior is _____ . Unlike _____ therapy, behavior is not seen as the symptom of an underlying problem; in behavior therapy the behavior *is* the problem.

8. A token-economy system is based on the basic learning principle of _____ _____ ; people must perform certain behaviors in order to receive tokens, or rewards.

9. There are two elements in systematic desensitization: Working up a _____ of threatening situations and training in _____ . These two elements are joined by getting the person to practice relaxing in the presence of more and more threatening stimuli.

10. _____ and _____ _____ are are the core of the social learning approach to therapy.

11. One difference between insight and behavior therapies is the amount of time the person spends in therapy; a person generally would spend much less time in behavior therapy than in insight therapy.

T / F

Answers: 7. learned; insight 8. operant conditioning 9. hierarchy; relaxation 10. Modeling; observational learning 11. True

---

■ GROUP THERAPY

Up to this point, it has been implied that therapy is something that happens between one person (the client) and another person (the therapist). This need not be the case. There are many instances in which more than one person at a time receives therapy or counseling. In some cases, group treatment is critical because it is the social system formed by two or more people that is largely responsible for the problem or the maladaptive behavior.

The term **group therapy** usually refers to interactions between a therapist and 5 to 10 people. The members of the group are not related and usually share a common complaint (such as depression, anorexia, or anxiety). It is assumed that hearing other people describe their problems will help members of the group realize that they are not unique or as

---

Covert modeling. Technique used in the social learning approach in which the person imagines how someone else would act in a certain situation and imitates that behavior for the therapist.

Group therapy. A form of therapy in which clients meet regularly in a group with a therapist.

Group therapy usually refers to interactions between a therapist and a small group of people who share a common complaint.

"abnormal" as they might have thought. In addition, groups often develop an attitude of unconditional positive regard for members and provide the support necessary for a full discussion of the problems facing each member. There is also the hope that members may be exposed to new and useful ways of coping or adapting through the comments and behavior of other members of the group. As you might expect, group treatments can include person-centered strategies, social learning, reinforcement, and a wide range of other devices aimed at adaptation. In addition to formal therapeutic groups, there are informal or self-help groups that have similar

purposes in mind. Alcoholics Anonymous is an example of this type of group.

Couple therapy involves two people who are thinking about either ending or improving a relationship. Most often, the two people are husband and wife. Since the problem often involves serious communication problems as well as distorted perceptions, it is important for the therapist to observe the couple interacting rather than to see them individually. Although psychoanalysis is not available to more than one person at a time, many of the other insight therapies are suited to couples.

Family therapy is an extension of this idea. Since

Family therapy is a form of group therapy. Family therapists believe that because a family involves several members who contribute to a problem, it makes sense to treat the family together.

the family unit consists of several members usually including a mother, a father, and one or more children, it makes sense to deal with that unit rather than any single member individually. The logic of both couple and family therapy is that it doesn't make sense to take people out of an unstable or unrewarding environment, treat them, and place them back in the environment that may have contributed heavily to the original problem.

■ SOMATIC THERAPIES

The somatic therapies are direct biological interventions that attempt to effect a cure or to reduce abnormal behavior. There have been three major categories of somatic treatments over the years: psychosurgery, drugs (chemotherapy), and electroshock. We will consider each one individually.

Couple therapy. Therapy for two people who are thinking about either ending or improving a relationship.

Family therapy. Therapeutic approach that sees the family as part of the problem in an individual's treatment and treats the whole family rather than just the individual.

Psychosurgery

In 1935, a Portuguese psychiatrist named Moniz heard a scientific report of surgery that had been performed on chimpanzees, in which parts of their cerebral cortex (from the prefrontal area) were removed. The result of this surgery was a reduction in emotionality and violence in the chimps. Moniz thought that this might be a useful technique for humans who had emotional disorders. Moniz collaborated with a colleague in performing this operation on humans. The surgical technique was called a **prefrontal lobotomy** (the term *lobotomy* simply means that a lobe of the brain was involved.)

Between 1935 and 1955, hundreds of these operations were performed. In fact, Moniz was awarded a Nobel prize in medicine in 1949 for his development of this surgical technique. Figure 16–1 illustrates what is done in this surgery. In many respects, the surgical technique is successful. Many of the patients who are operated on *do* become less violent and emotional, but the side-effects are often catastrophic. In addition to the reduction in emotionality, there are often violent seizures, dramatic reductions in cognitive ability, loss of energy or motivation to do *anything,* and even in some instances, death. In addition, not everyone is cured. It is ironic that Moniz had to stop practicing medicine in 1944. He was partially paralyzed by a bullet in his spine. The bullet was fired by a patient who had undergone a prefrontal lobotomy! The emo-

tionality and violence had not been reduced in *that* patient (Valenstein, 1973).

From what you know about the structure and function of the brain, you must be amazed to look at Figure 16–1 and see what actually is done in a prefrontal lobotomy. The brain is scored or sliced with an instrument much like an icepick. Recall that in Chapter 2 we talked about the loss of neurons. If neurons are lost randomly throughout the nervous system, the effects on behavior might not be so serious. In the case of lobotomies, however, neurons along a particular pathway are destroyed. There is every reason to believe that the brain is damaged in the same way as it would be if a bullet ripped through it. Evaluations of the results of lobotomies show little long-term advantage to the technique (Robbin, 1958, 1959; Barahal, 1958). Fortunately, the introduction of new antipsychotic drugs in the late 1950s eliminated interest in lobotomies as forms of treatment for mental illness. There has been some renewed interest in surgical treatments, but these newer techniques involve very small and specific areas of the brain. Since so much more is now known about brain structure and function, there is little likelihood of a repeat of the psychosurgery tragedies of 30 years ago.

Chemotherapy

In Chapters 2 and 15, you learned that the brain is heavily involved in all aspects of behavior, in-

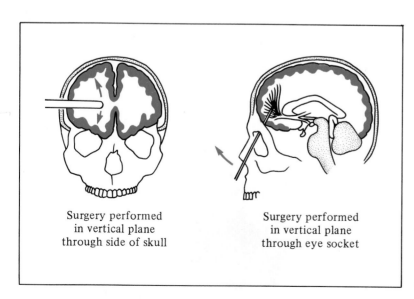

Surgery performed
in vertical plane
through side of skull

Surgery performed
in vertical plane
through eye socket

FIGURE 16–1

These two sketches show the two different methods of performing a prefrontal lobotomy. On the left the surgery was done through the side of the skull; on the right it was done through the eye socket. In both cases, large numbers of neurons were destroyed in certain areas, leading to many negative side effects of the surgery.

cluding abnormal patterns of action. The aim of drug therapy (chemotherapy) is to chemically alter brain function or action. As you may remember from the chapter on consciousness, every drug that affects brain function does it in one of four ways. The drug works on neurotransmission to: 1) block release, 2) block reception, 3) intensify or prolong release, or 4) imitate a natural neurotransmitter.

Some argue that drug therapy simply eliminates symptoms but doesn't really cure the individual. This argument is weakened by the data presented in the last chapter illustrating the heavy biological, and possibly even hereditary, component of serious disorders such as bipolar depression (manic-depressive disorder) and schizophrenia. It seems reasonable to argue that, in these cases, treating the symptoms *is* treating the disorder. If someone has an infection and a doctor prescribes an antibiotic, it would seem silly to say that the doctor was only treating the symptoms. More is known about the cause of infections than is known about the cause of mental disorders; nevertheless, the principle is the same. The belief is that biological factors are influencing behavior and that reducing these influences has the effect of normalizing behavior. For less serious disorders such as phobias, moderate depressions, and generalized anxiety, the objection may be more valid. Table 16–2 provides an illustration of the impact of one particular drug category, **phenothiazine,** on schizophrenic symptoms as compared to a placebo or neutral substance. There was improvement in thirteen of twenty-one categories, listed in Table 16–2. Phenothiazine is a chemical that blocks dopamine reception at the synapses of certain neurons in the brain. This is the result of the fact that phenothiazine is structurally similar to dopamine. It is a key that fits into the dopamine lock or receptor but will not open the lock. Nevertheless, it prevents the real substance, dopamine, from being received. Since schizophrenia has been hypothesized to result from too much dopamine, the reduction of dopamine reception should result in the reduction of schizophrenic symptoms.

This example is equally good for illustrating another aspect of drug therapy—unwanted side-

TABLE 16-2.

Effectiveness of Phenothiazines vs. a Placebo in Treating Schizophrenic Symptoms

Symptom or behavior	Placebo	Drug	Difference
Social participation	0.49*	1.51	1.02
Confusion	0.33	1.11	0.78
Self-care	0.13	0.88	0.75
Hebephrenic symptoms	−0.13	0.58	0.71
Agitation and tension	0.27	0.95	0.68
Slowed speed	−0.07	0.57	0.64
Incoherent speech	−0.17	0.43	0.60
Irritability	−0.20	0.40	0.60
Indifference to environment	−0.05	0.45	0.50
Hostility	0.09	0.54	0.45
Auditory hallucinations	0.18	0.62	0.44
Ideas of persecution	0.36	0.78	0.42
Disorientation	0.16	0.37	0.21

*The higher the score, the greater the improvement. A minus score indicates deterioration.
Source: Cole, 1964.

effects. As you may also remember from the biology chapter, certain disorders are the result of too *little* dopamine. An example of such a disorder is Parkinson's disease. This disease causes problems of movement, muscle tremors, and drooling, among other symptoms. This means that after extended use of phenothiazine, one set of symtoms may be eliminated (the schizophrenic symptoms) but other symptoms may appear to take their place (symptoms similar to Parkinson's disease). Unfortunately, it is impossible to limit the effects of drugs to a specific area or a particular group of neurons. Once the drug is introduced into the system, it will find its way to many sites and may act differently in each of those locations. At one location it may act as a blocker and at another location it may act to intensify neurotransmitter release.

Pretrontal lobotomy. An operation performed on the cerebral cortex to bring the violent behavior of patients under control. This turned out to have terrible side-effects with little long-term advantage and has been discontinued.

Phenothiazine. A drug given to schizophrenics—acts to block dopamine reception at the synapses of certain neurons in the brain.

In addition to these side-effects, other problems may arise as a result of phenothiazine use. These problems include constipation, low blood pressure, and blurred vision (Davison and Neale, 1982). These symptoms can often be treated with a second type of medication so that side-effects can be minimized. Nevertheless, there may be a price to pay—another group of side-effects—for the reduction of symptoms. This is one of the reasons drug therapy is questionable for disorders that are not particularly serious—the costs may outweigh the benefits. The new physiological symptoms will require new chemical treatments. All of these many different chemical substances—some to control symptoms and some to control side-effects—can take a toll on health and comfort.

As previously indicated, it doesn't always make sense to limit treatment to one approach alone. This is as true of drug therapy as it is of insight therapy. Particular drugs may be very useful in creating the conditions in which insight therapy might be more effective. As we saw, most of the insight therapies require verbal and logical competence. Drugs may be helpful in producing such behavior.

In the 50s and 60s, pride was taken in the fact that people showing drug-related improvement were coming out of hospitals and mental institutions and getting back on the street and into the community. It is now widely recognized that this was a misleading measure of "success." Without community follow-up and additional treatment-support systems, chemical interventions represent, at best, a delaying tactic. The streets of many cities have become flooded with homeless, helpless people with prescriptions in their pockets. There will never be a drug that can act as a substitute for a supportive family or a loving relationship or a satisfying job.

Electroconvulsive Therapy

Electroconvulsive therapy (ECT) (sometimes known as shock treatment) is another attempt to alter brain functioning. An electrical current of 70 to 130 volts is passed through the brain of the patient. This results in a major seizure or convulsion that is followed by deep sleep. This treatment is administered several times per week for several weeks (Davison and Neale, 1982) and has positive effects on the mood and activity level of severely depressed patients. As was the case with the other somatic therapies, there are negative side-effects. The most prominent of these side-effects is memory disturbance. It is common for the patient to have difficulties in remembering events that occurred before the treatment. These problems usually disappear within a few weeks after the treatments are completed, but they may last for years in some cases (Palmer, 1981). Once again, your knowledge of brain functioning and chemistry will help you understand both the intended and the unintended effects of ECT. You will remember that neurotransmission works on electrical principles. When a neuron fires, an action potential travels along the length of the axon. The action potential is equal to about 1/10 of a volt. An ECT treatment is 700 to 1,000 times stronger than an action potential. Furthermore, since the current travels across the entire surface of the brain, it causes a massive firing of neurons. It is no wonder that there are profound effects on both cognitive and emotional behaviors. All of this tells you something about *how* ECT works but not *why* it works. The answer to that question remains elusive. Further research may provide better understanding.

As was the case with punishment therapy described earlier in the chapter, ECT is controversial as a method of treatment. Critics argue that the costs far outweigh the benefits, the same argument that was made with respect to lobotomies. In Berkeley, California, an ordinance was passed making ECT illegal. There is no disagreement that ECT is radical. It is intended to interfere with neurotransmission. The seizures that are the side-effects can be handled effectively with little permanent aftereffect. Memory loss is more of a problem, although the problem appears to correct itself eventually in most patients. The real issue remains one of cost benefit. Is it better to leave the depression untouched? Is it better to maintain the patient on drugs that may have their own negative side-effects?

Progress has been made in reducing some of the undesirable side-effects of ECT, particularly those involving memory loss. ECT treatment can involve both hemispheres of the brain (called bilateral ECT) or only one hemisphere (called unilateral ECT) (Fisher, 1985). When the electrical current passes through only the right hemisphere of the brain, there seems to be markedly less memory impairment, and impairment that does occur seems to disappear more quickly than when both hemispheres are involved. We will need to know a great deal more about memory than we do currently in order to understand why these different effects occur. As it now stands, ECT is probably one of several reasonable alternatives for treatment of severe depression, but continued research is critical in order to understand the full range of effects of this approach.

REVIEW QUESTIONS

12. Psychosurgery consists of removing parts of the cerebral cortex, an operation called a _____ _____ .

13. Phenothiazine is a widely used drug given to schizophrenics to control their symptoms. It works by blocking the reception of the neurotransmitter _____ in the brain.

14. _____ therapy consists of passing an electrical current through a person's brain. This causes a major seizure or convulsion, followed by deep sleep. This type of therapy is used most often to treat _____ .

15. One of the worrisome side effects of ECT is its effect on _____ . Most problems connected with this disappear in a few weeks, but in some cases they may last for years.

Answers: 12. prefrontal lobotomy 13. dopamine 14. Electroconvulsive; depression 15. memory

---

■ THE RELATIVE EFFECTIVENESS OF ALTERNATIVE THERAPIES

As was indicated earlier in this chapter, there are inevitable comparisons to be made among the various types of therapy. These comparisons are made for obvious reasons. If one method achieves a higher cure-rate than another, this information is valuable to patient and therapist alike. Similarly, if

two methods of treatment are equally successful but one method works more quickly, or is substantially cheaper, or can be delivered with greater efficiency to a larger number of people, this is valuable information.

There are two types of comparisons that are frequently made. The first is a comparison of broad therapeutic categories. For example, one might compare chemotherapy with insight therapy, or behavior modification with ECT. The second type of comparison is among alternatives within a single broad category. For example, one might compare non-directive therapy with psychoanalysis. Let's consider these comparisons before coming to any final conclusion about the effectiveness of different approaches. We will first compare three different types of therapies and then compare various forms of psychotherapy.

Comparison of Broad Categories: An Example

The National Institutes of Mental Health sponsored a study of the effectiveness of three different types of therapy on depression (Boffey, 1986). The three broad therapies were congitive therapy, interpersonal therapy, and chemotherapy. The cognitive therapy involved changing patients' views of themselves and beliefs about their environment. The interpersonal therapy dealt with ineffective social functioning. The chemotherapy involved the use of the drug imipramine, a standard anti-depressant drug. Approximately 250 patients in three different locations were randomly assigned to one of the three treatment groups. Within 16 weeks, improvement was noted in all three treatment groups. In other words, it did not matter whether the patient received imipramine or one of the two forms of psychotherapy—they became less depressed. There did seem to be a difference in the early stages of treatment, however. The chemotherapy group seemed to improve almost immediately after beginning to

---

Electroconvulsive therapy (ECT). A type of somatic therapy used mostly in cases of major depression; an electrical current of 70 to 130 volts is passed through the brain, causing an alteration in brain functioning.

take the drug. Nevertheless, within 16 weeks there were no obvious differences among the treatment groups, suggesting that the psychotherapy patients "caught up" to the imipramine group quickly.

These results are preliminary. The patients will be followed for 18 months to see if the improvement is permanent. It may turn out that one form of therapy has longer-lasting effects than another. There are obviously differences in the actual treatments even though the results might be similar. For example, the use of imipramine is cheaper and less time consuming than psychotherapy. On the other hand, there are often undesirable physical side-effects to taking these anti-depressants. The good news seems to be that depression can be controlled to some extent by a wide range of treatments. Thus, the individual and the therapist are free to try a range of possible interventions and pick the one that is most effective for the individual.

Comparison of Psychotherapies

In the past decade, a considerable amount of attention has been paid to the comparison of particular types of psychotherapies. Many review articles have appeared on the topic (Smith and Glass, 1977; Bergin and Lambert, 1978; Smith, Glass, and Miller, 1980). For the most part, the reviews have come to the same conclusion: there are no differences in the effects produced by a wide variety of psychotherapies. This is difficult for many patients and therapists to accept. Patients, for their part, have clear preferences for what type of "treatment" they find acceptable. Therapists, for their part, have adopted a method of therapy that conforms to their views of personality and the probable causes of disordered or abnormal behavior. Thus, it is difficult for the therapist to embrace an alternative form of therapy because that would imply that the therapist is wrong about the dynamics of personality and abnormal behavior. A recent article by Stiles, Shapiro, and Elliott (1986) presents a clear picture of the problem of "equivalent" effects and its possible resolution.

There is little argument that there are real differences among various forms of psychotherapy. Some forms encourage the therapist to talk while others encourage the therapist to remain silent. Some encourage the therapist to make suggestions

and others forbid the therapist to offer any suggestions. If there really are different types of therapy, how then can we account for the equivalence of outcomes? Stiles and colleagues explore several possible explanations. I will list these explanations and consider them individually.

1. *The comparative studies are not well done.* The first possibility is that studies comparing the relative effectiveness of therapies are biased or distorted by the orientation of those doing the study. Similarly, many comparative studies are done with small samples and in unusual settings. This explanation cannot be completely dismissed, but preliminary results of well-done studies (e.g., the NIMH study described above), as well as statistical rather than narrative reviews of existing comparisons, make this an unlikely possibility.

2. *The "effects" examined are not specific enough.* Here, the argument is that it does not make sense to look at broad indexes of cure such as patients' reports of general improvement or therapists' evaluations of progress. Instead, we should concentrate on very specific changes in behavior patterns and very specific types of symptoms. In addition, we should consider the differences among settings in which the therapy occurs. For example, we should distinguish between treatment paid for by the patient and treatment paid for through use of public funds. In short, this argument says that if we cut the data fine enough, we will find differences. The reason that no differences appear now is because we have tried to analyze a basket containing apples and oranges and peaches all thrown together.

3. *The reason that no differences occur is because all therapists behave similarly.* Stiles and colleagues suggest that there might be a common core of therapist behaviors that is associated with "successful" therapy, regardless of the form of that therapy. They cite the work of Frank (1973), who proposed that all successful therapists used methods of persuasion for affecting change. They also suggest that successful psychotherapists a) genuinely care about the well-being of the patient, b) have a certain amount of power, and c) play a mediating role between the person and the outside world. They conclude that therapists from

many different perspectives probably share "such apparently desirable qualities as personal warmth, understanding and the ability to guide clients to new perspectives" (p. 172).

4. *The reason that no differences occur is because all clients behave similarly.* For the most part, clients approach therapy expecting to be "cured." They are "ready" to be treated, regardless of the form of treatment. In addition, most clients come to therapy ready to actively explore their problems with the therapist, using any ground rules that the therapist sets up. Further, the most common form of client verbal behavior, regardless of what the therapist says or does, is disclosure. They tell the therapist things about themselves that are "private" and subjective, things that they may never have told anyone else.

5. *The reason that no differences occur is because in successful therapeutic relationships, the client and the therapist form an alliance to effect a cure.* This perspective suggests that the actual behavior of the therapist and/or client is simply the raw material for forming a close personal bond. It is the successful establishment of a supportive relationship that produces the effect or "cure" regardless of the method necessary to establish that relationship.

There seems to be little doubt that very different forms of psychotherapy produce very similar results. From a practical point of view, this is encouraging. As indicated above, the implication is that a client and a therapist have a wide range of choices at their disposal, all equally promising. Nevertheless, this equivalence represents a substantial challenge for the science of psychology. We must learn *why* they all work equally well. It should be obvious that until we can answer that question, we do not understand the dynamics of abnormal behavior or behavioral change.

■ A FINAL WORD

The comparisons considered above seem to say that all forms of therapy are equally effective. To some extent, that seems to be true. But we have overlooked one important characteristic of those comparisons—for the most part they all deal with a common or uniform symptom, for example, depression or a phobic behavior. There is another broad question that might be asked: Are some forms of therapy more effective than others for *particular* problems? This is a different question than the one considered above and requires a different answer. For moderate disorders such as phobias, mild depression, and anxiety, insight and behavior therapies can be quite effective. This makes sense, since the disorders seem to have a substantial learning component. For serious disorders, a treatment that does not recognize the possible biological component of the disorder seems inadequate. For the most part, schizophrenics, manic depressives, and major depressives are not likely to be helped with traditional insight or behavior therapies. It may be possible to make the patients more manageable, but this is not the same as a "cure." As was noted earlier, sometimes combinations of approaches will be more effective than single treatments or therapies. More thought needs to be given to planning combinations that will be most effective for particular patients with particular problems.

■ SUMMARY

1. The general goals that all therapies share include: (a) changing maladaptive behavior patterns, (b) minimizing or eliminating environmental conditions contributing to such behaviors, (c) improving interpersonal and other competencies, (d) resolving inner conflicts and alleviating personal distress, (e) modifying individuals' inaccurate assumptions about themselves and their world, and (f) fostering a clearcut sense of self-identity. Differences among the therapies stem from the fact that each stresses one of these goals over the others. The *placebo effect* refers to the fact that the person's expectation that therapy will help can bring about positive results.

2. The goal of insight therapies is to help people understand how they are currently behaving, why these behaviors have developed, and how to modify these behaviors. Psychoanalysis works at uncovering conflicts that began in childhood through *free association* (allowing thoughts to run free and talking about anything that comes to mind) and

dream analysis. In psychoanalysis, dreams have two levels: the *manifest content,* or the surface components of the dream, and the *latent content,* or the dream's deeper meaning. For the psychoanalyst, *resistance* and *transference* indicate that the person is beginning to identify conflicts.

3. *Person-centered therapy* is a humanistic approach based on several assumptions: (a) the "real world" is the client's perception of the world, (b) people can be aware of their own behaviors and motives, (c) people are basically good and effective, (d) people are self-directing, and (e) the therapist should create an environment that enables the client to learn more about himself or herself and, as a result, grow and change. Characteristics of therapists that are important to clients' progress are openness, *unconditional positive regard,* and empathy.

4. *Gestalt therapy* is a humanistic approach that aims to uncover distortions in clients' perceptions and often involves role playing.

5. *Cognitive therapies* are based on the idea that problems arise from the way people think and the images they use to represent events in memory. Treatment involves replacing maladaptive thought processes with more rational thoughts that are more likely to lead to constructive actions.

6. *Behavior therapy* is based on the idea that all behaviors of significance can be eliminated and replaced by more effective patterns. Rather than unconditional positive regard, the behavior therapist follows a principle of conditional positive regard while trying to construct situations in which the patient can only succeed. There is no concern for unconscious conflicts or for attempting to identify underlying causes of maladaptive behavior.

7. *Applied behavior analysis* involves keeping a record of patients' behaviors, giving them tokens as secondary rewards, and allowing them to spend their tokens on the primary reinforcers they prefer. *Systematic desensitization* addresses the stress that results from certain associations by identifying a hierarchy of threat, providing training in relaxation, and linking increasing levels of threat on the hierarchy with relaxation. In *cognitive behavior therapy,* the patient learns to control irrational thinking. *Social learning* also emphasizes cognitive learning, rather than actual experience, and involves having a patient imagine acting out various behaviors.

8. *Behavior therapy* was developed in a laboratory setting, while *insight therapy* was developed in a clinical setting. The result of these different origins is that behavior therapists judge success of the therapy by changes in behavior, while insight therapists rely on patients' self-reports. Behavior therapists also try to specify exactly what the problem is and how they will treat it, while insight therapists do not. Behavior therapy is generally a much shorter treatment than insight therapy.

9. Besides individual therapy, there are also group, couple, and family therapies. These types have particular advantages, for some types of problems, over individual therapy.

10. *Somatic therapies* are direct biological interventions that attempt to effect a cure or to reduce abnormal behavior. These therapies include *psychosurgery,* or modifying some part of the brain; *chemotherapy,* or drug treatment for mental disorders; and *electroconvulsive shock therapy.*

11. *Scientific comparisons of therapies* are a means of finding out information about the relative speed, cost, and effectiveness of different treatments. One type of comparison that is often made is a comparison of broad therapeutic categories. A second type compares alternatives within a single category of therapy. While there are real differences among therapies, studies show that very different forms of therapy produce very similar results.

12. Another broad question is whether some forms of therapy are more effective than others for particular problems. It appears that sometimes combinations of approaches will be more effective than single therapies for particular kinds of problems.

■ ANSWERING QUESTIONS FOR THOUGHT

1. Psychologists use the term "placebo effect" in therapy to refer to the fact that expecting to be helped can have a positive effect. The very act of seeking therapy can relieve anxiety, and improvement often begins before there is even any direct contact between the therapist and the person.

2. Somatic therapies are usually most effective in treating major disorders such as schizophrenia or

depression, or in treating symptoms so that people are able to take part in other types of therapy. But besides this, there is no conclusive evidence to show that insight therapies are more effective than behavior therapies, or vice versa.

3. Insight therapists would say that abnormal behavior is the symptom of an underlying conflict, and would focus on determining the nature of that conflict. Behavior therapists, on the other hand, would say that the behavior itself is the problem and would direct their attention to getting people to replace maladaptive behaviors with more effective ones.

4. Freud referred to psychoanalysis as the "talk-ing cure." It really consists of more than just talking, but it is based on the assumption that an underlying conflict must be brought to the surface of consciousness, discussed, and worked through in order to rid oneself of it.

5. There are several benefits to group therapy: (1) hearing other people describe their problems may make you realize that you're not as unique or as abnormal as you thought, (2) the whole group can provide support and an attitude of unconditional positive regard, and (3) you may learn new and useful ways of coping from other members of the group.

17

Social Psychology

QUESTIONS FOR THOUGHT

1. If a well-known and popular sports figure appears on television and tells you to buy a certain brand of sports equipment, are you more likely to listen to the message?
2. How can smokers be well aware of the health risks involved yet still go on smoking? How do they justify their actions?
3. Is it true that people will attribute a woman's success to luck and a man's success to ability, even when the tasks performed are identical?
4. Why is it that at times people will ignore a stranger in distress and at other times go out of their way to be good Samaritans?
5. Do people work harder or do better as part of a group or do they do better on their own?

The answers to these questions are at the end of the chapter.

Since this course may well be your first in the behavioral sciences, let me be the first to inform you, "Humans are *social* animals." This description, which you will hear again if you take other behavioral science courses, does more than simply state the obvious. It implies that people, by nature, respond to the real or imagined influence of other people. Even the telephone company jingle, "Reach out, reach out and touch someone," emphasizes making contact—"touching *someone*"—and suggests that there is something uniquely satisfying about simply talking with other people (Brody, 1983).

The importance of social contact is apparent when we consider how people are sometimes punished: social isolation. Children are deprived of the company of others—sent to their rooms when they misbehave. Prisoners are placed in solitary confinement for breaking prison rules. Members of certain religious sects are shunned (treated as if they did not exist) for violating group principles. Several years ago, an Amish farmer in Pennsylvania became the object of shunning. The Amish, who are strict Mennonites, require that members adhere to church customs and beliefs. The farmer disagreed with some of these customs, and because he would not conform, the other members of the church (including his wife and children) shunned him. They would not speak to him or communicate with him in any way. The farmer eventually went to court to try to stop the shunning practice, but he lost his case. The court decided that social patterns were not subject to jurisprudence; people could not be required to interact with other people.

Social psychology is concerned with a wide range of social behavior, not only with extremes such as shunning. In its simplest form, **social psychology** is the study of how people perceive, influence, and are influenced by other people. Social psychology is the study of human behavior in the context of interpersonal relations. In that context, shunning is clearly a social phenomenon.

We have already explored some of the topics of social psychology, including the effects of mood on prosocial behavior (Chapter 12), equity theory (Chapter 12), crowding, and the effects of social support on stress (Chapter 14). To avoid repeating too much of what we covered earlier, this chapter will deal only with other aspects of behavior that clearly and overtly involve other people. We will first consider attitudes and how they affect people's behavior; then, how perceptions are involved in social action, helping, conformity, and obedience; and finally, the behavior of people in groups. Throughout the chapter, the role of cognitive factors in social action will be emphasized. This should be a familiar approach, since cognition has already been considered in several earlier chapters. Here we will look specifically at the effect of cognitions on interpersonal and group behavior.

Social psychology. The study of human behavior in the context of interpersonal relations.

People try to influence others' attitudes on issues in all sorts of ways, in the hope that attitudes will lead to action of some kind.

■ ATTITUDES

An **attitude** is a combination of feelings and beliefs about an object, person, or event. People have attitudes about guns, instructors, and concerts—in short, about many things. These attitudes help explain certain kinds of behaviors. For example, you would probably vote for the politician about whom you felt the best—toward whom you had the most favorable attitude. Most politicians attempt to create a favorable attitude toward themselves for this reason. Many groups, such as pro- and anti-abortion groups or anti-nuclear power groups, attempt to foster certain attitudes in others in the hope that these attitudes will eventually lead to action—in the form of marches, protests, letters to legislators, and so on.

It is important to remember that attitudes are made up of three distinct elements. There is the *be-*havioral element that we have just considered. There is also an *emotional* element and a *belief* element. The emotional element is what might be described as a "gut" reaction to an object or person: We "like" kittens; we "dislike" dentists. These emotional reactions exist in spite of the knowledge that kittens become cats (and we "don't like" cats) or that dentists are there to help us, not hurt us. The belief element refers to the collection of ideas, or cognitions, that we believe to be true about certain objects or people. We may believe that all movie stars lead glamorous lives; we may believe that breathing cold air will damage the lungs; we may believe that money will solve all of our problems. What we believe may not be true, and the *fact* that it may not be true may be irrelevant to our attitude—so long as we believe it. In fact, we often try to protect our beliefs from assault by discouraging the introduction of new information. This calls to mind a bumper sticker I once saw on a pickup truck:

TABLE 17-1. Components of an Attitude

Beliefs	Emotion	Behavior
Old people are helpless.	I like to help people.	I visit old people.
Old people are dull.	I don't like dull people.	I avoid old people.
Athletes are not intelligent.	I don't like unintelligent people.	I do not make friends with athletes.
Athletes are funny.	I like funny people.	I hang around with athletes.

The Bible Said It, I Believe It, and That's the End of It!

When you put the three elements of an attitude together—behavior, emotion, and belief—you have all the ingredients necessary for complex patterns of behavior. Consider the examples in Table 17-1. As you can see, the combination of elements results in behavior designed either to seek or avoid association with certain groups. Once again, we are reminded that psychologists with different specialties are all interested in the complexity of behavior. They simply approach behavior from different perspectives. Thus, what the biological psychologist might see as the actions of neurons, the learning theorist might see as the actions of reinforcers. The social psychologist, in turn, might see patterns of beliefs, emotions, and thinking. As a scientist, each is looking at the same behavior and trying to explain it.

How Are Attitudes Formed and Changed?

Attitudes are learned. This means that their formation follows the principles of learning discussed in Chapter 6. As those principles would suggest, attitudes can be learned in many ways. For example, our attitudes toward dentists are due, at least in part, to classical conditioning. Since a visit to a dentist often involves pain, we may develop attitudes toward dentists that were at first attitudes toward pain. The pain is the US, the dentist is the CS, and the attitude (particularly the emotional element) is the CR. Attitudes can also be learned through operant procedures: Our parents reinforce us for making positive statements about classmates who do well in school; our friends praise us for having negative attitudes about someone in a different

social group. In this chapter, we will concentrate on the influence that other people have on our attitudes.

From a social perspective, attitude formation and attitude change require communication. One person must send a message and another person must receive that message. It is not necessary for the first person to *intend* to send the message, or for the second person to *intend* to receive it. Furthermore, it is not necessary that the sender and receiver be personally or directly acquainted. Through his actions alone, the Indian leader Gandhi communicated a message to millions of people he never knew. His message, which was to adhere to a life of nonviolence, was known throughout the world.

The "Yale School," a group of researchers at Yale University who studied attitudes shortly after World War II, divided the communication through which attitudes are formed and changed into three parts: the communicator, the message, and the audience or target. The characteristics of each of these can affect the extent to which attitudes are formed or changed through communication. To illustrate, we will focus on the communicator, and particularly on three important characteristics of the communicator: expertise, trustworthiness, and liking (Sears, Freedman, and Peplau, 1985).

Expertise. People who are thought to be experts in a particular area will have a greater influence on attitudes regarding that area than people who are not thought to be experts. A race driver talks about

---

Attitude. A combination of behavior tendencies, feelings and beliefs a person has about another person, object, or event.

motor oil; a noted gourmet cook endorses a new brand of soup. We are more likely to form a positive attitude toward the motor oil or the soup by hearing about it from an expert than if we heard the same opinion from a plumber.

Often, attempts are made to take advantage of a person's perceived expertise in one area to influence attitudes in another area. For example, a famous movie actor speaks out about the environment; an eminent scientist speaks out against war. Little is known about the extent to which credibility will transfer from one situation to another, but these attempts to extend the range of influence are very common.

Trustworthiness. Sources of information that are perceived as trustworthy are more likely to influence attitudes than sources that are viewed with distrust. We often take the statements of others with a grain of salt, particularly if they have something to gain (such as a used-car salesman telling us about a car's reliability). Walster, Aronson, and Abrahams (1966) studied the effect of trustworthiness on persuasion. Two different types of communicators—a

prosecutor and a convicted criminal—tried to affect listeners' opinions about the power of the courts to deal with criminal behavior. There were two versions of the message: (1) an appeal for less powerful courts, and (2) an appeal for more powerful courts. As you can see from the results, which appear in Figure 17–1, the prosecutor was effective in both cases. The criminal was ineffective when arguing for *weaker* courts, because the audience believed that the criminal had a self-interest in the outcome. Although the criminal may be seen as having expertise about law enforcement, listeners were likely to believe that the statements were self-serving (that is, low on trustworthiness). On the other hand, when the criminal argued in favor of more *powerful* courts, his argument was even more effective than that of the prosecutor. Since more powerful courts would obviously be to the disadvantage of the criminal, the perceived trustworthiness of the communicator and the message increased dramatically. Why would the criminal be trying to mislead the listeners on such a personally important issue?

Together, expertise and trusthworthiness create **credibility**. A credible communicator is one who has the necessary expertise and is trustworthy.

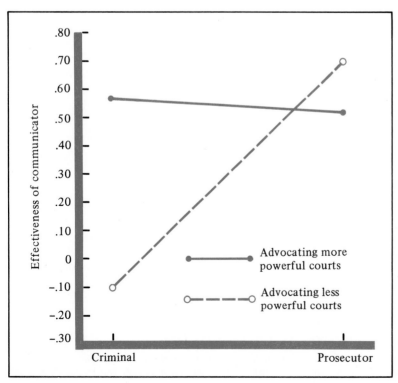

FIGURE 17–1

The graph shows the results of a study testing the effect of trustworthiness on persuasion. The prosecutor was effective in both conditions, arguing that there should be more powerful courts or less powerful courts. The criminal was ineffective when arguing for weaker courts because the audience believed that the criminal had a self-interest in the outcome. But the criminal was more effective than the prosecutor when he argued in favor of more powerful courts. Since he seemed to be arguing against his own advantage, his trustworthiness and that of the message increased dramatically. (Walster et al., 1966, p. 333)

A communicator can affect the extent to which attitudes are formed or changed by the communication. This communicator will be more persuasive if he is perceived to have the characteristics of expertise, trustworthiness, and likeability.

Liking. Communicators whom we like are more effective. There are several factors that influence liking. In general, we tend to like people who are in physical proximity to us, who are similar to us in background and interests, and who are physically attractive to us. Factors that increase liking also seem to increase attitude change. Communicators are more persuasive if they are attractive to and appear similar to the person who is the target of the message.

Why does liking increase attitude change? There are several reasons. One is that we often think that someone whom we like is similar to us in general values and perspectives. We are therefore inclined to think that he or she would be likely to make the same decision as we would, given the same information. Another reason is that liking fosters identification. We try to imitate people we like and admire in the hope of becoming more like them. This imitation may extend to adopting their attitudes. A third explanation is that we want those we like to like us too, and to spend time with us. We

are likely to believe that others will like us and want to be around us if we share similar attitudes.

Techniques of Attitude Change. Communicator expertise, trustworthiness, and liking influence both how we form attitudes and how our attitudes change. People who consciously attempt to persuade others both recognize and use these factors. Advertisers, for example, try to use spokespersons who are expert, trustworthy, and likeable. (It is rumored that Walter Cronkite, considered the most popular news anchor in broadcasting history, has been approached many times with lucrative offers to do TV commercials.)

In political elections, candidates routinely attack one another's expertise, trustworthiness, and likeability. Candidates raise questions about the "ex-

---

Credibility. A combination of expertise and trustworthiness in a person that promotes believability; a person thought to be credible will have a strong influence on listeners because they will tend to believe what he or she says.

pert" status of an opponent by suggesting that the opponent's ideas are mistaken, misguided, or out of touch with reality. An opponent's trustworthiness is another favored line of attack—any evidence of dishonesty in an opponent's past may be made a focal point of a campaign. A candidate may use the likeability factor by pointing out that an opponent is an unpleasant and unusual person with no similarities to the voter. While making all of these deliberate attempts to undermine any positive attitude the voter might have toward the opponent, the candidate's expertise, trustworthiness, and similarities to the voter are pointed out in an attempt to increase the candidate's own relative credibility. Presumably, if there are large shifts in perceived expertise, trustworthiness, and likeability, attitudes toward the candidate (and, it is hoped, voting behavior) will shift as well.

Before closing our discussion of communicator characteristics, it should be pointed out that the importance of expertise, trustworthiness, and liking may depend upon characteristics of the message and of the target. For instance, expertise may be relatively unimportant if the message is fairly similar to the target person's attitude, but it may be very important if the message is fairly discrepant from what the person presently believes. For example, if you believe that people typically need eight hours of sleep a night, a message that people need seven hours (little discrepancy) may be about equally effective whether it comes from a noted sleep researcher or from a friend. However, if the message is that only one or two hours of sleep a night are needed, then the more expert communicator may be much more persuasive (Bochner and Insko, 1966).

The Attitude-Behavior Relationship

When advertisers and politicians try to change our attitudes, they do so because they assume that changes in our behavior will follow. We, too, tend to assume that someone with a favorable attitude toward a candidate will be more likely to vote for that candidate. For years, most social psychologists have also tended to assume that people's behavior is directly caused by their attitudes. Then, many social psychologists began to question how well be-

havior could be predicted from attitudes. This questioning occurred largely as a result of an influential review of 31 studies by Wicker (1969), who concluded that in some instances attitudes and behavior have little or nothing to do with each other. Certainly we all know of instances in which people feel one way but act another, such as when a person acts pleasantly toward a much disliked boss.

The relationship between attitudes and behavior remains an active area of research in psychology. Since Wicker's (1969) review, numerous studies have found a strong relationship between attitudes and behavior especially under certain conditions. Now, more specifically, researchers have focused on the questions: Under what conditions *do* attitudes predict behavior? When are people's actions likely to be consistent with their attitudes?

A partial answer is that we can predict behavior from attitudes better if we measure a closely corresponding attitude (Fishbein and Ajzen, 1975). For example, we can predict church attendance better if we measure attitudes toward church attendance than if we measure a more general attitude, such as attitude toward religion. In addition, how closely attitudes and behavior correspond will depend on whether there are strong situational forces acting on the behavior. For instance, teenagers' attitudes toward drinking closely correspond with their drinking behavior at parties, but not with their drinking at home. At home, teens' drinking depends more on their parents' beliefs and allowances (Schlegel et al., 1977).

There is another important set of factors that determines how closely behaviors follow attitudes. These involve how accessible or salient the person's attitude is. In other words, behavior will generally follow from attitudes when people are aware of, or have been thinking about, their attitudes (Fazio, 1986). For this reason, behaviors correspond more closely to attitudes when any of the following occur:

a. the attitude is strong and clear (as opposed to weak and ambivalent);
b. the attitude is based on the person's own direct experience (as opposed to just hearing about something from other sources);
c. the person has some vested personal interest in the issue (as when 19-year-olds are asked to sign a petition to raise the minimum drinking age);

AN EXPERIMENT ON COGNITIVE DISSONANCE

Dissonance theory is based on the assumption that dissonant cognitions produce a state of unpleasant tension, and that a change in attitude results from a desire to reduce this tension. Recently, some researchers have been investigating the idea that attitude change may not be the only way of reducing this state of tension. It may be that stimuli that have nothing to do with the dissonant cognitions may serve to reduce tension and eliminate the need for attitude change. Drinking alcohol, for example, is one way that people try to reduce tension. Steele, Southwick, and Critchlow (1981) reasoned that because drinking alcohol reduces tension, it may also eliminate the need for attitude change when people experience dissonance.

They conducted an experiment in which some subjects were first asked to write essays in opposition to their own attitudes. Presumably, this should have caused them to be in a state of cognitive dissonance. The experimenters then asked this group of subjects to sample different kinds of vodka for ten minutes and afterwards to state their attitudes on a questionnaire. Actually, the vodka was used as a tension reducer. The researchers hypothesized that these subjects would not need to shift their attitudes into line with their essays because the alcohol would reduce the tension created by dissonance. Another group of subjects also wrote essays that opposed their own attitudes and then sampled different kinds of water. A third group sampled vodka and had their attitudes assessed by questionnaire but wrote no essays. The results confirmed the experimenters' hypothesis: Only those subjects in a state of dissonance who drank water shifted their attitudes into line with their essays. Subjects in the group that had drunk vodka but not written essays and those who had both written essays and drunk vodka had virtually the same attitudes as before. Steele and colleagues suggest that their findings may be a possible explanation for substance abuse. The uncomfortable experience of cognitive dissonance occurs relatively often. Some people may be seeking relief of this tension in the use—and abuse—of alcohol and drugs.

d. the person has recently been made to think about his or her attitude;

e. the person characteristically tends to pay more attention to his or her inner dispositions or feelings, rather than to situational cues or the preferences of others.

The point being made is a simple one. We can predict behavior from attitudes, at least some of the time. Furthermore, changing people's attitudes still appears to be a powerful way of changing their behavior—if the conditions are right. As we shall see in the following sections, the opposite is also true: Changing behavior can also be an important means of causing changes in attitude.

Cognitive Dissonance Theory

Like most people, on occasion you have probably felt uncomfortable about something you were doing. For example, perhaps you were drinking diet soda containing saccharin, an artificial sweetener suspected of causing cancer. On the one hand, you were aware of the potential health risks of drinking the diet soda and wanted to preserve your health. On the other hand, you wanted the soda, for the taste and the low calories. These two cognitions (thoughts) were in conflict with each other. Such conflict produces tension, and the tension must somehow be resolved. According to a theory proposed by Festinger (1957), we cannot hold dissonant, or conflicting, cognitions for any extended period of time. When our behavior is at odds with our beliefs, which Festinger calls **cognitive dissonance**, we will engage in some action to bring our behavior and our beliefs into agreement.

Festinger suggests three ways in which people

Cognitive dissonance. A conflict between belief and behavior or the incompatibility of two beliefs.

can reduce the experience of dissonance. In our diet soda example, you could change your behavior by switching to regular soda. You could change your belief by telling yourself that the research about cancer is based on white mice and probably doesn't apply to humans. Or, you could add supporting cognitions to balance your belief, by claiming that the diet soda keeps your weight down and therefore is healthy. In the latter two strategies, attitudes are revised or elaborated to deal with dissonant cognitions.

Dissonance theory is also at the heart of some theories of motivation. As you saw in Chapter 12, feelings of inequity often lead to action. These feelings are attitudes or beliefs. For example, you believe that you should be paid well if you work hard. You believe that you work hard but you are confronted with the fact of being poorly paid. These two beliefs are dissonant and produce tension. To reduce tension you can either take action (work less hard) or change beliefs (you didn't really work as hard as you thought). Dissonance theory has thus proven valuable to the study of both attitude formation and change and the effects of attitudes and behavior on each other.

It should be pointed out that not all inconsistencies are alike. Research shows that dissonance arises primarily in cases of conflict between a person's self-concept and a behavior that violates the self-concept (Aronson, 1968). For example, in the case of the diet soda, drinking a suspected cancer-causing agent may conflict with your self-concept—"I am a health-conscious person." Research also indicates that dissonance is greatest when the person feels personally responsible for the inconsistency (Wicklund and Brehm, 1976). If someone else had bought the diet soda for you, or had forced you to drink diet soda at gunpoint, you would probably not feel any dissonance.

An Alternative to Cognitive Dissonance Theory

Bem (1972) developed **self-perception theory** as an alternative explanation to the results of dissonance research. According to Bem, people *decide* what their attitudes are by observing their own behavior and the circumstances in which it occurred. For example, if in high school you smoked cigarettes (per-

haps because of peer pressure), you would probably conclude that you thought smoking was OK. Self-perception theory often makes the same predictions as dissonance theory, but it does not assume that distress from tension is always the result of inconsistencies. Instead, self-perception theory views people more as passive observers who figure out their own attitudes in the same way as they infer the attitudes of others—by watching themselves behave.

Dissonance theory is most applicable to actions that are attitude-discrepant, that is, when people do things that are clearly inconsistent with what they believe. Self-perception theory is most applicable when people do things that are fairly consistent with their attitudes or when they do not already have a relevant attitude. Behavior can influence attitudes in either case, but the unpleasant experience of dissonance should occur only if the behavior clearly violates an existing attitude.

Persuasive Techniques

Both cognitive dissonance theory and self-perception theory show that our behavior can influence our attitudes. One attitude-change technique that relies on this is known as the "foot-in-the-door-technique" (Freedman and Fraser, 1966). This approach assumes that getting people to comply with a small request makes them more likely to comply with a larger request. A sales representative must first get a prospective customer to listen before a sale can be made. This evokes an image of a door-to-door salesperson sticking his or her foot in the door to prevent the prospective customer from closing it. Indeed, salespeople usually try to get inside the front door before beginning the sale pitch. Pliner, Heather, Kohl, and Saari (1974) suggest that this technique works because it causes customers to think of themselves as "the kind of people who do this sort of thing" (listen to and buy products from a salesperson). In other words, they change their self-image as a result of a behavior. The many variations of this technique include 30-day free trials, test drives of automobiles, and getting a donor to make a small initial donation to a particular cause (in the hope that a larger one or a bigger commitment will follow).

A recent review of research on the foot-in-the-door technique suggests that it is not as uniformly effective as once thought (Beamon, Cole, Preston, Klenty, and Steblay, 1983). In particular, it may not be effective for very large (or painful) second requests such as donating blood.

On the other hand, research suggests that behavior might lead to attitude change even if it is only imagined, not real, behavior. For example, in one study some homeowners were asked to imagine using cable TV, while others were just given information about the service. A couple of months later, many more of the people who had imagined using cable TV had actually subscribed to it (47.4%), compared to those who had not imagined using it (19.5%). It seems that even imagined behavior can have an effect on our attitudes and our real behavior (Gregory, Cialdini and Carpenter, 1982).

REVIEW QUESTIONS

1. Social psychology is the study of human behavior as it is affected by _____ relations.

2. Attitudes are made up of three elements: _____, _____, and _____.

3. People who are thought to be experts in an area will have a great effect on attitudes; listeners tend to pay attention to them because they have a combustion of expertise and trustworthiness called _____ .

4. Festinger has theorized that when our behavior is at odds with our beliefs, a state he calls _____ _____, we will engage in some action to bring our behavior and beliefs into agreement.

5. One technique of attitude change, which depends on behavior to change attitudes, is used by door-to-door salespeople. It is called the _____ technique.

Answers: 1. interpersonal 2. behavior, emotion, belief. 3. credibility 4. cognitive dissonance 5. foot-in-the-door

---

■ SOCIAL COGNITION

In Chapter 4, you were introduced to Gestalt principles that define ways in which people group information or stimuli. Sometimes stimuli are grouped in terms of which ones are in close proximity. At other times, stimuli are grouped in terms of similarity of form, or in terms of some symmetry that is pleasing to the eye. People are stimuli, too. There is every reason to believe that we use rules for processing social information in the same way that we use rules, such as Gestalt principles, for processing other stimuli. People strive to make sense of what they see and to predict what might happen if they choose a particular course of action. Another name for this mental process of understanding and prediction is cognition. When social information is involved, we usually refer to **social cognition**. This is not to imply that social cognition is very different from other forms of cognition. Instead, it indicates that we limit our consideration to situations in which people or social groups are the stimuli for behavior.

Attribution theory is commonly used in discussions of social cognition. It refers to the guesses we make about the causes of our own and others' behavior. In other words, we *attribute* behavior to various causes. These guesses are what separate person-perception from ordinary perception. Who cares why a piece of pizza just sits there on the plate, not doing anything? But many people care to know why a friend looks at them in a strange way. Knowing the cause for an event or behavior seems to allow us, to an extent, to predict and control our environment.

Attribution Theory

Research has given a good deal of attention to how and why attributions are formed. It seems that people commonly analyze events to determine what caused them. Causes can be external, internal, or

---

Self-perception theory. A process of inferring one's own attitudes from observing one's own behavior.

Social cognition. The process of understanding and predicting social information.

Attribution theory. Making guesses about whether people's behavior is caused by their personality or by the situation they're in.

a combination of the two. For example, when you do well on a test, you may attribute that performance to intelligence and hard work (internal). When someone you don't like does well on a test, you might attribute it to luck or to an easy test (external).

Attributions may also depend on whether an observed behavior is expected or unexpected. Jones and Davis (1965) think that an observer decides whether or not a particular behavior is to be expected in a particular environment or social setting. If it is "normal" in that setting—that is, if most people would behave that way—then the situation is seen as the cause of the behavior. On the other hand, if the behavior is unexpected or not normal in that setting, then the person is thought to have a trait that caused the behavior. This is especially true if the behavior is extreme and no situational forces seem to be affecting the behavior. If you show up at a Halloween party dressed as a clown, people will assume that the situation demanded a costume and that you responded to the situational demand. If you show up at a dinner party and you are the only one wearing a costume, others at the party would be likely to see you as strange, an attention seeker, or a jerk.

Kelley (1967) has a similar explanation for how attributions are made. He proposes that most people are like scientists. We are presented with samples of information about others and we analyze those samples in order to come to some conclusions about why people behave in particular ways. Kelley suggests that when we evaluate the behavior of another person, we ask ourselves three questions: Do all people behave this way in similar situations? Does this person act this way in similar situations? Does this person act this way in other situations as well? Kelley thinks that the answers to these questions determine whether we attribute the behavior to internal or external causes (see Figure 17–2). If other people act the same way in similar situations, if the person in question acts this way in similiar situations, and if the person in question does not act this way in other types of situations, then we assume that the cause for the behavior is external. On the other hand, if few other people act this way in similar situations, if the person in question commonly acts this way in similar situations, and if the person acts this way in other situations as well, then the cause for the behavior is thought to be internal, something within the person, such as a personality trait.

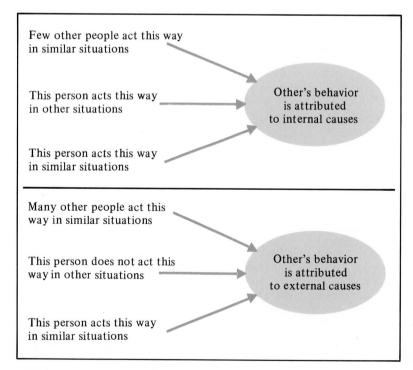

FIGURE 17-2

Whether we attribute other people's behavior to external or internal causes depends on a number of factors. (Kelley, 1967)

According to Kelley, behavior is thought to be caused by what it seems to vary with. If it varies from one occasion to another, then we think that the occasion is responsible for the behavior. If it varies from one person to another, then we attribute the behavior to the person.

The general point made by Kelley's theory is that behavior is thought to be caused by what it seems to vary with. If behavior varies from one situation or occasion to another, then we think that the situation or occasion is responsible for the behavior. If behavior varies from one person to another, then we attribute the behavior to the person.

The process of drawing attributions is not always as logical as Kelley's theory would suggest. In explaining our own behavior, we often make attributions in such a way as to protect our self-esteem. This **self-serving bias** causes people to make internal attributions for their successes and external attributions for their failures. You can see evidence of this in the sports pages. Winners tend to cite their own ability and preparation, and losers point out the unlucky breaks, bad calls, and so on that befell them. This self-serving bias is especially likely to occur when the person freely chooses to participate in an activity that is very important to the person (Weary, 1980). Sometimes, of course, people do take responsibility for their failures. This seems to be most likely if denying credit would be viewed negatively by others, or would deny credit for future success (Weary et al., 1982).

Attributions may go beyond simple internal–external judgments. We often make inferences about whether a successful performance is due to ability or effort. We see some people as having to work very hard to accomplish something, and others as having some natural talent that makes up for lack of effort. One often hears the latter observation made of athletes. A basketball player is described as a "natural" shooter, implying that the person possesses inborn reflexes and sensory skills that combine to yield high shooting accuracy. It is revealing to examine this distinction in attributions made about the successful performances of men and women. A number of studies (Deaux and Emswiller, 1974; Feldman-Summers and Kiesler, 1974; Taylor and Deaux, 1975) have demonstrated that a man's successful performance on a task is attributed to skill, which is a stable or enduring cause; by contrast, a woman's success is attributed to luck or effort, which are unstable causes that may change over time. This effect is exaggerated when the task is seen as a stereotyped masculine task (such as repairing an automobile).

Self-serving bias. The tendency to attribute one's successes to internal causes and one's failures to external causes.

Attribution research makes it clear that social behavior involves cognition. We use particular strategies for processing social information, and probably depend on such strategies to a much greater extent than with nonsocial information, since social stimuli are more complex than many other forms of stimuli. This means that objective reality may play much less of a role in analyzing social information than we might like to believe. Once again, we are struck with the difference between perception and reality.

Stereotypes

From what's been said it should not surprise you that distortions in social cognition sometimes occur. Distortions are not always unique to a single observor, but may be shared by many people. A common example of a group distortion is known as a **stereotype.** Stereotypes are beliefs about the characteristics of social groups. You might think of stereotypes as special cases of the representativeness mechanism described in Chapter 9. As soon as you are identified as a member of a group, all of the assumed characteristics of that group are attributed to you—both the positive and the negative. Stereotypes play an important role in behavior for two reasons. First, like other cognitive frameworks, stereotypes serve as guides for our behavior so we are not required to make new decisions about every individual. Second, stereotypes can be used to justify behavior toward a group. This is especially important if two groups are competing for a fixed resource such as jobs or money. The Protestant majority in Northern Ireland might contend that members of the Catholic minority have little skill, low motivation, and are not very smart. This justifies discrimination in jobs, housing, and elections to public office. White people might justify discriminatory actions toward black people by listing all the undesirable characteristics that they believe blacks possess and then, since the person in question is black, assume that he or she must have these negative characteristics.

Three different approaches have been developed to explain why stereotypes exist. The first is a trait or personality approach. This explanation emphasizes the fact that some people are more prone to form stereotypes then others. For example, Adorno (1950) suggests that one personality type, the

authoritarian personality, is particularly likely to form stereotypes. This implies that some people have a need to "put down" others, and that this need might be related to self-esteem. In other words, when you can identify a particular group of people as inferior, that makes the group to which you belong appear somehow better or special.

A second explanation for the formation of stereotypes is that they result from the threat of competition between groups for scarce and valuable resources. This approach, sometimes called realistic conflict theory, suggests that the reason some whites are prejudiced toward blacks is that blacks are seen as competition for jobs, education, and other valuable resources. Once formed, stereotypes are used to justify behavior toward the competing group, as mentioned earlier.

A third and more recent explanation of stereotypes is based on mechanisms of social cognition, such as those described above. It is assumed that each of us has a limited capacity to attend to and process information. Since social stimuli are so diverse, they require more processing time than we have available. As a result, we use shortcuts. One such shortcut is to organize social information based on groups or types of people. Once we have identified the group to which someone belongs, we can stop looking for more information about him or her. How many times have you felt you knew a great deal about someone just by knowing that he or she was a member of a particular group, such as the American Nazi Party or the Hare Krishna sect? Once the group is identified, the assumed characteristics of the group are transferred to the individual.

A number of studies have shown that we pay attention to salient characteristics (Taylor, 1980; Taylor and Crocker, 1980). **Salient characteristics** are those that stand out—are obvious. This should remind you of another mechanism described in the chapter on perception—figure-ground relationships. A woman in a crowd of men stands out. A tall person in a crowd of short people is immediately noticed. A black person in a group of white people receives close attention.

Keep in mind that the principles of social organization aren't radically different from the Gestalt principles of perception we've already outlined. In both cases we reorganize information in what we see as a more efficient manner. In some important respects, it does not matter whether the informa-

CAN STEREOTYPES BE REDUCED?

We have discussed some reasons for the existence of stereotypes and their persistence in social behavior. Social psychologists are also interested in how stereotypes can be reduced. Stereotypes and prejudice are closely related and eliminating them is clearly an important goal for society. Recent research suggests that promoting contact between separate groups, and getting people to respond to one another as individuals, are key factors in reducing stereotypes (Brewer and Kramer, 1985).

One theory of how people give up their prejudices is known as the contact hypothesis. The basic idea is that increased contact with an "outgroup"—that is, a group about which members of an "ingroup" have negative impressions—tends to reduce these negative impressions. For instance, if you, as a member of the purple-haired ingroup, consider the members of the green-haired outgroup to be a humorless bunch with poor table manners, being around a lot of green-haired people should rid you of your misconceptions. The contact hypothesis is one reason why legislators, educators, and parents are in favor of ideas like school desegregation. In important desegregation cases during the 1950's, social scientists testified that by going to the same schools, black and white children would be learning from an early age to be less hostile toward one another.

Other researchers, however, believe that simply increasing the amount of contact between ingroups and outgroups is not enough. In their view, only certain kinds of contact will help to reduce stereotypes. One condition that seems to be favorable is setting a goal that will be equally good for both groups. When members of two hostile groups are working together toward a common goal, prejudice seems to diminish. For example, white soldiers who had been in combat alongside black soldiers during World War II had fewer stereotyped beliefs about black soldiers than white soldiers who had not fought alongside blacks (Amir, 1969).

When contact between groups leads to an increase in awareness of particular members' characteristics, this, too, tends to reduce prejudice. This process is called *individuation*. As the name suggests, it involves learning about group members as individual people. When we see that the behavior of individuals we have come to know personally doesn't fit with our generalized beliefs about their group, our stereotypes begin to break down. If this happens frequently enough, we tend to give up the stereotype altogether. We can also see this process in reverse. During wartime, for example, soldiers learn to look upon the enemy not as individuals like themselves but as a group with universally negative traits that might include viciousness, heartlessness, sneakiness, bloodthirstyness, and so on.

In general, the reduction of stereotypes can best be achieved by increasing contact in situations where group members must work together toward a common goal and where they can come to know one another as individuals.

---

tion consists of the numbers and symbols on playing cards, or the skin color, gender, or accent of a person.

The Maintenance of Stereotypes

Stereotypes, by nature, have little objective basis. At best, they are overgeneralizations that are not confirmed by external evidence. How then, are stereotypes maintained? Several aspects of social cognition serve to sustain stereotypes, even though stereotypes are largely unfounded. First, people tend to perceive, interpret, and remember information in a biased way that confirms their stereotypes. Imagine that you see a person having a disagreement with a store clerk. If you believe that members of

---

Stereotype. A belief about the characteristics of a social group that is shared by many people; also, a preconceived idea about how a group or a person will behave.

Salient characteristics. Characteristics of a person or an object that stand out—are obvious.

a certain group are hostile, and the person is a member of that group, you are more likely to see the disagreement as hostile. Your interpretation would then serve to confirm your stereotype of that group.

In addition, people tend to seek out and remember evidence that confirms their stereotypes. If we believe someone is hostile, we might ask others questions that provide evidence of the person's unfriendly behavior. When we do encounter evidence *against* a stereotype, we often refuse to give up the stereotype. Sometimes we create a category of subtypes that maintains the stereotype; in other words, we say that some (but only a rare few) members of the group don't fit the stereotype and consider them "the exception that proves the rule." Alternatively, we may make attributions that explain away the disconfirming evidence. For example, we might attribute the success of a member of a disliked group to luck, but we would be sure to attribute any negative behavior to the fact that he or she belong to the disliked group.

Another reason stereotypes persist is **behavior confirmation of stereotypes,** a form of self-fulfilling prophecy (Snyder, Tanke, and Berscheid, 1977). When we believe that someone will act a certain way, through our own behavior we often cause them to act that way. If you believe that redheads are friendly, you will probably approach and be sociable to redheads. This may make them react in a friendly way to you. You would have created evidence in support of your stereotype, even if it had no objective accuracy apart from your influence.

REVIEW QUESTIONS

6. Match the following terms with the correct definition:

___ social cognition

___ self-serving bias

___ theory attribution

A. attributing one's successes to internal causes and failures to external causes.

B. judgments we make about whether people's behavior is caused by their personality characteristics or by the situation they're in.

C. trying to make sense of what is going on in a social situation.

7. According to one theory, unusual behavior tends to be attributed to the person/the situation, and expected or common behavior tends to be attributed to the person/the situation.

8. According to Kelley, if behavior varies from one situation to the other or one occasion to another, we think that the behavior is due to the _____ . If behavior varies from one person to another, it is attributed to the _____ .

9. _____ are beliefs about the characteristics of social groups. Such beliefs are often used to justify discriminatory behavior toward their members.

10. In forming impressions, we tend to pay attention to _____ characteristics, those that stick out or are obvious.

Answers: 6. social cognition, C; self-serving bias, A; attribution theory, B. 7. person; situation 8. situation; person 9. Stereotypes 10. salient

■ HELPING BEHAVIOR

Late one evening in New York City in 1964, a young woman named Kitty Genovese was attacked and murdered. The attack took place on a neighborhood street and lasted for over 30 minutes. During this time, the victim screamed repeatedly for help. A total of 38 people either saw or heard her struggling with her murderer; not one came to her aid or called the police. In fact, at one point her attacker fled the scene due to her screams, but when no one responded, he returned. Even the most hardened observers of the human condition were shocked. Why had no one helped?

From the interviews later conducted with the 38 witnesses, it became apparent that they were aware of one another. Social psychologists wondered if the fact that the witnesses *were* aware of one another's presence played a role in the tragedy. Since 1964, there have been dozens of **bystander intervention studies** of this phenomenon. The question is a simple one. Under what circumstances will one person be willing to help another person in distress? A series of experiments by Latané and Darley (1968, 1970) have provided some answers.

The experimental design was a simple one. Subjects were brought individually into a laboratory to complete a questionnaire before taking part, supposedly, in an interview. In fact, there was to be no interview. This was a deception study in which the subjects were intentionally misled. While a subject filled out the questionnaire, heavy smoke began to pour into the room through some air vents. Any normal person would have assumed that there was a serious fire somewhere in the building. The experimenters watched to see what their subjects would do. Latané and Darley hypothesized that the presence of others in the room would affect the behavior of the subjects, so the study was done with two experimental conditions. In condition A, a subject was left alone in the room. In condition B, there were other people in the room also filling out questionnaires. These other people were really assistants of the experimenters who had been instructed to acknowledge that smoke was coming out of the vents but to continue filling out the questionnaire. The hypothesis proved correct—the presence of other people made a difference in the behavior of the subjects. In the solitary condition, a subject was much more likely to look for someone in authority to alert that person about the smoke. About 75 percent of the solitary subjects reported the smoke within 6 minutes. However, in condition B, when the other people remained passive, so did the subject. In fact, in some trials the percentage of subjects in condition B who tried to warn authorities of the smoke was as low as 10 percent. Figure 17–3 presents a graph of the results of this study. As you can see, there was a dramatic difference between the two conditions.

In a second study, Latané and Darley (1970) brought subjects into an experimental room and told them that they would be taking part in a study of group problem-solving. Subjects were told that the experimenters were interested in the role that communication plays in solving problems, so subjects would only be allowed to communicate over an intercom. This would allow the experimenters to "control" communication. Subjects were then taken

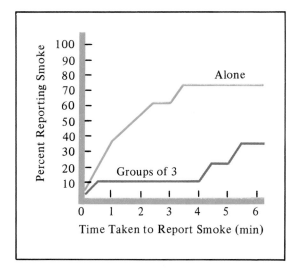

FIGURE 17–3
In this study, the time taken to report smoke in the room and the percent of people who reported smoke were both a function of how many people there were in the room when the smoke was seen. (Lantané and Darley, 1968)

singly to an experimental booth and told to work on solving a problem over the intercom. As was the case in the earlier study, there was really no "group." The voices over the intercom were really just tape-recorded messages. At some point, the subject heard another "group member" (actually a tape recording) confide that he was an epileptic, subject to occasional seizures, and that he felt one coming on and needed help.

Once again, the experimenters varied the size of the "group" by leading the subjects to believe that the "group" consisted of 2, 3, or 6 members (including the subject). It was hypothesized that the size of the group would affect the behavior of the subject. In the group of 2, the subject believed that no one else had heard the message. In the group of 3, the subject believed that one other person had heard the request for help. In the group of 6, presumably 4 others had heard the request. Once again, the results were clear. The 3- and 6-member groups had

---

Behavior confirmation of stereotypes. A form of self-fulfilling prophecy in which a person's expectations and behavior toward another person influence how the second person behaves; creates evidence in support of stereotypes.

Bystander intervention studies. Studies focusing on what conditions are necessary for a person to be willing to show helping behavior.

a much lower response rate than the 2-member group. Subjects were less likely to help in the presence of others, even others they could not see.

As a result of these experiments and others like them, there is now greater understanding why no one intervened while Kitty Genovese was being murdered. There seem to be two major factors. The first involves the diffusion of responsibility. When no one else is around, it is obvious that there is only one person able to help—you. But as more observers are added, the belief that "someone else" will intervene gets stronger. As the group grows in size, any single individual in that group feels less responsible.

The second factor has to do with the appearance of the situation. There is an old saying: When all those around you are losing their heads and you're not losing yours, you probably don't understand the situation. The reverse also seems to be seen as true: If all those around you are calm, then there may be no emergency. You may have misinterpreted what you saw. We use the behavior of others to come to conclusions about what is going on in ambiguous situations (situations that can be interpreted in several different ways). You are less likely to intervene if the situation is ambiguous and the inaction of those around you leads you to decide that nothing is seriously wrong. In contrast, Clark and Word (1974) found that help was offered more than 90 percent of the time when the situation was a clear-cut emergency, no matter how many people were present.

When an emergency situation arises, there are many variables besides group size that will influence the probability that a bystander will help. First, the bystander must *notice* that something has actually happened. Next, the bystander must *interpret* the situation as one in which help is needed. This is where ambiguity plays a role—a person stretched out on the sidewalk could just as easily be a drunk as a heart-attack victim. In addition, the bystander must assume *personal responsibility* for helping. As discussed above, the smaller the group, the greater the personal responsibility that is felt. The bystander must also decide on some form of assistance and be capable of giving it. If the bystander knows life-saving techniques, such as the Heimlich maneuver, used to aid someone choking on food, or cardiopulmonary resuscitation (CPR), used to restore breathing, he or she would be more likely to intervene in

such an emergency. Finally, the bystander may weigh the costs and benefits of helping and ask whether the time and inconvenience of helping someone change a flat tire, for example, is worth the good feeling that might result (also see Chapter 12).

The research on helping reminds us of attribution theory, social cognition, and perceptual processes in general. The way an individual perceives and interprets a situation is extremely important. Shotland and Straw (1976) demonstrated that people reacted very differently to a fight staged between a man and a woman, depending on what they perceived the couple's relationship to be. Of those who thought the couple was married, only 19 percent intervened. Of those who thought them to be strangers, 65 percent intervened. Interpretations matter.

If there is a moral or an application to these results, it is that someone must take the first step. Once a signal has been given that there is an emergency situation, the probability of intervention increases. Even if the person who sounds the alarm doesn't know how to help, someone else may. But someone must sound the alarm!

■ SOCIAL INFLUENCE

The research on helping shows that people's beliefs or behaviors can be greatly influenced by the (real or imagined) presence of others. This is a form of social influence. Two important areas of social influence are conformity and obedience.

Conformity

Conformity is yielding to perceived group pressure. In other words, when a person says or does something because other people are saying or doing it, the person is conforming. Social psychologists have been interested in the issue of conformity for some time. One of the first demonstrations of conformity was provided by Sherif (1935) in a study built around an illusion called the **autokinetic effect.** If you sit in a dark room and stare at a light source, the light will *appear* to move (it doesn't really). Curiously, people tend to make different estimates about such movement. One person might estimate that the light moved 15 feet; another might estimate that it moved 10 inches. Sherif noticed that when two subjects were in a room together and made independent estimates of the movement of the light source, their estimates gradually became closer, almost as if they were trying to conform to a norm of some kind.

Sherif decided to look at this phenomenon more carefully. He designed an experiment using fake subjects to provide estimates in the presence of real subjects. Both a real and a fake subject were placed together in a darkened room and told that the light would move a certain distance. Their task was to estimate how far it moved. The light was turned on and the real subject was asked to estimate the movement and state that estimate aloud. The fake subject would then typically estimate a value that was substantially lower or higher than the estimate of the real subject. After several trials, the estimates of the real subjects were very close to the estimates of the fake subjects. The real subjects had "conformed" to the estimates of the fake subjects.

It is not too difficult to understand why conformity occurred in this situation. Remember, the real subjects had been led to believe that the light actually moved. If the light did move, then there had to a "correct" answer. Since the real subjects did not know what that correct answer was and had never made estimates like this before, the estimates of the fake subjects were perceived as more "correct" and the real subjects used these estimates to make adjustments.

But what happens when the stimulus is not ambiguous and we should be able to trust our own judgment? Another social psychologist carried out a series of experiments that showed that knowledge of the "correct" answer does not eliminate the tendency to conform. In Asch's experiment (1951), subjects were brought into a room and told that they would be taking part in a perception experiment. They were asked to judge the lengths of various lines by comparing them to a standard line. Figure 17-4 gives an example of this type of task. The judgments were easy to make, since one of the target lines usually matched the standard line exactly and the other choices were much longer or shorter. The

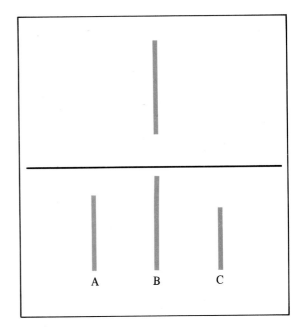

FIGURE 17-4
These were the cards used in the Asch experiment on conformity. Subjects were asked to judge the lengths of various lines by comparing them to the three lines on the bottom card. The line on the top card quite obviously matches line B on the bottom card; all of the judgments were this simple.

judgments were made in a group setting of five people. As you might have guessed by now, four of these people were actually experimental assistants; only one of the five was a real subject.

The group of five was given one judgment task after another. These tasks were arranged so that the real subject was always the last to judge. Each person announced the judgment aloud. The first few trials were without incident. The fake subjects picked the correct alternative on each trial, as did the real subject. Then the fake subjects all began to choose the same obviously incorrect alternative. As you might expect, this resulted in some discomfort for the real subjects. Would they "stick to their guns," or would they conform to the group and announce an incorrect choice? Averaging across subjects, conformity to the group choice occurred in 35 percent of the trials. About 30 percent of the sub-

---

Conformity. Behaving in a certain way in response to group pressure.

Autokinetic effect. A visual illusion; in a darkened room a stationary light will appear to be moving.

These photos were taken during the Asch conformity experiment. The man in the middle (Number 6) is the subject; the two others are confederates of Asch.

jects never conformed. In contrast, about 15 percent conformed nearly all of the time and most subjects, 55 percent, conformed at least once.

Why did these subjects conform? They had all the necessary information to make a correct choice and had made several correct choices in the previous trials, before the fake subjects began to make incorrect choices. Perhaps the subjects in the Asch research felt that the others in the group somehow knew better. This is possible, but it applies more to Sherif's study using the autokinetic effect. Another reason people conform is to gain acceptance from others and to avoid their disapproval. Thus, Asch's subjects may have known what was correct but answered incorrectly in spite of this knowledge. In a similar study, Deutsch and Gerard (1955) showed that conformity seemed to be related to what others in the group might *think* of the nonconformer. When subjects were allowed to respond anonymously, there was almost no conformity to incorrect choices. This showed that subjects do not want to appear deviant. When they cannot be identified, they are willing to make the correct choice.

Numerous variables affect conformity. These variables can be related to the two reasons people conform given above (because others provide useful information and because we desire social approval). For instance, we are more likely to conform to judgments of others when we consider them to be experts and when we are unsure of our own judgments. In these circumstances, others are likely to be seen as a more valid and useful source of information (Kiesler and Kiesler, 1969). We are also more likely to conform to a group that is cohesive. A group is cohesive if its members feel close allegiance to the group and really want to remain members of it. When a group is cohesive, people are more likely to worry about being rejected as a deviant.

Another variable that seems to affect conformity is the presence of a nonconforming ally. To test this, Asch (1956) set up an experiment similar to the ones just described, but in this case, one of the fake subjects was instructed to make the correct choice rather than to go along with the other fake subjects. This time, there was very little conformity on the part of the real subjects. It was almost as if a group had been formed within a group. Most of us have had similar experiences. If we can find one other person to agree with us, we behave quite differently than if we are alone in our opinion. One deviant judge seems foolish; two deviant judges seem brave. This is the same kind of reaction that seems to operate in bystander intervention. You don't want to be the first to summon help—that would be embarrassing if there were no real emergency. You would seem foolish. But if even one other person seems to notice the same emergency, the "embarrassment potential" drops considerably. Indeed, conformity drops off even if the dissenter (the fake subject) gives the wrong answer (Allen and Levin, 1971).

Willis and Hollander (1964) have added an interesting refinement to the concept of conformity. They distinguish among conformity, independence, and anticonformity. As you saw before, conformity means choosing a course of action that meets some expectation of another person or group. Independence means being aware of those expectations but not necessarily conforming to them. Anticonformity means being aware of expectations and doing exactly the opposite. It is interesting to note that in both the conformity and anticonformity patterns of behavior, the person is being controlled by a group expectation. In the anticonformity pattern, the group leads the individual to do the opposite of what the group expects.

Obedience

Conformity involves authority that is indirect. It becomes apparent to us that the group feels differently about a situation than we do. We can choose to go along with the group or to deviate from the group. Pressures may be brought to bear to get us back into line, but even these pressures are often subtle rather than direct. There are some situations in which social-influence pressures are much more direct. In many instances, we are expected to obey a command or a rule presented by an authority.

Obedience usually involves legitimate authority of some kind. We are told to do something by someone who seems to have the right to direct our activities. Do we comply with direct requests in the same way as we conform to group standards? It seems as though we do. In fact, it seems as if the tendency to obey is so great that we are even willing to harm others on command. A common defense offered by Nazi war criminals is that they were only following orders. In fact, historically, military training has stressed the importance of responding immediately and without question to a direct order. There appear to be circumstances in which right and wrong can be defined in a relative rather than an absolute sense. When told to do something by someone in authority, it seems as though that makes the action "right" by definition.

Deviant. Refusing to behave as the group demands or expects you to behave.

Obedience. Following the instructions or commands of a legitimate authority-figure.

In order to understand the circumstances surrounding obedience, Stanley Milgram (1963) conducted a famous series of experiments in New Haven, Connecticut. These experiments were described briefly in the first chapter. As was pointed out, these experiments revealed that experimenters are considered authorities by subjects. In this chapter, we will consider the extent of this power in some detail.

Milgram's experiment involved electric shock. Subjects were recruited through a newspaper ad and told that they would be paid to take part in a learning experiment. As subjects arrived, they were paired off with another subject, who was actually an assistant to the experimenter. The two subjects were told that in the experiment one person would learn a series of verbal associations and the other person would teach those associations. The real subject was always the teacher and the fake subject was always the learner. The task was to remember which words had been paired together during a training session, for example: *white/shoe, bright/sun,* and *loud/color.* In the test phase, the teacher could hear but not see the learner, since the learner was placed in a room with shock apparatus and the teacher was in a separate room with a shock panel. The teacher presented words from the list, such as the word *bright* and four additional words: *sun, car, color,* and *sound.* The learner had to choose the word that had been paired with *bright* before. Each time the learner made an incorrect response, the teacher had to administer electric shock by flipping a switch on the shock panel. There was a series of switches arranged in a graded sequence from a low voltage (15 volts) to a very high voltage (450 volts). The first incorrect response was to be punished with a 15-volt shock, the second mistake with the next level—30 volts—and so on, until the highest level of 450 volts was reached. The switches were identified both by their voltage and by printed descriptions (Slight Shock; Moderate Shock; Danger: Severe Shock). Above the 450-volt level was the ominous label XXX. The implication was clear that high levels were dangerous.

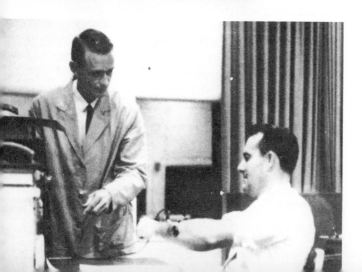

These photos show the apparatus and basic setup used in the Milgram experiment—the shock generator, the "learner" with electrodes attached to his wrist, and the subject receiving a sample shock from the generator.

Before the experiment began, the real subject—the teacher—saw the learner being hooked up to the shock apparatus. During the experiment, the learner actually read from a script and made a fixed number of errors in responding. Each time an error occurred, the teacher had to administer a shock to the learner. When a shock was administered by the teacher, the learner delivered a predetermined message over the intercom system: a shout of pain, a request to stop the experiment, or a complaint about shortness of breath.

Put yourself in the position of the teacher. When the learner began to protest, would you continue? Probably not, if you were left alone. But these subjects always had an experimenter in the room with them. As the shouts and protests of the learners grew more intense, the subjects expressed a desire to stop the experiment, but the experimenter urged them to go on with such prods as "Please continue" and "It is absolutely essential that you continue."

When the experiment was over, approximately 65 percent of the subjects had flipped all of the switches, going well beyond what they believed to be the danger level. They had continued to administer shocks even after hearing the learner bang the wall, scream out, gasp, and make no more responses of any kind at 315 volts! Keep in mind that these were normal people, no different from you or me, yet they were persuaded to harm another person. As was the case in the conformity studies, not everyone obeyed. But almost everyone administered some shock even after the learner began to protest.

The experimenter exerted a very powerful influence over the subjects. In interviews after the experiment was over, subjects (teachers) consistently reported wanting to stop but being afraid of ruining the experiment. The experimenter was considered a legitimate authority-figure who knew what was going on. In these circumstances, the subjects suspended their own judgment and submitted to the experimenter as the expert. The importance of the experimenter as an authority-figure can be seen in a variation of this study, in which the experimenter left the room and gave further instructions by phone. Obedience dropped by two-thirds.

The reactions of the subjects in the shock experiments were very similar to the reactions of the subjects in some of the conformity studies we discussed. Additional obedience studies using shock showed other similarities. In one study (Milgram, 1974), the subject was in the company of two people who seemed to be peers. These peers either encouraged the subject to continue the shocks or encouraged them to defy the experimenter and stop giving the shocks. These peers had a substantial effect. When they encouraged the subject to continue the shocks, the subject usually did. When they discouraged the shocks, the subject nearly always stopped. As was the case with conformity, it seems as if an ally can make an enormous difference in behavior and that group pressures can have either positive or negative effects.

These obedience studies have shown that in spite of the fact that people are capable of high-level moral reasoning, some situations are so powerful that these reasoning mechanisms are ignored or modified. You may remember the discussion of locus of control in the personality chapter. There are circumstances in which people seem to pass control from an internal to an external source. When that occurs, internal controlling mechanisms such as morals or conscience no longer have any meaning. Meaning is provided by an external agent: an experimenter, a prison guard, or another authority figure. Further, people believe that the authority figure—not they—will be responsible for their actions. Milgram (1974) has referred to this replacement of internal control with external control as a state of **agency**, in which an individual adopts the morals or conscience of a group or external agent. This may partially account for some bizarre antisocial behaviors such as gang rape and group persecution. Another contributing factor is that in obedience situations, such as the Milgram experiment, people obey in small, gradual steps, as in the foot-in-the-door technique.

Situational influences are not always obvious to us, nor are we aware of the possibility that conscience will give way to external forces. The shock experiments are a case in point. Before these experiments were actually begun, they were described to various groups of people who were asked if they would continue to give shocks until they had reached the limit. Very few people reported that they would give all of the shocks. But 65 percent of the experimental subjects did give shocks all the

---

Agency. A state in which an internal source of control is replaced by an external agent and the person adopts the morals of that external agent.

way up to 450 volts. This inconsistency between what people expected to do and what people actually did illustrates an interesting attributional phenomenon. We often underestimate how important and how powerful situational influences, like the presence of the experimenter in the Milgram research, really are.

GROUP DYNAMICS

You have probably heard it said that a group is more than a collection of its members. A group has a force that is unlike that of an individual. Have you ever skipped class rather than come in late and have 200 sets of eyes follow you to your seat? In several of the earlier chapters, you have seen much evidence of the effects of groups on behavior. You saw that groups can aid problem solving by helping to come up with ideas. You examined the mechanics of group therapy and its effect on behavior change. And you considered what it means to be of a particular gender—a member of a group called female or male. In each of these instances, groups influence individual behavior. In social psychology, this is known as **group dynamics**—the push and pull among group members. Group-dynamics researchers study topics such as leadership and decision-making. Another topic of investigation is how performance is affected by the presence of others.

The Positive Effects of Groups on Members

The discussion of obedience and conformity implied that group influences are mostly negative. Of course they can be, but group pressures are not, by definition, harmful to the individual. There are occasions when a group can be used as a source of support and encouragement. Attraction, liking, and loving are all positive emotions that depend on other people. No one can deny the pleasure that parents get from children and children from parents. Sometimes conformity and obedience lead us to act in positive, desirable ways.

Groups can also have a positive effect on our performance of a task. Hackman (1976) has considered the ways groups might affect the performance of their members and cites several possibilities. The first type of influence is on knowledge and skills.

When you join a new group, one or more members of that group will affect your knowledge or skill by:

1. giving you specific instructions in some task
2. giving you feedback about how well or poorly you are doing
3. giving you a model to observe and thus improve your skill

It doesn't matter whether the group is of fellow workers, fellow students, or fellow joggers; someone in the group is likely to be able to offer help that can lead you to improve some aspect of technique or knowledge.

Performance and the Presence of Others

Another way group members can affect member performance is through increased arousal. You recall from Chapter 5 that increased arousal can lead to increased performance, up to a certain point. Beyond that optimal point, however, increased arousal can hurt performance. Either way, arousal level makes a difference. At one time, it was thought that the mere presence of others made a difference in performance. It was hypothesized that just having someone else in the immediate vicinity increased arousal (and motivation to perform) This effect is called **social facilitation**. For example, joggers increase their speed when they run by a person sitting on a park bench (Worrington and Messick, 1983). A more recent view is that performance arousal is increased only when people think others may be evaluating them. This is sometimes called **evaluation apprehension**.

A second way arousal can be affected is through direct intervention. Group members may exhort other members to try harder. In sports, those exhortations are organized by cheerleaders, so that the players get the message. Spectators at a marathon will urge the runners to "go for it." Often, spectators make the difference between an outstanding or a mediocre performance. Many track stars credit the crowd for a record-breaking performance. Often, it seems as if the runner wants to pay the crowd back for the effort put into cheering. A bond is formed between runner and spectators. The following incident is an example of how this can happen:

Mary Decker set a world indoor record for 1500 meters before the largest crowd in indoor track history at Madison Square Garden in 1980. Her time was 4 minutes, 0.8 seconds. The crowd ... had booed the

The presence of others can act to increase arousal which in turn can lead to increased performance. For example, the crowd watching a race directly intervene to affect arousal when they cheer the runners on.

slow pace of the men's mile before her race, but began a steadily mounting crescendo of applause and cheering after Miss Decker's quarter-mile split was announced. By the time Miss Decker hit the finish, the noise was almost painful to the ears. "The crowd helped me tremendously," she said. "I would never have run that fast without it." (New York Times, 2/10/80)

High levels of arousal seem to help in performance tasks that are simple and in which the person can easily execute the correct response. However, there are certain situations in which increased arousal can hurt performance. High arousal seems to hurt in difficult, complex tasks, and in tasks where new responses must be learned to new stimuli. A recent

Group dynamics. The push and pull among members of a group that influences individual and group behavior.
Social facilitation. The positive effect of the presence of others on performance due to increased arousal and motivation.

Evaluation apprehension. Effect in which increased effort is shown because people think that those around them may be watching or judging them.

review of over 200 studies verifies that the presence of others does have the effect of improving performance on simple tasks and decreasing performance on complex tasks. However, this effect was relatively small (Bond and Titus, 1983).

The literature on social facilitation emphasizes that groups increase arousal. But the other side of the coin is just as important. Groups can sometimes lower arousal by providing support, comfort, and immunity from criticism. Consider what might happen if the offensive unit of a football team came off the field and told the defensive players as they went onto the field to "take it easy, have a good time, get to know the other guys, and feel free to express yourself in any way you like." Many coaches would be bothered by this type of exchange between the team's defensive and offensive units. At the very least, it would make for a very different type of game. Some possible combinations of arousal and performance are presented in Figure 17–5.

If you have ever helped others to carry a heavy object, you might have felt that your load was a little heavier than you expected. You may even have thought that someone was not carrying a fair share. You were probably correct. This phenomenon—that people work less hard in a group than they do working alone—has been labeled **social loafing**, and

has been demonstrated in several different ways. One way was through the measurement of how loudly people shout (Latané et al., 1979). After measuring the loudness of individual subjects shouting alone, it was found that the same subjects only shouted at 82 percent of capacity when they thought they were paired with one other person, and at 74 percent when they thought they were shouting in a group of six. Latene and his colleagues have found similar effects in tasks as diverse as handclapping, typing, swimming, and evaluating poems.

What causes social loafing? One explanation is that people may feel that their individual efforts are buried in those of the group. As a result, they see less likelihood that they will receive individual rewards for their efforts. Research has also shown that if people working in groups feel that their individual contributions are identifiable, social loafing will not occur (Williams, Harkins, and Latané, 1981). This finding clarifies why social loafing, rather than social facilitation, sometimes occurs. Social loafing is a result of feeling "lost in the crowd." Social facilitation is a result of feeling that one's performance is being evaluated by others.

Another explanation of social loafing is tied to the concepts of equity theory and expectation. According to this explanation, people may expect

FIGURE 17–5
This matrix shows the effects on learning and performance when the group tries to increase or decrease arousal. It appears that increased arousal can hinder the learning of new tasks but can help the performance of well-known tasks. On the other hand, while decreased arousal may be better for learning new tasks, it hinders the performance of well-known tasks.

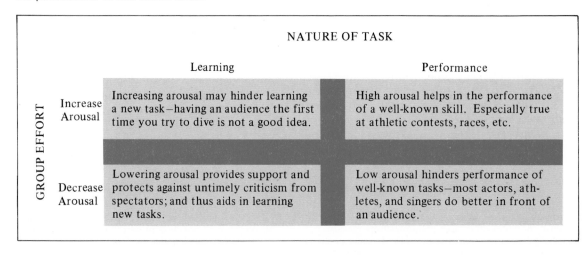

GROUP EFFORT	NATURE OF TASK	
	Learning	Performance
Increase Arousal	Increasing arousal may hinder learning a new task—having an audience the first time you try to dive is not a good idea.	High arousal helps in the performance of a well-known skill. Especially true at athletic contests, races, etc.
Decrease Arousal	Lowering arousal provides support and protects against untimely criticism from spectators; and thus aids in learning new tasks.	Low arousal hinders performance of well-known tasks—most actors, athletes, and singers do better in front of an audience.

that others will "slack off" on group tasks. This creates a sense of inequity, and the person responds by reducing his or her own efforts (Jackson and Harkins, 1985). The degree of social loafing is reduced when people are really interested in the task at hand and when the work group is cohesive.

The implications for group projects are clear: Try to get everyone interested. Build a cohesive group. Try to create expectations that all group members will work equally hard. And, perhaps most important, make sure everyone has a specific responsibility that can be identified and evaluated.

REVIEW QUESTIONS

11. There have been a number of studies of why people do or do not get involved in helping someone in distress. These studies are called _____ _____ studies.

12. One of the conditions that seems to determine whether or not people will help someone else is the _____ of the group involved.

13. Most groups put pressure on their members to behave in certain ways or _____ to the group standards.

14. In the Asch experiment, the presence of an ally who agreed with the subject caused the subject to conform to/deviate from the rest of the group's opinions.

15. When being part of a group makes everyone work harder it is called _____ _____; when being part of a group makes people do less than their fair share it is called _____ _____.

Answers: 11. bystander intervention 12. size 13. conform 14. deviate from 15. social facilitation; social loafing

■ SUMMARY

1. *Social psychology* is the study of human behavior in the context of interpersonal relations, or the examination of how an individual is influenced by and tries to influence the behavior of other individuals.

2. An *attitude* is a combination of three elements: behavioral tendencies, feelings, and beliefs about an object, event, or person. Research on attitudes emphasizes the potential relationship between attitudes and behaviors. An early view was that attitudes were simply behavior tendencies. The current view is that besides the behavior elements, an attitude also has an emotional element and a belief element, or a collection of cognitions that we hold to be true about objects or people.

3. Attitude formation and attitude change require communication, although it is not necessary for the communication to be intentional. Certain characteristics of the communicator affect the likelihood that he or she will change others' attitudes: expertise, or the fact that experts in an area are more influential than nonexperts; trustworthiness, or perceived honesty; and liking, or the fact that people are more easily influenced by those they like.

4. Festinger has theorized that when our actions are at odds with our behavior, or when we hold two conflicting beliefs at the same time, a state he calls *cognitive dissonance*, we will engage in some action to bring our beliefs and/or actions into agreement again. An alternative explanation to the results of dissonance research is *self-perception theory*. Bem has theorized that people decide what their attitudes are by observing their own behavior and the circumstances in which it occurred.

5. *Social cognition* is the mental activity involved in processing social information. *Attribution theory* refers to the inferences each of us makes about the causes of our own and others' behavior. Causes can be external, internal, or a combination of the two, and can also depend on whether the behavior is expected or unexpected.

6. Attribution theorists Jones and Davis believe that people tend to attribute unique behavior to the individual and common behavior to the situation. Kelley theorizes that behavior is thought to be caused by what it seems to vary with. According to the *self-serving bias*, people tend to make internal attributions for their successes and external attributions for their failures.

7. Stereotypes are beliefs about the characteristics of a group that serve as cognitive frameworks and can be used to justify behavior toward a group.

Social loafing: A condition in which being part of a group causes individuals to do less than their fair share.

Explanations of stereotypes include the trait or personality approach, which states that some people are more prone to form stereotypes than others, and realistic conflict theory, which states that stereotypes result from competition for valued resources. A more current explanation states that stereotypes result from the need to form a cognition on the basis of limited information. People tend to focus more attention on people's salient, or distinctive, characteristics. Stereotypes also persist because of *behavioral confirmation of stereotypes*, whereby we cause others to act as we expect them to.

8. *Bystander intervention studies* focus on the conditions under which a person is willing to help someone in distress. Latané and Darley have found that subjects were most likely to offer help when they believed that no one else was around; if they believed others were around, subjects were unlikely to offer help. Also, people use others' behavior to judge whether a situation is an emergency or not. Other variables that influence bystander intervention include: observing the event; interpreting the situation as one in which help is needed; assuming personal responsibility; and choosing a form of assistance and being capable of giving it.

9. *Conformity* results from a group's pressure on its members to behave in particular ways. In Sherif's experiments with the *autokinetic effect*, an ambiguous stimulus situation, subjects tended to conform to a norm. Asch's experiment showed that many subjects will choose an obviously incorrect alternative when all the other group members make this choice. Other researchers have shown that subjects make choices that they know are wrong so that they won't appear *deviant* to other group members. In the presence of an ally, or another person willing to make an inconsistent choice, subjects are much less likely to conform with those making the incorrect choice.

10. *Obedience* usually involves a legitimate authority, or someone who seems to have the power to define a particular action as right or wrong. In Milgram's obedience experiment, most subjects followed the experimenter's instructions to give shocks to another person. The subjects suspended their own judgment and obeyed the experimenter's authority. These experiments show that some situations are so powerful that internal controlling mechanisms can be ignored or modified. In what Milgram refers to as a state of *agency*, an individual

adopts the conscience of an external agent or group.

11. Group interaction can also have benefits. Group members can improve one another's performance by providing specific instructions, giving feedback, or serving as models for one another. The presence of others can also influence a person's arousal level, resulting in either positive or negative effects on performance. This is known as *social facilitation*. A more recent view of social facilitation is that arousal is increased only when people feel that others may be watching them. Further, if one's individual efforts seem lost in the group, *social loafing* may occur.

■ ANSWERING QUESTIONS FOR THOUGHT

1. Advertisers are well aware that the communicator can have an important influence on the success of the message. Thus, they go to great lengths to choose spokespeople who appear expert, trustworthy, and likeable. In this particular case, the gamble is that an audience is likely to believe the "expert" opinion of a well-known sports figure on which brand of sports equipment to buy. For example, a popular tennis star is considered a good spokesperson for what kind of tennis racket ensures a better game.

2. One explanation lies in the theory of cognitive dissonance. This theory states that dissonant, or conflicting, thoughts cause tension. In order to reduce the tension, people will attempt to bring their thoughts into agreement with their actions. In our example, smokers are aware of the potential health risks (one cognition), but are equally aware of continuing to smoke (dissonant cognition). Smokers could quit smoking, but it may be easier to convince themselves that smoking isn't so dangerous after all. There are various ways to go about this—associating with other smokers who support this attitude; avoiding literature that links smoking to cancer; or adopting an "It won't happen to me" kind of attitude.

3. Attribution research has helped identify some practical problems, including this curious double standard for men and women. A significant number of studies have demonstrated that both men and women attribute male success largely to skill and

female success mainly to luck. Such findings suggest that we probably depend on cognitive strategies to a large extent when processing complex social stimuli. As a result, objective reality may play much less of a role in processing social information than we would like to admit. The male-versus-female-success attribution is a particularly strong reminder of the difference between perception and reality.

4. People's willingness to help depends on several factors. One very important factor is the size of the group present at the time. The smaller the group size, the more likely people are to take on the responsibility of helping behavior. Other factors that affect the decision to help are correctly interpreting the situation as an emergency, choosing some form of assistance, and being capable of giving it.

5. It depends. A group can be helpful in some cases, but not in others. For example, in a situation that involves learning a new task, you'd probably be better off working alone. But athletes often perform much better in front of a crowd than when they are practicing alone—the social facilitation effect. At other times social loafing occurs, in which the presence of a group keeps each member from doing his or her fair share.

18 Industrial and Organizational Psychology

QUESTIONS FOR THOUGHT

1. Could you drive a car without a dashboard full of lights, knobs, and dials?
2. Do people work hard because they are happy, or are they happy because they work hard?
3. Are working people today more or less satisfied with their jobs than their parents were?
4. Can a highly complicated job, such as assembling an automobile, be successfully completed without a supervisor?
5. What can be done about unfair discrimination in hiring practices?

The answers to these questions are at the end of the chapter.

In the seventeen chapters preceding this one, you have learned a good deal about the study of psychology. You might assume that by now there's not much left to talk about. In a sense, you are right. You have been introduced to most of the important concepts in the field and to the major areas in which psychologists work. But concepts are only the raw materials for much of the practice of psychology, not the finished product. As you have seen in preceding chapters, applications add luster to concepts.

One broad area of application is found in the work of the industrial psychologist. You read in Chapter 1 that industrial and organizational psychology forms one of the eight major divisions of the field of psychology. There are over 2,000 industrial psychologists who belong to the American Psychological Association and who work in government and industry, do private consulting, conduct research for private and government agencies, and teach in university settings. Their specialty is the study of behavior in the work setting and their knowledge is in demand. This should come as no surprise—after adolescence, most of us spend many years in the work force. Except for time spent sleeping, more time is spent at work than at almost any other activity on a day-to-day basis. This means we do a lot of "behaving" in work settings. Furthermore, it is likely that our experiences at work have a major impact on the life we lead outside of work.

For many people, work can be the source of major joys and frustrations. The frustrations of workers in unsatisfying jobs have always been well-documented in popular songs. One I find especially compelling is the song called "Millworker" by James Taylor:

Millwork ain't easy,
Millwork ain't hard,
Millwork it ain't nothin but an awful boring
* job.*
I'm waitin' for my daydream,
To take me through the morning,
and put me in my coffee break,
where I can have a sandwich and remember.
Then it's me and my machine for the rest of
* the morning,*
and the rest of the afternoon,
and the rest of my life.

Work can clearly be a negative experience, but in many cases it offers opportunities for enjoyment as well. The sense of accomplishment from completing a difficult task, the pride of being identified as the person "responsible" for a successful product or a good job, and the stimulation of working closely with and depending on fellow workers or being part of a team are all rewards of work. There is little doubt that work has a major impact on our emotional lives. Sometimes this impact is not really felt until we are no longer able to work. This usually happens to people in one of two ways—sudden layoffs or planned retirement. People who lose their jobs without warning may be devastated by the experience. They may become depressed and suffer reduced self-esteem (Maurer, 1979). This can also be true for those who have planned to leave work but have not really prepared themselves. Thus, work—its performance and its absence—can be a central anchor in a person's self-evaluation.

Besides its effect on our emotional life, there are two more good reasons to examine work behavior. One is very practical. Most of us have worked at some point in our lives, and therefore should be able to relate to the application of some of the important concepts we have studied thus far to the workplace. The second reason, I must confess, is strictly personal. Let me explain with the following anecdote. Joe Paterno, the present coach of the Penn State University football team, was asked at an interview why he had substituted a fourth-string inexperienced player in a particular game. Paterno is Italian and proud of it. The player in question was also Italian. So the interviewer asked Paterno, "Did you put the player in because he was Italian?" Paterno answered, "Of course not! We don't make decisions based on the ethnic background of players." After a pause coach Paterno added, "I put him in because *I'm* Italian!" I'm afraid I'm guilty of Joe Paterno reasoning. One reason this chapter is here is because I am an industrial psychologist.

■ A BRIEF OVERVIEW AND SOME RELEVANT HISTORY

Modern **industrial and organizational (IO) psychology** has three main branches: human factors psychology, industrial social and organizational psychology, and personnel psychology. Each of these branches is concerned with a different aspect of, and a different approach to, work behavior.

Human Factors Psychology. In highly simplified terms, **human factors psychology** views the individual as a machine with certain capacities and limitations. Some examples of human capacities are the sense of vision, certain motor skills such as hand-eye coordination, and certain cognitive abilities such as memory. But with each human capacity comes a limitation. For example, we can only see light of certain wavelengths—we cannot see ultraviolet or infrared light. Similarly, there are limits to how quickly we can move our hands in response to visual stimuli. The human factors psychologist attempts to apply what is known about the capacities and limitations of human beings to the design of work tasks and environments.

Human factors psychology has its roots in **industrial engineering**. Some of its early practitioners were engineers, not psychologists. Frank and Lillian Gilbreath, a husband-and-wife team of industrial

engineers, developed principles of time and motion study and applied them to family life (they had 12 children). An amusing and popular book, called *Cheaper by the Dozen*, resulted from their efforts. In their book the Gilbreaths describe how they managed to make the performance of such tasks as taking baths, eating meals, and cleaning rooms more "efficient" by applying time and motion study. Their humorous book is also quite informative. In spite of the fact that we are amused by their descriptions of the "efficiency" of doing ordinary tasks, the fact is the Gilbreaths were as serious about their principles of efficient household arrangement as the modern human factors psychologist is about the design of a control room for a nuclear-power plant or the instrument panel of a supersonic jet. The Gilbreaths demonstrated that certain time and motion principles could be applied to almost any type of organization. (See the box.)

Time and motion study involves a careful observation of a work process in order to determine how much time is expended in each motion that makes up a work task. The time and motion analyst actually uses a stopwatch to break down each component of a complex action into its elements. Once that is done, attempts are made to find "wasted" or inefficient motion that can be eliminated, thus making the action more efficient.

Many of the principles of time and motion study were adopted in industry in the late 19th and early 20th centuries. Perhaps the best-known example is the early work of Taylor at Bethlehem Steel (Taylor, 1947). Taylor developed what he considered to be the most workable combination of equipment, labor incentives, and work/rest schedules for shoveling pig iron. His system included a special shovel designed to fit the strength and body type of the typical Bethlehem Steel laborer. Along with this special equipment, he called for specific rest pauses that required the worker to stop at particular intervals to allow his muscles to recover. Finally, Taylor told the steel workers that their earnings could increase greatly if they were to follow his instructions without question. There is little doubt that Taylor's technique (called **scientific management**) resulted in more pig iron being shoveled, but we do not know what the psychological cost of being controlled as a machine was to the industrial workers. This was not the concern of the industrial engineer in Taylor's time.

WHAT WORKS IN THE FACTORY SHOULD WORK IN THE HOME

In their foreword to *Cheaper by the Dozen,* a unique account of their family life, the Gilbreath children note that their parents were among the first in the scientific management field and the very first in motion study. In this excerpt from the book, they describe how their parents "managed" a houseful of children:

"So it was Mother the psychologist and Dad the motion study man and general contractor, who decided to look into the new field of the psychology of management, and the old field of psychologically managing a houseful of children. They believed that what would work in the home would work in the factory, and what would work in factory would work in the home.

Dad put the theory to a test shortly after we moved to Montclair. The house was too big for Tom Grieves, the handyman, and Mrs. Cunningham, the cook, to keep in order. Dad decided we were going to have to help them, and he wanted us to offer the help of our own accord. He had found that the best way to get cooperation out of employees in a factory was to set up a joint employer-employee board, which would make work assignments on a basis of personal choice and aptitude. He and Mother set up a Family Council, patterned after an employer-employee board. The council met every Sunday afternoon, immediately after dinner.

No one wanted to divide the work or otherwise be associated with it in any way, shape, or form. No one said anything.

"I think," Jack said slowly, "that Mrs. Cunningham and Tom should do the work. They get paid for it."

"Sit down," Dad hollered. "You are no longer recognized."

Dan was next recognized by the chair.

"I think Tom and Mrs. Cunningham have enough to do," he said, as Dad and Mother beamed and nodded agreement. "I think we should hire more people to work for us."

"Out of order," Dad shouted. "Sit down and be quiet!"

Dad saw things weren't going right. Mother was the psychologist. Let her work them out.

"Your chairman recognizes the assistant chairman," he said, nodding to Mother to let her know he had just conferred that title upon her person.

"We could hire additional help," Mother said, "and that might be the answer."

We grinned and nudged each other.

"But," she continued, "that would mean cutting the budget somewhere else. If we cut out all desserts and allowances, we could afford a maid. And if we cut out moving pictures, ice cream sodas, and new clothes for a whole year, we could afford a gardener, too."

"Do I hear a motion to that effect?" Dad beamed. "Does anybody want to stop allowances?"

No one did. After some prodding by Dad, the motion on allotting work finally was introduced and passed. The boys would cut the grass and rake the leaves. The girls would sweep, dust and do the supper dishes. Everyone except Dad would make his own bed and keep his room neat. When it came to apportioning work on an aptitude basis, the smaller girls were assigned to dust the legs and lower shelves of furniture; the older girls to dust table tops and upper shelves. The older boys would push the lawnmowers and carry leaves. The younger ones would do the raking and weeding."

Modern human factors psychology is considerably more complicated (and sympathetic to workers) than the scientific management technique.

Human factors psychologists of the 1980s are involved in designing systems that could affect the health and well-being of millions of people. For ex-

---

Industrial and organizational (IO) psychology. Specialized area of psychology that studies behavior in the work setting; branches into human factors psychology, industrial social and organizational psychology, and personnel psychology.

Human factors psychology. A branch of industrial psychology concerned with designing work tasks and equipment to suit human capacities and limitations.

Industrial engineering. The application of engineering principles to maintaining high productivity at minimum cost in industrial settings.

Scientific management. A work method developed by Taylor. Included many aspects of traditional time and motion study, plus a unique feature—workers were promised bonuses if they followed his work method instructions exactly.

ample, following the Three-Mile-Island nuclear accident in 1979, human factors research was recognized as a much more critical component in the design of nuclear-power-plant control rooms. After the recent Soviet accident at Chernobyl, it is likely that there will be increased attempts to understand the bases of the "human error" factor and find ways to compensate for it.

Regardless of whether we are considering the work of a manual laborer or the work of a control room operator in a nuclear-power plant, the goals of the human factors psychologist are the same—to develop work environments and methods that best suit the capacities and limitations of human beings.

Industrial Social and Organizational Psychology.

Early human factors psychology had focused on improving the physical environment. There was a firm belief that heat, light, and noise were the major factors influencing productive effort, and many lab and field studies were undertaken to explore these relationships. One series of such studies resulted in the formation of the second major branch of industrial psychology, **industrial social and organizational psychology**. The studies were as follows.

On the outskirts of Chicago, there was a major Western Electric production facility known as the Hawthorne plant. The workers in this plant made various components for electric motors and relays for telephone-switching equipment. In 1929, plant management decided to do their own study of the effect of light on production. Their first step was a sound one. As any good experimental psychologist would do, they identified an experimental group and a control group. Unfortunately, efforts went downhill from there. Every new study that was done confused them more. It was first found that the experimental groups did not show any effect from the changed lighting; however, the *control* groups did show measurable effects. Next, it was found that some experimental groups did better with more light, but others did worse. Finally, it was found that *both* experimental and control groups had increased their level of production, regardless of the lighting conditions.

A whole new series of studies was begun. In this later series, it was found that even in cases where lighting was reduced to a level of 70 percent below normal (to the equivalent of candle light!), production levels were maintained. In order to pinpoint what was going on, the experiment designers decided to try something that was common in experimental psychology at the time. They built in what is called a "catch trial" to determine if the subjects were acting in a reasonable manner. The experimenters changed some light bulbs in the plant, and told the workers that the old bulbs were being replaced with brighter ones. In fact, the "new" bulbs were bulbs of the same intensity as before. Many of the workers thanked the experimental team for their consideration and production once again increased!

A final set of studies at the Hawthorne plant clearly demonstrated that production was the result of many more things than just the physical characteristics of the environment. After gradually introducing rest pauses, shortened work days, and shortened work weeks, the experimenters found that overall production increased. These improvements in the work schedule were then gradually withdrawn until the workers were back on their original work schedule. Even as the work week was being lengthened, the work pauses eliminated, and the work day increased, production went up.

After examining diaries the workers had kept during the experiment and holding lengthy conversations with them, it became obvious that worker *attitudes* were the major influences on productive efforts. Over the course of the experiment, the workers had become more positive toward fellow workers and supervisors. It was this change that seemed to be the critical one. As a result of these findings, a major effort was begun to identify the personal and social elements of work behavior that fostered productivity. Industrial counseling became more common, studies of job satisfaction began to appear with greater frequency, and the whole area of leadership and supervisor/subordinate relationships attracted attention.

Modern IO psychologists are just as concerned with worker attitudes, job satisfaction, leadership, and group dynamics as their predecessors were. To these have been added modern concerns about stress and individual counseling. Many IO psychologists are involved in administering drug and alcohol counseling programs and stress-reduction training. The goal of this branch of IO psychology is to coordinate the needs of the individual employee with the needs of the organization. The assumption is that a well-adjusted employee is the most important resource an organization can have.

Personnel Psychology. For every psychologist chiefly interested in identifying the ways people are alike, there is another psychologist chiefly interested in showing how people differ. In spite of how this sounds, these two approaches are not incompatible. One can easily develop sophisticated and general laws of behavior based on the observation of individual differences. For example, you are well aware of the effect of studying on peoples' test performances: Those who study do better than those who don't. If you were to measure the amount of time each member of your introductory-psychology class spent studying, you would find wide variations (individual differences). If you were to measure differences in test performances as indicated by test grades, you would have another set of individual differences. If you were then to compare one set of differences with the other set of differences (through the correlation method, perhaps), you would probably find that those who had spent more time studying tended to receive the higher test scores. Thus, it is possible to induce a general principle from a comparison of individual differences.

The growing interest in measuring individual differences, and thus being able to "map" people's competencies, was put to good use with the outbreak of Word War I. The United States' armed forces had to be staffed. It was necessarily assumed that not all people would be capable of doing service, so there was need of a method to separate the competent from the incompetent. In addition, once the competent people had been identified, they would have to be placed in positions suited to their skills. Some people would be officers and others enlisted personnel; some people would ride horses and some would dig trenches. A group of psychologists volunteered to help the army and the navy make these decisions about personnel, and they set up

One of the early concerns of industrial psychologists was what elements in the environment affected rate of production. After extensive testing at the Hawthorne Works, shown here, it became obvious that worker attitudes were the major influences on productive efforts. As a result of these findings, a major effort was begun to identify the personal and social elements of work behavior.

tests and other measures of individual differences as the tools.

The same pressures for qualified personnel reappeared with the start of World War II, but in an even more exaggerated form. War-related jobs had become quite complex due to technological advances in the conduct of war. Planes, ships, weapons, and equipment of all kinds, demanded greater talent for effective use. To accommodate this need, a new wave of test development and measurement began. But the same goal remained. Put the best people in positions for which they are best suited. This concern for identifying individual differences has broadened into modern-day **personnel psychology**. In this branch of IO psychology, attempts are made to collect information about individuals with respect to their probability of success in a particular job or environment.

Industrial social and organizational psychology. A branch of industrial psychology that focuses on how factors such as job satisfaction, leadership, motivation, stress, and group dynamics affect job performance.

Personnel psychology. A branch of industrial psychology interested in individual differences—how to measure them and their probable effects on job performance.

Three Branches or One?

The previous section provided an overview of what is included in the broad scope of industrial and organizational psychology. It may have sounded as though its three branches have no relation to each other, but this is not the case. In many situations, psychologists from all three branches work together to design a physical and psychological environment that is best suited to the individuals who have been selected to work in that environment. In fact, in actual practice, these three branches are usually combined by one psychologist who considers proposed industrial or organizational programs from each of these three unique perspectives.

An excellent example of the interaction of the three branches of industrial psychology is to be seen in the introduction of computer technology to the workplace. There are few jobs or work settings today that have not been touched by the computer revolution. Figure 18–1 illustrates just a few of the jobs that have been adapted to computer technology. The pervasiveness of this revolution has demanded that many aspects of work and work-life be considered simultaneously. For example, computers change the social climate of work. The secretary who previously sat in the middle of a room of other secretaries may now sit in isolation in a work-cubicle housing a computer keyboard and printer. Opportunities to chat with fellow workers are much more limited. As we saw in the chapter on stress this may eliminate one of the factors involved in reducing stress—social support. Computers also place different demands on the skill-levels of workers. Computers are perfectly literal, meaning that they will do *exactly* what you tell them to do. So your programming of the computer must be exact. If you make even a "slight" error in a command (such as putting a comma in the wrong place or mispelling a word in a command), you could be in for hours of frustration until you discover your error. Clearly, operating a computer and solving the problems that arise are not for everyone. As a result, the type of tests that are used to hire employees for a computer-driven workplace are different from those used for hiring into more traditional (non-computer) settings. Fortunately, computer systems can be designed to be "friendly" (that is, easy for the novice to use) and ergonomically efficient (that is, not resulting in excessive fatigue for the user). Thus, the industrial psychologist who is involved in introducing a computer system to a workplace must be concerned with industrial-social aspects (for example, how the computer may change the opportunities for interaction with co-workers), personnel aspects, (for example, hiring job-applicants who have the unique skills demanded by computer-controlled production methods), and human factors aspects (for example, minimizing glare from the video-screen).

Basic Psychology in Industry

As you can gather from even this short introduction to the history and current status of industrial and organizational psychology, each one of the three branches draws upon important concepts of basic psychology. Human factors psychology must take into account sensation and perception (reading and interpreting dials or gauges), cognitive psychology (memorizing sequences of operations in starting a piece of equipment), and learning theory (designing tasks so that associations can be easily formed). Industrial social and organizational psychology may involve consciousness (daydreaming on the job), emotion and stress (anxiety resulting from production deadlines), motivation (getting workers to show up on time), social psychology (supervisor/subordinate relations), and abnormal behavior (drug use in the work setting). Personnel psychology relies on knowledge of learning (training new workers who need particular skills), testing (identifying those applicants who have abilities that are likely to lead to success on the job), and cognitive behavior (identifying aspects of jobs that require decision-making by the worker). The workplace is clearly an environment to which the science of modern psychology is applicable. Our next step in this chapter is to examine each branch of industrial and organizational psychology in greater detail.

■ HUMAN FACTORS PSYCHOLOGY

You may not be aware of this, but many aspects of your environment have been influenced by the work of human factors psychologists. Examples of this influence can be found in highway road markers, automobile seats and dashboards, personal computer keyboards and automatic teller machines. The

FIGURE 18-1
As you can see from this panel of photographs, jobs and work settings of various kinds are being adapted to computer technology.

human factors psychologist helps to design environments that are compatible with the behavioral characteristics of the human inhabitants of that environment.

In the area of human factors psychology, three issues are of central concern. First we'll list them and then discuss each in turn.

1. The equipment that people use to perform various simple and complex tasks.
2. The capacities and limitations that people bring to a job.
3. The characteristics of situations or environments that have an impact on human behavior.

Equipment Design

In some circles, human factors psychologists are known as "knobs and dials people." There is more than a grain of truth in this description. If you take a man-machine system view of the world, the human being is an operator who receives information from certain displays (dials), and takes action by activating certain control devices (knobs). A simple example of a man–machine system is a person who looks at the temperature recorded on the thermostat in the living room and then turns up the heat a few degrees. Figure 18–2 diagrams this man-machine interaction. The thermostat is a display

FIGURE 18-2
A diagram of man-machine interaction. (Taylor, 1957)

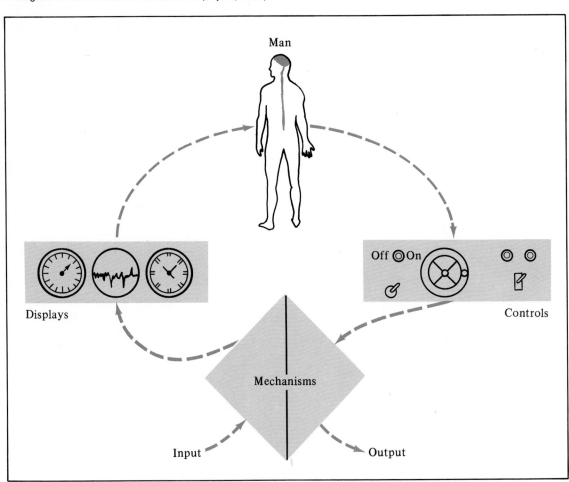

CAR MODELS OF THE FUTURE

What kinds of tests are being done to make future cars more comfortable and efficient to drive? At a subsidiary of the Ford Motor Company, the design staff experimented with different colors for lighted instrument panels. Subjects sat behind the wheel of a model car interior with an instrument panel that could be lighted in different colors by means of filters. The test colors were red, orange, yellow, green, and blue-green. The "drivers" used the brake and clutch pedals and the steering wheel according to the roadway conditions that were projected in front of them on a screen. Each driver was instructed to state the speedometer reading at the sound of a beep and was also asked to state whether the speedometer speed was within the speed limit shown on the screen. In the performance test, the color red yielded the most accurate readings. However, when drivers stated their color preferences, red was at the bottom of the list. Blue-green, the color ranked third for accuracy, was the color preference of most drivers. Researchers concluded that drivers associate the color red with warning lights, which explains their dislike of red for instrument lights.

For fighter aircraft, special display instruments have been designed so that the pilot does not have to look away from a target during combat. This kind of display is called the heads-up display—the pilot can read it without looking down. Heads-up displays operate by means of a small holographic mirror. An image is projected onto that mirror from within the instrument panel. True heads-up displays involve an image that appears to be somewhere other than its true physical location.

Researchers are now experimenting with this idea for use in cars—one study has shown that the average driver looks down at the speedometer between 40,000 to 80,000 times a year. How much information should be included in these automobile heads-up displays is the next question for researchers in this area. The speedometer reading seems essential, but it is less clear whether heads-up fuel-gauge readings and turn signals would be helpful or confusing for drivers.

General Motors Corporation has experimented with yet another aspect of the car interior—seat position. Designers of small, compact cars have looked for ways to provide more space for back seat passengers by moving the driver's seat forward. Researchers tested 60 people of different heights and weights in a model car interior, asking them to adjust 10 different wheel and pedal positions until each felt comfortable. The critical factor for most drivers appeared to be the distance between the seat and foot pedals. Far less important was steering wheel position. If the foot pedals were moved 45 millimeters, drivers moved the seat forward by 20 to 24 millimeters to compensate. For a similar change in wheel position, drivers moved the seat only 5 to 10 millimeters. These findings suggest that pedals and steering wheels might be positioned differently in cars of the future, but for the comfort of the driver, not the back seat passengers.

(often a dial of some kind), and the temperature-advance mechanism is a control device (often a knob or wheel).

Human factors psychologists have devoted a good deal of time to studying the most efficient design of displays and control devices. A ready example of a complicated display is a modern airplane cockpit. Another is an automobile dashboard. A typical automobile dashboard displays a number of different pieces of information that call for some action on the part of the driver. The most obvious of these is the speedometer. When the needle goes above a certain point (55 mph) in a speed zone, the operator takes a particular action (eases off the gas pedal). There are other similar dashboard displays, including the gas gauge, the oil indicator, and the engine-temperature indicator. These displays may be of two types: all-or-none displays or graduated displays. For example, your car may either have an engine-temperature light that comes on when the engine has gone above some critical temperature (an all-or-none display), or it may have a dial that moves

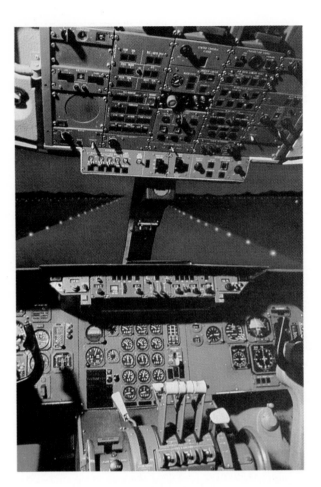

Human factors psychologists have devoted considerable time to studying the most efficient design of displays and control devices. Shown here are two examples of complicated information displays—an automobile dashboard and the cockpit of a commercial jetliner.

from cold to hot as the engine changes in temperature (a graduated display). In either case, information of a specific kind is conveyed by the display.

In addition to displays, there are any number of controlling devices in an automobile—the gas pedal, the brake pedal, and the steering wheel, to mention only three. The operator manipulates these controls in order to achieve a certain performance from the system. In driving a car, this performance is defined as getting from point A to point B in the safest and quickest manner.

The standard automobile dashboard is only one of several ways that systems information could have been displayed. For example, instead of having a standard gas gauge, an automobile could have a gas light that simply signals when it is about to run out of gas. The engine-temperature gauge could be placed on the far right of the dashboard in front of the passenger's seat. The controls of the automobile also could have been designed differently. Instead of a gas pedal, an automobile could have a nob on the dashboard that is turned clockwise to increase speed and counterclockwise to reduce speed. The steering wheel could be designed as a stick instead of a round, column-mounted device. However, many of these alternative displays and controls might not work well. Clearly, a gas gauge that tells you that you are about to run out of gas in the next few minutes is not very helpful. Most modern automobile dashboards represent efficient arrangements and presentations of information. Some may be slightly more efficient than others, but all are more efficient than arbitrary information displays. An interesting application of this design principle that relates to the second concern of human factors psychology—capacities and limitations—is the design of automobiles for the handicapped. Consider the way in which the vehicle in Figure 18–3 has been modified to make use of the capacities and work around the limitations of the handicapped passenger.

FIGURE 18-3
This van has been modified to make use of the capacities and work around the limitations of the handicapped passenger. Human factors psychologists have also been involved in the design of automobiles for the handicapped driver.

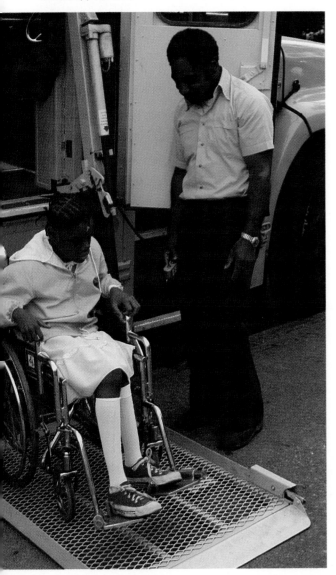

It is the job of the human factors psychologist to design a system of displays and controls that is compatible with the demands of the task and the characteristics of human operators. In carrying out these design studies, the human factors specialist typically uses all of the "tools" of the experimental psychologist. Experimental and control groups are identified, experimental treatments are carried out, data are gathered, and alternative designs are considered. As an example of a "knob" study, consider one operational problem of the pilot of an airplane. The two most critical times in a flight are takeoff and landing, and during those times the pilot must carefully monitor an array of displays or dials. Certainly, the pilot does not want to mistake the landing-gear control for the flap control at either of these times. As a result, it is necessary to have knobs that are easily identified as landing gear and flap controls. Jenkins (1947) carried out a series of studies that showed the extent to which certain knob shapes are seen as unique and not likely to be confused with other knob shapes (see Figure 18–4).

In addition to airplane-control knobs being easily identified by shape, these shapes are also designed to be readily associated with their use so as to en-

FIGURE 18-4
In one experiment, Jenkins allowed blindfolded subjects to grasp one of the knobs for one second. The tray of knobs was then spun and the person was asked to find the knob that had been originally grasped. The study identified a set of 11 knobs (shown here) that were not likely to be confused with one another. (Jenkins, 1947)

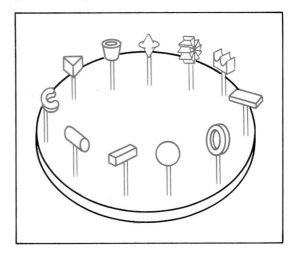

sure greater accuracy. An example of this appears in Figure 18-5. As you can see, the controls for the flaps and the landing gear are shaped like a flap and a wheel respectively.

There is one piece of equipment that you are very familiar with which has undergone a radical design transformation—your watch. The traditional watch has a dial or face with numbers representing hours and minutes. The newer digital watch has no face; instead, it simply displays hours and minutes as numerical digits. At first glance, both types of display seem to provide identical information—the current time. The traditional watchface, however, allows you to see at a glance both how much time has elapsed and how much time you have left. We often time our actions in terms of elapsed versus remaining time. A quick glance at the face of a traditional watch tells you that it is almost time to leave or that time is running out. The digital watch calls for additional cognitive activity on your part. To know how much time remains, you must take the current digital time and compare it relative to some other time that is not displayed. The effects of these two different types of time displays are not yet known, but they do seem to offer very different types of information. As a result, one type of display might be more effective in one situation than another. Watch manufacturers seem to be aware of the advantages and disadvantages of both types of designs. There are now many watches available that have both a traditional *and* a digital display.

The Concept of Capacities and Limitations

If you ever find yourself in a first-grade classroom, you will probably notice some strange things right away. First, you may trip on the steps leading up to the floor the room is on. This is because the steps are not as high as you are used to; they were designed for little legs, not big ones. Next, you will notice that your knees don't fit under the desk if you try to sit down. The desks were also designed for little bodies. If you look for the light switches, they will all be positioned lower on the wall than they are in your home. The blackboards and window sills will also be lower to the ground. In short, the environment was designed with the capacities and limitations of first-graders in mind.

The question of what an individual is capable of

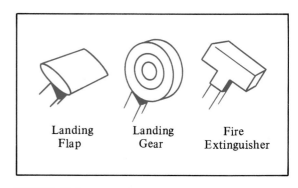

| Landing Flap | Landing Gear | Fire Extinguisher |

FIGURE 18-5
Airplane controls often have particular shapes that are associated with their use, as shown here.

is an essential one for the human factors psychologist. Let's go back to Figure 18-2 for a moment. This model suggests that there are three things to consider when designing equipment:

1. How a person brings in information.
2. How a person deals with or processes that information.
3. What responses are made after the information is processed.

A watch designed with both a traditional and a digital display.

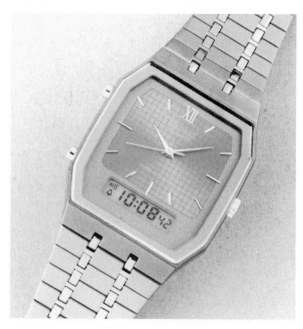

Information Input. We first discussed information input in the chapters on sensation and perception. Each of us has a certain capacity to receive information. Most of us can see certain wavelengths, hear certain sounds, feel certain temperatures, and distinguish certain odors. We know that each sense has an absolute and a difference threshold and that equipment should be designed with these thresholds in mind. For example, people react more quickly to sounds than to sights. Among other reasons, this is because we must be looking at something in order to process visual information from it, while it is not necessary to have our ears "turned" toward a sound source to hear a signal. Therefore, emergency signals should probably be designed to be heard, not seen. Furthermore, to be most useful those sounds should be within a particular frequency range and of a particular intensity. However, the larger consideration is the total work environment. If you happen to work in an environment that has lots of noises and you have to monitor a number of devices one after the other, it might be better to use visual displays to transmit information since they are relatively unaffected by environmental noise. In designing for the workplace, the human factors psychologist depends heavily on information that is provided from experiments in sensation and perception.

Information Processing. Information processing has appeared as a topic in the chapters on consciousness, memory, and cognition, so we won't go over the same ground again. In brief, information processing involves taking information that has been provided through the senses, grouping it in some way, analyzing this grouped information, and acting on the basis of that analysis. In addition, the information is stored in long-term memory for later retrieval and use. The human factors psychologist tries to determine the way a person is most likely to process particular information and what response systems are available for carrying out an appropriate action.

An important concern here is to avoid information overload. A person can only process so much information at once. Workers often receive information from several sources at the same time, so care must be taken to ensure that overload does not occur. As the amount of incoming information increases beyond an optimal level, performance begins to deteriorate. The consequences can be serious. In the movie *The China Syndrome*, a systems failure occurs in a nuclear-power plant. As the emergency grows, bells ring, horns sound, needles spin, people shout, and sweat pours. These are not the best circumstances for making decisions and taking action. The task of the human factors psychologist is to simplify and logically arrange the flow of information so that a person can make the best possible decision or take the most appropriate course of action.

Still another concern has to do with information processing and actual performance. Many disasters occur because human operators simply do not believe the displays or dials in front of them. As we saw in the perception chapter, airplane crashes have occurred because pilots would not believe what was indicated on their altitude gauges. One of the contributing factors in the Three-Mile-Island disaster was the fact that the control-room operators would not accept the information provided by certain dials. Actually, they chose to believe the information on one dial rather than another, and the dial they selected was malfunctioning. The point is that no matter how sophisticated our equipment gets, there will always be humans processing the information and making the final decisions. For that reason, the recognition given information processing is critically important in human factors psychology.

Response Selection and Execution. Once information has been received and processed, the next step is to choose a response of some kind and to carry it out. Information input and information processing depend primarily on human sensory and cognitive abilities. Actual responses, however, often depend on perceptual-motor or physical abilities. An example of a perceptual-motor ability would be hand–eye coordination. An example of a physical ability would be upper-body strength or speed of limb movement. The point to keep in mind is that the human factors psychologist must design work tasks and environments in ways that are compatible with these three different processes—information input, information processing, and response selection and execution.

The human factors psychologist usually works from a well-developed **taxonomy**, or list of human

---

Taxonomy. In psychology, often a list of human abilities and response capacities.

abilities and response capacities, when designing work environments. A simple list might include some cognitive abilities, such as memory, creativity, and problem solving, and some physical abilities, such as coordination, strength, and flexibility. With the taxonomy to refer to, it is less likely that a work environment or task will be ill-designed for the "average" worker. If you know that the reaction time of the average worker in a particular task is .5 seconds, you will not design a system that requires a reaction time of .1 seconds. There are several well-developed ability taxonomies. We will consider one of these taxonomies later in the chapter. Let's now consider the workplace from a very different perspective—the social and emotional perspective.

REVIEW QUESTIONS

1. Human factors psychology is concerned with human _____ and _____ and designing tasks and equipment to suit them.

2. The studies at the Hawthorne plant showed that workers' _____ were the major influence on their productivity.

3. Match the following terms with the correct definition:

___ human factors psychology

A. interested in adjustment; in particular how job satisfaction, leadership, and group dynamics affect job performance.

___ personnel psychology

B. focuses on individual differences, how to measure them, and how they affect job performance.

___ industrial social and organizational psychology

C. concerned with designing tasks and equipment to suit human capacities and limitations.

4. In an automobile, we receive information from _____ devices such as a speedometer, and we take action through _____ devices such as the gas pedal or brake.

5. Human factors psychologists draw on what is known of our sensory capacities to design emergency signals that will be heard rather than seen.   T / F

Answers: 1. capacities; limitations 2. attitudes 3. human factors psychology, C; personnel psychology, B; industrial social/industrial clinical, A. 4. display; control 5. True

■ INDUSTRIAL SOCIAL AND ORGANIZATIONAL PSYCHOLOGY

You might say that the person is taken "as is" in human factors psychology. The idea is to design an environment, a process, or a piece of equipment around the person's capacities and limitations. Industrial social and organizational psychology is somewhat different in orientation. Here the issue is adjustment—how organizations and individuals adjust to one another. The organization has certain expectations, such as a fair day's work for a fair day's pay. The worker also has certain expectations, such as suitable compensation and pleasant co-workers. In addition, the organization has certain survival needs—to produce enough goods or services of high enough quality to ensure that it will not be beaten or outsold by competitors. The worker has certain skills and abilities that might help the organization meet this need. Thus, organizations and the people they employ need to adjust to one another's needs. It is how the adjustment is carried out that interests the IO psychologist. There are two general areas of concern: job satisfaction and work motivation.

Job Satisfaction

As you saw in the chapter on social psychology, attitudes are complex cognitive reactions to various stimuli in an environment. Job satisfaction is a total collection of a person's attitudes about a job, or the sum of the emotional responses to specific elements of a person's work. Job satisfaction is an important consideration because of its implications for both the well-being of the worker (physical and psychological) and work behavior (productivity). Most organizations believe that happy workers are productive workers. While there is some logic to this assumption, there are notable exceptions to that way of thinking. There are workers who are productive but unhappy, and there are many workers who are happy but not productive. Research indicates that the relationship between satisfaction and productivity can go in both directions: People may become more productive when they are happy or they may be happy as a result of their successful or productive efforts (Landy, 1985). Regardless of the direction of the relationship between satisfaction and productivity, the industrial social and organizational psychologist is concerned with understanding the roots of job satisfaction and, if possible, helping workers and organizations to adjust to one another's needs.

There is general agreement about what aspects of a job most affect a person's satisfaction (Landy, 1985). These aspects are the work itself, the style of supervision, co-workers, pay, and promotional opportunities (Smith et al., 1969).

Relevant to the work itself are such factors as how interesting the job is, how much responsibility is involved, the extent to which a person has authority to make work-related decisions, and the importance of the job in the total effort of the organization. Generally, people are more satisfied with interesting, responsible, important, and autonomous work (work that allows them to make decisions on their own instead of checking out every action with a supervisor). It might surprise you to learn that one of the most satisfying jobs—at least in terms of autonomy—is that of garbage collector (Locke, 1976). Garbage collectors have a reasonable amount of control over their activities and schedules. They trade off jobs, one day emptying cans and another day driving the truck. They seldom see a supervisor after leaving the dispatch point and they can control the pace of their work themselves. Contrast this with assembly-line work, which leaves little or no opportunity for decision-making or discretionary action. The work itself is not a source of satisfaction.

The supervision factor pertains to whether or not people are satisfied with the style in which they are supervised. Some supervisors are personal and involved while others are impersonal and aloof; some are goal- and deadline-oriented while others are not; some allow workers to share in decisions while others do not. All of these factors can influence how satisfied a person is with supervision. A pleasant supervisor can turn a job into an opportunity for satisfying and supportive experiences. An unpleasant supervisor can create stress, prevent people from using their skills and abilities efficiently, and create disharmony (Fiedler and Lester, 1977).

Co-workers are a fact of life. They can be pleasant or unpleasant, helpful or in the way, boring or stimulating. Most of us have some emotional reaction to the people we work with and are aware of their capacity to make work a pleasure or a pain.

The factor of pay is really a broader category than the size of the weekly paycheck. It involves the general pay package, which might include wages, bonuses and incentives, paid vacation days and holidays, and fringe benefits such as health insurance and retirement benefits. As you saw in Chapter 12, pay is subjective as well as objective in character. You may be dissatisfied because someone you know is paid more than you, in spite of the fact that you are well-paid by objective standards and even may earn enough to live a life of luxury. Both the absolute and the relative amount of pay are important factors, and discrepancies can seriously affect job satisfaction.

An excellent example of this can be seen in the arguments surrounding the comparable-worth issue that has been raised by female workers. This issue concerns the relative compensation levels of men and women. It is clear that the average payscale of females is substantially lower than the average payscale of males. Traditionally, the explanation has been that women hold less demanding jobs and should, therefore, be paid less. Recently, there has been an attempt to demonstrate to the courts that this apparent difference in job demands is only a superficial one—more a difference in job titles than in the nature of the work (Landy, 1985). Women have organized to pursue a strategy for pay adjustment that will bring them closer to the pay rates for men. This strategy involves showing that even though certain jobs may have different job titles, the ability requirements and actual tasks are very similar. For example, a loading-dock supervisor (traditionally a male-dominated position) may fill out forms, schedule shipments, and coordinate the activities of a crew of five workers. The pay rate for this job may be $11.00 per hour. In contrast, a supervisor of an accounts-receivable department (a position commonly held by a female) may also fill out forms, schedule customer billing, and coordinate the efforts of five clerks, yet be paid $7.50 per hour. The argument is that since the work demands of the loading-dock supervisor and the accounts-receivable supervisor are comparable, the payscale should also be comparable.

The promotional opportunities factor involves the extent to which people feel they can get ahead in the organization if they so desire. People may become frustrated in their attempts to move up the organizational ladder because the number of available positions typically decreases as one moves up. There can only be one president. Many middle-aged executives find themselves in need of counseling to help cope with the reality of diminishing opportunities for advancement. On the other hand, not everyone wants to be president; some people may be unhappy with the pressure to move upward in an organization. The increased responsibility in higher-level positions may frighten them. Both these circumstances take their toll in the form of stress. As we saw in Chapter 14, stress has its own consequences in terms of its effects on health and behavior.

Are Some People Happier Than Others? A question that typically comes up in considerations of job satisfaction is whether certain groups of people are more satisfied than others. Are men happier than women, white people happier than black people, college graduates happier than high-school graduates, or older employees happier than younger ones? A partial answer is that some of these comparison groups show differences, while others do not. The mean results of seven annual surveys of job satisfaction are presented in Table 18–1. As you can see from the yearly tabulations, black workers are consistently less satisfied with their jobs than are white workers. This may say less about the general satisfaction tendencies of black workers than it does about the kinds of jobs blacks typically hold. Black workers, as a group, tend to earn less than white workers, to have lower-level jobs, and to have fewer promotional opportunities. There is little doubt that to a large extent these discrepancies in rewards and working conditions between black and white workers are the result of prejudice and discrimination. Given these differences, the results of the satisfaction surveys make sense. If satisfaction is related to rewards, there is every reason to expect lower satisfaction among black workers. If access to

a full range of jobs and rewards improves for black workers, it is reasonable to assume that the difference in job-satisfaction levels between black and white workers will gradually diminish.

In the same table, however, notice the satisfaction statistics comparing men and women as against those comparing blacks and whites. Women, like blacks, have traditionally been viewed as a minority group in employment settings and have been similarly subject to employment discrimination. Surprisingly, Table 18–1 shows that women tend to be just as satisfied with their jobs as men and considerably more satisfied with their jobs than black workers. This suggests either that women have not been as adversely affected by employment discrimination as blacks, or that the women surveyed are a special "survivor" group of women—those who attained satisfactory employment in the first place. It might also be that women show less job dissatisfaction because they had lower expectations to begin with than other worker groups—upon first entry into the work force, women as a group did not expect substantial rewards of money, prestige, or responsibility. As indicated earlier, however, such expectations are changing, at least with respect to pay compensation. As women become more unwilling to accept differential treatment and become more sensitive to male–female discrepancies in areas such as pay and promotion, we may find their satisfaction levels systematically declining and the difference between the satisfaction levels of men and women increasing. (Parenthetically, we can point to the potential effect of the survey questions themselves on the conclusions drawn. If the question asked of those surveyed was "Are you happy with your work?" we might still have gotten the results shown in Table 18–1. On the other hand, had the question been "Are you happy with your pay relative to other workers in your company?" the male–female differences might have been dramatically greater.)

Table 18–1 also shows that older workers report higher levels of satisfaction than younger workers. Is this because as people grow older they are better rewarded and their jobs are more interesting and important? Or does this mean that modern workers are less happy than the workers of one or two generations ago? We can rule out the second explanation; surveys of worker satisfaction have been taken since 1935, and the percentage of workers reporting dis-

TABLE 18-1.   Mean Job Satisfaction among Full-Time Workers in the United States, 1972–1978.*

| | Year of Survey | | | | | | | |
Variable	1972	1973	1974	1975	1976	1977	1978	Mean
Race								
White	2.36	2.34	2.38	2.43	2.44	2.37	2.43	2.39
Black	2.09	2.32	2.17	2.34	2.13	2.36	2.01	2.19
Sex								
Male	2.32	2.31	2.35	2.44	2.41	2.33	2.38	2.36
Female	2.28	2.40	2.36	2.40	2.42	2.42	2.39	2.38
Education								
Grade school	2.32	2.22	2.28	2.32	2.32	2.33	2.35	2.31
High school	2.25	2.28	2.38	2.46	2.39	2.38	2.37	2.36
Some college	2.26	2.45	2.35	2.52	2.38	2.36	2.31	2.37
College degree or more	2.44	2.52	2.41	2.37	2.54	2.46	2.49	2.46
Age								
Less than 20	1.43	1.95	2.25	2.08	1.73	2.17	2.14	1.95
20–29	2.06	2.18	2.18	2.24	2.25	2.19	2.67	2.20
30–39	2.37	2.39	2.26	2.48	2.53	2.33	2.35	2.38
40–49	2.36	2.34	2.41	2.48	2.45	2.39	2.43	2.41
50 or more	2.51	2.46	2.55	2.55	2.53	2.55	2.55	2.53
Personal income[a]								
Less than $5,000	—	—	2.23	2.23	2.21	2.21	2.21	2.22
$5,000–$6,999	—	—	2.21	2.47	2.44	2.46	2.14	2.35
$7,000–$9,999	—	—	2.26	2.38	2.37	2.32	2.31	2.33
$10,000–$14,999	—	—	2.42	2.44	2.47	2.35	2.43	2.42
$15,000 or more	—	—	2.58	2.60	2.55	2.48	2.50	2.53
Occupation								
Professional-technical	2.48	2.45	2.48	2.50	2.61	2.46	2.55	2.50
Managerial-administrative	2.51	2.65	2.59	2.64	2.56	2.52	2.55	2.57
Sales	2.24	2.35	2.33	2.71	2.41	1.96	2.48	2.33
Clerical	2.27	2.32	2.25	2.47	2.37	2.33	2.28	2.33
Craftsmen-foremen	2.34	2.19	2.44	2.33	2.56	2.42	2.50	2.39
Operatives	2.13	1.99	2.12	2.15	2.14	2.26	2.18	2.14
Laborers	1.89	2.21	2.29	2.50	2.16	2.36	1.89	2.16
Service	2.20	2.42	2.24	2.42	2.30	2.41	2.31	2.33

*Higher numbers mean higher satisfaction.
[a]Not available for 1972 and 1973.
Source: Weaver, 1980.

satisfaction has remained the same. This leaves the first explanation: As people get older they are paid more and their jobs are more interesting. In fact, older workers on the whole are better paid and have more interesting jobs.

What this and similar studies suggest is that job satisfaction is not the result of group tendencies or personality characteristics. More likely, it is the result of the external environment in which people work and how they perceive this environment. This is yet another example of the fact that perception is, to some extent, based on real-world characteristics. People do respond—favorably or unfavorably—to their objective environment. Thus, job satisfaction is not a by-product of sex or race or age; it is a by-product of the jobs themselves, which are occupied by people of different genders, ages, and races. Work conditions are likely to have the greatest influence on job satisfaction, not variables such as race, sex, or age.

Work Motivation

You were introduced to different theories of motivation in Chapter 12. Work motivation is no different in principle from any other kind of motivation and so we approach it in the same way. We are interested in understanding what conditions lead to the initiation, direction, intensity, and termination of behavior. In regard to work, this usually means understanding conditions that affect job performance. We are interested in knowing why some people work hard and others less so, or why some people come to work every day and others call in sick regularly. The various theories presented in Chapter 12 can be applied to explain work motivation (or the lack of it). We will not review these theories again here, but instead, we will consider three different approaches that have been taken by IO psychologists to *increase* work motivation.

Tie Rewards to Performance. This should be a familiar concept. You first saw in the learning chapters that when behaviors were reinforced, they tended to occur again. You saw this relationship again in Chapter 12 as part of the expectancy theory of human motivation.

This approach to increasing the motivation of industrial workers has been very popular in the past decade (Landy, 1985). As the model in Figure 18–6 shows, linking rewards to performance increases satisfaction, maintains or increases the value of desired rewards, confirms the person's belief that effort is worthwhile, and leads to a greater effort and eventually better performance. The critical link is between *successful* performance and rewards. This model of motivation is a cognitive one in that it emphasizes the fact that the person notices and remembers how the environment responds to effective performance. If the environment ignores it or does not distinguish between good and bad performance, bad performance is more likely to occur

FIGURE 18–6

In this model of what determines job performance and job satisfaction, the critical link is the reward that follows successful performance.

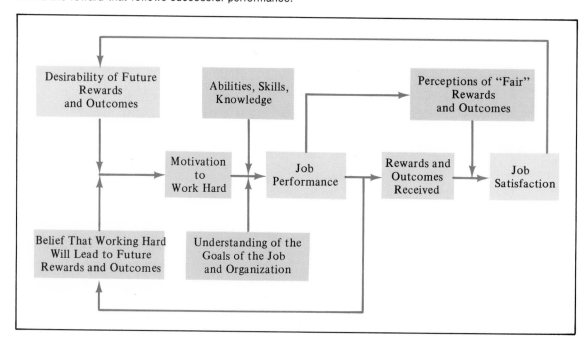

since it requires less effort. It is also clear from the model that effort alone is not always sufficient for reward. The person must also have an understanding of what is required and have the abilities, skills, and knowledge to meet those requirements.

REVIEW QUESTIONS

6. The IO psychologist usually works from a _____ , or list of human abilities and response capacities, when designing work environments.

7. In _____ _____ _____ _____ psychology, there are two major areas of concern: job satisfaction and work motivation.

8. Older/younger workers report higher levels of job satisfaction than older/younger workers.

9. One way to increase work motivation is to tie _____ to successful _____ .

Answers: 6. taxonomy   7. industrial social and organizational   8. Older; younger   9. rewards; performance

---

Job Design/Job Enrichment. For some time, many researchers in the field have believed that motivation is directly affected by the way a job and a work environment are set up. Their thinking is that certain environments allow or encourage people to initiate and direct their own efforts, while others discourage what we generally think of as motivated behavior. A series of experiments begun in 1969 by Volvo, the Swedish auto manufacturer, aptly demonstrated the point. In the mid-1960s, Volvos were being made like most American cars—put together bit by bit using long assembly lines of workers. Each assembly-line worker had about 1 minute to do some specific thing to the car—tighten 7 bolts, insert a windshield, grind down 6 spot-welds, or some other simple activity. Supervisors walked up and down the line making sure that everything moved along quickly.

Volvo then decided to do things a little differently. The factory-floor layout and work distribution were completely overhauled. In place of the typical assembly-line workflow that you can see in Figure 18-7A, Volvo instituted a new design of workflow similar to that shown in Figure 18-7B. Instead of standing in one spot along the assembly line and waiting for one car after another to pass, workers now were assigned to particular locations or stations where work was done together by groups instead of piecemeal by individuals. Each group worked on a single car for 45 to 60 minutes, performing many different operations. In addition, each group was given control over production. They pulled a new car into their work location only when they were finished with the one they were working on; in that way they controlled the speed of the line. A long line of cars circled the work stations, and each workgroup pulled a new car into their location as ready and sent finished cars out to be shipped. In addition, supervisors were retrained as advisers; they no longer gave orders and set schedules. The supervisor was available to help and answer questions if asked, but the workers directed their own work. The satisfaction of the workers improved substantially after these redesign efforts. Surprisingly, production levels did not change much. After an early decrease in production due to the need for learning the new techniques and equipment, output came back up to the original level.

At about the same time Volvo was experimenting with assembly redesign, so were American auto manufacturers. General Motors built a new plant in Lordstown, Ohio, which was thought at the time to house the most efficient assembly line in the world. Robot-like equipment was installed to help the workers complete their tasks. In effect, the robots became co-workers who never got tired. The reaction to this innovation was quite different from the reaction to Volvo's changes, as is evident from some comments of Lordstown workers:

I asked a young wife, "What does your husband tell you about his work?"
"He doesn't say what he does. Only if something happened like 'My hair caught on fire' or 'Something fell in my face.'"

"There's a lot of variety in the paint shop," says a dapper twenty-two-year-old, up from West Virginia. "You clip on the color hose, bleed out the old color, and squirt. Clip, bleed, squirt, think; clip, bleed, squirt, yawn; clip, bleed, squirt, scratch your nose. Only now the Gee-Mads [robots] have taken away the time to scratch your nose."

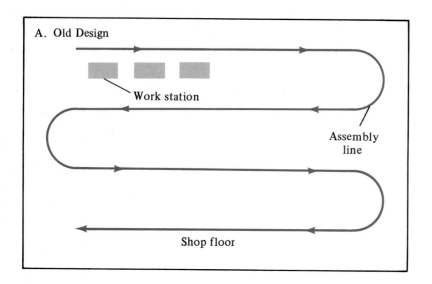

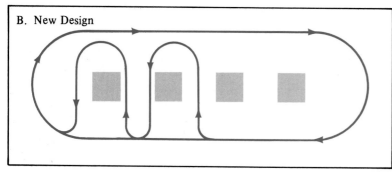

FIGURE 18-7
Two types of assembly lines are shown here. In part A (top) is the standard assembly-line work flow where the workers stand in one spot and wait for one car after another to pass them. In B is shown the new design put into effect by Volvo, with work stations where work is done by groups that might work on one car for an hour, performing many different operations.

A long-hair reminisced, "Before the Gee-Mads, when I was on door handles, I could get a couple of cars ahead and get myself a whole minute of relax."

I asked about diversions. "What do you do to keep from going crazy?"

"Well, certain jobs like the pit you can light up a cigarette without them seeing."

"I go to the wastepaper basket. I wait a certain number of cars then find a piece of paper to throw away."

"I have fantasies. You know what I keep imagining? I see a car coming down. It's red. So I know it's gonna have a black seat, black dash, black interiors. But I keep thinking what if somebody up there sends down the wrong color interiors—like orange, and me putting in yellow cushions, bright yellow!"

"I don't do anything any more," says an old-timer (twenty-four years with four years seniority, counting nineteen months in the Army). "I think the time passes fastest if you let your mind just phase out and blend in with the speed of the line."

"But everyone has the same hope: "You're always waiting for the line to break down." (Garson, 1975, p. 88)

It is pretty hard to detect any increased satisfaction or motivation in these comments.

Change Methods of Supervision. The Swedes got rid of traditional supervisors in the Volvo experiments. That was a radical move, and, it points up one of the key elements in work motivation—the first-level supervisor. Some recent experimental approaches have suggested that the supervisor is the key to the motivation puzzle. These approaches in turn suggest a number of strategies. The most popular is to have the supervisor play a cheerleader role. The supervisor helps set hard but realistic goals for the workers and then provides feedback to let

most active researchers has been Ed Locke. He has recently reviewed research on the effect of goal-setting on performance and has demonstrated quite clearly that an individual who sets or accepts high goals will perform more effectively than an individual who sets or accepts lower goals (Locke, Shaw, Saari and Latham, 1981). This will come as no surprise to serious athletes or to others who have dedicated a part of their lives to being the best at anything. It may very well be that the most motivating thing any supervisor can do is to work with a subordinate in setting hard but achievable goals. If you doubt the effect of goals on your own behavior, reflect for a moment on the "magical" qualities of a "things-to-do" list. There is nothing like a list of objectives to blast you out of terminal laziness. Much to my dismay, my wife is acutely aware of the value of such a list in accomplishing household chores. If we make up a list of these chores, and she can keep this list in front of my face, they will get done. On the other hand, if we simply "talk" about what needs to be done, or if I am lucky enough to lose the list, I find myself with more free time.

The real challenge to the supervisor (and my wife) is to get the individual to set or accept the goals in the first place. Goal-setting theory says that once hard goals are accepted, a sort of self-motivation process takes over. Both goal setting and goal acceptance can be greatly aided by pointing out to the individual the probable rewards for accomplishing the goals and the high probability of meeting the goals if certain behaviors are chosen. At first glance, this may seem no different from the motivation model in Figure 18–6—but it is. In that model, there is no mention of goals at all. Locke and his colleagues would contend that the only reason such a model would work at all would be because the individual had set personal goals for performance.

Another role that supervisors can play is that of a design agent. Supervisors can make jobs more stimulating by having them involve varying duties. In addition, supervisors can see when someone is getting bored in a position and change that person's duties.

This photo of an assembly-line worker was taken in the Volvo automobile assembly plant in Sweden. Beginning in 1969, Volvo began experimenting with assembly redesign as an approach to increasing the motivation of industrial workers. Since that time, more than 500 companies in Sweden have conducted experiments aimed at increasing job satisfaction by giving employees more control over their work.

them know if they are meeting the goals or not. The general technique is often called **Management By Objectives (MBO)**, and it encourages people to be self-directing and to set specific goals for themselves.

Psychologists have been studying the effects of goals on performance for many years. One of the

---

Management by objectives (MBO). A system in which supervisors set goals for workers and then provide feedback as to whether goals are being met; designed to encourage people to be self-directing and to set realistic goals for themselves.

Finally, supervisors can encourage workers to make recommendations about work procedures. Ouchi (1981) has suggested the idea of **quality circles** to solve organizational problems. Quality circles are groups of employees who meet on a regular basis to discuss how aspects of jobs might be changed and procedures improved. The presumed benefits of quality circles are increased participation in decision-making, and increased commitment once a decision has been made. For example, in an urban fire department, firefighters assigned to a given firehouse met every few weeks during a slow time of their shift to discuss possible changes and improvements. Their discussions resulted in some noticeable changes: The geographic sectors of the city covered by different firehouses were rearranged; the type of protective clothing worn by firemen was changed; and a new type of two-way radio that performed better inside burning buildings was purchased by the department. As a result of these innovations, job safety was increased and the response-time to various geographic sectors of the city was improved. In a more traditional fire department, innovations such as these described would depend on the time and willingness of an administrator. In addition, if changes were instituted without input from the firefighters, there is a strong chance that there would be resistance. The quality circle mechanism can provide a steady flow of ideas and, when changes are instituted, a higher degree of enthusiasm and acceptance.

The idea behind quality circles is not welcomed by some organizations. Often the attitude is that production workers are there to produce, not to think; the thinking should be done by engineers and managers. These are the very organizations that would probably show the greatest improvements in motivation if quality circles were introduced.

■ PERSONNEL PSYCHOLOGY

The human factors psychologist is described as one who accepts the capacities and limitations of humans as constants or givens, and designs tasks, environments, and equipment around those givens. The orientation of the personnel psychologist is almost the exact opposite. Personnel psychologists assume that there are important individual differences among workers that will ultimately add to or detract from work performance. Some workers have good memories and some have poor memories; some workers are better than others at estimating lengths and times and weights; some workers can process information from many sources at the same time while others cannot. Each of these differences may have implications for how well a worker can perform in a particular job. Further, it is assumed that the characteristics of the work environment are fixed or constant. Thus, the tasks of the personnel psychologist are to identify the demands of particular jobs, to determine which human capacities are likely to be used in meeting those demands, and to identify people with the capacities to perform successfully.

Training employees is also a major part of the personnel psychologist's job. Current employees are provided with special training to increase particular capacities such as coordination, memory, reasoning, or spatial orientation; this training enables employees to assume new responsibilities. As a rule, new employees receive some sort of initial training as well. The general point is that any improvements to be made in the match between employee and job are accomplished by selecting and training the right person for the job.

The work of the personnel psychologist does not stop once the person is placed on the job. The worker needs feedback about the effectiveness of his or her efforts. If performance is good, this tells the worker to continue with the same behavior. If performance is poor, this tells the worker that adjustments are necessary. It is up to the personnel psychologist to develop systems of performance evaluation that will provide the worker with this type of information.

The general goal of the personnel psychologist is to place a worker who is well suited for a particular job in that job. The steps toward that goal are as follows:

1. Completing a *job analysis*. A job analysis is a careful examination of a job in terms of the knowledges and abilities it demands from the worker.
2. Developing a test or assessment technique that will identify those workers who are most likely to succeed at the job as defined by the job analysis.
3. Administering the test or assessment device to applicants for the job in question.

TABLE 18-2.   Job Analysis of New York City Police Officer and Major
Abilities Necessary

Task groups	Major skill
Apprehending suspects	Verbal expression
Dealing with vehicle accidents	Verbal expression
Investigating specific criminal charges	Deductive reasoning
First aid	Verbal comprehension
Interacting with prisoners	Verbal expression
Recognizing dangerous situations	Memorization
Operating a patrol vehicle	Multilimb coordination
Providing information	Verbal expression
Providing security	Verbal expression
Research	Verbal comprehension
Promoting public safety	Verbal expression
Interacting with juveniles	Verbal expression
Issuing traffic summons	Verbal expression
Crowd control	Verbal expression
Clerical duty	Verbal comprehension

4. Providing any necessary training as indicated by the job analysis.
5. Providing feedback to the worker on a periodic basis regarding the effectiveness of his or her work.

Let's look at each of these activities in more detail. We will begin with the job analysis.

Identifying Performance Demands: Job Analysis

Suppose someone came up to you and offered you a job as a metrocruncher. Your first reaction would probably be, "What's a metrocruncher?" For most jobs there is usually a job description that provides prospective employees with information about the typical duties of the job. After carefully reading the job description for metrocruncher, you find that you would spend your work time on a subway platform, shoving passengers into the cars of crowded subway trains (the metro) so that the conductors could close the doors.

A job description is the product of long hours of observing and interviewing. The personnel psychologist uses the methods of field observation and survey research to accomplish this task. The actual procedure of gathering information about the demands of a job is called **job analysis**. In analyzing a job, the psychologist identifies the most important and frequently performed activities of a job. The left-hand column of Table 18-2 presents the results of a job analysis of the position of police officer that I completed for the New York City Police Department. In order to develop this job description, several hundred hours were spent riding around with patrol officers and watching them perform their duties. In addition, several thousand

---

Quality circles. Groups of employees who meet on a regular basis to discuss how jobs might be changed and procedures improved.

Job analysis. Process of identifying the most important and most frequently performed activities of a job; information is gathered by means of field observation and survey research.

questionnaires were completed by actual patrol officers and supervisors who provided information on particular questions asked about the job.

Test Development and Administration

Job analysis is the first step toward identifying those persons most likely to be successful in a job. Once a job analysis has been completed, it is possible to identify the *particular* skills and abilities involved in successful performance of the job. The value of an ability taxonomy in designing a job was mentioned earlier in the chapter—a job should be designed with the performance capacities and limitations of the potential operator in mind. When it comes to choosing among applicants, you need to know what abilities to look for. This is best done by determining which abilities might be needed to carry out the individual tasks that comprise a particular job. Fleishman (1975) has developed a very sophisticated taxonomy of cognitive, perceptual, and motor abilities that each of us possess to greater or lesser degrees and that could be used to complete various job tasks. This taxonomy and its respective definitions are presented in Table 18–3. Clearly, it is a very exhaustive, detailed list which serves principally as a reference. Now go back to the right-hand column of Table 18–2, under the heading "major skill," and you will find some of the abilities listed in Fleishman's taxonomy. These were determined using the data collected from actual police officers. This type of analysis of abilities then permits the selection or development of tests that can measure these abilities. Table 18–2 suggests that the tests for police officer should contain measures of verbal comprehension, verbal expression, reasoning, memorization, and coordination.

Now consider the information presented in Table 18–4, which shows a comparison of the ability requirements of a police officer, a bartender, and a college professor on Fleishman's taxonomy of abilities. In parentheses are examples of specific tasks involving those abilities. As you probably can gather from examining this table, the test used to hire a police officer would differ from one used to hire a bartender or a college professor. This is because the required abilities are substantially different for each job.

You may be surprised to see that the job of police

officer demands less physical strength than you might have thought. However, you will probably not be surprised that the job involves a great deal of unplanned communication. A police officer spends a good part of the day talking with and listening to people, but does not know from one day to the next what the nature of that communication will be. Several years ago, many police departments started to become aware of this large verbal component of the job and took steps to deal with it. In one department, officers had been required to fill out many different forms at the end of the day and to write out long and complicated reports. They objected to the fact that it took them off the street (or made their shifts longer). It also placed demands on them for writing skills that they felt were unrelated to success on the job. The solution was a simple one. Officers were instructed to call the information in by telephone to a bank of clerks, who filled out the forms and prepared the reports. At the end of a shift, an officer would simply check the forms and reports for accuracy. This solved two problems: Officers spent less time filling out reports and they delegated writing to those more able to handle it. There was also an interesting side-effect. Many officers reported that they were now able to use words they couldn't spell! This suggested that prior to this change the quality of the officers' communications had been artificially limited by their spelling ability. Previously, rather than spending several minutes looking up the correct spelling for a preferred word they would choose a less appropriate word—but one that they could spell!

The job description of college professor probably comes closer to your expectations. This job requires little physical effort of any kind. On a day-to-day basis, the major demands are for information ordering (course design and lecture preparation), reasoning (deciding rules and examples to illustrate course material), and verbal expression (lecturing)

Both in song and in popular mythology, good bartenders are reputed to be good listeners. The surprising thing is that they need not actually *comprehend* or understand what is being said (verbal comprehension), they only need to be willing to listen for long periods without showing fatigue or boredom. In addition, there is a certain physical side to bartending—lots of time spent moving up and down the bar, standing and talking, and reaching for bottles, glasses, and empty drinks.

TABLE 18-3. Fleishman's Taxonomy

Ability	Description
Verbal comprehension	Ability to understand language, either written or spoken; the ability to hear a description of an event and understand what happened.
Verbal expression	This ability involves using either oral or written language to communicate information or ideas to other people; includes vocabulary, knowledge of distinctions among words, and knowledge of grammar and the way words are ordered.
Fluency of ideas	The ability to produce a number of ideas about a given topic. Concerns only the *number* of ideas, not the quality of those ideas.
Originality	This is the ability to produce unusual or clever responses to a given topic or situation; the ability to improvise solutions in situations where standard operating procedures do not apply.
Memorization	This is the ability to memorize and retain new information that occurs as a routine part of the task or job.
Problem sensitivity	This is the ability to recognize or identify the existence of problems; involves both the recognition of the problem as a whole and the elements of the problem but does not include the ability to solve the problem.
Deductive reasoning	The ability to apply general rules or regulations to specific cases or to proceed from stated principles to logical conclusions.
Inductive reasoning	The ability to find a rule or concept that fits the situation; would include coming up with a logical explanation for a series of events that seem to be unrelated.
Information ordering	The ability to apply rules to a situation for the purpose of putting the information in the best or most appropriate sequence; involves the application of previously specified rules and procedures to a given situation.
Category flexibility	The ability to produce alternative groupings or categories for a set of things. These "things" might be people, cars, ideas, theories, etc.
Spatial orientation	The ability to keep a clear idea of where you are in relation to the space you happen to be in; helps you keep from getting lost in a particular space, whether it is a city, a building, a park, or a subway system.
Visualization	This ability involves forming mental images of what objects look like after they have been changed or transformed in some way.
Speed of closure	This ability involves the speed with which a large number of elements can be combined and organized in a meaningful pattern when you do not know what the pattern is or what is to be identified. Means having to combine lots of information quickly.
Flexibility of closure	This ability involves the skill of finding an object that is somehow hidden in a bunch of other objects; would involve picking out a particular face in a crowd of faces. Speed not important.
Selective attention	This is the ability to complete a task in the presence of distraction or monotony.
Perceptual speed	This ability involves the speed with which the features of a person, place, or thing can be compared with other features of another person, place, or thing to determine how similar the two objects are.
Time sharing	This is the ability to pay attention to two sources of information at the same time. The information that is received from these two sources may be either combined or used separately. Important aspect is the ability to deal with information that is coming *rapidly* from several different sources.
Static strength	Ability we generally think of when we hear the word "strength." It is the amount of force exerted against a fairly heavy object—can involve pushing, pulling, or lifting.

(continued on next page)

TABLE 18-3. Fleishman's Taxonomy (*Continued*)

Ability	Description
Explosive strength	Ability to use energy in one or a series of explosive muscular acts—what is needed is a burst of muscular energy rather than a steady effort.
Dynamic strength	Involves using your arms and trunk in moving your own body weight for some period of time or across some distance—example is climbing a rope.
Stamina	Ability to maintain physical activity over a long period of time. Extent to which the cardio-vascular system (heart and lungs) is exercised.
Extent flexibility	Ability involves stretching or extending arms and legs and their particular muscle groups.
Dynamic flexibility	Ability to make repeated or continuous arm and leg flexing movements with some speed—example is pulling in a rope hand over hand in a short time.
Gross body equilibrium	Ability to maintain the body in an upright position and keep one's balance.
Choice reaction time	Ability to choose the correct response quickly when two or more responses are possible; important aspect is how quickly the response is begun.
Reaction time	Ability concerned with the speed with which a single response can be begun—no choice of reaction involved here, as above.
Speed of limb movement	Ability involves the speed with which arms and legs can be moved—the speed to carry out an arm or leg movement after it has been chosen and begun—example would be how quickly a boxer could throw a punch or a quarterback release a football.
Wrist–finger speed	Ability deals with how quickly wrists, fingers, and hands can be moved—example would be speed with which someone could tie complicated knots or sew an intricate pattern.
Gross body coordination	Ability to coordinate movement of trunk, arms, and legs—example might be running on an uneven or slanted surface and keeping your balance.
Multilimb coordination	Ability to use two limbs together—example is driving, where arms must be used in coordinated fashion with feet or legs.
Finger dexterity	Ability to make skillful and coordinated use of fingers—example, threading a needle.
Manual dexterity	Ability to make skillful use of hand, or arm and hand together.
Arm–hand steadiness	Ability to make precise, steady arm–hand movements (neither speed nor strength are important). Includes the elimination of shaking or tremors—example might be taking aim with a gun or stitching a wound.
Rate control	Ability to make timed movements in response to changes in the speed of continuously moving object—example is catching a ball thrown to you, ducking a punch or thrown object.
Control precision	Ability to make controlled muscular movements to adjust or position a piece of equipment—example is working the controls of a radio.

Source: Adapted from Fleishman, 1975.

In each case, once the job demands have been translated into ability requirements, it is then possible to select or develop a test that will measure the ability levels of candidates for the job. In addition to measuring the ability of applicants, an employer might also be interested in the applicants' general knowledge or vocational interests. In fact, there are many different types of tests that can be administered once a job analysis has been completed. There are two main categories of tests: administrative and content. These will be discussed in the next section.

TABLE 18-4. Comparison of Jobs of Police Officer, College Professor, and Bartender on Fleishman's Abilities.

Police Officer	College Professor	Bartender
Verbal comprehension (understanding the message on the patrol car radio)	Verbal comprehension (reading a research article)	Verbal expression (chatting with customers)
Verbal expression (giving directions to a motorist)	Verbal expression (giving a lecture)	Memorization (recognizing the faces of regular customers)
Deductive reasoning (deciding on whether to charge a suspect with breaking and entering or trespassing)	Deductive reasoning (advising a student on rules governing a course drop)	Problem sensitivity (knowing when to give advice and when to keep quiet)
Inductive reasoning (realizing that the same person may be responsible for a series of purse snatchings)	Memorization (remembering the faces of students in class)	Time sharing (being aware of the needs of the people at the bar as well as filling orders brought by waitresses)
Problem sensitivity (recognizing that paramedics should be called to deal with a person who is short of breath)	Information ordering (arranging a lecture so that there is a logical progression from one point to the next)	Selective attention (hearing a drink order as a winning touchdown is scored and people go wild)
Memorization (making a mental note of an automobile that may be an abandoned vehicle)	Fluency of ideas (giving examples of topics for term papers to students)	Perceptual speed (comparing faces at different locations at the bar to get drink orders correct)
Information ordering (making sure that a recovered stolen car is checked for fingerprints before it is taken to the storage area)	Originality (giving examples from literature to make a point about abnormal behavior in a psychology class)	Extent flexibility (taking an empty glass off the bar with the left hand while reaching under the bar for a clean glass with the right hand)
Static strength (pushing a stalled vehicle by hand)	Problem sensitivity (identifying students who seem to need help in understanding certain course material)	Gross body equilibrium (moving back and forth behind the bar while several other bartenders are doing the same)
Reaction time (swerving to miss an object on the roadway when involved in a high speed chase)	Manual dexterity (using a typewriter to prepare lectures and tests)	Stamina (standing for 8 hours)
Explosive strength (kicking in a door on a raid)		Manual dexterity (working the cash register, the electric mixer, and bottles)
		Arm–hand steadiness (serving full glasses of liquid without spilling any)

REVIEW QUESTIONS

10. One of the most radical parts of the Volvo experiment was the elimination of the traditional role of the _____.

11. Another approach to increasing motivation is called _____ _____, in which groups of employees meet on a regular basis to discuss how jobs might be changed and procedures improved.

12. In personnel psychology, the assumption is that there are _____ _____ among workers that are important to a successful performance of a job.

13. In _____ _____ psychology, human capacities and limitations are considered constant, and the tasks and equipment are designed around them. In _____ psychology, the tasks and equipment are considered constant, and the point is to find

the right person to fit them or change the person through training.

14. A _____ _____ consists of identifying the most important and most frequently performed job activities. This is done through field observation and survey research.

Answers: 10. supervisor 11. quality circles
12. individual differences 13. human factors;
personnel 14. job analysis

TYPES OF TESTS

Administrative Categories

Tests are administered in different ways. For example, there are group tests and individual tests. **Group tests** are given to many people at the same time and are designed for efficiency. When large companies or government agencies advertise job openings and hundreds of individuals apply, group ability tests (such as the written, multiple-choice civil service test) are usually administered. **Individual tests** are administered to only one person at a time and are designed to provide in-depth information. An applicant for the position of computer operator might be asked to demonstrate appropriate skills by operating a real computer.

Some tests are **paper-and-pencil tests** and others are **performance tests**. A paper-and-pencil test requires written answers on an answer sheet. The civil service test described above is a paper-and-pencil test. A performance test requires making a behavioral response of some type (other than putting a mark on an answer sheet with a pencil). The applicant described above who is asked to demonstrate operator skills on a real computer is being given a performance test. Another very common form of performance test in employment testing is the interview. Since the interview is often used to determine the oral communication skills of the applicant, it qualifies as a performance test.

There are also **speed tests** and **power tests**. In a speed test, your score is the number of items you can answer correctly in a specific period of time. The time period is usually too short to complete all of the items on the test. For example, an applicant for a clerical position might be asked to look up as many addresses as possible in a directory in 3 minutes' time. The person's score would be the number of addresses correctly recorded. In a power test, the time limits are more liberal, but the questions are more difficult than in a speed test. Again, the score is the number of items answered correctly. Speed tests and power tests may require different operations on the part of the test-taker and may therefore test different abilities.

A final administrative category of tests has to do with the way the test scores will be used. **Achievement tests** are designed to measure how much learning has already taken place. **Aptitude tests**, on the other hand, measure a person's capacity or future potential to learn something. For example, if you were asked to memorize a page of the phone book and then given a test on that particular page, the test would be an achievement test. In contrast, the memory scale on a general-intelligence test is an aptitude test, because it measures the more general capacity to memorize all sorts of material, not a particular body of information. In some respects, this distinction betwen achievement and aptitude is really an arbitrary one. The identical test could be either an achievement test (if it was intended to measure past accomplishment) or an aptitude test (if it was intended to predict future performance), and both types of tests would actually be measuring present levels of some behavior.

Content Categories

In addition to administrative categories of tests, there are categories of test content. **Mental ability** represents one major content category. There are literally hundreds of individual and group mental-ability tests covering everything from mechanical aptitude to memory (see Figure 18–8). What they all have in common is a concern for mental operations involving relationships and the application of abstract principles.

Another content category includes **psychomotor tests**. These tests usually involve some sort of physical manipulation. If you apply for a job as an assembler at a computer factory, you may be asked to sit at a mock work station and put together specific pieces of equipment in a given amount of time. This would be considered a psychomotor test, since it measures motor skills as opposed to strictly intellectual skills.

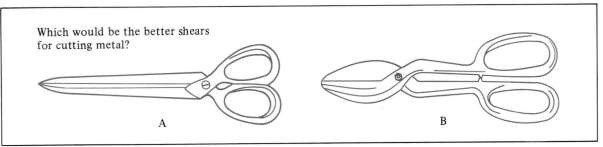

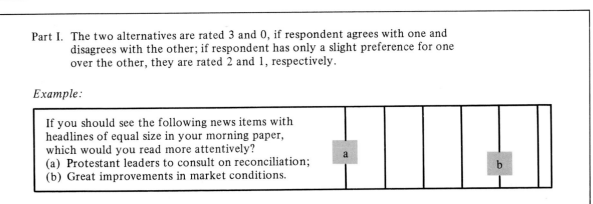

FIGURE 18-8
Two examples of the wide range of tests covering everything from mechanical aptitude to interests and values. On the top is shown an example from the Bennett Mechanical Comprehension Test. On the bottom is an example from the Allport-Vernon-Lindzey Study of Values.

One very broad content category is that of **personality tests.** We considered several of these tests in some detail in Chapter 13. There are really two types of personality tests. One type is used to measure or describe the unique aspects of an individual's style of behavior; another type is designed to help in diagnosing behavioral problems. On the basis of these diagnostic tests, guesses are made regarding why the problem appeared, as well as what course of action or therapy to follow.

Another content category is called **interest** or **motivation tests.** These tests assess the extent to which a person is interested in various categories of activity. This is often useful in determining

Group tests. Tests that are administered to many people at the same time; examples are multiple choice civil service tests.

Individual tests. Tests that are administered to only one person at a time; an example is the driving portion of the driver's licensing exam.

Paper-and-pencil tests. Tests in which answers are written out or marked on a specific answer sheet; an example is the SAT.

Performance tests. Tests that involve a behavioral response of some kind rather than a written answer; an example would be putting a puzzle together.

Speed tests. Tests with a time limit; one's score is the number of items answered correctly within a specific period of time.

Power tests. Tests with more liberal time limits but also more difficult questions than speed tests; one's score is the number of items answered correctly.

Achievement tests. Tests designed to measure how much learning has already taken place.

Aptitude tests. Tests designed to measure someone's future potential to learn as well as his or her present state of learning.

Mental ability tests. Tests for mental operations that involve relationships and the application of abstract principles.

Psychomotor tests. Tests designed to measure a person's physical ability or motor skills in manipulating objects.

Personality tests. Tests that serve one of two purposes: (1) to measure or describe unique aspects of a person's style of behavior; or (2) to help in diagnosing behavioral problems.

Interest or motivation tests. Assess the extent to which a person is interested in various categories of activity; can be useful in determining whether someone is suited to a particular occupation or course of study.

whether someone is suited motivationally for a particular occupation or course of study. The person's responses are compared to the responses of others who are already in the occupation or course of study and who are satisfied and successful. If a person's answers are similar to those of the "successful" group, then the prospects are favorable for that person entering that field. If, on the other hand, the person's responses are quite different from those of the "successful" group, another line of work or study might be more appropriate.

In most employment testing multiple forms of tests are used. For example, a person applying for a production job in a factory might first be given a short written test of math and mechanical comprehension, followed by an interview with the personnel director, followed by a short manual-dexterity test. Each one of the tests should be able to provide information about one or more important aspects of the person in relation to the job in question. This is the property of validity that we considered in Chapter 13.

REVIEW QUESTIONS

15. _____ tests are given to many people at the same time; _____ tests are administered to only one person at a time.

16. In _____ tests, you write answers to questions on paper or on a specific answer sheet. In _____ tests, you are asked to do certain tasks, such as assembling blocks in a certain way.

17. In _____ tests you must answer as many questions as you can in a certain amount of time. In _____ tests there is no strict time limit for answering, but the questions are very difficult to answer correctly.

18. _____ tests measure how much learning has already occurred; _____ tests are concerned with measuring someone's future potential to learn.

Answers: 15. group; individual 16. paper-and-pencil; performance 17. speed; power 18. Achievement; aptitude

■ DISCRIMINATION IN HIRING

Without question, the most serious issue in hiring today is the issue of unfair employment discrimination. Over 20 years ago, in 1964, the landmark Civil Rights Act was passed. Title VII of this act prohibits employers from discrimination in hiring and promotion decisions on the basis of sex, race, creed, color, or national origin. Equal employment opportunity laws are part of the larger Civil Rights Act, which also deals with housing, education, and other areas of potential discrimination. Several years ago, the federal agency that administers the equal employment opportunity law (the Equal Employment Opportunity Commission or EEOC) was also given responsibility for guarding against age discrimination in employment.

Literally thousands of court cases have revolved around attempts to question the validity of selection procedures. The arguments in these cases are quite straightforward: The applicant claiming discrimination in hiring usually argues that the job does not demand what the test for the job measures. A perfect example is verbal ability. If we are screening applicants for the job of fire warden in the middle of the Boundary Water Canoe Area in northern Minnesota, a test of vocabulary would be out of place. Instead, we might look for evidence of good vision, long attention span, and good judgment. The personnel psychologist tries to identify selection devices that will be perfectly matched to job demands, and this requires that the psychologist be very familiar with the job and its demands. In addition, the personnel psychologist must be skilled in identifying important skills for a job, and then in measuring how much of a particular skill an applicant possesses.

Most experts believe the solution to many discrimination problems is not to be found through better tests but through more accurate job analyses. An example might help to demonstrate this. In the mid-1960s, there were few female officers on state police forces. This was because most states had height and weight requirements that automatically excluded most women. Gradually, these height and weight requirements were replaced with performance tests. Instead of having to be at least 5'6" tall and having to weigh at least 135 pounds, applicants were required to demonstrate physical strength.

This was presumably a fairer selection procedure. In one northeastern state, applicants were asked to drag a 140-lb. weight 100 yards in a certain number of seconds. This was thought to be a representative task of a state police officer in that state, since many deer were killed by cars on the road and had to be removed from the highway by the state police. Not many women were able to successfully complete the test. A job analysis, however, revealed some interesting discrepancies between beliefs and reality. In fact, very few state police officers actually dragged a dead deer from the highway—this was usually done by road maintenance crews. When it *was* necessary for an officer to remove a deer carcass, the weight to be dragged was often closer to 100 lbs., and the distance closer to 10 yards. Furthermore, it didn't really matter if removal was completed in 10 seconds or 3 minutes. The point is that the test was only vaguely related to the job—in other words, it was not sufficiently valid.

We have reached the end of the chapter and have really only scratched the surface of industrial and organizational psychology. We have not considered such issues as training programs and their relationship to learning theory, substance-abuse at work and its relationship to abnormal behavior, or the extent to which work settings produce stress in workers that does damage to physical and psychological well-being. Similarly, I have not presented detailed information about particular tests or testing techniques or about the different uses and techniques of performance evaluation. Fortunately, there are other courses and texts (Landy, 1985) that explore these many facets of the field. Given our limits as an introductory text, I have tried to take one broad area of application with which most of us are familiar—work—and to show how the study of psychology relates to it.

■ SUMMARY

1. *Industrial* and *organizational psychology* is the area of psychology that studies behavior in the work setting. The three main branches of industrial and

Most experts believe the solution to many discrimination problems is to be found through more accurate job analyses. For example, more accurate job analyses have led to the redesign of performance tests for the selection of police officers.

organizational psychology are human factors psychology, industrial social and organizational psychology, and personnel psychology. The goals of modern human factors specialists are to develop work environments and methods that are optimally suited to the capacities and limitations of human beings. Industrial social and organizational psychologists aim at coordinating the needs of the individual employee and the needs of the organization. Personnel psychology is concerned with individual differences. This branch attempts to collect information about individuals with respect to their probability of success in a particular job or environment.

2. The area of *human factors* is especially concerned with issues like equipment design and ways to make equipment, such as displays and controls, as efficient and safe as possible. To design a system of displays and controls that is compatible with the demands of the task and the characteristics of human operators, human factors specialists use the methods of the experimental psychologist: experimental and control groups, experimental treatment, and gathering and analysis of data on alternative designs. Human factors psychologists also focus on people's capacities and limitations: how people take in information, how people process information, and what responses result from processing. A third area of concern for human factors specialists is the behavioral demands on a worker made by a particular job or environment.

3. *Industrial social and organizational psychologists* are concerned with the adjustment of organizations and individuals to one another. One particular area of concern is job satisfaction, or the sum of a worker's emotional responses to specific elements of the job. Characteristics of a job that affect satisfaction include the work itself, supervision, co-workers, pay, and promotional opportunities. Work conditions have a greater influence on job satisfaction than any other variable, including race, sex, and age.

4. IO psychologists are also interested in understanding work motivation. One approach to increasing work motivation is to tie rewards to performance in order to increase satisfaction, to maintain or increase the value of desired rewards, to confirm the individual's belief that effort is worthwhile, and to increase energy expenditure. Job design/job enrichment is an approach based on the view that certain environments encourage individuals to initiate and direct their own energy. A third approach to increasing motivation is to change methods of supervision.

5. *Personnel psychologists* attempt to identify the performance demands of particular jobs in order to determine which human capacities are likely to be used in meeting those demands and to identify individuals who have sufficient amounts of those capacities to perform the job successfully. Gathering information about the demands of the job, or *job analysis*, enables psychologists to identify the particular skills and abilities that are necessary for successful job performance. Additionally, personnel psychologists develop and administer tests, provide training that may be necessary, and provide feedback to the worker on a periodic basis.

6. *Group tests* are tests given to many people at the same time and are designed to provide limited information in the most efficient manner. *Individual tests* are administered to one person at a time and are intended to provide deeper and broader information. Other test-administration categories include *paper-and-pencil, performance, speed,* and *power tests. Achievement tests* are designed to measure the amount of learning that has already occurred; *aptitude tests* are designed to measure a person's potential abilities as well as present state of learning. Tests are also grouped into content categories such as *mental ability, psychomotor, personality,* and *interest* or *motivation tests.*

7. The most serious issue in employment hiring today is unfair discrimination. Many discrimination problems can be solved through an accurate job analysis.

ANSWERING QUESTIONS FOR THOUGHT

1. You could, but in a sense you would be driving "blind" or by guesswork—you wouldn't know how fast you were going, whether you were about to run out of gas, or how to turn on the windshield wipers if it started to rain. The feedback the driver gets from the displays on a dashboard are an important part of safe driving. Modern human factors specialists are involved in the efficient design of displays and control devices.

2. Research seems to indicate that this relationship can work both ways. People may be more productive when they are happy, or they may be

satisfied as a result of their successful or productive efforts.

3. The overall level of job satisfaction has changed very little over the last 50 years. However, older workers are, on the whole, paid better and have more interesting jobs, which is why older workers report higher levels of satisfaction than younger workers.

4. At the Volvo plant the job of the supervisor was eliminated. The supervisor was retrained to be an advisor, and the workers directed their own production. Another less radical approach to supervision roles is Management by Objectives. With this system the supervisor does set goals and provide feedback to workers as to whether those goals are being met, but basically just encourages workers to be self-directing.

5. The solution to unfair discrimination in hiring practices is not only to improve tests but also to conduct more accurate job analyses. This task falls to personnel psychologists, who, through observation and surveys, finds out what a job actually consists of and what skills are required to perform it well.

Appendix: Statistics

DESCRIPTIVE STATISTICS
Distribution and Graphs □ Shape of Distributions □
Central Tendency □ Variability □ Position □
Normal Distribution

CORRELATION AND PREDICTION
Correlation □ Prediction

STATISTICS FOR EXPERIMENTS
Probability □ Other Inferential Procedures

SUMMARY

Chapter 1 on history and methods discussed four goals of psychology: description, prediction, control, and understanding. Statistics is a branch of mathematics that helps achieve these goals. There are three types of statistical procedures that we will discuss: **Descriptive statistics** organize a set of data so that the basic characteristics of the data can be seen easily and communicated. **Correlational and prediction statistics** uncover relationships among different independent and dependent variables. Finally, **experimental statistics** assist in testing various hypotheses.

This appendix is divided into three sections; each section corresponds to one of the three types of procedures listed above. Even though each class of pro-

cedures is treated separately, you should realize that there is seldom any clear separation among the procedures in actual research and data analysis. A typical study is very likely to use all three types of procedures: Some data might be described, show the relationship between two or more variables, and—at the same time—test one or more hypotheses. For example, in Chapter 1, TV watching and aggression was used as an example of a psychological study. In analyzing the data gathered in this study, you might calculate the average age of the children observed (a descriptive statistic), calculate the association between hours of watching TV and amount of aggression in play (a correlational statistic), and calculate a number on which to base a decision on whether to accept or reject the hypothesis that watching violent TV shows leads to aggressive play in children (an experimental statistic).

To make the discussion a bit easier, we will use two different sets of data. Both sets of data relate to the general problem of TV violence and aggressive behavior. The first set of data is used for the descriptive and correlational statistics, while the second set is used in the context of an experiment. In spite of the fact that these data do not come from an actual experiment, they are similar to what you might find in this type of research.

◼ DESCRIPTIVE STATISTICS

Distribution and Graphs

A researcher takes a random sample of 24 fifth-grade students to study the relationship between the number of violent TV shows watched and the amount of aggressive behavior that occurs. Table A-1 presents a listing of the data. The information on the sex of the student and the number of violent TV shows watched per week was collected by asking the students about their TV-watching habits.

TABLE A-1.
Data from Relationship Study

Subject	Sex: 1 = Male 0 = Female	Variables	
		1: Number Violent TV Shows Watched	2: Incidence of Aggressive Behavior
1	1	4	10
2	0	6	2
3	0	4	1
4	1	16	12
5	1	9	5
6	0	11	4
7	1	2	3
8	0	7	3
9	1	21	9
10	1	14	4
11	1	11	14
12	0	7	10
13	1	12	7
14	0	13	4
15	0	11	13
16	0	14	9
17	1	6	3
18	1	6	4
19	0	21	12
20	1	10	3
21	1	3	0
22	1	5	1
23	0	2	5
24	0	9	2
Mean		9.33	5.83
Standard Deviation		5.23	4.12

Descriptive statistics. Statistics that organize a set of data so that the basic characteristics of the data can be easily seen and communicated.

Correlational and prediction statistics. Statistics that uncover relationships among different independent and dependent variables.

Experimental statistics. Statistics that assist in testing various hypotheses.

TABLE A-2.
Frequency Distribution for Variables 1 and 2

Score Interval	(1)	(2)
20–21	2	0
18–19	0	0
16–17	1	0
14–15	2	1
12–13	2	3
10–11	4	2
8–9	2	2
6–7	5	1
4–5	3	6
2–3	3	6
0–1	0	3
	N = 24	N = 24

The frequency and intensity of aggressive behavior was measured in a controlled one-hour observation session.

First we can organize the data. One or two procedures are commonly used; either a frequency distribution (table) is made or a frequency polygon (graph). Table A-2 presents frequency distributions for variables 1 and 2 for all 24 children. A **frequency distribution** arranges the scores from high to low values, showing how often each score occurred. At the bottom of the columns, the total number of scores is given, which in this case is 24. In research descriptions, the number of observations is usually indicated by the letter N which stands for N(umber), so in this case, N = 24. Figure A-1 presents the same information in a graphic way. This is called a **frequency polygon,** a diagram that represents the patterns of the scores.

By examining either the frequency distribution (Table A-2) or the frequency polygon (Figure A-1), you can notice some things that were not so obvious in the unordered data that appeared in Table A-1. First, there are more scores on the lower end of the score scale than on the higher end. This is true for both variables, but it is especially evident for Variable 1. Also, the concentration point for Variable 2 appears to be several points lower (around 2–4) than for Variable 1 (around 6–10). In addition, the scores on Variable 1 seem to spread out farther along the scale (from about 2 to 21) than do scores on Variable 2 (from about 0 to 14). Thus, from the frequency distribution and frequency polygon, it becomes more evident what the "typical" score and "spread" are for the data.

Shape of Distributions

In some cases we want to communicate the characteristics of a set of data without having to

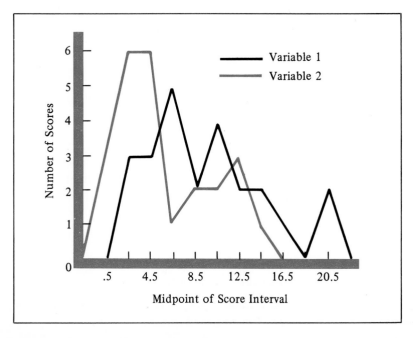

FIGURE A-1
A frequency polygon.

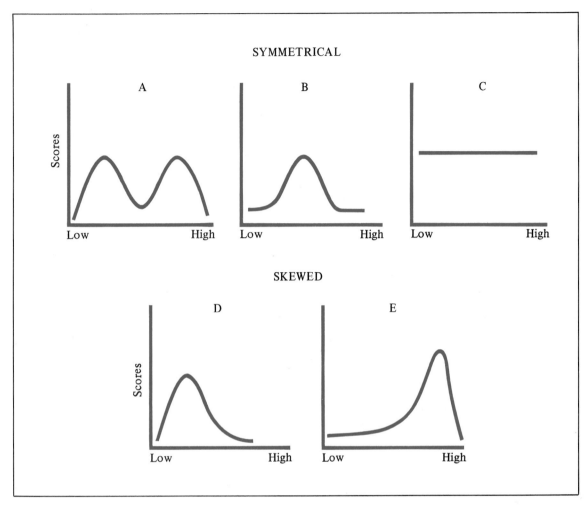

FIGURE A-2
Symmetrical and skewed distributions.

show a table or a graph. Fortunately, there are terms we can use to do this. Two features of a distribution are symmetry and the number of concentration points. A **symmetrical distribution** is one where the left side (from the middle) has the same pattern as the right side. An asymmetrical or **skewed distribution** is unbalanced around the middle point; the left side is not identical to the right side. Figure A-2 shows several symmetrical and skewed distributions.

For A, B, and C, a vertical line in the middle could be used to fold one side over exactly onto the other side. Graph B is sometimes called a "normal" curve and is a very important distribution in statistics. More will be said about that pattern later. Graphs D and E are skewed: D is a typical pattern for the results of a very difficult test in a course, and E reflects the distribution of a very easy test. Note that the + or − sign depends on the end of the graph

---

Frequency distributions. Scores are arranged from high to low values, showing for each score how often it occurred.
Frequency polygon. A closed diagram that represents the patterns of the frequencies (how often each score occurs).

Symmetrical distribution. A distribution in which the left and right sides have a similar pattern.
Skewed distribution. An unbalanced distribution, in which left and right sides are not similar.

that trails off. If you look again at Figure A-1, it appears that both distributions have some degree of positive skew.

A second characteristic of ordered data is how many concentration or peak points there are in a distribution. A peak point is called a mode. The **mode** is the score that occurs most often. Since distributions can have several peak points, they can have several modes. For A, there are two peak points; this is referred to as a *bi*modal distribution. Graphs B, D, and E have only one peak point and are called *uni*modal. Graph C is described as having no modal (peak) values. In Figure A-1, although the pattern is clearer for the aggressive behavior variable, statisticians would probably describe both of them as unimodal, since the largest peak points are toward the lower end of the score scale. Thus, one quick way to give a description of both distributions would be to say that they are unimodal, positively skewed. Note that the "normal" distribution could be described as unimodal, symmetrical.

Central Tendency

What if someone asked you about the average score on the two variables in the TV study? In statistics, the average is called a **measure of central tendency**. There are many different possible measures of central tendency. You are probably familiar with one of these measures—the **mean**. The mean is the value obtained by adding together all the scores and dividing by the number of scores.

In Table A-1, the mean for variable 1 is 9.33, and the mean for variable 2 is 5.83. Therefore, reporting that the means are 9.33 and 5.83 communicates quickly what the typical or average person scored. Incidentally, if you are curious about how boys compared to girls, the two means for boys are 9.15 and 5.77; for girls they are 9.55 and 5.91. From our data, girls tended to watch somewhat more violent TV shows and also exhibited somewhat more aggressive behavior.

In statistics there is often more than one way to indicate the same concept—in this case, central tendency. Two other measures frequently used are the mode and median. Above, we considered the mode in terms of describing the shape of a distribution. It can also be used to provide information about central tendency. As we saw earlier, the *mode* is the score that occurs most often—for Variable 1 that is *both* scores of 11 and 6 with three scores each, and for Variable 2 the modes are 3 and 4 with four scores each. The **median** is the midpoint in the distribution—half the scores fall above it, half fall below it. The values for the medians in Variables 1 and 2 are 9 and 4.25 respectively.

As you can see, the measures of central tendency do not always give the same results. In general, skewness has an important effect on how close the three different measures (mean, median, mode) are to being the same. In positively skewed distributions, the mean tends to be largest, next comes the median, and the mode is usually lowest. The reverse is generally true of negatively skewed distributions. In unimodal symmetric distributions like the normal curve, all three are the same value or very close. Unless there is a compelling reason *not* to use the mean, it is the most commonly reported measure of central tendency.

Variability

Another important statistical concept is the spread of scores. This is called *variability*. Two different distributions could have similar averages but differ considerably as to the spread of the scores. As was true with central tendency, there are also several measures of variability.

Figure A-3 shows several distributions with equal means but different variabilities. The term **range** is used to broadly describe variability among scores in a distribution; it is defined as the difference between the highest and lowest scores in a distribution. In Figure A-3, the range of scores for A is about half that of C. Clearly, some sets of scores vary more than others.

Range is a *total* variability measure. For Variable 1, the highest score is 21 and the lowest is 2; therefore, the range is 19 points. For Variable 2, the range is 14 to 0, or 14 points. Based on the range, Variable 2 seems to spread out less than Variable 1. As a quick estimate of variability, the range is acceptable. However, the range is only based on the end points and says nothing about the clustering of data between these points.

The one most widely used measure of variability is the **standard deviation**. The best way to think about standard deviation is in terms of the way scores tend to cluster close to the mean. If we are considering several distributions, the distribution

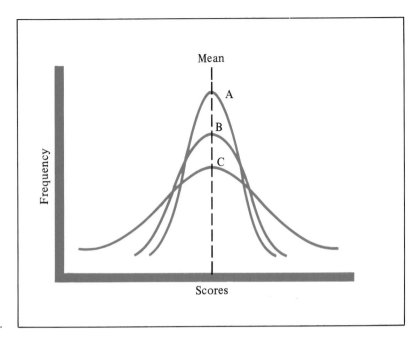

FIGURE A-3
Distributions with
different variabilities.

with the smallest standard deviation value is made up of scores that tend to be closer to the mean than in the other distributions. That is, scores in a distribution with a smaller standard deviation value deviate *less* from the mean compared to scores in another similar distribution. As long as the score scales among several distributions are comparable (for example, distribution of grade-point averages for three different universities), then the standard deviation provides an excellent way to indicate the variability of the scores.

Position

On occasions, psychologists want to pinpoint where a particular score value falls within a distribution. We could say, for example, that some children

watched more violent TV shows than the average, or exhibited less instances of aggressive behavior than the average; however, how would we indicate how *much* higher or how *much* lower? Two measures used frequently in statistical work to describe position are called percentile ranks and *z scores*.

A **percentile rank** is a number that represents the *percentage* of all the scores that fall *below* a certain value. For example, if 60 percent of the scores fall below *x*, that X value has a percentile rank of 60. When central tendency was discussed, it was noted that the median has half of N above and below. Therefore, the *median* score always has a percentile rank of 50. Since the mean is not always the same as the median, it is incorrect to say that the mean also has a percentile rank of 50; in some distributions (symmetrical) it does, but in many cases

---

Mode. The score that occurs most often (the score with the highest frequency).

Measure of central tendency. The average. There are many different possible measures that can be used to express this, such as mean, median, and mode.

Mean. The value obtained by adding together all the scores and dividing by the number of scores.

Median. The midpoint of the distribution—half the scores fall above it, half fall below it.

Range. The difference between the highest and lowest scores in a distribution.

Standard deviation. A measure of the variability of a group of scores; based on the deviations of scores from the mean.

Percentile rank. The percentage of all the scores that fall below a certain score value.

(skewed distributions) it does not. Several illustrations of percentile rank will be presented without the calculations. For example, the percentile rank for a value of 13 TV shows on Variable 1 is 77, which means that 77 percent of the 24 children reported watching less than 13 violent TV programs per week. For Variable 2, a value of 3 has a percentile rank of 29.

There are two common problems when interpreting percentile rank. First, since a percentile rank is a percentage number, it is often misinterpreted as the percent *correct* on a test. Percentile ranks do *not* represent the percentage of correct answers on an exam, but rather the percentage of people obtaining scores less than some score value. Second, there also is a tendency to think that high percentile ranks represent good performance and low values poor performance. This is not always true. For example, on an easy test, a fairly high test score (good performance) may have a low percentile rank because almost every other person did even better. It is best to interpret percentile ranks as indicating where a score is within a distribution rather than the quality of a performance.

A second way to indicate position is by using a *z score*. A **z score** indicates how many standard deviations a score is away from the mean. Note that *z*'s can be positive or negative. The sign tells whether the score is above (+) or below (−) the mean. In most distributions, *z* values will not exceed ± 3. The real advantage of measuring position using a *z* value is that *z* incorporates the best measure of central tendency (the mean) and variability (standard deviation). From our own data, a score of 9 would have a $z = -.06$ on the first variable, but the *same* data point would have a $z = .77$ on Variable 2. Put into words, this means that 9 is just slightly below the mean on Variable 1, but almost a full standard deviation *above* the mean on Variable 2. Obviously, a score of 9 needs to be interpreted differently for the two variables.

One of the applications of the *z score* is in the area of standardized test scales. Perhaps you are familiar with test scores such as IQ (intelligence) and SAT (college entrance exam). Most IQ scales, for example, have a mean = 100 and a standard deviation = 15. These are not natural characteristics of the scales, but are rather arbitrarily chosen. You may think that this is a little unusual, but it really isn't. We do the same thing for lots of variables that you

are familiar with. For example, the Fahrenheit and Centigrade (Celsius) temperature scales are arbitrary. On one (Fahrenheit), the temperature must reach 212° before water will boil; on the other (Centigrade), water boils at 100°. To return to the example of intelligence tests, the mean value from the raw score distribution is arbitrarily called 100. The standard deviation is 15. Then, an X score with a $z = 1.00$ is called 115 on the IQ scale; one unit of 15 points above an arbitrary mean of 100. Since distributions generally do not go beyond *z* values of ± 3, the range on the IQ scale would be, for all practical purposes, 100 ± 45 (3×15), or 55 to 145. Very few IQ values are lower or higher than these extreme values. SAT scores are produced in a similar manner. The mean value of the actual raw score distribution is changed to 500 (for each section on the SAT test—verbal and quantitative) and the standard deviation set = 100. Therefore, if you had a raw score that had a $z = -2$ on the SAT, your transformed score would be 300.

Normal Distribution

One of the most widely used concepts in statistical work is that of the normal curve (NC). As was mentioned earlier, an NC is both unimodal and symmetrical. From left to right, the scores increase in number to a maximum in the middle, and then taper off again at the right side. The reason the NC is so useful is that the frequency distributions for many types of variables tend to approximate the pattern of an NC.

Figure A-4 presents the NC pattern with several pieces of information labeled concerning the X, *z* and percentile rank scales. If the mean = 40 and the standard deviation = 5, then the raw score scale would have 40 in the middle and spacings of 5 points on either side out to ± 3 standard deviation units. The *z* values would range from − 3 through 0 (mean) in the middle to about + 3. Also, notice the values inside the NC. These numbers represent the approximate *percentage* of the total area (= 100 percent) of the curve. For example, there is approximately 34 percent of the area from the mean value to a $z = 1$ *or* from the mean to $z = -1$. Thus, approximately 68 percent of the test scores fall within the boundaries of mean ± 1 standard deviation units. On our raw score scale, if the raw scores are normally distributed, we can say that about two

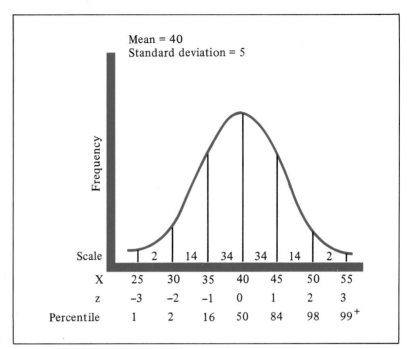

FIGURE A-4
A normal distribution.

thirds (68 percent) of all the scores fall between 35 and 45. Now look at the percentile rank scale. Remember, a percentile rank is the percentage of scores *below* some point. At the mean, this value is obviously 50, since half the area is below. What about at a score of 35? Since 34 percent is between the mean and a $z = -1$, that means that $50 - 34$, or 16 percent is below a score of 35. For a score of 45, the percentile rank is 84.

■ CORRELATION AND PREDICTION

Correlation

The first section of this appendix presents several basic ways for describing a distribution. Now let's look further into the question of what effect watching violent TV shows has on aggressive behavior.

Someone might wonder if there is any relationship between how many violent TV programs children watch and the amount of aggressive behavior they exhibit. The television industry may believe or argue that there is no systematic relationship, but teachers and parents may feel differently. How could we determine who is right?

In statistics, there is a popular way to examine the relationship between two variables; it is done by computing a statistic called a **correlation**. The easiest way to understand correlation is through the use of scatterplots. A **scatterplot** is a graph showing how two variables relate. Figure A-5 illustrates several different possible "relationships" between the "number of violent TV shows watched" (X) and "incidence of aggressive behavior" (Y) variables.

Graphs A and B show positive relationships, because the trend is uphill. An uphill trend, looking from left to right on the graph, means that as values increase on X, values also increase on Y. With our variables, a positive relationship would be where increases in the number of violent TV shows watched is associated with more aggressive behavior. Graphs D and E show the opposite or negative relationships,

---

Z score. Shows how many standard deviations a score is away from the mean.

Correlation. The relationship between two variables.
Scatterplot. A graph showing the relationship between two variables (see Figure A-5).

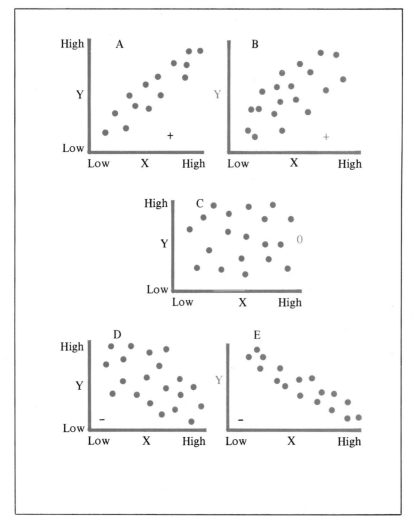

FIGURE A-5
Scatterplots.

because the trend is downhill. This indicates that an increase in the number of violent shows watched is associated with *less* aggressive behavior—a pattern that many would find hard to believe. Graph C indicates no noticeable relationship.

Graphs A and B, and D and E differ, however, even though each pair of graphs shows the same trend. Graph A seems to show a stronger trend than B, and E seems to be stronger than D. These scatterplots show another important characteristic of correlation, that of the magnitude or strength of the relationship. Correlations are numbers that can range from 0.00 (meaning no relationship) to 1.00 (meaning a perfect or exactly straight-line trend). In the case of 1.00, all the data points would be on an

uphill line (+ 1.00) or a downhill line (− 1.00). Graph C has a correlation of approximately 0.00. Thus, Graph A has a correlation closer to + 1.00 than Graph B, while Graph E has a correlation closer to − 1 than Graph D. It is very important to understand that the strength of the correlation is determined only by the number (0.00 to 1.00) and has nothing to do with the sign. The sign only indicates the direction or trend but says nothing about the strength of the relationship. For example, a correlation of − .60 is just as strong as a correlation of + .60.

Let's make a scatterplot of our data from Table A-1 using Variables 1 and 2 (Figure A-6). For the moment, ignore the straight line in the graph. Each dot

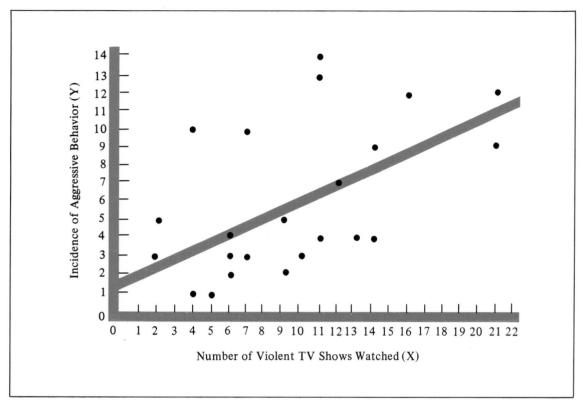

FIGURE A-6
Scatterplots for Variables 1 and 2.

represents the scores on both variables for *each* person. For example, subject 1 watched 4 violent TV shows (along the X axis) and exhibited 10 aggressive acts (along the Y axis). The intersection of these two positions (up from X and sideways from Y) is subject 1's data point. Since there are 24 subjects, there are 24 data points. What would you say about the trend? If you said it was uphill, you are correct. There is a *positive* correlation between the two variables. Our data seem to show that the greater the number of violent TV shows watched, the greater the amount of aggressive behavior exhibited. While the pattern is far from perfect, the positive trend is unmistakable.

There is one important thing to keep in mind about correlation coefficients. No matter how high they are, they do not indicate cause-and-effect relationships. As an example, the correlation between height and weight is usually above +.50 in a sample of adults. This does not mean that weight *causes* height. If that were the case, every time you gained

some weight, you would get taller. To take our TV and aggression example, the fact that a correlation exists between TV watching and aggression does not imply causality. If we simply asked children about the TV shows they watched and asked their parents about their aggressiveness, a positive correlation could mean that aggressive children watch violent TV shows rather than meaning that watching TV violence leads to aggression.

Prediction

There is one important thing that we can do when two variables are correlated: We can predict levels of one variable from information about the other variable. Someone might make the statement: "If you see a guy on an elevator with food spots on his tie, don't bother to look at his shoes—they'll be dirty." This is a sarcastic example of prediction. Knowledge provided by the condition of a person's tie could be used to predict the condition of that person's shoes. A more common (and useful) example of prediction from correlation is the use of SAT scores to predict the probability that a student will earn a college degree. There is a positive correlation between these two variables. Since SAT scores can be produced before the student enters college, they can be used to predict whether or not that student is likely to graduate.

To the extent that correlations are not 1.00 (that is, perfect), there will be error in prediction. The lower the correlation, the more the error of prediction. This is why high correlations are so attractive in research and application. In research, it means a better understanding of a relationship between two variables; in application, a high correlation means less error in prediction.

■ STATISTICS FOR EXPERIMENTS

One of the most common research activities of psychologists is conducting experiments. In general, the purpose of doing an experiment is to show that manipulations of an independent variable (X) produce some predictable and systematic effect on the dependent variable (Y). Here, the researcher wants to demonstrate cause and effect. In order to do so, the investigator sets up situations where the independent variable is controlled. By doing this, it is assumed that variations in the dependent variable (Y) are *caused* by the manipulations of X, the independent variable.

Instead of doing a relationship study, we could have designed an experiment. For example, assume that we set up two groups of children: An experimental group watched TV shows of which a certain percentage of shows were considered violent; the control group watched the same number of TV shows, but the percentage of violent programs was close to 0. After the viewings were complete, the researcher measured the incidence of aggressive behavior during a controlled observational session. Data from this experiment are presented in Table A-3. The means for the two groups appear to be clearly different, with the experimental group producing more aggressive behavior.

Although, on the surface, there appears to be a difference, we must remember that these data are

TABLE A-3
Results from Experiment

	Experimental Group	Control Group
	17	9
	12	7
	13	10
	10	13
	18	8
	9	5
	20	14
	4	10
	16	3
	14	5
	10	11
	11	7
	16	8
	15	9
Mean	13.21	8.5
Standard Deviation	4.23	3.06

from *samples*. If we did this experiment again with other samples, would we find the *same* results, that is, the experimental group having a higher mean value? This leads us to the problem of sampling error. Sampling error refers to the fact that chance can produce different results regardless of whether our independent variable does or does not have any effect. In our study, we only want to say that watching more TV violence produces more aggressive behavior if the results cannot be explained just by sampling error.

Probability

Since two means could be different as a result of sampling error, we must have some way of separating real differences from chance differences. The concept that is used to separate these two kinds of differences is *significance*. We examine a difference (for example, between two means) and ask whether or not that difference is "significant." In other words, we are asking if the difference is the result of sampling error, or whether the difference is a real one that we would find in other samples as well. Significance is usually described in terms of a **probability statement.** We might say that the probability of finding a difference between two means as large as the one that we observed as a result of sampling error is 5/100. In other words, we would expect to find a difference this large in only 5 samples of 100 if the difference were due solely to sampling error. If you should read an actual experimental report, the significance of the difference will be expressed as follows: $p = .05$. This would mean that the probability of finding such a difference as a result of chance (that is, sampling error) would be 5/100.

Other Inferential Procedures

The procedure outlined comparing two means in an experiment is called an *inferential statistical technique* because we want to generalize the results to a larger group, that is, the population. In fact, the only real interest in the sample means is that they accurately represent the type of performance to be expected if these treatments or methods were applied to other similar groups.

Although this brief appendix on statistical procedures only illustrates comparing two means, it needs to be emphasized that there are many other techniques useful for other hypothesis-testing situations. For example, perhaps you formulated a research hypothesis that there is a positive correlation between two variables. The first step is to select a sample and obtain information on both the X and Y variables. Then it is possible to estimate the amount of error in the size of the correlation that is likely to appear if we took other similar samples and repeated the study. Based on this estimate of error, we can compare it to the magnitude of the correlation we obtain in our sample. If the size of the correlation could easily be explained by sampling error (that is, close to 0), then our research hypothesis is not supported. However, if sampling error cannot easily explain the size of the correlation we obtain, our data then support our research hypothesis. Not only can this strategy be used with correlations, it can also be used with single means, standard deviations, and percentages, or differences in percentages. A course or book in statistics will provide you with the information you need to use these other statistical procedures.

■ SUMMARY

1. *Descriptive statistics* organize a set of data so that the basic characteristics can be easily seen and communicated. *Correlational and prediction statistics* uncover relationships among different independent and dependent variables. *Experimental statistics* assist in testing various hypotheses.

2. *Frequency distributions* (tables) arrange scores from high to low values with the frequencies in each score interval listed. A *frequency polygon* (graph) is a closed diagram that represents the patterns of the frequencies. A *skewed* distribution is one in which the left side is not identical to the right. A *mode* is a peak point in the distribution.

3. Measures of central tendency include the *mean*, or average; the *mode*, or the score with the highest frequency; and the *median*, the score at which half the frequencies are above and half are below.

4. *Variability* is the spread of the scores. The *standard deviation* is based on deviations from the mean.

5. *Percentile rank* describes the percentage of all scores that fall below a certain score value. A *z score* indicates how many standard deviation units a score is from the mean. A *normal curve* (NC) is unimodal and symmetrical. Many types of variables tend to approximate the pattern of an NC.

6. *Correlation* indicates a positive or negative relationship between two variables. A *scatterplot* is a graph showing how variables relate; a prediction line involves fitting a straight line through the scatterplot to predict behavior on one variable based on information about another variable.

7. Experiments attempt to show that manipulations of an independent variable produce predictable and systematic changes in the dependent variable, or *cause and effect. Sampling error* refers to the fact that chance can produce different results regardless of whether the independent variable has any effect. Statistical significance means that the difference between two tested groups is not the result of sampling error.

Probability statement. A statement estimating the likelihood that an observed experimental effect was due to chance or a sampling error.

Glossary Index

References

ABEL, E.L. Behavioral teratology of alcohol. *Psychological Bulletin*, 1981, *90*, 564-581.

ABRAMSON, L.Y., SELIGMAN, M.E.P. AND TEASDALE, J.D. Learned helplessness in humans: Critique and reformulation *Journal of Abnormal Psychology*, 1978, *87*, 49-74.

ADAMS, J.L. *Conceptual Blockbusting*. San Francisco: Freeman, 1974.

ADAMS, J.S. Inequity in Social Exchange in L. Berkowitz (Ed.), *Advances in experimental social psychology (Vol. 2)*, New York: Academic Press, 1965, 1976, 267-299.

ADORNO, T.W., FRENKEL-BRUNSWICK. E., LEVINSON, D.J. AND SANFORD, R.N. *The authoritarian personality*, New York: Harper and Row, 1950.

AGNEW, H.W. JR., WEBB, W. AND WILLIAMS, R.L. The effects of stage four sleep deprivation. *Electroencephalography and Clinical Neurophysiology*, *17*, 68-70.

AKELAITIS, A.J. A study of praxis and language following section of the corpus callosum. *Journal of Neurosurgery*, 1944, *1*, 94-102.

AKHTER, S., WIG, N.N., VARMA, V.K., PERSHAD, D., AND VERMA, S.K. A phenomenological analysis of symptoms in obsessive-compulsive neurosis. *British Journal of Psychiatry*, 1975, *127*, 342-348.

ALLEN, V.L., & LEVIN, J.M. (1971). Social support and conformity: The role of independent assessment of reality. *Journal of Experimental Social Psychology*, *7*, 48-58.

ALLYON, T., AND AZRIN, N.H., (1968) The token economy: A motivational system for therapy and rehabilitation. Englewood Cliffs, NJ. Prentice-Hall.

ALTMAN, I. *The environment and social behavior*, Monterey, Ca.: Brooks, Cole, 1975.

AMERICAN PSYCHIATRIC ASSOCIATION (1980). Diagnostic and statistical manual of mental disorders (3rd ed.) Washington, D.C., American Psychiatric Association.

AMERICAN PSYCHOLOGICAL ASSOCIATION. *Careers in Psychology*. Washington, D.C.: 1976.

AMERICAN PSYCHOLOGICAL ASSOCIATION. Ethical Principles of Psychologists. *American Psychologist*, 1981, *36*, 633-638.

AMERICAN PSYCHOLOGICAL ASSOCIATION. *Graduate Study in Psychology: 1983-1984 (16th Ed.)*, Washington, D.C.: 1982.

AMIR, Y. Contact hypothesis in ethnic relations. *Psychological Bulletin*, 1969, *71* 319-342.

ANAND, B.K. AND BROBECK, J.R. Hypothalamic control of food intake by rats and cats. *Yale Journal of Biology and Medicine*, 1951, *24*, 123-140.

ANASTASI, A. Coaching, test sophistication and developed abilities. *American Psychologist*. 1981, *36*, 1086-1093.

ANASTASI, A. *Psychological Testing* (5th Ed.), New York: Macmillan, 1982.

ANDERSON, A., AND LYNN, R. Japanese children and intelligence. *Nature*, May 1982.

ANDERSON, R.C. AND ORTONY, A. On putting apples into bottles—a problem of polysemy. *Cognitive Psychology*, 1975, *7*, 167-180.

ANDREWS, L.B. Mind control in the courtroom. *Psychology Today*, March 1982, 66-73.

ANGOFF, W.H. (ED.) *The College Board Admission Testing Program: A technical report on research and development activities relating to the Scholastic Aptitude Test and achievement tests*. New York: College Entrance Examination Board, 1971.

ARGYLE, M. *Bodily communication*. New York: International Universities Press. 1975.

ARONSON, E. (1968). Dissonance theory: Progress and problems. In R.P. Abelson, E. Aronson, W. J. McGuire, T.M. Newcomb, M.J. Rosenberg, (Eds.), *Theories of cognitive consistency: A sourcebook*. Chicago: Rand McNally.

ASCH, S.E. Effects of group pressure upon the modification and distortion of judgements. In H. Guetzkow (Ed.) *Groups, leadership and men*. Pittsburgh, Pa.: Carnegie Press, [1951].

ASCH, S.E. Studies of independence and conformity: I. a minority of one against a unanimous majority. *Psychological Monographs*. 1956, *70*, 9 (Whole #416).

ATKINSON, R.C., AND SHIFFRIN, R.M. Human memory: A proposed system and its control processes. In K.W. Spence J.T. Spence (Eds). *The psychology of learning and motivation* (Vol. 2). New York: Academic Press, 1968.

ATKINSON, R.C., AND SHIFRIN, R.M. The control of short-term memory. *Scientific American*, 1971 *225*, 82-90.

ATKINSON, R.C., AND RAUGH, M.R. An application of the mnemonic keyword method to the acquisition of a Russian vocabulary. *Journal of Experimental Psychology: Human Learning and Memory*, 1975, *104*, 126-133.

AYLLON, T. AND MICHAEL, J. The psychiatric nurse as a behavioral engineer. *Journal of the Experimental Analysis of Behavior*, 1959, *2*, 323-334.

AYLLON, T. AND AZRIN, N.H. The measurement and reinforcement of the behavior of psychotics. *Journal of the Experimental Analysis of Behavior*. 1965, *8*, 357-383.

BAHRICK, H.P.M. Maintenance of knowledge: Questions about memory we forgot to ask. *Journal of Psychology: General*, 1979, *108*, 296-308.

BAKER, T.L. AND DEMENT, W.C. Canine narcolepsy-cataplexy syndrome: evidence for an inherited monoamenergic-cholinergic imbalance. In. *Brain Mechanisms of Sleep*, D.J. McGinty (Ed.). New York: Raven Press, 1985.

BALTES, P.B. AND SCHAIE, K.W. On the plasticity of intelligence in adulthood and old age. *American Psychologist*. 1976, *31*, 720-725.

BANDURA, A. *Principles of behavior modification*. New York: Holt, Rinehart, and Winston, 1969.

BANDURA, A. (1971). Social learning theory. New York: General Learning Press.

BANDURA, A. AND WALTERS, R.H. *Adolescent aggression*. New York: Ronald Press, 1959.

BARAHAL, H.S. 1000 prefrontal lobotomies: Five to ten year follow up study. *Psychiatric Quarterly*. 1958, *32*, 653-678.

BARASH, D.P. Human ethology: Displacement activities in a dental office. *Psychological Reports*, 1974, *34*, 947-949.

BARBER, T.F.X. Suggested (hypnotic) behavior. The trance paradigm vs. an alternative paradigm. In E. Fromm and R.E. Shorr (eds.) *Hypnosis: research developments and perspectives*. Chicago: Aldine-Atherton, 1972.

BARD, P. (1934) On emotional expression after decortication with some remarks on certain theoretical views *Psychological Review*, *41*.

BARNES, V., POTTER, E.H., AND FIEDLER, F.E. Effect of interpersonal stress on the prediction of academic performance *Journal of Applied Psychology* 1983, *68*, 686-694.

BARON, R.A., AND BELL, P.A. Sexual arousal and aggression by males: Effects of type of erotic stimuli and prior provocation. *Journal of Personality and Social Psychology*. 1977, *35*, 79-87.

BARTLETT, F.C. Remembering; A study in experimental and social psychology. London: Cambridge University Press, 1932.

BATSON, C.D., COKE, J.S., CHARD, F., SMITH, D., AND TALIAFERRO. A. Generality of the ''glow of goodwill.'' Effects of mood on helping and information acquisition. *Social Psychology Quarterly*, 1979, *42*. 176-179.

BAUMRIND, D. Principles of ethical conduct in the treatment of subjects: Reactions to the draft report of the committee on ethical standards in psychological research. *American Psychologist*, 1971, *26*, 887-896.

BEAMAN, A.L., BARNES, COLE, C.M., PRESTON, M., KLENTZ, B., AND STEBLAY, N.M. (1983). Fifteen years of foot-in-the-door research: A meta-analysis. *Personality and Social Psychology Bulletin*, *9*, 181-196.

BEAR, D.M. AND FEDIO, P. Quantitative analysis of interictal behavior in temporary lobe epilepsy. *Archives of Neurology*, 1977, *34*, 454-467.

BEATTIE, G.W., CUTLER, A., AND PEARSON, M. Why is Mrs. Thatcher interrupted so often? *Nature*, 1982, *300*, 744-747.

BECK, A.T. *Cognitive therapy and the emotional disorders*. New York: International University Press, 1976.

BECK, A.T., AND YOUNG, J.E. (September, 1978). College Blues. *Psychology Today*, 80-92.

BELSKY, J. AND STEINBERG, L.D. The effects of day care: a critical review. *Child Development*, 1978, *49*, 929-949.

BEM, D.J. (1972). Self-perception theory. In L. Berkowitz (Ed.), *Advances in experimental social psychology*, (Vol. 6). New York: Academic Press.

BEM, S.L. The measurement of psychological androgyny. *Journal of Consulting and Clinical Psychology*. 1974, *42*, 155-162.

BENSON, H. *The relaxation response*. New York: Avon, 1975.

BERCHEID, E., DION, K., WALSTER, E., AND WALSTER, G.W. Physical attractiveness and dating choice: A test of the matching hypothesis. *Journal of Experimental Social Psychology*. 1971, *7*, 173-189.

BERCHEID, E., AND WALSTER, E. A little bit about love. In T.L. Huston (Ed). *Foundations of interpersonal attraction*. New York: Academic Press, 1974.

BERCHEID, E., AND WALSTER, E. *Interpersonal Attraction*. Reading, Mass.: Addison-Wesley, 1978.

BERGER, K.S. *The developing person*. New York: Worth, 1980.

BERGIN, A.E. AND LAMBERT, M.J. The evaluation of therapeutic outcomes. In S.L. Garfield and A.E. Bergin (Eds.) Handbook of psychotherapy and behavior change: an empirical analysis, 2nd Ed., pp. 139-189. New York, Wiley, 1978.

BERK, L.E. (1986) Private speech: Learning out loud. *Psychology Today* May, 1986, pp. 34-42.

BERMANT, G. AND DAVIDSON, J.M. *Biological bases for sexual behavior*. New York: Harper and Row, 1974.

BERSTEIN, I.I. Learned taste aversions in children receiving chemotherapy. *Science*, 1978, *200*, 1302-1303.

BEST, M.R., BROWN, E.R., AND SOWELL, M.K. Taste-mediated potentiation of noningestional stimuli in rats. *Learning and Motivation*, 1984, *15*, 244-258.

BEXTON, W.H., HERON, W. AND SCOTT, T.H. Effects of decreased variation in the sensory environment. *Canadian Journal of Psychology*, 1954, *8*(2), 70-76.

BIRDWHISTELL, R.L. The language of the body; The natural environment of words. In A. Silverstein (Ed.), *Human communication: Theoretical explorations*. Hillsdale, NJ: Erlbaum, 1974.

BIRREN, J.E. CUNNINGHAM, W.R., AND YAMAMATO, K. Psychology of adult development and aging. *Annual Review of Psychology*. 1983, *34*, 543-575.

BLANCHARD, E.B., AND EPSTEIN, L.H. *A biofeedback primer*. Reading, Mass. Addison-Wesley, 1978.

BLOCK, J. *Lives through time*. Berkeley, Calif.: Bancroft, 1971.

BLOCK, V. HENNEVIN, E. AND LECONTE, P. Interaction between post-trial reticular stimulation and subsequent paradoxical sleep in memory consolidation processes. In R.R. Dricker-Collin and J.L. McGaugh (Eds.) *Neurobiology of Sleep and Memory*, New York: Academic, 1977.

BLOUNT, B.G. Elicitation strategies in parental speech acts. In P.S. Dale and D. Ingram (Eds.) *Child language: an international perspective*. Baltimore: University Park Press, 1981.

BLUMENTHAL, A.L. *The Process of Cognition*. Englewood Cliffs, N.J.: Prentice-Hall, 1977.

BOCHNER, S., AND INSKO, C.A. (1966). Communicator discrepancy, source credibility, and opinion change. *Journal of Personality and Social Psychology, 4*, 614-621.

BOFFEY, P.M. Psychotherapy is as good as drug in curing depression, study finds. New York Times, May 14, 1986 p. A1 and A17.

BOGEN, J.E. Some educational implications of hemispheric specialization. In Wittrock, M.C. (Ed.) *The human brain.* Englewood Cliffs: Prentice-Hall, 1977.

BOLLES, R.C. Species-specific defense reactions and avoidance learning. *Psychological Review, 1970, 77*, 32-48

BOND, C.F., JR., AND TITUS, L.J. (1983). Social facilitation: A meta-analysis of 241 studies. *Psychological Bulletin, 94*, 265-292.

BOOTZIN, R. AND NICASSIO, P.M. Behavioral treatments for insomnia. In M. Hersen, R. Eisler, and P. Miller (eds.) *Progress in behavior modification.* New York: Academic Press. 1978.

BORHOVEC, T.D. (1982). Insomnia. *Journal of Consulting and Clinical Psychology, 50*, 880-895.

BORKOVEC, T.D., ROBINSON, E., PRUZINSKY, T. AND DePREE, J. Preliminary exploration of worry: Some characteristics and processes. *Behavior Research and Therapy, 1983, 21*, 9-16.

BORKOVEC, T., WILKINSON, L. FOLKENSBEE, R., AND LERMAN, C. Stimulus control applications to the treatment of worry. Unpublished manuscript, the Pennsylvania State University, 1983.

BOURNE, L. DOMINOWKI, R. AND LOFTUS, E. *Cognitive Processes.* Englewood Cliffs: Prentice-Hall, 1979.

BOURNE, L., DOMINOWSKI, R.L., LOFTUS, E. AND HEALY, A. *Cognitive processes (2nd Ed.).* Englewood Cliffs, N.J.: Prentice-Hall, 1986.

BOWER, G.H. AND GILLIGAN, S.G. Remembering information related to one's self. *Journal of Research in Personality, 1979, 13*, 420-432.

BOWER, G. AND KARLIN, M.B. Depth of processing pictures of faces and recognition memory. *Journal of Experimental Psychology, 1974, 103*, 751-757.

BOWER, G.H., AND TRABASSAO, T.R. Reversals prior to solution in concept identification. *Journal of Experimental Psychology, 1963, 66*, 409-418.

BOWER, G.H., AND WINZENZ, D. Comparison of associative learning strategies. *Psychonomic Science, 1970, 20*, 119-120.

BOWER, G.L. Mood and memory. *American Psychologist, 1981, 36*, 129-148.

BOWER, G.L., MONTEIRO, K.P., AND GILLIGAN, S.G. Emotional mood as a context for learning and recall. *Journal of Verbal Learning and Verbal Behavior, 1978, 17*, 573-585.

BOWER, G.L., AND HILGARD, E.R. *Theories of Learning.* Englewood Cliffs, Prentice-Hall, 1981.

BOWER, T.G.R. *A primer of infant development,* San Francisco: Freeman, 1977.

BRANSFORD, J.D., AND FRANKS, J.J. (1971) The Abstraction of linguistic ideas. *Cognitive Psychology, 2*, 331-350.

BRANSFORD, J.D., AND JOHNSON, M.K. Contextual prerequisites for understanding. Some investigations of comprehension and recall. *Journal of Verbal Learning and Verbal Behavior. 1972, 11*, 717-726.

BRANSFORD, J.D., AND JOHNSON, M.K. Considerations of some problems of comprehension. In W.G. Chase (Ed.), *Visual information processing.* New York: Academic Press, 1973.

BRANSFORD, J.D. AND McCARRELL, N.S. A cognitive approach to comprehension: some thoughts about what it means to comprehend. In W.B. Weimer and D.S., Palermo (Eds.) *Cognition and the symbolic processes.* Hillsdale, N.J. Erlbaum and Associates, 1974.

BRESNITZ, S. A study of worry. *British Journal of Social and Clinical Psychology, 1971, 10*, 271-279.

BREWER, M.B. AND KRAMER, R.M. The Psychology of Intergroup attitudes and behavior. *Annual Review of Psychology 1, 1985, 36*, 219-243.

BRIGHAM, C.C. *A study of American intelligence.* Princeton, N.J.: Princeton University Press, 1923.

BRODY, J. Personal Health. *New York Times,* April 6, 1983.

BROVERMAN, I.K., VOGEL, S.R., BROVERMAN, D.M., CLARKSON, F.E., AND ROSENKRANTZ, P.S. Sex role stereotypes: A current appraisal. *Journal of Social Issues, 1972, 28*, 59-78.

BROWMAN, C.P., SAMPSON, M.G., GUJAVARTY, K.S., AND MITLER, M.M. The drowsy crowd. *Psychology Today,* August 1982, 35-38.

BROWN, G.W., BONE, M. DALISON, B. AND WING, J.K. *Schizophrenia and social care.* London: Oxford University Press. 1966.

BROWN, P. AND JENKINS, H. Autoshaping of the pigeon's key-peck. *Journal of the Experimental Analysis of Behavior, 1968, 11*, 1-8.

BROWN R., AND HULK, J. (1977). Flashbulb memories. *Cognition, 5*, 73-99.

BROWN, R., AND McNEILL, D. The "tip of the tongue" phenomenon. *Journal of Verbal Learning and Verbal Behavior, 1966, 5*, 325-337.

BROWN, R.W. The first sentences of child and chimp. In R.W. Brown (Ed.) *Psycholinguistics: Selected Papers.* New York: Free Press, 1970.

BROWN, S.S., LIEBERMAN, E.W., AND MILLER, W.B. Young adults as partners and planners. Paper presented to Public Health Association, 1975.

BROWNMILLER, S. Feminism confronts pornography. *Los Angeles Times.* August 5, 1979.

BRUCE, R.L. *Fundamentals of Physiological Psychology.* New York: Holt, Rinehart and Winston, 1977.

BRUNER, J.S. *Beyond the information given. Studies in the psychology of knowing.* J.M. Anglin (Ed.), New York: Norton, 1973.

BURNASHA, R.F. The effects of behavior modeling training upon manager's behaviors and employee's perceptions. *Personnel Psychology, 1976, 29*, 329, 335.

BUSCHBAUM, M.S., AND HAIER, R.J. (1983). Psychopathology: Biological Approaches. *Annual Review and Psychology, 34*, 401-430.

BUTLER, N. Late postnatal consequences of fetal malnutrition. In M. Winick (Ed.), *Nutrition and fetal development.* New York: Wiley, 1974.

BUTLER, R.A. The effect of deprivation of visual incentives on visual exploration motivation in monkeys. *Journal of Comparative and Physiological Psychology, 1957, 50*, 177-179.

BUTTER, C.M. Contrasting effects of lateral striate and superior colliculus lesions on visual discrimination performance in rhesus monkeys. *Journal of Comparative and Physiological Psychology, 1979, 93*, 522-537.

BUTTERFIELD, F. School's use of physical punishment therapy is challenged. New York Times, November 18.

BYRNE, D. *The attraction paradigm.* New York: Academic Press, 1971.

CAMPBELL, J.P., AND PRITCHARD, R.D. Motivation theory in industrial and organizational psychology. In M.D. Dunnette (Ed.) *Handbook of Industrial and Organizational Psychology.* Chicago: Rand-McNally.

CARLSON, N.R. *The physiology of behavior.* (2nd Ed.). Boston: Allyn and Bacon. 1981.

CARTWRIGHT, R. *A primer on sleep and dreaming.* Reading. Mass.: Addison-Wesley, 1978.

CHASE, M. Every 90 minutes a brainstorm. *Psychology Today,* 1979. p. 172.

CHERRY, E.C. Some experiments on the recognition of speech, with one and two ears. *Journal of the Acoustical Society of America,* 1953, *25*, 975-979.

CHI, J. DOOLING, E., AND GILES, F. Left-Right Asymmetrics in the temporal Speech Areas of the Human Fetus. *Archives of Neurology, 1972. 34*, 346-348.

CHILMAN, C.S. Adolescent Sexuality in a Changing American Society. (2nd. Ed.). New York: John Wiley & Sons. 1983.

CHOMSKY, N. A review of B.F. Skinner's *Verbal Behavior Language,* 1959, *35*, 26-58.

CHUKOVSKY, K.I. *From two to five.* Berkeley: University of California Press, 1968.

CLARK, H.H., AND CLARK, E.V. *Psychology and language.* New York: Harcourt Brace Jovanovich, 1977.

CLARK, R.D., III AND WORD, L.E. Where is the apathetic bystander? Situational characteristics of the emergency. *Journal of Personality and Social Psychology.* 1974, *29*, 279-287.

CLARKE-STEWART, K.A. And daddy makes three: The father's impact on mother and young child. *Child Development.* 1978, *49*, 466-478.

CLARKE-STEWART, K.A., AND FEIN, G.G. Early childhood programs. In P.H. Mussen (Ed) Handbook of child psychology (4th ed.) Vol. 2, N.M. Maith and J.J. Campos (Eds.) Infancy and Developmental psychobiology. New York: Wiley, 1983.

COHEN. S., GLASS, D.C., AND SINGER, J.E. Apartment noise, auditory discrimination, and reading ability in children. *Journal of Experimental Social Psychology, 9*, 1973, 407-422.

COHEN, S., EVANS, G.W., KRANTZ, D.S., AND STOKOLS, D. Physiological, motivational and cognitive effects of aircraft noise on children: Moving from the laboratory to the field. *American Psychologist, 35*, 231-243, 1980.

COHEN, S., AND WEINSTEIN, N. Nonauditory effects of noise on behavior and health. *Journal of Social Issues.* 1981, *37*, 36-70.

COLBY, K. Computer-aided language development in non-speaking children. *Archives of General Psychiatry, 1968. 19*, 641-651.

COLEMAN, J.C. (1980). Contemporary Psychology and Effective Behavior (4th ed.) Glenview, IL: Scott, Foresman.

COLEMAN, J., BUTCHER, J.N., AND CARSON, R.C. (1984) Abnormal Psychology and Modern Life (7th ed.), Glenview, IL: Scott Foresman.

COLEMAN, S.J. Comments on responses to youth: Transition to adulthood. *School Review, 1974, 83*, 96-97, 139-144.

COLLINS, G. Stranger's stare: baleful or beckoning? *New York Times,* April 11, 1983, A22.

COMBS, B. AND SLOVIC, P. Newspaper Coverage of Causes of Death 1979 *Journalism Quarterly,* Vol. 56, No. 4, 837-843.

CONRAD, R. Acoustic confusions in immediate memory. *British Journal of Psychology, 1964, 55*, 75-84.

COOK, S.W., AND HARRIS, R.E. The verbal conditioning of the galvanic skin response. *Journal of Experimental Psychology, 1937, 21*, 202-210.

COREN, S. PORAC, C., AND WARD, L.M. *Sensation and Perception.* Academic Press, 1979, pp. 112, 120

COX, T. (1978). Stress. Baltimore, MD: University Park Press.

CRAIGHEAD, W.D., KENNEDY, R.E., RACZYNSKI, J.M., AND DOW, M.G. Affective disorders—unipolar. In S.M. Turner and M. Hersen (Eds.). *Adult psychopathology: A behavior perspective* New York: Wiley, 1982.

CRAIGHEAD, W.E., KAZDIN, A.E., AND MAHONEY, M.J. *Behavior modification: Principles, issues, and applications.* Boston: Houghton Mifflin, 1976.

CRAIK, F.I.M., AND LOCKHART, R.S. Levels of processing: A framework for memory research. *Journal of Verbal Learning and Verbal Behavior, 1972, 11*, 671-684.

CRAIK, F.I.M., AND WATKINS, M.J. The role of rehearsal in short-term memory. *Journal of Verbal Learning and Verbal Behavior, 1973, 12*, 599-607.

CRAIK, F.I.M., AND TULVING, E. Depth of processing and the retention of words in episodic memory. *Journal of Experimental Psychology: General, 1975, 104*, 268-294.

CRAIN, W.C. *Theories of development,* Englewood Cliffs: Prentice-Hall, 1980.

CRESPI L.P. Quantitative variation of incentive and performance in the white rat. *American Journal of Psychology.* 1942, *55*, 467-517.

CROOK, T.H. AND MILLER, N.E. The challenge of Alzheimer's disease. pp. 1245-1250. *American Psychologist,* 1985, Vol. 40, no. 11.

DARWIN, C. *The expression of emotion in man and animals.* Chicago: University of Chicago Press, 1965. (Originally published in 1862.)

DAVIS, M., ESHELMAN, E.R., AND McKAY, M. *The relaxation and stress reduction workbook.* Oakland, Ca.: New Harbinger Publications, 1982.

DAVISON, G.C. AND NEALE, J.M. *Abnormal psychology: An experimental approach.* 3rd Ed. New York: Wiley, 1982.

DEAUX, K. AND EMSWILLER, T. Explanations of successful performance on sex-linked tasks: What is skill for the male is luck for the female. *Journal of Personality and Social Psychology,* 1974, *29*, 80-85.

DeCharmes, R., and Muir, M.S. Motivation: social approaches. *Annual Review of Psychology*, 1978, *29*, 91-113.

Deci, E.L. The effects of contingent and non-contingent rewards and controls on intrinsic motivation. *Organizational Behavior and Human Performance*. 1972, *8*, 217-229.

Deci, E.L. *Intrinsic Motivation*. New York: Plenum, 1975.

Decker, P.J., and Nathan, B.R. Behavior modeling training. New York: Praeger, 1985.

Deffenbacher, J.L. Worry and emotionality in test anxiety. In I.G. Sarason (Ed.). *Test anxiety: Theory, research, and application*. Hillsdale, N.J.: Erlbaum, 1980.

DeLongis, A., Coyne, J.C., Dakoe, G., Folkman, S., and Lazarus, R.S. Relationship of daily hassles, uplifts, and major life events to health status. *Health Psychology*. 1982, *1*, 119-136.

Dement, W. The effect of dream deprivation. *Science, 131*, 1705-1707.

DeNike, L.D., and Speilberger, C.D. Induced mediating states in verbal conditioning. *Journal of Verbal Learning and Verbal Behavior*, 1963, *1*, 339-345.

DePaulo, B.M., and Bonvillian, J.D. The effect of the language development of special characteristics of speech addressed to children. *Journal of Psycholinguistic Research*, 1978, *7*, 189-211.

Deregowski, J.B. (1972, November). Pictorial perception and culture *Scientific American*, 82-83.

Desor, J.A., Maller, D. and Turner, R.E. Taste acceptance of sugars by human infants. *Journal of Comparative and Physiological Psychology*, 84, 1973, 496-501.

Deutsch, M. and Gerard, H.B. A study of normative and informational social influences upon individual judgment. *Journal of Abnormal and Social Psychology*. 1955, *51*, 629-636.

Dewan, E. The programming (P) hypothesis for REM sleep. In E. Hartmann (Ed.). *Sleep and Dreaming*. Boston: Little Brown, 1970.

Diamond, S., Baldwin, R., and Diamond, R. *Inhibition and choice*. New York: Harper and Row, 1963.

Doherty, W., and Jacobson, N. (1982). Marriage and the Family. In B. Wolman (Ed.), *Handbook of developmental psychology*. Englewood Cliffs, N.J.: Prentice-Hall.

Donnerstein, E. Donnerstein, M., and Evans, R. Erotic stimuli and aggression. Facilitation or inhibition. *Journal of Personality and Social Psychology*, 1975, *32*, 237-244.

Donnerstein, E., and Wilson, D.W. Effects of noise and perceived control on ongoing and subsequent aggressive behavior. *Journal of Personality and Social Psychology*. 1976, *34*, 774-781.

Douvan, E.A., and Adelson, J. (1966). *The adolescent experience*. New York: Wiley.

Dubos, R. *Man adapting*. New Haven, Conn.: Yale University Press, 1965.

Duffy, E. *Activation and Behavior*. New York: Wiley, 1962.

Duncker, K. On problem solving. *Psychological Monographs*, 1945. 58:5, Whole Number 270.

Dutton, D.G., and Aron, A.P. Some evidence for heightened sexual attraction under conditions of high anxiety. *Journal of Personality and Social Psychology*, 1974, *30*, 510-517.

Dworetzhy, T. Old dog, new trick. *Psychology Today*, January 1985, p. 57.

Eimas, P.D. Speech perception in early infancy. In L.B. Cohen and P. Salapatek (Eds.), *Infant perception from sensation to cognition* (Vol. 11). New York: Academic Press, 1975.

Ekman, P., Levenson, R.W., and Friesen, W.V. Autonomic nervous system activity distinguishes among emotions. *Science*, vol. 221, September 1983, pp. 208-210.

Ekman, P. and Oster, H. Facial expressions of emotion. *Annual Review of Psychology*. 1979, *30*, 527-554.

Elkind, D. Egocentrism in adolescence. *Child Development*, 1967, *38*, 1025-1033.

Elkind, D., and Weiner, I.B. *Development of the child*. New York: Wiley, 1978.

Ellis, A. *Reason and emotion in psychotherapy*. New York: Lyle Stuart, 1962.

Endler, N., and Magnusson, D. *Interactional psychology and personality*. Washington, D.C.: Hemisphere, 1976.

Epstein, R. Kirshnit, C.E., Lanza, R.P., and Rubin, L.C. "Insight" in the pigeon: antecedents and determinants of an intelligent performance. Nature, 308 larch, 1984, pp 61-62. This was not cited, nor was any study with pigeons mentioned.

Ericsson, M.A., and Chase, W.G. (1982). Exceptional memory. *American Scientist, 70*, 607-615.

Erikson, E. *Childhood and society*. (rev. Ed.) New York: Norton, 1963.

Erikson, E. *Identity, youth and crisis*. New York: Norton, 1968.

Exner, J.E., Jr. *The Rorschach: a comprehensive system*. New York: Wiley, 1974.

Exner, J.E., Jr. *The Rorschach: a comprehensive system. Volume 2: current research and advanced interpretations*. New York: Wiley Interscience, 1978.

Eysenck, H.J. *The biological basis of personality*. Springfield, Ill.: Charles C. Thomas, 1967.

Fazio, R.H. (1986). How do attitudes guide behavior? In R.M. Sorrentino and E.T. Higgins (Eds.), *Motivation and cognition: Foundations of social behavior*, (204-243). New York: Guilford Press.

Fearn, R.W. Hearing loss caused by amplified pop music. *Journal of Sound and Vibration*. 1976, *46*, 462-464.

Fearn, R.W. Hearing loss caused by different exposures to amplified pop music. *Journal of Sound and Vibration*. 1976, *47*, 454-456.

Fechner, G. Elemente der psychophysik. 1860. Translated by H.E. Alder. *Elements of psychophysics*. New York; Holt, 1966.

Feldman-Summers, S., and Kiesler, S.B. Those who are number two try harder. The effect of sex on attributions of causality. *Journal of Personality and Social Psychology*, 1974, *30* 846-855.

Ferster, C.B., and Skinner, B.F. *Schedules of reinforcement*. New York: Appleton-Century Crofts, 1957.

Feshbach, S. and Malmuth, N. Sex and aggression: Proving the link. *Psychology Today*, November 1978.

Festinger, L. *A theory of cognitive dissonance*. Stanford, California: Stanford University Press, 1957.

Festinger, L., Schachter, S., and Back, K. *Social pressures in informal groups: A study of human factors in housing*. New York: Harper, 1951.

Fiedler, F.E. and Lestier, A.F. Leader intelligence and task performance: A test of the multiple screen model. *Organizational Behavior and Human Performance*. 1977, *20* 1-14.

Fincher, J. *Sinister people: The looking glass world of the lefthander: scientific shaggy-dog story*. New York: Putnam, 1977.

Fischer, R. A cartography of the ecstatic and meditative states. *Science*. 1971, *174*, 897-904.

Fishbein, M., and Ajzen, I. (1975). *Belief, attitude, intention, and behavior: An introduction to theory and research*. Reading, MA: Addison-Wesley.

Fisher, K. DSM-III-R Protest: Critics say psychiatry has been stonewalling. *Monitor, 17*, July 1986, pp. 4-5.

Fisher, R.P., and Craik, F.I.M. Interaction between encoding and retrieval operations in cued recall. *Journal of Experimental Psychology: Human Learning and Memory*, 1977, *3*, 701-711.

Flavell, J. and Wohlwill, J. Formal and functional aspects of cognitive development. In D. Elkind and J. Flavell (Eds.). *Studies of cognitive development: Essays in honor of Jean Piaget*. New York: Oxford University Press.

Flavell, J.H. and Wellman, H.M. Metamemory. In R.V. Kail and J.W. Hagen (eds.). *Memory in cognitive development*. Hillsdale, N.J.: Erlbaum, 1976.

Fleishman, E.A. Toward a taxonomy of human performance. *American Psychologist*, 1975, *30*, 1127-1149.

Flood, R. and Seager, C. A retrospective examination of psychiatric case records of patients who subsequently commit suicide. *British Journal of Psychiatry*. 1968, *114*, 443-450.

Fodor, J.A. and Garrett, M. Some reflections on competence and performance. In J. Lyons and R. Wales (Eds), *Psycholinguistics Papers*. Edinburgh: Edinburgh University Press, 1966.

Ford. D.H. and Urban, H.B. *Systems of psychotherapy: A comparative study*. New York: Wiley, 1963.

Foss, D.J., and Mahes, D.T. Psycholinguistics. Englewood Cliffs, N.J.: Prentice-Hall, 1978.

Fouts, R. Acquistion and testing of gestural signs in four young chimpanzees. *Science*, 1973, *180*, 978-980.

Fouts, R.S. Capacity for language in great apes. In R.H. Tuttle (Eds.), *Socioecology and Psychology of Primates*. The Hague: Mouton, 1975b. 371-390.

Fox, R. and McDaniel, C. The perception of biological motion by human infants. *Science, 218*, 486-487.

Fox, S.S. Self-maintained sensory input and sensory deprivation in monkeys: a behavioral and neuropharmacological study. *Journal of Comparative and Physiological Psychology*, 1962, *55*, 438-444.

Fozard, J.L., Wolf, E., Bell, B., McFarland, R.A. and Podolsky, S. Visual perception and communication. In J.E. Birren and K.W. Schaie (Eds.), *Handbook of the Psychology of Aging*. New York: Van Nostrand. 1977.

Frank, J.D. 1973 Persuasion and healing: a comparative study of psychotherapy. (revised edition) Baltimore, Md. Johns Hopkins University Press.

Frankenhauser, M. Overstimulation—a threat to the quality of life. In *Man in the communications system of the future*. Swedish Cabinet Office. Secretariat for Future Studies. Stockholm, 1974.

Franhenhaeuser, M. The psychoendocrine response to challenge. In T.M. Dembroski, T.H. Schmidt, and G. Blümchen (Eds.), *Biobehavioral Bases of Coronary Heart Disease*. Basel, New York: 1982.

Frankenhaeuser, M. Psychobiological aspects of life stress. In S. Levine and H. Usrin, *Coping and Health*. New York: Plenum, 1980, pp. 203-223.

Frankenhaeuser, M. Coping with stress at work, *International Journal of Health Services*, vol. 11, 4, 1981, pp. 491-510.

Frankenhaeuser, M; Lundberg, U., Forsman, L. Dissociation between sympathetic-adrenal and pituitary-adrenal responses to an achievement situation characterized by high controllability. *Biol. Psychol. 10*, 79-91 (1980).

Freedman, J.L. *Crowding and behavior*. San Francisco: W.H. Freeman, 1975.

Freedman, J.L. and Fraser, S.C. Compliance without pressure: The foot-in-the-door technique. *Journal of Personality and Social Psychology*, 1966, *4*, 195-202.

Freedman, J.L., Sears, D.O. and Carlsmith, J.M. *Social Psychology* (Fourth Edition) Englewood Cliffs: Prentice-Hall, 1981.

Friedman, M. and Rosenman, R.H. *Type A behavior and your heart*. New York: Alfred A. Knopf, 1974.

Friedrich, L.K. and Stein, A.H. Aggressive and prosocial television programs and the natural behavior of preschool children. *Monographs of the Society for Research in Child Development*, 1973, *38*, No. 151.

Fritsch, G.T. and Hitzig, E. Uber die elektrische Erregbarkeit des Grosshirns. Arch. Anat. Physiol. Wiss. Med. (Leipzig) 1870, *37*, 30.

Fromkin, V.A., Krashen, S., Curtiss, S., Rigler, D., and Rigler, M. The development of language in Genie: A case of language acquisition beyond the "critical period." *Brain and Language*. 1974, *1*, 81-108.

Garcia, J. and Koelling, R.A. Relation of cue to consequence in avoidance learning. *Psychonomic Science*. 1966, *4*, 123-124.

Gardner, B.T., and Gardner, R.A. Evidence for sentence constituents in the early utterances of child and chimpanzee. *Journal of Experimental Psychology: General*, 1975, *3*, 244-267.

Gardner, R.C., and Lambert, W.E. *Attitudes and motivation in second-language learning*, Rowley, Mass: Newbury House, 1972.

GARSON, B. *All the livelong day.* New York: Penguin, 1975.

GAZZANIGA, M.S. Review of the split brain. In M.C. Wittrock (Ed.). *The Human Brain*, Englewood Cliffs: Prentice-Hall, 1977.

GEEN, R., AND O'NEAL, E. Activation of cue elicited aggression by general arousal. *Journal of Personality and Social Psychology*, 1969, *11*, 289-292.

GELDARD, F.A. *The Human Senses.* New York: Wiley, 1972 p. 23.

GELLER, E. Study: Less is drunk when it's in a glass. Paper presented at the American Psychological Association meeting, 1984.

GEOFFRION, L.D. AND GEOFFRION, O.P. Computers and reading instruction. Reading, MA.: Addison-Wesley, 1983.

GERGEN, K.J. The codification of research ethics: views of a Doubting Thomas. *American Psychologist.* 1973, *28*, 907-912.

GESCHWIND, N. The anatomical basis of hemispheric differentiation. In S.J. Diamond and J.G. Beaumont (eds.). *Hemisphere Function in Human Brain.* London: Paul Elek, 1974, pp. 7-24.

GETZELS, J.W. AND JACKSON, P.W. The highly intelligent and the highly creative adolescent. A summary of some research findings. In C.W. Taylor and F. Barron (Eds.). *Scientific Creativity.* New York: Wiley, 1963.

GIBBS, J.C. Kohlberg's stages of moral judgment: A constructive critique. *Harvard Educational Review.* 1977. *47*, 43-61.

GIRDANA, D. AND EVERLY, G. *Controlling stress and tension: a holistic approach.* Englewood Cliffs,: Prentice-Hall, 1979.

GLASER, R. Education and thinking: the role of knowledge. *American Psychologist*, 1984, *39*, 93-102.

GLASER, R. All's well that begins and ends with both knowledge and process: a reply to Sternberg. *American Psychologist*, 1985, *40*, 573-574.

GLASS, D.C. *Behavior patterns, stress, and coronary disease.* Hillsdale, N.J.: Lawrence Erlbaum, 1977.

GLASS, D.C., AND SINGER, J. *Urban stress,* New York: Academic Press. 1972.

GLICK, P.C. The future of the American family. *Current Population Reports (Special Studies Series P-23, #78).* Washington, D.C. U.S. Govt. Printing Office, 1978.

GLUCKSBERG, S., AND COWEN, G.N., JR. Memory for nonattended auditory material. *Cognitive Psychology*, 1970. *1*, 149-156.

GODDARD, H.H. Mental tests and the immigrant. *Journal of Delinquency*, 1917, *2*. 243-277.

GOLDFRIED, M.R. 1980. Toward the delineation of therapeutic change principles *American Psychologist, 35*, 991-999.

GOLEMAN, D.A. A taxonomy of meditation-specific altered states. *Journal of Altered States of Consciousness.* 1978, *4*, 203-213.

GOODMAN, P.S. An examination of referents used in the evaluation of pay. *Organizational Behavior and Human Performance.*, 1974, *12*, 170-195.

GOULD, S.J. *The mismeasure of man.* New York: Norton, 1981.

GREEN, S.G., AND MITCHELL, T.R., Attributional processes of leaders in leader-member interactions. *Organizational Behavior and Human Performance*, 1979, *23*, 429-458.

GREENBERG, J.H., OSGOOD, C.E. AND JENKINS, J.J. Memorandum concerning language universals. In Greenberg, J.H. (Ed.), *Universals of Language (2nd Ed.)*, Cambridge: MIT Press, 1966.

GREGORY, R. The intelligent eye. New York. McGraw-Hill, 1970.

GREGORY, W.L., CIALDINI, R.B., AND CARPENTER, K.M. (1982). Self-relevant scenarios as mediators of likelihood estimates and compliance: Does imagining make it so? *Journal of Personality and Social Psychology, 43*, 89-99.

GRIBBIN, K., SHAIE, K.W., AND PARHAM, I.A. Complexity of life style and maintenance of intellectual abilities. *Journal of Social Issues.* 1980, *36*, pp. 47-61.

GRINDER, J.J., AND ELGIN, S.H. *Guide to transformational grammar.* New York: Holt, Rinehart and Winston. 1973.

GROSSMAN, S.P. *A textbook of physiological psychology.* New York: John Wiley, 1967.

GROSSMAN, S.P. The biology of motivation. *Annual Review of Psychology*, 1979, *30*, 209-242.

GUILFORD, J.P. The three faces of intellect. *American Psychologist*, 1959, *14*, 469-479.

GUILFORD, J.P. Factorial angles to psychology. *Psychological Review.* 1961, *68*, 1-20.

GUILFORD, J.P. *The nature of human intelligence.* New York: McGraw-Hill. 1967.

GUILFORD, J.P. The structure of intelligence. In D.K. Whitla (Ed.), *Handbook of measurements and assessment in the behavioral sciences.* Reading. Mass.: Addison Wesley. 1968.

GUNNER-SWENSON, F. AND JENSEN, K. Frequency of mental disorders in old age. *Acta Psychiatrica Scandinavia.* 1976, *53*, 283-297.

GUNTER, B., CLIFFORD, B.R., AND BERRY C. Release from proactive interference with television news items. Evidence for encoding dimensions within televised news. *Journal of Experimental Psychology: Human Learning and Memory*, 1980, *6*, 216-223.

GYNTHER, R.A. The effects of anxiety and of situational stress on communicative efficiency. *Journal of Abnormal and Social Psychology*, 1957, *54*, 274-276.

HACKMAN, J.R. Attributes of organizations and their effects on organization members. In M.D. Dunnette (Ed.). *Handbook of Industrial and organizational psychology.* Chicago: Rand-McNally. 1976.

HALL, G.S. Adolescence. New York: Appleton, 1904,

HALL, J.F. *An invitation to learning and memory.* Boston: Allyn and Bacon, 1982.

HAMILTON, R.G. AND ROBERTSON, M.H. Examiner influence on the Holtzman inkblot technique. *Journal of Projective Techniques and Personality Assessment*, 1966, *30*, 553-558.

HARLESTON, B.W. Test anxiety and performance in problem-solving situations. *Journal of Personality*, 1962, *30*, 557-573.

HARLOW, H. Learning to learn. In S. Koch (Ed.). *Psychology; a study of science, Vol. 11.* New York: McGraw-Hill, 1959.

HARLOW, H. AND HARLOW, M. Social deprivation in monkeys. *Scientific American*, 1962, *207*, 136-146.

HASTORF, A., AND CANTRIL, H. They saw a game: a case study. *Journal of Abnormal and Social Psychology.* 1954, *49*, 129-134.

HAYES, K.J., AND HAYES, C. The intellectual development of a home-raised chimpanzee. *Proceedings of the American Philosophical Society*, 1951, *95*, 105-109.

HAYES, J.R. *The complete problem solver.* Philadelphia: Franklin Institute Press, 1981.

HECKLER, M.M. The fight against Alzheimer's disease. pp. 1240-1244. *American Psychologist*, 1985, Vol. 40, no.11.

HEFFERLINE, R.F. AND KEENAN, B. Amplitude—induction gradient of a small-scale (covert) operant. *Journal of the Experimental Analysis of Behavior*, 1963, *6*, 307-315.

HEIDER, E.R. Universals in color naming and memory. *Journal of Experimental Psychology*, 1972, *93*, 10-20.

HEINONEN, O.P., SLONE, D. AND SHAPIRO, S. *Birth defects and drugs in pregnancy.* Littleton. Mass.: Publishing Sciences Group, 1976.

HERGENHAHN, B.R. *An introduction to theories of learning.* (2nd Ed.). Englewood Cliffs: Prentice-Hall, 1982.

HERON, W. The pathology of boredom. *Scientific American*, 1957, *196*, 52-56.

HERSHENSON, M., KESSEN, W. AND MUNSINGER. H. Ocular orientation in the human newborn infant: a close look at some positive and negative results. In Wather-Dunn (Ed.), *Models for the perception of speech and visual form.* Cambridge. Mass.: MIT Press, 1967: 282-290.

HESS, ECHARD, H. Attitude and pupil size. *Scientific American*, 1965, *212*, 46-54.

HESTON, L.L. Psychiatric disorders in foster home reared children of schizophrenic mothers. *British Journal of Psychiatry*, 1966, *112*, 819-825.

HETHERINGTON, A.W. AND RANSON, S. W. Hypothalmic lesions and adiposity in the rat. *Anatomical Record.* 1940, *78*, 149-172.

HIGHAM, E. Sexuality in the infant and neonate: Birth to two years. In B.B. Wolman, and J. Money (Eds.). *Handbook of Human Sexuality.* Englewood Cliffs, N.J.: Prentice-Hall, 1980.

HILGARD, E.R. Hypnosis. *Annual Review of Psychology*, 1975, *26*, 19-44.

HILGARD, E.R. *Divided Consciousness.* New York: Wiley, 1977.

HIRSCH, H.V.B., AND SPINELL, D.N. Modification of the distribution of receptive field orientation in cats by selective visual exposure during development. *Experimental Brain Research*, 1971, *13*, 509-527.

HJELLE, L.A., AND ZIEGLER, D.J. *Personality theories.* New York: McGraw-Hill, 1981.

HOBSON, J.A., MCCARLEY, R.W., AND WYZINSKI, P.W. Sleep cycle oscillation: Reciprocal discharge by two brainstem neuronal groups. *Science*, 1975, *189*, 55-58.

HOCHBERG, J. *Perception.* Englewood Cliffs: Prentice-Hall, 1978.

HOKANSON, J.E. *The physiological bases of motivation.* New York: Wiley, 1969.

HOLMES, T.H., AND RAHE, R.H. (1967). The social readjustment rating scale. *Journal of Psychosomatic Research*, *11*, 213-218.

HOLUSHA, J. Rethinking Designs of Car Dashboards. New York Times, March 7, 1985, pp. C1, C12.

HOLZMAN, T.E., GLASER, R. AND PELLEGRINO, J.W. Process training derived from a computer simulation theory. *Memory and Cognition*, 1976, *4*, 349-356.

HOPKINS, J.D. AND STANLEY, J.C. *Educational and psychological measurement and evaluation* (6th ed.). Englewood Cliffs: Prentice-Hall, 1981.

HORN, J.L. Human abilities: A review of research and theory in the early 1970s. *Annual Review of Psychology*. 1976, *27*, 437-485.

HUBEL, D.H., AND WIESEL, T.N. Receptive fields, binocular interaction, and functional architecture in the cat's visual cortex. *Journal of Physiology*, 1962, *160*, 106-154.

HUGHS, J., SMITH, T.W., KOSTERLITZ, H.W., FORTHERGILL, L.A., MORGAN, G.A., AND MORRIS, H.R. Identification of two related peptides from the brain with potent opiate agonist activity. *Nature*, 1975, *258*. 577.

HULL, C. *Principles of behavior.* New York: Appleton-Century-Crofts, 1943.

HUNT, R.R., AND ELLIOT, J.M. The role of nonsemantic information in memory: Orthographic distinctiveness effects on retention. *Journal of Experimental Psychology: General*, 1980, *109*, 49-74.

HURVITCH, L.M., AND JAMESON, D. An opponent process theory of color vision. *Psychological Review*, 1957, *64*, 384-404.

HUXLEY, A. *The Doors of Perception.* New York: Harper & Row, 1954.

HYDE, T.S., AND JENKINS, J.J. The differential effects of incidental tasks on the organization of recall of a list of highly associated words. *Journal of Experimental Psychology*, 1969, *82*, 472-481.

INHELDER, B. AND PIAGET, J. *The growth of logical thinking from childhood to adolescence.* New York: Basic Books, 1958.

ISAACS, W., THOMAS, J., AND GOLDIAMOND, I. Application of operant conditioning to reinstate verbal behavior in psychotics. *Journal of Speech and Hearing Disorders.* 1960, *25*, 8-12.

ISEN, A.M. Success, failure, attention and reaction to others: The warm glow of success. *Journal of Personality and Social Psychology*, 1970, *15*, 294-301.

ISEN, A.M., AND LEVIN, P.F. Effect of feeling good on helping: cookies and kindness. *Journal of Personality and Social Psychology*, 1972, *21*, 384-388.

ISEN, A.M., CLARK, M. AND SCHWARTZ, M.F. Duration of the effect of good mood on helping: "Footprints on the sands of time." *Journal of Personality and Social Psychology*, 1976, *34*, 385-393.

JACKSON, J.M., AND HARKINS, S.G. (1985). Equity in effort: An explanation of the social loafing effect. *Journal of Personality and Social Psychology*, 49, 1199-1206.

JACOBS, B.L. AND TRULSON, M.E. (1979) Mechanism of action of LSD. *American Scientist,* 67, 396-404.

JACOBSON, E. *Progressive relaxation.* 2d ed. Chicago: Chicago Press, 1938.

JAMES, W. *Principles of Psychology,* New York: Holt, Rinehart and Winston, 1890.

JAMESON, D., AND HURVICH L.M. Note on factors influencing the relation between stereoscopic acuity and observation distance. *Journal of the Optical Society of America,* 1959, 49, 639.

JANIS, I. *Victims of groupthink.* Boston: Houghton-Mifflin, 1972.

JENKINS, J.G., AND DALLENBACH, K.M. (1924). Oblivescence during sleep and waking. American Journal of Psychology, 35, 605-612.

JENKINS, W.C. The tactual discrimination of shapes of coding aircraft type controls. In P.M. Pitts (Ed.). *Psychologcal research on equipment design.* Washington, DC. U.S. Govt. Printing Office, 1947.

JOHNSON-LAIRD, P.N. AND STEEDMAN, M. The psychology of Syllogisms. *Cognitive Psychology,* 1978, 10, 64-69.

JOHNSTON, L.D., BACHMAN, J.G., AND O'MALLEY, P.M. *Student drug use in America: 1975-1980.* Rockville, Maryland: National Institute on Drug Abuse, 1980.

JONES, E. *The life and work of Sigmund Freud.* New York: Basic Books, 1955.

JONES, E.E. AND DAVIS, K.E. From acts to dispositions: The attribution process in person perception. In L. Berkowitz (Ed.), *Advances in experimental social psychology (Vol. 2)* New York: Academic Press, 1965.

JONES, H.H., AND COHEN, A. Noise as a health hazard at work, in the community, and in the home. *USPHS, Public Health Reports,* 1968, 83, 533-536.

JONES, K.L. The Fetal Alcohol Syndrome. In R.D. Harbison (Ed.), *Perinatal addiction.* New York: Halsted, 1975.

JULIEN, R.M. A Primer of Drug Action. (4th ed.) San Francisco: Freeman, 1984

KAGAN, J., KEARSLEY, R.B. AND ZELAZO, P.R. *Infancy: Its place in Human Development.* Cambridge: Harvard University Press, 1978.

KALAT, J.W. Biological Psychology (2nd ed.) Belmont, Ca: Wadsworth, 1984

KALE, R.J., KAYE, J.H., WHALEN, P.A. AND HOPKINS, B.L. The effects of reinforcement on the modification, maintenance and generalization of social responses of mental patients. *Journal of Applied Behavior Analysis,* 1968, 1, 307-314.

KALES, A. AND KALES, J. Recent advances in the diagnosis and treatment of sleep disorders. In G. Usdin (Ed.) *Sleep research and clinical practice.* New York: Brunner Mazel, 61-94.

KALISH, H.I. The relationship between discriminability and generalization: A re-evaluation. *Journal of Experimental Psychology,* 1958, 55, 637-644.

KAMIN, L. The science and politics of IQ. Hillsdale: Erlbaum, 1974.

KAPLAN, H.S. *The new sex therapy.* New York: Brunner/Mazel, 1974.

KAPLAN, P. *A child's odyssey: Child and adolescent development.* St. Paul: West Publishing Co., 1986.

KARASEK, R.A. Job demands, job decision latitude and mental strain: implications for job redesign. Administrative Science Quarterly, 1979, 24, 285-308.

KASAMATSU, T. Visual cortical neurons influenced by the oculomotor input: Characterization of their receptive field properties. *Brain Research,* 1976, 113, 271-292.

KASTENBAUM, R. *Humans developing.* Boston: Allyn and Bacon, 1979.

KATONA, G. *Organizing and memorizing.* New York: Columbia University Press, 1940.

KATZMAN, R. (ED.) Biological Aspects of Alzheimer's disease. Banbury Report #15. Cold Spring Harbor Laboratory, 1983.

KEESEY, R.E. AND POWLEY, T.L. Hypothalmic regulation of body weight. *American Scientist,* 1975, 63, 558-565.

KELLOGG, W.N., AND KELLOGG, L.A. *The ape and the child.* New York: McGraw-Hill, 1933.

KELLY, G.A. *The psychology of personal constructs.* New York: Norton, 1955.

KELLEY, H.H. Attribution theory in social psychology. *Nebraska Symposium on Motivation.* Lincoln: University of Nebraska Press, 1967.

KENDLER, H.H. AND KENDLER, T.S. Vertical and horizontal processes in problem solving. *Psychological Review,* 1962, 69, 1-16.

KENDLER, H.H. AND KENDLER, T.S. From discrimination learning to cognitive development: A nonbehavioral odyssey. In W.K. Estes (Ed.). *Handbook of learning and cognitive process.* Vol. 1. Hillsdale, NJ: Erlbaum, 1975.

KENDLER, T.S. AND KENDLER, H.H. Reversal and nonreversal shifts in kindergarten children. *Journal of Experimental Psychology,* 1959, 58, 56-60.

KESSLER, K.A., AND WALETSKY, J.P. Clinical use of the antipsychotics. *American Journal of Psychiatry, 138,* 202, 1981.

KEUTHEN, N. Subjective probability estimation and somatic structures in phobic individuals. Unpublished manuscript cited in Davison, G.C. and Neale, J.M., *Abnormal psychology: An experimental approach,* 3rd Ed. New York: Wiley, 1982.

KHACHATURIAN, Z.S. Progress of research on Alzheimer's disease: Research opportunities for behavioral scientists. pp. 1251-1255. *American Psychologist,* 1985. Vol. 40, no.11.

KIESLER, C.A., AND KIESLER, S.B. (1969). *Conformity.* Reading, MA: Addison-Wesley.

KINSEY, A.C. POMEROY, W.B., AND MARTIN, C.E. *Sexual behavior in the human male.* Philadelphia: Saunders. 1948.

KINSEY, A.C., POMEROY, W.B., MARTIN, C.E. AND GEBHARD, P.H. *Sexual behavior in the human female.* Philadelphia: Saunders, 1953.

KLAUS, M.H., AND KENNELL, J.H. (1976). Parent-Infant Bonding. St. Louis, Mosby.

KLINGER, E. Fantasy need achievement as a motivational construct. *Psychological Bulletin,* 1966, 291-308.

KLOPPER, B. *Advances in Rorschach technique, Vol. 1.* Yonkers on the Hudson: World Book Co., 1954.

KOHLBERG, L. The development of modes of thinking and choice in the years 10 to 16. Unpublished doctoral dissertation, the University of Chicago, 1958.

KOHLBERG, L. (1969). The cognitive-developmental approach to socialization. In A. Goslin (Ed.), Handbook of Socialization theory and research. Chicago: Rand McNally.

KOHLBERG, L. The development of children's orientations toward a moral order. I. Sequence in the development of moral thought. *Vita Humana,* 6, 11-35.

KÖHLER, W. *The mentality of apes.* New York: Harcourt Brace, 1925.

KOLATA, C. (1982). Food affects human behavior. *Science,* 218, 1209-1210.

KONORSKI, J. *Integrative activity of the brain.* Chicago: University of Chicago Press, 1967.

KOTELCHUCK, M., ZELAZO, P.R., KAGAN, J. AND SPELKE, E. Infant reaction to parental separations when left with familiar and unfamiliar adults. *Journal of Genetic Psychology,* 1975, 126, 255-262.

KOTOVSKY, K. AND SIMON, H.A. Empirical tests of a theory of human acquistion of concepts for sequential patterns. *Cognitive Psychology,* 1973, 4, 399-424.

KRAFT, C. A psychophysical contribution to air safety; simulator studies of visual illusions in night visual approaches. In H. Pick, H. Leibowitz, J. Singer, A. Steinschneider and H. Stevenson (Eds.), *Psychology from research to practice.* New York: Plenum, 1978.

KRAMER, M., TAUBE, C.A., AND REDDICK, R.W. Patterns of use of psychiatric facilities by the aged: Past, present and future. In C. Eisdorfer and M.P. Lawton, (Eds.). *The psychology of adult development and aging.* Washington, D.C. American Psychological Association. 1973.

KRIPKE, D.F., AND SONNENSCHEIN, D. A biological rhythm in waking fantasy. In K.S. Pope and J.L. Singer, (Eds.). *The stream of consciousness: Scientific investigations into the flow of human experience.* New York: Plenum. 1978.

KÜBLER-ROSS, E. (1969). On death and dying. New York: Macmillan.

KÜBLER-ROSS, E. *Death: The final stage of growth.* Englewood Cliffs: Prentice-Hall, 1975

KUFFLER, S.W. Discharge patterns and functional organization of mammalian retina. *Journal of Neurophysiology,* 1953, 16, 37-68.

KUHN, D., NASH, S.C.,AND BRUCKIN, L. Sex role concepts of two- and three-year olds. *Child Development,* 1978, 49, 445-451.

KURTINES, W. AND GREIF, E.B. The development of moral thought: Review and evaluation of Kohlberg's approach. *Psychological Bulletin,* 1974, 81, 453-470.

LABOV, W. Linguistic change as a form of communication. In A. Silverstein (Ed.), *Human communication: Theoretical explorations.* Hillsdale, N.J.: Erlbaum, 1974.

LAING, R.D. Is schizophrenia a disease? *International Journal of Social Psychiatry.* 1964, 10, 184-193.

LAMM, H., AND TROMMSDORF, G. Group versus individual performance on tasks requiring ideational proficiency (Brainstorming): A Review. *European Journal of Social Psychology,* 1973, 3, 361-388.

LANDY, F.J., ROSENBERG, B.G. AND SUTTON-SMITH, B. The effect of limited father absence on cognitive development. *Child Development,* 1969, 40, 941-944.

LANDY, F. *The psychology of work behavior.* Homewood, Illinois: Dorsey Press, 1985.

LANDY, F.J. (ED.) Readings in Industrial and Organizational Psychology. Chicago: The Dorsey Press, 1986, pp. 309-312.

LANDY, F.J., AND TRUMBO, D.A. *The psychology of work behavior.* (2nd Ed.) Homewood, Ill.: Dorsey Press, 1980.

LATANÉ, B., AND DARLEY, J.M. Group inhibition of bystander interventions in emergencies. *Journal of Personality and Social Psychology,* 1968, 10, 215-221.

LATANÉ B., AND DARLEY, J.M. *The unresponsive bystander: Why doesn't he help?* New York: Appleton-Century-Crofts, 1970.

LATANÉ, B., WILLIAMS, K. AND HARKINS, S. Many hands make light the work: The causes and consequences of social loafing. *Journal of Personality and Social Psychology.* 1979, 37, 822-832.

LATHAM, G.P., AND SAARI, L.M. *The application of social learning theory to training supervisors through behavior modeling.* Unpublished manuscript. University of Washington, 1978.

LAZARUS, R.S. Little hassles can be hazardous to health. *Psychology Today,* July, 1981, 58-62.

LEAHEY, T.H. *A History of Psychology.* Englewood Cliffs, N.J.: Prentice-Hall, 1980.

LEBO, C., AND REDDELL, R. The prebycusis component in occupational hearing loss. *Laryngoscope.* 1972, 82, 1399-1409

LEIBOWITZ, H. A behavioral and perceptual analysis of grade crossing accidents. Unpublished manuscript. The Pennsylvania State University 1982.

LEIBOWITZ, H.W., AND OWENS, D.A. We drive by night. *Psychology Today,* January, 1986, pp. 55-58.

LEIFER, A.D., AND ROBERTS, D.F. Children's responses to television violence. In J.P. Murray, E.A. Rubinstein, and G.A. Comstock (Eds.), *Television and social behavior* (Vol. 2). Washington, DC: U.S. Govt. Printing Office, 1972.

LEVINSON, D.J., DARROW, C.M., KLEIN, E.B. LEVINSON, M.H., AND MCKEE, B. *The seasons of a man's life.* New York: Knopf, 1978.

LEVINTHAL, C.F. *The physiological approach in psychology.* Englewood Cliffs, Prentice-Hall, 1979.

LEVISON, C., LEVISON, P. AND NORTON, H. Effects on early visual conditions on stimulation seeking behavior in infant Rhesus monkeys. *Psychonomic Science,* 1968, 11(3), 101-102.

LEWIN, R. Unexpected progress in photoreception. *Science,* 1985, vol. 227, pp. 500-503.

LIBOW, L.S. Senile dementia and senile ''pseudo-senility'': Clinical diagnosis. In C. Eisdorfer and R.O. Friedel (Eds.) *Cognitive and emotional disturbance in the elderly.* Chicago: Yearbook Medical Publishers, 1977.

LIEBERT, R.M. AND WICKES-NELSON, R. *Developmental psychology,* Englewood Cliffs: Prentice-Hall, 1981.

LIEM, J.H. Effects of verbal communications of parents and children: A comparison of normal and schizophrenic families. *Journal of Consulting and Clinical Psychology.* 1974, *42*, 438-450.

LIPTON, S. Dissociated personality: a case report. *Psychiatric Quarterly*, 1943, 17, 35-36.

LOCKE, E.A. Nature and causes of job satisfaction. In M.D. Dunnette (Ed.), *Handbook of industrial and organizational psychology.* Chicago: Rand-McNally, 1976.

LOFTUS, E.F. Leading Questions and the eyewitness report. *Cognitive Psychology*, 1975, 7, 560-572.

LOFTUS, E.F. (1979) *Eyewitness testimony.* Cambridge, Mass: Harvard University Press.

LUBORSKY, L. AND SPENCE, D.P. *Quantitative research on psychoanalytic therapy.* In S.L. Garfield and A.E. Bergin, (Eds.), *Handbook of psychotherapy and behavior change: An empirical analysis (2nd Ed.).* New York: Wiley, 1978.

LUCERO, M.A. Lengthening of REM sleep duration consecutive to learning in the rat. *Brain Research,* 1970, *20*, 319-322.

LUCHINS, A.S. Mechanization in problem solving. *Psychological Monographs*, 1942, *54:6*, Whole No. 248.

LUNNEBORG P.W. *Why study psychology?* Monterey, California: Brooks Cole, 1978.

LUNNEBORG P.W. *What can you do with a BA in Psychology?* Seattle, Washington: Dept. of Psychology, University of Washington, 1982.

McCAUGH, J.L. (1983) Hormonal Influences on memory, Annual Review of Psychology, 34, 297-323.

McCLELLAND, D.C. Inhibited power motivation and high blood pressure in men. *Journal of Abnormal Psychology*, 1979, *88*, 182-190.

MacCOBY, E. AND JACKLIN, C. *The psychology of sex differences.* Stanford, California: Stanford University Press, 1974.

McLEAN, A. *Occupational stress.* Springfield, Ill.: Charles C. Thomas.

McLEAN, A.A. *Work Stress.* Reading, Mass. Addison-Wesley, 1979.

MAGUIRE, W.J. A syllogistic analysis of cognitive relationships. In M.J. Rosenberg, C.I. Hovland, W.J. Maguire, R.P. Abelson and J.W. Brehm, (Eds.) *Attitude organization and change.* New Haven: Yale University Press, 1960.

MAHONEY, M.J. *Cognition and behavior modification.* Cambridge, Mass.: Ballinger, 1974.

MAIER, S.F. AND SELIGMAN, M.E.P. Learned helplessness: theory and evidence. *Journal of Experimental Psychology: General*, 1976. *105*, 3-46.

MALINA, R.M. (1979). Secular changes in size and maturity: Causes and effects. *Monographs of the Society of Research in Child Development*, 44 (3-4, Serial No. 179), 59-120.

MALMO, R.B. Emotions and muscle tension: the story of Anne. *Psychology Today*, 1970, 3(10)64-67, 83.

MARCIA, J.E. Development and validation of ego identity status. *Journal of Personality and Social Psychology*, 1966, *3*, 551-558.

MARCIA, J.E. Identity six years after: A follow-up study. *Journal of Youth and Adolescence*, 1976, *5*, 145-160.

MARKS, I., AND LADER, M. Anxiety states (anxiety neurosis): A review. *Journal of Nervous and Mental Disease*, 1973, *156*, 3-18.

MARSHALL, A.G., AND IZARD, C.E. Depression as a pattern of emotions and feelings: factor analytic investigations. In Carroll E. Izard (Ed.), *Patterns of emotions*, New York: Academic Press, 1972.

MARTIN, G., AND PEAR, J. *Behavior modification,* Englewood Cliffs: Prentice-Hall, 1978.

MARTINDALE, C. *Cognition and Consciousness.* Homewood Ill.: Dorsey Press, 1981.

MARTINSON, F.M. Childhood sexuality. In B.B. Wolman and J. Money (Eds.) *Handbook of human sexuality.* Englewood Cliffs, N.J.: Prentice-Hall, 1980.

MASTERS, W.H. AND JOHNSON, V. *Human sexual response.* Boston: Little, Brown, 1966.

MASTERS, W.H. AND JOHNSON, V. *Human sexual inadequacy.* Boston: Little, Brown, 1970.

MASTERS, W.H. AND JOHNSON, V. *Homosexuality in perspective.* Boston: Little, Brown, 1979.

MASTERSON, R.B., JANE, J.A., AND DIAMOND, I. T. Role of the brainstem auditory structures in sound localization. II. Inferior colliculus and its brachium. *Journal of Neurophysiology, 1968, 31,* 96-108.

MATHEWS, K.E., AND CANON, L.K. Environmental noise level as a determinant of helping behavior. *Journal of Personality and Social Psychology*, 1975, *32*, 571-577.

MAURER, H. *Not working.* New York: Holt, Rinehart and Winston, 1979.

MAY, P.R.A. (1968) Treatments of schizophrenia: A comparative study of five treatment methods. New York: Science House.

MAYER, R.E. *Thinking Problem Solving, Cognition.* San Francisco: Freemont, 1983.

MEICHENBAUM, D. *Cognitive behavior modification: an integrative approach.* New York: Plenum Press, 1977.

MEICHENBAUM, D., AND CAMERON, R. Modifying what clients say to themselves. In M.J. Mahoney, and C.E. Thorenson (Eds.). *Self-control: Power to the person.* Monterey, Ca.: Brooks Cole, 1974.

MELLOR, C.S. First rank symptoms of schizophrenia. *British Journal of Psychiatry*, 1970, *117*, 15-23.

MELTZOFF, A., AND MOORE, M.K. Imitation of facial and manual gestures by human neonates. *Science*, October 7, 1977, 75-78.

MENZEL, E.M. Cognitive mapping in chimpanzees. In S.H. Hulse, H. Fowler and W.K. Honig (Eds.), *Cognitive processes in animal behavior.* Hillsdale: Erlbaum, 1978

MESSICK, S. The effectiveness of coaching for the SAT: Review and reanalysis of research from the fifties to the FTC. Princeton: *Educational and Psychological Measurement.* 1965, *25*, 707-726.

MEYER-BAHLBERG. H. Sex hormones and female homosexuality: A critical evaluation. *Archives of Sexual Behavior*, 1979, *8*, 101-119.

MILGRAM, S. Behavioral study of obedience. *Journal of Abnormal and Social Psychology*, 1963, *67*, 371-378.

MILGRAM, S. *Obedience to authority.* New York: Harper, 1974.

MILLER, G.A. The magical number seven, plus or minus two: Some limits on our capacity for processing information. *Psychological Review*, 1956, *63*, 81-97.

MILLER, N.E. Liberalization of basic S-R concepts: extensions to conflict behavior, motivation, and social learning. in S. Koch (Ed.), *Psychology: a study of a science (Vol. 2).* New York: McGraw-Hill, 1959.

MILLER, P.Y., AND SIMON, W. Adolescent sexual behavior: Context and change. *Social Problems*, 1974, *22*, 58-75.

MILLMAN J., BISHOP, C.H., AND EBEL, R. An analysis of test-wiseness.Educational Testing Service, 1980.

MILNER, B. The memory defect in bilateral hippocampal lesions. *Psychiatric Research Reports*, 1959, *11*, 43-58.

MILNER, B., CORKIN, S. AND TEUBER, H.L. Further analysis of the hippocampal amnesic syndrome: 14 year follow up study of H.M. *Neuropsychologia*, 1968, *6*, 215-234.

MISCHEL, W. *Personality and assessment.* New York: Wiley, 1968.

MITCHELL, T.R. Expectancy models of job satisfaction, occupational preference and effort: a theoretical, methodological and empirical approach. *Psychological Bulletin*, 1974, *81*, 1053-1077.

MOLDOFSKY, H. AND SCARASRICK, P. Induction of neurasthenic musculoskeletal pain syndrome by selective sleep stage deprivation. *Psychosomatic Medicine*, 1976, 35, 38, 44.

MONEY, J., AND ERHARDT, A. *Man and woman, boy and girl: The differentiation and dimorphism of gender identity from conception to maturity.* Baltimore: John Hopkins University Press, 1972.

MOOK, D. In defense of external validity. *American Psychologist*, 1983, 38, 379-388.

MOORE, K.L. *Before we are born*, 3rd Ed. W.B. Saunders, 1983.

MOOS, R.H., AND BILLINGS, A.G. Conceptualizing and measuring coping resources and processes. In L. Goldberger, and S. Breznitz (Eds.), *Handbook of stress: Theoretical and clinical aspects.* New York: The Free Press, 1982.

MORAY, N. Attention in dichotic listening: Affective cues and the influence of instructions. *Quarterly Journal of Experimental Psychology*, 1959, *11*, 56-60.

MORGAN, J.J.B. AND MORTON, J.T. The distortion of syllogistic reasoning produced by personal convictions. *Journal of Social Psychology*, 1944, *20*, 39-59.

MORRISON, H.K., AND HANSON, G.D. Clinical psychologist in the vanguard *Professional Psychology*, 1978, *9*, 240-248.

MORUZZI, G., AND MAGOUN, H.W. Brain stem reticular formation and activation of the EEG. *Electroencephalography and clinical neurophysiology.* 1949, *1*, 455-473.

MURRAY D. *A history of western psychology.* Englewood Cliffs: Prentice-Hall, 1983

MURRAY, H. *Explorations in personality.* New York: Oxford University Press, 1938.

MURSTEIN, B.I. *Who will marry whom? Theories and research in marital choice.* New York: Springer Publishing Co., 1976.

MURSTEIN, B.I. Marital choice. In B. Wolman (Ed.). *Handbook of Developmental Psychology.* Englewood Cliffs: Prentice-Hall, 1982. pp. 652-666.

MUSSEN, P., AND EISENBERG-BERG, N. *Roots of caring, sharing and helping.* San Francisco: W.H. Freeman, 1977.

NARANJO, C., AND ORNSTEIN, R.E. *On the psychology of meditation.* New York: Viking, 1971.

NASBY. W., AND YANDO, R. Selective encoding and retrieval of affectively valent information: Two cognitive consequences of children's mood states. *Journal of Personality and Social Psychology*, 1982, *43*, 1244-1253.

NATALE, M. AND HANTAS, M. Effect of temporary mood state on selective memory about the self. *Journal of Personality and Social Psychology*, 1982, *42*, 927-934.

NATIONAL CENTER FOR HEALTH STATISTICS. Profile of chronic illness in nursing homes. In *Vital and health statistics* (Series 13, No. 29) Hyattsville, Md.: U.S. Dept. of Health, Education, and Welfare, 1977.

NATSOULAS, T. Consciousness. *American Psychologist*, 1978, *33*, 906-914.

NAVTA, W.J.H., AND FEIRTAG, M. The organization of the brain. *Scientific American*, 1979, *88*, 111.

NELSON, B. Why are earliest memories so fragmentary and elusive? *New York Times*, December 7, 1982, C1 and C7.

NELSON, K.E., DENNINGER, M.M., BONVILLIAN, J.D., KAPLAN, B.J. AND BAKER, N. Maternal input adjustments and non-adjustments as related to children's linguistic advances and to language acquisition theories. In A.D. Pelligrini and T.W. Yawkey (Eds.) *The development of oral and written languages: readings in developmental and applied linguistics.* Ablex, 1983

NEWELL, A., AND SIMON, H.A. *Human problem solving.* Englewood Cliffs. N.J. Prentice-Hall, 1972.

NISBETT, R., AND ROSS, L. Human inference: Strategies and shortcomings of social judgment. Englewood Cliffs: Prentice-Hall, 1980.

NORD. W.B. Beyond the teaching machine: The neglected area of operant conditioning in the theory and practice of management. *Organizational Behavior and Human Performance*, 1969, *4*, 375-401.

NOVAK, M.A. AND HARLOW, H.F. Social recovery of monkeys isolated for the first year of life. I. Rehabilitation and therapy. *Developmental Psychology*, 1975, *11*, 453-465.

NUCKOLLS, K., CASSEL, J., AND KAPLAN, B. Psychosocial assets, life crisis, and the prognosis of pregnancy. *American Journal of Epidemiology*, 1972, 95, 431-441.

NUNNALLY, J.C. *Popular conceptions of mental health.* New York: Holt, Rinehart and Winston. 1961.

NUSSBAUM, P. Drinking and walking don't mix either. *Philadelphia Inquirer*, May 28, 1983. p. 1-A.

O'BRIEN, C.P. Experimental analysis of conditioning factors in human narcotic addiction. Pharmacological Reviews, 1975, 27, 533.

O'BRIEN, C.P., TESTA, T., O'BRIEN, T.J. BRADY, J.P., AND WELLS, B. Conditioned narcotic withdrawal in human. *Science*, 1977, 195, pp. 1000-1002.

OFFER, D. AND OFFER, J. (1975) Normal adolescent males: the high school and college years. *Journal of the American College Health Association*, 22, 209-215.

ORNE, M. Demand characteristics and the concept of quasi controls. In R. Rosenthal and R. Rosnow (Eds.), *Artifact in behavioral research*. New York Academic Press, 1969.

ORNE, M.T., DUNGES, D.F., AND ORNE E. On the Diagnosis of Multiple Personality in the Forensic Context. The Institute of Pennsylvania Hospital and University of Pennsylvania. Unpublished Paper.

OSTERHOUSE, R.A. Group systematic desensitization of test anxiety. In J.D. Krumboltz and C.E. Thoreson (Eds.), *Counseling Methods*. New York: Holt, Rinehart and Winston, 1976.

OUCHI, W.G. *Theory Z: How American business can meet the Japanese challenge*. Boston: Addison Wesley, 1981.

PACKARD, R.G. The control of "classroom attention: a group contingency for complex behavior. *Journal of Applied Behavior Analysis*. 1970, 3, 13-28.

PAIVIO, A. Coding distinctions and repetition effects in memory. In G.H. Bower (Ed.) *Psychology of learning and motivation* (Vol. 9). New York: Academic Press, 1975.

PAIVIO, A., SMYTHE, P.E., AND YUILLE, J. C. Imagery versus meaningfulness of nouns in paired-associate learning. *Canadian Journal of Psychology*, 1968, 22, 427-441.

PALAZOLLI, M. (1978). Self starvation. Jason Aronson.

PALMER, R.L. (ED.) *Electroconvulsive therapy: An appraisal*. Oxford: Oxford University Press, 1981.

PARLOFF, M.B. 1976, Shopping for the right therapy. Saturday Review, February 21, 1976, pp. 14-16.

PAUK, W. *How to study in college (2nd Ed.)* Boston: Houghton Mifflin, 1974.

PAUL, G. *Insight vs. desensitization in psychotherapy*. Stanford, California: Stanford University Press, 1966.

PAUL, G. Chronic mental patient: Current status—future directions. *Psychological Bulletin*, 1969, 71, 81-94.

PAUL, G.L., AND ERIKSEN, C.W. Effects of test anxiety on "real-life" examinations. *Journal of Personality*, 1964, 32, 480-494.

PAUL, G., AND LENTZ, R.J. *Psychosocial treatment of chronic mental patients*. Cambridge: Harvard University Press, 1966.

PAUL, G., AND LENTZ, R. (1977). Psychosocial treatment of chronic mental patients. Mileau vs. social learning programs. Cambridge, MA: Harvard University Press.

PEAK, H. Attitude and Motivation. *Nebraska Symposium on Motivation*. 1955, 149-188.

PENDERY, M., MALTZMAN, I. AND WEST, L.J. Science, July 9, 1982.

PENFIELD, W., AND MILNER, B. Memory deficit produced by bilateral lesions in the hippocampal zone. *A.M.A. Archives of Neurology and Psychiatry*. 1958, 79, 475-497.

PETERSON, L.R., AND PETERSON, M.J. Short-term retention of individual verbal items. *Journal of Experimental Psychology*. 1959, 58, 193-198.

PIAGET, J. *Genetic epistemology*. New York: Norton, 1970.

PINKER, S. Visual cognition: an introduction. *Cognition*, 1984, 18, 1-63.

PLINER, P., HEATHER, H., KOHL, J. AND SAARI, D. Compliance without pressure: Some further data on the foot-in-the-door technique. *Journal of Experimental Social Psychology*. 1974, 10, 17-22.

POLYA, G. *How to solve it*. Garden City, N.Y. Doubleday, Anchor, 1957.

POLYA, G. *Mathematical discovery*. New York: Wiley, 1968.

PORTER, L.W., AND LAWLER, E.E. *Managerial attitudes and performance*. Homewood, Illinois: Dorsey, 1968.

PRANGE, A.J., WILSON, I.C., LYNN, C.W., ALLTOP, L.B., STIKELEATHER, R.A., AND

RALEIGH, N.C. 1-Tryptophan in mania. *Archives of General Psychiatry*. 1974, 30, 56-62.

PREMACK, D. *Intelligence in ape and man*. Hillsdale, N.J.: Erlbaum, 1976.

PRESSEY, S.L. A simple apparatus which gives tests and scores and teaches. *School Sociology*, No. 586, 1926, 23, 323-376.

PRESSEY, S.L. Development and appraisal of devices providing immediate automatic scoring of objective tests and commitant self-instruction. *Journal of Psychology*. 1950, 29, 417-447.

PRESSLEY, M., LEVIN, J.R., AND DELANEY, H.D. The mnemonic keyword method. *Review of Educational Research*. 1982, 52, 61-91.

RABKIN, J. Criminal behavior of discharged mental patients: A critical appraisal of research. *Psychological Bulletin*, 1979, 86, 1-27.

RACHLIN, H. *Introduction to modern behaviorism*. San Francisco: W.H. Freeman, 1970.

RECHTSCHAFFEN, A., WOLPERT, E.A., DEMENT, W.C., MITCHELL, S.A. AND FISHER, C. Nocturnal sleep of narcoleptics. *Electroencephalography and Clinical Neurophysiology*. 1963, 15, 599-609.

RESCORLA, R.A. Pavlovian Conditioning and Its Proper Control Procedures. *Psychological Review*, 1967, 74, 71-80.

RESCORLA, R.A. AND WAGNER, A.R. A theory of Pavlovian conditioning: variations in the effectiveness of reinforcement and non-reinforcement. In A.H. Black and W.F. Prokasy (Eds.) Classical Conditioning II: Current theory and research. New York: Appleton Century Crofts, 1972.

RESNICK, J.H., AND SCHWARTZ, T. Ethical standards as an independent variable in psychological research. *American Psychologist*, 1973, 28, 134-139.

REVLIS, R. Two models of syllogistic reasoning: Feature selection and conversion. *Journal of Verbal Learning and Verbal Behavior*, 1975, 104, 192-233.

REYNOLDS, G.S. *A primer of operant conditioning*. (Rev. Ed.) Glenview, Ill.: Scott Foresman, 1975.

RICKARDS, L.D. ZUCKERMAN, D.M. AND WEST, P.R. Alzheimer's disease: Current Congressional Response, pp. 1256-1261. *American Psychologist*, 1985. Vol. 40, 11.

RIDEOUT, B. Non-REM sleep as a source of learning deficits induced by REM sleep deprivations. *Physiology and Behavior*, 1979, 22, 1043-1047.

ROBBIN, A.A. A controlled study of the effects of leucotomy. *Journal of Neurology, Neurosurgery, and Psychiatry*. 1958, 21, 262-269.

ROBBINS, A.A. The value of leucotomy in relation to diagnosis. *Journal of Neurology, Neurosurgery, and Psychiatry*. 1959, 22, 132-136.

ROBINS, E. AND GUZE, S.B. Classification of affective disorders: The primary-secondary, endogenous-reactive, and the neurotic-psychotic concepts. In T.A. Williams, M.M. Katz, and J.A. Shield (Eds.), *Recent advances in the psychobiology of the depressive illness (DHEW Publication No. HSM 70-9053)*. Washington, D.C.: U.S. Govt. Printing Office, 1972.

ROBINSON, F.P. *Effective study*, 4th Ed. New York: Harper Row, 1970.

RODIECK, R.W., AND STONE, J. Response of cat retinal ganglion cells to moving visual patterns. *Journal of Neurophysiology*, 1965, 28, 819-832.

ROGERS, C., AND DYMOND, R.F. (Eds.) *Psychology and personality change*. Chicago: University of Chicago Press, 1954.

RORER, L.G., AND WIDIGER, T.A. Personality structure and assessment. *Annual Review of Psychology*, 1983, 34, 431-464.

RORSCHACH, H. *Psychodiagnostics*. Berne: Hans Huber, 1921.

ROSCH, E.H. (1973) Natural categories. Cognitive Psychology, 4, 328-350.

ROSENHAN, D.L. (1973) On being sane in insane places. Science, 179, 250-258.

ROTTER, J. The role of the psychological situation in determining the direction of human behavior. *Nebraska Symposium on Motivation*. 1955, 245-268.

ROTTER, J.B. (1966). Generalized expectancies for internal versus external control of reinforcement. *Psychological Monographs, 80* (Whole No. 609).

ROZIN, P. The psychobiological approach to mem-

ory. In M.R. Rosenzweig and E.L. Bennett, (Eds.). *Neural Mechanisms of Learning and Memory*. Cambridge: MIT Press, 1976.

RUBENSTEIN, C. Psychology's fruit flies. *Psychology Today*, July 1982, 83-84.

RUBIN, Z. Measurement of romantic love. *Journal of Personality and Social Psychology*, 1970, 16, 265-273.

RUBIN, Z. *Liking and loving: An invitation to social psychology*. New York: Holt, Rinehart & Winston. 1973.

RUMBAUGH, D.M. AND SAVAGE-RUMBAUGH, E.S. Chimpanzee language research: status and potential. *Behavioral: Research Methods and Instrumentation*, 1978, 10, No. 2, 119-131.

RUMBAUGH, D.M., VON GLASERSFELD, E., WARNER, H., PISANI, P., AND GILL, T.V. Lana (chimpanzee) learning language: A progress report, *Brain and Language*, 1974, 1 205-212.

RUNDUS, D., Analysis of rehearsal processes in free recall. *Journal of Experimental Psychology*, 1971, 89. 63-77.

RUSSO, J.E. Eye fixations can save the world: A critical evaluation and a comparison between eye fixations and other information processing methodologies. In H. Keith Hunt (Ed.). *Advances in consumer research*. Ann Arbor: Association for Consumer Research, 1978. pp. 561-570.

SACHS, J. Recognition memory for syntactic and semantic aspects of connected discourse. *Perception and Psychophysics*. 1967, 2 437-442.

SAGAN, C. *Dragons of Eden*. New York: Random House, 1977.

SAKITT, B. Iconic Memory. *Psychological Review*, 1976, 83, 257-276.

SANDERS, A.F., AND SCHROOTS, J.J.F. Cognitive categories and memories span: III. Effects of similarity on recall, *The Quarterly Journal of Experimental Psychology*, 1969, 21, 21-28.

SARASON, I.G. (Ed.) *Test anxiety: Theory, research, and application*. Hillsdale, N.J.: Erlbaum, 1980.

SARASON, I.G., AND SARASON, B.R. *Abnormal Psychology* (3rd Ed.) Englewood Cliffs: Prentice-Hall, 1980.

SASMOR, R. Operant conditioning of a small-scale muscle response. *Journal of the Experimental Analysis of Behavior*, 1966, 9, 69-85.

SAVAGE-RUMBAUGH, E.S., D.M. RUMBAUGH, AND S. BOYSEN Do apes use language? *American Scientist*, 1980, 68, 49-61.

SAXON, L, AND RAPOLA, J. *Congenital defects*. New York: Holt, 1969.

SCHACHTER, J. Pain, fear and anger in hypertensives and normotensives: a psychophysiologic study. *Psychosomatic Medicine*, 1957, 19, 17-29.

SCHACHTER, S. Obesity and eating. *Science*, 1968, 161, 751-756.

SCHACHTER, S. Some extraordinary facts about obese humans and rats. *American Psychologist*, 1971, 26, 129-144.

SCHACHTER, S., AND SINGER, J.E. Cognitive, social and physiological determinants of emotional state. *Psychological Review*, 1962, 69, 379-399.

SCHACHTER, S. AND RODIN, J. *Obese humans and rats*. New York: Wiley, 1974.

SCHAIE, H.W. (1980). Age Changes in Intelligence. In R.L. Sprott (Ed.), Age, learning, ability, and intelligence. New York: Van Nostrand Reinhold.

SCHAIE, H.W. (Ed.) (1983). Longitudinal studies of adult psychological development. New York: The Guilford Press.

SCHIFF, W. *Perception: An Applied Approach*. Houghton Mifflin, 1980, pp. 46-47.

SCHLAADT, R. et. al. Drugs of choice: Current Perspectives on Drug Use. Prentice-Hall, 1986.

SCHLEGEL, R.P., CRAWFORD, C.A. AND SANBORN, M.D. (1977). Correspondence and mediational properties of the Fishbein model: An application to adolescent alcohol use. *Journal of Experimental Social Psychology, 13*, 421-430.

SCHNEIDER, A.M., AND TARHIS, B. *An introduction to physiological psychology*. New York: Random House, 1975.

SCHNEIDER, A.M., AND TARHIS, B. *Physiological Psychology*. (2nd Ed.) New York: Random House, 1980.

SCHNEIDER, G.E. Two Visual Systems. *Science*, 1969, 163, 895-902.

SCHOFIELD, M. *The sexual behavior of young people.* Boston: Little Brown, 1965.

SCOVILLE, W.B. The limbic lobe in man. *Journal of Neurosurgery*, 1954, *11*, 64-66.

SCOVILLE, W.B., AND MILNER, B. Loss of recent memory after bilateral hippocampal lesions. *Journal of Neurology, Neurosurgery, and Psychiatry,* 1957, *20*, 11-21.

SEARS, D.O., FREEDMAN, J.L. AND PEPLAU, L.A. (1985). *Social psychology.* Englewood Cliffs, N.J.: Prentice-Hall.

SECUNDO, R. FRIEDMAN, R.J. AND SCHUYLER, D. *Special report, 1973: The depressive disorders (DHEW) Publications No. HSM73-9125).* Washington, D.C.: U.S. Govt. Printing Office, 1973.

SEKULER, R. AND BLAKE, R. (1985). *Perception.* New York: Alfred A. Knopf.

SELIGMAN, M.E.P. On the generality of laws of learning. *Psychological Review*, 1970, *77*, 406-418.

SELIGMAN, M.E.P. *Helplessness: On depression, development and death.* San Francisco: Freeman, 1975.

SELIGMAN, M.E.P., AND MAIER, S.F. Failure to escape traumatic shock. *Journal of Experimental Psychology.* 1967, *74*, 1-9.

SELYE, H. *The physiology and pathology of exposure to stress.* Montreal, Canada: Acta, 1950.

SELYE, H. *Stress without distress.* Philadelphia: Lippincott, 1974.

—1976 *The stress of life.* 2nd ed. New York: McGraw-Hill.

—1978. On the real benefits of stress. *Psychology Today, 2*, 60-64.

—1982. History and present status of the stress concept. In L. Goldberger. and S. Breznitz (Eds.). *Handbook of Stress: Theoretical and clinical aspects.* New York: The Free Press.

SERIFICA, F. The development of attachment behaviors: An organismic-developmental perspective. *Human Development.* 1978, *21*, 119-140.

SHAPIRO, A.P., SCHWARTZ, G.E., FERGUSON, C.E., REDMOND, P.P., AND WEISS, S.M. Behavioral Methods in the treatment of hypertension: A review of their clinical status. *Annals of Internal Medicine*, 1977, *86*, 626-636.

SHATZ, M., AND GELMAN, R. The development of communication skills: The modification in the speech of young children as a function of listener. *SRCD Monographs.* 1973 *38*, (5 serial No. 152).

SHEEHY, G. *Passages: The predictable crises of adult life.* New York: E.P. Dutton, Inc., 1976.

SHERIF, M. A study of some social factors in perception. *Archives of Psychology*, 1935, No. 187.

SHERRINGTON, C.S. *Integrative action of the nervous system.* New Haven, Conn.: Yale University Press, 1906.

SHOTLAND, R.L. AND STRAW, M.K. (1976). Bystander response to an assault: When a man attacks a woman. *Journal of Personality and Social Psychology, 34*, 990-999.

SIMMONS, R. The relative effectiveness of certain incentives in animal learning. *Comparative Psychology Monographs*, 1924, *2*.

SIMON, H.A., AND KOTOVSKY, K. Human acquisition of concepts for sequential patterns. *Psychological Review*, 1963, *70*, 534-546.

SIMON, H.A., AND KOTOVSKY, K. *The sciences of the artificial.* Cambridge, Mass.: MIT Press, 1969.

SIMON, W., AND GAGNON, J.H. *Sexual conduct: The sources of human sexuality.* Chicago: Aldine. 1973.

SKINNER, B.F. *Verbal behavior.* New York: Appleton Century Crofts, 1957.

SKINNER, B.F. *Cumulative Record.* New York: Appleton Century Crofts, 1959

SLOBIN, D.I. *Psycholinguistics.* Glenview, Ill.: Scott Foresman, 1971

SMITH, M.L. AND GLASS, G.V 1977 Meta-analysis of psychotherapy outcomes studies. American Psychologist, 32, 752-760.

SMITH, M.L., GLASS, G.V AND MILLER, T.I. 1980. The benefits of psychotherapy. Baltimore, Maryland: Johns Hopkins University Press.

SMITH, P.C., KENDALL, L.M., AND HULIN, C. *The measurement of satisfaction in work and retirement: a strategy for the study of attitudes.* Chicago: Rand-McNally, 1969.

SNYDER, M., TANKE, E.D., AND BERSCHEID, E. (1977). Social perception and interpersonal behavior: On the self-fulfilling nature of social stereotypes. *Journal of Personality and Social Psychology, 35*, 656-666.

SOBELL, M.B. AND SOBELL, L.C. *Individualized behavioral treatment of alcohol problems.* New York: Plenum, 1978.

SOLOMON, R.L. The opponent process theory of acquired motivation. *American Psychologist,* 1980, *35*, 691-712.

SOLOMON, R.L., AND CORBIT, J.D. An opponent process theory of motivation: II. cigarette addiction. *Journal of Abnormal Psychology.* 1973, *81*, 158-171.

SORENSON, R.C. *Adolescent sexuality in contemporary America: Personal values and sexual behavior ages thirteen to nineteen.* New York: World, 1973.

SPERRY, R.W. The great cerebral commisure. *Scientific American*, 1964, *210*, 42-62.

SPERRY, R.W. (1968) Hemisphere deconnection and unity in conscious awareness. *American Psychologist, 23*, 723-733.

SPITZER, R.L., FOREMAN, J.B.W., AND NEE, J. DSM field trials. *American Journal of Psychiatry,* 1979, *136*, 815-817.

SRAIFE, L.A. Attachment and the Roots of competence. *Human Nature*, 1977, 50-57.

STAPP, J., FULCHER, R., NELSON, S.D., PALLAK, M., AND WICHERSKI, M. The employment of recent doctorate recipients in psychology: 1975 through 1978. *American Psychologist*, 1981, *36*, 1211-1254.

STARR, V.H. AND McCORMICK, M. 1985. *Jury Selection.* Boston: Little Brown & Co.

STEELE, C.M., SCUTHWICK, L.L., AND CRITCHLOW, B. Dissonance and alcohol: Drinking your troubles away. *Journal of Personality and Social Psychology.* 1981, *41*, 831-846.

STEIN, A. AND FRIEDRICH, L.K. Impact of television on children and youth. In E.M. Heatherington (Ed.) *Review of Child Development Research.* Chicago: University of Chicago Press, 1975, 5.

STEIN, B.S., AND BRANSFORD, J.D. Constraints of effective elaboration: Effects of precision and subject generation. *Journal of Verbal Learning and Verbal Behavior*, 1979, *18*, 769-777.

STEIN, L. AND WISE, D. Dopamine-B-Hydroxylase deficits in the brains of schizophrenic patients. *Science*, 1973, *181*, 344-347.

STEIN, M. Psychosocial perspectives on aging and the immune response. Paper presented at the annual meeting of the Academy of Behavioral Medicine Research, Reston Virginia.

STEIN, M.I. *Stimulating creativity.* (Vol. 2). New York: Academic Press, 1972.

STEINEM, G. Erotica and pornography: A clear and present difference. *Ms.*, November, 1978, 7.

STERN, R.M., AND LEWIS, N.L. Ability of actors to control their GSRs and express emotions. *Psychophysiology.* 1968, *4*, 294-299.

STERN, R.M., BOTTO, R.W. AND HERRICK, C.D. Behavioral and physiological effects of false heart rate feedback: a replication and extension. *Psychophysiology*, 1972, *9*, 21-29.

STERNBERG, R., All's well that ends well, but its a sad tale that begins at the end: a reply to Glaser. *American Psychologist, 1985, 40,* 571-572.

STERNBERG, R. The nature of mental abilities. *American Psychologist*, 1979, *34*, 214-230.

STERNBERG, R., AND KETRON, H.L. Selection and implementation of strategies in reasoning by analogy. *Journal of Educational Psychology*, 1982, *74*, 300-414.

STEVENS, S.S. The Psychophysics of Sensory Function. In W.A. Rosenblith (Ed.). *Sensory Communication.* Cambridge, Mass.: MIT Press, 1961, pp. 1-33.

STILES, W.A., SHAPIRO, DAVID A. AND ELLIOTT, R. Are all psychotherapies equivalent? *American Psychologist*, 1986, *41*, 165-180.

STOKOLS, D. Environmental psychology. *Annual Review of Psychology*, 1978, *29*, 253-295.

STROEBEL, C.F., AND GLUECK, B.C. Passive meditation: Subjective, clinical and electrographic comparison with biofeedback. In G. Schwartz and D. Shapiro (Eds.). *Consciousness and self-regulation* (Vol. 2). New York: Plenum, 1978.

SUTTON-SMITH, B. The effect of limited father absence on cognitive development. *Child Development*, 1969, *40*, 941-944.

SWINTON, S.S., AND POWERS, D.E. A study of the effects of special preparation on GRE analytical scores and item types. *Journal of Educational Psychology*, 1983, *75*, 104-115.

SZASZ, T.S. The myth of mental illness. *American Psychologist*, 1960, *15*, 113-118.

SZASZ, T.S. *Sex by prescription.* Garden City, N.Y.: Anchor Press Doubleday, 1980.

TANNER, J.M. Physical Growth. In P. Mussen (Ed.). *Carmichael's Manual of child psychology (3rd Ed.) (Vol. II).* New York: Wiley, 1970, pp. 77-155.

TANNER, J.M. Growing up. *Scientific American.* 1973. Sept. 1973, 34-43.

TANNER, O. *Stress.* New York: Time-Life Books, 1976, *The world almanac and book of facts 1983.* New York: Newspaper Enterprise Association, Inc., 1981.

TART, C.T. (1975). States of Consciousness. New York: Dutton.

TAUSCH, R. Optische Tauschungen als artifizielle effekte der gestaltungsprozesse von grossen und formerkonstanz in der naturlichen raumwahrnehmung. *Psychologische Forschung.* 1954, *24*, 299-348. Cited in Hochberg. 1978.)

TAYLOR, C.W., BERRY, P.C., AND BLOCK, C.H. Does group participation when using brainstorming facilitate or inhibit creative thinking? *Administrative Science Quarterly*, 1958, *3*, 23-47.

TAYLOR, F.W. *Principles of scientific management.* New York: Harper, 1947.

TAYLOR S.E. The interface of cognitive and social psychology. In J. Harvey (Ed.). *Cognition, social behavior and the environment.* Hillsdale, N.J.: Erlbaum, 1980.

TAYLOR S.E. AND CROCKER, J. Schematic bases of social information processing. In E.T. Higgins, P. Herman and P. Zanna, (Eds.). *Social cognition, cognitive structure and processes underlying person perception.* Hillsdale, N.J.: Erllbaum, 1980.

TAYNOR, J., AND DEAUX, K. Equity and perceived sex differences: Role behavior as defined by the task, the mode and the actor. *Journal of Personality and Social Psychology.* 1975, *32*, 381-390.

TERMAN, L.M. AND MERRILL, M.A. *Measuring intelligence.* Boston: Houghton-Mifflin, 1937.

TERRACE, H.S., PETITTO, L.A., SANDERS, R.J., AND BEVER, T.G. Can an ape create a sentence? *Science*, 1979, *206*, 891-902.

THEORELL, T. AND SCHWARTZ, J.E. Article published in two (journal) sources. July 1981, *American Journal of Public Health* and March, 1982 in *Social Science Medicine*.

THOMAS, D.R., AND MITCHELL, K. The role of instructions and stimulus categorizing in a measure of stimulus generalization. *Journal of the Experimental Analysis of Behavior.* 1962, *5*, 375-381.

THOMPSON, T. AND SCHUSTER, C.R. (EDS.) *Behavioral pharmacology.* Englewood Cliffs, N.J. 1968.

THORESEN, C.E. AND MAHONEY, M.J. *Behavioral self control.* New York: Holt, Rinehart and Winston, 1974.

THORNDIKE, E.L. *Animal Intelligence.* New York: MacMillan, 1911.

TOFANI, L. Rape in the county jail: Prince George's hidden horror. *Washington Post*, 9, 26, 82.

TOLMAN, E.C. *Purposive behavior in animals and man.* New York: Century, 1932.

TOLMAN, E.C. AND HONZIK, C.H. "Insight" in rats. *University of California Publications in Psychology.* 1930. (Cited in Bower and Hilgard, 1981.)

TOMKINS, S. Affect as the primary motivational system. In M.B. Arnold (Ed.) *Feelings and emotions.* New York: Academic Press, 1970.

TRABASSO, T.R. AND BOWER, G.H. Presolution reversal and dimensional shifts in concept identification. *Journal of Experimental Psychology.* 1964, *67*, 398-399.

TRABASSO, T.R., AND BOWER, G.H. *Attention in Learning.* New York: Wiley, 1968.

TRAPOLD, M.A., AND FOWLER, H. Instrumental escape conditioning as a function of noxious stimulation. *Journal of Experimental Psychology.* 1960, *60*, 323-326.

TUCKER, D.M. Lateral brain function, emotion and conceptualization. *Psychological Bulletin*, 1981, *89*, 19-46.

TULVING, E., AND THOMPSON, D.M. Encoding specificity and retrival processes in episodic memory. *Psychological Review*, 1973, *80*, 352-373.

TVERSKY, A., AND KAHNEMAN, D. Judgment under uncertainty: Heuristics and biases. *Science*, 1974, *185*, 1124-1131.

ULLMAN, S. Visual routines. *Cognition*, 1984, 18, 97-159.

ULRICH, R.F., AND PINHEIRO, R.L. Temporary hearing losses in teenagers attending repeated rock and roll sessions. *Acta Otolarying.* 1974, 77, 51-55.

U.S. BUREAU OF THE CENSUS. Characteristics of children and youth: *Current Population Reports (Special Studies Series P-23, No. 66)*. Washington, D.C. U.S. Govt. Printing Office, 1978.

VALENSTEIN, E.S. *Brain control.* New York: Wiley, 1973.

VALINS, S. Cognitive effects of false heart-rate feedback. *Journal of Personality and Social Psychology.* 1966, *4,* 400-408.

VANDENBOS, G., STAPP, J. AND PALLAK, M.. Editorial about the Human Resources in Psychology Special Issue. *American Psychologist*, 1981, *36*, 1207-1210.

VETERAN'S ADMINISTRATION. *Drug Treatment in Psychiatry.* U.S. Gov't Printing Office, Washington, D.C., 1970.

VICTOR, J.S. *Human sexuality.* Englewood Cliffs, N.J.: Prentice Hall, 1980.

VINACKE, E. Motivation as a complex problem. *Nebraska Symposium on Motivation*, 1962, *10*, 1-45.

VISOTSKY, H.M., HAMBURG, D.A., GOSS, M.E., AND LEBOVITZ, B.A. Coping under extreme stress: Observations of patients with severe poliomyelitis. *Archives of General Psychiatry*, 1962, *5*, 423-448.

VOEVODSKY, J. Evaluations of a deceleration warning light for reducing rear-end automobile collisions. *Journal of Applied Psychology, 1974, 59,* 270-273.

vonBÉKÉSY, G. Hearing theories and complex sounds. *Journal of the Acoustical Society of America.* 1963, *35*, 588-601.

vonBÉKÉSY, G. (1964) Olfactory analogue to directional hearing. Journal of Applied Physiology 19 (3), 369-373.

VROOM, V. *Work and Motivation.* New York: Wiley, 1964.

WACTHEL, P. *Psychoanalysis and behavior therapy: Toward an integration.* New York: Basic Books, 1977.

WAGNER, A.R. AND RESCORLA, R.A. Inhibition in Pavlovian Conditioning: Application of a theory. In R.A. Boakes and M.S. Halliday (Eds.) *Inhibition and Learning.* New York: Academic Press, 1972.

WAID, W.M., ORNE, M.T., AND WILSON, S.K. Effects of level of socialization on electrodermal detection of deception. *Psychophysiology*, 1979, *16*, 15-22.

WAID, W.M., ORNE, E.C., COOK, M.R., AND ORNE, M.T. Meprobamate reduces accuracy of physiological detection of deception. *Science*, 1981, *212*, 71-73.

WAID, W.M., AND ORNE, M.T. The physiological detection of deception. *American Scientist*, 1982, *70*, 402-409.

WALD, G. 1959, The photoreceptor process in vision. In Field, J., Magoun, H.W., and Hall, V.E. (ed.) Handbook Physiology, Vol. 1, pp. 671-691. Washington, D.C. American Physiological Society.

WALK, R.D. Can the duckling respond adequately to depth? Paper presented at the 33rd meeting of the Eastern Psychological Association. Atlantic City, April, 1962, (Cited in Coren, Porac, and Ward, 1979).

WALK, R.D. Class demonstration of visual depth perception with the albino rabbit. *Perceptual and Motor Skills*, 1964, *18*, 219-224.

WALKER, C.E., HEDBERG, A.G., CLEMENT, P.W., AND WRIGHT, L. *Clinical procedures for behavior therapy.* Englewood Cliffs, N.J.: Prentice Hall, 1981.

WALSTER, E., ARONSON, E., AND ABRAHAMS, D. On increasing the persuasiveness of a low prestige communicator. *Journal of Experimental Social Psychology*, 1966, *2*, 325-342.

WATKINS, J.G. AND WATKINS, H.H. Ego states and hidden observers. *Journal of Altered States of Consciousness.* 1979, *5*, 3-18.

WATSON, J.B., AND RAYNER, R. Conditioned emotional reactions. *Journal of Experimental Psychology.* 1920, *3*, 1-14.

WEARY, G. (1980). Examination of affect and egotism as mediators of bias in causal attributions. *Journal of Personality and Social Psychology*, 38, 348-357.

WEARY, G., HARVEY, J.H., SCHWIEGER, P., OLSEN, C.T., PERLOFF, R., AND PRITCHARD, S. (1982). Self-presentation and the moderation of self-serving attributional biases. *Social Cognition*, *1*, 140-159.

WEATHERLEY, D. Self-perceived rate of physical maturation and personality in late adolescence. *Child Development*, 1964, *35*, 1197, 1210.

WEBB, W.B. Paper presented at a symposium of the First International Congress of the Association for the Psychophysiological Study of Sleep. Bruges, Belgium, 1971.

WEBSTER, E.C. *The employment interview: a social judgment process.* Schomberg, Ontario, Canada, S.I.P. Publications, 1980.

WEICK, K.E. How do I know what I mean until I see what I say. Paper presented at the meetings of the Midwest Psychological Association, Chicago, May, 1966.

WEIMER, W. Psycholinguistics and Plato's paradoxes of the Meno. *American Psychologist*, 1973, *28*, 15-33.

WERNER, H., AND KAPLAN, E. Development of word meaning through verbal context: An experimental study. *Journal of Psychology*, 1950, *29*, 251-257.

WERTHEIMER, M. (1959). *Productive Thinking.* New York: Harper.

WHIMBY, A., AND LOCHHEAD, J. *Problem solving and comprehension* (2nd Ed.). Philadelphia: Franklin Institute Press, 1980.

WHITE, R.W. Motivation reconsidered: the concept of competence. *Psychological Review*, 1959, *66*, 233-297.

WHORF, B.L. (1956). Language, thought and reality. New York: MIT Press-Wiley.

WICKENS, D.D., BORN, D.G. AND ALLEN C.K. Proactive inhibition and item similarity in short-term memory. *Journal of Verbal Learning and Verbal Behavior.* 1963, *2*, 440-445.

WICKER, A.W. (1969). Attitudes versus action: The relationship of verbal and overt behavior responses to attitude objects. *Journal of Social Issues, 25,* (4), 41-78.

WICKLUND, R.A., AND BREHM, J.W. (1976). *Perspectives on cognitive dissonance.* Hillsdale, N.J.: Lawrence Erlbaum.

WIENER, S.L. AND GOODENOUGH, D.R. A move toward a psychology of conversation. In R.O. Freedle (Ed.). *Discourse production and comprehension. Vol. 1.* Norwood, N.J.: Ablex, 1977.

WIENER-LEVY, D., AND EXNER, J.E. JR. The Rorschach comprehensive system: an overview. In P. McReynolds (Ed.) *Advances in psychological assessment (Vol. 5).* San Francisco: Jossey Bass, 1981.

WILDER, D. Reduction of intergroup discrimination through individuation of the outgroup. *Journal of Personality and Social Psychology*, 1978, 36, 1361-1374.

WILKINS, W. Placebo problems in psychotherapy research. American Psychologist, 1986, 41, 551-556.

WILLIAMS, K., HARKINS, S., AND LATANE, B. (1981). Identifiability as a deterrent to social loafing: Two cheering experiments. *Journal of Personality and Social Psychology, 40,* 303-311.

WILLIS, R.H. AND HOLLANDER, E.P. An experimental study of three response modes in social influence situations. *Journal of Abnormal and Social Psychology*, 1964, *69*, 150-156.

WILSON, J. Hers: On succumbing to shrewishness. New York Times. June 16, 1983, p. C2.

WINCH, R.F. The theory of complementary needs in male selection: A test of one kind of complementariness. *American Sociological Review*, 1955, *20*, 52-56.

WINCH, R.F. *Mate-selection: A study of complementarity needs.* New York: Harper & Row, 1958.

WOLPE, J. *Psychotherapy by reciprocal inhibition.* Stanford: Stanford University Press, 1958.

WOODS, P.J. (Ed.) *Career opportunities for psychologists: expanding and emerging areas.* Washington, D.C.: American Psychological Association, 1976.

WOODS, P.J. *The psychology major: training and employment strategies.* Washington, D.C.: American Psychological Association, 1979.

WORLD HEALTH ORGANIZATION. *Report of the international pilot study of schizophrenia.* Geneva: World Health Organization, 1973.

WORRINGTON, C.J. AND MESSICK, D.M. (1983). Social facilitation of running: An unobtrusive study. *Journal of Social Psychology*, *121*, 23-29.

YARBUS, A.L. (Ed.). *Eye movements and vision.* New York: Plenum, 1967.

YARBUS, A.L. In Schiff, W. (Ed.). *Perception: An applied approach.* Boston: Houghton-Mifflin, 1980.

YERKES, R.M. (Ed.) *Psychological examining in the United States Army.* Washington, D.C.: Memoirs of the National Academy of Sciences (No. 15), 1921.

YERKES, R.M., AND DODSON, J.D. The relation of strength of stimulus to rapidity of habit formation. *Journal of Comparative and Neurological Psychology.* 1908, *18*, 459-482.

YIN, R.K. Face Recognition by Brain-Injured Patients: A Dissociable Ability? *Neuropsychologia*, *8*, 395-402, 1970.

ZAJONC, R.B. Attitudinal effects of mere exposure. *Journal of Personality and Social Psychology.* 1968. Monograph Supplement 9, (2), 1-29.

ZAPOROZHETS, A.V. The development of P.H. Mussen (Ed.). European research in cognitive development: *Monographs of the Society for the Research in Child Development*, 1965, *30*, 82-101.

ZELNICK, M., AND KATNER, J.F. Sexual and contraceptive experience of young unmarried women in the United States. 1976 and 1971. *Family Planning Perspectives, 9*, March-April 1977, pp. 55-71.

ZILBERGELD, B., AND EVANS, M. The inadequacy of Masters and Johnson. *Psychology Today*, August 1980, *14* (3), 28-43.

ZIMBARDO, P. Introduction in P.N. Middlebrook, *Social psychology and modern life.* New York: Knopf, 1974.

ZUBIN, J. Classification of the behavior disorders. *Anual Review of Psychology*, 1967, *18*, 373-401.

ZUBIN, J. AND SPRING, B. Vulnerability—a new view of schizophrenia. *Journal of Abnormal Psychology*, 1977, *86*, 103-126.

ZUCKERMAN, M. The sensation-seeking motive. In B. Maher (Ed.) *Progress in Experimental Personality Research (Vol. 7).* New York: Academic Press, 1974.

641

Acknowledgments

Figures, Tables

Table 1-1 Reid, Don. *Info World*, (Dec. 1982) p. 46, **Table 1-2:** American Psychological Association, Vandenbos et al., "About the human resources in psychology: Special issue, *American Psychologist*, Vol. 36, No. 11 (Nov. 1981), p. 1281. **Figures 1-1 and 1-2:** American Psychological Association, Stapp et al., *American Psychologist*, Vol. 36, No. 11 (Nov. 1981), p. 1285. **Table 1-3:** Lunneborg, P.W. "What can you do with a B.A. in psychology?" Seattle, Washington: Department of Psychology, University of Washington, 1982. Grateful acknowledgment is made for permission to reprint by Patricia W. Lunneborg, Department of Psychology, University of Washington, Seattle, Washington. **Table 1-4:** Lunneborg, P.W. "Why study psychology?" Monterey, California: Brooks Cole, 1978, pp. 53-54. Grateful acknowledgment is made for permission to reprint by Patricia W. Lunneborg, Department of Psychology, University of Washington, Seattle, Washington.

Table 2-1: Adapted from Neil R. Carlson, Physiology of Behavior, Second Edition. Copyright © 1981 by Allyn and Bacon, Inc. Used with permission. **Figure 2-4:** Adapted from an illustration by Jane Hurd for *the Washington Post*, (9/6/82). **Figure 2-12:** Reprinted with permission of Macmillan Publishing Company, from *The Cerebral Cortex of Man* by Wilder Penfield and Theodore Rasmussen. Copyright 1950 by Macmillan Publishing Company, renewal by Theodore Rasmussen.

Table 3-1: Galanter, E. Contemporary psychophysics. In R. Brown et al. (eds.), *New directions in psychology*. New York: Holt, Rinehart & Winston, 1962, 89-156. **Figure 3-2:** Stevens, S.S. On the psychophysical law. *Psychological Review*, 1957, *64*, 153-181. © 1957 by the American Psychological Association. Reprinted by permission of the author. **Figure 3-7:** From A.L. Yarbus (Ed.), *Eye movements and vision*, 1967. Plenum Publishing Company. **Figure 3-10;** Adapted from Dartnall, Bowmaker, and Mollon, 1983. Human visual pigments: Microspectrophometric results from the eyes of seven persons. Proceedings of the Royal Society of London, Series B, 220, 115-130. Box art p. 98 Adapted from R. Sekuler and R. Blake, *Perception*, New York: Alfred A. Knopf, pp 131-133. **Table 3-3:** Deatherage, B.H. Auditory and other sensory forms of information presentation, in H.P. Van Cott and R.G. Kinkade (Eds.), *Human engineering guide to equipment design*, rev. ed. (Washington, D.C. U.S. Government Printing Office, 1972), p. 159. **Figure 3-12:** Brody, J.E. Noise poses a growing threat affecting hearing and behavior. *New York Times*, (Nov. 16, 1982) pp C1 and C5. **Figures 3-14 and 3-16:** Barrett, J. et al. *Biology*. Englewood Cliffs, NJ: Prentice-Hall, 1986 pp 458 and 451. Box art, p. 119: Redrawn from Georg von Békésy. (1964) Olfactory analogue to directional hearing Journal of Applied Physiology 19(3), 369-373. Box art, p. 139: Deregowski, J.B. Pictorial perception and culture, *Scientific American*, (Nov. 1972).

Figure 4-12: Adapted from *The psychology of visual perception* by Ralph Norman Haber, Maurice Hershenson. Copyright © 1973 by Holt Rinehart and Winston, Inc. Reprinted by permission of Holt, Rinehart and Winston. **Figure 4-15:** After The origin of form perception, by Robert L. Fantz, *Scientific American*, (May 1961). Text page 151: Huxley, Aldous. *The Doors of Perception*. New York: Harper & Row (1954).

Table 5-1: Schlott and Shannon. *Drugs of Choice*, Englewood Cliffs, New Jersey: Prentice-Hall, (1982) pp. 260-262. **Figure 5-1:** Smith and Gay, 1972, p. 216. **Figure 5-3:** Catman, C.W. and J.L. McCaugh. *Behavioral Neuroscience*, New York, Academic Press (1980), p. 612. **Figure 5-4:** Reproduced from *Some must watch while some must sleep* by William C. Dement. By permission of W.W. Norton & Company, Inc. Copyright © 1972, 1974, 1976 by William C. Dement. **Figure 5-5:** Fischer, R. A cartography of the Ecstatic and meditative states. *Science, 174,* (1971) p. 898 Copyright 1971 by the American Association for the Advancement of Science.

Figure 7-3: The Source. The Source is a service mark of Source Telecomputing Corporation, a division of the Reader's Digest Association, Inc. **Figure 7-4:** Allyon, T. and N.H. Azrin. The measurement and reinforcement of behavior of psychotics. *Journal of the Experimental Analysis of Behavior*, (1965), 8, 357-383. Copyright 1965 by the Society for the Experimental Analysis of Behavior, Inc. **Table 7-1:** Adapted from R.G. Packard. The control of classroom attention: a group contingency for complex behavior. *Journal of Applied Behavior Analysis*, (1970), 3, pp. 13-28. **Figure 7-6:** Adpated from S.F. Maier and M.E.P. Seligman. Learned helplessness: Theory and evidence. *Journal of Experimental Psychology: General*, (1976), 105, 3-46. Copyright © 1976 by the American Psychological Association. Reprinted by permission. **Table 7-2:** Adapted from L.Y. Abramson, M.E.P. Seligman, and J.D. Teasdale. Learned helplessness in humans: Critique and reformulation. *Journal of Abnormal Psychology, 87,* (1978), p. 69.

Figure 8-1: Atkinson, R.C. and R.M. Shiffrin. The control of short-term memory. *Scientific American*, (1971), 225, 82-90. **Table 8-2:** Craik, F.I.M. and R.S. Lockhart. Levels of processing: A framework for memory research. *Journal of Verbal Learning and Verbal Behavior*. (1972), *11*, 671-684. **Figure 8-2:** From short-term retention of individual verbal items. By L.R. Peterson and M.J. Peterson. In *Journal of Experimental Psychology*. (1959) 58 193-198. Copyright 1959 by the American Psychological Association. Reprinted by permission.

Figure 9-1: Liberman, A.M. The grammars of speech and language. *Cognitive Psychology*, (1970), *1*, 301-323. Copyright 1970 Academic Press, Inc. Used by permission. **Table 9-1:** Brinder, J.J. and S.H. Elgin. *Guide to transformational grammar*. New York: Holt, Rinehart and Winston. **Figure 9-2:** Smith (1926); Lenneberg, 1967. **Figures 9-3, 9-4, and 9-5:** From J.L. Adams *Conceptual blockbusting*. San Francisco: Freeman (1974). **Table 9-2:** Luchins, A.S. Mechanization in problem solving. *Psychological Monographs*. (1942), 54:6, Whole No. 248. **Table 9-4:** Rosch, 1975. **Figure 9-7:** From J.P. Guilford, Factorial Angles to Psychology. *Psychological Review* (1961), 68, 1-20. Copyright © 1961 by the American Psychological Association. Reprinted by permission.

Table 9-6: Adapted from L.M. Terman and M.A. Merrill. *Measuring intelligence*. Boston: Houghton Mifflin, 1937. Reproduced by permission of the publisher, the Riverside Publishing Company.

Figure 9-8: Copyright 1961 by Institute of Personality and Ability Testing. Reproduced by permission.

Figure 10-3: From Keith L. Moore. *Before We Are Born*, Third Edition. Courtesy of W.B. Saunders Company. (1983)

Figure 11-1: From Nancy Bayley. Individual pattern of development. *Child Development* (1956), *27*, 45-74. Reprinted with the permission of the Society for Research in Child Development, Inc.

Figure 11-2: From *Growing up* by J.M. Tanner. Copyright © 1973 by Scientific American, Inc. All rights reserved.

Table 11-2: Bourne, L. et al. *Cognitive Processes*. Englewood Cliffs, New Jersey: Prentice-Hall. (1978B)

Table 11-3: Levinson, D.J., C.M. Darrow, E.B. Klein, M.H. Levinson, and M. Braxton. The psycho-social development of men in early adulthood and the mid-life crisis. In D.F. Ricks, A. Thomas, and M. Roff (Eds.), *Life History Research in Psychopathology*, Minneapolis: University of Minnesota Press, (1974), *3*, 243-258.

Table 11-5: Adapted from Bem. *Journal of Consulting and Clinical Psychology*. (1974) Copyright by the American Psychological Association and reproduced by permission.

Table 11-6: Bem. *Journal of Consulting and Clinical Psychology*. (1974) Table 1, p. 156 in original. Copyright by the American Psychological Association and reproduced by permission.

Figure 11-3: National Center for Health Statistics, *Health United States 1975*. Health examination survey.

Table 11-7: Adapted with permission of Macmillan Publishing Company from *On Death and Dying* by Elisabeth Kübler-Ross. Copyright © 1969 by Elisabeth Kübler-Ross.

Figure 12-3: Redrawn from P. Eckman. Autonomic nervous system activity distinguishes among emotions. *Science*, Vol. 221 (Sept. 1983), p. 1208.

Figure 12-7: Bower, G.L. Mood and Memory. *American Psychologist* (1981), *36*, 133.

Figure 12-8: Bower, G.L. and S.G. Gilligan. Emotional mood as a context for learning and recall. *Journal of Verbal Behavior*. (1978), *17*, 573-585.

Figure 12-10: Zuckerman. The search for high sensations. *Psychology Today*. (1978), p. 46. F.J. Landy and D.A. Trumbo. *The Psychology of Work Behavior*, Second Edition. Honewood, Illinois: Dorsey Press, 1980.

Figure 12-14: Porter, L.W. and E.E. Lawler. *Managerial Attitudes and Performance*. Honewood, Illinois: Irwin-Dorsey, (1968).

Figure 13-3: Catell, R.B. The scientific analysis of personality. Harmondsworth, England: Penguin Books (1965).

Table 13-1: Based on Peruin, (1976) p. 470.

Table 13-3: The Psychological Corporation (1970).

Table 14-1: Holmes, T.H. and R.H. Rahe. Social readjustment rating scale. *Journal of Psychosomatic Research*, Vol. II, © 1967, Pergamon Press, Ltd. Reprinted with permission.

Figure 14-1: Columbia University Department of Industrial Engineering and Operations Research.

Figure 14-2: Marianne Frankenhauser. The sympathetic-adrenal and pituitary adrenal response to challenge: Comparison between the sexes. In T.M. Dembroski, T.H. Schwartz, and G. Blümchen (Eds.), *Biobehavioral Bases of Coronary Heart Disease*. Basel, New York: Karger (1982).

Figure 14-3: Fiedler, F.E. and A.F. Leister. Leader intelligence and task performance: A test of a multiple screen model. *Organizational Behavior and Human Performance*. New York: Academic Press (1977) *20*, 1-14. Reprinted with permission.

Table 14-2: From R. S. Lazarus and A. Monat. *Personality*. Englewood Cliffs, New Jersey: Prentice-Hall (1979) p. 163.

Table 14-3: By C. David Jenkins, Ph.D., Stephen J. Zyanski, Ph.D., Ray H. Rosenman, M.D. Copyright © 1979, 1969, 1966, 1965 by the Psychological Corporation, a subsidiary of Harcourt Brace Jovanovich, Inc. All rights reserved. Reprinted with permission.

Tables 15-1 and 15-2: Based on Langer and Abelson, 1974.

Table 15-3: American Psychiatric Association. *Diagnostic and Statistical Manual of Mental Disorders,* Third edition. Washington (1980).

Tables 15-4 and 15-5: American Psychiatric Association. *DSM-III.* Washington, D.C.: APA (1980).

Table 15-6: Marks, I. and M. Lader. Anxiety states (anxiety neurosis): A review. *Journal of Nervous and Mental Disease* (1973), *156,* 3-18. Case Study p. 496 from Phobic in New York. Susan Berman, *New York* magazine (January 24, 1983).

Table 15-7: *Diagnostic and Statistical Manual, Vol. III,* (1980), p. 214. Copyright by the American Psychiatric Association.

Table 16-1: Walker, E.E., A.G. Hedberg, P.W. Clement, and L. Wright. *Clinical Procedures for Behavior Therapy.* Englewood Cliffs, New Jersey: Prentice-Hall, (1981).

Table 16-2: Cole, J.O. Phenothiazine treatment in acute schizophrenia: Effectiveness. *Archives of General Psychiatry* (1964), *10,* pp. 246-261.

Figure 17-1: Walster, Aronson, and Abrahams. On increasing the persuasiveness of a low prestige communicator. *Journal of Experimental Social Psychology.* (1966), *2,* p. 333.

Figure 17-2: Kelley, H.H. Attribution theory in social psychology. Nebraska Symposium on Motivation. Lincoln: University of Nebraska Press, (1967).

Figure 17-3: Latané, B. and J.M. Darley. Group inhibition of bystander interventions in emergencies. *Journal of Personality and Social Psychology* (1968), *10,* pp. 215-221. Text p. 585: From ''Millworker,'' words and music by James Taylor, © 1979 Country Road Music, Inc. All rights reserved. Used by permission. Box text p. 587: Gilbreath and Gilbreath. *Cheaper by the Dozen.*

Figure 18-2: Taylor, R.V. Psychology and the design of machines. *American Psychologist.* (1957) *21,* 249-258.

Figure 18-4: Jenkins, W.O. Tactual discrimination of shapes for coding aircraft-type controls. In P.M. Fitts, *Psychological Research on Equipment Design.* Washington, D.C.: Government Printing Office (1947).

Table 18-1: Weaver, C. Job satisfaction in the United States in the 1970s. *Journal of Applied Psychology.* (1980), *65,* pp. 365-366.

Figure 18-6: Porter, L.W. and E.E. Lawler. *Managerial Attitudes and Performance.* Homewood, Illinois: Irwin-Dorsey (1968). Excerpt on p. 642 from *All the Live-Long Day* by Barbara Garson. Copyright © 1972, 1973, 1974, 1975 by Barbara Garson. Reprinted by permission of Doubleday and Co., Inc.

Table 18-3: Fleishman, E.A. Toward a taxonomy of human performance. *American Psychologist* (1975), *30,* 1127-1149.

Photos

5 Will McIntyre/Photo Researchers 10 Laimute E. Druskis 17 R. Rowan/Photo Researchers 19 Bettmann Archive 21 Bettmann Archive 23 John Curtis/Taurus Photos 34 Mimi Forsyth/Monkmeyer Press 70 United Press International 72 Lester V. Bergman & Associates 83 Petit-Format and Larry Mulvehill both of Science Source/Photo Researchers 94 Bernard Asset/Photo Researchers 104 Grace Moore/Taurus Photos. 105 A.L. Yarbus (Ed) Eye movement and vision (1967) Plenum Publishing Company. 107 Nancy Ploeger/Monkmeyer 108-9 Courtesy of Inmont Corporation 116 Eric Kroll/Taurus Photos 122 Mimi Forsyth/Monkmeyer 128 Howard Weinberg/Photo Researchers 129 George Haling/Photo Researchers 133 Russ Kinne/Photo Researchers 136 Peter Buckley 137 Georg Gerster/Photo Researchers 142 William Vandivert 146 William Vandivert 159 Bruce Roberts, Rapho/Photo Researchers 168 Martin M. Rotker/Taurus Photos 171 Teri Leigh Stratford. Courtesy Sleep-Wake Disorders Center, Montefiore Medical Center. 179 Alex Von Koschembahr/Photo Researchers 182 Arthur Tress/Photo Researchers 197 Miami Dade Community College 205 Eliot Elisofon, Life Magazine © 1958 Time, Inc. 206 Daniel Zirinsky/Photo Researchers 208 Ken Karp 218 Alec Duncan/Taurus Photos 230 Menschenfreund/Taurus Photos 233 (top) Photo History Division, Department of Photography and Cinema, the Ohio State University (bottom) Mimi Forsyth/Monkmeyer Press 234 Courtesy Grumman Data Systems Corp. 240 Sybil Shackman/Monkmeyer Press 252 Bettmann Archive 254 UPI/Bettmann Archive 258 Boeing Photo 268 NASA 270 UPI/Bettmann Newsphotos 286 Laimute Druskis 291 United Nations 293 R.A. and B.T. Gardner 303 Sygma Paris 311 Resorts International Hotel Casino 318 National Archives 331 Dr. Landrum Shettles 338 Ken Karp 339 Suzanne Szasz 342 Suzanne Szasz/Photo Researchers 343 Mimi Forsyth/Monkmeyer Press 347 Ken Karp 348 Courtesy of Harry F. Harlow, Univ. of Wisconsin Primate Laboratory 350 Bandura and Walters (1959) 365 Mimi Forsyth/Monkmeyer Press 370 Gary Guisinger/Photo Researchers 373 Craig Blovin/Taurus Photos 381 Eric Kroll/Taurus Photos 384 Ken Karp/Sirovich Senior Center 393 (top) Marc Anderson 395 Dr. Paul Ekman, SCIENCE, Vol. 221 (Sept. 1983) p. 1208. 399 Bettye Lanel Photo Researchers 404 Laimute Druskis 411 Author supplied 412 George Goodwin/Monkmeyer Press 430 (top left) Frank Siteman/Taurus; (bottom left) Christopher Lukas/Photo Researchers (right) Ray Ellis/Taurus 434 Ray Ellis/Photo Researchers 437 Richard Hutchings/Photo Researchers 443 Geoffrey Baris 450 Russ Kinne/Photo Researchers 464 (left) John Huber; (right) *The New York Times* 466 Martin M. Rotker/Taurus Photos 469 Philip Jon Bailey/Taurus Photos 474 Susan Berkowitz/Taurus Photos 478 Porterfield/Chickering, Photo Researchers 482 Menschenfreund/Taurus Photos 489 Walker Bros. Creations/Photo Researchers 499 James Wilson/Woodfin Camp & Associates 501 Ellis Herwig/Stock, Boston 517 Dr. Jay Weisberg/Photo Researchers 520 Mimi Forsyth/Monkmeyer Press 532 Van Bucher/Photo Researchers 535 Bettmann Archive 540 David Gonzales, Camarillo State Hospital 546 Ken Karp 547 Ann Chwatsky/Leo de Wys 558 A. Tannenbaum/Sygma 561 Marc Anderson 567 Helena Kolda/Photo Researchers 574 William Vandivert 576 Copyright 1965 by Stanley Milgram. From the film ''Obedience,'' distributed by the New York University Film Library. 579 Alain Nogues/Sygma 589 Courtesy Western Electric 591 (top left) Courtesy Honeywell, Inc; (bottom left) Courtesy Texas Instruments; (top right) Courtesy IBM, (bottom right) Courtesy System Development Corp. 594 (left) Courtesy Chrysler Corporation (right) Courtesy Delta Airlines 595 Bernard Pierre Wolf/Photo Researchers 596 Courtesy Seiko 605 ILO Photo by J. Mohr distributed by U.N. 615 Freda Leinwand/Monkmeyer Press

Index

About the Author

Frank Landy is a Professor of Psychology at The Pennsylvania State University. He received his B. A. from Villanova University and his M. A. and Ph.D. degrees from Bowling Green State University. Although he specializes in the area of industrial and organizational psychology, he has conducted research in many other areas as well. His early research was related to the effect of father absence on the emotional and intellectual development of children. He has also published research in the measurement of phobias, hypnotic suggestibility, and the capacity of individuals to identify physiological changes which accompany strong emotions.

In the area of industrial and organizational psychology, Frank has a leading textbook in industrial psychology called *The Psychology of Work Behavior* (Dorsey Press, 1985). In addition, Frank has just published two books in the measurement of human performance. He has been conducting research in the area of performance rating and evaluation for over 18 years. In the context of work behavior, he has published research on the topics of employee selection, interviewing, job satisfaction, work motivation, and age discrimination. He is an Associate Editor of the *Journal of Applied Psychology* and the Editor of the journal *Human Performance*.

The text reflects Frank's vast experience in teaching introductory psychology at Penn State, a teaching assignment that he has accepted with enthusiasm for 18 years. In fact, he was teaching introductory psychology while revising the book. He is known among undergraduate students for his sense of humor and interesting lectures.

In addition to his university duties, he has been an active industrial consultant. Among other settings, he has applied psychological principles in an iron ore mine above the Arctic Circle, in a police squad car in lower Manhattan, in the Three Mile Island nuclear facility, and on the production floor of a hot rolling steel mill. Many of the applied examples in the text come directly from his consulting projects.

Outside of his interest in students and his professional work, Frank and his family are involved

in swimming. He and his wife are swim officials and his two daughters are competitors in summer and winter swim leagues as well as interscholastically. In addition, Frank is an avid runner, averaging 70 miles per week. He has completed 10 marathons, two while revising this book.